Strategic Management

AN INTEGRATED APPROACH

2ND AUSTRALASIAN EDITION

Strategic Management

AN INTEGRATED APPROACH

2ND AUSTRALASIAN EDITION

Charles W. L.
Hill
UNIVERSITY
OF WASHINGTON

Gareth R.
Jones
TEXAS
A&M UNIVERSITY

Peter
Galvin
CURTIN UNIVERSITY
OF TECHNOLOGY

Ali
Haidar
MONASH
UNIVERSITY

BICENTENNIAL
1807
WILEY
2007
BICENTENNIAL

John Wiley & Sons Australia, Ltd

Houghton
Mifflin

Second edition published 2007 by
John Wiley & Sons Australia, Ltd
42 McDougall Street, Milton Qld 4064

First edition published 2004

Typeset in 10.5 pt Dante MT Regular

Adapted with permission from *Strategic management: an integrated approach*,
5th edn, published by Houghton Mifflin Company, Boston, USA.

National Library of Australia
Cataloguing-in-Publication data

Galvin, Peter, 1970– .
Strategic management: an integrated approach.

  2nd Australasian ed.
  Bibliography.
  Includes index.
  For tertiary students.
  ISBN 978 0 470 80929 7.

  1. Business planning — Case studies. 2. Management — Case studies.
  3. Strategic planning — Case studies. I. Haidar, Ali. II. Title.

658.4012

Cover and internal design images: © Brand X Pictures

Wiley Bicentennial Logo: Richard J. Pacifico

Edited by David Rule

Printed in Singapore by
Fabulous Printers Pte Ltd

10   9   8   7   6   5   4   3

About the authors

Peter Galvin, Curtin University of Technology

Dr Galvin received his PhD from the University of Western Australia. He has previously held positions at the Queensland University of Technology and California Polytechnic State University. He has also held visiting positions at the State University of New York (Stony Brook) and ESC Toulouse in France. Today, Dr Galvin teaches in the MBA and DBA programs at the Graduate School of Business at Curtin University of Technology, Western Australia. He has published in international journals and contributed chapters to the textbook *Management*. Dr Galvin was awarded Curtin University Excellence in Teaching awards in 2003 and 2004.

Ali Haidar, Monash University

Dr Haidar is a senior lecturer in management in the Department of Management, Faculty of Business and Economics, Monash University, Australia. He has a PhD in public administration from the Victoria University of Wellington, New Zealand and a background in public management research. His current research interests are public manager values, employment relationships, power and politics in organisations, strategies and commitment of hospitals for the care of older adults, and assimilation of elite athletes back into the society. He has published in the *International Employment Relations Review*, the *Journal of Malaysian Studies*, the *Indian Journal of Public Administration*, *Public Sector* (New Zealand), the *Asia Pacific Journal of Human Resources*, the *Employment Relations Record*, *Local Government Studies*, *International Journal of Employment Studies*, and the *International Journal of Public Sector Management*. He also has several chapters published in textbooks.

About the contributors

Chapters 2 and 4 — Jeremy Galbreath, Curtin University of Technology

Dr Galbreath has 15 years' business experience, mainly in hi-tech manufacturing and professional services firms. He has held positions in engineering, consulting, sales and business development and corporate strategy. Currently, he is a Curtin Business School Research Fellow, having completed his PhD in strategic management at the Graduate School of Business, Curtin University of Technology in 2004. In addition, he holds a master of science in information and communication sciences, a bachelor of science in telecommunications and an MBA, all earned in the United States. He has published extensively, with more than 40 articles in print.

New Zealand 'Strategy in action' examples — Paul Knott, University of Canterbury

Dr Knott is a lecturer in strategic management at the University of Canterbury, New Zealand. His research interests are in firm-level competence and in the practical application of strategy tools. He completed his PhD at Manchester Business School in 1997, having earlier worked in the aerospace industry. He moved in 1999 to Canterbury, where he teaches the core undergraduate and MBA strategy papers. He directed the BCom Honours program in management from 2001 to 2005.

New Zealand 'Strategy in action' examples — Achinto Roy, Christchurch Polytechnic Institute of Technology

Dr Achinto Roy lectures for the BBIE program at the School of Business, CPIT and as guest lecturer for MBA and MEM programs at University of Canterbury.

His research areas include Business Ethics, Management Strategy, International Business, CRDM (corruption-related decision-making) and corruption in business. His work has been presented, among others, at international conferences such as ISBEE (World Congress on Business Ethics) Melbourne 2004 and EBEN (European Business Ethics) Research Conference 2005. He has several academic journal publications and book contributions to his credit and over 20 years of professional, consulting and business experience.

Brief contents

Contents

PART 3 Strategies 127

Preface

This book is designed to be a comprehensive text on strategic management for students in Australia and New Zealand. It adopts a traditional perspective on the strategy process, presenting a detailed coverage of all the major areas within it, including the different theoretical paradigms that exist. The first half of the text covers the appropriate theory, starting with 'content' issues and moving on to 'implementation' issues. Given the state of flux in the field of strategy, we have attempted to incorporate recent advances in the field while retaining the core theory. As well as incorporating new theory, this text contains examples of how different strategy concepts work in practice. This second edition introduces a chapter that specifically deals with strategy issues in the public sector and for not-for-profit organisations.

With the additional theory, examples, cases and teaching resources, we hope that this text will be even more effective as a central text in strategy-related subjects in Australia and New Zealand.

The use of examples and cases

To illustrate the theory component of the text, each chapter contains examples of how the theory may operate in different settings. In addition, detailed cases appear at the end of the text. Most of these cases are longer than those developed for other sources, and they are designed to be multidimensional as a way of illustrating the complexity involved in strategic management. These cases, along with the Strategy in action boxes, the end-of-chapter questions and the opening cases, encourage discussion among students, as well as with the instructor.

Strategy is quite different from many functional areas in the field of management. No single framework exists for choosing the best strategy under different circumstances — not in the same way, for example, that a human resources manager can take a structured approach to choosing the best method of remuneration (such as basing a team's remuneration on performance and a public service employee's pay on the characteristics of his or her job). Rather, for determining strategy, a series of frameworks and tools are available to break down large chunks of information and analyse them coherently. For this reason, discussion is a key part of developing a detailed appreciation of the subject, which is why this text includes extensive examples and detailed cases.

Adaptation of the US edition for Australia and New Zealand

The US text *Strategic management: an integrated approach* by Charles WL Hill and Gareth R Jones is widely used around the world. For years, it has been the principal text for thousands of Australian and New Zealand students. It is clear, accessible and logical in its approach. As with many US texts written primarily for the North American market, however, it lacks cases relevant to the Asia-Pacific region. Our students regularly highlighted the need for local cases, and this need for local context was the original driver for the first edition of the Australian and New Zealand adaptation of the Hill and Jones text. More recently, the need for serious coverage of strategy issues in the public sector and our engagement with the Asia-Pacific region have created the stimulus for a significantly revised second edition.

As with the first edition, the text has taken a global rather than a purely regional orientation. Australia and New Zealand operate in a regional context, but our era of globalisation means that local managers increasingly interact with people from outside their region. Furthermore, students studying at Australian and New Zealand institutions come from a range of countries. We were mindful, therefore, of the need to keep global examples in the text. We kept some US examples and added many Australian and New Zealand examples, as well as introducing Asian and European examples. We have continued to introduce a range of contemporary theory. Some major additions to the original text include a revisiting of Porter's generic strategies material, to discuss whether low-cost and differentiation strategies are necessarily mutually exclusive. Furthermore, chapter 4 introduces a more thorough review of the role of resources and capabilities: this area of theory is changing rapidly and remains the 'hot topic' in the strategy field. Chapter 13 reviews the strategy process in the public and not-for-profit sectors; and also reflecting the changes in society, the revised chapter 12 on evaluation discusses the balanced scorecard and triple bottom line reporting. We hope you find that these theory additions are a useful extension to the original text.

Features

- A brand new chapter on strategic management in public sector organisations
- Chapter opening cases and Strategy in action boxes highlight strategic management applications within each chapter
- A wealth of end-of-chapter material including review, discussion and applied questions, small-group exercises, exploring the Web activities, and a strategic management project
- High-quality end-of-book case studies covering small, medium and large companies, both domestic and international. Each case study is accompanied by extensive teaching notes.

A complete teaching and learning package

- Additional cases are provided on the website, allowing instructors to incorporate more recently written cases in their teaching program. The website also contains support materials for students.
- A simulation is available to complement the text. It allows students to apply the contents of the subject in an interactive manner.
- An instructor resource guide (prepared by John Thornton from the University of South Australia) includes a chapter synopsis, lecture outlines, teaching objectives and answers to all the chapter questions.
- A case study resource guide (developed by the authors of the different cases) covers different questions that can be asked about each case, along with the major points relevant to the cases. Most importantly, the guide provides a structure for teaching each case, so that instructors can build the discussion logically and sequentially.
  - A test bank written by Paul Corcoran of the University of the Sunshine Coast, includes multiple-choice, true/false and essay questions for each chapter, all of which are referenced by page number and teaching objective.
  - PowerPoint presentation material includes slides summarising the key points in each chapter.

Peter Galvin and Ali Haidar
June 2006

Acknowledgements

Charles Hill and Gareth Jones deserve special mention for their original work, which formed the basis for this adaptation. Our thanks go also to Jeremy Galbreath, for his work on chapters 2 and 4, and to Paul Knott and Achinto Roy for the New Zealand boxed feature examples provided throughout the text. For contributing cases, we thank Bishnu Sharma, Paul Corcoran, Kerry Scott and Wayne Graham from the University of the Sunshine Coast; Ingrid Bonn of Bond University; Sussie Morrish of the University of Auckland; Bob Hamilton and Paul Knott of the University of Canterbury; Tatiana Zalan of the University of Melbourne; Mark Dibben of Lincoln University and Phil Garrett of Flying Kiwi Productions; and Stephane Tywoniak of Queensland University of Technology. Thanks also to previous students of Peter Galvin who have contributed case material: Celia Dunlop, Corlia Kruger, Mark McPherson and Allen Smyth. We thank also the authors of the cases included on the website, as well as John Thornton from the University of South Australia for his work on the instructor's resource guide and Paul Corcoran for his work on the test bank.

We gratefully acknowledge the following reviewers, who provided extensive comments and highlighted vital points to be included in the text: Nigel Munro-Smith (RMIT University), Mark Dibben (Lincoln University), Alan Singer (University of Canterbury), Peter Smith (The University of Auckland), Paul Waight (Griffith University) and James Lockhart (Massey University).

Finally, we must thank two other groups of people. First, the users of the first edition who supported the concept of an Asia-Pacific edition of the text and provided feedback on how it could be improved in a second edition. The other group are those people in our life whose support made this project possible: our families. Thank you to all these people.

The authors and publisher would like to thank the following copyright holders, organisations and individuals for their permission to reproduce copyright material in this book.

Images

Administrative Science Quarterly: **15**, reprinted from 'Strategy formation in an adhocracy' by Henry A. Mintzberg and Alexandra McGugh, published in *Administrative Science Quarterly*, vol. 30, no. 2, June 1985, by permission of Administrative Science Quarterly, Cornell University • Pearson Education US: **36** based on *Defining the business: the starting point of strategic planning* by Derek F. Abell, © 1980 • Harvard Business School Publishing Corporation: **65** adapted and reprinted by permission of *Harvard Business Review*. From 'How competence forces shape strategy' by Michael E. Porter (March–April 1979). © 1979 by the Harvard Business School Publishing Corporation; all rights reserved; **218** (fig. 7.7) reprinted by permission of Harvard Business School Press. From *Competing for the future* by G. Hamel & C. K. Prahalad. Boston, MA, 1994, p. 227. © 1994 by Gary Hamel and C. K Prahalad; all rights reserved • The Boston Consulting Group: **215** adapted with permission from *Perspectives*, no. 66, 'The product portfolio' by Bruce D. Henderson, Copyright The Boston Consulting Group 1970 • Australian Beverages Council: **C19**, **C20** © www.australianbeverages.org/ AC Nielsen • © Virgin Blue Airlines: **C37** (exhibit 9) • Australian Automotive Aftermarket Association: **C43** from *Aftermarket*, February–March 2000. Reproduced with permission from the Australian Automotive Aftermarket Association • Ray Della-Polina: **C44**, **C46** / Marlows • © Bloomberg L.P.: **C89** • © Phil Garrett: **C100**.

Text

Courtesy of Rio Tinto: **35** (figure 2.2) • Emerald: **48** (table 2.2) 'Corporate social responsibility strategy: strategic options, global considerations', by J. Galbreath, *Corporate Governance: International Journal of Business in Society*, issue 3, June 2006 • Journalists Copyright: **229** © David James/*BRW*, vol. 27, 22–28 September 2005 • East Grampians Health Service: **391** © East Grampians Health Service 'Strategic plan 2001–2005' • Sage Publications USA: **404** (table 13.2) Gregory Streib and Theodore Poister, *American Review of Public Administration*, vol. 20, no. 1, March 1990, p. 37 • Kleenmaid St George: **C14** reproduced with kind permission of

Kleenmaid St George • Commonwealth Copyright Administration: **C34** (exhibit 3) Australian Domestic Market, 2003, adapted from Bureau of Transport and Regional Economics, *Digest of statistics 2002–03*, copyright Commonwealth of Australia reproduced by permission • Qantas: **C35** (exhibits 4 and 5), **C36** (exhibits 6 and 7) reproduced with the permission of Qantas Airways Limited • © Virgin Blue Airlines: **C37** (exhibit 8) • Allen Smyth: **C40–C50** case study reprinted by permission of Allen Smyth, Celia Dunlop, Mark McPherson and Corlia Kruger © 2003 • Bank of Queensland: **C53** (figures C5.1 and C5.2) © Bank of Queensland *Annual Report 2000–2001*; **C59** © adapted from Bank of Queensland *Annual Report* 2004 • © Australian Bureau of Statistics: **C57** (exhibits 1 and 2) Australian National Accounts: Financial Accounts 5232.0 • Australian Prudential Regulatory Authority: **C58** (exhibit 3) list of authorised deposit-taking institutions © APRA, www.apra.gov.au • IGD: **C60** (figure C6.1) IGD appears on link http://www.igd.com/cir.asp?cirid=463&search=1 • © Aldi: **C62** (table C6.2) • Michael A. Roberto: **C86–7** reprinted by permission of Harvard Business Review. From 'The changing structure of the global wine industry', by Michael A. Roberto, vol. 2, 2003. Copyright © 2003 by the Harvard Business School Publishing Corporation; all rights reserved.

Every effort has been made to trace the ownership of copyright material. Information that will enable the publisher to rectify any error or omission in subsequent editions will be welcome. In such cases, please contact the Permissions Section of John Wiley & Sons Australia, Ltd who will arrange for the payment of the usual fee.

Introduction to strategic management

part 1

The strategic management process

learning objectives

After studying this chapter, you should be able to:

- discuss why strategy is an important element of an organisation's planning process
- identify the key elements of the basic strategic planning process
- identify the key elements of strategic leadership
- differentiate between intended and emergent strategies
- discuss the cognitive biases that affect strategic decisions.

opening case

iiNet

Perth-based iiNet started in 1993, well before the technology boom of the late 1990s. Ironically, it was this insatiable appetite for technology stocks that allowed iiNet to list on the Australian Stock Exchange in 1999. The stock eventually traded at more than $1 before falling to less than 50 cents in 2001. However, unlike most technology — and especially Internet — companies, iiNet managed to survive and today is the fourth-largest Internet service provider (ISP) behind Telstra, Optus and Primus.

Founded by Michael Malone, iiNet has grown very quickly over the past ten years — with revenues growing at around 80 per cent per year over this period. This is not unique in this industry, in which growth tends to come relatively easily but profits are a lot rarer because much of the growth tends to come about from acquisitions. To achieve this, Malone, as CEO, has a clear vision of the strategy that will build the company further.

Success in the ISP business is heavily reliant upon achieving economies of scale. Most firms do not have their own network and therefore purchase bandwidth (essentially the use of the network) from the owners, such as Telstra. The more bandwidth purchased, the greater the discount. Therefore, to make money in a market in which prices tend not to vary very much, it is imperative that the company get as many customers as quickly as possible to achieve these economies of scale — particularly in relation to buying bandwidth. iiNet's strategy has therefore called for appropriate acquisitions, such as Froggy in New South Wales and iHug in New Zealand. These have pushed the number of customers to about 400 000. Growing the customer base quickly is critical as most growth occurs in the first two years of the general rollout of particular Internet technologies. Malone predicts for example that the fight for broadband customers will be virtually over by the end of 2006 and, therefore, it is a fine line between building the business quickly and not paying too much for each new customer.

The other side of the business is keeping the customer. The ISP business tends not to allow for significant differentiation and so price is often the basis of the initial decision whom to use. However, for most people, it is how the staff at the ISP respond to questions and deal with problems that ultimately determine the customer satisfaction levels, and, therefore, whether the customer stays with the same provider. For this reason, Malone's strategy has been to employ people with customer service skills. After all, teaching people the technical side of the business is relatively easy but teaching people customer service skills tends to be more difficult. For this reason, many of the customer support staff have a background in the hospitality industry, as these are more likely to appreciate the necessity of good customer service. Customer service and rapid growth through appropriate acquisitions are the two fundamental strategies that have helped iiNet's earnings per share to grow by 3990 per cent over the past three years.

Source: Treadgold, T 2005, 'Service first', *Business Review Weekly*, 17–23 February, p. 52.

Overview

Why do some organisations succeed while others fail? In the fast-changing world of digital communications, for example, why have companies such as iiNet succeeded but OneTel failed? Globally, why have companies such as Yahoo! done well but Netscape has been losing market share? In video games, why did Sega outperform Atari, only to be outdone by the Sony Play-Station? And how will the next generation of PlayStation hold off challenges from Microsoft's Xbox 360? In airlines, why did Qantas make profits and Ansett go broke? Why has Singapore Airlines consistently outperformed other regional carriers such as Thai Airways and Malaysian Airways? In the retail industry in Australia, what factors have made Woolworths such a popular stock while Coles-Myer shares have been a relative underperformer for a number of years? And in the fashion industry, what made Levi's a success in the 1980s and early 1990s, yet it struggles today?

This book argues that the strategies that an organisation pursues have a major impact on its performance relative to that of its peers. A **strategy** is an action that an organisation takes to attain one or more of its goals. For most organisations, an overriding goal is to achieve superior performance, so a strategy can often be defined more precisely as *an action a company takes to attain superior performance*. This same notion can be applied to not-for-profit and government organisations. Superior performance may be measured relative to past performance because most organisations today are attempting to do more with less.

Much of this book is devoted to identifying and describing the pros and cons of the various strategies that a company can pursue. Many of these strategies are generic — that is, they apply to all organisations, large or small, manufacturing or service, and profit seeking or not for profit. The aim is to give you a thorough understanding of the analytical techniques and skills necessary to identify and exploit strategies successfully. The first step towards achieving this objective is to give you an overview of the **strategic management process** — that is, the process by which managers choose a set of strategies for the enterprise. By the end of this chapter, you will understand the processes that managers use to select strategies for their company, and you will appreciate the strengths and weaknesses of these processes.

strategy
An action that an organisation takes to achieve its goals

strategic management process
The set of processes used to determine the strategies for the organisation

Strategic planning

Asked how an organisation chooses its strategy, the average person in the street would probably answer that the strategy is the result of a rational planning process that is orchestrated, if not dominated, by the top management of the organisation. To an extent, this emphasis reflects the military roots of strategy, with its imagery of generals and their staff clustered around a map table, plotting a strategy for defeating the enemy. A number of writers in the business literature have propagated this imagery. They have emphasised that strategy is the outcome of a formal planning process and that top management plays the most important role in this process.[1]

Although the view of strategy as the product of a rational planning process driven by top management has some basis in reality, it is not the whole story. As we shall see later in the chapter, not all of an organisation's strategies result from formal strategic planning exercises. Valuable strategies often emerge from deep within the organisation without prior planning. In addition, the strategy development process is not always rational, either because the strategist is guessing what the future holds or because he/she may be acting in self-interest. Nevertheless, a consideration of planning is a useful starting point for our journey into the world of strategy. Accordingly, in this section, we consider what may be described as a stereotypical strategic planning model.

A basic planning model

The strategic planning process can be broken into six steps, as illustrated in figure 1.1. You may want to think of figure 1.1 as a plan of the book, for it also shows how the different chapters relate to the different steps of the strategic planning process. The six steps are: (1) selection of the corporate mission and major corporate goals; (2) analysis of the organisation's external competitive environment to identify the organisation's opportunities and threats; (3) analysis of the organisation's internal operating environment to identify the organisation's strengths and weaknesses; (4) selection of strategies that build on the organisation's strengths and correct its weaknesses, to take advantage of external opportunities and counter external threats; (5) strategy implementation; and (6) strategy evaluation (as part of the feedback process).

The task of analysing the organisation's external and internal environment and then selecting an appropriate strategy is normally referred to as **strategy formulation**. In contrast, **strategy implementation** typically involves designing appropriate organisational structures and control systems to put the organisation's chosen strategy into action.

Each component illustrated in figure 1.1 constitutes a sequential step in the strategic planning process. Each cycle of the planning process begins with a statement of the corporate mission and major corporate goals. The mission statement is followed by external analysis, internal analysis and strategic choice. The process continues with the design of the organisational structure and control systems necessary to implement the organisation's chosen strategy. To facilitate the feedback process, the final step in the process is strategy evaluation, which can be used as the starting point for the next strategic planning process.

Some organisations go through this kind of process every year, although this should not be taken to imply that the organisation chooses a new strategy each year. Often, it simply reaffirms a strategy and structure that are already in place. The strategic plans generated by this kind of process generally cover a period of one-to-five years, with the plan being updated or 'rolled forwards' every year. The appropriateness of whether to maintain or fundamentally alter an existing strategic direction depends on the evaluation process. Even if the organisation makes only minor changes to its strategic direction, the planning process is important because it normally feeds into the budgetary processes of the organisation. Strategic planning thus shapes resource allocation within the organisation.

Mission and major goals

The first component of the strategic management process is defining the **mission** and **major goals** of the organisation. This topic is covered in depth in chapter 2. The mission and major goals of an organisation provide the context within which strategies are formulated.

The mission sets out why the organisation exists and what it should be doing. The mission of an international airline, for example, may be to satisfy the needs of individual and business travellers for high-speed transportation at a reasonable price to major population centres in the Asia Pacific, European and north American regions. Similarly, the mission of Yahoo! may be defined as 'connecting anyone to anybody or anything'. The mission must reflect what the organisation really wants to do. Too often, the mission statement becomes a broad statement of values that has no real worth in helping the organisation determine its priorities. Examples of these broad statements are 'to provide superior value to the customers', 'to be a responsible employer', 'to conduct business in an ethical manner' and 'to be the best in the field'. A mission statement needs to provide direction. Without direction, the organisation could drift and conflict could arise between decision makers as to which option would best fulfil the mission statement. PepsiCo has a mission statement along the lines of 'Beat Coke!'. Before he died, the Coca-Cola CEO through much of the 1980s and 1990s, Robert Goisueta, expressed his vision for the company in terms of putting Coke within arm's reach of every consumer to the extent that you could turn on a tap in your home and Coke would come out.

strategy formulation
The analysis process used to determine which strategies an organisation should use

strategy implementation
How strategies are executed, managed and reviewed

mission
An organisation's unique purpose and the scope of its activities

major goals
Organisationwide goals for the medium term to long term

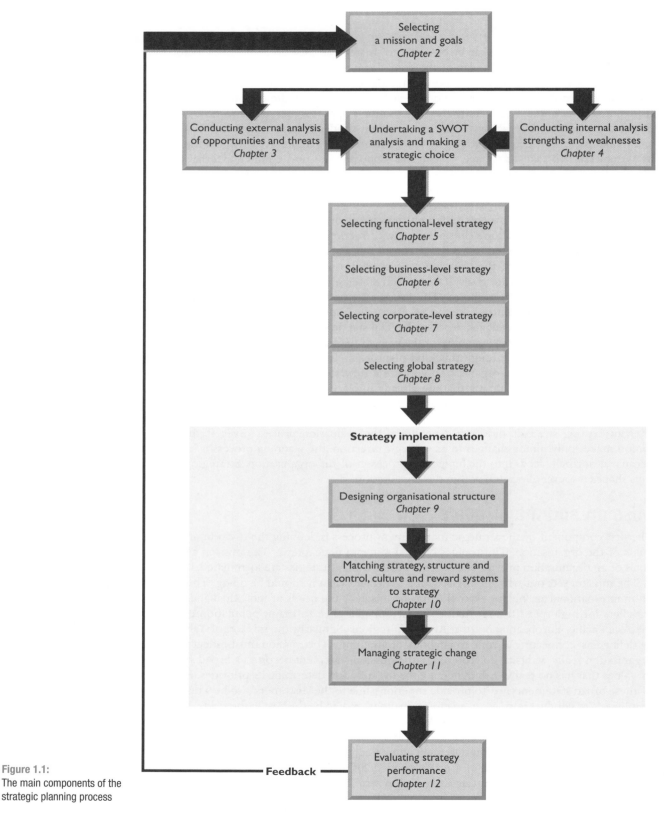

Figure 1.1:
The main components of the
strategic planning process

Major goals specify what the organisation hopes to fulfil in the medium to long term. Most profit-seeking organisations operate with a hierarchy of goals, in which attaining superior performance is placed at or near the top. Secondary goals are objectives that the organisation judges necessary to attain superior performance. Under the leadership of Jack Welch, General Electric operated with a secondary goal of being first or second in every major market in which it competes. This secondary goal reflected Welch's belief that building market share is the best way in which to achieve superior performance.

External analysis

The second component of the strategic management process is the analysis of the organisation's external operating environment. This topic is covered in detail in chapter 3. The objective of external analysis is to identify strategic *opportunities* and *threats* in the organisation's operating environment. Three interrelated environments should be examined at this stage: (1) the immediate (or industry) environment in which the organisation operates, (2) the national environment and (3) the wider macroenvironment.

Analysing the industry environment requires an assessment of the competitive structure of the organisation's industry (including the competitive position of the focal organisation and its major rivals) as well as the stage of industry development. Many markets are now global markets, so analysing the industry environment also means assessing the impact of globalisation on competition within an industry. Analysing the national environment requires an assessment of whether the national context within which an organisation operates facilitates the attainment of a competitive advantage in the global marketplace. If it does not, then the organisation may have to consider shifting a significant part of its operations to countries where the national context does facilitate the attainment of a competitive advantage. Analysing the macroenvironment consists of examining macroeconomic, social, government, legal, international and technological factors that may affect the organisation.

Internal analysis

Internal analysis, the third component of the strategic management process, serves to pinpoint the *strengths* and *weaknesses* of the organisation. Issues such as identifying the quantity and quality of resources available to the organisation, and how these resources are deployed, are considered in chapter 4, where the sources of competitive advantage are probed. The chapter looks at how companies can attain a competitive advantage, and discusses the role of distinctive competencies (unique company strengths), resources and capabilities in building and sustaining a company's competitive advantage. One conclusion reached in chapter 4 is that building and maintaining a competitive advantage requires a company to achieve superior efficiency, quality, innovation and customer responsiveness. Company strengths lead to superiority in these areas, whereas company weaknesses translate into inferior performance.

SWOT analysis and strategic choice

The next component requires generating a series of strategic alternatives, given the organisation's internal strengths and weaknesses, and its external opportunities and threats. The comparison of strengths, weaknesses, opportunities and threats is normally referred to as a SWOT analysis.[2] The central purpose of the SWOT analysis is to identify strategies that *align*, *fit* or *match* a company's resources and capabilities to the demands of the environment in which the company operates. To put it another way, the purpose of the strategic alternatives generated by a SWOT analysis should be to build on the organisation's strengths so as to exploit opportunities and counter threats, and to correct the organisation's weaknesses.

SWOT
Strengths, weaknesses, opportunities and threats

Strategic choice is the process of choosing from the strategic alternatives generated by a SWOT analysis. The organisation has to evaluate alternatives against each other, in terms of their ability to achieve major goals. The strategic alternatives generated can encompass business-level, functional-level, corporate-level and global strategies. The process of strategic choice requires the organisation to identify the set of strategies at different levels that would best enable it to survive and prosper in the fast-changing and globally competitive environment that characterises most modern industries.

Business-level strategy

The business-level strategy of an organisation encompasses the overall competitive theme that the organisation chooses to stress, how it positions itself in the marketplace to gain a competitive advantage, and the different positioning strategies that can be used in different industry settings. The various strategic options available are first introduced in chapter 5 and then discussed in more detail in chapter 6. Chapter 6 reviews the pros and cons of three generic business-level strategies: a cost-leadership strategy, a differentiation strategy and a focus strategy for a particular market niche.

Chapter 6 also considers the relationship between business-level strategy and industry structure. It concentrates on the different strategic options confronting companies in radically different industry settings, such as the benefits and drawbacks of establishing a first-mover advantage in a newly formed or embryonic industry. It also discusses the role of market signalling, price leadership and product differentiation for sustaining a competitive advantage in mature industries, and explores the different strategic options that a company can choose in a declining industry.

Functional-level strategy

Competitive advantage stems from an organisation's ability to attain superior efficiency, quality, innovation and customer responsiveness — a point made in chapter 4. Chapter 5 examines the different functional-level (operations) strategies that can be employed to achieve these four crucial aims. Functional-level strategies are strategies directed at improving the effectiveness of operations within a company, such as manufacturing, marketing, materials management, product development and customer service.

Corporate-level strategy

Chapter 7 deals with the issue of corporate-level strategy. An organisation's corporate-level strategy must answer this question: what businesses should we be in to maximise the long-run profitability of the organisation? For many organisations, competing successfully often means vertical integration — that is, integrating operations either backwards into the production of inputs for the organisation's main operation or forwards into the disposal of outputs from the operation. Beyond this, organisations that succeed in establishing a sustainable competitive advantage may find that they are generating resources in excess of their investment requirements within their primary industry. For such organisations, maximising long-run profitability may entail diversification into new business areas. Accordingly, chapter 7 looks closely at the costs and benefits of different diversification strategies. In addition, we examine the role of strategic alliances as alternatives to diversification and vertical integration. It also reviews the different vehicles that companies use to achieve vertical integration and diversification, including acquisitions and new ventures. It also considers how diversified companies can restructure their portfolio of businesses to improve company performance.

Global strategy

In today's world of global markets and global competition, achieving a competitive advantage and maximising organisational performance increasingly require an organisation to expand its operations outside its home country. Accordingly, an organisation must consider the various global strategies that it can pursue. Chapter 8 assesses the benefits and costs of global expansion and examines four different strategies — multidomestic, international, global and transnational — that a company can adopt to compete in the global marketplace. In addition, that chapter explores the benefits and costs of strategic alliances between global competitors, the different entry modes that can be used to penetrate a foreign market, and the role of host-government policies in influencing a company's choice of global strategy.

Strategy implementation

Once a company has chosen a strategy to achieve its goals, that strategy then has to be put into action. This book breaks down the topic of strategy implementation into four main components: (1) designing appropriate organisational structures; (2) designing control systems; (3) matching strategy, structure and controls; and (4) managing conflict, politics and change.

Designing organisational structure

Implementing a strategy requires the allocation of roles and responsibilities for different aspects of that strategy to different managers and subunits within the company. A company's organisational structure maps out roles and responsibilities, along with reporting relationships. In this sense, strategy is implemented through structure. The telecommunications company Telstra, for example, has four major profit centres: domestic retail (which includes domestic landline services, mobile services and country services); Telstra wholesale (such as sales to other carriers); Telstra International (which includes TelstraClear in New Zealand); and the Infrastructure Services Group. The managing director of each group reports directly to the CEO and is responsible for ensuring the group appropriately implements its component of the company's overall strategy. If an organisation's existing structure is not appropriate, given the company's strategy, then a new structure may have to be designed. Chapter 9 discusses the different types of organisational structure that managers can use to implement strategy.

Designing control systems

Besides choosing a structure, an organisation must also establish appropriate organisational control systems. It must decide how best to assess the performance and to control the actions of subunits. The options range from market and output controls to bureaucratic controls and control through organisational culture, all of which are tackled by chapter 10. An organisation also needs to decide what kind of reward and incentive system to set up for employees. Chapter 10 reviews these options as well.

Managing strategic change

We live in a world in which the only constant is change. Much of this change is the result of technological progress. In recent years, the rise of the Internet and the associated World Wide Web has illustrated the way in which technological change can have an impact on established markets. Web-based commerce is providing a host of new opportunities, while simultaneously threatening to make established business models obsolete. In the brokerage industry, for example, the use of the Internet by individuals to buy and sell shares directly without the aid of a broker has propelled the growth of companies such as E*Trade, Access Brokerage and ComSec (a subunit of the Commonwealth Bank). Simultaneously, this change has threatened the established business model of 'full-service' brokerage companies such as JB Were & Sons and Merrill Lynch, which have traditionally employed brokers to buy and sell stocks for individuals. Because change is so pervasive, companies that succeed in the long run are those that are able to adapt their strategy and structure to a changing world. In 1999, for example, Merrill Lynch embraced an online strategy, even though this effectively reduces the need for its vast network of brokers. Chapter 11 takes a close look at the process of managing strategic change and discusses the different tactics that managers can use to successfully implement such change.

Strategy evaluation and the feedback loop

In the same way that the best strategies in the world will not work if not appropriately implemented, successful strategies will not remain successful as conditions change both inside and outside the firm. To determine whether a strategy is successful, every organisation should undertake a regular formal evaluation of its strategic performance. The evaluation process, therefore, is the first step in the feedback loop. This feedback process (see figure 1.1) is ongoing, with the results of the evaluation helping to inform the next strategic planning process in terms of what may need to be changed.

Once an organisation has implemented a strategy, it must monitor its execution to determine how well it is achieving strategic objectives. This monitoring should be supplemented at least annually with a formal evaluation process that considers performance along several dimensions. The performance data are fed into the next round of strategy formulation and implementation. In this way, the evaluation process is a vital step in determining whether to maintain the existing strategic direction or undertake a significant shift in direction. In many cases, the evaluation process may simply identify that performance targets were simply a little too ambitious or that a gradual shift in the competitive dynamics of the industry requires a greater emphasis on one particular part of the strategy. The strategic direction of an organisation is rarely altered fundamentally on a regular basis, but the evaluation process and the subsequent feedback provide the necessary information on when and why change needs to take place.

Strategic leadership

A key strategic role of managers is to provide strategic leadership for their subordinates. Strategic leadership refers to the ability to articulate a strategic vision for the organisation, or a part of the organisation, and to motivate others to follow that vision. An enormous amount has been written about leadership, and it is beyond the scope of this book to review this complex topic in detail. A few key characteristics of good leaders that several authors have identified are discussed though[3]: (1) vision, eloquence and consistency; (2) commitment; (3) being well informed; (4) willingness to delegate and empower; (5) astute use of power and (6) emotional intelligence.

Vision, eloquence and consistency

A key task of leadership is to give the organisation a sense of direction. Strong leaders seem to have a vision of where the organisation should go. Moreover, they are eloquent enough to communicate this vision to others within the organisation in terms that can energise people, and they consistently articulate their vision until it becomes part of the organisational culture.[4] John F Kennedy, Winston Churchill and Gough Whitlam have all been held up as examples of visionary leaders. All three had their own clear vision of the society they would like to see, and all were able to communicate it eloquently to people using evocative language that energised the audience. Think of the impact of Kennedy's challenge, 'Ask not what your country can do for you; ask what you can do for your country'. Whitlam was able to use his position of prime minister of Australia to push for government action that was consistent with his vision, whereas others such as Winston Churchill have been able to unite a country during periods of hardship. In the world of business, examples of strong business leaders include Microsoft's Bill Gates, Michael Chaney of Wesfarmers and Stephen Tindall of The Warehouse Group.

Commitment

A strong leader is someone who demonstrates commitment to his or her particular vision, often leading by example. Consider some of the best-known companies. McDonald's is famous for its focus on quality management and service. The processes that have made McDonald's famous came about because Ray Kroc was committed to instituting standardised practices for all aspects of store management. Anita Roddick of The Body Shop is committed to social responsibility. This commitment affects all aspects of the business — where products are sourced, what products are sold and how The Body Shop undertakes its marketing. All employees thus perceive social responsibility as a key component of The Body Shop's strategy. When Paul Anderson set out to reduce BHP's cost structure there was a review of all discretionary expenditure. As a result, everybody through to the CEO travelled economy class. Management thus showed that it was committed, so the rest of the organisation realised that cost management was not just another fad. When top managers show a commitment to a vision that is especially strong, the resulting organisational culture can survive long after the tenure of those managers.

Being well informed

Good leaders do not operate in a vacuum. Rather, they develop a network of formal and informal sources that keep them well informed about what is going on within their organisation. They develop backchannel ways of finding out what is going on so they do not have to rely on formal information channels. Graham Turner at Flight Centre, for example, was able to find out a lot about the health of his company by regularly visiting different stores. Using informal and unconventional means of gathering information is wise, because formal channels can be captured by special interests within the organisation or by gatekeepers, who may misrepresent the true state of affairs within the organisation to the leader. People such as Turner who are constantly interacting with their employees at all levels within the organisation are better able to build informal information networks than are leaders who closet themselves in remote corporate headquarters and never interact with lower-level employees.

Willingness to delegate and empower

Good leaders are skilled delegaters. They recognise that unless they delegate they can quickly become overloaded with responsibilities. They also recognise that empowering subordinates to make decisions is a good motivational tool. Delegating also makes sense when it results in decisions being made by those who must implement them. At the same time, good leaders recognise that they need to maintain control over certain key decisions. They will not, therefore, delegate those decisions that they judge to be critical to the future success of the organisation under their leadership.

Astute use of power

In a now classic article on leadership, Wrapp notes that good leaders tend to be astute in their use of power.[5] By 'astute', he means three things. First, good leaders play the power game with skill, preferring to build consensus for their ideas rather than use their authority to force the implementation of ideas. They act as members or democratic leaders of a coalition, rather than as dictators. Second, good leaders often hesitate to commit themselves publicly to detailed strategic plans or precise objectives, because the emergence of contingencies will probably require adaptation of those plans or objectives. A successful leader may thus commit the organisation to a particular vision — such as minimising costs or boosting product quality — without stating precisely how or when this will be achieved. Good leaders often have precise private objectives and strategies that they would like the organisation to pursue but they recognise the futility of public commitment, given the likelihood of change and the difficulties of implementation. Third, good leaders possess the ability to push through programs piecemeal. They recognise that it may be useless, on occasion, to try to implement total packages or strategic programs when significant objections to at least part of the package program are likely to arise. The successful leader may be willing to take less than total acceptance to achieve modest progress towards a goal. He or she tries to push through ideas one piece at a time, so that they seem to be incidental to other ideas yet are part of a larger program or hidden agenda that moves the organisation in the direction of the manager's objectives.

Pfeffer has articulated a similar vision of the politically astute manager who gets things done in organisations by intelligent use of power.[6] In Pfeffer's view, power comes from control over resources, including budgets, positions, information and knowledge that is important to the organisation. Politically astute managers use these resources to acquire another critical resource: allies. Allies can then help the managers attain their strategic objectives. Pfeffer stresses that one does not need to be a CEO to assemble power in an organisation. Quite junior operations managers can build a surprisingly effective power base and use it to influence organisational outcomes.

Emotional intelligence

Goleman coined the term 'emotional intelligence' to describe a bundle of psychological attributes that many strong leaders exhibit.[7] The attributes include self-awareness, self-regulation, motivation, empathy and social skills. *Self-awareness* refers to the ability to understand one's moods, emotions and drives, as well as their effect on others. *Self-regulation* is the ability to control or redirect disruptive impulses or moods — that is, to think before acting. *Motivation* refers to a passion for work that goes beyond money or status, and a propensity to pursue goals with energy and persistence. *Empathy* means understanding the feelings and viewpoints of subordinates and taking those into account when making decisions. Goleman defines *social skills* as 'friendliness with a purpose'.

According to Goleman, leaders who possess these attributes — that is, those who exhibit a high degree of emotional intelligence — tend to be more effective than those who lack them. Their self-awareness and self-regulation help elicit the trust and confidence of subordinates. In Goleman's view, people respect leaders who recognise their own limitations through self-awareness and, because of self-regulation, do not 'shoot from the hip' but carefully consider decisions. Goleman also argues that self-aware and self-regulating individuals tend to be more self-confident and consequently better able to cope with ambiguity and more open to change. A strong motivation exhibited in a passion for work can also be infectious, persuading others to join together in pursuit of a common goal or organisational mission. Finally, strong empathy and social skills can help leaders earn the loyalty of subordinates. Empathetic and socially adept individuals tend to be more skilled at managing disputes between managers, better able to find common ground and purpose among diverse constituencies, and more likely to move people in a desired direction than leaders who lack these qualities. In short, Goleman argues that the psychological make-up of a leader matters.

Strategy as an emergent process

The planning model reviewed earlier in the chapter suggests that an organisation's strategies are the result of a plan, that the strategic planning process is rational and highly structured, and that the process is orchestrated and dominated by top management. In recent years, several scholars have advocated an alternative view of strategy making, which questions the traditional view centred on planning.[8] These scholars have three main criticisms of the planning model: (1) the unpredictability of the real world; (2) the role that lower level managers can play in the strategic management process; and (3) the fact that many successful strategies are often the result of serendipity, not rational strategising.

Strategy making in an unpredictable world

Critics of formal planning systems argue that we live in a world in which uncertainty, complexity and ambiguity dominate, and in which small chance events can have a large and unpredictable impact on outcomes.[9] In such circumstances, these critics claim, even the most carefully thought-out strategic plans are prone to being rendered useless by rapid and unforeseen change in the environment. Military historians and thinkers have long recognised this problem. Carl von Clausewitz, the famous Prussian military strategist of the early 1800s, once noted that 'the principles, rules, or even systems of strategy must always fall short, undermined by the world's endless complexities ... in strategy most things are uncertain and variable'.[10] Although von Clausewitz was talking about military strategy, his observations are just as relevant to business strategy. One reason that strategy creation is so difficult is that it involves planning for the future, which is inherently uncertain. In most cases, the very act of implementing a strategy creates changes. Think of airlines in the months after the terrorist attacks in the United States on 11 September 2001. No airline subsequently expected such a radical drop-off in passenger numbers and many airlines ordered new aircraft for future demands. Then one airline suffering a cashflow problem lowered fares to attract new customers in the short term. Strategy is interactive: competitors watched these fare reductions and probably countered in some particular way, perhaps offering further fare reductions or double frequent flyer points for customers who may not have been as price sensitive (such as business travellers). Strategies by one company, therefore, may be counteracted by the strategies of other companies. The process can become similar to a chess game, except that the competition is not limited to a single opponent. In a study of major oil companies, Grant has shown that many firms are moving away from rational design models.[11]

Strategy making by lower-level managers

Another criticism of the rational planning model of strategy is that it attaches too much importance to the role of top management.[12] Hamel certainly builds on this idea, suggesting that top management teams tend to be very homogeneous, and may therefore be incapable of devising truly innovative strategies. Although this is possibly something of an extreme view, it certainly is very common for the members of the top-management team to have similar backgrounds and experiences and, consequently, similar ideas. This is likely to limit the number of different approaches that top management uses to analyse and assess issues. To overcome such problems, Hamel suggests that top management should specifically include three groups of people in the strategic planning process. These are young people, those on the periphery and newcomers into the industry.[13] All of these groups provide an alternative perspective to issues. Young people and newcomers to an industry have not been heavily exposed to unspoken mental models that may dominate top management ranks. People on the periphery, such as those working in locations remote from headquarters or those in a different field to the dominant group (e.g. a technical person in a marketing-driven firm) also bring new perspectives because they see the world through a different lens, such as seeing design problems rather than marketing problems.

The result is that the strategy process is most effective when it is not entirely dominated by top management. Indeed, some firms owe their success to strategies that were developed by people outside of the top management team. EDS, for example, saw a group of middle managers essentially develop a strategy to reposition the firm away from centralised data storage. With a supportive top-management team, they were given the freedom to do the analysis and then build a new strategy that was later adopted by top management. Interestingly, the people involved in the process were diverse in terms of positions and came from a range of geographical locations, rather than being headquarters dominated.

Serendipity and strategy

Business history is replete with examples of accidental events that helped push companies in new and profitable directions. These examples suggest that many successful strategies are not the result of well-thought-out plans, but of serendipity. One such example occurred at 3M during the 1960s. At that time, 3M was producing fluorocarbons for sale as coolant liquid in air-conditioning equipment. One day, a researcher working with fluorocarbons in a 3M lab spilled some of the liquid on her shoes. Later that day, the same researcher spilled coffee over her shoes. She watched with interest as the coffee formed into little beads of liquid and then ran off her shoes without leaving a stain. Reflecting on this phenomenon, she realised that a fluorocarbon-based liquid may turn out to be useful for protecting fabrics from liquid stains. The idea for Scotch Gard was thus born. Subsequently, Scotch Gard became one of 3M's most profitable products and took the company into the fabric protection business, in which it had never planned to participate.[14]

Serendipity can also play a role in determining the industries in which companies end up doing business. As shown in Strategy in action 1.1, Aristocrat, has grown enormously as some gambling has been legalised and deregulated.

The point is that serendipitous discoveries and events are commonplace and can open up all types of profitable avenue for an organisation. As a result, the strategy of many profitable firms is less the product of planning and more the exploitation of serendipity. By the same token, some organisations have missed out on profitable opportunities because serendipitous discoveries or events were inconsistent with their prior (planned) conception of what their strategy should be.

strategy in action 1.1

Aristocrat's gamble pays off

Aristocrat is Australia's largest manufacturer of poker machines and the second-largest in the world behind IGT of the United States. Founded in 1952 by Len Ainsworth, the initial focus was upon servicing New South Wales clubs. Aristocrat's early strategy was to create economies of scale by capturing a large slice of the market. So through the 1950s and into the 1960s Aristocrat took over most of the small players in Australia. In time, this move towards mass manufacturing led the company to overseas markets, including the huge US market.

These international moves were not always easy. Entry into the United States involved changing the board structure and limiting the Ainsworth's family's voting stock. However, in many ways, the biggest growth was to come, not from carefully managed organic growth but rapidly from the legalising and deregulating of poker machines in Australia and elsewhere in the world. For example, in Australia, Tasmania was the only state with a legal casino in the 1970s. However, from the 1980s through to the 1990s, Tasmania was joined by Queensland, South Australia, Western Australia and, more recently, Victoria, then New South Wales. Aristocrat captured much of the new market, to the extent that in 1999, three-quarters of all machines sold in Australia were made by Aristocrat, including the vast bulk of the machines bought by the new big players, Star City Casino, Crown Casino and Tabcorp. Other markets outside Australia, particularly in South America and Europe, were also growing.

This very rapid period of growth did create some problems from having excess inventory and staff. A large sale of machines to Colombia ran into trouble. The shares dived to about 80 cents in late 2002. However, a new CEO in the form of Paul Oneile, a review of some business processes, a reduction in control of the company by Ainsworth family members and further growth in the global market have allowed this company to rise again to see its shares trading at more than $10.

Sources: Masters, R 2005, 'Head of the game', *Sydney Morning Herald*, 15 January, accessed 10 January 2006, www.smh.com.au/news/Business/Head-of-the-game/2005/01/14/1105582714216.html; Dettre, A 2005, 'New broom is sweeping Aristocrat back to the top', *Australasian Gaming Magazine*, February, accessed 10 January 2006, www.australasian-gaming.com.au/articles/23-newbroomsweeping.html.

Intended and emergent strategies

Mintzberg incorporated the ideas discussed so far into a model of strategy development that provides a more encompassing view of what strategy is. According to this model (see figure 1.2), a company's **realised strategy** is the product of any **intended strategies** (those that are planned) that are put into action and of any **emergent strategies** (those that are not planned). In Mintzberg's view, emergent strategies are the unplanned responses to unforeseen circumstances. They often arise from autonomous action by individual managers deep within the organisation (such as Richard Drew at 3M) or from serendipitous events (such as those that led Nokia into mobile phones). They are not the product of formal top-down planning mechanisms.

Mintzberg maintains that emergent strategies are often successful and may be more appropriate than intended strategies. Pascale described how this was the case for the entry of Honda Motor into the US motorcycle market.[15] When Honda executives arrived in Los Angeles from Japan in 1959 to establish a US subsidiary, their original aim (intended strategy) was to focus on selling 250-cc and 350-cc machines to confirmed motorcycle enthusiasts, rather than 50-cc Honda Cubs, which were a big hit in Japan. Their instinct told them that the Honda 50s were not suitable for the US market, where everything was bigger and more luxurious than in Japan.

realised strategy
Strategy that is implemented. It may be a combination of intended and emergent strategies.

intended strategy
Planned strategy for the future that an organisation develops on the basis of a series of analyses

emergent strategy
Strategy that evolves (that is, it is not planned) in an organisation on the basis of actions that the organisation takes in reaction to internal and external pressures

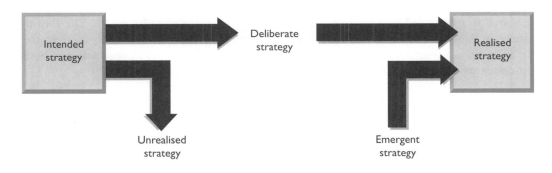

Figure 1.2:
Intended and emergent strategies

Source: H Mintzberg & A McGugh, 'Strategy formation in an adhocracy', *Administrative Science Quarterly*, vol. 30, no. 2, 1985. Reprinted by permission of *Administrative Science Quarterly*.

Sales of the 250-cc and 350-cc bikes were sluggish, however, and the bikes were plagued by mechanical failure. It looked as though Honda's strategy was going to fail. At the same time, the Japanese executives were using the Honda 50s to run errands around Los Angeles, attracting a lot of attention. They received a call from a Sears Roebuck buyer, who wanted to sell the 50-cc bikes to a broad market of Americans who were not necessarily already motorcycle enthusiasts. The Honda executives were hesitant to sell the small bikes for fear of alienating serious bikers, who might then associate Honda with 'wimpy' machines. In the end, they were pushed into doing so by the failure of the 250-cc and 350-cc models. The rest is history. Honda had stumbled onto a previously untouched market segment that was to prove huge: the average American who had never owned a motorbike. Honda had also found an untried channel of distribution: general retailers rather than specialty motorbike stores. By 1964, nearly every motorcycle sold in the United States was a Honda.

The conventional explanation of Honda's success is that the company redefined the US motorcycle industry with a brilliantly conceived intended strategy. The truth was that Honda's intended strategy was a near disaster. The emergent strategy was not a result of planning but an unplanned action taken in response to unforeseen circumstances. Nevertheless, the Japanese management can be credited with recognising the strength of the emergent strategy and pursuing it with vigour.

The critical point demonstrated by the Honda example is that successful strategies can emerge — in contrast to the view that all strategies are planned — without prior planning, often in response to unforeseen circumstances. As Mintzberg noted, strategies can take root in strange places, virtually wherever people have the capacity to learn and the resources to support that capacity.

In practice, the strategies of most organisations are probably a combination of intended (planned) and emergent strategies. The message for management is that it needs to recognise the process of emergence and intervene when appropriate, killing off poor emergent strategies but nurturing potentially good ones.[16] To make such decisions, however, managers must be able to judge the worth of emergent strategies. They must be able to think strategically. Even though emergent strategies arise from within the organisation without prior planning — that is, without sequentially moving through the steps illustrated in figure 1.1 — top management still has to evaluate emergent strategies. Such evaluation involves comparing each emergent strategy with the organisation's goals, external environmental opportunities and threats, and internal strengths and weaknesses. The objective is to assess whether the emergent strategy fits the organisation's needs and capabilities. In addition, Mintzberg stresses that an organisation's capability to produce emergent strategies is a function of the kind of corporate culture fostered by the organisation's structure and control systems.

In other words, the different components of the strategic management process are just as important from the perspective of emergent strategies as they are from the perspective of intended strategies. The essential differences between the strategic management process for intended strategies and that for emergent strategies are illustrated in figure 1.3. The formulation of intended strategies is basically a top-down, planning-driven process, whereas the formulation of emergent strategies is a bottom-up process. In successful organisations, both processes are often at work.[17]

Strategic planning in practice

Even the most vocal critics of formal strategic planning concede that it has a role. Mintzberg's model of strategy making (see figure 1.3), for example, maintains a role for formal strategic planning, while simultaneously pointing to the importance of unplanned emergent strategies. Given that formal strategic planning is still widely practised, and rightly so, it is pertinent to ask whether formal planning systems help an organisation attain superior performance.

The research evidence seems to indicate that formal planning systems help companies make better strategic decisions. A study analysed in detail the results of 26 previously published studies of the relationship between strategic planning and company performance.[18] The authors concluded that strategic planning, on average, has a positive impact on company performance, suggesting that strategic planning is a valuable activity.

Despite such results, many informed observers have increasingly questioned the use of formal planning systems as an aid to strategic decision-making. Peters and Waterman, authors of the bestseller *In search of excellence*, were among the first to question the usefulness of formal planning systems. The anti-planning rhetoric continues to be a theme in the more recent works of Peters.[19] Similarly, Mintzberg argues that business history is filled with examples of companies that have made poor decisions on the basis of supposedly comprehensive strategic planning.[20] The fundamental criticisms of formalised strategic planning systems come down to four basic reasons, of which three are considered here: (1) planning under uncertainty, (2) top-down ivory tower planning and (3) planning for the present, as opposed to the future, and ways offered of dealing with them. The fourth explanation, which focuses on decision-making biases among managers, is taken up in the next section.

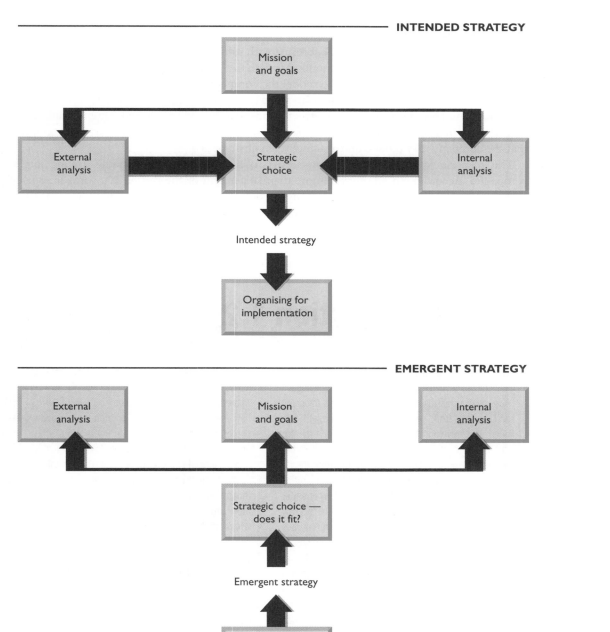

Mission
and goals

External
analysis

Strategic
choice

Internal
analysis

Intended strategy

Organising for
implementation

EMERGENT STRATEGY

External
analysis

Mission
and goals

Internal
analysis

Strategic choice —
does it fit?

Emergent strategy

Organisational
grassroots

Figure 1.3:
The strategic management
process for intended and
emergent strategies

Planning under uncertainty

One reason for the poor reputation of strategic planning is that many executives, in their initial enthusiasm for planning techniques, forget that the future is inherently unpredictable. In the real world, the only constant is change. Even the best-laid plans can fall apart if contingencies occur and, as noted, unforeseen events occur all the time.

Scenario planning

Recognising that the future cannot be forecast with sufficient accuracy in an uncertain world, Royal Dutch/Shell pioneered the scenario approach to planning. Rather than trying to forecast the future, Shell's planners attempt to model the company's environment and use that model to predict possible scenarios. Executives are asked to devise strategies to cope with the different scenarios. The objective is to get managers to understand the dynamic and complex nature of their environment, to think through problems strategically, and to generate strategic options that the company may pursue under different circumstances.[21]

The scenario approach to planning seems to have spread quite rapidly among large companies. According to one survey, more than 50 per cent of the *Fortune* 500 companies use some form of scenario planning.[22] Although a detailed evaluation of the pros and cons of scenario planning has yet to appear, Schoemaker of the University of Chicago suggests that scenario planning expands people's thinking and, as such, may lead to better plans, as seems to have occurred at Shell. Schoemaker cautions, however, that forcing planners to consider extreme scenarios that are unbelievable can discredit the approach and create resistance from the planners.

strategy in action 1.2

Scenario planning in action

The Scenario Planning and Research Unit (SPARU) at Curtin University of Technology (in Western Australia) undertakes projects for both for-profit and not-for-profit organisations. One project has been the development of possible scenarios for the future of the City of Mandurah. Mandurah is the fastest-growing region in Australia but this growth is creating a large social divide. Traditionally, many people have been attracted to Mandurah by cheaper land prices than those in nearby Perth. More recently though, it has seen a huge influx of wealthy retirees and lifestyle-oriented people, which has driven up house prices enormously in some areas. SPARU worked with a range of different stakeholder groups to generate scenarios to help in planning for the future. It collected information in seven main areas: the impact of technology, sustainable economic development, leadership and governance, resource management, social issues, training and education, and community identity.

The result was the creation of four scenarios. SPARU did not try to predict the future but rather provided alternative scenarios against which major planning decisions could be tested. The four scenarios were:

- *Southern Comfort — a dynamic city*. The city would develop an economy distinct from Perth's,

and simultaneously keep its present distinct 'feel'.
- *Tale of Two Cities — a dormitory suburb of Perth*. Few new businesses are created and growth comes from people working in Perth and relying upon the new train link to allow them to have a coastal lifestyle at a cheaper price. The city takes on a suburban feel with social divides between those with money and those without becoming more pronounced.
- *Winds of Change — a regional city*. Without any industrial land for heavy industry, the city ends up with many small businesses. Economically, the city never really takes off and it moves towards attracting people (including retirees) as a lifestyle location.
- *Downward Spiral — growth slows*. The major employer in the area closes and the region faces environmental problems including a resurgence of the algal bloom problem. The local housing bubble bursts and social problems grow as the economy stalls and local services are cut.

Source: Scenario Planning and Research Unit (Curtin University of Technology) 2000, *Future Perth: scenarios for our future*, Report for the Western Australian Planning Commission, Perth.

Ivory tower planning

A serious mistake made by many companies in their initial enthusiasm for planning is to treat planning as an exclusively top-management function. This ivory tower approach can result in strategic plans that are formulated in a vacuum by planning executives who have little understanding or appreciation of operating realities. Consequently, the executives formulate strategies that do more harm than good. When demographic data indicated that houses and families were shrinking, planners at General Electric's appliance group concluded that smaller appliances were the wave of the future. Because the planners had little contact with home builders and retailers, they did not realise that kitchens and bathrooms were the two rooms that were not shrinking. Furthermore, they did not appreciate that consumers wanted big refrigerators to cut down on trips to the supermarket. The result was that General Electric wasted a lot of time designing small appliances for which there was only limited demand.

Involving operating managers

Correcting the ivory tower approach to planning involves recognising that strategic planning, to succeed, must encompass managers at all levels of the organisation. Operating managers can and should do much of the best planning. They are closest to the facts. The role of corporate-level planners should be to help operating managers to plan by both setting the broad strategic goals of the organisation and providing operating managers with the resources required to identify the strategies to attain those goals.

Procedural justice

It is not enough just to involve lower-level managers in the strategic planning process. They also need to perceive that the decision-making process is just and fair. Kim and Mauborgne have written extensively about the importance of procedural justice in strategic decision making.[23] They define procedural justice as the extent to which the dynamics of a decision-making process are judged to be fair. If people perceive the decision-making process to be unjust, then they are less likely to be committed to any resulting decisions and to cooperate voluntarily in activities designed to implement those decisions. Consequently, their performance is likely to be below par. In short, a strategy based on a decision-making process that is perceived to be procedurally unjust may fail for lack of support among those who must implement it at the operating level (see 'Strategy in action 1.3', page 20).

Three criteria have been found to influence the extent to which strategic decisions are perceived as just: engagement, explanation and clarity of expectations.[24] *Engagement* means involving individuals in the decision-making process, both by asking them for their input and by allowing them to refute the merits of each other's ideas and assumptions. *Explanation* means telling everyone involved the underlying rationale for strategic decisions, and explaining why a decision might have overridden the ideas and inputs of individuals. *Clarity of expectations* means ensuring — before, during and after strategic decisions are made — managers have a solid understanding of what is expected of them and what the new 'rules of the game' are. By paying close attention to engagement, explanation and clarity of expectations, managers can greatly increase the likelihood that the strategic decision-making process is perceived as just, even when it overrides individuals' ideas and input. This perception increases the probability that individuals will cooperate as fully as possible in implementing those decisions. Consequently, company performance is likely to be higher than would have otherwise been the case.

strategy in action 1.3

The concept of implementing decisions that are perceived to be fair, or that run the risk of failure, is not new. The elements of procedural justice as defined by Kim and Mauborgne can explain Napoleon Bonaparte's initial success and later downfall. Some of Napoleon's best-known battle successes were Lodi (1796), Marengo (1800) and Austerlitz (1805). In these battles, Napoleon tended to consult with his senior officers, even changing his plans because of their input. Given that he had less experience, in many cases he relied on his officers to provide him with information such as enemy troop formations and likely tactics. This process of engagement created trust, loyalty and respect among the senior officers. Even when he rejected ideas, he explained why the idea was not going to be implemented, to ensure people did not feel rejected and thus unwilling to contribute again. Before battles, Napoleon would wander among his troops, talking with them about the upcoming battle. He was the first to explain a strategy to his regular troops. Before Austerlitz, for example, he explained how the troops on the right were to feign weakness and withdraw whenever they encountered the Russian and Austrian troops. The advancing enemy would then expose its extended line to Napoleon's cavalry, so he could cut their army in two.

With Napoleon controlling much of Europe from northern Italy to Poland and large parts of Germany, he crowned himself emperor and shut down the French legislative assembly. He withdrew from his generals, who received all orders from Napoleon's chief-of-staff, Berthier. By the time Napoleon set off on his Russian campaign in 1812, he had no direct contact with any of his generals and he overruled all of their suggestions passed on from Berthier, whom Napoleon criticised. Soldiers had no idea what to expect and were throwing away heavy items (including ammunition) to maintain the pace required to achieve their goals before the Russian winter. While Napoleon theoretically won the battles, he lost two-thirds of his force and was forced to withdraw. By the time Napoleon faced the allies at Waterloo, he had not learned from the disastrous Russian campaign. He did not inform generals of the details of his strategy, and dismissed the information that Wellington and Blücher's armies were planning to converge as trivial. Although Napoleon's strategy was superior and could have led to a French win, Napoleon's generals failed to understand it as a whole and thus never appropriately implemented it. Napoleon was exiled to the island of Saint Helena in the South Atlantic, where he died less than six years later.

Sources: Sinha, SA 1999, 'Napoleon Bonaparte: victim of an inferior strategy?', INSEAD case, Fontainebleau, France; Chandler, DG 1973, *The campaigns of Napoleon: the mind and methods of history's greatest soldier*, Macmillan, Basingstoke, UK.

Planning for the present

The traditional strategic planning model reviewed earlier has been characterised as the *fit model* of strategy making because it tries to achieve a fit between the internal resources and capabilities of an organisation, and the external environmental opportunities and threats. Hamel and Prahalad have attacked the fit model as being too static and limiting.[25] They argue that adopting the fit model to strategy formulation leads to a mindset in which management focuses too much on the degree of fit between the *existing* resources of a company and *current* environmental opportunities, and not enough on building *new* resources and capabilities to create and exploit *future* opportunities. Strategies based on the fit model, say Hamel and Prahalad, tend to be more concerned with today's problems than with tomorrow's opportunities. As a result, companies that rely exclusively on the fit approach to strategy formulation are unlikely to be able to build and maintain a competitive advantage. This is particularly true in a dynamic competitive environment, in which new competitors are continually arising and new ways of doing business are constantly being invented.

Hamel and Prahalad note that US companies using the fit approach have been surprised by the ascent of foreign competitors that initially seemed to lack the resources and capabilities to be a real threat. They cite Xerox, which ignored the rise of Canon and Ricoh in the photocopier market until they had become serious global competitors; and General Motors, which initially overlooked the threat posed by Toyota and Honda in the 1970s.

Strategic intent

The secret of the success of companies such as Toyota, Canon and Komatsu, according to Hamel and Prahalad, is that they all had bold ambitions that outstripped their existing resources and capabilities. All wanted to achieve global leadership and they set out to build the resources and capabilities that would enable them to attain this goal. Consequently, the top management of these companies created an obsession with winning at all levels of the organisation, then sustained that obsession over a ten- to 20-year quest for global leadership. Hamel and Prahalad refer to this obsession as strategic intent. At the same time, they stress that strategic intent is more than simply unfettered ambition; they argue that strategic intent also encompasses an active management process, which includes 'focusing the organisation's attention on the essence of winning; motivating people by communicating the value of the target; leaving room for individual and team contributions; sustaining enthusiasm by providing new operational definitions as circumstances change; and using intent consistently to guide resource allocations'.[26] Underlying the concept of strategic intent, therefore, is the notion that strategy formulation should involve setting ambitious goals that stretch a company, then finding ways in which to build the resources and capabilities necessary to attain those goals.

strategic intent
The process of leveraging resources and capabilities to achieve a vision that is precise but very ambitious

Although Hamel and Prahalad aptly criticise the fit model, they note that the two approaches to strategy formulation are not mutually exclusive. All the components of the strategic management process that we discussed earlier (as summarised in figure 1.1) are important. Managers have to analyse the external environment to identify opportunities and threats. They have to analyse the company's resources and capabilities to identify strengths and weaknesses. They need to be familiar with the range of functional-level, business-level, corporate-level and global strategies that are available to them. And they need to have an appreciation for the structures required to implement different strategies. What Hamel and Prahalad seem to be saying is that the strategic management process should begin with challenging goals — such as attaining global leadership — that stretch the organisation. The emphasis then should be on finding the means (strategies) to develop the resources and capabilities necessary to achieve these goals, rather than on exploiting existing strengths to take advantage of existing opportunities. The difference between strategic fit and strategic intent, therefore, may simply be one of emphasis. Strategic intent is more internally focused and concerned with building new resources and capabilities. Strategic fit focuses more on matching existing resources and capabilities to the external environment.

Improving strategic decision making

Even the best-designed strategic planning systems fail to produce the desired results if strategic decision makers do not effectively use the information at their disposal. A good deal of evidence shows that many managers are poor strategic decision makers.[27] The reasons have to do with two related psychological phenomena: cognitive biases and groupthink. Each is discussed in turn, then techniques for improving decision making are considered.

Cognitive biases and strategic decisions

The rationality of human decision makers is bounded by our own cognitive capabilities.[28] We are not supercomputers, and it is difficult for us to absorb and process large amounts of information effectively. As a result, we tend to fall back on certain rules of thumb, or heuristics, when making decisions. Many of these rules of thumb are actually quite useful because they help us to make sense of a complex and uncertain world. Sometimes, however, they lead to severe and systematic errors in the decision-making process.[29] Systematic errors are errors that reappear. They seem to arise from a series of cognitive biases in how human decision makers

cognitive biases
The decision-making errors that arise from how information is processed

groupthink
A process in which all members of a group overlook important elements of information or contradictory views

process information and reach decisions. Cognitive biases lead many managers to make poor strategic decisions. Figure 1.4 presents five well-known cognitive biases. These biases have been verified repeatedly in laboratory settings, so we can be reasonably sure that they exist and that we are all prone to them.[30] The **prior hypothesis bias** refers to the fact that decision makers who have strong beliefs about the relationship between two variables tend to make decisions on the basis of these beliefs, even when presented with evidence that their beliefs are wrong. Moreover, they tend to seek and use information that is consistent with their prior beliefs, while ignoring contradicting information. To put this bias in a strategic context, it suggests that a CEO who has a strong belief that a certain strategy makes sense may continue to pursue that strategy, despite evidence that it is inappropriate or failing.

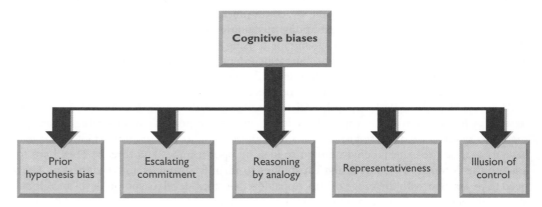

Another well-known cognitive bias is referred to as **escalating commitment**.[31] Escalating commitment occurs when decision makers, having already committed significant resources to a project, commit even more resources if they receive feedback that the project is failing. This may be an irrational response; a more logical response would be to abandon the project and move on (that is, to cut your losses and run), rather than escalate commitment. Feelings of personal responsibility for a project apparently induce decision makers to stick with a project, despite evidence that it is failing. A good example of escalating commitment is the US involvement in Iraq from 2003. A relatively small force was originally used to topple the regime of Saddam Hussein. The real problems began later when insurgents came together in a semi-organised manner to engage in attacks on US-led coalition forces. Other coalition partners withdrew (such as Spain) while the US significantly increased its troop numbers through 2004 and 2005. In business, escalating commitment often occurs in relation to large capital projects, especially complex imformation technology (IT) projects. For example, one Australian steel manufacturer recently implemented an enterprisewide IT system such that all data were linked and updated in real time. The system initially failed to produce the expected results and so more money was spent reorganising the work processes. More and more changes were made, along with changes to the software, until after almost two years and millions of dollars spent, the company gave up and went back to their collection of different nonintegrated IT systems.

The bias of **reasoning by analogy** involves the use of simple analogies to make sense of complex problems. US, Australian and New Zealand policy towards Vietnam in the 1960s, for example, was guided by the analogy of falling dominoes. Policy makers believed that if Vietnam fell to the Communists, the rest of South-East Asia also would fall. The danger of using such analogies is that oversimplifying a complex problem can mislead. Several companies have relied on the analogy of a three-legged stool to justify diversifying into business areas about which they had little prior knowledge. The analogy suggests that a stool with fewer than three legs — and, by extension, a company that is active in fewer than three different businesses — is unbalanced.

Representativeness is a bias rooted in the tendency to generalise from a small sample or even a single vivid anecdote. This bias, however, violates the statistical law of large numbers, which says that it is inappropriate to generalise from a small sample, let alone from a single case. Representativeness may partly explain much of the copycat behaviour by organisations. If one company makes price cuts or vertically integrates, and it is successful, then other companies, which often are in very different situations, may copy these actions. There may be no logic behind the move, other than having seen the first company profit from such a move.

The final cognitive bias is the illusion of control, which is the tendency to overestimate one's ability to control events. Top-level managers seem to be particularly prone to this bias. Having risen to the top of an organisation, they tend to be overconfident about their ability to succeed. According to Roll, such overconfidence leads to what he has termed the 'hubris hypothesis' of takeovers.[32] Roll argues that senior managers are typically overconfident about their abilities to create value by acquiring another company. They end up making poor acquisition decisions, often paying far too much for the companies they acquire. Servicing the debt taken on to finance such an acquisition makes it all but impossible to profit from the acquisition.

Groupthink and strategic decisions

The biases just discussed are individual biases. Most strategic decisions are made by groups, however, not individuals. The group context within which decisions are made is clearly an important variable in determining whether cognitive biases will have an adverse effect on the strategic decision-making processes. Janis argues that many groups are characterised by a process known as groupthink — when a group of decision makers embarks on a course of action without questioning underlying assumptions — that results in many groups making poor strategic decisions.[33] Typically, a group coalesces around a person or policy. It ignores or filters out information that can be used to question the policy and it develops after-the-fact rationalisations for its decision. Commitment is based on an emotional, rather than an objective, assessment of the correct course of action. The consequences can be poor decisions.

This phenomenon may partly explain why companies often make poor strategic decisions despite sophisticated strategic management. Garvin and Roberto suggest that President John F. Kennedy's inner circle suffered from groupthink when it supported the decision to launch the Bay of Pigs invasion of Cuba even though available information showed that it would be an unsuccessful venture and damage US relations with other countries.[34] It has been suggested that Australia's decision to participate in the 'War on terror' in Afghanistan and Iraq may be another example in the way that contrary evidence and public opinion were ignored to support a single view.

Janis observes that groupthink-dominated groups are characterised by strong pressures towards uniformity, which make their members avoid raising controversial issues, questioning weak arguments or calling a halt to softheaded thinking. Examples of groupthink are hard to find because, without access to the actual decision-making process, it is difficult to ascertain when groupthink occurs as opposed to another cognitive bias or when it is just poor decision making.

Techniques for improving decision making

The existence of cognitive biases and groupthink raises the issue of how to bring critical information to bear on the decision mechanism so strategic decisions are realistic and based on thorough evaluation. Two techniques for counteracting groupthink and cognitive biases are devil's advocacy and dialectic inquiry (see figure 1.5), which have been proposed as two means of improving decision making.[35]

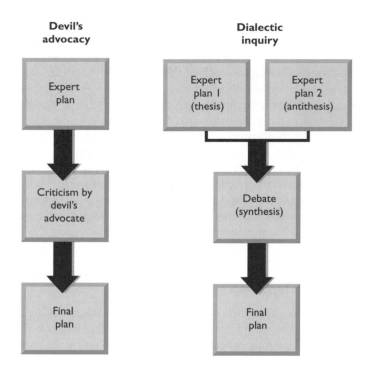

Devil's advocacy

Dialectic inquiry

Figure 1.5:
Two decision-making processes that counteract biases and groupthink

devil's advocacy
The critical analysis of a decision by considering all the potential downsides of the decision

dialectic inquiry
The process of debating two opposing approaches to an issue, so as to generate a single solution from the opposing views

Devil's advocacy requires the generation of both a plan and a critical analysis of the plan. One member of the decision-making group acts as the devil's advocate, noting all the reasons that may make the proposal unacceptable. In this way, decision makers can become aware of the possible perils of recommended courses of action. **Dialectic inquiry** is more complex, because it requires the generation of a plan (a thesis) and a counterplan (an antithesis). According to Mason, one of the early proponents of this method in strategic management, the plan and the counterplan should reflect plausible but conflicting courses of action.[36] Corporate decision makers consider a debate between advocates of the plan and counterplan. The purpose of the debate is to reveal problems with definitions, recommended action and assumptions. As a result, corporate decision makers and planners are able to form a new and more encompassing conceptualisation of the problem, which becomes the final plan (a synthesis).

Summary

This chapter has introduced the basic concept of strategic management. In doing so, it has covered what strategic management is, who develops strategy and what it takes to be successful in implementing strategy. As such, this chapter covered the following important points.

▶ A strategy is an action that a company takes to attain one or more of its goals.

▶ A central objective of strategic management is to identify why some organisations succeed while others fail.

▶ Traditional definitions of strategy stress that an organisation's strategy is the outcome of a rational planning process.

▶ The major components of the strategic management process include: (1) defining the mission and major goals of the organisation; (2) analysing the external and internal environments of the organisation; (3) choosing strategies that align (or fit) the organisation's strengths and weaknesses with external environmental opportunities and threats; (4) adopting organisational structures and control systems to implement the organisation's chosen strategy and (5) evaluating strategy as part of the feedback process.

▶ The key characteristics of good leaders include: vision, eloquence and consistency; commitment; being well informed; a willingness to delegate and empower; astute use of power; and emotional intelligence.

▶ A more recent conceptualisation of strategy suggests that strategy can emerge from deep within an organisation, in the absence of formal plans, as lower-level managers respond to unpredicted situations.

▶ Strategic planning often fails because executives do not plan for uncertainty and because ivory tower planners lose touch with operating realities.

▶ Hamel and Prahalad criticise the fit approach to strategy making because it focuses too much on the degree of fit between existing resources and current opportunities, and not enough on building new resources and capabilities to create and exploit future opportunities.

▶ Strategic intent refers to an obsession with achieving an objective that stretches the company and requires it to build new resources and capabilities.

▶ Despite systematic planning, companies may adopt poor strategies if their decision-making processes are vulnerable to groupthink and if individual cognitive biases are allowed to intrude on the decision-making process.

▶ Techniques for increasing the effectiveness of strategic decision making include devil's advocacy and dialectic inquiry.

Practising strategic management

Review questions

1. What is a company's mission?
2. What is a SWOT analysis?
3. Why does strategic planning often fail?
4. What are the five major cognitive biases?

Discussion questions

5. What do we mean by 'strategy'?
6. When do you think emergent strategies will be more dominant than the intended strategies within the realised strategies? Why?
7. What are the characteristics of a good leader? Using these criteria, assess two political leaders.
8. Why do you think groupthink might be a significant problem within top management teams?

Applied questions

9. Strategy in action 1.2 details a scenario planning exercise conducted for Mandurah. Information was collected on seven main trend areas. Thinking of the town or city where you live, discuss the major trends that are likely to affect that place in each of the seven main areas.
10. Conduct a basic SWOT analysis on an organisation that you know.

Small-group exercise

Designing a planning system

Break into groups of three to five people and discuss the following scenario:

You are a group of senior managers working for a fast-growing computer software company. Your product allows users to engage in interactive role-playing games over the Internet. In the past three years, your company has gone from being a start-up enterprise with ten employees and no revenue to a company with 250 employees and revenue of $60 million. The company has been growing so rapidly that you have not had time to create a strategic plan for where the company is headed, but now your board of directors tells you that it wants to see a plan and that it wants the plan to drive decision making and resource allocation at the company. The board wants you to design a planning process with the following attributes.

1. It will be democratic, involving as many key employees as possible in the process.
2. It will help build a sense of shared vision within the company about how to continue to grow rapidly.
3. It will lead to the generation of three to five key strategies for the company.
4. It will drive the formulation of detailed action plans, which will be linked to the company's annual operating budget.

Design a planning process to present to your board of directors. Think carefully about who should be included in this process. Outline the strengths and weaknesses of the approach you choose, and be prepared to explain why your approach may be superior to alternative approaches.

Article file

At the end of every chapter in this book, you will find an Article file task. The task requires you to search newspapers, journals or magazines in the library for an example of a real company that satisfies the task question or issue. (You may find that you can access articles on the Internet if relevant publications have a website.) Your first Article file task is to find an example of a company that recently changed its strategy. Identify whether this change was the outcome of a formal planning process or an emergent response to unforeseen events occurring in the company's environment.

Exploring the Web

Visiting Foster's

Go to the website of Foster's (www.fosters.com.au) and visit the sections that describe its history. Using the information contained here, map the evolution of strategy at Foster's from a small beer producer to a major alcoholic beverage company. To what degree do you think that this evolution was the result of detailed long-term strategic planning? To what degree was it the result of unplanned actions taken in response to unpredictable circumstances?

Additional resource

Mintzberg, H 1994, 'The rise and fall of strategic planning', *Harvard Business Review*, January–February, pp. 107–14.

Strategic management project

Module 1

To give you a practical insight into the strategic management process, a strategic module is provided at the end of every chapter in this book. Each module asks you to collect and analyse information relating to the material discussed in that chapter. By completing these strategic modules, you will gain a clearer idea of the overall strategic management process. The first step in this project is to pick a company to study. It is recommend that you focus on the same company throughout the book. You will be asked for information about the corporate and international strategy of your company, as well as its structure, so choose a company for which such information is likely to be available.

You can use one of two approaches to select a company to study: your instructor will tell you which one to follow. The first approach is to pick a well-known company that has a lot of information written about it — for example, a large publicly held company such as IBM, Microsoft or Qantas. By going to the library at your university, you should be able to track down a great deal of information on such companies. Many libraries now have electronic data search facilities such as ABI/Inform, Wall Street Journal Index, F&S Index and Nexis. These enable you to identify any article that has been written in the business media on the company of your choice within the past few years. If you do not have electronic data search facilities at your university, ask your librarian about data sources. Nonelectronic data sources are also available. You will also want to collect full financial information on the company that you pick. Again, this can be accessed from electronic databases. Alternatively, your library may have the annual financial reports or other statements pertaining to the company you pick. Again, ask your librarians; they are the best source of information.

A second approach is to pick a smaller company in your town or city to study. Although small companies are not routinely covered in the national business media, they may be covered in the local media. More importantly, this approach can work well if the management of the company agrees to talk to you at length about the strategy and structure of the company. If you happen to know somebody in such a company, or if you have worked there at some point, then this approach can be very worthwhile. It is not recommended, however, that you use this approach unless you can obtain a substantial amount of guaranteed access to the company. If in doubt, ask your instructor before making a decision. The key issue is to ensure you have access to enough interesting information to complete the strategic modules.

Your assignment for module 1 is to choose a company to study and to obtain enough information about that company to carry out the following instructions and answer the following questions.

1. Give a short account of the history of the company, and trace the evolution of its strategy over time. Try to determine whether the strategic evolution of your company is the product of intended strategies, emergent strategies or a combination of the two.
2. Identify the mission and major goals of the company.
3. Do a preliminary analysis of the internal strengths and weaknesses of the company, and of the opportunities and threats that it faces in its environment. On the basis of this analysis, identify the strategies that you think the company should pursue. (*Note:* You will need to perform a much more detailed analysis later in the book.)
4. Who is the CEO of the company? Evaluate his or her leadership capabilities.

End notes

1. Andrews, KR 1971, *The concept of corporate strategy*, Dow Jones Irwin, Homewood, Illinois; Ansoff, HI 1965, *Corporate strategy*, McGraw-Hill, New York; Hofer CW & Schendel, D 1978, *Strategy formulation: analytical concepts*, West, St Paul, Minnesota.
2. ibid.
3. For a summary of research on strategic leadership, see Hambrick, DC 1989, 'Putting top managers back into the picture', *Strategic Management Journal*, Special issue, vol. 10, pp. 5–15. See also Goleman, D 1998, 'What makes a leader?', *Harvard Business Review*, November–December, pp. 92–105; Mintzberg, H 1998, 'Covert leadership', *Harvard Business Review*, November–December, pp. 140–8.
4. Tichy, NM & Ulrich, DO 1984, 'The leadership challenge: a call for the transformational leader', *Sloan Management Review*, Fall, pp. 59–68; Westley, F & Mintzberg, H 1989, 'Visionary leadership and strategic management', *Strategic Management Journal*, Special issue, vol. 10, pp. 17–32.
5. Wrapp, E 1967, 'Good managers don't make policy decisions', *Harvard Business Review*, September–October, pp. 91–9.
6. Pfeffer, J 1992, *Managing with power*, Harvard Business School Press, Boston, Massachusetts.
7. Goleman, op. cit.
8. For details, see Burgelman, RA 1991, 'Intraorganizational ecology of strategy making and organizational adaptation: theory and field research', *Organization Science*, vol. 2, pp. 239–62; Mintzberg, H 1978, 'Patterns in strategy formulation', *Management Science*, vol. 24, pp. 934–48; Hart, SL 1992, 'An integrative framework for strategy making processes', *Academy of Management Review*, vol. 17, pp. 327–51; Hamel, G 1996, 'Strategy as revolution', *Harvard Business Review*, July–August, pp. 69–83.
9. This is the premise of those who advocate that chaos theory should be applied to strategic management. See Stacey, R & Parker, D 1994, *Chaos, management and economics*, Institute for Economic Affairs, London; Courtney, H, Kirkland, J & Viguerie, P 1997, 'Strategy under uncertainty', *Harvard Business Review*, November–December, pp. 66–79.

10. von Clausewitz, C 1976, *On war*, translated and edited by M Howard & P Paret, Princeton, New Jersey, pp. 134, 136.

11. Grant, R 2003, 'Strategic planning in a turbulent environment: evidence from the oil majors', *Strategic Management Journal*, vol. 24, pp. 491–517.

12. Hart, op. cit.; Hamel 1991, op. cit.

13. Hamel, G 1996, 'Strategy as revolution', *Harvard Business Review*, July–August, pp. 69–82.

14. Story was related to Charles Hill by George Rathmann, the head of 3M's research activities at the time.

15. Pascale, RT 1984, 'Perspectives on strategy: the real story behind Honda's success', *California Management Review*, vol. 26, pp. 7–72.

16. This viewpoint is strongly emphasised by Burgelman, RA and Grove, AS 1996, 'Strategic dissonance', *California Management Review*, Winter, pp. 8–28.

17. ibid.

18. Miller, CC & Cardinal, LB 1994, 'Strategic planning and firm performance: a synthesis of more than two decades of research', *Academy of Management Journal*, vol. 37, pp. 1649–65. See also Rogers, PR, Miller, A & Judge, WQ 1999, 'Using information processing theory to understand planning/performance relationships in the context of strategy', *Strategic Management Journal*, vol. 20, pp. 567–77.

19. Peters, TJ & Waterman, RH 1982, *In search of excellence*, Harper & Row, New York; Peters, TJ 1992, *Liberation management: necessary disorganization for the nanosecond nineties*, Knopf, New York.

20. Mintzberg, H 1990, 'The design school: reconsidering the basic premises of strategic management', *Strategic Management Journal*, vol. 11, pp. 171–96; —— 1994, *The rise and fall of strategic planning*, Free Press, New York.

21. Courtney, Kirkland & Viguerie, op. cit.

22. Schoemaker, PJH 1993, 'Multiple scenario development: its conceptual and behavioral foundation', *Strategic Management Journal*, vol. 14, pp. 193–213.

23. Kim, WC & Mauborgne, R 1998, 'Procedural justice, strategic decision making, and the knowledge economy', *Strategic Management Journal*, vol. 19, pp. 323–38; —— 1997, 'Fair process: managing in the knowledge economy', *Harvard Business Review*, July–August, pp. 75, 65–76.

24. ibid.

25. Hamel, G & Prahalad, CK 1994, *Competing for the future*, Free Press, New York.

26. Hamel, G & Prahalad, CK 1989, 'Strategic intent', *Harvard Business Review*, May–June, p. 64.

27. For a review of the evidence, see Schwenk, CR 1984, 'Cognitive simplification processes in strategic decision making', *Strategic Management Journal*, vol. 5, pp. 111–28; Eisenhardt, KM & Zbaracki, M 1992, 'Strategic decision making', *Strategic Management Journal*, Special issue, vol. 13, 17–37.

28. Simon, H 1957, *Administrative behavior*, McGraw-Hill, New York.

29. The original statement about this phenomenon was made by Tversky, A & Kahneman, D 1974, 'Judgment under uncertainty: heuristics and biases', *Science*, vol. 185, pp. 1124–31.

30. Schwenk, op. cit.

31. Staw, BM 1981, 'The escalation of commitment to a course of action', *Academy of Management Review*, vol. 6, pp. 577–87.

32. Roll, R 1986, 'The hubris hypotheses of corporate takeovers', *Journal of Business*, vol. 59, pp. 197–216.

33. Janis, IL 1982, *Victims of groupthink*, 2nd edn, Houghton Mifflin, Boston. For an alternative view, see Fuller, SR & Aldag, RJ 1998, 'Organizational tonypandy: lessons from a quarter century of the groupthink phenomenon', *Organizational Behavior and Human Decision Processes*, vol. 73, pp. 163–84.

34. Garvin, DA & Roberto, MA 2001, 'What you don't know about making decisions', *Harvard Business Review*, vol. 19, iss. 8, pp. 108–16.

35. See Mason, RO 1969, 'A dialectic approach to strategic planning', *Management Science*, vol. 13, pp. 403–14; Cosier, RA & Aplin, 'JC 1980, A critical view of dialectic inquiry in strategic planning', *Strategic Management Journal*, vol. 1, pp. 343–56; Mintroff, II & Mason, RO 1980, 'Structuring III — structured policy issues: further explorations in a methodology for messy problems', *Strategic Management Journal*, vol. 1, pp. 331–42.

36. Mason, op. cit.

Corporate mission, stakeholders, ethics and social responsibility

learning objectives

After studying this chapter, you should be able to:

- identify stakeholders, both internal and external, and conduct a stakeholder impact analysis

- describe the key elements of a vision or mission statement and explain why organisations use these statements

- identify the three key components that can help in defining a business

- describe the corporate governance problem and explain the main corporate governance mechanisms that an organisation can use to counter the problem

- identify the principal philosophical approaches for determining what constitutes an ethical decision

- identify the four basic approaches to corporate social responsibility (CSR) and describe what influences whether a CSR strategy can be applied in the same manner across multiple countries.

opening case

James Hardie

James Hardie is a major producer of building products ranging from concrete pipe to particle board. In the past, it has also been a significant producer of asbestos for internal use, such as insulation, and external use, such as in fences and roofs. However, the deadly nature of asbestos has raised questions whether James Hardie is liable for the products that it has produced. Many believe that James Hardie should be required to pay out many millions, or even billions, of dollars as people who have been exposed to asbestos fibres get the disease mesothelioma.

In 2004, a New South Wales special commission of inquiry heard how James Hardie had restructured its operations in 2001 and moved its headquarters to the Netherlands. This corporate change program saw James Hardie leave Australia but before it did so, it set up a foundation fund that was supposed to be fully funded to pay for all current and future asbestos-related disease claims. Questions were raised in the media about what was the fundamental logic for leaving Australia but the more immediate problem was that the fund was considerably underfunded and, in 2004, it was already approaching the NSW Supreme Court to continue operating even though it was moving towards insolvency.

The special commission of inquiry heard six months of damning evidence against James Hardie, regarding how it had managed its move offshore, used inappropriate models for gauging the required size of the compensation fund and secretly dismantled much of the funds that it put in place. By 17 August 2004, James Hardie's new chair, Meredith Hellicar, had officially apologised for many of the recent actions by James Hardie but there is still the possibility of both criminal and civil charges been brought against some company officers, including a previous chairman and chief financial officer.

While the inquiry was going on, unions and past employees (especially sufferers of asbestos-related diseases) waged a very public campaign against James Hardie. This included a call by Victorian construction unions to place a ban on using any James Hardie products, as well as a broader call to the community at large for all James Hardie products to be boycotted. The political fallout proved to be very costly for James Hardie. They acknowledged the need to provide more funds to compensate current and future victims of asbestos-related diseases. Their reputation was in tatters after having made headlines for all the wrong reasons.

In December 2004, James Hardie signed a heads of agreement with the Australian Council of Trade Unions, Unions of New South Wales and the New South Wales State government. A legally binding principal agreement was due to be subsequently signed in March 2005 — subject to certain conditions. This principal agreement was then delayed to 1 December 2005 due to the complexities of the legal document. While nothing is legally binding until this document is signed, it is likely that given all of the bad publicity James Hardie received in 2004, it will want to try and keep its name out of the press as much as possible in the future.

Sources: Bannerman, J 2004, 'James Hardie apologises for compensation shortfall', *7:30 Report* (transcripts), 17 August, accessed 15 January 2006, www.abc.net.au/7.30/content/2004/s1178820.htm; James Hardie 2005, 'Update on tax condition precedent to final funding agreement', company statement, 16 December; Alderton, R & Robinson, P 2004, 'James Hardie denies all', *The Age*, 30 July, accessed 16 January 2006, www.theage.com.au/articles/2004/07/29/1091080379591.html?oneclick=true; Sexton, E 2005, 'Delays in Hardie compensation', *Sydney Morning Herald*, 31 March, accessed 6 May 2005, www.smh.com.au/news/Business/Delays-in-Hardie-compensation/2005/03/30/1111862462755.html.

stakeholders
Individuals or groups that have an interest, claim or stake in an organisation as a result of either their ability to affect, or their potential to be affected by, the organisation

corporate governance
The mechanisms used within an organisation to determine its strategic direction and ensure that it is consistent with the desires of key stakeholders

Overview

The opening case details how James Hardie has suffered enormous reputational damage because of the six-month special inquiry into compensation of asbestos-related disease sufferers. Different stakeholders in the form of unions, past employees (and their families), the government and the general community was able to place pressure on James Hardie to agree to a compensation scheme that it may not have otherwise agreed to. The case also raises some interesting issues in relation to ethics, such as how responsible is a company, especially if it was unaware at the time of the health risks faced by their employees, customers and general public. The agreement to be signed will cover disease sufferers for a period of 40 or more years. Would an ethical company sign up to such a scheme, especially given the drain on corporate profits that this will produce for present shareholders (many of whom would not have been shareholders when much of the asbestos-based product was sold)?

This chapter is concerned with a series of contextual factors that influence the development of an organisation's strategy from its stakeholders to values, to ethics and finally to CSR. In addition, it considers the role of the organisation's mission or vision and how stakeholder considerations are often incorporated in setting this basic statement that guides what the organisation seeks to achieve. A company's stakeholders are individuals or groups that have an interest, claim or stake in the company, in what it does and in how well it performs.[1] The chapter begins by looking at the relationship between stakeholders and a company. Then it considers the corporate mission statement, which is the first key indicator of how a company views the claims of its stakeholders. The purpose of the mission statement is to establish the guiding principles for strategic decision making. It also explores the issue of corporate governance, that is, the set of mechanisms that are used to 'govern' managers and ensure that the actions they take are consistent with the interests of key stakeholder groups.

The chapter closes with a look at the ethical dimension of strategic decisions and at the growing field of CSR.

Stakeholders

A company's stakeholders can be divided into internal stakeholders and external stakeholders (see figure 2.1). Internal stakeholders are shareholders and employees, including senior management and board members. External stakeholders are all other individuals and groups that have some claim on the company. This group typically comprises customers, suppliers, governments, unions, local communities and the general public.

All stakeholders are in an exchange relationship with the company. Each of the stakeholder groups listed in figure 2.1 supplies the company with important resources (or contributions); in exchange, each expects its interests to be satisfied (by inducements).[2] Shareholders provide the enterprise with capital and, in exchange, expect an appropriate return on their investment. Employees provide appropriate labour and skills and, in exchange, expect commensurate income, job satisfaction, job security and good working conditions. Customers provide a company with its revenue and, in exchange, want high-quality, reliable products that represent value for money, and so on.

A company must take these claims into account when formulating its strategies or stakeholders may withdraw their support. Shareholders may sell their shares, employees may leave their jobs and customers may buy elsewhere. Suppliers may seek more dependable buyers. Unions may engage in disruptive labour disputes. Communities may oppose the company's attempts to locate its facilities in their area, and the general public may form pressure groups, demanding action against companies that impair the quality of life. Any of these reactions can have a serious effect on an enterprise, as Strategy in action 2.1 illustrates.

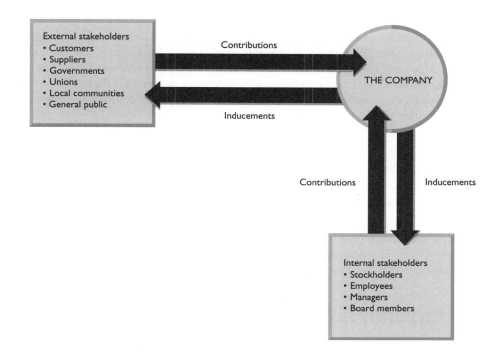

Figure 2.1:
Stakeholders and the
enterprise

strategy in action 2.1

The International Olympic Committee (IOC) is probably unlike just about any other organisation on the planet. It has an annual turnover in the billions of dollars but its accounts are not scrutinised, it has no shareholders and it perceives itself above governments; it is a case of governments pleading their case with the IOC, not the other way round. The IOC is not run along the lines of a United Nations-style organisation, in which each country gets some representation; rather, existing members elect new members and the committee reports to no-one externally. The lack of a need to balance the demands of conflicting stakeholders led to certain IOC members engaging in what many would consider to be unethical practices.

Starting in 1999, details started to emerge about the events surrounding Salt Lake City in the United States being awarded the 2002 Winter Olympics. Investigations found that the children of certain IOC members had been given jobs or college scholarships on the understanding that votes would flow to the Salt Lake City bid. Investigations found that previous bids, such as Sydney 2000, had also involved dubious activities, such as the provision of gifts to IOC members and the creation of 'scholarships' for sporting organisations in poorer countries.

When this scandal first broke with specific details, the IOC was reluctant to do anything about it. It tried to cover up the story and ensure that as few details emerged as possible. It was widely known within the sporting community that these practices had been going on for years and that they were generally considered to be part of doing business with the IOC. As an official investigation of the Salt Lake City bid uncovered more details, however, the pressure on the IOC mounted. This pressure came not from governments or other potential stakeholders — because these groups have never had any power with the IOC — but from the major sponsors of Olympic events, such as McDonald's, IBM and Visa. Not wanting to be associated with an organisation that the average Olympic viewer perceives as corrupt, these sponsors essentially forced the IOC to start its own investigation. Dick Pound of Canada led the investigation, which resulted in seven IOC members being expelled and others being reprimanded. The complete details of the investigation were never released but a code of conduct was put in place for IOC members. This investigation and code of conduct were enough for the major sponsors, which have remained with the IOC. Whether the IOC would have acted without the pressure of the sponsors is an interesting question. Irrespective of the answer, however, this case shows how stakeholders can fundamentally affect how an organisation does business.

A company cannot always satisfy the claims of all stakeholders. The goals of different groups may conflict and, in practice, few companies have the resources to manage all stakeholders.[3] Union claims for higher wages can conflict with, for example, consumer demands for reasonable prices and shareholder demands for acceptable returns. Often, the company must make choices. To do so, it must identify the most important stakeholders and give the highest priority to pursuing strategies that satisfy their needs. Stakeholder impact analysis can provide such identification. It typically follows these steps:

1. identifying stakeholders
2. identifying stakeholders' interests and concerns
3. as a result, identifying the claims that stakeholders are likely to make on the company
4. identifying the stakeholders that are most important from the company's perspective
5. identifying the resulting strategic challenges.[4]

This enables a company to identify the stakeholders most critical to its survival and to make sure the satisfaction of their needs is paramount. Most companies that go through this process quickly reach the conclusion that they must satisfy three stakeholder groups to survive and prosper: customers, employees and stakeholders.

The mission statement

As noted, the corporate mission statement is a key indicator of how a company views the claims of its stakeholders. It describes how a company intends to incorporate stakeholder claims into its strategic decision making and, by doing so, reduce the risk of losing stakeholder support. In its mission statement, therefore, a company makes a formal commitment to its stakeholders, sending out the message that its strategies will be formulated with the claims of those stakeholders in mind.

Most corporate mission statements are built around three main elements: (1) a declaration of the overall vision, or mission, of the company; (2) a summary of the key philosophical values that managers are committed to and that influence the decisions they make and (3) the articulation of key goals to which management believes the company must adhere to attain the vision, or mission, which are consistent with the values to which managers are committed.[5]

Vision (or mission)

The vision, or mission, of a company is what the company is trying to achieve over the medium to long term as formally declared in its mission statement. In practice, the terms 'vision' and 'mission' are often used interchangeably and some companies use the term 'purpose' instead. Boeing states that its mission is 'to be the number one aerospace company in the world and among the premier industrial concerns in terms of quality, profitability, and growth'.[6] BHP Billiton aims 'to create value through the discovery, development and conversion of natural resources, and the provision of innovative customer- and market-focused solutions.'[7] Many companies refer to being a dominant player in their particular industries. This ambition can be part of the process of creating strategic intent. Lesser-known organisations (including not-for-profit organisations) can also set themselves ambitious long-term goals that create a strategic intent. Fosters perceives itself as a global player with a vision of 'being the leading premium branded beverage company'[8] and the Royal New Zealand Foundation for the Blind has a vision of 'New Zealand [being] a country where the rights and responsibilities of blind citizens are equal to the rights and responsibilities of sighted citizens'.[9]

Strategic intent

The concept of strategic intent is introduced in chapter 1. As you recall, its underlying notion is that managers should set an overarching ambitious goal that stretches a company.[10] Often, the vision, or mission, statement articulates the company's strategic intent. Boeing's strategic intent is thus to remain the number one aerospace company in the world, while that of Foster's is to become a global company. To create strategic intent, the company needs to be clear about what it wants to do and where it is aiming. Often, companies tend to put together vision, or mission, statements that say little about their overall goals. As indicated in chapter 1, these generalist statements about creating good returns for shareholders, looking after employees and working with local communities do not create an overarching direction that unites employees in working towards a particular goal. Some companies specifically keep their mission statements broad, to allow them flexibility in what they do, whereas other companies have not thought through exactly where they want to be and how they will get there. For an example of a broad vision statement, see figure 2.2.

Rio Tinto's vision

Rio Tinto is a world leader in finding, mining and processing the earth's mineral resources.
In order to deliver superior returns to our shareholders over many years, we take a long term and responsible approach to exploring for first-class orebodies and developing large, efficient operations capable of sustaining competitive advantage.
In this way, we help to meet the global need for minerals and metals which contribute to essential improvements in living standards, as well as making a direct contribution to economic development and employment in those countries in which we invest.
Wherever we operate, we aim to work as closely as possible with our hosts, and strive to respect laws and customs, minimise adverse impacts, and ensure transfer of benefits and enhancement of opportunities.
We believe that our competitiveness and future success depend not only on the unrivalled quality and diversity of our assets but also on our record as good neighbours and partners around the world.
Accordingly, we set ourselves high environmental and community standards.
Our commitment to health, safety and the enhancement of the skills and capabilities of our employees is second to none.
We seek to make lasting contributions to local communities and to be sensitive to their culture and way of life.

Figure 2.2:
Rio Tinto's vision

Source: Rio Tinto, *Annual report*, Melbourne, 2002.

Strategic intent requires, however, that companies are precise in their goals where the targets are ambitious. The arguments for setting an overarching stretch goal are that (1) it gives a sense of direction and purpose to those within the company; (2) it helps drive strategic decision making and resource allocation; and (3) it forces managers within the company to look for significant improvements in how they run the business because that is the only way to attain stretch goals. Put differently, as Jack Welch, former CEO of General Electric, observed:

> If you don't demand something out of the ordinary, you won't get anything but ordinary results ... We used to say nudge the peanut along, moving from, say, 4.73 inventory turns to 4.91. Now we want big stretch results like ten turns or fifteen turns.[11]

Managers must also ensure, however, that the vision does not become so grandiose that it cannot be realised and thus loses credibility among employees. A stretch goal has to be attainable, even though it may require managers to strive for extraordinary performance improvements.

Customer orientation and business definition

An important first step in the process of formulating a mission statement is to define the company's business. Essentially, the definition should answer these questions: what is our business? What will it be? What should it be?[12] The responses guide the formulation of a mission statement.

To answer the first question — what is our business? — Abell suggests that a company should define its business in terms of three dimensions: who is being satisfied (what customer groups), what is being satisfied (what customer needs) and how are customer needs being satisfied (by what skills or distinctive competencies)?[13] Figure 2.3 illustrates these three dimensions.

Figure 2.3:
Abell's framework for defining the business

Source: Based on *Defining the business: the starting point of strategic planning* by Derek F. Abell, © Pearson Education.

consumer-oriented
Focusing on the consumer, in terms of who they are, what they seek and how their needs are satisfied

product-oriented
Focusing on the product, in terms of what products are sold into which markets

Abell's approach stresses the need for a **consumer-oriented**, rather than a **product-oriented**, business definition. A product-oriented business definition focuses just on the products sold and the markets served. Abell maintains that this approach obscures the company's function, which is to satisfy consumer needs. A product is only the physical manifestation of applying a particular skill to satisfy a particular need for a particular consumer group. In practice, that need can be served in different ways. A broad consumer-oriented business definition that identifies these ways can safeguard companies from being caught unaware by major shifts in demand. By helping anticipate demand shifts, Abell's framework can help companies capitalise on the changes in their environment. It can help answer the second question: what will our business be?

The need to take a consumer-oriented view of a company's business has often been ignored. History is littered with the wreckage of once great corporations that did not define their business or that defined it incorrectly. Kodak, for example, was very slow to move into the digital photography area because its concept of photography was built around chemical film. It was only as its sales started to drop in relation to film that it made any serious attempts to move to digital technology. If Kodak had used Abell's framework to appreciate that customers sought to capture an image, rather than conceptualising the industry in terms of cameras and film, it might have moved more quickly into digital photography, as well as into related imagery-based areas such as video cameras. Instead, Kodak was left behind and is still trying to catch up to many digital camera specialists.

In contrast, Foster's has been willing to change because it has perceived that customer demands are changing. Initially, it based its international growth strategy on lagers, which were increasing in popularity relative to ales and bitters in the prime export market of the UK. Once entrenched in the UK, Foster's expanded throughout the world. Since the mid-1980s, however, the demand for beer has been decreasing in many of Foster's' key markets, while the demand for wine has been rapidly increasing. The company's response was to make a series of acquisitions in the wine industry, including the purchase of Beringer Wines Estates in California and Southcorp in Australia. With these acquisitions, Foster's has more than half of its business in wine and has redefined itself away from being a beer company to being an alcoholic beverages company (beer and wine).

The third question — 'what should our business be?' — can also be answered using Abell's framework. Foster's decided it should be in wine as well as beer. Other firms have fundamentally altered the business they were in to cater for changing customer demands. IBM has moved from making most of its revenue in computer hardware to being primarily in consulting. Telstra is moving into data services, away from just basic telecommunications. Kodak is moving from chemical-based photography products into digital photography. Nokia has gone from manufacturing commodity-style products into mobile telecommunications.

Values

The values of a company state how managers intend to conduct themselves, how they intend to do business, and what kind of organisation they want to build. Insofar as they direct behaviour within a company, values are seen as the bedrock of a company's organisational culture and a driver of its competitive advantage.[14] (Chapter 12 deals in depth with the issue of organisational culture.) Figure 2.2 shows the vision statement of Rio Tinto. Dissimilarly to many organisations that seem to focus almost entirely on success — where success is defined by market position (preferably at the top of an industry) or returns to shareholders — Rio Tinto has a vision that extends to employees, local communities and the environment. The company has articulated this vision by ensuring its standards are consistent around the world, that is, its safety and environmental standards are the same in Indonesia as in Australia. To reinforce this approach, up to 30 per cent of a manager's salary is determined by the implementation and achievement of established safety levels. This shift to more uniform approaches to nonbottom-line items is becoming more widespread but mining companies still more commonly adopt one set of rules for safety and environmental issues in a developed country and another less strict set for their operations in less-developed countries. These dual standards open up a company to considerable criticism and it can take years for a business's public image to recover from such criticism (as experienced by Nike).

A set of values does not have to be articulated in formal documents to determine fundamentally how a company operates. It is possible to establish the inherent values of an organisation by looking at the strategies that it puts in place, the behaviour of rapidly rising stars in the organisation or the behaviour of the top managers. Strategies built around a low-cost position, involving a high level of use of casual workers as opposed to full-time employees and regular layoffs, give clues to the underlying values of the company. Similarly, if managers rapidly moving up the company demonstrate a strong team orientation, a willingness to share information and a desire to help those around them to improve their skills, then this behaviour also indicates the organisation's underlying values.

The values that operate within an organisation can have a major impact on how various stakeholders view the company and organisations often make mention of how they wish to interact with key stakeholders such as employees, customers, government and the local community in which they operate.

In one study of organisational values, researchers identified a set of values associated with 'high-performing organisations' that help companies, through an impact on employee behaviour, to achieve superior financial performance.[15] Not surprisingly, these values include respect for the interest of key stakeholders, particularly customers, employees, suppliers and shareholders. They also include respect for, and encouragement of, the assumption of leadership and entrepreneurial behaviour by mid-level and lower-level managers, and respect for, and a willingness to support, efforts at change within the company. According to the authors of such studies, Hewlett-Packard and PepsiCo are among the companies that emphasise such values consistently.

The study mentioned also identified the values of poorly performing companies. These values, as may be expected, are not articulated in company mission statements. They include: arrogance, particularly towards ideas from outside the company; a lack of respect for key shareholders such as customers, employees, suppliers and shareholders and a history of resisting efforts at change and 'punishing' mid-level and lower-level managers who show 'too much leadership'. The authors depict General Motors as one such company, noting that mid-level and lower-level managers there who showed too much leadership and initiative were not promoted.

Goals

goal
An objective that an organisation seeks to achieve at some point in the future

Having stated a vision founded on a consumer-oriented definition of the company's business and having articulated some key values, the company can take the next step in the formulation of a mission statement: establishing major goals. A **goal** is a desired future state that a company attempts to realise. In this context, the purpose of setting goals is to specify with precision what must be done if the company is to attain its mission. Qantas has managed to be one of the more successful international airlines of late, largely due to its ability to cut costs as part of its Sustainable Future Program. In 2003, Qantas set itself the goal of cutting costs by $350 million in 2003–04 and by a further $500 million in 2004–05. The savings were to come from a reduction in staff numbers (both voluntary and involuntary redundancy) and retirement of some older, more inefficient aircraft.[16] The program has since been extended and a further $1.5 billion in savings is sought in the 2005–06 and 2006–07 financial years.

Goal characteristics

To be meaningful, goals should have four main characteristics.[17] First, well-constructed goals are *precise and measurable*. If a goal cannot be stated precisely and measured, then the company will be unable to assess its progress towards attaining that goal. Measurable goals give managers a yardstick for judging their performance.

Second, well-constructed goals *tackle important issues*. To maintain focus, a company should operate with a limited number of major goals. Therefore, the goals that are selected should all be important ones. In the case of Coles-Myer, the need to cut head-office expenses was perceived as critical. Given that head-office staff are inherently support staff and consequently create no value by themselves, reducing their number was considered to be one way to make the organisation more 'lean' and improve the bottom line.

Third, well-constructed goals are *challenging but realistic*. Challenging goals give managers an incentive to look for ways of improving the operations of a company. If, however, a goal is unrealistic in the challenges it poses, then employees may give up, whereas a goal that is too easy may fail to motivate managers and other employees.[18] Again, Coles-Myer can serve as an example. Achieving cost savings through more efficient supply chain management of $90 million is a challenging goal but one that managers within the company perceive to be realistic.

Fourth, well-constructed goals should, when appropriate, *specify a period* in which they ought to be achieved. As discussed, Qantas set out to achieve cost savings of close to $1 billion through their Sustainable Future Program. The result was actually greater than anticipated with the company saving $1.5 billion over three years.[19] Time constraints are important because they tell employees that success requires a goal to be attained by a given date, not after that date. Deadlines can inject a sense of urgency into the pursuit of a goal and act as a motivator.

Not all goals, however, require time constraints. Coles-Myer's goal of restoring and growing shareholder returns does not have a timeframe attached to it. It is a permanent goal (at least among current management) that will help to focus all of the other activities undertaken by the company.

To this point, the chapter has considered the goals of companies that seek to make a profit. In many respects, these are relatively simple examples because it is far easier to create definable, measurable goals when there is a clear desired objective: profit. What about goals for organisations that are not designed to make a profit? How do you construct goals for government organisations, schools or social justice organisations? The goals for these types of organisation still need to have the characteristics discussed (that is, be precise, tackle important issues, be challenging and occur over a specific period). Working out an overarching direction, however, is more difficult. Coles-Myer sought to increase shareholder returns but the Brisbane City Council has a vision that is not as singularly focused. In its Living in Brisbane — 2010 plan, the council has specific goals in different areas, such as 'a clean and green city' and 'a prosperous city'. In relation to 'a clean and green city', the council has goals that relate to specific improvements in air and water quality, waste management and land use. These goals are mostly written in a measurable format, such as to increase journeys taken using public transport by 7 per cent. Goals for not-for-profit organisations are therefore just as necessary and need to have the characteristics of all good goals; their focus, however, reflects a lack of emphasis on achieving a profit.

As discussed in chapter 10, goals provide a useful way of evaluating the performance of managers. Goals tend to be built into a company's control systems through mechanisms such as key performance indicators, allowing stakeholders to assess the company's performance in relation to the company's key objectives.

Maximisation of shareholder returns

Although most profit-seeking organisations operate with a variety of corporate goals, within a public corporation — at least in theory — many of these goals are directed towards maximising shareholder returns. A company's shareholders are its legal owners. Consequently, an overriding goal of most corporations is to maximise shareholder returns, which means increasing the long-term returns earned by shareholders from owning shares in the corporation.

Shareholders receive returns in two ways: from dividend payments and from capital appreciation in the market value of a share (that is, by increases in stock market prices). A company can best maximise shareholder returns by pursuing strategies that maximise its own profitability, as measured by the rate of return that the company achieves on its investments in plant, equipment, research and development (R&D), and the like, that is, its rate of return on investment (ROI). In general, the more efficient a company becomes, the higher will be its ROI; moreover, its future prospects will look better to shareholders, and it will have a greater ability to pay dividends. Furthermore, a higher ROI leads to greater demand for a company's shares, bidding up the share price and leading to capital appreciation.

The short-term problem

There is an important danger associated with overemphasising a return on investment goal.[20] The overzealous pursuit of ROI can encourage managers to maximise short-term rather than long-term returns. A short-term orientation may encourage such misguided managerial action as cutting expenditures that are judged to be nonessential in the short term, for example expenditures for R&D, marketing and new capital investments, which are vital in the long term. Although cutting current expenditures increases current ROI, the resulting underinvestment, lack of innovation and poor market awareness jeopardise long-term ROI. Despite these negative consequences, managers may make such decisions because the adverse effects of a short-term orientation may not materialise and become apparent to shareholders for several years, or because they are under extreme pressure to achieve short-term ROI goals.

In a famous *Harvard Business Review* article, Hayes and Abernathy argue that the historically widespread focus on short-term ROI was a major contributing factor in the loss of international competitiveness by US companies.[21] Massachusetts Institute of Technology economist Thurow likewise faulted the short-term orientation of many US businesses for some of their problems. Thurow claims that many US companies are unwilling to make long-term investments for fear of depressing their short-term ROI. He cites declining expenditures for R&D and reduced innovative activity within US enterprises as evidence of this orientation.[22] Similarly, after a detailed study of productivity problems in US industry, the MIT Commission on Industrial Productivity concluded that the short time horizons of many corporations placed them at a competitive disadvantage to their foreign rivals.[23]

Most economies that have structural characteristics similar to those of the US economy in terms of the operation of share markets also face this short-term problem. Australia, New Zealand and the UK, for example, have similar problems. Management tends to take a perspective that long-term investments are not going to benefit the company in their tenure and with constant pressures for results now rather than years down the track, that success means success today. As we discuss in the coming pages, managers do not always do what is best for the company because they can be directed by self-interest to make decisions that benefit themselves. Companies' response to this problem has been to make a significant part of managers' salaries dependent on measurables such as increases in the share price and level of profits. In fixing one problem (ensuring managers' actions are consistent with the best interests of shareholders), however, the company may increase the short-term problem. The quickest way to drive up profits and the share price is to reduce investments that pay off only in the long term (such as expenditure on R&D, new product development and even staff training). In comparison, this short-term problem is not always prevalent in many Asian economies, such as Japan's. Most shares in Japan are held by other companies. In many cases, there are cross-holdings among companies, with the most famous examples being the *keiretsus*, in which a group of companies closely affiliate with each other (often centred round a major bank). There are six major *keiretsus* in Japan, with 60 per cent of all companies listed on the Tokyo stock exchange being affiliated with or part of these *keiretsus*.[24] Compared with individual shareholders who are often after immediate profits, companies that hold shares tend to take a very long-term view. They cannot buy into and out of other shares easily, given the relationships that underpin the cross-ownership patterns, so they tend to be interested in ensuring a long-term profit maximisation approach to decision making at the companies in which they own shares. At one extreme, therefore, are US, Australian, UK and New Zealand CEOs, who have a tenure of three to five years, whereas companies in Japan are known to have 20-, 50-, or, in the case of Matsushita, 100-year plans. Even companies that are not part of *keiretsus* have a long-term perspective, with top management rarely changing. Sharp Corporation (which does not belong to a *keiretsu*) has had only four presidents (the position equivalent to CEO) since starting in 1912.

Long-term goals

To guard against short-term behaviour, managers need to ensure they adopt goals whose attainment will increase the long-term performance and competitiveness of their enterprise. Long-term goals are related to such issues as customer satisfaction, employee productivity and efficiency, product quality, and innovation. The thinking here is that companies, to attain such goals, have to make long-term investments in plant, equipment, R&D, people and processes. Only by doing so can a company improve its customer satisfaction, productivity, product quality and innovation. Moreover, insofar as the attainment of these goals increases a company's competitive position and boosts its long-term profitability, the company will be better able to maximise the returns from holding its shares.

Corporate governance and strategy

As noted, one of a company's major goals is to give its shareholders a good rate of return on their investment. In most publicly held corporations, however, shareholders delegate the job of controlling the company and selecting its strategies to corporate managers, who become the agents of the shareholders.[25] In this role, managers should pursue strategies that maximise long-term returns for shareholders. Although most managers do this diligently, not all do, and this failure gives rise to the corporate governance problem: managers pursuing strategies that are not in the interest of shareholders.

The corporate governance problem

Why should managers want to pursue strategies other than those consistent with maximising shareholder returns? Some writers have argued that managers are motivated by the desire for status, power, job security and income, as are many other people.[26] By virtue of their position within the company, certain managers, such as the CEO, can use their authority and control over corporate funds to satisfy this desire. CEOs may use their position to invest corporate funds in perks that increase their status — executive jets, lavish offices and an extensive support staff — instead of investing those funds in ways that increase shareholder returns. Economists have termed such behaviour 'on-the-job consumption'.[27]

In Australia, many would consider HIH to be a classic case of on-the-job consumption. The company's executives were still authorising large company-funded parties and gold watches to top managers just days before the company entered liquidation. In the HIH royal commission, it was alleged that fraud, insider trading, misleading the market and using senior company positions for personal benefit took place.[28] HIH collapsed in late 2001 with more than $5.3 billion in debt.

Besides engaging in on-the-job-consumption, CEOs and other senior managers may satisfy their desire for greater income by awarding themselves excessive pay increases. Critics claim that extraordinary pay has now become endemic. They point out that the pay of CEOs has been increasing far more rapidly than that of average workers. For example, in 2004, the average Australian CEO was paid $1.7 million (up from $1.35 million in 2003).[29] In comparison, the average wage for Australian (including all bonuses and overtime) full-time workers hit $53 000 by the end of 2005.[30]

What rankles critics is that the size of some CEO pay packages apparently lacks any relationship to company performance.[31] For example, when National Australia Bank saw its profits drop 52.5 per cent, CEO Frank Cicutto received an increase of 24.7 per cent in remuneration. Similarly, when television broadcaster the Ten Network saw profits dive by more than 80 per cent, the remuneration of its CEO, John McAlpine, increased by 19.3 per cent.[32]

A further concern is that in trying to satisfy the desire for status, security, power and income, a CEO may engage in 'empire building', that is, buying many new businesses to increase the size of the company through diversification.[33] Although the growth may do little to increase the company's profitability, and consequently shareholder returns, it increases the size of the empire under the CEO's control and, by extension, his or her status, power, security and income. (There is a strong correlation between company size and CEO pay.)

Instead of maximising shareholder returns, some senior managers may trade long-term profitability for greater company growth by buying new businesses. Figure 2.4 graphs profitability against a company's growth rate. A company that does not grow is probably missing out on some profitable opportunities.[34] A growth rate of G_0 in figure 2.5 is not consistent with maximising profitability (P_1 is less than P_{max}). A moderate growth rate of G_1, on the other hand, does allow a company to maximise profits, producing profits equal to P_{max}. Achieving a growth rate in excess of G_1, however, requires diversification into areas that the company knows little about. Consequently, it can be achieved only by sacrificing profitability, that is, past G_1, the investment required to finance further growth does not produce an adequate return, and the company's profitability declines. Yet G_2 may be the growth rate favoured by an empire-building CEO, for it will increase his or her power, status and income. At this growth rate, profits are equal to only P_2. Because P_{max} is greater than P_2, a company growing at this rate is clearly not maximising its profitability or the wealth of its shareholders. A growth rate of G_2, however, may be consistent with attaining managerial goals of power, status and income.

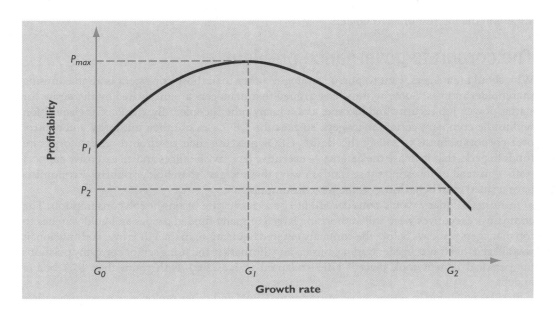

Figure 2.4:
The trade-off between profitability and growth rate

Corporate governance mechanisms

By no means do all managers behave as just outlined. Most act relatively consistently with shareholder interests. Moreover, although some CEOs are overpaid, it could be argued that some deserve their high pay. For some companies, as performance increases, so too do the expectations that are set before some share options or other bonuses become available; so good performance does not always lead to a pay increase. For example, the consistently high-performing Wesfarmers saw its earnings increase 18 per cent and its share price 27 per cent in 2003/04, yet its CEO — Michael Chaney — took home less pay than the previous year. At BHP Billiton, CEO Chip Goodyear received a 13 per cent pay increase, yet for the year the company delivered an 81 per cent increase in profit and its shares increased by 45 per cent.[35]

Nevertheless, given that some managers put their own interests first, the problem facing shareholders is how to govern the corporation to check managerial desire for on-the-job consumption, excessive salaries or empire-building diversification. There is also a need for mechanisms that allow shareholders to remove incompetent or ineffective managers. **Governance mechanisms** allow shareholders to exert some control over managers. They include the board of directors, share-based compensation schemes and corporate takeovers.

Board of directors

governance mechanisms
Mechanisms used within an organisation to ensure the direction set by top management matches that of key stakeholders

The board of directors looks after shareholders' interests within a company. Shareholders elect board members, so, under corporate law, the board represents the shareholders' interests in the company. The board can be held legally accountable for the company's actions. Its position at the apex of decision making within the company allows the board to monitor corporate strategy decisions and ensure they are consistent with shareholders' interests. If the board's sense is that corporate strategies are not in the best interest of shareholders, then it can apply sanctions, such as voting against management nominations to the board or submitting its own nominees. In addition, the board has the legal authority to employ, fire and compensate corporate employees, including the CEO.[36]

The typical board of directors comprises a mix of inside and outside directors. Inside directors are senior employees of the company, such as the CEO. They are required on the board because they have valuable information about the company's activities. Without this information, the board cannot adequately perform its monitoring function. Given, however, that insiders are full-time employees of the company, their interests tend to be aligned with those of management. Outside directors are therefore needed to bring objectivity to the monitoring and evaluation processes. Outside directors are not full-time employees of the company. Many of them are full-time professional directors who hold positions on the boards of several companies. The need to maintain a reputation as competent outside directors gives them an incentive to perform their tasks as objectively and effectively as possible.[37] Critics charge, however, that inside directors may be able to dominate the outsiders on the board. Insiders can use their position within the management hierarchy to exercise control over the kind of company-specific information that the board receives. Consequently, insiders can present information in a way that puts them in a favourable light. In addition, insiders have the advantage of intimate knowledge of the company's operations. Superior knowledge and control over information are sources of power, so insiders may be better positioned than outsiders to influence boardroom decision making. The board may become the captive of insiders and merely rubber stamp management decisions, instead of guarding shareholders' interests.

There are clear signs that many corporate boards are moving away from doing this and beginning to play a much more active role in corporate governance. In Australia, the Corporations Law places considerable expectations upon directors to ensure that they act in the best interests of shareholders (as discussed later). In other jurisdictions, shareholders may sue board members who have not fulfilled their obligations to the shareholders adequately. For example, in 1985 a Delaware (US) court ruled that Trans Union Corporation directors had been too quick to accept a takeover bid. The court held the directors personally liable for the difference between the offer they accepted and the price that the company might have fetched in a sale. The directors then agreed to make up the US$23.5 million difference. Therefore, today, boards rarely recommend against a takeover bid that is launched at a premium to the prevailing share price, unless they are confident of improved company performance in the future. If the takeover bid falls through because a board recommends against the bid, and the share price does not increase to around the level offered in the takeover, then the shareholders could sue the board for recommending a financially inferior option.

Another catalyst has been the growing willingness of some institutional investors (such as the managers of large superannuation/pension funds or mutual funds) to use their shareholding in a company, and the voting power it gives them, to gain seats on the board of directors, or to simply replace existing board members. In Australia, the Australian Shareholders Association occasionally run a campaign against the re-election of certain directors in companies that have performed particularly poorly. By applying large numbers of proxy votes, they are sometimes able to force new directors onto particular companies.

Spurred by the threat of legal action and pressures from powerful institutional shareholders, an increasing number of boards have started to assert their independence from company management in general and from corporate CEOs in particular. Relatively recently, boards of directors have engineered the removal or resignation of CEOs at a number of major companies, including AMP, BHP, Southcorp, Coles-Myer and NRMA, and today the boards of most public companies are dominated by outside directors.

Share-based compensation

As another way in which to align the interests of managers with those of shareholders, and thus solve the corporate governance problem, shareholders have urged many companies to introduce share-based compensation schemes for their managers. In addition to their regular salary, managers are given share options in the company. These options give managers the right to buy the company's shares at a predetermined (strike) price, which may turn out to be less than the market price of the share. The idea behind share options is to motivate managers to adopt strategies that increase the share price of the company, for in doing so they will also increase the value of their own options.

Many top managers earn huge bonuses by exercising share options that were granted several years earlier. While not denying that these options do motivate managers to improve company performance, critics claim that the options are often too generous. A particular concern is that options are often granted at such low strike prices that chief executive officers can hardly fail to make a significant amount of money by exercising them, even if the companies they run underperform the share market by a significant margin. Other critics complain that huge share option grants, by increasing the outstanding number of shares in a company, unjustifiably dilute the equity of shareholders and, accordingly, should be shown in company accounts as a charge against profits.

On the other hand, several academic studies suggest that share-based compensation schemes for executives — such as options — can align management and shareholder interests. One study found that managers were more likely to consider the effects of their acquisition decisions on shareholder returns if they themselves were significant shareholders.[38] According to another study, managers who were significant shareholders were less likely to pursue strategies that would maximise the size of the company rather than its profitability.[39]

Regulations and financial statements

In Australia, the Corporations Law makes it necessary for all company directors to act in the best interests of the company at all times. This lessens the potential for directors to act in their own interest when it is contrary to shareholder interests. The Australian government watchdog for this area is the Australian Securities and Investments Commission. It has pursued several cases of late — such as the action against people involved in the HIH collapse — in which it feels the Corporations Law has been broken. Similar legislation exists elsewhere, such as in the UK and New Zealand.

The Corporations Law is also very strong in relation to the financial information that must be provided to the market. As with most countries, an audited set of accounts must be provided at least annually for all listed companies. However, there are additional regulations that cover the need for firms not to trade while insolvent. Furthermore, firms that look as though they may be heading towards insolvency are often requested to provide quarterly updates regarding their financial position and answer additional questions to show how their cash position is likely to improve. These audited financial statements can then be used by shareholders to determine whether changes are required to realign the interests of the board and its representatives, such as a change in board membership, or whether the executive remuneration system needs to be altered.

Strategy and ethics

Any strategic action taken by a company inevitably affects the welfare of its stakeholders: employees, suppliers, customers, shareholders, the local communities in which it does business and the general public. Although a strategy may improve the welfare of some stakeholder groups, it may harm others. Faced with falling demand and out-of-date technology, BHP

Billiton decided to close its steel mill at Newcastle in New South Wales. The company was a major source of employment in Newcastle, so closing the steel mill set the local community back considerably. Keeping the mill open through cross-subsidisation, however, was not consistent with maximising shareholder returns. Was the closure the right thing to do? Was the decision ethical? Managers must balance these competing benefits and costs. They must decide whether to proceed with a proposed strategy in the light of not only its economic benefits but also its ethical implications, given the potentially adverse effect on some stakeholder groups.[40]

The purpose of business ethics

The purpose of business ethics is not so much to teach the difference between right and wrong as to give people the tools for dealing with moral complexity — tools that they can use to identify and think through the moral implications of strategic decisions.[41] Most of us already have a good sense of what is right and wrong. We already know that it is wrong to lie, cheat and steal. We know that it is wrong to take actions that put the lives of others at risk. These moral values are instilled in us at an early age through formal and informal socialisation. The problem is that although most managers adopt the moral principles, some fail to apply them in their professional life, occasionally with disastrous consequences.

The task of business ethics, therefore, is to make two central points: (1) business decisions have an ethical component and (2) managers must weigh the ethical implications of strategic decisions before choosing a course of action.

Shaping the ethical climate of a company

To encourage an awareness that strategic decisions have an ethical dimension, a company must establish an organisational climate that emphasises the importance of ethics. This requires at least three steps. First, top managers have to use their leadership position to incorporate an ethical dimension into the values they stress. At Hewlett-Packard, Bill Hewlett and David Packard, the company's founders, propagated a set of values known as 'the HP way'. These values, which shape the way in which business is conducted both within and by the corporation, have an important ethical component. Among other things, they stress the need for confidence in, and respect for, people; open communication and concern for the individual employee.

Second, ethical values must be incorporated into the company's mission statement. Third, the company must act on ethical values. Top managers have to implement employment, firing and incentive systems that explicitly recognise the importance of adhering to ethical values in strategic decision making. At Hewlett-Packard, it has been said that it is difficult to lose your job (given the concern for individual employees) but that nothing gets you fired more quickly than violating the ethical norms of the company as articulated in the HP way.[42]

Thinking through ethical problems

Besides establishing the right kind of ethical climate in a company, managers must be able to think through the ethical implications of strategic decisions systematically. Philosophers have debated for centuries about the specific criteria that should be used to determine whether decisions are ethical. Three models of what determines whether a decision is ethical — the *utilitarian*, *moral rights* and *justice* models — are summarised in table 2.1. In theory, each model offers a different and complementary way of determining whether a decision or behaviour is ethical, and all three models should be used to sort out the ethics of a particular course of action. Ethical issues, however, are seldom clear-cut, and the interests of different stakeholders often conflict, so it is frequently extremely difficult for a decision maker to use these models to ascertain the most ethical course of action.

Table 2.1: Comparing utilitarian, moral rights and justice models

Model	Managerial implications	Problems for managers
Utilitarian model: an ethical decision is one that produces the greatest good for the greatest number of people.	Managers should compare and contrast alternative courses of action based on the benefits and costs of these alternatives for different organisational stakeholder groups. They should choose the course of action that provides the most benefits to stakeholders. For example, managers should locate a new manufacturing plant at the place that will most benefit its stakeholders.	How do managers decide on the relative importance of each stakeholder group? How are managers to measure the benefits and harms to each stakeholder group precisely? For example, how do managers choose among the interests of stockholders, workers and customers?
Moral rights model: an ethical decision is one that best maintains and protects the fundamental rights and privileges of the people affected by it. For example, ethical decisions protect people's rights to freedom, life and safety, privacy, free speech, and freedom of conscience.	Managers should compare and contrast alternative courses of action based on the effect of these alternatives on stakeholders' rights. For example, decisions that would involve significant harm to the safety or health of employees or customers are unethical.	If a decision will protect the rights of some stakeholders and hurt the rights of others, how do managers choose which stakeholder rights to protect? For example, in deciding whether it is ethical to snoop on an employee, does an employee's right to privacy outweigh an organisation's right to protect its property or the safety of other employees?
Justice model: an ethical decision is one that distributes benefits and harm among stakeholders in a fair, equitable or impartial way.	Managers should compare and contrast alternative courses of action based on how far the action will promote a fair distribution of outcomes. For example, employees who are similar in their level of skill, performance and responsibility should receive about the same pay. The allocation of outcomes should not be based on arbitrary differences such as gender, race or religion.	Managers must learn not to discriminate among people because of observable differences in their appearance or behaviour. Managers must also learn how to use fair procedures to determine how to distribute outcomes to organisational members. For example, managers must not give people they like bigger raises than they give to people they do not like or bend the rules to help their favourites.

For this reason, many experts on ethics propose a guide to determine whether a decision or behaviour is ethical.[43] A decision is probably acceptable on ethical grounds if a manager can answer yes to each of these questions:

1. Does my decision fall within the accepted values or standards that typically apply in the organisational environment?
2. Am I willing to see the decision communicated to all stakeholders affected by it, for example, by having it reported in newspapers or on television?
3. Would the people with whom I have a significant personal relationship, such as family members, friends or even managers in other organisations, approve of the decision?

strategy in action 2.2

Price fixing at Sotheby's and Christie's

Sotheby's and Christie's are two of the largest fine art auction houses in the world. In the mid-1990s, the two companies controlled 90 per cent of the fine art auction market, which at the time was worth some US$4 billion a year. Traditionally, auction houses make their profit by the commission they charge on auction sales. In good times, these commissions can range as high as 10 per cent on some items but in the early 1990s, the auction business was in a slump, with the supply of art drying up. With Sotheby's and Christie's desperate for works of art, sellers played the two houses off against each other, driving commissions down to 2 per cent or even lower.

To try to control this situation, Sotheby's CEO, Dede Brooks, met with her opposite number at Christie's, Christopher Davidge, in a series of clandestine meetings held in car parking lots that began in 1993. Brooks claims she was acting on behalf of her boss, Alfred Taubman, the chairman and controlling shareholder of Sotheby's. According to Brooks, Taubman had agreed with the chairman of Christie's, Anthony Tennant, to work together in the weak auction market and limit price competition. In their meetings, Brook and Davidge agreed to a fixed and nonnegotiable commission structure. Based on a sliding scale, the commission structure would range from 10 per cent on a US$100 000 item to 2 per cent on a US$5 million item. In effect, Brooks and Davidge were agreeing to eliminate price competition between them, guaranteeing both auction houses higher profits. The price-fixing agreement started in 1993 and continued unabated for six years until federal investigators uncovered the arrangement and brought charges against Sotheby's and Christie's.

With the deal out in the open, lawyers filed several class action lawsuits on behalf of sellers who had been defrauded by Sotheby's and Christie's. Ultimately, some 100 000 sellers signed on to the class action lawsuits, which the auction houses settled with a US$512 million payment. The auction houses also pleaded guilty to price fixing and paid US$45 million in fines to US antitrust authorities. As for the key players, the chairman of Christie's, as a British subject, was able to avoid prosecution in the United States (price fixing is not an offence for which someone can be extradited). Christie's CEO, Davidge, struck a deal with prosecutors and in return for amnesty handed over incriminating documents to the authorities. Brooks also cooperated with federal prosecutors and avoided jail (in April 2002 she was sentenced to three years' probation, six months' home detention, 1000 hours of community service, and a US$350 000 fine). Taubman, ultimately isolated by all his former co-conspirators, was sentenced to a year in jail and fined US$7.5 million.

Sources: Tully, S 2000, 'A house divided', *Fortune*, 18 December, pp. 64–75; Chaffin, J 2002, 'Sotheby's ex CEO spared jail sentence', *Financial Times*, 30 April, p. 10; Thorncraft, T 2001, 'A courtroom battle of the vanities', *Financial Times*, 3 November, p. 3.

Corporate social responsibility

CSR is the sense of obligation on the part of companies to build certain social criteria into their strategic decision making. The concept implies that when companies evaluate decisions from an ethical perspective, they should presume in favour of courses of action that increase the welfare of society at large. The goals selected may be quite specific: to increase the welfare of communities in which a company is based, to improve the environment or to empower employees to give them a sense of self-worth, for example.

In his groundbreaking book on corporate strategy, Kenneth Andrews of the Harvard Business School argues that with respect to developing strategy, strategists consider what the firm might and can do as well as what the firm wants to do.[44] However, he also argues that strategists must address what the firm *ought* to do. The 'ought to do', in Andrews' parlance, refers to CSR. Therefore, CSR is ultimately a strategic issue, one that can not be separated from a firm's overall strategy.[45] Indeed, ignoring CSR can have dire consequences. For example, the total social costs that must be borne by US businesses because socially irresponsible behaviour (e.g. pollution, faulty or dangerous products resulting in consumer injuries, worker accidents caused by poor safety conditions) is estimated at two and half trillion US dollars per year.[46]

Given that CSR and strategy are integral, and if ignoring one's social responsibilities can bring deep financial consequences, then firms have important decisions to make. That is, firms need to decide on the type of CSR strategy they will pursue. Therefore, first, as with any good decision-making exercise, a firm needs to understand what its options are with respect to CSR strategies. However, making a choice with respect to a CSR strategy in one's home base does not necessarily translate into a 'global' CSR platform. Therefore, secondly, firms need to consider the nation of operation in relation to the home country as differences might occasion different approaches from host country CSR strategies.

CSR strategy: what are the options?

Although there are no precise definitions, Archie Carroll, of the University of Georgia, conceptualises CSR in the context of economic, legal, ethical and discretionary (or philanthropic) responsibilities.[47] Georges Enderle suggests firms have three responsibilities to society: (1) economic, (2) social and (3) environmental. The work of Carroll and Enderle is important in that it offers insight into what a firm's responsibilities are. However, their work offers little guidance on what types of strategies a firm might choose to pursue with respect to CSR, so this section describes four strategic options: (1) the shareholder strategy; (2) the altruistic strategy; (3) the reciprocal strategy and (4) the citizenship strategy (see table 2.2).

Table 2.2: CSR strategic options

	Goal	Vehicles	Measurement	Benefactors	Benefits	Time frame
Shareholder Strategy	Profit	Rationalisation; Self-interest	Financial results	Shareholders; Others indirect	Financial	Short-term vision
Altruistic Strategy	Give back	'Check-book' philanthropy	Donations	Community Groups and Causes	Benefits may not be measured	Intermittent; Possibly timed (e.g. annually)
Reciprocal Strategy	Mutual benefits	Public Relations; Sponsorship; Partnerships; Community activity; Volunteering; Cause Related Marketing	Activity-based reporting	The Firm and the Community	Performance; Market Goals; Human Resources	Medium- to long-term planning
Citizenship Strategy	Responsibility; Transparency; Sustainability; Accountability	Governance; Applied Ethics; Stakeholder dialogue; Input to/outflow of Corporate Strategy	Triple Bottom Line; Holistic	To firm: Survival, position role; To partners of all sectors; To wider society	Tangible plus potentially Intangible	Long-term horizon

Used with permission of *Corporate Governance: International Journal of Business in Society.* Galbreath, J 2006, 'Corporate social responsibility strategy: strategic options, global considerations', *Corporate Governance: International Journal of Business in Society*, iss. 3, June.

CSR strategic option 1: the shareholder strategy

The shareholder strategy represents an approach to CSR as a component of an overall profit motive, one that is focused exclusively on maximising shareholder returns. This strategic option is connected with the economist Milton Friedman. Although the rise of investor capitalism and the responsibility to shareholders as the focal concern of managers gained strong momentum in the 1980s, Friedman, concerned with the growth of unchecked and unquestioned demands of CSR, argued decades ago that the only responsibility of business is to provide jobs, make goods and services that are demanded by consumers, pay taxes and make a profit by obeying minimum legal requirements for operation and by engaging in open and free competition without deception or fraud.[48] According to Friedman, by pursuing maximum profit and strict accountability to the owners of capital, the wealth created is sufficient to meet any social responsibilities. Therefore, a business firm that fulfils its profit-maximising obligations not only secures its own survival but also contributes to the overall wealth and prosperity of society. Friedman's argument represents the neoclassical economic concept of self-interest, by the agency of the 'invisible hand', at work in society. However, regulations (e.g. environmental, labour) or legal actions (e.g. shareholder lawsuits) may force firms with a pure profit motive into reactive strategies for CSR.[49] Last, given its pure economic focus, the shareholder strategy is predominantly based on a short-term vision, in that it is primarily concerned with producing better financial results over any given previous period.

Is the shareholder strategy a legitimate strategic option with respect to CSR? Certainly, as individuals who place their capital at risk, shareholders have a right to expect a return on their investment. However, Friedman argues that any use of shareholder funds beyond the means of making a profit is a misuse of those funds. Indeed, if a business is viewed from a property rights perspective, a human rights case may be made against CSR, in that any use of shareholder funds for noncommercial goals means 'robbing' shareholders of the full value of their property rights. Friedman himself offers a caveat in that initiatives focused on social responsibility may be possible but only if they *improve* the *profits* of the firm.

Echoing Milton Friedman's position, some executives plainly see their responsibility to society as nothing more than maximising shareholder value.[50] Furthermore, if a company is small or just starting out, any activity that diverts attention away from making a profit may endanger its survival.[51] Evidence does suggest that smaller firms are not as engaged in socially responsible behaviours (beyond profit maximisation) as larger firms.[52] Although perhaps seen as shortsighted by many, a shareholder strategy, one based on the classic 'Friedmanite' argument, is nonetheless a strategic option with respect to CSR.

CSR strategic option 2: the altruistic strategy
It has been suggested that business *firms* are not responsible to society but rather that the obligation of social responsibility falls upon the *managers* of business firms.[53] That is, although the firm can be viewed as an artificial person,[54] which therefore has the ability to do harm or good, it is ultimately managers that guide the firm's social responsiveness. In this sense, the personal values of managers and even their religious convictions influence strongly how a firm is predisposed toward social responsibility beyond profit maximisation.[55]

In this CSR strategic option, the interwoven relationship between the firm and its community is acknowledged and understood. Furthermore, as a member of the community, the firm recognises that it must 'give something back', in the form of philanthropy, to make a positive contribution to that community. Typically, philanthropic giving comes from a firm's surplus profits and is distributed according to social value and social and moral precepts; surpluses may be channelled to various kinds of social, educational, recreational or cultural enterprises. Although it is hard to identify the real underlying motives, this strategy encompasses 'doing the right thing' by giving back to the community without expecting anything in return. Largely, the altruistic strategy might best be represented as an act of goodwill on the part of the firm, and direct benefits may not be measured. Last, firms adopting this CSR strategy might contribute to social causes on an ad-hoc or intermittently (e.g. after a natural disaster in the community) or they might make recurring contributions (e.g. giving to annual charity events).

CSR strategic option 3: the reciprocal strategy
Perhaps best viewed as 'enlightened self-interest', this CSR strategic option is pragmatic in that it seeks to resolve the conflicts between economic objectives and the intense social, moral and environmental expectations of society. Indeed, based on the public's recent view of business, a firm's survival in modern society seems to require an awareness of social responsibility as an indispensable part of strategy.[56] Therefore, the reciprocal strategy has an interconnected, twofold purpose: (1) to benefit society, while (2) providing an economic benefit to the firm.

In this strategy, firms are more active with respect to social responsibility. For example, an industrial firm that implements environmentally sound manufacturing that goes beyond minimum legal requirements may not only offer improved benefits to society but may also lead to reduced regulatory intervention, which can result in positive economic benefits.[57] Similarly, a pharmaceuticals firm may give to a specific health-related cause (e.g. AIDS research) not only to make a positive contribution to society but to signal that they are a caring employer, benefiting their recruiting efforts, for example.[58]

nongovernmental organisation:
Nonprofit group that combines resource mobilisation, information provision and activism to advocate for changes in certain areas

CSR strategy in this option may also be tied to partnerships, such as between the firm and a specific community group or a nongovernmental organisation (NGO) for the purpose of benefiting social welfare while at the same time benefiting the firm's sales or reputation. Cause-related marketing is also a technique in this strategy and is helpful in that it not only benefits community-based nonprofit organisations and social causes but is designed to increase the firm's product sales or corporate identity.[59]

Recognised as an investment that requires a medium- to long-term horizon to accrue benefits, be they financial or other benefits, such as improved recruitment and retention, CSR in this strategic option has a clear rationale, is generally tied to core business activities and is managed for both firm benefit and positive social returns. To measure the results, activity-based reporting is a requirement in this CSR strategy because firms are more interested in specific bottom-line benefits than in the altruistic strategy.[60] Although not necessarily used for disclosure to the public, activity-based reporting is beneficial in that it allows a firm to track a given CSR investment to an actual return.

CSR strategic option 4: the citizenship strategy

The citizenship strategy takes on a broader scope than the previous strategic options for CSR. Here, a business firm recognises that various stakeholders have different interests and expectations, including customers, employees, suppliers, specific communities, shareholders, the environment and so on. Indeed, this strategy perhaps is best described from a stakeholder perspective.[61] Interestingly, as far back as the 1940s, some scholars suggested that a business firm should be viewed 'as a citizen in society', which has responsibilities to other citizens.[62] Consequently, the citizenship strategy not only recognises its responsibilities to potential external constituents beyond its shareholders but to its internal constituents as well.

To be sure, balancing the competing demands of the various groups that are affected by or have an interest in a firm is a feature of this strategy. However, the reality is stakeholder demands are often mutually exclusive and a firm cannot necessarily treat all stakeholders as equals; therefore, firms may categorise their stakeholders as *primary* and *secondary*.[63] To settle this tension while at the same time trying to be a good corporate citizen, sorting out how to reconcile the various economic and social objectives of stakeholders, although fraught with difficulty, seems to move the firm in the right direction.

By way of example, if a chemical manufacturer implements environmental production standards beyond those that are required by law but, in the process, has to lower wages to its employees to cover the costs, is this good citizenship? In another example, if a financial services firm lays off information technology (IT) employees in its home base of operation to move jobs overseas where IT labour is cheaper but in the process improves the socioeconomic conditions of an emerging foreign economy, is this good citizenship? These examples illustrate the tensions involved in trying to meet the demands of all the firm's stakeholders, particularly in a global context.

To be sure, a key feature of the citizenship strategy is that firms enter into a dialogue with their stakeholders and integrate their findings into decision making. Indeed, in this strategy, stakeholder needs are integral to corporate strategy (as both an input and output) and social objectives are integrated with economic goals. However, given the complexity of managing multiple stakeholder needs, it is recognised that the potential benefits of the citizenship may not quickly materialise; therefore, the citizenship strategy has a long-term focus, even at the expense of weaker short-term results. Furthermore, citizenship strategies develop means of managing and measuring their accountability (e.g. triple bottom line) to those stakeholders. In other words, be it through annual reports, corporate website disclosure or separate triple bottom line reports, firms adopting a citizenship approach are transparent with respect to CSR. Evidence does suggest that a citizenship-type strategy of CSR can offer tangible rewards such as improved financial results as well as intangible rewards, such as outstanding reputations.[64]

strategy in action 2.3

The British-based retailer The Body Shop International is often viewed as a prime example of a company that is committed to being ethical and socially responsible in its business dealings. The company's founder, Anita Roddick, has become an energetic spokesperson for the importance of ethics and social responsibility. The Body Shop competes in the international cosmetics and toiletries market but it offers unique products derived from natural ingredients. The company has based its success on the claim that none of its products is tested on animals or elaborately packaged. The products appeal to consumers who are concerned about animal rights and the environment. Under a program called the Community Trade Program, The Body Shop purchases many of the ingredients for its products from third-world producers at a fair price. It also makes a point of putting money back into the communities where its suppliers are based, to support a variety of health and educational projects. This company commitment to social responsibility helped propel The Body Shop from a single store in 1976 to a global enterprise with more than 2000 stores in more than 50 countries and annual revenue of more than £700 million in 2005.

Roddick's philosophy helped turn The Body Shop into the darling of the business ethics community. The good feeling, however, was rudely shattered in 1994 when a journalist, Jon Entine, published an article highly critical of The Body Shop in *Business Ethics* magazine. Among other things, Entine made the following claims:

- The Body Shop uses many outdated, off-the-shelf product formulas filled with nonrenewable petrochemicals.
- Many of its products are contaminated and contain formaldehyde, which is an artificial ingredient.
- The Body Shop has used ingredients in its products that have been tested on animals.
- Contrary to its claims, The Body Shop sources only a tiny amount of ingredients through its Community Trade Program. Moreover, The Body Shop does not pay 'first world wages for third world products', as it claims in its publicity.
- The company's charitable contributions and progressive environmental standards fall short of its claims. Until 1994, the company never contributed more than 1.24 per cent of its pretax profits to charitable organisations.
- The company invented stories about the exotic origins of some of its products.

Entine's article drew a vigorous response from Gordon Roddick, the chair of Body Shop International. In a ten-page letter sent to all subscribers of *Business Ethics* magazine, Roddick claimed that Entine's article was filled with 'many lies, distortions, and gross inaccuracies ... I am at a loss to find anything balanced or fair in this article'. Roddick went on in the letter to give a detailed rebuttal of Entine's charges. With regard to the Community Trade Program, for example, Roddick observed that Entine's article:

> ... goes after our Community Trade Program, building its attack around an utterly irrelevant statistic — the percentage of our ingredients that come from ... projects. What is this number supposed to reveal? It certainly tells us nothing about the effectiveness of our efforts. Or the amount of time we have put into nurturing these projects. Or the obstacles we have had to overcome due to the lack of infrastructure in disenfranchised Third World communities. ... One single ingredient, such as Brazil nut oil or cocoa butter, may take two years or more to source and develop. Believe me, there are much easier ways to do business than by taking on the problems of such projects. ... We do it because we are asked to help by the disenfranchised communities themselves. The only significant measure of our success is the number of people who are directly beneficially affected by our activities. That is a number, I am proud to say, that runs into the thousands.

The Body Shop followed up Entine's attack by commissioning an independent 'ethics audit' by the New Economics Foundation, a London-based ethics business consultant. Issued in January 1996, the audit reported that 93 per cent of The Body Shop's employees feel the company lives up to its mission to be socially and environmentally responsible and that the purchases from suppliers in developing countries or poor communities increased by more than 30 per cent during 1995. The audit also noted that less than 2 per cent of the company's raw material inputs came from the Community Trade Program in 1995, although about 17.8 per cent of the accessories sold in The Body Shop stores — such as brushes and sponges — came from the program. The company donated 2.3 per cent of its pretax profits to charity in 1995.

Sources: Poe, TP 1996, 'Body Shop comes clean about audit of its operation', *Wall Street Journal*, 26 January, p. B12; *The Economist* 1994, 'Storm in a bubble bath', 3 September, p. 56; Entine, J 1994, 'Shattered image', *Business Ethics*, September–October, pp. 23–8; Roddick, G 1994, The Body Shop International letter to *Business Ethics* subscribers, 22 September; The Body Shop International 2005, *Annual reports and accounts*, accessed 16 December 2005, www.thebodyshopinternational.com/epages/wizard/images/CLIENT811131363170388_lg.pdf.

Although there may be various permutations to these strategic options, they serve as a good guide. Certainly, however, not every firm will develop CSR strategies that perfectly match these options nor will they necessarily maintain the same CSR strategy over time. Furthermore, choosing a strategic option with respect to CSR in one's base of operation does not necessarily translate to equivalent CSR strategies for operating in a global environment.

From home country to host country: global considerations for CSR strategy

Choosing an option with respect to setting the policy for CSR in the home country is one thing. However, although in many cases the drivers (e.g. regulatory, ethical, economic) that serve as the impetus for the development of CSR strategies are the same worldwide, the context of CSR can vary considerably between countries, reflecting the distinctive traits of countries themselves. Furthermore, regional — if not local community — differences all bear on what constitutes socially responsible behaviour of a business firm. Meeting the challenges of CSR in a global context is much more difficult than it seems. Without careful consideration of host country differences, firms might make poor decisions regarding what constitutes appropriate CSR strategies in foreign lands and cultures. This can ultimately undermine both financial results and the firm's reputation.

Within a global context, business firms around the world share common language with respect to products, production, marketing, finance, profits and so on. However, they are inevitably embedded in a specific city, city-state, city-province, city-nation. For example, firms such as Coca-Cola, Sony and Shell are all based in a particular city-state but they have production facilities, suppliers, and subcontractors operating in quite different city-states around the world. Here, aspects of the location of various stakeholders may vary widely which consequently affects CSR differently.[65] Therefore, businesses are embedded within the various traditions of the particular setting of their location. To consider CSR strategy in a broader, global context, four key aspects are discussed: (1) culture; (2) regulatory environment; (3) NGOs and (4) global standards.

Culture

Just as business firms develop their own unique cultures in a home country, if they plan global expansion, they must operate within the context of national and even regional cultures of another country.[66] According to Burton and colleagues: 'Different cultures will emphasize different values; what is important to one culture at one time may not be important to another culture or even to the first culture at some time in the future. These values may affect both the role institutions assume within society and what society expects of those institutions.'[67]

Based on the assessment of Burton and colleagues, understanding the cultures of the countries and regions a firm is seeking to operate in is very important. By way of example, in India, ten-year-olds work 12-hour days weaving rugs. In Honduras, 15-year-old girls work 80 hours per week producing sweaters. In Bangladesh, incidents of nine-year-olds working in shoe factories with imposed production quotas occur.[68] In many countries, these activities would not only be seen as appalling and quite contrary to culturally accepted norms of socially responsible behaviour but would also be in criminal violation of labour laws. However, the reality is that in some countries the use of very young workers is a necessity because this keeps them off the street begging for survival or from committing criminal acts to obtain money.[69] Research does show that individuals view CSR differently from country to country.[70]

The examples given do raise a fundamental issue: should the culture of a particular region or nation or should the firm's own standards (in the home country) form the basis of CSR strategy in international locations? For example, if a firm adopts a shareholder strategy with respect to CSR in the home country, will the same approach translate into an acceptable strategy in a different country of operation? Therefore, firms must consider whether to adapt to the norms of a national or regional culture (a 'relativism' approach) or to impose an international standard of CSR (a 'universalism' approach) regardless of the local cultural norms.[71]

The reality is firms must apply ethical and moral standards to cultural differences with respect to CSR. In some cases, firms might choose *not* to do business in a given country or region because of its suspect norms of socially responsible behaviour. In other cases, they might compromise and conduct CSR so that it opposed the policy set in the home base of operation. In still other cases, firms might act to offer their CSR leadership in the home base to the foreign base of operation, setting the standard for domestic businesses operating in that community. By way of example, Sony recently announced that its environmental targets and policies will be standardised, implemented and enforced in all of its global locations. In another example, in 1997, Mattel announced the creation of its Global Manufacturing Principles, a set of standards applied to all of the company-owned and contract manufacturing facilities around the world.

Last, understanding culture is important with respect to CSR because social — if not stakeholder — concerns vary from country to country. For example, in Australia, Canada and China, environmental concerns take centre stage within society. In Indonesia, Turkey and the United States, improving education ranks highest among social concerns. Finally, in Brazil, Chile and South Africa, reducing poverty and homelessness are the most important social concerns.[72] Based on this information, while having a 'universal' policy with respect to CSR globally may be an ideal in some areas (e.g. workers rights, the environment), firms that understand the intricacies of a national or regional culture are better equipped to meet local concerns of social responsibility when and where necessary (e.g. through philanthropic giving or strategic partnerships).

Regulatory environment

According to Archie Carroll, the regulatory environment, in the form of an enforceable legal framework, is a key component of CSR.[73] In general, laws and regulations have been theorised as necessary in an economy as a response to inefficient or inequitable behaviour.[74] Indeed, a widely held view is that federal and state bodies impose laws where the marketplace has failed to ensure fair competition, safe products, fair and equitable working conditions and a clean and healthy environment.

Although firms are expected to operate within the overall regulatory framework of the land, since the 1970s, the development of laws with respect to specific facets of social responsibility have been growing, especially those operating at a global level. In November 1997, for example, 34 nations signed the OECD Convention on Combating Bribery of Foreign Public Officials in International Business Transactions. The convention now makes bribery of foreign public officials a criminal act on an extraterritorial basis. Although in many ways seen as something unnecessarily imposed on business by the government, the regulatory environment under which a firm must operate in a given country is yet another area of consideration with respect to global CSR strategy. Here, firms are again faced with ethics decisions regarding home versus host country considerations. For example, if a firm faces a very strict set of environmental regulations in its home country, should these same standards naturally be applied to its operations in another country?

NGOs

Historically, associations of private individuals (e.g. churches) have come together for public purposes, typically to provide services (e.g. education, health and welfare) in the community not available from the state, long before the establishment of democratic government and the concept of the welfare state. In more recent times, particularly since the 1950s, a new class of private 'association' has been established, which generally focuses directly on changing public policy. These local, regional and international NGOs now number more than 50 000 in number, almost double the number just 25 years ago, up from just more than 1000 in 1956.[75]

A general definition of NGOs is 'non-profit groups that combine resource mobilisation, information provision and activism to advocate for changes in certain areas'.[76] NGOs are generally based either on ideas: human rights, education, equality, environmental sustainability and so on, or on identity: indigenous, female, gay and the like. However, these lines may be blurring, with many NGOs integrating ideas- and identity-based causes.[77]

With respect to what NGOs actually do, there are three approaches to classification: (1) operational; (2) advisory and (3) advocacy. Operational NGOs act to provide social services such as education, health and disaster relief. Advisory NGOs are involved in providing information and consulting services, for example, to mutual funds focused on socially responsible investing. Advocacy NGOs are directly involved in lobbying governments and local, national and international organisations for changes or adoption of socially responsible policies for businesses. They may also file resolutions on behalf of shareholders to pressure businesses into acting more socially responsible. Although sometimes seen as questionable and unaccountable, NGOs are causing substantial changes in corporate management, strategy and governance. Of particular interest is discerning the role and impact of NGOs in the host country to ascertain whether CSR policy set in the home country needs to be customised to the local environment.

Global standards

Last, just as NGOs can add pressure to businesses to act on behalf of society in many different ways, global standards, many coming from NGOs themselves, are another source of institutional pressure. Most CSR-related global standards are voluntary, asking firms to develop and implement policies and practices on various CSR issues.[78] The standards help users to establish a systematic process that generates indicators, targets and reporting systems necessary for effective implementation and monitoring of various CSR programs and activities. In essence, global standards are instruments designed for corporate self-regulation.

A variety of global standards have emerged over the years and the Business and Social Initiatives database, established by the International Labour Office, now lists more than 400 different standards, principles and codes of conduct. Some of the more recognised standards, however, include the International Standards Organisation's ISO14000 and ISO14031 for the environment; Social Accountability's SA8000 for labour-related issues; the United Nations Declaration on Human Rights and the Environment; and the Caux and Sullivan principles for economic, social and political justice and general CSR. With these and a host of other global standards covering every conceivable aspect of social responsibility, firms are faced with increasing pressure to evaluate a cadre of external benchmarks strategically as they establish CSR policy. Of course, strategic decisions here can become complicated when firms operate, or plan to operate, in more than one location, as noted.

Summary

The primary purpose of this chapter has been to identify the factors that influence and shape the organisational context within which strategies are formulated. Strategy is often encapsulated within a firm's mission or vision statement. The specifics of what is achieved and the principles that guide the firm are described in the firm's goals and values. The overall management system that enables a firm's strategy to be set is partly determined by the corporate governance procedures in place. In addition, in determining the strategic direction of a firm, management must increasingly consider ethical issues as well as CSR. Specifically, this chapter makes the following points in covering the contextual factors influencing strategy development.

▶ Stakeholders are individuals or groups, either within or outside a company, that have some claim on the company. They include customers, suppliers, employees and shareholders. If a company is to survive and prosper, then it must attend to the interests of these different stakeholder groups.

- The mission statement describes how a company intends to incorporate stakeholder claims into its strategic decision making and thereby reduce the risk of losing stakeholder support.

- An important step in the process of formulating a mission statement is to define the company's business. Defining the business involves focusing on consumer groups to be served, consumer needs to be satisfied and the technologies with which those needs can be satisfied.

- The values of a company state how managers intend to conduct themselves, how they intend to do business and what kind of organisation they want to build. Values can become the bedrock of a company's organisational culture and a major component of its competitive advantage.

- The goals of a company specify what must be done if the company is to attain its mission.

- Well-constructed goals are precise and measurable, tackle important issues, are challenging but realistic and specify a period within which they should be achieved.

- Shareholders are among a profit-oriented company's most important stakeholders. Maximising shareholder wealth is one of the most important goals of a business. A corporate governance problem arises when managers pursue strategies that are not consistent with this goal.

- Some governance mechanisms serve to limit the ability of managers to pursue strategies that are at variance with maximising shareholder wealth. These include shareholder meetings, the board of directors, share-based compensation schemes and, in some jurisdictions, appropriate Corporations Law.

- Many strategic decisions have an ethical dimension. Any action by a company inevitably has an impact on the welfare of its stakeholders.

- The purpose of business ethics is not so much to teach the difference between right and wrong as to give people the tools for dealing with moral complexity, for identifying and thinking through the moral implications of strategic decisions.

- CSR is the sense of obligation on the part of companies to build certain social criteria into their strategic decision making to meet the needs of various stakeholders.

- Businesses have four CSR strategic options to consider: (1) the shareholder strategy; (2) the altruistic strategy; (3) the reciprocal strategy and (4) the citizenship strategy.

- Choosing a CSR strategy in the home base does not necessarily translate into a 'global' program. Firms need to consider the impact of four key factors to determine whether a standard (i.e. global) or customised CSR approach should be adopted for other countries: local cultures, regulatory environments, NGOs and applicable global standards.

Practising strategic management

Review questions

1. What are the key steps in conducting a stakeholder impact analysis?
2. What is a mission statement?
3. What are the different philosophical bases for determining whether a decision is ethical and what is their underlying position?
4. What are the key issues to consider in determining the appropriateness of applying one CSR strategy to a range of different countries?

Discussion questions

5. What are the benefits of having a highly defined mission statement? In comparison, what are the benefits of having a broad mission statement?
6. Why is it important for a company to define its values explicitly?
7. Do the corporate governance problems identified in the text apply to not-for-profit organisations? Which elements do apply? Why? Which do not apply? Why?
8. When is it appropriate to adopt different CSR approaches to a single firm's operations in different parts of the world?

Applied questions

9. Does James Hardie (see opening case) have an ethical responsibility in relation to people suffering from mesothelioma who were never employed by James Hardie and came across a James Hardie product by way of buying a house in which James Hardie asbestos products were previously installed?
10. Consider the goals of a company that you know. Evaluate these goals in terms of the characteristics of effective goals that are discussed in the text.

Small-group exercise

Constructing a mission statement

Break into groups of three to five people, and perform the following tasks.
1. Define the business of your educational institution.
2. Use this business definition to guide the construction of a mission statement for your educational institution. Be

sure the mission statement contains a long-term vision, a set of values and precise and measurable goals. Be prepared to articulate the logic behind your choice of vision, values and goals.
3. Try to identify key strategies that your educational institution needs to pursue to attain the vision and goals outlined in your mission statement. Be sure these strategies are consistent with the values that you set down in the mission statement.

Article file

Find an example of a company that ran into trouble because it failed to account for the rights of one of its stakeholder groups when making an important strategic decision.

Exploring the Web

Visiting Merck

Go to the website of Merck, the world's largest pharmaceutical company (www.merck.com) and find the mission statement posted there.
1. Evaluate this mission statement in light of the material contained in this chapter. Does it state clearly what Merck's basic strategic goal is? Do the values listed provide a good guideline for managerial action at Merck?
2. Read the section on corporate responsibility, then answer the following question: how does Merck try to balance the goals of (a) providing shareholders with an adequate ROI and (b) developing medicines that benefit humanity and that can be acquired by people in need at an affordable price? For further information, consider Merck's role in helping stop river blindness and the Vioxx case. See:
   (a) www.merck.com/about/cr/mectizan/home.htm
   (b) www.consumeraffairs.com/news04/vioxx_justice.html
   Do you think that Merck does a good job of balancing these goals?

Strategic management project

Module 2

This module deals with the relationships that your company has with its major stakeholder groups. With the information you have at your disposal, perform the following tasks and answer the following questions.

1. Find out whether your company has a formal mission statement. Does this statement define the business, identify major goals and articulate the corporate philosophy?

2. (a) If your company lacks a mission statement, what do you think its mission statement should be? or

   (b) If your company has a mission statement, do you consider it appropriate, given the material discussed in this chapter?

3. Identify the main stakeholder groups in your company. What claims do they place on the company? How is the company trying to satisfy those claims?

4. Evaluate the performance of the CEO of your company from the perspective of (a) shareholders, (b) employees, (c) customers and (d) suppliers. What does this evaluation tell you about the ability of the CEO and the priorities to which he or she is committed?

5. Try to establish whether the governance mechanisms that operate in your company do a good job of aligning the interests of top managers with those of stockholders.

6. Pick a major strategic decision made by your company in recent years and consider the ethical implications of that decision. In the light of your review, do you think that the company acted correctly?

End notes

1. Freeman, RE 1984, *Strategic management: a stakeholder approach*, Pitman, Boston, Massachusetts.

2. Hill, CWL & Jones, TM 1992, 'Stakeholder–agency theory', *Journal of Management Studies*, vol. 29, pp. 131–54; March, JG & Simon, HA 1958, *Organizations*, John Wiley & Sons, New York.

3. Hill & Jones, op. cit.

4. Macmillan, IC & Jones, PE 1986, *Strategy formulation: power and politics*, West, St Paul, Minnesota.

5. Abell, DF 1980, *Defining the business: the starting point of strategic planning*, Prentice Hall, Englewood Cliffs, New Jersey; Andrews, K 1971, *The concept of corporate strategy*, Dow Jones Irwin, Homewood, Illinois; Pearce, JA 1982, 'The company mission as a strategic tool', *Sloan Management Review*, Spring, pp. 15–24.

6. Boeing, www.boeing.com.

7. BHP Billiton 2001, *BHP Billiton Limited annual report*, www.bhpbilliton.com.

8. Foster's, accessed 2 February 2006, www.fosters.com.au/aboutus.htm.

9. Royal New Zealand Foundation for the Blind, accessed 2 February 2006, www.rnzfb.org.nz/aboutus/visionandmissionstatements.

10. Hamel, G & Prahalad, CK 1994, *Competing for the future*, Harvard Business School Press, Boston. Also see Collins, JC & Porras, JI 1996, 'Building your company's vision', *Harvard Business Review*, September–October, pp. 65–77.

11. Quoted in Tully, S 1995, 'Why go for stretch targets', *Fortune*, 14 November, pp. 145–58.

12. These three questions were first proposed by Drucker. See Drucker, PF 1974, *Management — tasks, responsibilities, practices*, Harper & Row, New York, pp. 74–94.

13. Abell, op. cit.

14. Collins & Porras, op. cit.

15. See Kotter, JP & Heskett, JL 1992, *Corporate culture and performance*, Free Press, New York. For similar work, see Collins & Porras, op. cit.

16. Rochfort, S 2004, 'How's that for a cracker result?', *Sydney Morning Herald*, 20 February, accessed 15 December 2005, www.smh.com.au/articles/2004/02/19/1077072783993.html?from=storyrhs.

17. Richards, MD 1986, *Setting strategic goals and objectives*, West, St Paul, Minnesota.

18. Locke, EA, Latham, GP & Erez, M 1988, 'The determinants of goal commitment', *Academy of Management Review*, vol. 13, pp. 23–39.

19. Jackson, M 2005, 'Obligation, Responsibility and Respect', The 20th Foenander lecture (University of Melbourne), 23 August, p. 5, accessed 15 December 2005, www.management.unimelb.edu.au/downloads/2005_Foenander_Transcript.pdf.

20. Hoskisson, RE, Hitt, MA & Hill, CWL 1993, 'Managerial incentives and investment in R&D in large multiproduct firms', *Organization Science*, vol. 3, pp. 325–41.

21. Hayes, RH & Abernathy, WJ 1980, 'Managing our way to economic decline', *Harvard Business Review*, July–August, pp. 67–77.

22. Thurow, LC 1985, *The zero sum solution*, Simon & Schuster, New York, pp. 69–89.

23. Dertouzos, ML, Lester, RK & Solow, RM 1989, *Made in America*, MIT Press, Cambridge, Massachusetts.

24. Laserre, P & Schutte, H 1995, *Strategies for Asia Pacific*, Macmillan Education Australia, Melbourne.

25. Jensen, MC & Meckling, WH 1976, 'Theory of the firm: managerial behavior, agency costs and ownership structure', *Journal of Financial Economics*, vol. 3, pp. 305–60.

26. See, for example, Marris, R 1964, *The economic theory of managerial capitalism*, Macmillan, London; Galbraith, JK 1970, *The new industrial state*, Houghton Mifflin, Boston, Massachusetts.

27. Fama, EF 1980, 'Agency problems and the theory of the firm', *Journal of Political Economy*, vol. 88, pp. 375–90.

28. 'HIH report goes to government', media release, accessed 1 April 2003, http://news.ninemsn.com.au/Business/story-3253.asp.

29. Riggs, P 2004, 'Executive remuneration: thriving under observation', accessed 2 May 2005, www.ceoforum.com.au/200412_remuneration.cfm.

30. AAP News 2005, 'Average Aussie annual wage hits $53,000', 17 November, accessed 16 December 2005, http://au.biz.yahoo.com/051114/30/d5jy.html.

31. For academic studies that look at the determinants of CEO pay, see Jensen, MC & Murphy, KJ 1990, 'Performance pay and top management incentives', *Journal of Political Economy*, vol. 98, pp. 225–64; Hill, CWL & Phan, P 1991, 'CEO tenure as a determinant of CEO pay', *Academy of Management Journal*, vol. 34, pp. 07–17; Tosi, HL & Gomez-Mejia, LR 1994, 'CEO compensation monitoring and firm performance', *Academy of Management Journal*, vol. 37, pp. 1002–16; Porac, JF, Wade, JB &

Pollock, TG 1999, 'Industry categories and the politics of the comparable firm in CEO compensation', *Administrative Science Quarterly*, vol. 44, pp. 112–44.

32. Owen, C 2005, 'Salaries high, performance low', accessed 2 May 2005, http://bosswatch.labor.net.au/campaigns/general/1031717447_28193.php.

33. For recent research on this issue, see Lane, PJ, Cannella, AA & Lubatkin, MH 1998, 'Agency problems as antecedents to unrelated mergers and diversification: Amihud and Lev reconsidered', *Strategic Management Journal*, vol. 19, pp. 555–78.

34. Penrose, ET 1958, *The theory of the growth of the firm*, Macmillan, London.

35. Dabkowski, S & Porter I 2004, 'Climbing aboard the gravy train', *Sydney Morning Herald*, 16 October, accessed 2 May 2005, www.smh.com.au/articles/2004/10/15/1097784048594.html?from=storylhs.

36. Williamson, OE 1985, *The economic institutions of capitalism*, Free Press, New York.

37. Fama, op. cit.

38. Lewellen, WG, Eoderer, C & Rosenfeld, A 1985, 'Merger decisions and executive stock ownership in acquiring firms', *Journal of Accounting and Economics*, vol. 7, pp. 209–31.

39. Hill, CWL & Snell, SA 1988, 'External control, corporate strategy, and firm performance', *Strategic Management Journal*, vol. 9, pp. 577–90.

40. Freeman, RE & Gilbert, D 1988, Corporate strategy and the search for ethics, Prentice Hall, Englewood Cliffs, New Jersey.

41. Solomon, RC 1992, *Ethics and excellence*, Oxford University Press, Oxford.

42. Hanson, KO & Velasquez, M 1988, 'Hewlett-Packard Company: managing ethics and values', in *Corporate ethics: a prime business asset*, The Business Roundtable, February.

43. For example, see Freeman, RE & Gilbert, D 1988, *Corporate strategy and the search for ethics*, Prentice Hall, Englewood Cliffs, New Jersey. Jones, T 1991, 'Ethical decision making by individuals in organisations,' *Academy of Management Review*, vol. 16, pp. 366–95. Rest, JR 1986, *Moral development: advances in research and theory*, Praeger, New York.

44. Andrews, KR 1971, *The concept of corporate strategy*, Dow-Jones Irwin, Homewood, Illinois.

45. Carroll, AB & Hoy, F 1984, 'Integrating corporate social policy into strategic management', *Journal of Business Strategy*, vol. 4, pp. 48–57.

46. Estes, R 1996, *Tyranny of the bottom line*, Berrett-Koehler, San Francisco, California. See also Frooman, J 1997, 'Socially irresponsible and illegal behaviour and shareholder wealth', *Business and Society*, vol. 36, pp. 221–49.

47. Carroll, AB 1979, 'A three-dimensional conceptual model of corporate performance', *Academy of Management Review*, vol. 4, pp. 497–505.

48. Friedman, M 1970, 'The social responsibility of business is to increase its profits', *New York Times Magazine*, 13 September, pp. 32–3, 122, 124, 126. See also Friedman, M 1962, *Capitalism and freedom*, University of Chicago Press, Chicago, Illinois.

49. Walton, CC 1982, 'Corporate social responsibility: the debate revisited', *Journal of Economics and Business*, vol. 34, pp. 173–87; Kok, P, van der Wiele, T, McKenna, R & Brown, A 2001, 'A corporate social responsibility audit within a quality management

framework', *Journal of Business Ethics*, vol. 31, pp. 285–97; Waddock, SA, Bodwell, C & Graves, SB 2002, 'Responsibility: the new business imperative', *Academy of Management Executive*, vol. 16, pp. 132–48.

50. Centre for Corporate Public Affairs 2000, *Corporate community involvement: establishing a business case*, Centre for Corporate Public Affairs in Association with the Business Council of Australia, Melbourne.

51. Spence, LJ, Schmidpeter, R & Habisch, A 2003, 'Assessing social capital: Small and medium sized enterprises in Germany and the UK', *Journal of Business Ethics*, vol. 47, pp. 17–29.

52. Waddock, SA & Graves, SB 1997, 'The corporate social performance-financial performance link', *Strategic Management Journal*, vol. 18, pp. 303–19.

53. Murray, KB & Vogel, CM 1997, 'Using a hierarchy-of-effects approach to gauge the effectiveness of corporate social responsibility to generate goodwill toward the firm: financial versus nonfinancial impact', *Journal of Business Research*, vol. 38, pp. 141–59.

54. Wokutch, RE 1990, 'Corporate social responsibility Japanese style', *Academy of Management Executive*, vol. 4, pp. 56–74.

55. Joyner, BE & Payne, D 2002, 'Evolution and implementation: A study of values, business ethics and corporate social responsibility', *Journal of Business Ethics*, vol. 41, pp. 297–311; Angelidis, J & Ibrahim, N 2004, 'An exploratory study of the impact of degree of religiousness upon an individual's corporate social responsiveness orientation', *Journal of Business Ethics*, vol. 51, pp. 119–28; Hemingway, CA & Maclagan, PW 2004, 'Managers' personal values as drivers of corporate social responsibility', *Journal of Business Ethics*, vol. 50, pp. 33–44.

56. Environics International 1999, 'Executive brief', *The Millennium Poll on corporate social responsibility*, Environics International Ltd, Toronto.

57. Murray, KB & Vogel, CM 1997, 'Using a hierarchy-of-effects approach to gauge the effectiveness of corporate social responsibility to generate goodwill toward the firm: financial versus nonfinancial impact', *Journal of Business Research*, vol. 38, pp. 141–59; Hemingway & Maclagan, op. cit.

58. Turban, DB & Greening, DW 1997, 'Corporate social performance and organizational attractiveness to prospective employees', *Academy of Management Journal*, vol. 40, pp. 658–72; Waddock, SA, Bodwell, C & Graves, SB 2002, 'Responsibility: The new business imperative', *Academy of Management Executive*, vol. 16, pp. 132–48; Rosen, S, Simon, J, Vincent, JR, MacLeod, W, Fox, M & Thea, DM 2003, 'AIDS is your business', *Harvard Business Review*, vol. 81, pp. 80–7.

59. File, KM & Prince, RA 1998, 'Cause-related marketing and corporate philanthropy in the privately held enterprise', *Journal of Business Ethics*, vol. 17, pp. 1529–39.

60. See, for example, Demmy, S & Talbott, J 1998, 'Improve internal reporting with ABC and TOC', *Management Accounting*, vol. 80, pp. 18–24.

61. Freeman, op. cit.

62. Drucker, P 1946, *The concept of the corporation*, The John Day Co, New York.

63. Clarkson, MBE 1995, 'A stakeholder framework for analyzing and evaluating corporate social performance', *Academy of Management Review*, vol. 20, pp. 92–117.

64. Margolis, JD & Walsh, JP 2003, 'Misery loves companies: rethinking social initiatives by business', *Administrative Science Quarterly*, vol. 48, pp. 265–305.

65. Burton, BK, Farh, J-L & Hegarty, WH 2000, 'A cross-cultural comparison of corporate social responsibility orientation: Hong Kong vs. United States students', *Teaching Business Ethics*, vol. 4, pp. 151–67.

66. Hofstede, G 1980, *Culture's consequences: international differences in work-related values*, Sage, Beverly Hills, California.

67. ibid., p. 153.

68. Quindlen, A 1994, 'Out of the hands of babes', *New York Times*, 23 November, p. A15.

69. Greenfield, WM 2004, 'In the name of corporate social responsibility', *Business Horizons*, vol. 47, pp. 19–28.

70. Orpen, C 1987, 'The attitudes of United States and South African managers to corporate social responsibility', *Journal of Business Ethics*, vol. 6, pp. 89–96; Burton, Farh & Hegarty, op. cit.

71. Smeltzer, LR & Jennings, MM 1998, 'Why an international code of business ethics would be good for business', *Journal of Business Ethics*, vol. 17, pp. 57–66; Carroll, AB 2004, 'Managing ethically with global stakeholders: a present and future challenge', *Academy of Management Executive*, vol. 18, pp. 114–20.

72. Environics International 2002, 'Executive brief', *Corporate social responsibility monitor 2002*, Environics International Ltd, Toronto.

73. Carroll 2004, op. cit.

74. Posner, RA 1974, 'Theories of economic regulation', *The Bell Journal of Economic and Management Science*, vol. 5, pp. 335–58.

75. Gordenker, L & Weiss, TG 1996, 'Pluralizing global governance: analytical approaches and dimensions', in Weiss, TG & Gordenker, L (eds), *NGOs, the UN and global governance*, Rienner Publishers, London.

76. Spar, DL & La Mure, LT 2003, 'The power of activism: Assessing the impact of NGOs on global business', *California Management Review*, vol. 45, p. 79.

77. van Tuijl, P 1999, 'NGOs and human rights: sources of justices and democracy', *Journal of International Affairs*, vol. 52, pp. 493–512.

78. Neergaard, P & Pedersen, ER 2003, 'Corporate social behaviour: Between the rules of the game and the law of the jungle', *Journal of Corporate Citizenship*, vol. 12, pp. 43–57.

The nature of competitive advantage

part 2

External analysis: industry opportunities and threats

learning objectives

After studying this chapter, you should be able to:

- apply Porter's five forces model
- discuss elements to consider in analysing the business environment
- understand when and why you may need to use the concept of strategic groups
- appreciate the weaknesses of industry analysis techniques
- understand how the stage of an industry's evolution affects industry conditions
- appreciate how network economics can affect the attractiveness of industries.

Exporting New Zealand education

The international education industry in New Zealand, comprising all universities, polytechnics, language schools, secondary schools and private training institutions, exceeded a turnover of more than NZ$2 billion for the second consecutive year in April 2005. The growth experienced by this industry has been phenomenal if one takes into account that until 1999, it contributed just a few hundred million dollars (the industry foreign exchange earnings amounted to NZ$438 million in 1999 as against NZ$2187 million in 2004). Before 1999, the industry lacked a unified marketing strategy and concerted industry effort. Today, New Zealand is considered as a major education exporter in the league of international players such as the United States, the UK, Canada and Australia. There are other smaller players in the international market, such as Germany, France, Malaysia, Greece, Cyprus and South Africa, but New Zealand has surpassed these countries in earnings from international student recruitment in just a few years.

How did this transformation take place? Serious efforts to promote New Zealand's international education industry started during 1998/99. The New Zealand government provided incentives to the industry to unify its marketing efforts and entrusted Trade New Zealand with the task of developing overseas markets in collaboration with the education industry. Between the years 1999 and 2000, a number of steps were taken by the education institutions, Trade New Zealand and the Ministry of Education to bring about the creation of an 'Educated in New Zealand' brand, which provided a platform for a global marketing thrust. A new marketing body was created in September 2000 to act as the industry's representative with the responsibility of coordinating all onshore efforts to promote New Zealand as a destination for education. This body is now called Education New Zealand and is managed by a group of professionals who work consistently on a whole range of issues including careful management of the 'Educated in New Zealand' brand image. The task of coordinating the offshore marketing effort is allotted to Trade New Zealand and its offices around the world. Today, as a result of the concerted efforts of Education New Zealand, Trade New Zealand, the education institutions and the Ministry of Education, the country receives international students from 40 different markets ranging from China to the Maldives. Trade New Zealand, in collaboration with the New Zealand education institutions has developed, 'education export networks' of institutions, which focus on a particular country to market the New Zealand label in that country. The purpose is to ensure that the features peculiar to that specific market are better dealt with. This is achieved by creation of strong student recruitment agency networks in those markets. These networks provide market intelligence, raise the country's profile and provide ground support with services such as counselling, choice of course and institution, student visa processing and resettlement advice. In this way they act as a vital link between the market and institutions in New Zealand.

Sources: Education New Zealand 2005, 'Student immigration policy review is good news for international educators', press release, 11 April; New Zealand Ministry of Education, www.minedu.govt.nz; Education New Zealand, www.educationnz.org.nz.

industry
A group of companies that offer products or services that are the same or close substitutes for each other

Overview

The world higher education **industry** is very competitive, with many countries seeking to attract fee-paying international students. A range of different approaches are taken by different countries, resulting in a nonhomogenous industry, evolving in different ways in different parts of the world. This chapter introduces a range of tools for analysing industry dynamics and appreciating how they affect the success of organisations within an industry. These tools include understanding the macroenvironmental forces present and how an organisation can take advantage of conditions in its macroenvironment by developing and implementing appropriate strategies. This chapter also covers industry analysis to appreciate why some industries are naturally more attractive than others. Third, because industries are rarely homogenous, it introduces techniques such as strategic grouping and strategic blocking for analysing the competitive dynamics of having groups of companies with strategic similarities within an industry. The remainder of this chapter considers the nature of industry evolution and discusses how the globalisation of the world's economy is affecting the competitive forces at work within an industry's environment. Industry analysis is just one part of understanding how the external environment can affect the success of an organisation. By the end of this chapter, you will understand how the industry environment can determine profitability levels, requiring companies to change either the industry environment (to make it more attractive) or themselves (to fit with the competitive dynamics created by the industry environment).

Analysing industry structure

An industry can be defined as a group of companies offering products or services that are close substitutes for each other. Close substitutes are products or services that satisfy the same basic consumer needs: for example, the metal and plastic body panels used in motor vehicle construction are close substitutes for each other. Despite different production technologies, motor vehicle supply companies manufacturing metal body panels are in the same basic industry as that of companies manufacturing plastic body panels. They serve the same consumer need: that of vehicle assembly companies for body panels.

Nevertheless, defining where the boundaries of an industry lie is very inexact because one can define an industry broadly or narrowly. What is important is that the definition is useful for the purposes of the analysis being conducted. For example, a firm that wants to understand industry dynamics in the MP3 player industry may only focus on purpose-built MP3 player manufacturers and not include mobile phone manufacturers, even though they may have MP3 capabilities.

The task facing managers is to analyse competitive forces in an industry environment to identify the opportunities and threats confronting a company. Porter, of the Harvard School of Business Administration, developed a framework that helps managers in this analysis.[1] Porter's framework, known as the five forces model, appears in figure 3.1. This model focuses on five forces that shape competition within an industry: (1) the threat of new entrants; (2) the degree of rivalry among established companies within an industry; (3) the bargaining power of buyers; (4) the bargaining power of suppliers and (5) the threat of substitute products.

Porter argues that the stronger that each of these forces are, the more limited is the ability of established companies to raise prices and earn greater profits. Within Porter's framework, a strong competitive force can be regarded as a threat because it depresses profits. A weak competitive force can be viewed as an opportunity because it allows a company to earn greater profits. The strength of the five forces may change as industry conditions change. The tasks facing managers are to recognise how changes in the five forces give rise to new opportunities and threats, and to formulate appropriate strategic responses. In addition, a company can, through its choice of strategy, alter the strength of one or more of the five forces to its advantage. This notion is discussed in the following chapters. This section focuses on understanding the impact of each of the five forces on a company.

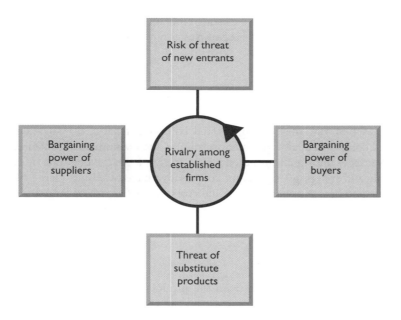

Figure 3.1:
The five forces model

Source: Adapted from Porter, ME 1979, 'How competence forces shape strategy', *Harvard Business Review*, March–April. Adapted and reprinted by permission of *Harvard Business Review*. © 1979 by the Harvard Business School Publishing Corporation; all rights reserved.

Threat of new entrants

Theories of perfect competition suggest that new firms will try to enter highly profitable industries until the increased level of competition eventually drives profits down to at least the average profit levels for an economy. However, this obviously does not always occur because there are barriers to entry in many industries. If there are low **barriers to entry**, then new companies will continually enter the industry while the industry is doing well. This new entry will invariably increase the level of competition as more companies compete for the same market. In turn, the increased competition is likely to lead to lower levels of profitability for all companies in the industry. Conversely, if there are significant barriers to entry for potential new companies, then existing companies have greater opportunities for profit maximisation, without the threat of having to face many new competitors.

Bain did the original work on barriers to entry. He identified three main sources of barriers to new entry: brand loyalty, absolute cost advantages and economies of scale.[2] Two further barriers of significance can be added to Bain's list in many situations: switching costs and government regulation.

barriers to entry
Factors that make it costly for companies to enter an industry

Brand loyalty

Buyers' preference for the products of incumbent companies is termed **brand loyalty**. A company can create it through continual advertising of brand and company names, patent protection of products, product innovation achieved through company research and development programs, an emphasis on high product quality and good aftersales service. Significant brand loyalty makes it difficult for new entrants to take market share away from established companies. It thus reduces the threat of entry by potential competitors because they may perceive the task of breaking down well-established consumer preferences as too costly.

brand loyalty
Buyers' willingness to stay with a particular company's product for the brand and not the superior product attributes

Absolute cost advantages

Sometimes, incumbent companies have an **absolute cost advantage** over potential entrants. Absolute cost advantages seem to derive from three main sources: (1) superior production operations, which owe to past experience, patents or secret processes; (2) control of particular inputs required for production, such as labour, materials, equipment and management skills;

absolute cost advantage
A superior cost position that is not related to the volume of product produced

and (3) access to cheaper funds because existing companies represent lower risks than do those that are not yet established. If incumbent companies have an absolute cost advantage, then the threat of entry decreases.

Economies of scale

The cost advantages of large company output are known as economies of scale. Their sources include cost reductions gained through mass producing a standardised output, discounts on bulk purchases of raw material inputs and component parts, the advantages gained by spreading fixed costs over a large production volume and economies of scale in advertising. If these cost advantages are significant, then a new entrant faces the dilemma of either entering on a small scale and suffering a significant cost disadvantage or taking a large risk by entering on a large scale and bearing significant capital costs. A further risk of large-scale entry is that the increased supply of products will depress prices and result in vigorous retaliation by established companies. When established companies have economies of scale, therefore, the threat of entry is reduced.

Switching costs

When it costs a consumer to switch from the product offering of an incumbent company to the product offering of a new entrant, switching costs arise. When these costs are high, consumers can be locked in to the product offerings of incumbents, even if new entrants offer better products.[3] For example, consumers may stick with existing DVD formats for their movies when newer higher-definition versions such as Sony's Blu-Ray system become publicly available. This system can produce five times as many pixels, creating a much sharper and clearer image but consumers will need a new DVD player and probably a more upmarket television as well to notice any difference. In addition, replacing existing DVDs with new Blu-Ray DVDs will be expensive. Therefore, the switching costs may simply be too great for many consumers, who will stay with traditional DVDs.

Switching costs do not just occur in relation to products. Frequent-flyer programs were initially devised to minimise regular flyers switching between airlines because the possibility of free travel or other products is supposed to make consumers stay with one airline, even when it is not offering the lowest prices. Similarly, frequent-shopper programs such as the FlyBuys card from the Coles-Myer group make it more attractive to patronise stores in this group of companies by creating a cost (missing out on possible points) by shopping elsewhere.

Government regulation

Historically, government regulation has constituted a major barrier to entry in many industries. The Australian domestic airline industry, for example, was regulated until 1990, limiting the industry to two interstate carriers. The effect of this government regulation did not immediately disappear in 1990, in that new entrants had considerable difficulty entering the airline industry. The Commonwealth Government had previously owned airports indirectly, which were set up to cater for two domestic carriers. The airports were privatised, and Ansett and Australian (which later merged with Qantas) came to own their own terminal buildings. New carriers were effectively given the least attractive space within the airport, with the terminal gates furthest from the airport entry and exit point. The byproduct of this government regulation was still evident in 2002 when Virgin Blue started operating out of Perth. Although the Ansett terminal was hardly being used, because Ansett was in receivership, passengers for Virgin Blue had to go to the international terminal and gain access to their aircraft through a service corridor for a cafeteria (to avoid immigration procedures). A long history of government intervention and regulation had essentially set up the industry to work around two carriers. When new entrants tried to enter the industry, they faced not just two well-established competitors but a whole industry that seemed to conspire against their success.

Entry barriers and competition

If established companies have built brand loyalty for their products, have an absolute cost advantage over potential competitors, have significant economies of scale, are the beneficiaries of high switching costs or enjoy regulatory protection, then the risk of entry by potential competitors is greatly diminished. When this risk is low, established companies can charge higher prices and earn greater profits than would otherwise have been possible. It is therefore in the interest of companies to pursue strategies consistent with raising entry barriers. Empirical evidence suggests that the height of barriers to entry is one of the most important determinants of profit rates in an industry.[4] This can be seen in Strategy in action 3.1, which discusses the barriers to entry in the soft-drink industry.

strategy in action 3.1
Barriers to entry in the soft-drink industry

The soft-drink industry is highly profitable for the key players of Coca-Cola and PepsiCo. With two firms dominating the industry and (pretax) profits running at around 35 per cent of sales, it is clear that the barriers to entry in this industry are very high to keep new players from competing. To appreciate the extent of the barriers to entry in this industry, it is worth considering where you can purchase soft drinks and what options are available at these different locations. Coca-Cola and PepsiCo have contracts with fountain outlets, such as McDonald's, Hungry Jack's and KFC, that exclude all other competitors. A new entrant would simply not be able to sell their product in any major fast-food chain. The major companies also have long-term leases with the owners of relevant sites (universities, airports, hotels) making it difficult for smaller competitors to operate in this area as well. The greatest opportunity for new competitors is entry through supermarkets (where the margins are lowest). Even here, however, most shelf space (including all of the prime space) is allocated to well-known brands.

Beyond these challenges in distributing the product, new entrants also suffer from the exclusive contracts that Coca-Cola and PepsiCo have with bottlers, which mean that the most efficient bottlers would be unavailable in most cases because of their exclusive contracts with the major producers. The inability to use bottlers that can provide economies of scale would increase costs for the new entrant. In addition, there is incredible brand loyalty within the soft-drink market. People tend to identify themselves as a Coke or Pepsi (or another brand) drinker and rarely switch brands. To overcome this, a new entrant would need to engage in a significant marketing campaign to overshadow the already very large marketing efforts of Coca-Cola and PepsiCo.

The power of these barriers to entry was witnessed when Richard Branson released Virgin Cola. He was unable to penetrate the market effectively, because Coca-Cola and PepsiCo blocked most of the distribution channels by instituting long-term contracts. Even though the Virgin group had significant financial resources, it simply did not have the capital to fight a protracted cola war with Coca-Cola and PepsiCo.

Source: Yoffie, D 2004, 'Cola wars continue: Coke and Pepsi in the twenty-first century', Harvard Business School Case 9-702-442.

Rivalry among established companies

The second of Porter's five competitive forces is the extent of rivalry among established companies within an industry. If this rivalry is weak, then companies have an opportunity to raise prices and earn greater profits. If rivalry is strong, however, then significant price competition (including price wars) may result, as seen in Strategy in action 3.2. Price competition limits profitability by reducing the margins that can be earned on sales. Intense rivalry among established companies thus constitutes a strong threat to profitability. The determinants of interfirm rivalry are detailed in the following sections.

strategy in action 3.2

Vodafone vs Telecom in New Zealand

Vodafone is a leading international mobile communications company controlling one-fourth of the world's mobile phone market, with 139 million customers worldwide (as in October 2004). The company's entry into the New Zealand market in 1998 led to intense competition with Telecom New Zealand. Vodafone's entry resulted in both companies battling constantly to woo customers and retain them. The competition between the two brought innovation and higher levels of investment into New Zealand. The biggest beneficiary of this relentless price war and the desire to outdo each other is the New Zealand consumer. Wholesale mobile rates went down by 30 per cent over the five years to 2005. Mobile call rates have fallen as reflected in offers to consumers with 'no lock-in contracts, per second billing and no hidden nasties (costs)'. The greater investment in the telecommunications sector by both rivals has resulted in price benefits to residential and business customers with land lines as well.

In 2003, Vodafone announced that they had 1.3 million mobile customers in New Zealand, which amounted to 51 per cent of the market, overtaking Telecom in the mobile sector. In the same year, Telecom introduced unlimited text messaging for NZ$10 per month with a view to capturing the youth market segment (the greatest users of text messages). Vodafone did not immediately retaliate but by April 2005 had announced free text messaging (Vodafone to Vodafone mobiles) during weekends (Friday evening–Sunday midnight) for all Vodafone customers. The rivalry thus benefited New Zealand customers once again.

Source: Vodafone, accessed 4 May 2005, www.vodafone.com.

Concentration

Rivalry tends to intensify as the number of competitors increases and as competitors become more equal in size and capacity. With fewer firms, greater opportunities for collusion or at least an implicit understanding of how each major competitor operates exist. This lessens the likelihood of companies competing on profit-destroying dimensions such as price. Approximately 75 per cent of the Australian concrete industry, for example, is controlled by Boral, Pioneer and CSR. Price competition is limited because a price cut by one competitor is simply matched by the others. In the past, this implicit collusion has been more tightly controlled, with the former Trade Practices Commission fining these three companies on more than one occasion for price fixing. Similarly, when a single company dominates an industry, that company often adopts the position of price leader and others follow this lead, limiting the opportunities for price-based competition.

Industry growth and demand

Industries that have very slow growth or even declining demand tend to exhibit higher levels of rivalry because companies fight vigorously for every percentage point of market share, because growth can normally occur only at the expense of rivals. Similarly, when an industry has overcapacity because of too rapid expansion, competition also becomes fierce. The wine industry is a good example of how overcapacity without a rapidly growing market can lead to high levels of rivalry. Since the mid-1990s, new vineyards have been planted across Australia. Local demand has increased, as have exports, but industry observers have long been predicting a glut of grapes. Prices for well-known brands are in many cases lower than they were a year ago and many wine companies felt the fallout from this rivalry, with the poorly performing Southcorp being taken over by Foster's, and Evans Tate having an administrator appointed in 2005. These difficult conditions also saw players exerting further pressure on suppliers to minimise the negative fallout from the overcapacity; and in one well-publicised case, McGuigan Simeon Wines had cancelled their contracts with up to 170 grape growers for 2006.[5]

Product or service differentiation

Rivalry is stronger when the products and services of competitors are so weakly differentiated that customers incur low costs in switching from one supplier to another. Certain industries, such as milk and supermarkets, are naturally oriented towards competition on the basis of price. Even though supermarkets may try to differentiate and create switching costs through the use of frequent-shopper programs (such as the FlyBuys program) and petrol discounts, these programs have limited effect because their rewards are not great and in the case of petrol discounting, every major chain has a similar offer in place. The more that products or services take on the characteristics of commodities, the greater the propensity for companies to use price as the primary competitive weapon. When price reductions become the dominant strategic move, the industry has limited opportunities to achieve very high rates of return. For example, over the past two decades, Australian and New Zealand banks eliminated many features that created customer loyalty, in an effort to reduce operating costs. As a result, the major banks now have less opportunity to differentiate themselves, so most consumers shop around for the best interest rates for major commitments (such as home mortgages), rather than remaining loyal to their present bank.

Ratio of fixed costs to variable costs

When an industry faces excess capacity or demand either plateaus or starts to decrease, the degree to which price discounting may occur is partly a function of the extent of fixed costs relative to the industry's overall cost structure. When fixed costs are high, the temptation for companies in struggling industries is to take any price higher than existing variable costs because this will ensure some cash flow and at least cover some fixed costs. In comparison, when variable costs are high, there is far less benefit to selling a product at a loss, potentially alleviating extreme forms of price discounting.

High exit barriers

Rivalry tends to be more vigorous when it costs more to get out of a business than to stay and compete. **Exit barriers** can derive from existing contracts (such as termination payments owed to employees if made redundant), specialised assets (the business needs to retain a hold over valuable assets), strategic interrelationships (the business links to others within a conglomerate) and the emotions of decision makers. The airline industry is highly volatile worldwide, yet competitors remain in the industry during downturns in the market, even when making losses, because they cannot easily sell their assets and relocate to another industry. Instead, competitors discount their fares to try to cover as many fixed costs as possible, as they wait for an upswing in demand.

exit barriers
Factors that make it costly for companies to leave an industry

Diversity of competitors

Rivalry becomes more volatile and unpredictable as competitors are more diverse in their strategies, resources and corporate priorities. Companies with similar resources, backgrounds and strategic approaches are less likely to engage in competitive activities that can be mutually destructive. If four firms dominate an industry, then the likelihood of extended price-based competition is low because no company will consider it likely that a price war would have a positive effect (more likely, decreased profits would result). Further, given the similar size of the competitors, it would be difficult to force a company to leave the industry completely. When companies are of different sizes and contain quite different resources, however, it is possible to knock a smaller competitor out of the industry. When companies are considerably different in their resources base and size, competition is likely to revert to the lowest common denominator: price.

High strategic stakes

When a successful strategic move has significant flow-on effects, the initial strategic battle is likely to be far more intense than the importance of the market at a point in time would seem to deserve. When the VHS and Beta formats of video players and recorders were competing, the battle was not just for the limited number of machines being sold at the time. Rather, it was a battle to create an international standard. The companies behind the two formats (JVC and Sony) therefore spent heavily on product development to create incremental innovations and kept prices at levels that did not return profits, to try to attract the initial group of consumers. In the same way, companies may compete vigorously within an industry when there is an opportunity to upset the present status quo. New companies will be willing to take losses to gain market share when entering an industry. Large companies may also weather losses to try to displace a competitor from a particular segment or force them entirely from the industry. The video game industry is one of high strategic stakes where there tends to be only one winner and for this reason games consoles such as the Xbox 360 and PlayStation 3 are often sold at below production cost in the hope of attracting more users.

The bargaining power of buyers

The third of Porter's five competitive forces is the bargaining power of buyers. A company's buyers may be the customers who consume its products (its end-users) but also the companies that distribute its products to end-users, such as retailers and wholesalers. Although Unilever sells its soap powder to end-users, the major buyers of its products are supermarket chains, which resell the product to the end-users. Buyers can be viewed as a competitive threat when they are in a position to demand lower prices from the company or when they demand better service (which can increase operating costs). On the other hand, when buyers are weak, a company can raise its prices and earn greater profits. The end result is that if there is a certain amount of profit to be made in any transaction, the one with the greatest level of power is the one that will appropriate the vast majority of that profit. Therefore, whether buyers are able to make demands on a company depends on their power relative to that of the company. According to Porter, buyers are most powerful in the following circumstances.

- If buyers are few and they purchase in large quantities, they can bargain for lower prices. No company within the industry would be willing to lose a large account when there are few possible buyers and the output may not be able to be sold if the company does not accept the discounted offer. Woolworths and Coles dominate the supermarket industry in Australia. As the primary buyers for products such as IXL jams, they are able to bargain for lower prices, ask for discounts for prompt payment or extend traditional 30-day payment periods to 60 or even 90 days. Most suppliers are in no position to bargain with Coles and Woolworths because they cannot afford to lose such a large customer.

- If a single buyer's purchases represent a sizeable percentage of the industry's sales, every company will compete for at least part of this account, leading to extensive rivalry within the industry. Continuing with the supermarket example, Coles and Woolworths have only limited shelf space for jams, so they can carry only limited varieties. Given the size of the market that Woolworths and Coles can reach, every significant jam manufacturer in Australia would compete vigorously to become a selected brand for at least one of the major supermarket chains.

- If the industry comprises many relatively small sellers, the seller would be unable to exert pressure on buyers. Instead, buyers probably switch easily between companies, ensuring high levels of competition. Today, there are hundreds of small Australian and New Zealand wineries, yet most distribution channels (the bottle shops) are owned by just a few companies. Unless a particular winery is very large or quite famous, the owners of the bottle shops can push for lower prices, longer payment terms and advertising support should they decide to carry a particular winery's product.

- If an item is sufficiently standardised among sellers, buyers can not only find alternative sellers but also switch suppliers at low cost, ensuring that the latter compete vigorously to maintain existing accounts. Manufacturers of nondifferentiated products, such as standard printing and photocopy paper, have the problem that their customers can switch suppliers at no cost, making competition among these standardised suppliers very intense.

- If buyers pose a credible threat of backward integration, the industry is unlikely to exhibit very high rates of return over time. If it does, then buyers will integrate backwards, increasing competition and driving down returns. Coffee-roasting companies have found that most consumers cannot differentiate between different coffees, making their products highly price competitive. As a result, some roasters have forward integrated by setting up their own coffee shops. This is a way of moving in on the relatively high profits that are earned as a result of an increase in premium coffee consumption. The most famous example is the US store Starbucks (now international), which opened its first two stores under the name of Il Giornale because coffee shops were perceived to have greater potential than coffee roasting for high profits.

- If it is economically feasible for buyers to purchase the item from several suppliers rather than from just one, the level of competition among companies will heighten, driving down profit margins. Very large companies such as General Motors are well known for having multiple suppliers for various components. Each supplier's desire to keep its contract (or increase the size of its contract) ensures high levels of price-based competition.

The bargaining power of suppliers

The fourth of Porter's competitive forces is the bargaining power of suppliers. Suppliers can be viewed as a threat when they are able to force up the price that a company must pay for its inputs or able to reduce the quality of the inputs they supply, depressing the company's profitability. On the other hand, if suppliers are weak, then a company has the opportunity to force down prices and demand higher input quality. As with buyers, the ability of suppliers to make demands on a company depends on their power relative to that of the company. The factors that determine the bargaining power of suppliers tend to be the same as those that determine the bargaining power of buyers and according to Porter, suppliers are most powerful in the following circumstances.

- If an input is important to the buyers — that is, when an industry needs an input for which there is no realistic substitute — they have no option but to purchase supplies at whatever price and quality level are set by the suppliers. In this scenario, the purchasing companies become price takers.

- If the supplier industry is dominated by a few large producers, the likelihood of these suppliers being highly rivalrous is reduced. If suppliers do not compete extensively, then they are unlikely to adopt tactics such as price reductions to try to increase market share. Software on Internet-oriented mobile phones, for example, is developed for the major companies of Nokia, Ericsson and Motorola. The dominant players in the software industry are Microsoft (through its Windows CE package) and the British company Psion (through its Java-based Symbian systems). The small number of software developers, the demand for innovative (as opposed to low-cost) software and the rapid growth of the mobile phone industry limit the competition between the two main producers and provide them with significant power, allowing them to charge high prices for their software.

- If suppliers' respective products are so much differentiated that it is difficult or costly for buyer companies to switch from one supplier to another, the suppliers have the upper hand in the relationship. Many computer assemblers, for example, continue to use Intel-produced processors rather than cheaper equivalents because prestige is attached to the Intel brand name.

- If buying companies are not important customers of the suppliers, the suppliers are unlikely to conform to the demands of companies in the focus industry.
- If there is a significant threat of forward integration, suppliers have less power. An industry that achieves high rates of return will be an attractive proposition for many firms outside the industry. Barriers may limit the entry of new companies but if suppliers can forward integrate, then the industry will be subjected to increased levels of competition. Higher levels of competition could either drive the nonintegrated (and most likely smaller) companies out of business or increase competition to the point that returns from operations return to average.

Substitute products

The final force in Porter's model is the threat of substitute products. Substitute products and services fulfil a similar function and may form a realistic alternative to the products or services produced by an industry. When realistic substitutes exist, they create an upper limit to the prices that the industry can charge because prices beyond a particular point will lead to customer defection to substitutes. Within Australia, most air routes do not have realistic transport substitutes because the distances involved make ground-based travel unfeasible for most travellers. Very fast trains (VFTs), however, may become a realistic substitute for air travel between major centres such as Sydney and Canberra. The time required to go from a city centre to the airport, wait at the airport, fly to the destination and catch a taxi to the destination city centre may be only slightly less than the time required to go between city centres on a VFT. If the train is cheaper by an amount that equates to the value of the extra time taken, then it could capture a significant part of the market.

In the soft-drink industry, many substitutes exist for soft drinks, including water, juice and sports drinks. The ability of soft-drink manufacturers to differentiate their product and continue to expand their market indicates that many consumers do not perceive the substitutes as realistic options most of the time. In the container area, however, there are many substitutes. Aluminium cans are more expensive to purchase but have superior characteristics to those of steel cans. Various sizes of recyclable bottles are a more recent substitute that threaten to make significant inroads into the soft-drink bottling industry, which is a major market for aluminium can producers.

A sixth force: complementors

complementors
Companies that supply complementary products or services that increase the inherent value of the focal product

Andrew Grove, former CEO of Intel and a part-time teacher at Stanford's Graduate School of Business, argues that Porter's five forces model ignores a sixth force: the power, vigour and competence of **complementors**.[6] Complementors are companies that sell complements to the enterprise's own product offerings. The complementors to Sony's popular home video game system, the PlayStation 3, are the companies that produce and sell games that run on the PlayStation 3. Grove's point is that an industry, without an adequate supply of complementary products, will face weak demand and low revenue and profits. No-one would purchase the PlayStation if there were not enough games to play on it. For another example, consider the early motor vehicle industry. When the motor car was first introduced at the beginning of the twentieth century, demand for the product was very limited. One reason was the lack of important complementary products, such as a network of paved roads and petrol stations. A car was of limited use when there were few paved roads to drive on, and when petrol stations were few and far between. As the supply of complementary products increased — as roads and petrol stations started to spring up — so did the attractiveness of owning a car. With roads and an adequate supply of petrol, owning a car became more practical and demand started to rise. In turn, this created a demand for more roads and petrol stations, setting up a self-reinforcing positive feedback loop.

Grove's argument has a strong foundation in economic theory. Most economic textbooks have long argued that both substitutes and complements influence demand in an industry.[7] Moreover, recent research has emphasised the importance of complementary products in determining demand and profitability in many hi-tech industries, such as the computer industry, in which Grove made his mark.[8] The basic point, therefore, is that when complements are an important determinant of demand in an industry, the health of the industry depends on complementors existing and producing an adequate supply of complementary products. It follows that if complementors are weak and lack attractive product offerings, then this situation can be a threat to the industry. (The converse also holds true.)

The importance of this potential sixth force would seem to depend on the extent to which the existence of complementary products and services determines the value of the focus product. The examples mentioned — namely, computer game consoles and cars — increase in value to the consumer as complementary products and services are more numerous. The attractiveness of these industries (in terms of profitability) is thus affected by the extent of the relevant complementors. Some industries, however, are not so dependent on complementary goods and services for value creation. The value that a consumer gains from a soft drink, for example, does not depend on the existence of any complementary products and services. This potential sixth force, therefore, has no bearing on the soft-drink industry. To appreciate how and when this sixth force of complementors may operate, see the discussion on network economics (pp. 85–6).

The role of the macroenvironment

So far industries have been treated as self-contained entities. In practice, they are embedded in a wider **macroenvironment**: the broader economic, technological, social, demographic, political and legal environment (see figure 3.2). Changes in the macroenvironment can have a direct impact on any one of the forces in Porter's model, altering the relative strength of the force and, with it, the attractiveness of an industry.

macroenvironment
The broader environment that can affect a company through political, legal, technological, economic, sociocultural and demographic forces

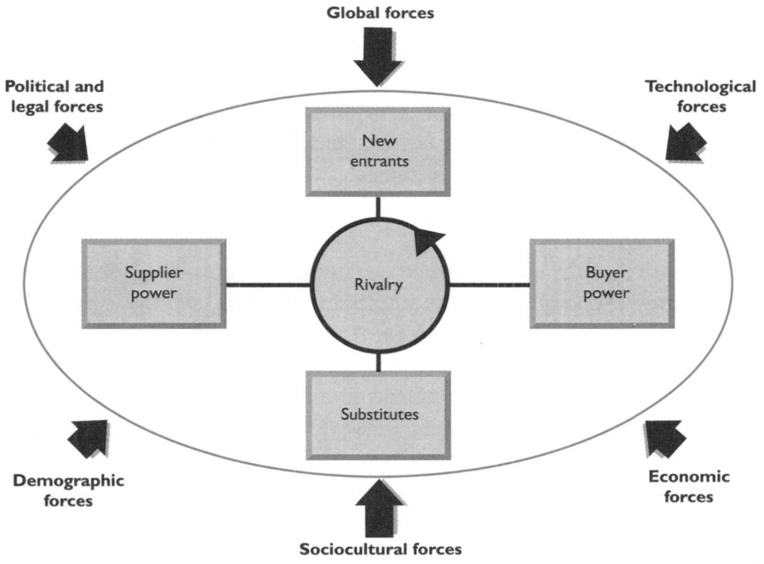

Figure 3.2:
The role of the macroenvironment

Understanding the overall environment in which a company operates involves scanning, monitoring and forecasting possible forces and assessing how they may affect the company. A company should regularly *scan* the macroenvironment for signals of environmental change or general trends. On observing a trend that may lead to a relevant environmental change, the company needs to *monitor* the change so it has a better understanding of the exact nature of the change and whether it applies to the organisation. If the monitoring process suggests the change is relevant, then the company needs to *forecast* how the change will affect its operations in the future. It is then necessary to *assess* the forecast implications to determine whether the environmental change will make a change in the company's strategy necessary.

To appreciate what a company should scan, macroenvironmental factors can be grouped into segments. The segments provide a checklist that a company can use to ensure it considers all factors that may affect its industry. These segments and their potential effects on an industry are discussed in the following sections.

Political and legal forces

Political and legal forces, through measures such as taxation laws, deregulation, monopolies legislation, environmental laws, employment laws and general government policy, can significantly affect the present or future operations of companies. In Australia, there has been a trend over the past decade towards deregulating more aspects of the economy and reducing trade barriers. The result has been that manufacturers (as the prime benefactors of tariffs and other trade barriers) have needed to become more efficient or develop alternative strategies if they cannot compete on the basis of price relative to imported goods. Similarly, deregulation in trading hours for shops (in all but one state) has meant that where deregulation has not occurred, comprehensive public awareness campaigns have been adopted to pressure the government to avoid taking this path.

Demographic forces

Most Western nations had declining population growth rates over the past two decades. Simultaneously, a 'greying of the population' has occurred because people are living longer. This combination of very low birth rates and longer lifespans has led to an increase in the average age of the population. The real effect of this 'greying' is likely to be felt as the baby boomers start retiring in large numbers in the next decade. In Australia and New Zealand, people continue to move away from regional areas into major population centres. While the size of major regional centres has remained constant, many of the smaller towns have virtually disappeared. The ageing of Western nations is providing opportunities for private hospitals, manufacturers of certain pharmaceutical products and providers of income-oriented investment products. The move by banks out of many smaller regional areas is a direct response to the declining profit opportunities in these areas and the technology-related opportunities to replace personal services with electronic services.

Economic forces

Various industries are highly susceptible to general economic conditions. Inflation rates, interest rates, currency exchange rates, unemployment levels, average disposable income and personal savings rates can affect industries to a greater or lesser extent. The home-building industry, for example, is closely tied to interest rates. Lower interest rates signal an ability for people to borrow more money, tending to lead to a boom in home construction. Conversely, every time interest rates rise, home builders know that demand for their services will fall.

General economic conditions affect some industries far more than others. During periods of recession, discretionary items are purchased far less frequently. In the most recent recessionary period in Australia and New Zealand, the sale of new cars dropped as people held on to their cars for longer or purchased second-hand vehicles. The reverse is also true in that 2005 saw a glut of second-hand cars as people moved into new cars. Hi-fi equipment sales and restaurant expenditure also increased. Other industries, such as power generation and many foodstuffs, remained relatively unchanged. In relation to exchange rates, when the Australian dollar or New Zealand dollar falls in value relative to other currencies, exporters are more competitive because their prices fall for overseas buyers. The cost of imports, however, increases, making local assembly operations of foreign manufactured goods less price competitive. Companies that are involved with highly discretionary products or services must therefore constantly scan the environment for changes in the general state of the economy.

Technological forces

The spread of computers in the latter part of the twentieth century affected almost every industry. Even basic industries were affected by new stock and human resource management systems, improved communications and greater access to information. The widespread uptake of computers has rarely led, however, to any company obtaining a sustainable competitive advantage. Instead, most companies simply have to keep up with the constant technological advances to remain competitive. More recently, many companies have invested in developing an Internet presence, often as the first step in developing an e-commerce capability.

Computers have been just one technology to be introduced. Incredible technological advances have been made since World War II. Technological change has fundamentally changed many industries and led to the creation of others. The mobile phone industry, for example, has emerged from nothing in the early 1980s. Now calling it the mobile phone industry may soon be obsolete as mobile communications become the norm, replacing fixed lines. Technological innovations will continue to change the competitive landscape in many industries, with new companies emerging on the basis of an innovation and others dropping out as they fail to adapt to the new environment that such discontinuous innovations create. Scanning the environment for appropriate technological advances becomes a necessity, because it provides a short-term competitive advantage for some. The slowest adapters are often left in a position that threatens their viability.

Sociocultural forces

The rise in the number of women in the workforce, greater levels of health consciousness and the environmental movement are examples of sociocultural forces that have had major effects on certain industries. The greater availability of highly trained women, who are taking less time out of their careers for family responsibilities, has been a boon for many industries that have faced greater demand than the labour pool can supply. High demand for skilled labour and a general move to higher levels of efficiency have created a range of professionals who are 'time poor'. This trend, in turn, has created enormous opportunities for industries that cater to the demands of people without enough time, for example, housekeeping and gardening services.

Inner-city living has increased the demand for small (though relatively luxurious) cars, smaller appliances and better-quality takeaway food. The demographic of the single or unmarried couple living in an inner-city apartment working long hours but with a very high disposable income has created a raft of opportunities for companies that can cater to this group's needs from tropical holidays to wine bars.

Global forces

Global factors such as changes in the financial status of major overseas markets, trade boycotts, wars, new political regimes and the creation of trade blocs can have a major impact on companies. In the mid-1990s, the 'bubble economy' of Japan burst, leaving the country in its longest recession. Soon after, in 1997, the Asian 'currency crisis' hit many Asian countries (including Thailand, Malaysia, Indonesia and South Korea) as companies and governments defaulted on loans and currency values plummeted. In 2002, the euro was introduced as a floating currency for many western European nations, with the intention of trying to create a more unified trading bloc by limiting transaction costs. Each of these events created opportunities for some companies but had a negative outcome for others. More recently, there has been a trend to negotiate free-trade agreements between certain countries. Australia instituted a free-trade deal with the United States in 2004 and started negotiating a similar deal with China in 2005. These deals could have significant ramifications for different industry sectors. In the US deal, it was widely expected that many primary producers would be better off because of increased access to the US market but television and film companies would be worse off because of the relaxation of limits in terms of local content required by Australian television stations.

Strategic groups and strategic blocks within industries

Industries are not homogeneous in most industries because they differ considerably in terms of the level of rivalry among companies, the strategies that companies use and even the market segment that companies target. In the motor vehicle, cosmetics and clothing industries, for instance, many companies do not even see themselves as competitors. High-end car companies such as Ferrari, for example, do not actively compete with companies such as Hyundai. In other industries, significant differences in strategies (such as being a low-cost producer rather than an innovative market leader) can mean that companies apply Porter's five forces model very differently, potentially resulting in the industry being viewed as attractive for one company, yet relatively unattractive for another. Given that it is often not possible to conceptualise industries as homogeneous entities, the concept of a **strategic group** can be used to appreciate how industry dynamics (as understood in the five forces model) can affect different groups of companies within an industry.

strategic group
A cluster of companies in an industry that follow similar strategies on the basis of similar resource endowments

Strategic groups can be conceptualised as a group of companies in an industry that follow the same or similar strategy in terms of the way that the firms compete.[9] Other approaches to conceptualising strategic groups are based around companies' similarities in resource endowments.[10] These two approaches to understanding strategic groups are similar because companies that have similar resources are likely to adopt similar strategies. As an example of how strategic groups can be created, it is useful to examine research in the area. In a study of the international airline industry servicing Australian ports, Davies, Galvin and Simmons looked at two dimensions to understand the strategic groups operating in the industry: (1) the extent of route structure and (2) ownership (private or majority government).[11] The aim was to capture the differences in the general size of airlines to differentiate between the megacarriers (such as British Airways) and smaller airlines (such as Malaysian Airlines and Qantas). The other dimension, ownership, was perceived as being important because governments run some airlines at a loss to maximise the more important tourist income or generate foreign currency reserves. In comparison, privately owned carriers are more likely to feel the full weight of economic realities and act accordingly (that is, withdraw from a route if it is unprofitable or not engage in price rivalry). Plotting each airline in the sample across these two dimensions created three clear clusters (see figure 3.3). The megacarriers are industry leaders and have extensive resources but generally face very high costs. Consequently, they try to minimise price-based competition and offer superior services, including benefits for frequent travellers and integrated services that can take passengers to almost anywhere in the world. The privately owned midsized carriers tend to have lower costs, rely more on their alliance partners to be able to get their passengers to many destinations and are wary of price-based competition. At times, however, airlines in this group instigate a price war when they cut fares to maintain capacity on a particular route. The government-owned airlines rarely have significant resources because many are unprofitable but governments keep them afloat for a variety of reasons, including the desire to earn 'hard' currency. With few resources, these airlines often engage in price wars to stimulate demand for travel to their home country or increase their passenger load.

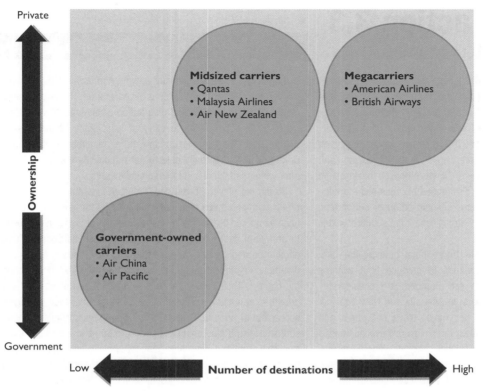

Figure 3.3:
Strategic groups in the international airline industry

Strategic groups can be useful in understanding how the five forces model will influence the different groups within an industry. In the pharmaceutical industry, for example, the companies that focus on the development and marketing of recently developed proprietary drugs (such as Merck, Pfizer and Eli Lilly) are much more attractive (and earn much higher rates of return) than the companies that produce generic drugs (such as Marion Labs and Carter Wallace). For a further example of strategic groups in action, see Strategy in action 3.3.

The other use of strategic groups is to appreciate patterns of rivalry within an industry, that is, who competes with whom. It is logical that companies within the same strategic group compete against each other because they target the same customers using similar strategies. The similar nature of the companies in the same group, however, is more likely to lead to higher levels of collusion, in which the companies work to stop new competitors from entering their group. This behaviour was evident in the pharmaceutical industry, in which companies in the same strategic group aimed their strategies at companies outside the group, implicitly colluding.[13] It is suggested that the companies within a strategic group recognise their mutual interdependence and so act to minimise the negative effects of intense rivalry with similar competitors.[14]

In much the same way, it is suggested that the more strategic groups that compete within an industry, the more intense the rivalry will be. One strategic group is likely to lead to implicit collusion; the existence of two strategic groups is likely to lead to competition between the companies of these groups; for more groups, this competition will increase exponentially. In the airline study by Galvin, Davies and Simmons, the level of price discounting was expected to increase as the number of airlines on a route increased (because increasing the number of competitors tends to increase the level of rivalry, as suggested in the five forces model).[15] The number of groups on a route also had a significant effect on the level of price discounting, even when controlling for the number of airlines on the route. Where, for example, three airlines from a single strategic group operated on a route, implicit collusion limited price discounting; on other routes, where the three airlines operating came from different strategic groups, intense price discounting was used as a competitive mechanism.

strategy in action 3.3

Strategic groups in the beer industry

The theory of strategic groups was initially tested through studies in the beer industry. Porter's five forces model suggests that attractive industry structures will tend to lead to higher levels of profitability and unattractive industries will see lower levels of profitability across all firms within an industry. This, however, was not observed in the beer industry, in which there were both very successful and considerably less successful players.[12] It was proposed that strategic groups could help explain these differences because some groups would be high performers and others would be lower performers. There was some, not particularly strong, empirical support for this position.

More than 25 years on from these initial studies, the beer industry around the world continues to produce both winners and losers. However, now, the raw numbers are considerably lower because of many takeovers. In Australia and New Zealand, the industry is dominated by two major players: Foster's and Lion Nathan. Over recent decades, both players have purchased many breweries to become global players. For example, Lion Nathan acquired XXXX, Swan Brewery and Tooheys.

Outside these big players, with their huge resources, are players of much smaller size, such as the family-run business of Coopers in South Australia, down to boutique brewers such as Little Creatures in Fremantle. With very different resources on hand, these smaller players compete in different ways, rarely on price. Coopers has managed to survive a significant downturn in its fortunes and now that premium beer is a rapidly growing market, it has prospered to the extent of establishing distribution arrangements with most major bottle-shop chains to carry at least some of their range. Boutique brewers, however, are in a more precarious position. Little Creatures was eventually able to get nationwide distribution only after winning national and international awards.

So the big players in the beer industry constitute one strategic group, with enormous resources, but their performance of late has been hampered by the decline in demand for traditional (as opposed to premium) beers. Medium-sized players such as Coopers form another strategic group because they are large enough to achieve distribution nationally and be placed 'on tap' in many hotels around the country. Their limited range is somewhat detrimental but the growth in demand for premium beers ensures that they are highly successful at present. Finally, boutique brewers struggle to attain sufficient distribution channels. Little Creatures is a success story from this group but, even here, its beer tends to be available to just one or two hotels in most states (if at all) and certainly cannot be found in the vast majority of bottle shops. The demand for different premium beer makes this an attractive industry to enter but most players in this last strategic group will often remain marginal because they have difficulty in selling their beer beyond a few outlets.

---

strategic block
A cluster or network of companies that are somehow linked by alliances or other cooperative arrangements

The concept of strategic groups has been in existence since the mid-1970s. The notion of a **strategic block** is a more recent approach to understanding patterns of rivalry and who competes with whom. Strategic blocks are groups of companies within an industry that exhibit denser strategic links among themselves than with other companies in the industry.[16] With the proliferation of intercompany alliances and interorganisational alliances, patterns of rivalry may be best understood by considering which companies are linked together in an industry. In the airline industry, major alliance blocks include OneWorld, Sky Team and Star Alliance. Airlines in these alliance blocks undertake a code-sharing arrangement (in which one airline operates a route for its partners as well as itself), share executive lounges, coordinate the time of their flights and allow frequent flyer points to be earned and redeemed on each other's networks. It does not make sense for two airlines in the same alliance block to compete vigorously with each other; rather, they compete with airlines in different alliance blocks. Alliance blocks have been identified in several industries, including motor vehicles, semiconductors, banks, telecommunications hardware and chemicals.[17] The validity of using strategic blocks rather than strategic groups is not clear but one study of the airline industry showed that price discounting on a route increased as the number of strategic blocks increased.[18] There was strong collaboration when only one strategic block was present on a route, moderate levels of competition when there were two blocks and relatively intense competition when there were three blocks. These patterns of competition occurred irrespective of the number of airlines on a route.

Overall, the work on segmenting industries into groups shows that some strategic groups are more attractive than others in terms of the five forces model but that competition among groups is likely to be more intense than competition within groups. Moving to a new group may be difficult, not just because the competitive force creates a barrier but also because a company requires a different set of resources to operate in a new group. The notion of strategic groups may need to be complemented with the concept of strategic blocks where extensive alliances within an industry are seen, because companies that are somehow linked are likely to compete with each other far less vigorously than unconnected companies do.

Limitations of the five forces and strategic group models

The five forces and strategic group models provide useful ways of thinking about and analysing the nature of competition within an industry to identify opportunities and threats. Managers need to be aware of their shortcomings, however, because both models (1) present a static picture of competition that slights the role of innovation and (2) de-emphasise the significance of individual company differences while overstressing the importance of the industry and groups within the industry as determinants of company profit rates.

Innovation and industry structure

Over any reasonable length of time, competition in many industries can be viewed as a process driven by innovation.[19] Companies that pioneer new products, processes or strategies can earn enormous profits. This prospect gives companies a strong incentive to seek innovations. Consider, for example, the growth of Nokia, Cochlear, Lonely Planet and Dell Computer Corporation. All of these companies have been innovators. Nokia was a major innovator in mobile phones, Cochlear took hearing aids to a new level of sophistication, Lonely Planet introduced an independent travel guide for backpackers and Dell developed a new system for selling computers through an online ordering system.

Successful innovation can revolutionise industry structure. In recent decades, one of the most common consequences of innovation has been the lowering of fixed costs of production, reducing barriers to entry and allowing new, smaller enterprises to compete with large, established organisations. Take the steel industry as an example. Two decades ago, BHP operated a number of steel mills in Australia. Around the world, large integrated manufacturers dominated the steel industry. Each industrialised country tended to have a limited number of producers, creating a type of oligopoly in which tacit price collusion was practised. The first threat to this structure came from new plants in Asia, which use more advanced and efficient technologies. Then along came a series of efficient minimill producers, such as Nucor and Chapman Steel, which used scrap metal and electric arc furnaces. Over the past 25 years, these developments have completely changed the industry structure. What was once a consolidated industry is now much more fragmented and price competitive. In Australia, BHP Billiton has a reduced presence from its operations of even a decade ago; in the United States, the successor company to US Steel, USX, has a 15 per cent market share, down from 55 per cent in the 1960s. Other major steel mills in the United States, such as Bethlehem and LTV, have been through Chapter 11 bankruptcy proceedings. In comparison, new plants in countries such as South Korea and China have continued to grow, and minimills now hold more than 30 per cent of the market. These changes have reshaped the nature of competition in the steel industry. A five forces analysis done 25 years ago would have shown a very attractive industry, whereas an analysis today (at least from the perspective of integrated mills) would show an industry that is relatively unattractive.

In more recent work, Porter, the originator of the five forces and strategic group concepts, explicitly recognises the role of innovation in revolutionising industry structure. Porter talks of innovations as 'unfreezing' and 'reshaping' industry structure.[20] He argues that after a period of turbulence triggered by innovation, the structure of an industry again settles into a fairly stable pattern. When the industry stabilises in its new configuration, the five forces and strategic group concepts can once more be applied. This view of the evolution of industry structure is often referred to as 'punctuated equilibrium'.[21] The punctuated equilibrium view holds that long periods of equilibrium, when an industry's structure is stable, are punctuated by periods of rapid change, when innovation revolutionises industry structure, that is, there is an unfreezing and refreezing process.

Figure 3.4 shows how punctuated equilibrium may look for one key dimension of industry structure: competitive structure. From time t_0 to t_1, the competitive structure of the industry is a stable oligopoly, with a few companies sharing the market. At time t_1, either an existing company or a new entrant pioneers a major innovation. The result is a period of turbulence between t_1 and t_2. After a while, however, the industry settles into a new state of equilibrium but the competitive structure is now far more fragmented. Note that the opposite could have happened: the industry could have become more consolidated, although this seems to be less common. In general, innovations seem to lower barriers to entry, allow more companies into the industry and, as a result, lead to fragmentation rather than consolidation.

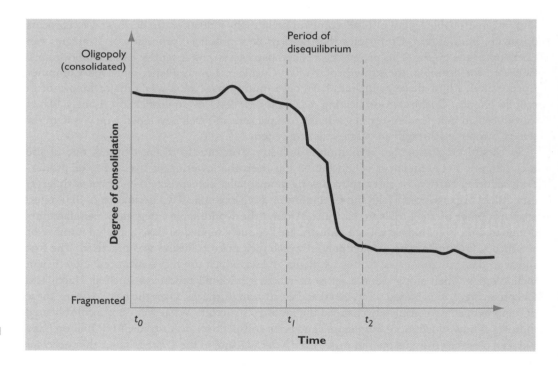

Figure 3.4:
Punctuated equilibrium and competitive structure

It is important to understand that during periods of rapid change, when innovation industry revolutionises structure, value typically migrates to new business models.[22] In brokerage, for example, value is currently migrating from the full-service broker model towards the online share trading model. In the steel industry, the introduction of electric arc technology led to a migration of value from large integrated enterprises towards small minimills. In the bookselling industry, value may be beginning to migrate from 'brick and mortar' booksellers towards online bookstores such as Amazon (although it is still too early to state definitively how successful the online retail model will be).

Because the five forces and strategic group models are static, they cannot adequately capture what occurs during periods of rapid change in the industry environment when value is migrating. They are useful tools, however, for analysing industry structure during periods of stability. Some scholars, though, question the validity of the punctuated equilibrium approach. D'Avani has argued that many industries are in a state of **hypercompetition**.[23] Hypercompetitive industries are characterised by permanent and ongoing innovation. (The computer industry is often cited as an example of a hypercompetitive industry.) The structure of this type of industry is constantly being revolutionised by innovation; there are no periods of equilibrium. When this is the case, the five forces and strategic group models may be of limited value because they represent no more than snapshots of a moving picture.

hypercompetition
Rapidly developing industries that do not achieve periods of maturity, so that patterns of competition are constantly changing

Industry structure and company differences

The second criticism of the five forces and strategic group models is that they overemphasise the importance of industry structure as a determinant of company performance and understress the importance of differences between companies within an industry or strategic group.[24] As pointed out in the next chapter, the profit rates of individual companies within an industry can vary enormously. Research by Rumelt and others suggests that industry structure explains only about 10 per cent of this variance, whereas individual company differences explain approximately 40 per cent.[25] Other studies put the explained variance closer to 20 per cent, which is still not a large figure.[26] Similarly, a growing number of studies have found only weak evidence of a link between strategic group membership and company profit rates, despite the strategic group model predicting a strong link.[27] Collectively, these studies suggest that the individual resources and capabilities of a company are far more important determinants of its profitability than is the industry or strategic group of which the company is a member. Although these findings do not make the five forces and strategic group models irrelevant, they do mean that the models have limited usefulness. A company will not be profitable just because it is based in an attractive industry or strategic group. As discussed in chapters 4 and 5, more is required.

Competitive changes during an industry's evolution

Most industries pass through stages from growth through maturity and eventually into decline. These stages have different implications for the form of competition. The strength and nature of each of Porter's five competitive forces typically changes as an industry evolves.[28] This is particularly true regarding potential competitors and rivalry, and this discussion focuses on those two forces. The changes in their strength and nature give rise to different opportunities and threats at each stage of an industry's evolution. The tasks facing managers are to anticipate how the strength of each force will change with the stage of industry development, and to formulate strategies that take advantage of opportunities as they arise, which counter emerging threats.

The **industry lifecycle model** is a useful tool for analysing the effects of industry evolution on competitive forces. With it, five industry environments can be identified, each linked to a distinct stage of an industry's evolution: (1) an embryonic industry environment, (2) a growth industry environment, (3) a shakeout environment, (4) a mature industry environment and (5) a declining industry environment (see figure 3.5).

industry lifecycle model
A stylised model of how industries go through stages

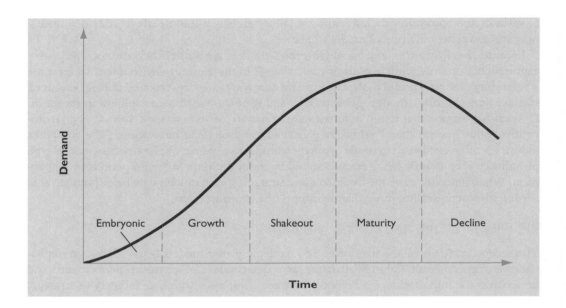

Figure 3.5:
Stages of the industry
lifecycle

Embryonic industries

An embryonic industry is one that is just beginning to develop (for example, third-generation mobile phone systems — with video phone capabilities — are probably still in the embryonic stage in Australia). Growth at this stage is slow as a result of factors such as buyers' unfamiliarity with the industry's product, high prices caused by the inability of companies to reap any significant economies of scale, and poorly developed distribution channels. Barriers to entry at this stage in an industry's evolution tend to be based on access to key technological know-how rather than on costs or brand loyalty. If the core know-how required to compete in the industry is complex and difficult to grasp, then barriers to entry can be quite high and incumbent companies will be protected from potential competitors. Rivalry in embryonic industries is based not so much on price as on educating customers, opening up distribution channels and perfecting the design of the product. The rivalry can be intense, and the company that is the first to solve design problems often has the opportunity to develop a significant market position. An embryonic industry may also be the creation of one company's innovative efforts, as happened with desktop computers (Apple), vacuum cleaners (Hoover) and photocopiers (Xerox). In these circumstances, the company has a major opportunity to capitalise on the lack of rivalry and build a strong hold on the market.

Growth industries

Once demand for the industry's product begins to take off, the industry develops the characteristics of a growth industry. In a growth industry, first-time demand expands rapidly as many new consumers enter the market. Typically, an industry grows when consumers become familiar with the product, when prices fall because experience and economies of scale have been attained and when distribution channels develop. In the Asia-Pacific region, the mobile phone industry has been growing at a rapid rate. In New Zealand, for example, only 18 per cent of households had a mobile phone in 1997 but this proportion had risen to more than 65 per cent by 2004 (with many households now having more than one mobile phone). Accompanying this growth have been price wars as new entrants try to gain market share.

Normally, the importance of control over technological knowledge as a barrier to entry has diminished by the time an industry enters its growth stage. Because few companies have yet achieved significant economies of scale or differentiated their product sufficiently to guarantee brand loyalty, other barriers to entry tend to be relatively low as well, particularly early in the growth stage. The threat from potential competitors is therefore generally highest at this point. Paradoxically, high growth usually means that an industry can absorb new entrants without a marked increase in competitive pressure.

During an industry's growth stage, rivalry tends to be relatively low. Rapid growth in demand allows companies to expand their revenue and profits without taking market share from competitors. A company has the opportunity to expand its operations. In addition, a strategically aware company takes advantage of the relatively benign environment of the growth stage to prepare itself for the intense competition of the coming industry shakeout.

Industry shakeout

Explosive growth of the type experienced by the mobile phone and PC industries in the 1990s cannot be maintained indefinitely. Sooner or later, the rate of growth slows and the industry enters the shakeout stage, when demand approaches saturation levels. In a saturated market, few potential first-time buyers remain, and demand is mostly limited to replacement demand.

At this stage, rivalry between companies becomes intense. Companies that have become accustomed to rapid growth during an industry's growth phase typically continue to add capacity at rates consistent with it. Managers use historic growth rates to forecast future growth rates and they plan expansions in productive capacity accordingly. As an industry approaches maturity, however, demand no longer grows at historic rates, so excess productive capacity emerges. This condition is illustrated in figure 3.6, in which the solid curve indicates the growth in demand and the broken curve indicates the growth in productive capacity. Past point t_1, demand growth becomes slower as the industry becomes mature. Capacity continues to grow, however, until time t_2. The gap between the solid line and the broken line signifies excess capacity. In an attempt to use this capacity, companies often cut prices. The result can be a price war, which drives many of the most inefficient companies into bankruptcy. This scenario is enough to deter any new entry.

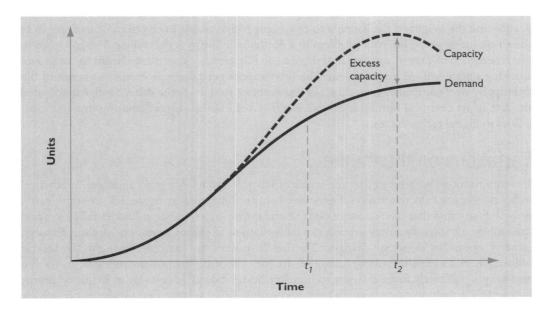

Figure 3.6:
Growth in demand and capacity

Mature industries

The shakeout stage ends when the industry enters its mature stage. In a mature industry, the market is totally saturated and demand is limited to replacement demand. During this stage, growth is low or even zero. The little growth that occurs comes from population expansion bringing new consumers into the market.

As an industry enters maturity, barriers to entry increase and the threat of entry from potential competitors decreases. As growth slows during the shakeout, companies can no longer maintain historic growth rates merely by holding on to their market share. Competition for market share develops, driving down prices. Often the result is a price war.

To survive the shakeout, companies begin to focus on both minimising costs and building brand loyalty. Breweries for example have ramped up their spending on advertising to try to create brand loyalty across the mature beer industry. They have also invested in developing new beers, particularly in the still growing premium beer market, or have invested offshore in ventures such as Lion Nathan's expansion into China. As a result of the shakeout, most industries in the maturity stage have consolidated and become oligopolies, like the soft-drink and beer industries. In mature industries, companies tend to recognise their interdependence and try to avoid price wars. Stable demand gives them the opportunity to enter into price-leadership agreements. The net effect is to reduce the threat of intense rivalry among established companies, allowing greater profitability. As noted earlier, however, the stability of a mature industry is always threatened by further price wars. A general slump in economic activity can depress industry demand. As companies fight to maintain their revenues when demand flags, price-leadership agreements break down, rivalry increases and prices and profits fall. The periodic price wars that occur in the airline industry seem to follow this pattern.

Declining industries

Eventually, most industries enter a decline stage. In this stage, growth becomes negative for a variety of reasons, including technological substitution (e.g. air travel for rail travel), social changes (e.g. greater health consciousness hitting tobacco sales), demographics (e.g. the declining birthrate hurting the market for baby and child products) and international competition (e.g. the decline of the Australian steel industry). Within a declining industry, the degree of rivalry among established companies usually increases. Depending on the speed of the decline and the height of the barriers to exit, competitive pressures can become as fierce as in the shakeout stage.[29] The main problem in a declining industry is that falling demand leads to the emergence of excess capacity. In trying to use this capacity, companies begin to cut prices, sparking a price war. As noted, the steel industry experienced these problems as a result of the attempt by steel companies to use their excess capacity. Kodak, on the other hand, has accepted the fate of its chemical film business and has invested enormously, attempting to build capabilities in digital technologies.

Variations on the theme

It is important to remember that the industry lifecycle model is a generalisation. In practice, industry lifecycles do not always follow the pattern illustrated in figure 3.5. In some cases, growth is so rapid that the industry skips the embryonic stage. Other industries fail to get past the embryonic stage. Industry growth can be revitalised after long periods of decline, through either innovations or social changes. The health boom, for example, brought the bicycle industry back to life after a long period of decline. The time span of the different stages can also vary significantly from industry to industry. Some industries can stay in maturity almost indefinitely if their products become basic necessities of life, as is the case for the motor vehicle industry. Others skip the mature stage and go straight into decline, as occurred in the vacuum tube industry: transistors replaced vacuum tubes as a major component in electronic products while the industry was still in its growth stage. Still other industries may go through not one but several shakeouts before they enter full maturity.

Network economics as a determinant of industry conditions

In recent years, there has been a growing realisation that network economics are a primary determinant of competitive conditions in many hi-tech industries, including computer hardware and software, consumer electronics, home video games, telecommunications and Internet service providers.[30] Network economics arise in industries in which the size of the 'network' of complementary products is a primary determinant of demand for the industry's product. As argued, the demand for cars early in the twentieth century was a function of the increasing network of paved roads and petrol stations. Similarly, the demand for telephones is a function of the increasing number of other numbers that can be called with that telephone, that is, it is a function of the size of the telephone network. In other words, the telephone network is the complementary product. In the stereo equipment industry, the network is the availability of recorded music. CDs long held their dominance over other types of digital recorded music (mini-discs, digital cassettes etc). Initially, the creation of MP3 files from CDs did not threaten the CD as a format (only the amount of CDs that may be purchased) because these files could realistically only be played on a computer. Consequently, there were few opportunities to buy legal MP3 files from well-known artists. This all changed with Apple's iPod and a range of other MP3 players. On-line distribution of music as MP3 files became a realistic business and online stores such as iTunes were created. With these complementary hardware products (MP3 players) and distribution outlets for complementary products in the form of music being in place, it is likely to only be a matter of time before the CD as a format starts its decline.

The same type of positive feedback loop is now at work with the Internet. The value of an Internet connection to individual users is a function of (1) the supply of useful information that they can access over the Internet and (2) the opportunity for engaging in commercial transactions through the medium of the Internet. The number of people with Internet connections drives forward the supply of information and commercial services. The increase in services, in turn, increases the value of an Internet connection, which drives forward the demand for Internet connections, leading to a further increase in the supply of information and services, and so on.

Why do network economics affect industry conditions? For a start, a positive feedback loop can help generate rapid growth in demand, as can now be seen with the Internet. The demand for Internet services has been expanding exponentially. These exponential surges in demand cannot go on forever but they create very attractive industry conditions while they are at work. Second, the operation of positive feedback loops can result in an industry becoming very concentrated and potential competitors being locked out by high switching costs. To understand this process, consider the history of the personal computer industry.

The value of a PC is a function of (1) the amount of software used on that computer and (2) how many other complementary products can be used with that computer, including printers, modems and Internet connections. In other words, the value of a PC is a function of the 'network' of complementary products.

As a result of network economics, the markets for PC operating systems and microprocessors have become very concentrated. Microsoft and Intel have tremendous bargaining power over their suppliers and buyers, while switching costs have produced high barriers to entry. Given

network economics
The economic effects of a product's value being determined by the existence of complementary products or services

these factors, Microsoft and Intel enjoy high profit margins. Despite several attempts, new competitors have struggled to gain much of a foothold in these profitable markets. It would be wrong, however, to assume that Microsoft and Intel are consequently immune to competition. If a new competitor should arise, offering an operating system or microprocessor that is so superior that consumers are willing to bear switching costs, then Microsoft and Intel could lose market share. That this has not happened yet is partly a testament to the ability of Microsoft and Intel to improve continually the performance capabilities of the Windows operating systems and Intel's microprocessors, respectively (see figure 3.7).

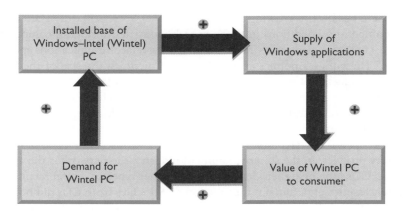

Figure 3.7:
Positive feedback in the computer industry

In summary, a consideration of network economics leads to important conclusions. First, in industries where network economics are important, positive feedback loops tend to operate. Once initiated, a positive feedback loop can lead to a rapid increase in demand. Second, markets in which positive feedback loops operate tend to be winner-takes-all markets, with second- or third-string competitors being marginalised. This has occurred in the market for computer operating systems. Third, enterprises that benefit from network economics tend to be in a powerful position relative to buyers and suppliers and tend to be protected from potential competitors by barriers to entry arising from switching costs. From the perspective of an individual company, the trick is to find the right strategy to allow it to grow the installed base of its product rapidly to set up a positive feedback loop. To see how this works, see Strategy in action 3.4.

Globalisation and industry structure

A fundamental change is occurring in the world economy.[31] We seem to be witnessing the globalisation of production and of markets. With regard to the globalisation of production, individual companies are increasingly dispersing parts of their production process to different locations around the globe, to take advantage of national differences in the cost and quality of factors of production such as labour, energy, land and capital. The objective is to lower costs and boost profits.

Boeing's most recent addition to its commercial jet aircraft range — the 777 — involves 132 500 engineered parts, which are produced around the world by 545 different suppliers. Eight Japanese suppliers make parts of the fuselage, doors and wings; a supplier in Singapore makes the doors for the nose landing gear; three suppliers in Italy manufacture wing flaps and so on. Part of Boeing's rationale for outsourcing so much production to foreign suppliers is that these various suppliers are the best in the world at performing their particular activity. The result of having foreign suppliers build specific parts is a better final product.[32] Similarly,

strategy in action 3.4

Network economics in the video game industry

Sony's Playstation is the clear market leader in the home video game industry, with the latest version, the Playstation 3, being released in early 2006. Its most recent challenger comes from Microsoft, now on its second-generation product, the Xbox 360. The video game industry is a classic example of an industry subject to network economics. The value that a user of a video game system receives is largely dependent upon the range and quality of the games that are available. However, most games are developed by external developers, rather than by the hardware manufacturers. An average game now costs more than $5 million to develop, with blockbuster games easily exceeding $25 million per title. With this sort of money put at risk every time developers start to create a new game, they want to ensure that their game is available to the largest possible group of consumers. In this case, it makes sense for them to develop their games for the most popular system (in this case, Playstation) to maximise the probability of receiving a good return on their investment. Therefore, whichever gaming system achieves dominance early is likely to remain the market leader because of the existence of more, and probably better, games.

In addition to these hardware–software complementarities, the network economics of this industry are reinforced by customer-to-customer links. The dominant demographic for home video game systems are 12-to-25-year-olds. They have social pressures to conform, in that if most of a potential new customer's friends and classmates own one type of system, then they are likely to purchase the same system. This is not only seen as being socially acceptable but it also increases the ability of this group to swap games and play against each other.

To build this initial dominant position can be very difficult. Technological superiority is a key factor, but it is also necessary to institute a low price to get players to move to a new system. This may mean selling the product at a loss initially. For example, the original Playstation retailed for about $200 but it is estimated that it cost Sony more than $450 to produce. Economies of scale, learning and greater efficiencies eventually reduced its manufacturing cost to about $80. In addition, it is often necessary to develop an initial range of games internally or finance external developers to do so to ensure that a range of games is on the market for the new hardware. With Playstation such a dominant force in the market, it will be a challenge for the Xbox to overcome the network economics of the industry to wrest market leadership from Sony.

Sources: Schilling, M 2003, 'Technological leapfrogging: lessons from the US video game console industry', *California Management Review*, vol. 45, no. 3, pp. 6–32; Cool, K & Paranikas, P 2003, 'Playstation 2 vs Xbox: video game consoles in the US in 2002', INSEAD case 304-038-1.

Hollywood-sponsored films are being shot in Sydney, on the Gold Coast and in New Zealand; major software houses often have software development offices in India and US cartoons are often drawn and coloured in Asia.

As for the globalisation of markets, it has been argued that we are moving away from an economic system in which national markets are distinct entities, isolated from each other by trade barriers and barriers of distance, time and culture, and towards a system in which national markets are merging into one huge global marketplace. Increasingly, consumers around the world demand and use the same basic product offerings. Consequently, in many industries, it is no longer meaningful to talk about the German market, the US market or the Japanese market; there is only the global market. The global acceptance of Coke, Sony Play-Stations, McDonald's hamburgers, Nokia mobile phones and Microsoft's Windows operating system exemplifies this trend.[33]

The trend towards the globalisation of production and markets has several important implications for competition within an industry. First, it is crucial for companies to recognise that an industry's boundaries do not stop at national borders. Because many industries are becoming global in scope, actual and potential competitors exist not only in a company's home market but also in other national markets. Companies that scan just their home market can be caught unprepared by the entry of efficient foreign competitors. The globalisation of markets and production implies that companies around the globe are finding their home markets under attack from foreign competitors. To illustrate, Australian wines outsell French and Italian wines in parts of Europe; Nokia has taken the lead from Motorola in mobile phones in the United States; and Japanese bicycle components manufacturer Shimano outperforms the combined operations of European component manufacturers Sachs, Campagnolo and Mavic.

Second, the shift from national to global markets during the past 20 years has intensified competitive rivalry in industry after industry. National markets that were once consolidated oligopolies, dominated by three or four companies and subjected to relatively little foreign competition, have been transformed into segments of fragmented global industries, in which a large number of companies battle each other for market share in country after country. This rivalry has driven down profit rates and made it all the more critical for companies to maximise their efficiency, quality, customer responsiveness and innovative ability. Not all global industries are fragmented though. Many remain consolidated oligopolies, except that now they are consolidated global, rather than national, oligopolies.

Third, as competitive intensity has increased, so has the rate of innovation. Companies strive to gain an advantage over their competitors by pioneering new products, processes and ways of doing business. The result has been to compress product lifecycles and make it vital for companies to stay on the leading edge of technology. The criticism that Porter's five forces model is too static may be particularly relevant to highly competitive global industries, in which the rate of innovation is accelerating.

Finally, even though globalisation has increased both the threat of entry and the intensity of rivalry within many formerly protected national markets, it has also created enormous opportunities for companies based in those markets. The steady decline in trade barriers has opened up many once protected markets to companies based outside them. In recent years, companies of industrialised countries have accelerated their investments in eastern Europe, Latin America and parts of South-East Asia as they try to take advantage of growth opportunities in those areas.

Summary

This chapter details a framework that managers can use to analyse the external environment of their company, enabling them to identify opportunities and threats. The following major points are made in the chapter.

- For a company to succeed, either its strategy must fit the environment in which the company operates, or the company must be able to reshape this environment to its advantage through its choice of strategy. Companies typically fail when their strategy no longer fits the environment in which they operate.

- The main technique used to analyse competition in the industry environment is the five forces model. The five forces are: (1) the risk of new entry by potential competitors, (2) the extent of rivalry among established firms, (3) the bargaining power of buyers, (4) the bargaining power of suppliers and (5) the threat of substitute products. The stronger each force, the more competitive is the industry and the lower is the rate of return that can be earned.

- The risk of entry by potential competitors is a function of the height of barriers to entry. The higher they are, the lower is the risk of entry and the greater are the profits that can be earned in the industry.

- The extent of rivalry among established companies is a function of an industry's competitive structure, demand conditions and barriers to exit. Strong demand conditions moderate the competition among established companies and create opportunities for expansion. When demand is weak, intensive competition can develop, particularly in consolidated industries with high barriers to exit.

- Buyers are most powerful when a company depends on them for business but they are not dependent on the company. In these circumstances, buyers are a threat.

- Suppliers are most powerful when a company depends on them for business but they are not dependent on the company. In such circumstances, suppliers are a threat.

- Substitute products are the products of companies serving consumer needs that are similar to the needs served by the industry being analysed. The greater the similarity of the substitute products, the lower is the price that companies can charge without losing customers to the substitutes.

- Some argue that there is a sixth competitive force of some significance: the power, vigour and competence of complementors. Powerful and vigorous complementors may have a strong positive impact on demand in an industry.

- Most industries comprise strategic groups, which are groups of companies pursuing the same or a similar strategy. Companies in different strategic groups pursue different strategies.

- The members of a company's strategic group constitute its immediate competitors. Given that different strategic groups are characterised by different opportunities and threats, a company may benefit from switching strategic groups. The feasibility of switching is a function of the height of mobility barriers.

- The five forces and strategic group models have been criticised for presenting a static picture of competition that de-emphasises the role of innovation. Innovation can revolutionise industry structure and completely change the strength of different competitive forces.

- The five forces and strategic group models have been criticised for de-emphasising the importance of individual company differences. A company will not be profitable just because it is based in an attractive industry or strategic group; much more is required.

- Industries go through a well-defined lifecycle, from an embryonic stage, through growth, shakeout and maturity, and eventually into decline. Each stage has different implications for the competitive structure of the industry, and each has its own opportunities and threats.

- In many hi-tech industries, network economics are important and positive feedback loops tend to operate. Once initiated, a positive feedback loop can lead to a rapid increase in demand. Markets in which positive feedback loops operate tend to be winner-takes-all markets. Enterprises that benefit from network economics tend to be in a powerful position relative to buyers and suppliers, and tend to be protected from potential competitors by entry barriers arising from switching costs.

- A fundamental change is occurring in the world economy: the globalisation of production and markets. The consequences of this change include more intense rivalry, more rapid innovation and shorter product lifecycles.

Practising strategic management

Review questions

1. What are the five forces in Porter's five forces model?
2. What are the key macroenvironment forces?
3. What are strategic groups?
4. What are the major stages in an industry product lifecycle?

Discussion questions

5. (a) Under what environmental conditions are price wars most likely to occur in an industry?

   (b) What are the implications of price wars for a company?

   (c) How should a company try to deal with the threat of a price war?

6. Discuss Porter's five forces model with reference to what you know about your local hotel industry. What does the model tell you about the level of competition in this industry?

7. Explain what impact network effects may have on demand and industry structure in the market for mobile phone handsets.

8. Which macroenvironmental forces are likely to have the greatest impact upon the building industry in the future?

Applied questions

9. Using the material from Strategy in action 3.3, complete a five forces analysis for the video game industry. How important is the role of complementors in this industry?

10. Go to your local supermarket to find out which manufacturers operate in the laundry/detergent industry (e.g. major players such as Unilever and Procter & Gamble). Using this information, segment the industry into strategic groups along the lines of the example in Strategy in action 3.2 (covering the beer industry), indicating the dimensions that you use in your decision making and showing examples of companies that fall into each strategic group.

Small-group exercise

Competing with Microsoft

Break into groups of three to five people, and discuss the following scenario.

You are a group of managers and software engineers at a small start-up. You have developed a revolutionary new operating system for PCs. This operating system offers distinct advantages over Microsoft's Windows operating system. It takes up less memory space on the hard drive of a PC. It takes full advantage of the power of the PC's microprocessor and, in theory, can run software applications much faster than Windows can. It is much easier to install and use than Windows. It also responds to voice instructions with an accuracy of 99.9 per cent, in addition to input from a keyboard or mouse. The operating system is the only product offering that your company has produced.

1. Analyse the competitive structure of the market for PC operating systems. On the basis of this analysis, identify factors that may inhibit the adoption of your operating system by consumers.

2. Can you think of a strategy that your company may pursue, either alone or in conjunction with other enterprises, to beat Microsoft? What will it take to successfully execute that strategy?

Article file

Find an example of an industry that has become more competitive in recent years. Identify the reasons for the increase in competitive pressure.

Exploring the Web

Visiting Boeing and Airbus

Visit the websites of Boeing (www.boeing.com) and Airbus Industrie (www.airbus.com). Go to the news features of both sites and read through the media releases issued by both companies. Also look at the annual reports and company profile (or history features) contained on both sites. With this material as your guide, perform the following tasks.

1. Use Porter's five forces model to analyse the nature of competition in the global commercial jet aircraft market.

2. Assess the likely outlook for competition during the next ten years in this market. Try to establish (a) whether new entry into this industry is likely, (b) whether demand will grow or shrink, (c) how powerful buyers are likely to become and (d) what the implications of all this may be for the nature of competition ten years from now.

Strategic management project

Module 3

This module requires you to analyse the industry environment in which your company is based. Using the information you have at your disposal, perform the following tasks and answer the following questions.

1. Apply the five forces model to the industry in which your company is based. What does this model tell you about the nature of competition in the industry?
2. Are any changes taking place in the macroenvironment that may have an impact, either positive or negative, on the industry in which your company is based? If so, what are these changes? How will they affect the industry?
3. Identify any strategic groups that may exist in the industry. How does the intensity of competition differ across the strategic groups you have identified?
4. How dynamic is the industry in which your company is based? Is there any evidence that innovation is reshaping competition or has done so in the recent past?
5. In what stage of its lifecycle is the industry in which your company is based? What are the implications of this stage for the intensity of competition, both now and in the future?
6. Is your company based in an industry that is becoming more global? If so, what are the implications of this change for competitive intensity?
7. Analyse the impact of the national context on the industry in which your company is based. Does national context help or hinder your company in achieving a competitive advantage in the global marketplace?

Additional resources

Porter, M 2001, 'Strategy and the Internet', *Harvard Business Review*, vol. 79, no. 3, pp. 62–78. (A discussion regarding how the five forces model may apply to Internet business.)

Shapiro, C & Varian, HR 1999, 'The art of standards wars', *California Management Review*, vol. 41, no. 2, pp. 8–32. (A discussion of network economics.)

End notes

1. Porter, ME 1980, *Competitive strategy: techniques for analyzing industries and competitors*, Free Press, New York.
2. Bain, JE 1956, *Barriers to new competition*, Harvard University Press, Cambridge, Massachusetts. For a review of the modern literature on barriers to entry, see Gilbert, RJ 1989, 'Mobility barriers and the value of incumbency', in Schmalensee, R & Willig, RD (eds), *Handbook of industrial organization*, North Holland, Amsterdam, chapter 1.
3. A detailed discussion of switching costs and lock-in can be found in Shapiro, C & Varian, HR 1999, *Information rules: a strategic guide to the network economy*, Harvard Business School Press, Boston, Massachusetts.
4. Most of this information on barriers to entry can be found in the industrial organisation economics literature. See especially Bain, op. cit.; Mann, M 1966, 'Seller concentration, barriers to entry and rates of return in 30 industries', *Review of Economics and Statistics*, vol. 48, pp. 296–307; Comanor, WS & Wilson, TA 1967, 'Advertising, market structure and performance', *Review of Economics and Statistics*, vol. 49, pp. 423–40; Gilbert 1989, op. cit.; Cool, K, Roller, LH & Leleux, B 1999, 'The relative impact of actual and potential rivalry on firm profitability in the pharmaceutical industry', *Strategic Management Journal*, vol. 20, pp. 1–14.
5. *The Advertiser* (online) 2005, 'Glut hits growers', 3 December, accessed 21 December 2005.
6. Grove, AS 1996, *Only the paranoid survive*, Doubleday, New York.
7. In standard microeconomic theory, the concept used for assessing the strength of substitutes and complements is the cross-elasticity of demand.
8. For details and further references, see Hill, CWL 1997, 'Establishing a standard: competitive strategy and technology standards in winner take all industries', *Academy of Management Executive*, vol. 11, pp. 7–25; Shapiro & Varian, op. cit.
9. Porter, op cit., p. 129.
10. Cool, K & Dierickx, I 1993, 'Rivalry, strategic groups and firm profitability', *Strategic Management Journal*, vol. 14, pp. 47–59.
11. Davies, J, Galvin, P & Simmons, R 2002, 'Strategic groups versus strategic blocks as an explanation for patterns of rivalry in the international airline industry', Paper presented at 22nd Annual Strategic Management Society Conference, Paris, September.
12. Hatten, K, Schendel, D & Cooper, 1978 'A strategic model of the US brewing industry: 1925–1971', *Academy of Management Journal*, vol. 21, pp. 592–619.
13. Cool, K & Schendel, D 1987, 'Strategic group formation and performance: the case of the US pharmaceutical industry, 1963–1982', *Management Science*, vol. 33, pp. 1102–24.
14. Cool & Dierickx, op. cit.
15. Davies, Galvin & Simmons, op. cit.
16. Nohria, N & Garcia-Pont C 1991, 'Global strategic linkages and industry structure', *Strategic Management Journal*, vol. 12, pp. 105–24.
17. Vanhaverbeke, W & Noorderhaven, N 2001, 'Competition between alliance blocks: the case of the RISC microprocessor technology', *Organization Studies*, vol. 22, no. 1, pp. 1–30.
18. Davies, Galvin & Simmons, op. cit.
19. This perspective is associated with the Austrian school of economics. The perspective goes back to Schumpeter. For a recent summary of this school and its implications for strategy, see Jacobson, R 1992, 'The Austrian school of strategy', *Academy of Management Review*, vol. 17, pp. 782–807; Hill, CWL & Deeds, D 1996, 'The importance of industry structure for the determination of industry profitability: a neo-Austrian approach', *Journal of Management Studies*, vol. 33, pp. 429–51.
20. Porter, ME 1990, *The competitive advantage of nations*, Free Press, New York.

21. The term 'punctuated equilibrium' is borrowed from evolutionary biology. For a detailed explanation of the concept, see Tushman, ML, Newman, WH & Romanelli, E 1985, 'Convergence and upheaval: managing the unsteady pace of organizational evolution', *California Management Review*, vol. 29, pp. 29–44; Gersick, CJG 1991, 'Revolutionary change theories: a multilevel exploration of the punctuated equilibrium paradigm', *Academy of Management Review*, vol. 16, pp. 10–36.

22. Slywotzky, AJ 1996, *Value migration: how to think several moves ahead of the competition*, Harvard Business School Press, Boston, Massachusetts.

23. D'Avani, R 1994, *Hypercompetition*, Free Press, New York.

24. Hill & Deeds, op. cit.

25. Rumelt, RP 1991, 'How much does industry matter?' *Strategic Management Journal*, vol. 12, pp. 167–85. See also Mauri, AJ & Michaels, MP 1998, 'Firm and industry effects within strategic management: an empirical examination', *Strategic Management Journal*, vol. 19, pp. 211–19.

26. See Schmalensee, R 1989, 'Inter-industry studies of structure and performance', in Schmalensee, R & Willig, RD (eds), *Handbook of industrial organization*, vol. 1, North Holland, Amsterdam. Similar results were found by McGahan, AN & Porter, ME 1997, 'How much does industry matter, really?', *Strategic Management Journal*, vol. 18, pp. 15–30.

27. See, for example, Cool, K & Schendel, D 1987, 'Strategic group formation and performance: the case of the US pharmaceutical industry 1932–1992', *Management Science*, September, pp. 1102–24.

28. Hofer has argued that lifecycle considerations may be the most important contingency when formulating business strategy: see Hofer, CW 1975, 'Toward a contingency theory of business strategy', *Academy of Management Journal*, vol. 18, pp. 784–810. There is also empirical evidence to support this view: see Anderson, CR & Zeithaml, CP 1984, 'Stages of the product life cycle, business strategy, and business performance', *Academy of Management Journal*, vol. 27, pp. 5–24; Hambrick, DC & Lei, D 1985, 'Towards an empirical prioritization of contingency variables for business strategy', *Academy of Management Journal*, vol. 28, pp. 763–88. Also see Miles, G, Snow, CC & Sharfman, MP 1993, 'Industry variety and performance', *Strategic Management Journal*, vol. 14, pp. 163–77.

29. The characteristics of declining industries have been summarised by Harrigan, KR 1980, 'Strategy formulation in declining industries', *Academy of Management Review*, vol. 5, pp. 599–604.

30. For details, see Hill, op. cit.; Shapiro & Varian, op. cit.; Arthur, B 1996, 'Increasing returns and the new world of business', *Harvard Business Review*, July–August, pp. 100–9.

31. Dicken, P 1992, *Global shift*, Guilford Press, New York.

32. Metthee, I 1994, 'Playing a large part', *Seattle-Post Intelligencer*, 9 April, p. 13.

33. Levitt, T 1983, 'The globalization of markets', *Harvard Business Review*, May–June, pp. 92–102.

Internal analysis: resources, capabilities, competencies and competitive advantage

learning objectives

After studying this chapter, you should be able to:

- discuss the concept of value creation and how it links to competitive advantage

- discuss the generic building blocks of competitive advantage

- describe how the value chain may be used to determine the basis of a company's competitive advantage

- discuss how distinctive competencies, resources and capabilities can be used to build a competitive advantage

- describe what creates a sustainable or durable competitive advantage

- identify why companies fail and what they can do to limit their chances of failure.

David Jones and the store wars

In Australia, there are only two major department store chains that have a truly national footprint: Myer and David Jones. As part of the Coles-Myer group, Myer dwarfs David Jones. It has 61 stores and for the six months to January 2005, it reported sales of $1.66 billion and net earnings of more than $60 million. In comparison, David Jones has only 36 stores and its sales for the same period were $946 million with a net profit of $53 million.

Size is obviously not everything, with the net profit figures for these two chains being much closer than the number of stores (or even the total revenue). In this respect, David Jones has become something of a star performer in recent years. After having a share price that had sat about $1.20 in the early 2000s, the share price took off midway through 2003 and now consistently sits above the $2 mark.

So why has David Jones been the winner in what have been termed the 'store wars' of the past few years? The key changes started in February 2003 when David Jones appointed a new CEO, Mark McInnes. He started to actively institute what has become known as the 'house of brands' strategy.

The house of brands strategy sees David Jones stock many top-name brands and advertise them aggressively (rather than simply advertise David Jones). Wherever possible, it seeks to be the exclusive stockist of that brand in Australia. In many respects, the strategy is about partnerships in which the brand and David Jones are important to each other, rather than the brand simply representing just one competitor within the department store mix. McInnes uses the example of the Sass & Bide label, which was nurtured by David Jones, eventually allowing it to achieve global prominence. The result is that David Jones contains a veritable 'who's who' of major fashion brands.

The house of brands strategy contradicts the trend towards using less recognised brands to allow department stores to leverage their bargaining power over suppliers to achieve better margins. This involves using a brand that is specifically designed for a particular department store in the same way that supermarkets are moving more and more towards their own store brands and offering fewer proprietary brands.

How far David Jones can take its house of brands strategy remains to be seen. As the number of brands increase there will inevitably be some cannibalisation of sales. Although it can drop poor-performing brands, how many brands can be adequately stocked and managed within David Jones would seem to have a limit, although McInnes suggests that some years of growth remain in this strategy. In the meantime, David Jones is back to a position of strength after having spent much of the past decade largely fighting for survival against its larger and much more powerful competitor, Myer.

Sources: Lloyd, S 2005, 'Big plans in store', *Business Review Weekly*, vol. 27, no. 24, 23–29 June, pp. 36–8; Jones, T, Ross, T & Arcus, M 2004, 'David Jones: there's no store like it', in Hill, C, Jones, G & Galvin, P, *Strategic management: an integrated approach*, John Wiley & Sons, Brisbane, pp. C61–C76.

Overview

Chapter 3 focuses on factors outside the boundaries of the firm that aid an understanding of why some firms consistently outperform other firms. But what about firms operating in the same industry? In the opening case, it is shown that David Jones is outperforming Myer, because of what is occurring within the respective firms. This internal focus sees this chapter focus on analysing the resources and capabilities of the companies. This approach helps us to explain why Lonely Planet has outperformed Let's Go, why Toyota has outperformed Ford and General Motors (GM), why Woolworths has outperformed Coles and why Sharp and Sony have outperformed RCA and Philips.

Both Myer and David Jones have their own set of strengths and weaknesses. In many respects they are not necessarily any better or worse than those of the competitor; they are simply different. More important is how companies can make use of their strengths and overcome their weaknesses to gain a **competitive advantage** in their industry. This is what David Jones has done: it has taken the strengths that formed the basis of its competitive advantage and built strategies around them that have been successful. That is, its existing reputation at the high end of the market and appropriate store locations have enabled it effectively to adopt a house of brands strategy to sell to customers that are likely to be highly brand conscious.

This chapter and the next look inside a company at the strengths and weaknesses that determine its efficiency, innovative capability, product quality and responsiveness to customers. They explore how the strengths of a company are grounded in its resources, capabilities and distinctive competencies, and discuss how these help a company attain a competitive advantage based on superior efficiency, innovation, quality and responsiveness to customers. They also discuss three critical questions. First, once it is obtained, what factors influence the durability of competitive advantage? Second, why do successful companies lose their competitive advantage? Third, how can companies avoid competitive failure and sustain their competitive advantage? When you have finished this chapter, you will have a good understanding of the nature of competitive advantage, which will help you make better strategic decisions as a manager.

competitive advantage
When a company is able to outperform its rivals, as commonly measured by the attainment of profits above the industry norm

Competitive advantage, value creation and profitability

An underlying aspiration of companies when formulating a business strategy is the attainment — and sustainability — of competitive advantage. Generally, competitive advantage is manifested in a source (cause) of superior performance. The potential sources are many, but the dominant marker, or anchor, for developing and sustaining a competitive advantage is value creation.

The concept of value creation is broad and can take on many definitions. Does value creation mean the wealth created for shareholders from a higher share price? Does it mean the high levels of customer satisfaction derived from more or differentiated product attributes? Does it mean a rise in profits from the use of lower cost manufacturing processes? Value creation can mean all of these things. The principal focus of this section, however, is on value creation in light of two fundamental sources: (1) customers and (2) the company.

This discussion considers that there are largely two battlegrounds for the creation of value that can lead to competitive advantage. First, and most important, is the concept of customer value. Customer value is largely concerned with what constitutes value from the customer's perspective. Research reveals that consumers (customers) equate value with four basic categories: (1) low price, (2) what is wanted in a product or service, (3) the quality received for the price paid and (4) that which is received (benefits) for what is given (price).[1] Each of these four categories is briefly explained here.

1. *Value is low price*. Customers in this category largely perceive value as something that increases as the price they pay for a product or service decreases.

2. *Value is what is wanted in a product or service*. Customers in this category focus on the benefits received as the most important component of value. That is, the benefits received, rather than the price paid, are most important to the customers.

3. *Value is the quality received for the price paid*. Customers in this category tend to equate value with the trade-off between price and quality. In other words, value is created for the customer when he or she receives quality at a fair price (but not necessarily the lowest price).

4. *Value is that which is received for what is given*. Customers in this category equate value with all the benefits that they will receive in relation to price. Research suggests that value creation can be defined by the ratio of attributes (weighted by their evaluations) to price (weighted by its evaluations).[2] That is, value is defined as the highest amount of possible benefit received divided by the price paid. If, for example, a customer can get more from a litre of frozen juice than a litre of milk (assuming both cost the same) because the juice can be watered down and thus more drinks can be made, then he or she receives higher value from the juice relative to price.

Viewing value from the customer's perspective highlights that companies exist to satisfy customers. Drucker wrote that 'to satisfy the customer is the mission and purpose of every business'.[3] Recognising customers' value and then being able to provide that value, however, are highly complex issues, which involve the company's full attention. The second battleground in the value creation process is the company's creation and delivery of the things that customers value. This effort entails attending to the strategic choices that let the company satisfy the needs of the customer. These include, but are not limited to, questions such as the following:

- What market segment or segments should the company serve?
- What resources and capabilities are required to create, produce and continually innovate around the products and services that will meet the needs of the market segment or segments served?
- How will the company position itself against its rivals?
- What business model (that is, how the company will make a profit) should the company pursue?

Companies seek to develop a source or sources of competitive advantage to meet customer needs in a way that rivals cannot, which in turn brings superior performance. This discussion is elaborated in the following by a representation of the concepts of competitive advantage, value creation and profitability.

At the most basic level, how profitable a company becomes (which is a measurement of whether it has a competitive advantage) depends on three factors: (1) the amount of *value* that customers place on the company's products; (2) the *price* that a company charges for its products and services and (3) the *costs* of creating that value.

Note the important distinction between *value* and *price*. Value is something that customers assign to a product. It is a function of the attributes of the product, such as its performance, design, quality and point-of-sale and aftersales service. Most customers would place a much higher value on a top-end Lexus car from Toyota than on a low-end basic economy car from GM Holden, precisely because they perceive the Lexus to have better performance and superior design, quality and service. A company that strengthens the value of its products in the eyes of customers gives itself more pricing options: it can raise prices to reflect that value or hold prices lower, which induces more customers to purchase its product and expand unit sales volume.

Whatever pricing option a company chooses, however, the price that a company charges for a good or service is typically less than the value the customer places on that good or service. This is so because the customer captures some of that value in what economists call a 'consumer surplus'.[4] The customer is able to do this because the company is competing with other companies for his or her business, so it must charge a lower price than it could if it had a monopoly. Moreover, it is normally impossible to segment the market to such a degree that the company can charge each customer a price that reflects that individual's unique assessment of the value of a product (what economists refer to as a customer's 'reservation price'). For these reasons, the price charged tends to be less than the value that many customers place on the product. Nevertheless, remember the basic principle: *the more value a company creates, the more pricing options it has.*

These concepts are illustrated in figure 4.1: V is the average value per unit of a product to a customer, P is the average price per unit that the company decides to charge for that product and C is the average unit costs of producing that product (including actual production costs and the cost of capital investments in production systems). The company's average profit per unit is equal to $P - C$, and the consumer surplus is equal to $V - P$. The company makes a profit so long as P is more than C, and its profitability will be greater, the lower C is relative to P. The difference between V and P is partly determined by the intensity of competitive pressure in the marketplace; the lower the intensity, the higher is the price that can be charged relative to V. The difference between V and P also reflects the company's pricing choice.[5] A company may choose to keep prices low relative to volume because lower prices enable the company to sell more products, attain economies of scale and boost its profit margin by lowering C relative to P.

Note also that the value created by a company is measured by the difference between perceived value (V) and costs of production (C), that is, $V - C$. A company creates value by converting factors of production that cost C into a product on which customers place a value of V.

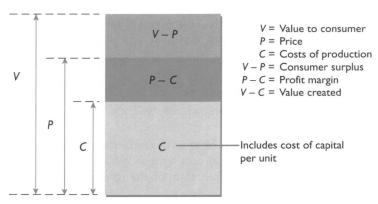

A company can create more value by either lowering its production costs (C) or increasing the value to the customer (V) by making the product more attractive through superior design, performance, quality, service and the like. When customers place a greater value on the product (V increases), they are willing to pay a higher price (P increases). This discussion suggests that a company has a competitive advantage and high profitability when it creates more value for its customers than rivals do.

The company's pricing options are captured in figure 4.2. Suppose a company's current pricing option is the one pictured in the middle column of figure 4.2. Imagine that the company decides to pursue strategies to increase the perceived value of its product offering from V to $V^\star$, to boost its profitability. Increasing value initially raises production costs because the company has to spend money to increase product performance, quality, service and other factors.

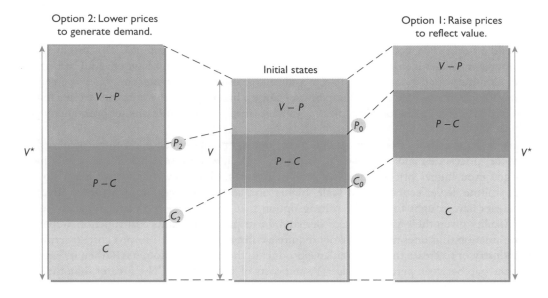

Option 2: Lower prices to generate demand.

Option 1: Raise prices to reflect value.

Figure 4.2:
Value creation and pricing options

Now the company can pursue two different pricing options. Option 1 is to raise prices to reflect the higher value: the company raises prices more than its costs increase, and profit margins $(P - C)$ increase. Option 2 is very different: the company lowers prices to expand unit volume. Customers recognise that they are getting a great bargain because price is now much lower than value (the consumer surplus has increased), so they rush out to buy more (demand has increased). As unit volume expands to meet increased demand, the company is able to realise economies of scale and reduce its average unit costs. The net result, although prices are lowered and creating the extra value initially costs more, is that the average unit costs of production fall as volume increases and economies of scale are attained, so profit margins widen.

There are more pricing options than those illustrated in figure 4.2. The company could hold prices constant, raise prices by less than is illustrated in option 1, or expand profit margins by simultaneously raising prices and realising some economies of scale on cost from a higher unit volume. What a company does depends on its industry environment and its business model, which are issues considered in the following chapters.

For now, the important point is that managers must understand the dynamic relationships among *value*, *pricing*, *demand* and *costs*, and make decisions based on that understanding to maximise competitive advantage and profitability. Option 2 in figure 4.2, for example, may not be a viable strategy if demand does not increase rapidly with lower prices or if few economies of scale will arise from increasing volume. Managers must understand the impact of value creation and pricing decisions on demand, and how unit costs change with increases in volume. In other words, they must have a good grasp of the demand for the company's product and its cost structure at different levels of output if they are to make decisions that maximise profitability.

Consider the motor vehicle industry. According to the 2005 Harbour Report, Toyota made US$1488 profit on every vehicle it manufactured in North America in 2004. GM, in contrast, made a loss of more than $2000 per vehicle, although before 2004, it had consistently made a little more than $100 per vehicle. What accounts for the difference? First, Toyota has the best reputation for quality in the industry. According to annual surveys issued by JD Power, Toyota consistently tops the list in terms of quality, while GM cars are, at best, in the middle of the pack. The higher quality translates into higher value created and delivered to customers, and allows Toyota to charge 5–10 per cent higher prices than GM charges for equivalent cars.

Second, Toyota has a lower cost per vehicle than that of GM, partly because of superior labour productivity. In Toyota's North American plants, it took an average of 27.9 employee hours to build a car in 2004, compared with 34.3 at GM plants in North America. This productivity advantage translates into lower labour costs for Toyota and therefore a lower overall cost structure. As summarised in figure 4.3, Toyota's advantage over GM derives from greater perceived value (V), which has allowed the company to charge a higher price (P) for its cars, from a lower cost structure (C). Taken together, these advantages imply significantly greater profitability per vehicle (P – C).[6]

Toyota's pricing decisions are guided by its managers' understanding of the relationship of value, prices, demand and costs. Given its ability to create more value, Toyota could have charged even higher prices than illustrated in figure 4.3 but they might have led to lower sales volume, fewer economies of scale, higher unit costs and lower profit margins. Toyota's managers have sought to find the pricing option that enables the company to maximise its profitability given their assessment of demand for its products and its cost function. Superior value creation thus does not necessarily require a company to have the lowest cost structure in an industry or to create the most valuable product in the eyes of customers. Rather, it requires that the gap between perceived value (V) and costs of production (C) be greater than the gap attained by competitors.

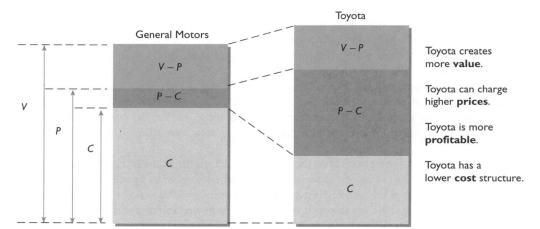

Figure 4.3:
Comparing Toyota and General Motors

Differentiation and cost structure

Note that Toyota has differentiated itself from GM by its superior quality, which allows it to charge higher prices, and its lower cost structure. Its competitive advantage over GM is, therefore, the result of strategies that have led to distinctive competencies resulting in greater differentiation and a lower cost structure.[7]

At the heart of any company's business model is the combination of strategies aimed at creating distinctive competencies that (1) differentiate its products in some way so it can create and deliver more value for customers (which gives it more pricing options) and (2) result in a lower cost structure (which also gives it a broader range of pricing choices).[8] Achieving a sustained competitive advantage and superior profitability requires the right choices with regard to value creation through differentiation and pricing given the demand conditions in the company's market, and the company's cost structure at different levels of output. This issue is considered in detail in the following chapters and captured in figure 4.4. See also Strategy in action 4.1 for an example of differentiation creating competitive advantage.

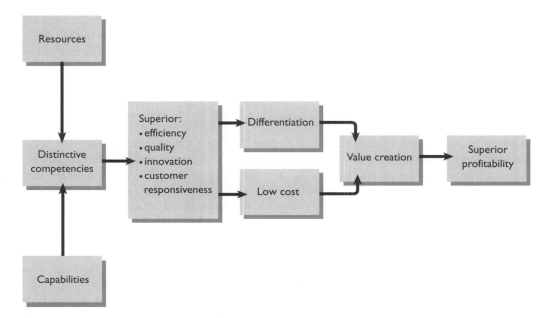

strategy in action 4.1

Lonely Planet's competitive advantage

Lonely Planet is arguably the most successful travel information company at present. Its guidebooks cover every continent, with about 650 on sale and an increasing range of associated products from calendars to television shows produced under the Six Degrees name. Interestingly, Lonely Planet was a relative latecomer to the travel guidebook industry but has managed to overtake its more seasoned rivals such as The Rough Guide, Frommers and Let's Go.

At the heart of Lonely Planet's success is a strategy of differentiation. The company was started by Tony and Maureen Wheeler in 1972 after they had travelled overland across Asia as part of the journey from London to Australia. Responding to questions from others who were interested in their experiences and wanting to know how they might do something similar, the Wheelers decided to publish a book about their experiences and how they did it. The result was *Across Asia on the cheap*. From these early days, Lonely Planet guidebooks have maintained a philosophy inspired by the Wheelers of engaging with local cultures through responsible travel and 'getting off the beaten track' where possible.

However, for the consumer, the Lonely Planet product filled an important niche for independent travellers. The Let's Go guides tended to dominate the budget end of the market. Written and updated by university students in their summer holidays, these guides covered how to get around cheaply but their impartiality was not always obvious, especially because they included advertisements throughout the book. At the other end, Frommers tended to cater to a money-conscious but less budget-oriented travel market. Lonely Planet publications have moved more into the gap between these two sets of publications, although the accommodation and food sections do cover the whole spectrum of options.

Perhaps more importantly, the quality of the material (using professional travel writers who work incognito), the level of detail, the impartiality and the regular updates have been important points of differentiation. More recently, the support materials supplied through their website to give up-to-the-minute travel hints and advice have made Lonely Planet a popular option for customers from backpackers through to well-off independent travellers.

The generic building blocks of competitive advantage

Figure 4.4 shows the four factors that influence a company's ability to build and sustain a competitive advantage: efficiency, quality, innovation and responsiveness to customers. In turn, the four factors allow a company to (1) differentiate its product offering and thus create greater perceived customer value and (2) lower its cost structure. These factors are generic building blocks of competitive advantage, that is, any company, regardless of its industry or its products or services, can pursue them. Although they are discussed sequentially in the following sections, the factors are highly interrelated. You should note the important ways in which they affect each other. Superior quality can lead to superior efficiency, for example, and innovation can increase efficiency, quality and responsiveness to customers.

Efficiency

In one sense, a business is simply a device for transforming inputs into outputs. Inputs are basic factors of production such as labour, land, capital, management and technological know-how. Outputs are the goods and services that the business produces. The simplest measure of efficiency is the quantity of inputs that it takes to produce a given output; that is, efficiency = outputs/inputs. The more efficient a company, the fewer the inputs required to produce a given output. If, for example, GM Holden in Australia takes 30 hours of employee time to assemble a car and Ford takes 25 hours, then we can say that Ford is more efficient than GM Holden. Moreover, so long as other things are equal, such as wage rates, we can assume from these data that Ford will have a lower cost structure than that of GM Holden. Efficiency thus helps a company attain a low-cost competitive advantage.

The most important component of efficiency for many companies is employee productivity, which is usually measured by output per employee. Holding all else constant, the company with the highest employee productivity in an industry typically has the lowest costs of production. In other words, that company will have a cost-based competitive advantage.

The interesting issue is how to achieve superior productivity. Later chapters examine in detail how a company can achieve high productivity (and quality, innovation and customer responsiveness). For now, it is enough to note that to achieve high productivity, a company must adopt the appropriate strategy, structure and control systems.

Quality

A product can be thought of as a bundle of attributes.[9] The attributes of many physical products include the form, features, performance, durability, reliability, style and design of the product.[10] A product is said to have *superior quality* when customers perceive greater value in its attributes than in rival products'. A Rolex watch, for example, has attributes — such as design, styling, performance and reliability — that customers perceive as superior to the same attributes in many other watches. We can therefore refer to a Rolex as a high-quality product: Rolex has differentiated its watches by these attributes.

Among the various attributes of products, one in particular has taken on special significance in the past two decades: *reliability*. A product can be said to be reliable when it consistently does the job that it was designed for, does it well and rarely, if ever, breaks down. Increasing product reliability has been the central goal of an influential management philosophy that came out of Japan in the 1980s and is commonly referred to as 'total quality management'. Given its unique role in the overall perception of quality, reliability is separated from other attributes of a product in our discussion of product quality. Quality products are defined as goods and services that are reliable, in the sense that they do the job that they were designed for and do it well, which increases perceived value but that also are differentiated by attributes that customers perceive to have a higher value.

The position of a product against these two dimensions — reliability and other attributes — can be plotted on a figure similar to figure 4.5. A Lexus, for example, has attributes (design, styling, performance and safety features) that customers perceive as superior to those of most other cars. The Lexus is also a very reliable car. The overall level of quality of the Lexus, therefore, is very high, which creates an impression of value in the minds of customers and gives

Toyota the option of charging a premium price for the Lexus. Toyota also produces another very reliable vehicle — the Toyota Corolla — but aims this car at less wealthy customers. The Corolla lacks many of the superior attributes of the Lexus, so although it is also a high-quality car in the sense of being reliable, it is not as high quality as a Lexus. At the other end of the spectrum can be found poor-quality products that have both low reliability and inferior attributes, such as poor design, performance and styling. An example is the Yugo, a car that was made in the former Yugoslavia in the 1980s. The Yugo was a boxy, low-powered vehicle aimed at the budget segment of the market, and it had a dismal reputation for styling, reliability and safety. Its overall quality was very low. A car (or any other product) may also have a collection of superior attributes but nevertheless suffer from very poor reliability, which would damage its overall quality.

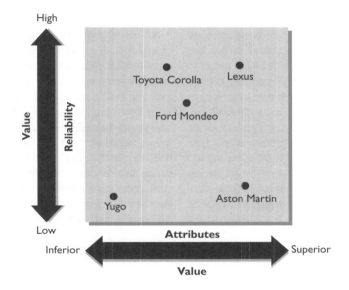

Figure 4.5:
A quality map for motor vehicles

The concept of quality applies whether one is talking about Toyota vehicles, clothes designed and sold by Billabong, the customer service department of ANZ or the ability of Air New Zealand to have its planes arrive on time. Quality is just as relevant to services as it is to goods.[11] The impact of high product quality on competitive advantage is twofold.[12] First, providing high-quality products increases the value of those products in the eyes of customers. This increased perception of value gives the company the option of charging a higher price for its products. In the motor vehicle industry, for example, Toyota can charge a higher price for its cars as a result of the higher quality of its products. Compared with GM, Toyota in the United States has both lower costs and the ability to charge higher prices. As a result, historically it has operated with a bigger profit margin than that of GM.

The second impact of high quality on competitive advantage comes from the greater efficiency and the lower unit costs associated with reliable products. When products are reliable, less employee time is wasted making defective products or providing substandard services and less time has to be spent fixing mistakes, which translate into higher employee productivity and lower unit costs. High product quality thus not only enables a company to differentiate its product from that of rivals but also, if the product is reliable, lowers costs.

The importance of reliability in building competitive advantage has increased dramatically over the past decade. So crucial is reliability to many companies that achieving high product reliability can no longer be viewed as just one way of gaining a competitive advantage. In many industries, it has become an absolute imperative for survival.

In the airline industry, companies used to be able to differentiate themselves on their reliability (such as on-time arrivals and safety records). Today, however, many major international carriers have similar reliability ratings, so no single carrier has an advantage. They are having to differentiate themselves, therefore, in terms of superior attributes, as shown in Strategy in action 4.2.

strategy in action 4.2

Quality developments in the airline industry

Not all that many years ago, economy passengers on international routes were given relatively few services. The focus was on keeping costs low. Business- and first-class passengers received much higher levels of personalised service and larger seats that generally reclined much further to allow the passengers to sleep more easily. In these upper classes, each airline has been attempting to outdo the others to achieve some differentiation. Executive lounges are now commonplace, as are seats that can be turned into flat beds in first class. Some airlines now allow you to order any meal in advance and an on-board chef will cook it for you whenever you request it. Malaysia Airlines offers limousine service to and from the airport, as well as Dom Perignon champagne on board. Today, almost all major full-service airlines have flat bed-style seats at least in first class and now in many of their business-class cabins.

Not all changes have been limited to the expensive seats at the front end of the plane. In economy class, Singapore Airlines started a move to install individual monitors so customers can choose their own movies from a large selection. More and more airlines are starting to install these monitors after seeing the positive response to the Singapore Airlines' initiative. Even the food has improved. Celebrity chef Neil Perry has helped design all of the Qantas menu offerings, from first class to economy class. Today, quality offerings are expected of any international airline that wishes to compete in the full-service airline segment.

Innovation

Innovation can be defined as anything new or novel about a company's operations or its products or services. Innovation includes advances in the types of product, production process, management system, organisational structure and strategy developed by a company. All of the following can be viewed as innovations: Intel's development of the microprocessor; the discounting strategy of Toys 'R' Us in the retail toy business; Toyota's lean production system for manufacturing cars and Dell's pioneering approach to online selling and customer service. Successful innovation is about developing new products or managing the enterprise in a novel way that creates value for consumers.[13]

Innovation is perhaps the single most important building block of competitive advantage. In the long run, competition can be viewed as a process driven by innovation. Although not all innovations succeed, those that do can be a major source of competitive advantage because, by definition, they provide a company with a **uniqueness**, that is, something that its competitors lack (until they imitate the innovation). Uniqueness lets a company differentiate itself from its rivals and either charge a premium price for its product or reduce its unit costs far below those of competitors.

As with efficiency and quality, the issue of innovation is explored more fully later in the book. A few examples can highlight the importance of innovation as the bedrock of competitive advantage. Consider Xerox's development of the photocopier, Cisco's development of the router, Intel's development of new microprocessors, Hewlett-Packard's development of the laser printer, Nike's development of hi-tech athletic shoes, Bausch & Lomb's development of

uniqueness
The ability of a company to gain a competitive advantage by either differentiating itself from its rivals and charging a premium for its product, or reducing its unit costs far below those of competitors

contact lenses and Sony's development of the Walkman. All these product innovations helped build a competitive advantage for the pioneering companies. In each case, the company, being the sole supplier of a new product, could charge a premium price. By the time competitors succeeded in imitating the innovator, the innovating company had built up such strong brand loyalty and supporting management processes that its position proved difficult for imitators to attack. Sony is still known for its Walkman, Hewlett-Packard for its laser printers and Intel for its microprocessors.

Responsiveness to customers

To achieve superior customer responsiveness, a company must be able to do a better job than competitors of identifying and satisfying the needs of its customers. Consumers will then place more value on its products, creating a differentiation-based competitive advantage. Improving the quality of a company's product offering is consistent with achieving responsiveness, as is developing new products with features that existing products lack. In other words, achieving superior quality and innovation are an integral part of achieving superior customer responsiveness.

Another factor that stands out in any discussion of customer responsiveness is the need to customise goods and services to the unique demands of individual customers or customer groups. The proliferation of different types of soft drink and beer in recent years can be viewed partly as a response to this trend.

Levi's similarly allows customers to have their jeans custom designed. By having their measurements fed into a computer system and choosing the style of jeans desired, customers can have their jeans altered in the cut and the size of panels.[14]

An aspect of customer responsiveness that has drawn increasing attention is **customer response time**, which is the time that it takes for a good to be delivered or a service to be performed.[15] For a manufacturer of machinery, response time is the time that it takes to fill customer orders. For a bank, it is the time that it takes to process a loan or the time that a customer must stand in line to wait for a free teller. For a supermarket, it is the time that customers must stand in checkout lines. Many customer surveys have revealed that slow response time is a major source of customer dissatisfaction.[16]

customer response time
The time that it takes for a good to be delivered or a service to be performed

Besides quality, customisation and response time, other sources of improved customer responsiveness are superior design, service and aftersales service and support, all of which allow a company to differentiate itself from its less responsive competitors. In turn, differentiation enables a company to build brand loyalty and charge a premium price for its products. Consider, for example, how much people are prepared to pay for Express Post services in Australia. In 2006, the cheapest Express Post Platinum service (guaranteed delivery to business addresses in a defined network covering major cities by 12 noon the following day) was $11.90 for post weighing up to 500 grams. A standard letter was 50 cents. The price premium was $11.40, or 2280 per cent over the regular price.

Summary

Efficiency, quality, innovation and responsiveness to customers are all important elements of a competitive advantage. Superior efficiency enables a company to lower its costs; superior quality lets it both charge a higher price and lower its costs; superior responsiveness to customers allows it to charge a higher price; and superior innovation can lead to higher prices or lower unit costs (see figure 4.6). Together, these four factors help a company create more value by lowering costs or differentiating its products from those of competitors, which enables the company to outperform its competitors.

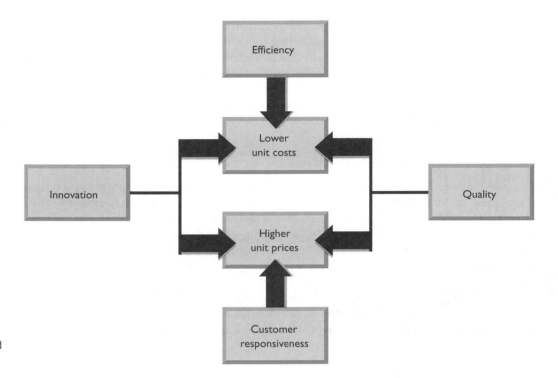

Figure 4.6:
The impact of efficiency,
quality, customer
responsiveness and
innovation on unit costs and
prices

Business functions, the value chain and value creation

This section considers the role played by the different functions of a company — such as production, marketing, research and development (R&D), service, information systems, materials management and human resources — in the value creation process. Specifically, it briefly reviews how the different functions of a company can help in the process of driving down costs and increasing the perception of value through differentiation. As a first step, consider the concept of the **value chain**, which is illustrated in figure 4.7.[17] It refers to the idea that a company is a chain of activities for transforming inputs into outputs that customers value. The process of transforming inputs into outputs comprises a number of primary and support activities. Each activity adds value to the product.

value chain
The activities that are necessary for transforming inputs into outputs that customers value

Primary activities

Primary activities have to do with the design, creation and delivery of the product, as well as its marketing and its support and aftersales service. In the value chain illustrated in figure 4.7, the primary activities are broken into four functions: R&D, production, marketing and sales, and service.

research and development (R&D)
The activities necessary for the design of products and production processes

Research and development (R&D) is concerned with the design of products and production processes. Although we think of R&D as being associated with the design of physical products and production processes in manufacturing enterprises, many service companies also undertake research and development. Banks, for example, compete with each other by developing new financial products and new ways of delivering those products to customers. Online banking and smart debit cards are two recent examples of new product development in the banking industry. Earlier examples of innovation in the banking industry include automatic teller machines (ATMs), credit cards and debit cards.

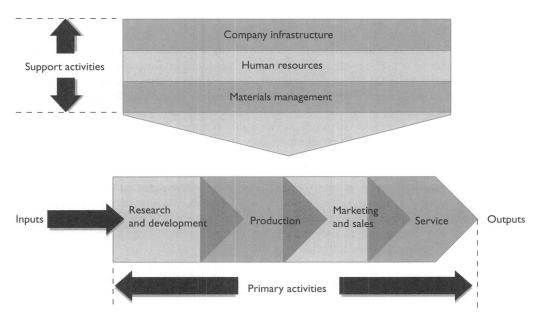

Figure 4.7:
The value chain

By superior product design, R&D can increase the functionality of products, which makes them more attractive to consumers. Alternatively, the work of R&D may result in more efficient production processes, lowering production costs. Either way, the R&D function of an enterprise can create value. At Intel, for example, R&D creates value both by developing ever more powerful microprocessors, and by helping to pioneer ever more efficient manufacturing processes (in conjunction with equipment suppliers).

Production is concerned with the creation of a good or service. For physical products, when we talk about production, we generally mean manufacturing. For services such as banking or retail operations, production typically takes place when the service is delivered to the customer, for example, when a bank originates a loan for a customer, it is engaged in production of the loan. The production function of a company creates value by performing its activities efficiently so that lower costs result. Production can also create value if a company performs its activities consistently with high product quality, which leads to differentiation and lower costs.

production
The activities necessary for the creation of a good or service

The **marketing and sales** functions of a company can help create value in several ways. Through brand positioning and advertising, the marketing function can increase the value that consumers perceive in a company's product. If these activities help create a favourable impression of the company's product in the minds of consumers, they increase value. For example, a Ben Sherman T-shirt retails for up to ten times more than other T-shirts in a department store. The marketing department for Ben Sherman has created a strong brand, which increases the value that consumers ascribe to the product.

marketing and sales
The activities necessary for the positioning, promotion and sale of the company's products and services

Marketing and sales can also create value by discovering consumer needs and communicating them back to the R&D function of the company, which can then design products that better match those needs.

The role of the **service** function of an enterprise is to provide aftersales service and support. This function can create a perception of superior value in the minds of consumers by solving customer problems and supporting customers after they have purchased the product. Caterpillar, the US-based manufacturer of heavy earthmoving equipment, can get spare parts to any point in the world within 24 hours, minimising the downtime that its customers have to suffer if their Caterpillar equipment malfunctions. This is an extremely valuable support capability in an industry in which downtime is very expensive. It has helped to increase the value that customers associate with Caterpillar products and thus the price that Caterpillar can charge for those products.

service
The activities necessary for the provision of aftersales service and support

Support activities

The **support activities** of the value chain provide inputs that allow the primary activities to take place (see figure 4.7). The **materials management** (or logistics) function controls the transmission of physical materials along the value chain, from procurement through production and into distribution. The efficiency with which this is carried out can significantly lower costs, creating more value.

Similarly, the **human resources** function can help an enterprise create more value. The human resources function ensures the company has the right mix of skilled people to perform its value creation activities effectively. It also ensures people are adequately trained, motivated and compensated to perform their value creation tasks.

Information systems refer to the (largely) electronic systems for managing inventory, tracking sales, pricing products, selling products, dealing with customer service enquiries and so on. Information systems, when coupled with the communications features of the Internet, hold the promise of being able to alter the efficiency and effectiveness with which a company manages its other value creation activities.

The final support activity is the **company infrastructure**. This has a somewhat different character from the other support activities. Infrastructure is the companywide context within which all the other value creation activities take place. The infrastructure includes the organisational structure, control systems and culture of the company. Given that top management can exert considerable influence on these aspects of a company, it should also be viewed as part of a company's infrastructure. Through strong leadership, it can consciously shape a company's infrastructure and, through it, the performance of all other value creation activities within the company.

Unique value chains and customer value

The previous section presents a generic description of the activities that constitute the value chain. In the pursuit of meeting customer needs, however, each company has to develop unique value chains to some extent. The bank Westpac, for example, places emphasis on marketing and service activities for creating value, rather than on activities such as R&D or materials management. On the other hand, the mining company Rio Tinto emphasises R&D activities to stay ahead of the competition.

From a practical perspective, the value chain serves as a guide for categorising the broad activities necessary to run a company. The real importance of the value chain, however, is its ability to help executives and managers focus attention on the value-based activities, both actual and potential, needed to develop and deliver a product or service. By understanding where value is created and why it is created at each stage in the development and delivery of a product or service, the company can link value-based strategies to customer needs and sources of advantage. In the quest to develop a unique position in the market, the company can map competitive advantage to specific value chain activities or a combination of those activities.

Distinctive competencies, resources and capabilities

Companies acquire, develop and deploy a variety of resources to build a competitive advantage. Building a competitive strength in superior efficiency, quality, innovation or customer responsiveness, however, requires a **distinctive competency**, that is, either the unique skill to manage resources better than competitors do, or the possession of a uniquely valuable resource and the ability to exploit that resource effectively. A company with a distinctive competency can differentiate its products or achieve substantially lower costs than those of its rivals. It thus creates more value than its rivals and will earn a profit rate substantially above the industry average.

It can be argued that Toyota has distinctive competencies in the development and operation of manufacturing processes. Toyota has pioneered a range of manufacturing techniques, such as just-in-time inventory systems, self-managing teams and reduced set-up times for complex equipment. These competencies have helped Toyota attain superior efficiency and product quality, which are the basis of its competitive advantage in the global motor vehicle industry.[18]

Resources and capabilities

The distinctive competencies of a company arise from two complementary sources: its **resources** and its **capabilities** (see figure 4.8). Resources are factors that a company owns, controls and uses for the purpose of creating value.[19] Generally, resources are divided into those that are tangible and those that are intangible. *Tangible resources* include assets that are financial in nature (e.g. cash, debt and equity) or have physical properties (e.g. buildings, equipment, inventory, land and raw materials). They include those assets that the company measures and presents on its statement of financial position for accounting purposes; as such, they are the fixed and current assets of the company.

Intangible resources include those nonphysical assets that the company uses to produce goods or provide services, or expects to generate future productive benefits.[20] These resources are assets that are rarely, if at all, recorded on the company's statement of financial position.[21] Such assets include:

- legal assets, for example contracts, copyrights, patents, designs and trademarks
- human assets, for example individual employee knowledge, skills and expertise
- informational assets, for example competitor, customer and market intelligence
- organisational assets, for example organisational structure and culture
- relational assets, for example, customer, distributor, alliance, partner and supplier relationships
- reputational assets, for example brand name, company and product or service reputations that reduce perceived risk or have symbolic value.

These resources are considered to be what the company has as opposed to what the company does or can do.[22]

In the context of creating value, tangible and intangible resources are not very productive on their own. The CEO, for example, is unlikely to create the value necessary to build and sustain a company's market position without financial capital, physical property, marketing and sales staff, technology systems and other tangible and intangible resources. The capacity to deploy resources productively to create value in excess of the cost of production requires capabilities. Because a company develops and uses capabilities to create value in conjunction with other resources, they are also considered a specialised, intangible resource.[23]

Capabilities can be identified and defined in terms of the types of activity that companies perform to create value. Organisational capabilities may be thought of as a hierarchy — not an administrative hierarchy but a hierarchy of knowledge integration.[24] First, individual employees hold specialised knowledge (individual capabilities). Second, the company integrates these individual capabilities to deal with specialised tasks. Third, the company integrates these specialised tasks to construct broader activity-based capabilities (such as a manufacturing capability) and functional capabilities (such as a research, a design or a sales and marketing capability). Finally, the company integrates these broad capabilities to span cross-functional capabilities, such as a new product development, a strategic planning or a customer support capability. While identifying a hierarchy of capabilities is relatively simple, however, understanding how a company builds and adopts a capability to fit within its organisational context and market strategy is more complex.

resources
Factors that a company owns, controls and uses for the purpose of creating value

capabilities
A company's capacity to productively deploy resources, usually in combination, to bring about a desired end

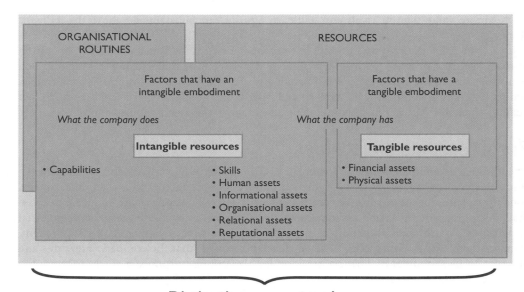

Distinctive competencies

Superior:
- efficiency
- quality
- innovation
- customer responsiveness

Differentiation

Low cost

Value creation

Higher profits

Figure 4.8:
The roots of competitive advantage

Why is Cisco able to create rapid shareholder value through acquisitions when the failure rate for most acquisitions is more than 70 per cent? How is it that Australia-based Ramsay Health Care is able to use a decentralised approach to management that allows it to out-perform the largest (centrally managed) competitor in the industry financially? Why are many Japanese manufacturing firms (e.g. Canon, Casio and Sony) able to consistently create some of the world's most innovative products while maintaining low costs? It is difficult, if not impossible, to explain why some companies are capable of performing some activities better than others. Nevertheless, it is possible to formulate ideas and hypothesise how a company builds a capability and modifies it, and why some companies perform capabilities better than others do. Capabilities constitute the various skills, knowledge and expertise of the employees. Those skills, knowledge and expertise must be integrated with other resources (tangible and intangible resources) to create value. The closely coordinated actions of individuals and teams within the company allow this integration of resources. This requires organisational routines, which are all the regular and predictable patterns of activity that make up the coordinated actions of a company's employees.[25]

organisational routines
All the regular and predictable patterns of activity that make up the coordinated actions of a company's employees

Organisational routines are the organising processes and decision rules for completing company-level activities. How does a company process and fulfil a customer order received over the Internet? How does a company take raw materials and manufacture a finished product? Companies organise and carry out such activities with standardised, complementary routines.

Companies develop capabilities when they match and integrate knowledge from standardised, complementary routines to specific organisational activities (such as fulfilling a customer order) that are bound by context and history. Further, capabilities are subject to learning, that is, they may evolve as companies learn from their experiences in the market and adjust to changes that follow from economic and market shifts and changing consumer demand. Companies that are able to learn from changes in the environment have a stronger potential to understand which resource combinations are required for new value-creating strategies. This adaptive approach to business change affords the opportunity continually to redeploy or reconfigure resources to meet changing market conditions. The ability to reconfigure other resources and even organisational routines to adapt to changing competitive and market dynamics reflects a 'dynamic' capability.[26]

Gaining a distinctive edge (such as differentiation or low unit cost) over rivals, however, requires a distinctive competency. A competency is distinctive when it contributes disproportionately to the provision of superior value creation or enables the company to create value in a more cost-effective way.

An example is Nucor, the US-based steel minimill that is consistently able to produce its steel at a lower cost than that of its rivals despite having the same resources (plant, equipment, skilled employees, know-how) as other minimills. Nucor does this by managing its resources more highly productively. Canon, on the other hand, has valuable expertise in microelectronics, precision mechanics and fine optics. It exploits this valuable resource in a variety of product markets, including cameras, calculators, fax machines, photocopiers and laser printers. For both Nucor and Canon, distinctive competencies are critical to creating value and achieving an advantage in the market.

In summary, companies are a nexus or bundle of tangible and intangible resources. Productively deploying tangible and intangible resources requires firmwide capabilities, which are developed and exercised through organisational routines. This causal chain of activity can be thought of as the necessary steps for any company to create, implement and fulfil a value-creating market strategy. Every company has capabilities, of which some are performed better than others. To find a unique strength in the market, however, each company must develop distinctive competencies. To have a distinctive competency, a company must (1) possess a valuable resource and the capabilities necessary to exploit that resource uniquely (as illustrated by Canon) or (2) be able to manage resources better than competitors can (as illustrated by Nucor). A distinctive competency is most differentiated when a company possesses both uniquely valuable resources and the skill capabilities to manage those resources better than competitors.

Strategy and competitive advantage

The primary objective of strategy is to achieve a competitive advantage. Attaining this goal demands a two-pronged effort. A company needs to pursue strategies that build on its existing resources, capabilities and distinctive competencies, as well as strategies that build additional resources and capabilities (and even new distinctive competencies) and so improve the company's long-term competitive position.[27] Figure 4.9 illustrates the relationship between a company's strategies and its resources and capabilities. By 'strategies' is meant all types of strategy: functional-level, business-level, corporate-level and international strategies and, more typically, some combination of them. The various strategies available to a company are discussed in detail throughout part 3. Here, it is stressed that successful strategies often either build on a company's existing distinctive competencies or help a company develop new ones.

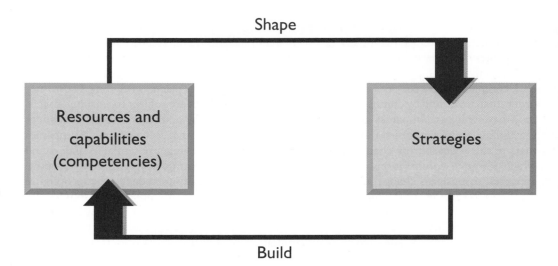

Shape

Resources and capabilities (competencies)

Strategies

Build

Figure 4.9
The relationship between
strategies and resources
and capabilities

The history of The Walt Disney Company during the 1980s exemplifies the need to pursue strategies that build on a company's resources and capabilities.[28] In the early 1980s, Disney suffered a string of poor financial years. This culminated in a 1984 management shakeup, when Michael Eisner was appointed CEO. Four years later, Disney's sales had increased from US$1.66 billion to US$3.75 billion, its net profits had risen from US$98 million to US$570 million and its stock market valuation had risen from US$1.8 billion to US$10.3 billion. This transformation was the result of the company's deliberate attempt to exploit its existing resources and capabilities more aggressively. These resources and capabilities included Disney's enormous film library, its brand name and its in-house film-making skills, particularly in animation. Under Eisner, many old Disney classics were rereleased, first in movie theatres and then on video, earning the company millions of dollars. The company also started a cable television channel, the Disney Channel, to use this library and capitalise on the Disney brand name. In addition, under Eisner, the film-making arm of Disney flourished, first with a string of low-budget box-office hits under the label Touchstone and then with the reintroduction of the product that had originally made Disney famous: the full-length animated feature. Putting together its brand name and in-house animation capabilities, Disney produced three major box-office hits in four years: *The Little Mermaid*, *Beauty and the Beast* and *Aladdin*. In sum, Disney's transformation was based primarily on strategies that exploited the company's existing resource base.

Other companies that have successfully exploited their resources and capabilities to create profitable opportunities include 3M and Honda. The former exploited its distinctive competency in sticky tape to create businesses as diverse as Post-it notes, pressure-sensitive tapes and coated abrasives. The latter exploited its distinctive competency in the design and manufacture of high-powered lightweight engines to move from motorcycles to cars, lawnmowers and four-wheel off-road buggies. On the other hand, some of the most striking strategic failures have occurred at companies that strayed too far from their distinctive competencies. Pacific Dunlop initially made its name in tyres before branching into other rubber products (latex gloves, condoms and so on) and other automotive products (such as car batteries). By the 1980s, however, the company had moved into a range of food products, medical equipment manufacturers and clothing. These diversification attempts failed and today Ansell has been spun off as a separate company after long being Pacific Dunlop's most profitable division.

To understand the process of building resources and capabilities through strategies, consider Xerox. During the late 1970s, its market share in the photocopier business slumped by 50 per cent because its main Japanese competitors, Canon and Ricoh, were paying close attention to their distinctive competencies, whereas Xerox was not. As a result, by the early 1980s, Canon and Ricoh were selling high-quality, technologically superior copiers at a price approximating that of Xerox's. To recapture its lost market share, Xerox had to rethink how it did business fundamentally. It launched a series of functional-level strategies designed to improve quality and product design, eliminate unnecessary inventory and reduce new product development time (cycle time). The goal of these strategies was to develop the kind of resources and capabilities that had enabled Canon and Ricoh to take its market share. Xerox was reasonably successful in this endeavour: its share of the US copier market increased from a low of 10 per cent in 1985 to 31 per cent in 2001.[29] The company's renaissance stemmed from the successful implementation of functional-level strategies to build new distinctive competencies.

The role of luck

Some scholars argue that luck plays a critical role in determining competitive success and failure.[30] In its most extreme version, the luck argument devalues the importance of planned strategy. It states that some companies, in coping with uncertainty, just happen to stumble on the correct strategy. Put another way, companies happen to develop or possess the right resources and capabilities by accident rather than by design.

Although luck may be the reason for a company's success in particular cases, it is an unconvincing explanation for the persistent success of a company. Recall the argument that the generic building blocks of competitive advantage are superior efficiency, quality, innovation and customer responsiveness. Keep in mind also that competition is a process in which companies are continually trying to outdo each other in their ability to achieve those building blocks. It is possible to imagine a company getting lucky and coming into possession of resources that allow it to achieve excellence in one or more of these dimensions. It is difficult to imagine, however, how sustained excellence in any of the four dimensions could result from anything other than conscious effort (i.e. by strategy). Luck may play a role in success. To argue, however, that success is entirely a matter of luck is to strain credibility.

Other conditions for gaining a competitive advantage

As mentioned, the primary objective of strategy is to achieve an advantage in the market. Resources (including the possible distinctive competencies that develop from the resources) underpin the ability of a firm to create a competitive advantage. In addition to strategy and luck, three additional conditions can have an impact on the attainment of a competitive advantage: (1) there must be ex ante limits to resource competition; (2) the company must have resources that are valuable and (3) the company must have resources that are rare.[31]

Ex ante limits to competition

For a company to attain a competitive advantage, *ex ante* **limits to competition** must exist, that is, before a company establishes a superior resource position, competition for those resources must be limited. If, for example, mining companies BHP Billiton and Rio Tinto both know in advance that the acquisition of a certain piece of land will endow them with an inimitable resource position over current and future rivals — for example, the land contains rich iron ore deposits — then the two companies may compete for the land so that any expected returns to the company that acquires the land are eliminated. That is, the two companies keep increasing the amount that they will pay for the land until the cost is so high that no profit from the land can be made. In other words, resources have to be acquired below their discounted net present value to yield profits; otherwise, the price paid for the resource will absorb future profits.

ex ante limits to
competition
Limited competition for
resources before the
company establishes a
competitive advantage
based on those resources

Valuable resources

resource value
The value of a resource in helping a company to create or implement strategies that improve the company's efficiency, improve the ratio of value to cost of a product or service, or allow the company to either exploit its opportunities or neutralise threats arising from the external environment

Resources that are valuable allow a company to create or implement strategies that improve the company's efficiency, improve the ratio of value to cost of a product or service, or allow the company to either exploit its opportunities or neutralise threats arising from the external environment. **Resource value** is important to competitive advantage. The bundle of resources that a company accumulates or acquires to execute a given market strategy must be more valuable than the resources of competitors in the market, for the firm to enjoy a competitive advantage and superior performance. Sony, for example, has developed valuable resources in miniaturisation, which distinguish the company from its competitors and enable it to attain a sustainable competitive advantage.

Rare resources

resource rareness
Possession of a resource by a few competitors (current or potential) or, ideally, by only one company

Resources are rare if they are possessed by a few competitors (current or potential) or, ideally, by only one company. **Resource rareness** is a matter of degree. It is a function of how many other companies have the same resource out of the overall number in the industry. If many companies in the industry have the same specific resource (even if it is valuable), then the resource's ability to generate a competitive advantage for any one company is diminished. If few companies possess a particularly valuable resource, then that resource is generally considered rare and has the potential to generate a competitive advantage. Many companies around the world produce a variety of cola drinks, for example, but Coca-Cola and PepsiCo have the most recognisable brand names of all the producers. They are the world's leading cola-drink producers and have been for many years. Their brand names are, therefore, a rare (intangible) resource that affords the companies a competitive advantage in the global cola-drink market.

The durability of competitive advantage

Resources (the company's competencies) underpin the ability of a company to create a competitive advantage. Gaining a competitive advantage, however, is not the same as sustaining a competitive advantage. Rivals within the market compete for a unique, sustainable position, but not all will achieve a competitive advantage let alone sustain one. The question is, how long will a competitive advantage last once it has been created? That is, what is the durability of competitive advantage given that other companies also seek to develop distinctive competencies that will give them a competitive advantage? The answer depends on: (1) resource position barriers, (2) the capability of competitors and (3) the general dynamism of the industry environment.

Resource position barriers

resource position barrier
A barrier that enables companies to sustain a resource-based competitive advantage

While luck, *ex ante* limits to competition and resources that are valuable and rare provide opportunities to gain a competitive advantage, a company must prevent other competitors from imitating those resources. To do so, it needs a **resource position barrier**. The sustainability of a competitive advantage is, therefore, predicated on two additional conditions known as resource position barriers: resource inimitability and resource nonsubstitutability.

Inimitability

resource inimitability
How hard it is for competitors to imitate a resource

Resource inimitability means competitors cannot imitate a resource. The easiest way to imitate or replicate the resource or resources of a competitor is to buy them. If a company's strategy is based on resources that competitors can readily and easily buy, then that company's ability to build and sustain a competitive advantage will be considerably diminished and probably shortlived. The ability to buy a resource depends on its availability. Resources such as buildings, equipment and even personnel with standardised skills (such as data entry clerks or wordprocessing temps) are generally readily available, being able to be bought and even transferred from one company to another. Other resources are not so mobile. Some resources are highly context specific (and therefore not mobile), depreciate on transfer or may not, despite considerable effort, offer the same benefits to the acquiring company that were enjoyed by the seller company. Resource inimitability largely results from the following factors.

- *Causal ambiguity*. For competitors trying to imitate successful companies' resources, causal ambiguity may limit their understanding of exactly what makes successful companies successful. In other words, causal ambiguity exists when the link between resources and a sustained competitive advantage is not understood or understood only imperfectly.[32] Capabilities and distinctive competencies are deeply embedded within a company, so outsiders may have difficulty understanding why companies such as Canon or Honda are so successful at continually developing highly innovative products in such a range of product markets. In Australian banking, the Commonwealth Bank and the National Australia Bank consistently outperform Westpac and ANZ, yet the resources or distinctive competencies that drive this superior performance are unclear.

- *History*. Resource inimitability may result from path dependencies, such as historical events or unique historical circumstances. Some companies may gain inimitable advantages through the historical acquisition of a physical location. Disney's historical purchase of land in an underdeveloped part of Florida allowed it to create a sprawling theme park and entertainment complex — and thus a favourite vacation destination for families — unmatched by any competitor in the world. In the wine industry, Penfolds Grange occupies a prestige position as the premier wine in Australia. It is unlikely that it is the best wine in Australia every year but after being named the best wine in the world (the 1990 vintage) by the US publication *Wine Spectator*, it has been able to command a significant price premium. Other wine companies could try to replicate the wine using similar grapes, extraction and maturation techniques, yet the Penfolds product would still have an advantage because its success at least partly depends on a singular historical event.

- *Legal property rights*. In some cases, competitors may clearly identify and understand a resource. The legal system of property rights, however, may prevent them from imitating the resource. Legal (intangible) assets such as patents, trademarks and copyrights are protected by intellectual property law. The patent protection of Australian-based Cochlear's hearing device and the technologies in Fisher & Paykel Healthcare's respiratory humidifiers, for example, have helped to maintain these two companies' formidable position in the healthcare industry.

- *Social complexity*. Some resources are based on complex social phenomena. It may be possible, therefore, to specify how a socially complex resource, such as culture, adds value to a company but not to replicate or 'engineer' a similar culture to attain similarly valuable benefits. Competitors may commit significant amounts of time and money to replicate a competitor's resource or resources without ever achieving similar benefits. While individually the many physical assets (aircraft, spare parts, reservation systems and so on) of Singapore Airlines, for example, may be imitable, the complexity of the interconnectedness of Singapore Airlines' history, culture, processes and relationships with customers and suppliers and its physical assets has allowed it to be consistently rated one of the world's best airlines. Competitors may be able to match the physical assets required to run Singapore Airlines but they have been unable to match the complexity of the resource interconnectedness that makes this airline so successful (see Strategy in action 4.3).

- *Cost of compressing time*. Time is needed to develop resources through learning, experience, company-specific knowledge or trained proficiency in a skill. Honda, for example, has distinctive competencies in combustion engines and power train technology, which enable the company to develop a wide range of world-class products, including cars, motorcycles and lawnmowers, that have taken decades to build. Companies wishing to imitate Honda's world-class expertise, given how much it would cost to cut the time it would need, would face years of development time, learning and considerable capital investment.[33]

strategy in action 4.3

Key resources in airlines

Each successful airline has behind it a set of resources that allows it to achieve a competitive advantage. The airline industry has performed terribly over the past 10 years with the increased number of new (primarily low-cost) airlines as well as because of a general slowing of growth in passenger numbers. This trend was partly caused by the fall-out from the September 11 terrorist attacks but also because of other, smaller, more temporary events including the first few months following the United States-led invasion of Iraq and the outbreak of SARS in Asia.

Nevertheless, some airlines have continued to do well and are producing good profits. These airlines have resources or competencies that underpin their competitiveness that cannot be easily imitated or replicated. For example, Virgin Blue has a culture of helpfulness and irreverence. While this may seem to be easy to replicate, the challenge of changing a culture in an airline, in which job security is not what it used to be and staff could be cut, is virtually impossible. Singapore Airlines has built up a reputation for using very modern aircraft and

exceptional customer service. However, in this case, the cost of upgrading a large fleet is beyond most local competitors and so they will continue to purchase new aircraft but not as regularly as Singapore Airlines.

Other airlines seem to have lost control of their most important resources. British Airways evolved from the combination of two UK-based carriers into a national (government-owned) carrier. It became what is known as the national flag carrier and maintained a large amount of UK custom simply on that basis. In the late 1990s, it replaced its tail design of the red, white and blue with different patterns so that every aircraft would have a different tail design. In doing so, it came to be seen less as the national carrier and this made it easier for competitors such as Virgin Atlantic to gain a substantial foothold in the market. On the basis of the British Airways experience, Qantas (which was previously part owned by British Airways) will never replace its 'flying kangaroo' symbol, which forms an important part of its brand.

Nonsubstitutability

nonsubstitutability
How difficult it is to find a substitute for a resource

The final test of a resource's ability to sustain a competitive advantage is its degree of **nonsubstitutability**. In other words, for a resource to be a source of sustained competitive advantage, it must have no equivalent. Similar to the rare condition (described in the section 'Other conditions for gaining a competitive advantage' on page 113), however, nonsubstitutability is a matter of degree. Perfect substitutes would undermine the profit-generating capacity of another resource but they rarely exist. As such, the rent-generating capacity of a given resource is lessened only to the extent that an alternative resource can provide strategically equivalent benefits.

If two resources are equivalents and provide the same strategic benefits, but are also rare, then they can still give both companies profit-generating capacity and be sources of sustainable competitive advantage. In this sense, similar to the rareness condition, nonsubstitutability has degrees of difference. Fashion designers, for example, are a substitutable resource but they cannot be exactly substituted because each designer brings a different approach and style to the collection. In addition, designers are rare, so an international fashion label would be willing to risk its name with only a limited number of designers.

Say a company has developed a highly complex decision support system, encompassing information technology that is deeply embedded in the company's formal and informal decision-making processes. This socially complex technology allows the company to consistently perform at the highest levels among its peers. On the other hand, a different company relies on a tightly knit, highly experienced management team to make concomitant adjustments to its strategies. This company is also one of the highest performing in the market. The sophisticated decision support system and the highly experienced management team may be considered substitutes but if they are also both rare, then they may still afford the two companies a sustainable competitive advantage.

Capability of competitors

According to work by Ghemawat, a major determinant of the capability of competitors to rapidly imitate a company's competitive advantage is the nature of the competitors' prior strategic commitments.[34] By **strategic commitment**, Ghemawat means a company's commitment to a particular way of doing business, that is, to developing a particular set of resources and capabilities. Ghemawat's point is that a company, once it has made a strategic commitment, will find it difficult to respond to new competition if doing so requires a break with this commitment. When competitors already have long-established commitments to a particular way of doing business, therefore, they may be slow to imitate an innovating company's competitive advantage. That competitive advantage will therefore be relatively durable.

The US motor vehicle industry offers an example. From 1945 to 1975, the industry was dominated by the stable oligopoly of GM, Ford and Chrysler, all of which geared their operations to the production of large cars (which was what US consumers demanded at the time). When the market shifted from large cars to small, fuel-efficient ones during the late 1970s, US companies lacked the resources and capabilities required to produce these cars. Their commitments had built the wrong kind of skills for this new environment. As a result, foreign producers, particularly the Japanese, stepped into the market breach by providing compact, fuel-efficient, high-quality and low-cost cars. The failure of US manufacturers to react quickly to the distinctive competency of Japanese companies gave the latter time to build a strong market position and brand loyalty, which subsequently proved difficult to attack.

Another determinant of the ability of competitors to respond to a company's competitive advantage is their **absorptive capacity**, that is, the ability of an enterprise to identify, value, assimilate and use new knowledge.[35] In the 1960s and 1970s, Toyota developed a competitive advantage based on its innovation of lean production systems. Competitors such as GM were slow to imitate this innovation, primarily because they lacked the necessary absorptive capacity. GM was such a bureaucratic and inward-looking organisation that it was difficult for the company to identify, value, assimilate and use the knowledge underlying lean production systems. Long after GM identified and understood the importance of lean production systems, the company was still struggling to assimilate and use that new knowledge. Put differently, internal inertia can make it difficult for established competitors to respond to a rival whose competitive advantage is based on new products or internal processes, that is, competitive advantage based on innovation.

Taken together, factors such as existing strategic commitments and low absorptive capacity limit the ability of established competitors to imitate the competitive advantage of a rival, particularly when that competitive advantage derives from innovative products or processes. This is why, when innovations reshape the rules of competition in an industry, value often migrates away from established competitors and towards new enterprises that are operating with new business models.

strategic commitment
The level of resources and capabilities that a company commits to a particular strategic decision

absorptive capacity
A company's ability to identify, value, assimilate and use new knowledge

Industry dynamism

A dynamic industry environment is one that is changing rapidly. The factors that determine the dynamism and intensity of competition in an industry are examined in chapter 3 in discussing the external environment. The most dynamic industries tend to be those with a high rate of product innovation, such as the consumer electronics industry and the PC industry. In dynamic industries, the rapid rate of innovation means that product lifecycles are shortening and competitive advantage can be transitory. A company that has a competitive advantage today may find its market position outflanked tomorrow by a rival's innovation.

In the past two decades, the financial industry has become far more turbulent, with new competitors entering the market and many new innovations being introduced. Financial investments used to be limited to a direct investment in shares, interest-bearing bank accounts of different types and a few specialist investments (such as linking returns to the money market). This range expanded enormously with the takeup of retail managed or mutual funds. These funds invested in a range of companies to allow investors to diversify their portfolio easily and simultaneously to get the benefits of experts in share selection. Different types of fund developed, such as index funds, which attempt to track the performance of a major index (such as the Dow Jones in the United States or the All Ordinaries Top 200 in Australia). Imputation credit-oriented funds were introduced for people looking more for tax minimisation rather than capital growth, and funds that invest in only socially responsible companies are a recent addition to the options available. With banks and other financial institutions developing new funds every year, fund lifecycles are shortening and the easy movement of fund managers between different funds has made the maintenance of a competitive advantage difficult. Other dynamic industries include the computer software, consumer electronics, general retail and speciality services industries.

Summary

The durability of a company's competitive advantage depends on these factors: resource position barriers, strategic commitments, the absorptive capacity of other competitors and the general dynamism in the industry environment. When resource position barriers are low, capable competitors abound and the environment is dynamic, with innovations being developed all the time, then competitive advantage is likely to be transitory. On the other hand, even within such industries, companies can achieve a more enduring competitive advantage if they are able to make investments that build resource position barriers. During the 1980s, Apple Computer built a competitive advantage based on the combination of a proprietary disk operating system and an intangible product image. (As noted, intangible resources are difficult to imitate.) The resulting brand loyalty enabled Apple to carve out a fairly secure niche in an industry in which competitive advantage has otherwise proved to be fleeting. By the mid-1990s, however, its strategy had been imitated, primarily with the introduction of Microsoft's Windows operating system, which had most of the features that had enabled Apple to build brand loyalty. As a result, Apple was in financial trouble by 1996, providing yet another example that no competitive advantage lasts forever. Ultimately, anything can be imitated. (Interestingly, Apple has shown remarkable resilience. Most recently, its success has come from the Apple iPod, but again Apple faces considerable threats from manufacturers of similar products.)

Why do companies fail?

This section expands the issue of why a company may lose its competitive advantage and asks why companies fail. A failing company is defined as one whose profit rate is substantially lower than the average profit rate of its competitors. A company can lose its competitive advantage but still not fail; it may just earn average profits. Failure implies something more drastic. Failing companies typically earn low profits or make losses; in other words, they are at a competitive disadvantage.

The question is particularly pertinent given that some of the most successful companies of the twentieth century have seen their competitive position deteriorate at times. Companies such as IBM, GM, American Express, BHP and Pacific Dunlop, at one time held up as examples of managerial excellence, have gone through periods of poor financial performance, when they clearly lacked any competitive advantage. Three related reasons for failure are explored: inertia, prior strategic commitments and the Icarus paradox.

Inertia

The inertia argument says that companies find it difficult to change their strategies and structures to adapt to changing competitive conditions.[36] IBM is a classic example of this problem. For 30 years, it was viewed as the world's most successful computer company. Then in the space of a few short years, its success turned into a disaster, with a loss of US$5 billion in 1992 leading to layoffs of more than 100 000 employees. IBM's troubles were caused by a dramatic decline in the cost of computing power as a result of innovations in microprocessors. With the advent of powerful low-cost microprocessors, the locus of the computer market shifted from mainframes to small, low-priced PCs. This left IBM's huge mainframe operations with a diminished market. Even though IBM had, and still has, a significant presence in the PC market, it had failed to shift the focus of its efforts away from mainframes and towards PCs. This failure meant deep trouble for one of the most successful companies of the twentieth century, although IBM has now executed a successful turnaround, primarily by repositioning the company as a provider of e-commerce infrastructure and solutions.

Why do companies find it so difficult to adapt to new environmental conditions? One factor that seems to stand out is the role of a company's capabilities in causing inertia. This chapter earlier argues that capabilities can be a source of competitive advantage; their downside, however, is that they are difficult to change. Recall that capabilities are the ways in which a company makes decisions and manages its processes. IBM always emphasised close coordination of different operating units and favoured decision processes that stressed consensus among interdependent operating units as a prerequisite for a decision to go forwards.[37] This capability was a source of advantage for IBM during the 1970s, when coordination among its worldwide operating units was necessary to develop, manufacture and sell complex mainframes. But the slow-moving bureaucracy that it had spawned was a source of failure in the 1990s, when companies had to adapt readily to rapid environmental change.

Capabilities are difficult to change because a certain distribution of power and influence is embedded within the established decision-making and management processes of a company. Those who play key roles in a decision-making process clearly have more power. It follows that changing the established capabilities of a company means changing its existing distribution of power and influence, and those whose power and influence would diminish resist the change. Proposals for change trigger turf battles. The power struggle and the political resistance associated with trying to alter how a company makes decisions and manages its process — that is, trying to change its capabilities — bring on inertia. This is not to say that companies cannot change but because change is so often resisted by those who feel threatened by it, it has to be induced by a crisis in most cases. By then, the company may already be failing, as happened at IBM.

Prior strategic commitments

Ghemawat argues that a company's prior strategic commitments not only limit its ability to imitate rivals but may also cause competitive disadvantage.[38] IBM had made major investments in the mainframe computer business. As a result, when the market shifted, it was stuck with significant resources that were specialised to that particular business. The company had manufacturing facilities geared to the production of mainframes, research organisations that were similarly specialised and a mainframe sales force. These resources were not well suited to the newly emerging PC business, so IBM's difficulties in the early 1990s were inevitable in a sense. Its prior strategic commitments locked IBM into a business that was shrinking. Shedding these resources was bound to cause hardship for all stakeholders.

The Icarus paradox

Miller postulated that the roots of competitive failure can be found in what he terms the Icarus paradox.[39] Icarus is a figure in Greek mythology, who used a pair of wings — made for him by his father — to escape from an island where he was being held prisoner. He flew so well that he went higher and higher, ever closer to the sun, until the heat of the sun melted the wax that held his wings together and he plunged to his death in the Aegean Sea. The paradox is that his greatest asset — his ability to fly — caused his demise. Miller argues that the same paradox applies to many once successful companies. According to Miller, many companies become so dazzled by their early success that they believe more of the same type of effort is the way to future success. As a result, however, a company can become so specialised and inwardly directed that it loses sight of market realities and the fundamental requirements for achieving a competitive advantage. Sooner or later, this leads to failure.

Miller identifies four major categories among the rising and falling companies. The 'craftsmen', such as Texas Instruments and Digital Equipment Corporation (DEC), achieved early success through engineering excellence. The companies became so obsessed with engineering details, however, that they lost sight of market realities. The 'builders', such as Gulf & Western and ITT, are successful, moderately diversified companies that became so enchanted with diversification for its own sake that they continued to diversify beyond the point at which it was profitable to do so. The 'pioneers', such as Wang Labs, became so enamoured of their own originally brilliant innovations that they continued to search for additional brilliant innovations. They ended up producing novel but completely useless products. The 'salesmen', exemplified by Procter & Gamble and Chrysler, became so convinced of their ability to sell anything that they paid scant attention to product development and manufacturing excellence; as a result, they spawned a proliferation of bland, inferior products. Although all of Miller's examples are United States-based, it is easy to relate his categories to companies all over the world that have failed.

Avoiding failure and sustaining competitive advantage

How can a company avoid the traps that have snared so many once successful companies? How can it build a sustainable competitive advantage? A complete answer is not given here because much of the remaining text deals with these issues but key points can be made (see also Strategy in action 4.4 for an example).

Focus on the building blocks of competitive advantage

First, maintaining a competitive advantage requires a company to continue focusing on its four generic building blocks — efficiency, quality, innovation and customer responsiveness — and to develop distinctive competencies that contribute to superior performance in these areas. One of the messages of Miller's Icarus paradox is that many successful companies become unbalanced in their pursuit of distinctive competencies. DEC, for example, focused on engineering

strategy in action 4.4

Sustaining competitive advantage in The Warehouse Group

New Zealand's first The Warehouse store was launched in 1982 with starting capital of NZ$40 000. In 2002, The Warehouse invested NZ$10 million in its two-hundred-and-thirty-fourth store. During 2004, it achieved sales of NZ$2.24 billion, with a profit of NZ$61.2 million, while clocking 53.2 million customer transactions in one of the world's least-populated regions.

What is the secret of The Warehouse's outstanding growth? 'Innovative price driven retailing' the company and its founder believe. The Warehouse's catchy television jingle 'Where everyone gets a bargain' conveys the price advantages of buying at The Warehouse. This is supported by a consistent money back guarantee without a question in the event of goods being returned. The Warehouse sustains its innovative price-driven retailing with low-cost sourcing of products from different parts of the world, including in recent times New Zealand. It also prides itself on its efficient distribution infrastructure.

Although these factors contribute to a competitive advantage over other retailers, the company chairman Keith Smith believes 'no single competitive advantage is sustainable in the long-term […] retailing is a very dynamic sector'. Therefore, the company is signalling its intention to continue innovating to retain advantage as the competition and market evolve. The 'Kiwi Made' label is one such effort, in which the combination of The Warehouse's buying power and an enterprising New Zealand manufacturer work towards replacing imports with New Zealand-made product at the same or lower cost. The label aims to create local jobs and appeal to New Zealand consumers to support their local industries.

Sources: The Warehouse Group, accessed 6 August 2005, www.thewarehouse.co.nz; Smith K 2003, 'Presentation by Keith Smith, chairman, The Warehouse Group Limited', annual meeting, 28 November, accessed 2 January 2006, www.thewarehouse.co.nz/Content.aspx?id=100009244.

quality at the expense of almost everything else, including, most importantly, customer responsiveness. Other companies forget to focus on any distinctive competency. This was the case at Pacific Dunlop, where an empire-building CEO, John Gough, focused on diversification but lost sight of a focus on achieving excellence in efficiency, quality, innovation and customer responsiveness at the level of business units within Pacific Dunlop.

Institute continuous improvement and learning

The only constant in the world is change. Today's source of competitive advantage may soon be rapidly imitated by capable competitors or made obsolete by the innovations of a rival. In such a dynamic and fast-paced environment, a company can maintain a competitive advantage only by continually improving its efficiency, quality, innovation and customer responsiveness. The way to achieve this improvement is to recognise the importance of learning within the company.[40] The most successful companies are not those that stand still, resting on their laurels; they are those that continually seek out ways of improving their operations and, in the process, constantly upgrade the value of their distinctive competencies or create new competencies. Companies such as Nokia and Toyota have a reputation for being learning organisations. This means that they are continually analysing the processes that underpin their efficiency, quality, innovation and customer responsiveness. Their objective is to learn from prior mistakes and seek ways of improving their processes over time. This approach has enabled Toyota, for example, to upgrade its employee productivity and product quality continually, allowing the company to stay one step ahead of imitators.

Track best industrial practice and use benchmarking

One of the best ways in which to develop distinctive competencies is to identify **best industrial practice** and adopt it. Only by so doing will a company be able to build and maintain the resources and capabilities that underpin excellence in efficiency, quality, innovation and customer responsiveness. Chapter 5 discusses what constitutes best industrial practice.

best industrial practice
Guidelines, or metrics, that define a best practice within a specific industry — for example, defects per million parts for manufacturing companies

It requires tracking the practice of other companies, which is perhaps best done through **benchmarking**, that is, the process of measuring the company against the products, practices and services of its most efficient global competitors.

Benchmarking does not need to occur in just the competitor's industry. A company may look to Sony to study its R&D processes, to Australia Post for distribution systems and to Coca-Cola for brand management issues.

benchmarking
The process of measuring a company against the products, practices and services of some of its most efficient global competitors

Overcome inertia

A further reason for failure is an inertia-related inability to adapt to changing conditions. Overcoming the barriers to change within a company is a key requirement for maintaining a competitive advantage and a whole chapter (chapter 11) is devoted to this issue. Identifying barriers to change is an important first step. Once this step has been taken, implementing change requires good leadership, the judicious use of power and appropriate changes in organisational structure and control systems. These issues are discussed later in the book.

Summary

The principal objective of this chapter is to identify the basis of competitive advantage by examining why, within a given industry, some companies outperform others. Competitive advantage is the product of at least one of the following: superior efficiency, quality, innovation or customer responsiveness. Achieving superiority requires that a company develop appropriate distinctive competencies, which are a product of the kind of resources and capabilities that a company possesses. The chapter also examines issues related to the durability of competitive advantage. This durability is determined by resource position barriers, the capability of competitors to imitate a company's advantage, and the general level of environmental turbulence. Finally, the discussion of why companies fail and what they can do to avoid failure indicates that failure is due to factors such as organisational inertia, prior strategic commitments and the Icarus paradox. Avoiding failure requires that a company constantly try to upgrade its distinctive competencies in accordance with best industrial practice and that it take steps to overcome organisational inertia. The main points made in this chapter can be summarised as follows.

▶ The source of a competitive advantage is superior value creation.

▶ To create superior value, a company must lower its costs, differentiate its product so it can charge a higher price or do both together.

▶ The four generic building blocks of competitive advantage are efficiency, quality, innovation and customer responsiveness.

▶ Superior efficiency allows a company to lower its costs; superior quality allows it to both charge a higher price and lower its costs; and superior customer service allows it to charge a higher price. Superior innovation can lead to higher prices, particularly in the case of product innovations; alternatively, it can lead to lower unit costs, particularly in the case of process innovations.

▶ Distinctive competencies are the unique strengths of a company. Valuable distinctive competencies enable a company to earn a profit rate that is above the industry average.

▶ The distinctive competencies of a company arise from its resources and capabilities.

▶ Resources refer to the tangible and intangible assets of a company, including financial, physical, legal, human, informational, organisational, relational and reputational assets.

▶ Capabilities refer to a company's skills at coordinating resources and putting them to productive use.

- To achieve a competitive advantage, companies need to pursue strategies that build on their existing resources, capabilities and distinctive competencies and they need to formulate strategies that build additional resources and capabilities (and even new distinctive competencies).

- The durability of a company's competitive advantage depends on resource position barriers, the capability of competitors and environmental dynamism.

- Failing companies typically earn low or negative profits. Three factors seem to contribute to failure: (1) organisational inertia in the face of environmental change; (2) the nature of a company's prior strategic commitments and (3) the Icarus paradox.

- Avoiding failure requires having a constant focus on the basic building blocks of competitive advantage: continuous improvement, identification and adoption of best industrial practice and victory over inertia.

Practising strategic management

Review questions

1. What are the primary activities and support activities within the value chain?
2. What are the resource position barriers that enable a company to sustain a competitive advantage that is based on its resources?
3. What are some of the main reasons why companies fail?
4. What are organisational routines?

Discussion questions

5. What are the main implications of the material on strategy formulation discussed in this chapter?
6. When is a company's competitive advantage most likely to endure?
7. Is it possible for a company to be the lowest-cost producer in an industry and simultaneously have an output that is the most valued by customers? Discuss.
8. What is the difference between organisational routines and capabilities?

Applied questions

9. Consider the opening case of David Jones and explain why you think the company attained a competitive advantage. Use the terms from the text and identify the specific resources, capabilities, strategies and even instances of luck that have helped David Jones develop its enviable position.
10. Go to your local bookshop and look at the range of travel guides available (including the Let's Go and Lonely Planet ranges). What drives the competitive advantage of each of these publications and which do you think will be the most successful and why?

Small-group exercise

Analysing competitive advantage

Break into groups of three to five people. Drawing on the concepts introduced in this chapter, analyse the competitive position of your business school or university in the market for business education. Then answer the following questions.

1. Does your business school or university have a competitive advantage?
2. If so, on what is this advantage based? Is it sustainable?
3. If your school does not have a competitive advantage in the market for business education, what inhibiting factors are holding it back?
4. How may the Internet change the way in which business education is delivered?
5. Does the Internet pose a threat to the competitive position of your school in the market for business education or is it an opportunity for it to improve its competitive position? (*Note:* It can be both.)

Article file

Find an example of a company that has sustained its competitive advantage for more than ten years. Identify the source of the competitive advantage and describe why it has lasted so long.

Exploring the Web

Visiting Lonely Planet

Visit the website of Lonely Planet (www.lonelyplanet. com). Read through the material contained on the site, paying particular attention to the material in the 'About Lonely Planet' section. On the basis of this information, answer the following questions.

1. Do you think that Lonely Planet has a distinctive competency?
2. What is the nature of this competency? How does it help the company attain a competitive advantage?
3. What are the resources and capabilities that underpin this competency? From where do these resources and capabilities arise?
4. How imitable do you think Lonely Planet's distinctive competency is?

General task

Search the Internet for a company site that goes into depth about the history, products and competitive position of that company. On the basis of the information you collect, answer the following questions.

1. Does the company have a distinctive competency?
2. What is the nature of this competency? How does it help the company attain a competitive advantage?

3. What are the resources and capabilities that underpin this competency? Where do these resources and capabilities come from?

4. How imitable is the company's distinctive competency?

Strategic management project

Module 4

This module deals with the competitive position of your company. With the information you have at your disposal, perform the following tasks and answer the following questions.

1. Identify whether your company has a competitive advantage or disadvantage in its primary industry. (Its primary industry is the one in which it has the most sales.)

2. Evaluate your company against the four generic building blocks of competitive advantage: efficiency, quality, innovation and customer responsiveness. How does this exercise help you understand the performance of your company relative to that of its competitors?

3. What are the distinctive competencies of your company?

4. What role have prior strategies played in shaping the distinctive competencies of your company? What role has luck played?

5. Do the strategies currently pursued by your company build on its distinctive competencies? Are they an attempt to build new competencies?

6. What are the barriers to imitating the distinctive competencies of your company?

7. Is there any evidence that your company finds it difficult to adapt to changing industry conditions? If so, why do you think this is the case?

Additional resources

Grant, R 1991, 'The resource-based theory of competitive advantage: implications for strategy formulation', *California Management Review*, vol. 33, no. 3, pp. 114–35. (An alternative explanation of how resources lead to a competitive advantage.)

Zahra, SA 1999, 'The changing rules of global competitiveness in the 21st century', *Academy of Management Executive*, vol. 13, no. 1, pp. 36–42. (Coverage of how resources and capabilities are driving modern-day competitiveness.)

End notes

1. Zeithaml, VA 1988, 'Consumer perceptions of price, quality, and value: a means-end model and synthesis of evidence', *Journal of Marketing*, pp. 2–22.

2. Sawyer, AG & Dickson, P 1984, 'Psychological perspectives in consumer response to sales promotion', in Jocz, K, ed., *Research on sales promotion: collected papers*, Marketing Science Institute, Cambridge, Massachusetts.

3. Drucker, PF 1973, *Management*, Harper & Row, New York, p. 79.

4. The concept of consumer surplus is an important one in economics. For a more detailed exposition, see Besanko, D, Dranove, D & Shanley, M 1996, *Economics of strategy*, John Wiley & Sons, New York.

5. $P - V$ only in the special case in which the company has a perfect monopoly and it can charge each customer a unique price that reflects the value of the product to that customer (that is, where perfect price discrimination is possible). More generally, except in the limiting case of perfect price discrimination, even a monopolist will see most consumers capture some of the value of a product in the form of a consumer surplus.

6. Harbour Consulting 2005, press release, 2 June, accessed 22 December 2005, www.harbourinc.com/pdf/2005%20Press%20Release.pdf.

7. Priddle, A 2001, 'Efficiency by the numbers', *Ward's Auto World*, July, pp. 57–9; Smith, DC 2001, 'Power surveys set standards for measuring quality', *Ward's Auto World*, July, pp. 34–5.

8. Porter, ME 1985, *Competitive advantage*, Free Press, New York.

9. This approach goes back to the pioneering work by Lancaster, K 1971, *Consumer demand, a new approach*, Columbia University Press, New York.

10. Garvin, D 1987, 'Competing on the eight dimensions of quality', *Harvard Business Review*, November–December, pp. 101–19; Kotler, P 2000, *Marketing management*, Millennium edn, Prentice Hall, Upper Saddle River, New Jersey.

11. Prahalad, CK & Krishnan, MS 1999, 'The new meaning of quality in the information age', *Harvard Business Review*, September–October, pp. 109–18.

12. See Garvin, D 1984, 'What does product quality really mean?', *Sloan Management Review*, vol. 26, pp. 25–44; Crosby, PB 1980, *Quality is free*, Mentor, New York; Gabor, A 1990, *The man who discovered quality*, Times Books, New York.

13. Chan Kim, W & Mauborgne, R 1997, 'Value innovation: the strategic logic of high growth', *Harvard Business Review*, January–February, pp. 102–15.

14. Pine, BJ 1993, *Mass customization: new frontiers in business competition*, Harvard Business School Press, Boston, Massachusetts.

15. Stalk, G & Hout, TM 1990, *Competing against time*, Free Press, New York.

16. ibid.

17. Porter, op cit.

18. Cusumano, M 1989, *The Japanese automobile industry*, Harvard University Press, Boston, Massachusetts.

19. Resources described in this chapter are largely internal to the company. Some scholars argue, however, that the resources necessary to implement a market strategy, if not to gain a competitive advantage, may reside at the country level or even in external companies. See, for example, Porter, ME 1990, *The competitive advantage of nations*, Free Press, New York; Dyer, JH & Singh, H 1998, 'The relational view: cooperative strategy and sources of interorganizational competitive advantage', *Academy of Management Review*, vol. 23, pp. 660–79.

20. Lev, B 2001, *Intangibles: management, measurement, and reporting*, Brookings Institution Press, Washington DC.

21. A dozen or so nations, including the UK and France, permit the recognition of brand names as assets on the statement of financial position.

22. What the company has may be considered assets, while what it does or can do may be considered a skill. See Hall, R 1992, 'The strategic analysis of intangible resources', *Strategic Management Journal*, vol. 13, pp. 135–44.

23. From the perspective of terminology, there is disagreement over whether capabilities are a resource. Some scholars define capabilities as distinct from resources. Other scholars argue that capabilities are clearly resources and should be defined as such. For the former view, see Amit, R & Shoemaker, P 1993, 'Strategic assets and organizational rents', *Strategic Management Journal*, vol. 4, pp. 33–47. For the latter view, see Foss, NJ & Robertson, PL 2000, 'Introduction: resources, technology and strategy', in *Resources, technology and strategy*, Routledge, London, pp. 1–10. This chapter holds to the view that capabilities are a specialised resource that a company employs in implementing a market strategy. For a corroborating view, see Makadok, R 2001, 'Toward a synthesis of the resource-based and dynamic-capability views of rent creation', *Strategic Management Journal*, vol. 22, pp. 387–401.

24. Grant, RM 1996, 'Prospering in dynamically-competitive environments: organizational capability as knowledge integration', *Organization Science*, vol. 7, pp. 375–87.

25. Nelson, RR & Winter, SG 1982, *An evolutionary theory of economic change*, Harvard University Press, Cambridge, Massachusetts.

26. See, for example, Teece, DJ, Pisano, G & Shuen, A 1997, 'Dynamic capabilities and strategic management', *Strategic Management Journal*, vol. 18, pp. 509–33; Eisenhardt, KM & Martin, JA 2000, 'Dynamic capabilities: what are they?', *Strategic Management Journal*, vol. 21, pp. 1105–21.

27. Grant, RM 1991, *Contemporary strategic analysis*, Blackwell, Oxford. See also Chan Kim & Mauborgne, op. cit.

28. Business Week 1987, 'Disney's magic', 9 March; *Business Week* 1988, 'Michael Eisner's hit parade', 1 February.

29. Kearns, D 1990, 'Leadership through quality', *Academy of Management Executive*, vol. 4, pp. 86–9; Sheridan, J 1990, 'America's best plants', *Industry Week*, 15 October, pp. 27–40; Corporation for American Banking 2001, 'Xerox dominates US digital copier placements for third consecutive year', 7 March, accessed 22 December 2005, www.aba.com/CAB/CAB_xeroxdigitalcopierrel.htm.

30. The classic statement of this position was by Alchain, AA 1950, 'Uncertainty, evolution, and economic theory', *Journal of Political Economy*, vol. 84, pp. 488–500.

31. Barney, JB 1991, 'Firm resources and sustained competitive advantage', *Journal of Management*, vol. 17, pp. 99–120; Peteraf, MA 1993, 'The cornerstones of competitive advantage: a resource-based view', *Strategic Management Journal*, vol. 14, pp. 179–91.

32. Barney, op. cit.

33. A company may attempt to acquire competencies similar to Honda's through a merger or acquisition transaction, rather than develop them in-house. Given that most mergers and acquisitions fail to achieve shareholder value, however, the payoff of acquiring a specific competency is not guaranteed.

34. Ghemawat, P 1991, *Commitment: the dynamic of strategy*, Free Press, New York.

35. Cohen, WM & Levinthal, DA 1990, 'Absorptive capacity: a new perspective on learning and innovation', *Administrative Science Quarterly*, vol. 35, pp. 128–52.

36. Hannah, MT & Freeman, J 1984, 'Structural inertia and organizational change', *American Sociological Review*, vol. 49, pp. 149–64.

37. See Anon. 1985 'IBM Corporation', Harvard Business School Case no. 180-034, Boston, Massachusetts.

38. Ghemawat, op. cit.

39. Miller, D 1990, *The Icarus paradox*, HarperBusiness, New York.

40. Senge, PM 1990, *The fifth discipline: the art and practice of the learning organization*, Doubleday, New York.

Strategies

part 3

Building competitive advantage through functional-level strategy

learning objectives

After studying this chapter, you should be able to:

- understand the role of economies of scale and learning effects in achieving superior efficiency

- discuss flexible manufacturing, mass customisation and modular product architectures as alternatives to mass production

- appreciate how the different functional areas may operate in achieving improved efficiency

- discuss how customer responsiveness can help a company attain a competitive advantage

- understand the role of quality in improving a company's competitive position

- describe how a total quality management (TQM) system can be implemented in a company

- appreciate why innovation can be so valuable to a company

- understand why some companies profit from their innovations but, in other cases, the imitator profits instead.

opening case

The growth of Aussie

Aussie Home Loans was founded by John Symond in February 1992. At the time, traditional banks dominated the home loan industry and high barriers to entry made this attractive industry difficult to enter. Banks were able to rely upon their large base of cheap (household) deposits and then use their extensive branch system to service potential home loan customers. With a long history of operating in a highly regulated market, there was little attempt to innovate and minimal pressure to cut costs actively because all players had operated within a stable oligopoly for decades.

The industry provided excellent returns for those involved because the generally uncompetitive market structure, low default rates on loans and the appreciation of house prices, meaning that banks would generally get their money back should a default occur, meant that this was a stable, low-risk and relatively profitable business to be in. This system was put under considerable pressure with the entry of Aussie, RAMS and PUMA in the early 1990s.

While banks rely upon household deposits for the capital to provide home loans, new lenders went straight to the capital markets. Using a process called 'securitisation', loans are pooled together and bundled into trusts or units (i.e. securities), which are then sold off to professional investors. The future income stream for investors came from interest payments and the low default rate made these securities relatively popular for some superannuation fund managers. Finally, although the banks were required to manage their loan portfolio actively, once bundled into a security, Aussie home loans did not remain on the balance sheet and were simply managed by Aussie (for a fee) on behalf on the owners of the security.

The result was a more efficient system, which meant that in April 1996 the banks had an average standard variable home loan rate of 10.5 per cent but Aussie offered a rate of 9.0 per cent. These sorts of differentials fuelled enormous growth in nonbank home loans such that in 1995, Aussie went from managing 356 000 mortgages to 1 352 000. Although the traditional banks have been able to fight back with a range of new products that are today every bit as competitive as the products from nonbanks, the damage was already done and the banks' virtual monopoly over residential home loans had been broken.

With Aussie having lost any natural advantage in home loans by 2000, in 2002 the company undertook a major review of its business. Not only did it outsource departments such as information technology (IT), call centres, loan processing and servicing but it also fundamentally changed their business, moving from mortgage originator to mortgage broker. Using a new IT system, the now Aussie Group sought to leverage the Aussie brand as a broker of different mortgage products rather than just of its stable of products. It also provided the springboard for entering into new markets, which would also allow for effective use of the Aussie brand.

Although Aussie has made a move into home insurance through a strategic alliance with CGU Insurance, its most significant new product has been the Aussie Mastercard. Entering as a low-cost product (in direct competition with the Virgin credit card), Aussie saw this as the new arena in which there could be a significant price differential relative to the major players (again the banks). This new product also uses the antibanks slogan of 'we'll save you' (from the banks), although it actually turns out to be a joint venture with the ANZ Bank. This new product has again had success relatively early: in 2005, it already had more than 50 000 customers.

Sources: Ross, E 2005, 'In-house entrepreneurs', *Business Review Weekly*, vol. 27, no. 28, 21–27 July, pp. 58–62; Hanratty, P 1995, 'Mortgage originators: new financial stars', Parliamentary Library, Parliament of Australia, research note 51 1995–96, accessed 12 November 2005, www.aph.gov.au/library/pubs/rn/1995-96/96rn51.htm.

Overview

Chapter 4 discusses the central role played by resources and capabilities as the building blocks for developing a competitive advantage. This chapter considers how managers can use their resources and capabilities at a functional level within the company to attain superior efficiency, quality, innovation and customer responsiveness. Functional-level strategies are directed at improving the effectiveness of basic operations within a company, such as production, marketing, materials management, research and development (R&D) and human resources. Even though these strategies may focus on a given function, they often embrace two or more functions and require close cooperation among functions to attain companywide efficiency, quality, innovation and customer responsiveness goals.

The opening case describes how Aussie Home Loans and later the Aussie Group were initially innovative and could provide a mortgage product that was significantly cheaper than those offered by the major banks, then became more customer responsive to offer a range of mortgage products as a mortgage broker and most recently have launched a low-cost credit card, again with the aim of taking market share away from the big banks.

To explore the issue of functional-level strategies, this chapter looks at how companies can increase their efficiency, quality, innovation and customer responsiveness. In some cases, it focuses on the contribution of a given function — such as production or marketing — to attaining these goals but it also emphasises the importance of strategies and policies that cut across functions. After reading this chapter, you should have a much clearer understanding of the actions that managers can take at the operating level to attain superior efficiency, quality, innovation and customer responsiveness.

Achieving superior efficiency

A company is a device for transforming inputs into outputs. Inputs are basic factors of production such as labour, land, capital, management and technological know-how. Outputs are the goods and services that a company produces. The simplest measure of efficiency is the quantity of inputs that it takes to produce a given output: that is, efficiency = outputs/inputs. The more efficient a company is, the fewer the inputs required to produce a given output and, therefore, the lower its costs. Put another way, an efficient company has higher productivity than that of its rivals and, therefore, lower costs.

The steps that companies can take at the functional level to boost their efficiency and thus lower their unit costs are reviewed here. After considering the primary functions of production and marketing, the various support functions of the enterprise are examined. It must be stressed, however, that achieving superior quality plays a major role in achieving superior efficiency. How to achieve it is discussed in the next section.

Production and efficiency: economies of scale

Economies of scale are unit-cost reductions associated with a large scale of output. One source of economies of scale is the ability to spread fixed costs over a large production volume. Fixed costs must be incurred to produce a product regardless of the level of output; they include the costs of purchasing machinery, the costs of setting up machinery for individual production runs, the costs of facilities and the costs of advertising and R&D. It cost Microsoft approximately US$1 billion to develop Windows XP but Microsoft can realise substantial economies of scale by spreading the fixed costs of developing a new operating system over the enormous sales volume that it expects for this operating system (given that 90 per cent of the world's PCs use a Microsoft operating system). In Microsoft's case, these economies of scale are even more significant because the incremental (or marginal) cost of producing additional copies of Windows XP is trivial: once the master copy has been produced, additional CDs containing the operating system can be produced for just a few cents.

Many hi-tech companies face a similar cost structure: high fixed costs and trivial marginal costs. Telecommunications companies spend billions of dollars in infrastructure to build their networks but almost nothing to transmit additional signals down those networks. For these companies, the key to their efficiency and profitability is to increase sales rapidly enough so the company can spread fixed costs over a large unit volume, and realise substantial economies of scale.

Another source of economies is the ability of companies producing in large volumes to achieve a greater **division of labour** and specialisation. Specialisation has a favourable impact on productivity, mainly because it enables employees to become very skilled at performing a particular task. The classic example of such economies is Ford's Model T. The world's first mass-produced car, the Model T was introduced in 1923. Until then, Ford had made cars using an expensive hand-built 'craft production' method. By introducing mass-production techniques, the company achieved greater division of labour (that is, it split assembly into small, repeatable tasks) and specialisation, which boosted employee productivity. Ford was also able to spread the fixed costs of developing a motor vehicle and setting up production machinery over a large volume of output. As a result of these economies, the cost of manufacturing a car at Ford fell from US$3000 to less than US$900 (in 1958 dollars).

Economies of scale are not relevant only to manufacturing enterprises. Service organisations such as banks and universities can also benefit from economies of scale. Universities can gain economies of scale in several ways, such as by having more students per class or by spreading the cost of central computer systems (such as those that handle student records) over a larger number of students. Banks also spread the cost of their centralised computer systems over a larger customer base and they can also achieve economies of scale in areas such as marketing, new product development and legal activities. On a global scale, Australia has a relatively efficient banking sector. The four largest banks (National Australia Bank, Commonwealth Bank, Westpac and ANZ Bank), which dominate as part of the 'four pillar policy', have had to be efficient at an international level since deregulation of the financial industry started in 1983. With the Australian market opening up to foreign competitors, and the four pillar policy ensuring none of the four banks merges with another, the major banks have had to work to ensure their survival by taking over smaller banks (to increase customer numbers as the first step towards achieving economies of scale) and reducing the number of branches to maximise the number of customers per branch. Having just four major banks ensures the customer base is large enough for the banks to realise economies of scale. In comparison, Malaysia had more than 15 significant banks in 2003. With its financial industry gradually opening up to international competitors, the Malaysian banking industry is going through considerable change as many of the banks merge or the larger banks take over the smaller. Both the government and the banking industry realise that local banks will only survive if they can achieve greater efficiencies, including those attained by economies of scale.

Some experts argue that after a certain **minimum efficient scale** of output is reached, few, if any, additional economies of scale can be had from expanding volume.[1] (Minimum efficient scale is the minimum plant size necessary to gain significant economies of scale.) For an example of minimum efficient scale, see Strategy in action 5.1, which looks at the Australian motor vehicle industry. As shown in figure 5.1, the long-term unit-cost curve of a company is L shaped. At outputs beyond the minimum efficient scale in figure 5.1, additional cost reductions are hard to find. Another point worth noting is that diseconomies of scale can arise when large enterprises build up a substantial corporate bureaucracy, which increases corporate overheads without reducing unit costs.

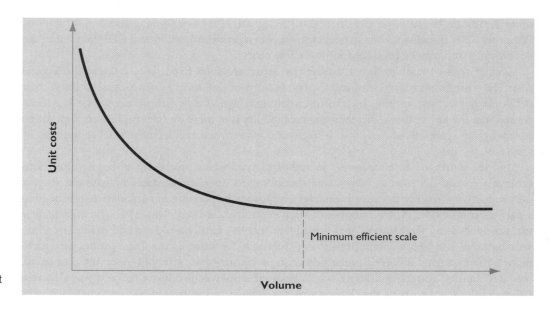

Figure 5.1:
A typical long-term unit-cost
curve

Production and efficiency: learning effects

learning effects
The efficiencies that arise
from employees learning,
through repetition, to
complete their tasks more
efficiently

Learning effects are cost savings that come from learning by doing. Labour, for example, learns by repetition how best to carry out a task. In other words, labour productivity increases over time and unit costs fall as individuals learn how to perform a particular task most efficiently. Equally important, in new manufacturing facilities, management typically learns over time how best to run the new operation. Production costs thus decline as a result of increasing labour productivity and management efficiency.

Learning effects tend to be more significant when a technologically complex task is repeated, because there is more to learn. Learning effects will, therefore, be more significant in an assembly process involving 1000 complex steps than in one with 100 simple steps. Although learning effects are normally associated with the manufacturing process, there are reasons for believing that they are just as important in many service industries. One famous study of learning in the context of the healthcare industry found that more experienced medical providers posted significantly lower mortality rates for some common surgical procedures, suggesting that learning effects are at work in surgery.[2] The authors of this study used the evidence to argue for the establishment of regional referral centres to provide highly specialised medical care. These centres would perform many specific surgical procedures (e.g. heart surgery), replacing local facilities with lower volumes and presumably higher mortality rates.

In terms of the long-term average cost curve of a company, while economies of scale imply a movement along the curve (say, from A to B in figure 5.3), the realisation of learning effects implies a downward shift of the entire curve (B to C in figure 5.3) as both labour and management become more efficient over time at performing their tasks at each and every level of output. No matter how complex the task, however, learning effects typically peter out after a time. It has been suggested that they are important only during the startup of a new process and that they cease after two or three years.[3]

Production and efficiency: the experience curve

experience curve
The curve showing the
reduction in unit cost
for each additional unit
produced, in which the
efficiencies come from
experience gained in
producing the product

The **experience curve** refers to the systematic unit-cost reductions that have been observed over the life of a product.[4] According to the experience curve concept, unit manufacturing costs for a product typically decline by some characteristic amount each time the accumulated output of the product (the total output of a product since its introduction) is doubled. The rela-

strategy in action 5.1

The struggle facing the Australian motor vehicle industry

In 1997, the former Industry Commission in Australia released a major report on the state of the Australian motor vehicle industry to determine its efficiency and whether the Commonwealth Government should support it through further tariffs. Although it found that the industry was a major employer (employing more than 70 000 people directly and a further 300 000 indirectly) and had made significant improvements in efficiency, it determined that it was still not very competitive on the world stage and, therefore, tariffs should be phased out.

A major reason for the inefficiencies is that the Australian producers do not produce enough vehicles to achieve minimum efficient scale. A recent Australian Productivity Commission suggested that volumes of at least 250 000 cars are necessary to achieve economies of scale in mass-produced, low-margin segments of the market. Australian plants produce between 40 000 and almost 115 000 cars per year, meaning that even the largest plants struggle to compete at an international level. Holden, for example, produced just more than 110 000 cars at its Elizabeth plant in South Australia. In comparison, the Mitsubishi plant produced only 33 000 units of the Magna. Toyota produces about 75 000 cars (a mix of Camrys and Corollas at its Altona plant in Victoria), yet the Toyota Georgetown plant in the United States has a capacity for 400 000 Camrys alone. Similarly, the Ford plant at Broadmeadows in Victoria has a total capacity of 120 000 units per year, whereas the Ford plant in Chicago has a capacity for 300 000 Tauruses per year (see figure 5.2).

Given that the entire capacity of Australian plants is slightly less than 400 000 units, the local industry can probably support only two (maybe three) plants if exports can be increased. Any attempts to maintain more operations are likely to lead to inefficiencies, because the industry cannot realise full economies of scale.

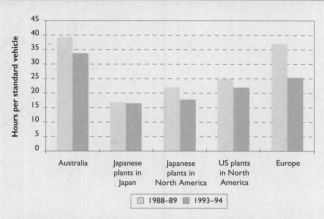

Australian figures are for 1988 and 1993. Figures for other countries are for early 1989 and 1993–94. Figures are for entire (unmatched) samples of assembly plants.

Figure 5.2:
International comparisons of productivity across motor vehicle plants

Source: MacDuffie, JP & Pil, FK 1996, *Performance findings of the international automotive assembly plant study*, International Motor Vehicle Program, Massachusetts Institute of Technology, Cambridge, Massachusetts.

Source: Based on Industry Commission (now Productivity Commission) 1997, *The automotive industry overview: recommendations and findings*, Report no. 58, Commonwealth of Australia, Canberra. Reproduced by permission. Australian Productivity Commission 2002, *Review of Automotive Assistance*, Report 25, Commonwealth of Australia, Canberra.

tionship was first observed in the aircraft industry, where it was found that each time the accumulated output of airframes was doubled, unit costs declined to 80 per cent of their previous level.[5] The fourth airframe, therefore, typically cost only 80 per cent of the second airframe to produce, the eighth airframe cost only 80 per cent of the fourth, the sixteenth cost only 80 per cent of the eighth and so on. The outcome of this process is a relationship between unit manufacturing costs and accumulated output similar to that illustrated in figure 5.4.

Economies of scale and learning effects create the experience curve phenomenon. Put simply, as a company increases the accumulated volume of its output over time, it is able to realise both economies of scale (as volume increases) and learning effects. Consequently, unit costs fall with increases in accumulated output.

The strategic significance of the experience curve is clear. It suggests that increasing a company's product volume and market share will also bring cost advantages over the competition. Company A in figure 5.4, because it is further down the experience curve, has a clear cost advantage over company B. The concept is perhaps most important in those industries

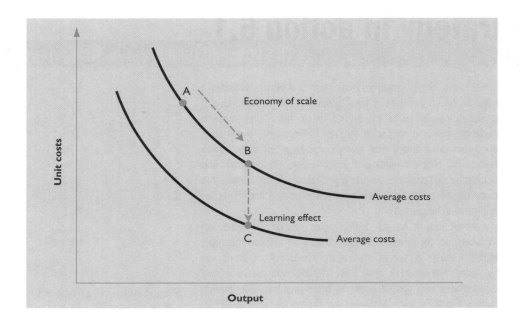

where the production process involves the mass production of a standardised output (e.g. the manufacture of semiconductor chips). If a company wishes to become more efficient and so attain a low-cost position, it must try to ride down the experience curve as quickly as possible. This means constructing efficient large-scale manufacturing facilities even before the company has the demand and aggressively pursuing cost reductions from learning effects. The company may also need to adopt an aggressive marketing strategy, cutting prices to the bone and stressing heavy sales promotions to build up demand — and thus accumulated volume — as quickly as possible. Once down the experience curve, the company is likely, given its superior efficiency, to have a significant cost advantage over its competitors. It has been argued, for example, that Intel uses these tactics to ride down the experience curve and gain a competitive advantage over its rivals in the market for microprocessors.[6]

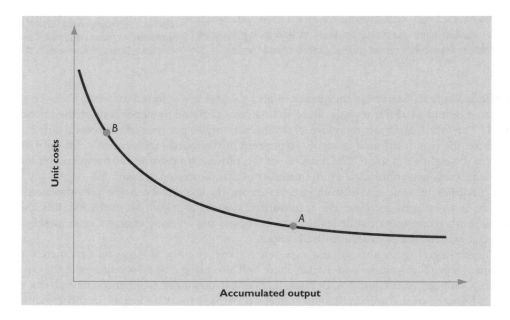

The company farthest down the experience curve must not become complacent about its cost advantage for three reasons. First, because neither learning effects nor economies of scale last forever, the experience curve will bottom out at some point; it must do so by definition. When this occurs, further unit-cost reductions from learning effects and economies of scale will be hard to find. In time, therefore, other companies can catch up with the cost leader. Once this happens, several low-cost companies can have cost parity with each other. In such circumstances, a sustainable competitive advantage must rely on strategic factors other than minimising production costs by using existing technologies, such as better customer responsiveness, product quality and innovation.

Second, cost advantages gained from experience effects can be made obsolete by the development of new technologies. The price of television picture tubes, for example, followed the experience curve pattern from the introduction of television in the late 1940s until 1963. The average unit price dropped from US$34 to US$8 (in 1958 dollars) in that time.[7] Technology then changed to colour televisions and more recently to plasma and LCD screens. But the same cost reduction pattern has occurred each time. For example a 19-inch LCD monitor was more than $1500 in 2004, but was down to about $700 (for a well-recognised brand) by 2005 and at the start of 2006 the same size monitor from Compaq was available for $460. In short, technological change can alter the rules of the game, requiring that former low-cost companies take steps to re-establish their competitive edge.

A further reason for avoiding complacency is that high volume does not necessarily give a company a cost advantage. Some technologies have different cost functions. The steel industry, for example, has two alternative manufacturing technologies: an integrated technology, which relies on the basic oxygen furnace, and a minimill technology, which depends on the electric arc furnace. As illustrated in figure 5.5, the minimum efficient scale of the electric arc furnace is located at relatively low volumes but that of the basic oxygen furnace is located at relatively high volumes. Even when both operations are producing at their most efficient output levels, steel companies with basic oxygen furnaces do not have a cost advantage over minimills.

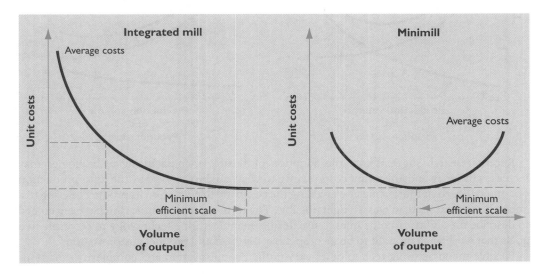

Figure 5.5:
Unit production costs in an integrated steel mill and a minimill

Consequently, the pursuit of economies from experience by an integrated company using basic oxygen technology may not bring the kind of cost advantages that a naive reading of the experience curve phenomenon would lead the company to expect. This is an example of how in many industries new flexible manufacturing technologies hold out the promise of allowing small manufacturers to produce at unit costs comparable with those of large assembly line operations — an issue discussed in the following section.

Production and efficiency: flexible manufacturing and mass customisation

Central to the concept of economies of scale is the idea that the best way to achieve high efficiency, and thus low unit costs, is to mass produce standardised output. The trade-off implicit in this idea is between unit costs and product variety. Producing greater product variety from a factory implies shorter production runs, which imply an inability to realise economies of scale. That is, wide product variety makes it difficult for a company to increase its production efficiency and thus reduce its unit costs. According to this logic, the way to increase efficiency and drive down unit costs is to limit product variety and produce a standardised product in large volumes (see figure 5.6a).

The rise of **flexible manufacturing** technologies has challenged this view of production efficiency. The term flexible manufacturing technology — or lean production, as it is often called — covers a range of manufacturing technologies designed to (a) reduce setup times for complex equipment, (b) increase the use of individual machines through better scheduling and (c) improve quality control at all stages of the manufacturing process.[8] Flexible manufacturing technologies allow the company to produce a wider variety of end-products at a unit cost that at one time it could achieve only through the mass production of a standardised output (figure 5.6b).

flexible manufacturing
A system that allows a company to both attain economies of scale and customise the product somewhat

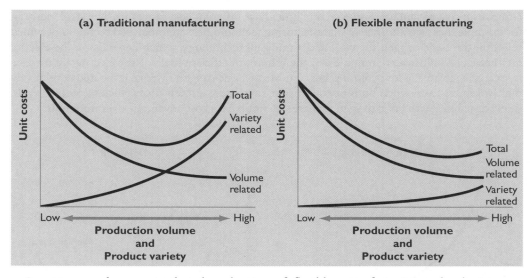

Figure 5.6:
The trade-off between costs and product variety

Recent research suggests that the adoption of flexible manufacturing technologies may increase efficiency and lower unit costs relative to what can be achieved by the mass production of a standardised output, while also enabling the company to customise its product offering to a much greater extent than was thought possible. The term mass customisation has been coined to describe the ability of companies to use flexible manufacturing technology to reconcile two goals that were once thought to be incompatible: low cost and product customisation.[9]

Flexible manufacturing technologies vary in their sophistication and complexity. A famous example of a flexible manufacturing technology, Toyota's production system, is relatively unsophisticated but it has been credited with making Toyota the most efficient company in the global motor vehicle industry. Because it lacked capital, Toyota was unable to use traditional mass production techniques, which relied on making a very large number of different parts. This approach tied up capital and was expensive in terms of inventory storage and the waste costs involved if the initial machine settings were wrong. Engineers at Toyota developed a series of levers and pulleys that allowed workers to change the machine settings rapidly, thus

mass customisation
Flexible manufacturing that allows a company to both attain economies of scale and customise the product to meet consumer preferences

making it economical to manufacture in much smaller batches. Toyota required a full day to change the dies on a stamping machine in 1950 but only three minutes in 1971. Not only did this make Toyota more efficient, it also allowed for greater customisation of the product to meet different customer needs.[10]

A major advance in developing flexible manufacturing strategies has been the move towards using modular product architectures to produce **modular products**. These exist when the interfaces of the various components that make up the product are kept constant. This means that a company can upgrade components without having to redesign the entire product. Bicycle pedals, for example, come in more than 200 different models and makes around the world but they all screw into the crank in the same way (using the same length screw with the same thread). In the same way, Sony released more than 160 versions of its Walkman by mixing and matching different components but retaining the basic architecture (that is, how the components fit together).[11]

Modular architectures are used for a whole range of products, including personal computers, workstations, motor vehicles, bicycles, stereo equipment, aircraft, various microelectronic goods and cameras.[12] Companies such as Chrysler have used modular architecture extensively as a way of producing a greater range of cars using many of the same components. The 'quad 4' engine, for example, is used across much of the production line for small to midsized vehicles. Computer assemblers such as Dell are able to meet the demands of different consumers by plugging together different components in various combinations. Modularity allows for cheaper and more rapid product upgrades because a company can replace components without having to redesign the entire product.

Besides improving efficiency and lowering costs, flexible manufacturing technologies also enable companies to customise products to the unique demands of small consumer groups at

> **modular products**
> Products for which the parts or components fit together in the same way over versions of the product

strategy in action 5.2

Mass customisation

Mass customisation has previously been viewed as the new way forward for many consumer-oriented firms that seek to serve a heterogeneous market. Levi's introduced custom-made jeans, which were individually cut to fit the individual's body shape perfectly. National Bicycle Company of Japan provided customised bicycles that cost only slightly more than a similar mass-produced bicycle because it was able to move beyond the hand-built approach that most custom bicycle manufacturers are forced to use. Possibly most famous of all, Dell offers a range of different combinations and permutations of PCs that are then individually made to order.

More recent examples come from Adidas and Proctor & Gamble. When they go to buy shoes with the label of Mi-Adidas, consumers visit an Adidas store and have their feet measured. They then select the materials and colours for their shoes. In roughly three weeks, their customised shoes are available, for about $40 more than standard Adidas shoes in the same range. While this move into mass customisation has been successful in terms of uptake and the loyalty it has created, many others have failed to create an impact. The Levi's experiment provided data on common body shapes and how they had changed over the past 20 years but the poor uptake of customised jeans did not warrant the costs of establishing and maintaining the system supporting customisation. National Bicycle Company of Japan was a one-off operation that was slowly outclassed as consumers wanting high-end bicycles turned more and more to carbon-fibre monocoques and other alternative materials that could not be cut and welded in the same way as traditional bicycles can. In 2005, one of the most successful mass customisation efforts was shut down: Reflect.com. Part of the Procter & Gamble empire, Reflect.com sold individually developed and personally labelled hair, skin and cosmetic products. As an example of the level of customisation, Elixir Custom Gloss (a lipstick) came in more than 10 000 shades. The site attracted over one million unique visitors a month and formed an important source of customer data for other Procter & Gamble brands such as Cover Girl and Olay. Yet, in June 2005, Reflect.com was shut down without reason and few firms are engaging in mass customisation.

Sources: Kotha, S 1996, 'From mass production to mass customization: the case of the National Industrial Bicycle Company of Japan', *European Management Journal*, vol. 14, pp. 442–50; Shoebridge, N 2005, 'One size does not fit all' *Business Review Weekly*, vol. 27, no. 26, 7–13 July, p. 63.

a cost that once could be achieved only by mass producing a standardised output. They thus help a company achieve mass customisation, which increases its customer responsiveness. For a discussion of mass customisation, see Strategy in action 5.2.

Marketing and efficiency

marketing strategy
A company's approach to its product pricing, promotion, design and distribution (or placement)

The **marketing strategy** that a company adopts can have a major impact on the efficiency and cost structure of an enterprise. Marketing strategy refers to the company's approach to pricing, promotion, product design and distribution. It can play a major role in boosting a company's efficiency. Some of the steps leading to greater efficiency are obvious. How aggressive pricing, promotions and advertising — all of which are the task of the marketing function — can help a company ride down the experience curve to gain a low-cost position have already been discussed. Other aspects of marketing strategy, however, have a less obvious, although not less significant, impact on efficiency. One important aspect is the relationship between customer defection rates and unit costs.[13]

customer defection rate
The percentage of customers who move to a competitor each year

The **customer defection rate** is the percentage of a company's customers who defect every year to competitors. Defection rates are determined by customer loyalty, which is a function of a company's ability to satisfy its customers. Because acquiring a new customer entails one-time fixed costs for advertising, promotions and the like, defection rates and costs are directly rated. The longer a company holds on to a customer, the greater is the volume of customer-generated unit sales that can be set against these fixed costs, and the lower is the average unit cost of each sale. Lowering customer defection rates thus allows a company to achieve substantial cost economies. This is illustrated in figure 5.7, which shows that high defection rates imply high average unit costs (and vice versa).

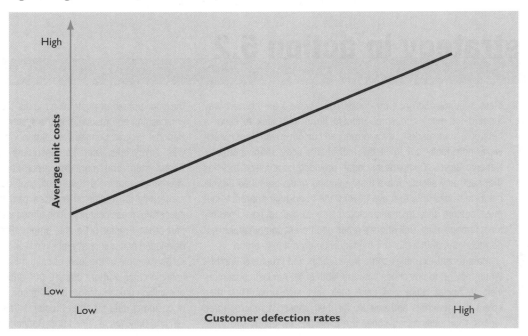

Figure 5.7:
The relationship between average unit costs and customer defection rates

One consequence of the relationship summarised in figure 5.7 is a correlation between the length of time that a customer stays with the company and profit per customer (see figure 5.8). Given the fixed costs of acquiring new customers, serving customers who stay with the company for only a short time before switching to competitors often yields a negative profit. The longer a customer stays with the company, however, the more the fixed costs of acquiring that customer can be spread over repeat purchases, which boosts the profit per customer.

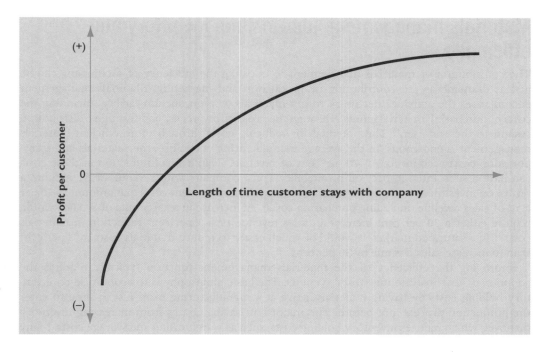

For an example of this phenomenon, consider the credit card business.[14] In 1990, most credit card companies spent an average of US$51 to recruit a customer and set up a new account. These costs came from the advertising required to attract new customers, credit checks required for each customer and the mechanics of setting up an account and issuing a card. These one-time fixed costs can be recouped only if a customer stays with the company for at least two years. Moreover, when customers stay a second year, they tend to increase their use of the credit card, which raises the volume of revenue generated by each customer over time. As a result, the average profit per customer in the credit card business increases from –US$51 in year one (that is, a loss of US$51) to US$44 in year three and US$55 in year six.

Another economic benefit of long-time customer loyalty is the free advertising that customers provide for a company. Loyal customers do a lot of talking and can dramatically increase the volume of business through referrals. A striking example is The Body Shop. Its success is built on social responsibility at a reasonable price. The company has generated considerable customer loyalty and such a well-known brand name that it does not need to advertise, which is a major source of cost saving.

The key message is that reducing customer defection rates and building customer loyalty can be a major source of cost saving. By leading to lower unit costs, a reduction in customer defection rates of just 5 per cent can increase profits per customer by 25–85 per cent, depending on the industry. A 5 per cent reduction in customer defection rates leads to the following increases in profits per customer over the average customer life: a 75 per cent increase in profit per customer in the credit card business; a 50 per cent increase in profit per customer in the insurance brokerage industry; a 45 per cent increase in profit per customer in the industrial laundry business and a 35 per cent increase in profit per customer in the computer software industry.[15]

How can a company reduce customer defection rates? It can do so by building brand loyalty, which requires that the company be responsive to the needs of its customers. The issue of customer responsiveness is considered later in the chapter. For now, note that a central component of developing a strategy to reduce defection rates is to spot customers who defect, find out why they defected and act on that information so other customers do not defect for similar reasons. To take these measures, the marketing function must have information systems capable of tracking customer defections.

Materials management, just-in-time inventory and efficiency

The contribution of materials management to boosting the efficiency of a company can be just as dramatic as the contribution of production and marketing. Materials management encompasses the activities necessary to get materials to a production facility (including the costs of purchasing material inputs), through the production process and through a distribution system to the end-user.[16] The potential for reducing costs through more efficient materials management is enormous. In the average manufacturing enterprise, the materials and transportation costs account for 50–70 per cent of revenue. Even a small reduction in these costs can have a substantial impact on profitability. For a company with revenue of $1 million, a return on investment rate of 5 per cent and materials management costs that amount to 50 per cent of sales revenue (including purchasing costs), an increase in total profits of $15 000 would require either a 30 per cent increase in sales revenue or a 3 per cent reduction in materials costs.[17] In a saturated market, it would be much easier to reduce materials costs by 3 per cent than to increase sales revenue by 30 per cent.

Improving the efficiency of the materials management function typically requires the adoption of **just-in-time inventory systems**. The basic philosophy is to economise on inventory holding costs by having materials arrive at a manufacturing plant just in time to enter the production process, not before. The major cost saving comes from increasing inventory turnover, which reduces inventory holding costs, such as warehousing and storage costs. Many online stores (especially those selling CDs and books) go one step further by not holding any stock other than top-selling items) and ordering the item from the supplier only once a customer submits an order and pays for the product.

The drawback of just-in-time systems is that they leave a company without a buffer stock of inventory. Although buffer stocks of inventory are expensive to store, they can tide a company over shortages of inputs caused by disruption among suppliers (such as a labour dispute at a key supplier). Buffer stocks can also help a company respond quickly to increases in demand. There are ways around these limitations, however. To reduce the risks of dependence on one supplier for an important input, for example, the company may source inputs from multiple suppliers.

just-in-time inventory systems
The delivery of supplies just as they are needed for the production process

R&D strategy and efficiency

The role of superior R&D in helping a company achieve greater efficiency is twofold. First, the R&D function can boost efficiency by designing products that are easy to manufacture. Making a product with fewer parts can dramatically decrease the required assembly time, which translates into higher employee productivity and lower unit costs. Design for manufacturing requires close coordination between the production and R&D functions of the company. Cross-functional teams that contain both sets of personnel, so they can work on the problem jointly, best achieve such coordination.

The second way the R&D function can help a company achieve greater efficiency is by pioneering process innovations, that is, new ways of operating that improve efficiency. Process innovations have often been a major source of competitive advantage. In the motor vehicle industry, Toyota's competitive advantage is partly based on the company's invention of new flexible manufacturing processes, which dramatically reduced setup times. This process innovation enabled Toyota to obtain, years ahead of its competitors, efficiency gains associated with flexible manufacturing systems.

Human resources strategy and efficiency

Employee productivity is one of the key determinants of an enterprise's efficiency and cost structure. The more productive the employees, the lower will be the unit costs. The challenge for a company's human resources function is to devise ways to increase employee productivity. It has three main choices: (1) training employees, (2) organising the workforce into self-managing teams and (3) linking pay to performance.

Employee training

Individuals are a major input into the production process. A company that employs workers with higher skills is likely to be more efficient than one employing less skilled personnel. Those who are more skilled can perform tasks faster and more accurately, and are more likely than less skilled individuals to learn the complex tasks associated with many modern production methods. Training can upgrade employee skill levels, bringing productivity-related efficiency gains.[18]

Self-managing teams

Self-managing teams are a relatively recent phenomenon. Few companies used them until the mid-1980s but they have since spread rapidly. The growth of flexible manufacturing cells, which group workers into teams, has undoubtedly facilitated the spread of self-managing teams among manufacturing enterprises. The typical team comprises five to 15 employees who produce an entire product or undertake an entire task. Team members learn all team tasks and rotate from job to job. A more flexible workforce is one result. Team members can fill in for absent co-workers. Teams also take over managerial duties such as scheduling work and vacation time, ordering materials and employing new members. The greater responsibility thrust on team members and the empowerment that it implies are seen as motivators. (Empowerment is the process of giving lower-level employees decision-making power.) People often respond well to being given greater autonomy and responsibility. Performance bonuses linked to team production and quality targets work as an additional motivator.

self-managing teams
Semiautonomous teams that manage themselves within the boundaries set by management

Pay for performance

People work for money, so it is hardly surprising that linking pay to performance can help increase employee productivity. The issue is not quite so simple as just introducing incentive pay systems, however; it is also important to define what kind of performance is to be rewarded and how. Some of the most efficient companies in the world — mindful that cooperation among employees is necessary to realise productivity gains — do not link pay to individual performance. Instead, they link pay to group or team performance. In other cases, where quality is a central aim, the bonus systems are based on quality, not output. Here, bonuses may be paid according to reductions in faulty product returns or a similar measure.

Information systems, the Internet and efficiency

Computers, the Internet and new software programs are allowing many organisations to undertake many of their processes more efficiently. For example, Dell has been able to avoid paying for a large sales force through the use of an extensive online ordering system. In addition, much of the customer support is Internet based and the result is that some 200 000 people access Dell's troubleshooting tips online. Each of these hits at Dell's website saves the company US$15, which is the average cost of a technical support call. If just 10 per cent of these people were to call Dell using a telephone, then they would cost the company US$15.6 million per year.[19]

More generally, companies such as Dell are using Web-based information systems to reduce the costs of coordination between the company and its customers, and the company and its suppliers. By using Web-based programs to automate customer and supplier interactions, a company can substantially reduce the number of people required to manage these interfaces, decreasing costs and increasing productivity. This trend is not limited to hi-tech companies because financial services companies are finding that they can substantially reduce costs by moving customer accounts and support functions online. This reduces the need for customer service representatives, bank tellers, brokers, insurance agents and so on. Because the cost of conducting a transaction online is likely to be a matter of cents, services are now differently priced depending on how the transaction is conducted. For example, some Australian banks will charge $2 for a branch transaction, either $0.30 or $0.50 for an ATM, EFTPOS or automated phone banking transaction and nothing for Internet transactions. In essence, the high cost of operating branches is why Australian and New Zealand banks are doing everything possible to move customers away from using branches to using telephone and Internet banking. Similarly, the whole idea behind Internet-based retailers such as Amazon.com is that the retail system can remove significant costs by replacing physical stores and their supporting personnel with an online virtual store and automated ordering and checkout processes. Companies can also realise cost savings by using Web-based information systems to automate many internal company activities, from managing expense reimbursements to planning benefits and employing staff, reducing the need for internal support personnel.

Infrastructure and efficiency

The infrastructure sets the context within which all other value creation activities take place. It follows that the infrastructure can help a company achieve efficiency goals. Above all, the infrastructure can foster a companywide commitment to efficiency and promote cooperation among different functions in pursuit of efficiency goals.

The leadership of top management can build companywide commitment to efficiency. The leadership task is to articulate a vision that recognises the need for all functions of the company to focus on improving their efficiency. It is not enough to improve just the efficiency of production or marketing, for example. Achieving superior efficiency requires a companywide commitment to this goal and only top management can articulate this commitment.

A further leadership task is to facilitate the cross-functional cooperation needed to achieve superior efficiency. Designing products that are easy to manufacture, for example, requires production and research personnel to communicate; integrating just-in-time systems with production scheduling requires close communication between material management and production; designing self-managing teams to perform production tasks requires close cooperation between human resources and production and so on.

Summary: achieving superior efficiency

Table 5.1 summarises the primary roles that various functions must take to achieve superior efficiency. It is not something that can be tackled function by function, however; it requires companywide commitment and an ability to ensure close cooperation among functions. Top management, by exercising leadership and influencing the infrastructure, plays a major role in this process.

Achieving superior quality

total quality management (TQM)
A philosophy that focuses on constantly improving the quality of a company's products and services

Superior quality gives a company two advantages: (1) the increased reputation for quality allows the company to charge a premium price for its product and (2) the elimination of defects from the production process increases efficiency and thus lowers costs. This section examines the means to achieve superior quality. The main approach is **total quality management** (TQM), which is a management philosophy that focuses on improving the quality of a company's products and services, and stresses that all company operations should be oriented towards this goal.[20] A companywide philosophy, it requires the cooperation of all the different functions if it is to be successfully implemented. This section first considers the TQM concept, then discusses the steps needed to implement TQM programs. Throughout, the roles that different functions must play in this process are highlighted.

Table 5.1: The primary roles of different value creation functions in achieving superior efficiency

Value creation function	Primary roles
Infrastructure (leadership)	1. Provides companywide commitment to efficiency. 2. Facilitates cooperation among functions.
Production	1. Where appropriate, pursues economies of scale and learning economics. 2. Implements flexible manufacturing systems.
Marketing	1. Where appropriate, adopts aggressive marketing to ride down the experience curve. 2. Limits customer defection rates by building brand loyalty.
Materials management	Implements just-in-time systems.
R&D	1. Designs products for ease of manufacture. 2. Seeks process innovations.
Information systems	1. Uses information systems to automate processes. 2. Uses information systems to reduce the costs of coordination.
Human resources	1. Institutes training programs to build skills. 2. Implements self-managing teams. 3. Implements pay for performance.

The concept of TQM

A number of US consultants, including Deming, Juran and Feigenbaum, first developed the TQM concept.[21] Originally, these consultants won few converts in the United States. In contrast, the Japanese embraced them enthusiastically and even named their premier annual prize for manufacturing excellence after Deming. The philosophy underlying TQM, as articulated by Deming, is based on the following five-step chain reaction.

1. Improved quality means that costs decrease as a result of less reworking, fewer mistakes, fewer delays and better use of time and materials.

2. As a result, productivity improves.

3. Better quality leads to higher market share and allows the company to raise prices.

4. This increases the company's profitability and allows the company to stay in business.

5. The company thus creates more jobs.[22]

He identified fourteen steps that should be part of any TQM program (see figure 5.9). Deming continually changed these steps in line with his belief in the importance of continuous quality improvement. The steps given here are the latest (1990) version.

In essence, Deming urged a company to have a definite strategic plan for where it is going and how it is going to get there. He argued that management should embrace the philosophy that mistakes, defects and poor-quality materials are not acceptable and should be eliminated. Quality of supervision should be improved by allowing more time for supervisors to work with employees and giving them appropriate skills for the job. Furthermore, management should create an environment in which employees will not fear reporting problems or recommending improvements. Deming also believed that work standards should be defined not only as numbers or quotas but also by some notion of quality, to promote the production of defect-free output. He argued that management has the responsibility to train employees in new skills to keep pace with changes in the workplace and that achieving better quality requires the commitment of everyone in the company.

It took the rise of Japan to the top rank of economic powers to alert Western business to the importance of the TQM concept. Since the early 1980s, TQM practices have spread rapidly throughout Western industry. Despite its spectacular success, TQM practices are still not universally accepted. A study by the American Quality Foundation found that only 20 per cent of US companies regularly review the consequences of quality performance, compared with 70 per cent of Japanese companies.[23] Another study of 500 US companies using TQM found that only 36 per cent believed that TQM was increasing their competitiveness.[24] A prime reason for this finding, according to the study, was that many companies had not fully understood or embraced the TQM concept.

1. Create constancy of purpose towards improvement of product and service, with the aim of becoming competitive and staying in business, and providing jobs.

2. Adopt the new philosophy. We are in a new economic age. Western management must awaken to the challenge, must learn their responsibilities and take on leader-ship for change.

3. Cease dependence on inspection to achieve quality. Eliminate the need for inspection on a mass basis by building quality into the product in the first place.

4. End the practice of awarding business on the basis of price tag. Instead, minimise total cost.

5. Improve constantly and forever the system of production and service, to improve quality and productivity, and thus constantly decrease costs.

6. Institute training on the job.

7. Institute leadership. The aim of leadership should be to help people and machines and gadgets do a better job. Leadership of management is in need of an overhaul, as well as leadership of production workers.

8. Drive out fear, so everyone may work effectively for the company.

9. Break down barriers between departments. People in research, design, sales and production must work as a team, to foresee problems of production and in use that may be encountered with the product or service.

10. Eliminate slogans, exhortations and targets for the workforce asking for zero defects and new levels of productivity. Such exhortations only create adversarial relationships. The bulk of the causes of low quality and low productivity belong to the system and thus lie beyond the power of the workforce.

11. (a) Eliminate work standards on the factory floor. Substitute leadership. (b) Eliminate management by objective. Eliminate management by numbers, numerical goals. Substitute leadership.

12. (a) Remove barriers that rob hourly workers of their right to pride of workmanship. The responsibility of supervisors must be changed from sheer numbers to quality. (b) Remove barriers that rob people in management and in engineering of their right to pride of workmanship.

13. Institute a vigorous program of education and self-improvement.

14. Put everybody in the company to work to accomplish the transformation. The transformation is everybody's job.

Figure 5.9: Deming's 14 points to quality

Source: Gabor, A 1990, *The man who discovered quality: Howard W Edwards Deming brought the quality revolution to America — the stories of Ford, Xerox, & GM*, Random House, New York. Used by permission of Times Books, a division of Random House, Inc.

Implementing TQM

Among companies that have successfully adopted TQM, certain imperatives stand out. They are discussed in the order in which they are usually tackled in companies implementing TQM programs, and the role of functions in regard to each precept is highlighted. What cannot be stressed enough, however, is that implementing TQM requires close cooperation among all functions in the pursuit of the common goal of improving quality; it is a process that cuts across functions. The roles played by the different functions in implementing TQM are summarised in table 5.2.

Build organisational commitment to quality

Evidence shows that TQM does little to improve the performance of a company unless it is embraced by everyone in the organisation.[25] Both top management and the human resources function of the company can play a major role in this process. Top management has the responsibility of exercising the leadership required to make a commitment to quality a companywide goal. The human resources function must take on responsibility for company-wide training in TQM techniques.

Focus on the customer

TQM practitioners see a focus on the customer as the starting point — even the *raison d'être* — of the whole quality philosophy.[26] The marketing function, because it provides the primary point of contact with the customer, should play a major role here. It needs to identify what the customers want from the good or service that the company provides; what the company provides to customers; and the gap between what customers want and what they get, which could be called the quality gap. Then, together with the other functions of the company, it needs to formulate a plan for closing the quality gap.

Table 5.2: The roles of different value creation functions in implementing TQM

Value creation function	Primary roles
Infrastructure (leadership)	1. Provides leadership and commitment to quality. 2. Finds ways of measuring quality. 3. Sets goals and creates incentives. 4. Solicits input from employees. 5. Encourages cooperation among functions.
Production	1. Shortens production runs. 2. Traces defects back to the source.
Marketing	1. Focuses on the customer. 2. Provides customer feedback on quality.
Materials management	1. Rationalises suppliers. 2. Helps suppliers implement TQM. 3. Traces defects back to suppliers.
R&D	Designs products that are easy to manufacture.
Information systems	Uses information systems to monitor defect rates.
Human resources	1. Institutes TQM training programs. 2. Organises employees into quality teams.

Find ways of measuring quality

Another imperative of any TQM program is to create some metric that can be used to measure quality. This is relatively easy in manufacturing companies, where quality can be measured by criteria such as defects per million parts. It tends to be more difficult in service companies but suitable metrics can be devised with a little creativity. Some banks, for example, use the key measures of the number of customer defections per year and the number of statement errors per thousand customers. The theme of these examples is identifying what quality means from a customer's perspective and devising a method to gauge it. Top management should take primary responsibility for formulating different metrics to measure quality. To succeed in this effort, however, it must receive input from the various functions of the company.

Set goals and create incentives

Once a metric has been devised, the next step is to set a challenging quality goal and create incentives for reaching that goal. One way of creating incentives to attain the goal is to link rewards — such as bonus pay and opportunities for promotion — to it. Within many companies that have adopted self-managing teams, the bonus pay of team members is partly determined by their ability to attain quality goals. The task of setting goals and creating incentives is a key task of top management.

Solicit input from employees

Employees can be a vital source of information regarding the sources of poor quality. The company must establish a framework for soliciting employee suggestions of the improvements that can be made. Quality circles, which are meetings of groups of employees, are often used to achieve this goal. Other companies use self-managing teams as forums for discussing quality improvement ideas. Whatever the forum, soliciting input from lower-level employees requires that management be open to receiving, and acting on, bad news and criticism from employees. According to Deming, one problem with management is that it has grown used to 'killing the bearer of bad tidings'. But, he argues, managers who are committed to the quality concept must recognise that bad news is a gold mine of information.[27]

Identify defects and trace them to the source

Product defects most often occur in the production process. TQM preaches the need to identify defects during the work process, trace them to their source, find out what caused them and make corrections so that they do not recur. The production and materials management functions typically have primary responsibility for this task.

To uncover defects, Deming advocates the use of statistical procedures to pinpoint variations in the quality of goods or services. Deming views variation as the enemy of quality.[28] Once a company has identified variations, it must trace them to their source and eliminate them. One technique that helps greatly in tracing defects to their source is reducing lot sizes for manufactured products. With short production runs, defects show up immediately. Consequently, they can be quickly traced to the source and the problem can be fixed. Reducing lot sizes also means that when defective products are produced, their number will not be large, thus decreasing waste. Flexible manufacturing techniques, discussed earlier, can be used to reduce lot sizes without raising costs. Consequently, adopting flexible manufacturing techniques is an important aspect of a TQM program.

Just-in-time inventory systems also play a part. In these, defective parts enter the manufacturing process immediately; they are not warehoused for several months before use, so they can be quickly spotted. The problem can then be traced to the supply source and corrected before more defective parts are produced. Under a more traditional system, the practice of warehousing parts for months before they are used may mean that a supplier produces large numbers of defects before they enter the production process and are recognised.

Build relationships with suppliers

Poor-quality component parts are a major source of poor-quality finished goods. To decrease product defects, a company has to work with its suppliers to improve the quality of the parts they supply. The primary responsibility in this area falls on the materials management function because it interacts with suppliers.

Two steps are necessary to implement just-in-time systems with suppliers and to get them to adopt their own TQM programs. First, the company has to reduce its suppliers to a manageable number. Second, the company must commit to building cooperative long-term relationships with the suppliers that remain. Asking suppliers to invest in just-in-time and TQM systems is asking them to make major investments that tie them to the company. To implement a just-in-time system fully, for example, the company may ask a supplier to relocate its manufacturing plant so that it is next door to the company's assembly plant. Suppliers are likely to be hesitant about making such investments unless they feel that the company is committed to an enduring relationship with them.

Design for ease of manufacture

The more assembly steps a product requires, the more opportunities there are for making mistakes. Designing products with fewer parts should make assembly easier and result in fewer defects. Both R&D and manufacturing functions need to be involved in designing products that are easy to manufacture.

Break down barriers among functions

Implementing TQM requires companywide commitment and substantial cooperation among functions. The R&D function has to cooperate with the production function to design products that are easy to manufacture; the marketing function has to cooperate with the production and R&D function so that customer problems identified by marketing can be acted on; the human resources function has to cooperate with all other functions of the company to devise suitable quality training; and so on. The issue of achieving cooperation among subunits within a company is explored in chapter 11. What needs stressing at this point is that top management is responsible for ensuring the cooperation occurs.

Achieving superior innovation

In many ways innovation is the single most important building block of competitive advantage. Successful innovation of products or processes gives a company something unique that its competitors lack. This uniqueness may allow a company to charge a premium price or lower its costs below those of its rivals. Competitors, however, will try to imitate successful innovations. They often will succeed, although high barriers can slow the speed of imitation. Maintaining a competitive advantage requires, therefore, a continuing commitment to innovation. Importantly, innovation does not have to be limited to product innovation. Process innovation can be just as important. For example, Rio Tinto spends many millions of dollars on R&D each year, part of which goes to better understanding what causes the rails of train tracks to buckle. When a rail buckles and a train is derailed, it costs more than a million dollars a time to rectify the problem. Therefore, finding a way to move iron ore from the mines to the ports without derailments has nothing to do with the quality or attributes of the final product but innovations in rail tracks could save the company many millions of dollars every year.

The high failure rate of innovation

Although innovation can be a source of competitive advantage, the failure rate of innovative new products is high. One study of product development in 16 companies in the chemical, drug, petroleum and electronics industries suggested that only about 20 per cent of R&D projects result in a commercially successful product or process.[29] Another in-depth case study of product development in three companies (one in chemicals and two in drugs) reported that about 60 per cent of R&D projects reached technical completion, 30 per cent were commercialised and only 12 per cent earned an economic profit that exceeded the company's cost of capital.[30] Similarly, a famous study by the consulting division of Booz, Allen & Hamilton found that more than one-third of 13 000 new consumer and industrial products failed to meet company-specific financial and strategic performance criteria.[31] In sum, this evidence suggests that many R&D projects do not result in a commercial product and that 33 per cent to 60 per cent of all new products that reach the marketplace fail to generate an adequate economic return. Although many explanations have been advanced for this, five appear on most lists: (1) uncertainty, (2) poor commercialisation, (3) poor positioning strategy, (4) technological myopia and (5) a lack of speed in the development process.[32]

Uncertainty

New product development is an inherently risky process. It requires testing a hypothesis whose answer is impossible to know before market introduction: namely, is there sufficient market demand for this new technology? Although good market research can minimise the uncertainty about likely future demand for a new technology, the uncertainty cannot be eradicated altogether. A certain failure rate is to be expected.

That failure rate would be expected to be higher for quantum product innovations than for incremental innovations. A quantum innovation represents a radical departure from existing technology, that is, the introduction of something that is new to the world. In comparison, the Fisher & Paykel drawer-style dishwasher, for example, is an incremental innovation in that it uses the same dishwashing technology used in most other dishwashers but arranged in such a way that a drawer system can be used.

The uncertainty of future demand for a new product is much greater if that product represents a quantum innovation that is new to the world than if it is an incremental innovation designed to replace an established product with a well-known demand profile. Consequently, the failure rate tends to be higher for quantum innovations.

quantum innovations
Innovations that represent a completely new approach to solving a problem

incremental innovations
Innovations that build on existing technologies to improve them in some way

Poor commercialisation

A second reason frequently cited to explain the high failure rate of new product introductions is poor commercialisation, a condition that occurs when there is an intrinsic demand for a new technology but the technology is not suited to consumer needs as a result of factors such as poor design and poor quality. For example, digital video cameras have developed quickly from digital tape-based products to systems in which the images are stored directly onto a hard drive. In between these product generations were a series of video cameras that transferred the image directly to a DVD. Although these products had a select following with high-end enthusiasts, their increased size and lack of noticeable improvement in quality meant that most consumers moved straight from the mini DV tape-based systems to the hard-disk products.

Poor positioning strategy

Sometimes a company introduces an intrinsically attractive new product but sales fail to materialise because the product is poorly positioned in the marketplace. Positioning strategy is the position that a company adopts for a product on four main dimensions of marketing: price, distribution, promotion and product features. Poor positioning strategy might have affected the introduction of recordable DVDs (see Strategy in action 5.3), which suffered from high prices, poor promotion and a failure by the innovating companies to produce products for the portable and car market.

Technological myopia

Another reason for the failure of many new product introductions is that companies often make the mistake of marketing a technology for which there is not enough consumer demand. Technological myopia occurs when a company is blinded by the wizardry of a new technology and fails to consider whether there is consumer demand for the product. This problem might have been a factor in the failure of the desktop computer introduced by NeXT in the late 1980s. (NeXT was founded by Steve Jobs, the founder of Apple Computer.) Technologically, the NeXT machines were clearly ahead of their time, with advanced software and hardware features that most PCs would not incorporate for another decade. Consumer acceptance was very slow, however, primarily reflecting the complete lack of applications software (such as spreadsheet and word-processing programs) to run on the machines. Management at NeXT was so enthusiastic about the technology of the new computer that it ignored this basic market reality. After several years of slow sales, NeXT eventually withdrew the machines from the marketplace.

technological myopia
When companies believe entirely in their technology and do not consider the market for the technology or alternative technologies

strategy in action 5.3

Analogue and digital recording media

There is a significant jump in technology between analogue and digital technologies. We used to listen to prerecorded music from records or cassettes. Then in the 1980s Sony and Philips released the CD, which quickly became the de facto standard for recorded music. However, the major drawback to CDs was that they could not easily be recorded upon until the late 1990s (almost 20 years after their release). Therefore, there was a gap in the technology for a different digital media that would allow for people to record their own material. One offering was the digital compact cassette (DCC) by Philips. The DCC was designed to replace analogue cassette tapes and even though it stored and recorded digital signals, it also allowed users to play their analogue cassette tapes, making it backward compatible. However, the product never really broke into the market and was eventually withdrawn from the market in the 1990s. Other recordable digital media entered the market including the mini-disc by Sony and the DAT system but, with the exception of mini-discs in Japan, none of these ever succeeded in breaking the stranglehold of the CD. It was not until 2003 that the Apple iPod and other similar memory-based devices created a realistic alternative to CDs.

A similar situation has developed in the visual media. Video cassette recorders (VCRs) long dominated the way that we recorded programs from television and the media we used to watch movies in our own homes. Video cassettes were quickly replaced by DVDs as the preferred medium for movies for home use in around 2000 (depending upon which country you resided in). But similarly to the CD, early DVD players did not provide an option for recording and so most households ended up with both a DVD and a VCR player. Recordable DVD systems are now becoming affordable for the average consumer. But will they become successful? The new alternative is a system that uses an enormous hard drive to record television programs in a digital format. These systems are capable of recording more than 200 hours of television and as the price of hard drives drops further they are likely to become similar to iPods, for which the amount of recordable space eventually becomes so large it becomes potentially meaningless. The next five years will provide a new winner in this industry with other rival innovations invariably failing as was seen in the systems supporting prerecorded and recordable music.

Slowness in marketing

Finally, companies fail when they are slow to deliver their products to market. The longer the time between initial development and final marketing, that is, the slower the 'cycle time', the more likely it is that someone else will beat the firm to market and gain a first-mover advantage.[33] Slow innovators usually update their products less frequently than do fast innovators. Consequently, they can be perceived as laggards to the fast innovators. For example, Qantas is never the first to move to a new aircraft such as the Airbus A380; it is often years behind other innovations such as individual screens for economy-class passengers and seats that can convert into fully flat beds in business class.

Why do some innovations fail to make money?

The preceding discussion explains why many innovations fail. In many cases, however, companies develop groundbreaking innovations that are appropriate for the market, yet fail to make much money. This problem often arises when competitors imitate the product and take a leadership position within the industry. The Comet by de Havilland was the world's first commercial jet aircraft, for example, yet the Boeing 707 came to dominate the industry. The CAT scanner by EMI was probably the most important medical imaging device innovation of the twentieth century (just as the x-ray machine was the most important in the nineteenth century), yet EMI had exited the market within ten years and companies such as GE and Siemens dominate the scanner industry today. In comparison, Pilkington dominates the float glass production method and NutraSweet dominates the artificial sweetener industry, showing that it is possible for innovators to profit from an innovation. Teece suggests three fundamental factors that can help predict whether an innovator will profit from an innovation or whether an imitator will be the primary beneficiary: appropriability regimes, complementary assets and the dominant design paradigm.[34]

Appropriability regimes

Appropriability regimes refer to how well a company can protect the knowledge that underpins the innovation. If a company can protect an innovation so that competitors cannot easily copy it, then the innovator company is much more likely to benefit from the innovation. Protection can be gained through patents, copyrights, trademarks and other legal mechanisms. These legal approaches tend to work best where the innovation can be clearly defined by its process (such as the float glass method) or its product characteristics. The NutraSweet product, for example, has a mix of particular chemicals that was relatively easy to patent. Patents have a limited lifespan (depending on the country) but innovators often maintain their dominance even after the patents expire because they have had many years in the marketplace, building up a brand name and developing further innovations (which often build on the initial patent). Other companies are so far behind in terms of their research and their position in the market that they rarely manage to mount realistic threats to the innovator.

Many innovations, however, can be reverse engineered or altered. These cases tend to be more difficult to protect and the company often relies on trade secrets or keeping the knowledge in tacit forms. It is often necessary to keep innovating to stay ahead of the competition, to have systems that cannot be copied (such as complex purpose-built production technologies that create product complexity) or to ensure the key knowledge holders of the technology remain with the company and are not poached by competitors.

Complementary resources

Once a company develops an innovation, it needs a series of **complementary resources** to be able to profit from the innovation. These resources can include the money to produce and distribute the product, appropriate human resources to market and service the product, access to distribution channels and complementary products that add value to the innovation. One reason for EMI's lack of success in the CAT scanner business was that it did not have people who had the hospital connections that had the authority to buy million-dollar pieces of equipment. In addition, EMI did not have the staff to train customers properly in the scanner's use, or the service team to repair machines when problems arose. In the case of alternative digital music formats (the DCC, mini-discs, DAT systems and even DVD audio) to the CD, none has been very successful, often because the range of prerecorded music on CD has not also been available on these other formats, that is, the complementary products that make the innovation valuable to the consumer were not available.

Dominant design paradigm

Chapter 3 discusses the role of network economics. Various products increase in value to consumers in proportion to the number (and possibly variety) of complementary products. Products such as computers need software, peripherals (such as printers) and repair shops. DVD players need a range of DVD movies, DVD rental stores and receivers that decode the various digital formats (such as Dolby 5.1) to send appropriate signals to the speakers. Producers of complementary products often do not want to invest heavily in developing these complementary products until they know that there will be a significant market. Innovators of products that are subject to network economies thus find it difficult to sell their product given a lack of complementary products. This is particularly problematic when competing versions of a particular product are on the market. In this case, the product that captures a significant share of the early market is likely to completely dominate the market. Once a product has achieved a critical mass in terms of consumers, then producers of complementary goods will increase their production range. More people will thus be attracted to this product, enticing even more producers to provide complementary products. These innovations that attract a critical mass of customers become the **dominant designs**, and the companies that produce them almost always become the leaders in their industries.

To achieve a dominant design, a company sometimes must relinquish some control over the product to achieve a critical mass. When mobile phones, for example, were first sold, there were many different standards for analogue systems, for example, the Nordic countries, France, Germany, Italy and the UK used different standards. When second-generation systems (digital) were introduced, therefore, Nokia and Ericsson made a lot of their technology available for free, so that a pan-European standard (their GSM standard) could be adopted. As a result, 103 countries adopted the GSM standard, while only three countries picked up the proprietary standard developed by Qualcomm. Nokia and Ericsson made no money from developing the GSM standard but they became leaders in producing mobile phones for countries that use GSM and thus were able to achieve incredible economies of scale by producing phones for most countries in the world.[35]

Network economic effects make it highly desirable to achieve the dominant design and thus control the market. To do this, a company often must cede some control over the innovation because it is better to make a small amount of money per unit in an enormous market than a large amount of money per unit in a very small one.

Building competencies in innovation

Companies can take steps to build a competency in innovation and avoid failure. Three of the most important seem to be: (1) building skills in basic and applied scientific research; (2) developing a good process for project selection and project management; and (3) integrating the different functions of the company through cross-functional product development teams and partly parallel development processes.[36]

Building skills in basic and applied research

Building skills in basic and applied research requires the employment of research scientists and engineers, and the establishment of a work environment that encourages creativity. A number of top companies try to achieve this environment by setting up university-style research facilities, in which scientists and engineers are given time to work on their own research projects, in addition to projects that are linked to ongoing company research. The Hewlett-Packard company labs, for example, are open to engineers around the clock. Hewlett-Packard even encourages its corporate researchers to devote 10 per cent of company time to exploring their own ideas, and does not penalise them if they fail. Similarly, 3M has a '15 per cent rule', which allows researchers to spend 15 per cent of the work week researching any topic they want to investigate, as long as there is the potential of a payoff for the company. The most famous outcome of this policy is the ubiquitous yellow Post-it Notes product. The idea evolved from a researcher's desire to find a way of keeping the bookmark from falling out of his hymn book. Post-it Notes are now a major 3M consumer business, with revenue of about US$300 million.

Developing a process for project selection and management

Project management is the overall management of the innovation process, from generation of the original concept, through development, and into final production and shipping. Project management requires three important skills: (1) the ability to encourage as much generation of ideas as possible; (2) the ability to select from competing projects at an early stage of development so the most promising receive funding and the potential costly failures are halted and (3) the ability to minimise time to market. The concept of the development funnel, illustrated in figure 5.10, summarises what is required to build these skills.[37]

As figure 5.10 shows, the development funnel is divided into three phases. The objective in phase 1 is to widen the mouth of the funnel to encourage as much idea generation as possible. To this end, a company should solicit input from all its functions, as well as from customers, competitors and suppliers.

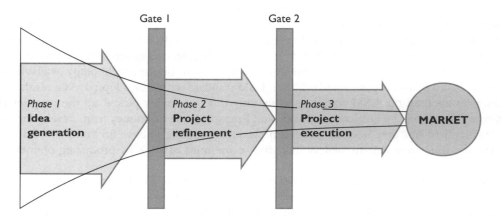

At gate 1, the funnel narrows. Here ideas are reviewed by a cross-functional team of managers who were not involved in the original concept development. Those concepts that are ready to proceed then move to phase 2 of the funnel, where the company works out the details of the project proposal. Note that gate 1 is not a go/no-go evaluation point; at this screen, ideas may be sent back for further concept development to be resubmitted for evaluation.

During phase 2, which typically lasts only one or two months, the data and information developed during phase 1 are put into a form that will enable senior management to evaluate proposed projects against competing projects. This process normally requires the development of a careful project plan, complete with details of the proposed target market, attainable market share, likely revenue, development costs, production costs, key milestones and the like. The next main selection point, gate 2, is a go/no-go evaluation point. Senior managers review the various projects under consideration. Their task is to select those projects that seem likely winners and that make most sense from a strategic perspective, given the long-term goals of the enterprise. The overriding objective at this gate is to select projects whose successful completion will help maintain or build a competitive advantage for the company. A related objective is to ensure the company does not spread its scarce capital and human resources too thinly over too many projects; instead, the company wants to concentrate resources on those projects where the probability of success and potential returns are most attractive. Any project selected to proceed at this stage will be funded and staffed, being expected to move forwards to market introduction. In phase 3, a cross-functional product development team executes the project development proposal.

Setting up cross-functional integration

Tight cross-functional integration between the R&D, production and marketing functions can help a company ensure that:

- customer needs drive product development projects
- new products are designed for ease of manufacture
- development costs are kept in check
- time to market is minimised.

Close integration of the R&D and marketing functions is required to ensure the needs of customers drive product development projects. A company's customers can be one of its primary sources of new product ideas. Identification of customer needs (particularly unmet needs) can set the context within which successful product innovation takes place. As the point of contact with customers, the marketing function of a company can provide valuable information. Moreover, the integration of R&D, and marketing is crucial for a new product to be properly commercialised. Without this integration, a company runs the risk of developing products for which there is little or no demand.

The integration of the R&D and production functions can help a company ensure that products are designed with manufacturing requirements in mind, which lowers manufacturing costs and leaves less room for mistakes, increasing product quality. Such integration can also reduce development costs and speed products to market. If a new product is not designed with manufacturing capabilities in mind, then it may prove too difficult to build, given existing manufacturing technology. In that case, it would have to be redesigned, increasing both overall development costs and the time it takes to bring the product to market. Making design changes during product planning could raise overall development costs by 50 per cent and add 25 per cent to the time needed to bring the product to market.[38] Moreover, many quantum product innovations require new processes to manufacture them. That makes it all the more important to integrate R&D and production because minimising time to market and development costs may require the simultaneous development of new products and new processes.[39]

Product development teams

One of the best ways to achieve cross-functional integration is to establish cross-functional product development teams. These are teams composed of representatives from R&D, marketing and production. The objective of a team should be to take a product development project through from the initial concept development to market introduction. Certain attributes seem particularly important for a product development team if it is to function effectively and meet all its development milestones.[40]

First, the team should be led by a 'heavyweight' project manager, who has both high status within the company and the power and authority to obtain the financial and human resources that the team needs to succeed. This leader should be dedicated primarily, if not entirely, to the project. The leader should be someone who believes in the project — that is, a champion of the project — and who is skilled at integrating the perspectives of different functions and at helping personnel from different functions work together for a common goal. Moreover, the leader must be able to act as the team's advocate to senior management.

Second, the team should include at least one member from each key function. The team members should have an ability to contribute functional expertise, high standing within their function, a willingness to share responsibility for team results, and an ability to put functional advocacy aside. It is usually preferable for core team members to be 100 per cent dedicated to the project for its duration, so their focus is on the project, not on the ongoing work of their function.

Third, the team members should be physically located together to create a sense of camaraderie and allow communication.

Fourth, the team should have a clear plan and clear goals, particularly for critical development milestones and development budgets. The team should have incentives to attain those goals, such as pay bonuses when major development milestones are hit.

Fifth, each team needs to develop its own processes for communication and conflict resolution. Most companies build their communication processes around holding regular meetings of the people involved but some extend this participation to include people outside those who are directly involved.

Partly parallel development processes

One way a product development team can develop a product and bring it to market quicker is to use a partly parallel development process. Traditionally, product development processes have been organised sequentially, as illustrated in figure 5.11(a). A problem with this kind of process is that product development proceeds without consideration of manufacturing issues. Most significantly, because the basic design of a product is completed before the design of a manufacturing process and full-scale commercial production, no early warning system can indicate manufacturability. Consequently, the company may find that it cannot manufacture the product cost-efficiently and must send it back to the design stage for redesign. The result is that the cycle time lengthens as the product iterates back and forth between stages.

To solve this problem, companies typically use a process similar to that illustrated in figure 5.11(b). In the partly parallel development process, development stages overlap, so that, for example, work starts on the development of the production process before the product design is finalised. By reducing the need for expensive and time-consuming product redesigns, this sort of process can significantly reduce the time that it takes to develop a new product and bring it to market.

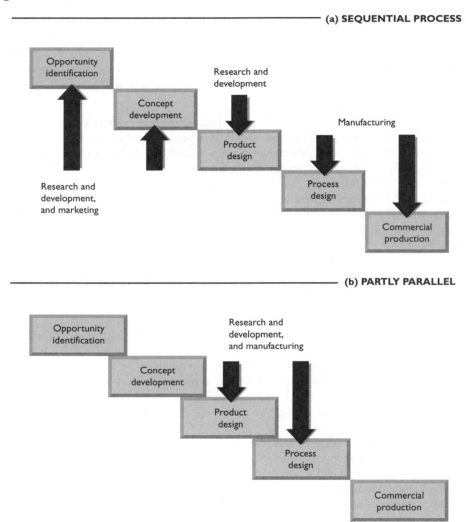

Figure 5.11:
Sequential and partly parallel development processes

Summary: achieving superior innovation

Table 5.3 summarises the primary role of the various functions in achieving superior innovation. Two matters, especially, need noting. First, top management must bear primary responsibility for overseeing the whole development process. This entails both managing the development funnel and facilitating cooperation among functions. Second, while the R&D function plays a central role in the innovation process, its effectiveness in developing new products and processes depends on its ability to cooperate with the marketing and production functions. Although there are likely to be formalised roles and responsibilities, it is important that employees are given a high degree of latitude for 'thinking outside of the box' should a company wish to avoid stifling innovation.

Table 5.3: The roles of various value creation functions in achieving superior innovation

Value creation function	Primary roles
Infrastructure (leadership)	1. Manages overall project (i.e. manages the development function). 2. Encourages cross-functional cooperation.
Production	1. Cooperates with R&D to design products that are easy to manufacture. 2. Works with R&D to develop process innovations.
Marketing	1. Provides market information to R&D. 2. Works with R&D to develop new products.
Materials management	No primary responsibility.
R&D	1. Develops products and processes. 2. Cooperates with other functions, particularly marketing and manufacturing, in the development process.
Information systems	Uses information systems to coordinate cross-functional and cross-company product development work.
Human resources	Employs talented scientists and engineers.

Achieving superior responsiveness to customers

To achieve superior responsiveness to customers, a company must give them what they want when they want it, so long as the company's long-term profitability is not compromised in the process. The more responsive a company is to the needs of its customers, the greater is the brand loyalty that it can command. In turn, strong brand loyalty may allow a company to charge a premium price for its products or to sell more goods and services to customers. Either way, the company that is responsive to its customers' needs will have a competitive advantage.

Achieving it means giving customers value for money. Steps taken to improve the efficiency of a company's production process and the quality of its output should be consistent with this aim. In addition, giving customers what they want may require the development of new products with new features. In other words, achieving superior efficiency, quality and innovation are all part of achieving superior responsiveness to customers. The two other prerequisites for attaining this goal are: (1) to focus on the company's customers and their needs and (2) to find ways of better satisfying those needs.

Focusing on the customer

A company cannot be responsive to its customers' needs unless it knows what those needs are. The first step in building superior responsiveness to customers, therefore, is to motivate the whole company to focus on the customer. The means to this end are demonstrating leadership, shaping employee attitudes and using mechanisms for bringing customers into the company.

Demonstrating leadership

Customer focus must start at the top of the company. A commitment to superior customer responsiveness brings attitudinal changes throughout a company that can ultimately be built only through strong leadership. A mission statement (see chapter 2) that puts customers first is one way to send a clear message to employees about the desired focus. Another avenue is top management's own actions. Spending time interacting with customers is just one way of showing that customers matter and that understanding their needs is critical to the business.

Shaping employee attitudes

Achieving a superior customer focus requires that all employees see the customer as the focus of their activity. Leadership alone is not enough to attain this goal. All employees must be trained to focus on the customer, whether their function is marketing, manufacturing, R&D or accounting. The objective should be to make employees think of themselves as customers, that is, to put themselves in the customers' shoes. At that point, employees are better able to identify ways to improve the quality of a customer's experience with the company. To reinforce this mindset, incentive systems within the company should reward employees for satisfying customers.

Bringing customers into the company

'Know thy customer' is one of the keys to achieving superior customer responsiveness. This approach not only requires that employees think like customers themselves but also demands that they listen to what their customers have to say and, as much as possible, bring them into the company. While this effort may not involve physically bringing customers into the company, it does mean collecting customers' opinions by soliciting feedback on the company's goods and services, and by building information systems that communicate the feedback to the relevant people.

Satisfying customer needs

Once a focus on the customer has been achieved, the next task is to satisfy the customer needs that have been identified. As noted, efficiency, quality and innovation are all crucial to satisfying those needs. Beyond these, companies can provide a higher level of satisfaction if they customise the product, as much as possible, to the requirements of individual customers and if they minimise the time that it takes to respond to customer demands.

Customising the product

Varying the features of a good or service to tailor it to the unique needs of groups of customers or, in the extreme case, individual customers is known as customisation. It used to be thought that customisation raised costs. As noted earlier in this chapter, however, the development of flexible manufacturing technologies has made it feasible to produce a far greater variety of products without suffering a substantial cost penalty. Companies can now customise their products to a much greater extent than they could ten to 15 years ago, particularly when they link flexible manufacturing technologies to Web-based information systems. Strategy in action 5.2 illustrates how some companies are trying to move towards mass customisation. The same is true of service companies. Online retailers such as Amazon.com have used Web-based technologies to develop a home page that is customised for each individual user. When customers access Amazon.com, they are confronted by a list of recommendations for books or music to purchase that is based on an analysis of their buying history.

The trend towards customisation has fragmented many markets, particularly consumer markets, into ever smaller niches. The classic example is the motor vehicle industry. Sixty or 70 years ago, most car companies manufactured just one or two models. By the 1970s, most large manufacturers produced at least three or four models (often including small, midsized and family cars). Today, many large manufacturers produce at least one car for each major market segment, along with options for that particular model. The Holden Commodore (in the family car market), for example, comes with a range of engine options (from a basic V6 to a V8 sports model), as a ute, as a four-wheel-drive sedan (Adventra) and until recently as a two-door coupe (the Monaro). In addition, the models range in terms of interior luxury, from the basic Executive model through to the leather and wood-panelled Statesman model.

Minimising the response time

Giving customers what they want when they want it requires speed of response to customer demands. To gain a competitive advantage, a company must often respond to consumer demands very quickly, whether the transaction is a furniture manufacturer's delivery of a product once it has been ordered, a bank's processing of a loan application, a car manufacturer's delivery of a spare part for a car that broke down, or the wait in a supermarket checkout line. We live in a fast-paced society, in which time is a valuable commodity. Companies that can satisfy customer demands for rapid response can build brand loyalty and set a higher price for the product or service.

Increased speed allows a company to charge a significant premium, as the mail delivery industry illustrates. The air express delivery niche of the industry is based on the notion that customers are often willing to pay considerably more for overnight express mail than for regular mail. Another example of the value of rapid response is Caterpillar (the manufacturer of heavy earthmoving equipment), which can get a spare part to any point in the world within 48 hours. Given that downtime for heavy construction equipment is very costly, Caterpillar's ability to respond quickly in the event of equipment malfunction is of prime importance to its customers. As a result, many customers have remained loyal to Caterpillar despite the aggressive low-price competition from Komatsu of Japan.

In general, reducing response time requires: (a) a marketing function that can quickly communicate customer requests to production; (b) production and materials management functions that can quickly adjust production schedules in response to unanticipated customer demands and (c) information systems that can help production and marketing in this process.

Summary: achieving superior responsiveness to customers

Table 5.4 summarises the roles that different functions must take if a company is to achieve superior responsiveness to customers. Although marketing plays the critical role in helping a company attain this goal (primarily because it represents the point of contact with the customer), table 5.4 shows that the other functions also have major roles to perform. Moreover, achieving superior responsiveness to customers requires top management to lead in building a customer orientation within the company, just as achieving superior efficiency, quality and innovation do.

Table 5.4: The roles of different value creation functions in achieving superior responsiveness to customers

Value creation function	Primary roles
Infrastructure (leadership)	Through leadership by example, builds a companywide commitment to customer responsiveness.
Production	1. Achieves customisation by implementing flexible manufacturing. 2. Achieves rapid response through flexible manufacturing.
Marketing	1. Knows the customer. 2. Communicates customer feedback to appropriate functions.
Materials management	Develops logistics systems capable of responding quickly to unexpected customer demands (just-in-time systems).
R&D	Brings customers into the product development process.
Information systems	Uses Web-based information systems to increase customer responsiveness.
Human resources	Develops training programs that get employees to think like customers.

Summary

This chapter discusses the role that functional-level strategies play in achieving efficiency, quality, innovation and responsiveness to customers. It examines in detail the different steps that lead to this end and makes the following main points:

▶ A company can take steps to increase efficiency, including exploiting economies of scale and learning effects; adopting flexible manufacturing technologies, using a modular architecture; reducing customer defection rates; implementing just-in-time systems; getting the R&D function to design products that are easy to manufacture; upgrading the skills of employees through training, introducing self-managing teams; linking pay to performance; building a companywide commitment to efficiency through strong leadership and designing structures that facilitate cooperation among different functions in pursuit of efficiency goals.

▶ Superior quality can help a company to lower its costs or differentiate its product and charge a premium price.

▶ Achieving superior quality demands a companywide commitment to quality and a clear focus on the customer. It also requires metrics to measure quality goals; incentives that emphasise quality; employee input on how quality can be improved; a method of tracing defects to their source and correcting the problems that produce them; rationalisation of the company's supply base; cooperation with the suppliers that remain to implement TQM programs; products that are designed for ease of manufacturing and substantial cooperation among functions.

▶ The failure rate of new products is high, as a result of factors such as uncertainty, poor commercialisation, poor positioning strategy, technological myopia and slow cycle time.

▶ To achieve superior innovation, a company must build skills in basic and applied research; design good processes for managing development projects and achieve close integration among the different functions of the enterprise, primarily by adopting cross-functional product development teams and partly parallel development processes.

▶ Whether a company profits from an innovation depends on the existence of appropriability regimes, its ability to access complementary resources and whether the product is a dominant design.

▶ Achieving superior responsiveness to customers often requires the company to achieve superior efficiency, quality and innovation.

▶ To achieve superior responsiveness to customers, a company needs to give customers what they want when they want it. It must ensure a strong customer focus, which can be attained through leading by example; training employees to think like customers; bringing customers into the company by means of superior market research; customising the product to the unique needs of individual customers or customer groups and responding quickly to customer demands.

Practising strategic management

Review questions

1. What are three products that would be subject to learning effects?
2. What are Deming's five steps for creating better organisations through the use of TQM?
3. What are the key elements to being more responsive to customers?
4. Why can innovations fail?

Discussion questions

5. How far do the reasons innovations fail apply not just to product innovations but also to process innovations?
6. What role can top management play in helping a company achieve (a) superior efficiency, (b) quality, (c) innovation and (d) responsiveness to customers?
7. In the long run, will adoption of TQM practices give a company a competitive advantage, or will it be required just to achieve parity with competitors?
8. Countries outside the United States, Japan and the European Union have traditionally been seen as relatively poor at innovation. Why might this be the case?

Applied questions

9. In the opening case, Aussie has succeeded through creating innovative products that has allowed it to be more customer responsive. How sustainable is its competitive advantage?
10. Strategy in action 5.1 shows how a lack of economies of scale was undermining the ability of the Australian motor vehicle industry to compete at an international level. If you were managing a car plant operation within Australia, what could you do to improve efficiency?

Small-group exercise

Identifying excellence

Break into groups of three to five people, and discuss the following scenario.

You are the management team of a startup company, which will produce disk drives for the personal computer industry. You will sell your product to manufacturers of PCs (original equipment manufacturers). The disk drive market is characterised by rapid technological change, product lifecycles of only six to nine months, intense price competition, high fixed costs for manufacturing equipment, and substantial manufacturing economies of scale. Your customers — the original equipment manufacturers — issue demanding technological specifications with which your product has to comply. The original equipment manufacturers also pressure you to deliver your product on time, to fit in with their own product introduction schedule. In this industry, what functional competencies are the most important for you to build? How will you design your internal processes to ensure those competencies are achieved within the company?

Article file

Find an example of a company that is widely regarded as excellent. Identify the source of its excellence and relate it to the material discussed in this chapter. Pay particular attention to the roles of the various functions in building excellence.

Exploring the Web

Visiting Airbus

Visit the website of Airbus, the world's largest manufacturer of commercial aircraft, at www.airbus.com. Read various materials provided on the website from the section for analysts to customers, the materials under corporate information (where you will find their mission) and the section headed 'my airbus'. How important are efficiency, quality, innovation and customer responsiveness to this company? Do you think they value any of these four building blocks above the others? Finally, how well has Airbus been doing in achieving its goals?

General task

Search the Internet for a company whose home page describes in some detail its approach to achieving one of the following: superior productivity, product quality, innovation or responsiveness to customers. Using this information, document the company's functional-level strategy and assess whether the strategy makes sense, given what you have learned so far in this book.

Strategic management project

Module 5

This module deals with the ability of your company to achieve superior efficiency, quality, innovation and responsiveness to customers. With the information you have at your disposal, answer the following questions and perform the following tasks:

1. Is your company pursuing any of the efficiency-increasing practices discussed in this chapter?
2. Is your company pursuing any of the quality-increasing practices discussed in this chapter?
3. Is your company pursuing any of the innovation-increasing practices discussed in this chapter?
4. Is your company pursuing any of the customer responsiveness-increasing practices discussed in this chapter?
5. Evaluate the competitive position of your company in the light of your answers to questions 1–4. Explain what, if anything, the company needs to do to improve its competitive position.

Additional resources

Horan, J 1996, 'Building the invisible quality corporation: the executive guide to transcending TQM', *The Academy of Management Executive*, vol. 10, no. 4, pp. 119–21. (Details about building a TQM culture in an organisation.)

Kim, WC & Mauborgne, R 2005, 'Blue ocean strategy: from theory to practice', *California Management Review*, vol. 47, no. 3, pp. 105–21. (This looks at developing strategy around innovation.)

End notes

1. See, for example, Scherer, FM, Beckenstein, A, Kaufer, E & Murphy, RD 1975, *The economies of multiplant operations*, Harvard University Press, Cambridge, Massachusetts.
2. Luft, H, Bunker, J & Enthoven, A 1979, 'Should operations be regionalized?' *New England Journal of Medicine*, vol. 301, pp. 1364–9.
3. Hall, G & Howell, S 1985, 'The experience curve from an economist's perspective', *Strategic Management Journal*, vol. 6, pp. 197–212; Lieberman, M 1984, 'The learning curve and pricing in the chemical processing industries', *RAND Journal of Economics*, vol. 15, pp. 213–28.
4. Boston Consulting Group 1972, *Perspectives on experience*, Boston, Massachusets; Hall & Howell, op. cit.; Hirschmann, WB 1964, 'Profit from the learning curve', *Harvard Business Review*, January–February, pp. 125–39.
5. Alchian, AA 1963, 'Reliability of progress curves in airframe production', *Econometrica*, vol. 31, pp. 679–93.
6. Borrus, M, Tyson, LA & Zysman, J 1986, 'Creating advantage: how government policies create trade in the semi-conductor industry', in Krugman, PR (ed.), Strategic trade policy and the new international economics, MIT Press, Boston, Massachusetts; Ghoshal, S & Bartlett, CA 1988, 'Matsushita Electrical Industrial (MEI) in 1987', *Harvard Business School* Case no. 388–144, Boston, Massachusetts.
7. Abernathy, WJ & Wayne K 1980, 'Limits of the learning curve', *Harvard Business Review*, pp. 109–19.
8. See Nemetz, P & Fry, L 1988, 'Flexible manufacturing organizations: implications for strategy formulation', *Academy of Management Review*, vol. 13, pp. 627–38; Greenwood, N 1986, *Implementing flexible manufacturing systems*, Halstead Press, New York; Womack, JP, Jones, DT & Roos, D 1990, The machine that changed the world, Rawson Associates, New York; Parthasarthy, R & Seith, SP 1992, 'The impact of flexible automation on business strategy and organizational structure', *Academy of Management Review*, vol. 17, pp. 86–111.
9. Pine, BJ 1993, *Mass customization: the new frontier in business competition*, Harvard Business School Press, Boston; Kotha, S 1995, 'Mass customization: implementing the emerging paradigm for competitive advantage', *Strategic Management Journal*, vol. 16, pp. 21–42; Gilmore, JH & Pine, BJ II 1997, 'The four faces of mass customization', *Harvard Business Review*, January–February, pp. 91–101.
10. Cusumano, MA 1989, *The Japanese automobile industry*, Harvard University Press, Cambridge, Massachusetts; Taiichi O 1990, *Toyota production system*, Productivity Press, Cambridge, Massachusetts; Womack, Jones & Roos, op. cit.
11. Sanderson, S & Uzumeri, M 1997, *Managing product families*, Irwin, Chicago.
12. Galvin, P 1999, 'Product modularity, information structures and the diffusion of innovation', *International Journal of Technology Management*, vol. 17, pp. 467–79.
13. Reichheld, FF & Sasser, WE 1990, 'Zero defections: quality comes to service', *Harvard Business Review*, September–October, pp. 105–11.
14. The example comes from ibid.
15. ibid.
16. Narasimhan, R & Carter, JR, 'Organization, communication and coordination of international sourcing', *International Marketing Review*, vol. 7, 1990, pp. 6–20.
17. Busch, HF 1990, 'Integrated materials management', *IJDP & MM*, vol. 18, pp. 28–39.
18. Sorge, A & Warner, M 1980, 'Manpower training, manufacturing organization, and work place relations in Great Britain and West Germany', *British Journal of Industrial Relations*, vol. 18, pp. 318–33; Jaikumar, R 1986, 'Postindustrial manufacturing', *Harvard Business Review*, November–December, pp. 72–83.
19. Gates, op. cit.
20. See the articles published in the special issue on total quality management, *Academy of Management Review*, vol. 19, 1994. The following paper provides a good overview of many of the issues involved from an academic perspective: Dean, JW & Bowen, DE 1994, 'Management theory and total quality', *Academy of Management Review*, vol. 19, pp. 392–418. Also see Powell, TC 1995, 'Total quality management as competitive advantage', *Strategic Management Journal*, vol. 16, pp. 15–37.

21. For general background information, see *The Economist* 1989, 'How to build quality', 23 September, pp. 91–2; Gabor, A 1990, *The man who discovered quality*, Penguin, New York; Crosby, PB 1980, *Quality is free*, Mentor, New York, 1980.

22. Deming, WE 1982, 'Improvement of quality and productivity through action by management', *National Productivity Review*, vol. 1, pp. 12–22.

23. Bowles, J 1992, 'Is American management really committed to quality?', *Management Review*, April, pp. 42–6.

24. Port & G Smith 1992, 'Quality', *Business Week*, 30 November, pp. 66–75. See also *The Economist* 1995, 'The straining of quality', 14 January, pp. 55–6.

25. Bowles, op. cit; *The Economist* 1995, 'The straining of quality', 14 January 1995.

26. Gabor, op. cit.

27. Deming, op. cit.

28. Deming, WE 1986, *Out of the crisis*, MIT Center for Advanced Engineering Study, Cambridge, Massachusetts.

29. Mansfield, E 1981. 'How economists see R&D', *Harvard Business Review*, November–December, pp. 98–106.

30. ibid.

31. Booz Allen Hamilton 1982, 'New products management for the 1980s', Melbourne.

32. See Brown, SL & Eisenhardt, KM 1995, 'Product development: past research, present findings, and future directions', *Academy of Management Review*, vol. 20, pp. 343–78; Lieberman, MB & Montgomery, DB 1988, 'First mover advantages', *Strategic Management Journal*, special issue 9, Summer, pp. 41–58; Teece, DJ 1987, 'Profiting from technological innovation: implications for integration, collaboration, licensing and public policy', *Research Policy*, vol. 15, pp. 285–305; Tellis, GJ & Golder, PN 1996, 'First to market, first to fail?', *Sloan Management Review*, Winter, pp. 65–75.

33. Stalk, G & Hout, TM 1990, Competing against time, Free Press, New York.

34. Teece, op. cit.

35. Galvin, P & Rice, J 2001, 'Information structures in the mobile telephone industry: a case study of knowledge protection and diffusion for innovation', paper presented at the Academy of Management Conference, Washington DC, 3–8 August.

36. Clark, KB & Wheelwright, SC 1993, *Managing new product and process development*, Free Press, New York; Schilling, MA & Hill, CWL 1998, 'Managing the new product development process', *Academy of Management Executive*, vol. 12, August, pp. 67–81.

37. Clark & Wheelwright, op. cit.

38. Port, O 1992, 'Moving past the assembly line', Business Week, Special issue: 'Reinventing America', pp. 177–80.

39. Pisano, GP & Wheelwright, SC 1995, 'The new logic of high tech R&D', *Harvard Business Review*, September–October, pp. 93–105.

40. Clark, KB & Fujimoto, T 1990, 'The power of product integrity', *Harvard Business Review*, November–December, pp. 107–18; Clark & Wheelwright, op. cit.; Brown & Eisenhardt, op. cit.; Stalk & Hout, op. cit.

Competitive business-level strategy and industry environment

learning objectives

After studying this chapter, you should be able to:

- understand what a business-level strategy means
- discuss the advantages and disadvantages of cost-leadership strategies
- appreciate the advantages and disadvantages of differentiation strategies
- discuss the advantages and disadvantages of focus strategies
- discuss how a company may achieve a leadership position in a fragmented industry
- understand how a company may prosper in a mature industry
- discuss the different strategies that a company may use in a declining industry.

opening case

Innovation as a pathway to success

The ResMed story started in 1982 when University of Sydney medical specialist, Professor Colin Sullivan developed a machine to treat a sleeping disorder known as apnoea. People with this disease stop breathing sometimes when they are asleep and have to jolt themselves awake to restart the breathing process. This may need to happen hundreds of times per night for severe sufferers but before the machine was developed, the only other option was an involved and highly invasive procedure. Sullivan's machine required a mask and early versions have been described as a reverse vacuum cleaner.

The innovation itself, however, was just the first step to success in the medical devices industry, in which Australian firms have not had much success. ResMed chairman and CEO, Peter Farrell, became involved with the company in 1989, when he led a management buyout of Baxter (where he was a senior executive) and also purchased patents from the University of Sydney, including those behind the breathing machine for apnoea sufferers. From here, he has sought out markets for the product, developed linkages with the medical community and overseen an innovation process that has led to continual innovations in respect of the machine.

While the initial innovation provided the starting point for ResMed, Farrell has had to work hard to maintain an innovative culture in the firm. 'You have to make sure that the culture encourages entrepreneurship and innovation. Having a good idea isn't enough ... innovation is only real when someone pays for it, when you have turned the idea into something you can make and sell,' he says. Farrell is a big believer that a lot of innovations fail because of poor management practices. This includes incomplete or poor analysis, a lack of detailed planning and setting up structures that do not allow top management to hear bad news and consequently make the necessary changes.

Luckily for ResMed, the market analysis seems to have significantly understated the potential market rather than have overstated it. Initial estimates were that approximately 2 per cent of the adult population suffers from apnoea but real numbers are hard to come by because it is poorly researched and poorly understood by most of the medical community. More recent estimates suggest that as much as 20 per cent of the population may suffer apnoea and although many of these do not need treatment, the market is potentially huge. Furthermore, the disease is highly correlated with obesity, a disease whose number of sufferers continues to grow.

Since 1995, the company has had 35 consecutive quarters of revenue and profit growth: an incredible result for any firm. Today, ResMed has about 33 per cent of the global market. A US company, Respironics, is the major competitor but new, smaller players are also entering the market with innovative products. As a result, ResMed will need to continue to innovate to make its device smaller, quieter, simpler and more patient friendly.

Source: Quinlivan, B 2004, 'Sleep, perchance to profit', *Business Review Weekly*, vol. 26, no. 24, 17–23 June, pp. 48–9.

Overview

On the basis of different functional strategies, organisations are able to build different business strategies. In the case of ResMed, its innovative functional strategy has allowed it to pursue a niche-oriented strategy built around differentiation from its competitors. Chapters 4 and 5 discussed how a company develops functional-level strategies to build internal strengths and distinctive competencies to achieve a competitive advantage. The purpose of this chapter is to consider the business-level strategies that a company can use to exploit its competitive advantage and compete effectively in an industry. This includes specific strategies for particular situations including those facing firms in fragmented, mature or declining industries.

What is business-level strategy?

business-level strategy
The plan of action that a company follows to gain a competitive advantage over other companies

Business-level strategy refers to the plan of action that strategic managers adopt for using a company's resources and distinctive competencies to gain a competitive advantage over rivals in a market or industry. Chapter 2 discusses Abell's view that the process of business definition entails decisions about (a) customers' needs, or what is to be satisfied; (b) customer groups, or who is to be satisfied and (c) distinctive competencies, or how customer needs are to be satisfied.[1] These three decisions are the basis for choosing a business-level strategy because they determine how a company will compete in a business or industry. Consequently, how a company makes these three decisions to gain a competitive advantage over its rivals needs to be considered.

Customers' needs and product differentiation

product differentiation
When a product competes on the basis of some type of difference relative to other products in the market

Customers' needs are desires, wants or cravings that can be satisfied by means of the characteristics of a product or service. **Product differentiation** is the process of creating a competitive advantage by designing products (goods or services) to satisfy customers' needs. All companies must differentiate their products to a certain degree to attract customers and satisfy some minimal level of need. Some companies, however, differentiate their products to a much greater degree than others do, and this difference can give them a competitive edge.

Some companies offer the customer a low-priced product without engaging in much product differentiation. Others seek to create something unique about their product so they satisfy customers' needs in ways that other products cannot. The uniqueness may relate to the physical characteristics of the product, such as quality or reliability, or it may lie in the product's appeal to customers' psychological needs, such as the need for prestige or status.[2] A Japanese car, therefore, may be differentiated by its reputation for reliability, and a Porsche may be differentiated by its ability to satisfy customers' needs for status.

Customer groups and market segmentation

market segmentation
The process of subdividing the market into customer groups based on customer preferences

Market segmentation is how a company decides to group customers, based on important differences in their needs or preferences, to gain a competitive advantage.[3] Toyota, for example, groups its customers according to the amount of money they want to spend and can afford to buy a car; for each group, it builds different cars, which range from the low-priced Toyota Echo to the high-priced Lexus SC-430. In addition, it produces a different range for different markets such that the Uncer model (which is made in Indonesia) is a much more basic and so low-priced car, which is not sold in first-world countries.

A company can generally adopt three alternative strategies towards market segmentation.[4] First, it can choose not to recognise that different customer groups have different needs and, instead, adopt the approach of serving the average customer. Second, a company can choose to segment its market into different constituencies and develop a product to suit the needs of each. Third, a company can choose to recognise that the market is segmented but concentrate on servicing only one market segment, or niche, such as the luxury-car niche pursued by BMW.

Why would a company want to make complex product/market choices and create a different product tailored to each market segment rather than create a single product for the whole market? The answer is that the decision to provide many products for many market niches allows a company to satisfy customers' needs better. As a result, customers' demand for the company's products rises and generates more revenue than would be the case if the company offered just one product for the whole market.[5] Sometimes, however, the nature of the product or the nature of the industry does not allow much differentiation, as is true, for example, of bulk chemicals and cement.[6] These industries afford little opportunity for obtaining a competitive advantage through product differentiation and market segmentation because there is little opportunity for serving customers' needs and customer groups in different ways. Price is the main criterion by which customers evaluate the product and the competitive advantage lies with the company that has superior efficiency and can provide the lowest-priced product.

Distinctive competencies

The third issue in business-level strategy is deciding which distinctive competencies to pursue to satisfy customers' needs and customer groups.[7] As discussed in chapter 5, companies can obtain a competitive advantage in four ways: superior efficiency, quality, innovation and responsiveness to customers. The Pan Pacific hotel chain, for example, attempts to do all it can to provide its customers with the highest-quality accommodation and the best customer service possible. In making business strategy choices, a company must decide how to organise and combine its distinctive competencies to gain a competitive advantage.

Choosing a generic business-level strategy

Companies pursue a business-level strategy to gain a competitive advantage that allows them to outperform rivals and achieve above-average returns. They can choose from three basic generic competitive approaches: cost leadership, differentiation and focus, although these can be combined in different ways.[8] These strategies are *generic* because all businesses or industries can pursue them regardless of whether they are manufacturing, service or not-for-profit enterprises. Each of the generic strategies results from a company's consistent choices on product differentiation, market segmentation and distinctive competencies — choices that reinforce each other. Table 6.1 summarises the choices appropriate for each of the three generic strategies.

Table 6.1: Product/market/distinctive-competency choices and generic competitive strategies

	Cost-leadership strategy	Differentiation strategy	Focus strategy
Product differentiation	Low (principally by price)	High (principally by uniqueness)	Low to high (price or uniqueness)
Market segmentation	Low (mass market)	High (many market segments)	Low (one or a few segments)
Distinctive competency	Manufacturing and materials management	Research and development, sales and marketing	Any kind of distinctive competency

Cost-leadership strategy

A company's goal in pursuing a cost-leadership strategy is to outperform competitors by doing everything that it can to produce goods or services at a cost lower than theirs. Two advantages accrue from a cost-leadership strategy. First, its lower costs means the cost leader can charge a lower price than that of its competitors yet make the same level of profit. If companies in the industry charge similar prices for their products, then the cost leader still makes a higher profit than its competitors because it has lower costs. Second, if rivalry within the industry increases and companies start to compete on price, then the cost leader will be able to withstand competition better than the other companies can because it has lower costs. For both these reasons, cost leaders are likely to earn above-average profits. How does a company become the cost leader? It achieves this position by means of the product, market or distinctive-competency choices that it makes to gain a low-cost competitive advantage (see table 6.1).

Strategic choices

The cost leader chooses a low level of product differentiation. Differentiation is expensive; if the company expends resources to make its products unique, then its costs rise.[9] The cost leader aims for a level of differentiation not markedly inferior to that of the differentiator (a company that competes by spending resources on product development) but a level obtainable at low cost.[10] The cost leader does not try to be the industry leader in differentiation; it waits until customers want a feature or service before providing it. A cost leader does not introduce stereo sound in television sets, for example; it adds stereo sound only when it is obvious that consumers want it.

The cost leader also normally ignores the different market segments and positions its product to appeal to the average customer. The reason that the cost leader makes this choice is, again, that developing a line of products tailored to the needs of different market segments is an expensive proposition. A cost leader normally engages in only a limited amount of market segmentation. Even though no customer may be totally happy with the product, the lower price attracts customers.

In developing distinctive competencies, the overriding goal of the cost leader must be to increase its efficiency and lower its costs compared with those of its rivals. The development of distinctive competencies in manufacturing and materials management is central to achieving this goal. Companies pursuing a low-cost strategy may attempt to ride down the experience curve so that they can lower their manufacturing costs.

Achieving a low-cost position may also require that the company develop skills in flexible manufacturing and adopt efficient materials management techniques. (Table 5.1 outlines how a company's functions can be used to increase efficiency.) Consequently, the manufacturing and materials management functions are the centre of attention for a company pursuing a cost-leadership strategy; the other functions shape their distinctive competencies to meet the needs of manufacturing and materials management.[11] The sales function, for example, may develop the competency of capturing large, stable sets of customers' orders. In turn, manufacturing can make longer production runs and thus achieve economies of scale and reduce costs. The human resources function may focus on instituting training programs and compensation systems that lower costs by increasing employees' productivity, and the research and development (R&D) function may specialise in process improvements to lower the manufacturing costs. For example, Dell Computer Corporation uses the Internet to lower the cost of selling its computers because its Internet orders limit costs associated with resellers or agents, allow the company to build only computers for which they have already been paid and limit how many people are employed to support the whole process.

Many cost leaders gear all their strategic product, market and distinctive-competency choices to the single goal of squeezing out every cent of costs to sustain their competitive advantage. A company such as HJ Heinz is another excellent example of a cost leader. Because beans and canned vegetables do not permit much of a markup, the profit comes from the large volume of cans sold. Heinz goes to extraordinary lengths to try to reduce costs — by even one-twentieth of a cent per can — because this will lead to large cost savings and thus bigger profits over the long term.

Advantages and disadvantages

The advantages of each generic strategy are best discussed in terms of Porter's five forces model, which is introduced in chapter 3.[12] The five forces are threats from competitors, powerful suppliers, powerful buyers, substitute products and new entrants. The cost leader is protected from *industry competitors* by its cost advantage. Its lower costs also mean that it will be (a) less affected than its competitors by increases in the price of inputs if there are *powerful suppliers* and (b) less affected by a fall in the price that it can charge for its products if there are *powerful buyers*. Moreover, because cost leadership usually requires a big market share, the cost leader purchases in relatively large quantities, increasing its bargaining power over suppliers. If *substitute products* start to come into the market, then the cost leader can reduce its price to compete and retain its market share. Finally, the leader's cost advantage constitutes a *barrier to entry*, because other companies are unable to enter the industry and match the leader's costs or prices. The cost leader is relatively safe, therefore, as long as it can maintain its cost advantage and as long as price is the key for a significant number of buyers.

The principal dangers of the cost-leadership approach lurk in competitors' ability to find ways of producing at a lower cost and beating the cost leader at its own game. If, for example, technological change makes experience-curve economies obsolete, then new companies may apply lower cost technologies that give them a cost advantage over the cost leader. Competitors may also draw a cost advantage from labour cost savings. Wage costs in the Western world, for example, are often much higher than those found in parts of Asia, central America and south America. For many countries that manufacture products that require a high level of labour (particularly unskilled labour), carrying out production in a country with low labour costs is almost a necessity for adopting a cost-leadership strategy.

Competitors' ability to imitate easily the cost leader's methods is another threat to the cost-leadership strategy. For example, low-cost airlines have proliferated around the world, often competing vigorously with other low-cost players.

Finally, the cost-leadership strategy carries a risk that the cost leader, in its single-minded desire to reduce costs, may lose sight of changes in customers' tastes. A company may make decisions that decrease costs but drastically affect demand for the product. Since the mid-1990s, Myer (Grace Brothers) has been cutting back the level of staff (particularly from the shop-floor) to reduce costs, but its reputation has suffered significantly from the subsequent lack of customer service. The cost leader cannot lose sight of customer needs and thus be significantly inferior to the differentiators if the low-cost, low-price policy is to succeed.

Differentiation strategy

The objective of the generic differentiation strategy is to achieve a competitive advantage by creating a product (good or service) that customers perceive to be unique in some important way. The differentiated company's ability to satisfy a customer's need in a way that its competitors cannot means that it can charge a premium price (a price considerably above the industry's average). The ability to increase revenue by charging premium prices (rather than by reducing costs as the cost leader does) allows the differentiator to outperform its competitors and gain above-average profits. The premium price is usually substantially above the price charged by the cost leader, and customers pay it because they believe the product's differentiated qualities are worth the difference. Consequently, the product is priced on the basis of what the market will bear.[13] For example, Rolex watches do not cost much to produce; their design has not changed much for years and their gold content represents only a fraction of the price. Customers buy a Rolex, however, because they perceive the unique quality in its ability to confer status on its wearer. In stereos, the name Bang & Olufsen of Denmark stands out; in jewellery, Tiffany; in hotels, Ritz Carlton. All these products command premium prices as a result of their differentiated qualities.

Strategic choices

As table 6.1 shows, a differentiator chooses a high level of product differentiation to gain a competitive advantage. Product differentiation can be achieved in three principal ways, which are discussed in detail in chapter 4: quality, innovation and responsiveness to customers. To appreciate the most appropriate way to achieve differentiation, firms need to fully understand what drives the buying decisions of their customers. It is also important to note that these factors can change over time such as being small and lightweight in relation to mobile phones was important when the market was dominated by larger phones but today the mix of features and reliability are more likely to be important. So depending upon what customer attributes are desired, different firms will focus upon different points of differentiation. Mt Barker Free Range Chickens, for example, advertises that its chickens are not only free range but also free of artificial hormones and antibiotic growth promoters. Maytag stresses reliability and the best repair record of any washing machine on the market. IBM promotes the quality service provided by its well-trained sales force.

Innovation is important for technologically complex products, for which new features are the source of differentiation, and many people pay a premium price for new and innovative products, such as a state-of-the-art computer, stereo or car. Consumers in Australia, for example, will pay a premium for an LG air-conditioning system that they can switch on remotely by telephone so that their house will be cool by the time they arrive home.

When differentiation is based on responsiveness to customers, a company offers comprehensive aftersales service and product repair. This is an especially important consideration for complex products such as cars and domestic appliances, which are likely to break down periodically. Companies such as Dell and BMW excel in responsiveness to customers. In service organisations, lawyers and accountants stress the service aspects of their operations to clients: their knowledge, professionalism and reputation.

Finally, a product's appeal to customers' psychological desires can become a source of differentiation. The appeal can manifest itself in terms of prestige or status (such as a Rolex watch or XO Cognac), in nationalist pride (such as the Proton car range in Malaysia), in the safety of one's family (such as Volvo cars), in being different from other people (which may account for the popularity of many exotic imported beers) or simply in providing value for money (such as Kmart in Australia and The Warehouse in New Zealand). Differentiation can also be tailored to age groups or socioeconomic groups. The bases of differentiation are endless.

A company that pursues a differentiation strategy strives to differentiate itself along as many dimensions as possible. The less it resembles its rivals, the more it is protected from competition and the wider is its market appeal. Ferraris do not offer only prestige; they also offer technological sophistication, speed and handling. All these bases of differentiation, plus the success of the Ferrari Formula 1 team, help increase sales.

A differentiator generally chooses to segment its market into many niches. Now and then, a company offers a product designed for each market niche and decides to be a **broad differentiator** but it may choose to serve only those niches in which it has a specific differentiation advantage. Sony, for example, produces many models of television, filling all the niches from midpriced to high-priced sets. Its lowest-priced model, however, is always priced about $100 above that of its competitors, bringing into play the premium price factor: you have to pay extra for a Sony. Similarly, although Mercedes-Benz has filled niches below its old

broad differentiators
Companies that compete in a range of niche markets using a differentiation strategy

high-priced models with its S and C series, until recently it made no attempt to produce a car for every market segment. This all changed when the Mercedes A class was released in 1999, which was designed to appeal to a younger and more price-conscious market, and the slightly more upmarket B class tourer in late 2005.

Finally, in choosing which distinctive competency to pursue, a differentiated company concentrates on the organisational function that provides the sources of its differentiation advantage. Differentiation on the basis of innovation and technological competency depends on the research and development function, as discussed in chapter 5. Efforts to improve service to customers depend on the quality of the sales function. A focus on a specific function does not mean, however, that the control of costs is not important for a differentiator. A differentiator does not want to increase costs unnecessarily and tries to keep them somewhere near those of the cost leader. Given, however, that developing the distinctive competency needed to provide a differentiation advantage is often expensive, a differentiator usually has higher costs than those of the cost leader.

Still, it must control all costs that do not contribute to its differentiation advantage, so the price of the product does not exceed what customers are willing to pay. Given that bigger profits are earned by controlling costs and maximising revenues, it pays to control costs, although not to minimise them to the point of losing the source of differentiation.[14]

Advantages and disadvantages

The advantages of the differentiation strategy can now be discussed in the context of the five forces model. Differentiation can lead to brand loyalty either because the brand means something to consumers (such as implications of superior performance) or because of high switching costs to alternative products or services. In either case, brand loyalty is a valuable asset because it protects the company on all fronts. Powerful suppliers, for example, are rarely a problem because the company's strategy is geared more towards the price that it can charge than towards the costs of production. A differentiator can, therefore, tolerate moderate increases in input prices better than the cost leader can. Differentiators are unlikely to experience problems with powerful buyers because the company offers the buyer a unique product. Only it can supply the product. Differentiators can pass on price increases to customers because customers are willing to pay the premium price. Differentiation and brand loyalty also create a barrier to entry for other companies seeking to enter the industry. New companies are forced to develop their own distinctive competency to be able to compete, and doing so is very expensive.

Finally, the threat of *substitute products* depends on the ability of competitors' products to meet the same customers' needs as met by the differentiator's products, and to break customers' brand loyalty. In the case of microprocessors, Intel has spent considerable sums on its 'Intel Inside' campaign, so that consumers will actively look for an Intel microprocessor in any PC that they may consider purchasing. With its strong brand recognition, Intel has been able to charge a premium price for its products, even though competitors such as AMD have often produced faster microprocessors before Intel. Given Intel's strength in brand name but weakness in matching the clock speeds of AMD microprocessors, an important question is how much of a premium price Intel can charge before it will lose customers to its major competitors.

The main problems with a differentiation strategy centre on the company's long-term ability to maintain its perceived uniqueness in customers' eyes. Patents expire and what may originally seem exotic, such as the inclusion of multiple airbags in family cars, eventually becomes the norm across all competing products.

A strategy of differentiation, then, requires the company to develop a competitive advantage by making choices about its product, market and distinctive competency that reinforce each other and together increase the value of a good or service in the eyes of consumers. When a product has uniqueness in customers' eyes, differentiators can charge a premium price. The disadvantages of a differentiation strategy are the ease with which competitors can imitate a differentiator's product and the difficulty of maintaining a premium price. When differentiation stems from the design or physical features of the product, differentiators are at great risk because imitation is easy. When differentiation stems from quality of service or reliability, or from any intangible source, such as the prestige of a Rolex, a company is much more secure. It is difficult to imitate intangibles, and the differentiator can reap the benefits of this strategy for a long time. Nevertheless, all differentiators must watch for imitators and be careful that they do not charge a price higher than the market will bear.

Cost leadership and differentiation

Recently, changes in production techniques — particularly the development of flexible manufacturing technologies (discussed in chapter 5) — have made the choice between cost-leadership and differentiation strategies less clear. With technological developments, companies have found it easier to obtain the benefits of both strategies. The reason is that the new flexible technologies allow companies to pursue a differentiation strategy at a low cost: that is, companies can combine these two generic strategies.

Traditionally, differentiation was obtainable only at high cost because the necessity of producing different models for different market segments meant that companies had to have short production runs, which raised manufacturing costs. In addition, the differentiated company had to bear higher marketing costs than the cost leader because it was serving many market segments. As a result, differentiators had higher costs than those of cost leaders, which produced large batches of standardised products. Flexible manufacturing may, however, enable a company pursuing differentiation to manufacture a range of products at a cost comparable to that of the cost leader. The substantial reduction of the costs of differentiation by flexible manufacturing is promoting the current trend towards market fragmentation and niche marketing in many consumer goods industries, such as mobile phones, computers and appliances.

Another way a differentiated producer may be able to realise significant economies of scale is by standardising many of the component parts used in its end-products. In the 1990s, Chrysler began to offer more than 20 different models of cars and minivans to different segments of the motor vehicle market. Despite their different appearances, all 20 were based on only three different platforms. Moreover, most of the cars used many of the same components, including axles, drive units, suspensions and gearboxes. As a result, Chrysler was able to realise significant economies of scale in the manufacture and bulk purchase of standardised component parts.

A company can also reduce both production and marketing costs if it limits the number of models in the product line by offering packages of options rather than letting consumers decide what options they require. It is increasingly common for car manufacturers, for example, to offer an economy package, a luxury package and a sports package to appeal to the principal market segments. Package offerings substantially lower manufacturing costs because long production runs of the various packages are possible. At the same time, the company is able to focus its advertising and marketing efforts on particular market segments, so these costs are also decreased. Again, the company is gaining from differentiation and low cost at the same time.

Just-in-time inventory systems, too, can help reduce costs, as well as improve the quality and reliability of a company's products. This benefit is important to differentiated firms, for whom quality and reliability are essential ingredients of the product's appeal. Improved quality control improves a company's reputation and thus allows it to charge a premium price, which is one object of total quality management (TQM) programs.

Taking advantage of the new production and marketing developments, some companies are managing to reap the gains from cost-leadership and differentiation strategies simultaneously. Because they can charge a premium price for their products compared with the price charged by the pure cost leader and because they have lower costs than those of the pure differentiator, they obtain at least an equal (and probably a higher) level of profit than do companies pursuing only one of the generic strategies. The combined strategy is thus the most profitable to pursue, and companies are quickly moving to take advantage of the new production, materials management and marketing techniques.

Focus strategy

The third generic competitive strategy, the focus strategy, differs from the other two chiefly because it is directed towards serving the needs of a limited customer group or segment. A focus strategy concentrates on serving a particular market niche, which can be defined by geographic region, type of customer or segment of the product line. A geographic niche, for example, can be defined by region or even locality. Selecting a niche by type of customer may mean serving only the very rich, the very young or the very adventurous. Concentrating on a segment of the product line means focusing on only vegetarian foods, very fast cars, designer clothes or sunglasses, for example. In following a focus strategy, a company is specialising in some way.

Once it has chosen its market segment, a company pursues a focus strategy through either a differentiation approach or a low-cost approach. Figure 6.1 shows these two different kinds of focused strategy and compares them with a pure cost-leadership strategy and a pure differentiation strategy.

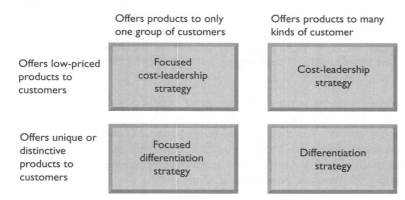

Figure 6.1:
Types of business-level strategy

In essence, a focused company is a specialised differentiator or a cost leader. If a company uses a focused low-cost approach, then it competes against the cost leader in the market segments in which it has no cost disadvantage. In local timber or cement markets, for example, the focuser has lower transportation costs than those of the low-cost national company. The focuser may also have a cost advantage because it is producing complex or custom-built products that do not lend themselves easily to economies of scale in production and, therefore, offer few experience-curve advantages. With a focus strategy, a company concentrates on small-volume custom products, for which it has a cost advantage, and leaves the large-volume standardised market to the cost leader. Pacific Blue (see Strategy in action 6.1) is such a company.

If a company uses a focused differentiation approach, then all the means of differentiation that are open to the differentiator are available to the focused company. The point is that the focused company competes with the differentiator in only one or a few segments. Lotus, for example, is a focused company that competes against competitors in the sports car segment of the car market, not in other market segments. Focused companies are likely to develop differentiated product qualities successfully as a result of their knowledge of a small customer set (such as sports car buyers) or their knowledge of a region.

strategy in action 6.1

Pacific Blue finds a niche

Part of Virgin Blue, the airline Pacific Blue is well known for its trans-Tasman and Pacific Island passenger operations. Commercial cargo business is complementary to passenger services of this type because of the freight capacity available in the holds of the aircraft. Early in 2005 Pacific Blue launched a trans-Tasman freight service based in Christchurch. The competitive positioning of this business differed from that of the passenger operations.

Pacific Blue recognised a market niche that was not well served by existing competitors, namely direct freight services from Christchurch serving South Island exporters. Direct services had earlier been withdrawn by Air New Zealand and Qantas in favour of an Auckland-based service. In seeking to fill this niche, Pacific Blue aligned its offering with the value drivers of potential customers including exporters of fresh produce such as flowers and seafood. Because these products had previously been flown to Auckland, the new service cut a day from the transit time, which represented a day of extra shelf life. Pacific Blue's aircraft had a relatively low cargo capacity of three tonnes,

whereas its competitor Emirates could carry 14 tonnes. By having frequent flights and more regional destinations, however, Pacific Blue was well positioned to carry time-sensitive but smaller cargoes. It therefore promoted its service in terms of speed of delivery.

Perhaps mindful of the limitations of a narrow market niche, in March 2005, the company indicated further extension of its business model. Areas for development included corporate and government sectors (complementary to Pacific Blue's existing leisure market), and 'ancillary revenues' including holidays, insurance and catering.

Sources: Keown J 2005, 'Pacific targeting a Tasman niche', *Lloyd's List Daily Commercial News (ABIX Abstracts)*, 10 February; McCarthy, P 2005, 'Exporters relish new air freighter', *The Southland Times*, 5 February; Godfrey, B 2005, 'Virgin Blue interim financial results', presentation by Brett Godfrey, managing director, 31 March; Virgin Blue 2005, 'Pacific Blue takes on international freight', press release, 4 February, accessed 2 September 2005, www.virginblue.com.au/about_us/news/index.php?co=vb&artdate=022005#news040205b.

Furthermore, concentration on a small range of products sometimes allows a focuser to develop innovations faster than a large differentiator can. The focuser does not attempt to serve all market segments, however, because doing so would bring it into direct competition with the differentiator. Instead, a focused company concentrates on building market share in one market segment and, if successful, may begin to serve more and more market segments, chipping away the differentiator's competitive advantage.

Strategic choices

Table 6.1 illustrates the specific product, market and distinctive-competency choices made by a focused company. Differentiation can be high or low because the company can pursue a low-cost approach or a differentiation approach. As for customer groups, a focused company chooses specific niches in which to compete rather than going for a whole market, as a cost leader does, or filling a large number of niches, as a broad differentiator does. The focused company can pursue any distinctive competency because it can seek any kind of differentiation or low-cost advantage. It may find a cost advantage and develop a superior efficiency in low-cost manufacturing within a region. Alternatively, it may develop superior skills in responsiveness to customers, based on its ability to serve the needs of regional customers in ways that a national differentiator would find very expensive.

The many avenues for developing a competitive advantage explain why there are so many small companies in relation to large ones. A focused company has enormous opportunity to develop its own niche and compete against low-cost enterprises and differentiated enterprises, which tend to be larger. A focus strategy provides an opportunity for an entrepreneur to find and then exploit a gap in the market by developing an innovative product that customers cannot do without.[15]

Advantages and disadvantages

A focused company's competitive advantages stem from the source of its distinctive competency: efficiency, quality, innovation or responsiveness to customers. The company is protected from rivals to the extent that it can provide a product or service that they cannot provide. This ability also gives the focuser power over its *buyers* because they cannot get the same thing from anyone else. With regard to *powerful suppliers*, however, a focused company is at a disadvantage, because it buys in small volume and consequently is in the suppliers' power. But as long as the company can pass on price increases to loyal customers, this disadvantage may not be a significant problem. Potential competitors face the barrier to entry of trying to overcome the customer loyalty that the focuser has generated. The development of customers' loyalty also lessens the threat from *substitute products*. This protection from the five forces allows the focuser to earn above-average returns on its investment. Another advantage of the focus strategy is that it permits a company to stay close to its customers and respond to their changing needs. The difficulty that a large differentiator sometimes experiences in managing many market segments is not an issue for a focuser.

Because a focuser produces a small volume, its production costs often exceed those of a low-cost company. Higher costs can also reduce profitability if a focuser is forced to invest heavily in developing a distinctive competency, such as expensive product innovation, to compete with a differentiated company. Nonetheless, flexible manufacturing systems are opening up new opportunities for focused firms because small production runs become possible at a lower cost. Increasingly, small specialised companies are competing with large companies in specific market segments in which their cost disadvantage is much reduced.

A second problem is that the focuser's niche can suddenly disappear as a result of technological change or changes in consumers' tastes. Unlike the more generalist differentiator, a focuser cannot move easily to new niches, given its concentration of resources and competency in one or a few niches. A clothing manufacturer that focuses on heavy metal music enthusiasts, for example, would find it difficult to shift to other segments if heavy metal lost its appeal. And a Mexican restaurant would find it difficult to move to Chinese food if customers' tastes change. The disappearance of niches is one reason that so many small companies fail.

Finally, differentiators may compete for a focuser's niche by offering a product that can satisfy the demands of the focuser's customers. Many magazines target highly specific niches, such as *Scoop* magazine, which specifically targets high-spending men and women in the 28–54-year-old age group, living in or visiting Western Australia. Federal Publishing Company and ACP Publishing, however, continue to expand their range of similarly targeted magazines beyond offerings such as *GQ*, *Vogue Australia* and *Gourmet Traveller* to target the same readers as *Scoop*. A focuser is vulnerable to attack and, therefore, has to defend its niche constantly.

Stuck in the middle

Each generic strategy requires a company to make consistent product, market and distinctive-competency choices to establish a competitive advantage. In other words, a company must achieve a fit among the three components of business-level strategy. A low-cost company, for example, cannot strive for a high level of market segmentation (as a differentiator does) and provide a wide range of products, because doing so would raise production costs too much and the company would lose its low-cost advantage. Similarly, a differentiator with a competency in innovation cannot try to reduce its expenditures on R&D, and one with a competency in responsiveness to customers through aftersales service cannot seek to economise on its sales force to decrease costs because it will lose its competitive advantage as its distinctive competency disappears.

Successfully choosing a business-level strategy means giving serious attention to all elements of the competitive plan. Many companies, through ignorance or mistakes, do not conduct the planning necessary for success in their chosen strategy. These companies are said to be **stuck in the middle** because they have made product or market choices that make them unable to obtain or sustain a competitive advantage.[16] As a result, they have no consistent business-level strategy, experience below-average performance and suffer when industry competition intensifies.

It is not clear that the stuck in the middle concept is valid though. The generic strategies are based on earlier work done in the field of economics, which mapped profitability against the level of production. This previous work found that the most profitable companies were those that either produced in relatively small quantities or produced in very large quantities.[17] In some ways, these two positions are similar to the generic strategies of differentiation (relatively low volumes but with a high value-added component, such as a Rolex watch) and cost leadership (high volumes with smaller margins, such as a Ford Falcon). Between these two extremes, empirical studies found that companies tended to be considerably less profitable. Being stuck in the middle represents this less profitable area.

While being stuck in the middle was obviously not a profitable situation for companies during the 1950s and 1960s (when the economic studies were conducted) and the 1970s (when Porter first developed his generic strategies), the implications in terms of profitability may now be considerably less. Developments such as TQM and flexible manufacturing have allowed small companies to be as efficient in small production runs as the largest companies in the same industry. For example, Toyota has always manufactured in short runs compared with the largest car manufacturers such as General Motors and Ford. Today, however, it is considered to be one of the most efficient companies in the industry. In addition, markets have considerably fragmented, so that demand is entirely homogeneous in only a few industries (outside of commodities). The result is that many companies have to undertake some level of customisation or small batch work to be able to meet the divergent needs of different market segments. To demonstrate that it is no longer a recipe for disaster, consider how some of today's best-known and most successful firms are stuck in the middle, for example, Honda, Myer (which operates in between the differentiated David Jones and Kmart and Target in the low-cost position) and Sony.

Although it is possible to be successful while being stuck in the middle, not many strategists generally recommend it. The reason is that the fundamental ways of managing companies oriented towards achieving cost leadership are quite different from those for companies seeking to differentiate themselves. Cost leadership often involves more mechanistic structures. These companies are likely to be characterised by tight cost controls, detailed reporting, highly structured systems and processes and quantitative targets. This approach (and underlying culture) is likely to avoid any extraneous expenditure, such as nonessential R&D or brand development. In comparison, companies seeking to differentiate their product may be more organic in nature. They often spend considerable sums to differentiate their product, through advertising, R&D and customisation. They tend to be flatter and more decentralised and have looser reporting relationships and looser control systems. Combining the structures, cultures and control systems to allow a company to adopt a stuck in the middle strategy, in which it has elements of both cost leadership and differentiation, can therefore be very difficult.

Strategic groups and business-level strategy

As implied by the preceding discussion, companies in an industry can pursue many different kinds of business-level strategy that differ in terms of the choice of market segments to serve, product quality, technological leadership, customer service, pricing policy and advertising policy. As a result, within most industries, strategic groups emerge, each composed of companies pursuing the same generic strategy.[18] All the companies inside an industry pursuing

strategy in action 6.2

Flight Centre gets stuck in the middle

The Flight Centre has been a real success story in the travel agency business. Entering an industry that was highly fragmented, it has created the largest travel agent chain in Australia and New Zealand and now has operations in over 20 countries. It entered the market in the low-cost position, seeking to create volume as a way to achieve lower costs than existing competitors and to then pass some of the savings on to price-sensitive customers, further increasing volume. This approach has been successful and although there have been hiccups along the way, such as the need to change the slogan from 'Lowest Airfares Guaranteed' after concerns were raised by the Australian Competition and Consumer Commission (ACCC), Flight Centre has now opened more than 1000 stores.

However, in recent years, Flight Centre has had its market position eroded by various Internet operations. Without a physical infrastructure to maintain and by forcing customers to do their own bookings to get the absolute cheapest fare, these players have taken the low-cost position away from the Flight Centre, leaving it 'stuck in the middle'. Nevertheless, Flight Centre has minimised its loss of customers by establishing its own Internet operation, and this position seems to be highly profitable. Certainly, the performance of the Flight Centre has been better than that of other travel chains such as Harvey Travel or Jetset, and that of the online players such as travel.com.au, zuji and webjet. As with other 'stuck in the middle' operators, such as Toyota in motor vehicles and Sony in electronic goods, this position may well be the most profitable of all in this specific industry.

a low-cost strategy form one strategic group; all those seeking to pursue a broad differentiation strategy constitute another strategic group and all those pursuing a focused differentiation strategy or a focused low-cost strategy form yet other strategic groups.

In the pharmaceutical industry, for example, there are two main strategic groups.[19] One group includes such companies as Merck, Eli Lilly and Pfizer, which pursue a differentiation strategy characterised by heavy research and development spending and a focus on developing new proprietary blockbuster drugs. The other strategic group may be characterised as the low-cost strategic group because it focuses on the manufacture of low-priced generic drugs. Companies in this group are pursuing a low-cost strategy because they are not investing millions of dollars in R&D, and, as a result, cannot expect to charge a premium price.

The concept of strategic groups has implications for business-level strategy. First, a company's immediate competitors are those companies pursuing the same strategy in its strategic group. Consumers tend to view the products of such enterprises as being direct substitutes for each other. A major threat to a company's profitability may consequently arise primarily from within its own strategic group, not necessarily from the other companies in the industry pursuing different generic business-level strategies. The main competition for megaplex type cinemas such as those operated by Greater Union (Birch, Carroll & Coyle), for example, comes from Hoyts and not from smaller chains and independent cinemas featuring arthouse movies.

Second, different strategic groups can have a different standing in terms of each of Porter's five competitive forces because, as discussed, the five forces affect companies in different ways. In other words, the risk of new entry by potential competitors, the degree of rivalry among companies within a group, the bargaining power of buyers, the bargaining power of suppliers, and the competitive force of substitute products can all vary in intensity among different strategic groups within the same industry.

The previous section examined the different types of generic business-level strategy that companies can adopt to obtain a competitive advantage and outperform their rivals. If strategic managers succeed in developing a successful generic business-level strategy, they face still another crucial task: choosing an appropriate competitive strategy to position their company so it can sustain its competitive advantage over time in different industry environments. This section of the chapter explores the issue. First, it focuses on how companies in fragmented industries try to develop competitive strategies that support their generic strategies. Second, it considers the challenges of developing a competitive advantage in *mature industries*. It concentrates on how a set of companies that have been pursuing successful generic competitive strategies can use a variety of competitive tactics and gambits to manage the high level of competitive interdependence found in such industries. Finally, it assesses the problems of managing a company's generic competitive strategy in *declining industries*.

Strategies in fragmented industries

A fragmented industry consists of many small and midsized companies. The video rental industry, for example, is still very fragmented, as are the restaurant industry, the health club industry and the legal services industry. An industry may consist of many small companies rather than a few large ones for several reasons.[20] Some industries offer few economies of scale, so large companies do not have an advantage over smaller enterprises. In some industries, size is a disadvantage, for example, many home buyers prefer to deal with local real estate agencies, which they perceive as having better local knowledge than national chains have. Because they lack economies of scale, fragmented industries are often characterised by low barriers to entry (and new entries keep the industry fragmented). That is the situation in the restaurant industry because the costs of opening a restaurant are very moderate and can be borne by a single entrepreneur. High transportation costs can also keep an industry fragmented because regional production may be the only efficient way of satisfying customers' needs, as in the cement business. Finally, an industry may be fragmented because customers' needs are so specialised that only small job lots of products are required, and so there is no room for a large mass production operation to satisfy the market.

For some fragmented industries, these factors dictate the competitive strategy to pursue, and the focus strategy stands out as the principal choice. Companies may specialise by customer group, customer need or geographic region; consequently, many small specialty companies operate in local or regional market segments. All kinds of custom-made products — furniture, clothing, hats, boots and so on — fall into this category, as do all small service operations that cater to particular customers' needs, such as laundries, restaurants, health clubs and furniture rental stores. Service companies make up a large proportion of the enterprises in fragmented industries because they provide personalised service to clients and, therefore, need to be responsive to their needs.

Strategic managers, however, are eager to gain the cost advantages of pursuing a low-cost strategy or the sales and revenue-increasing advantages of differentiation by circumventing the problems of a fragmented industry. Because returns from consolidating a fragmented industry are often huge, during the past few years many companies have developed competitive strategies to achieve it. Among these companies are the large retailers such as Myer (Grace Bros), fast-food chains such as McDonald's and Pizza Hut, video rental chains such as Blockbuster Video and Video Ezy, and chains of health clubs, repair shops, and even lawyers and consultants. To grow, consolidate their industries and become the industry leaders, these companies use three main competitive strategies: (1) chaining, (2) franchising and (3) using the Internet.

Chaining

Companies such as Coles-Myer and Woolworths pursue a chaining strategy to obtain the advantages of cost leadership. They establish networks of linked merchandising outlets so interconnected that they function as one large business entity. The amazing buying power that these companies possess through their nationwide store chains allows them to negotiate large price reductions with their suppliers, which in turn promotes their competitive advantage.

They overcome the barrier of high transportation costs by establishing sophisticated regional distribution centres, which can economise on inventory costs and maximise responsiveness to the needs of stores and customers. Last but not least, they realise economies of scale from sharing managerial skills across the chain and from advertising nationally rather than locally.

Franchising

For differentiated companies in fragmented industries, such as McDonald's or Century 21 Real Estate, the competitive advantage comes from a business strategy that employs franchise agreements. In franchising, the franchisor (parent) grants the franchisee the right to use the parent's name, reputation and business skills at a particular location or in a particular area. Because the franchisee acts as the manager, he or she is strongly motivated to control the business closely and make sure that quality and standards are consistently high so that customers' needs are always satisfied. Such motivation is particularly critical in a strategy of differentiation, for which a company's ability to maintain its uniqueness is very important. One reason that industries fragment is the difficulty of controlling the many small outlets that must be operated, while at the same time retaining their uniqueness. Franchising solves this problem.[21] In addition, franchising lessens the financial burden of swift expansion, so permits rapid growth of the company. Finally, a differentiated large company can reap the advantages of large-scale advertising, as well as economies in purchasing, management and distribution, as McDonald's does very efficiently. McDonald's is able to pursue cost leadership and differentiation simultaneously only because franchising allows it to control costs locally and achieve differentiation by marketing on a national level.

franchising
Selling a brand name, systems and other aspects of a company's operations to others to be used in the same way, creating another business of the same type operating in the same way

Using the Internet

The Internet is the latest means by which companies have been able to consolidate a fragmented industry. Before eBay, for example, the auction business was extremely fragmented and local auctions in cities were the usual way in which people could dispose of their antiques and collectibles. With the advent of eBay, sellers using the website know that they are getting wide visibility for their collectibles and, therefore, are likely to receive a higher price for their product.

The challenge in a fragmented industry is to choose the most appropriate means — franchising, chaining or using the Internet — of overcoming a fragmented market to realise the competitive advantages of the different business-level strategies. It is difficult to think of any major service activities — from consulting and accounting firms, to businesses satisfying the smallest consumer need, such as beauty parlours and car repair shops — that have not been merged or consolidated by chaining, franchising or using the Internet.

Strategies in mature industries

As a result of fierce competition in the shakeout stage, an industry becomes consolidated. A mature industry is thus often dominated by a small number of large companies. Although a mature industry may also contain many midsized companies and a host of small specialised ones, the large companies determine the nature of the industry's competition because they can influence the five competitive forces. These are the companies that have developed the most successful generic business-level strategies in the industry.

By the end of the shakeout stage, strategic groups of companies pursuing similar generic competitive strategies have emerged in the industry. Companies in an industry constantly analyse each other's business-level strategies and they know that if they move to change their strategies, then their actions are likely to stimulate a competitive response from rivals in their strategic group and from companies in other groups that may be threatened by the change in strategy.

A differentiator that starts to lower its prices because it has adopted a more cost-efficient technology not only threatens other differentiators in its group but also threatens low-cost companies, which see their competitive edge being eroded. These other companies may change their strategies in response, most likely by reducing their prices, too, as is happening in the PC industry. How one company changes or finetunes its business-level strategy over time thus affects how other companies in the industry pursue theirs. By the mature stage of the industry lifecycle, therefore, companies have learned how interdependent their strategies are.

The main challenge facing companies in a mature industry is to adopt a competitive strategy that simultaneously allows each individual company to protect its competitive advantage and preserves industry profitability. No generic strategy will generate above-average profits if competitive forces in an industry are so strong that companies are at the mercy of each other, potential entrants, powerful suppliers, powerful customers and so on. As a result, in mature industries, competitive strategy revolves around understanding how large companies collectively try to reduce the strength of the five forces of industry competition to preserve both company and industry profitability.

Interdependent companies can help protect their competitive advantage and profitability by adopting competitive moves and tactics to reduce the threat of each competitive force. The next sections examine the various price and nonprice competitive moves and tactics that companies use, first, those used to deter entry into an industry and second, those used to reduce the level of rivalry within an industry. Methods that companies can employ to gain more control over suppliers and buyers are then discussed.

Strategies to deter entry in mature industries

Companies can use three main methods to deter entry by potential rivals and thus maintain and increase industry profitability. As figure 6.2 shows, these methods are product proliferation, price cutting and the maintenance of excess capacity.

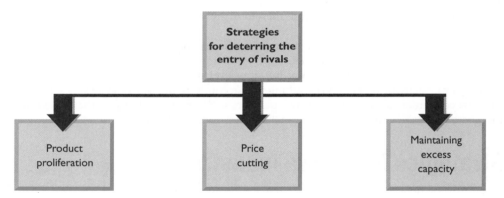

Figure 6.2:
Strategies for deterring the entry of rivals

Product proliferation

Companies seldom produce just one product. Most commonly, they produce a range of products aimed at different market segments so that they have broad product lines. Sometimes, to diminish the threat of entry, companies expand the range of products they make to fill a wide variety of niches. This creates a barrier to entry because potential competitors find it harder to break into an industry in which all the niches are filled.[22] This strategy of pursuing a broad product line to deter entry is known as **product proliferation**.

Levi's had a long history of making value-for-money, long-lasting jeans. Through the 1970s, and much of the 1980s, Levi's held on to its number one position against competitors such

product proliferation
When a company produces a range of products and services aimed at capturing different segments of the same market

as Lee, which produced very similar jeans. Starting in the 1970s, Levi's entered the fashion market with hipster jeans, featuring flares. By the 1980s, it was covering the fashion end of business only in terms of a working-class style (replicating the style of people such as Bruce Springsteen during his *Born in the USA* period). At all times, Levi's never covered more than the fashion end of streetwear. Starting in the late 1980s, however, small manufacturers started to produce jeans with a focus on designer fashion rather than street credibility and value for money. Brands such as Guess, Jordano and Calvin Klein started producing jeans that were sold through high-end fashion stores and did not aim to be streetwear in the same way that Levi's jeans were. This market niche was totally untapped. Being sold through just about any department or clothing store, however, Levi's was unable to position itself in the fashion segment of the market. While Levi's should have seen that this market segment was untapped, it had been slowly moving away from fashion trends since the hipster and flare styles went out of style. It has started fighting back with high-fashion wear that is cutting edge but, by the company's own admission, not expected to sell well. Rather, the new lines are designed to gain credibility for Levi's as a fashion brand and enable the company to compete in a range of market segments. Although Levi's failed to use product proliferation to counter new entrants, the major mobile phone manufacturers such as Nokia, Sony-Ericsson and Motorola have proliferated the market with a huge range of products, making it more difficult for the smaller manufacturers such as Samsung, LG and Panasonic.

Price cutting

In some situations, **price cutting** can be used to deter entry by other companies, protecting the profit margins of companies already in an industry. One price-cutting strategy is to charge a high price initially for a product and seize short-term profits but then cut prices aggressively to build market share *and* deter potential entrants simultaneously.[23] The incumbent companies thus signal to potential entrants that if they enter the industry, the incumbents will use their competitive advantage to drive down prices to a level at which new companies will be unable to cover their costs.[24] This pricing strategy also allows a company to ride down the experience curve and obtain substantial economies of scale. Because costs fall with prices, profit margins can still be maintained. This strategy, however, is unlikely to deter a strong potential competitor, such as an established company that is trying to find profitable investment opportunities in other industries.

price cutting
A company's reduction of prices for strategic reasons (as opposed to simply discounting)

Most evidence suggests that companies first skim the market and charge high prices during the growth stage, maximising short-run profits.[25] They then move to increase their market share and charge a lower price to expand the market rapidly, develop a reputation and obtain economies of scale, driving down costs and barring entry. As competitors enter the market, the incumbent companies reduce prices to hinder entry and give up market share to create a stable industry context: one in which they can use nonprice competitive tactics (such as product differentiation) to maximise long-term profits. At that point, **nonprice competition** becomes the main basis of industry competition and prices are likely to rise as competition stabilises. Competitive tactics such as pricing and product differentiation are thus linked in mature industries; competitive decisions are taken to maximise the returns from a company's generic strategy.

nonprice competition
When companies compete on nonprice dimensions

Maintenance of excess capacity

The third competitive technique that allows companies to deter entry involves maintaining excess capacity, that is, producing more of a product than customers currently demand, as is done in the diamond industry (see Strategy in action 6.3). Existing industry companies may deliberately develop some limited amount of excess capacity because it serves to warn potential entrants that if they enter the industry, existing firms can retaliate by increasing output and forcing down prices until entry would become unprofitable. The threat to increase output has to be credible though, that is, companies in an industry must collectively be able to raise the level of production quickly if entry appears likely.

Strategies to manage rivalry in mature industries

Beyond seeking to deter entry, companies also wish to develop a competitive strategy to manage their competitive interdependence and decrease rivalry. As noted, unrestricted competition over prices or output reduces the level of company and industry profitability. Several competitive tactics and gambits are available to companies to manage industry relations. The most important are price signalling, price leadership, nonprice competition and capacity control.

strategy in action 6.3

The artificial market for diamonds

Most first-year economic texts introduce the concepts of supply and demand: when demand is high and supply is low, prices increase. The diamond industry, however, through the efforts of the Central Selling Organisation (CSO), has largely avoided the effects of supply and demand curves by carefully controlling the number of diamonds that are available for sale each year.

Established in the 1930s by Sir Ernest Oppenheimer as a way of controlling the flow of diamonds onto the market and, therefore, the prices that they sell for, the CSO was born out of the dominance of the South African diamond mines controlled by De Beers. Its success has been enviable because there was no price reduction for any category of diamond until 1995, when a 'realignment' of prices affected only small and low-grade diamonds.

The CSO, through the De Beers operations, used to control almost half of the world's high-end, gem-quality diamonds. In addition, it built up a significant stockpile, worth more than US$4 billion through the 1990s. The effect is that De Beers has the financial clout to be able to flood the market and make even the largest production operations in the world unprofitable. This excess capacity and the ability to price everybody else out of the market makes the CSO an incredibly powerful player in the diamond industry, limiting how much producers will operate independently of the CSO. Rather than compete on price, it makes more sense for mines to sell their production to the CSO, which will pay fair prices for different diamond grades. This way, the market for diamonds is not affected and the prices received are probably higher than those that would be paid in a free market.

The power of the CSO was demonstrated in the early 1980s when a sharp downturn in the industry forced De Beers to continue to buy large quantities of diamonds at preset prices but then stockpile almost all of the diamonds because it lacked buyers. Rather than cut prices, De Beers rode out the lack of demand, accumulating almost US$2 billion worth of diamonds in the process.

While the power of the CSO to affect market prices is obvious, various operators have tried to operate outside of the CSO in an attempt to gain market prices for their diamonds rather than the CSO price. These attempts by Israel (through its booming diamond-cutting business), the Democratic Republic of Congo, Australia (through the Rio Tinto-owned Argyle Diamonds) and, more recently, Russia have had mixed success. As more of the De Beers-operated mines close, however, and as new countries such as Australia, the Democratic Republic of Congo, Russia and Namibia come to dominate the world trade, the CSO may lose its control of the industry and volatility will return to diamond prices. If too much of the world's diamond production ends up on the world market without the controls implemented by the CSO, then the rapidly growing number of diamond mines could lead the whole system to fall apart and diamond prices could freefall as supply overshadows demand.

The increasingly large number of players in the world diamond industry, especially those operating outside the CSO, can be seen in the development of the Kimberley Process. Designed to stop the trade in 'blood diamonds' (diamonds that support different groups engaged in civil wars), the Kimberley Process has 45 country participants that provide certification that diamonds mined or processed in that country are not 'blood diamonds'.

Price signalling

Most industries start out fragmented, with small companies battling for market share. Over time, the leading players emerge and companies start to interpret each other's competitive moves. **Price signalling** is the first means companies use to attempt to structure competition within an industry to control rivalry among competitors.[26] Companies increase or decrease product prices to convey their intentions to other companies and thus influence how they price their products.[27] Companies use price signalling in two ways to help defend their generic competitive strategies.

First, companies may use price signalling to announce that they will respond vigorously to hostile competitive moves that threaten them. Companies may signal, for example, that if one company starts to cut prices aggressively, then they will respond in kind. The term **tit-for-tat strategy** is often used to describe this kind of market signalling. The outcome of a tit-for-tat strategy is that nobody gains. Similarly, as noted in the last section, companies may signal to potential entrants that if the latter do enter the market, then they will fight back by reducing prices and the new entrants may incur significant losses.

A second and very important use of price signalling is to allow companies to coordinate their actions indirectly and avoid costly competitive moves that lead to a breakdown in the pricing policy within an industry. One company may signal that it intends to lower prices because it wishes to attract customers who are switching to the products of another industry, not because it wishes to stimulate a price war. On the other hand, signalling can be used to improve profitability within an industry. The airline industry is a good example of the power of price signalling because competitors are able to signal their intentions through the electronic reservation systems that all airlines use. When Australia had a duopoly on its major domestic routes, Qantas and Ansett were able to signal their prices to each other. During periods of intense competition after deregulation, such as when Impulse Airlines and Virgin Blue entered the industry, each player in the industry was able to view the others' prices to determine whether to match the latest round of discounts. When the duopoly returned — this time between Qantas and Virgin Blue — signalling limited the chances of either firm being drawn into a price war. If one airline increased its prices for all fares after a certain date, then the other could quickly follow. With additional information such as the number of seats available at a particular price point, the airlines were able to tell if a new price was a competitive move to try to capture additional market share or simply a way of disposing of otherwise unsold seats. In sum, price signalling allows companies to give one another information (indirectly) so that they understand each other's competitive moves. Coordinated competitive moves can thus occur across the industry.

price signalling
When companies make their pricing decisions known to competitors

tit-for-tat strategy
When companies retaliate against the pricing decision of one competitor, so that enough iterations of retaliation can lead to a price war

Price leadership

Price leadership, in which one company assumes responsibility for setting industry prices, is a second tactic used to increase the profitability of companies in a mature industry.[28] Formal price leadership, or joint price setting by companies, is illegal in many countries, so the process of price leadership is very subtle. In the Australian concrete industry, for example, the big three competitors, CSR, Boral and Pioneer, set amazingly similar prices. To some extent, this similarity would be expected because concrete is essentially an undifferentiated product and these big three competitors are likely to have achieved certain economies of scale. The former Trade Practices Commission, however, found collusive activity among these three players on different occasions, fining each of them A$10 million in the last instance. How price leadership works is difficult to say, however, because companies do not openly admit to engaging in it, even when charged with doing so. It is thought that the weakest company (that is, the one with the highest costs) sets the price, which competitors use as a basis for their pricing decisions. The more efficient firms are happy with this arrangement because they know that they will make a

price leadership
Where a company sets prices for the entire industry on the basis of its pricing decision

profit regardless what price is set. The other possibility is that an obvious leader in the industry (in terms of size and capacity) makes its pricing decision, which its competitors then follow. The big competitor often knows that there is no use in trying to knock the smaller players out of the industry because regulating bodies (such as the ACCC in Australia and the Commerce Commission in New Zealand) and antimonopoly legislation would not allow the company to expand. Under these conditions, the big player sets a price at which it will make good profits and the remaining companies simply follow this pricing decision.

Although price leadership can stabilise industry relationships by preventing head-to-head competition and so raising the level of profitability within an industry, it has its dangers. Price leadership helps companies with high costs, allowing them to survive without becoming more productive or more efficient. It may as a consequence encourage complacency; companies may keep extracting profits without reinvesting any to improve their productivity. In the long term, this will make companies vulnerable to new entrants that have lower costs because they have developed new productive techniques.

Nonprice competition

A third and important aspect of product or market strategy in mature industries is the use of nonprice competition to manage rivalry within an industry. Using various tactics and manoeuvres to try to prevent costly price cutting and price wars does not preclude competition by product differentiation. In many industries, product differentiation is the principal competitive tactic used to prevent competitors from obtaining access to a company's customers and attacking its market share. In other words, companies rely on product differentiation to deter potential entrants and manage rivalry within their industry. Product differentiation allows industry rivals to compete for market share by offering products with different or superior features or by applying different marketing techniques. In figure 6.3, product and market segment dimensions are used to identify four nonprice competitive strategies based on product differentiation: market penetration, product development, market development and product proliferation. (Notice that this model applies to new market segments, not new markets.)[29]

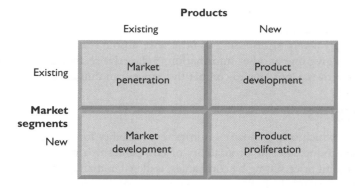

Figure 6.3:
Four nonprice-competitive strategies

Market penetration

When a company concentrates on expanding market share in its existing product markets, it is engaging in a strategy of **market penetration**.[30] Market penetration involves heavy advertising to promote and build product differentiation. In a mature industry, the thrust of advertising is to influence consumers' brand choice and create a brand reputation for the company and its products. In this way, a company can increase its market share by attracting the customers of its rivals. Because brand products often command premium prices, building market share in this situation is very profitable. In some mature industries, for example soap and detergent,

market penetration
The process of actively seeking to increase a company's market share

disposable nappies and brewing, a market penetration strategy becomes a way of life.[31] In these industries, all companies advertise intensively and battle for market share.

Product development

Product development is the creation of new or improved products to replace existing ones.[32] The wet-shaving industry is another that depends on product replacement to create successive waves of consumer demand, which then create new sources of revenue for companies in the industry. Gillette, for example, periodically comes out with a new and improved razor (such as the Sensor shaving system), which often gives a massive boost to its market share.

product development
The process of creating new or improved products

Product development is important for maintaining product differentiation and building market share.[33] For example, Coca-Cola has gone from one standard product to Cherry Coke, Vanilla Coke, Coke with Lemon, Coke with Lime and a variety of diet versions (Diet Coke, Coke Zero and so on). Refining and improving products is an important competitive tactic in defending a company's generic competitive strategy in a mature industry but this kind of competition can be as vicious as a price war because it is expensive and raises costs dramatically.

Market signalling to competitors can also be an important part of a product development strategy. One company may let the others know that it is proceeding with product innovations that will provide a competitive advantage that the others will be unable to imitate effectively because their entry into the market will be too late. Sony, for example, made it clear that it had a new product coming for both the Playstation 2 and Playstation 3 over a year out from the eventual release of the new system.

Market development

Market development finds new market segments for a company's products. A company pursuing this strategy wants to capitalise on one aspect of its operations that it has developed in one market segment by locating new market segments in which to compete. In this way, it can leverage its strengths into multiple market segments. Sharp, for example, was one of the first companies to use liquid crystal displays (LCDs) commercially when it tried to make lighter, less power-hungry calculators during the early years in the calculator industry. Sharp has since been looking at ways of exploiting its world leadership in LCDs. This meant that Sharp introduced LCDs into microwaves, was the first to produce the Handycam with the flip-out viewfinder and also became involved with Apple to produce the screens for the ill-fated Apple Newton. Most recently, Sharp released a range of LCD-screen televisions, in direct contrast to the early leaders in flat screen televisions, which used plasma technology.

market development
The process of finding new markets for a company's products

Product proliferation

Product proliferation can be used to manage rivalry within an industry and deter entry. The strategy of product proliferation generally means that large companies in an industry have a product in each market segment or niche and compete head to head for customers. If a new niche develops, such as customised golf balls, then the leader has a first-mover advantage but all the other companies soon catch up; again, competition is stabilised and rivalry within the industry is reduced. Product proliferation thus allows the development of stable industry competition based on product differentiation, not price, that is, nonprice competition based on the development of new products. The battle is over a product's perceived quality and uniqueness, not its price.

Capacity control

Although nonprice competition helps mature industries avoid the cutthroat price reductions that shrink both company and industry levels of profitability, price competition does periodically break out in some industries. This occurs when there is industry overcapacity, that is, when companies collectively produce too much output and lowering the price is the only way to dispose of it. If one company starts to cut prices, then the others quickly follow because they fear that the price cutter will be able to sell all its inventory and they will be left holding unwanted goods. Capacity control strategies are the last set of competitive tactics and manoeuvres for managing rivalry within an industry that are discussed in this chapter.

Excess capacity may be caused by a shortfall in demand, as when a recession lowers the demand for cars and causes car companies to give customers price incentives to purchase a new car. In this situation, companies can do nothing except wait for better times. Mostly, however, excess capacity results from companies within an industry simultaneously responding to favourable conditions: they all invest in new plants to be able to take advantage of the predicted upsurge in demand. Paradoxically, each individual company's effort to outperform the others means that collectively the companies create industry overcapacity, which hurts them all. Figure 6.4 illustrates this situation. Although demand is rising, the consequence of each company's decision to increase capacity is a surge in industry capacity, which drives down prices.

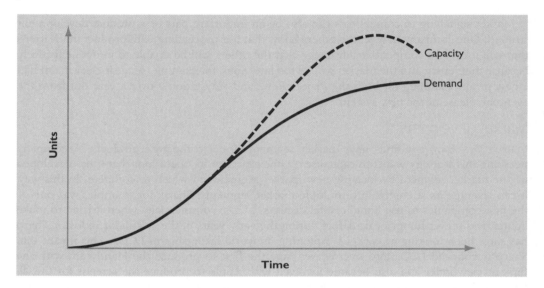

Figure 6.4:
Changes in industry
capacity and demand

To prevent the accumulation of costly excess capacity, companies must devise strategies that let them control — or at least benefit from — capacity expansion programs. Before examining these strategies, however, the factors that cause excess capacity need to be considered in greater detail.[34]

Factors causing excess capacity

The problem of excess capacity often derives from technological factors. Sometimes, new, low-cost technology is the culprit because all companies, to prevent being left behind, introduce the technology simultaneously. Excess capacity occurs because the new technology can produce more than the old could. In addition, new technology is often introduced in large increments, which generate overcapacity. An airline, for example, that needs more seats on a route must add another plane, so adding hundreds of seats even though only 50 are needed.

Overcapacity may also be caused by competitive factors within an industry, such as entry into an industry. Sometimes, the age of a company's plant is the source of the problem. In the hotel industry, given the rapidity with which the quality of hotel furnishings declines, customers are attracted to new hotels. Building new hotel chains alongside the old chains can cause excess capacity. Companies are often simply making simultaneous competitive moves based on industry trends but those moves eventually lead to head-to-head competition. Most fast-food chains, for example, establish new outlets whenever demographic data show population increases. The companies do not seem to care that all chains use the same data. A locality that has no fast-food outlets may as a consequence see several being built at the same time. Whether they can all survive depends on the growth rate of demand relative to the growth rate of the fast-food chains. And, sometimes, excess capacity is simply caused by too many companies wanting to become involved in a rapidly growing industry. The Australian wine industry, for example, is facing a glut of midpriced product as new vineyards get to market faster than demand (locally and through exports) increases.

Choosing a capacity control strategy

Given the various ways capacity can expand, companies clearly need to find some means of controlling it. If they are always plagued by price cutting and price wars, then companies will be unable to recoup the investments in their generic strategies. Low profitability within an industry caused by overcapacity forces not just the weakest companies but sometimes the major players as well to leave the industry. In general, companies have two strategic choices. Either (1) each company individually must try to pre-empt its rivals and seize the initiative or (2) the companies collectively must find indirect means of coordinating with each other so that they are all aware of the mutual effects of their actions.

To *pre-empt* rivals, a company must foresee a large increase in demand in the product market and then move rapidly to establish large-scale operations that will be able to satisfy the predicted demand. By achieving a first-mover advantage, the company may deter other companies from entering the market because the pre-emptor will usually be able to move down the experience curve, reduce its costs and, therefore, its prices as well, and threaten a price war if necessary.

This strategy is extremely risky though because it involves investing resources in a generic strategy before the extent and profitability of the future market are clear. A pre-emptive strategy is also risky if it does not deter competitors and they decide to enter the market. If the competitors have a stronger generic strategy or more resources, then they can make the pre-emptor suffer. For the strategy to succeed, the pre-emptor must generally be a credible company with enough resources to withstand a possible price war.

To *coordinate with rivals* as a **capacity control strategy**, companies must exercise caution because collusion on the timing of new investments is illegal in most capitalist countries. Tacit coordination is practised in many industries, as companies attempt to understand and forecast the competitive moves of each other. Generally, companies use market signalling and engage in a kind of tit-for-tat strategy to secure coordination. They make announcements about their future investment decisions in trade journals and newspapers. A coordination strategy thus reduces the risks associated with investment in the industry.

capacity control strategies
Alternative ways of managing capacity that do not lead to price-based competition

Strategies in declining industries

Sooner or later, many industries enter into a decline stage, in which the size of the total market starts to shrink. The railroad, tobacco and steel industries are at this stage. Reasons for industry decline include technological change, social trends and demographic shifts. The railroad and steel industries began to decline when technological changes brought viable substitutes for the products that these industries manufactured. The advent of the internal combustion engine drove the railroad industry into decline and the steel industry fell into decline with the rise of plastics and composite materials. As for the tobacco industry, changing social attitudes towards smoking, which are themselves a product of growing concerns about its health effects, have caused a decline in demand.

There are four main strategies that companies can adopt to deal with decline: (1) a *leadership strategy*, in which a company seeks to become the dominant player in a declining industry; (2) a *niche strategy*, which focuses on pockets of demand that are declining more slowly than the industry as a whole; (3) a *harvest strategy*, which optimises cash flow and (4) a *divestment strategy*, in which a company sells off the business to others. Before examining each of these strategies in detail, note that the choice of strategy partly depends on the intensity of the competition.

The severity of decline

When the size of the total market is shrinking, competition tends to intensify in a declining industry and profit rates tend to fall. The intensity of competition in a declining industry depends on four critical factors, which are indicated in figure 6.5. First, the intensity of competition is greater in industries in which decline is rapid as opposed to industries in which decline is slow and gradual, such as tobacco.

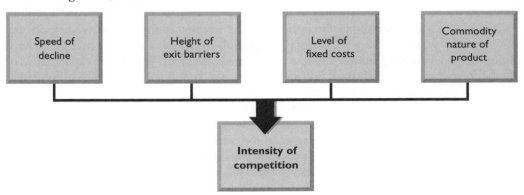

Figure 6.5:
Factors that determine the intensity of competition in declining industries

Second, the intensity of competition is greater in declining industries in which barriers to exit are high. As you recall from chapter 3, high barriers to exit keep companies locked into an industry even when demand is falling. The result is the emergence of excess productive capacity and an increased probability of fierce price competition.

Third, and related to the previous point, the intensity of competition is greater in declining industries in which fixed costs are high (as in the steel industry). The reason is that the need to cover fixed costs, such as the costs of maintaining productive capacity, can make companies try to use any excess capacity by slashing prices, an action that can trigger a price war.

Finally, the intensity of competition is greater in declining industries in which the product is perceived as a commodity (as it is in the steel industry) than it is in industries in which differentiation gives rise to significant brand loyalty (as is true of the declining tobacco industry). Companies therefore continue to advertise widely in declining industries if they believe they can create significant brand loyalty because this approach can minimise price-based competition.

Not all segments of an industry typically decline at the same rate. In some segments, demand may remain reasonably strong, despite decline elsewhere. The steel industry illustrates this situation. Although bulk steel products, such as sheet steel, have suffered a general decline, demand has risen for speciality steels, such as those used in high-speed machine tools. Nurseries may be another example, as shown in Strategy in action 6.4.

Choosing a strategy

As noted, four main strategies are available to companies in a declining industry: leadership, niche, harvest and divestment. Figure 6.6 provides a simple framework for guiding strategic choice. Note that the intensity of competition in the declining industry is measured on the vertical axis and a company's strengths relative to remaining pockets of demand are measured on the horizontal axis.

strategy in action 6.4

The Australian nursery industry faces decline

Family houses on large blocks is an enduring image of Australian life that pervades the collective Australian conscious. The reality is somewhat different as the number of persons per household drops and more and more people move to medium-density or even inner-city, high-density housing. This in itself has hampered the growth of the nursery industry but what sparked its decline was the introduction of water restrictions. Starting in Perth in 2001 and finally joined by Brisbane in May 2005 (as the last of the Australian capital cities to put in place some form of water restrictions), these restrictions have caused a massive rethink as to how Australians use their front, and particularly, their back yards. More paved areas and a greater reliance upon waterwise plants have been the typical responses.

From December 2003 (soon after the restrictions were introduced in Sydney, Melbourne and Adelaide) through to July 2005, a total of 43 nursery suppliers, 57 wholesale nurseries and 61 retail nurseries have closed down across Australia. In addition to these 161 closures, it is estimated that 10 000 to 12 000 people have lost their jobs in the irrigation and reticulation industries in New South Wales alone. Richard de Vos, CEO of the Nursery and Garden Industry of Australia, suggests that there has been a downturn in the industry to the tune of $200 million in the past 12 months. It is not just the plant sales that are suffering. All garden-related equipment and products such as reticulation systems have also been hit. The one bright spot on the horizon is that demand in the market in Perth, which has faced water restrictions for the longest period of all the capitals, has plateaued. People seem to be coming to terms with water restrictions and adjusting accordingly. Although the decline has stabilised in Perth, it is unlikely to grow again for both environmental and demographic reasons.

Source: Wahlquist, A 2005, 'No water, no growth', *The Australian*, 7 September, p. 11.

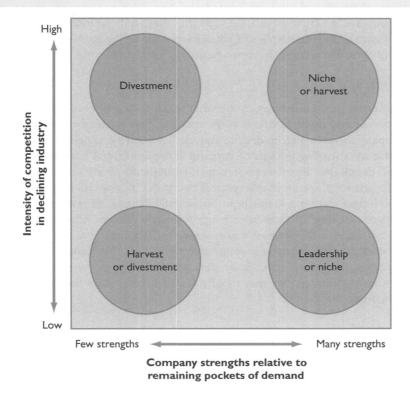

Figure 6.6: Strategy selection in a declining industry

Leadership strategy

A **leadership strategy** aims at growing in a declining industry by picking up the market share of companies that are leaving the industry. A leadership strategy makes most sense when (a) the company has distinctive strengths that allow it to capture market share in a declining

leadership strategy
Strategy of capturing the market share of companies leaving the industry

industry and (b) the speed of decline and the intensity of competition in the declining industry are moderate. Philip Morris has pursued this strategy in the tobacco industry. By aggressive marketing, Philip Morris has increased its market share in a declining industry and earned enormous profits in the process.

The tactical steps that companies may use to achieve a leadership position include undertaking aggressive pricing and marketing to build market share; acquiring established competitors to consolidate the industry and raising the stakes for other competitors, such as making new investments in productive capacity. These competitive tactics signal to other competitors that the company is willing and able to stay and compete in the declining industry. These signals may persuade other companies to leave the industry, which would further improve the competitive position of the industry leader.

Niche strategy

niche strategy
Strategy of focusing on a potentially profitable niche in an otherwise declining industry

A **niche strategy** focuses on those pockets of demand in the industry in which demand is stable or declining less rapidly than for the industry as a whole. The strategy makes sense when the company has some unique strengths related to those niches in which demand remains relatively strong. As an example, consider Naval, a company that manufactures whaling harpoons, as well as small guns to fire them, and makes money doing so. This may be considered rather odd because the world community has outlawed whaling. Naval survived the terminal decline of the harpoon industry, however, by focusing on one group of people who are still allowed to hunt whales, although only in very limited numbers: North American Inuits. Inuits are permitted to hunt bowhead whales, provided that they do so only for food and not for commercial purposes. Naval is the sole supplier of small harpoon whaling guns to Inuit communities, and its monopoly position allows it to earn a healthy return in this small market.[35]

Harvest strategy

harvest strategy
Strategy of maximising returns in an industry by eliminating investment and waiting for operations to become unprofitable

As noted, a **harvest strategy** is the best choice when a company wishes to get out of a declining industry and perhaps optimise cashflow in the process. This strategy makes the most sense when the company foresees a steep decline and intense future competition or when it lacks strengths relative to remaining pockets of demand in the industry. A harvest strategy requires the company to cut all new investments in capital equipment, advertising, R&D and the like. As illustrated in figure 6.7, the inevitable result is that the company will lose market share but, because it is no longer investing in this business, initially increase its positive cashflow. Essentially, the company is taking cashflow in exchange for market share. Ultimately, however, cashflow will start to decline: at this stage, it makes sense for the company to liquidate the business. Although this strategy is appealing in theory, it can be difficult to put into practice. Employee morale in a business that is being run down may suffer. Furthermore, if customers catch on to what the company is doing, they may rapidly defect. Market share may then decline much faster than the company expected.

Divestment strategy

divestment strategy
Strategy of selling a business before an industry enters a severe decline

A **divestment strategy** rests on the idea that a company can maximise its net investment recovery from a business by selling it early, before the industry has entered a steep decline. This strategy is appropriate when the company has few strengths relative to whatever pockets of demand are likely to remain in the industry and when the competition in the declining industry is likely to be intense. The best option may be to sell out to a company that is pursuing a leadership strategy in the industry. The drawback of the divestment strategy is that it depends for its success on the ability of the company to spot its industry's decline accurately before it becomes serious and to sell out while the company's assets are still valued by others.

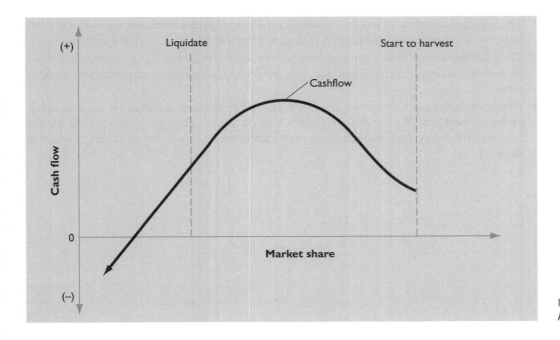

Figure 6.7:
A harvest strategy

Summary

The purpose of this chapter is to discuss the factors that must be considered if a company is to develop a business-level strategy that allows it to compete effectively in the marketplace. The formulation of business-level strategy means matching the opportunities and threats in the environment to the company's strengths and weaknesses by making choices about products, markets and distinctive competencies, as well as the investments necessary to pursue the choices. Once a generic business strategy has been chosen, specific strategies may be undertaken to account for specific industry conditions, including operating in fragmented, mature and declining industries. Each of these scenarios pose particular challenges to the strategic manager which often require action of a particular type. The chapter makes the following points.

- Business-level strategy refers to how strategic managers devise a plan of action for using a company's resources and distinctive competencies to gain a competitive advantage over rivals in a market or industry.

- At the heart of developing a generic business-level strategy are choices concerning product differentiation, market segmentation and distinctive competency. The combination of those three choices results in the specific form of generic business-level strategy that a company employs. A company must constantly manage its strategy; otherwise, it risks being stuck in the middle.

- Companies can also adopt two forms of focus strategy: a focused low-cost strategy and a focused differentiation strategy.

- Most industries are composed of strategic groups, which are groups of companies pursuing the same or a similar business-level strategy. The members of a strategic group constitute a company's immediate competitors.

- In fragmented industries composed of many small and midsized companies, the principal forms of competitive strategy are chaining, franchising and using the Internet.

- Mature industries are composed of a few large companies whose actions are so highly interdependent that the success of one company's strategy depends on the responses of its rivals.

- The principal competitive tactics and moves used by companies in mature industries to deter entry are product proliferation, price cutting and the maintenance of excess capacity.

- The principal competitive tactics and manoeuvres used by companies in mature industries to manage rivalry are price signalling, price leadership, nonprice competition and capacity control.

- Four main strategies that a company can pursue when demand is falling are the leadership, niche, harvest and divestment strategies. The choice of strategy is determined by the severity of industry decline and the company's strengths relative to the remaining pockets of demand.

Practising strategic management

Review questions

1. What is a cost-leadership strategy?
2. What does being 'stuck in the middle' mean? Why is it considered to be a negative position?
3. What are the most common strategies that firms can use to deter new entrants in a mature industry?
4. When a firm faces a declining industry, when will a niche strategy be appropriate?

Discussion questions

5. Why does each generic competitive strategy require a different set of product/market/distinctive-competency choices? Give examples of pairs of companies in (a) the computer industry and (b) the motor vehicle industry that pursue different competitive strategies.
6. What are some of the different ways that firms can seek to achieve a differentiated position within an industry? Give examples where possible.
7. Why are industries fragmenting and how can firms move to consolidate industries?
8. How can companies use (a) product differentiation and (b) capacity control to manage rivalry and increase an industry's profitability?

Applied questions

9. Are focus strategies destined to ensure that companies that use them remain forever comparatively small or can they become large firms in their own right? Use examples where possible.
10. The breakfast cereal industry is relatively mature. If you were managing Kellogg's or a similarly large company in this industry, what would you do to try to deter new entrants?

Small-group exercise

Finding a strategy for a restaurant

Break into groups of three to five people, and discuss the following scenario.

You are a group of partners contemplating opening a new restaurant in your city. You are trying to decide what business-level strategy would provide your restaurant with the best competitive advantage to make it as profitable as possible.

1. Create a strategic group of the restaurants in your city and define their generic strategies.
2. Identify which restaurants you think are the most profitable and why.
3. On the basis of this analysis, decide what kind of restaurant you want to open and why.

Article file

Find an example (or several examples) of a company pursuing one or more of the three generic business-level strategies. Which strategy is being pursued? On which product, market and distinctive-competency choices is it based? What are advantages and disadvantages of this strategy for the company?

Exploring the Web

Visiting Foster's

Enter the website of Foster's (www.fosters.com.au). Study how Fosters has changed its competitive focus over the past decade, by searching the 'Companies', 'Brands' and 'News' sections of the website.

General task

Search the Internet for a company pursuing a low-cost strategy, a differentiation strategy or both. What product, market and distinctive-competency choices has the company made to pursue this strategy? How successful has the company been in its industry using this strategy?

Strategic management project

Module 6

This part of the project focuses on the nature of your company's business-level strategy. If your company operates in more than one business, then concentrate either on its core (most central) business or its most important businesses. Using all the information you have collected on your company, answer the following questions.

1. How differentiated are the products or services of your company? What is the basis of their differentiated appeal?

2. What is your company's strategy towards market segmentation? If it segments its market, on what basis does it do so?

3. What distinctive competencies does your company have? (To answer this question, use the module 5 information on functional-level strategy.) Is efficiency, quality, innovation, responsiveness to customers or a combination of these factors the main driver in your company?

4. Based on the product, market and distinctive-competency choices, what generic business-level strategy is your company pursuing?

5. What are the advantages and disadvantages of your company's choice of business-level strategy?

6. How could you improve the company's business-level strategy to strengthen the company's competitive advantage?

7. Is your company a member of a strategic group in an industry? If so, which group?

8. In what kind of industry environment (for example embryonic, mature) does your company operate? (Use the information from module 3 to answer this question.)

9. How has your company attempted to develop a competitive strategy to protect its business-level strategy? If your company is operating in an embryonic industry for example, discuss how it has attempted to increase its competitive advantage. If it is operating in a mature industry, discuss how it has tried to manage the five forces of industry competition.

10. What new strategies would you advise your company to pursue to increase its competitive advantage?

Additional resources

Gottfredson, M & Aspinall, K 2005, 'Innovation versus complexity: What is too much of a good thing?', *Harvard Business Review*, vol. 83, no. 11, 2005, pp. 62–73. (This is an article that considers the trade-off between differentiation and low costs.)

Kim, W & Mauborgne, R 1999, 'Creating market space', *Harvard Business Review*, vol. 77, no. 1, pp. 83–93.

End notes

1. Abell, DF 1980, *Defining the business: the starting point of strategic planning*, Prentice Hall, Englewood Cliffs, New Jersey, p. 169.

2. Kotler, R 1984, *Marketing management*, 5th edn, Prentice Hall, Englewood Cliffs, New Jersey; Darby, MR & Karni, E 1973, 'Free competition and the optimal amount of fraud', *Journal of Law and Economics*, vol. 16, pp. 67–86.

3. Abell, op. cit.

4. Porter, ME 1985, *Competitive advantage: creating and sustaining superior performance*, Free Press, New York.

5. Buzzell, RD & Wiersema, FD 1981, 'Successful share building strategies', *Harvard Business Review*, January–February, pp. 135–44; Phillips, LW, Chang, DR & Buzzell, RD 1983, 'Product quality, cost position and business performance: a test of some key hypotheses', *Journal of Marketing*, vol. 47, pp. 26–43.

6. Porter, ME 1980, *Competitive strategy: techniques for analyzing industries and competitors*, Free Press, New York, p. 45.

7. Abell, op. cit.

8. Although many other authors have discussed cost leadership and differentiation as basic competitive approaches, for example, Scherer, F 1980, *Industrial market structure and economic performance*, 2nd edn, Houghton Mifflin, Boston, Massachusetts, Porter's model (Porter 1980, op. cit.) has become the dominant approach. Consequently, this model is the one developed here and the discussion draws heavily on his definitions. The basic cost-leadership/differentiation dimension has received substantial empirical support: see, for example, Hambrick, DC 1983, 'High profit strategies in mature capital goods industries: a contingency approach', *Academy of Management Journal*, vol. 26, pp. 687–707.

9. Porter 1985, op. cit.

10. ibid., pp. 13–14.

11. Miller, D 1986, 'Configurations of strategy and structure: towards a synthesis', *Strategic Management Journal*, vol. 7, pp. 217–31.

12. Porter 1985, op. cit.

13. Hofer, CW & Schendel, D 1978, *Strategy formulation: analytical concepts*, West, St Paul, Minnesota.

14. Hall, WK 1980, 'Survival strategies in a hostile environment', *Harvard Business Review*, vol. 58, pp. 75–85; Hambrick 1983, op. cit.

15. Drucker, PF 1954, *The practice of management*, Harper, New York.

16. Porter 1985, op. cit.

17. Bain, JS 1968, *Industrial organization*, 2nd edn, John Wiley & Sons, New York.

18. The development of strategic group theory has been a strong theme in the strategy literature. Important contributions include Caves, RE & Porter, M 1977, 'From entry barriers to mobility barriers', *Quarterly Journal of Economics*, May, pp. 241–62; Harrigan, KR 1985, 'An application of clustering for strategic group analysis', *Strategic Management Journal*, vol. 6, pp. 55–73; Hatten, KJ & Schendel, DE 1976, 'Heterogeneity within an industry: firm conduct in the US brewing industry, 1952–1971', *Journal of Industrial Economics*, vol. 26, pp. 97–113; Porter, ME 1979, 'The structure within industries and companies' performance', *Review of Economics and Statistics*, vol. 61, pp. 214–27.

19. For details on strategic group structure in the pharmaceutical industry, see Cool, K & Dierickx, I 1993, 'Rivalry, strategic groups, and firm profitability', *Strategic Management Journal*, vol. 14, pp. 47–59.

20. Porter 1980, op. cit., pp. 191–200.

21. Shane, SA 1996, 'Hybrid organizational arrangements and their implications for firm growth and survival: a study of new franchisors', *Academy of Management Journal*, vol. 1, pp. 216–34.

22. Brander, J & Eaton, J 1985, 'Product line rivalry', *American Economic Review*, vol. 74, pp. 323–34.

23. Milgrom, P & Roberts, J 1982, 'Predation, reputation, and entry deterrence', *Journal of Economic Theory*, vol. 27, pp. 280–312.

24. Oster, SM 1990, *Modern competitive analysis*, Oxford University Press, New York, pp. 262–4.

25. Hay, DA & Morris, DJ 1979, *Industrial economics: theory and evidence*, Oxford University Press, New York, pp. 192–3.

26. Porter 1980, op. cit., pp. 76–86.

27. Heil, O & Robertson, TS 1991, 'Towards a theory of competitive market signaling: a research agenda', *Strategic Management Journal*, vol. 12, pp. 403–18.

28. Scherer, FM 1980, *Industrial market structure and economic performance*, 2nd edn, Houghton Mifflin, Boston, chapter 8.

29. The model differs from Ansoff's model for this reason. See Ansoff, HI 1984, *Corporate strategy*, Penguin Books, London.

30. ibid, pp. 97–100.

31. Buzzell, RD, Gale, BT & Sultan, RGM 1975, 'Market share — a key to profitability', *Harvard Business Review*, January–February, pp. 97–103; Jacobson, R & Aaker, DA 1985, 'Is market share all that it's cracked up to be?', *Journal of Marketing*, vol. 49, pp. 11–22.

32. Ansoff, op. cit., pp. 98–9.

33. Brown, SL & Eisenhardt, KM 1995, 'Product development: past research, present findings, and future directions', *Academy of Management Review*, vol. 20, pp. 343–78.

34. The next section draws heavily on Lieberman, MB 1987, 'Strategies for capacity expansion', *Sloan Management Review*, vol. 8, pp. 19–27; Porter 1980, op. cit., pp. 324–38.

35. Willoughby, J 1987, 'The last iceman', *Forbes*, 13 July, pp. 46–7.

Corporate strategy: vertical integration, diversification and strategic alliances

learning objectives

After studying this chapter, you should be able to:

- appreciate the strategic differences between focusing on a single business and being involved in more than one business

- understand the factors that may influence the success or otherwise of a strategy of vertical integration

- describe how a company may use cooperative relationships and strategic outsourcing as alternatives to vertical integration

- discuss how and when diversification may lead to superior performance, and what constrains a company's level of diversification

- understand the different portfolio-planning techniques and their inherent strengths and weaknesses

- discuss different entry strategies including internal new venturing, acquisitions and joint ventures.

opening case

Fonterra's bid for National Foods

Fonterra Co-operative Group processes some 96 per cent of the milk produced in New Zealand and is owned by about 12 000 milk suppliers. It regards its home base as Australia and New Zealand, and in line with this in late 2004, it announced a takeover offer for National Foods Ltd.

At the time of the bid, National Foods had 43 per cent of the fresh milk market in Australia (Fonterra had 16 per cent). Importantly for Fonterra, it also had 33 per cent of the Australian yoghurt and dessert market and owned the rights to the strong Yoplait brand. Yoghurt is a growing segment, in which Fonterra has not had a strong presence. National Foods also had valuable channel access through a deal with the major supermarket Woolworths. However, it also faced an Australian milk-processing market that was very competitive because of deregulation and overcapacity.

There was a clear relationship between the National Foods business and Fonterra's existing business, expertise and strategy. However, some commentators expressed concern that the takeover might reduce Fonterra's payouts to its farmers. This concern reflected the well known tendency for companies to pay more for a company than the value of its projected profits.

Fonterra's initial offer in October 2004 was $5.45 per share, representing a premium over the price before the announcement of just less than 22 per cent and an implied price/earnings ratio of just less than 20 per cent: higher than that of many food and dairy companies. Fonterra could justify this premium to its shareholders due to potential synergies with its existing ownership of Australian dairy companies Bonlac Foods and Peters and Browne.

However, a higher offer for National Foods was then made by the San Miguel Corporation, a Philippines-based food and beverage company that started as a brewer and whose flagship product is still its San Miguel beer. In response to its $6.00 bid, the share price rose still higher because of market expectations of a further bid from Fonterra.

In the meantime, Fonterra had carried out more detailed due diligence on National Foods and made the case for higher projected synergy gains. After a takeover, it was argued that cost savings could be achieved by removing duplication and value could be generated by selling extra products through National Foods channels. It was on this basis that in March 2005, Fonterra justified its new offer of up to $6.20 per share. This represented a 35 per cent premium over the National Foods share price on the day before Fonterra announced its original offer. One concern expressed at this time was that the synergy gains might be handed to the existing National Foods shareholders rather than accruing to the shareholders of Fonterra.

After this, San Miguel offered $6.40 per share. Fonterra pulled out of the bidding and instead accepted San Miguel's offer for the shares it already owned. It argued that the price meant other growth opportunities in Australia were now more attractive. Some of the acquisition premium was paid to Fonterra because of its existing shareholding in National Foods, giving it a gross profit of $210 million. This sum was then available for alternative acquisitions: subsequently, Fonterra announced its intention to increase its shareholding in Bonlac Foods from 50 per cent to full ownership and to integrate its Australian operations under the Fonterra name.

Sources: van der Hayden, H & Stuart, G 2004, Fonterra presentation, 28 October; *The Press (Christchurch)* 2005, 'The great Australian yoghurt grab', 29 January; *National Business Review* 2005, 'Fonterra urged to stay sober on takeover', 11 February; *Fonterra News* 2005, 'Fonterra lifts bid for National Foods', 2 March; *Stuff/NZPA* 2005, 'Fonterra pulls out of bidding for Nat Foods', 11 April; *Fonterra News* 2005, 'Fonterra ends National Foods offer and divests stake', 11 April; *Fonterra News* 2005, 'Fonterra takes next steps in Australian growth strategy', 7 June; San Miguel Corporation n.d., corporate information.

Overview

The principal concern of corporate strategy is to identify the business areas in which a company should participate to maximise its long-term profitability. When choosing business areas in which to compete, a company has several options. It can focus on one business (such as milk), it can diversify into different businesses (as San Miguel did by moving from beer into dairy products) or it can vertically integrate either upstream or downstream (as Fonterra did in moving from milk into yoghurts and other dessert products). This chapter explores the options in depth and examines their advantages and disadvantages. It also considers strategic alliances and joint ventures as alternatives to outright ownership of other businesses.

This chapter repeatedly stresses that to succeed, corporate-level strategies should create value. Understanding what this means requires going back to the concept of value creation and the value chain, introduced in chapter 4: that is, to create value, a corporate strategy should enable a company, or one or more of its business units, to perform one or more of the value creation functions at a lower cost or perform one or more of the value creation functions in a way that allows for differentiation and a premium price. A company's corporate strategy should therefore help in establishing a distinctive competency and competitive advantage at the business level. There is, therefore, a very important link between corporate-level strategy and competitive advantage at the business level.

> **corporate-level strategy**
> Determining the businesses in which a company should be involved

Concentration on a single business

For many companies, the appropriate corporate-level strategy does not involve vertical integration or diversification. Instead, corporate strategy entails concentrating on competing successfully within the confines of a single business (that is, focusing on a single industry or market). Examples of companies that pursue such a strategy include Mushroom, with its focus on the music industry; Coca-Cola, with its focus on the soft-drink business; Fisher & Paykel, which split in 2002 to form two businesses (Appliances, focusing on whitegoods, and Healthcare); and Allied Pickfords, with its focus on being an international removalist company. Interestingly, Coca-Cola and other once focused companies at one time pursued diversification strategies. Coca-Cola once owned Columbia Pictures and a wine-producing business. Southcorp (which was taken over by Foster's in 2005) was a wine company but it used to be involved in packaging and water heaters. Those companies that have moved from being diversified to having a single business focus have tended to do so because diversification did not create any real value for them; in many cases, diversification reduced the profitability of the company. Focusing on a single business has some clear advantages.

One advantage is that the company can focus its total managerial, financial, technological and physical resources and capabilities on competing successfully in a single area. This strategy can be important in fast-growing industries, in which demands on the company's resources and capabilities are likely to be substantial but the long-term profits that flow from establishing a competitive advantage are also likely to be significant.

Neither do only fast-growing companies benefit from focusing their resources and capabilities on one business activity. Some diversified companies that are active in more mature businesses have also stretched scarce resources too thinly over too many activities, and their performance has declined as a consequence. CSR, for example, used to be a diversified industrial and minerals company in the 1980s. The ability of top management to manage all of the different operations actively, however, was limited by the number and breadth of the businesses within the group. Through the 1980s, management made an effort to focus on building and construction materials, with some holdings in timber, aluminium and sugar. By 1989, CSR had around two-thirds of its assets in the building and construction materials area (including offshore holdings) compared with just 14 per cent in 1986. Although the business is now subject to the cyclical effects of the building industry, the long-term return on equity has been much higher than the sub-10 per cent being achieved before the company rationalised its divisions.

Another advantage of concentrating on a single business is that in doing it the company 'sticks to its knitting'.[1] What this means is that the company sticks to doing what it knows best and does not make the mistake of diversifying into areas that it knows little about and in which its existing resources and capabilities add little value. Companies undertaking this sort of diversification are likely to discover after the event that they are involved in a business they do not understand and that their uninformed decision making may have a serious and perhaps detrimental effect.

Concentrating on one business area also has disadvantages though. As the next section shows, a certain amount of vertical integration may be necessary to create value and establish a competitive advantage within a company's core business. Moreover, companies that concentrate on one business may be missing out on opportunities to create value and increase profits by using resources and capabilities more broadly.

Vertical integration

A strategy of **vertical integration** means a company is producing its own inputs (figure 7.1).

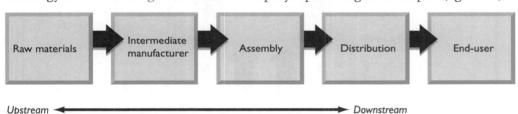

Upstream ◄─────────────────────► Downstream

Figure 7.1:
Stages in the raw materials-to-consumer value chain

As an example of the value-added concept, consider the production chain in the PC industry (see figure 7.2). In this industry, the raw materials companies include the manufacturers of speciality ceramics, chemicals and metals, such as Kyocera of Japan, which makes the ceramic substrate for semiconductors. These companies sell their output to the manufacturers of intermediate products. The intermediate manufacturers, which include Intel, Seagate and Micron Technology, transform the ceramics, chemicals and metals that they purchase into computer components such as microprocessors, memory chips and disk drives. In doing so, they add value to the purchased raw materials. They sell these components to assembly companies such as Apple, Dell Computer and Compaq, which transform the components into PCs, that is, add value to the purchased components. Many of the completed PCs are then sold to distributors such as Officeworks and Tandy or value-added resellers, which in turn sell them to final customers. The distributors also add value to the product by making it accessible to customers and providing service and support. Value is thus added by companies at each stage in the raw materials-to-consumer chain.

vertical integration
The process by which an organisation controls either its own inputs (backward integration) or the distribution of its product or service (forward integration)

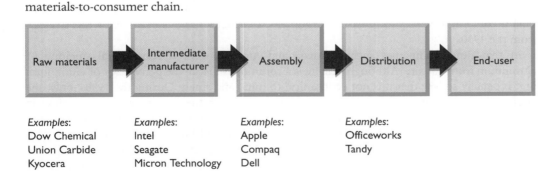

Examples:	Examples:	Examples:	Examples:
Dow Chemical	Intel	Apple	Officeworks
Union Carbide	Seagate	Compaq	Tandy
Kyocera	Micron Technology	Dell	

Figure 7.2:
The raw materials-to-consumer value chain in the PC industry

full integration
Producing all of one input of the company entirely within the company, or disposing of all product output through company-owned channels

taper integration
Buying input from independent suppliers as well as company-owned suppliers, or disposing of product output through independent channels as well as company-owned channels

Besides forward and backward integration, it is also possible to distinguish between full integration and taper integration (figure 7.3).[2] A company achieves full integration when it produces all of a particular input needed for its processes or when it disposes of all its output through its own operations. Taper integration occurs when a company buys from independent suppliers in addition to company-owned suppliers or when it disposes of its output through independent outlets in addition to company-owned outlets. The advantages of taper integration over full integration are discussed later in the chapter.

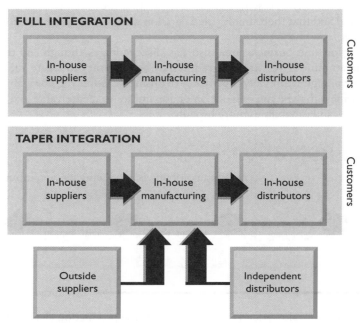

Figure 7.3:
Full and taper integration

Creating value through vertical integration

A company pursuing vertical integration is normally motivated by a desire to strengthen the competitive position of its original or core business.[3] The four main arguments for pursuing a vertical integration strategy are that it (a) enables the company to build barriers to new competition, (b) facilitates investments in efficiency-increasing specialised assets, (c) protects product quality and (d) results in improved scheduling.

Building barriers to entry

By vertically integrating backwards to gain control over the source of critical inputs or vertically integrating forwards to gain control over distribution channels, a company can build barriers to entry into its industry. If this strategy is effective, it limits competition in the company's industry, enabling the company to charge a higher price and make greater profits than it could otherwise.[4] To grasp this argument, consider a famous example of this strategy from the 1930s.

At that time, companies such as Alcoa and Alcan pioneered commercial smelting of aluminium from bauxite. Although bauxite is a common mineral, the percentage of aluminium in it is usually so low that it is not economical to mine and smelt. During the 1930s, only one large-scale deposit of bauxite had been discovered in which the percentage of aluminium in the mineral made smelting economical. This deposit was on the Caribbean island of Jamaica. Alcoa and Alcan vertically integrated backwards and acquired ownership of this deposit. This action created a barrier to entry into the aluminium industry: potential competitors were deterred from entry because they could not get access to high-grade bauxite, which was all owned by Alcoa and Alcan. Because they had to use lower-grade bauxite, those that did enter the industry found themselves at a cost disadvantage. This situation persisted until the 1950s, when new high-grade deposits were discovered in Australia and Indonesia. However, this is a rare example. Unless a natural monopoly exists, therefore, barriers to entry are a poor reason to integrate vertically. A natural monopoly (of a temporary form) may also occur when a firm holds critical patents that restrict the entry of other firms. The success stories, however, from building barriers to entry in the context of vertical integration are few and the failures many. For example, during an acquisition phase in the 1980s, Kodak purchased FX and Fox Photo Labs to go with its existing Kodak store operations. The opportunity to reduce Fuji's market share by selling only Kodak film in all of these stores never worked because Fuji just set up its own stores and developed alliances with other chains, in which these stores would sell only the Fuji product.

Facilitating investments in specialised assets

A **specialised asset** is an asset that is designed to perform a specific task and whose value is significantly reduced in its next best use.[5] A specialised asset may be a piece of equipment that has very specialised uses or it may be the know-how or skills that an individual or company has acquired through training and experience. Companies (and individuals) invest in specialised assets because these assets allow them to lower the costs of value creation or to better differentiate their product offering from that of competitors, facilitating premium pricing. A company may invest in specialised equipment because that enables it to lower its manufacturing costs and increase its quality, or it may invest in developing highly specialised technological knowledge because doing so lets it develop better products than those of its rivals. Specialisation can thus be the basis for achieving a competitive advantage at the business level.

A company may find it very difficult, however, to persuade other companies in adjacent stages in the raw materials-to-consumer production chain to undertake investments in specialised assets. To realise economic gains, the company may have to integrate vertically into the adjacent stages and make the investments itself. Imagine that Ford has developed a new, high-performance, high-quality and uniquely designed fuel-injection system. This fuel injection system will increase fuel efficiency, which in turn will help differentiate Ford's cars from those of its rivals, that is, it will give Ford a competitive advantage. Ford has to decide whether to make this product in-house (vertical integration) or contract out manufacturing to an independent supplier (outsourcing). In-house manufacturing will require substantial investments in equipment that can be used only for this purpose. Its unique design means the equipment cannot be used to manufacture any other type of fuel-injection system for Ford or any other motor vehicle manufacturer. The investment in this equipment thus constitutes an investment in specialised assets.

An independent supplier that Ford asked to make this investment may reason that it would become dependent on Ford for business because Ford is the only possible customer for the output of this equipment. The supplier perceives the situation as putting Ford in a strong bargaining position and worries that Ford may use the position to squeeze down prices for the carburettors. Given this risk, the supplier declines to make the investment in specialised equipment.

Ford may also fear excessive dependence. By contracting out production of this fuel-injection system to an independent supplier, it may have to rely on that supplier for a vital input. Given the specialised equipment needed to produce the product, Ford would not be able to switch its orders easily to other suppliers because they would lack that equipment. Ford perceives the situation as increasing the bargaining power of the supplier and worries that the supplier may use its bargaining strength to demand higher prices.

The condition of **mutual dependence** that would be created by the investment in specialised assets makes Ford hesitant to contract out and makes any potential suppliers hesitant to

specialised asset
An asset that is designed to perform a particular task and whose value is significantly reduced if it is used for an alternative task

mutual dependence
When two or more companies rely on each other to act in each other's best interests, so the companies both benefit in the long term

undertake such investments. The real problem here is a lack of trust. Neither Ford nor the supplier completely trusts the other to play fair in this situation. The lack of trust arises from the **risk of holdup**, that is, the risk that a trading partner will take advantage of a company after the investment in specialised assets has been made.[6] Given this risk, Ford may reason that the only safe way of obtaining the new fuel-injection system is to manufacture it itself.

To generalise from this example, when achieving a competitive advantage requires one company to make investments in specialised assets so as to trade with another company, the risk of holdup may serve as a deterrent and the investment may not take place. In those circumstances, the potential for competitive gains from specialisation would be mostly lost. To prevent such loss, companies vertically integrate into adjacent stages in the value chain. This consideration has, for example, driven aluminium companies to integrate backwards vertically into bauxite mining.

Protecting product quality

By protecting product quality, vertical integration lets a company become a differentiated player in its core business. The Australian wine industry has traditionally been vertically integrated, as has that of New Zealand. This is not always the norm in other locations though. On the central coast of California, the industry includes wineries that buy their fruit. In Australia, all of the major labels grow their own fruit. In many cases, they buy grapes from other growers as a supplement but then use the bought fruit primarily in lower-priced wines. The wineries' own fruit tends to be the base of the more expensive wines. The reason is that the winemakers like to have significant control over when the fruit is picked, as a way of ensuring maximum quality. Without vertical integration, the quality of the final wine may be compromised as a result of mistakes made by growers. Similarly, when McDonald's decided to open its first restaurant in Moscow, it was initially dismayed to find that to serve food and drink indistinguishable from that served in McDonald's restaurants elsewhere, it had to vertically integrate backwards and supply its own inputs. The quality of Russian-grown potatoes and meat was simply too poor. To protect the quality of its product, therefore, McDonald's set up its own dairy farms, cattle ranches, vegetable plots and food-processing plant within Russia.

Companies can gain quality in ways other than closely managing the supply chain. Kodak, for example, has long been vertically integrated through owning Eastman Chemical. The benefits are not that Eastman can provide better quality chemicals but rather that Kodak does not want anybody to know the processes (including the chemicals) used in its film production. By using a vertically integrated structure to control and protect the underlying knowledge about its film, Kodak is able to produce a superior product to that of its competitors.

Improving scheduling

It is sometimes argued that strategic advantages arise from the easier planning, coordination and scheduling of adjacent processes made possible in vertically integrated companies.[7] These advantages can be particularly important to companies trying to realise the benefits of just-in-time inventory systems, discussed in detail in chapter 5. In the 1920s, Ford profited from the tight coordination and scheduling that is possible with backward vertical integration. Ford integrated backwards into steel foundries, iron ore shipping and iron ore mining. Deliveries at Ford were coordinated to such an extent that iron ore unloaded at Ford's steel foundries on the Great Lakes was turned into engine blocks within 24 hours. Ford substantially lowered its costs by eliminating the need to hold excessive inventories.

The improved scheduling that vertical integration makes feasible may also enable a company to respond better to sudden changes in demand or to deliver its product into the marketplace faster. Nevertheless, modern enterprisewide computing systems, long-term supplier relationships and well-constructed contracts can normally provide similar benefits without having to integrate vertically. Today, security of supply may be more important than the benefits that can be gained in scheduling. Japanese steel mills, for example, invested in Australian coal firms to ensure supply and have at times also tried to gain greater control of iron ore deposits.

Arguments against vertical integration

Vertical integration has its disadvantages. Most important among them are (a) cost disadvantages, (b) disadvantages that arise when technology is changing fast and (c) disadvantages that arise when demand is unpredictable. These disadvantages imply that the benefits of vertical integration are not always as substantial as they initially seem.

Cost disadvantages

Although often undertaken to gain a production cost advantage, vertical integration can raise costs if a company becomes committed to purchasing inputs from company-owned suppliers when low-cost external sources of supply exist. Vertical integration tends to lock a company into using its own supplies, which can be a disadvantage when a company's own sources of supply have higher operating costs than those of independent suppliers.

Company-owned suppliers may have high operating costs compared with those of independent suppliers because they know that they can always sell their output to other parts of the company. Not having to compete for orders lessens the incentive to minimise operating costs. The managers of the supply operation may be tempted to pass on any cost increases to other parts of the company in the form of higher transfer prices, rather than looking for ways of lowering those costs. The lack of incentive to reduce costs can thus raise operating costs. The problem may be less serious, however, when the company pursues taper, rather than full, integration, because the need to compete with independent suppliers can produce a downward pressure on the cost structure of company-owned suppliers.

Technological change

When technology is changing fast, vertical integration poses the hazard of tying a company to an obsolescent technology.[8] Take for example the case of Philips, the giant Dutch consumer electronics company. Philips was one of the co-developers of the CD and is still heavily involved in the manufacture of different components that are used within CD players. Possibly for this reason, it has been slow to move into memory-based music systems (first popularised by the Apple iPod). Although most other consumer electronics companies from Sony to BenQ had products on the market, Philips was a little slower to respond with similar MP3 players. For example, with a similar styling to the original Apple iPod, the Philips Micro Jukebox had only six gigabytes of memory in early 2006, compared with the 60-gigabyte iPods that were available from Apple at the same time.

Demand uncertainty

Vertical integration can also be risky in unstable or unpredictable demand conditions. When demand is stable, higher degrees of vertical integration may be managed with relative ease. Stable demand allows better scheduling and coordination of production flows among different activities. When demand conditions are unstable or unpredictable, achieving close coordination among vertically integrated activities may be difficult.

The problem is to balance capacity among different stages of a process. A motor vehicle manufacturer, for example, may vertically integrate backwards to acquire a supplier of engine cooling systems that has a capacity exactly matching the car manufacturer's needs. If demand for cars subsequently falls, however, the carmaker will find itself locked into a business that is running below capacity. Clearly, this would be uneconomical. The car manufacturer could avoid this situation by continuing to buy cooling systems on the open market rather than making them itself. If demand conditions are unpredictable, then taper integration may be somewhat less risky than full integration. When a company obtains only part of its total input requirements from company-owned suppliers, in times of low demand it can keep its in-house suppliers running at full capacity by ordering exclusively from them.

Bureaucratic costs and the limits of vertical integration

As noted, although vertical integration can create value, it may also result in substantial costs caused by a lack of incentive on the part of company-owned suppliers to reduce their operating costs; a possible lack of strategic flexibility in times of changing technology; or uncertain demand. Together, these costs form a major component of what are referred to as the bureaucratic costs of vertical integration. Bureaucratic costs are simply the costs of running a company. They include the costs that stem from bureaucratic inefficiencies, such as those we have just discussed. Bureaucratic costs place a limit on the amount of vertical integration that can be profitably pursued: it makes sense for a company to vertically integrate only if the value created by such a strategy exceeds the bureaucratic costs of expanding the boundaries of the company to incorporate additional upstream or downstream activities.

Common sense suggests that not all vertical integration opportunities have the same potential for value creation. Although vertical integration may initially have a favourable impact, the value created by additional integration into areas more distant from a company's core business is likely to become increasingly marginal. The more marginal the value created by a vertical integration move, the more likely it is that the bureaucratic costs of expanding into new activities will outweigh the value created. Once this occurs, a limit to profitable vertical integration has been reached.[9]

Note, however, that the pursuit of taper integration rather than full integration may decrease the bureaucratic costs of vertical integration. The reason is that taper integration creates an incentive for in-house suppliers to reduce their operating costs and increases the company's ability to respond to changing demand conditions. It thus reduces some of the inefficiencies that increase bureaucratic costs.

Alternatives to vertical integration: cooperative relationships and strategic outsourcing

The disadvantages of vertical integration raise the question whether it is possible to reap the benefits of vertical integration without having to bear the associated bureaucratic costs. Can the benefits of vertical integration be captured through outsourcing activities to other companies? The answer seems to be a qualified 'yes'. Under certain circumstances, companies can realise the gains linked with vertical integration, without having to bear the bureaucratic costs, if they enter into long-term cooperative relationships with their trading partners. These are typically referred to as strategic alliances. In many cases, these strategic alliances have been able to provide the benefits of vertical integration but in a much more efficient manner. Australian wineries, for example, rely on their own grapes to produce many of their better wines but this reliance is reducing every year as wineries source grapes elsewhere. The most expensive and prestigious wine from Australia, Penfolds Grange, is made entirely by grapes sourced through the use of long-term contracts. With modern communications technology, too, there is no reason to be vertically integrated to achieve improved scheduling. Just-in-time systems and computer systems that are integrated with those of key suppliers can make scheduling with external suppliers just as efficient as any entirely internal system. The right type of alliance can even allow the effective management of specialised assets.

strategy in action 7.1

Icebreaker is a New Zealand-based company producing and marketing outdoor performance clothing based on pure merino wool. Founded in 1995, its innovation was to introduce strong branding and design to exploit the inherent properties of the fibre, which was otherwise being exported unprocessed. Its turnover in 2005 was more than NZ$20 million. Icebreaker adds value by managing a supply chain starting with the merino growers and ending with the retail outlet. However, it limits the activities it actually owns and operates, concentrating on design and marketing. The supply chain starts with the merino growers in the Southern Alps. To control the quality of the fibre and ensure consistent supply, Icebreaker works directly with a select group of high-country farmers. It measures ten different fibre attributes to ensure the highest level of suitability for its products. The direct supplier links also maintain the authenticity of its product as being from the mountains of New Zealand.

Icebreaker does not manufacture clothing itself but instead contracts out its production to local manufacturers. In the future, it may also make use of offshore production. Much of the company's product is sold internationally in North America, Europe and Asia. For the US market it maintains a small office intended to localise the global Icebreaker brand. It recently made a deal with the Sole Survivor distribution company, which supplies major outdoor clothing stores including the largest US chain, REI. One of the things that helped it secure this deal was hosting representatives of the distribution company on one of the merino farms back in New Zealand.

Sources: National Business Review 2004, 'World class style — Icebreaker carves a path', 27 February; *The Press (Christchurch)* 2005, 'Icebreaker masters', 24 March; *Sunday Star-Times* 2003, 'Really breaking the ice', 31 August; *Otago Daily Times* 2003, 'Icebreaker signs $6.6 million wool deal', 17 March; *Sunday Star-Times* 2002, 'Down-under wonder hit in US', 27 January.

However, companies will generally be unable to realise the gains associated with vertical integration if they enter into short-term contracts with their trading partners. To see why this is so, we first discuss the problems with short-term contracts. Then, we look at strategic alliances and long-term contracts as alternatives to vertical integration, and discuss how companies can build enduring, long-term relationships with their trading partners.

Strategic alliances and long-term contracting

Long-term contracts are long-term cooperative relationships between two companies. These are often referred to as strategic alliances. Typically in these arrangements, one company agrees to supply the other, which agrees to continue purchasing from that supplier; both make a commitment jointly to seek ways of lowering the costs or raising the quality of inputs into the downstream company's value creation process. If their goal is achieved, such a stable long-term relationship allows the participating companies to share the value created by vertical integration while avoiding many of the bureaucratic costs linked to ownership of an adjacent stage in the raw material-to-consumer production chain. Long-term contracts can thus substitute for vertical integration.

The cooperative relationships that many Japanese car companies have with their component parts suppliers (the *keiretsu* system) exemplify successful long-term contracting. These relationships often go back decades. Together, the car companies and their suppliers work out ways of increasing the value added, for example, by implementing just-in-time inventory systems or cooperating on part designs to improve quality and lower assembly costs. As part of this process, the suppliers make substantial investments in specialised assets to better serve the needs of the car companies. The Japanese carmakers have thus been able to capture many benefits of vertical integration without having to bear the associated bureaucratic costs. The parts suppliers also benefit from these relationships because they grow with the company that they supply and they share in its success.[10]

In contrast to their Japanese counterparts, US car companies historically tended to pursue formal vertical integration.[11] According to several studies, the increased bureaucratic costs of managing extensive vertical integration helped place General Motors and Ford at a disadvantage to their Japanese competition.[12] Moreover, when US car companies decided not to integrate vertically, they did not necessarily enter into cooperative long-term relationships with independent component suppliers. Instead, they tended to use their powerful position to pursue an aggressive competitive bidding strategy, playing off component suppliers against each other.[13] This mindset seems to be changing.

strategy in action 7.2

Woodside's alliances

Woodside Petroleum has grown significantly since it first became involved in the North-West Shelf project in the 1980s as one of six joint owners of the resource. The company has moved from being primarily a small gas-oriented firm that operated the North-West Shelf venture to one that covers both oil and gas. At the same time, its field of interest has moved beyond the waters of northwest Australia to the Timor Sea and now there are exploration efforts occurring in west Africa, the Gulf of Mexico and the east coast of Australia. Some of Woodside's success has no doubt occurred because of its close relationship with its biggest shareholder, Royal Dutch/Shell Group, which maintains a 34 per cent shareholding. Woodside and Shell have long had a synergistic relationship involving the transfer of technology, knowledge and particular skills. Although Shell had a bid to acquire Woodside outright in 2001 blocked on the grounds of national interest by Treasurer Peter Costello, the strong relationship between Shell and Woodside remains (no doubt strengthened by the part-ownership aspect).

More recently, part ownership of the North West Shelf gas reserves is being sold to China National Offshore Oil Company (CNOOC). In 2004, a liquefied natural gas (LNG)-buying consortium contracted to purchase a minimum of 3.3 million tonnes of LNG a year for 25 years to supply China's first LNG project in Guangdong Province. This long-term contract goes beyond a standard buy-and-sell relationship because associated with this project is the purchase of equity in the venture by CNOOC as well as support components, including the training of oil and gas executives from China in Western Australia for a period of one year each. This case illustrates taper integration, long-term contracts and elements of strategic alliances.

Source: Ferguson, A 2005, 'Woodside at full throttle', *Business Review Weekly*, vol. 27, no. 34, 1–7 September, pp. 40–3.

Building long-term cooperative relationships

Given the lack of trust and the fear of holdup that arise when one company has to invest in specialised assets to trade with another, how can companies achieve stable long-term strategic alliances? How have companies such as Toyota managed to develop enduring relationships with their suppliers?

Companies can take specific steps to ensure a long-term cooperative relationship will work and to lessen the chances of a partner reneging on an agreement. A common approach is to make investments in specialised assets and thus establish a credible commitment on both sides to build a trusting long-term relationship.[14]

Credible commitments

credible commitment
A commitment by two companies to an alliance in the form of a contract or expenditure that demonstrates their obligation to the alliance

A **credible commitment** is a believable commitment to support the development of a long-term relationship between companies. To understand the concept of credibility in this context, consider the following relationship between General Electric and IBM. General Electric is one of IBM's major suppliers of advanced semiconductor chips and many of the chips are customised to IBM's requirements. To meet IBM's specific needs, General Electric has had to make substantial investments in specialised assets that have little other value. Consequently, General Electric depends on IBM and faces the risk that IBM will take advantage of this dependence to demand lower prices. Theoretically, IBM could back up its demand with the threat to switch to another supplier. General Electric reduced this risk, however, by having IBM enter a contractual agreement that committed IBM to purchase chips from General Electric for a ten-year period. In addition, IBM agreed to share in the costs of developing the customised chips, reducing General Electric's investment in specialised assets. By publicly committing itself to a long-term contract and putting money into the development of the customised chips, IBM has essentially made a credible commitment to continue purchasing those chips from General Electric. In Australia and New Zealand, some wineries will commit to long-term contracts with selected vineyards to encourage those vineyards to adopt new processes (such as organic processes) or plant new varieties.

Maintaining market discipline

A company that has entered into a long-term relationship can become too dependent on an inefficient partner. Given that it does not have to compete with other companies in the marketplace for the company's business, the partner may lack the incentive to be cost efficient. Consequently, a company entering into a cooperative long-term relationship must be able to apply some kind of **market discipline** to its partner.

The company holds two strong cards. First, even long-term contracts are periodically renegotiated (generally every four to five years). A partner knows that if it fails to live up to its commitments, then the company may refuse to renew the contract. Second, some companies engaged in long-term relationships with suppliers use a **parallel sourcing policy**, that is, they enter into a long-term contract with two suppliers for the same part (as is the practice at Toyota, for example).[15] Although parallel sourcing normally involves two independent suppliers, some companies maintain some level of internal production of key components that may be sold internally. This approach means that the internal supplier faces competition from the market and the buyer of components can ensure that both suppliers are competitive. This arrangement gives the company a hedge against a defiant partner because each supplier knows that if it fails to comply with the agreement, then the company can switch all its business to the other. This threat is rarely made explicit because that would be against the spirit of building a cooperative long-term relationship. But the mere awareness of parallel sourcing serves to inject an element of market discipline into the relationship, signalling to suppliers that they can be replaced at short notice if the need arises.

By establishing credible commitments or maintaining market discipline, companies may be able to use long-term contracts to realise much of the value associated with vertical integration, yet not have to bear the bureaucratic costs of formal vertical integration. Note that the growing importance of just-in-time inventory systems as a way of reducing costs and increasing quality is increasing the pressure on companies to enter into long-term agreements in a wide range of industries. These agreements may become much more popular. When such agreements cannot be reached, however, formal vertical integration may be required.

Strategic outsourcing and the virtual corporation

The opposite of vertical integration is the **outsourcing** of value creation activities to subcontractors. In recent years, many enterprises have outsourced noncore activities.[16] This process typically begins with a company identifying those value creation activities that form the basis of its competitive advantage (its distinctive or core competencies). The idea is to keep performing these core value creation activities within the company. The company then reviews the remaining activities to determine whether independent suppliers could perform them more

market discipline
Instituting a process that ensures any supplies purchased through an alliance are comparable in price and quality with what is available in the market

parallel sourcing policy
The acquisition of identical inputs from different suppliers

outsourcing
The contracting out of activities normally undertaken by the company to outside suppliers

effectively and efficiently. If they can, these activities are outsourced to those suppliers. The relationships between the company and the suppliers are often structured as long-term contractual relationships, although it may make sense in some instances to manage relationships on the basis of competitive bidding. The term **virtual corporation** has been coined to describe companies that have pursued extensive strategic outsourcing.[17]

Strategic outsourcing offers several advantages.[18] First, by outsourcing a noncore activity to a supplier that is more efficient at performing that particular activity, the company may be able to reduce its own costs. Second, it may also be able to better differentiate its final product. Finally, it has been argued that strategic outsourcing enables a company to be more flexible and responsive to changing market conditions. The belief is that a company that is unencumbered by commitments to internal suppliers can switch more easily between providers of noncore value creation activities in response to changing market conditions than can a comparable company that undertakes those activities itself.

The most common activities that are outsourced are the information technology (IT) and human resources areas. Outsourcing IT activities can make sense in that they are core activities of few companies outside the IT field, yet just about all midsized and large companies have an IT function. Having experts purchase and maintain servers and software, and using an offsite help desk can significantly decrease the cost of the information technology function for many companies. Aspects of the human resources function have been outsourced for many years. Recruitment agencies find employees for all types of company. Specialist trainers conduct much of the training and development for select companies and many small to midsized companies outsource their pay function. Companies can outsource just about any activity that is not core.

The disadvantages of strategic outsourcing also need to be recognised. By outsourcing an activity, a company loses both the ability to learn from that activity and the opportunity to transform it into a distinctive competency. A further drawback of outsourcing is that the company may become too dependent on a particular supplier. In the long term, this can hurt the company if the performance of that supplier starts to deteriorate or if the supplier starts to use its power to demand higher prices from the company. Another concern is that in its enthusiasm for strategic outsourcing, a company may go too far and outsource value creation activities that are central to the maintenance of its competitive advantage. By doing so, the company may lose control over the future development of a competency and, as a result, its performance may decline. Finally, outsourcing can have a negative effect on the ability of firms to develop innovations or integrate innovations into their products. When the innovations that dominate an industry do not have to integrate with other products, then a virtual organisation can be very successful. When, however, an innovation's success is tied to changes being made in other products (such as a car manufacturer changing from a standard combustion engine to a rotary or orbital engine and then requiring changes in the exhaust system), then highly decentralised or virtual companies can be slow to change or simply not innovate. 'Virtual' may not be as virtuous as first thought when it comes to innovation.[19] Furthermore, outsourcing activities completely can leave a company unable to assess its own suppliers to make suggestions. Rolls Royce, for example, is one of the world's major suppliers of jet engines. Suppliers make much of each engine but Rolls Royce continues to conduct research into all areas of the engine to maintain a distinctive competency across the entire engine. The result is that Rolls Royce maintains patents for parts of the engine that are outsourced. By completing its own research, Rolls Royce is able to converse with suppliers knowledgeably, monitor their quality and make suggestions that will improve the product.[20] None of this is meant to imply that companies should not pursue strategic outsourcing but it does indicate that managers should carefully weigh the pros and cons of the strategy before pursuing it.

Diversification

Diversification is the third major option for a company choosing business areas in which to compete. The two main types of diversification are related diversification and unrelated diversification. Related diversification is diversification into a new business activity that is linked to a company's existing business activity (or activities) by commonality between one or more components of each activity's value chain. These links are normally based on manufacturing, marketing or technological commonalities. The diversification of Philip Morris into the brewing industry with the acquisition of Miller Brewing is an example of related diversification because there are marketing commonalities between the brewing and tobacco businesses. (Both are consumer product businesses in which competitive success depends on brand-positioning skills.) Unrelated diversification is diversification into a new business area, which has no obvious connection with any of the company's existing areas.

This section first considers how diversification can create value for a company, then examines the reasons that so much diversification apparently dissipates rather than creates value. It also accounts for the bureaucratic costs of diversification. Finally, it discusses factors that determine the choice between related and unrelated diversification.

Creating value through diversification

Most companies first consider diversification when they are generating financial resources in excess of those necessary to maintain a competitive advantage in their original or core business.[21] The question they must tackle is how to invest the excess resources to create value. The diversified company can create value in three main ways: (1) through superior internal governance, (2) by transferring competencies among businesses and (3) by realising economies of scope.

Superior internal governance

The term internal governance refers to how the top executives of a company manage (or 'govern') subunits and individuals within the company. In the context of a diversified company, governance has to do with the effectiveness of senior managers in managing businesses. Diversification can create value when the senior executives of a company manage its different business units so well that the units perform better than they would if they were independent companies.[22] That is not easy to accomplish but certain senior executives seem to have a skill for managing businesses and pushing the heads of those business units to achieve superior performance.

An examination of companies that succeed at creating value through superior internal governance reveals shared features. First, the company's different business units tend to be placed into self-contained divisions. Second, these divisions tend to be managed by senior executives in a very decentralised fashion. The executives do not get involved in the day-to-day operations of the divisions; instead, they set challenging financial goals for each division, probe the general managers of each division about their strategy for attaining these goals, monitor divisional performance and hold the general managers accountable for that performance. Third, these internal monitoring and control mechanisms are linked with progressive incentive pay systems, which reward divisional personnel for attaining or surpassing performance goals. Although this strategy sounds relatively easy to pursue, few companies have been able to do it successfully, although in Australia, Wesfarmers seems able to create value across seemingly disparate businesses with no obvious synergy.

The idea that certain executives have a 'Midas touch', with which they can achieve success time and time again, is not universally supported, even when the executives devolve authority and implement the abovementioned management practices. Certain executives may have a run of luck as much as a run of good management. Those managers who devolve considerable authority simply maximise their chances of success because they create incentives for high performance among the managers of the different divisions. For example, AMP, BHP, Mayne and Coles-Myer have faced situations in which their CEOs were considered to be underperforming and in most cases these CEOs were forced out very publicly. Yet when the largest companies appoint CEOs from outside, they appoint only people with highly successful backgrounds and still their success is not uniformly high. People who rise to this rank are intelligent, hard working and astute. The idea that certain individuals are so outstanding, even in comparison with other CEOs, that they could create value simply by managing better than other intelligent, hard-working and astute people seems a difficult concept to accept. More likely, certain managers are well suited to particular situations and roles or have a run of luck over time, which leads some people to think of them as super-CEOs.

Transfer of competencies

Companies that base their diversification strategy on transferring competencies seek out new businesses related to their existing business by one or more value creation functions, for example, manufacturing, marketing, materials management, and research and development. They may want to create value by drawing on distinctive skills in one or more of their existing value creation functions to improve the competitive position of the new business. Alternatively, they may acquire a company in a different business area in the belief that some of the skills of the acquired company can improve the efficiency of their existing value creation activities. If successful, competency transfers can lower the costs of value creation in one or more of a company's diversified businesses or enable one or more of these businesses to perform their value creation functions in a way that leads to differentiation and a premium price. The Virgin group run by Richard Branson uses competencies in marketing and cost management to build a successful business quickly. Virgin Blue airlines and Virgin Mobile are very different businesses but they have been successful on the basis of successful marketing (including the Virgin brand name) and a careful cost management approach that allows them to undercut their major competitors.

For this strategy to work, the competencies being transferred must involve activities that are important for establishing a competitive advantage. Too often, companies assume that any commonality (such as similarity in distribution channels) is sufficient for creating value.

A group of technology companies have made using competencies more broadly a way of life. Sharp, for example, was one of the first to spend large sums of money to perfect liquid crystal display (LCD) technology. The LCD was initially designed for use in the Sharp range of calculators. As it became more proficient with the technology, Sharp sought other products through which it could use its competency in LCDs. It established a joint venture with Apple to produce the Apple Newton (which subsequently failed as a result of software problems originating from Apple's side of the joint venture). It was the first to introduce a camcorder with a flip-out LCD screen on the side of the machine. It produces laptop computers in which the primary component supplied by Sharp is the LCD screen, and more recently has been a major producer of LCD televisions. Similarly, Canon has competencies in the areas of precision mechanics, fine optics and microelectronics, and every one of its products builds on at least two of these competencies (cameras, digital cameras, photocopiers, faxes, laser printers, bubble jet printers and laser copiers).[23] As a final example, Honda's competency in the area of engines led it away from producing low-powered motorcycles and into producing cars, lawnmowers, generators and other products that rely on internal combustion engines.

Economies of scope

The sharing of resources such as manufacturing facilities, distribution channels, advertising campaigns and R&D costs by two or more business units gives rise to **economies of scope**.

economies of scope
The benefits that are derived when more than one business unit in the company can use the operations of a component of the value chain

Each business unit that shares resources has to invest less in the shared functions.[24] The ANZ Bank, for example, achieves economies of scope from selling a range of products (banking services, insurance, superannuation, financial advice) through its branch network using the ANZ brand name. Similarly, some of the different parts of Coles-Myer (Target, Coles, Kmart, Myer) use the same stock management software. Strategy in action 7.3 shows how the Commonwealth Bank has used economies of scope to create value among their different businesses.

It is important to understand that economies of scope are related to economies of scale. By producing the components for the assembly operations of two distinct businesses, for example, a component manufacturing plant may be able to operate at greater capacity, realising economies of scale in addition to economies of scope. A diversification strategy based on economies of scope can therefore help a company attain a low-cost position in each of the businesses in which it operates. Diversification to realise economies of scope can be a valid way of supporting the generic business-level strategy of cost leadership.

Similarly to competency transfers, however, diversification to realise economies of scope is possible only when there are significant commonalities between one or more of the value creation functions of a company's existing and new activities. Moreover, managers need to be aware that the bureaucratic costs of coordination necessary to achieve economies of scope within a company often outweigh the value that can be created by such a strategy.[25] Consequently, the strategy should be pursued only when sharing is likely to generate a significant competitive advantage in one or more of a company's business units.

strategy in action 7.3

Commonwealth Bank

The Commonwealth Bank is the largest provider of home loans in Australia. Compared with the other three major banks in Australia, the Commonwealth Bank has always been more heavily focused on retail customers. However, the Commonwealth Bank has successfully diversified beyond traditional banking products into a range of other products that allow it to draw upon its extensive customer base. Credit cards were initially the realm of specialty companies such as American Express, Bankcard and Diners Club. However, the Commonwealth Bank, with its large customer base, has been very successful in building this business. Its Comm Insure division offers a range of insurance products and, in many cases, people with home loans through the bank are eligible to receive discounts on both home and contents insurance. In the late 1990s, CommSec was launched as a discount online share-trading facility. Since the takeover of Colonial Mutual, the Commonwealth Bank has moved much more aggressively into a range of financial investment products including managed funds, as well as superannuation.

Many of these products are unrelated in terms of the back-office operations involved or the competencies needed to be successful in each different market space. However, the basis for success in many cases comes from the economies of scope that exist by having a very large client base. Many financial products such as credit cards and share-trading accounts operate on relatively low margins. The cost of acquiring a new customer in terms of the advertising involved and the administration of setting up a new account often eat up any potential profits in the first year. However, by tapping into an existing base of customers, these costs can be minimised. Furthermore, the attractiveness of a suite of products with a single contact point (along with some discounts for high-value customers who take out multiple products) can maximise the probability of customers that are with the Commonwealth Bank for one product using other products from the bank when the time comes. It is partly for this reason that the Commonwealth Bank's diversification moves into new businesses such as share trading have been very successful.

Bureaucratic costs and the limits of diversification

Although diversification can create value for a company, it often ends up doing just the opposite. In a study that examined the diversification of 33 major US corporations over 35 years, Porter observed that the track record of corporate diversification had been dismal.[26] Porter found that most of the companies had divested many more diversified acquisitions than they had kept. He concluded that the corporate diversification strategies of most companies had dissipated value instead of creating it. More generally, a large number of academic studies support the conclusion that extensive diversification tends to depress rather than improve company profitability.[27]

One reason for the failure of diversification to achieve its aims is that the bureaucratic costs of diversification often exceed the value created by the strategy. The level of bureaucratic costs in a diversified company is a function of two factors: (1) the number of businesses in a company's portfolio and (2) how much coordination is required among the different businesses for the company to realise value from a diversification strategy.

Number of businesses

The more businesses in a company's portfolio, the more difficult it is for corporate management to remain informed about the complexities of each business. Management simply does not have the time to process all the information needed to assess objectively the strategic plan of each business unit. The information overload in extensively diversified companies may lead corporate-level management to base important resource allocation decisions on only the most superficial analysis of each business unit's competitive position. As a result, for example, a promising business unit may be starved of investment funds, while other business units receive far more cash than they can profitably reinvest in their operations. Furthermore, corporate-level management's lack of familiarity with operating affairs increases the chances that business-level managers may deceive corporate-level managers. Business-unit managers may, for example, blame poor performance on difficult competitive conditions, even when it is the consequence of poor management. Information overload within extensively diversified companies can thus result in substantial inefficiencies that cancel out the value created by diversification. These inefficiencies include the suboptimal allocation of cash resources within the company and a failure by corporate management to successfully encourage and reward aggressive profit-seeking behaviour by business-level managers.

The inefficiencies arising from information overload can be viewed as one component of the bureaucratic costs of extensive diversification. These costs can be reduced to manageable proportions if a company limits the scope of its diversification. A desire to decrease these costs was at least part of the logic behind the divesture of divisions by large companies such as CSR, Southcorp and Pacific Dunlop through the 1980s and 1990s.

Coordination among businesses

The coordination required to realise value from a diversification strategy based on competency transfers or economies of scope can also be a source of bureaucratic costs. Both the transfer of distinctive competencies and the achievement of economies of scope demand close coordination among business units. The bureaucratic mechanisms needed for this coordination give rise to bureaucratic costs.

A more serious matter, however, is that substantial bureaucratic costs can result from a company's inability to identify the unique profit contribution of a business unit that is sharing resources with another unit in an attempt to realise economies of scope. Consider a company that has two business units: one producing household products (such as liquid soap and laundry detergent) and another producing packaged food products. The products of both units are sold through supermarkets. To lower the costs of value creation, the parent company decides to pool the marketing and sales functions of each business unit. Pooling allows the business units to share the costs of a sales force (because one sales force can sell the products of both divisions) and gain economies from using the same physical distribution system. The organisational structure required may be similar to that illustrated in figure 7.4. The company is organised into three divisions: household products, food products and marketing.

Although this arrangement may create value, it can also give rise to substantial control problems and consequent bureaucratic costs. If, for example, the performance of the household products business begins to slip, then identifying who is to be held accountable — the management of the household products division or the management of the marketing division — may prove difficult. Each may blame the other for poor performance. The management of the household products division may blame the marketing policies of the marketing division, and the management of the marketing division may blame the poor quality and high costs of products produced by the household products division. Although this kind of problem can be resolved if corporate management directly audits the affairs of both divisions, doing so is costly in terms of both the time and the effort that corporate management must expend.

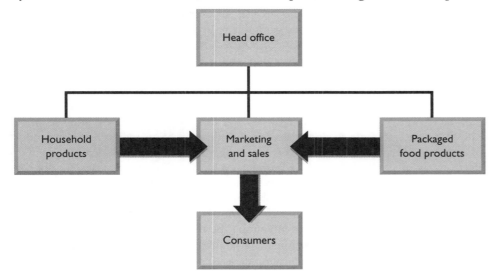

Figure 7.4:
Structure of a company sharing marketing between two business units

Now imagine the situation within a company that is trying to create value by sharing marketing, manufacturing and R&D resources across ten businesses rather than just two. The accountability problem could become far more severe in such a company. It may become so acute that the effort involved in trying to tie down accountability may create a serious information overload for corporate management. When this occurs, corporate management effectively loses control of the company. If accountability cannot be sorted out, then the consequences may include poor resource allocation decisions, a generally high level of organisational slack and an inability by corporate management to encourage and reward aggressive profit-seeking behaviour by business-level managers. All these inefficiencies can be considered part of the bureaucratic costs of diversification to realise economies of scope.

Limits of diversification

Although diversification can create value for a company, it inevitably involves bureaucratic costs. As in the case of vertical integration, the existence of bureaucratic costs places a limit on the amount of diversification that the company can profitably pursue. It makes sense for a company to diversify only as long as the value created exceeds the bureaucratic costs.

It bears repeating that the more business units there are within a company and the greater the need for coordination among them, the larger the bureaucratic costs are likely to be. A company that has 20 businesses, all trying to share resources, incurs much larger bureaucratic costs than does a company that has ten businesses with none trying to share resources. The implications of this relationship are quite straightforward: the more businesses already in a company's portfolio and the greater the need for coordination among them, the more probable it is that the value created by diversification will be outweighed by the resulting increase in bureaucratic costs. Once this occurs, the company has reached a profitable limit to the diversified scope of the enterprise.

Practising strategic management: diversification that dissipates value

The failure of so much diversification to create value is also caused by many companies diversifying for the wrong reasons. This is particularly true of diversification to pool risks or achieve greater growth, both often given by company managers as reasons for diversification.

In the case of risk pooling, the benefits arise from merging imperfectly correlated income streams to create a more stable income stream. An example of risk pooling may be a steel company's diversification into the oil and gas industry in an effort to offset the adverse effects of cyclical downturns in the steel industry. According to advocates of risk pooling, the more stable income stream reduces the risk of bankruptcy and is in the best interests of the company's shareholders.

This simple argument ignores two facts. First, shareholders can easily eliminate the risks inherent in holding an individual stock by diversifying their own portfolios, and they can do so at a much lower cost than the company can. Far from being in the best interests of stockholders, therefore, attempts to pool risks through diversification represent an unproductive use of resources. Second, research on this topic suggests that corporate diversification is not an effective way of pooling risks.[28] The business cycles of different industries are not easy to predict and, in any case, tend to be less important than a general economic downturn (which hits all industries simultaneously) in terms of their impact on profits.

As for diversification to achieve greater growth, it is not a coherent strategy because growth on its own does not create value. Growth should be the byproduct, not the objective, of a diversification strategy. Similarly, remaining a large diversified company is not reason enough to avoid divesting divisions. BHP, for example, as Australia's largest company through the 1980s and much of the 1990s, came under the threat of a takeover by Robert Holmes à Court in the late 1980s. Holmes à Court planned to dismantle the company and sell off the individual divisions (oil and gas, steel and so on). Even though such a move would have led to shareholders gaining value, the board of BHP treated it as a hostile takeover. Why? Could it have been that those in power wanted to keep the 'Big Australian' exactly that, not allowing it to be sold off to form a series of much smaller companies?

Related versus unrelated diversification

One issue that a company must resolve is whether to diversify into totally new businesses or businesses related to its existing business by value chain commonalities. The distinction is between related diversification and unrelated diversification. By definition, a related company can create value by sharing resources and transferring competencies among businesses. It can also carry out some restructuring. In contrast, because there are no commonalities between the value chains of unrelated businesses, an unrelated company cannot create value by sharing resources or transferring competencies. Unrelated diversifiers can create value only by pursuing an acquisition and restructuring strategy.

Given that related diversification can create value in more ways than unrelated diversification can, it could perhaps be the preferred strategy. In addition, related diversification is normally perceived as involving fewer risks because the company is moving into business areas top management has some knowledge of. Probably as a result of those considerations, most diversified companies display a preference for related diversification.[29] Research suggests, however, that the average related company is, at best, only marginally more profitable than the average unrelated company.[30] How can this be, if related diversification is associated with more benefits than unrelated diversification?

The answer is simple. Bureaucratic costs arise from (a) the number of businesses in a company's portfolio and (b) how much coordination is required among the different businesses to realise value from diversification. An unrelated company does not have to achieve coordination between business units, so it has to cope only with the bureaucratic costs that arise from the number of its businesses. In contrast, a related diversified company has to achieve coordination between business units to realise the value that comes from skill transfers and resource sharing. Consequently, it has to cope with the bureaucratic costs that arise both from the number of business units in its portfolio and from coordination among business units. Therefore, although related diversified companies can create value in more ways than unrelated companies can, they have to bear higher bureaucratic costs to do so. These higher costs may cancel out the higher benefits, making the strategy no more profitable than unrelated diversification.

An alternative to diversification: strategic alliances

How then is a company to choose between these strategies? The choice depends on a comparison of the relative value added and the bureaucratic costs associated with each strategy. In making this comparison, it should be noted that the opportunities for creating value from related diversification are a function of the extent of commonalities between the skills required to compete in the company's core business and the skills required to compete in other industrial and commercial areas. Few companies have been very successful using a strategy of undertaking unrelated diversification, although it could be argued that Virgin, for example, has competencies in terms of cost management and economies of scope in using its brand name broadly or that Philip Morris (cigarettes and beer) has competencies in terms of brand management.

So a company benefits from concentrating on related diversification when (a) the company's core skills are applicable to a wide variety of industrial and commercial situations and (b) the bureaucratic costs of implementation do not exceed the value that can be created through resource sharing or skill transfers. The second condition is likely to hold only for companies that are moderately diversified.

By the same logic, a company benefits from concentrating on unrelated diversification when (a) the company's core functional skills have broad application outside the company's core business; (b) the company's top management is skilled at acquiring and increasing the profitability of different businesses and (c) the bureaucratic costs of implementation do not exceed the value attained in operating this new conglomerate. The third condition, however, is unlikely to hold for companies that are highly diversified.

One way of trying to realise the value associated with diversification, without having to bear the same level of bureaucratic costs, is to enter into a strategic alliance with another company to start a new business venture. In this context, strategic alliances are agreements between two or more companies to share the costs, risks and benefits of developing new business opportunities. Many strategic alliances are constituted as formal joint ventures, in which each party has an equity stake. Other alliances take the form of a long-term contract between companies, whereby they agree to undertake some joint activity that benefits both. Agreements to work together on joint R&D projects often take this form.

Strategic alliances seem to be a particularly viable option when a company wishes to create value from transferring competencies or sharing resources among diversified businesses to realise economies of scope. Alliances offer companies a framework within which to share the resources required to establish a new business. Alternatively, alliances enable companies to swap complementary skills to produce a new range of products without a large increase in bureaucratic costs.

There is a downside to alliances. For one thing, profits must be split with an alliance partner, whereas full diversification allows a company to keep all the profits. Another problem with an alliance is that the company runs the risk of giving away critical know-how to its alliance partner, which may then use it to compete with the company. By entering into a formal joint venture, rather than a more loosely structured alliance, firms are able to provide a credible commitment because both parties will need to invest substantial amounts of capital. Finally, alliances tend not to last forever and there needs to be an appropriate exit strategy. Because circumstances will have probably changed considerably from when the initial agreement was developed, disengagement can be difficult, particularly if intellectual property is involved.

Reviewing the corporate portfolio

A central concern of corporate strategy is identifying which business opportunities a company should pursue. A common starting point is to review a company's existing portfolio of businesses activities. The purpose of such a review is to help a company determine the existing businesses in which it should continue to participate, those it should cease and those it should take up. This section discusses two different approaches to the review.

The first approach uses a set of techniques known as portfolio planning matrices.[31] Developed primarily by management consultants, these techniques are meant to compare the competitive position of the different businesses in a company's portfolio on the basis of common criteria. These techniques contain some flaws and their application has produced some bad decisions, as is shown in the following.

The second approach considered is to reconceptualise a company as a portfolio of core competencies, as opposed to a portfolio of businesses. It has been championed by Hamel and Prahalad.[32] **Corporate development** is oriented towards maintaining existing competencies, building new competencies and using them by applying them to new business opportunities.

corporate development
Decisions concerned with which business opportunities a company should pursue and how it should pursue these opportunities, including how to exit from inappropriate businesses

Portfolio planning

One of the most famous portfolio planning matrices is referred to as the growth-share matrix. The Boston Consulting Group (BCG) developed it, principally to help senior managers identify the cash flow requirements of different businesses in their portfolio and determine whether they need to change the mix of businesses in the portfolio. Reviewing the growth-share matrix illustrates both the value and the limitations of portfolio planning tools. The growth-share matrix has three main steps: (1) dividing a company into strategic business units (SBUs); (2) assessing the prospects of each SBU and comparing them by means of a matrix and (3) developing strategic objectives for each SBU.

Identifying SBUs

According to the BCG, a company must create an SBU for each economically distinct business area in which it competes. Normally, a company defines its SBUs in terms of its product markets. For example, Coles-Myer may see Coles, Myer, the variety stores (such as Kmart and Target), Officeworks and the liquor outlets (such as Liquorland, Vintage Cellars and 1st Choice) each as strategic business units.

Assessing and comparing strategic business units

Having defined SBUs, top managers then assess each according to two criteria: (1) the SBU's relative market share and (2) the growth rate of the SBU's industry. Relative market share is the ratio of an SBU's market share to the market share held by the largest rival company in its industry. If SBU X has a market share of 10 per cent and its largest rival has a market share of 30 per cent, then SBU X's relative market share is 10/30, or 0.33. Only if an SBU is a market leader in its industry will it have a relative market share greater than 1.0. If SBU Y has a market share of 40 per cent and its largest rival has a market share of 10 per cent, then SBU Y's relative market share is 40/10, or 4.0. According to the BCG, market share gives a company cost advantages from economies of scale and learning effects. An SBU with a relative market share greater than 1.0 is assumed to be farther down the experience curve and thus have a significant cost advantage over its rivals. By similar logic, an SBU with a relative market share smaller than 1.0 is assumed to lack the economies of scale and low-cost position of the market leader.

The growth rate of an SBU's industry is assessed according to whether it is faster or slower than the growth rate of the economy as a whole. BCG's position is that high-growth industries offer a more favourable competitive environment and better long-term prospects than those of slow-growth industries.

Given the relative market share and industry growth rate for each SBU, management compares SBUs by way of a matrix similar to that illustrated in figure 7.5. The horizontal dimension of this matrix measures relative market share; the vertical dimension measures industry growth rate. The centre of each circle corresponds to the position of an SBU on the two dimensions of the matrix. The size of each circle is proportional to the sales revenue generated by each business in the company's portfolio. The bigger the circle, the larger is the SBU's revenue relative to total corporate revenue.

relative market share
The ratio of an SBU's market share to the market share held by the largest rival company in the industry

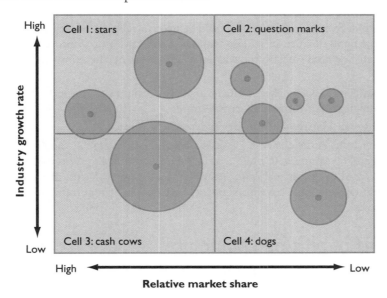

Figure 7.5:
The BCG matrix
The matrix is divided into four cells: SBUs in cell 1 are stars; those in cell 2 are question marks; those in cell 3 are cash cows; and those in cell 4 are dogs. BCG argues that these different types of SBU have different long-term prospects and different implications for cash flows.

Source: Adapted with permission from Henderson, BD 1970, 'The product portfolio', *Perspectives*, no. 66. The Boston Consulting Group 1970.

Stars

The leading SBUs in a company's portfolio are the stars. Stars have a high relative market share and are based in high-growth industries. Accordingly, they offer attractive long-term profit and growth opportunities.

Question marks

Question marks are SBUs that are relatively weak in competitive terms (that is, they have low relative market shares) but are based in high-growth industries and thus may offer opportunities

stars
Businesses that have a high relative market share and are in high-growth industries

question marks
Businesses that have a low relative market share and are in high-growth industries

for long-term profit and growth. A question mark can become a star if nurtured properly. To become a market leader, a question mark requires substantial net injections of cash: it is cash hungry. The corporate head office has to decide whether a particular question mark has the potential to become a star and is therefore worth the capital investment necessary to achieve stardom.

Cash cows

SBUs that have a high market share in low-growth industries and a strong competitive position in mature industries are **cash cows**. Their competitive strength comes from being farthest down the experience curve. They are the cost leaders in their industries. BCG argues that this position enables such SBUs to remain very profitable, although low growth implies a lack of opportunities for future expansion. BCG thus argues that the capital investment requirements of cash cows are not substantial and these businesses are depicted as generating a strong positive cash flow.

Dogs

SBUs that are in low-growth industries but have a low market share are **dogs**. They have a weak competitive position in unattractive industries and so are viewed as offering few benefits to a company. BCG suggests that such SBUs are unlikely to generate much in the way of a positive cashflow and may become cash hogs. Although offering few prospects for future growth in returns, dogs may require substantial capital investments just to maintain their low market share.

Strategic implications

The objective of the BCG portfolio matrix is to identify how corporate cash resources can best be used to maximise a company's future growth and profitability. BCG recommendations include the following approaches.

- The cash surplus from any cash cows should be used to support the development of selected question marks and nurture stars. The long-term objective is to consolidate the position of stars and turn favoured question marks into stars, making the company's portfolio more attractive.

- Question marks with the weakest or most uncertain long-term prospects should be divested to reduce demands on a company's cash resources.

- The company should leave any industry where the SBU is a dog.

- If a company lacks sufficient cash cows, stars or question marks, then it should consider acquisitions and divestments to build a more balanced portfolio. A portfolio should contain enough stars and question marks to ensure a healthy growth and profit outlook for the company and enough cash cows to support the investment requirements of the stars and question marks.

Limitations of portfolio planning

Although portfolio planning techniques may sound reasonable, if we take the BCG matrix as an example, there are at least four main flaws. First, the model is simplistic. An assessment of an SBU in terms of just two dimensions — market share and industry growth — is bound to be misleading because a host of other relevant factors should be taken into account. Although market share is undoubtedly an important determinant of an SBU's competitive position, companies can also establish a strong competitive position by differentiating their product to serve the needs of a particular segment of the market. A business having a low market share can be very profitable and have a strong competitive position in certain segments of a market. The motor vehicle manufacturer BMW is in this position but the BCG matrix would classify BMW as a dog because it has a low market share in a low-growth industry. Similarly, industry growth is not the only factor determining industry attractiveness. Many factors besides growth determine competitive intensity in an industry and thus its attractiveness.

Second, the connection between relative market share and cost savings is not as straightforward as BCG suggests. High market share does not always give a company a cost advantage. Industries in which economies of scale are not prevalent can lead to larger companies having a higher cost structure. There are other cases in which the histories of different companies lead them to have significantly different cost structures that are independent of size. Virgin Blue, for example, is considerably smaller than Qantas but universally recognised as having a much lower cost structure for several reasons, such as the aircraft used, the staff numbers required for each flight and the level of unionism. The BCG matrix would classify Virgin Blue as a dog, whereas it is relatively profitable (at least for an airline). Finally, the technologies used by big and small companies can differ. In the steel industry, minimills would be classified as dogs, yet they are often more efficient than the much larger integrated steel mills.

Third, a high market share in a low-growth industry does not necessarily result in the large positive cashflow characteristic of cash cow businesses. The BCG matrix would classify most large car manufacturers as cash cows. Yet the capital investments needed to remain competitive are so substantial in the car industry that the reverse is more likely to be true. Low-growth industries can be very competitive and staying ahead can require substantial cash investments.

Several companies and management consulting enterprises have recognised the limitations of the BCG approach and developed alternative approaches that address the above weaknesses. One better-known approach is that of McKinsey and Company, which developed a portfolio matrix that uses a much wider range of factors to assess the attractiveness of an industry in which an SBU competes, as well as the competitive position of an SBU (see figure 7.6). Included in the assessment of industry attractiveness are factors such as industry size, growth, cyclicality, competitive intensity and technological dynamism. The assessment of competitive position relies on factors such as market share and an SBU's relative position in terms of production costs, product quality, price competitiveness, distribution and innovation.

Although the approaches adopted by McKinsey represent a distinct improvement over the original BCG model, all portfolio planning techniques generally suffer from significant flaws. Most important, they fail to pay attention to the source of value creation from diversification. They treat business units as independent, whereas the units may be linked by the need to transfer skills and competencies, or to realise economies of scope. Moreover, portfolio planning approaches tend to trivialise the process of managing a large diversified company. They suggest that success is simply a matter of putting together the right portfolio of businesses, whereas success comes from managing a diversified portfolio to create value, whether by using distinctive competencies across business units, sharing resources to realise economies of scope or achieving superior governance. In diverting top management's attention away from these vital tasks and legitimising underinvestment in core business areas designated as cash cows, portfolio management techniques might have done a great disservice to the corporations that adopted them.

The corporation as a portfolio of core competencies

According to Hamel and Prahalad, a more fruitful approach to identifying different business opportunities is to reconceptualise the company as a portfolio of **core competencies** (as opposed to a portfolio of businesses) and then consider how the company may develop those competencies to sustain existing businesses and leverage them to create new business opportunities.[33] The concept of a competency is introduced in chapter 4, in discussing how distinctive competencies can form the bedrock of a company's competitive advantage. According to Hamel and Prahalad, a core competency is a central value-creating capability, that is, a core skill. They argue, for example, that Canon has core competencies in precision mechanics, fine optics, microelectronics and electronic imaging.

core competencies
The central set of knowledge in a company that, when applied, allows the company to create superior value than can competitors

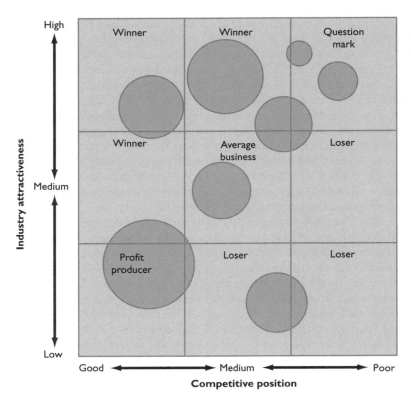

High

Medium

Low

Industry attractiveness

Winner | Winner | Question mark

Winner | Average business | Loser

Profit producer | Loser | Loser

Good ⟷ Medium ⟷ Poor

Competitive position

Figure 7.6
The McKinsey matrix

Hamel and Prahalad maintain that identifying current core competencies is the first step for a company engaged in deciding which business opportunities to pursue. Once a company has identified its core competencies, then Hamel and Prahalad advocate using a matrix similar to that shown in figure 7.7 to establish an agenda for building and using core competencies to create new business opportunities. This matrix distinguishes between existing and new competencies, and between existing and new-product markets. Each quadrant in the matrix has a title, of which the strategic implications are discussed in the following paragraphs.

New

Core competence

Existing

Premier plus 10
What new core competencies will we need to build to protect and extend our franchise in current markets?

Mega-opportunities
What new core competencies would we need to build to participate in the most exciting markets of the future?

Fill in the blanks
What is the opportunity to improve our position in existing markets by better leveraging our existing core competencies?

White spaces
What new products or services could we create by creatively redeploying or recombining our current core competencies?

Existing

New

Market

Figure 7.7:
Establishing a core competency agenda

Source: Hamel, G & Prahalad, CK 1994, *Competing for the future*, Harvard Business School Press, Boston, Massachusetts, p. 227.

Fill in the blanks

The lower left quadrant represents the company's existing portfolio of competencies and products. Fifteen years ago, Canon had competencies in precision mechanics, fine optics and microelectronics, and was active in two basic businesses: producing cameras and producing photocopiers. The company used its competencies in precision mechanics and fine optics to produce basic mechanical cameras. These two competencies plus an additional competency in microelectronics were required to produce plain-paper copiers. The phrase 'fill in the blanks' refers to the opportunity to improve the company's competitive position in existing markets by using existing core competencies. Canon was able to improve the position of its camera business by using micro-electronics skills from its copier business to support the development of cameras with electronic features, such as autofocus capabilities, as well as a range of printers (both bubble-jet and laser printers).

Premier plus 10

The upper left quadrant is referred to as 'premier plus 10'. The term is meant to suggest another important question: what new core competencies must be built today to ensure the company remains a premier provider of its existing products in ten years? Canon decided that to maintain a competitive edge in its copier business, it was going to have to build a new competency in electronic imaging (the ability to capture and store images in a digital format, as opposed to using more traditional, chemical-based photographic processes). This new competency has subsequently helped Canon to extend its product range to include laser copiers, colour copiers, scanners and digital cameras.

White spaces

The lower right quadrant is referred to as 'white spaces'. The question to be answered here is how best to fill the white space by creatively redeploying or recombining current core competencies. In Canon's case, the company has been able to recombine its established core competencies to move into micrographics products and photoprinters. The company also recently started to move into medical imaging products.

Mega-opportunities

Opportunities represented by the upper right quadrant of figure 7.7 do not overlap with the company's current market position or current competency endowment. Nevertheless, a company may choose to pursue such opportunities if they are seen as particularly attractive, significant or relevant to the company's existing business opportunities. For Canon, such a space is likely to involve the convergence of various communication and digital storage devices. Cameras and mobile phones are now combined as are video-playback and portable music devices, and phones and personal organisers. At some point, many more technologies are likely to converge in a single product, which may well represent a 'mega-opportunity'.

Similarly to more traditional tools for reviewing the corporate portfolio, such as the portfolio planning matrices discussed earlier, the framework advocated by Hamel and Prahalad helps to identify business opportunities and has clear implications for allocating resources. Its great advantage, however, is that it focuses on how a company can create value by building new competencies or recombining existing ones to enter new business areas (as Canon did with fax machines and bubble jet printers). Whereas traditional portfolio tools treat businesses as independent, Hamel and Prahalad's framework recognises the interdependencies between businesses and focuses on the opportunities for creating value by building and using competencies. In this sense, their framework is far more 'strategic' than the frameworks once advocated by BCG and others like them.

Entry strategy

Having reviewed the different businesses in the company's portfolio, corporate management may decide to enter a new business. Companies use three vehicles to enter new business areas: internal ventures, acquisitions and joint ventures. They are reviewed in the next sections.

Internal new venturing as an entry strategy

Internal new venturing is typically employed as an entry strategy when a company possesses a set of valuable competencies (resources and capabilities) in its existing businesses that it can use or recombine to enter the new business area.

As a rule, science-based companies that use their technology to create market opportunities in related areas tend to favour internal new venturing as an entry strategy, as seen in the example concerning Canon.

Even if it lacks the competencies required to compete in a new business area, a company may pursue an internal new-venturing strategy when it is entering a newly emerging or embryonic industry in which there are no established players that possess the competencies required to compete in that industry. In such a case, the option of acquiring an established enterprise possessing those competencies is ruled out, and the company may have no choice but to enter through an internal new venture.

Pitfalls of internal new venturing

Despite the popularity of the internal new-venturing strategy, its failure is reportedly high. The evidence on the failure rate of new products indicates the scope of the problem because most internal new ventures are associated with new product offerings. According to the evidence, 33–60 per cent of all new products that reach the marketplace fail to generate an adequate economic return.[34]

Acquisitions as an entry strategy

Companies often use **acquisitions** to enter a business area that is new to them when they lack important competencies (resources and capabilities) required to compete in that area, and when they can purchase at a reasonable price an incumbent company that has those competencies. Companies also have a preference for acquisitions as an entry mode when they feel the need to move fast.

The advantages of acquisitions is that a company can purchase a market leader in a strong cash position overnight, rather than spend years building up market leadership through internal development. Acquisitions are also often perceived to be somewhat less risky than internal new ventures, primarily because they involve less uncertainty. Given the nature of internal new ventures, large uncertainties are associated with projecting future profitability, revenue and cashflow. In contrast, when a company makes an acquisition, it is acquiring known profitability, revenue and market share, which reduce the uncertainty. An acquisition allows a company to buy an established business with a track record; for this reason, many companies favour acquisitions. This approach has been at the heart of Foster's' expansion from beer into the wine industry as detailed in Strategy in action 7.4.

Finally, acquisitions may be the preferred entry mode when the industry to be entered is well established and incumbent enterprises enjoy significant protection from barriers to entry. As you may recall from chapter 3, barriers to entry arise from factors associated with product differentiation (brand loyalty), absolute cost advantages and economies of scale. When these barriers are substantial, a company finds that entering an industry through internal new

strategy in action 7.4

Foster's first brewed in 1888. As part of a wave on consolidations that struck the industry in the early twentieth century after a long economic recession, Foster's merged with Carlton Brewery and four other breweries to form Carlton and United Breweries (CUB). Through much of the twentieth century, CUB (renamed Foster's in 1990) continued to grow as further consolidation in the industry occurred, becoming the premier brewer in Australia.

Beer consumption in Australia peaked in 1977–78 at 138.8 litres per person. By 1993, this figure had dropped to less than 100 litres per person. With further decline predicted, Foster's decided to take the bold move of entering the rapidly growing wine industry. However, with a history in beer, CUB entered the wine industry entirely through acquisition. The Mildara Winery was established in the late nineteenth century and merged with Wolf Blass Wines in 1991. Foster's acquired this new entity — Mildara Blass — in

1996. Next was its acquisition of Beringer Wine Estates in California for US$1.5 billion in 2001. This made Foster's a true multinational in the wine industry and catapulted it into the top ten wine companies in the world. Then in 2005, it acquired Southcorp for $3.1 billion to make it the largest quality wine company in the world. The result is that today the wine side of Foster's operations is considerably larger than the beer operations, and the vast majority of this growth in the wine operations has come not from internal growth but through acquisition.

Sources: Foster's 2005, 'History', accessed 13 October 2005, www.fosters.com.au/about/history.htm; Chessell, J 2005, 'Foster's still has some to convince', *The Age*, 22 January, accessed 13 October 2005, www.theage.com.au/news/Business/Fosters-still-has-some-to-convince/2005/01/21/1106110940311.html.

venturing can be difficult. To enter, a company may have to construct an efficient-scale manufacturing plant, undertake massive advertising to break down established brand loyalties, and quickly build up distribution outlets, all goals that are hard to achieve and likely to involve substantial expenditures. In contrast, by acquiring an established enterprise, a company can circumvent most barriers to entry. It can purchase a market leader, which already benefits from substantial economies of scale and brand loyalty. The greater the barriers to entry, the more likely it is that acquisitions will be the favoured entry mode. (The attractiveness of an acquisition is predicated, however, on the assumption that an incumbent company can be acquired for less than it would cost to enter the same industry by way of an internal new venture; something that is often not possible.)

For the reasons noted, acquisitions have long been a popular vehicle for expanding the scope of a company into new business areas. Despite their popularity, however, many acquisitions fail to add value for the acquiring company and often end up dissipating value. A study by Mercer Management Consulting looked at 150 acquisitions (worth more than US$500 million each) that were undertaken between January 1990 and July 1995.[35] The Mercer study concluded that 50 per cent of these acquisitions ended up eroding or substantially eroding shareholder value, while another 33 per cent created only marginal returns. Just 17 per cent of the acquisitions were judged to be successful.

More generally, there is a wealth of evidence from academic research suggesting that many acquisitions fail to realise their expected benefits.[36] In a major study of the postacquisition performance of companies, Ravenscraft and Scherer conclude that many good companies were acquired and, on average, their profits and market shares declined following acquisition.[37] They also note that a smaller but substantial subset of those good companies experienced traumatic difficulties, which ultimately led to the acquiring company selling them. In other words, Ravenscraft and Scherer's evidence suggests that many acquisitions destroy rather than create value, as does that presented by Mercer Management Consulting.

Why do so many acquisitions apparently fail to create value? There seem to be four major reasons: (a) companies often experience difficulties when trying to integrate divergent corporate cultures; (b) companies overestimate the potential economic benefits from an acquisition; (c) acquisitions tend to be very expensive and (d) companies often do not adequately screen their acquisition targets.

Postacquisition integration

Having made an acquisition, the acquiring company has to integrate the acquired business into its own organisational structure. Integration can entail the adoption of common management and financial control systems, the joining of operations from the acquired and the acquiring company, or the establishment of links to share information and personnel. When integration is attempted, many unexpected problems can occur. They stem from differences in corporate cultures. After an acquisition, many acquired companies experience high management turnover, possibly because their employees do not like the acquiring company's way of doing things.[38] Research evidence suggests that the loss of management talent and expertise — to say nothing of the damage from constant tension between the businesses — can materially harm the performance of the acquired unit.[39]

Overestimation of the economic benefits

Even when companies achieve integration, they often overestimate the potential for creating value by joining together different businesses. They overestimate the strategic advantages that can be derived from the acquisition and so pay more for the target company than it is probably worth. Roll has attributed this tendency to hubris on the part of top management: according to Roll, top managers typically overestimate their ability to create value from an acquisition, primarily because rising to the top of a corporation has given them an exaggerated sense of their own capabilities.[40]

The expense of acquisitions

Acquisitions of companies whose stock is publicly traded tend to be expensive. When a company bids to acquire the stock of another enterprise, the stock price is frequently bid up in the acquisition process. This is particularly likely to occur in the case of contested bids, where two or more companies simultaneously bid for control of a single target company. The acquiring company must consequently often pay a premium over the current market value of the target. For example, Foster's paid $4.26 per share for Southcorp in 2005 after the shares spent most of 2004 between $3 and $3.50. Given this premium of about 30 per cent, Foster's will have to find significant synergies or additional value in the business to make the takeover worthwhile.

Inadequate preacquisition screening

After researching acquisitions made by 20 different companies, Haspeslagh and Jemison concluded that one reason for the failure of acquisitions is management's inadequate attention to preacquisition screening.[41] It found that many companies decide to acquire other companies without thoroughly analysing the potential benefits and costs. After the acquisition has been completed, the companies discover that instead of a well-run business, they have bought a troubled organisation. Alternatively, though less commonly, they find that their customers have moved to new suppliers. Takeovers of service companies are particularly susceptible here because often some of the most senior employees move elsewhere. With consultancies, advertising agencies, law firms and the like, clients are more likely to follow the people they know rather than remain with the acquired company, where they will need to develop new relationships.

Joint ventures as an entry strategy

joint venture
A business that involves two or more companies operating in a cooperative manner

The most common reason for using **joint ventures** to enter a business is to use the resources and competencies held by the partner company. To illustrate, consider how News Corporation has regularly used joint ventures to expand its business. The Fox Studios in Sydney are the largest movie production centre in Australia. News Corporation had filmmaking capacity through its subsidiary 20th Century Fox, but was not experienced in the real estate side of the business. For the real estate component of the Fox Studios business (including all of the buildings on site), News Corporation established a joint venture with one of Australia's largest real estate firms, Lend Lease. Lend Lease is well known for its specialist buildings capability because it offers services in project management, construction, development and capital structuring. The project has been a success, producing hit movies including *Superman returns* and *Star Wars: Revenge of the Sith*. In much the same way, News Corporation entered into a joint venture, under the name of Foxtel, for its cable television operations in Australia. Its partner is Telstra, which provides the cable. News Corporation, through its various Fox subsidiaries, provides the content. For Telstra, the benefits accrue because its cable infrastructure can generate rents far in excess of what it would generate if it just supplied high-speed Internet access. At the same time, News Corporation is able to focus on being a media company and not have to involve itself in infrastructure projects.

Beyond particular resources and competencies that each party contributes to the venture, joint ventures may also be formed as part of an effort to create a standard in the market, to leverage key knowledge of one firm to gain economies of scale, to help speed up market entry and to limit the potential for overcapacity in the market (should both players enter the market).

Joint ventures often fail because of the incompatibility of partners in terms of their respective goals, level of commitment to the venture, internal culture capacity for risk and resources and capabilities. In addition, firms often take a different perspective to learning and how knowledge should be shared. Finally, circumstances change and sometimes the venture is simply made untenable or at least impracticable.

Summary

The purpose of this chapter is to examine the different corporate-level strategies that companies pursue to maximise their value. The chapter makes the following main points.

▶ Corporate strategies should add value to a corporation, enabling it — or one or more of its business units — to perform one or more of the value creation functions at a lower cost or in a way that allows differentiation and brings a premium price.

▶ Concentrating on a single business allows a company to focus its total managerial, financial, technological and physical resources and capabilities on competing successfully in one area. It also ensures the company sticks to doing what it knows best.

▶ Vertical integration can enable a company to achieve a competitive advantage by helping build barriers to entry, facilitating investments in specialised assets, protecting product quality and helping improve scheduling between adjacent stages in the value chain.

▶ The disadvantages of vertical integration include (a) cost disadvantages if a company's internal source of supply is high cost and (b) lack of flexibility when technology is changing fast or demand is uncertain.

▶ The strategic outsourcing of noncore value creation activities may allow a company to lower its costs, better differentiate its product offering and make better use of scarce resources, while also enabling it to respond rapidly to changing market conditions. Strategic outsourcing may have a detrimental effect, however, if the company outsources important value creation activities or becomes too dependent on key suppliers of those activities.

▶ Diversification can create value through the pursuit of a restructuring strategy, competency transfers and the realisation of economies of scope.

- The bureaucratic costs of diversification are a function of (a) how many independent business units are within the company and (b) the extent of coordination among them.

- Diversification motivated by a desire to pool risks or achieve greater growth is often associated with the dissipation of value.

- Strategic alliances can enable companies to realise many of the benefits of related diversification without having to bear the same level of bureaucratic costs. When entering an alliance, however, a company runs the risk of giving away key technology to its partner. This risk can be minimised if a company obtains a credible commitment from its partner.

- A common way of starting to identify which business opportunities to pursue is to review a company's existing portfolio of business activities. One approach to this uses a set of techniques known as portfolio planning matrices. The purpose of these techniques is to compare the competitive position of the different businesses in a company's portfolio on the basis of common criteria.

- A second approach to the corporate development process, championed by Hamel and Prahalad, reconceptualises a company as a portfolio of core competencies (as opposed to a portfolio of businesses). In this approach, corporate development is oriented towards maintaining existing competencies, building new competencies and leveraging competencies by applying them to new business opportunities.

- The advantage of Hamel and Prahalad's framework is that it focuses explicitly on how a company can create value by building new competencies or by recombining existing competencies to enter new business areas. Traditional portfolio planning matrices treat businesses as independent but Hamel and Prahalad's framework recognises the interdependencies among businesses and focuses on the opportunities for creating value by building and leveraging competencies.

- To enter a new business area, acquisitions may be favoured when the company lacks important competencies (resources and capabilities) required to compete in an area, but when it can purchase, at a reasonable price, an incumbent company that has those competencies.

- Many acquisitions fail as a result of poor postacquisition integration, an overestimation of the value that can be created from an acquisition, the high cost of acquisition and poor preacquisition screening. Guarding against acquisition failure requires structured screening, good bidding strategies and positive attempts to integrate the acquired company into the acquiring company.

- Joint ventures may be the preferred entry strategy when (a) the risks and costs of setting up a new business unit are more than the company is willing to assume on its own and (b) the company can increase the probability of successfully establishing a new business by teaming up with another company that has skills and assets complementing its own.

Practising strategic management

Review questions

1. Under what conditions might a firm wish to vertically integrate?
2. What are some of the disadvantages associated with diversification?
3. How can companies limit the potential for opportunistic behaviour by a trading partner when they engage in a strategic alliance as an alternative to vertical integration?
4. What are some of the advantages of joint ventures?

Discussion questions

5. Why do barriers to entry rarely form a good reason to vertically integrate? Use an example (real or hypothetical) to illustrate your answer.
6. What are some of the problems using portfolio planning techniques?
7. If Qantas or Air New Zealand were to enter the car rental business, what entry strategy would you recommend it pursue? Do you think such a diversification move could or would make sense?
8. When is a company likely to choose related diversification and when is it likely to choose unrelated diversification? Discuss with reference to an electronics manufacturer and an ocean shipping company.

Applied questions

9. Strategy in action 7.3 discusses using a common customer base as the primary basis for diversification within the Commonwealth Bank. How far do you think this diversification can go? What are potential business areas into which the Commonwealth Bank could move? Could it move beyond basic consumer-oriented financial products? What will limit how far the Commonwealth Bank can diversify?
10. Microsoft has moved from operating systems software (i.e. Windows) to application software (such as Microsoft Word and Excel) to gaming hardware (Xbox). Using Hamel and Prahalad's framework shown in figure 7.7, how might the firm move into the 'white space' quadrant?

Small-group exercise

Comparing vertical integration strategies

Break into a group of three to five people. Then read the following description of the activities of Quantum Corporation and Seagate Technologies, both of which manufacture computer disk drives. On the basis of this description, outline the pros and cons of a vertical integration strategy. Which strategy do you think makes most sense in the context of the computer disk drive industry?

Quantum Corporation and Seagate Technologies are both major producers of disk drives for personal computers and workstations. The disk drive industry is characterised by sharp fluctuations in the level of demand, intense price competition, rapid technological change and product lifecycles of 12 to no more than 18 months. In recent years, Quantum and Seagate have pursued very different vertical integration strategies. Seagate is a vertically integrated manufacturer of disk drives, both designing and manufacturing the bulk of its own disk drives. Quantum specialises in design, while outsourcing most of its manufacturing to independent suppliers, including, most importantly, Matsushita Kotobuki Electronics (MKE) of Japan. Quantum makes only its newest and most expensive products in-house. Once a new drive is perfected and ready for large-scale manufacturing, Quantum turns over manufacturing to MKE. MKE and Quantum have cemented their partnership over eight years. At each stage in designing a new product, Quantum's engineers send the newest drawings to a production team at MKE. MKE examines the drawings and is constantly proposing changes that make new disk drives easier to manufacture. When the product is ready for manufacture, eight to ten Quantum engineers travel to MKE's plant in Japan for at least a month to work on production ramp-up.

Article file

Find an example of a company whose vertical integration or diversification strategy appears to have dissipated rather than created value. Identify why this has happened and what the company should do to rectify the situation.

Exploring the Web

Visiting Woolworths

Visit the Woolworths website (www.woolworthslimited.com.au). Using the information contained within that website, answer the following questions.

1. Review Woolworth's portfolio of major businesses. Does this portfolio make sense from a value creation perspective? Why?

2. What (if any) changes would you make to Woolworth's portfolio of businesses? Why would you make these changes?

3. What (if any) core competencies do you think are held in common by one or more of Woolworth's major business units? Is there any evidence that Woolworths creates new businesses by leveraging its core competencies?

General task

By searching through information sources on the Internet, find an example of a company that has recently restructured its portfolio of businesses. Identify and evaluate the strategic rationale behind this restructuring. Does it make sense?

Strategic management project

Module 7

This module requires you to assess the vertical integration and diversification strategy being pursued by your company. With the information you have at your disposal, undertake the following tasks and answer the following questions.

1. How vertically integrated is your company? If your company does have vertically integrated operations, is it pursuing a strategy of taper or full integration?

2. How diversified is your company? If your company is already diversified, is it pursuing a related diversification strategy, an unrelated diversification strategy or a mix of the two?

3. Assess the potential for your company to create value through vertical integration. In reaching your assessment, also consider the bureaucratic costs of managing vertical integration.

4. On the basis of your assessment in question 3, do you think your company should (a) outsource some operations that are performed in-house or (b) bring some operations in-house that are outsourced? Justify your recommendations.

5. Is your company involved in any long-term cooperative relationships with suppliers or buyers? If so, how are these relationships structured? Do you think that these relationships add value to the company? Why?

6. Is there any potential for your company to enter into (additional) long-term cooperative relationships with suppliers or buyers? If so, how might these relationships be structured?

7. Assess the potential for your company to create value through diversification. In reaching your assessment, also consider the bureaucratic costs of managing diversification.

8. On the basis of your assessment in question 7, do you think your company should (a) sell off some diversified operations or (b) pursue additional diversification? Justify your recommendations.

9. Is your company trying to transfer skills or realise economies of scope by entering into strategic alliances with other companies? If so, how are these relationships structured? Do you think that these relationships add value to the company? Why?

10. Is there any potential for your company to transfer skills or realise economies of scope by entering into (additional) strategic alliances with other companies? If so, how might these relationships be structured?

Additional resources

Chesbrough, H & Teece, D 1996, 'When is virtual virtuous? Organizing for innovation', *Harvard Business Review*, January–February, pp. 65–73. (A discussion of virtual organisations.)

Dyer, JH 2001, 'How to make strategic alliances work', *MIT Sloan Management Review*, vol. 42, no. 4, pp. 37–43. (A discussion of strategic alliances.)

Roberts, E 2001, 'Ally or acquire?', *MIT Sloan Management Review*, vol. 43, no. 1, 2001, pp. 26–34. (A discussion of alliances versus acquisitions.)

End notes

1. Peters, TJ & Waterman, RH 1982, *In search of excellence*, Harper & Row, New York.

2. Harrian, KR 1984, 'Formulating vertical integration strategies', *Academy of Management Review*, vol. 9, pp. 638–52.

3. This is the essence of the argument made by Chandler, AD 1962, *Strategy and structure*, MIT Press, Cambridge, Massachusetts. The same argument is made by Pfeffer, J & Salancik, GR 1978, *The external control of organizations*, Harper & Row, New York. See also Harrigan, KR 1985a, *Strategic flexibility*, Lexington Books, Lexington, Massachusetts; —— 1985b, 'Vertical integration and corporate strategy', *Academy of Management Journal*, vol. 28, pp. 397–425; Scherer, FM 1981, *Industrial market structure and economic performance*, Rand McNally, Chicago.

4. This section is based on the transaction cost approach popularised by Williamson, OE 1985, *The economic institutions of capitalism*, Free Press, New York.

5. Williamson, op. cit. For recent empirical work that uses this framework, see Poppo, L & Zenger, T 1998, 'Testing alternative theories of the firm: transaction cost, knowledge-based, and measurement explanations for make or buy decisions in information services', *Strategic Management Journal*, vol. 19, pp. 853–78.

6. Williamson, op. cit.

7. Chandler, AD 1977, *The visible hand*, Harvard University Press, Cambridge, Massachusetts.

8. Harrigan 1985a, op. cit., pp. 67–87.

9. For a detailed theoretical rationale for this argument, see Jones, GR & Hill, CWL 1988, 'A transaction cost analysis of strategy-structure choice', *Strategic Management Journal*, vol. 9, pp. 159–72.

10. Martin, X, Mitchell, W & Swaminathan, A 1995, 'Recreating and extending Japanese automobile buyer-supplier links in North America', *Strategic Management Journal*, vol. 16, pp. 589–619; Hill, CWL 1995, 'National institutional structures, transaction cost economizing, and competitive advantage', *Organization Science*, vol. 6, pp. 119–31.

11. Standard & Poor's 1993, 'Autos — auto parts', *Industry Surveys*, New York, 24 June.

12. See Womack, J, Jones, D & Roos, D 1990, *The machine that changed the world*, Rawson Associates, New York; Richardson, J 1993, 'Parallel sourcing and supplier performance in the Japanese automobile industry', *Strategic Management Journal*, vol. 14, pp. 339–50.

13. Mudambi, R & Helper, S 1998, 'The close but adversarial model of supplier relations in the US auto industry', *Strategic Management Journal*, vol. 19, pp. 775–92.

14. Williamson, op. cit. See also Dyer, JH 1997, 'Effective inter-firm collaboration: how firms minimize transaction costs and maximize transaction value', *Strategic Management Journal*, vol. 18, pp. 535–56.

15. Richardson, op. cit.

16. Davidow, WH & Malone, MS 1992, *The virtual corporation*, Harper & Row, New York.

17. ibid.

18. ibid; Chesbrough, HW & Teece, DJ 1996, 'When is virtual virtuous? Organizing for innovation', *Harvard Business Review*, January–February, pp. 65–74.

19. ibid.

20. Brusoni, S, Prencipe, A & Pavitt, K 2001, 'Knowledge specialization, organizational coupling, and the boundaries of the firm: why do firms know more than they make?', *Administrative Science Quarterly*, vol. 46, pp. 597–621.

21. This resource-based view of diversification can be traced to Penrose, E 1959, The theory of the growth of the firm, Oxford University Press, Oxford.

22. See, for example, Jones & Hill, op. cit.; Williamson, OE 1975, *Markets and hierarchies analysis and antitrust implications: a study in the economics of internal organizations*, Free Press, New York, pp. 132–75.

23. Prahalad, CK & Hamel, G 1990, 'The core competence of the corporation', *Harvard Business Review*, vol. 68, pp. 79–91.

24. Teece, DJ 1980, 'Economies of scope and the scope of the enterprise', *Journal of Economic Behavior and Organization*, vol. 3, pp. 223–47. For recent empirical work on this topic, see St John, CH & Harrison, JS 1999, 'Manufacturing based relatedness, synergy and coordination', *Strategic Management Journal*, vol. 20, pp. 129–45.

25. Thomas, T 2000, 'Big five insist low audit fees are not baits', *Business Review Weekly*, 7 July, p. 83.

26. Porter, ME 1987, 'From competitive advantage to corporate strategy', *Harvard Business Review*, May–June, pp. 43–59.

27. For reviews of the evidence, see Ramanujam, V & Varadarajan, P 1989, 'Research on corporate diversification: a synthesis', *Strategic Management Journal*, vol. 10, pp. 523–51; Dess, G, Hennart, JF, Hill, CWL & Gupta, A 1995, 'Research issues in strategic management', *Journal of Management*, vol. 21, pp. 357–92.

28. For evidence, see Hill, CWL 1983, 'Conglomerate performance over the economic cycle', *Journal of Industrial Economics*, vol. 32, pp. 197–212; Mueller, DTC 1977, 'The effects of conglomerate mergers', *Journal of Banking and Finance*, vol. 1, pp. 315–47.

29. For example, see Hill, CWL 1985, 'Diversified growth and competition', *Applied Economics*, vol. 17, pp. 827–47; Rumelt, RP 1974, *Strategy, structure and economic performance*, Harvard Business School Press, Boston, Massachusetts. See also Jones & Hill, op. cit.

30. See Christensen, HK & Montgomery, CA 1981, 'Corporate economic performance: diversification strategy versus market structure', *Strategic Management Journal*, vol. 2, pp. 327–43; Jones & Hill, op. cit.; Dess et al., op. cit.; Hill, CWL 1994, 'The role of headquarters in the multidivisional firm', in Rumelt, R, Teece, DJ & Schendel, D (eds), *Fundamental issues in strategy research*, Harvard Business School Press, Boston, pp. 297–321.

31. Hofer, CW & Schendel, D 1979, *Strategy formulation: analytical concepts*, West, St Paul, Minnesota; Bettis, RA & Hall, WK 1981, 'Strategic portfolio management in the multibusiness firm', *California Management Review*, vol. 24, pp. 23–8.

32. Hamel, G & Prahalad, CK 1994, *Competing for the future*, Harvard Business School Press, Boston, Massachusetts.

33. ibid.

34. See Booz Allen & Hamilton 1982, 'New products management for the 1980s'; Page, AL 1991, 'PDMA's new product development practices survey: performance and best practices', paper at PDMA 15th Annual International Conference, Boston, Massachusetts, 16 October; Mansfield, E 1981, 'How economists see R&D', *Harvard Business Review*, November–December, pp. 98–106.

35. Warner, J, Templeman, J & Horn, R 1995, 'The case against mergers', *Business Week*, 30 October, pp. 122–34.

36. For evidence on acquisitions and performance, see Caves, RE 1989, 'Mergers, takeovers, and economic efficiency', *International Journal of Industrial Organization*, vol. 7, pp. 151–74; Jensen, MC & Ruback, RS 1983, 'The market for corporate control: the scientific evidence', *Journal of Financial Economics*, vol. 11, pp. 5–50; Roll, R 1989, 'Empirical evidence on takeover activity and shareholder wealth', in Coffee, JC, Lowenstein, L & Rose, S (eds), *Knights, raiders and targets*, Oxford University Press, Oxford; Shleifer, A & Vishny, R 1991, 'Takeovers in the 60s and 80s: evidence and implications', *Strategic Management Journal*, vol. 12, pp. 51–9; Brush, TH 1996, 'Predicted changes in operational synergy and post-acquisition performance of acquired businesses', *Strategic Management Journal*, vol. 17, pp. 1–24.

37. Ravenscraft, DJ & Scherer, FM 1987, *Mergers, selloffs, and economic efficiency*, Brookings Institution, Washington DC.

38. See Walsh, JP 1988, 'Top management turnover following mergers and acquisitions', *Strategic Management Journal*, vol. 9, pp. 173–83.

39. See Cannella, AA & Hambrick, DC 1993, 'Executive departure and acquisition performance', *Strategic Management Journal*, vol. 14, pp. 137–52.

40. Roll, R 1986, 'The hubris hypothesis of corporate takeovers', *Journal of Business*, vol. 59, pp. 197–216.

41. Haspeslagh, P & Jemison, D 1991, *Managing acquisitions*, Free Press, New York.

Strategy in the global environment

learning objectives

After studying this chapter, you should be able to:

- appreciate how the national environment in which a company operates affects the company's competitiveness

- understand why companies can profit from global expansion

- describe the pressures for centralisation and the pressures for local responsiveness

- discuss the types of entry strategy available to companies, along with the benefits of each type

- appreciate when and why to use strategic alliances.

BlueScope Steel in China

BlueScope Steel initially entered China in the 1990s when it was part of BHP. It has slowly moved aspects of its operations away from Australia and in 2004–05, its Asian sales were about $1 billion (approximately one-eighth of the company's total), with these Asian sales being roughly evenly split between South-East Asia and China. The strategy for China is based around being a premium niche player, primarily in the areas of providing customer roofing or walling sheets.

The initial ambitions of the steel group within BHP were put on hold following the Tiananmen Square massacre in 1989. Then in 1998, its fledgling operations were again slowed with the Asian currency crisis, and most recently the merger of BHP and Billiton put a temporary hold on developments for a year or so. However, BlueScope sees Asia, and especially China, as a critical market for the future, and so is moving quickly to develop a strong position in the region. BlueScope has attained manufacturing facilities thus far in Indonesia, Malaysia and Thailand. In 2004, BlueScope bought Butler Manufacturing for $144 million. Central to this purchase were Butler's Chinese operations, which focused on production of pre-engineered buildings, including custom roofing and wall sheet products. This made China the first market for BlueScope in which they sought to sell both steel components as well as pre-engineered buildings. The next step is to pursue other opportunities more aggressively, which include a $280 million investment in Suzhou that was starting to get under way in late 2005.

Even though BlueScope Steel is very much an Australian company, it has adopted a multidomestic strategy whereby each regional market is treated as discrete. This means that steel is sourced locally wherever possible from local suppliers and each country has its own distribution and sales network. The other outcome of this country-by-country approach is that management takes place at a country level rather than specific activities being managed in the value chain. Country managers have the ability to develop specific strategies for that particular country, and the acquisition of Butler and its pre-engineered buildings operations (making this a company first for BlueScope) is a classic example.

With an orientation on local operations, the focus on Australia has also lessened through the company. For example, all training used to be conducted in Australia. However, specialised training for BlueScope's 1300-strong Chinese workforce in now conducted in Malaysia. Training is cheaper in Malaysia and just as convenient because there are Malaysian manufacturing facilities. Furthermore, it produces local synergies for the different Asian operations.

China is now the largest producer of steel in the world (though it still lacks the capacity to produce very high-value, thin rolled steel and strip casting). Companies such as Baoshan Steel are aligning themselves with world leaders such as POSCO (from Korea) and Nippon Steel (from Japan) as part of a process to improve their ability to manufacture high-value-added steel. More and more companies are likely to move into the downstream operations in terms of steel coating and fabrication: the core business of BlueScope. Consequently, BlueScope will need to continue to either maintain a very distinct niche position, increase in size considerably to attain significant economies of scale or seek to differentiate its product in several ways.

Source: James, D 2005, 'Strategy in steel', *Business Review Weekly*, vol. 27, no. 37, 22–28 September.

Overview

This chapter covers issues of an international nature that affect the strategy process. Initially, it considers the national environment and how this affects the ability of companies to be competitive in particular locations. By considering four attributes of the national environment, it is possible to show why many industries tend to cluster in particular locations, such as ceramic tiles in Italy, consumer electronics in Japan and software development in parts of the United States. The implication is that some countries provide better opportunities than others do for different types of activity.

After covering the role of the national environment in affecting a company's performance, the chapter examines the strategies companies adopt when they expand outside their domestic marketplace. At one extreme, a company can centralise its operations and sell the same basic product worldwide. A company such as Coca-Cola does this with its global brands. At the other extreme, companies can account for the tastes and preferences of consumers in different countries and customise their products for each different national market, which is more the approach being taken by BlueScope as it expands through Asia. This sort of strategy is likely to limit the ability for companies to attain significant economies of scale, however, because customisation tends to lead to rising costs. This tension between how much to standardise and how much to customise is a fundamental issue that companies need to resolve.

This issue leads to further considerations of the choice of foreign markets to enter, when to enter them and on what scale. The choice of entry mode is also an issue, with companies being able to enter foreign markets using different means, including exporting, licensing, establishing joint ventures or setting up wholly owned subsidiaries. The chapter closes with a review of the benefits and costs of entering strategic alliances with global competitors.

The nation-state and competitive advantage

Despite the globalisation of production and markets, many of the most successful companies in certain industries are still clustered in a few countries. Many of the world's most successful biotechnology and computer companies, for example, are based in the United States, many of the world's most successful consumer electronics companies are based in Japan and many of the world's most successful chemical and engineering companies are based in Germany. This suggests that the nation-state within which a company is based may have an important bearing on the competitive position of that company in the global marketplace.

Companies need to understand how national factors can affect competitive advantage, because then they will be able to identify (a) where their most significant competitors are likely to be and (b) where they may want to locate certain productive activities. Seeking to take advantage of US expertise in biotechnology, many foreign companies have set up research facilities in US locations such as San Diego, Boston and Seattle, where US biotechnology companies tend to be clustered. Similarly, in an attempt to take advantage of Japanese success in consumer electronics, many electronics companies have set up research and production facilities in Japan, often in conjunction with Japanese partners.

In a study of national competitive advantage, Porter identified four attributes of a nation-state that have an important impact on the global competitiveness of companies located within that nation:

- *factor endowments:* a nation's factors of production, such as skilled labour or the infrastructure necessary to compete in a given industry
- *local demand conditions:* the nature of domestic demand for the industry's product or service
- *competitiveness of related and supporting industries:* the presence or absence of supplier industries and related industries that are internationally competitive

- *strategy, structure and rivalry:* the conditions in the nation governing how companies are created, organised and managed, and the nature of domestic rivalry.[1]

Porter speaks of these four attributes as constituting 'the diamond' (see figure 8.1). He argues that firms are most likely to succeed in industries or industry segments in which conditions in terms of the four attributes are favourable. He also argues that the diamond's attributes form a mutually reinforcing system, in which the effect of one attribute depends on the state of others.

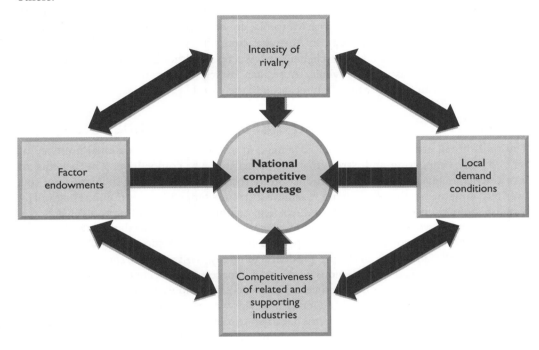

Figure 8.1:
National competitive advantage

Factor endowments

Porter follows basic economic theory in stressing that **factor conditions** — the cost and quality of factors of production — are a prime determinant of the competitive advantage that certain nations may have in certain industries. Factors of production include basic factors, such as land, labour, capital and raw materials, and advanced factors, such as technological know-how (i.e. managerial sophistication) and physical infrastructure (roads, railways, ports and so on). The competitive advantage that the United States enjoys in biotechnology may be explained by the presence of certain advanced factors of production — technological know-how, for example — in combination with some basic factors, such as a pool of relatively low-cost venture capital that can be used to fund risky startups in industries such as biotechnology. In much the same way, Australian wine companies have been internationally successful on the basis of the right agricultural conditions, a knowledgeable workforce in the domestic industry and support via extensive scientific input from the Australian Grape and Wine Research Council.

factor conditions
The factors of production, such as skilled labour and infrastructure, that a nation has to support an industry

Local demand conditions

Porter emphasises the role of **local demand conditions** in providing the impetus for 'upgrading' competitive advantage. Companies are typically most sensitive to the needs of their closest customers. The characteristics of home demand are particularly important in shaping the attributes of domestically made products and creating pressures for innovation and quality. Porter argues that a nation's companies gain competitive advantage if their domestic

local demand conditions
The nature and level of demand for the industry's product or service

consumers are sophisticated and demanding. Sophisticated and demanding consumers pressure local companies to meet high standards of product quality and produce innovative products. Porter notes that Japan's sophisticated and knowledgeable buyers of cameras helped stimulate the Japanese camera industry to improve product quality and introduce innovative models. A similar example can be found in the cellular phone equipment industry, in which sophisticated and demanding local customers in Scandinavia helped push Nokia of Finland and Ericsson of Sweden to invest in cellular phone technology long before demand for cellular phones took off in other developed nations. As a result, Nokia and Ericsson (now merged with Sony to constitute Sony-Ericsson), together with Motorola, are dominant players in the global cellular telephone equipment industry today. In Australia, compulsory bicycle helmet legislation has led to a high level of demand for bicycle helmets. As a result, although Australia has an almost negligible bicycle industry as a whole, Australian bicycle helmet manufacturers (such as Rosebank) successfully export their helmets around the world.

Competitiveness of related and supporting industries

related and supporting industries
Industries that are either upstream or downstream of the focus industry or link to the focus industry through other means such as complementary technologies

The third broad attribute of national advantage in an industry is the national presence of related and supporting industries that are internationally competitive. The benefits of investments in advanced factors of production by related and supporting industries can spill over into an industry, thereby helping it achieve a strong competitive position internationally. Swedish strength in fabricated steel products (e.g. ball bearings and cutting tools) has drawn on strengths in Sweden's speciality steel industry. Technological leadership in the US semi-conductor industry until the mid-1980s provided the basis for US success in PCs and several other technically advanced electronic products. Similarly, Switzerland's success in pharma-ceuticals is closely linked to its previous international success in the technologically related dye industry. One consequence of this process is that successful industries within a country tend to be grouped into 'clusters' of related industries. This was one of the most pervasive findings of Porter's study. One such cluster is the German textile and apparel sector, which includes high-quality cotton, wool, synthetic fibres, sewing machine needles and a wide range of textile machinery. Another example occurs in Australia's software industry, which is strong in a few areas. One of those is mine control software, which has developed in line with Australia's extensive mining operations.

Strategy, structure and rivalry

The fourth broad attribute of national competitive advantage in Porter's model is the strategy, structure and rivalry of companies within a nation. Porter makes two important points here. First, different nations are characterised by different 'management ideologies', which either help them or do not help them build national competitive advantage. Porter notes the predom-inance of engineers in the top management of German and Japanese companies. He attributes this to the companies' emphasis on improving manufacturing processes and product design. In contrast, Porter notes a predominance of people with finance backgrounds in the top manage-ment of many US companies. He links this to the lack of attention that many US companies paid to improving manufacturing processes and product design, particularly during the 1970s and 1980s. He also argues that the dominance of finance has led to a corresponding over-emphasis on maximising short-term financial returns. According to Porter, one consequence of these different management ideologies has been a relative loss of US competitiveness in those engineering-based industries in which manufacturing processes and product design issues are all important (such as motor vehicles).

Porter's second point is that there is a strong association between vigorous domestic rivalry and the creation and persistence of competitive advantage in an industry. Vigorous domestic rivalry induces companies to look for ways of improving efficiency, which in turn makes them better international competitors. Domestic rivalry creates pressures to innovate, improve quality, reduce costs and invest in upgrading advanced factors. All this helps create world-class competitors. As an illustration, Porter cites the case of Japan:

> Nowhere is the role of domestic rivalry more evident than in Japan, where it is all-out warfare in which many companies fail to achieve profitability. With goals that stress market share, Japanese companies engage in a continuing struggle to outdo each other. Shares fluctuate markedly. The process is prominently covered in the business press. Elaborate rankings measure which companies are most popular with university graduates. The rate of new product and process development is breathtaking.[2]

In sum, Porter's argument is that how likely a nation is to achieve international success in a certain industry is a function of the combined impact of factor endowments, domestic demand conditions, related and supporting industries and domestic rivalry. He argues that for this 'diamond' to have a positive impact on competitive performance usually requires the presence of all four components (although there are exceptions). Porter also contends that government can influence each of the four components of the diamond either positively or negatively. Government can affect factor endowments through subsidies, policies on capital markets, policies on education and the like, and it can shape domestic demand through local product standards or regulations that mandate or influence buyer needs. Government policy can also influence supporting and related industries through regulation, and rivalry through such devices as capital market regulation, tax policy and anticompetitive legislation.

As an example of Porter's theory, consider the Australian wine industry. Factor conditions in the form of relatively cheap farming land, appropriate weather conditions and a well-trained labour force through the university and TAFE systems all provide a conducive environment for the industry. Although local demand is not as high as that in France or Italy per capita, it is increasing and is predominantly for ready-to-drink styles that do not require an extensive knowledge of wine to appreciate the product — something that the 'new world' producers such as Australia are famous for. Related and supporting industries are found in the research concerning everything from grapes to the final product through the Australian Grape and Wine Research Council. However, possibly even more important is the business rather than lifestyle orientation of Australian agricultural industries, in that wine production is viewed by most in the industry as a serious business. Finally, under strategy, structure and rivalry, the number of wineries creates strong local competition, but at the same time, the industry's ability to operate unrestricted has allowed Australia to produce some of the largest wine companies in the world. The other important factor here is that the large international players are run by serious businesspeople (often with a strong grounding in marketing and finance), who could possibly run a range of other businesses and are not exclusively wine focused.

Perhaps the most important implication of Porter's framework is its message about the attractiveness of certain locations for performing certain productive activities. Many Japanese computer companies have moved much of their research and development (R&D) activity to the United States so that they can benefit from the international competitiveness of the United States in this industry. Most US financial service companies have substantial operations in London so that they can take advantage of its central position in the world financial services industry. Many international textile companies have design operations in Italy so that they can take advantage of Italian style and design know-how. French wine companies have invested in Australian and Californian operations so that they can learn about new approaches being used in wine production. In all these cases, companies are trying to build a competitive advantage by establishing critical productive activities in the optimal location, as defined by the elements highlighted in Porter's framework.

Profiting from global expansion

Expanding globally allows companies, large or small, to increase their profitability in ways not available to purely domestic enterprises. Companies that operate internationally can (a) earn a greater return from their distinctive competencies; (b) realise location economies by dispersing individual value creation activities to those locations where they can be performed most efficiently and (c) ride down the experience curve ahead of competitors, lowering the costs of value creation.

Transferring distinctive competencies

In chapter 4, where the concept is first considered, a distinctive competency is defined as a *unique strength that allows a company to achieve superior efficiency, quality, innovation or responsiveness to customers.* These strengths typically find their expression in product offerings that other companies find difficult to match or imitate. Distinctive competencies thus form the bedrock of a company's competitive advantage. They enable a company to lower the costs of value creation or perform value creation activities in ways that lead to differentiation and premium pricing.

Companies with valuable distinctive competencies can often realise enormous returns by applying those competencies — and the products they produce — to foreign markets in which indigenous competitors lack similar competencies and products. McDonald's, for example, has expanded rapidly overseas in recent years to exploit its distinctive competencies in managing fast-food operations. These competencies have proved to be just as valuable in markets as diverse as France, Russia, China, Germany and Brazil as they have been in the United States. Before the entry of McDonald's, none of these nations had US-style fast-food chains, so McDonald's introduced unique skills and a unique product. The lack of indigenous competitors with similar competencies and products has greatly enhanced the profitability of this strategy for McDonald's.

Realising location economies

Location economies are the economies that arise from performing a value creation activity in the optimal location for that activity, wherever in the world that may be (transportation costs and trade barriers permitting). Locating a value creation activity in the optimal location for that activity can have one of two effects: (a) lower the costs of value creation, helping the company achieve a low-cost position or (b) enable a company to differentiate its product offering and charge a premium price. Efforts to realise location economies are thus consistent with the generic business-level strategies of low cost and differentiation. In theory, a company that realises location economies by dispersing each of its value creation activities to its optimal location should have a competitive advantage over a company that bases all its value creation activities at a single location. It should be better able than its single-location competitor to differentiate its product offering and lower its costs. In a world where competitive pressures are increasing, this strategy may become an imperative for survival.

Consider the businesswear manufacturer and retailer Fletcher Jones. A long-term competitor in the Australian and New Zealand markets, Fletcher Jones has come under increasing pressure because these two nations have reduced clothing tariffs, and as cost-competitive garments from Asian manufacturers have entered the markets. Even in the relatively high end of the market, Fletcher Jones has not been immune to these challenges. As a result, it has moved some of its production offshore. Fletcher Jones still uses Australian and New Zealand wools (some of the finest in the world) for its suits but the manufacture of many of its cheaper suits now occurs in parts of eastern Europe, such as the Czech Republic. By using cheaper skilled labour, Fletcher

location economies
The economies that arise from either lowering the company's cost structure or creating a point of differentiation as a result of undertaking activities in the most conducive location in the world

Jones has been able to remain competitive in Australia and New Zealand while many other local companies have been forced out of the industry by the flood of cheap imports.

Boeing's strategy for manufacturing its commercial jet aircraft, the 777, also illustrates location economies. The 777 uses 132 500 engineered parts produced around the world by 545 different suppliers. Eight Japanese suppliers make parts of the fuselage, doors and wings; a supplier in Singapore makes the doors for the nose landing gear; and three suppliers in Italy manufacture wing flaps. Part of Boeing's rationale for outsourcing so much production to foreign suppliers is that these various suppliers are the best in the world at performing their particular activity when measured on the basis of cost and quality. The result of having foreign suppliers build specific parts is a better final product and a competitive advantage for Boeing in the global marketplace.[3] Generalising from the Fletcher Jones and Boeing examples, it can be said that one result of this kind of thinking is the creation of a **global web** of value creation activities, with different stages of the value chain being dispersed to those locations around the globe where value added is maximised or where the costs of value creation are minimised.

global web
The dispersal of different stages of a company's value chain around the world

Moving down the experience curve

As you recall from chapter 5, the experience curve refers to the systematic decrease in production costs that has been observed to occur over the life of a product. Chapter 5 points out that learning effects and economies of scale underlie the experience curve and that moving down the experience curve allows a company to lower the costs of value creation. The company that moves down the experience curve most rapidly will have a cost advantage over its competitors. Moving down the experience curve is therefore consistent with the business-level strategy of cost leadership.

Sources of experience-based economies can derive from spreading the fixed costs of building productive capacity over a large output. It follows that the key to riding down the experience curve as rapidly as possible is to increase the accumulated volume produced by a plant as quickly as possible. Given that global markets are larger than domestic markets, companies that serve a global market from a single location are likely to build up accumulated volume faster than can companies that focus on serving their home market or serving multiple markets from multiple production locations. Serving a global market from a single location is consistent with moving down the experience curve and establishing a low-cost position.

In addition, to get down the experience curve quickly, companies need to price and market aggressively so that demand rapidly expands. They also need to build production capacity capable of serving a global market. Another point to bear in mind is that the cost advantages of serving the world market from a single location will be all the more significant if that location is also the optimal one for performing that value creation activity, that is, if the company is simultaneously realising economies from experience-curve effects *and* from location.

Using business-level strategy to profit from global expansion

It is important to recognise that the different ways of profiting from global expansion are all linked to the generic business-level strategies of cost leadership and differentiation. Companies that transfer distinctive competencies to other nations are trying to realise greater gains from their low-cost or differentiation-based competitive advantage. Companies such as Fletcher Jones that attempt to realise location economies are trying to lower their costs or increase the value added so that they can better differentiate themselves from their competitors. Companies that serve a global market to ride down the experience curve more quickly are trying to build a competitive advantage based on low cost.

Pressures for centralisation and local responsiveness

Companies that compete in the global marketplace typically face two types of competitive pressure: (a) pressures to centralise and (b) pressures to be locally responsive (see figure 8.2).[4] These competitive pressures place conflicting demands on a company. Pressures for centralisation normally come about due to a need or at least an opportunity to reduce costs through centralising all operations in one location. This normally involves a company basing its productive activities at the most favourable low-cost location, wherever in the world that may be. It may also have to offer a standardised product to the global marketplace, so as to ride down the experience curve as quickly as possible. On the other hand, responding to pressures to be locally responsive requires a company to differentiate its product offering and marketing strategy across markets in an effort to accommodate the diverse demands arising from national differences in consumer tastes and preferences, business practices, distribution channels, competitive conditions and government policies. Because differentiation across countries can involve significant duplication and a lack of product standardisation, it may raise costs.

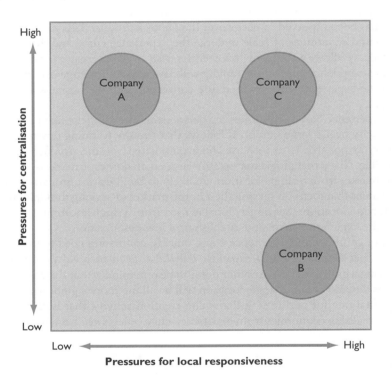

Figure 8.2:
Pressures for centralisation and local responsiveness

Whereas some companies, such as company A in figure 8.2, face high pressures for centralisation and low pressures for local responsiveness, and others, such as company B, face low pressures for centralisation and high pressures for local responsiveness, many companies are in the position of company C: they face high pressures for both centralisation and local responsiveness. Dealing with these conflicting and contradictory pressures is a difficult strategic challenge for a company, primarily because being locally responsive tends to raise costs. The remainder of this section considers the sources of pressures for centralisation and local responsiveness. The next section examines the strategies that companies adopt to deal with these pressures.

Pressures for centralisation

Pressures for centralisation arise from a desire to reduce costs on the basis of economies of scale, scope and learning, and because of a need to access resources that are unique to a firm's home base or an inability to use existing organisational capabilities.

Pressures for cost reductions

Increasingly international companies must cope with pressures for cost reductions. Pressures for cost reductions can be particularly intense in industries producing commodity-type products, where meaningful differentiation on nonprice factors is difficult and price is the main competitive weapon. Products that serve universal needs tend to fall into this category. Universal needs exist when the tastes and preferences of consumers in different nations are similar, if not identical. This applies to conventional commodity products, such as bulk chemicals, petroleum, steel and sugar. It also tends to be true for many industrial and consumer products, such as handheld calculators, semiconductor chips and PCs. In essence, companies that can centralise their operations tend to produce products that have a global product design. Pressures for cost reductions are also intense in industries in which major competitors are based in low-cost locations, where there is persistent excess capacity and consumers are powerful and face low switching costs. Many commentators have also argued that the liberalisation of the world trade and investment environment in recent decades has generally increased cost pressures by facilitating greater international competition.[5] As a result, a well-known international company such as Fuji manufactures all of its film in a single location to gain the economies of scale that Kodak is unable to achieve with manufacturing facilities spread out all over the globe.

Unique resources

On occasion, a firm may have unique resources that are simply not available in other locations and for this reason there is a natural pressure to centralise. An obvious example of this would be a primary producer for which the right agricultural conditions exist in only one location and, therefore, international expansion in any areas other than marketing and distribution is simply not realistic (as shown in Strategy in action 8.1). There may also be an inability to use the unique resources of a firm in a particular country. Trading companies such as Li and Fung, for example, must continue to operate in Hong Kong because of the complex web of interpersonal relationships that they have built up over decades of trading.

strategy in action 8.1

The New Zealand timber industry

The creation of New Zealand's sustainable forestry industry is linked to the government's economic reforms in 1987. Until then, the government owned more than half the forests and two large sawmills, administered forestry encouragement loans and controlled log exports with the simple objective of generating employment. The private forestry industry was subsidised, removing much of the incentive for innovation. As part of its economic reforms, the government sold its planted forests (not the land ownership) to private timber companies. At the same time, it withdrew all subsidies, generating domestic competition for access to designated timber forests and creating the conditions that generated production and marketing efficiencies.

Today, the New Zealand timber industry is based on planted forests that cover 1.8 million hectares or 6.6 per cent of New Zealand's land area. In 2002, the industry accounted for NZ$2.5 billion in exports,

contributing 3.9 per cent to the nation's GDP. The NZ forestry industry is research based, with continual improvements being made to the genetic quality of the wood and to value-adding processing techniques. This in turn is creating a new base of skilled human resources. At the same time, related upstream and downstream industries have developed, such as processing and pulp industries and panel board industries. The industry now comprises four pulp companies, two paper manufacturing companies, eight panel board companies, 362 saw-millers and 50 re-manufacturers. The New Zealand timber industry is expected to keep growing with global demand, which is forecast to rise 40 per cent by year 2010.

Source: Ministry of Agriculture and Forestry 2005, accessed on 27 December 2005, www.maf.govt.nz.

Pressures for local responsiveness

Pressures for local responsiveness arise from differences in consumer tastes and preferences, differences in infrastructure and traditional practices, differences in distribution channels and host government demands.

Differences in consumer tastes and preferences

Strong pressures for local responsiveness emerge when consumer tastes and preferences differ significantly between nations, as they may for historical or cultural reasons. If they do, the product and marketing messages have to be customised to appeal to the tastes and preferences of local consumers. This typically creates pressures for the delegation of production and marketing functions to national subsidiaries.

The success of McDonald's partly relies on customisation of menus to cater to local needs. Small changes have been made in Europe, such as the inclusion of beer and wine as beverage choices (given that alcoholic drinks are a standard component of any meal in countries such as France, Germany and Italy). More radical changes have been made in Arab countries, where it offers halal menus, and in India, where lamb replaces beef in the burgers. Even in markets that are similar to the United States, McDonald's is constantly refining its operations to compete in the increasingly competitive fast-food industry.

As a counterpoint, in a now famous article, Levitt argued that consumer demands for local customisation are on the decline worldwide.[6] According to Levitt, modern communications and transport technologies have created the conditions for a convergence of the tastes and preferences of consumers from different nations. The result is the emergence of enormous global markets for standardised consumer products. As evidence of the increasing homogeneity of the global marketplace, Levitt cites worldwide acceptance of McDonald's hamburgers, Coca-Cola and Sony television sets, all of which are sold as standardised products.

Levitt's argument, however, has been characterised as extreme by many commentators. Bartlett and Ghoshal observe that buyers in the consumer electronics industry reacted to an overdose of standardised global products by showing a renewed preference for products that are differentiated for local conditions.[7] For example, even though large multinationals such as AXA tend to dominate the insurance industry, insurance products are still developed country by country to account for specific needs and differences.

Differences in infrastructure and traditional practices

Pressures for local responsiveness arise from national differences in infrastructure or traditional practices, creating a need to customise products accordingly. Fulfilling this need may require the delegation of manufacturing and production functions to foreign subsidiaries. Power supplies, for example, vary across nations, being 110-, 220- or 240-volt systems. Cars need to be made in either left-hand drive or right-hand drive configurations according to the market for which they are destined. With wide open spaces, large distances between population centres and wide lanes on the road, the most popular cars in Australia are the family-sized Holden Commodore and Ford Falcon. In comparison, tight traffic conditions and small distances between population centres have meant that cars such as the VW Beetle, the Mercedes A class and the Opel Astra are popular in western Europe. Traditional practices can also create pressures for local responsiveness. In the UK, most bottles of wine are purchased by relatively inexperienced wine drinkers at the supermarket. Many Australian and New Zealand producers have consequently had to redesign their labels for the UK market, to make the labels more visually appealing and recognisable so that they stand out among hundreds of other competitors.

In comparison, French wines, particularly those destined for the French market, rely less upon labels because they are catering to a more informed market.

Differences in distribution channels

A company's marketing strategies may have to be responsive to national differences in distribution channels. This may necessitate the delegation of marketing functions to foreign subsidiaries. While the trend is slowly changing, a considerable portion of meat at the retail level in Australia and New Zealand is still sold through butchers. This is not the case in the United States, where there are virtually no speciality meat stores. The US industry is dominated by supermarket chains, so Australian and New Zealand producers of lamb and beef have to negotiate with supermarket chains if they wish to export their product to North America. The marketing focus of these producers has to change, therefore, because supermarkets are primarily interested in price and continuity of supply, whereas family-owned butchers in Australia and New Zealand may be more interested in quality and terms of credit.

Host government demands

Economic and political demands imposed by host country governments may necessitate a degree of local responsiveness. The politics of healthcare around the world, for example, requires pharmaceutical companies to manufacture in multiple locations. Pharmaceutical companies are subject to local clinical testing, registration procedures and pricing restrictions, all of which require the manufacturing and marketing of a drug to meet local requirements. Moreover, since governments and government agencies control a significant proportion of the healthcare budget in most countries, they are in a powerful position to demand a high level of local responsiveness.

More generally, threats of protectionism, economic nationalism and local content rules (which require that a certain percentage of a product should be manufactured locally) dictate that international businesses manufacture locally. As an example, consider Bombardier, the Canadian-based manufacturer of railcars, aircraft, jet boats and snowmobiles. Bombardier has 12 railcar factories across Europe. Critics of the company argue that the resulting duplication of manufacturing facilities leads to high costs and helps explain why Bombardier makes lower profit margins on its railcar operations than on its other business lines. In reply, managers at Bombardier argue that Europe's informal rules regarding local content favour those that use local workers. To sell railcars in Germany, Bombardier claims, you must manufacture in Germany. The same goes for Belgium, Austria and France. To try to rationalise its cost structure in Europe, Bombardier centralised its engineering and purchasing functions but it has no plans to centralise manufacturing.[8] This is certainly not unusual.

Implications

Pressures for local responsiveness imply that it may not be possible for a company to realise the full benefits from experience-curve effects and location economies. It may not be possible, for example, to serve the global marketplace from a single low-cost location, producing a globally standardised product and marketing it worldwide to achieve experience-curve economies. In practice, the need to customise the product offering to local conditions may work against the implementation of this strategy. So Australian and New Zealand beef and lamb exporters have to customise their approach to selling overseas: in North America, the distribution channels require a different marketing message to be successful; in Japan, the preference is for fattier meat, requiring different cuts of '-marbled' meat; in Germany, the 'green' movement has led to a consumer preference for meats that are guaranteed to be farm animals that were not fed genetically modified foods and were 'free range'; and in Arab countries, buyers want live exports so they can be slaughtered in line with halal requirements. The need for customisation may limit the ability of a company to achieve economies of scale, generate experience-curve effects, take full advantage of location economies or gain the benefits of transferring established competencies. Concessions to local requirements are nevertheless generally required if companies wish to succeed outside their home country.

Strategic choice

Companies use four basic strategies to enter and compete in the international environment: international, multidomestic, global and transnational.[9] Each strategy has its advantages and disadvantages. For a company, the appropriateness of each strategy varies with the extent of pressures for cost reductions and local responsiveness (see figure 8.3). This section describes each strategy, identifies when it is appropriate and discusses its pros and cons.

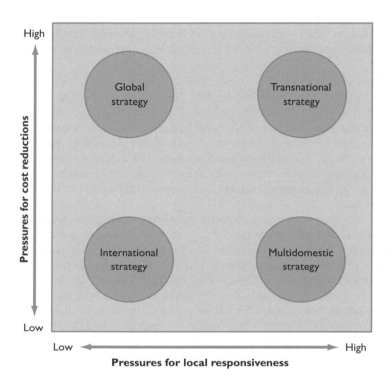

Figure 8.3:
Four basic strategies for
entering the international
environment

International strategy

Companies that pursue an international strategy try to create value by transferring valuable skills and products to foreign markets where indigenous competitors lack those skills and products. Most international companies have created value by transferring differentiated product offerings developed at home to new markets overseas. Accordingly, they tend to centralise product development functions (e.g. R&D) at home. They also tend, however, to establish manufacturing and marketing functions in each major nation in which they do business. Although they may undertake some local customisation of product offering and marketing strategy, this effort tends to be limited in scope. Ultimately, in most international companies, the head office retains tight control over marketing and product strategy.

Many international consulting companies take on this type of strategy. Australia has many companies that consult on aspects of mining and oil and gas exploration and extraction, such as Clough Engineering. Most conduct a considerable portion of their business in Asia, where specific technical skills are required to establish a new mine or plant. They establish offices in the target nation and either transfer skilled consultants to the new office or train locals. The fundamental operations of the business do not change, but some of the local operations (such as dealings with governments and organisational structures) need to be customised.

An international strategy makes sense if a company has a valuable distinctive competency that indigenous competitors in foreign markets lack and if the company faces relatively weak pressures for local responsiveness and cost reductions. In such circumstances, an international strategy can be very profitable. When pressures for local responsiveness are high, however, companies pursuing this strategy lose out to companies that place a greater emphasis on customising the product offering and market strategy to local conditions. Moreover, given the duplication of manufacturing facilities, companies that pursue an international strategy tend to incur high operating costs. This strategy is often inappropriate in industries in which cost pressures are high.

Multidomestic strategy

Companies pursuing a multidomestic strategy orient themselves towards achieving maximum local responsiveness. The key distinguishing feature of multidomestic companies is that they extensively customise both their product offering and their marketing strategy to match different national conditions. Consistent with this approach, they tend to establish a complete set of value creation activities — including production, marketing and R&D — in each major national market in which they do business. As a result, they generally cannot realise value from experience-curve effects and location economies. Accordingly, many multidomestic companies have a high-cost structure. They also tend to do a poor job of using core competencies broadly within the firm.

A multidomestic strategy makes most sense when there are high pressures for local responsiveness and low pressures for cost reductions. The high costs associated with duplicating production facilities makes this strategy inappropriate in industries in which cost pressures are intense. Another weakness of this strategy is that many multidomestic companies have developed into decentralised federations, in which each national subsidiary functions largely autonomously. Consequently, they begin to lose the ability to transfer the skills and products derived from distinctive competencies to their various national subsidiaries around the world. In a famous case that illustrates the resulting problems, the failure of Philips to establish its V2000 video cassette format as the dominant design in the video recording industry during the late 1970s — as opposed to JVC's VHS format — was caused by the refusal of its US subsidiary company to adopt the V2000 format. Instead, the subsidiary bought video recorders produced by JVC and put its own label on them.

Global strategy

Companies that pursue a global strategy focus on increasing profitability by reaping the cost reductions that come from experience-curve effects and location economies. That is, they pursue a low-cost strategy. The production, marketing, and research and development activities of companies pursuing a global strategy are concentrated in a few favourable locations. Global companies tend not to customise their product offering and marketing strategy to local conditions. The reason is that customisation raises costs because it involves shorter production runs and the duplication of functions. Instead, global companies prefer to market a standardised product worldwide so that they can reap the maximum benefits from descending the experience curve. They also tend to use their cost advantage to support aggressive pricing in world markets.

This strategy makes most sense when there are strong pressures for cost reductions and demands for local responsiveness are minimal. Increasingly, these conditions prevail in many industrial goods industries. In the semiconductor industry, for example, global standards have emerged, creating enormous demands for standardised global products. Accordingly, companies such as Intel and Motorola pursue a global strategy. As noted, however, these conditions are not found in many consumer goods markets, where demands for local responsiveness remain high (as in the markets for stereo systems, motor vehicles and processed food products). The strategy is inappropriate when demands for local responsiveness are high.

Transnational strategy

Bartlett and Ghoshal argue that competitive conditions in today's environment are so intense that companies, to survive in the global marketplace, must exploit experience-based and location economies, transfer distinctive competencies within the company and at the same time pay attention to pressures for local responsiveness.[10] Moreover, they note that distinctive competencies in the modern multinational enterprise do not reside just in the home country but can develop in any of the company's worldwide operations. They maintain that the flow of skills and product offerings should not be all one way, from home company to foreign subsidiary, as in the case of companies pursuing an international strategy. Rather, the flow should also be from foreign subsidiary to home country and from foreign subsidiary to foreign subsidiary, a process that Bartlett and Ghoshal refer to as global learning. They term the strategy pursued by companies trying to achieve all of these objectives simultaneously a transnational strategy.

A transnational strategy makes sense when a company faces high pressures for cost reductions and high pressures for local responsiveness. Companies that pursue a transnational strategy are trying to achieve low-cost and differentiation advantages simultaneously. As attractive as this sounds, the strategy is not easy to pursue. As mentioned, pressures for local responsiveness and cost reductions place conflicting demands on a company. Being locally responsive raises costs, which obviously makes cost reductions difficult to achieve. How, then, can a company effectively pursue a transnational strategy?

Some clues can be derived from the example of Australian-based wine companies. In many ways, BRL Hardy (as part of the Constellation Brands) and Orlando Wyndham (as part of the Pernod Ricard Group) used a transnational strategy. Needing to compete with low-cost products from nations such as Chile and South Africa, forced both winemakers to constantly look for cost reductions — generally through a process of attaining economies of scale in their operations. However, at the same time, they have customised aspects of their operations to deal with market-level product preferences. As a result, these companies were two of the first to develop global brands in the wine industry (Banrock Station for BRL Hardy and Jacobs Creek for Orlando Wyndham) that could be cost efficiently produced from an Australian base by relying on significant economies of scale. At the same time, additional products were developed specifically for the UK market that were better designed to meet the supermarket-dominated distribution channels in the UK.

Nonetheless, Bartlett and Ghoshal admit that building a company capable of supporting a transnational strategic posture is a complex and difficult task. The core of the problem is that simultaneously trying to achieve cost efficiencies, global learning and local responsiveness places contradictory demands on a company. What tends to happen is that different parts of an organisation's operations will either be centralised or decentralised to allow for local responsiveness. Rarely is a firm entirely centralised or decentralised at a global level. For example, a firm such as Canon may achieve significant economies of scale by manufacturing all of their digital cameras in a single location but activities further down the value chain, such as marketing and distribution, are often localised so that appropriate marketing campaigns can be developed that will suit the local market. To see how Qantas faces both pressures to centralise as well as be locally responsive can be seen in Strategy in action 8.2.

Summary

The advantages and disadvantages of each of these four strategies are summarised in table 8.1. Although a transnational strategy seems to offer the most advantages, its implementation raises organisational issues. More generally, the appropriateness of each strategy depends on the relative strength of pressures for cost reductions and local responsiveness.

strategy in action 8.2

Qantas questions its centrality

Qantas is one of the world's oldest airlines and operates a significant fleet serving both a domestic as well as an extensive international market. Traditionally the company has been highly centralised, probably more because of history than because of any significant pressures to either be centralised or locally responsive. As an Australian company, all aircrew were Australia-based, all heavy maintenance occurred within Australia and all high-level administration in terms of route determination, load management and pricing were done within Australia.

Recently, however, greater levels of competition and the need to reduce costs further have led to a review of which of these areas can and should be done locally. One of the first areas to come under scrutiny was whether to engage non-Australian cabin-crew. This initially involved hiring some non-Australians but, more recently, discussions have been held with the relevant unions to locate a significant number of crew initially in London (and possibly some in Singapore) as a way to

reducing costs. Interestingly here, cost reductions are likely to be achieved not by centralising but by decentralising this function. The next step, apparently, is to have Singapore-based pilots. In terms of maintenance, a significant portion of the work is likely to be outsourced to an Asia-based heavy maintenance group. A few global players have well-respected aircraft maintenance facilities in Asia that are considerably cheaper than Qantas' own operations (which are spread out between Sydney, Melbourne and Brisbane) and, therefore, this component of Qantas' operations is likely to be centralised in a single low-cost location.

However, although local offices engage in basic advertising and managing support staff on the ground, important administrative and strategic decisions will be kept in Australia (remaining in Sydney). This means that there is uniformity in brand management, pricing and arrangements with alliance partners, and that the route structure reflects the best use of Qantas aircraft for the given global economic environment.

Table 8.1: The advantages and disadvantages of different strategies for competing globally

Strategy	Advantages	Disadvantages
International	• Transfer of distinctive competencies to foreign markets	• Lack of local responsiveness • Inability to realise location economies • Failure to exploit experience-curve effects
Multidomestic	• Ability to customise product offerings and marketing in accordance with responsiveness	• Inability to realise location economies • Failure to exploit experience-curve effects to foreign markets • Failure to transfer distinctive competencies to foreign markets
Global	• Ability to exploit experience-curve effects • Ability to exploit location economies	• Lack of local responsiveness
Transnational	• Ability to exploit experience-curve effects • Ability to exploit location economies • Ability to customise product offerings and marketing in accordance with local responsiveness • Reaping of benefits of global learning	• Difficulties in implementation as a result of organisational problems

Basic entry decisions

This section looks at three basic decisions that a company contemplating foreign expansion must make: (a) which markets to enter; (b) when to enter those markets and (c) on what scale to enter.

Which foreign markets?

Not all of the more than 160 different nation states in the world hold the same profit potential for a company contemplating foreign expansion. The choice from among different foreign markets must be based on an assessment of their long-term profit potential. The attractiveness of a nation as a potential market for an international business depends on the balance of benefits, costs and risks of doing business there. The long-term economic benefits of doing business in an overseas market are a function such things as the size of the market (in terms of demographics), the present wealth (purchasing power) of consumers in that market and the likely future wealth of consumers. While some markets are large when measured by consumer numbers (e.g. China and India), lower average living standards may cause limited purchasing power and, therefore, a somewhat smaller market in economic terms. The costs and risks of doing business in a foreign market are typically lower in economically advanced and politically stable democratic nations and greater in less-developed and politically unstable nations.

The benefit–cost–risk calculator is complicated by the potential long-term benefits bearing little relationship to a nation's current stage of economic development or political stability. Rather, they depend on likely future economic growth rates, and economic growth seems to be a function of a free market system and a nation's capacity for growth (which may be greater in less-developed nations). Other factors being equal, therefore, the benefit–cost–risk tradeoff is likely to be most favourable in politically stable developed and developing nations that have free market systems and do not have a dramatic upsurge in either inflation rates or private sector debt. It is likely to be least favourable in politically unstable developing nations that operate with a mixed or command economy, or in developing nations in which speculative financial bubbles have led to excess borrowing.

By applying this reasoning, a company can rank countries in terms of their attractiveness and long-term profit potential.[11] It would give preference to entering markets that rank highly. In considering the potential of various markets relative to their risk, a company should note that risk profiles differ according to products. It is possible to obtain professionally prepared risk profiles for most nations. These reports try to quantify the level of risk of selling in one market relative to another. Some products, however, are more susceptible than others to certain risks. Consider products that have relatively inelastic demand curves (such as foodstuffs), that is, those that are unlikely to be affected by economic downturns. These products tend to be the domain of smaller firms, limiting the risk of the operation being nationalised. An Australian or New Zealand dairy products company that conducts some final-stage production and sales of cheeses and yoghurts in a tropical nation is unlikely to suffer a significant drop in demand if the economy falters or to be nationalised if there was a political coup. In comparison, Iran nationalised the oil wells of several multinationals after the overthrow of the shah; nevertheless, given the enormous profits that can be made in the oil business, many of the same multinationals again queued up in the mid-1990s when Iran sought foreign investment and joint-venture partners to develop its oil reserves.

Companies need to consider carefully all the possible ways they can set up their operations to minimise risk. Ericsson, for example, sells a lot of mobile telecommunications networking equipment to less developed countries. The governments often cannot pay for the equipment, so Ericsson installs it for free and then collects the revenue generated by the network for a period to recoup its investment. This arrangement means the government cannot incur a bad debt and is unlikely to nationalise the operation because the network would falter without Ericsson's maintenance.

Timing of entry

Once a company identifies attractive markets, it must consider the **timing of entry**. Entry is early when an international business enters a foreign market before other foreign companies do, and late when it enters after other international businesses have already established themselves in the market. Several first-mover advantages are frequently associated with entering a market early.[12] One is the ability to pre-empt rivals and capture demand by establishing a strong brand name. A second advantage is the ability to build up sales volume in that market and ride down the experience curve ahead of rivals. If this is possible, the early entrant has a cost advantage over later entrants. This cost advantage may enable the early entrant to respond to later entry by cutting prices below the (higher) cost structure of later entrants, driving them out of the market. A third advantage is the ability of early entrants to create switching costs that tie customers to their products or services. These make it difficult for later entrants to win business. Innovative companies that are comparatively small often need to be the first to market to have any reasonable chance at capturing a significant part of the market which is part of Whisper Tech's strategy to enter the UK, as discussed in Strategy in action 8.3.

timing of entry
When a company enters an international market relative to the entry of international competitors

strategy in action 8.3

Whispering success

Whisper Tech is a small startup company based in Christchurch, New Zealand. It was founded to exploit the commercial potential of a new technology that enables domestic boilers to generate electricity at the same time as producing heat. The result is very efficient use of energy, so the unit both pays back the initial higher investment and reduces carbon dioxide emissions from household energy consumption. Whisper Tech has been developing its WhisperGen system for more than ten years and owns worldwide patents on its key components.

The company put aside other applications and markets to focus on use by UK households. There, natural gas is piped to most homes and provides lower cost energy than mains electricity. It is normally used to heat the house using a hot-water boiler and a network of water-filled radiators. Consequently, the market needs are closely matched with the characteristics of the product: the WhisperGen replaces the boiler but saves the household money by also generating electricity.

Whisper Tech obtained market access by signing a joint development agreement with the electricity and gas supplier Powergen, which has more than eight million electricity and gas customers. After successful trials, in 2004, Powergen ordered 80 000 units on condition that it be given exclusive rights to market the product in the UK.

The Powergen order required Whisper Tech to deliver significant product volumes at low cost. To achieve this, it looked globally for partners with existing capabilities in the mass production of similar types of consumer product. At the same time, it planned to continue manufacturing certain components itself to protect key intellectual property.

Sources: Whisper Tech 2004, 'More success for Whisper Tech in the UK', media release, 21 October; *Christchurch Press* 2004, report, 21 August.

It is important to realise that there can also be disadvantages in entering a foreign market before other international businesses, often referred to as **first-mover disadvantages**.[13] These may give rise to pioneering costs, which an early entrant has to bear but a later entrant can avoid. These arise when the business system in a foreign market is so different from that in the company's home market that the enterprise has to devote considerable effort, time and expense to learning the rules of the game. Pioneering costs include the costs of business failure if the company, as a result of its ignorance of the foreign environment, makes major mistakes. Put differently, there is a liability associated with being a foreigner, and this liability is greater for foreign companies that enter a national market early.[14] Recent research evidence confirms that the probability of survival increases if an international business enters a national market after several other foreign companies have already done so.[15] The late entrant would seem to benefit by observing and learning from the mistakes made by early entrants.

first-mover disadvantages
The problems and costs that a company must bear as a result of being the first to enter an international market

Pioneering costs also include the costs of promoting and establishing a product offering, including educating customers. These can be significant when local consumers are not familiar with the product being promoted. In many ways, what the De Beers-controlled Central Selling Organisation (CSO) did in terms of creating a demand for diamonds in many countries paved the way for others to follow. In the 1950s, for example, Japanese had no word for 'diamond'. A marketing campaign based on the *yuino* ceremony (in which a bride and a groom exchange gifts), however, led to more than 60 per cent of Japanese brides receiving diamond rings by 1980. A similar marketing campaign in Germany (based on adding a diamond ring to the traditional two interlinked gold rings) made Germany the third-largest market for diamonds in the world. These campaigns have been at considerable expense to the CSO, yet in many ways the new producers that do not sell all of their production through the CSO (such as Argyle Diamonds) benefit most from the enormous increase in demand.

Scale of entry and strategic commitments

The final issue that an international business needs to consider when contemplating market entry is the scale of entry. Entering a market on a large scale involves committing significant resources to that venture. While not all companies have the resources necessary to enter on a large scale, even some large enterprises prefer to enter foreign markets on a small scale and then build their presence slowly over time as they become more familiar with the foreign market.

The consequences of entering on a significant scale are associated with the value of the resulting strategic commitments.[16] A **strategic commitment** is a decision that has a long-term impact and is difficult to reverse. Deciding to enter a foreign market on a significant scale is a major strategic commitment. Strategic commitments can have an important influence on the nature of competition in a market. By entering a market on a significant scale, a company signals its commitment to the market, potentially making it easier for the company to attract customers because they are more likely to believe that the company will remain in the market. Large-scale entry also provides the opportunity for the company to achieve economies of scale, although it potentially opens the industry to higher levels of competition. A significant commitment by a foreign company entering a market is likely to lead to retaliatory moves by existing competitors, whereas a minor commitment by the new entrant may be perceived as relatively inconsequential and thus not attract retaliatory moves.

Significant strategic commitments are neither unambiguously good nor bad. Rather, they tend to change the competitive playing field and unleash changes, some of which may be desirable and some of which will not be. It is therefore important for a company to think through the implications of large-scale entry into a market and act accordingly. Particularly important is the attempt to identify how actual and potential competitors may react to large-scale entry into a market. Companies also need to consider the connection between large-scale entry and first-mover advantages. Specifically, the large-scale entrant is more likely than the small-scale entrant to capture the first-mover advantages associated with demand pre-emption, economies of scale and switching costs.

Balanced against the value and risks of large-scale entry are the benefits of small-scale entry. Small-scale entry has the advantage of allowing a company to learn about a foreign market while simultaneously limiting the company's exposure to that market. Small-scale entry can be seen as a way of gathering more information about a foreign market before deciding whether to enter on a significant scale and how best to enter that market. By giving the company time to collect information, therefore, small-scale entry reduces the risks of a subsequent large-scale entry. On the other hand, the lack of commitment associated with small-scale entry may make it more difficult for the small-scale entrant to build market share and capture first-mover or early-mover advantages. The risk-averse company that enters a foreign market on a small scale may limit its potential losses but it may also miss the chance to capture first-mover advantages.

strategic commitment
The level of resources and capabilities that a company commits to a particular strategic decision

Summary

There are no 'right' decisions here, just decisions that are associated with different levels of risk and reward. Entering a large developing nation such as Indonesia or India before most other international businesses in the company's industry, and entering on a large scale, will be associated with high levels of risk. At the same time, the potential long-term rewards of such a strategy are great. The early large-scale entrant into a major developing nation may be able to capture significant first-mover advantages, which will bolster its long-term position in that market. In contrast, entering developed nations such as Germany or Canada after other international businesses in the company's industry, and entering initially on a small scale to first learn more about those markets, will be associated with much lower levels of risk. The potential long-term rewards are also likely to be lower, however, because the company is forgoing the opportunity to capture first-mover advantages, and because the lack of commitment to the market (as signalled by small-scale entry) may limit the company's future growth potential.

The choice of entry mode

Considering entry into a foreign market raises the question of the best mode of such entry. There are five main choices: (a) exporting, (b) licensing, (c) franchising, (d) entering into a joint venture with a host-nation company and (e) setting up a wholly owned subsidiary in the host nation. Each entry mode has its advantages and disadvantages, and managers must weigh these carefully when deciding on which mode to use.[17]

Exporting

Most manufacturing companies begin their global expansion as exporters and only later switch to one of the other modes for serving a foreign market. Exporting has two distinct advantages: (a) it avoids the costs of establishing manufacturing operations in the host nation, which are often substantial, and (b) it may be consistent with realising experience-curve and location economies. By manufacturing the product in a centralised location and then exporting it to other national markets, the company may be able to realise substantial economies of scale from its global sales volume.

On the other hand, there are drawbacks to exporting. First, exporting from the company's home base may not be appropriate if there are lower-cost locations for manufacturing the product abroad (that is, if the company can realise location economies by moving production elsewhere). Particularly in the case of a company pursuing a global or transnational strategy, it may pay, therefore, to manufacture in a location where conditions are most favourable from a value creation perspective and then export from that location to the rest of the globe. This is not so much an argument against exporting as an argument against exporting from the company's home country. Many electronics companies have moved some of their manufacturing to Asia because low-cost but highly skilled labour is available there. From that location, they export to the rest of the globe.

Another drawback is that high transport costs can make exporting uneconomical, particularly in the case of bulk products. One way of getting around this problem is to manufacture bulk products regionally. This enables the company to realise some economies from large-scale production while limiting transport costs. Many multinational chemical companies manufacture their products on a regional basis, serving several countries in a region from one facility.

Tariff barriers can also make exporting uneconomical. The threat by the government of an importing nation to impose tariff barriers can make the strategy very risky. The general move towards free trade, however, has led to less use of tariffs, quotas and other anti-import mechanisms. There are exceptions, such as the Bush Administration's policy to protect the US steel industry, but more national governments are reducing tariffs than are increasing them.

wholly owned subsidiary
A company that is
completely owned by its
parent company

Finally, a common practice among companies that are just beginning to export — that is, delegating marketing activities in each overseas market to a local agent — also poses risks. There is no guarantee that the agent will act in the company's best interest. Foreign agents often also carry the products of competing companies and thus have divided loyalties. Consequently, they may not do as good a job as the company would if it managed its own marketing. One way of solving this problem is to set up a **wholly owned subsidiary** in the host nation to handle local marketing. By so doing, the company can both reap the cost advantages of manufacturing the product in a single location and exercise tight control over marketing strategy in the host nation.

Licensing

International licensing is an arrangement in which a foreign licensee buys the rights to produce a company's product in the licensee's country for a negotiated fee (normally, royalty payments on the number of units sold). The licensee then puts up most of the capital necessary to get the overseas operation going.[18]

The advantage of licensing is that the company does not have to bear the development costs and risks of opening up a foreign market. Licensing, therefore, can be a very attractive option for companies that lack the capital to develop operations overseas. It can also be an attractive option for companies that are unwilling to commit substantial financial resources to an unfamiliar or politically volatile foreign market where political risks are particularly high.

Licensing has three serious drawbacks though. First, it does not give a company the tight control over manufacturing, marketing and strategic functions overseas that it needs to realise experience-curve and location economies (as companies pursuing both global and transnational strategies try to do). Typically, each licensee sets up its own manufacturing operations, so the company stands little chance of realising experience-curve and location economies by manufacturing its product in a centralised location. When these economies are likely to be important, licensing may not be the best way of expanding overseas.

Second, competing in a global marketplace may make it necessary for a company to coordinate strategic moves across nations so the profits earned in one market can be used to support competitive attacks in another. Licensing, by its very nature, severely limits a company's ability to coordinate strategy in this way. A licensee is unlikely to let a multinational company take its profits (beyond those due in the form of royalty payments) and use them to support an entirely different licensee operating in another market.

A third problem with licensing is the risk associated with licensing technological know-how to foreign companies. For many multinational companies, technological know-how forms the basis of their competitive advantage and they want to maintain control over its use. By licensing its technology, a company can quickly lose control over it. For example, to avoid this becoming a problem, Nippon Steel negotiated a 50:50 joint venture with Baoshon Steel as part of the process of licensing certain steel making technologies that can be used to make steel for auto manufacturers.

There are ways of reducing this risk, however, including a cross-licensing agreement with a foreign company. Under a cross-licensing agreement, a company may license some valuable intangible property to a foreign partner and request, in addition to a royalty payment, that the foreign partner license some of its valuable know-how to the company. These agreements are reckoned to reduce the risks of licensing technological know-how because the licensee realises that if it violates the spirit of a licensing contract (by using the knowledge obtained to compete with the licensor), then the licensor can do the same to it. Cross-licensing agreements enable companies to hold each other hostage, which reduces the probability that they will behave opportunistically towards each other.[19] These agreements are increasingly common in hi-tech industries.

Franchising

In many respects, franchising is similar to licensing, although it tends to involve longer-term commitments than does licensing. Franchising is a specialised form of licensing, in which the franchisor not only sells intangible property (normally a trademark) to the franchisee but also insists that the franchisee agree to abide by strict rules for doing business. The franchisor often also assists the franchisee in running the business. As with licensing, the franchisor typically receives a royalty payment, which amounts to some percentage of the franchisee's revenue.

Whereas licensing is a strategy primarily pursued by manufacturing companies, franchising is a strategy that service companies usually employ. McDonald's is an example of a company that has grown by using a franchising strategy. It has set strict rules as to how franchisees should operate a restaurant. These rules extend to control over the menu, cooking methods, staffing policies, and the design and location of a restaurant. McDonald's also organises the supply chain for its franchisees and provides management training and financial assistance for them.[20]

The advantages of franchising are similar to those of licensing. Specifically, the franchisor does not have to bear the development costs and risks of opening up a foreign market on its own, because the franchisee typically assumes those costs and risks. Using a franchising strategy, a service company can thus build a global presence quickly and at a low cost.

The disadvantages, however, are less pronounced than in the case of licensing. Given that franchising is a strategy used by service companies, a franchisor does not have to consider the need to coordinate manufacturing to achieve experience-curve and location economies. Nevertheless, franchising may inhibit a company's ability to achieve global strategic coordination.

A more significant disadvantage of franchising is the lack of quality control. The foundation of franchising arrangements is the notion that the company's brand name conveys a message to consumers about the quality of the company's product. Business travellers booking into a Hilton International hotel in Hong Kong can thus reasonably expect the same quality of room, food and service as they would receive in New York. The Hilton brand name is a guarantee of the consistency of product quality. Foreign franchisees, however, may not be as concerned about quality as they should be, and poor quality may mean not only lost sales in the foreign market but also a decline in the company's worldwide reputation. A bad experience at the Hilton in one location may cause the business traveller to never go to another Hilton hotel anywhere and steer colleagues away as well. The geographic distance separating the franchisor from its foreign franchisees, along with the sheer number of individual franchisees — tens of thousands in the case of McDonald's — can make it difficult for the franchisor to detect poor quality. Consequently, quality problems may persist.

To obviate this drawback, a company can set up a subsidiary wherever it is expanding. The subsidiary may be wholly owned by the company or a joint venture with a foreign company. The subsidiary then assumes the rights and obligations to establish franchisees throughout that particular market. The combination of proximity and the few independent franchisees that have to be monitored reduces the quality control problem. Furthermore, because the subsidiary is at least partly owned by the company, the company can place its own managers in the subsidiary to ensure the kind of quality monitoring it wants. This organisational arrangement has proved popular, being used by McDonald's, KFC and Hilton Hotels to expand their international operations, to name just three examples.

Joint ventures

Establishing a joint venture with a foreign company has long been a favoured mode for entering a new market. The split of sponsorship of the new joint venture may be 50/50 but some companies set up arrangements in which one party has a majority shareholding. This permits tighter control by the dominant partner.

Joint ventures have advantages. First, a company may feel that it can benefit from a local partner's knowledge of a host nation's competitive conditions, culture, language, political systems and business systems. Second, when the development costs and risks of opening up a foreign market are high, a company may gain by sharing these costs and risks with a local partner. Third, political considerations in some nations make joint ventures the only feasible entry mode.[21] While they are an ever reducing minority, some governments do not allow wholly owned subsidiaries to operate in their nations. In the places they govern, any foreign-owned operations must take place through a joint venture with a local partner.

Despite these advantages, two main drawbacks mean joint ventures can be difficult to establish and run. First, as in the case of licensing, a company that enters into a joint venture risks losing control over its technology to its venture partner. To minimise this risk, a company can seek a majority ownership stake in the joint venture because, as the dominant partner, it would be able to exercise greater control over its technology. The trouble with this strategy is that it may be difficult to find a foreign partner willing to accept a minority ownership position.

The second disadvantage is that a joint venture does not give a company the tight control over its subsidiaries that it may need to realise experience-curve or location economies, as both global and transnational companies try to do, or to engage in coordinated global attacks against its global rivals.

Wholly owned subsidiaries

A wholly owned subsidiary is one in which the parent company owns 100 per cent of the subsidiary's stock. To establish a wholly owned subsidiary in a foreign market, a company can either set up a completely new operation in that nation or acquire an established host-nation company and use it to promote its products in the host market.

Setting up a wholly owned subsidiary offers three advantages. First, when a company's competitive advantage is based on its control of a technological competency, a wholly owned subsidiary is normally the preferred entry mode because it reduces the company's risk of losing this control. Consequently, many hi-tech companies prefer wholly owned subsidiaries to joint ventures or licensing arrangements. Wholly owned subsidiaries tend to be the favoured entry mode in the semiconductor, electronics and pharmaceutical industries. Second, a wholly owned subsidiary gives a company the kind of tight control over operations in different countries that it needs to engage in global strategic coordination, so it can take profits from one market to support competitive attacks in another. Third, a wholly owned subsidiary may be the best choice if a company wants to realise location economies and experience-curve effects. As you saw earlier, when cost pressures are intense, it may pay a company to configure its value chain to maximise the value added at each stage. A national subsidiary may, therefore, specialise in manufacturing only part of the product line or certain components of the end-product, exchanging parts and products with other subsidiaries in the company's global system. Establishing this system requires a high degree of control over the operations of national affiliates. Different national operations have to be prepared to accept centrally determined decisions on how they should produce, how much they should produce and how their output should be priced for transfer between operations. A wholly owned subsidiary would have to comply with these mandates, whereas licensees or joint-venture partners would most likely shun such a subservient role.

On the other hand, establishing a wholly owned subsidiary is generally the most costly method of serving a foreign market. The parent company must bear all the costs and risks of setting up overseas operations; in contrast to joint ventures, in which the costs and risks are shared, or licensing, in which the licensee bears most of the costs and risks. The risks of learning to do business in a new culture diminish, however, if the company acquires an established host-nation enterprise. These acquisitions raise additional problems, such as the difficulty of marrying divergent corporate cultures, which may more than offset the benefits. (The

strategy in action 8.4

Third time lucky for Mallesons

Mallesons Stephens Jaques is an Australian commercial law firm with a focus on the Asia-Pacific region. The present structure is the result of the 1987 merger between the Melbourne-based firm Mallesons and the Sydney-based firm of Stephen Jaques Stone James. This merger made the firm one of the leading commercial law firms in Australia.

Since the merger, Mallesons has made forays into Asia. One of the principal areas of focus has been China. As a fast-moving and rapidly growing economy, which is very open to foreign investment, the opportunities in China are just as great for service firms as they are for manufacturers: the traditional focus for direct foreign investment. However, with this growth and opportunity comes risk, and the present operations of Mallesons in relation to the Chinese market are literally its third attempt to capitalise on the growing Chinese market: the first attempt being in the early 1990s, the second in the late 1990s, the most recent being defined by a takeover in 2004. The first attempt saw Mallesons establish a branch but it failed to appreciate that this in itself would not be sufficient and that they had to bring something to their potential clients that could be attained from existing Hong Kong operations. Since then, an effort has been made to understand the opportunities more thoroughly and this included the efforts to allow Mallesons to become the first Australian firm to get a licence to practise international law in Beijing. The financial crisis of the late 1990s ended this foray.

The most recent move saw Mallesons take over the Hong Kong law firm of Kwok & Yih giving Mallesons a top ten presence in Hong Kong. Although there has been a push to make Shanghai the financial hub of China, the relatively undeveloped capital markets, uncertain regulatory environment and a lack of transparency have seen most of the major financial institutions take a position just outside of China in Hong Kong. As such, Hong Kong remains a focus for Mallesons. However, Kwok & Yih also provided a Shanghai licence (to add to the Beijing licence obtained in the 1990s) and offices in both Beijing and Shanghai.

The focus for Mallesons is now on providing legal services for foreign direct investments and trade flows into and out of China. Their client base includes many large financial institutions. Although this latest venture into China through a takeover, using primarily local staff, has been successful and has allowed it much greater access to China, Robert Milliner, CEO of Mallesons, suggests that considerable challenges are still ahead, including English not being commonly spoken and the regulatory environment being quite changeable.

Sources: Mallesons n.d., accessed 1 November 2005, www.mallesons.com.au; James, D 2005, 'Lawyers try again', *Business Review Weekly*, vol. 27, no. 37, 22–29 September, p. 40.

problems associated with acquisitions are discussed in chapter 7.) An example of how risky and difficult using the wholly owned subsidiary approach can be seen in Strategy in action 8.4, concerning the law firm Mallesons Stephens Jaques.

Choosing from among entry modes

The advantages and disadvantages of the various entry modes are summarised in table 8.2. Inevitably, there are tradeoffs in choosing one entry mode over another. When considering entry into an unfamiliar nation with a track record of nationalising foreign-owned enterprises, a company may favour a joint venture with a local enterprise. Its rationale may be that the local partner will help it establish operations in an unfamiliar environment and will speak out against nationalisation if that risk arises. If, however, the company's distinctive competency is based on proprietary technology, then entering into a joint venture may mean risking loss of control over that technology to the joint venture partner, which would make this strategy unattractive. Despite these hazards, some generalisations can be made about the optimal choice of entry mode.

Table 8.2: The advantages and disadvantages of different strategies for competing globally

Entry mode	Advantages	Disadvantages
Exporting	• Ability to realise location and experience-curve economies	• High transport costs • Trade barriers • Problems with local marketing agents
Licensing	• Low development costs and risks	• Inability to realise location and experience-curve economies • Inability to engage in global strategic coordination • Lack of control over technology
Franchising	• Low development costs and risks	• Inability to engage in global strategic coordination • Lack of control over quality
Joint ventures	• Access to local partner's knowledge • Shared development costs and risks • Political dependency	• Inability to engage in global strategic coordination • Inability to realise location and experience-curve economies • Lack of control over technology
Wholly owned subsidiaries	• Protection of technology • Ability to engage in global strategic coordination • Ability to realise location and experience-curve economies	• High costs and risks

Impact of distinctive competencies on entry mode

When companies expand internationally to earn greater returns from their distinctive competencies, transferring the skills and products derived from their competencies to foreign markets in which indigenous competitors lack those skills, the companies are pursuing an international strategy. The optimal entry mode for such companies depends somewhat on the nature of their distinctive competency. In particular, companies with a distinctive competency in technological know-how need to be distinguished from those with a distinctive competency in management know-how.

If a company's competitive advantage — its distinctive competency — derives from its control of proprietary technological know-how, then the company should avoid licensing and joint venture arrangements, if possible, to minimise the risk of losing control of that technology. If a hi-tech company is considering setting up operations in a foreign market to profit from a distinctive competency in technological know-how, then it should probably do so through a wholly owned subsidiary.

This rule, however, should not be viewed as hard and fast. A licensing or joint-venture arrangement may be structured in such a way as to reduce the risks of a company's technological know-how being expropriated by licensees or joint venture partners (as was the case with the Fuji–Xerox venture). This kind of arrangement is considered in more detail later in the chapter in discussing the issue of structuring strategic alliances. Another exception to the rule is when a company perceives its technological advantage as being only transitory and expects rapid imitation of its core technology by competitors. In this case, the company may want to license its technology as quickly as possible to foreign companies to gain global acceptance of its technology before imitation occurs.[22] This strategy has some advantages. By licensing its technology to competitors, the company may deter them from developing their own, possibly superior, technology. It also may be able to establish its technology as the dominant design in the industry, ensuring a steady stream of royalty payments. The attractions of licensing are probably outweighed in most cases by the risks of losing control of technology, so companies with proprietary technological know-how should avoid licensing.

The competitive advantage of many service companies, such as McDonald's or Hilton Hotels, is based on management know-how. For these companies, the risk of losing control of their management skills to franchisees or joint-venture partners is not that great. The reason is that the valuable asset is the brand name, which international trademark laws generally protect. Given this, many of the issues that arise in the case of technological know-how do not arise in the case of management know-how. As a result, many service companies favour a combination of franchising and subsidiaries to control franchisees within a particular country or region. The subsidiary may be wholly owned or a joint venture. In most cases, however, service companies have found that entering into a joint venture with a local partner to set up a controlling subsidiary in a country or region works best because a joint venture is often politically more acceptable and brings a degree of local knowledge to the subsidiary.

Impact of pressures for cost reduction on entry mode

The greater the pressures for cost reductions, the more likely it is that a company will want to pursue some combination of exporting and wholly owned subsidiaries. By manufacturing in the locations where factor conditions are optimal and then exporting to the rest of the world, a company may be able to realise substantial location economies and experience-curve effects. The company may then want to export the finished product to marketing subsidiaries based in various overseas markets. Typically, these subsidiaries would be wholly owned and responsible for overseeing distribution in a particular country. Setting up wholly owned marketing subsidiaries is preferable to using a joint-venture arrangement or a foreign marketing agent because it gives the company the tight control over marketing that it may require to coordinate a globally dispersed value chain. In addition, tight control over a local operation enables the company to use the profits generated in one market to improve its competitive position in another market. Companies pursuing global or transnational strategies prefer to establish wholly owned subsidiaries.

Global strategic alliances

Strategic alliances are cooperative agreements between companies that may also be competitors. This section deals specifically with strategic alliances between companies from different nations. Strategic alliances run the range from formal joint ventures (in which two or more companies have an equity stake) to short-term contractual agreements (in which two companies may agree to cooperate on a particular problem, such as developing a new product).

Advantages of strategic alliances

Companies enter into strategic alliances with actual or potential competitors to achieve a number of strategic objectives.[23] First, as noted in this chapter, strategic alliances may be a way of facilitating entry into a foreign market. Second, many companies have entered into strategic alliances to share the fixed costs (and associated risks) that arise from the development of new products or processes. Third, many alliances can be seen as a way of bringing together complementary skills and assets that neither company could easily develop on its own. Finally, it may make sense to enter into an alliance if it helps the company set technological standards for its industry and if those standards benefit the company. The small Western Australian company Orbital Engine Corporation needed an alliance to be able to enter the automotive parts industry, as detailed in Strategy in action 8.5.

strategy in action 8.5

Orbital Engine Corporation was founded in Western Australia to develop and sell the orbital engine developed by Ralph Sarich. After many years of development work and many attempts to sell the engine to major car manufacturers, Sarich realised that his ambition of being a major player in the engine development and production field was unrealistic. Orbital has since focused on elements of the engine that provide superior performance, seeking to develop these into components that could be used with standard combustion engines. To date, the company has mostly focused on an innovative fuel injection system that atomises fuel into tiny droplets that are essential for efficient combustion and, more importantly, low exhaust emissions. Orbital is banking on this capability to reduce exhaust emissions to provide the company with a major break.

Orbital is aware that Perth is a remote location from which to try to break into the global motor vehicle industry, which tends to be centred in the United States, Europe and Japan. Furthermore, as a small company, it does not have the reputation to become a tier-one supplier to the motor vehicle industry. Its limited success in supplying fuel injector systems for some two-stroke and four-stroke engines (such as outboard manufacturer Mercury Marine and motorcycle manufacturer Aprilia) does not provide the launchpad for supplying major car companies such as General Motors (GM), Ford and BMW.

As a result, Orbital has established an equal joint venture — known as Synerject — with the giant German company Siemens. With manufacturing facilities in Virginia and other offices in France, the Synerject operation has a global reach far beyond what Orbital could hope to develop alone. The joint venture is committed to developing and manufacturing air injectors that supply additional low-pressure air to the cylinder. These air injectors are used within the larger Orbital fuel injection systems and sold separately under the Siemens brand. It is hoped that Orbital's technology and Siemens' brand and distribution capabilities will encourage a major car manufacturer to take up the Orbital technology.

Disadvantages of strategic alliances

The advantages discussed can be significant. Nevertheless, some commentators have criticised strategic alliances for giving competitors a low-cost route to gain new technology and market access. Reich and Mankin studied strategic alliances between US and Japanese companies and argued that there is an implicit Japanese strategy to keep higher paying, higher value-added jobs in Japan while gaining the project engineering and production process skills that underpin the competitive success of many US companies.[24] They view Japanese success in the machine tool and semiconductor industries as largely built on US technology acquired through strategic alliances. They also assert that US managers are increasingly aiding the Japanese in achieving their goals by entering alliances that channel new inventions to Japan and provide a US sales and distribution network for the resulting products. Although such deals may generate short-term profits, Reich and Mankin argue that the long-term result is a 'hollowing out' of US companies, leaving them with no competitive advantage in the global marketplace.

Reich and Mankin have a point: alliances do have risks. Unless it is careful, a company can give away more than it receives in return. On the other hand, there are so many examples of apparently successful alliances between companies, including alliances between US and Japanese companies, that Reich and Mankin's position seems more than a little extreme. Nevertheless Reich and Mankin have a point, and so the question emerges: why do some alliances benefit the company, whereas others lead to the company giving away technology and market access, and getting little in return? The next section provides an answer to this question.

Making strategic alliances work

The failure rate for international strategic alliances seems to be high. One study of forty-nine international strategic alliances found that two-thirds run into serious managerial and financial troubles within two years of their formation and, although many of these problems are eventually solved, that 33 per cent are ultimately rated as failures by the parties involved.[25] Here, we argue that the success of an alliance seems to be a function of three main factors: (a) partner selection, (b) alliance structure and (c) the manner in which the alliance is managed.

Partner selection

One of the keys to making a strategic alliance work is to select the right kind of partner. A good partner has three principal characteristics. First, a good partner helps the company achieve its strategic goals, whether the goals are to achieve market access, share the costs and risks of new product development or gain access to critical core competencies. In other words, the partner must have capabilities that the company lacks and that it values.

Second, a good partner shares the company's vision for the purpose of the alliance. If two companies approach an alliance with radically different agendas, then the chances are great that the relationship will not be harmonious and will end. This seems to have been the case with the alliance between GM and Daewoo. GM's agenda was to use Daewoo as a source of cheap labour to produce cars for the Korean and US markets, whereas Daewoo wanted to use GM's know-how and distribution systems to grow its own business not just in Korea and the United States but also in Europe. Different perceptions of the strategic role of the venture contributed to the dissolution of the alliance.

Third, a good partner is unlikely to try to exploit the alliance for its own ends, that is, to expropriate the company's technological know-how while giving little in return. Companies that have a reputation for fair play and want to maintain it probably make the best partners. IBM, for example, is involved in so many strategic alliances that it would not benefit from trampling roughshod over alliance partners. Opportunistic action would tarnish IBM's hard-won reputation of being a good partner and make it more difficult for IBM to attract alliance partners in the future. Similarly, Japanese companies such as Sony, Toshiba and Fuji, which have a history of alliances with non-Japanese firms, have reputations that lessen the likelihood that they would exploit an alliance partner.

To select a partner with these three characteristics, a company needs to conduct comprehensive research on potential alliance candidates. To increase the probability of selecting a good partner, the company should collect as much pertinent, publicly available information about potential allies as possible; collect data from informed third parties, including companies that have had alliances with the potential partners, investment bankers who have had dealings with them, and some of their former employees; and get to know potential partners as well as possible before committing to an alliance. This last step should include face-to-face meetings between senior managers (and perhaps middle-level managers) to ensure the chemistry is right.

Alliance structure

Having selected a partner, the company should structure the alliance to reduce the risk of giving too much away to the partner. Figure 8.4 depicts four safeguards against opportunism by alliance partners. (Opportunism includes the 'theft' of technology or markets that Reich and Mankin describe.) First, alliances can be designed to make it difficult (if not impossible) to transfer technology not meant to be transferred. Specifically, the design, development, manufacture and service of a product manufactured by an alliance can be structured so as to 'wall off' sensitive technologies and thus prevent their leakage to the other participant. In the alliance between General Electric and Snecma to build commercial aircraft engines, for example, General Electric reduced the risk of 'excess transfer' by walling off certain sections of the production process. The modularisation effectively cut off the transfer of what General Electric regarded as key competitive technology, while permitting Snecma access to final assembly.[26]

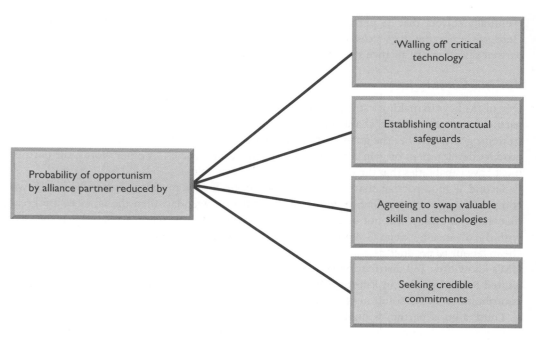

Figure 8.4:
Structuring alliances to
reduce opportunism

Second, contractual safeguards can be written into an alliance agreement to guard against the risk of opportunism by a partner. Australian engineering consulting companies entering certain African and Asian countries, for example, are forced to work with a local partner. To ensure their existing market is not attacked, however, these consulting companies often include in the agreements a clause that forbids the partner organisation from providing services to their present client base for a period of time (generally two to five years).

Third, both parties to an alliance can agree in advance to swap skills and technologies, ensuring a chance for equitable gain. Cross-licensing agreements are one way of achieving this goal. In the alliance between Motorola and Toshiba, for example, Motorola has licensed some of its microprocessor technology to Toshiba, which has licensed some of its memory chip technology to Motorola.

Fourth, the risk of opportunism by an alliance partner can be reduced if the company extracts a significant credible commitment from its partner in advance. The long-term alliance between Xerox and Fuji to build photocopiers for the Asian market perhaps best illustrates this approach. Rather than entering an informal agreement or licensing arrangement (which Fuji Photo initially wanted), Xerox insisted that Fuji invest in a 50/50 joint venture to serve Japan and east Asia. This venture constituted such a significant investment in people, equipment and facilities that Fuji Photo was committed from the outset to making the alliance work to earn a return on its investment. By agreeing to the joint venture, Fuji made a credible commitment to the alliance and Xerox felt secure in transferring its photocopier technology to Fuji.[27]

Management of the alliance

Once the company has selected a partner and agreed on an appropriate alliance structure, it needs to maximise the benefits from the alliance. One important ingredient of success appears to be a sensitivity to cultural differences. Differences in management style can often be attributed to cultural differences. Managers need to make allowances for these when dealing with their partner. In addition, managing an alliance successfully means building interpersonal relationships among managers from the different companies. Developing personal friendships can help build trust and facilitate harmonious relations between the companies. Moreover, personal relationships can create an informal management network between the companies, which can then be used to help solve problems that arise in more formal contexts, such as joint committee meetings between personnel from both companies.

A major factor determining how much a company gains from an alliance is its ability to learn from alliance partners. Hamel, Doz and Prahalad reached this conclusion after a five-year study of 15 strategic alliances between major multinationals. They focused on alliances between Japanese companies and Western (European or US) partners. In every case in which a Japanese company emerged from an alliance stronger than its Western partner, the Japanese company had made a greater effort to learn. Few Western companies seemed to want to learn from their Japanese partners; they tended to regard the alliance purely as a cost-sharing or risk-sharing device, rather than as an opportunity to learn how a potential competitor does business.[28] As a counterpoint, however, Xerox used the Fuji–Xerox joint venture to learn about Japanese manufacturing practices, such as total quality management and design for manufacturing.

On the other hand, the joint effort of GM and Toyota to build the Chevrolet Nova exemplifies an alliance that reveals a clear learning asymmetry.[29] Structured as a formal joint venture, called New United Motor Manufacturing, this alliance gives both parties a 50 per cent equity stake. The venture owns a motor vehicle plant in Fremont, California. According to one of the Japanese managers, Toyota achieved most of its objectives from the alliance: 'We learned about US supply and transportation. And we got the confidence to manage US workers.' All that knowledge was then quickly transferred to Georgetown, Kentucky, where Toyota opened their first US plant. By contrast, although GM got a new product (the Chevrolet Nova), some GM managers complained that their new knowledge was never put to good use inside GM. They say that they should have been kept together as a team to educate GM's engineers and workers about the Japanese system; instead, they were dispersed to different GM subsidiaries.

When entering an alliance, a company must take some measures to ensure it learns from its alliance partner and then puts that knowledge to good use within its own organisation. One suggested approach is to educate all operating employees about the partner's strengths and weaknesses, and make clear to them how acquiring particular skills will bolster their company's competitive position. For such learning to be of value, the knowledge acquired from an alliance has to be diffused throughout the organisation (as did not happen at GM). To spread this knowledge, the managers involved in an alliance should be used as a resource in familiarising others within the company about the skills of an alliance partner.

Summary

This chapter examines the various ways companies can profit from global expansion and reviews the strategies that companies engaged in global competition can adopt. It also discusses the optimal choice of entry mode to serve a foreign market and explores the issue of strategic alliances. The chapter makes the following main points.

▶ There is a link between the national environment (constituting factors such as conditions, strategy, structure and rivalry, demand conditions and the competitiveness of related and supporting industries) and the ability of a company to develop a competitive advantage.

▶ For some companies, international expansion represents a way of earning greater returns by transferring the skills and product offerings derived from their distinctive competencies to markets in which indigenous competitors lack those skills.

▶ Given national differences, it pays a company to base each of its value creation activities at the location where conditions are most conducive to the performance of that activity. This strategy focuses on the attainment of location economies.

▶ By building sales volume more rapidly, international expansion can help a company to move down the experience curve.

- The best strategy for a company to pursue may depend on the kind of pressures it takes: pressure for cost centralisation or pressure for local responsiveness. Pressure for centralisation tends to be greatest in industries producing commodity-type products, in which price is the main competitive weapon. Pressure for local responsiveness arises from differences in consumer tastes and preferences, differences in national infrastructure and traditional practices, differences in distribution channels and host government demands.
- Companies pursuing an international strategy transfer the skills and products derived from distinctive competencies to foreign markets, while undertaking some limited local customisation.
- Companies pursuing a multidomestic strategy customise their product offering, marketing strategy and business strategy to national conditions.
- Companies pursuing a global strategy focus on reaping the cost reductions that come from experience-curve and location economies.
- Many industries are now so competitive that companies must adopt a transnational strategy. This involves a simultaneous focus on cost reduction, skills and products transfer and local responsiveness. Implementing this strategy, however, may not be easy.
- Entering a national market early, before other international businesses have established themselves, has several advantages, but these advantages must be balanced against the pioneering costs that early entrants often have to bear, including the greater risk of business failure.
- Large-scale entry into a national market constitutes a major strategic commitment, which is likely to change the nature of competition in that market and limit the entrant's future strategic flexibility. The company needs to think through the implications of such commitments before embarking on a large-scale entry. Although making major strategic commitments can yield many benefits, such a strategy also involves risks.
- The five different ways of entering a foreign market are exporting, licensing, franchising, entering into a joint venture and setting up a wholly owned subsidiary. The optimal choice of entry mode depends on the company's strategy.
- Strategic alliances are cooperative agreements between actual or potential competitors. The advantages of alliances are that they facilitate entry into foreign markets, enable partners to share the fixed costs and risks of new products and processes, facilitate the transfer of complementary skills between companies and help companies establish technical standards.
- The drawback of a strategic alliance is that the company risks giving away technological know-how and market access to its alliance partner while receiving little in return.
- A company can reduce the disadvantages of alliances if it selects partners carefully, paying close attention to reputation, and if it structures the alliance to avoid unintended transfers of know-how.

Practising strategic management

Review questions

1. The attractiveness of a country and its ability to support certain industries are determined by what factors?
2. What are some potential benefits of global expansion?
3. What factors increase the pressure on a firm to centralise? What factors increase the pressure on a firm to be more locally responsive?
4. What are some benefits of strategic alliances?

Discussion questions

5. Are the following global industries or multidomestic industries: (a) bulk chemicals, (b) pharmaceuticals, (c) branded food products, (d) film making, (e) television manufacture, (f) PCs and (g) airline travel?
6. How might a firm decide where and how to engage in international operations?
7. How much can or should the role of government be incorporated into Porter's diamond model of national competitive advantage?
8. What type of company stands to gain most from entering strategic alliances with potential competitors? Why?

Applied questions

9. Strategy in action 8.1 discusses the success of the New Zealand timber industry. Can this be explained using Porter's diamond model of national competitive advantage? Map out this industry to justify your answer.
10. Recently, Australian-based wine companies (such as Fosters and BRL Hardy) have established alliances with overseas wine companies to source grapes and make wine. Why do you think these companies entered into these arrangements? What are some of the risks to which they exposed themselves?

Small-group exercise

Developing a global strategy

Break into a group of three to five people and discuss the following scenario.

You work for a company in the soft-drink industry that has developed a line of carbonated fruit-based drinks. You have established a significant presence in your home market and you are planning the global strategy development of the company. You need to decide on:

1. an overall strategy to pursue: global, multidomestic, international or transnational
2. markets to enter first
3. an entry strategy to pursue, for example franchising, joint venture or wholly owned subsidiary.

What information do you need to make these decisions? Based on what you do know, what strategies would you recommend?

Article file

Find an example of a multinational company that has switched its strategy in recent years from a multidomestic, international or global strategy to a transnational strategy. Identify why the company made the switch and any problems that the company may be encountering while it tries to change its strategic orientation.

Exploring the Web

Visiting IBM

IBM is the acronym of International Business Machines. Using the significant resources located at IBM's corporate website, including annual reports and company history, explain what 'International' means in 'IBM'. Specifically, in how many nations is IBM active? How does it create value by expanding into foreign markets? What entry mode does it adopt in most markets? Can you find any exceptions? How would you characterise IBM's strategy for competing in the global marketplace: international, multidomestic, global or transnational?

General task

Search the Internet for a company website that has a good description of that company's international operations. On the basis of this information, try to establish how the company enters foreign markets and what overall strategy it is pursuing (international, multidomestic, global or transnational).

Strategic management project

Module 8

This module requires you to identify how your company may profit from global expansion, the strategy that your company should pursue globally and the entry mode that it may favour. With the information you have at your disposal, answer the questions regarding the following two situations.

(a) Your company is already doing business in overseas markets

1. Is your company creating value or lowering the costs of value creation by realising location economies, transferring distinctive competencies abroad or realising cost economies from the experience curve? If not, does it have the potential to do so?

2. How responsive is your company to differences between nations? Does it vary its product and marketing message from one national market to another? Should it?

3. What are the pressures for cost reduction and local responsiveness in the industry in which your company is based?

4. What strategy is your company pursuing to compete globally? In your opinion, is this the correct strategy, given pressures for cost reduction and local responsiveness?

5. What major foreign market does your company serve? What mode has it used to enter this market? Why is your company active in these markets and not others? What are the advantages and disadvantages of using this mode? Might another mode be preferable?

(b) Your company is not yet doing business in overseas markets

1. What potential does your company have to add value to its products or lower the costs of value creation by expanding internationally?

2. On the international level, what are the pressures for cost reduction and local responsiveness in the industry in which your company is based? What implications do these pressures have for the strategy that your company might pursue if it chose to expand globally?

3. What foreign market might your company enter? What entry mode should it use if it were to enter this market? Justify your answer.

Additional resources

Bartlett, C & Ghoshal, S 2000, 'Going global: lessons from late movers,' *Harvard Business Review*, March–April, pp 132–42. (A discussion of how companies that are late to a market can still achieve a global presence.)

Gupta, A & Govindarajan, V 2001, 'Converting global presence into global competitive advantage', *Academy of Management Executive*, vol. 15, no. 2, pp. 45–56. (A discussion of how developing a global strategy can lead to a competitive advantage.)

End notes

1. Porter, ME 1990, *The competitive advantage of nations*, Free Press, New York.

2. ibid., p. 121.

3. Metthee, I 1994, 'Playing a large part', *Seattle-Post Intelligencer*, 9 April, p. 13.

4. Prahalad, CK & Doz, YL 1987, *The multinational mission: balancing local demands and global vision*, Free Press, New York; also see Birkinshaw, J, Morrison, A & Hulland, J 1995, 'Structural and competitive determinants of a global integration strategy', *Strategic Management Journal*, vol. 16, pp. 637–55.

5. Prahalad & Doz, op. cit.

6. Levitt, T 1983, 'The globalization of markets', *Harvard Business Review*, May–June, pp. 92–102.

7. Bartlett, CA & Ghoshal, S 1989, *The transnational solution: managing across borders*, Harvard Business School Press, Boston, Massachusetts.

8. Chipello, CJ 1998, 'Local presence is key to European deals', *Wall Street Journal*, 30 June, p. A15.

9. Bartlett & Ghoshal, op. cit.

10. ibid.

11. See Hill, CWL 2000, *International business: competing in the global marketplace*, McGraw-Hill, Burr Ridge, Illinois.

12. For a discussion of first-mover advantages, see Liberman, M & Montgomery, D 1988, 'First mover advantages', *Strategic Management Journal*, vol. 9, special issue: 'Strategy content', Summer, pp. 41–58.

13. Shaver, JM, Mitchell, W & Yeung, B 1997, 'The effect of own firm and other firm experience on foreign direct investment survival in the United States 1987–92', *Strategic Management Journal*, vol. 18, pp. 811–24.

14. Zaheer, S & Mosakowski, E 1997, 'The dynamics of the liability of foreignness: a global study of survival in the financial services industry', *Strategic Management Journal*, vol. 18, pp. 439–64.

15. Shaver, Mitchell & Yeung, op. cit.

16. Ghemawat, P 1991, *Commitment: the dynamics of strategy*, Free Press, New York.

17. This section draws on several studies including Hill, CWL, Hwang, P & Kim, WC 1990, 'An eclectic theory of the choice of international entry mode', *Strategic Management Journal*, vol. 11, pp. 117–28; Hill, CWL & Kim, WC, 'Searching for a dynamic theory of the multinational enterprise: a transaction cost model', *Strategic Management Journal*, vol. 9, special issue: 'Strategy content', 1988, pp. 93–104; Anderson, E & Gatignon, H 1986, 'Modes of foreign entry: a transaction cost analysis and propositions', *Journal of International Business Studies*, vol. 17, pp 1–26; Root, FR 1980, *Entry strategies for international markets*, DC Heath, Lexington, Massachusetts; Madhok, A 1997, 'Cost, value and foreign market entry: the transaction and the firm', *Strategic Management Journal*, vol. 18, pp. 39–61.

18. Contractor, FJ 1982, 'The role of licensing in international strategy', *Columbia Journal of World Business*, Winter, pp. 73–83.

19. Williamson, OE 1985, *The economic institutions of capitalism*, Free Press, New York.

20. Serwer, AE 1994, 'McDonald's conquers the world', *Fortune*, 17 October, pp. 103–16.

21. Bradley, DG 1977, 'Managing against expropriation', *Harvard Business Review*, July–August, pp. 78–90.

22. Hill, CWL 1992, 'Strategies for exploiting technological innovations', *Organization Science*, vol. 3, pp. 428–41.

23. See Ohmae, K 1989, 'The global logic of strategic alliances', *Harvard Business Review*, March–April, pp. 143–54; Hamel, G, Doz, YL & Prahalad, CK 1988, 'Collaborate with your competitors and win!', *Harvard Business Review*, January–February, pp. 133–39; Burgers, W, Hill, CWL & Kim, WC 1993, 'Alliances in the global auto industry', *Strategic Management Journal*, vol. 14, pp. 419–32.

24. Reich, RB & Mankin, ED 1986, 'Joint ventures with Japan give away our future', *Harvard Business Review*, March–April, pp. 78–90.

25. Bleeke, J & Ernst, D 1991, 'The way to win in cross-border alliances', *Harvard Business Review*, November–December, pp. 127–35.

26. Roehl, W & Truitt, JF 1987, 'Stormy open marriages are better', *Columbia Journal of World Business*, Summer, pp. 87–95.

27. McQuade, K & Gomes-Casseres, B 1992, 'Xerox and Fuji–Xerox', Harvard Business School Case no. 9-391-156, Boston, Massachusetts.

28. Hamel, Doz & Prahalad, op. cit.

29. Wysocki, B 1990, 'Cross border alliances become favorite way to crack new markets', *Wall Street Journal*, 4 March, p. A1.

Implementing strategy

part 4

Designing organisational structure

learning objectives

After studying this chapter, you should be able to:

- understand the role of organisational structure in terms of its effect on company profitability

- appreciate how the basic organisational design building blocks of vertical and horizontal specialisation affect organisational structure

- discuss in which situations centralisation or decentralisation is deemed more appropriate

- describe the characteristics, advantages and disadvantages of simple, functional, multidivisional, product team and matrix structures

- appreciate how and why companies need different integrating mechanisms.

Restructuring at the National

The National, established by Alexander Gibb in Melbourne in 1858 as the National Australasia Bank, became the National Australia Bank when it merged with Commercial Banking Company of Sydney. The group works in an environment that is fast changing and increasingly becoming fiercely competitive. The rapid development of the Internet and other technological advancements has powered the globalisation of the financial services industry. The industry has many traditional and new players, such as financial conglomerates, mutual societies, investment or merchant banks, specialist retail and wholesale fund managers, building societies, credit unions and finance companies.

Before the current restructure, the organisational structure of the group was aligned with customers — as opposed to along product lines — to focus on and meet the needs of its millions of customers, rather than focusing internally on the preferences of its managers. Based on this philosophy, the group organised its businesses into six areas: business and personal financial services, specialist and emerging businesses, national shared services, wholesale financial services, wealth management and HomeSide Lending Inc. HomeSide, based in Jacksonville, Florida, operates a loan servicing and origination business. The National also had another division during this time called the Corporate Centre. This centre determined the strategic direction of the group. In addition, it also had the following units: risk management, people and culture, finance and planning, and the office of the CEO. The operations of the group within Australia, regionally and internationally all worked under this customer-focused structure.

During early 2004, the company had a serious crisis when it lost $360 million in foreign currency options. There was a dispute in the board between directors over the independence of the investigation into the unauthorised trading of foreign currency. This was followed by the resignations of the CEO and several members of the board of directors. The company was in serious trouble. Many parts of its business were in nosedive and out of control. Market share was declining, customers were defecting, costs were increasing and the earnings of many businesses had virtually stalled.

John Stewart, the new CEO, identified four causes of underperformance of the group. He argued that the business structure of the company was complex and management lacked ownership and accountability for costs. Second, the company was operating in silos and there was lack of interdivisional cooperation. In the 2004 *Concise annual report*, he said: 'The customer segment approach reduced the focus on providing competitively priced products. Lending processes became progressively more complex. The outcome of this was poor cross-sell performance, customer churn and attrition and lower margins.' Third, the company had a very weak compliance framework. In many cases, policies and procedures were not clear and individual responsibilities were not clearly defined. Managers were not aware of the policies nor of their responsibilities. To make matters worse, the too complex monitoring process largely failed to bring the issues out into the open. Last, although the National had a set of agreed values, managers were neither assessed based on them nor held accountable when in breach of them.

On 11 August 2004, the National announced a change in its organisational design, moving the group away from a divisional to a regional business model. The three regions were: Australia, Europe and New Zealand. The Australian division incorporates retail and business banking (Financial Service Australia), wealth management, Australian corporate banking services, transactional solutions, custody services and Asian business. The European division coordinates the operations of Clydesdale Bank, Yorkshire Bank, National Irish Bank and Northern Bank. This division also looks after wealth management services in Europe. The National operates in New Zealand through the Bank of New Zealand, which operates retail and corporate banking as well as custody and wealth management services. This restructure came into effect at the beginning of 2005. It also included a division called institutional markets and services, covering this line of business in all National's regions. It deals with such matters as markets, portfolio management and syndications, credit products, structured products, financial institutions, services and the New York branch. The National continued with the Corporate Centre in a much streamlined form. It supports all the regional businesses in areas including technology, people and culture, finance and risk management, major projects, corporate strategy and corporate affairs.

Sources: National Australia Bank 2004, *Concise annual report;* National Australia Bank 2001, *Annual financial report;* Gluyas, R 2005, 'Stable NAB stays on reforms path', *The Australian*, 29 September.

organisational design
The combination of organisational structure and control systems that allows a company to implement its strategy effectively

organisational structure
The reporting relationships, communication channels and form of hierarchy within a company

Overview

As the opening case suggests, this chapter considers how a company should organise its activities to create the most value. Chapter 1 defines *strategy implementation* as the way a company creates the organisational arrangements that allow it to pursue its strategy most effectively. Strategy is implemented through organisational design. **Organisational design** means selecting the combination of **organisational structure** and control systems that allows a company to pursue its strategy most effectively, that is, that lets it create and sustain a competitive advantage.

The primary role of organisational structure and control is twofold: (1) to *coordinate* the activities of employees so they work together most effectively to implement a strategy that increases competitive advantage and (2) to *motivate* employees and provide them with the incentives to achieve superior efficiency, quality, innovation or responsiveness to customers. National's strategy, as it seems from the opening case, is that it hopes to regain customer confidence by creating a transparent structure that clearly identifies and locates points of responsibility. National believes that this division of work along geographic lines will help with monitoring performance and with communicating within the company.

Organisational structure and control shape how people behave and determine how they will act in the organisational setting. If a new CEO wants to know why it takes a long time for people to make decisions in a company, why there is a lack of cooperation between sales and manufacturing or why product innovations are few and far between, he or she needs to look at the design of the organisational structure and control system, and analyse how it coordinates and motivates employees' behaviour. An analysis of how structure and control work makes it possible to change them to improve both coordination and motivation. Good organisational design allows a company to improve its ability to create value and obtain a competitive advantage.

This chapter examines the organisational structures available to strategic managers to coordinate and motivate employees. Chapter 10 considers the strategic control systems that managers use in conjunction with their organisational structures to monitor, motivate and reward corporate, divisional and functional performance. This chapter also traces how different strategy choices lead to the use of different types of structure and control system. After reading these chapters, you will be able to understand the principles behind National's redesign of its organisational structure and control system, and you will be able to choose the right organisational design for implementing a company's strategy.

The role of organisational structure

Organisational structure is one of the most important requirements for company strategy. As a matter of fact, strategy and structure are integrally intertwined: they are mutually reinforcing. Structure helps companies in strategy formulation and implementation, and strategies influence the type of organisational structure a company has.[1] The value creation activities of organisational members are meaningless unless some type of structure is used to assign people to tasks, and connect the activities of different people and functions.[2] As discussed in chapters 4 and 5, each organisational function needs to develop a distinctive competency in a value creation activity to increase efficiency, quality, innovation or responsiveness to customers. Each function, therefore, needs a structure designed to allow it to develop its skills and become more specialised and productive. As functions become increasingly specialised, however, they often begin to pursue their own goals exclusively and lose sight of the need to communicate and be coordinated with other functions. The goals of the research and development (R&D) function, for example, centre on innovation and product design, whereas the goals of the manufacturing function often revolve around increasing efficiency. Left to themselves, the functions may have little to say to one another, and value creation opportunities will be lost.

The role of organisational structure is to provide the vehicle through which managers can coordinate the activities of the various functions or divisions to exploit their skills and capabilities fully. To pursue a cost-leadership strategy, for example, a company must design a structure that facilitates close coordination between the activities of manufacturing and those of R&D to ensure that innovative products can be produced both reliably and cost effectively. To achieve gains from synergy among divisions, managers must design mechanisms that allow divisions to communicate and share their skills and knowledge. In pursuing a global or multidomestic strategy, managers must create the right type of organisational structure for managing the flow of resources and capabilities among domestic and foreign divisions. Chapter 10 examines how managers match their strategies to different types of structure and control system. The goal here is to examine the basic building blocks of organisational structure to understand how structure shapes the behaviour of people, functions and divisions.

Building blocks of organisational structure

As Strategy in action 9.1 shows, the basic building blocks of organisational structure are **division of work** and **integration**. Division of work is how a company allocates people and resources to organisational tasks so as to create value.[3] Generally, the greater the number of different functions or divisions in a company and the more skilled and specialised they are, the higher is the level of specialisation. A multinational company such as General Motors (GM), with more than 300 different divisions and a multitude of different sales, R&D, and design departments, has a much greater level of specialisation than that of a local manufacturing company or restaurant. In deciding how to divide work in the company to create value, strategic managers face two choices.

First, strategic managers must choose how to distribute *decision-making authority* in the organisation to control value creation activities best; these are **vertical specialisation** choices.[4] Corporate managers must decide, for example, how much authority to delegate to managers at the divisional or functional level. Second, corporate managers must choose how to divide people and tasks into functions and divisions to increase their ability to create value; these are **horizontal specialisation** choices. Should there be separate sales and marketing departments, for example, or should the two be combined? What is the best way of dividing the sales force to maximise its ability to meet customers' needs: by type of customer or by region in which customers are located?

Integration is how a company seeks to coordinate people and functions to accomplish organisational tasks.[5] As noted, when separate and distinct value creation functions exist, they tend to pursue their own goals and objectives. A company has to create an organisational structure that allows the different functions and divisions to coordinate their activities to pursue a strategy effectively. A company uses integrating mechanisms, as well as the various types of control system discussed in the next chapter, to promote coordination and cooperation between functions and divisions. To speed innovation and product development, companies establish teams so employees can work together to exchange information and ideas effectively. Similarly, establishing organisational norms and values and a common culture that supports innovation promotes integration.

In short, division of work refers to how a company divides itself into parts (functions and divisions) and integration refers to how the parts are then combined. Together, the two processes determine how an organisational structure will operate and how successfully strategic managers will be able to create value through their chosen strategies.

division of work
How a company allocates people and resources to different tasks

integration
How a company coordinates people and functions to accomplish organisational tasks

vertical specialisation
Division and allocation of authority among managers

horizontal specialisation
Division and allocation of functions or tasks among managers

strategy in action 9.1

Division and coordination of work in Vodafone

Vodafone became one of the largest mobile phone operators under the leadership of Sir Chris Gent. Gent built an empire. Hundreds of thousands of operators spread all over the world needed to be integrated. The task fell to Arun Sarin, who became the CEO of Vodafone in July 2003. Sarin's mission was to bring these pieces together so that they fitted with one another and also to achieve economies of scale. This required redrawing organisation charts, rationalising back offices and cutting costs among other things. These types of activities rarely generate publicity. This task of bringing harmony between disparate tasks is dull but necessary. With the rollout of the third-generation (3G) mobile services, Mr Sarin wants to demonstrate that a big organisation such as

Vodafone can also work as an unified entity. He wants to make sure Vodafone users use the same technology the world over. To achieve coordination among the different parts of the company, under a reformed organisational structure, Mr Sarin requires all regional managers to report directly to him. Under this functional arrangement, marketing executives from different international locations report directly to the head of the marketing function rather than to their local or regional head. This allows Mr Sarin to have more direct contact and control over the whole of Vodafone.

Source: The Economist 2004, 'Foundation and empire; face value', vol. 373, iss. 8403, 27 November, p. 88.

Division of work, integration and bureaucratic costs

bureaucratic costs
The costs of running a company that tend to increase as the company grows, reflecting coordination costs (as more management is required) and the costs of inefficiencies that occur

Implementing a structure to coordinate and motivate task activities is expensive. Bureaucratic costs are the costs of operating an organisational structure and control system. The more complex the structure — that is, the higher the level of specialisation and integration — the higher are the bureaucratic costs of managing it. In more differentiated companies — for example, those with more managers in specialised roles — each manager requires more resources to perform his or her role effectively. Managers are expensive, so the more managers a company employs, the higher are its bureaucratic costs.

Similarly, the more integrated the company, the more managerial time is spent in face-to-face meetings to coordinate task activities. Managerial time also costs money, so the higher the level of integration, the more costly it is to operate the structure. A large company such as IBM or GM spends billions of dollars a year to operate its structures, that is, to pay its managers and employees, and to provide them with the resources (offices, computers, equipment, laboratories and so forth) they need to create value.

The high bureaucratic costs of strategy implementation can reduce a company's profits as fast or faster than poor strategy formulation can, so they directly affect bottom-line organisational performance. This is why good organisational design is so important. Chapter 4 notes that profit is the difference between revenue and costs. Bureaucratic costs are a large component of the cost side of the equation. A poor organisational design (for example, one that has too many levels in the hierarchy or a poorly constructed pattern of work relationships) results in high costs, which reduce profits. By contrast, good organisational design, which economises on bureaucratic costs, can give a company a low-cost advantage, which raises profits.

Organisational design also affects the revenue side of the equation. If strategic managers choose the right structure to coordinate value creation activities, then they increase the company's ability to create value, charge a premium price and thus increase revenue. John Stewart hoped that the National's new structure would increase its ability to create value and improve its image among the different customer groups. Good design thus affects both the revenue side and the cost side of the profit equation, as figure 9.1 illustrates. This is why strategy implementation is such a vital issue. In today's competitive environment, more and more companies are restructuring or re-engineering their organisations to improve bottom-line performance through good organisational design. Consequently, it is necessary to understand the principles behind organisational design, beginning with differentiation.

Vertical division of work

The aim of **vertical division of work** is to specify the reporting relationships that link people, tasks and functions at all levels of a company. This means that management chooses the appropriate number of hierarchical levels and the correct **span of control** for implementing a company's strategy most effectively.

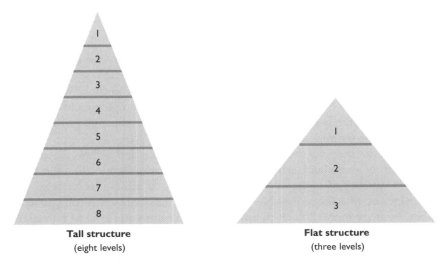

vertical division of work
How authority is devolved within a company, creating tall or flat structures

span of control
The number of subordinates that a manager directly manages

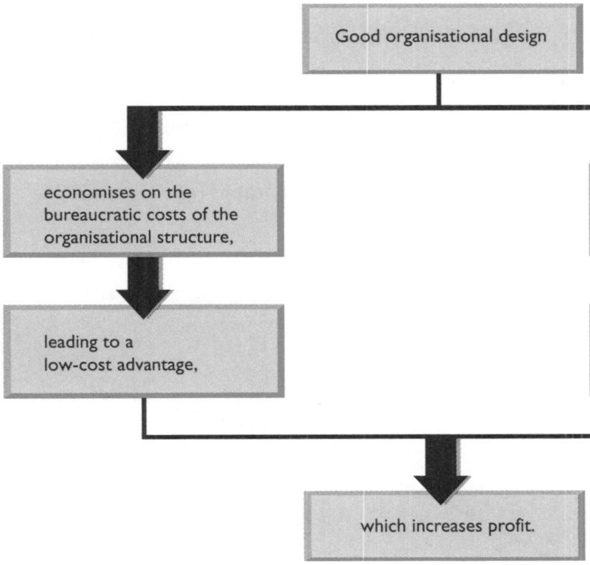

Figure 9.1:
How organisational design increases profitability

The organisational hierarchy establishes the authority structure from the top to the bottom of the company. The span of control is defined as the number of subordinates that a manager directly manages.[6] The basic choice is whether to aim for a flat structure, with few hierarchical levels and therefore a relatively wide span of control, or a tall structure, with many levels and therefore a relatively narrow span of control (see figure 9.2). Tall structures have many hierarchical levels relative to size; flat structures have few levels relative to size.[7] Research suggests that the average hierarchical levels for a company employing 3000 persons is seven. A company with nine levels would consequently be tall and one with four would be flat. With its 30 000 employees and five hierarchical levels, Microsoft has a relatively flat structure.

Tall structure
(eight levels)

Flat structure
(three levels)

Figure 9.2:
Tall and flat structures

Companies choose the number of levels they need on the basis of their strategy and the functional tasks necessary to achieve this strategy.[8] Hi-tech companies, for example, often pursue a strategy of differentiation based on service and quality. Consequently, these companies usually have flat structures, giving employees wide discretion to meet customers' demands without having to refer constantly to supervisors.[9] (This subject is discussed further in chapter 10.) The crux of the matter is that the allocation of authority and responsibility in the company must match the needs of corporate-, business- and functional-level strategies.[10]

Problems with tall structures

As a company grows and diversifies, the number of levels in its hierarchy of authority increases to allow it to monitor and coordinate employee activities efficiently. Research shows that the number of hierarchical levels relative to company size is predictable (see figure 9.3).[11]

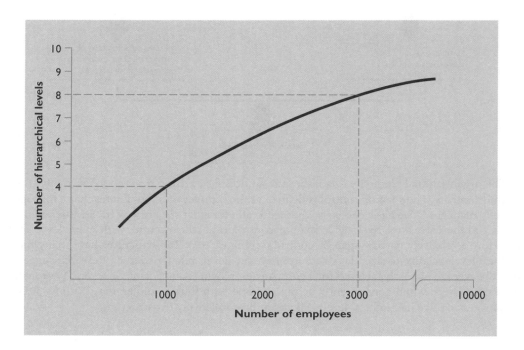

Figure 9.3:
Relationship between company size and the number of hierarchical levels

Companies with approximately 1000 employees usually have four levels in the hierarchy. Those with 3000 employees have increased their level of vertical specialisation by raising the number of levels to eight. Something interesting happens to those with more than 3000 employees, however. Even when companies grow to 10 000 employees or more, the number of hierarchical levels rarely increases beyond nine or ten. As companies grow, managers apparently try to limit the number of hierarchical levels.

Managers try to keep the company as flat as possible and follow the principle of the minimum chain of command, which states that a company should choose a hierarchy with the minimum number of levels of authority necessary to achieve its strategy. Managers try to keep the hierarchy as flat as possible because problems occur when companies become too tall, making strategy more difficult to implement and raising the level of bureaucratic costs.[12] Several factors that raise bureaucratic costs are illustrated in figure 9.4 and discussed in the following paragraphs.

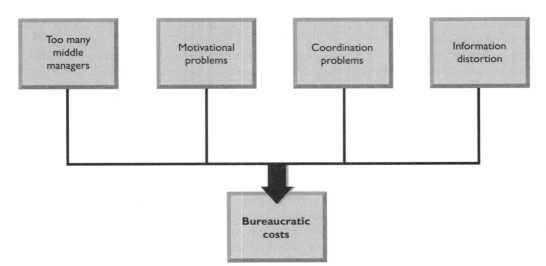

Coordination problems

Too many hierarchical levels impede communication and coordination between employees and functions, and raise bureaucratic costs. Communication between the top and the bottom of the hierarchy takes much longer as the chain of command lengthens. This leads to inflexibility, and valuable time is lost in bringing a new product to market or keeping up with technological developments.[13] For the US company Federal Express, for example, communication and coordination are vital. To avoid problems with them, the company allows a maximum of only five layers of management between the employee and the CEO.[14] Companies regularly take measures to flatten their structures so as to speed communication and decision making.

Information distortion

More subtle, but just as important, are the problems of information distortion that occur as the hierarchy of authority lengthens. Going down the hierarchy, managers at different levels (for example, divisional or corporate managers) may misinterpret information — either through accidental garbling of messages or on purpose — to suit their own interests. In either case, information from the top may not reach its destination intact. A request to share divisional knowledge to achieve gains from synergy, for example, may be overlooked or ignored by divisional managers who perceive it as a threat to their autonomy and power.

Information transmitted upwards in the hierarchy may also be distorted. Subordinates may transmit to their superiors only information that improves their own standing in the company. The greater the number of hierarchical levels, the more scope subordinates have to distort facts, so the bureaucratic costs of managing the hierarchy increase. Similarly, bureaucratic costs increase if managers start to compete with each other. When they are free of close corporate supervision, they may hoard information to promote their own interests at the expense of the company's interest. This problem also reduces coordination.

Motivational problems

As the number of levels in the hierarchy increases, the amount of authority possessed by managers at each hierarchical level lessens. Consider the situation of two identically sized companies: one with three levels in its hierarchy and the other with seven. Managers in the flat structure have much more authority, which increases their motivation to perform effectively and take responsibility for the company's performance. Furthermore, where there are fewer managers, their performance is more visible and they can expect greater rewards when the business does well.

By contrast, the ability of managers in a tall structure to exercise authority is limited. Furthermore, their decisions are constantly scrutinised by their superiors. As a result, managers tend to offload blame and responsibility and refuse to take the risks that are often necessary in pursuing new strategies. The bureaucratic costs of managing the company consequently rise because more managerial time is spent coordinating task activities. The shape of the company's structure thus strongly affects the motivation of people within it and how strategy is implemented.[15]

Too many middle managers

Another drawback of tall structures is that having many hierarchical levels implies having many middle managers, who are expensive. As noted, managerial salaries, benefits, offices and secretaries are a huge expense for a company. If the average middle manager costs a company a total of $200 000 per year (salary, superannuation, travel, computer, office space and so on), then employing ten surplus managers costs $2 million per year. Most large companies have recognised this and, in the 1990s, companies such as IBM, the Commonwealth Bank and Coles-Myer downsized their hierarchies, terminating thousands of managers. When these companies made billions of dollars in profits, they had little incentive to control the number of levels in the hierarchy and the number of managers. Once they grew aware of the cost of these managers, however, the companies ruthlessly purged the hierarchy, reducing the number of levels and consequently the number of managers to lower bureaucratic costs and restore profitability.

To offer another example, when companies grow and are successful, they often hire personnel and create new positions without much regard for the effect on the organisational hierarchy. Later, when managers review that structure, they often reduce the number of levels in response to the disadvantages just discussed. Deregulation also prompts a reduction in levels and personnel. In a deregulated environment, companies must respond to increased competition. Since the deregulation of the banking and airline industries in Australia, companies such as the Commonwealth Bank and Qantas have reduced their costs and streamlined their structures so that they can respond to change more rapidly and cope more effectively with increased competition. Since the deregulation of the banking industry in the United States, Bank of America has laid off 20 per cent of its workforce.[16]

In sum, many problems arise when companies become too tall and the chain of command becomes too long. Strategic managers tend to lose control over the hierarchy, which means that they lose control over their strategies. Disaster often follows because a tall organisational structure decreases, rather than promotes, motivation and coordination between employees and functions and, as a result, bureaucratic costs escalate. One way of overcoming such problems (at least partly) and lessening bureaucratic costs is to decentralise authority, that is, to vest authority in the hierarchy's lower levels as well as at the top. This is one of the most important implementation decisions a company can make, so it is discussed next in more detail.

Many others argue that it is wiser to adopt a contingency approach in designing organisational structure. The contingency approach argues that there is no one best way to design an organisation's structure. Managers should consider the strategy they are pursuing while designing their organisational structure and align the two. If the strategy they are pursuing requires a tall structure, they should design their organisation hierarchically. It is fashionable to have a flatter organisation with fewer layers in the hierarchy, which is credited with a long list of virtues. Flatter organisations are less bureaucratic, less authoritarian, less bound by rules and regulations and more flexible, more democratic, more innovative, better at internal communication and more customer responsive and achieve higher degrees of satisfaction for employees. General Electric under Jack Welch cut entire layers of management across the corporation.

However, such Japanese firms as Toyota, Honda and Sony are very hierarchical, yet renowned for their competitive success. A typical Japanese firm will have two to three times as many middle managers as an American one. These organisations are hierarchical, yet they are flexible and innovative. Honda, for example, creates cross-functional, self-managed teams that come together for a particular project and disband again. This occurs inside the confines of a large hierarchical organisation.[17]

Centralisation or decentralisation?

Centralisation occurs when upper levels of the organisational hierarchy make all of the important decisions. Decentralisation allows divisions, functions and managers and workers at lower levels in the company to make decisions. By allowing lower- and mid-level managers to make decisions, companies can economise on bureaucratic costs and avoid communication and coordination problems because information does not have to be constantly sent to the top of the company for decisions to be made. There are three advantages to decentralisation.

First, when strategic managers delegate operational decision-making responsibility to middle and first-level managers, they reduce information overload, enabling themselves to spend more time on strategic decision making. Consequently, they can make more effective decisions.

Second, when managers in the bottom layers of the company become responsible for adapting the company to suit local conditions, their motivation and accountability increase. The result is that decentralisation promotes organisational flexibility and reduces bureaucratic costs because lower-level managers are authorised to make on-the-spot decisions.

The third advantage of decentralisation is that when lower-level employees are given the right to make important decisions, fewer managers are needed to oversee their activities and tell them what to do. Having fewer managers means lower bureaucratic costs.

If decentralisation is so effective, why do not all companies decentralise decision making and avoid the problems of tall hierarchies? The answer is that centralisation also has advantages. Centralised decision making allows easier coordination of the organisational activities needed to pursue a company's strategy. If managers at all levels can make their own decisions, then overall planning becomes extremely difficult and the company may lose control of its decision making.

Centralisation also means that decisions fit broad company objectives. As companies grow, their different parts may operate differently. Centralisation can limit the problems this might bring. One of the greatest strengths of McDonald's, for example, is how it centralises some of its operations, including the development of procedures. Customers are sure they will receive the same quality of product and level of service around the world. Centralisation can provide consistency, cost savings and rapid decision making (because a small group of people make all decisions). It can also, however, lead to a disenfranchising of employees because some of their autonomy is removed.

Horizontal division of work

Managing the strategy–structure relationship when the number of hierarchical levels becomes too great is difficult and expensive. Depending on a company's situation, decentralisation can reduce the bureaucratic costs of tall hierarchies. As company size increases, however, decentralisation may become less effective. How then, as companies grow and diversify, can they economise on bureaucratic costs without becoming too tall or too decentralised? How can a company such as Coles-Myer control 160 000 employees without becoming too bureaucratic

centralisation
When decisions are made at the upper levels of the organisational hierarchy

decentralisation
When decisions are made at different levels within the organisational hierarchy

and inflexible? There must be alternative ways of creating organisational arrangements to achieve corporate objectives. The first of these is to choose the appropriate form of horizontal division of work, that is, to decide how best to group organisational activities and tasks to create value.

Whereas vertical division of work concerns the division of authority, horizontal division of work focuses on the division and grouping of tasks to meet the objectives of the business.[18] Given that a company's tasks are largely a function of the company's strategy, the dominant view is that companies choose a form of horizontal division of work or structure to match their organisational strategy. Perhaps the first person to address this issue formally was the Harvard business historian Alfred D Chandler.[19] After studying the organisational problems experienced in large US companies such as DuPont and GM as they grew and diversified in the early decades of this century, Chandler reached two conclusions: (1) in principle, organisational structure follows the growth strategy of a company (in other words, it follows the range and variety of tasks that the company chooses to pursue); and (2) US companies' structures change in a predictable way over time as their strategy changes.[20] The types of structure that companies adopt are discussed in this section.

Simple structure

The simple structure is normally used by the small, entrepreneurial company producing a single product or a few related ones for a specific market segment. In this situation, one person, the entrepreneur, usually takes on most of the managerial tasks. No formal organisational arrangements exist and horizontal specialisation is low because employees perform multiple duties. A classic example is a cafe or small retail shop. The owner normally organises all of the necessary tasks, from ordering supplies, employing staff and arranging advertising to managing the financial side of the business. As soon as the business grows larger than a few staff, however, it starts to outgrow the simple structure. Once it exceeds ten staff, it generally requires some level of specialisation among the staff and more formalised reporting relationships; otherwise, the owner/manager could suffer from an information overload. Although developing a more complex structure raises bureaucratic costs, this effect is acceptable as long as the structure also increases the amount of value that a company can create.

Functional structure

As companies grow, two things happen. First, the range of tasks that must be performed expands. It becomes apparent that the services of a professional accountant, a production manager or marketing expert, for example, are needed to take control of specialised tasks. Second, no one person can successfully perform more than one organisational task without becoming overloaded. The founder, for example, can no longer simultaneously make and sell the product. So what group of activities — or what form of horizontal specialisation — can most efficiently handle the needs of the growing company at least cost? The answer for most companies is a functional structure.

A functional structure groups people on the basis of their common expertise and experience, or because they use the same resources.[21] Engineers, for example, would be grouped in a function because they perform the same tasks and use the same skills or equipment. Figure 9.5 shows a typical functional structure. Each rectangle represents a different functional specialisation — R&D, sales and marketing, manufacturing and so on — and each function concentrates on its own specialised task.

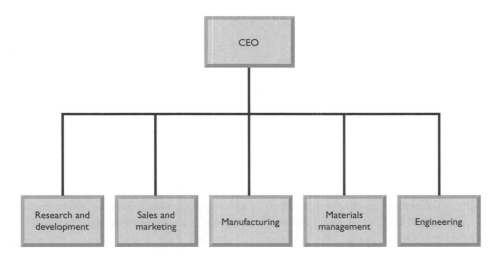

Advantages of a functional structure

Functional structures have several advantages. First, if people who perform similar tasks are grouped together, then they can learn from one another and become better — that is, more specialised and productive — at what they do.

Second, they can monitor each other to make sure everyone is performing tasks effectively and not shirking responsibilities. As a result, the work process becomes more efficient, reducing manufacturing costs and increasing operational flexibility.

Third, managers have greater control of organisational activities. As noted, many difficulties arise when the number of levels in the hierarchy increases. If people are grouped into different functions, however, each with their own managers, then several different hierarchies are created and the company can avoid becoming too tall. There will be one hierarchy in manufacturing, for example, and another in accounting and finance. Managing the business is much easier when different groups specialise in different organisational tasks and are managed separately.

strategy in action 9.2

Fisher & Paykel focuses on function

Fisher & Paykel Appliances is a New Zealand-based company that designs and manufactures kitchen appliances. Its largest markets are Australia and New Zealand.

In 2001, Fisher & Paykel faced intense price competition in its home market and consequently looked for ways to improve the efficiency of its business. Part of its strategy to improve performance involved changing its structure from what it called a 'product-focused divisional structure' to an 'integrated business unit managed on a functional basis'. The old structure had divisions focusing on particular types of appliance, each employing its own set of specialists in the various functional areas involved in design and development.

The new structure was simpler, required fewer people and was less costly to operate. At the same time it made it easier to manage production centrally, resulting in better use of capacity and lower finished goods inventory. These factors combined to lower the company's capital expenditure requirements.

As well as reducing costs, the company also needed to maintain its effectiveness at launching innovative products. Fisher & Paykel reported that its new unitary structure helped them to pursue common priorities and practices across the business as a whole. Previously, these efforts would have been fragmented by the need to work through the product divisions. With the new structure, the risk is a new form of fragmentation by specialist function. Because an efficient product pipeline requires good coordination of activities across functions, Fisher & Paykel would have had to put in place effective integrating mechanisms to encourage close collaboration between the functional areas.

Source: Fisher & Paykel 2001, *Annual report*.

Disadvantages of a functional structure

In adopting a functional structure, a company increases its level of horizontal differentiation to handle more complex tasks. The structure allows it to keep control of its activities as it grows. This structure serves the company well until it starts to grow and diversify. If the company becomes geographically diverse and begins operating in many locations, or if it starts producing a wide range of products, then control and coordination problems arise that lower a company's ability to coordinate its activities and that increases bureaucratic costs.[22]

Communication problems

As separate functional hierarchies evolve, functions grow more remote from one another. As a result, it becomes increasingly difficult to communicate across functions and to coordinate their activities. This communication problem stems from functional orientations.[23] With greater specialisation, the various functions develop different orientations to the problems and issues facing the company. Different functions have different time or goal orientations. Some, such as manufacturing, work to a short timeframe and concentrate on achieving short-term goals, such as reducing manufacturing costs. Others, such as R&D, operate with a long-term perspective, with goals (that is, innovation and product development) that may have a time horizon of several years. These factors may cause each function to develop a different view of the strategic issues facing the company. Manufacturing, for example, may consider that the strategic issue is the need to reduce costs; sales may consider it to be the need to increase customer responsiveness, and R&D may consider it to be the need to create new products. In such cases, the functions have trouble communicating and coordinating with one another, and bureaucratic costs increase.

Measurement problems

As its products proliferate, a company may find it difficult to gauge the contribution of a product (or a group of products) to its overall profitability. Consequently, the company may turn out some unprofitable products without realising it and also may make poor decisions about resource allocation. This means that the company's measurement systems are not complex enough to serve its needs. Dell Computer's explosive growth in the early 1990s, for example, caused it to lose control of its inventory management systems; it could not accurately project supply and demand for the components that go into its PCs. Problems with its organisational structure plagued Dell, reducing efficiency and quality. As one manager commented, designing its structure to keep pace with its growth was like 'building a high performance car while going around the race track'.[24] Dell nevertheless succeeded and today enjoys a 10 per cent cost advantage over competitors such as Compaq, partly as a result of its innovative organisational design.

Location problems

Location factors may also hamper coordination and control. If a company is producing or selling in many different regional areas, then the centralised system of control provided by the functional structure no longer suits it because managers in the various regions must be flexible enough to respond to the needs of these regions. The functional structure is, therefore, not complex enough to handle regional diversity.

Strategic problems

Sometimes the combined effect of all these factors is that long-term strategic considerations are ignored because management is preoccupied with solving communication and coordination problems. As a result, a company may lose direction and fail to take advantage of new opportunities while bureaucratic costs escalate.

Experiencing these problems is a sign that the company does not have an appropriate level of division of work to achieve its objectives. A company must change its mix of vertical and horizontal division of work if it is to perform effectively the organisational tasks that will enhance its competitive advantage. These problems indicate that the company has outgrown its structure. The company needs to invest more resources in developing a more complex structure, which can meet the needs of its competitive strategy. Again, this is expensive but as long as the value that a company can create is greater than the bureaucratic costs of operating the structure, the adoption of a more complex structure makes sense. Many companies choose a multidivisional structure, discussed towards the end of this chapter.

Product structure

In a product structure, a company divides organisational work among its managers and employees based on the types of products it produces. The functional structure does not take into account the types of products a company produces and a company may use the same functional structure to produce many different products. Companies following the functional structure and producing many products may find that their different functional units do not pay equal attention to all their products. The structure that organisations most commonly adopt to cater for the production of many different products for many different market segments is called the product structure. The intent behind the change to a product structure is to break up a company's growing product line into a number of smaller, more manageable subunits to reduce bureaucratic costs in communication, measurement and the other areas noted.

An organisation that decides to group activities by product first decides how to group its overall product line into product groups or categories so that each product group can be developed, manufactured, distributed and sold at the lowest cost consistent with permitting the differentiation needed to create value for customers. Each product group is targeted at satisfying the needs of a particular customer group and is managed by its own team of managers, who focus their efforts on that group. To keep costs as low as possible, the decision is made to centralise support value functions such as R&D, marketing, sales and accounting at the top of the organisation, with the different product groups sharing their services. Each support function, in turn, is divided into product-oriented teams of functional specialists, who focus on the needs of one particular product group. This arrangement allows each team to specialise and become expert in managing the needs of its product group. However, because all of the R&D teams belong to the same centralised function, they can share knowledge and information with each other that allows them to build their competencies over time.

Strategy in action 9.3 illustrates how Kodak uses product structure. As figure 9.6 shows, each of Kodak's product lines uses the services of the central support functions. The expense of creating separate functions for each product line could be justified only if the needs of the different product lines were so different that different sets of functional specialists were required for each group of products. Normally this happens only when a company enters new industries and markets and its range of product offerings becomes increasingly diverse and unrelated. When this happens, a company requires an even more complex structure, a multidivisional structure, which is discussed later in this chapter.

multidivisional structure
An organisational structure in which employees are grouped into divisions on the basis of common product markets or geographic markets

strategy in action 9.3

Kodak's product structure

The Eastman Kodak company is one of the oldest and best-known companies in the world. For decades, Kodak monopolised the global film market but, starting in the 1970s, new low-cost competitors such as Fuji began to take market share from Kodak.

To respond to this challenge, Kodak decided to strengthen its core photographic business by bringing out new and improved products but it had to find a low-cost way to do so because it was already at a cost disadvantage to Fuji. Kodak's CEO, Daniel Carp, decided it would be necessary to move to a product structure, shown in figure 9.6.

Carp decided to streamline Kodak's structure by dividing all its products into different product categories, such as consumer photographic products, digital imaging and digital cameras, health imaging products and commercial imaging products. Each product group is headed by a separate team of managers responsible for managing the value chain functions necessary to develop advanced new products for customers. However, to reduce costs, each product line shares the services of R&D, imaging, marketing, sales, accounting and so on, which remain centralised. In essence, the responsibility for strategy making is decentralised to managers inside each product line, but support value chain activities are kept centralised to defray costs and because developments can be quickly spread among and shared by Kodak's different imaging groups. For example, the R&D team that focuses on medical imaging can share discoveries about new methods for digitising images with the R&D team for commercial products. As a result, Kodak is able to transfer its skills and leverage its competencies across product groups and market segments, and advances in digital imaging technology can be quickly communicated to each group to speed product development. Also, by keeping sales centralised, a single national sales force can sell the complete range of Kodak's imaging products. So far, this grouping of organisational activities by product as well as function has helped Kodak lower its cost structure and overcome many of its old problems of handing off or transferring its knowledge and skills across its many different product lines.

Sources: Eastman Kodak 2000, www.kodak.com; Johannes, L 2000, 'Kodak streamlines units to be nimbler in digital age', *Wall Street Journal*, 3 November, p. B1.

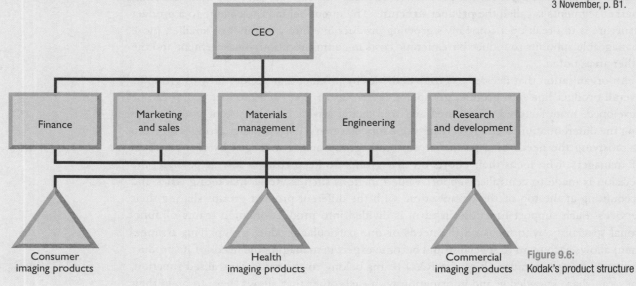

Figure 9.6: Kodak's product structure

Market structure

In a market structure, a company divides work among its managers and employees in terms of the various groups of customers it serves.

Suppose the source of competitive advantage in an industry depends on the ability to meet the needs of distinct and important sets of consumers or different customer groups. What is the best way of implementing strategy now? Many companies develop a market structure that is conceptually quite similar to the product structure, except that the focus is on customer groups instead of product groups.

For a company pursuing a strategy based on increasing responsiveness to customers, it is vital that the nature and needs of each different customer group be identified. Then people and functions are grouped by customer or market segment, and a different set of managers becomes responsible for developing the products that each group of customers wants and tailoring or customising products to the needs of each particular customer group. In other words, to promote superior responsiveness to customers, companies design a structure around their customers and a market structure is adopted. A typical market structure is shown in figure 9.7.

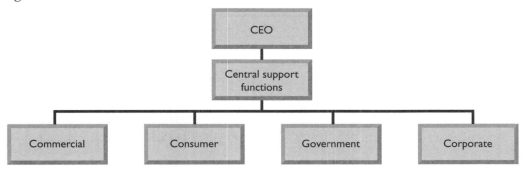

Figure 9.7:
Market structure

A market structure brings customer group managers and employees closer to specific groups of customers. These people can then take their detailed knowledge and feed it back to the support functions, which are kept centralised to reduce costs. For example, information about changes in customers' preferences can be quickly fed back to R&D and product design, so that a company can protect its competitive advantage by supplying a constant stream of improved products for its installed customer base. This is especially important when a company serves well-identified customer groups.

In the market structure, in dividing work among managers and employees most attention is given to the customer that buys products from a company. In this structure, various divisions may actually make similar or even identical products but they are concerned with providing services to different types of customers.[25]

Multidivisional structure

The multidivisional structure possesses two main innovations over a functional structure — innovations that allow a company to grow and diversify, yet overcome problems that stem from loss of control. First, each distinct product line or business unit is placed in its own self-contained unit or division, with all support functions. PepsiCo, for example, has two major divisions — soft drinks and snack foods — and each has its own functions, such as marketing and R&D. The result is a higher level of horizontal differentiation.

Second, the office of corporate headquarters staff is created to monitor divisional activities and exercise financial control over each of the divisions.[26] These staff include corporate managers who oversee the activities of divisional and functional managers and they constitute an additional level in the organisational hierarchy. A higher level of vertical division of work thus occurs in a multidivisional structure than in a functional structure.

Figure 9.8 presents a typical multidivisional structure found in a large chemical company such as DuPont. Although this company may easily have 70 operating divisions, only three — the oil, pharmaceuticals and plastics divisions — are represented here. As a self-contained business unit, each division possesses a full array of support services; for example, each has self-contained accounting, sales and personnel departments. Each division functions as a profit centre, making it much easier for corporate headquarters staff to monitor and evaluate each division's activities.[27]

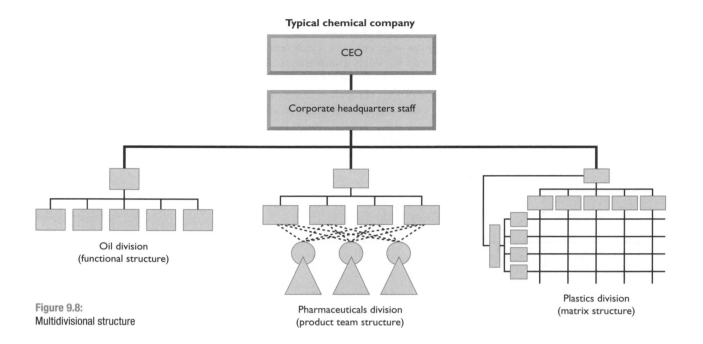

Typical chemical company

Oil division
(functional structure)

Figure 9.8:
Multidivisional structure

Pharmaceuticals division
(product team structure)

Plastics division
(matrix structure)

The bureaucratic costs of operating a multidivisional structure are high compared with those for a functional structure. The size of the corporate staff brings a major expense, with companies such as GM and IBM having thousands of managers on their corporate staff, even after their massive downsizing. Similarly, the use of product divisions — each with its own specialist support functions (such as R&D and marketing) — is a major expense. Nevertheless, if a higher level of value creation offsets higher bureaucratic costs, then adoption of a more complex structure makes sense.

Each division is also able to adopt the structure that best suits its needs. Figure 9.8 shows that the oil division has a functional structure because its activities are standardised; the pharmaceuticals division has a product team structure; and the plastics division has a **matrix structure**. (The latter two structures are discussed in detail later in this chapter.) Similarly, GM operates the whole corporation through a multidivisional structure but each vehicle division organises itself into different product groups, based on the type of vehicle made.

In the multidivisional structure, the day-to-day operations of a division are the responsibility of divisional management; that is, divisional management has operating responsibility. Corporate headquarters staff (the board of directors, as well as top executives), however, are responsible for overseeing long-term plans and providing guidance for interdivisional projects. This staff has strategic responsibility. This combination of self-contained divisions with a centralised corporate management represents a higher level of both vertical and horizontal specialisation, as noted. These two innovations provide the extra control necessary to coordinate growth and diversification.

Advantages of a multidivisional structure

When managed effectively at both the corporate and the divisional levels, a multidivisional structure offers several advantages. Together, these advantages can raise profitability to a new peak because they allow the company to operate more complex types of corporate-level strategy.

matrix structure
An organisational structure in which employees are grouped by both function and product orientation, resulting in two sets of reporting relationships

Increased corporate financial control

The profitability of different business divisions is clearly visible in the multidivisional structure.[28] Because each division is its own profit centre, the company can apply financial controls to each business on the basis of profit criteria. Typically, these controls cover establishing targets, monitoring performance regularly and selectively intervening when problems arise. Corporate headquarters is also in a better position to allocate corporate financial resources among competing divisions. The visibility of divisional performance means that corporate headquarters can identify the divisions in which investment of funds will yield the greatest long-term returns. In a sense, the corporate office is in a position to act as the investor or banker in an internal capital market, channelling funds to high-yield uses.

Increased strategic control

The multidivisional structure frees corporate staff from operating responsibilities. The staff consequently gain time for contemplating wider strategic issues and developing responses to environmental changes. The multidivisional structure also enables corporate headquarters to obtain the proper information for performing strategic planning functions. Separating individual businesses is a necessary prerequisite for portfolio planning, for example.

Growth

The multidivisional structure allows the company to overcome an organisational limit to its growth. By reducing information overload at the centre, corporate managers can handle more businesses. They can consider opportunities for further growth and diversification. Communication problems are reduced because all divisions can use the same set of standardised accounting and financial control techniques. Also, corporate managers are able to implement a policy of management by exception, which means that they intervene only when problems arise.

Stronger pursuit of internal efficiency

Within a functional structure, the interdependence of functional departments means that the individual performance of each function inside a company cannot be measured by objective criteria. The company cannot assess the profitability of the finance function, marketing function or manufacturing function, for example, in isolation because these functions are only part of the whole. This often means that considerable degrees of organisational slack — that is, use of unproductive functional resources — can go undetected within the functional structure. The head of the finance function, for example, might employ a larger staff than required to reduce work pressures inside the department and to assume higher status.

In a multidivisional structure, however, the company can observe and measure the individual efficiency of each autonomous division in terms of the profit it generates. Autonomy makes divisional managers accountable for their own performance; they can have no excuses for poor performance. The corporate office is consequently in a better position to identify inefficiencies.

In a multidivisional company such as Coles-Myer, it is easy to see that Coles out-performs Myer (Grace Bros), which in turn outperforms Target. Even within the divisions, it is possible to see whether one division's accounting group is more or less efficient than those in the other divisions just in terms of productivity.

Disadvantages of a multidivisional structure

Probably because a multidivisional structure has powerful advantages, it seems to be the preferred choice of most large diversified enterprises today. Research suggests that large companies that adopt this structure outperform those that retain the functional structure.[29] A multidivisional structure has its disadvantages as well though. Good management can eliminate some of them but others are inherent in the structure and require constant managerial attention. These disadvantages are discussed next.

The divisional–corporate authority relationship

The authority relationship between corporate headquarters and the divisions must be correctly established. The multidivisional structure introduces a new level in the hierarchy: the corporate level. The problem lies in deciding how much authority and control to assign to the operating divisions and how much to retain at corporate headquarters.

This problem was first noted by Alfred Sloan, the founder of GM. He introduced the multidivisional structure at GM — which was the first company to adopt it — and created five vehicle divisions: Chevrolet, Pontiac, Oldsmobile, Buick and Cadillac.[30] What Sloan found, however, was that when headquarters retained too much power and authority, the operating divisions lacked sufficient autonomy to develop the business strategy that might best meet their particular needs. On the other hand, when too much power was delegated to the divisions, they pursued divisional objectives with little heed to the needs of the whole corporation. As a result, for example, not all of the potential gains from synergy discussed could be achieved.

The central issue in managing the multidivisional structure is, therefore, to determine how much authority should be centralised at corporate headquarters and how much should be decentralised to the divisions. Each company must resolve this issue in reference to the nature of its business- and corporate-level strategies. There are no easy answers and, over time, the balance between corporate and divisional control changes as the environment changes or the company alters its strategies.

Distortion of information

If corporate headquarters overemphasises divisional return on investment (ROI) — for example, by setting high and stringent return-on-investment targets — then divisional managers may choose to distort the information that they supply top management, painting a rosy picture of the present situation at the expense of future profits. That is, divisions may maximise short-term profits, perhaps by cutting product development, new investments or marketing expenditures. This approach may cost the company in the future. The problem stems from too tight financial control.

Competition for resources

The third problem with managing a multidivisional structure is that the divisions may compete for resources, setting up a rivalry that prevents synergy gains or economies of scope. The amount of money that corporate personnel have to distribute to the divisions is fixed. The divisions that can demonstrate the highest ROI generally receive the major share of the money. Because that large share strengthens them in the next time period, the strong divisions grow stronger. Consequently, divisions may actively compete for resources and, by so doing, reduce interdivisional coordination.

Transfer pricing

transfer prices
Prices that one division or department within a company charges to supply inputs to another division or department in the same company

Divisional competition may also lead to battles over transfer prices, which are one problem with vertical integration or related diversification. Rivalry among divisions increases the difficulty of setting fair prices. Each supplying division tries to set the highest price for its outputs to maximise its own ROI. Such competition can completely undermine the corporate culture and make a company a battleground. Many companies have a history of competition among divisions. Some may encourage competition if managers believe that it leads to maximum performance.

Short-term R&D focus

If corporate headquarters set extremely high targets for return on investment, then the divisions may cut back on R&D expenditure to improve their financial performance. Although this approach inflates divisional performance in the short term, it reduces a division's ability to develop new products and leads to a fall in the stream of long-term profits. Corporate headquarters, therefore, must carefully control its interactions with the divisions, to ensure both the short- and long-term goals of the business are being achieved.

Bureaucratic costs

As noted, because each division possesses its own specialised functions, such as finance or R&D, multidivisional structures are expensive to run and manage. R&D is especially costly, so some companies centralise it and other like functions at the corporate level to serve all divisions. The duplication of specialist services is not a problem if the gains from having separate specialist functions outweigh the costs. Again, strategic managers must decide whether duplication is financially justified. Activities are often centralised in times of downturn or recession, particularly advisory services and planning functions; divisions, however, are retained as profit centres.

The advantages of divisional structures must be balanced against their disadvantages; as noted, however, the disadvantages can be managed by an observant, professional management team that is aware of the issues involved. The multidivisional structure is dominant today, which suggests its usefulness as the means of managing the multibusiness corporation.

Matrix structure

A matrix structure differs from the structures discussed so far in that it is based on two forms of horizontal differentiation rather than one, as in the functional structure.[31] In the matrix design, activities on the vertical axis are grouped by *function*, so there is a familiar differentiation of tasks into functions such as engineering, sales and marketing and R&D. Superimposed on this vertical pattern is a horizontal pattern based on differentiation by *product* or *project*. The result is a complex network of reporting relationships among projects and functions, as depicted in figure 9.9.

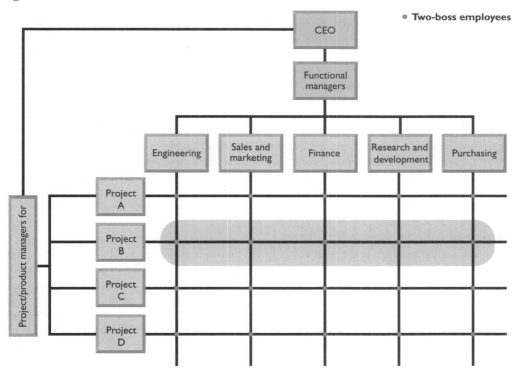

Figure 9.9:
Matrix structure

This structure also employs an unusual kind of vertical differentiation. Although matrix structures are flat, with few hierarchical levels, employees inside the matrix have two bosses: a functional boss, who is the head of a function, and a project boss, who is responsible for managing the individual projects. Employees work on a project team with specialists from other functions and report to the project boss on project matters and to the functional boss on functional issues. All employees who work in a project team are called two-boss employees and are responsible for managing coordination and communication among the functions and projects.

Matrix structures were first developed by companies in hi-tech industries such as aerospace and electronics, for example TRW and Hughes Aircraft. These companies were developing radically new products in uncertain, competitive environments and speed of product development was the crucial consideration. They needed a structure that could respond to this need but the functional structure was too inflexible to allow the complex role and task interactions necessary to meet the requirements of new product development. Moreover, employees in these companies tend to be highly qualified and professional and they perform best in autonomous, flexible working conditions, which the matrix structure provides.

This structure requires a minimum of direct hierarchical control by supervisors. Team members control their own behaviour and participation in project teams allows them to monitor other team members and learn from each other. Furthermore, as the project proceeds through its different phases, it requires different specialists from different functions. At the first stage, the services of R&D specialists may be needed; at the next stage, engineers and marketing specialists may be needed to make cost and marketing projections. As the demand for the type of specialist changes, team members can move to other projects that require their services. The matrix structure, therefore, can make maximum use of employees' skills as existing projects are completed and new ones come into existence.

Finally, the freedom given by the matrix not only provides the autonomy to motivate employees but also leaves top management free to concentrate on strategic issues because they do not have to become involved in operating matters. On all these counts, the matrix is an excellent tool for creating the flexibility necessary for quick reactions to competitive conditions.

The matrix structure does have disadvantages though.[32] First, the bureaucratic costs of operating this structure are high compared with those of operating a functional structure. Because employees tend to be highly skilled, both salaries and overhead are high. Second, the constant movement of employees around the matrix means that time and money are spent establishing new team relationships and getting the project off the ground. Third, the two-boss employee's role, balancing the interests of the project with those of the function, is difficult to manage, and care must be taken to avoid conflict between functions and projects over resources. Over time, project managers may take the leading role in planning and goal setting, in which case the structure would work more like a product or multidivisional structure. If function and project relationships are left uncontrolled, then they can lead to power struggles among managers, resulting in stagnation and decline rather than increased flexibility. Finally, the larger the company, the more difficult it is to operate a matrix structure, because task and role relationships become complex. Then changing to a multidivisional structure may be the only option.

Given these advantages and disadvantages, the matrix is generally used only when a company's strategy warrants it. There is no point in using a more complex structure than necessary because it will only cost more to manage. In dynamic product or market environments, such as biotechnology and computers, the benefits of the matrix in terms of flexibility and innovation are likely to exceed the high bureaucratic costs of using it, so the matrix becomes an appropriate choice of structure. Companies in the mature stage of an industry's lifecycle or those pursuing a low-cost strategy would rarely choose this structure, however, because it is expensive to operate. The matrix structure is discussed further in chapter 10.

Product team structure

A major structural innovation in recent years has been the product team structure. Its advantages are similar to those of a matrix structure, but it is much easier and far less costly to operate because people are organised into permanent cross-functional teams (see figure 9.10).

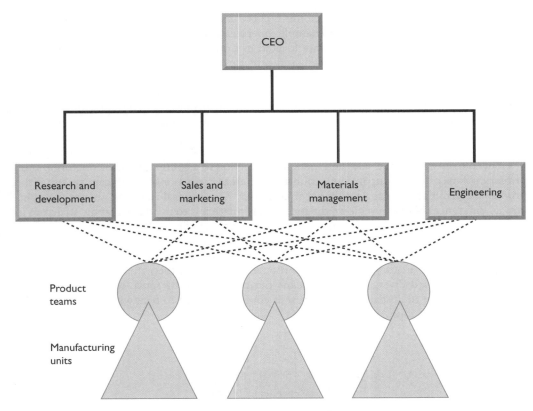

In the product team structure, as in the matrix structure, tasks are divided along product or project lines to reduce bureaucratic costs and increase management's ability to monitor and control the manufacturing process. Instead of being assigned only temporarily to different projects as in the matrix structure, however, functional specialists are placed in permanent cross-functional teams. As a result, the costs of coordinating activities are much lower than in a matrix structure, in which tasks and reporting relationships change rapidly.

Cross-functional teams are formed at the beginning of the product development process, so any difficulties can be fixed early, before they lead to major redesign problems. When all functions have direct input from the beginning, the company can keep design costs and subsequent manufacturing costs low. Moreover, the use of cross-functional teams speeds innovation and customer responsiveness because decisions can be made more quickly when authority is decentralised to the team.

Geographic structure

When a company operates as a geographic structure, geographic regions become the basis for grouping organisational activities. A company may divide its manufacturing operations and establish manufacturing plants in different regions of the country. This allows it to be responsive to the needs of regional customers and reduces transportation costs. Similarly, service organisations such as store chains or banks may organise their sales and marketing activities on a regional, rather than national, level to get closer to their customers. The National, as shown in the opening case, has moved from a market structure to geographic structure.

A geographic structure provides more control than a functional structure because several regional hierarchies carry out the work previously performed by a single centralised hierarchy. A company such as Federal Express needs to operate a geographic structure to fulfil its corporate goal: next-day delivery. Some holiday and hotel businesses also need to use a geographic structure. Club Med, for example, operates different styles of business around the world. While many of its businesses are located in tropical locations, some are designed for operation only in winter to offer snow-based activities. Even those in tropical locations vary considerably — from basic thatched huts to more upmarket resort accommodations — and consequently require a certain level of decentralisation to allow for different resorts to operate differently. Similarly, many pharma-ceutical companies incorporate a geographic element into their structures. They sell different drugs to different countries on the basis of ability to pay. Many developing countries have access to a more limited range of generally cheaper drugs compared with those sold in many Western countries. In addition, pharmaceutical companies often need to customise the sales and marketing function to a country, because doctors are the primary means of marketing in some countries, whereas the national health care system is the primary determinant of drug use in other countries. As a general rule, the greater the operational differences between regions, the more appropriate it is to use a geographic structure in a company. An example of a geographic structure is shown in figure 9.11.

The usefulness of the bases of dividing organisational work, however, depends on the size of the company and its range of products and regions. If a company starts to diversify into unrelated products or integrate vertically into new industries, then these structures cannot handle the increased diversity, which means the company must move to a multidivisional structure. Only the multidivisional structure is complex enough to deal with the needs of the large, multibusiness company.

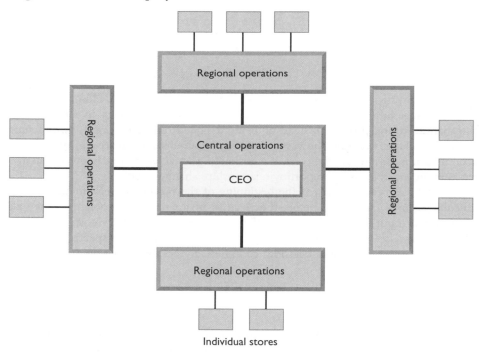

Figure 9.11:
Geographic structure

Integration and integrating mechanisms

As discussed, a company must choose the appropriate form of structure to match its strategy. Greater diversification, for example, requires that a company move from a functional structure to a multidivisional structure. Division of work is only the first organisational design decision to be made. The second decision concerns the level of integration necessary to make an organisational structure work effectively. As noted, integration refers to how far a company seeks to coordinate its value creation activities and make them interdependent. The design issue can be summed up simply: the higher a company's level of specialisation, the higher is the level of integration needed to make the organisational structure work effectively.[33] If a company adopts a more complex form of structure, it will require a more complex form of integration to accomplish its goals. Federal Express, for example, needs an enormous amount of integration and coordination to fulfil its promise of next-day package delivery. It is renowned for its innovative use of integrating mechanisms — such as customer liaison personnel — to manage its transactions quickly and efficiently.

Forms of integrating mechanism

A series of integrating mechanisms is available for a company to use to increase its level of integration as its level of specialisation increases.[34] These mechanisms (on a continuum from simple to complex) are listed in table 9.1, together with examples of the individuals or groups that may perform these integrating roles. As is the case when a company increases its level of differentiation, however, increasing the level of integration is expensive. There are high bureaucratic costs arising from using managers to coordinate value creation activities. A company therefore uses more complex integrating mechanisms to coordinate its activities only to the extent necessary to implement its strategy effectively.

Table 9.1: Types and examples of integrating mechanism

Type	Example
Direct contact	Sales and production managers
Liaison roles	Assistant sales and plant managers
Task forces	Representatives from sales, production and R&D
Teams	Organisational executive committee
Integrating roles	Assistant vice-president for strategic planning or vice-president without a portfolio
Matrix	Integrating roles for all positions

Direct contact

The aim of establishing direct contact among managers is to set up a context within which managers from different divisions or functions can work together to solve mutual problems. Managers from different functions have different goals and interests but equal authority, so they may tend to compete rather than cooperate when conflicts arise. In a typical functional structure, for example, the heads of each of the functions have equal authority; the nearest common point of authority is the CEO. Consequently, if disputes arise, no mechanism exists to resolve the conflicts, apart from the authority of the boss.

One sign of conflict is the number of problems sent up the hierarchy for upper level managers to solve. This wastes management time and effort, slows strategic decision making and makes it difficult to create a cooperative culture in the company. For this reason, companies generally choose more complex integrating mechanisms to coordinate interfunctional and divisional activities.

Interdepartmental liaison roles

A company can improve its interfunctional coordination through the interdepartmental liaison role. When the volume of contacts between two departments or functions increases, one way to improve coordination is to give one manager in each division or function the responsibility for coordinating with the others. These managers may meet daily, weekly, monthly or as needed. Figure 9.12(a) depicts the nature of the liaison role, with the small dot representing the manager inside the functional department who has responsibility for coordinating with the other function. The responsibility for coordination is part of a manager's full-time job, but these roles allow the managers involved to form a permanent relationship, which greatly eases strains between departments. Further, liaison roles offer a way of transferring information across the company, which is important in large, anonymous companies, whose employees may know no-one outside their immediate department.

Temporary task forces

When more than two functions or divisions share common problems, direct contact and liaison roles are of limited value because they do not provide enough coordination. The solution is to

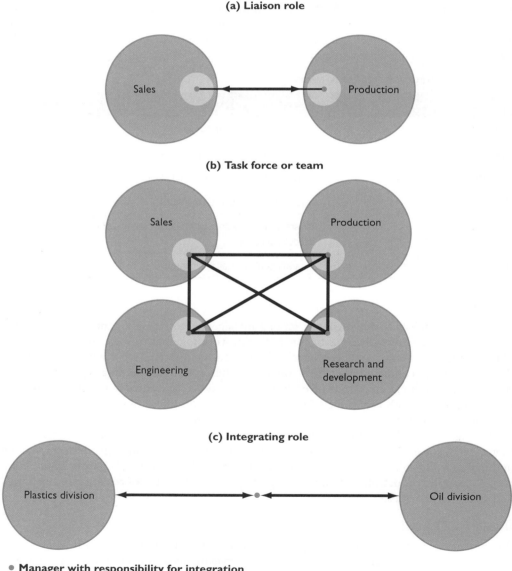

• **Manager with responsibility for integration**

adopt a more complex form of integrating mechanism called a task force. The nature of the task force is represented diagrammatically in figure 9.12(b). One member of each function or division is assigned to a task force created to solve a specific problem. Essentially, task forces are *ad hoc* committees whose members are responsible for reporting back to their departments on the issues dealt with and solutions recommended. Task forces are temporary because once the problem has been solved, members return to their normal roles in their own departments or are assigned to other task forces. Task force members also perform many of their normal duties while serving on the task force.

Permanent teams

In many cases, the issues dealt with by a task force recur. To settle these issues effectively, a company must establish a permanent integrating mechanism, such as a permanent team. An example of a permanent team is a new product development committee, which is responsible for the choice, design and marketing of new products. This requires a great deal of integration among functions if the company is to introduce new products successfully and a permanent integrating mechanism accomplishes this level of integration. Intel, for instance, emphasises teamwork. It formed a council system based on approximately 90 cross-functional groups, which meet regularly to set functional strategy in areas such as engineering and marketing and to develop business-level strategy.

The importance of teams in the management of the organisational structure cannot be overemphasised. Permanent teams are the company's standing committees, and much of the company's strategic direction is formulated in their meetings. Mintzberg, in a study of how the managers of corporations spend their time, discovered that they spend more than 60 per cent of their time in these committees.[35] The reason is not bureaucracy but, rather, that integration is possible only in intensive, face-to-face sessions, in which managers can understand others' viewpoints and develop a cohesive organisational strategy. The more complex the company, the more important these teams become. Westinghouse, for example, established a whole new task force and team system to promote integration among divisions and improve corporate performance.

Integrating roles

The only function of the integrating role is to prompt integration among divisions or departments; it is a full-time job. As figure 9.12(c) indicates, the role is independent of the subunits or divisions being integrated. It is staffed by an independent expert, who is normally a senior manager with a great deal of experience in the joint needs of the two departments. The job is to coordinate the decision process among departments or divisions so the company can obtain synergetic gains from cooperation. One study found that DuPont had created 160 integrating roles to provide coordination among the different divisions of the company and improve corporate performance.[36] Again, the more differentiated the company, the more common are these roles. People in these roles often take the responsibility for chairing task forces and teams, providing additional integration.

Integrating departments

The number of integrating roles sometimes becomes so high that the company establishes a permanent integrating department at corporate headquarters. This normally occurs only in large, diversified corporations that see the need for integration among divisions. This department consists mainly of strategic planners and may be called the strategic planning department. Corporate headquarters staff in a divisional structure can also be viewed as an integrating department from the divisional perspective.

Matrix structure

Finally, when differentiation is very high and the company must be able to respond quickly to the environment, a matrix structure becomes the appropriate integrating device. The matrix contains many of the integrating mechanisms already discussed. The subproject managers integrate functions and projects, and the matrix is built on the basis of temporary task forces.

Integration and control

Companies have many options when they increase their level of specialisation as a result of increased growth or diversification. The implementation issue for managers is to match specialisation with the level of integration to meet organisational objectives. While too much specialisation and not enough integration leads to a failure of implementation, the converse is also true. That is, the combination of low specialisation and high integration leads to an overcontrolled, bureaucratised organisation, in which the level of integration reduces rather than increases flexibility and speed of response. Further, too much integration is expensive for the company because it raises bureaucratic costs. For these reasons, the goal is to decide on the optimum amount of integration necessary for meeting organisational goals and objectives. A company needs to operate the simplest structure consistent with implementing its strategy effectively. In practice, integrating mechanisms are only the first means by which a company seeks to increase its ability to control and coordinate its activities; modern information systems are a second.

Information systems and organisational structure

As discussed throughout this book, advances in software information systems and Internet technology are having important effects on managers and companies. By improving the ability of managers to coordinate and control company activities, and by helping managers make more effective decisions, modern computer-based information systems have become a central component of any company's structure. Evidence is growing, too, that information systems can be a source of competitive advantage; companies that do not adopt leading-edge information systems are likely to be at a competitive disadvantage. This section examines how the rapid growth of computerised information systems is affecting organisational structure and competitive advantage.

Until the development of modern computer-based information systems, no viable alternative to the organisational hierarchy existed, despite the information problems discussed earlier. The rapid rise of computer-based information systems has been associated with a 'delayering' (flattening) of the organisational hierarchy and a move towards greater decentralisation and horizontal information flows.[37] By electronically providing managers with high-quality, timely and relatively complete information, modern information systems have reduced the need for tall management hierarchies. They have reduced the need for a hierarchy to function as a means of controlling the activities of the company or to coordinate organisational activities.

Email systems, the development of software programs for sharing documents electronically and the development of the Internet have increased horizontal information flows within companies. The development of companywide computer networks is breaking down the barriers that traditionally separated departments and the results have been improved performance and superior efficiency, quality, innovation and customer responsiveness.[38] One reason for an increase in efficiency is that the use of advanced information systems can reduce the number of employees required to perform activities. At one time, for example, 13 layers of management separated Eastman Kodak's general manager of manufacturing and factory workers. Now, with the help of information systems, the number of layers has been reduced to four.

Moreover, by increasing horizontal information flows and helping to break down the barriers that separate departments, computer networks are allowing managers to boost quality, innovation and responsiveness to customers. The experience of Lotus Development, the company that developed Lotus Notes, illustrates how information systems can speed product development. Using its own Notes technology, Lotus managers found that software writers in Asia, the United States and Europe can work almost in parallel, sharing documentation and messages on a real-time basis. As a result, a Japanese version of a new product can be introduced within three or four weeks of its English-language release, instead of the three or four months that were necessary before the adoption of Notes.[39] New computer-aided design (CAD) systems can indirectly assist in flattening organisational structures. By using advanced design technologies such as CAD, companies are able to develop modular products, in which a product is made from subsystems that join together in a defined way.

A company can alter and improve these subsystems without changing the overall structure of the product because the same subsystems continue to fit together in the same way. The groups working on the different subsystems can as a consequence operate relatively independently, limiting the amount of integration required and keeping the company structure flat. Before the introduction of the IBM PC in 1981, for example, computers were designed with components and software completely integrated. This approach made for very tall organisational structures because whole departments were needed to coordinate the different activities and ensure the product was appropriately integrated. The creation of modular architecture across PCs in 1981 allowed departments to work on different components independently because all the components fit together in a defined way. The microprocessor or software or monitor could be improved independently and because the final product was modular, no coordination was required to ensure the product was operational. Today, many companies use advanced design technologies to create a modular architecture, so that they can then allow different departments (or even other companies) to make the components without being concerned about whether the final product will be operational. Strategy in action 9.4 illustrates the benefit that Nestlé received out of the introduction of information technology (IT) in its operations.

strategy in action 9.4

Nestlé and e-chocolate

Nestlé of Switzerland is one the largest food and drink makers in the world. It has grown enormously in the past 20 years and now the challenge is to integrate its unwieldy operations, which expand into several continents. In the 1980s, Nestlé steadfastly refused to introduce IT solutions to its operations and had always been committed to decentralisation to adapt to local tastes and preferences. Nestlé's operations became quite costly because of these policies and the first to go was its commitment to decentralisation. Nestlé centralised the management of its factories in individual countries into regions and established strategic business units that cut across many countries. Nestlé ended its aversion to IT and decided to establish one technology platform for the entire company to standardise the codes of the various inputs it purchased. Under the decentralised structure, Nestlé ran three different accounting systems for Zone Europe, Zone Americas and Zone Asia, Oceania and Africa. This is in addition to several other systems that the company inherited from many of its acquisitions. A bag of sugar, for example, used to be identified by 50 different codes within Nestlé. Nestlé America paid more than 20 different prices for

vanilla to the same supplier because each factory identified vanilla with a different code. An IT system would standardise these inputs and should reduce costs. Nestlé IT strategy can be illustrated by 'e-chocolate'. Under this system, US storeowners, for example, would order Nestlé chocolates through a new website called NestléEZOrder instead of using thousands of faxes and telephones. Nestlé factories would buy raw materials for chocolates over the Internet and pick suppliers that offer the best prices. Nestlé factories, under the new IT system, would have the option of outsourcing the making of chocolates or they could make their own. Instead of stocking chocolates unnecessarily, Nestlé factories would monitor the sales of their products through their electronic links with supermarkets and retailers. Nestlé plans to market its products through chocolate lovers' websites that provides them advice, recipes and the pleasures of eating chocolates.

Sources: The Economist 2004, 'Special report: Daring, defying, to grow – Nestlé, Nestlé', 7 August; Echikson, W & Weintraub, A 2000, 'Nestlé: an elephant dances", *Business Week*, 12 November.

State-of-the-art IT can thus improve the competitiveness of a company. The search for competitive advantage is driving much of the rapid development and adoption of such systems. By improving the decision-making capability of managers, modern information systems help a company improve its competitive position. To make information software systems usable and to make organisational structure work, a company must create a control and incentive structure to motivate people and subunits to raise organisational performance. The next chapter discusses the various types of strategic control system that companies can use to make their organisational structures work effectively.

Summary

This chapter discusses the issues involved in designing a structure to meet the needs of a company's strategy. Companies can adopt many structures to match changes in their size and strategy over time. The company must match its form of horizontal division of work to vertical division of work. That is, it must choose a structure and then make choices about the number of levels in the hierarchy and the degree of centralisation or decentralisation. The combination of both types of division of work produces internal organisational arrangements.

Once a company has divided itself into parts, however, it then must integrate itself. A company must choose the appropriate level of integration to match its level of specialisation if it is to coordinate its value creation activities successfully. Specialisation and integration are expensive, so a company's goal is to economise on bureaucratic costs by adopting the simplest structure consistent with achieving its strategy. The following points are stressed:

▶ Implementing a strategy successfully depends on selecting the right organisational structure to match a company's strategy.

▶ Organisational design is one of the basic tools of strategy implementation. Good organisational design increases profits in two ways. First, it economises on bureaucratic costs and lowers the costs of value creation activities. Second, it increases the ability of a company's value creation functions to achieve superior efficiency, quality, innovation and responsiveness to customers and to obtain a differentiation advantage.

▶ Division of work and integration are the two design concepts that govern how a structure will work. The higher the level of specialisation and integration, the higher are bureaucratic costs.

▶ Division of work has two aspects: (1) vertical specialisation, which refers to how a company chooses to allocate its decision-making authority at different levels, and (2) horizontal specialisation, which refers to how a company groups organisational activities into functions, departments or divisions at the same level in organisation.

▶ The basic choice in vertical division of work is whether to have a flat or a tall structure. Tall hierarchies have a number of disadvantages, such as problems with communication and information transfer, motivation and cost. Decentralisation or delegation of authority can solve some of these problems though.

▶ As a company grows and diversifies, it adopts a multidivisional structure. Although a multidivisional structure has higher bureaucratic costs than those of a functional structure, it overcomes the control problems of a functional structure and gives a company the capability to handle its value creation activities effectively.

▶ Other specialised kinds of structure include the matrix, product team, geographic, product and market structures. Each has a specialised use and, to be chosen, must match the needs of the organisation.

▶ The more complex the company and the higher its level of differentiation, the higher is the level of integration needed to manage its structure.

▶ The types of integrating mechanism available to a company range from direct contact to matrix structure. The more complex the mechanism, the greater are the costs of using it. A company should take care to match these mechanisms to its strategic needs.

Practising strategic management

Review questions

1. How are structure and strategy interlinked?
2. Compare and contrast multidivisional structure and geographic structure.
3. Compare and contrast market structure and functional structure
4. Discuss various mechanisms of coordination
5. Discuss the type of structure that the National has introduced (see opening case).

Discussion questions

6. A matrix structure is an improvement over a product team structure. Discuss.
7. Divided work areas coordinate themselves. Coordination does not require any deliberate effort. Do you agree? Argue your case.
8. The introduction of IT centralises decision making. Discuss.
9. Flat organisations are not necessarily more efficient. Discuss.
10. What is the difference between vertical and horizontal division of work? Rank the various structures discussed in this chapter along these two dimensions.

Applied questions

11. Using annual reports, company documents or other appropriate sources to find organisational charts, classify a minimum of five companies as having tall or flat structures. Based on the characteristics of these five organisations, describe some factors that seem to be associated with tall structures versus flat structures.
12. Strategy in action 9.4 describes the benefits of introducing IT into company operations. Find another large company that has introduced IT in its operations and evaluate the consequences of its introduction.

Small-group exercise

Speeding up product development

Break into groups of three to five people and discuss the following scenario.

You are the top functional managers of a small greeting card company, whose new lines of humorous cards for every occasion are selling as fast as they reach the stores. Currently, your employees are organised into different functions, such as card designers, artists and joke writers, as well as functions, such as marketing and manufacturing. Each function works on a wide range of different types of card: birthday, Christmas, marriage and so on. The design department sometimes comes up with the initial idea for a new card and sends the idea to the artists, who draw and colour the picture. The card is then sent to the joke writers, who write the joke to suit the card. At other times, the process starts with the writers, who send a joke to the design department to find the best use for the idea.

The problem is that your current functional structure does not allow you to produce new cards fast enough to satisfy customers' demands. It typically takes a new card one year to reach the market, and you want to halve this time to protect and expand your market niche.

1. Discuss ways in which you can improve the operation of your current functional structure to speed the product development process.
2. Discuss the pros and cons of moving to an (a) multidivisional, (b) matrix and (c) product team structure to reduce card development time.
3. Which of these structures, do you think, is most appropriate? Why?

Article file

Find an example (or examples) of a company that has recently changed its organisational structure. What changes did it make? Why did it make these changes? What effect did these changes have on the behaviour of people and subunits?

Exploring the Web

What kind of organisational structure?

Find a website that displays a company's organisational chart or explains a company's method of managing its structure (such as whether the company uses a centralised or decentralised approach). What kind of structure does the company use to manage its activities?

Strategic management project

Module 9

This module asks you to identify the type of organisational structure used by your company and explain why your company has selected this form of specialisation and integration. If you are studying a company in your area, you will probably have more information about the company's structure than if you are studying a company using published sources. You can make many inferences about the company's structure from the nature of its activities. Furthermore, if you write to the company, it may provide you with an organisational chart and other information. Based on the information that you gather, answer the following questions.

1. How large is the company as measured by number of employees? How many levels in the hierarchy does it have from the top to the bottom?

2. Based on these two measures and any other information you have, would you say your company operates with a relatively tall or flat structure? What effect does this have on people's behaviour?

3. Does your company have a centralised or a decentralised approach to decision making? How do you know?

4. How do the company's vertical differentiation choices affect the behaviour of people and subunits? Do you think the company's choice of vertical differentiation is appropriate for its activities? Why?

5. What changes (if any) would you make to the way in which the company operates in a vertical direction?

6. Draw an organisational chart showing the main way in which your company groups its activities. Based on this chart, with what kind of structure (functional or divisional) does your company operate?

7. Why did your company choose this structure? In what ways is the structure appropriate for its business? In what ways is it not appropriate?

8. What changes (if any) would you make to how your company operates in a horizontal direction?

9. Given this analysis, does your company have a low or a high level of differentiation?

10. What kind of integration or integration mechanisms does your company use? Why? Does the company's level of integration match its level of differentiation?

11. Based on the analysis of your company's level of specialisation and integration, is your company coordinating and motivating its people and subunits effectively? Why?

12. What changes would you make in the company's structure to increase the company's effectiveness? What changes has the company made to improve effectiveness? Why?

Additional resources

Bartlett, C & Ghoshal, S 1990. 'Matrix management: not a structure, a frame of mind', *Harvard Business Review*, July, pp. 138–45. (A discussion of matrix structures.)

Campbell, A & Goold, M 2002, 'Do you have a well designed organisation?', *Harvard Business Review*, March, pp. 117–24. (A discussion of general organisational design principles.)

End notes

1. Engdahl, RA, Keating, RJ & Aupperle, KE 2000, 'Strategy and structure: chicken or egg? Reconsideration of Chandler's paradigm for economic success', *Organizational Development Journal*, vol.18, pp. 21–33.

2. Galbraith, JR 1973, *Designing complex organizations*, Addison-Wesley, Reading, Massachusetts.

3. Child, J 1977, *Organization: a guide for managers and administrators*, Harper & Row, New York, pp. 50–72.

4. Miles, RH 1980, *Macro organizational behavior*, Goodyear, Santa Monica, California, pp. 19–20.

5. Galbraith, op. cit.

6. Graicunas, VA 1937, 'Relationship in organization', in Gulick, L & Urwic, L (eds), *Papers on the science of administration*, Institute of Public Administration, New York, pp. 181–5; Worthy, JC 1950, 'Organizational structure and company morale', *American Sociological Review*, vol. 15, pp. 169–79.

7. Child, op. cit.

8. Jones, GR 1987, 'Organization–client transactions and organizational governance structures', *Academy of Management Journal*, vol. 30, pp. 197–218.

9. Mintzberg, H 1979, *The structuring of organizations*, Prentice Hall, Englewood Cliffs, New Jersey, p. 435.

10. Woolridge, B & Floyd, SW 1990, 'The strategy process, middle management involvement, and organizational performance', *Strategic Management Journal*, vol. 11, pp. 231–41.

11. Child, op. cit.

12. Carzo Jr, R & Yanousas, JN 1969, 'Effects of flat and tall organization structure', *Administrative Science Quarterly*, vol. 14, pp. 178–91.

13. Gupta, A & Govindardan, V 1984, 'Business unit strategy, managerial characteristics, and business unit effectiveness at strategy implementation', *Academy of Management Journal*, vol. 27, pp. 25–41; Lenz, RT 1981, 'Determinants of organizational performance: an interdisciplinary review', *Strategic Management Journal*, vol. 2, pp. 131–54.

14. Wagel, WH 1984, 'Keeping the organization lean at Federal Express', *Personnel*, March, p. 4.

15. Jones, GR 1984, 'Task visibility, free riding and shirking: explaining the effect of organization structure on employee behavior', *Academy of Management Review*, vol. 4, pp. 684–95.

16. Bank of America 1999, media release, September, www. BankofAmerica.com.

17. Witzel, M 2005, 'Flatter is not necessarily fitter', *Financial Times*, 22 August.

18. Daft, RL 1986, *Organizational theory and design*, 3rd edn, West, St Paul, Minnesota, p. 215.

19. Chandler, AD 1962, *Strategy and structure*, MIT Press, Cambridge, Massachusetts.

20. This discussion draws heavily on Chandler, op. cit.; Scott, BR 1971, *Stages of corporate development*, Intercollegiate Clearing House, Harvard Business School, Boston, Massachusetts.

21. Galbraith, JR & Kazanjian, RK 1986, *Strategy implementation: structure system and process*, 2nd edn, West, St Paul, Minnesota; Child, op. cit.; Duncan, R 1979, 'What is the right organizational structure?', *Organizational Dynamics*, Winter, pp. 59–80.

22. Williamson, OE 1975, *Markets and hierarchies: analysis and antitrust implications*, Free Press, New York.

23. Lawrence, PR & Lorsch, J 1967, *Organization and environment*, Division of Research, Harvard Business School, Boston, Massachusetts.

24. Pope, K 1993, 'Dell refocuses on groundwork to cope with rocketing sales', *Wall Street Journal*, 18 June, p. B5.

25. Litterer, JA 1965, *The analysis of organisations*, John Wiley & Sons, New York, p.174.

26. Chandler, op. cit.; Williamson, op. cit.; Wrigley, L 1970, 'Divisional autonomy and diversification', PhD thesis, Harvard Business School, Boston, Massachusetts.

27. Rumelt, RP 1974, *Strategy, structure, and economic performance*, Division of Research, Harvard Business School, Boston, Massachusetts; Scott, op. cit.; Williamson, op. cit.

28. The discussion draws on each of the sources cited in end notes 19–21; Jones, GR & Hill, CWL 1988, 'Transaction cost analysis of strategy–structure choice', *Strategic Management Journal*, vol. 9, pp. 159–72.

29. Armour, HO & Teece, DJ 1978, 'Organizational structure and economic performance: a test of the multidivisional hypothesis', *Bell Journal of Economics*, vol. 9, pp. 106–22.

30. Sloan, A 1983, *My years at General Motors*, Doubleday, New York, chapter 3.

31. Davis, SM & Lawrence, RR 1977, *Matrix*, Addison-Wesley, Reading, Massachusetts; Galbraith, JR 1971, 'Matrix organization designs: how to combine functional and project forms', *Business Horizons*, vol. 14, pp. 29–40.

32. Duncan, op. cit; Davis & Lawrence, op. cit.

33. Lawrence & Lorsch, op. cit., pp. 50–5.

34. Galbraith 1973, op. cit., chapter 1; Galbraith & Kazanjian 1986, op. cit., chapter 7.

35. Mintzberg, H 1973, *The nature of managerial work*, Prentice Hall, Englewood Cliffs, New Jersey, chapter 10.

36. Lawrence & Lorsch, op. cit., p. 55.

37. Davidow, W & Malone, M 1996, *The virtual corporation*, Irwin, Homewood, Illinois.

38. ibid.

39. Stewart, TA 1998, 'Managing in a wired company', *Business Week*, 16 September, pp. 40–4.

Matching structure and control, culture and reward systems to strategy

learning objectives

After studying this chapter, you should be able to:

- discuss strategic control, organisational culture, strategic reward systems and organisation structure as components of strategy implementation

- discuss various types of control and relationship between control, culture and structure

- discuss issues related to matching the components of strategy implementation with functional, business and corporate strategies

- discuss implementation of cross-national strategies

- appreciate new organisational forms that represent a compromise in the strategy–structure choice.

Strategy implementation at Dell

Dell Computer Corporation was one of the fastest-growing companies of the 1990s and its stock price increased at the rate of 100 per cent a year. One of Michael Dell's challenges has been to manage and change Dell's organisational structure, control systems and culture as his company grows.

Dell was 19 when in 1984, he took US$1000 and spent it on the computer parts he assembled himself into PCs that he then sold over the phone.

By 1993, Dell employed 4500 workers and was hiring over a hundred new workers each week. He soon realised that he had to recruit and hire managers. He recruited executives from IBM and Compaq and with their help created a functional structure.

Dell's functional structure worked well and under its new management team, the company's growth continued to soar. By 1993, the company had sales of more than US$2 billion, twice as much as in 1992.

Dell soon realised that new and different kinds of problems were arising. Dell was now selling huge numbers of computers to different kinds of customers, for example, home, business and educational customers and the different branches of government. Because customers now demanded computers with very different features or different amounts of computing power, its product line broadened rapidly. It started to become more difficult for employees to meet the needs of these different kinds of customers efficiently because each employee needed information about all product features or all of Dell's thousands of different sales offers across its product range.

In 1995, Dell changed his company to a market structure and created separate divisions, each geared to the needs of the different groups of customers: a consumer division, business division and so on. This move to a market structure allowed employees to obtain in-depth knowledge about the needs of their market that helped them to respond better to their customer needs. So successful was this change in structure and culture that by 2001, Dell's revenues were more than US$31 billion, and its profits were in excess of US$3.6 billion, a staggering increase from 1984. Despite its growth rate slowing slightly since 2001, Dell's annual revenues are still impressive — pulling in over US$49 billion in 2005.

Dell has continued to alter his company's structure to respond to the changing nature of its customers' needs and to fully exploit its own distinctive competencies. To leverage his company's strengths in materials management, manufacturing and Internet sales over a wider range of computer hardware products, Dell decided to begin assembling servers, workstations and storage devices to compete with IBM, Sun and Compaq. The increasing importance of the Internet led him to split the market division into 35 smaller subunits that focus on more specialised groups of customers, and they all conduct most of their business over the Internet. Today, for example, Dell can offer large and small companies and private buyers a complete range of PCs, workstations and storage devices that can be customised to their needs.

To help coordinate its growing activities, Dell is increasingly making use of its corporate intranet and using information technology (IT) to standardise activities across divisions to integrate across functions. Dell's hierarchy is shrinking as managers are increasingly delegating everyday decision making to employees who have access through IT to the information they need to provide excellent customer service.

Sources: McWilliams, G 2000, 'Dell looks for ways to rekindle the fire it had as an upstart', *Wall Street Journal*, 31 August, pp. A.1, A.8; *Houston Chronicle* 2000, 'Dell hopes to lead firm out of desert', 3 September, p. 4D; Dell Computer Corporation 2002, www.dell.com; ——, *Fiscal 2005 in review*, www.dell.com.

Overview

As the story of Dell suggests, this chapter examines how managers can best implement their strategies to achieve a competitive advantage and superior performance. It must be borne in mind that strategies, no matter how brilliant they are, do not implement themselves. A well-thought-out strategic plan becomes profitable only if it can be implemented. In practice, strategy implementation is a difficult, challenging and never ending task. For example, managers cannot just create an organising framework for a company's value chain activities and then assume it will keep working efficiently and effectively, just as they cannot select strategies and assume that these strategies will work as intended in the future when the environment changes. The previous chapter discusses organisational design, which is one of the most important components of strategy implementation. Strategy implementation requires selecting the right combination of structure, control, reward systems and culture for achieving a company's strategy. This chapter discusses the remaining three components of strategy implementation and also discusses issues of alignment between the components of strategy implementation on the one hand and implementation of different levels and types of strategies on the other.

Noble identifies two contrasting views of strategy implementation: the structural and the interpersonal process. The structural view focuses on the impact of formal organisational structure and control mechanisms on strategy implementation. The interpersonal process view concentrates on the impact of strategic consensus, leadership styles, implementation styles and methods and communication among others on strategy implementation.[1] This book adopts the structural perspective of strategy implementation and takes the view that strategy implementation refers to how a company should create, use and combine organisational structure, control systems, reward systems and culture to pursue strategies that lead to a competitive advantage and superior performance. Four components of strategy implementation are identified: structure, control systems, reward systems and culture.

This chapter first looks at the nature of **strategic control** and describes the main steps in the control process. It then discusses the main types of strategic control system available to managers to shape and influence employees: financial controls, output controls, behaviour controls. Second, it discusses the ways **organisational culture**, manifested through values and norms, influences managers to work for company strategies. Finally, it discusses the alignment of three levels of strategies — functional, business and corporate — on the one hand and the four elements of strategy implementation on the other. The approach is taken that there is no one best way to implement strategies. Rather, the chapter argues that different types of strategies require different types of mixes in strategy components.

Components of strategy implementation

Taking the structural perspective, four components of strategy implementation can be identified. They are organisation structure, control systems, reward systems and culture. An organisational structure, discussed in the previous chapter, assigns people to tasks and roles (specialisation) and specifies how these are to be coordinated (integration). Nevertheless, organisational structure does not provide or contain the mechanism through which people can be influenced to make it work, giving rise to the need for control systems, reward systems and culture. The purpose of these is to provide managers with (a) a means of influencing employees to work towards organisational goals and (b) specific feedback on how well a company and its employees are performing. Structure provides a company with a skeleton but control and culture give it the muscles, sinews, nerves and sensations that allow managers to regulate and govern its activities. Organisational culture is the specific collection of values, norms, beliefs and attitudes shared by people and groups in an organisation and that control

strategic control
The process by which top management monitors the performances of managers implementing strategies on an ongoing basis

organisational culture
The collection of values and norms that are shared within a company, which influence the behaviour of company employees

the way they interact with each other and with stakeholder groups.[2] As discussed in detail in the following, top managers can influence which beliefs and values develop in an organisation and how. Values and beliefs are the most important determinants of how an organisation's members will work towards achieving organisational goals.[3] While organisational control has an impact on how a particular kind of organisational structure will work, organisational culture determines how both structure and control will work in practice. Strategic reward systems link various incentives that are provided to managers with their performances.

Figure 10.1 sums up the argument so far. Organisational structure, control and culture are the means by which an organisation motivates, coordinates and 'incentivises' its members to work towards achieving the building blocks of competitive advantage. Top managers who wish to find out why it takes a long time for people to make decisions in a company, why there is a lack of cooperation between sales and manufacturing or why product innovations are few and far between need to understand how the design of a company's structure and control system and the values and norms in its culture affect how its employees are coordinated and motivated and rewarded by working together. Organisational structure, control systems, reward systems and culture shape how people behave and their values and attitudes, and determine how they will implement an organisation's business model and strategies.[4] On the basis of this analysis, top managers can devise a plan to restructure or change their company's structure, control systems, reward systems and culture to improve coordination and motivation. Effective strategy implementation allows a company to obtain a competitive advantage and achieve above-average profitability.

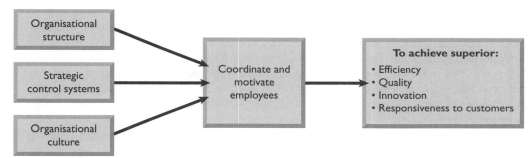

Figure 10.1:
Implementing strategy

Finally, the chapter discusses how the design of reward systems becomes an important part of the strategic control process. By the end of this chapter, you will appreciate the rich variety of different control systems available to managers and understand why developing an appropriate control system is vital to maximising the performance of a company and its employees.

What is strategic control?

Strategic control is the process by which top management monitors the performances of managers implementing strategies on an ongoing basis. Please note that the concepts of strategic control and strategy evaluation have many similarities in their meanings. In this book, strategic control focuses on the performances of managers while strategy evaluation focuses on the performances of strategies. In setting up strategic control, first, top management chooses the strategy that it hopes will allow the company to use its resources most effectively to create value for its customers. Second, it creates the structure: dividing the work related to that strategy among managers. Third, strategic managers create control systems to monitor and evaluate (a) whether managers who are implementing strategies are working as intended, (b) how their performances could be improved if they are not performing as intended. Strategic control does not just mean reacting to events; it also means keeping managers on track, anticipating potential events and responding swiftly to new opportunities that present themselves. To understand the vital importance of strategic control, consider how it helps managers to obtain superior efficiency, quality, innovation and responsiveness to customers, that is, the four basic building blocks of competitive advantage. An example of how strategic control can help achieve a competitive advantage is shown in Strategy in action 10.1.

strategy in action 10.1

Strategic control at China Haier Group

When CEO Zhang Ruimin took over a refrigerator-producing company called Haier from the Chinese government in 1984, it had assets of US$300 000. In less than 20 years (in 2003), the company accumulated assets of US$2 billion. The company opened its US factory in California at a cost of US$35 million in 2000 and its American headquarters in 2002. The company enjoys a greater than 30 per cent market share in the air-conditioner and refrigerator industry in the United States and 10 per cent of the European air-conditioner market. The Haier group has also established a university called the Haier University to teach employees about its philosophy and values.

One of the management methods that helped the company to achieve such a phenomenal success is its management control strategy, called the OEC, in which 'O' stands for 'Overall', 'E' stands for 'Everyone, Everything, Everyday' and 'C' stands for 'Control' and 'Clear'. Lin says: 'The OEC management control system aims at overall control of everything that every employee finishes on his or her job everyday with a 1% increase over what was done the previous day.' The OEC management control system has three aspects: target setting; control, checking and clearance; and incentive mechanism. In December every year, the company executives set the next year's goals and ways to achieve those goals for each of its divisions. Divisions submit 'divisional management accounts' showing the actions they plan to adopt to achieve the goals. Every employee submits an 'employee management account', which identifies daily activities that they intend to carry out to achieve monthly departmental goals.

The second aspect — control, checking and clearance — includes the 6-S daily routine, which is an adaptation of the Japanese 5-S quality control movement. It includes the initials of five Japanese words — *seiri*, *seiton*, *seiso*, *seiketsu* and *shitsuke* — and the English word 'safety'. *Seiri* asks employees to discard the unnecessary, *seiton* asks to arrange tools in the order of use, *seiso* asks to keep the worksite clean, *seiketsu* asks employees to keep themselves clean and *shitsuke* asks employees to follow workshop discipline. Another part of the control, checking and clearance subsystem is briefing by supervisors every morning before the work starts and on-site tours of supervisors every two hours. As part of the incentive system, at the end of the day, every employee fills out the 3E (Everyone, Everything and Everyday) card, on which they calculate their wages using the following formula: wage = rate × quantity + award − penalty. These 3E cards are evaluated by supervisors who grade employee performance A, B or C. An employee receiving an A gets a bonus, while an employee receiving a C is penalised and is paid less than his or her normal wage. This 3E card is then evaluated by successive levels of higher management. Employees are also rewarded based on the quality of their work, which is gauged by red 'reward' and yellow 'penalty' cards. Employees are informed about their progress towards achieving their targets. Promotion is awarded based on an open bidding system. Employees bid for job openings based on their skills and managers decide who should get the job.

Source: Lin, TW 2005, 'OEC management system helps China Haier Group achieve competitive advantage', *Management Accounting Quarterly*, vol. 6, no. 3, pp. 1–11.

Control and efficiency

To determine how *efficiently* they are using organisational resources, managers must be able to measure accurately how many units of inputs (raw materials, human resources and so on) are being used to produce a unit of output. They must also be able to measure the number of units of outputs (goods and services) that they produce. A control system contains the measures or yardsticks that allow managers to assess how efficiently they are producing goods and services. Moreover, if managers experiment with changing how they produce goods and services to find a more efficient production method, then these measures tell managers how successful they have been. Strategy in action 10.1 describes an example of an efficiency measurement system.

Control and quality

Today, much of the competition between companies revolves around increasing the *quality* of goods and services. In the car industry, for example, cars within each price range compete against one another in terms of their features, design and reliability over time. Whether a customer buys a Ford Falcon, a Holden Commodore, a Toyota Camry or a Honda Accord depends significantly on the quality of each company's product. Organisational control is important in determining the quality of goods and services because it gives managers feedback on product quality. If managers of a company such as Toyota consistently measure the number of customers' complaints and the number of new cars returned for repairs, then they have a good indication of the quality built into their product.

Control and innovation

Strategic control can also help to raise the level of *innovation* in a company. Successful innovation takes place when managers create an organisational setting in which employees feel empowered to be creative and in which authority is decentralised to employees so they feel free to experiment and take risks. Deciding on the appropriate control systems to encourage risk taking is a major management challenge and a company's control system is important in this regard. At Chrysler, for example, top managers encourage each product team to perform by monitoring each team's performance (by examining how each team reduced costs or increased quality, for example) and then paying each team a bonus related to its performance. The product team manager then evaluates each team member's individual performance, and the most innovative employees receive promotions and rewards based on their performance level.

Control and responsiveness to customers

Finally, strategic managers can help make their companies more *responsive* to *customers* if they develop a control system that allows them to evaluate how well employees with customer contact are performing their jobs. When employees know their behaviour is being monitored, they may have more incentive to be helpful and consistent towards customers. To help improve customer service, for example, the taxi industry in many cities runs a 'taxi driver of the year' competition. Customers who receive exemplary service are invited to nominate a driver and explain why they felt the service was special. In the same way, too many complaints about a driver can lead to that driver's licence being reviewed.

Strategic control systems

Strategic control systems are the formal target-setting, measurement and feedback systems that allow strategic managers to evaluate whether other managers in a company are achieving superior efficiency, quality, innovation and responsiveness to customers, and implementing its strategy successfully. An effective control system should have three characteristics: (1) it should be *flexible* enough to allow managers to respond as necessary to unexpected events; (2) it should provide *accurate information*, giving a true picture of managers' performances; and (3) it should supply managers with the information in a *timely manner* because making decisions on the basis of outdated information is a recipe for failure.[5] As figure 10.2 shows, designing an effective strategic control system requires four steps.

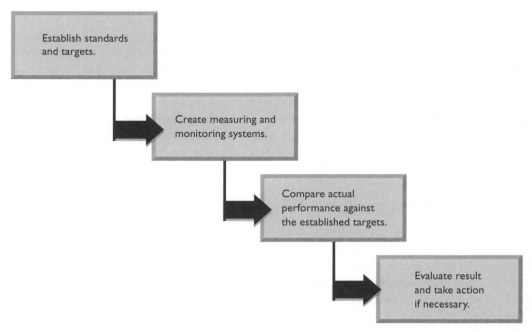

Figure 10.2:
Steps in designing an
effective control system

1. *Establish the standards and targets against which performance is to be evaluated.* Specific performance targets for managers are derived from the strategy pursued by the company. These targets are likely to differ depending on the levels at which managers work. If a company is pursuing a low-cost strategy, then reducing costs by 7 per cent a year may be a target. If the company is a service organisation, such as ANZ Bank or McDonald's, then its standards may include time targets for serving customers or guidelines for food quality.

2. *Create the measuring and monitoring systems that indicate whether the standards and targets are being reached.* The company establishes procedures for assessing whether targets set for managers at various levels are being achieved. In some cases, measuring performance is fairly straightforward. Managers can measure quite easily, for example, how many customers are served by counting the number of receipts from the cash register. In many cases, however, measuring performance is a difficult task because a strategy may involve many complex activities. How can managers judge how well their research and development (R&D) department is doing when it may take five years to develop products? The answer is that managers need to use various types of control system, which are discussed later in this chapter.

3. *Compare actual performance against the established targets.* Managers evaluate whether and how much performance of managers deviates from the standards and targets developed in step 1. If performance is higher, then management may decide that it has set the standards too low and may raise them for the next time period. On the other hand, if performance is too low, then managers must decide whether to take remedial action. This decision is easy when the reasons for poor performance (such as high labour costs) can be identified. More often, however, the reasons for poor performance are hard to uncover. They may stem from involved external factors (such as a recession) or from internal ones (such as the R&D laboratory's underestimation of problems that it would encounter or the extra costs of doing unforeseen research). For any form of action, however, step 4 is necessary.

4. *Initiate corrective action when the standards and targets are not being achieved.* The final stage in the control process is to take the corrective action that will allow the company to meet its goals. The types of corrective action to be taken depend on finding the reasons behind poor performance when, for example, a strategy has not done well.

Levels of strategic control

Strategic control systems are developed to measure performances of managers at four levels in a company: the corporate, divisional, functional and individual levels. Managers at all levels must develop the most appropriate set of measures to evaluate corporate-, business- and functional-level performance. These measures should be tied as closely as possible to the goals of achieving superior efficiency, quality, innovativeness and responsiveness to customers. Care must be taken, however, to ensure the standards used at each level do not cause problems at the other levels, for example, that divisional attempts to improve performance do not conflict with corporate performance. Furthermore, controls at each level should provide the basis on which managers at lower levels can select their control systems. Figure 10.3 illustrates these links.

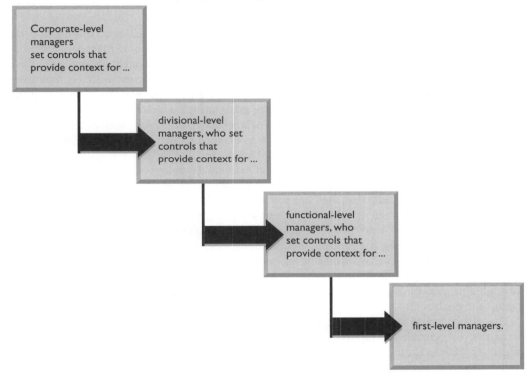

Figure 10.3:
Levels of organisational control

Types of strategic control

Three types of control — personal, output and behaviour control — can be used by managers to monitor activities of managers in relation to strategies.

Personal control

Personal control is the desire to shape and influence the behaviour of a manager in a face-to-face interaction in the pursuit of a company's strategies. The most obvious kind of personal control is direct supervision from a manager further up in the hierarchy. The personal approach is useful because managers can question subordinates about problems or new issues they are facing to better understand the situation, as well as to ensure that subordinates are performing their work effectively and not hiding any information that could cause problems down the line. Personal control also can come from a group of peers, such as occurs when people work in teams. Once again, personal control at the group level means more possibility for learning to occur and competencies to develop, as well as greater opportunities to prevent free-riding or skirting.

personal control
The desire to shape and influence the behaviour of a manager in a face-to-face interaction in the pursuit of a company's strategies

Output control

output control
A control system in which strategic managers estimate or forecast appropriate performance goals for managers at division, department and individual levels and then measure actual performance relative to these goals

In **output control**, strategic managers estimate or forecast appropriate performance goals for managers at division, department and individual levels and then measure actual performance against these goals.

Goals for managers at divisional levels state corporate managers' expectations for each division concerning performance on such dimensions as efficiency, quality, innovation and responsiveness to customers. Generally, corporate managers set challenging divisional goals to encourage divisional managers to create more effective strategies and structures in the future. General Electric, for example, set the goal for each division to be number one or two in its industry in terms of market share. Divisional managers are given considerable autonomy to formulate a strategy to meet this goal (to find ways of increasing efficiency, innovation and so on) and the company divests itself of divisions that fail.

Output control for managers at the functional and individual levels is a continuation of control at the divisional level. Divisional managers set goals for functional managers that will allow the division to achieve its goals. As at the divisional level, functional goals are established to encourage managers to develop competencies that provide the company with a competitive advantage. The same four building blocks of competitive advantage (efficiency, quality, innovation and responsiveness to customers) act as the goals against which functional performance is evaluated. In the sales function, for example, goals related to efficiency (such as cost of sales), quality (such as number of returns) and responsiveness to customers (such as the time needed to respond to customer needs) can be established for the whole function.

Finally, functional managers establish goals that individual employees are expected to achieve to allow the function to achieve its goals. Sales personnel, for example, may have specific goals (related to functional goals) that they are required to achieve. Functions and individuals are then evaluated on the basis of achieving or not achieving their goals; in sales, compensation is commonly pegged to achievement. The achievement of these goals is a sign that the company's strategy is working and meeting organisational objectives.

management by objectives
A system of measuring the performance of employees against established goals

Management by objectives (MBO) is an example of output control. In this arrangement, managers establish goals for managers at corporate, divisional, functional and individual levels through a process of participation, and performances of managers are periodically reviewed against the goals set.[6]

The inappropriate use of output control can also promote conflict among divisions and managers. In general, setting across-the-board output targets (such as return-on-investment targets) for divisions can lead to destructive results if divisions single-mindedly try to maximise divisional profits at the expense of achieving corporate objectives. Moreover, to reach output targets, divisions may engage in strategic manipulation of the figures to make their divisions look good.[7] In sum, strategic managers need to design the set of output controls that will best promote long-run profitability. In practice, output controls must be used in conjunction with behaviour controls and organisational culture if the right strategic behaviour is to be encouraged.

Behaviour control

The first step in strategy implementation is for managers to design the right kind of organisational structure. To make the structure work, however, employees must learn the behaviours that they are expected to perform. Using managers to tell employees what to do lengthens the organisational hierarchy, is expensive and raises bureaucratic costs; consequently, strategic managers rely on behaviour control. Behaviour control involves the establishment of a comprehensive system of rules and procedures to direct the actions or behaviour of divisions, functions and individuals.[8]

The intention in using behaviour controls is not to specify the goals but to standardise how to reach them. Rules standardise behaviour and make outcomes predictable. If employees follow the rules, then actions are performed and decisions are handled the same way each time. The results are predictability and accuracy — the aims of all control systems. The main types of behaviour control are operating budgets and standardisation.

Operating budgets

Once managers at each level have been given a goal to achieve, the company establishes operating budgets that regulate how managers and workers are to attain those goals. An **operating budget** is a blueprint that states how managers intend to use organisational resources to achieve organisational goals most efficiently. Most commonly, managers at one level allocate to managers at a lower level a specific amount of resources to use to produce goods and services.

Once they have been given a budget, managers must decide how they will allocate certain amounts of money for different organisational activities. These lower-level managers are then evaluated on the basis of their ability to stay within the budget and make the best use of it. Managers within Foster's' beer division, for example, may be allocated $5 million to develop a new premium beer that attracts female drinkers. The management team has to then decide how much to allocate to R&D or to marketing and sales, so the beer generates as much revenue as possible.

Most commonly, large companies treat each division as a stand-alone profit centre, and corporate managers evaluate each division's performance by its relative contribution to corporate profitability.

Standardisation

Standardisation refers to how much a company specifies how decisions are to be made so employees' behaviour becomes predictable.[9] In practice, a company can standardise three elements: *inputs*, *conversion activities* and *outputs*.

1. *Standardisation of inputs*. A company can control the behaviour of both people and resources by standardising its inputs. This means that managers screen inputs according to established criteria or standards, and then decide which inputs to allow. If employees are the input in question, for example, then one way of standardising them is to specify required qualities and skills and then select only those applicants who possess them.

2. *Standardisation of conversion activities*. The aim of standardising conversion activities is to program work activities so they are done the same way each time. The goal is predictability. Behaviour controls, such as rules and procedures, are among the chief means by which companies can standardise throughputs. Fast-food restaurants such as McDonald's and Pizza Hut, for example, standardise all aspects of their restaurant operations, resulting in standardised fast food.

3. *Standardisation of outputs*. The goal of standardising outputs is to specify the desired performance characteristics of the final product or service: what dimensions or tolerances the product should conform to, for example. To ensure their products are standardised, companies apply quality control and use various criteria to measure this standardisation. One criterion may be how many goods customers return or the number of customers' complaints. On production lines, periodic sampling of products can indicate whether they are meeting performance characteristics.

As with other types of control, the use of behaviour control is accompanied by potential pitfalls that the company must manage to avoid strategic problems. Rules constrain people and lead to standardised, predictable behaviour but they are always easier to establish than to remove, and the number of rules that a company uses tends to increase. As new developments lead to additional rules, often the old rules are not discarded and the company becomes overly bureaucratised. Consequently, the company and the people in it become inflexible and slow to react to changing or unusual circumstances. This inflexibility can reduce a company's competitive advantage by lowering the pace of innovation and reducing customer responsiveness.

operating budget
A blueprint that states how managers intend to use organisational resources to achieve organisational goals most efficiently

standardisation
How much a company specifies how decisions are to be made so employees' behaviour becomes predictable

Inside the company, too, integration and coordination may fall apart as rules impede communication between functions. Managers must be continually on the alert, therefore, for opportunities to reduce the number of rules and procedures necessary to manage the business; they should always prefer to discard a rule than add a new one.

Organisational culture

The first function of strategic control is to shape the behaviour of company employees to ensure they are working towards organisational goals and prompt managers to take corrective action if those goals are not being met. The second function, however, is to keep company employees focused on thinking about what is best for the company in the future and keep them looking for new opportunities to use organisational resources and competencies to create value. Organisational culture is an important strategic control system that serves this dual function.

Organisational culture is the collection of values and norms that people and groups in a company share, which control how they interact with each other and with external stake-holders.[10] **Organisational values** are beliefs and ideas about the goals that employees should pursue and about the appropriate types or standards of behaviour that employees should use to achieve these goals.

Organisational values

Organisational values are beliefs that help us to distinguish between what is preferable and what is not preferable. From organisational values develop **organisational norms**: guidelines or expectations that prescribe appropriate behaviour by employees in particular situations and control the behaviour of organisational members towards one another. The norms of behaviour for software programmers at Microsoft, the world's largest manufacturer of computer software, include working long hours and weekends, wearing whatever clothing is comfortable (but never a suit and tie), consuming junk food and communicating with other employees via e-mail and the company's state-of-the-art intranet. Strategy in action 10.2 shows how organisational culture can affect performance.

strategy in action 10.2

Sony's organisational culture

Sony is renowned the world over for its innovations. However, it seems to be failing to keep up with its competitors. Howard Stinger, CEO, Sony Corporation announced that he would cut 10 000 employees and shut several factories worldwide. Many commentators believe that this may not be enough to revitalise Sony. They argue that the problem with Sony lies in its culture. Sony's culture is an engineering-driven one, which is not too responsive to customers. Sony refuses to take cues from the market. Even when it does, it seems that Sony listens more to its domestic consumers rather than its overseas consumers. This explains why Sony's products often feature complex software that its Japanese consumers prefer but is disliked by its overseas customers. On the contrary, Samsung, one of its competitors, sends its designers and engineers to many different parts of the world to find out the preferences of consumers. No wonder Samsung was the first to pack digital cameras and music players into mobile phones, which became an instant success. Sony seems to believe that its engineers can dream up products behind closed doors and release them to markets and charge premium prices. Factionalism is rife in Sony and the top management has not done much so far. For example, its music, movie and gadgets businesses have agendas that often clash and they refuse to cooperate with one another. Many fear that because of this factionalism and its fear of piracy, Sony will lose in the portable video player market. Sony's content engineers and managers have already made sure that consumers can play only expensive Sony-formatted disks on its PlayStation.

Source: Cliff E et al. 2005, 'The lessons for Sony at Samsung', *Business Week*, 10 October.

Organisational culture functions as a type of control in that strategic managers can influence the values and norms that develop in the company: values and norms that specify appropriate and inappropriate behaviour, and shape and influence how employees behave.[11] Microsoft has a culture of performance in the form of innovation. As noted, employees are encouraged to work when it suits them, wear what they want and act informally but only so long as they respond by exhibiting innovation and efficiency in their work.

Other managers, however, may cultivate values that encourage employees to always be conservative and cautious in their dealings with others, consult with their superiors before they make important decisions and record their actions in writing so they can be held accountable for what happens. Managers of chemical and oil companies, financial institutions and insurance companies, for example — or any company in which caution is needed — may encourage a conservative, wary approach to making decisions.[12] In a bank or mutual fund, for example, the risk of losing all of the investors' money makes a cautious approach to investing highly appropriate. It may, therefore, be expected that managers of different types of company will deliberately try to cultivate and develop the organisational values and norms best suited to their strategy and structure.

Organisational socialisation is the term used to describe how people learn organisational culture. Through socialisation, people internalise and learn the norms and values of the culture so that they become members of the organisation.[13] Control through culture is so powerful because, once these values have been internalised, they become a part of the individual's values and the individual follows the organisational values without thinking about them.[14] The values and norms of a company's culture are often transmitted to its employees through the stories, myths and language that people in the company use, as well as by other means (see figure 10.4). The founder of Domino's Pizza, Tom Monaghan, used stories about his own rise from rags to riches as a way of indicating that anybody can achieve success. A failure at school and a university dropout, Monaghan eventually succeeded with his Domino's Pizza franchises. Employees are encouraged to follow Monaghan to the extent that they start off in pizza delivery, working their way up to being a store manager and eventually being offered the chance to purchase a franchise.

Figure 10.4:
Ways of transmitting organisational culture

Culture and strategic leadership

Given that both organisational structure (the design of the company's task and reporting relationships) and organisational culture shape employees' behaviour, it is crucial to match the structure and culture to implement strategy successfully. How companies design and create their structures is discussed in chapter 9 but how do they design and create their cultures? In general, strategic leadership is one of the most important determinants of organisational culture.

The influence of the founder

First, a company's founder and top managers provide the strategic leadership that creates organisational culture. The founder is particularly important in determining culture because he or she imprints his or her values and management style on the company. In New Zealand, Dick Hubbard, founder of Hubbards Foods, promotes values of people friendliness and social responsibility. Walt Disney exerted a conservative influence on the company he established until well after his death. Managers were afraid to experiment with new forms of entertainment because they were afraid Walt Disney would not like them. The installation of a new management team under Michael Eisner was needed to turn around the company's fortunes and allow it to deal with the realities of the new entertainment industry.

The leadership style established by the founder is transmitted to the company's managers and, as the company grows, it typically attracts new managers and employees who share the same values. Moreover, managers typically recruit and select only those who share their values. A company's culture thus becomes more and more distinct as its employees become more similar. The virtue of these shared values and common culture is that they increase integration and improve coordination among staff. The common language that typically emerges in a company, for example, aids cooperation among managers. Similarly, rules and procedures and direct supervision are less important when shared norms and values control behaviour and motivate employees. When a company's employees take on the company's cultural norms and values, this bonds them to the company and increases their commitment to finding new ways to help it succeed. That is, employees are more likely to commit themselves to organisational goals and work actively to develop new skills and competencies to help achieve those goals.

Strategic leadership also affects organisational culture through the way in which managers design organisational structure, that is, how managers delegate authority and divide up task relationships. Michael Dell, for example, has always tried to keep his company as flat as possible and has decentralised authority to lower-level managers and employees, who are charged with striving to get 'as close to the customer' as they can. As a result, he has created a customer service culture at Dell, in which employees go out of their way to provide high-quality customer service.

Adaptive and inert cultures

adaptive cultures
Company cultures that are innovative and able to respond to change on the basis of giving middle management more responsibility

inert cultures
Company cultures that do not change easily and are cautious and conservative

Few environments are stable for long. If a company is to survive, managers must help it adapt to environmental changes. If they do not, they may find themselves faced with declining demand for their products. In a study of 207 companies, Kotter and Heskett distinguished between adaptive cultures and inert cultures.[15] Adaptive cultures are innovative and encourage and reward initiative by middle- and lower-level managers. Inert cultures are cautious and conservative, do not value initiative on the part of middle- and lower-level managers and may even discourage such behaviour.

According to Kotter and Heskett, managers in companies with adaptive cultures are able to introduce changes in the company's operations (including changes in strategy and structure) that allow the company to adapt to changes in the external environment. This does not occur in companies with inert cultures. As a result, companies with adaptive cultures are more likely to survive in a changing environment and should have a higher performance, which is exactly what Kotter and Heskett found among the 207 companies they examined.

When a company has an inert culture, strategic problems can result. If, for example, all top managers accept the same set of norms and values, then they may be unable to steer the company in a new strategic direction if the environment changes and new competitors or technology demand that the company change. Furthermore, having designed their structures, managers become used to how they operate and rarely recognise the important effect of structure on cultural norms and values. Organisational culture can thus promote inertia.

As noted, cognitive biases can prevent a company from developing an adaptive culture by distorting the decision-making process. Over time, the norms and values of a company's culture can bias decision making and cause managers to misperceive the reality of the situation facing their company. To prevent these strategic leadership problems from arising, great care needs to be taken in composing the top management team.

A homogenous team of top managers can also stand in the way of developing an adaptive culture. Researchers have found that when a company has a diverse top management team, with managers drawn from different functional backgrounds, different company types or different national cultures, the threats of inertia and faulty decision making are reduced and the culture becomes adaptive. Hamel suggests that homogeneous top management teams are one reason for companies becoming so entrenched in a single mode of operation.[16] He suggests that managers, to become promoted, find it necessary to fit in with the existing culture and way of doing things. Through a process of natural selection, managers tend to replace themselves with similar people, who have the same ideas and a similar worldview on important issues. Rule-breakers and radicals within organisations tend not to reach the top. This process ensures — even though people come and go within the top management team — enormous consistency in how things are done and decisions are made.

Strategic reward systems

Companies also strive to influence employees' behaviour by linking reward systems to their control systems.[17] Based on a company's strategy (low cost or differentiation, for example), strategic managers must decide which behaviour to reward. They then create a control system to measure the behaviour types and link the reward structure to them. Determining how to relate rewards to performance is a crucial strategic decision because it sets the incentive structure, which affects how managers and employees at all levels behave.

Top managers could be encouraged to work in the shareholders' interests by being rewarded with share options linked to the company's long-term performance. Furthermore, companies such as Coles-Myer encourage managers to buy company shares. When managers are made shareholders, they are more motivated to pursue long-term rather than short-term goals. Similarly, in designing a pay system for salespeople, the choice is whether to motivate salespeople through a straight salary or a salary plus a bonus based on sales. Some companies pay employees a straight salary because they want to encourage high-quality service and discourage a hard-sell approach. They offer no incentives based on quantity sold. On the other hand, the pay system for rewarding car salespeople encourages high-pressure selling by typically containing a large bonus for the number and price of cars sold.

Because the design of a company's reward system affects how managers and employees behave, the reward system also affects the types of norm, value and culture that develop in a company. Top management teams rewarded by a salary alone and those rewarded by a salary and share options linked to performance are likely to have different norms and values. Specifically, top management teams rewarded with share options may be more entrepreneurial and more concerned with increasing quality and innovation than those managers who lack this reward.

What types of reward system are available to strategic managers?[18] Generally, reward systems are found at the individual, group and company-wide levels. They are often used in combination, for example, merit for individual performance, accompanied by a bonus based on divisional or corporate performance. Within each type of system, several forms of reward are available.

Individual reward systems

The main means of rewarding individuals are piecework plans, commission plans, bonus plans and promotion.

Under the piecework plan, employees are paid on the basis of some set amount for each unit or piece of output produced. Piecework plans are most commonly used for employees who work alone and whose performance can be directly measured. This system encourages quantity rather than quality.

Commission systems resemble piecework systems, except that they are normally tied to how much is sold, rather than what is produced. They are therefore most commonly found in sales situations.

Bonus plans at the individual level generally reward the performance of a company's key individuals, such as the CEO and senior managers.[19] A company must proceed carefully, however, if it is to avoid problems such as an emphasis on short-term rather than long-term objectives. Paying, for example, bonuses based on quarterly or yearly return on investment (ROI), rather than on five-year growth, can have a markedly different effect on the behaviour of strategic managers.

Last, but not least, promotion is an important source of reward for individuals at all organisational levels. Managers compete for promotion to the next level in the hierarchy. Promotion is so important because salary and bonuses rise sharply as managers ascend the hierarchy. In addition, increased prestige and decision-making power can be attractive for many managers who have devoted years of hard work to climbing the corporate hierarchy.

Group and companywide reward systems

The increasing use of product-team structures and cross-functional teams has led many companies to develop some form of group-based rewards system to encourage high team performance. The most common reward systems at the group and company levels are group bonuses, profit sharing, employee share options and companywide bonuses.

Group-based bonus systems reward teams or project groups for their performances. These are becoming quite popular and possible because increasingly many companies are establishing project teams or workgroups to perform all the operations needed to turn out a product or provide a service.

Profit sharing is designed to reward employees on the basis of the profit that a company earns in any one period. It encourages employees to take a broad view of their activities and feel connected to the company as a whole.

Rather than reward employees on the basis of short-term profits, a company sometimes establishes an employee share ownership plan and allows employees to buy its shares at below-market prices, heightening employees' motivation. As shareholders, the employees focus not only on short-term profits but also on long-term capital appreciation because they are now the company's owners.

Companywide bonus systems

Profit is not the only basis on which a company can reward companywide performance. Rewards are also commonly based on cost savings, quality increases and production increases obtained in the most recent time period. Because these systems usually require that the company measures outputs accurately, they are most commonly used in assembly-line companies and service companies, where it is possible to cost the price of the services of personnel. The systems are mainly a backup to other forms of pay systems. In rare situations, however, they become the principal means of control. That is the case at Lincoln Electric, which is a company renowned for the success of its cost savings-based group plan.

Control through organisational reward systems complements all the other forms of control discussed in this chapter. Rewards act as the oil that makes a control system function effectively. To ensure the right strategic behaviours are being rewarded, rewards should be closely linked to a company's strategy. Moreover, they should be designed so that they do not lead to conflicts among divisions, functions or individuals. Given that organisational structure and organisational control and reward systems are not independent dimensions of organisational design but are highly interrelated, they must be compatible for the company to implement its strategy successfully. Matching structure and control to strategy is the issue focused on in the next part of this chapter.

Using information technology

Information technology (IT) is playing an increasing role in strategy implementation at all organisational levels. It is making it much easier for organisations cost-effectively to develop output and behaviour controls that give strategic managers much more and much better information to monitor the many aspects of their strategies and to respond appropriately. IT, which provides a way of standardising behaviour through the use of a consistent, often cross-functional software platform, is a form of behaviour control. It is also a form of output control because all employees or functions using the same software platform to provide up-to-date information on their activities codifies and standardises organisational knowledge and makes it easier to monitor progress towards strategic objectives. It is also a form of integrating mechanism because it provides people at all levels in the hierarchy and across all functions with more of the information and knowledge they need to perform their roles effectively. For example, today, functional-level employees are able to access information easily from other functions using cross-functional software systems that keep them all informed about changes in product design, engineering, manufacturing schedules and marketing plans that will have an impact on their activities. In this sense, IT overlays the structure of tasks and roles that is normally regarded as the 'real' organisation structure.

Matching strategy, structure and control

Now that the main components of strategy implementation have been outlined, the issue of creating the structure, control systems, reward systems and culture to put a company's strategies into action can be discussed. Chapter 1 emphasised that strategic managers have to match strategy formulation with strategy implementation. All the tools of strategy formulation and implementation are discussed in previous chapters. This chapter puts the two sides of the equation together and examines how strategic managers match strategy and structure to build competitive advantage.

First, the chapter considers how functional-level strategy and the attempt to achieve superior efficiency, quality, innovation and responsiveness to customers affect structure and control. Second, it examines how a company's choice of generic business-level strategy influences the choice of structure and control for implementing the strategy. Third, it focuses on the implementation of a global strategy and discusses how to match different global strategies with different global structures. Finally, it takes up the special problems that different types of corporate-level strategy pose for strategic managers in designing a structure, and notes how changes in corporate-level strategy over time affect the form of structure and control systems adopted by a company. By the end of this chapter, you will understand how to match strategy to structure to create a high-performing company.

Implementing functional strategies

The chapter on functional-level strategy discusses how a company's functions can help it achieve superior efficiency, quality, innovation and responsiveness to customers: the four building blocks of competitive advantage. It also discusses how strategic managers can help each function to develop a distinctive competency. This section examines how strategic managers can combine the four components of strategy implementation to encourage the development of distinctive functional competencies or skills.

Decisions at the functional level fall into two categories: choices about the level of vertical specialisation and choices about monitoring and evaluation systems. (Choices about horizontal specialisation are not relevant here in considering each function individually.) The choices depend on the distinctive competency that a company is pursuing. To see how the different components of the strategy implementation process work together to implement functional strategy, consider how it works in three functions: manufacturing, R&D and sales.

Manufacturing

In manufacturing, functional strategy usually centres on improving efficiency, quality and responsiveness to customers. A company must create an organisational setting in which managers can learn from experience-curve effects how to economise on costs. Traditionally, to move down the experience curve quickly, companies have exercised tight control over work activities and employees and developed tall, centralised hierarchies to squeeze out costs wherever possible. As part of their attempt to increase efficiency, companies have also made great use of behaviour and output controls to reduce costs. Activities are standardised, such as human inputs being standardised through the recruitment and training of skilled personnel, the work process being standardised or programmed to reduce costs and quality control being used to ensure outputs are produced correctly. In addition, managers use output controls such as operating budgets to monitor and contain costs continuously.

Following the lead of Japanese companies such as Toyota and Sony, which operate total quality management (TQM) and flexible manufacturing systems, many companies have moved to change the way in which they design the manufacturing setting. Under TQM, the company creates work teams, workers are involved in the decision-making process and authority is decentralised and gives workers the responsibility and authority to discover and implement improved work procedures. Quality control circles are formed to exchange information and suggestions about problems and work procedures. Frequently, the company establishes a bonus system or employee share ownership plan to motivate workers and allow them to share in the increased value that TQM often produces.

Under TQM, components of strategy implementation take a new twist. No longer are managers employed purely to supervise workers and make sure they are doing the job. Managers assume the role of coach and facilitator, and team members jointly take on the supervisory burden, reducing bureaucratic costs. Work teams are often given the responsibility of controlling and disciplining their members; they may even have to decide who should work in their team. Frequently, work teams develop strong norms and values, and work group culture becomes an important means of control. This type of control matches the new decentralised team approach. Although workers are given more freedom to control their activities, the extensive use of output controls and the continual measurement of efficiency and quality ensure the work team's activities meet the goals that management sets for the function. Efficiency and quality increase as the company develops new and improved work rules and procedures to raise the level of standardisation. The aim is to find the right match between structure and control and a TQM approach, so that manufacturing develops distinctive competency leading to superior efficiency and quality.

R&D

The functional strategy for an R&D department is to develop a distinctive competency in innovation and to develop technology that results in products that fit customers' needs. Consequently, the R&D department's structure and control systems should be designed to provide the coordination necessary for scientists and engineers to bring products quickly to market. Moreover, these systems should motivate researchers and developers to develop innovative products or processes.

R&D departments typically have flat, decentralised structures, which group their staff into teams. Flat structures give R&D personnel the freedom and autonomy to be innovative. Furthermore, because the performance of scientists and engineers can typically be judged only over the long term (because they may take several years to complete a project), adding layers of hierarchy would simply raise bureaucratic costs and waste resources.[20]

By using teams, strategic managers can take advantage of scientists' ability to work jointly in solving problems and improve each other's performance. In small teams, too, the professional values and norms that highly trained employees bring to the situation promote coordination. A culture for innovation frequently emerges to control employees' behaviour, as has occurred at Intel, where the race to be first energises the R&D teams.

To spur teams to work effectively, the reward system should be linked to the performance of the team. If scientists, individually or in a team, do not share in the profits that a company obtains from its new products or processes, then they may have little motivation to contribute wholeheartedly to the team. To prevent the departure of their key employees and encourage high motivation, many companies give their researchers share options and rewards tied to their individual performance, their team performance and the company's performance.

Sales

Similarly to R&D, the sales function usually has a flat structure. Most commonly, three hierarchical levels — sales director, regional or product sales managers and individual salespeople — can accommodate even large sales forces. Flat structures are possible because the company does not depend on direct supervision for control. Salespeople's activities are often complex; moreover, because they are dispersed in the field, these employees are difficult to monitor. Rather than depend on the hierarchy, the sales function usually employs output and behaviour controls.

Supervisors can easily establish and monitor output controls, such as specific sales goals or goals for increasing responsiveness to customers. The output controls can be linked to a bonus reward system to motivate salespeople. Supervisors can also use behaviour controls — for example, salespeople's detailed reports on their interactions with customers — to standardise salespeople's behaviour and make it easier to review their performance.[21]

Similar design considerations apply to the other functions, such as accounting, finance, engineering and human resources management. Managers must select the right combination of structure and control mechanisms to allow each function to contribute to achieving superior efficiency, quality, innovation and responsiveness to customers. When, as now, reducing costs is required for survival, more and more companies flatten their functional hierarchies and decentralise control to reduce bureaucratic costs. Strategic managers must develop control and incentive systems that align employees' interests with those of the company and that motivate employees.

Implementing business-level strategies

This section considers the strategy implementation issues for a company seeking to implement one of the generic, competitive business-level strategies to build and sustain its competitive advantage. Building competitive advantage through structure, control, rewards and culture starts at the functional level. The key to successful strategy implementation, however, is designing the right mix of these four components of strategy implementation that links and combines the skills and competencies of a company's value creation functions, allowing it to pursue a business-level strategy successfully.

Because the focus is on managing cross-functional relationships, the choice of horizontal specialisation (the grouping of organisational activities) and integration for achieving business-level strategies becomes important.[22] Control systems must also be selected with the monitoring and evaluating of cross-functional activities in mind. Table 10.1 summarises the appropriate organisational structure and control systems (two components of strategy implementation) that companies can use when following a low-cost, differentiation or focus strategy.

Table 10.1: Generic strategy, structure and control

	Strategy		
	Cost leadership	Differentiation	Focus
Appropriate structure	Functional	Product team or matrix	Functional
Integrating mechanisms	Focus on manufacturing	Focus on research and development or marketing	Focus on product or customer
Output controls	Great use (for example, cost control)	Some use (for example, quality goals)	Some use (for example, cost control, quality goals)
Behaviour controls	Some use (for example, budgets, standardisation)	Great use (for example, rules, budgets)	Some use (for example, budgets)
Organisational culture	Little use (for example, quality control circles)	Great use (for example, norms and values)	Great use (for example, norms and values)

Implementing cost-leadership strategy

The aim of pursuing the cost-leadership strategy is to make the company the lowest-cost producer in the market.[23] At the business level, this means reducing costs, not just in production but across all functions in the company, including R&D and sales and marketing. The company should take every opportunity to minimise costs, which may involve using low-cost labour, minimising the number of managers and keeping down marketing costs.

If a company is pursuing a cost-leadership strategy, then its R&D efforts probably focus on product and process development rather than on the more expensive product innovation, which carries no guarantee of success. In other words, the company stresses research that improves product characteristics or lowers the cost of making existing products. Similarly, the company tries to decrease the cost of sales and marketing by offering a standard product to a mass market rather than offering different products aimed at different market segments, which is also more expensive.[24]

To implement a cost-leadership strategy, the company combines the components of the strategy implementation in such a way that keeps the costs down. The structure chosen is normally a functional structure, which is relatively inexpensive to operate because it is based on a low level of differentiation and integration. Even in a functional structure, cross-functional teams can be organised around the manufacturing function. A company can develop, for example, a TQM program implemented through task forces and teams, so as to integrate the activities of manufacturing and the other functions. This approach allows for continuous improvements in the rules and procedures for standardising task activities, which is a major source of cost saving.[25]

A cost-leadership company also tries to keep its structure as flat as possible to reduce bureaucratic costs and functional structures are relatively flat. The cost leader constantly evaluates whether it needs that extra level in the hierarchy and whether it can decentralise authority (perhaps to the workgroup) to keep costs low.

To further reduce costs, cost-leadership companies try to use the cheapest and easiest forms of control available: output controls. For each function, a company adopts output controls that allow it to monitor and evaluate functional performance closely. In the manufacturing function, for example, the company imposes tight controls and stresses meeting budgets based on production, cost or quality targets.[26] R&D personnel, eager to demonstrate their contribution to cost savings, may focus their efforts on improving process technology, in which savings are calculable.

In short, pursuing a successful cost-leadership strategy requires close attention to the design of structure and control to limit bureaucratic costs. Managers, rules and organisational control mechanisms cost money and low-cost companies must try to economise when implementing their structures. When a company's competitive advantage depends on building and sustaining a low-cost advantage, adopting the right organisational arrangements is vital.

Implementing differentiation strategy

To make its product unique in the eyes of the customer, a differentiated company must design the components of strategy implementation around the particular source of its competitive advantage.[27] If the differentiator's strength lies in its superior knowledge, then the design of the company's structure, for example, should account for this factor. Ernst & Young has made considerable steps towards becoming a knowledge-based company, building its competitive position around how well it can generate, codify, store and transfer knowledge within the company. This knowledge increases the value of the services that it offers. Because the company works on a series of generally unconnected projects for different clients, it uses a project team structure. Consultants move from one team to another as they are needed and each project features at least one senior staff member who manages the team. Beyond the billable hours measure used by many professional service companies, Ernst & Young also measures how much new knowledge is added to the computer-based knowledge management system, and how extensively a project team uses that system. In the same way that a manufacturing company may continually refine its manufacturing process to keep ahead of competitors, Ernst & Young perceives this knowledge-based approach as a way of guaranteeing its future competitiveness.

In other situations, a more standard form or structure may be appropriate. If the source of the differentiator's competitive advantage is superior quality or responsiveness to customers, for example, then a product-team or geographic structure may fit best. In a product-team structure, each product group can focus on the needs of a particular product market. Support functions such as research and development, and sales are organised by product and task forces and teams have a product, not a research, orientation.

If a company's differentiation strategy is based on serving the needs of a number of different market segments, then a geographic structure becomes appropriate. If a differentiated company focuses on types of customer, then it may use a geographic structure designed according to a regional logic or even different types of customer, such as businesses, individual consumers or the government. CSR, for example, has operations outside its core area of Australia and

New Zealand. Each continent represents a division in the CSR structure, allowing the company to be more responsive to the needs of specific groups of customers.

The control systems used to match the structure can also be geared to the company's distinctive competency. The differentiator needs to ensure its various functions do not pull in different directions; cooperation among the functions is vital for cross-functional integration. When functions work together, however, output controls become much harder to use. It is generally more difficult to measure the performance of people in different functions when they are engaged in cooperative efforts. Consequently, a company must rely more on behaviour controls and shared norms and values when pursuing a strategy of differentiation.

Companies pursuing a differentiation strategy consequently often have a markedly different culture from that of companies pursuing a low-cost strategy. Because human resources — scientists, designers or marketing people, for example — are often the source of differentiation, these companies have a culture based on professionalism or collegiality — a culture that emphasises the distinctiveness of the human resource rather than the high pressure of the bottom line.[28] Qantas, Lion Nathan and the ANZ Bank are examples of companies that emphasise some kind of distinctive competency and have professional cultures.

The bureaucratic costs of operating the structure and control system of the differentiator are higher than those of the cost leader but the benefits are also greater if companies can reap the rewards of a premium price. Companies are willing to accept a higher level of bureaucratic costs if their structure and control systems lead to superior efficiency, quality, innovation or responsiveness to customers. Samsung's approach to managing its businesses, described in Strategy in action 10.3, demonstrates how a company may operate when pursuing a differentiation strategy.

Implementing a combined differentiation and cost-leadership strategy

Pursuing a combined differentiation and low-cost strategy is the most difficult challenge for a company at the business level. On the one hand, the company has to coordinate its activities around manufacturing and materials management to implement a cost-reduction strategy. On the other hand, it must also coordinate its activities around the source of its differentiation advantage, such as R&D or marketing, to protect its competency in innovation or responsiveness to customers. For many companies in this situation, the answer has been the product-team structure. This structure is far less costly to operate than a matrix structure but provides a much higher level of cross-functional integration than is provided by the functional structure.

A product-team structure groups tasks by product and each product line is managed by a cross-functional team that provides all the support services necessary to bring the product to market. The role of the product team is to protect and increase a company's differentiation advantage and, at the same time, coordinate with manufacturing to lower costs. HomeStart Finance (South Australia), Westpac and Ford Australia are among the companies that have adopted a product-team structure so they can improve product development processes while controlling their operating costs.

In addition, team structures can make companies more flexible, because the composition or focus of a team can change rapidly compared with the speed of reorganising more standard functional or product-based structures. For this reason, the use of such teams is popular among professional services companies such as law, accounting and management consultants.

Focus strategy and structure

Focus strategy has been defined as a strategy directed at a particular market or customer segment. A company focuses on a product or range of products aimed at one type of customer

strategy in action 10.3

Samsung implementing a differentiation strategy

From being virtually nowhere half a decade ago, Samsung is emerging as a market leader in the electronics industry. In the global market, Samsung leads in LCD displays, big screen TVs, DRAM chips and microwave ovens. In these products, Samsung is ahead of such big players as Sony, Mitsubishi, Hitachi, Micron, Hynix, Infineon, LG, Galanz, Sharp, to name just a few. Samsung holds the second-largest global market in such products as flash memory, and takes third position in mobile phones, MP3 players and DVD players. Samsung has managed this because it is a lean corporation that focuses on its core business. In Samsung, there are fewer layers in the hierarchy to go through to get approval for new products, budgets and marketing plans. In Samsung, internal divisions compete with outsiders to get business. For example, Samsung buys half of its LCDs from the Sumitomo Chemical Co. and the other half from its own divisions. Samsung does its best to customise its products. In the memory chip business, Samsung charges prices that are 17 per cent above the industry average. Samsung does it by customising memory devices for products such as Dell servers, Nokia mobile phones and Microsoft Xbox game consoles. Samsung achieved its phenomenal success because of the speed at which it can transform a product concept into a concrete product. For Samsung, this is usually five months. For example, in April 2003, Samsung convinced T-Mobile, the German-US mobile phone carrier, to market a new camera phone. Very quickly, Samsung gathered 80 designers from its chip, display, telecom, computing and manufacturing operations. Within four months, this group produced a prototype camera phone named V205 with a lens that swivels 270 degrees and wirelessly transmits photos. Samsung then sent 30 engineers to Seattle to test the phone on the T-Mobiles servers and networks. By November, phones were rolling out of the Korean plant.

Source: Cliff, E, Moon, I & Pete, E 2003, 'The Samsung way', *Business Week*, 16 June, iss. 3837, pp. 56–64.

or region. This strategy tends to have higher production costs than those of the other two strategies because output levels are lower, making it harder to obtain substantial economies of scale. As a result, a company using a focus strategy must exercise cost control. On the other hand, because some attribute of its product — possibly the ability to provide customers with high-quality, personalised service — usually provides the company's unique advantage, a company using a focus strategy has to develop a unique competency. For both these reasons, the structure and control system adopted by a company following a focus strategy have to be inexpensive to operate but flexible enough to allow a distinctive competency to emerge.

A company using a focus strategy normally adopts a functional structure to meet these needs. This structure is appropriate because it is complex enough to manage the activities needed to serve the needs of the market segment or produce a narrow range of products. At the same time, the bureaucratic costs of operating a functional structure are relatively low, and there is less need for complex, expensive integrating mechanisms. This structure permits more personal control and flexibility than the other two do, so it reduces bureaucratic costs while fostering the development of a distinctive competency.[29] Given its small size, a company using a focus strategy can rely less on output and behaviour controls and more on culture, which is vital to the development of a service competency. Although output controls need to be used in production and sales, this form of control is inexpensive in a small organisation.

Companies should combine the four components of strategy implementation while they implement business-level strategies, as this chapter discusses. Companies should be flexible and creative in their approach to combine these four elements of strategy implementation. Business-level strategies work within one industry. In their attempt to implement strategies at the corporate level, companies face another set of challenges because these strategies cross many industries. These challenges are discussed in the next section.

Implementing corporate strategies

At the corporate level, strategic managers combine the four components of strategy implementation to operate different businesses efficiently.

A company's choice of corporate strategy implementation design depends on the degree to which a company must control the interactions among divisions. The more interdependent the divisions — that is, the more they depend on each other for resources — the more complex are the control and integration mechanisms required to integrate their activities and make the strategy work.[30] Consequently, as the need for integration increases, so too does the level of bureaucratic costs. A company is willing, however, to bear the increased bureaucratic costs stemming from a more complex strategy if the strategy creates more value.[31] This is illustrated in table 10.2, which also indicates what structures and controls companies should adopt to manage the three corporate strategies. These are examined in detail in the next sections.

Table 10.2: Corporate strategy, structure and control

Corporate strategy	Appropriate structure	Need for integration	Type of control		
			Financial control	Behaviour control	Organisational culture
Unrelated diversification	Multidivisional	Low (no exchanges among divisions)	Great use (for example, ROI)	Some use (for example, budgets)	Little use
Vertical integration	Multidivisional	Medium (scheduling of resource transfers)	Great use (for example, ROI, transfer pricing)	Great use (for example, standardisation, budgets)	Some use (for example, shared norms and values)
Related diversification	Multidivisional	High (synergies among divisions achieved through integration of roles)	Little use	Great use (for example, rules, budgets)	Great use (for example, shared norms and values, common language)

Implementing unrelated diversification strategy

Because there are no links among divisions, unrelated diversification is the easiest and cheapest strategy to manage. It is associated with the lowest level of bureaucratic costs. The main requirement of the structure and control system is that it allows corporate managers to evaluate divisional performance easily and accurately. Companies therefore use a multidivisional structure, with each division evaluated by financial controls such as ROI. A company also applies sophisticated accounting controls to obtain information quickly from the divisions so corporate managers can readily compare divisions on several dimensions.

Divisions normally have considerable autonomy, unless they fail to reach their return-on-investment objectives. Generally, corporate headquarters is not interested in the types of business-level strategy pursued by each division unless there are problems. If problems arise, corporate headquarters may take corrective action, perhaps replacing managers or providing additional financial resources, depending on the reason for the problem. If corporate personnel see no possibility of a turnaround, however, then they may decide to divest the division. The multidivisional structure allows the unrelated company to operate its businesses as a portfolio of investments that can be bought and sold as business conditions change. Usually, managers in the various divisions do not know one another and they may not know what companies are in the corporate portfolio.

The use of financial controls to manage a company means that no integration among divisions is necessary. This is why the bureaucratic costs of managing an unrelated company are low. The biggest problem facing corporate personnel is determining capital allocations to the various divisions so as to maximise the overall profitability of the portfolio. Corporate personnel also have to oversee divisional managers and ensure divisions are achieving return-on-investment targets.

Implementing vertical integration strategy

Vertical integration is more expensive to manage than unrelated diversification because sequential resource flows from one division to the next must be coordinated. The multidivisional structure allows this coordination. This structure provides the centralised control necessary for the vertically integrated company to achieve benefits from the control of resource transfers. Corporate personnel assume the responsibility for devising financial and behaviour controls to promote the efficient transfer of resources among divisions. Complex rules and procedures are instituted to manage interdivisional relationships and specify how exchanges are to be made; consequently, bureaucratic costs rise. As noted, complex resource exchanges can lead to conflict among divisions; corporate managers must try to minimise divisional conflicts.

Centralising authority at corporate headquarters must be done with care in vertically related companies. It carries the risk of involving corporate managers in operating issues at the business level to the point where the divisions lose their autonomy and motivation. Because their interests are at stake, divisions need to have input into scheduling and decisions regarding resource transfer. The plastics division in a chemical company, for example, has a vital interest in the activities of the oil division, because the quality of the products that it receives from the oil division determines the quality of its own products. Divisional integrating mechanisms can bring about direct coordination and information transfers among divisions.[32] To handle communication among divisions, a company sets up task forces or teams; it can also establish liaison roles. In hi-tech and chemical companies, for example, integrating roles across divisions is common. These integrating mechanisms also increase bureaucratic costs.

A strategy of vertical integration is thus managed through a combination of corporate and divisional controls. Although the organisational structure and control systems used for managing this strategy have higher bureaucratic costs than those used for unrelated diversification, the benefits derived from vertical integration often outweigh its extra costs.

Implementing related diversification strategy

In the case of related diversification, divisions share R&D knowledge, information, customer bases and goodwill to obtain gains from synergies. The process is difficult to manage, so a multidivisional structure is used to facilitate the transfer of resources to obtain synergies. Even with this structure, however, high levels of resource sharing and joint production by divisions make it hard for corporate managers to measure the performance of each individual division.[33] If a related company is to obtain gains from synergy, then it has to adopt more complicated forms of integration and control at the divisional level to make the structure work efficiently.

First, financial control is difficult to use because divisions share resources, so it is not easy to measure the performance of an individual division. A company needs, therefore, to develop a corporate culture that stresses cooperation among divisions and corporate, rather than purely divisional, goals. Second, corporate managers must establish sophisticated integrating devices to ensure coordination among divisions. Integrating roles and teams are crucial because they provide the context in which managers from different divisions can meet and develop a common vision of corporate goals. Hewlett-Packard, for instance, created three new high-level integrating teams to ensure the new products developed by its technology group made their way quickly to its product divisions. All this extra integration is expensive, however, and must be carefully managed.

A company with a multidivisional structure must have the right mix of incentives and rewards for cooperation if it is to achieve gains from sharing skills and resources among divisions.[34] With unrelated diversification, divisions operate autonomously and the company can quite easily reward managers on their division's individual performance. With related diversification, however, rewarding divisions is more difficult because they are engaged in joint production, and strategic managers must be sensitive and alert to achieving equity in rewards among divisions. The aim always is to design the structure so it can maximise the benefits from the strategy at the lowest bureaucratic cost.

Managing a strategy of related diversification also raises the issue of how much authority to centralise and how much to decentralise. Corporate managers need to take a close look at how their controls affect divisional performance and autonomy. If corporate managers get too involved in the day-to-day operations of the divisions, then they can endanger divisional autonomy and undercut divisional managers' decision making.[35] Corporate managers, after all, see everything from a corporate, rather than a divisional, perspective. Too much centralisation makes the corporate head office too large and slows decision making, whereas too little centralisation can lead companies to miss out on the benefits of cross-divisional synergies or learning.

Implementing strategy across countries

The strategies of most large companies have a global dimension if the companies produce and sell their products in international markets. Procter & Gamble and food companies such as HJ Heinz, Kellogg's and Nestlé Enterprises, for example, have production operations throughout the world, as do the large carmakers and computer makers. Companies having business across many countries face challenges that are fundamentally different from companies that implement strategies, including corporate strategies, in one country. Companies can use four basic strategies as they begin to market their products and establish production facilities abroad:

1. A *multidomestic strategy* is oriented towards local responsiveness, and a company establishes semiautonomous national units in each country in which it operates to produce and customise products to local markets.

2. An *international strategy* is based on R&D and marketing being centralised at home and all the other value creation functions being decentralised to national units.

3. A *global strategy* is oriented towards cost reduction, with all the principal value creation functions centralised at the optimal global location.

4. A *transnational strategy* focuses on achieving local responsiveness as well as global integration, so some functions are centralised at the optimal global location while others are decentralised, to both achieve local responsiveness and allow global learning.

If a company is to operate each strategy successfully, then the need to coordinate and integrate global tasks increases as the company moves from a multidomestic to an international to a global and then to a transnational strategy. The bureaucratic costs of managing a transnational strategy are much higher than those of managing a multidomestic strategy. To implement a transnational strategy, a company transfers its distinctive competencies to the global location where they can create the most value, and then it establishes a global network to coordinate its foreign and domestic divisions. This coordination involves managing global resource transfers to allow global learning. Compared with the other strategies, the transnational strategy requires more managerial time to be spent coordinating organisational resources and capabilities to achieve the global synergies that justify pursuing the strategy.

By contrast, pursuing a multidomestic strategy does not require coordination of activities on a global level because value creation activities are handled locally, by country or world region. The international and global strategies fit between the other two strategies. Although products have to be sold and marketed globally — and consequently global product transfers must be managed — there is less need to coordinate resource transfers than in the case of a transnational strategy.

The implication is that as companies change from a multidomestic to an international, global or transnational strategy, they require a more complex structure and control system to coordinate the value creation activities associated with that strategy. The bureaucratic costs, therefore, increase at each stage; they are low for a multidomestic strategy; medium for an international strategy; high for a global strategy; and very high for a transnational strategy (see table 10.3). In general, the choice of structure and control systems for managing a global business is a function of three factors:

1. the decision on how to distribute and allocate responsibility and authority among domestic and foreign managers so head office maintains effective control over a company's foreign operations
2. the selection of a level of horizontal differentiation that groups foreign operations with domestic operations in a way that allows the best use of resources and serves the needs of foreign customers most effectively
3. the selection of the right types of integration mechanism and organisational culture to make the structure function effectively.

Table 10.3 summarises the appropriate design choices for companies pursuing each of these strategies.

Table 10.3: Global strategy–structure relationships

	Multidomestic strategy	International strategy	Global strategy	Transnational strategy
Centralisation of authority	Decentralisation to national units	Core competencies centralised; others decentralised to national units	Centralised at optimal global location	Simultaneously centralised and decentralised
Horizontal differentiation	Global area structure	International division structure	Global product group structure	Global matrix structure, matrix in the mind
Need for complex integrating mechanisms	Low	Medium	High	Very high
Organisational culture	Not important	Quite important	Important	Very important

Implementing multidomestic strategy

When a company pursues a multidomestic strategy, it generally operates with a global area structure (see figure 10.5). When using this structure, a company duplicates all value creation activities and establishes a foreign division in every country or world area in which it operates. Authority is then decentralised to managers in each foreign division and they devise the appropriate strategy for responding to the needs of the local environment. Because corporate headquarters managers are so far away from the scene of operations, it makes sense to decentralise control and grant decision-making authority to managers in the foreign operations. Managers at global headquarters use market and output controls — such as rate of return, market share growth and operation costs — to evaluate the performance of foreign divisions. On the basis of these global comparisons, they can make decisions about capital allocation and orchestrate the transfer of new knowledge among divisions.

global area structure
A structure in which all value creation activities are duplicated by a foreign division established in every country or region in which the company operates

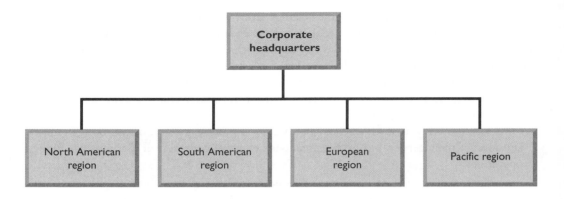

A company that makes and sells the same products in many different markets often groups its foreign subsidiaries into world regions to simplify the coordination of products across countries. Europe may be one region, Asia another and the Middle East a third. This allows the company to apply the same set of market and behaviour controls across all divisions inside a region. Companies can thus obtain synergies from dealing with broadly similar cultures because information can be more easily transmitted. Consumers' preferences regarding product design and marketing, for example, are likely to be more similar among countries in one world region than among countries in different world regions.

Because the foreign divisions have little or no contact with each other, no integrating mechanisms are needed. Furthermore, a global organisational culture does not develop, because there are no transfers of personnel or informal contacts among managers from the various world regions. Car companies such as Chrysler, General Motors (GM) and Ford all used to employ global area structures to manage their foreign operations. GM Holden, for example, has little or no contact with its US parent, and capital is the principal resource exchanged.

One problem with a global area structure and a multidomestic strategy is that the duplication of specialist activities raises costs. Moreover, the company is not taking advantage of low-cost manufacturing opportunities or opportunities to trade information and knowledge on a global basis. Multidomestic companies have chosen to keep behaviour costs low but they lose the many benefits of operating globally.

Implementing international strategy

A company pursuing an international strategy sells its domestically made products in foreign markets. Until recently, companies such as Mercedes-Benz and Jaguar made no attempt to produce in a foreign market; instead, they distributed and sold their domestically produced cars internationally. Companies like these usually just add a **foreign operations department** to their existing structure and continue to use the same control system. If a company is using a functional structure, this department has to coordinate manufacturing, sales, and research and development activities with the needs of the foreign market. Efforts at customisation are minimal though.

In the foreign country, the company usually establishes a subsidiary to handle sales and distribution. The Mercedes-Benz foreign subsidiaries, for example, allocate dealerships, organise supplies of spare parts and sell cars. Companies establish a system of behaviour controls to keep their home offices informed of changes in sales, spare parts requirements and so on.

A company with many different products or businesses operating from a multidivisional structure has the challenging problem of coordinating the flow of different products across different countries. To manage these transfers, many companies create an international division, which they add to their existing divisional structure (see figure 10.6).[36]

foreign operations department
The department that organises the distribution and sales of goods produced in the company's home base for sales in other countries

International operations are managed as a separate divisional business, whose managers are given the authority and responsibility for coordinating domestic product divisions and foreign markets. The international division also controls the foreign subsidiaries that market the products and decides how much authority to delegate to foreign management. This arrangement permits the company to engage in more complex foreign operations at relatively low bureaucratic cost. Managers in the foreign countries are though essentially under the control of managers in the international division, so if the domestic and foreign managers compete for control of operations in the foreign country, then conflict and lack of cooperation can result.

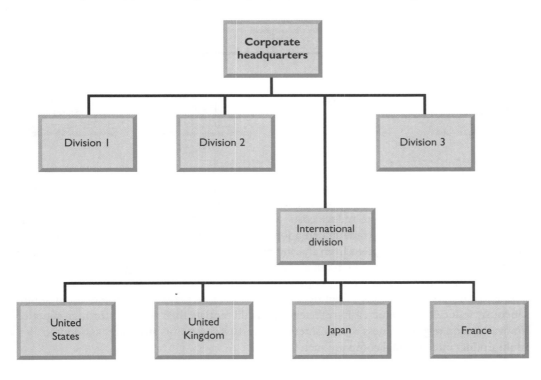

Figure 10.6:
International division structure

Implementing global strategy

A company embarks on a global strategy when it starts to locate manufacturing and all the other value creation activities in the lowest-cost global location to increase efficiency, quality and innovation. In seeking to obtain the gains from global learning, a company must cope with greater coordination and integration problems. It has to find a structure that can coordinate resource transfers between corporate headquarters and foreign divisions and, at the same time, provide the centralised control that a global strategy requires. The answer for many companies is a **global product group structure** (see figure 10.7).

In this structure, a product group headquarters (similar to a strategic business unit headquarters) is created to coordinate the activities of the domestic and foreign divisions within the product group. Product group managers in the home country are responsible for organising all aspects of value creation globally. The product group structure allows managers to decide how best to pursue a global strategy, for example, to decide which value creation activities, such as manufacturing or product design, should be performed in which country to increase efficiency. Increasingly, Western companies are moving manufacturing to low-cost countries such as China but keeping their product design centres in their country of origin to take advantage of local skills and capabilities.

global product group structure
A structure in which the distribution and sales of a product to different countries are controlled at a product and then a country level

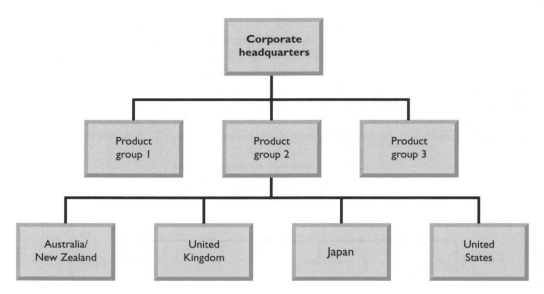

Implementing transnational strategy

The main failing of the global product group structure, while it allows a company to achieve superior efficiency and quality, is that it is weakly responsive to customers because the focus is still on centralised control to reduce costs. Moreover, this structure makes it difficult for the different product groups to trade information and knowledge, and to obtain the benefits of cooperation. The potential gains from sharing product, marketing or R&D knowledge among product groups are sometimes high but a company cannot achieve these gains because it lacks a structure that can coordinate the groups' activities.

Companies are increasingly adopting a **global matrix structure**, which lets them simultaneously reduce costs by increasing efficiency and differentiate their activities through superior innovation and responsiveness to customers. Figure 10.8 shows this structure, as adopted by a multiproduct international company such as Boral.

global matrix structure
A structure in which a company has simultaneous product- and region-based lines of reporting

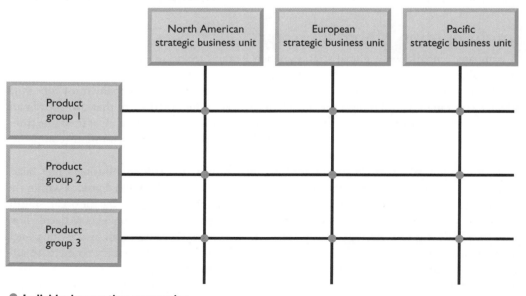

● **Individual operating companies**

The vertical axis shows, instead of functions, the company's product groups, which provide specialist services such as R&D, product design and marketing information to the foreign divisions, or strategic business units. These may be petroleum, plastics, pharmaceuticals or fertiliser product groups, for example. The horizontal axis shows the company's foreign divisions, or strategic business units, in the various countries or world regions in which it operates. Managers in the foreign subsidiary control foreign operations and through a system of behaviour controls report to divisional personnel at the head office. Together with local divisional personnel, they are also responsible for developing control and reward systems that promote the sharing of marketing or research and development information to achieve gains from synergies.

This structure both provides a great deal of local flexibility and gives divisional personnel in the headquarters considerable access to information about local affairs. The matrix structure also allows the company to transfer knowledge and experience among geographic regions and among divisions and regions. Given that it offers many opportunities for face-to-face contact between domestic and foreign managers, the matrix aids the transmission of a company's norms and values, and thus the development of a global corporate culture. This is especially important for an international company, for which lines of communication are longer and information is subject to distortion. Club Med, for example, exploits these synergies in how it manages its holiday resorts.

To make these matrix structures work, many companies strive to develop a strong international organisational culture to improve communication and coordination among managers. Companies are increasingly transferring managers between foreign and domestic operations, for example, so that they can develop a global view. Furthermore, to improve integration, companies are trying to form global networks of managers so they can turn to each other for help. The idea is to create a matrix in the mind, that is, an information network that allows the company to capitalise globally on the skills and capabilities of its personnel.[37]

To develop the matrix-in-the-mind concept and promote cooperation, companies are also using electronic integrating devices such as online teleconferencing, email and global intranets across different parts of their operations, both globally and domestically. Motorola, for example, is rapidly expanding its Australian operations so work on projects can continue for 24 hours per day. A project may go from a United States-based team to an Australian team to a European team in a single day. The teams contact each other only by electronic means and never meet, yet they all work on the same project sequentially.

These integration mechanisms provide the extra coordination that helps the global matrix structure work effectively. It is a complex structure to operate and carries a high level of bureaucratic costs but the potential gains for a company in terms of superior efficiency, quality, innovation and responsiveness to customers make these costs worthwhile. In the complicated game of international competition, companies must increasingly adopt many of these elements of a global matrix to survive.

Special issues in strategy implementation

Many companies are changing their corporate-level strategies and restructuring to find new ways of using their resources and capabilities to create value. In this section, we focus on three issues that arise during the management of rebuilding or restructuring process: (1) the implementation of mergers and acquisitions strategies; (2) the implementation of new ventures strategies and (3) the implementation of outsourcing through the development of a network structure.

Mergers, acquisitions and structure

Mergers and acquisitions are the principal vehicles by which companies enter new product markets and expand their operations.[38] Their implementation is important because many acquisitions are unsuccessful, often because many companies do a very poor job of integrating the new divisions into their corporate structure.[39]

The first factor that makes managing new acquisitions difficult is the nature of the businesses that a company acquires. If a company acquires businesses related to its existing businesses, then they should integrate into its corporate structure fairly easily. The controls already being used in the related company can be adapted to the new divisions. To achieve gains from synergies, the company can expand its task forces or increase the number of integrating roles, so that the new divisions are drawn into the existing divisional structure.

If managers do not understand how to develop connections among divisions to permit economies of scope, then the new businesses will perform poorly.[40] Some authors argue that this is why the quality of management is so important. A company must employ managers who have the ability to recognise synergies among apparently different businesses and thus derive benefits from acquisitions and mergers.[41] Porter cites the example of Philip Morris, the cigarette producer, which took over Miller Brewing.[42] On the surface, these seem to be very different businesses. When their products are viewed as consumer products that are often bought and consumed together, however, the possibility of sales, distribution and marketing synergies becomes clearer, and this merger was a great success. On the other hand, if companies acquire unrelated businesses only to operate them as a portfolio of investments, then they should have no trouble managing the acquisitions.

Implementation problems are likely to arise when corporate managers acquire businesses that they know little about or when they try to integrate unrelated companies with related ones. These mistakes explain why related acquisitions are sometimes more successful than unrelated ones.[43]

Strategic managers need to be sensitive to the problems involved in taking over new businesses through mergers and acquisitions. Similarly to other managers, they rarely appreciate the real issues inherent in managing the new business and the level of bureaucratic costs involved in managing a strategy until they have to deal with these issues personally. Even when acquiring closely related businesses, new managers must realise that each business has a unique culture or way of doing things. Such idiosyncrasies must be understood to manage the new company properly. Over time, new management can change the culture and alter the internal workings of the company but this is a difficult implementation task. Furthermore, the bureaucratic costs of changing a culture are often enormous because the top management team and the organisational structure have to be changed for people's behaviour to change. Strategy in action 10.4 provides an example of the difficulties encountered when two incompatible corporate cultures attempt to merge.

Implementing internal new venturing strategy

The main alternative to growth through acquisition and merger is for a company to develop new businesses internally. At the heart of new-venture design must be the realisation by corporate managers that internal new venturing is a form of entrepreneurship. The design should encourage creativity and give new-venture managers the opportunity and resources to develop new products or markets. Hewlett-Packard, for example, gives managers a great deal of latitude in this respect. To encourage innovation, it allows them to work on informal projects while they carry out their assigned tasks.[44] More generally, management must choose the appropriate structure and controls for operating new ventures.[45]

strategy in action 10.4

After the honeymoon; realities of joint ventures

The joint venture between France Télécom SA's mobile phone unit Orange and Thailand's Telecom Asia (TA) did not work out. This joint venture was set up with the belief that Orange would provide the marketing expertise and technological proficiency, while TA would provide the local knowledge and local connections. This joint venture ended within two years. This collapse is not unusual in the world of joint ventures. One argument was that the two partners had conflicting strategic visions: the Orange executives wanted to pursue a low-cost, wide customer-base strategy but TA executives wanted to focus on high-spending clientele with an emphasis on multimedia. TA executives argue that as the local partner they should have had a greater say in how products of the joint venture were advertised because they have the local knowledge. Instead, they argue, Orange executives rolled out the soft-sell, one size fits all global advertising campaign that they used mainly in the European market. TA is a fixed-line operator and its executives proposed to combine fixed-line and mobile phones in its services and products. Orange executives, however, wanted to concentrate just on the mobile phones. Although Thai executives freely expressed their opinion, Orange executives refused to be drawn into the debate about the failure of the joint venture.

The collapse of this TA–Orange joint venture is not new in Thailand. Other failures include the partnership between Danish brewer Carlsberg and Thai-owned Chang beverages, one between US investment bank Goldman Sachs and Dusit Thani Hotel group and, last but not least, that between Dutch-owned bank ABN Amro and Thai-owned Bank of Asia. Many Thai executives argue that these joint ventures end in failure because of philosophical differences between Western partners, who want quick profits, and Thai partners, who prefer to secure a safer base for the company by investing current profits. Many foreign business consultants differ and argue that Thai businesses, which are by and large owned by powerful families, want foreign capital but not foreign managers.

Source: Crispin, SW 2004, 'Thailand's rocky road', *Far Eastern Economic Review*, 23 September, vol. 167, no. 38, pp. 39–40.

One of the main design choices is the creation of a **new-venture division**. To provide new-venture managers with the autonomy to experiment and take risks, the company sets up a new-venture division separate from other divisions and makes it a centre for new product or project development. Away from the day-to-day scrutiny of top management, divisional personnel pursue the creation of new business as if they were external entrepreneurs. The division is operated by controls that reinforce the entrepreneurial spirit. Market and output controls are, therefore, inappropriate because they can inhibit risk taking. The company instead develops a culture for entrepreneurship in this division, so as to provide a climate for innovation. Care must be taken, however, to institute bureaucratic controls that somewhat limit freedom of action; otherwise, costly mistakes may be made and resources may be wasted on frivolous ideas.

In managing the new-venture division, the company must use integrating mechanisms such as task forces and teams to screen new ideas. Managers from R&D, sales and marketing, and product development are heavily involved in this screening process. The champions of new products generally need to defend their projects before a formal evaluation committee (consisting of proven entrepreneurs and experienced managers from the other divisions) to secure the resources for developing the product or project.

Care must be taken to preserve the autonomy of the new-venture division. As mentioned earlier, the costs of R&D are high and the rewards are uncertain. After spending millions of dollars, corporate managers often become concerned about the division's performance and introduce tight output controls or strong budgets to increase accountability. These measures hurt the entrepreneurial culture.

Sometimes, however, after creating a new invention, the new-venture division wants to reap the benefits by producing and marketing it. If this happens, the division becomes an ordinary operating division and entrepreneurship declines.[46] Strategic managers must take steps to provide a structure that can sustain the entrepreneurial spirit.[47]

> **new-venture division**
> A division that develops and trials new products and services away from existing operations

Internal new venturing is an important means by which large, established companies can maintain their momentum and grow from within.[48] The alternative is to acquire small businesses that have already developed some technological competency and to pump resources into them, which has been Microsoft's favoured strategy in recent years as it enters the many different niches of the Internet software market. This approach can also succeed and it obviously lessens management's burden if the company operates the new business as an independent entity.

Companies are likely to operate in both ways, acquiring some new businesses and developing others internally. As increasing competition from abroad has threatened their dominance in existing businesses, companies have been forced to evaluate opportunities for maximising long-term growth in new businesses, and many companies have made acquisitions.

Implementing outsourcing strategy: network structure, and the virtual corporation

The use of outsourcing is increasing rapidly as companies recognise the many opportunities that it offers to reduce costs and increase their flexibility. In an era when competition is intense, it makes sense to focus on your distinctive competencies and outsource noncore activities. Consequently, service companies often outsource their call centres, and manufacturing companies outsource their distribution activities.

network structure
A structure in which a company links (horizontally or vertically) with other companies as an alternative to owning the business of those companies

To implement outsourcing effectively, strategic managers must decide what organisational arrangements to adopt. Increasingly, a network structure, that is, the set of strategic alliances that a company creates with suppliers, manufacturers and distributors to produce and market a product, is becoming the structure of choice to implement outsourcing. An example of a network structure is the series of strategic alliances that Japanese car companies such as Toyota and Honda formed with their suppliers of inputs such as car axles, gear boxes and airconditioning systems. Members of the network work together long term to find new ways of reducing costs and increasing the quality of their products. Moreover, developing a network structure allows a company to avoid the high costs of operating a complex organisational structure (the costs of employing many managers, for example).

The ability of managers to develop a network structure to produce or provide the goods and services that customers want, rather than create a complex organisational structure to do so, has led many researchers and consultants to popularise the idea of the 'virtual corporation'. The virtual corporation is composed of people who are linked by computers, faxes, computeraided design systems and video teleconferencing, who may rarely (if ever) see one another. People come and go as and when their services are needed, much as in a matrix structure, but they are not formal members of a company, just functional experts who form an alliance with a company, fulfil their contractual obligations and then move on to the next project.

Summary

This chapter is an attempt to bring together strategy formulation and strategy implementation. It identifies four components of strategy implementation: organisational structure, strategic control, strategic reward systems and organisational culture. Issues related to organisational structure are discussed in the previous chapter. The remaining three components are discussed in this chapter. All managers must remember that the strategy process may not end with strategy formulation. Many would argue that implementation is much harder than formulation. Students of strategic management should remember that on many occasions it could be difficult to distinguish between formulation and implementation in the strategy process. It is commonly assumed that at a certain stage, one ends and the other begins but it may not always be so, because the distinction between them may largely be analytical rather than actual.

- Strategic control is the process of setting targets and monitoring, evaluating and rewarding organisational performance.

- Control takes place at all levels in the organisation: corporate, divisional, functional and individual.

- Effective control systems are flexible, accurate and able to provide quick feedback to strategic planners.

- Control systems range from those directed at measuring outputs to those measuring behaviour or actions.

- Output controls establish goals for divisions, functions and individuals. They can be used only when outputs can be objectively measured and they are often linked to a management by objectives system.

- Behaviour controls are achieved through budgets, standardisation, and rules and procedures.

- Organisational culture is the collection of norms and values that govern how people act and behave inside the company.

- A company's reward systems constitute the final form of control. A company designs its reward systems to provide employees with the incentives to make its structure work effectively and to align their interests with organisational goals and objectives.

- Companies use all these forms of control simultaneously. Management must select and combine those that are consistent with each other and with the strategy and structure of the company.

- Global area structure is a structure in which all value creation activities are duplicated by a foreign division established in every country or region in which the company operates.

- A foreign operations department organises the distribution and sales of goods produced in the company's home base for sale in other countries.

- A global product group structure is a structure in which the distribution and sales of a product to different countries are controlled at a product and then a country level.

- Global matrix structure is a structure in which a company has simultaneous product- and region-based lines of reporting.

- A new-venture division develops and trials new products and services away from existing operations.

- A network structure is a structure in which a company links (horizontally or vertically) with other companies as an alternative to owning the businesses of those companies.

- A global area structure is a structure in which all value creation activities are duplicated by a foreign division established in every country or region in which the company operates.

- At the functional level, each function requires a different kind of structure and control system to achieve its functional objectives.

- Cost-leadership and differentiation strategies each require a structure and control system that matches the source of the company's competitive advantage. Implementing a simultaneous cost-leadership and differentiation strategy is the problem facing many companies today.

- Unrelated diversification, vertical integration and related diversification require different combinations of the components of strategy implementation if the company is to realise the benefits of pursuing the strategy.

- As a company moves from a multidomestic to an international, global and transnational strategy, it needs to switch to a more complex structure that allows it to coordinate increasingly complex resource transfers. Similarly, it needs to adopt a more complex integration and control system that aids global learning. When there are gains to be derived from synergy, companies frequently adopt a global matrix structure to share knowledge and expertise.

- The profitability of mergers and acquisitions depends on the structure and control system that a company adopts to manage them and the way in which a company integrates them into its existing businesses.

- To encourage internal new venturing, companies must design a structure that gives the new-venture division the autonomy it needs to develop new products and to protect it from excessive interference by corporate managers.

- Increasingly, the growth of outsourcing has led companies to develop network structures. The virtual corporation is becoming a reality as computer information systems become more sophisticated.

Practising strategic management

Review questions

1. Define strategy implementation and identify the components of strategy implementation.
2. Identify different types of control and their effect on employees and the performance of companies.
3. What structures and control systems do companies use to pursue a cost-leadership strategy? How do these differ from those of companies pursuing a strategy based on differentiation?
4. How does the network structure differ from the market structure used by Dell discussed in the opening case?
5. What issues would you be faced with in implementing a transnational strategy?

Discussion questions

6. A performance-based executive compensation system is unfair. Discuss.
7. Organisational culture is a sophisticated method to control employees. Discuss.
8. Structure is just one of the many factors that influence successful strategy implementation. Discuss.
9. If a related company begins to buy unrelated businesses, then in what ways should it change its structure or control mechanisms to manage the acquisitions?
10. How would you design a structure and control system to encourage entrepreneurship in a large, established corporation?
11. Implementing an international strategy is as straight-forward as implementing a domestic strategy. Discuss.

Applied questions

12. Strategy in action 10.1 discusses the management control system used by Haier. What types of strategic control is it using?
13. Strategy in action 10.2 details the organisational culture currently existing in Sony. What type of culture is it?
14. Strategy in action 10.4 identifies a few factors associated with the collapse of joint ventures. Do you agree with the explanation given in the case?

Small-group exercise

Deciding on an organisational structure

Break into groups of three to five people, and discuss the following scenario.

You are a group of managers of a major soft-drinks company that is going head-to-head with Coca-Cola to increase market share. Your strategy is to increase your product range and offer a soft-drink in every segment of the market to attract customers. Currently, you have a functional structure. What you are trying to work out now is how best to implement your strategy so as to launch your new products. Should you move to a more complex kind of product structure? If so, which one? Alternatively, should you establish new venture divisions and spin off each kind of new soft-drink into its own company so each company can focus its resources on its market niche? There is also a global dimension to your strategy, because it is your intention to compete with Coca-Cola for market share worldwide, and you must consider what is the best structure globally as well as domestically.

1. Debate the pros and cons of the different possible organisational structures and decide which structure you are going to implement.
2. Debate the pros and cons of the different types of global structure and decide which is most appropriate and which will best fit in with your domestic structure.

Article file

Find an example of a company that has changed its structure and control systems to manage its strategy better. What were the problems with its old structure? What changes did it make to its structure and control systems? What effects does it expect these changes to have on performance?

Exploring the Web

Matching strategy and structure

Search the Internet for a company that is in the process of modifying or changing its organisational structure (domestic or global) to manage its new strategy. Towards which structure is it moving? Why is this structure more appropriate than the old one?

Strategic management project

Module 10

Ideally the structure, control and reward systems and culture of your company should be in alignment with the strategy it is pursuing. Identify areas in which it has achieved alignment and in which it has not. The following questions should help you answer this question.

1. What are the sources of your company's distinctive competencies? Which functions are most important to it? How does your company design its structure at the functional level to improve its (a) efficiency, (b) quality, (c) innovation and (d) responsiveness to customers?

2. What is your company's business-level strategy? How does the company design its structure and control systems to improve and support its business-level strategy? What steps does it take, for example, to further cross-functional integration? Does it have a functional, product or matrix structure?

3. How does your company's culture support its strategy? Can you determine any ways in which its top management team influences its culture?

4. What kind of international strategy does your company pursue? How does it control its global activities? What kind of structure does it use? Why?

5. At the corporate level, does your company use a multidivisional structure? Why? What crucial implementation problems must your company manage to implement its strategy effectively? What kind of integration mechanisms, for example, does it employ?

6. Based on this analysis, does your company have high or low bureaucratic costs? Is this level of bureaucratic costs justified by the value that the company can create through its strategy?

7. Can you suggest ways of altering the company's structure to reduce the level of bureaucratic costs?

8. Can you suggest ways of altering the company's structure or control systems to allow it to create more value? Would each change increase or decrease bureaucratic costs?

9. In summary, do you think your company has achieved a good fit between its strategy and structure?

Additional resources

Al-Ghamdi, SM 1998 'Obstacles to successful implementation of strategic decisions; the British experience', *European Business Review*, vol. 98, no. 6, pp. 322–7. (A discussion of obstacles to strategy implementation.)

Dobni, B, Dobni, D & Lufman, G 2001, 'Behavioral approaches to marketing strategy implementation', *Marketing Intelligence & Planning*, vol. 19, nos. 6/7, pp. 400–8. (Discusses the limitations of traditional strategy implementation approaches.)

Ghoshal, A & Bartlett, C 1994, 'Changing the role of top management: beyond structure to processes', *Harvard Business Review*, vol. 73, no. 1, pp. 86–96. (A discussion of a possible move away from structured control systems.)

Hambrick, DC & Connella, AA, Jr 1989, 'Strategy implementation as substance and selling', *Academy of Management Executive*, vol. 3, no. 4, pp. 278–85. (A discussion of why strategy implementation fails.)

Miller, D 1987, 'Strategy making and structure: analysis and implications for performance', *Academy of Management Journal*, vol. 30, no. 1, pp. 7–32. (A discussion of the link between strategy and structure.)

End notes

1. Noble, CH 1999, 'The eclectic roots of strategy implementation research', *Journal of Business Research*, vol. 45, pp. 119–34.
2. ibid.
3. Simmons, R 1991, 'Strategic orientation and top management attention to control systems', *Strategic Management Journal*, vol. 12, pp. 49–62.
4. Rodgers, R & Hunter, JE 1991, 'Impact of management by objectives on organizational productivity', *Journal of Applied Psychology*, vol. 76, pp. 322–6.
5. Ouchi, WG 1978, 'The transmission of control through organizational hierarchy', *Academy of Management Journal*, vol. 21, pp. 173–92; Newman, WH 1975, *Constructive control*, Prentice Hall, Englewood Cliffs, New Jersey.
6. Rodgers, R & Hunter, JE 1991, 'Impact of management by objectives on organizational productivity', *Journal of Applied Psychology*, vol. 76, pp. 322–6.
7. Flamholtz, E 1979, 'Organizational control systems as a managerial tool', *California Management Review*, Winter, pp. 50–8.
8. Williamson, OE 1975, *Markets and hierarchies*, Free Press, New York; Ouchi, WG 1980, 'Markets, bureaucracies, and clans', *Administrative Science Quarterly*, vol. 25, pp. 129–41.
9. Mintzberg, H 1979, *The structuring of organizations*, Prentice Hall, Englewood Cliffs, New Jersey, pp. 5–9.
10. Smircich, L 1983, 'Concepts of culture and organizational analysis', *Administrative Science Quarterly*, vol. 28, pp. 339–58
11. Ouchi, WG 1978, 'The transmission of control through organizational hierarchy', *Academy of Management Journal*, vol. 21, pp. 173–92.
12. Jones, GR 1997, *Organizational theory*, Addison-Wesley, Reading, Massachusetts.
13. Van Maanen, J & Schein, EH 1979, 'Towards a theory of organizational socialization', in Staw, BM (ed.), *Research in organizational behavior*, JAI Press, Greenwich, Connecticut, pp. 1, 209–64.
14. Jones, GR 1986, 'Socialization tactics, self-efficacy, and newcomers' adjustments to organizations', *Academy of Management Journal*, vol. 29, pp. 262–79.
15. Kotter, JP & Heskett, JL 1992, *Corporate culture and performance*, Free Press, New York.
16. Hamel, G 1996, 'Strategy as revolution', *Harvard Business Review*, vol. 74, no. 4, pp. 69–83.
17. Lawler, EE III 1973, *Motivation in work organizations*, Brooks/Cole, Monterey, California; Galbraith, J & Kazanjian, R 1992, *Strategy implementation*, West, St Paul, Minnesota, chapter 6.
18. Lawler, EE III 1987, 'The design of effective reward systems', in Lorsch, JW (ed.) *Handbook of organizational behavior*, Prentice Hall, Englewood Cliffs, New Jersey, pp. 386–422; Mathis, R & Jackson, J 1979, *Personnel*, 2nd edn, West, St Paul, Minnesota, p. 456.

19. Tosi, HL Jr & Gomez-Mejia, LR 1994, 'CEO compensation and firm performance', *Academy of Management Journal*, vol. 37, pp. 1002–16

20. Ouchi, WG 1977, 'The relationship between organizational structure and organizational control', *Administrative Science Quarterly*, vol. 22, pp. 95–113.

21. Eisenhardt, KM 1985, 'Control: organizational and economic approaches', *Management Science*, vol. 16, pp. 134–48.

22. Galbraith, JR 1973, *Designing complex organizations*, Addison-Wesley, Reading, Massachusetts; Lawrence, PR & Lorsch, JW 1967, *Organization and environment*, Harvard University Press, Cambridge, Massachusetts; Miller, D 1987, 'Strategy making and structure: analysis and implications for performance', *Academy of Management Journal*, vol. 30, pp. 7–32.

23. Porter, ME 1980, *Competitive strategy: techniques for analyzing industries and competitors*, Free Press, New York; Miller, D 1986, 'Configurations of strategy and structure', *Strategic Management Journal*, vol. 7, pp. 233–49.

24. Miller, D & Freisen, PH 1984, *Organizations: a quantum view*, Prentice Hall, Englewood Cliffs, New Jersey.

25. Woodward, J 1965, *Industrial organization: theory and practice*, Oxford University Press, London; Lawrence & Lorsch, op. cit.

26. White, RE 1986, 'Generic business strategies, organizational context and performance: an empirical investigation', *Strategic Management Journal*, vol. 7, pp. 217–31.

27. Porter, op. cit; Miller 1986, op. cit.

28. Deal, E & Kennedy, AA 1985, *Corporate cultures*, Addison-Wesley, Reading, Massachusetts; *Business Week* 1980, 'Corporate culture', 27 October, pp. 148–60.

29. Miller, D 1978, 'Configurations of strategy and structure', in Miles, RE & Snow, CC (eds), *Organizational strategy, structure, and process*, McGraw-Hill, New York.

30. Jones, GR & Hill, CWL 1988, 'Transaction cost analysis of strategy–structure choice', *Strategic Management Journal*, vol. 9, pp. 159–72.

31. D'Aveni, RA & Ravenscraft, DJ 1994, 'Economies of integration versus bureaucracy costs: does vertical integration improve performance?', *Academy of Management Journal*, vol. 5, pp. 1167–206.

32. Lawrence & Lorsch, op. cit.; Galbraith, op. cit.; Porter, ME 1985, *Competitive advantage: creating and sustaining superior performance*, Free Press, New York.

33. Nayyar, PR 1993, 'Performance effects of information asymmetry and economies of scope in diversified service firm', *Academy of Management Journal*, vol. 36, pp. 28–57.

34. Gomez-Mejia, LR 1992, 'Structure and process of diversification, compensation strategy, and performance', *Strategic Management Journal*, vol. 13, pp. 381–97.

35. Markides, CC & Williamson, PJ 1994, 'Related diversification, core competencies, and corporate performance', *Strategic Management Journal*, vol. 15, special issue, pp. 149–65.

36. Stopford, J & Wells, L 1972, *Managing the multinational enterprise*, Longman, London.

37. Bartlett, CA & Ghoshal, S 1991, *Managing across borders: the transnational solution*, Harvard Business School, Cambridge, Massachusetts.

38. Salter, MS & Weinhold, WA 1979, *Diversification through acquisition*, Free Press, New York.

39. Paine, FT & Power, DJ 1984, 'Merger strategy: an examination of Drucker's five rules for successful acquisitions', *Strategic Management Journal*, vol. 5, pp. 99–110.

40. Bruton, GD, Oviatt, BM & White, MA 1994, 'Performance of acquisitions of distressed firms', *Academy of Management Journal*, vol. 4, pp. 972–89.

41. Prahalad, CK & Bettis, RA 1986, 'The dominant logic: a new linkage between diversity and performance', *Strategic Management Journal*, vol. 7, pp. 485–501; Porter 1980, op. cit.

42. Porter 1980, op. cit.

43. Singh, H & Montgomery, CA 1984, 'Corporate acquisitions and economic performance', unpublished manuscript.

44. Fast, ND 1970, 'The future of industrial new venture departments', *Industrial Marketing Management*, vol. 8, pp. 264–79.

45. Burgelman, RA 1985, 'Managing the new venture division: research findings and the implications for strategic management', *Strategic Management Journal*, vol. 6, pp. 39–54.

46. Fast, op. cit.

47. Burgelman, op. cit.

48. Burgelman, RA 1983, 'Corporate entrepreneurship and strategic management: insights from a process study', *Management Science*, vol. 29, pp. 1349–64.

chapter 11

Managing strategic change

learning objectives

After studying this chapter, you should be able to:

- define strategic change
- explain approaches to the management of change
- describe how organisational conflict can limit organisational change
- discuss the political approach to the management of strategic change
- discuss how companies can monitor and evaluate change programs.

Lenovo: changing through joint ventures

Lenovo Group Limited, the biggest computer manufacturer in China, acquired IBM's PC business towards the end of 2004. With this acquisition, Lenovo has become the ninth-largest PC maker in the world with a revenue of more than US$12 billion. Lenovo was set up as Legend Group in 1984 by researchers from the Chinese Academy of Sciences. The Lenovo group, majority owned by the Chinese government, began its business as a distributor of AST computers, and in the 1990s, signed an agreement with Acer Computer to distribute its computers. They also sold such foreign brands as Hewlett-Packard and IBM. The company also manufactured keyboards and other simple devices for many multinational computer manufacturers.

Lenovo made its first major transformation when in 1990, it began manufacturing its own PCs. The Lenovo management did not waste any time in learning the ropes of manufacturing, marketing and distribution of computer business from its partnerships with large multinational firms. The company did not stop there though. It developed IT consulting services that included customer support and provision of integrated software services for thousands of small businesses in China. In addition to working with overseas firms, the company made the best possible effort to understand the Chinese computer market and built computers for domestic use only. Lenovo successfully integrated Chinese ideographs into computer software and appliances such as keyboards. Lenovo also designed computer software for Chinese accounting practices, which are different from those elsewhere.

Lenovo had always wanted to enter the international computer arena and it realised that one way to do it was to develop internationally known brands. With that strategy in mind, Lenovo signed an agreement to be exclusive provider of computing services for the Turin Winter Olympics in 2006 and Beijing Summer Olympics in 2008 at a cost of US$65 million to US$80 million. The change of its name from the Legend Group to Lenovo Group Limited was also a part of developing an internationally recognisable brand, and for this the company has increased its advertising expenditure by 20 per cent.

To distinguish itself from many others in the computing industry, Lenovo has begun manufacturing application-based PCs. For example, its Tianjiao series allows users to listen to music, view digital photos and download TV programs with a single button without booting up Microsoft's Windows. Computers, however, are not Lenovo's only business. It has moved into manufacturing mobile phones, MP3 players and digital cameras. Recently, Lenovo has presented a perfumed mobile phone that releases a fragrance whenever the phone is turned on.

Lenovo has successfully transformed itself from a firm that assembled and distributed computers in the mid-1980s into a company that is now one of the largest computer makers in the world. However, many challenges lie ahead for the company. Its acquisition of IBM's PC business has brought two companies together that are engaged in a radically different style of work. While IBM focuses on research and development (R&D), and targets the corporate sector, Lenovo focuses more on selling computers and servicing its individual customers.

Sources: Spooner, JG & Kanellos, M 2004, 'IBM sells PC group to Lenovo', *CNET News*, 8 December, accessed on 1 December 2005, www.news.com; Kanellos, M 2002, 'A legend in the making', 12 August 2002, accessed on 1 December 2005, www.news.com; Buckman, R, Dolven, B & Lawrence, SV 2003, 'Legend goes for the big league', *Far Eastern Economic Review*, 19 June, pp. 32–5; Biediger, J, Hoffman, G, Ojeda, J, Decicco, T, Lei, D, Slocum, J, Green, T, Mahadevan, K & Ward, K 2005, 'Learning from practice: strategic action at Lenovo', *Organizational Dynamics*, vol. 34, no. 1, pp. 89, 102.

Overview

In today's global environment, change rather than stability is the order of the day. Rapid changes in technology, competition and customers' demands have increased the rate at which companies need to alter their strategies to survive in the marketplace. As discussed, however, one of the principal reasons that companies fail is the organisational inertia that prevents them from changing and adapting to a new competitive environment.[1] Once a company has been created, and task and role relationships are defined, forces are put in operation that make a company resistant to change. In considering the Icarus paradox, for example, the tendency of companies to continue to rely on the skills and capabilities that made them successful even when those capabilities do not match the new competitive environment is noted.[2] Other causes of organisational inertia are the conflict and power struggles that occur at the top of a company as managers strive to influence decision making to protect and improve their own positions.

This chapter looks at the issues that strategic managers must deal with to overcome organisational inertia and change a company's strategy. It identifies two contrasting approaches for the management of changes in strategy: rational and political. You must remember that many other approaches can be taken to manage changes in strategies.[3] The rational perspective takes an impersonal, logical and cold view. In reality, this picture of how strategic managers change strategy is incomplete; it ignores how power and political processes influence the management of changes in strategy. The latter is the political approach to the management of changes in strategies.

This chapter discusses why it is difficult to change companies and outlines the issues and problems that managers must tackle and solve if they are to succeed in changing a company's strategy so that it matches new competitive environments. By the end of this chapter, you will understand the forces at play when strategic managers try to change their companies, and the role of power and politics in helping to manage change successfully.

Strategic change

The study of change in management is quite old. It has been studied under names such as organisational change, organisational development and organisational renewal. The meaning of change in strategic management is not straightforward either. Many competing terms exist in the area. Many authors refer to changes in strategy while others talk about **strategic change**. Quite simply, change means becoming different. But questions may arise whether a change that has been introduced by a company is really a strategic change or rather a minor adjustment. It is also necessary to know at what point a change becomes strategic. For example, was the introduction of Egg McMuffin by McDonald's strategic? One school of thought argues that it was because it brought McDonald's into a new market, the breakfast one, extending the use of existing facilities. Opponents argue that it was not a strategic change because nothing really changed but a few ingredients: Egg McMuffin was the same old McDonald's formula in a new package.[4] One way to understand whether a change is strategic is to develop a framework of interrelated terms.

This can be based on four interrelated terms: target of change, scope of change, amplitude of change and pace of change. Target of change refers to what is being changed, that is, structure, technology or process. Scope of change can be very wide or very narrow. It is considered wider when, for example, an attempt at change encompasses structure, processes and technology. It is considered narrower when the attempt encompasses, for example, only changes in the training policy for managers. Amplitude of change refers to the departures that are made compared with the current state of a company. It can be revolutionary when a radical

strategic change
Altering a company's present state or activities to improve its competitiveness

alteration has been made to the current structure or process. Amplitude can be considered a minor adjustment when the alterations that have been made are not a major departure from the current way of doing business. Pace of change refers to the speed at which changes are introduced. Some companies may introduce changes incrementally, while others may introduce change in sudden outbursts.[5] This framework can help identify the degree of change that has been introduced along several dimensions and can put a stop to the argument over whether a change is strategic.

Types of strategic change

In the past decade, most large companies have gone through some kind of strategic change as their managers tried to strengthen their existing core competencies and build new ones to compete more effectively.[6] Most of these companies pursued one of three major types of strategic change: (a) re-engineering and e-engineering (b) restructuring or (c) innovation (see figure 11.1).

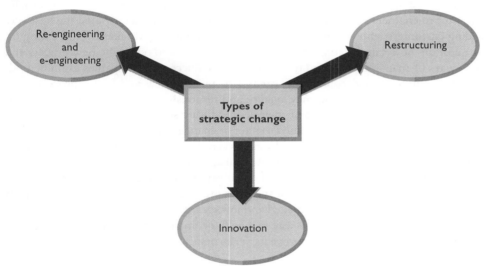

Figure 11.1:
Three major types of
strategic change

Re-engineering and e-engineering

Often, given drastic unexpected changes in the environment, such as the emergence of aggressive new competitors or technological breakthroughs, strategic managers need to develop a new strategy to raise the level of their business's performance. One way of changing a company to allow it to operate more effectively is by **re-engineering**. This is the 'fundamental rethinking and radical redesign of business processes to achieve dramatic improvements in critical, contemporary measures of performance such as cost, quality, service, and speed'.[7] As this definition suggests, strategic managers who use re-engineering must completely rethink how their company goes about its business. Instead of concentrating on a company's functions, strategic managers focus on business processes.

A **business process** is any activity (such as order processing, inventory control or product design) that is vital to delivering goods and services to customers quickly or that promotes high quality or low costs. Business processes are not the responsibility of any one function but cut across functions. Hallmark Cards, for example, re-engineered its card design process with great success. Before the re-engineering effort, artists, writers and editors worked in different functions to produce all kinds of card. After re-engineering, these same artists, writers and editors worked in cross-functional teams that each produce a specific type of card, such as birthday, Christmas or Mother's Day. As a result, the time it took to bring a new card to market dropped from years to months, and Hallmark's performance increased dramatically.

re-engineering
The fundamental redesign of organisational structure or business processes to achieve dramatic improvements in competitiveness

business process
Any company activity that is vital to delivering goods or services to customers quickly or promotes high quality or low costs

Because re-engineering focuses on business processes and not on functions, a company that re-engineers always has to adopt a different approach to organising its activities. Companies that take up re-engineering deliberately ignore the existing arrangement of tasks, roles and work activities. They start the re-engineering process with the customer (not the product or service) and ask how they can reorganise how they do their work — their business processes — to provide the best-quality and lowest-cost goods and services to the customer.

Frequently, when companies ask this question, they realise that there are more effective ways of organising their activities. After re-engineering, one person or a few people may perform a business process that used to involve members of ten different functions working sequentially to provide goods and services, and the smaller team may do so at a fraction of the original cost. Often, individual jobs become increasingly complex and people are grouped into cross-functional teams as business processes are re-engineered to reduce costs and increase quality. This occurred at Eastman Chemicals as it re-engineered itself to raise quality and responsiveness to customers.

Re-engineering and total quality management (TQM) are highly interrelated and complementary. After re-engineering has taken place and the company has determined the best way of providing customers with the goods or service they require, TQM takes over, focusing on the next question: how can the company continue to improve and refine the new process and find better ways of managing task and role relationships? Successful companies examine both questions simultaneously and continually attempt to identify new and better processes for meeting the goals of increased efficiency, quality and responsiveness to customers. They are always seeking to improve their visions of their desired future state.

The term 'e-engineering' has been coined to refer to change efforts centred on the introduction of new software systems. Internet-based systems can change the way in which a company's structure and control systems operate. Alcoa's Australian headquarters in Perth, for example, is the first site for the company's global rollout of an enterprise resource planning (ERP) system. This software will significantly alter many of the work practices in Alcoa, including the ways in which orders are processed, stock is managed and invoices are created. E-engineering is likely to gain more importance as it alters the way in which a company organises its value creation functions and links them together to improve its performance.

Restructuring

restructuring
Altering the form or management processes used within a business (in a corporate setting, sometimes reducing divisions, department or functional areas, as well as employees, to reduce operating costs)

Strategic managers also turn to **restructuring** as a means of managing strategic change aimed at improving performance. Restructuring has two basic steps. First, a company reduces its level of specialisation and integration by eliminating divisions, departments or levels in the hierarchy. Second, it downsizes by reducing employees to decrease operating costs.

Restructuring and sometimes downsizing can be necessary for many reasons.[8] Sometimes, an unforeseen change occurs in the business environment: perhaps a shift in technology makes a company's products obsolete or a worldwide recession reduces the demand for its products. A company may also find itself with excess capacity because customers no longer want its goods and services, viewing them as outdated or of poor value for money. Sometimes, too, companies downsize because they have grown excessively tall and bureaucratic, and their operating costs have skyrocketed. Even companies that hold a strong position may choose to restructure, simply to build and improve their competitive advantage and stay on top.

All too often, however, companies must downsize because they have failed to continually monitor the operation of their basic business processes and have not made the incremental changes in structures that would help them contain costs and adjust to changing conditions. Paradoxically, because they have not paid attention to the need to re-engineer themselves, they are forced into a position in which restructuring becomes the only way of surviving in an increasingly competitive environment (see Strategy in action 11.1).

strategy in action 11.1

Nissan, one of the largest Japanese carmakers was not doing very well. The company was losing domestic and international market share, factories in Japan were operating at 50 per cent of capacity and most of all it had US$20 billion in debt. Renault paid US$5 billion to acquire almost half of Nissan and sent Carlos Ghosn, an ethnic Lebanese, Brazil-born and France-educated restructuring specialist, commonly known as *le Cost killer*, as the CEO and president. When Ghosn arrived in Nissan, he found a company whose managers were apathetic, who did not care much about profit, routinely ignored customers and who were very good at fighting with one another. Ghosn set measurable targets that had to be achieved within a stipulated time. He adopted strategies to reduce purchasing costs by 20 per cent, general expenditure by 20 per cent and the workforce by 14 per cent; and to increase production capacity by 30 per cent. His measures also included getting rid of thousands of dealerships and divesting many affiliates. He also dumped cross-shareholdings in partners and sold noncore businesses. In the case of Nissan, this meant the sale of its aerospace operations. Most of all, his reforms at Nissan included attacking some of the fundamental norms and assumptions that underlay Japanese company culture. He disagreed with such Japanese norms as business is a collective enterprise in which no one should be left behind. He pushed the strategy that there would be losers and based on this idea he attacked such institutions as lifetime employment and promotion based on seniority. His prescriptions worked miraculously. Nissan reported record earnings, soaring stock prices and smash hits of some of its products. However, most important is the way a *gaijin*, through *Ghosn-ryu* or Ghosn style, influenced Japanese company culture. Many companies have since followed in the footsteps of Nissan, including such heavyweights as Canon and the Sumitomo Corporation.

Sources: Dawson, C 2002, 'Ghosn's way: why Japan Inc. is following a gaijin', *Business Week*, 20 May, iss. 3783; Murphy, C 2005, 'Review of *Shift: Inside Nissan's historic revival* by C Ghosn and P Ries, Currency/Doubleday', *Far Eastern Economic Review*, March, vol. 168, no. 3.

Innovation

As noted, restructuring may often be necessary because changes in technology make a company's technology or the goods and services that it produces obsolete. Changes in technology have made computers both much cheaper to manufacture and more powerful, and have affected what customers want. If companies are to avoid being left behind in the competitive race to produce new goods and services, then they must take steps to introduce new products or develop new technologies to produce those products reliably and at low cost.

You will recall from earlier discussions that in innovation, companies use their skills and resources to create new technologies or goods and services to change and respond better to the needs of their customers.[9] Innovation can bring a company spectacular success. Apple Computer, for example, changed the face of the computer industry when it introduced its PC. Honda changed the face of the small motorcycle market when it introduced 50-cc motorcycles, and Aussie Home Loans changed Australia's home loan industry by reducing home loan interest rates, ensuring that banks could no longer cross-subsidise other services from the profits they made from their mortgages.

Along with change generated by innovation, however, comes a high level of risk, because the outcomes of R&D activities are often uncertain.[10] Although innovation can lead to the kind of change that companies want, that is, the introduction of profitable new technologies and products, it can also bring undesirable change in the form of technologies that are inefficient and products that customers do not want. Sharp (which established a microprocessor plant) and IBM (which developed the System 360) are two well-known companies that bet the entire company on a new technology (a microprocessor plant and the System 360, respectively), and they could have gone bankrupt if they had failed.

Innovation is one of the most difficult change processes to manage. As discussed in previous chapters, when companies rely on innovation as the source of their competitive advantage, they need to adopt flexible structures such as matrix or cross-functional teams, which give people the freedom to experiment and be creative.[11] Functions need to coordinate their activities and work together if innovation is to be successful, and companies that rely on innovation have to facilitate the change effort and support the efforts of their members to be creative. The term 'skunkworks' was coined at Lockheed for a specialised unit it set up, separate from its regular functions, to pioneer the development of a new spy plane, the U2. Creating a separate unit allowed managers to act more flexibly and autonomously. To try to increase the success rate of innovation and new product development, many hi-tech companies have developed the role of 'product champion' and appointed an expert manager to head a new team and lead a new project from its beginning to commercialisation.[12] Of all the kinds of change programs that strategic managers can implement, innovation has the prospects for the greatest long-term success but also the greatest risks (see Strategy in action 11.2).

strategy in action 11.2

Sungho's digital shoes

Production factories all over the world are under challenge from cost-efficient Chinese companies. China is not only challenging the West but also its Asian competitors. The South Korean shoe industry was one of the pioneers of its industrialisation. It did the same type of work for Nike and Reebok that many companies in Asia are currently doing. However, Kwaon Dong Chil, president of Sungho Industrial is not giving up. Korean experience has taught him that cheap labour cannot sustain the long-term competitive advantage of a company. It needs to innovate. He has invested close to US$2.5 million in developing innovative shoes. When visitors go to the Sungho shoe factory they do not smell rubber or leather. Neither do they hear the constant noise of heavy industrial sewing machines. Instead, visitors see computers with flat-screen monitors. Sungho makes custom-designed shoes for its customers. Shop assistants from its outlets send foot measurements of their customers via the Internet directly to the factory, where the shoes are made and delivered to the customers' homes in three days. Sungho demonstrates that competitive advantage will increasingly come more from customisation, marketing and design and less and less from cost efficiency.

Source: Min, KJ 2003, 'A new spring in its step', *Far Eastern Economic Review*, 13 February, vol. 166, no. 6, pp. 30–3.

Approaches to managing change

Two contrasting approaches can be taken to the management of changes in strategy: rational and political. It should be remembered that there are many other approaches to the management of change. The rational approach is claimed to be logical and objective. It moves in sequential steps. The first is to determine the need for change, which comes from an analysis of the gap between desired and actual performance. The company, having analysed the obstacles to change, should take appropriate measures to implement it. The rational approach is rounded off by an evaluation of change. In many ways, it has many similarities with the intended mode of strategy formulation. The political approach recognises the interests of top-level decision makers and the uncertainty of future events, which mean that changes in strategies are managed by power struggles, coalition building, compromise, bargaining and negotiation. Many argue that the rational approach is normative, showing how a change process should be managed, while the political approach shows how in reality managers manage changes in strategies.

Rational approach

According to the rational approach, to understand the issues involved in implementing strategic change, it is useful to focus on the series of steps that strategic managers must follow if the change process is to succeed.[13] These steps are listed in figure 11.2 and discussed in the rest of this chapter.

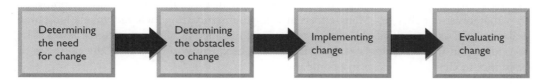

| Determining the need for change | → | Determining the obstacles to change | → | Implementing change | → | Evaluating change |

Figure 11.2:
Stages in the change process

Determining the need for change

The first step in the change process is for strategic managers to recognise the need for change. Sometimes, this need is obvious, as when divisions are fighting or when competitors introduce a product that is superior to anything that the company has in production. More often, however, managers have trouble determining that something is going wrong. Problems may develop gradually and organisational performance may slip for some years before the issues become obvious.

So the first step in the change process occurs when a company's strategic managers or others in a position to take action recognise that there is a gap between desired and actual company performance.[14] Using measures such as a decline in profitability, return on investment, share price or market share as indicators that change is needed, managers can start looking for the source of the problem. To discover it, they conduct an analysis of strengths, weaknesses, opportunities and threats (a SWOT analysis).

Strategic managers examine the company's strengths and weaknesses. They may conduct, for example, a strategic audit of all functions and divisions, examining their contribution to profitability over time. Perhaps some divisions have become relatively unprofitable because innovation has slowed without management's realising it. Perhaps sales and marketing have failed to keep pace with changes occurring in the competitive environment. Perhaps the company's product is simply outdated. Strategic managers also analyse the company's level of specialisation and integration to make sure it is appropriate for its strategy. Perhaps a company does not have the integrating mechanisms in place to achieve gains from synergy. Or perhaps the structure has become tall and inflexible, so bureaucratic costs have escalated. Perhaps it is necessary to quickly implement a product team structure to speed the process of product development.

Strategic managers then examine environmental opportunities and threats that may explain the problem. Intense competition may have arisen unexpectedly from substitute products or a shift in consumers' tastes or technology may have caught the company unawares.

Once the source of the problem has been identified using a SWOT analysis, strategic managers must determine the desired future state of the company, that is, how it should change its strategy and structure to achieve the new goals they have set for it. Alternatively, as happened at Merck and Foster's, the company may increase its R&D budget or diversify into new products to increase the rate of product innovation. Essentially, strategic managers work out the best strategy for maximising profitability. The choices they make are specific to each individual company and, as noted, managers cannot determine their correctness in advance.

In summary, the first step in the change process involves determining the need for change, analysing the company's current position and determining how to achieve (by implementing a re-engineering, restructuring or innovation program, for example) the desired future state that strategic managers would like the company to attain.

Determining the obstacles to change

Restructuring, re-engineering, innovation and other forms of strategic change are often resisted by people and groups inside a company. The decision to restructure and downsize a company often requires, for example, the establishment of a new set of task and role relationships among organisational employees. Because these changes may threaten the jobs of some employees, they may resist the changes. Many efforts at change, restructuring included, take a long time and often fail as a result of the strong resistance to change at all organisational levels. The second step in implementing strategic change is consequently to determine the obstacles or resistance to change that exists in a company.[15]

Types of obstacle to change

Strategic managers must analyse the factors that cause organisational inertia and prevent the company from reaching its ideal future state. Obstacles to change can be found at four organisational levels: corporate, divisional, functional and individual.

Corporate obstacles

At the corporate level, several potential obstacles must be considered. Changing strategy even in seemingly trivial ways may significantly affect a company's behaviour. Suppose that a company, aiming to reduce costs, decides to centralise all divisional purchasing and sales activities at the corporate level. This could severely damage each division's ability to develop a unique strategy for its own individual markets. Alternatively, suppose that a company, in response to low-cost foreign competition, decides to pursue a policy of differentiation. This action would change the balance of power among functions and lead to problems as functions start fighting to retain their organisational status. A company's present structure and strategy may constitute powerful obstacles to change. They produce a massive amount of inertia, which the company has to overcome before change can take place. This is why strategic change is usually a slow process.[16]

The type of structure that a company uses can be another impediment to change. It is much easier to change strategy if a company is using a matrix structure rather than a functional one, or if it is decentralised rather than centralised, or if it has a high rather than a low level of integration. Decentralised matrix structures are more flexible than highly controlled functional structures, and so have less potential for conflict between functions or divisions because people are used to cooperative cross-functional relationships.

Although some are easier to change than others, corporate cultures can present yet another obstacle to change. Change is notoriously difficult in the military, for example, because obedience and the following of orders are deemed sacrosanct. Some cultures, however, such as Hewlett-Packard's, thrive on flexibility or even change itself; they adapt much more easily when change becomes necessary.

Divisional obstacles

Similar factors operate at the divisional level. Change at this level is difficult if divisions are highly interrelated and trade resources because a shift in one division's operations affects other divisions. Consequently, it is harder to manage change if a company is pursuing a strategy of related, rather than unrelated, diversification. Furthermore, changes in strategy affect different divisions differently because change generally favours the interests of some divisions over those of others. Managers in the different divisions may therefore have different attitudes to change, with some being less supportive than others. Existing divisions may resist the establishment of new product divisions, for example, because they will lose resources and their status will diminish.

Functional obstacles

The same obstacles to change exist at the functional level. Different functions have different strategic orientations and goals and react differently to the changes that management proposes, just as divisions do. The manufacturing function generally has a short-term, cost-directed efficiency orientation; the R&D function is oriented towards long-term, technical goals and the sales function is oriented towards satisfying customers' needs. As a result, production may perceive the solution to a problem as one of reducing costs, sales as one of increasing demand and R&D as one of product innovation. Differences in functional orientation make it hard to formulate and implement a new strategy; they slow a company's response to changes in the competitive environment.

Individual obstacles

At the individual level, too, people often exhibit resistance to change because change implies uncertainty, which breeds insecurity and fear of the unknown.[17] Because managers are people, this individual resistance reinforces the tendency of each function and division to oppose changes that may have uncertain effects on them. Restructuring and re-engineering efforts can be particularly stressful for managers at all levels.

When David Jones took over the family-owned department store chain Aherns, for example, considerable resistance arose among many of the Aherns employees, who worried about keeping their jobs and, if they did, their promotion opportunities. Furthermore, Aherns staff had to learn new work practices in reporting, training techniques and staff management, and the threat of this significant change led some employees to become highly resistant to the takeover.

All these obstacles make it difficult to change organisational strategy quickly. That is why US car manufacturers took so long to respond to the challenge from Japanese competition and why companies such as Qantas and Ansett took so long to develop ways of countering the threat of low-cost airlines entering the Australian domestic market. Even though the industry has been deregulated, Qantas is still trying to restructure itself to become more competitive with Virgin Blue, and Ansett did not make enough changes to avoid going bankrupt in 2001. These companies were accustomed to complete dominance in their industries and had developed inflexible, centralised structures that inhibited risk taking and quick reaction.

Paradoxically, companies that experience the greatest uncertainty may become best able to respond to it. When companies have been forced to change frequently, strategic managers often develop the ability to handle change easily.[18] Strategic managers must understand potential obstacles to change as they design a new strategy. They must recognise obstacles and account for them in the strategic plan. The larger and more complex the company, the harder it is to manage change, because inertia is likely to be more pervasive.

Organisational conflict

The obstacles to change just discussed can also dramatically reduce a company's ability to change when they spawn **organisational conflict** among functions and divisions. Organisational conflict is the struggle that arises when the goal-directed behaviour of one organisational group thwarts another's achievement of its goals.[19] Different functions and divisions have different orientations, so if organisational change favours one division over another, organisational conflict can erupt, resulting in a failure to move quickly to exploit new strategic opportunities. A model developed by Pondy helps show how organisational conflict emerges and how it can become a powerful obstacle to change.[20]

The five stages in Pondy's model of the conflict process are summarised in figure 11.3. The first stage in the conflict process is latent conflict: potential conflict that can flare up when the right conditions arise. All the obstacles to change just discussed are potential sources of conflict. Latent conflicts are frequently activated by changes in organisational strategy that affect the relationships among functions or divisions. Suppose a company has been producing one major product type but then decides to diversify and produce different products. To overcome problems of coordinating a range of specialist services over many products, the company

organisational conflict
A struggle that occurs between two organisational groups

moves from a functional to a divisional structure. The new structure changes task relationships among divisional managers, changing the relative status and authority of the different functional and product managers. Conflict between functional and product managers or among product managers is likely to ensue.

Because every change in a company's strategy alters the organisational context, conflict can easily arise unless the situation is carefully managed to avoid it. Good strategic planning allows managers to anticipate problems that may emerge later, so that they can move early to prevent them.[21] When managers change a company's strategy, for example, they should also consider the effect of these changes on future group relationships. Similarly, when changing organisational structure, strategic managers should anticipate the effects of the changes on functional and divisional relationships. Because avoidance is not always possible, however, latent conflict may quickly lead to perceived conflict, which is the second stage of Pondy's model.

Perceived conflict occurs when managers become aware of the clashes. After a change in strategy, managers discover that the actions of another function or group obstruct the operations of their group. Managers start to react to the situation and, from the perceived stage, they go quickly to the third stage: felt conflict. At this point, managers start to personalise the conflict. Opinions polarise as one function or division starts to blame the others for causing the conflict. Production may blame the inefficiency of sales for a fall in orders, while sales may blame production for a fall in product quality. Typically, there is a marked lack of cooperation at this stage, and integration among functions or divisions breaks down as the groups start to develop an 'us' versus 'them' mentality. If not managed, this stage in the conflict process leads quickly to the fourth stage: manifest conflict.

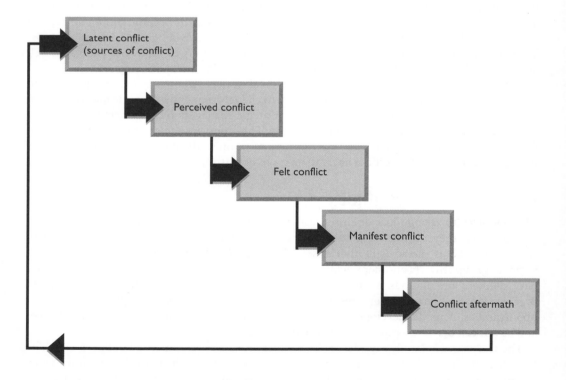

Figure 11.3:
Stages in the conflict process

At this point, the conflict among functions or divisions comes into the open and each group strives to thwart the goals of the other. Groups compete to protect their own interests and block the interests of other groups. Naturally, this behaviour blocks change and prevents a company from adapting to its environment. Manifest conflict can take many forms. The most obvious is fighting or a lack of cooperation among top managers as they start to blame the managers of other functions or divisions for causing the problem. Other forms of manifest conflict are transfer pricing battles between divisions and knowledge hoarding. If divisional managers refuse to share resources or information, then a company cannot develop synergy among divisions and all the benefits of changing to a strategy of related diversification will be lost.

At the functional level, the effects of conflict can be equally devastating. A company in trouble cannot change and pursue a low-cost strategy if its functions are competing. If, for example, sales makes no attempt to keep manufacturing informed about customers' demands, then manufacturing cannot maximise the length of production runs. Similarly, a struggling company trying to change and regain its differentiated appeal cannot do so if marketing does not inform R&D about changes in consumers' preferences, or if product engineering and R&D are competing over product specifications. Most companies have experienced each of these conflicts and suffered a loss in performance and competitive advantage when conflict has blocked their ability to change and quickly adapt to a changing environment. Manifest conflict is also common in top management. Top managers fight for promotion to high office or for resources to enhance their organisational status and prestige. If top managers are all fighting, however, how can a company re-engineer or restructure itself successfully?

The long-term effects of manifest conflict emerge in the last stage of the conflict process: conflict aftermath. Suppose a change in one company's strategy led to conflict among division managers over transfer prices. Divisional managers, with the help of corporate personnel, resolved the problem to everyone's satisfaction and re-established good working relationships. In another company, however, the conflict among divisions over transfer prices was settled only when corporate managers imposed a solution on divisional managers. A year later, a change in the environment makes the transfer pricing system in both companies inequitable and prices have to be renegotiated. How would the two companies react to the need to change again? The managers in the company in which the conflict was settled amicably would likely approach this new round of negotiations with a cooperative, not an adversarial, attitude. The company could consequently rapidly make the necessary changes. In the company in which divisions never really established an agreement, a new round of intense clashes would be likely and change would be difficult to achieve.

The aftermath of conflict is the scene for the next round of conflict, which will certainly occur because the environment is constantly changing and so must companies. The reason that some companies have a long history of bad relationships among functions or divisions is that their conflict has never been managed successfully. In companies in which strategic managers have resolved the conflict, a cohesive organisational culture develops. In these companies, managers adopt a cooperative, not competitive, attitude, when conflict occurs as a result of change. The question, then, is how best to manage conflict strategically to avoid its bad effects and to make changes in strategy and structure as smooth as possible. There are several tactics and techniques that strategic managers can use to overcome conflict and implement strategic change effectively. Perhaps the most important of these is how managers should use power and political tactics to manage strategic change.

Political approach

Management of changes in strategy does not always follow a rational approach for various reasons, including time and resource constraints, unpredictability and lack of information about future events. Decisions about how to change strategy are not made just by following a calculated, rational plan that considers only shareholders' interests. In reality, managing changes in strategy is quite different. When managing changes in strategies — evaluating alternative courses of action, choosing a new strategic direction, implementing and evaluating changes — managers often make decisions that will further their personal, functional or divisional

strategy in action 11.3

General Motors Europe resists changes

Frederick A Henderson, newly appointed CEO of General Motors (GM) Europe announced a plan to cut 12 000 jobs from its operations. The largest carmaker in the world, GM has lost considerably more than US$2 billion over the past four years from its European operations and its market share has fallen by 1 per cent.

GM's European factories include Opel plants at Ruesselsheim and Bochum in Germany, Saab's main production site at Trollhaettan in Sweden and the Vauxhall plant at Ellesmere Port in the UK. It also has operations in Belgium, Poland, Portugal, Russia and Spain, employing more than 63 000 workers across the whole of Europe. To turn its European operations around, GM has merged its European operations under a single regional chairman, located in Zurich, Switzerland. With this change, GM intends to do away with the old system of autonomous management teams, simplify its European operations and speed up decision making, centralise design teams to increase efficiency and develop a single corporate culture so that all its European operations work towards the same goals.

Downsizing was applied to its German operations in view of Germany having the second-highest labour costs in the world. In protest against the cuts, German workers walked out of their jobs in wildcat strikes, and GM Opel workers council chairman Kalus Franz claimed that the workers were not consulted in imposing the downsizing decision. About 50 000 workers from across Europe expressed solidarity with their German colleagues by staging rallies against the cutback decision. Unions demanded that GM must not close any of its plants, must not force redundancies, and should develop a long-term plan for its European operations and products. However, although the GM management promised that factories would not be shut down, it did not rule out plant closures.

In Berlin, Chancellor Gerhard Schroeder appealed to the workers to return to work, as did the finance minister. Negotiations began between the management and the employee representatives, and a few workers returned to work. All the workers returned to work when the company assured them they would make all possible efforts to avoid forced redundancies and preserve German production sites.

Sources: European Industrial Relations Observatory On-Line 2004, 'Day of action against GM job cuts', accessed 15 December 2005, www.eiro. eurofound.eu.int/2004/11/inbrief/eu0411201n.html; Welch, D, Edmondson, G & Boston, W 2004, 'Toughest job yet for this Mr Fixit', *Business Week*, 15 November, iss. 3908, pp. 72–4; *Deutsche Welle* 2004, 'GM's European workforce shows solidarity', accessed 15 December 2005, www.dw-world. de/popus/popup_printcontent,,1365945,00.html; *BBC News* 2004, 'GM to cut 12 000 jobs in Europe', 14 October, accessed 15 December 2005, http://news.bbc.co.uk/2/hi/business/3742154.stm; —— 2004, 'GM reviewing European operations', 22 September, accessed 15 December 2005, http://news.bbc.co.uk/1/hi/business/3680528.stm; —— 2004, 'GM creates Europe-wide management', 18 June, accessed 15 December 2005, http://news.bbc.co.uk/1/hi/business/3819585.stm; —— 2004, 'GM bosses start talks with unions', 18 October, accessed 15 December 2005, http://news.bbc.co.uk/1/hi/business/3752196.stm; —— 2004, 'Thousands protest at GM job cuts', 19 October, accessed 15 December 2005, http://news.bbc.co.uk/2/hi/business/3755040.stm.

---

organisational politics
The tactics that managers use to obtain and use power to influence organisational goals or organisational activities

interests. **Organisational politics** are tactics that strategic managers engage in to obtain and use power to influence organisational goals and change strategy to further their own interests.[22] Politics or power struggles also arise because in many situations it is almost impossible to determine the strategy that is objectively correct, and because changes in the environment do not indicate a strategy that is right for a company. Top-level managers constantly come into conflict over what the correct strategy should be, and power struggles and coalition building are a major part of strategy formation. In this political view of strategy formation, obstacles to change are overcome and conflicts over goals are settled by compromise, bargaining and negotiation between managers and coalitions of managers, and by the outright use of power.[23]

This section examines the relationship between strategic change and organisational politics and the process of strategy formation. First, it considers the sources of politics and why politics is a necessary part of managing the strategic change process. Second, it looks at how managers or divisions can increase their power so they can influence the company's strategic direction. Third, it explores how a company can manage politics to overcome inertia and implement strategic change.

Sources of organisational politics

To understand why politics is an integral part of strategic change, it is useful to contrast the rational view of strategy formation with the political view of how strategies are formed (see figure 11.4). The rational view assumes that complete information is available and no uncertainty exists about outcomes but the political view suggests that strategic managers can never be sure that they are making the best decisions. From a political perspective, strategy formation always takes place in a time of uncertainty, when the outcomes of strategic change are difficult to predict. According to the rational view, moreover, managers always agree about appropriate organisational goals and the appropriate means, or strategies, for achieving these goals. According to the political view, on the other hand, the choice of goals and means is linked to each individual, function or division's pursuit of self-interest. Disagreement over the best course of action is inevitable in the political view because strategic change necessarily favours some individuals or divisions over others. If managers decide, for example, to invest in resources to promote and develop one product, then other products will not be created. Some managers win; others lose.

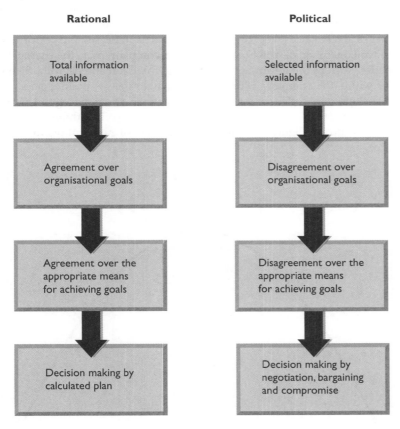

Figure 11.4:
Rational and political views of strategy formation

Given the political point of view, strategy choices are never right or wrong; they are simply better or worse. As a result, managers have to promote their ideas and lobby for support from other managers so they can build up backing for a course of action. Coalition building is therefore a vital part of managing strategic change.[24] Managers join coalitions to lobby for their interests because in doing so they increase their political muscle in relation to that of their organisational opponents.

Managers also engage in politics for personal reasons. Because companies are shaped like pyramids, individual managers realise that the higher they rise, the more difficult it is to climb to the next position.[25] If their views prevail and the company follows their lead, however, and if their decisions bear results, then they reap rewards and promotions. By being successful at politics and claiming responsibility for successful change, therefore, they increase their visibility in the company and make themselves contenders for higher organisational office.

The assumption that personal, rather than shareholder or organisational, interests govern strategic choice is what gives the word 'politics' bad connotations in many people's minds. Because no-one knows for certain what will happen as a result of strategic change, however, letting people pursue their own interests may in the long term mean that the company's interests are being pursued. This is because competition among managers stemming from self-interest may lead to better strategic decision making and an improved change plan, with successful managers moving to the top over time. If a company can maintain checks and balances in its top management (by preventing any particular manager or coalition from becoming too powerful), then politics can be a healthy influence, in preventing managers from becoming complacent about the status quo, promoting strategic change and thus averting organisational decline.

If politics grows rampant, however, and if powerful managers gain such dominance that they can suppress the views of managers who oppose their interests, then major problems may arise. Checks and balances fade, organisational inertia increases and performance suffers. When a dominant member of the board departs, a company may, for example, outsource noncore activities (such as the information technology function and payroll), then reintegrate these activities within the company. Ultimately, companies that let politics get so out of hand that shareholders' interests suffer are taken over by aggressive new management teams, which engage in major restructuring activities (often involving the layoff of thousands of employees) to turn around a company. Figure 11.5 illustrates the effect of rampant organisational politics on performance.

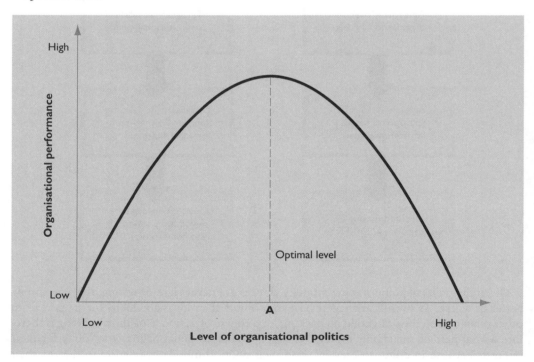

Figure 11.5:
Effect of rampant organisational politics on performance

The figure shows that up to point A, politics can increase organisational performance because it can overcome inertia and induce needed organisational change. After point A, however, an increase in the level of organisational politics can lead to a decline in performance because politics runs out of control and the company fragments into competing interest groups. Astute managers seek, therefore, to keep the level of political behaviour from passing the optimum point. If kept in check, politics can be a useful management tool for overcoming inertia and bringing about strategic change. The best CEOs recognise this and create a strategic context in which managers can fight for their ideas and reap the rewards from successfully promoting change in organisational strategy and structure. Rio Tinto and Wesfarmers are well known for their top management committee structure, in which divisional managers who request new funds and new-venture managers who champion new products must present their projects to the entire top management team and lobby for support for their ideas. All top managers in these companies experience this learning process; presumably, the top management comprises those who succeeded best at mobilising support and commitment for their concepts.

Formal power and politics

Politics is an exercise of power. Power, however, as are other social science concepts, is an essentially contested one. Weber, the historical sociologist, defines power thus: 'Within a social relationship power means any chance (no matter whereon that chance is based) to carry through one's (individual or collective) own will (even against resistance)'[26] One way of understanding power is to look at its sources: formal and informal power.

power
Carrying through one's will even against resistance

Formal power is the authority that a manager possesses by virtue of holding a position in the hierarchy. This is why the CEO is so powerful. As the top manager of a company, he or she decides whom to devolve power to and how much to delegate. Authority also allows a manager to resolve conflicts and decide what needs to be done. This is the power that gives a manager the ability to overcome obstacles to change. As discussed, conflict often occurs between functions and divisions because they have different goals and interests. Because functional managers have equal authority, they cannot control each other, so they often pass the problems they cannot solve to corporate managers or the CEO, who has the authority to impose a solution on the parties.

Informal sources of power and politics

Although a considerable amount of a strategic manager's power derives from his or her level in the hierarchy, many other informal sources of power are crucial in determining the types of change made in strategy and, consequently, in a company's future direction. To a large degree, how much informal power the managers of the different functions and divisions possess derives from a company's corporate- and business-level strategies. Different strategies make some functions or divisions, and their managers, more important than others in achieving the corporate mission, and consequently confer a greater ability to implement strategic change. Figure 11.6 lists the informal sources of power that are discussed next.

Ability to cope with uncertainty

A function or division gains power if it can reduce uncertainty for another function or division.[27] Suppose a company is pursuing a strategy of vertical integration. A division that controls the supply and quality of inputs to another division has power over it because it controls the uncertainty facing the second division. At the business level, in a company pursuing a low-cost strategy, the sales function has power over the production function because it provides information about customers' needs that is necessary to minimise production costs. In a company pursuing a differentiation strategy, the R&D function has power over the marketing function at the early stages in a product's lifecycle because it controls product innovations. Once innovation problems have been solved, however, marketing is likely to be the most powerful function because it supplies the R&D function with information on customers' needs. A function's power therefore depends on how much other functions rely on it.

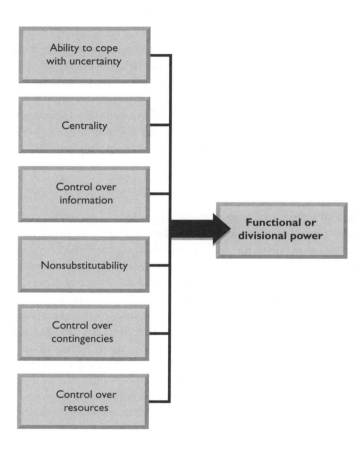

Figure 11.6:
Informal sources of power

The boxes in the figure read (top to bottom): Ability to cope with uncertainty; Centrality; Control over information; Nonsubstitutability; Control over contingencies; Control over resources — all pointing to **Functional or divisional power**.

Centrality

centrality
How central a department or division is to resource transfers or cross-divisional or cross-departmental activities

Power also derives from the centrality of a division or function.[28] **Centrality** refers to how central a division or function is to resource transfers among divisions. In a chemical company, for example, the division supplying specialised chemicals is likely to be central because its activities are critical to both the petroleum division, which supplies its inputs, and the end-using divisions, such as plastics or pharmaceuticals, which depend on its outputs. Its activities are central to the production process of all the company's businesses, so it can exert pressure on corporate headquarters to pursue policies in its own interest.

At the functional level, the function that has the most centrality and therefore power is the one that provides the distinctive competency on which a company's business-level strategy is based.[29] At Apple, the function with the greatest centrality is R&D because the company's competitive advantage rests on a technical competency. On the other hand, at Woolworths, the purchasing and distribution function is the most central because Woolworths' competitive advantage relies on its purchasing and logistics competencies.

Control over information

Functions and divisions are also central if they are at the heart of the information flow, that is, if they can control the flow of information to other functions or divisions (or both).[30] Information is a power resource because one function or division, by giving or withholding information, can cause others to behave in certain ways. The sales function, for example, can control how the production function operates. If it manipulates information to satisfy its own goals, for example, responsiveness to customers, then production costs will rise. The production function may be unaware that costs could be lowered with a different sales strategy. Similarly, the R&D function can shape managers' attitudes to the competitive prospects of different products by supplying favourable information about the products that it prefers and downplaying others.

Managers are engaging in a subtle information game when they form policies, set objectives and influence the change process. Divisions can disguise their performance by providing only positive information to corporate managers. The more powerful a division, the more easily it can do this. In both strategy formulation and implementation, divisions and functions, by using information to develop a power base, can strongly influence changes in strategies that favour their own interests.

Nonsubstitutability

A function or division can accrue power proportionately to its activities being nonsubstitutable (that is, not being duplicatable). If a company is vertically integrated, then supplying divisions are nonsubstitutable if the company cannot buy in the marketplace what they produce. The petroleum products division is not very powerful, therefore, if large quantities of oil are available from other suppliers. In an oil crisis, the opposite is true. On the other hand, the activities of a new venture division (a division in which new products are developed) are nonsubstitutable if a company cannot buy another company that possesses similar knowledge or expertise. If knowledge or information can be bought, then the division is substitutable.

The same holds true at the functional level. A function and the managers within it are powerful if no other function can perform their task. As in the case of centrality, which function is nonsubstitutable depends on the nature of a company's business-level strategy. If the company is pursuing a low-cost strategy, then production is likely to be the key function and the R&D function or marketing function has less power. If, however, the company is pursuing a strategy of differentiation, then the opposite is likely to be the case.

The power that a function or division gains by virtue of its centrality or nonsubstitutability thus derives from the company's strategy. Eventually, as a company's strategy changes, the relative power of the functions and divisions also changes. This is the next informal source of power that is discussed.

Control over contingencies

Over time, the contingencies, that is, the opportunities and threats, facing a company from the competitive environment change as the environment changes.[31] The functions or divisions that can deal with the problems confronting the company and allow it to achieve its objectives gain power. Conversely, the functions that can no longer manage the contingency lose power. Consider which functional executives rose to top management positions during the past 50 years. Generally, the executives who reached the highest posts did so from functions or divisions that were able to deal with the opportunities and threats facing the company.[32]

In the 1950s, for instance, the main contingent problem facing a company was to produce goods and services. Pent-up demand from the years of World War II led to a huge increase in consumer spending on motor vehicles, homes and durable goods. Goods needed to be produced quickly and cheaply to meet demand, and the managers who rose to the top during this period were from the manufacturing function or consumer products divisions.

In the 1960s, the problem changed. Most companies had increased their productive capacity and the market was saturated. Producing goods was not as difficult as selling them. Marketing and sales functions thus rose to prominence. The rise of executives in companies reflected this critical contingency, for greater numbers of them emerged from the sales function and marketing-oriented divisions than from any other groups.

In the 1970s, companies began to realise that competitive conditions were permanent. They had to streamline their strategies and structures to survive in an increasingly hostile environment. As a result, accounting and finance became the function that supplied most of the additions to the top management team. Today, a company's business- and corporate-level strategies determine which group gains pre-eminence.

Control over resources

The final informal source of power examined here is the ability to control and allocate scarce resources.[33] This source gives corporate-level managers their clout. The power of corporate managers largely depends on their ability to allocate capital to the operating divisions and to allot cash to or take it from a division on the basis of their expectations of its future success.

The power of resources is not merely a function of the ability to allocate resources immediately; it also comes from the ability to generate resources in the future. Individual divisions that can generate resources thus have power in the company. Divisions that can generate high revenue from sales to consumers, for example, have great power. At the functional level, the same considerations apply. The ability of sales and marketing to increase customers' demand and generate revenue explains their power in the company. In general, the function that can generate the most resources has the most power.

Summary of informal power

The most powerful division or function in a company is the one that can reduce uncertainty for others, is most central and nonsubstitutable, has control over resources and can generate them and is able to deal with the critical external strategic contingency facing the company. In practice, each function or division in a company has power from one or more of these sources, so there is a distribution of power among functions and divisions.

Individual managers have various informal ways of increasing their personal power. First, managers can try to make themselves irreplaceable.[34] They may develop specialised skills — such as a knowledge of computers or special relationships with key customers — that allow them to solve problems or limit uncertainty for other managers in the company. Second, they may specialise in an area of increasing concern to the company so that they eventually control a crucial contingency. Third, managers can also try to make themselves more central in a company by deliberately accepting responsibilities that bring them into contact with many functions or managers. Finally, another tactic to obtain power is to be associated with powerful managers who are on their way to the top. By supporting a powerful manager and being indispensable to him or her, it is possible to rise up the organisational ladder with that manager. Political managers cultivate both people and information, and they are able to build up a personal network of contacts that they can then use to pursue personal goals such as promotion.

Effects of power and politics on strategic change

Power and politics strongly influence a company's choice of strategy and structure because a company has to maintain an organisational context that is responsive to both the aspirations of the various divisions, functions and managers, and changes in the external environment.[35] The problem that companies face is that the internal structure of power always lags changes in the environment because the environment generally changes faster than companies can respond. Those in power never voluntarily give up engaging in politics but excessive politicking and power struggles reduce a company's flexibility, cause inertia and erode competitive advantage.

To use politics to promote effective change, a company must devise organisational arrangements that create a **power balance** among the various divisions or functions so no single one dominates the whole enterprise. If no power balance exists, power struggles proceed unchecked and change becomes impossible as divisions start to compete and to hoard information or knowledge to maximise their own returns. In these situations, exchanging resources among divisions becomes expensive and gains from synergy are difficult to obtain. These factors lower a company's profitability and reduce organisational growth.

power balance
When no single group dominates the direction or activities of a company

In the divisional structure, the corporate headquarters staff plays the balancing role because they can exert power over even strong divisions and force them to share resources for the good of the whole corporation. In a single-business company, a strong CEO is important because he or she must replace the corporate centre and balance the power of the strong functions against the weak. The forceful CEO takes the responsibility for giving weak functions an opportunity to air their concerns and interests, and tries to avoid being railroaded into decisions by the strong function pursuing its own interests. The CEO of a large corporation, therefore, has great potential for exercising power to bring about change. The CEO also plays another important role, however, as arbiter of acceptable political decision making.

Politics pervades all companies but the CEO and top-level managers can shape its character. In some companies, power plays are the norm because the CEOs gained their power in that way. Other companies — especially those founded by entrepreneurs who believed in democracy or in decentralised decision making — may not tolerate power struggles. In these cases, a different kind of political behaviour becomes acceptable: it is based on a function or division manager's competency or expertise rather than on his or her ability to form powerful coalitions.

To design an organisational structure that creates a power balance facilitating change, strategic managers can use the tools of implementation. First, they must create the right mix of integrating mechanisms, so that functions or divisions can share information and ideas. A multidivisional structure offers one means of balancing power among divisions and the matrix or product team structure offers a means of balancing power among functions. A company can then develop norms, values and a common culture that emphasise corporate, rather than divisional, interests and that stress the company's mission. In companies such as Wesfarmers or Sony, culture serves to harmonise divisional interests with the achievement of corporate goals.

Finally, as noted, strong hierarchical control by a gifted CEO can also create the organisational context in which politics can facilitate the change process. When CEOs use their expert knowledge as their power, they provide the strategic leadership that allows a company to overcome inertia and change its strategy and structure. The strategic manager's job should involve learning how to manage politics and power to further corporate interests because politics is an essential part of the process of strategic change.

One model of achieving a balance in power among members in an organisation is the constitutional theory of checks and balances that operates in such democratic governments as Australia's. In these arrangements, no one institution or person is given absolute power over anything. Any power that is given to an institution or to an individual is controlled by another institution or person. For example, a minister of government has power over a range of matters but is controlled informally by the party machine, by the cabinet through a range of conventions, formally by the parliament and also by the Australian Constitution that puts definite limits on what he or she can or cannot do.

Managing and evaluating change

Even with the political situation under control, managing change raises several questions. One concerns who should carry out the change: internal managers or external consultants? Although internal managers may have the most experience or knowledge about a company's operations, they may lack perspective because they are too much a part of the company's culture. They also run the risk of appearing to be politically motivated and having a personal stake in the changes they recommend. Companies, therefore, often turn to external consultants, who can view a situation more objectively. Outside consultants, however, must spend a lot of time learning about the company and its problems before they can propose a plan of action. For both these reasons, many companies — including BHP Billiton, Coles-Myer and AMP — have brought in CEOs from outside the company to spearhead their change efforts at different times. In this way, companies can reap the benefits of both inside information and external perspective.

Generally, a company can take two main approaches to managing change: top-down change or bottom-up change. With **top-down change**, a strong CEO or a top management team analyses how to alter strategy and structure, recommends a course of action, and then moves quickly to restructure and implement change. The emphasis is on speed of response and management of problems as they occur. **Bottom-up change** is much more gradual. Top management consults with managers at all levels in the company. Then, over time, it develops a detailed plan for change, with a timetable of events and stages through which the company will go. The emphasis in bottom-up change is on participation and on keeping people informed about the situation so uncertainty is minimised.

The advantage of bottom-up change is that it removes some of the obstacles to change by including them in the strategic plan. Further, the purpose of consulting with managers at all levels is to reveal potential problems. The disadvantage of bottom-up change is its slowness.

On the other hand, in the case of the much speedier top-down change, the problems may emerge later and may be difficult to resolve. Big bureaucratic companies such as Telstra often need top-down change because managers are so unaccustomed to, and threatened by, change that only a radical restructuring effort provides the momentum to overcome organisational inertia.

The last step in the change process is to evaluate the effects of the changes in strategy and structure on organisational performance. A company must compare how it operates after implementing change with how it previously did. Managers use indices such as changes in share price or market share to assess the effects of change in strategy. It is much more difficult, however, to assess the effects of changes in structure on a company's performance because they are so much harder to measure. Whereas companies can easily measure the increased revenue from increased product differentiation, they do not have any sure means of evaluating how a shift from a product to a divisional structure has affected performance. Managers can be surveyed, however, and it may become obvious over time that organisational flexibility and the company's ability to manage its strategy have increased. Managers can also assess whether the change has decreased the level of politicking and conflict, and strengthened cooperation among the divisions and functions.

Summary

Organisational change is a complex and difficult process for companies to manage successfully. The first hurdle is getting managers to realise that change is necessary and to admit that there is a problem. Once the need for change has been recognised, managers can go about analysing potential obstacles to change and recommending a course of action. Strategic managers need to appreciate, however, that companies are not just rational decision-making systems in which managers coldly calculate the potential returns from their investments. Companies are arenas of power, in which individuals and groups fight for prestige and possession of scarce resources. In the pursuit of their interests, managers compete and come into conflict. This is inevitable. Managers consequently have to deal with politics and conflict creatively to implement strategic change successfully and increase or restore a company's competitive advantage. The most successful companies are those in which change is regarded as the norm and managers are constantly seeking to improve organisational strengths and eliminate weaknesses so they can maximise future profitability. This chapter makes the following main points.

top-down change
A change process that is designed and implemented from the top of the company

bottom-up change
A change process that is designed and implemented with the participation of managers and employees at several levels of the company

- Strategic change is the movement of a company away from its present state to increase its competitive advantage. Three main types of strategic change are (a) re-engineering and e-engineering, (b) restructuring and (c) innovation.

- According to the rational approach, strategic change is managed through a series of steps that strategic managers must follow if the change process is to succeed.

- The first step in the change process is determining the need for change. Strategic managers must recognise a gap between actual performance and desired performance, use a SWOT analysis to define the company's present state and then determine its desired future state.

- The second step in the change process is identifying the obstacles to change that may prevent a company from reaching its desired future state. Obstacles to change are found at the corporate, divisional, functional and individual levels. Important obstacles include the inertia produced by a company's present strategy, structure, culture and differences in divisional and functional goals and interests.

- Organisational conflict results from fights between divisions, functions and individual managers pursuing different goals and interests. Conflict is also a major obstacle to change and managers must seek ways of resolving conflict to implement strategic change successfully.

- Strategic managers play organisational politics to overcome obstacles to change, resolve conflicts and bring about strategic change. Organisational politics are the tactics that strategic managers engage in to use power and to influence goals and change strategy to further their own interests.

- To play politics, managers must have power. Power is carrying through one's will even against resistance.

- Power available to strategic managers includes formal power and power from informal sources, such as coping with uncertainty, centrality, control over information, nonsubstitutability, and control over contingencies and resources.

- Power and politics influence a company's choice of strategy and the nature of the strategic changes that are implemented.

- Strategic managers need to evaluate the results of each change process and use this analysis to define the company's present condition so they can start the next change process. Well-run companies are constantly aware of the need to monitor their performance, and strategic managers institutionalise change so they can continually realign their strategy and structure to suit the competitive environment.

Practising strategic management

Review questions

1. Distinguish between strategic change and changes in strategies.
2. What are the four stages in the change process?
3. Distinguish between formal and informal power.
4. What is the difference between top-down change and bottom-up change?

Discussion questions

5. Compare and contrast re-engineering and restructuring types of changes.
6. Do actual processes of change rarely follow the steps that the rational model of change identifies. If so, why?
7. Why is conflict inevitable in all processes of change?
8. Informal power is ineffective in the face of formal power in implementing strategic change. Discuss this statement.

Applied questions

9. The opening case discusses the transformation of the Lenovo Group. Identify the strategies that you believe helped make this transformation. Do you believe that the company needs to introduce any more changes. What changes do you recommend for the Lenovo Group?
10. Why do you believe the Nissan executives in Japan accepted changes introduced by Ghosn as described in Strategy in action 11.1?

Small-group exercise

Handling change

Break into groups of three to five people and discuss the following scenario.

You are a group of top-level strategic managers of a large, well-established computer company that has traditionally pursued a strategy of differentiation based on R&D. As a result of intense competition, your company is pursuing a combined low-cost, differentiation strategy. You have been charged with preparing a plan to change the company's structure, and you have decided on two main changes. First, you plan to re-engineer the company and move from a multidivisional structure to one in which cross-functional product teams become responsible for developing each new computer model. Second, to decentralise decision making and reduce costs, you propose to restructure the company and severely cut the number of corporate and top divisional managers.

1. Discuss the nature of the obstacles to change at the organisational, functional and individual levels that you, as internal change agents, will encounter in implementing this new strategy and structure. Which do you think will be the most important obstacles to change?
2. Discuss some ways in which you can overcome obstacles to change to help your company move to its desired future state.

Article file

Find an example of a company that has been implementing a major change in its strategy. Why did managers think that change was necessary? What type of change was implemented? What were its effects?

Exploring the Web

Managing change

Search the Internet to find a company that has recently been involved in a major change process. What was the nature of the change? Why did the change take place? What problems did the company experience during the change process?

Strategic management project

Module 11

Your task is to examine how your company has managed the process of strategic change. Undertake the following tasks and answer the following questions.

1. Find examples of recent changes in your company's strategy or structure. What types of change did your company implement? Why did your company make these changes?
2. What, do you think, are the major obstacles to change in your company?
3. Given the nature of your company's strategy and structure, is conflict a likely obstacle to change in your company? Can you find any examples of conflicts that have occurred in your company?

4. Is there any evidence of political contests or struggles between top managers or between divisions or functions in your company? What can you find out about the power of the CEO and the top management team?

5. Using the informal sources of power discussed in the chapter (e.g. centrality and control over resources), draw a map of the power relationships among the various managers, divisions or functions inside your company. On the basis of this analysis, which are the most powerful managers or subunits? Why? How do managers in the powerful subunits use power to influence decision making?

6. How well do you think strategic managers have managed the change process? What other changes do you think your company should make in its strategy or structure?

Additional resources

Christensen, C & Overdorf, M 2000, 'Meeting the challenge of disruptive change', *Harvard Business Review*, vol. 78, no. 2, pp. 66–76. (A discussion of how to determine what can be changed.)

Meyerson, D 2001, 'Radical change, the quiet way', *Harvard Business Review*, vol. 79, no. 9, pp. 92–100. (A discussion of large-scale change.)

Snow, CS & Hambrick, DC 1980, 'Measuring organizational strategies: Some theoretical and methodological problems', *Academy of Management Review*, vol. 5, pp. 527–38. (A comparative discussion of change and minor adjustment.)

Zajac, EJ & Shortell, SM 1989, 'Changing generic strategies: likelihood, direction, and performance implications', *Strategic Management Journal*, vol. 10, pp. 413–30. (A discussion of strategic change and changes in strategy.)

End notes

1. Hannan, MT & Freeman, J 1984, 'Structural inertia and organizational change', *American Sociological Review*, vol. 49, pp. 149–64.

2. Miller, D 1990, *The Icarus paradox*, Harper Business, New York.

3. Quinn, B 1978, 'Strategic change: "Logical incrementalism"', *Sloan Management Review*, vol. 20, pp. 7–21; Gray, B & Ariss, SS 1985, 'Politics and strategic change across organizational life cycles', *Academy of Management Review*, vol. 10, pp. 707–23; Greenwood, R & Hinnings, CR 1988, 'Organization design types, tracks and the dynamics of strategic change', *Organization Studies*, vol. 9, 1988, pp. 293–316.

4. Ginsberg, A 1988, 'Measuring and modelling changes in strategy: theoretical foundations and empirical directions', *Strategic Management Journal*, vol. 9, p. 560.

5. De Witt, B & Meyer, R 2004, *Strategy: process, content, context*, 3rd edn, Thomson, London, pp. 168–70.

6. Thackray, J 1987, 'Restructuring in the name of the hurricane', *Euromoney*, February, pp. 106–8.

7. Hammer, M & Champy, J 1993, *Reengineering the corporation*, HarperCollins, New York.

8. Bruton, GD, Keels, JK & Shook, CL 1996, 'Downsizing the firm: answering the strategic questions', *Academy of Management Executive*, May, pp. 38–45.

9. Jones, GR, *Organizational theory*, Addison-Wesley, Reading, Massachusetts; Burgelman, RA & Maidique, MA 1988, *Strategic management of technology and innovation*, Irwin, Homewood, Illinois.

10. Jones, GR & Butler, JE 1992, 'Managing internal corporate entrepreneurship: an agency theory perspective', *Journal of Management*, vol. 18, pp. 733–49.

11. Burgelman, RA 1984, 'Designs for corporate entrepreneurship in established firms', *California Management Review*, vol. 26, pp. 154–66.

12. Frey, D 1991, 'Learning the ropes: my life as a product champion', *Harvard Business Review*, September–October, pp. 46–56.

13. Beckhard, R 1969, *Organizational development: strategies and models*, Addison-Wesley, Reading, Massachusetts; French, WL & Bell Jr, CH 1978, *Organizational development*, 2nd edn, Prentice Hall, Englewood Cliffs, New Jersey.

14. Beckhard, op. cit.

15. Coch, LC & French Jr, RP 1948, 'Overcoming resistance to change', *Human Relations*, August, pp. 512–32; Lawrence, PR 1969, 'How to deal with resistance to change', *Harvard Business Review*, January–February, pp. 4–12.

16. Huff, JO, Huff, AS & Thomas, H 1992, 'Strategic renewal and the interaction of cumulative stress and inertia', *Strategic Management Journal*, vol. 13, special issue, pp. 55–75.

17. Kotter, P & Schlesinger, LA 1979, 'Choosing strategies for change', *Harvard Business Review*, March–April, pp. 106–14.

18. Galbraith, JR 1982, 'Designing the innovative organization', *Organizational Dynamics*, Winter, pp. 5–25.

19. Litterer, JA 1966, 'Conflict in organizations: a reexamination', *Academy of Management Journal*, vol. 9, pp. 178–86; Schmidt, SM & Kochan, TA 1972, 'Conflict: towards conceptual clarity', *Administrative Science Quarterly*, vol. 13, pp. 359–70.

20. Pondy, LR 1967, 'Organizational conflict: concepts and models', *Administrative Science Quarterly*, vol. 2, pp. 296–320.

21. Amason, AC 1996, 'Distinguishing the effects of functional and dysfunctional conflict on strategic decision making: resolving a paradox for top management teams', *Academy of Management Journal*, vol. 1, pp. 123–48.

22. Miles, RH 1980, *Macro organizational behavior*, Goodyear, Santa Monica, California.

23. Pettigrew, AM 1973, *The politics of organizational decision making*, Tavistock, London.

24. March, JG 1962, 'The business firm as a coalition', *Journal of Politics*, vol. 24, pp. 662–78; Vredenburgh, DJ & Maurer, JG 1984, 'A process framework of organizational politics', *Human Relations*, vol. 37, pp. 47–66.

25. Burns, T 1961, 'Micropolitics: mechanisms of institutional change', *Administrative Science Quarterly*, vol. 6, pp. 257–81.

26. Walliman, I, Rosenbaum, H, Tatsis, N, & Zito, G 1980, 'Misreading Weber: the concept of "Macht"', *Sociology*, vol. 14, p. 266.

27. This section draws heavily on Hickson, DJ, Hinings, CR, Lee, CA, Schneck, RE & Pennings, DJ 1971, 'A strategic contingencies

theory of intraorganizational power', *Administrative Science Quarterly*, vol. 16, pp. 216–27; Hinings, CR, Hickson, DJ, Pennings, JM & Schneck, RE 1974, 'Structural conditions of intraorganizational power', *Administrative Science Quarterly*, vol. 19, pp. 2–44.

28. Hickson et al., op. cit.
29. Ibarra, H 1993, 'Network centrality, power, and innovation involvement: determinants of technical and administrative roles', *Academy of Management Journal*, vol. 36, pp. 471–501.
30. Pettigrew, op. cit.
31. Hickson et al., op. cit.
32. Landsberger, HA 1961, 'The horizontal dimension in bureaucracy', *Administrative Science Quarterly*, vol. 6, pp. 299–322.
33. Salancik, GR & Pfeffer, J 1974, 'The bases and use of power in organizational decision making: the case of a university', *Administrative Science Quarterly*, vol. 19, pp. 453–73.
34. Hickson et al., op. cit.
35. Pfeffer, J 1992, *Managing with power*, Harvard Business School Press, Boston, Massachusetts.

Evaluating strategy performance

learning objectives

After studying this chapter, you should be able to:

- describe strategy evaluation as a final step in the strategy process

- list the functions of strategy evaluation

- design a process for strategy evaluation

- discuss financial evaluation, the balanced scorecard and the triple bottom line as methods of strategy evaluation

- discuss options that managers can consider when they determine the outcomes of their strategies

- develop a framework to identify critical success factors

- compare and contrast intended and emergent processes of strategy evaluation.

Evaluation at Loy Yang Power

Loy Yang Power (*Loy Yang* is an Aboriginal phrase meaning 'big eel') operates Victoria's biggest power station (a 2000-megawatt power station) and the adjacent coal mine in the Latrobe Valley, Gippsland, 165 kilometres south-east of Melbourne. The company supplies about one-third of the power requirements of Victoria and also sells power to South Australia and New South Wales. The company burns brown coal, which is the most accessible and cost-efficient fuel for electricity generation. Established by the Victorian Government, the company was acquired by the Great Energy Alliance Corporation (GEAC), comprising the Australian Gas Light Company, the Tokyo Electric Power Company and an investor group consisting of Commonwealth Bank, Mitsui and Co., Westscheme Superannuation and Motor Trades Association of Australia Superannuation Fund, in April 2004 for $3.48 billion.

Loy Yang Power believes that economic performance is driven by operational performance, financial performance and company support for the local community. In 2004, it mined 30.33 million tonnes of brown coal, with coal supply reliability of 99.95 per cent. The electricity output in 2004 was about 17 625 gigawatt-hours and was available to generate full load 96.8 per cent of the time. Financially, the company remained profitable in 2004, helped by an 8 per cent increase in electricity revenue over 2003.

The company, as part of its community support program, made financial and in-kind contributions to 89 community groups. In association with other local power generating companies, the company is working on a three-year project to raise $300 000 for the Gippsland Cancer Care Centre based at the Latrobe Regional Hospital. Turnover is very low: more than 90 per cent of the 498 employees have been with the company for more than ten years. Women comprise a very small proportion of workers in the operational areas but a large proportion of the workforce is female in the nonoperational areas. The company encourages women into nontraditional areas by placing them in apprenticeships and by promoting the Guides Australia Women of Note Gippsland Dinner. In 2004, the company welcomed five managers from the Tokyo Electric Power company. In 2004, for the first time since 1967, the company failed to get a five-star rating from the National Safety Council of Australia, because of the many lost-time injuries recorded in 2003.

The brown coal that the company uses to generate electricity contributes to the increased greenhouse effect and climate change. By and large, the company complied with air emission, water discharge and dust emission regulations. However, 13 environmental incidents occurred in 2004: four of them related to water runoff, seven to chimney emissions, and two to chemical spills. None of these, the company claimed, resulted in significant environmental impact. The company, since 1997, has reduced greenhouse gas emissions by implementing a series of efficiency improvement projects. The company regularly informs the community about its environmental performance and continually endeavours to become an environmentally friendly power generation company. In addition to the many policies that it has adopted, the company has met all commitments under its voluntary membership of the Australian Federal Government's Greenhouse Challenge and Generation Efficiency Standards program

Sources: Based on Loy Yang Power n.d. 'Loy Yang Power: eport', 'Electricity Generation Company', 'History of Loy Yang', accessed 11 March 2003, www.loyangpower.com.au; —— 2002, 'Half year performance report 2002', accessed 4 April 2003, www.loyyangpower. com.au; —— 2004, '2004 report to the community', accessed 27 April 2005, www.loyyangpower.com.au/documents/pubrep/2004/lypbigad.pdf; Loy Yang Power 2004, '2003 public report', July, accessed 27 April 2005, www.loyyangpower.com.au/documents/pubrep/2003/lypcr2003.pdf.

Overview

Why do some companies succeed while others fail? This book starts with this question. In recent years, companies such as One.Tel, HIH Insurance, Kiwi Air and Impulse Airlines have failed, while other organisations such as Mitsubishi Motors Australia have had ups and downs in their performance. It is difficult to make accurate judgements about performances and even more difficult to identify factors that contribute to success or failure. Strategy is only one of many factors that contribute significantly to organisational success or failure. The discussion of organisational success refers to performance. Evaluating performance is difficult but is done because it provides information on the performances of strategies as well as other important information. Consider the opening case, which details how Loy Yang Power evaluates its performance in terms of three criteria: economic, social and environmental. This case indicates that evaluation performs many more functions than simply revealing the outcomes of company strategies; rather, evaluation identifies factors that could have contributed towards Loy Yang making less profit than it expected.

This book considers the strategy process as a cycle, involving the setting of the organisational mission, external and internal analysis, strategy formulation, strategy implementation and **strategy evaluation**. In this process, strategy evaluation occurs after strategies have been implemented. The results of strategy evaluation are fed back into the strategy process, closing the cycle. Strategy evaluation involves assessing the performances of strategies after implementation, as distinct from the evaluation of strategy options or alternatives (which occurs after internal and external analysis) before implementation. Having defined evaluation, functions that strategy evaluation performs are discussed, including (a) assessing the performances of strategies, (b) providing information for control over employees and managers and (c) providing information for public relations. Ideal strategy evaluation requires an evaluation design that allows managers to identify and operationalise strategy objectives; make decisions about matters such as the source of data collection and who should collect data; interpret the results of strategy evaluation and determine a timeframe for making conclusions about the performances of strategies.

Many methods can be employed to evaluate strategies. Three available methods discussed in this chapter are financial analysis, the balanced scorecard and triple bottom line reporting. It is argued that financial analysis provides simple but understandable information about performances of strategies. The balanced scorecard balances four aspects of business operations to assess strategy performance: the financial, customer, internal business process, and innovation and learning perspectives. The argument in this book is that the balanced scorecard focuses on only the internal aspects of a company and ignores that the business operations are affected by and affect social and environmental factors. Triple bottom line reporting, now being used by many large corporations, emphasises the economic, social and environmental bottom lines.

Managerial tasks do not end with finding out how strategies have performed. Managers need to decide what to do with the evaluation results. If strategies are successful, then the task facing managers is reasonably straightforward: they can continue to use those strategies. If, however, strategies do not perform well, then they need to be terminated. Many managers forget that strategies do not terminate themselves because vested interest grows around them. Companies need to watch for the managerial tendency to escalate strategies despite having negative information about their performances. It is difficult but top managers need to terminate unsuccessful strategies.

The idea of identifying factors that can ensure the success of strategies is attractive to managers. It is difficult, however, to identify critical success factors for strategies for a variety of reasons. This chapter presents a framework that can help you understand the degrees of critical importance of factors that can have an impact on strategy success. The chapter concludes by identifying intended and emergent processes of the strategy evaluation process.

strategy evaluation
Assessment of the performance of a strategy after it has been implemented

What is evaluation?

Ideally, the strategy process proceeds in several phases. The process begins with a decision on the missions and objectives of the company's strategies. This step is followed by an analysis of the external environment of the company, then an analysis of the internal environment to determine the strengths and weaknesses that the company possesses in responding to the opportunities and threats posed by the external environment. Top management then identifies a range of strategy alternatives. Management compares and evaluates the strategy alternatives to determine their appropriateness for achieving the mission and goals that have been fixed for the company. Companies are most likely to select the alternative that they believe is most suited to their mission and goals. The selected strategy alternative is then implemented. After implementation, the company evaluates the strategy's performance to determine whether it has satisfied the mission and goals that the company set out to achieve.

strategy alternatives
Options that management has identified to achieve strategy objectives

In the preceding paragraph, you may have noticed the word 'evaluate' occurred twice: the first mention refers to evaluating strategy alternatives to select the most appropriate and the second mention refers to evaluating the performance of the selected strategy. Rumelt called the first type of evaluation 'alternatives evaluation' and identified four criteria that managers need to use when selecting from strategic alternatives: (a) *consistency* (having coherence among the different strategies that a company follows); (b) *consonance* (adapting strategies to the dynamic external environment); (c) *advantage* (adopting only strategies that bring competitive advantage) and (d) *feasibility* (being able to implement strategies within the means of the company).[1]

This chapter is concerned with the second type of evaluation. Managers need to find out how a strategy is performing: is it on track to achieve the strategic goals? Is it within set budgetary limits? Does it require any change of direction? The focus is on evaluating the performance of a strategy after it has been implemented.

Evaluation is 'the determination of a thing's value'.[2] Managers can determine the value of a strategy before a strategy has been adopted (when managers compare competing strategic alternatives for selection) and after the selected one has been implemented (when managers judge whether the strategy has achieved what it was meant to achieve).[3] The latter — namely, performance evaluation of a strategy — should occur after the strategy has been implemented, but also continually in the company. This continual evaluation is commonly known as monitoring. This helps ensure any problem does not go unseen before it is too late to correct. It is particularly important to evaluate whether the assumptions underpinning a selected strategy continue to hold true. This issue is linked to the perspective on strategy evaluation that managers adopt. If managers adopt an 'intended' view of strategy, then they conduct evaluation mainly after the strategy has been implemented. If they adopt an 'emergent' perspective, however, then they conduct ongoing strategy evaluation. This issue is discussed later in the chapter.

monitoring
Checking continually whether a strategy that is being implemented is on the right track

Strategies look towards the future, so in formulating strategies, managers need to make certain assumptions about the future. Knowledge about the future is usually imperfect.[4] The external environment changes all the time and assumptions that managers make about this uncertain future are not always accurate. Consider Honda, described in chapter 1 of this book. When Honda executives went to the United States to sell their motorcycles, they made several inaccurate assumptions about the US market based on their own experiences and knowledge. The unpredictable nature of strategic situations requires managers to monitor the performances of their strategies continually so they can adapt those strategies to the changing circumstances.

Many managers may prefer not to evaluate their strategies when they are successful: the company is making a profit; customers are happy and employees are content. These managers are implying that strategies should be evaluated only when they are failing, so as to determine the reasons for the failure and turn around the company. The argument in this chapter, however, is that managers need to evaluate successful strategies too, because they need to determine the factors behind the success. Strategies may be successful for a temporary reason, such as the company's competitors being currently weak but preparing to bring new products to the market. In these situations, a company is successful as a result not of its own strategies, but of some external factors over which it has very little control. Such successes are likely to be short-lived. For a strategy to continue to succeed, the company needs to know the factors behind the strategy's success so it can replicate them and is not caught off guard when the competitors introduce new products.[5]

The opening case on Loy Yang Power demonstrates that a company can use evaluation for multiple purposes. Goldenberg argues that evaluation has at least three purposes: learning, control and public relations.[6] The manifest purpose of strategy evaluation is to learn about the performances of strategies so companies can repeat successes and avoid repeating mistakes. Learning is thus the most common purpose of evaluation. Even if evaluation does not serve this purpose, managers would still use evaluation because: 'Usually it provides the evaluating agency with the means for exercising greater control over those implementing the program. Occasionally evaluation also improves the ability of the evaluating agency to delay, deflect, or channel the interventions of outsiders'.[7] These three purposes of evaluation — learning, control and public relations — are mutually supportive. That is, a company can use what it learns about a strategy to control internal or external forces.

Learning

The most obvious function of strategy evaluation is to provide information and data about performances of strategies: whether strategies have failed or succeeded. Managers can use these data to analyse the internal and external factors that contributed to the success or failure of their strategies. This analysis provides occasions for managers to rethink the goals, evaluation methods used, evaluation criteria used and a range of other considerations that have gone into strategy evaluation and can help **learning** about the strategies, their organisations and the environment within which they work. This analysis provides lessons for managers and they can take appropriate actions about the directions of strategies. The learning perspective emphasises both strategy outcomes and processes (such as implementation practices) that lead to those outcomes. By looking at outcomes but not the process, managers will not come to understand the processes that lead to the outcomes, and thus they will not know why one strategy succeeded and another failed. Information about processes helps managers to make process improvements, that is, to modify a strategy when it veers from the directed course.

learning
Modifying a course of action after finding out about a strategy's outcomes and the processes that led to those outcomes

Control

Companies can use information from strategy evaluation to provide incentives and to **control** the behaviour of managers. They can pay bonuses to the managers involved in successful strategies, while penalising the managers of failed strategies (by reducing their salaries, for example). Information about strategy evaluation can also be used to channel managerial behaviour in the direction that top-level managers prefer. Linking strategy performance with reward and penalty can be difficult though. Telecommunications company Telstra links the fortunes of its management with those of the shareholders. The salary that Telstra executives receive is divided into fixed and variable components. The variable component is based on a range of financial and performance measures. Telstra executives are evaluated by their performances in relation to customer service, measures of employee attitude and ability to add value to the business. The executive pay packet is also linked to the performance of Telstra shares relative to the benchmark in Australia, the All Ordinaries Index.[8] It is not easy to establish clear links between organisational performance and strategy, or to isolate the contributions of individual

control
Using information gained through strategy evaluation to influence the behaviour of those implementing the strategy (by rewarding or punishing employees, for example)

strategy in action 12.1

The compensation packages of the most senior executives are related to the performances of their companies. Quite simply, from a strategic perspective, this policy demonstrates an alignment between executive pay and company performance. The idea behind this policy is to provide incentives to executives so that they work harder to achieve higher performance for their companies. Usually, there are two components in their pay packages: variable and fixed. Recent developments have, however, demonstrated several shortfalls in this policy. On occasions, executive pay did not decrease with decline in company performance. For example, the share price of the Singapore Assembly Test Service, a company that tests semiconductors, experienced six consecutive years of decline, yet its CEO resigned with US$1 million for his services. John Kirby, deputy chairman of Village Roadshow, Australia, was paid US$1.1 million for his services from 1999 to 2002, when the share price of the company just about halved. Between 2000 and 2001, the average compensation of most US executives rose from US$5.2 million to US$7 million, when the decline in share prices reduced the assets of shareholders by as much as 12 per cent. Another problem with this policy is that it pays executives based on the short-term

performance of companies. Quite often, companies do well in the short run but very badly in the long run. Sometimes, under this policy, executives are given targets to achieve a certain percentage of market share. This policy can demotivate when the target is not achievable or it may act against motivating executives to achieve a market share that is higher than the target. In the latter situation, the company is not achieving its potential. This pay-for-performance policy has also led to a growing gap between the compensation packages of senior executives and workers. For example, while in 1999, US CEOs' salaries were 140 times higher than that of the average worker, in 2003, they were 500 times higher. In Australia, in 2005, while the executive compensation increased by 30 per cent, wages of workers increased only by 3.5 per cent. John Howard, the Prime Minister of Australia argued that this growing disparity may motivate workers to ask for higher wages, leading to higher inflation, higher interest rates and higher unemployment.

Sources: Uren, D & Bachelard, M 2005, 'Curb your own pay', *The Australian*, 12 February; *The Economist* 2004, 'Business: CEOs and their Indian rope trick: executive pay', 11 December; Leemaster, T 2002, 'High pay, low performance', *Far Eastern Economic Review*, 28 November.

managers to a strategy and ultimately organisational success. Moreover, as Strategy in action 12.1 shows, these incentive payments may not always be aligned with the performances of companies.

Public relations

Most large companies have a public affairs division that interacts with the general public and manages the company's **public relations**. Companies cannot be as secretive about their operations as they could 50 years ago. Various environmental, human rights and other interest groups act as corporate watchdogs. One famous example is the global campaign that arose in response to concerns that footwear and apparel company Nike was exploiting its employees in Indonesia. Hardly any company can hide information. If companies regularly evaluate their operations, then they are likely to have objective data to defend their operations and deflect external criticism. Without such information, which can only come from systematic evaluation of the performance of strategies, companies have no means of rebutting the claims of outside groups.

A company's evaluation team can ask for other studies, conduct its own studies and publicise its own research. It can share evaluation designs with other companies and lobby groups, developing external understanding of the rationale behind its program. The evaluation team can become a treasure house of information by keeping track of the relevant strategies that other companies pursue. With a reputation for its evaluation approach, a company can attract the attention of external researchers, so having a chance to influence what those researchers publicly say about the company.

public relations
Using information gained through strategy evaluation to create a positive public image for a company

Evaluation teams can also organise and participate in conferences and other professional meetings. They can write articles and notes in professional national newspapers to deflect and influence criticism. ANZ Bank made changes after evaluating its strategies. ANZ Bank found that it was doing well in the corporate sector but not so well with noncorporate customers in the retail sector. ANZ Bank CEO John McFarlane noted that the bank has introduced changes to improve its image with general customers and the community, although the company faces sure financial loss in this strategy because there are many unprofitable customers in the retail sector. The changes included free opening of accounts for customers aged over 60 years, virtually free banking for welfare recipients and simplified accounts.[9]

The opening case on Loy Yang Power shows that the company has given more space to public relations exercises by publishing information on its 'environmental performance' (i.e. that it has not infringed legal limits in dust emissions) and 'social performance' (i.e. that it is raising funds for cancer victims). The company publishes this information in the local media.

Evaluation design

evaluation system design
Stipulation of matters that are important in evaluating the performance of strategies

For an effective evaluation of strategies, companies need to have an **evaluation system design**. This design requires the company to consider questions that are important in evaluating the performance of strategies. Managers must set and operationalise goals for strategies' outcomes, determine a timeframe during which strategies are to be evaluated, determine who will evaluate the strategies and who will judge the outcomes of strategies, and decide how to collect data about the performances of strategies. Designing an evaluation system poses several challenges.

The most important challenge is to clarify the goals and objectives of strategies. As part of clarifying goals, a company needs to define what it considers to be success and failure. It should also specify how much deviation from the goals is acceptable. Managers may face insurmountable hurdles, arising from many different areas, in clarifying the goals of their strategies. Senior managers may want to keep a strategic goal ambiguous so their performances cannot be judged against it. If their companies use a system of performance-based pay, then senior managers do not receive bonuses when their strategies do not perform well. Managers have a strong incentive, therefore, to ensure goals of strategies are unclear.[10] Cyert and March argue that organisations are political coalitions.[11] In such a situation, managers may find it easier to agree on goals that are vague and amorphous because vague goals can accommodate diverse views (some of which may be in conflict). Clear goals, on the other hand, may quickly generate opposition because they more easily subvert managers' agendas.

means–ends hierarchy
A series of actions to be undertaken to accomplish a goal

Managers need to identify actions that the company will take to achieve the goals. To do so, they develop a **means–ends hierarchy**, that is, an ordered set of actions that managers believe will achieve the goals they have set. To deal with unsatisfied employees, for example, a company may introduce a pay rise. Kaplan and Norton called such actions 'performance drivers'.[12]

Evaluation system design also requires managers to choose a method of data collection. They can collect information about the performances of strategies using qualitative methods, such as interviews, participant observations and case studies, and also quantitative methods, such as surveys and published information (company annual reports, statements of financial position and statements of financial performance). Managers need to remember that different methods are suitable for evaluating different types of strategy. When managers want to know customers' level of satisfaction with a product, for example, they may conduct a survey. When managers want to know about the financial performance of their company, they can evaluate the statement of financial performance.[13]

An evaluation system design must also specify the source from which the company will collect data to evaluate the performances of its strategies. Managers who were part of the group that formulated and implemented a strategy are more likely to view the performances of the strategy in favourable terms. If the company wants to know the real outcome of a strategy, then it should use data sources that were not involved in the strategy formulation or implementation. A related issue is the choice of evaluators. A common practice is to appoint outside consultants, on the assumption that they would provide an objective evaluation. This assumption may not always be true, however, because consultants may bias results so as to be employed for other work.

Ideally, an evaluation system design should also establish a monitoring system. Strategies are long-term, multifunctional decisions; they are not implemented in a day or two. As noted earlier, strategies look towards an uncertain, ever-changing future, so managers must continually monitor the implementation of strategies. Managers frequently need to adapt strategies to the changing circumstances.

How managers adapt to the changing strategy situations depends largely on their approach to evaluation. Later in the chapter, the concepts of intended and emergent methods of evaluation are introduced. As part of the evaluation design, managers need to specify actions that would be taken when, for example, strategies do not achieve the goals they were set to achieve. Managers with a rigid mind about the goals that they set would view such actions as deviations. Instead, other managers may re-examine the appropriateness of the goals that they set: they may need to refine or even change those goals.[14]

Methods of evaluation

Methods of evaluation deal with matters such as the stakeholders that strategy evaluation takes into account, the processes established to evaluate strategies, and the comprehensiveness of coverage of strategy evaluation issues. There are many methods for strategy evaluation, including financial evaluation, the balanced scorecard and triple bottom line reporting. Financial evaluation examines strategies from the perspective of shareholders, the balanced scorecard examines them from the perspectives of customers and employees, and triple bottom line reporting examines them from the perspectives of shareholders, communities and the natural environment.

Financial evaluation

Assessing the financial performances of strategies is simple and straightforward, and can be done in many ways. Measures include the statement of financial performance (formerly the profit and loss statement), the statement of financial position (formerly the balance sheet), economic value added and market value added. The use of these measures varies depending on the information that is required. The statement of financial performance is useful for showing the current financial condition of a company but it does not predict the future performance. The statement of financial position contains details of the assets that a company holds at a particular time. Similarly to the statement of financial performance, however, it does not predict future performance. An analysis of market value can indicate a company's future performance but possibly not the wealth of the company. Analysis of market share is a further evaluation approach but, again, is unlikely to indicate a company's profitability or wealth. One of the most important inadequacies of financial statements is that they rarely enable users to evaluate strategies comprehensively.

Financial statements show a company's earnings and how the company has spent these earnings over a period of time. Profit (or, technically, retained earnings) is calculated from a deduction from earnings of the cost of goods, depreciation, selling costs, administration costs, interest on loans, tax and dividends.[15] A commonly used method of financial evaluation is *return on investment*, which is calculated from a division of income before tax by total assets. Net income before tax equals sales (or turnover) less depreciation costs, selling costs, administrative costs and interest on loans. Assets include what a company owns, such as cash at the bank, property and a good reputation. *Earnings per share* are another accounting measure of a company's performance. Earnings per share are calculated from a division of the company's earnings by the number of shares on issue. If a company has earned $2 million and issued one million shares, then the earnings per share are $2. *Return on equity* is an accounting measure that divides net income by total equity. Equity is simply the company's shares that people buy. It is something like a loan to a company, in which buyers expect regular repayment in the form of interest.[16]

Among many recently used financial measures of corporate performance are *economic value added* and *market value added*, which are variants of the **shareholder value model**. The shareholder value model emerged as a reaction to companies being perceived as not remembering that their main duty is to create value for shareholders. Companies exist in the economy to generate wealth, which they do when they add value to the capital that they borrow from shareholders and others by combining it with other factors of production.[17] Many companies, instead, have focused on other goals such as maximised size, earnings, earnings growth, earnings per share and market share. For protecting shareholders, the shareholder value model is superior to accounting models because it assesses the riskiness of a company's operations by calculating the cost of capital. It evaluates corporate performance in terms of the *economic profit* generated by the company's operations. Economic profit is calculated from a deduction from after-tax operating profit of the cost of capital employed to produce that profit. Traditional accounting measures largely ignored the cost of capital investments used to generate earnings, whereas the shareholder value model concentrates on the cashflow — the amount of money that a company has at a given period in time — as the key measure of corporate performance.[18] The model involves calculating shareholder value by adding the value of the company if it is liquidated to the current value of the future stream of cashflow. The economic value added is the difference between after-tax operating income and the total annual cost of capital. The market value added is the difference between the company's market value and the capital contributed by its shareholders and lenders (i.e. what investors have paid into the company's shares and what they would receive if they were to sell those shares).[19] It demonstrates whether the management has increased or diminished the capital contributed by shareholders, so it is one of the best financial measures of the performances of corporate strategies. Market value may be quite different from the price paid for shares. Simply, the market value added reflects the market's estimate of the net present value of a company's past and expected capital investment projects.

shareholder value model
A model of evaluating corporate performance in terms of the value created for shareholders

The balanced scorecard

Traditionally, companies evaluated their performances in terms of financial criteria such as return on investment, profit, market share and so on. Many managers felt that evaluating businesses against only financial criteria produced part, out-of-date and, at times, misleading results. Financial measures are short term and they report past performances, so they are inadequate indicators of future performances.[20] Furthermore, they do not evaluate corporate performance in terms of learning. In response to these inadequacies, many managers have tried to improve and develop financial criteria, while others have abandoned financial criteria and instead emphasise operational criteria such as the level of customer service. Managers do not have to choose though; they can combine multiple criteria.

Kaplan and Norton suggest that companies should not evaluate the performances of their strategies in an imbalanced way by emphasising only a financial perspective because 'no single measure can provide a clear performance target or focus attention on the critical areas of business'.[21] They argue that companies can achieve balanced evaluation if they take four perspectives on the performances of their strategies: financial, customer, internal business process, and innovation and learning.

The **balanced scorecard** approach asks managers to evaluate their strategies in terms of these four important perspectives. It provides answers to four basic questions:

1. Has company performance been in the interests of the shareholders?
2. How do customers evaluate the company?
3. What are the internal resources and capabilities of the company?
4. In what areas does the company need to innovate?

These four criteria not only provide a balance among factors that companies should be using to evaluate their business but they also provide 'balance between short-term and long-term objectives, between desired outcomes and the performance drivers of those outcomes, and between hard objective measures and softer, more subjective measures'.[22]

In addition to these four perspectives, the balanced scorecard identifies performance drivers for each of the four perspectives; operationalises the four perspectives; develops outcome measures and performance drivers; establishes links among the four perspectives, outcomes measures and performance drivers; establishes cause-and-effect relationships among the four perspectives; organises perspectives and performance drivers in a strategic means–ends hierarchic chain; links the performances of businesses, functional units and individual managers with the scorecard; links long-term strategy with intermediate and short-term operational goals and integrates a system of monitoring with the overall framework. By linking outcome measures, performance drivers and rewards, the balanced scorecard ensures managers conform to the strategic vision of their company.[23]

Financial perspective

The **financial perspective** examines 'whether the company's strategy, implementation, and execution are contributing to bottom line improvement'.[24] Many managers criticise financial measures for their backward-looking focus. Others argue that instead of focusing on such outcomes as financial profit, it is important to focus on processes that drive these outcomes because taking care of the processes will automatically take care of the outcomes. Kaplan and Norton disagree for two reasons: 'A well-designed financial control system can actually enhance rather than inhibit an organization's total quality management program ... More important, however, the alleged linkage between improved operating performance and financial success is actually quite tenuous and uncertain'.[25]

Improvements in capabilities or processes such as delivery time or defect rates may not translate into increased profit. A company can improve its processes yet may release new products very slowly, fail to expand marketing to new and perhaps more demanding customers, or target customers who are not really profitable; all measures that may prevent the company from realising the financial benefits from improving its processes and capabilities.

From the financial perspective, a company can identify outcomes such as profitability, growth and market share. It can measure profitability by an annual increase in profits, growth by sales growth, and market share by an expansion of market share for the company as a whole or in market segment. Performance drivers of financial outcomes can be an expansion of the product and service offerings, marketing to new customers and markets, a change to the product and service and a reduction in the cost of production.

The financial objectives of a company may vary depending on its lifecycle, which can be divided into three stages. At the *growing* (rapid growth) *stage*, a company develops and improves

balanced scorecard
Evaluating strategies in terms of the financial, customer, internal business process, and innovation and learning perspectives

financial perspective
How shareholders evaluate the performances of a company

new products and services; constructs and expands production facilities; builds operating capabilities, infrastructure and distribution networks; and nurtures and develops customer relationships. At the *sustain stage*, a company wants to achieve returns on its investment and to maintain its market share by 'relieving bottlenecks, expanding capacity, and enhancing continuous improvement'.[26] At the *mature stage*, a company harvests its investments: it needs to invest only enough to maintain equipment and capabilities. It maximises cashflow and does not expand.

This approach of viewing financial objectives in terms of company lifecycle can greatly help companies to identify the strategies that they should be pursuing for themselves at different stages of their company lifecycle. This approach can also help a company anticipate the possible strategies that its rivals are likely to pursue when it knows the stage at which those rivals are in this company lifecycle.

Customer perspective

customer perspective
How customers evaluate company products

The **customer perspective** requires managers to 'identify the customer and market segments in which the business unit will compete and the measures of the business unit's performance in these targeted segments'.[27] Managers identify the outcomes they want to achieve and then the criteria by which to measure these outcomes. Outcome measures can include:

* customer satisfaction, as measured by customer loyalty, repeat purchasing behaviour and so on
* customer retention, as measured by the number of customers who are buying company products or the percentage growth of business with existing customers
* customer acquisition, as measured by the rate at which a business unit attracts or wins new customers or business, the number of new customers and the total sales to new customers
* customer profitability, as measured by a customer's level of purchasing from a company
* market share, as measured by sales
* account share, as measured by the amount of money that individual customers spend on company products.

Managers also need to identify the performance drivers of these customer perspective outcomes. The performance drivers could be short lead times, on-time delivery, a constant stream of innovation and the production of products and services that anticipate customer expectations. They vary across industries and markets, but those identified here are generic and broadly applicable.

Internal business process perspective

internal business process perspective
How processes related to cycle time, delivery speed, safety ratings and level of employee skills and knowledge, for example, match strategic requirements

Internal business processes are a means of achieving financial and customer objectives. From the **internal business process perspective**, managers concentrate on the processes that are most critical for strategy success. Improvements to internal business processes focus not only on improving current processes to serve current customers but also on creating new processes, products and services to meet the emerging needs of current and future customers.[28] Outcomes may include cycle time, product quality, employee skills, employee productivity, core competencies and critical technologies. Managers can measure these outcomes by the speed and rate at which employees produce products and the quality of such products, for example. A further measure includes comparative analysis of the current skills and competencies of the employees and the skills and competencies required for production of a new product.

Business process improvements need to be subdivided into contributions that are expected at division, branch, functional and individual levels. All the sections, departments, individual employees and managers are thus linked: 'This linkage ensures that employees at lower levels in the company have clear targets for actions, decisions and improvement activities that will contribute to the company's overall mission'.[29] Information systems play a very important role in encouraging these links by providing timely information about the levels of service, profitability and so on. If circulating information is not timely, then managers may not be aware of a problem until it is too late.

Innovation and learning perspective

While the customer perspective and internal business processes perspective ensure success in the current market, the **innovation and learning** (or learning and growth) **perspective** prepares the company for the future market. Ever increasing global and domestic competition and environmental turbulence require companies to improve their products, processes and capabilities. In such competitive times, companies can create and enter new markets — and consequently increase revenue and profit margins — only by launching new products, creating quality products and being more efficient.

Outcomes from innovation could be improvements in the number of new products launched, processes, the support system for making decisions, communication and so on. Managers can measure these outcomes by the speed at which the company introduces new products and the increased percentage sales from such products, for example. These measures help companies identify reasons for declining sales, for example, even after the introduction of a new product. Innovation usually focuses on product and process innovation but it can also focus on improvements to existing processes. A company can estimate specific rates of improvement for such customer-related and internal business process-related outcomes as on-time delivery, cycle time, defect rates and yield.

innovation and learning perspective
The sustainability of a company over a long period of time

The four balanced scorecard processes

The balanced scorecard identifies four processes in addition to the four perspectives. The processes are: translation of the vision, communication, business planning, and feedback and learning.

Translation of the vision

Managers formulate strategies to achieve objectives but lofty ideals formulated in attractive terms are not useful for strategy evaluation. Rather, the balanced scorecard suggests that top management operationalise the company's visions, goals and objectives in terms that are understandable, precise, measurable and agreed to by all relevant parties. When managers talk about a strategy, they often assume that everyone understands what it is and that everyone has the same meaning in mind, but this is not always the case.[30] Ideally, the company vision provides the guidelines for formulating the goals from the four perspectives.

Communication

The emphasis under the balanced scorecard is on everyone in the company knowing about the goals, outcome measures and performance drivers of company strategies. Both top-down and bottom-up approaches to communication help achieve this level of companywide knowledge. The balanced scorecard advocates participation in strategy formulation. Different levels in a strategy are allocated to different levels in the company: top management formulates the corporate-level strategies; business-level managers formulate business-level strategies within the corporate strategy; functional-level managers formulate functional-level strategies within the business-level strategies; and individual managers identify their responsibilities and tasks for implementing the functional-level strategies. Alternatively, the senior managers formulate financial and customer objectives, within which middle-level managers formulate internal business process and learning and growth objectives. Participative management has advantages: first, the company can gather a large amount of information that can be used in the strategy process and, second, managers come to know more about, feel a part of, and have increased commitment to the strategy.

The balanced scorecard approach communicates overall strategy throughout the company and requires that individual managers' performances are aligned with the overall strategy. To achieve this alignment, the company has to undertake three activities: (a) communicating and educating, (b) setting goals and (c) linking rewards to performance measures.

Through communication and education, top management shares information about strategies and critical objectives with all employees. High-level strategies are translated into objectives and measures for operating units and individuals through a process of goal setting.

Individual managers develop a personal scorecard on which they identify their objectives and then 'articulate which of their own objectives would be consistent with the business unit and corporate objectives, as well as what initiatives they would take to achieve their objectives. The scorecard also asks them to define up to five performance measures for their objectives and set targets for each measure'.[31] The personal scorecard not only clarifies objectives for each employee but also identifies measures by which their performance can be evaluated and aligns their personal objectives with the overall strategy of the company through their business unit's objectives.

It is always an attractive option for companies to link rewards to managers' performances. This link can be risky, however, if managers are rewarded or punished based on incorrect measures supported by invalid and unreliable data.

Business planning: linking short-term actions with long-term strategies

In most companies, the strategy process and the budget process are separate. Strategies involve major decisions for the long-term future of the company, while budgets span a year and involve short-term operational targets. This separation means that companies may work for conflicting goals, wasting valuable company resources and managerial time. In the periodic reviews (usually monthly or fortnightly), companies discuss the budget, not the strategies, because it provides quantitative figures that are measurable. The balanced scorecard, however, requires companies to integrate their strategy and budgeting processes, to ensure that their budgets support their strategies.

Managers can link the strategy and budget processes by establishing specific short-term targets. To do so, managers integrate short-term customer, internal business process, and innovation and learning targets with their budgets for short-term financial performance. This approach allows managers to assess continually both the assumptions underpinning the strategy and the strategy's implementation.[32]

Feedback and learning

The balanced scorecard approach advocates continual feedback and learning about the strategy process. Supporters of this approach believe that all strategies are theories, that is, strategies are based on assumed relationships among processes. When faced with high staff turnover, for example, managers who introduce a bonus assume that the bonus is negatively related to turnover. This assumption may be true or false. Using the balanced scorecard approach, managers have a feedback system to test the theories behind strategies and practices continuously, and so engage in strategic learning rather than single-loop learning.

In the *single-loop learning process*, managers do not question the assumptions behind their strategies; rather, they dogmatically adhere to their theories and refuse to re-examine the strategy or its implementation.[33] Managers following *strategic learning* re-examine their assumptions and make necessary adjustments in the light of changing circumstances. Evidence of a correlation between goals and performance drivers indicates that the theory behind the strategy is true; a lack of such correlation suggests the theory may not be true.[34] Strategic learning accepts that strategies look towards an unpredictable future and that managers must make strategic adjustments in the light of changing circumstances. A strategic feedback system encourages managers to question their assumptions and change their current strategy if they do not find expected correlations among action, performance drivers and objectives. See Strategy in action 12.2 for an example of the balanced scorecard at work.

strategy in action 12.2

Trent, the parent company of the Westside chain of retail stores of the Tata Group of companies was inducted into the balanced scorecard hall of fame by no other than Dr Robert Kaplan, one of the authors of the balanced scorecard. Trent is the second company in India to receive this award after Tata Motors, another company of the Tata Group.

The Tata Group, established by Jamsetji Tata in the 1860s, is one of the oldest business conglomerates in India. The group comprises 93 companies in seven business sectors that include information systems and communication, engineering, materials, services, energy, consumer products and chemicals. In 2004–05, the group had revenue of US$17.8 billion, employing considerably more than 215 000 people in its operations in 40 countries across six continents.

Induction of Trent into the balanced scorecard hall of fame was only a very insignificant part of the contributions of the tool. More important are the profitability, improved turnover and improved customer satisfaction that resulted from the implementation of the balanced scorecard. The Trent management was never happy with a one-dimensional performance management system that emphasised only the financial side. The company realised that it needed a tool that measures several dimensions of the business. Most importantly, the company management believed that profitability was largely a consequence of customer satisfaction. The company also believed that it needed an overarching strategy that provided coherence in its operations throughout its business. The company defined its key strategic objective as 'surprisingly, affordable style, quality and a great shopping experience for the entire family'.

To achieve this strategy, the company needed to work though its business processes. The company experienced almost an insurmountable obstacle in improving its business process because of the people who worked traditionally in the retail stores. The frontline workers of the retail sector are the college students who work in the stores for only a very short time, only to move to another job that offers them a career.

To overcome this hurdle, Trent developed an innovative learning and growth strategy. This emphasised training. As part of this program, the company identified its best employees in each store and designated them as coaches, who trained their own staff. Each store developed three types of coaches: in customer service, information technology skills and product knowledge. Trent emphasised that an integrated strategy to satisfy customers requires not only a group of trained and friendly staff but also a group of staff that have up-to-date knowledge and information about products that customers want.

Sources: Tata Group, www.tata.com; Kasbekar, G 2005, 'Tilting the balance', www.tata.com/trent/articles/20051129_tilting_balance.htm.

Assessing the balanced scorecard

The balanced scorecard provides an excellent framework for assessing whether a strategy is a success or a failure by evaluating the performances of strategies from both financial and nonfinancial perspectives, and from long-term and short-term perspectives. It involves a comprehensive assessment of a strategy from four different perspectives and provides information on whether a strategy is just a short-term financial success, whether a company is innovating and learning to make long-term successes, whether the internal processes of a company are aligned with the strategy that a company has adopted, and so on. The balanced scorecard approach can demonstrate, for example, that a company is in excellent financial health but not ready to face challenges in the external environment in five years because the company is not developing new products. These evaluation results may prompt the company to invest in research and development to design new processes and products.

The balanced scorecard can be described as a strategic control system that combines elements of boundary, diagnostic and interactive control systems. It focuses on boundary control by identifying visions, mission and strategic goals, and thus limiting the attention of managers to activities that the company has identified. It focuses on diagnostic control by comparing strategy implementation with goals, visions and missions that the company has chosen. Finally, the balanced scorecard focuses on interactive control by stressing feedback and learning, whereby managers are encouraged to continually learn and change their strategies as they implement them.[35]

Kaplan and Norton, however, give conflicting messages regarding the importance of their four criteria for evaluating strategy performance. They clearly state that the financial criterion is most important and the other three criteria are drivers of the financial criterion:

> Measures of customer satisfaction, internal business performance, and innovation and improvement are derived from the company's particular view of the world and its perspective on key success factors. But that view is not necessarily correct ... A failure to convert improved operational performance, as measured in the scorecard, into improved financial performance should send executives back to the drawing boards to rethink the company's strategy or its implementation plans.[36]

In the balanced scorecard, these four perspectives form a means–ends chain, with financial improvement as the ultimate end:

> A strategy is a set of hypotheses about cause and effect. Cause and effect relationships can be expressed by a sequence of if-then statements ... A properly constructed scorecard should tell the story of the business unit's strategy. The measurement system should make the relationships (hypotheses) among objectives (and measures) in the various perspectives explicit so that they can be managed and validated. The chain of cause and effect should pervade all four perspectives of a balanced scorecard.[37]

A company may identify increasing profitability as the financial goal but it then should identify how the other three perspectives are linked to the financial goal. The company can then identify that improving customer loyalty (an outcome from the customer perspective) may be one option for increasing profit. It may also identify that shortening delivery time (an outcome from the internal business process perspective) is a means of achieving the customer-related outcome. Furthermore, it may identify that training and improving the skills of employees (an outcome from the learning and innovation perspective) is a means of reducing delivery times.[38]

In other work, however, Kaplan and Norton seem to suggest that managers should not suboptimise, that is, managers should give equal importance to all four perspectives:

> ... the scorecard guards against suboptimization. By forcing managers to consider all the important operational measures together, the balanced scorecard lets them see whether improvement in one area may have been achieved at the expense of another. Even the best objective can be achieved badly.[39]

One of the simple, obvious and yet great benefits of the balanced scorecard is that it requires companies to bring together information that is usually scattered across separate and bulky documents, providing an integrated perspective of the four different areas of the business. The emphasis on four perspectives can be too rigid, however, and lead a company to ignore potentially important influences on its business. The balanced scorecard mostly ignores many stakeholders (such as suppliers, employees and the community) and the contributions they make to a company's performances.[40] Researchers found that several French companies that implemented the balanced scorecard added perspectives such as 'impact on society'.[41]

Use of the balanced scorecard increases the workload of employees. Companies conventionally collect information on financial measures, but the balanced scorecard requires them to collect information on three additional dimensions. Companies may not have established the processes to collect such information. Furthermore, managers who are usually overstretched with their current workload may delay in implementing the balanced scorecard. The proponents of the balanced scorecard seem to assume that strategies that companies follow are clear and easily developed. They forget that top management in many cases hold different views about their strategies.[42] Managers implementing the balanced scorecard at ABB experienced the overcomplexity of the task which generated far too many cause-and-effect chains and took more than four months, which the company considered to be far too long.[43]

In two case studies — on a motor vehicle company and a bank — with a link between balanced scorecard evaluation and employee rewards, Shih-Jen and Mackay found that the motor vehicle company has successfully implemented the balanced scorecard while the bank experienced difficulties and ultimately abandoned the approach. The authors argue that different results arose from implementation differences between these two companies. The feedback mechanism was much faster at the motor vehicle factory than at the bank, so the former could process individuals' performance data quickly and give them rewards. The bank, however, took months to pay managers and tellers their financial rewards. Furthermore, the bank had both subjective and objective measures in its balanced scorecard while the motor vehicle factory had only objective measures. The bank required much longer to come to a conclusion about the performances of managers because it had to interview managers in detail about their performances. Another issue was that different bank managers across the branches interpreted performance requirements differently, leading to the payment of inequitable rewards. These two case studies suggest that companies should develop the balanced scorecard gradually with the active participation of employees and managers at all levels. The motor vehicle factory developed measures for the company as a whole at top-management level, while departments developed their own scorecards and the links between the departmental and overall organisational scorecards. At the bank, however, the top management developed and defined measures without any input from the branches.[44]

More than 60 per cent of companies that have implemented the balanced scorecard link it with employee rewards. Many companies establishing such a link may engage in hypocritical behaviour, in which they ask their managers to be customer sensitive but reward them based on historical financial indicators.[45] A study of manufacturing companies in Australia found that more larger than smaller companies use the balanced scorecard. The study could not identify any reason for this bias and did not suggest that large companies use the balanced scorecard because they benefit from it. The authors speculated that large companies use the balanced scorecard because they can afford it or simply because it is a fashion.[46]

Triple bottom line reporting

The balanced scorecard emphasises a company's internal aspects for strategy evaluation but businesses exist in a multifaceted environment. In the language of systems theory, businesses import inputs from, and send outputs to, the environment. Inputs are natural and physical resources, and outputs are the products from the companies. The quality and quantity of outputs that a business sends to the environment largely depends on the quality and quantity of inputs that it imports from the environment. Most resources that businesses use to make their products are not infinite and need to be replenished. Similarly, businesses work in an environment that is supported by people (including their employees) and many visible and invisible, formal and informal institutions. These individuals and institutions cannot be taken for granted; they need to be nourished and supported. No-one can deny, however, that companies need to look after the survival of their businesses. In other words, they need to make sure that they remain economically viable.

The triple bottom line asks companies to evaluate their performances in terms of three bottom lines: the **environmental bottom line**, the **social justice bottom line** and the **economic bottom line**.[47] The concept responds to, and brings together, three main concerns of businesses in one integrated framework. Management as a discipline has always emphasised social responsibility and, since the 1960s, many pressure groups have emphasised the environmental responsibility of businesses. The triple bottom line approach regards a business as having responsibilities to society and the environment because these sustain business. That is, for a business to be sustainable, it needs to be socially and environmentally responsible. Failure to accept such responsibility will lead to an extinction of all, including businesses.

environmental bottom line
The impact of organisational performance on the natural environment

social justice bottom line
The impact of organisational operations on social institutions and people

economic bottom line
The impact of organisational performance on the company's economic viability

Elkington, arguably the founder of the triple bottom line concept, argues that this evaluation approach helps companies achieve what he calls 'sustainable capitalism'.[48] If companies do not ensure economic prosperity, improve environmental quality and make positive contributions to achieve social justice, then they face extinction. The proponents argue that triple bottom line reporting, in the long term, is entirely compatible with the profit motive of companies:

> [The triple bottom line] approach is merely an extension of the scope and time line over which a shareholder's interests are assessed. The underlying rationale is that companies emphasising the economic, social, and environmental dimensions of their businesses will be in a much better position to build competitive advantage, generate long term wealth creation, and sustain profitability than companies that do not.[49]

Others disagree. Hayward argues that companies such as Exxon Mobil that do not claim to be socially and environmentally responsible and do not waste capital on 'unproductive renewable technologies' earn more profit than earned by companies that are responsible on both bottom lines, such as British Petroleum (BP) and Royal Dutch/Shell.[50] Exxon Mobil's price–earnings ratio, profit margin and return on shareholder's equity are much higher than those of its greener competitors, BP and Royal Dutch/Shell.[51]

Three bottom lines

Triple bottom line reporting identifies three forms of capital that contribute to company success and thus, the proponents argue, should receive return on investment. The three forms are cash capital, natural capital and social capital. Traditional accounting practices recognise only cash capital. The fundamental emphasis of triple bottom line reporting is sustainability, which proponents argue can be achieved only if corporations place a balanced emphasis on all three forms of capital. Sustainability was first formally emphasised by the Brundtland Commission of the United Nations in 1987, which defined it as 'meeting the needs of the present without compromising the ability of future generations to meet their own needs'.[52]

Economic or *cash capital*, which includes all tangible assets, intellectual property and sometimes services, is widely understood and recognised by current accounting practices. Its contribution to the survival of corporations is well known and ways of measuring it are well established. A challenge for companies adopting triple bottom line reporting, however, is to make products that are equally competitive in the market. The economic bottom line therefore considers the impact of organisational performance on the company's economic viability.

Natural capital comes from the *natural environment* that sustains all forms of life on Earth. It represents the ecology, air, climate, plants, animals and raw materials that companies use as inputs. Natural capital appears limitless in the short term because those resources decay very slowly. Most companies therefore use this natural capital as if it were limitless but it is not. Although most companies replenish their cash capital — because they know that otherwise they would not survive — many companies do not view natural capital similarly. Rather, they have a cradle-to-grave philosophy, viewing raw materials as disposable items. Triple bottom line reporting calls for a cradle-to-cradle philosophy, asking companies to use and reuse raw materials.[53] The environmental bottom line therefore evaluates the impact of a company's activities on the natural environment.

What one measures for the social bottom line is hardly clear.[54] One proponent of triple bottom line reporting identifies two types of social capital: human capital and social system capital. Human capital represents the 'investment of intelligence, creativity, experience, skills, talents, passions, and education by employees and their families, suppliers, partners, advisors, and customers'.[55] Many companies view their employees — the most important source of human capital — as disposable items and terminate their employment as part of downsizing programs to gain short-term financial gains. The assumption of triple bottom line reporting is that most companies treat their employees inequitably and that top managers receive disproportionately high levels of benefits compared with the majority of employees. This treatment leads to high levels of turnover, lack of loyalty and employee discontent.

Social system capital refers to the institutional framework that supports company success. It includes infrastructural institutions such as transport and communication; legal institutions such as the justice system, organised police and a system of rule of law; political institutions such as parliament and regular, legitimate and orderly transfer of political power; financial institutions such as a regulated banking system and a safe investment environment; and educational institutions that supply skilled young people with proper values. Few managers recognise the contributions that the social system makes to businesses. Triple bottom line reporting encourages companies to appreciate and accept the contributions made by the social system and, in return, contribute to that social capital.

Drivers of the triple bottom line

The proponents of triple bottom line reporting argue that several recent developments require companies to be transparent, including the need to disclose information about their processes and strategies in publicly available reports. Governments and many not-for-profit organisations largely ensure social justice and look after the natural environment. Since the 1960s, however, governments command fewer resources and less legitimacy, requiring the private sector also to perform a guardianship role in relation to social and environmental matters.[56] Large companies are under pressure from interest groups to change their attitude towards softer values such as human rights and child labour, and to consult affected groups when establishing operations in many parts of the world (as BP had to do in Nigeria). Companies are increasingly living in fishbowls, under pressure to be publicly transparent about their plans, strategies, activities and commitments with the help of technologies such as the Internet and cable television. Companies are also under pressure to think in terms of the life cycles of their products rather than their products at the point of sale: 'Here we are seeing a shift from companies focusing on the acceptability of their products at the point of sale to a new emphasis on the performance from cradle to cradle — i.e., from extraction of raw materials right through to recycling or disposal'.[57] Many companies and many shareholders have a short-term focus on financial gains; they have little concern about the long-term sustainability of the company. Companies have to move away from their focus on quarterly profits and the short-term financial bottom line, to focus on stakeholder value rather than shareholder profits. Stakeholders include employees, creditors, suppliers, customers, the community at large and nature, all of which have long-term perspectives. In terms of corporate governance, consumers are increasingly asking questions about the appropriate balance between shareholder profits, fat salaries for top executives and the democratisation of board-level decision making.

Implementing triple bottom line reporting

There is little universal agreement about interpretation of the three bottom lines, particularly the social justice and environmental bottom lines.[58] This disagreement has been reflected in companies' operationalisation of the concept: a challenge is to develop universally accepted methods and accounting practices for evaluating the three bottom lines.

To evaluate strategies in terms of triple bottom line reporting, companies need to find 'accurate, useful and credible indicators of progress in terms of economic prosperity, environmental quality and social justice'.[59] They face not just a problem of data availability but also 'weaknesses in accounting theory and the fragmentation and standards and metrics in this field'.[60] In measuring the environmental bottom line, for example, how do companies calculate the costs of chopping down rainforests on which a whole range of animals, plants and weather patterns depended? Even in the case of renewable resources, a company can calculate the costs of cutting trees and catching fish but how do they calculate the costs of the 'ongoing capacity of such ecosystems to produce yields on a sustainable basis'?[61] It can also be extremely difficult to calculate the costs and liabilities of greenhouse gas emissions in the atmosphere. Similarly, for the social bottom line, companies need to measure knowledge or skills developed or lost, levels of resilience, mutuality and trust in communities, yet Elkington argues that 'the social accounting challenge has hardly begun to be addressed'.[62] Social issues such as human rights and child labour have hardly been tackled.

The opening case on the Loy Yang Power shows that the company uses triple bottom line reporting on its performances. Royal Dutch/Shell is a company that is trying hard to develop triple bottom line reporting. Its experience with this reporting is available at www.shell.com, and its report for 2000 identified key performance indicators for triple bottom line reporting. Rolltronics, a nonprofit electronics company, has also introduced triple bottom line reporting. The company is committed to developing a production process that is less harmful to the environment, by using lower temperatures to fabricate products, eliminating the need for lead solder connections and creating products and enabling technologies that help close the gap between its economic, digital and technology environments. The company is committed to designing products and technologies that serve the needs of the world populations not served by other companies. Employees and contractors are the shareholders and the company allows continual stakeholder participation in company processes. The company established the Rolltronics foundation with the purpose of developing sustainability in all aspects of human existence through research. It is also committed to implementing a comprehensive environment management system and it ensures its suppliers too conform to principles of triple bottom line awareness.[63]

In New Zealand, Hubbards Foods Limited and The Warehouse Group have produced triple bottom line reports.

Responses to strategy evaluation results

Having evaluated a strategy, a company has options that depend on the results of the evaluation. If the company accepts that a strategy is a success, then it can continue using the strategy. A company should not sit idle with a successful strategy because this success could merely be the result of sheer luck or poor performance by competitors. Ideally, it should determine the reasons for the success, so that it can replicate it for many years. Later, the chapter considers the idea of identifying the reasons for success: critical success factors. Here, the discussion focuses on possible company responses when the company concludes a strategy is a failure. Ideally, companies should terminate a failed strategy. Strategies do not terminate themselves, however, they need to be terminated. A common tendency is for managers to continue with a failed strategy, known as nonrational escalation of commitment.

Escalation

escalation
Continued use of a failed strategy

Escalation relates to a decision about one problem as a result of a previous decision.[64] What does a company do when one of its strategies fail: terminate the strategy or continue with it? It would be easy to make a decision if a company knew which course of action would be beneficial. Unfortunately, however, the correct decision is not always clear.

A common tendency is to continue with a failed course of action. Many argue that past decisions are history and should not be considered while making decisions for the future. The idea is that managers should forget a failed strategy and consider future costs and benefits. This is a normative position because, in actuality, managers do not forget their past decisions. When managers have spent money on a project, they do not forget that investment even when it fails; they try to recover at least something from pursuing that strategy. Others argue that it is rational to continue with a particular decision because giving up at the first sign of failure is a psychological deficiency. Our parents and schoolteachers advise us to 'try and try again'.

Psychologists have found that:

> ... decision makers who commit themselves to a particular course of action have a tendency to make subsequent decisions that continue that commitment beyond the level suggested by rationality. As a consequence, resources are often allocated in a way that justifies previous commitments, whether or not these initial commitments now appear valid.[65]

This is called nonrational escalation of commitment. Studies have shown that managers continue to allocate more and more resources even when they see that the strategies have failed. This behaviour also happens in other areas, such as when managers evaluate more positively the performances of subordinates whom they had hired than the performances of those subordinates whose hiring they were not involved in. Evidence from many studies suggests that managers find it difficult to separate their previous decisions from related future decisions. This nonrational escalation of commitment can occur for a variety of reasons. Identifying and understanding the reasons can help managers de-escalate or withdraw from a situation.

Perceptual bias

Individuals are biased about their previous decisions. They see only the positive information about their decisions and ignore negative information. In the case of strategies that they have formulated, they see only what the strategy has achieved and ignore what the strategy did not achieve. They may even actively seek information that supports their decisions and filter out information that does not support that commitment. Ways of correcting the occurrence of perceptual bias include searching vigilantly for disputing information as well as confirming information, and establishing monitoring systems that check managerial perceptions. An outside observer, for example, can evaluate managerial openness to disputing information.[66]

perceptual bias
Placing selective attention on the positive aspects of one's actions

Illusive expectations

The concept of illusive expectations suggests that managers expect that continuing with a strategy will lead to its success.[67] Suppose a manager has spent $50 000 setting up an overseas operation only to find a few months later that the operation has failed. Suppose the manager has two options: accept a sure loss of $50 000 or, by spending another $50 000, have a 50/50 chance of getting back the full $100 000. Research findings suggest that managers are more likely to allocate the second $50 000 with the hope of recovering all the investment.

illusive expectations
Managerial thinking that continuation with a failed strategy will lead to its success

Impression management

Managers want to demonstrate that they are successful. Impression management refers to actions that managers take to hide their failures. One such action is not to accept that a decision failed. When managers discontinue an action that is failing, they accept that they adopted the wrong strategies; continuing with the course of action saves face.[68]

Managers may also try to seem consistent, even when doing so increases commitment to wrong actions. Society perceives that managers who are 'consistent in their actions are better leaders than those who switch from one line of behaviour to another'.[69] Companies should inform managers that impression management at the cost of the company is not tolerable. The emphasis should be on results. This approach cuts down on escalation by discouraging decisions that are risky or that have not lived up to expectations.

impression management
Actions that managers adopt to hide their failures

Structural factors

Managers sometimes continue with a strategy because it may be difficult to undo a decision when an administrative structure has been created, when plants, machinery or people have been hired, and when a project has low salvage value and high closing costs.[70] When a multinational company sets up a subsidiary in another country, for example, it may be extremely difficult to withdraw those operations even if the company realises that the subsidiary will not make profit. The company might have rented office buildings for several years, hired managers on multiyear contracts and bought raw materials that would take several years to use.

Termination

When a company concludes that its strategy has failed or that it is not happy with its performance, it may terminate it. It may do so even when it is successful, to release money for another strategy or to change strategic direction.

There are many different types of strategy. Here, strategy termination in the area of intercompany relationships is discussed. An intercompany relationship can be a supplier–buyer relationship, a producer–distributor relationship, a partnership and so on. Not many studies of strategy termination have been done, except in the area of inter-company relationships. A rich tradition exists in the public sector literature on strategy termination discussed under the title of policy termination.[71]

An intercompany relationship 'can be considered terminated when no activity links or resource ties exist between the parties involved in the relationship'.[72] Strategy termination, particularly in the area of an intercompany relationship, moves through steps that end in termination. Social psychology literature identifies a four-stage process in relationship termination: first, parties privately evaluate their dissatisfaction and assess the costs and benefits in continuing with the relationship; second, when parties conclude that costs outweigh benefits, they decide to terminate the relationship and negotiate their 'unbonding'; third, they publicly announce their decision to terminate the relationship and finally, the parties attempt to recover psychologically from the termination.[73]

Parties can adopt a range of actions to terminate relationships. They can explicitly state their intention to leave the relationship or they can withdraw from the relationship silently by exhibiting avoidance behaviour. They can also unilaterally withdraw from or terminate the relationship by mutual agreement. They can also adopt self-oriented actions, in which they care little about hurting the other party, or they can adopt other-oriented actions, in which they avoid hurting the other party. These actions can work together in many different combinations. A party can, for example, withdraw unilaterally by using avoidance behaviour in a self-oriented way.

In a case study of a law partnership, Drummond found that a set of conditions is necessary for termination to occur.[74] Christine, a lawyer, established a partnership with two more lawyers stationed at a different place. On the first day of the partnership, Christine found that the partners were out of the office in the middle of the day and did not return until 3 pm. It soon became clear that long lunches were a regular phenomenon. Clients could rarely find her partners, and one day, a senior lawyer of a large law company who failed to find her partners said that he would complain to the Law Society. Christine realised that this complaint would mean negative publicity for her.

Drummond argues that termination occurs when clear and negative feedback exists about a business relationship. It was also clear in Christine's case that the perceived benefit of the relationship was unlikely to result. Christine soon realised that her partners would not contribute anything. They were lazy, irresponsible and rarely in their offices, spending most of their time in lunches. Drummond further argues that termination is easier when bonding is low because there is less social pressure to continue with the relationship. In Christine's case, bonding was low because the partners were working in separate offices and finances and client bases intermeshed little. Psychological and social pressure to continue was low because Christine did not have any feelings of responsibility to her partners. Furthermore, the cost of continuing the relationship was higher than the cost for discontinuing it because Christine feared that she would lose everything by staying in the partnership.

Duration of the relationship is important too. Christine's partnership was new and the negative information came quite early in the formation of the relationship, so termination was easy. If the information had arisen long after the partnership had been formed, it would have been difficult to withdraw. In the early stages of a relationship, vigilance tends to be higher, the decision is fresh in people's memory and any negative feedback can lead one party to withdraw. Drummond argues that perceptual bias can work in favour of withdrawal as well. Christine made her decision on the first day when she heard that her partners were not in the office; from then on, she was gathering data to help her terminate the partnership. This evidence suggests 'once decision makers tentatively decide to withdraw, they deliberately seek out data which confirms their decisions ... Having decided to withdraw, decision makers ignore information which disconfirms that decision'.[75]

Critical success factors

One purpose of strategy evaluation is to assess the success of strategies. A logical continuation of this evaluation is to identify factors that contribute to the success or failure of a strategy. Any manager would welcome a consultant who could outline the actions that would ensure the success of his or her strategies. For example, Strategy in action 12.3 suggests that one of the most important factors behind the success of Kia Carnival would be selling the car at a very low price.

Scholars of strategic management argue that there is a link between strategy and perform-ance.[76] Miles and Snow, for example, argue that a fit between strategy, external environment and internal environment leads to organisational success and that a misfit leads to failure[77]: 'Successful companies achieve strategic fit with their market environment and support their strategies with appropriately designed structures and management processes. Less successful companies typically exhibit poor fit externally and/or internally'.[78] Porter argues that the performances of companies depend on the degree of competition in an industry, with an inverse relationship existing between the degree of competition and the amount of profit that companies in the industry make.[79] Prahalad and Hamel, by comparing many global multi-national companies, have argued that successful companies are those that work with a strategic intent and marshal their core competencies to achieve that intent.[80]

Another popular topic among researchers is the empirical study of the **critical success factors** associated with company performances. There is a burgeoning literature on the identi-fication of these factors. Liu and Arnett identify the critical success factors in family businesses run by immigrant communities;[81] Nam and Herbert identify those in export businesses;[82] Katsikeas, Deng and Wotzel identify those for multinational professional service companies;[83] Dwyer, Hill and Martin identify those for personal selling;[84] and Yusof and Aspinwall identify those for small and medium-sized enterprises.[85]

> **critical success factors**
> Factors that invariably lead to the success of a strategy

The goal is to identify a set of factors that ensure success for a company. These factors have been called critical success factors, key success factors and simply success factors. Many scholars believe that this approach is an oversimplification of a highly complex situation because a host of factors influence performances of companies.[86] Critical success factors are defined as 'areas that a company must do well in order to succeed' but judging success and failure is not always easy. [87] One strategy could be judged as a success and a failure at the same time. Consider Honda's entry into the US market. Honda intended to sell large motorcycles but could not make many sales because its product did not work in the US market; the eventual success of Honda's smaller Supercubs was an accident. Honda thus failed in its strategy of selling large motorcycles but was successful in selling small motorcycles. Evaluation of success and failure also depends on the perceptions of people who judge the performances of strategies. These judgments may vary even from one generation to another. Evaluation of success and failure further depends on the time frame, so that a strategy may be considered a failure in the short but not in the long term. Judgements of success and failure also reflect the criteria used to evaluate performances. A company may be judged a failure on financial criteria, but a success in innovation. Criteria to judge success and failure may vary across sectors. In public sector activities, for example, equity is more important than effectiveness as a performance indicator. Consider the following examples where a range of critical success factors has been identified.

- Gordon Cairns, CEO of Lion Breweries, said that global branding and distribution are the key success factors for building an international wine business.[88]
- A study of 500 of the world's best unknown companies demonstrated that innovation is the most important success factor in the manufacturing industry.[89]
- Michael Chaney, managing director of Wesfarmers, said that the most important factor behind his company's success was that the management team worked as a close-knit team.[90]

Others, however, consider that the effort to identify success factors is not in vain. Through consistent effort and empirical studies refined by newer and newer concepts and frameworks, it should be possible to identify factors that will help lead companies to success. To achieve that, it is necessary to analyse current research findings on critical success factors and build a conceptual framework for judging how important the factors are to a strategy's success or failure.[91]

strategy in action 12.3

KIA Carnival's increasing market share

KIA Carnival is the highest-selling motor vehicle in the people-mover segment in Australia. Since its introduction in the late 1990s, the car has consistently increased its market share. In October 1999, the month when it was first introduced to the Australian market, KIA Carnival sold six more units than the market leader Toyota Tarago. Table 12.1 shows that between 2002 and 2004, KIA Carnival has not only doubled the number of units it sold but also has almost doubled its market share of the people-mover segment compared with Toyota Tarago.

Table 12.1: Comparative volume sale and market share of Toyota Tarago and KIA Carnival

	2002		2003		2004	
	Volume	Share (%)	Volume	Share (%)	Volume	Share (%)
Kia Carnival	2582	20.2	2634	22.2	5259	34.5
Toyota Tarago	2925	22.9	2736	23.1	2930	19.2

One of the main reasons of its popularity is its price. At a starting price of $29 990, which is two-thirds of the price of other competing people movers, the car offers all the space and features. This price, which is standard for most large family sedans, has made a people mover affordable to many Australian families. With a 2.5-litre, V6 engine, the car is powerful enough to carry its seven passengers and daily shopping. Many of the features, such as air-conditioning,

power mirrors, central locking, six-speaker stereo, that cost extra in family sedans come as standard in KIA Carnival. In terms of occupant safety, the car is also competitive. It comes with an energy-absorbing steering wheel, dual airbags, lap-sash seatbelts and child locks, to name only a few features. Versatility is one of the most important selling points of the KIA Carnival. Its second- and third-row seats can be completely removed for cargo space if necessary. Seats can also be adjusted to create extra legroom or folded down to convert them into tables. This expanding market share and success does not mean KIA is sitting idle. In January 2006, KIA will introduce an eight-seater Grand Carnival powered by a 3.8-litre V6 engine.

KIA, established in 1962, is the oldest carmaker in South Korea. It now exports more than 10 million cars to 147 countries. It has so far sold 110 000 vehicles in Australia. It has design centres in Detroit, Los Angles, Frankfurt, Tokyo and Seoul and has assembly plants in Europe, the Middle East and Asia.

Sources: Kia, www.kia.com.au; *Fastlane* 1999, 'All-new V6 Carnival dominates people mover sales', 8 November, accessed 25 January 2006, www.fastlane.com.au/news/Kia_Carnival_firstmonth.htm; Pettendy, M 2005, 'Kia Australia to launch new eight-seater Grand Carnival four months early in January,' *Carsales*, 23 December, accessed 25 January 2006, http://editorial.carsales.com.au/mellor/mellor.nsf/story/0046959B73C54DDFCA2570DF007F4474?OpenDocument&Highlight=2,kia%20carnival; L Polk Australia 2004, 'New vehicle sales — 2004', *Polk News*, accessed 25 January 2006, www.automotivepersonnel.com.au/news/2004/2004v.pdf#search='kia%20carnival%20market%20share'; —— 2003, 'New vehicle sales — 2003', *Polk News*, accessed 25 January 2006, www.automotivepersonnel.com.au/news/2003/2003.pdf.

The concept of 'criticality' has been defined loosely and subjectively in the literature, leading to considerable confusion in the use of the term. Managers and consultants do not clarify what they mean by 'criticality'. The importance of a factor to strategy success may occur to different degrees: a factor may be causally related to or only remotely associated with the success of a company. A company's understanding of its critical success factors is greatly improved if it can understand the different levels of criticality of those factors. Williams and Ramaprasad have developed a taxonomy based on four levels of criticality and three sets of dichotomous attributes.[92] The four levels of criticality (in descending order of strength) are: (1) factors that are linked to success by a known causal mechanism; (2) factors that are necessary and sufficient for success; (3) factors that are necessary for success and (4) factors that are associated with success.

A *causally related factor* ensures the success of a company. A causal relation, in addition, 'suggests that a series of events lead from the factor to success, and these events are governed by one or more known laws; we are not only able to claim the result but also able to explain the chain of events which leads to the result'.[93] A *sufficient factor* is that one whose presence guarantees success. A *necessary factor* is one that has to be present but that does not ensure success. The difference between a causal and a sufficient condition is that the company with the former would also know the mechanism and process through which factors work to bring success.

Williams and Ramaprasad's three pairs of dichotomous attributes of critical success factors are: (1) standing or instigating attributes; (2) direct or indirect attributes and (3) enhancing or inhibiting attributes.[94] They add that these six attributes represent six different possible relationships between the critical success factor and success. One can identify other attributes too.

A *standing critical success factor* is present over a long period of time and acts like an environment conducive to success, while an *instigating factor* provides the trigger, in conjunction with the standing factors, for success. A standing factor is necessary but not sufficient for success. A set of critical success factors would normally combine a number of standing and instigating factors. While *direct factors* are related to success, *indirect factors* affect success through their effect on other factors. A factor may affect strategy success both directly and indirectly. A company can develop a 'cause map' linking many direct and indirect factors with its performances. *Enhancing factors* aid success, while *inhibiting factors* prevent companies from achieving success. Commonly, this pair are also known as positive and negative factors. Managers and authors of strategic management place disproportionate emphasis on enhancers; emphasis should also be placed on identifying critical failure factors.

Managers would like to know the causal critical success factors but empirical studies have concentrated on factors that are associated only with company performances. In other words, current research has focused more on examining the weakest rather than the strongest type of criticality. One simple reason is that it is easier to establish the weakest relationship and most difficult to make conclusions about the strongest relationship.

In terms of attributes, researchers have preferred to focus more on factors that instigate, direct and enhance success. One explanation for such preferences is that the effects of these factors are easier to discern than the effects of factors that are standing, indirect and inhibiting. Moreover, managers are likely to be comfortable in taking action based on the former group of factors rather than on the latter group of factors.

The establishment of a causal relationship demonstrates the strongest relationship between factors and company performance and provides managers with the most certain knowledge about the course of action they should follow. Although current research focuses on studying associations between factors and company performance, 'it would again be logical to expect a progression from a simple association to complex causal mechanisms'.[95]

Intended and emergent processes of strategy evaluation

This book has emphasised the concepts of intended and emergent strategies. If you are a careful reader, you will have noticed that evaluation can also be logically viewed in these terms. In the intended strategy evaluation process, companies evaluate strategies in terms of the goals originally selected for the strategies. These goals are not subject to change: managers rigidly adhere to the goals selected at the time of the strategy formulation and make every effort not to deviate from this goal. A strategy that does not achieve its goal is considered a failure. The emergent strategy evaluation process is quite messy. Although managers have goals, they do not rigidly adhere to them while implementing strategies. Managers believe that strategies look towards an environment that is fast changing, unpredictable and distant, and that they must continually adapt to this changing environment by changing their goals. They thus evaluate strategies against the changed goals rather than the original goals. Considering the Honda case, you would come to two different conclusions if you followed these two different processes of evaluation. One of the Honda executives indicated that the goal was to sell motorcycles and that the company was not really concerned whether it sold large or small motorcycles.

Summary

This chapter discusses evaluation as an assessment of the performance of strategies, focusing on issues such as the significance of evaluation, challenges in designing an evaluation system and various methods of evaluation. Instead of identifying critical success factors for strategies, the chapter discusses a framework that can help managers understand factors that contribute to strategy success. The following are the main points of the chapter:

▶ Strategy evaluation performs multiple functions. In addition to the traditional function of providing information about the performances of strategies (that is, the learning function), strategy evaluation performs control and public relations functions.

▶ Evaluation design requires managers to set and operationalise goals, determine a time frame for evaluating strategies, determine who will evaluate the strategies and who will judge the results of strategies, and decide how data will be collected about the performance of strategies.

▶ There are many methods for strategy evaluation, each of which varies in the outcomes and measures used.

▶ Financial evaluation assesses strategies from the perspective of shareholders. It is simple and straightforward, often using standard accounting tools and techniques. Often, however, it does not provide much information about the likely future performance of a strategy.

▶ The balanced scorecard emphasises four perspectives that help a company evaluate its strategies both in the short term and long term. The four perspectives are the financial perspective, the customer perspective, the internal business process perspective and the innovation and learning perspective. The balanced scorecard approach involves the processes of (a) translation of the vision, (b) communication, (c) business planning and (d) feedback and learning.

▶ Triple bottom line reporting requires companies to evaluate their performances in terms of the environmental bottom line, the social justice bottom line and the economic bottom line, based on the argument that a business, in addition to its economic or financial roles, has responsibilities to society and the environment because these sustain the business.

▶ Managers have several options after they evaluate their strategies. They can continue with a strategy or terminate it.

▶ Managers sometimes continue with failed strategies in what is known as a nonrational escalation of commitment.

▶ The chapter argues that based on the current state of knowledge about strategic management, it is not possible to identify factors that determine the success of strategies. It therefore discusses a framework that is likely to help managers understand factors that influence the success or failure of their strategies.

▶ In the intended strategy evaluation process, managers evaluate strategies in terms of the goals originally selected for the strategies. Managers rigidly adhere to the goals selected at the time of strategy formulation.

▶ In the emergent strategy evaluation process, managers believe that strategies look towards an environment that is fast changing, unpredictable and distant, and that they must continually adapt to this changing environment by changing their goals. They evaluate strategies against the changed goals rather than the original goals.

Practising strategic management

Review questions

1. Distinguish between evaluation of strategic alternatives that occurs while strategies are being formulated and evaluation of strategies that occurs after strategies have been implemented.
2. How can strategy evaluation help improve public relations?
3. Describe some of the challenges of designing an evaluation system.
4. Discuss the importance of the four balanced scorecard processes.
5. What challenges are faced when implementing the triple bottom line reporting method of strategy evaluation?

Discussion questions

6. 'Strategy evaluation is a waste of company resources and managerial time.' Do you agree with this statement? Argue your case.
7. 'The emphasis of the balanced scorecard on its four perspectives is not balanced'. Discuss.
8. 'Companies following the triple bottom line reporting method are likely to make less profit than the companies that do not'. Discuss.
9. Do you think low price is the most critical factor for the success of products? Explain your position.

Applied questions

10. Discuss the evaluation method that Loy Yang Power (discussed in the opening case) uses for its performance evaluation.
11. Identify the factors for Kia Carnival's increased market share in Australia (discussed in Strategy in action 12.3).
12. Discuss the issues associated with pay for performance (discussed in Strategy in action 12.1).

Small-group exercise

Break into groups of three to five participants and assess the relative suitability of the balanced scorecard and the triple bottom line as methods of evaluating strategies. In your assessment, answer the following questions.
1. What are the basic features of the balanced scorecard and triple bottom line?
2. What are the advantages and disadvantages of each method?
3. Which method would you use to evaluate strategies if you were the manager of a company? Why?
4. Would you use any other method? Why?
5. What could be a few indicators to measure the social bottom line of a company?

Article file

Find an example of a company that recently successfully implemented a strategy. Identify the strategy's key success factors and how important they were to the success of the strategy.

Exploring the Web

Visiting Mitsubishi Australia

Visit the website of Mitsubishi Motor Corporation Australia (www.mitsubishi-motors.com.au) and review the company's Australian operations. Using the information available on the website, answer the following questions:
1. Identify the problems that the company has faced in recent years.
2. Do you think the company has escalated its commitment by continuing its operations in Australia?
3. Do you think that the company should have terminated its Australian operations? Argue your case.

Strategic management project

Module 12

Examine whether your company has a process in place to evaluate its strategies.
1. Identify a strategy that your company has implemented.
2. Find out whether your company has evaluated this strategy.
3. Identify the type of evaluation process — intended or emergent — that your company has followed.
4. Learn the results of this evaluation — that is, whether it was a success or failure.
5. Examine the criteria that your company used to reach its conclusion about the strategy.

Additional resources

Alajoutsijarvi, K, Moller, K & Tahtinen, J 2000, 'Beautiful exit: how to leave your business partner', *European Journal of Marketing*, vol. 34, pp. 1270–89. (An empirical study of terminating a buyer–seller relationship, expanding on the issues discussed in the chapter.)

Chia, A & Hoon, SS 2000, 'Adopting and creating balanced scorecards in Singapore-based companies', *Singapore Management Review*, vol. 22, pp. 1–15. (An empirical study on strategy evaluation, discussing the challenges of implementing the balanced scorecard in an Asian context.)

Dess, GG & Robinson, RB 1984, 'Measuring organizational performance in the absence of objective measures: the case of the privately-held firm and conglomerate business unit', *Strategic Management Journal*, vol. 5, pp. 265–73. (A discussion of the sources of data about the performances of strategies.)

Elkington, J 1997, *Cannibals with forks: the triple bottom line of 21st century business*, Capstone, Oxford. (A comprehensive account of aspects of the triple bottom line reporting such as social capital, environmental capital, implementation, accounting and accountability issues.)

Kloot, L & Martin, J 2000, 'Strategic performance measurement: a balanced approach to performance management issues in local government', *Management Accounting Research*, vol. 11, pp. 231–51. (A study of performance evaluation in terms of the balanced scorecard in the local governments of Victoria, examining issues generated by the application of concepts developed for the private sector to the public sector.)

Mair, A 1999, 'Learning from Honda', *Journal of Management Studies*, vol. 36, pp. 25–41. (An argument that there are many empirical inaccuracies in viewing the case of Honda's entry into the United States as a great success.)

End notes

1. Rumelt, R 1996, 'Evaluating business strategy', in Mintzberg, H & Quinn, JB (eds), *The strategy process: concepts, context and cases*, 3rd edn, Prentice Hall, New Jersey, pp. 55–63. For a recent discussion and development of this meaning see, Moroney, M 2000, Strategy evaluation: towards an updated paradigm, IBAR *Journal of the Irish Academy of Management*, vol. 21, no. 1, pp. 103–29.
2. Mason, EJ & Bramble, WJ 1997, *Research in education and the behavioral sciences: concepts and methods*, Brown & Benchmark, Madison, Wisconsin, p. 352.
3. Rose, J & Haynes, M 1999, 'A soft system approach to the evaluation of complex interventions in the public sector', *Journal of Applied Management*, vol. 8, pp. 199–216.
4. Hogwood, BW & Gunn, LA 1984, *Policy analysis for the real world*, Oxford University Press, Oxford, p. 218.
5. Viljoen, J & Dann, S 2000, *Strategic management: planning, implementing successful corporate strategies*, 3rd edn, Pearson, Sydney, p. 556.
6. Goldenberg, EN 1983, 'The three faces of evaluation', *Journal of Policy Analysis and Management*, vol. 4, pp. 515–25.
7. Goldenberg, op. cit., p. 516.
8. *Australian Financial Review* 2000, 'Shareholder value versus executive pay', 31 August.
9. Cornell, A 2002, 'The fixer', *Australian Financial Review*, 10 May.
10. Hogwood & Gunn, op. cit., p. 220.
11. Cyert, RM & March, JG 1963, *A behavioral theory of the firm*, Prentice Hall, Englewood Cliffs, New Jersey.
12. Kaplan, RS & Norton, DP 1992, 'The balanced scorecard — measures that drive performance', *Harvard Business Review*, January–February, pp. 71–9.
13. Cooper, DR & William Emory, C 1995 *Business research methods*, 5th edn, Irwin, Chicago, p. 115.
14. Hogwood & Gunn, op. cit., p. 221.
15. Thompson, JL 1997, *Strategic management: awareness and change*, 3rd edn, Thomson, London, p. 187.
16. Carew, E 1985, *The language of money*, George Allen & Unwin, Sydney.
17. Ehrbar, A 1999, 'Using EVA to measure performance and assess strategy', *Strategy and Leadership*, May–June, pp. 20–4.
18. Lehn, K & Makhija, AK, 1996, 'EVA and MVA as performance measures and signals for strategic change', *Strategy and Leadership*, May–June, pp. 34–8.
19. Wheelen, TL & Hunger, JD 2002, *Strategic management and business policy*, 8th edn, Prentice Hall, Upper Saddle River, New Jersey, p. 249
20. Voelker, KE, Rakich, JS & French, R, 'The balanced scorecard in healthcare organizations: a performance measurement and strategic planning methodology', *Hospital Topics*, vol. 3, 2001, pp. 13–24.
21. Kaplan & Norton, op. cit., p. 71.
22. Kaplan, RS & Norton, DP 1996a, 'Linking the balanced scorecard to strategy', *California Management Review*, vol. 39, p. 56.
23. Shih-Jen, K & McKay, RB 2002, 'Balanced scorecard: two perspectives', *The CPA Journal*, March, p. 21.
24. Kaplan & Norton 1992, op. cit., p. 77.
25. ibid.
26. Kaplan & Norton 1996a, op. cit., p. 57.
27. ibid., p. 58.
28. ibid., p. 63.
29. Kaplan & Norton 1992, op. cit., p. 75.
30. Kaplan, RS & Norton, DP 1996b, 'Using the balanced scorecard as a strategic management system', *Harvard Business Review*, January–February, p. 78.
31. ibid., p. 81.
32. ibid., pp. 83–4.
33. ibid., p. 84.
34. ibid.
35. Mootaj, S Oyon, D & Hostettler, D 1999, 'The balanced scorecard: a necessary good or an unnecessary evil', *European Management Journal*, vol. 17, pp. 481–91.
36. Kaplan & Norton 1992, op. cit., pp. 77–8.
37. Kaplan & Norton 1996, op. cit., p. 65.
38. ibid.
39. Kaplan & Norton 1992, op. cit., p. 73.
40. Atkinson, AA, Waterhouse, JH & Wells, RB 1997, 'A stakeholder approach to strategic performance measurement', *Sloan Management Review*, Spring, pp. 25–37.
41. Epstein, M & Manzoni, J-F 1998, 'Implementing corporate strategy: from tableaux de board to balanced scorecards', *European Management Journal*, vol. 16, pp. 190–203.
42. ibid.

43. Ahn, H 2001, 'Applying the balanced scorecard concept: an experience report', *Long Range Planning*, vol. 34, pp. 441–61.
44. Shih-Jen & McKay, op. cit., pp. 24–5.
45. Epstein & Manzoni, op. cit., p. 200.
46. Hoque, Z & James, W 2000, 'Linking balanced scorecard measures to size and market factors: impact on organizational performance', *Journal of Management Accounting Research*, vol. 12, pp. 1–17.
47. Sauvante, M 2001, 'The "triple bottom line": a boardroom guide', *Director's Monthly*, vol. 25, pp. 2–6.
48. Elkington, J 1999a, 'Triple bottom line reporting: looking for balance', *Australian CPA*, March, pp. 18–21.
49. Whittaker, M 1999, 'Emerging triple bottom line model for industry weighs environmental, economic and social considerations', *Oil and Gas Journal*, vol. 20, p. 23.
50. Hayward, SF n.d., 'The triple bottom line: authentic model or tripartite nonsense?', accessed 7 April 2003, www.cdfe.org/bottom_line.htm.
51. ibid.
52. Sauvante, op. cit., p. 3.
53. ibid., p. 4.
54. Wilson, M & Lombardi, R 2001, 'Globalization and its discontent: the arrival of triple-bottom-line reporting', *Ivey Business Journal*, September–October, pp. 69–72.
55. Sauvante, op. cit., p. 4.
56. Whittaker, op. cit., p. 23.
57. Elkington, J 1999b, 'The triple bottom line: implications for the oil industry', *Oil and Gas Journal*, vol. 13, p. 140.
58. O'Donovan, G 2002, 'Triple bottom line solution', *Australian CPA*, April, pp. 14–15.
59. Elkington 1999a, op. cit., p. 19.
60. ibid.
61. ibid.
62. ibid., p. 21.
63. Sauvante, op. cit., pp. 5–6.
64. Bazerman, M 1998, *Judgment in managerial decision making*, 4th edn, John Wiley & Sons, New York, 1998, p. 67.
65. ibid., p. 99.
66. ibid., pp. 73–4.
67. Brockner, J 1992, 'The escalation of commitment to a failing course of action: toward theoretical progress', *Academy of Management Review*, vol. 17, p. 40.
68. ibid., p. 41.
69. Bazerman, op. cit., p. 75.
70. Drummond, H 1995, 'De-escalation in decision making: a case of partnership', *Journal of Management Studies*, vol. 32, pp. 265–81.
71. See, for example, Daniels, MR 2001, 'Policy and organizational termination', *International Journal of Public Administration*, vol. 24, pp. 249–62; Geva-May, I 2001, 'When the motto is "till death do us part": the conceptualization and the craft of termination in the public policy cycle', *International Journal of Public Administration*, vol. 24, pp. 263–88; Norris-Tirrell, D 2001 'Organization termination or evolution: mergers in the nonprofit sector', *International Journal of Public Administration*, vol. 24, pp. 311–22; Harris, M 2001, 'Policy termination: the case of term limits in Michigan', *International Journal of Public Administration*, vol. 24, pp. 323–39.
72. Giller, C & Matear, S, 2001 'The termination of inter-firm relationships', *Journal of Business and Industrial Marketing*, vol. 16, p. 94.
73. ibid., p. 95.
74. Drummond, op. cit., pp. 269–73.
75. ibid., p. 275.
76. Parnell, JA, Wright, P & Tu, HS 1996, 'Beyond the strategy–performance linkage: the impact of the strategy–organization–environment fit on business performance', *American Business Review*, vol. 14, pp. 41–50.
77. Miles, R & Snow, CC 1984, 'Fit failure and the hall of fame', *California Management Review*, vol. 26, pp. 10–28.
78. ibid., p. 10.
79. Porter, ME 1996, 'How competitive forces shape strategy', in Mintzberg, H & Quinn, JB (eds), *The strategy process: concepts, context and cases*, 3rd edn, Prentice Hall, Englewood Cliffs, New Jersey, pp. 75–83.
80. Prahalad, CK & Hamel, G 1990, 'The core competence of the corporation', *Harvard Business Review*, May–June.
81. Liu, C & Arnett, KP 2000, 'Exploring factors associated with web site success in the context of electronic commerce', *Information and Management*, vol. 38, pp. 23–33.
82. Nam Y-H & Herbert, JI 1999, 'Characteristics and key success factors in family business: the case of Korean immigrant businesses in metro-Atlanta', *Family Business Review*, vol. 12, pp. 341–52.
83. Katsikeas, CS, Deng, SL & Wotzel, LW 1997, 'Perceived export success factors of small and medium-sized Canadian firms', *Journal of International Marketing*, vol. 5, pp. 53–72.
84. Dwyer, S, Hill, J & Martin, W 2000, 'An empirical investigation of critical success factors in the personal selling process for homogenous goods', *Journal of Personal Selling and Sales Management*, vol. 20, pp. 151–9.
85. Yusof, SM & Aspinwall, EM 2000, 'Critical success factors in small and medium enterprises: survey results', *Total Quality Management*, vol. 11, pp. 448–62.
86. Parnell, Wright & Tu, op. cit., p. 41.
87. Williams, JJ & Ramaprasad, A 1996, 'A taxonomy of critical success factors', *European Journal of Information Systems*, vol. 5, pp. 250–60.
88. Evans, S 2001, 'Lion stalks the wine purist's Petaluma', *Australian Financial Review*, vol. 6, October.
89. Charles, D 2002, 'Our rivals have jump on us over research', *Australian Financial Review*, vol. 17, October.
90. Klinger, P 2002, 'For business, the sun shines brighter in the east', *Australian Financial Review*, vol. 13, June.
91. Williams & Ramaprasad, op. cit., p. 251.
92. ibid., p. 250.
93. ibid., p. 252.
94. ibid., p. 253.
95. ibid., p. 257.

Strategic management in public organisations

learning objectives

After studying this chapter, you should be able to:

- appreciate the importance of strategic management in the public sector

- compare and contrast public organisations and business organisations

- debate the applicability of strategic management concepts to public organisations

- appreciate the challenges facing public organisations and measures that have been adopted

- compare the prescriptive and actual strategic planning processes of public organisations

- list the strategies that public organisations pursue

- apply a framework to study strategies adopted by public organisations.

opening case

Strategic planning at the EGHS

The East Grampians Health Service (EGHS), formed in 1995, is located in the Ararat Rural City Council, which is 202 km from Melbourne and 540 km from Adelaide. EGHS is a publicly funded organisation and also raises money from other sources. In 2003, it raised $700 000 from donations. EGHS is incorporated under the Health Services Act 1998, Victoria and is accountable to the minister of health of the state government of Victoria. It is governed by an eight-member board of management, which is equally divided between the two genders. These members are recommended by the minister of health and appointed by the governor-in-council of the state of Victoria. EGHS is obliged to comply with at least 34 acts, regulations and subordinate legislations.

EGHS has a nine member staff management group headed by a CEO.

Health services provided by EGHS include hospital services, aged-care services, allied health services, community health services, home nursing services, diagnostic services, support group services and acute bed services.

The strategic plan of EGHS is part of a three-tier EGHS strategic and operational planning framework. EGHS' strategic plan, spanning from 2001 to 2005, is at the top tier and encompasses four mid-tier plans. They are the EGHS Service and Human Resource Plan, EGHS Facilities Master Plan, EGHS Information Technology Plan and the EGHS Quality and Risk Management Plan. The EGHS Operational Plan 2001–2004, forming the third tier of the framework, is a short-term plan that details how the strategic plan should be accomplished. The plan identifies vision, core values and philosophy related to each objective, planned outcomes, strategies, evaluation mechanisms and key performance indicators for each objective. With a vision '…to be always moving forward', EGHS's core values include integrity, dignity, respect, empathy, creativity, individual and collective contribution and success. Organisational objectives include customer focus, quality services, partnership with stakeholders, equitable service access, skilled workforce, effective management and rural leadership. The strategic planning scheme is illustrated in table 13.1 with an example from the equitable service access objective, something specific to public organisations.

EGHS' operational plan also identifies targets and the roles of various functional units, such as top management, human resources and information systems, in achieving each of them.

Sources: East Grampians Health Service n.d., 'Strategic plan 2001–2005', accessed 8 January 2006, www.eghs.net.au/opplan/Strategic%20Plan.pdf.; —— n.d., 'Operational Plan 2001–2004', accessed 11 August 2005, www.eghs. net.au/; —— 2003, 'Newsletter', October, 2nd edn, accessed 11 August 2005, www.eghs.net.au.

Table 13.1: EGHS strategic planning for equitable service

Planned outcomes/strategies	Evaluation mechanism	Performance indicator
An EGHS marketing plan is developed and implemented	Evidence of raised community awareness of range of services provided or accessible through EGHS	A trend of higher scores for community awareness surveys
The service has single point of entry	Evidence of community awareness and satisfaction with the entry process	A trend of higher scores for community awareness and satisfaction with access
Cultural and disability issues relevant to community access to EGHS services are addressed	Evidence of community satisfaction with service access	Patient/customer satisfaction rates
There are transparent processes to prioritise community access to services	Evidence of policies defining processes and accountability related to prioritising waiting times and lists	Not identified
Relevant patient/customer information is available for all services	Evidence of regular review and evaluation processes for all patient and customer information	Rates of patient/customer satisfaction with information
Inclusion of health promotion and health status evaluation strategies in care pathways and/or guidelines	Evidence of evaluation of changes in health status resulting from identified services	Changes in patient health status assessment scores

Source: East Grampians Health Service n.d., 'Strategic plan 2001–2005', accessed 8 January 2006, www.eghs.net.au/opplan/Strategic%20Plan.pdf.

Overview

So far, the focus has been on strategic management of privately owned organisations or companies, also called business organisations. But there is also strategic management in public organisations. Many of you will find your employment in public organisations and all of you are affected by public organisations, which include, in Australia, federal, state and local governments. This discussion should also be applicable to nonprofit organisations because they display more similarity to public organisations than to business organisations. Nonprofit organisations in most cases, similarly to public organisations, do not work for profit and instead survive on revenues received from their sponsors rather than the recipients of their services. Business organisations, to the contrary, get their revenues from the sale of their products and services.

An understanding of strategic management in the public organisation requires an appreciation of the unique characteristics of public organisations as noted. This discussion should provide you with an appreciation why strategic management may not be applicable as it is applied in business organisations. It must be remembered that the concepts and theories of strategic management were developed mainly in the context of business organisations. Application of them makes sense only when one works in a competitive environment. Many public organisations face no competitors at all.

Since the end of World War II, public organisations have been under threat from many fronts. They are claimed to be inefficient, ineffective, full of red tape, customer unfriendly, procedure rather than results oriented, to name just a few shortcomings. Governments and sponsors who fund public organisations have in many countries risen to the challenge and introduced fundamental reforms. In this region, New Zealand is one of the countries that have taken this business-like reform to an extreme. Australia, however, has always followed a cautious path.

One aspect of this strategic reform is strategic planning. Having considered the reforms introduced by public organisations, the chapter discusses the linear strategic planning model proposed by Bryson. This discussion is followed by a few empirical studies that examine the experiences of implementing such linear planning models in public organisations. The result seems to be quite mixed.

The second aspect of strategic reforms introduced to the public organisations is the adoption of strategies. Unfortunately, there are not many studies in this area. Scholars seem to have focused more on the planning process rather than on strategies themselves, that is, the outcome of this planning process. Here the chapter looks at one study of strategies pursued by a few departments of state in the United States. This section closes with a discussion of a framework that has been developed to study strategies pursued by public organisations. The framework is interesting and promising because it brings Miles and Snow's framework (see page 408), which has been extensively applied in the research on business organisations into research in public organisations.

Importance of studying strategic management in the public sector

All students of business should know at least something about the public sector for several reasons. The public sector, with its three levels of government, is one of the largest employers in almost all countries, including Australia. The public sector spends a large portion of the nation's income. There is hardly any business or industry that is not somehow controlled or regulated by the government. An understanding of governmental processes greatly helps business managers to manage their relationship with the government. There is another conceptual advantage in assessing the applicability of strategic management concepts to the public sector.

Most theories of strategic management are concerned with private sector organisations, for which market-driven competition provides the basis for the conceptualisation of the discipline.[1] An attempt to discuss strategic management in the public sector brings out many underlying assumptions of the concepts of strategic management that most students of business take for granted.

Defining public organisations

Conventionally, two broad types of organisations are identified: **public organisations** and **business organisations**. Public organisations are publicly owned and are equated with government organisations while business organisations are privately owned. This dichotomous view is too simplistic because organisations vary not only in terms of their ownership but also on other dimensions. This dimensional approach to publicness argues that most organisations would have some elements of publicness and some characteristics of business organisations. In other words, most organisations are mixtures of public and private features. Very few organisations are purely public or purely business type. The dimensional approach assesses organisations, varying from the most to the least public along some dimensions and, therefore, is capable of understanding hybrid organisations in relation to public and business ideal types.[2]

> **public organisations**
> Organisations that provide services and products free of charge working in an environment that provides very little competition

> **business organisations**
> Organisations that sell their services and products in a competitive market environment

The following section discusses the dimensions of publicness to understand the distinct context within which public organisations, including government organisations and innumerable numbers of nonprofit organisations, work. These dimensions are discussed by systematically comparing public organisations and business organisations. In doing this, the essential features of business organisations are also clarified.

Markets

Business organisations are market organisations and they face two interrelated markets. In the input markets, they buy scarce resources to produce their output, that is, products and services. In the output markets, business organisations sell their products and services in a voluntary **quid pro quo** transaction to buyers, who pay money in return. In the case of business organisations, these two markets are interrelated because they get their revenues from those whom they sell their products and services to. Public organisations are not market organisations. They do not sell their products and services. The relationship between public organisations and their clients is neither voluntary nor of the quid pro quo type. Public organisations do not get their revenues directly from those whom they 'sell' their products and services to. They get their revenues from their sponsors, which could be from the government, private charities or donations. This situation indicates that, in the case of public organisations, the input and output markets are dissociated.[3] Public organisations exist in a triangular relationship, with recipients of their services on one side and the financiers of their operations on the other.

> **quid pro quo**
> An exchange relationship in which a buyer pays for the services or products received

For business organisations, sales provide information about their performance. Business organisations can tell from sales figures how are they doing. They provide an excellent source of measurable information to evaluate performance. There is no such information about the performances of public organisations because they do not sell their products or services, unless there is major complaint about the performances or actions of public organisations.[4] Business organisations come to know the preferences of their customers through their sales. Absence of performance data in the case of public organisations means that they organise public consultations, meetings, announcements, task forces to know and to refine the preferences of their clients. These consultations often lead to inertia, conflicts and clashes.[5] The services that clients receive from pure public organisations are free. Although these recipients of services do not directly pay for the services they receive, they do pay taxes. Currently, no mechanisms exist that can match the taxes paid by each citizen with the services they receive from public organisations.[6]

Dependence on nonmarket sources for revenue is therefore one of the criteria of public-ness. Pure public organisations are totally dependent on nonmarket sources for their income. Departments of defence and police are examples of these. However, their publicness would decline if they were allowed to raise funds in return for specific services provided to the public. For example, many public universities raise two-thirds of their revenues from fees (tuition) or from grants obtained by academic staff.[7]

Competition among providers

Business organisations operate in markets that are competitive. Several business organ-isations will be in one market, competing for buyers. In the fast-food market, for example, KFC, McDonald's and Red Rooster compete for buyers. Public organisations do not compete with one another. Rather, they are expected to collaborate in providing services. Creation of competition in the provision of public services is viewed as duplication of services and a waste of public money. Public organisations are required to provide services in a particular geographic area, and in that geographic area there would be only one public organisation. For example, a police department would have no competitor in a catchment area where it provides security services. Moreover, people who 'buy' products from public organisations are in most cases captive buyers. They have no option or choice to go elsewhere with regard to the services they receive.[8]

Autonomy

autonomy
The degree of freedom organisations have in pursuing their strategies

Public organisations are created by statutes, which limit the autonomy that they have in carrying out their work. Public organisations have less autonomy than business organisations in adding or carrying out services and even the methods and procedures they follow in delivering services. For example, statutes that create fire and law enforcement departments limit them to providing services in a particular geographic area and stipulate the services they must provide. Statutes do not allow them to market for new customers. For instance, a welfare administrator might know how to improve fund disbursement efficiency but, without petitioning a legis-lative body, has no way to initiate useful changes.[9]

Public organisations are not as free as business organisations to select their strategies from a wide range of available options. For example, business organisations can stop selling unprof-itable products and introduce a new one with a hope to earn more profit. They can change the quality of their products or change the prices of their products. Public organisations are unlikely to have this sort of autonomy, and are likely to have these strategic matters decided for them. For example, in recent years, local governments in Australia and the UK have been required to contract out specified proportions of their services as part of a quest for efficiency savings. Public organisations have their freedom to manoeuvre limited by the imposition of regulations.[10]

Coercion

coercion
A situation in which an organisation, for example the government, can force its 'clients' to comply with its policies

Public organisations, particularly many governmental ones, can exercise coercion. For example, individuals cannot decide whether to pay tax. Neither can they decide how much they want to pay.[11] Refusal to pay tax can lead to arrest because government has 'the monopoly of the legitimate use of physical force within a given territory'.[12] Consider the authority that the departments of police and immigration exercised in putting Cornelia Rau first in jail and then in a detention centre, as discussed in Strategy in action 13.1.

Scope of impact

Public organisations are expected to deal with a greater variety of social concerns than are business organisations. Schools, for example, are expected to deal with poverty, racism, child abuse, juvenile crime and many other social problems in addition to their normal work of provision of education. Communities have less expectation that business organisations should be concerned with these issues.[13] Actions of public organisations, particularly those of government organisations, make a broader impact than those of business organisations. The impact of the policies of the department of education would be felt throughout a country but a business organisation's actions, no matter how large it is, are unlikely to have as wide an effect.

Public scrutiny

Laws demand public organisations to be transparent in their plans, strategies and operations. Almost everything that public organisations do can be subject to scrutiny. The concept of 'fishbowl management' aptly describes the management style that public organisations work under. Their work is scrutinised by the parliament, the press, general public, interest groups and an army of judicial and quasi-judicial bodies. Many quasi-judicial bodies even possess the authority to question the basis of decisions made by public organisations.[14] Consider the public hue and cry that was raised about Cornelia Rau, as discussed in Strategy in action 13.1.

Ownership

Public organisations are owned by the whole society. Everyone owns them. They are expected to provide such services as police protection, sanitation, and social welfare for the maintenance of the social infrastructure, which is usually not provided by business organisations.[15] Public organisations are expected to conduct their business not only with efficiency but also with equity. Business organisations are privately owned and so are not under this obligation.[16] For example, one of the most important objectives of the East Grampians Health Service (see opening case) is the provision of equitable service.

Multiple goals

Public organisations usually have multiple goals, which are both vague and conflicting. There is no 'bottom line' that can be used as a proxy measure of success in public organisations. This provides opportunities for stakeholders of public organisations to develop expectations that are frequently conflicting. For example, public hospitals are judged using one set of standards by insurers, another by patients, another by medical staff and another by their board of trustees.[17] Along with the nonmarket characteristics of public organisations, goal ambiguity and goal multiplicity make performance expectations confused and difficult to specify. Public organisations generate multiple, therefore conflicting expectations about their performance. No one really knows for sure what to expect from public organisations.[18] Objectives that usually clash are efficiency and equity.[19] Public organisations have learnt to deal with this clash by carefully listing and wording their objectives. Consider the list of objectives identified by the East Grampians Health Service in the opening case.

Separation of powers

Power is concentrated at the top in business organisations; in public organisations, the opposite is true. Public organisations are characterised by what political scientists call **separation of powers**. The three arms of government — executive, legislature and judiciary — are independent from one another. None of these arms can impose its power on another. They have

separation of powers
A situation in which the power of the organisation is divided among its constituent parts

different functions too. The executive proposes strategies and policies, the legislature approves these, and the judiciary adjudicates on their implementation and judges their validity. Different countries vary in carrying this through. For example, in the United States this separation is much sharper and clearer than in the countries following the UK-type parliamentary constitution. Power is separated to ensure checks and balances in its exercise. The effect of this separation quite frequently creates conflict between these arms, resulting in slow decision making.[20] Usually the first casualty of such an arrangement is efficiency. Many political scientists argue that government has not been created to be efficient.

A pure public organisation is a nonmarket organisation with coercive powers, owned by a political community that provides 'collective' services under extensive public scrutiny. The more an organisation displays these characteristics, the more it fulfils the conditions of a pure public organisation. Departments of police and defence are good examples of a pure public organisation.

In contrast, a pure business organisation is owned by private shareholders, operates in a market environment and is guided by the profit motive, with efficiency as the main consideration for its business operations. The more an organisation displays these features, the more it is a business organisation. McDonald's is an example of a pure business organisation. Most nonprofit and third-sector organisations, such as hospitals, trade unions and professional societies, will display characteristics that are closer to those of a public organisation. Most organisations, however, would combine these characteristics in their actual operations in innumerable ways.

strategy in action 13.1

Exercising the coercive power of the state: the case of Cornelia Rau

Cornelian Rau, 39, of German extraction, came to live in Australia when she was 18 months old. She worked for Qantas as a flight attendant and spoke English with a distinct Australian accent. She suffered from schizophrenia and never wanted to be in a hospital. She disappeared from the Manly Hospital Psychiatric wing, Sydney on 17 March 2004 and headed towards Queensland. She went as far as Coen, one of the most northerly towns in Australia. She had been staying near an Aboriginal community in the Cape York Peninsula, whose inhabitants became concerned that she was ill and brought her to the Cairns police in April 2004. There she introduced herself as Anna Brockmeyer.

The police checked with a number of databases but could not find anyone by that name in their records. The police handed her to the immigration department as a 'suspected unlawful non-citizen' because 'all the information provided by the woman led the department [of Immigration] to believe she was an unlawful non-citizen'.[21] Under section 189 of the Immigration Act, someone believed to be an 'unlawful non-citizen' could be required to produce records of identity such as passports, birth or marriage certificates, or his or her visa status, and if he or she were not cooperative, it is possible that he or she might be detained. She was put into jail without being charged with a crime. She spent six months in a jail in Queensland, where she called herself Anna Schmidt, until September 2004. Then she was sent to Baxter Detention Centre for illegal immigrants in South Australia, where she was held for four months.

Having noticed her unusual behaviour, which included eating mud, asylum seekers in the Baxter Detention Centre agitated on her behalf and a story appeared in *The Age* about a mystery German-speaking woman held at Baxter. The newspaper received a photograph from Chris Rau, which revealed her to be his missing sister, and promptly faxed this to the Baxter authorities.

Andrew Bartlett of the Australian Democratic Party visited the Baxter Detention Centre but the authorities refused to talk to him about Cornelia. Dr Louise Newman, chairwoman of the Royal Australian and New Zealand College of Psychiatrists was also refused permission to see her because Cornelia was 'incapable of giving us written permission', which is a requirement under the Immigration Act. The Opposition Labor party accused the police and immigration departments of ineptitude adding that: 'It's pretty dangerous if you have Alzheimer's disease or you speak a second language right now.'[22] Civil libertarians called for the federal government to be more transparent about what happens inside Australian detention centres. Mike Rann, premier of South Australia, said that it was an extraordinary human tragedy and added: 'To have an Australian citizen who has lived here virtually all her life arrested in one state, listed as a missing person in another and put in a Commonwealth detention centre in a third is incredible.'

Senator Amanda Vanstone, the minister for immigration, instituted an inquiry into the Cornelia Rau case.

Sources: McGary, A 2005, 'Mentally ill Aussie in detention centre', *The Australian*, 5 February; www.safecom.org.au/2005/02/finding-anna-when-immigration-gets-it.htm; Jackson, A 2005, 'This could happen to you: warning', *The Age*, 7 February, www.safecom.org.au/2005/02/finding-anna-when-immigration-gets-it.htm; *Advertiser* 2005, 'Clues to woman's identity missed', 6 February, accessed 11 August 2005, www.safecom.org.au/2005/02/finding-anna-when-immigration-gets-it.htm; Daly H 2005, 'Cornelia Rau: a case of neglect', *Sunday*, 13 March, accessed 11 August 2005, http:/Sunday.ninemsn.com.au/Sunday/cover_stories; ABC News Online 2005, 'Secrecy blamed for Rau's ordeal', 6 February, accessed 11 August 2005, www.abc.net.au/news/newsitems/200502/s1296993.htm; Hudson P & Skelton, R 2005, 'Minister rules out apology', *The Age*, 6 February, accessed 11 August 2005, www.theage.com.au/articles/2005/02/05/1107476857884.html; Seccombe, M & Jackson, A 2005, 'We cannot say sorry, says PM', *Sydney Morning Herald*, 7 February, accessed 11 August 2005, http://smh.com.au/news/National/We-cannot-say-sorry-says-PM/2005/02/06/1107625065196.html; Jackson, A 2005, 'Solved: mystery of "Anna"', *The Age*, 5 January, accessed 11 August 2005, www.theage.com.au/articles/2005/02/04/1107476803813.html; *Sydney Morning Herald* 2005, 'My sister lost her mind, and Australia lost its heart', 7 February, accessed 11 August 2005, www.smh.com.au/articles/2005/02/06/1107625064599.html; *Sydney Morning Herald* 2005, 'She spoke German: Vanstone defends Rau lock-up', 7 February, accessed 11 August 2005, www.smh.com.au/news/Immigration/Rau-detention-understandable-says-Vanstone/2005/02/07/1107625090700.html; DIMA 2005, 'Cornelia Rau inquiry', vps 030/2005, accessed 11 August 2005, www.minister.immi.gov.au/media_releases/media05/v05030.htm; *Sydney Morning Herald* 2005, 'Rau case exposes flaws in the system', 7 February, accessed 11 August 2005, www.smh.com.au/news/National/Dont-destroy-the-evidence-Raus-sister/2005/02/07/1107625101810.html.

Challenges faced by the public sector

Public organisations, particularly governments, became interested in strategic management only recently. Their interest developed for several reasons. The government has faced challenges since the end of World War II, some quite recent. There was a time when public organisations faced a relatively placid and predictable environment but that is no longer the case.[23] Now, changes surround them: in technology, demography and peoples' values. Most important of all, there is pressure from globalisation. People are demanding more services and more efficient delivery, yet refuse to pay higher taxes.[24]

Many argue that instead of serving the public, public organisations instead pay more attention to internal aspects: managers, processes and procedures and operations. Institutional economists and public choice theorists argue that public managers focus more on building empires and in maximising the budgets of their departments, rather than on achieving the purposes for which a budget is provided. Politicians often accuse public managers of being more interested in serving their own interests rather than those of the public or of the ministers. Very rarely do public organisations develop new products and services because they work in a virtual monopoly, in which their survival is almost never at stake.

Managerialists argue that the public organisations cling to traditional organisational design with an emphasis on rules and procedures rather than adopting flexible organisational design that provides managers with discretion in their work (particularly in personnel management and budgetary matters). Under this traditional design, managers act according to rules and procedures rather than to achieve results. In turn, they are held accountable for compliance with rules rather than for results. Neoconservatives argue that government has involved itself in too many diverse types of work — in particular social welfare, free education and public housing, which they should not be doing because they cannot manage them well.[25] Many believe that practice of strategic management provides a set of tools, concepts and procedures that can be of great use to governments in their response to this changed environment.[26]

Strategic approach to public sector management

managerialism
Importation of tools and practices of business organisations into public organisations

Many suggestions have been put forward to overcome the challenges faced by public organisations. In the UK, Australia and New Zealand, these suggestions have come in the form of managerialism and new public management, In the United States, a solution has been offered in the name of **Reinventing government** (the title of a book by Osborne and Gaebler).[27] The authors of these new approaches to public management advise that governments adopt a series of strategies to overcome the challenges they are facing from the changes in the environment. These strategies include cutting down the size of government, introducing competition in the services provided by government and asking public organisations to work with goals and objectives, be customer driven and be entrepreneurial.

Osborne and Gaebler argue that governments have *involved themselves in too many activities*. They should be catalytic and reduce the size and scope of their activities. They should steer rather than row. Governments should adopt a very broad strategic role and engage in managing policies. Governments should make a distinction between management of strategies and policies and delivery of services. The details or the tactical aspects of governmental work should be privatised or outsourced to private operators to deliver governmental services. In this steering role, governments regulate deliverers of the services and evaluate their performances to make sure that they meet community needs.[28]

Many government agencies enjoy a *monopoly in the delivery of services*. This makes them complacent and in many cases inefficient and unresponsive to the demands and needs of their clients. To rectify these problems, competition should be introduced in the delivery of services. Government departments should not have monopoly over the delivery of services. They should be asked to compete with other government agencies or other nongovernmental agencies for the delivery of services. Competition should not only be between government and nongovernment organisations but also between different departments of the government in the delivery of services. This intragovernment competition could be in such services as printing, accounting, purchasing and telecommunications.[29]

Government agencies should be *mission driven rather than rule driven*. Rules encourage inefficiency, stand in the way of achieving missions and block innovation. Government agencies should define their mission and allow managers to pursue those missions. This strategy should be applied across all agencies but most importantly for budgeting. Traditionally, budgeting was line-item based, which locked managers into spending money on stipulated items. They had no freedom to move money from one item to another even if it was necessary. To encourage managers to be mission driven, these hurdles should be abolished.[30]

Government agencies should change their strategies from being *input oriented to results oriented*. Instead of funding inputs, government should fund outcomes. Traditionally, governments, in funding schools for example, emphasised how many children enrolled. Instead, schools should be funded based on how well the children do in the school. The strategy of results-oriented government requires that government agencies have a set of goals, a set of community condition indicators and a set of performance indicators. Sunnyvale City Council in California followed this results-oriented government strategy. It encourages getting things done, distinguishing success from failure, rewarding success, learning from failures, correcting failures, paying for performance and winning public support.[31]

Government agencies should be *customer driven* and meet the needs of the customer, not of the managers. Most government agencies are customer blind and they do not know who their customers are. Government agencies should listen to their customers though customer surveys and focus groups and take action based on those feedbacks. They need to provide customers with choices. The customer should be in the driver's seat. Governments should be providing resources to the customers rather than to the agencies so that customers can choose their service providers. Vouchers, cash grants and allocating set dollar amounts to customers are ways to empower customers rather than managers. Governments should make a system that motivates managers to chase customers rather than the other way round. Customer-driven government not only provides customers with choices but also ensures equitable distribution of services, providing everyone with equal funds or even by giving funds according to income.[32]

Government agencies spend money but they do not earn it. Public managers not only do not know how to earn money, they do not like the idea either. They think it is banal. Many public managers believe that they are doing 'God's work' and the public should be grateful. Government agencies can earn money by selling their products, by charging user fees. It is equitable too. Poor taxpayers subsidise the rich to play golf and moor their luxury boats. User fees raise money, lower demands and economise the use of public services.[33]

Politicians, to implement strategies of customer-driven, results-oriented and competitive government, need to have a human resources management strategy that ensures a responsive group of public managers. This requires changes in how public managers are recruited, selected, trained and managed.[34]

Strategic reforms introduced in public organisations

Reforms along the line proposed by the new approaches to public management have been introduced in the United States, the UK, Australia and New Zealand. For example, in Australia, markets have been established for a large range of products and services in which different government departments and providers from the private sector compete. Government departments are allowed to charge user fees, which they can retain and use for their programs. Many government agencies have been privatised (see Strategy in action 13.3) or corporatised with the government becoming one of the shareholders.[35]

A series of reforms have been introduced in the financial and budgeting sector since the 1970s. Their most important aspect was shifting the focus from inputs to outputs and outcomes. One central aspect was the introduction of **program management and budgeting** (PMB). PMB asked government agencies to define policy outcomes and objectives, with the establishment of a program structure to achieve the objectives and the establishment of performance indicators to evaluate the programs' success. PMB allowed government agencies more freedom and flexibility in the management of money than they were given by the parliament.[36]

These reforms also included changes in how the human resources aspect of public management was managed. Traditionally, in the Westminster system of government that Australia follows, public managers are quite independent from ministers. Ministers argued that this is absurd because as heads of departments they should have control over their departments so that they can have their policies implemented by government agencies. To establish political control over public managers, the public service board, which guarded the independence of public servants and stood between ministers and public managers, was abolished. Reforms were introduced to appoint senior public managers at all three levels of government on fixed-term performance-based contracts.[37] Human resources management of senior level public managers in Australia is very much under the control of ministers (see Strategy in action 13.2).[38]

program management and budgeting
A system in which an annual budget with clearly set out goals, programs, activities and tasks is formulated, and money allocated to these successive levels of budget

Strategic planning in public organisations

Many have argued that to correct this situation, public organisations should adopt strategic approaches. This involves not only adopting a different set of strategies but also a sophisticated strategic planning process. Bryson is one such proponent.[40] He argues that strategy in a public organisation must be technically workable and politically acceptable to key stakeholders and must accord with the organisation's philosophy and core values. It must also be ethical, moral and legal. He suggested that public organisations should adopt an eight-step planning process.

In the first step, stakeholders in the planning process agree on the usefulness of the planning effort, its purpose and roles and the functions of planning teams and committees that

strategy in action 13.2

Firing the head of the department of defence

Paul Barratt, head of the department of defence, while in the Philippines, was informed by Max Moore Wilton, the head of the department of cabinet and prime minister, that his job would be terminated because John Moore, the minister of defence, had lost confidence in him and could no longer work with him. Barratt had been appointed on a five-year contract with 20 per cent loading on his salary to compensate for the possibility that his job could be terminated at any time. He was one of the three highest-paid public servants in the Commonwealth Government, earning considerably more than $350 000 a year. Although John Howard was not supportive of the recommendation of sacking, he agreed to it to demonstrate his solidarity with his cabinet colleague. It was Howard who had asked Barratt to join the Commonwealth public service in 1966. He had left briefly to work for the Business Council of Australia, returning to the public service in 1996.

In the past, public servants usually accepted the termination decisions of governments. Barratt, however, challenged the government decision in the court and was successful in gaining an unprecedented injunction preventing his removal. Barratt resolved to fight all the way to retain his job. This hardened the government's resolve to fire him and, as a consequence, it rejected a proposal from Barratt to have the issue mediated by a retired judge. Lawyers for Barratt argued that the decision to terminate his job was unfair.

Lawyers for the government, however, argued that the laws of natural justice did not apply because these conditions were already built into Barratt's employment contract.

Barratt's dismissal was upheld by Justice Peter Hely of the Federal Court, who ruled that Prime Minister Howard:

> has complete power to fire senior public servants whenever he likes — but he must tell them why as he pushes them out the door... while Mr Howard has to give reasons, he doesn't have to find 'some fault or incapacity of a fundamental nature' in the work of a secretary. This is because the termination might have nothing to do with performance, but merely be triggered by a change in government or the availability of a person the prime minister wants to put in the job.[39]

Sources: McGregor, R 1999, 'Public service elite get pay rises', *The Australian*, 19 January; Garran, R 1999, 'Careers torpedoed by Collins fiasco', *The Australian*, 28 July; —— 1999, 'Paul, it's Max. You are fired. Defence boss fired by telephone', *Weekend Australian*, 24 July; McGregor, R 1999, 'Defence chief to test right to fire', *The Australian*, 27 July; McGregor, R & Garran, R 1999, 'PM seals Defence chief's fate', *The Australian*, 29 July; *The Age*, 'Defence chief wants $1 million to go', 21 August; McGregor, R 1999, 'Defence chief hits back with injunction', *The Australian*, 28 July; —— 1999, 'Barratt must go: Coalition', *Weekend Australian*, 31 July; —— 1999, 'Ruling ratifies PM's power to hire and fire', *The Australian*, 20 August.

coordinate planning effort. Public organisations are not as free as business organisations as argued. They work under an externally imposed framework, which comes from statutes, charters, conventions, regulations and various informal understandings. In the second step, participants in the planning process identify and clarify this framework and various constraints that arise out of the framework. Unless this framework is clarified, it is unlikely that public organisations would meet their legal obligations. Second, public organisations would likely be unaware of what they are allowed to pursue and what not.

Having clarified the framework, in the third step, public organisations develop and clarify their mission and values. Clarification of mission, values and the framework provide the social justification for their existence. External environmental assessment and internal environmental assessment constitutes the fourth and fifth step of the planning process. In the sixth step of the planning process, public organisations identify strategic issues or conflicts that arise over ends, means, and philosophy.

In the seventh step, public organisations develop strategies to deal with the issues identified in the previous step. In developing strategy, public organisations identify alternatives, enumerate the barriers to achieving those alternatives, prepare proposals for overcoming barriers, identify the actions needed over the next two years to implement the major proposals and, finally, spell out a detailed work program, covering the next six months to a year, to implement the actions. In the eighth step, the public organisation describes what it should look like if it successfully implements its strategies and achieves its full potential.

What Bryson has proposed has great similarity with what, as is noted in chapter 1 of this book, Mintzberg has described as the intended planning process. This model is a rational model of strategy process in which managers move through the steps sequentially. In this sense, it is hardly novel for public organisations. They have experienced various versions of this model at different times beginning from the early 1960s. It all began with performance and program budgeting in the US Department of Defense, when the department was asked to identify its goals so that it could measure its performance. The planning, programming and budgeting system (PPBS) applied this rational logic in a much more detailed way. The model of budgeting is hierarchical and asks government departments not only to identify goals but also programs that would be adopted to achieve those goals and, in turn, the procedures that would be followed to achieve those programs hierarchically.[41]

The implementation of rational modes of planning, including the one proposed by Bryson to the public sector, faces formidable challenges. Some have been identified here. One of the fundamental requirements of strategic planning is a goal that the organisation strives to achieve. Many argue that public organisations usually have multiple goals that often conflict. Rational models also face the challenge of measuring the performances of strategies in the absence of an agreed-upon goal. The following section discusses studies that report on experiences of public organisations with strategic planning.

Experiences of strategic planning in public organisations

One of the earliest studies on strategic planning on public organisations in Australia was conducted on the universities in 1995. The study examined the formal, published planning statements prepared by each of the 35 universities based on the Bryson (1999) model discussed

strategy in action 13.3

The New Zealand electricity industry

Before 1985, 61 electricity supply companies controlled the distribution and supply of electricity within New Zealand. They were government-subsidised, inefficient, regional statutory monopolies and the result was power shortages. To find solutions, Electricity Corporation of New Zealand (ECNZ) was established in 1987 as a commercial, profit-making organisation and the sole provider of electricity. ECNZ was to generate, transmit and supply electricity to retail electricity companies efficiently. Later, Transpower was created as a subsidiary to take over the electricity supply function but both ECNZ and Transpower failed to meet consumer expectations for a variety of reasons. Subsequent power shortages and price rises attracted further government action, such as the establishment of a wholesale electricity market (1993–96); separation of ownership of the electricity supply line and supply businesses (1996–99); customer choice for switching electricity retailers (1999); an electricity industry enquiry (2000); the *Electricity Industry Act* (2001); setting up the Electricity Complaints Commission (2002); government policy statements on electricity governance (2002, 2004); and, most recently, the Regulatory Framework for Transmission, Investment and Pricing (2004), which has a view to achieving the government's overall objective of delivering electricity in an 'efficient, fair, reliable and environmentally sustainable manner to all classes of consumers'. Today, the industry is regulated into four groups: generator companies that produce and supply electricity to the national grid; Transpower as owner of the national grid and seller of electricity in the wholesale market; distribution companies as owners of regional distribution lines to distribute electricity, and retailers (28 companies), which compete with each other to sell electricity to consumers by purchasing electricity from the wholesale market.

Sources: Ministry of Economic Development 2004, 'Government policy statement on electricity governance', accessed 29 August 2004, www.med.govt.nz; —— 2005, 'Chronology of New Zealand electricity reform: part three: 2002 to...', accessed 2 September 2005, www.med.govt.nz/ers/electric/chronology/chronology-02.html; Electricity Commission, accessed 4 September 2005, www.med.govt.nz/templates/MultipageDocumentPage_____6480.aspx

earlier). Of these universities, 71 per cent (25) had completed or draft plans, ten institutions (29 per cent) had no existing plans, including one university claiming that it was 'too busy to prepare a plan'. The planning processes was participative, combining top-down, bottom-up approaches.[42]

Of the 71 per cent (25) of universities that had completed, draft or incomplete plans, only 29 per cent (10) had undertaken any kind of comprehensive strategic analysis. Three universities (9 per cent) undertook some preliminary analysis. Twenty-six (74 per cent) out of the 35 universities had identified a mission; among them only three (9 per cent) universities actually referred to their founding charter or mandate outlined in state legislation. All universities with an articulated mission statement made reference to their products or services, which included undergraduate and postgraduate programs, flexible study patterns; continuing education; and technology transfer. About three quarters made reference to their beneficiaries, which included students, the government, the community, the professions, business, science, human services and staff. Twenty institutions (57 per cent) identified their core competencies as teaching; research, technologies; and consultancy.[43]

Less than half of the universities (43 per cent) included values and beliefs that are sometimes unrealistic and esoteric, rather than reality based. For most of the universities, plans were without any focus, and goals and objectives were vague, hazy and largely meaningless. For example, goals included: 'to explore ways'; 'to work towards enhancing quality'; 'to improve responsiveness'; 'to manage efficiently'; 'to have a plan' and 'to promote innovative research'. In most cases, actions that have been identified as strategies are really low-level activities. For example, the strategies outlined in many of the plans include activities such as: promoting discussion and understanding; reviewing a process, establishing a process and seeking information.[44]

Only six universities (17 per cent) had indicated what their priorities were and how resources would be allocated, indicating that very few universities integrated their planning with budgeting. Only nine (26 per cent) universities identified a set of performance indicators and even fewer than this had actually defined their performance indicators. For most of these universities, performance indicators included such items as the number of research papers completed and the number of enrolments. Very few institutions attempted either to differentiate or to focus their products competitively in relation to other universities.[45]

These findings portray a very messy picture about strategic planning in the Australian universities. Before we become too critical, we must make a number of qualifications. This study was done more than ten years ago and it is certain that the planning processes of these institutions has become much more sophisticated now. Second, the study is based on published formal planning documents. This does not mean that they did not have a sophisticated planning process. It is possible that they have not articulated their process in published documents. Neither do these findings indicate that universities did not have strategies. A formalised strategic planning process is not the only way to make correct strategies. The only conclusion that can be derived from these findings is that universities did not have a formalised strategic planning process.

Another explanation is that the universities were not experienced enough to engage in strategic planning. Before the period when this study was conducted, universities did not need to plan because they lived in a very predictable and stable environment.[46] Another factor that stood in the way of practising sophisticated strategic planning had been the amalgamation issue. During the period when this study was carried out, universities were under pressure from government to undergo mergers with other educational providers that were quite different from universities in fundamental ways. At times, these merger negotiations were bitter and protracted. Naturally, it was quite difficult to engage in such a sophisticated practice as strategic planning when universities were going through such complex negotiations.[47] More important, however, is whether any organisations, public or private, actually practise the linear model that has been proposed by Bryson. The next section examines a study conducted by Bryson (1988) himself with one of his colleagues into the strategic planning process in public organisations.

Bryson and Roering tracked strategic planning based on the steps discussed above by eight government units in the metropolitan area of Minnesota. Of these government organisations, five were suburban city governments, one was a county government, one was the county's executive director's office and the other was the county's public health nursing service.

The strategic planning process was a clear success in only two of the six cases: County A and — Nursing Service of County B. In the other cases, success was much more mixed. The process helped managers to focus on important issues but was less successful in setting priorities. The process almost collapsed during the strategic issue identification and strategy development phases for two reasons. First, the process generated so many issues and strategies that the teams had difficulty comprehending their implications and setting priorities in the issues and strategies.

Second, many of the issues and strategies generated by the process required the contribution of managers in authority but the latter were not part of the planning exercise. In other words, organisations participating in the study were not really serious about the exercise. That planning was done by a team rather than by the top management indicates that strategies were considered only of marginal importance.[48]

Meanings of strategic plans varied widely across units. To one set of organisations, a strategic plan consisted of a formal plan with mission statements, situation assessments, discussion of strategic issues, and strategies. For another organisation, a strategic plan consisted of typical governmental 'decision packages', which included discussion of issues, strategic options and recommendations of action. To another set of organisations, strategic plans are informal documents that deal with a single issue at a time. Planning teams involved in the process considered alternative strategic options in terms of informal rather than a set of formally agreed-upon criteria. Discussions to consider the strategic options were never orderly. They applied political, moral and legal criteria and many others but they settled on a proposal they could live with. 'Strategic planning became a kind of planning by argumentation.'[49]

They conclude that 'most efforts to produce fundamental decisions and policy changes in government through strategic planning will not succeed' because none of the organisations studied was able to follow the linear, sequential strategic planning models of the business policy textbooks. They advise that if a government unit wants to initiate strategic planning, it must have a powerful process sponsor to legitimise the process, an effective process champion who believes in the benefits of planning, facilitated and participated-in planning discussions without pushing his or her own agenda, a strategic planning team, an expectation of disruptions and delays, willingness to be flexible concerning what constitutes a strategic plan, and a willingness to construct and consider arguments geared to many different evaluative criteria.[50]

Bryson and Roering seem to assume that business organisations practise a linear, sequential and intended strategy process. Studies on the planning practices of business organisations conclude otherwise. Quinn and Voyer report that business organisations do not practise the linear model.[51] Business organisations practise what they called **logical incrementalism**. In this mode, business organisations do not muddle through; nor do they incrementally adjust to changing problems faced. Organisations have an objective but they remain largely flexible in adjusting goals and strategies to changing situations and occasionally take stock of things to make sure that they were not off the course of their objectives. You should also go back to chapter one of this book to have a second look at results of research on strategic planning practices of business organisations.

Strieb and Poister, based on a study of 451 senior officials of city councils in the United States, with a response rate of 42 per cent, examined how much strategic planning is used.[52] They found, as table 13.2 shows, that the most common use of the strategic planning process was to establish new goals and objectives. The least use was made for reorganising departmental structures.

logical incrementalism
A mode of strategic planning where organisations work with fixed goals and change their actions depending on the changes in the environment

Table 13.2: Strategic planning process uses

Reported strategic planning applications	
Established new goals and objectives	78%
Reorient departmental mission	44%
Identify major problems and issues	49%
Review programs for possible alteration	33%
Reorganize departmental structure	34%
Develop new strategies, policies and programs	67%
Improve communication within the jurisdiction	53%
Develop plans for community and economic development	66%

Source: Strieb, G & Poister, TH 1990, 'Strategic planning in US cities: pattern of use, perceptions of effectiveness, and assessment of strategic capacity', *American Review of Public Administration*, vol. 20, no. 1, p. 37, figure 3.

Berry and Wechsler in a survey of the agencies of all the state governments of the United States found that 60 per cent used strategic planning.[53] They introduced the practice of strategic planning because of the decision of top management, fiscal pressures on state agencies, their need to resolve competing resource allocation priorities, their desire to be responsive to constituents, and to emulate business practices from the private sector.

Most of the agencies used such techniques in their planning practice as the strength, weakness, threats and opportunities (SWOT) analysis and environmental scanning to identify and manage their stakeholders and their policy portfolios. In the public sector, there is a frequent complaint that public organisations do not integrate planning and budgeting. Berry and Wechsler found that most US state agencies coordinated their budgets and plan, and formulated their budgets within the strategic issues, goals and objectives of the plan.[54]

US state agencies found at least six benefits in order of their degree of importance of the use of strategic planning. Strategic planning:

1. helped in the clarification of agency direction and goals
2. assisted to make policy decisions to allocate resources, designating priority policies in the budget process
3. helped in increasing the support of the legislature, governor and constituents, and in increasing staff commitment to improving customer satisfaction
4. improved teamwork, internal communication and staff morale and increased corporate culture within the agency
5. helped in agency reorganisation
6. improved service delivery by realigning the agency's resources and structures with its priorities.[55]

This section has discussed the normative strategic planning model and experiences of public organisations with strategic planning. It has discussed the eight-step model of Bryson, which he originally developed in 1988, and argued that this model has great similarities with the intended strategy model identified by Mintzberg, discussed in chapter 1 of this book. It has also discussed the experiences of public organisations as described by empirical studies. These findings indicate that although public organisations found the model useful, many of them do not really practise the normative model identified by Bryson. It has also been argued that business organisations do not practise the linear model either. What they practise is logical incrementalism. It would be reasonable to conclude from these findings that it is better to view the linear model as an ideal and compare actual practices against this ideal. It is unlikely any organisation ever would fully practise a linear model.

Strategies public organisations pursue

So far, the context of strategies in the public sector, challenges faced by public organisations and various macrolevel strategies that public organisations should pursue have been discussed. The previous section discusses the process that is followed to develop strategies. It must distinguish between strategy process and strategy content or simply strategies. The term strategy process refers to the series of steps through which objectives are fixed, the internal and external environments are analysed and strategies are selected. This process results in strategy content or strategy. Strategies are actions with which organisations achieve their goals.[56]

Strategic management of the public sector is a relatively new field. In this field, there are more studies on strategy process that on strategies themselves. The following section discusses empirical studies that report on strategies that government agencies pursue. This section concludes with a conceptual framework that promises to provide an excellent set of concepts to do research on strategies of public organisations in the context of introduced changes.

Wechsler and Backoff studied four agencies of the state of Ohio in the United States: the Department of Natural Resources, the Department of Mental Retardation and Developmental Disabilities, the Department of Public Welfare and the Public Utilities Commission of Ohio, based on a framework with eight dimensions.[57]

- The first dimension assessed the extent of external influences on the departments.
- The second examined the strength of the departments in relation to these external forces
- The third examined whether departments were proactive or reactive.
- The fourth identified three types of orientations of agencies: agencies with strategic orientation pursue political interests of internal or external stakeholders; agencies with organisational orientation add resources, improve performance or develop capacity and agencies with policy orientation support policies of specific communities.
- The fifth classifies agencies into those oriented towards fundamental change and those that maintain status quo.
- The sixth assesses a range of concerns tackled by the agency's strategic management activity: whether they are broad or narrow.
- The seventh distinguishes agencies between those that devote significant effort to their strategic management activity from those that devote very low-level effort.
- The eighth and last dimension assesses agencies in terms of their internal or external focus.[58]

Based on the various combinations of these dimensions, they identify four patterns of strategies practised by Ohio state agencies: developmental strategy, transformational strategy, protective strategy and political strategy.[59]

Agencies pursuing *developmental strategy* are proactive: they anticipate future events and plan their actions. They develop the capacity of their organisations by adding resources. They tackle a very broad range of issues with specific strategic objectives and devote considerable effort to achieve them. Organisations pursuing this strategy have sufficient income to stand on their own two feet and, as a consequence, have the capability to resist control efforts from other organisations. The scope of change introduced by these organisations is quite narrow and they move incrementally rather than radically.

Among the US state departments studied, the Department of Natural Resources (DNR) was found to have pursued this strategy. DNR developed new programs, expanded old ones, purchased land for state nature preserves, initiated various programs to conserve nature and introduced litter control programs. The department integrated its diverse and often conflicting stakeholders under the core objectives of the department. The top management of the department agreed on a shared vision to be pursued by the department and it was successfully communicated throughout the department and among its stakeholders. The staff of the department were given training, and efforts were made to increase their commitment to the department. The stakeholders of the department, because they were too diverse, could not exercise effective control over the department. Moreover, the department was largely independent in terms of its funding sources.[60]

Agencies pursuing *transformational strategy* change their programs as a result of changes in the environment. Instead of resisting changes, they adapt to them. This transformation of organisations may not, however, always be planned. They react to the pressures for change as they come along. Among the departments studied by Wechsler and Backoff, the department responsible for caring for people with intellectual and developmental disabilities pursued this strategy. One of the most significant changes faced by the department was how people with intellectual disabilities should be cared for. Results of research showed that these people should be deinstitutionalised and be cared for in the community. In addition, various legal rights groups and professional experts in the treatment of people with intellectual disabilities advocated for more humane treatment of these patients. These pressures led to the reduction in the government-operated programs, closure of many residential centres and the handing over of care work to the community. These deinstitutionalisation measures transformed the department. The department became more of a regulator of the organisations that provided for people with intellectual disabilities rather than a direct service provider.[61]

Agencies pursuing *protective strategies* face a hostile and threatening external environment and they have very little power to resist such external pressures because they are dependent on these external forces for their funding. Organisations faced with these environmental conditions know well that investing time in planning would be futile and instead of changing their programs as agencies pursuing transformational strategy do, they devote all their effort to protecting what they have. Among the departments studied, the Department of Public Welfare was found to have pursued this strategy. The department faced budget cuts in welfare programs when there was increased need of funding in them. In this hostile environment, the department devoted all its energies to protecting its current programs and preventing further reductions in welfare benefit programs. Strategies adopted to achieve these goals included establishing good relationships with politicians, interest groups and constituents, and to make its internal operation more efficient.[62]

Agencies pursuing *political strategies* respond to the demands of the powerful political groups because they are largely dependent on them for political and financial support. They are so dependent on their political supporters that instead of engaging in setting their strategic plans, they just drift along in accordance with the whims of their political masters. Among the departments studied, the Public Utilities Commissions of Ohio (PUCO) pursued this strategy. For most of its history, PUCO was perceived by many as favouring the interests of the utility companies. But such changes in the industry as the Arab oil embargo, problems in the nuclear power industry and high rates of inflation made it difficult for PUCO to continue with this approach and it adopted a strategy that is more favourable to consumers .[63]

The Wechsler and Backoff study indicates the importance of the degree of freedom of public organisations to how much they engage in strategic planning. It clearly indicates that agencies that enjoy higher degrees of autonomy are more enterprising: they expand their market, increase their resources and provide better services for their clients. The departments that depend on external stakeholders for resources are more busy with establishing and maintaining relationships with them.

Strategies to increase budgets

Public organisations are nonmarket organisations. Recipients of their services and products do not directly pay them. They get their revenues from their sponsors. In the case of public organisations, their input market and output market are separate. This situation requires that public organisations adopt one set of strategic actions in relation to the recipients of their services and products and another set to get revenues.

Wildavski reported in his study of the budgetary process of the federal government of the United States the strategies that public organisations adopt to increase their budget.[64] He divided government departments into two groups. Most of the departments are spenders. They spend rather than earn: the Department of Defense is an example. Some other departments are guardians of the public purse. This group would include the Treasury, Office of Management and Budget, and Congress. Wildavski reported that spenders adopt two-pronged strategies to get money from the 'guardians'. One focuses on the clientele. This includes such tactics as expanding the client base, serving the clientele better and securing feedback from the clientele. The second set of strategies concentrate on building confidence among the guardians. This includes such tactics as playing straight, demonstrating integrity in developing estimates of funds and making friends. Public organisations that are totally dependent on the budget provided by the government can adopt a series of strategies. They can pad their estimates, hide the real cost of a project or engage in endless tactical battles with the finance and treasury departments to get more money.

Heclo and Wildavski found in their study of the budgetary process in the UK that spenders and guardians engage in bargaining and haggling over departmental budgets.[65] It is almost like a village life in which spenders and guardians conduct their negotiation over budget outside the public eye. Once public managers have finished their negotiation, the budgetary battle moves to ministers. These battles occur in cabinet committees and ultimately in the cabinet.

Haidar found in his study of the New Zealand budgetary process that the negotiation over the largest part of the departmental budget occurs within the rules, procedures and perimeters set by and agreed between the spenders, and guardians.[66] Spenders and savers engage in setting up this framework within which budgetary battles are fought. Approval for new projects involving large amounts of money takes place outside the rules and framework established by the departments. These projects are negotiated and bargained among ministers through various cabinet committees and ultimately in the cabinet.

Wheelen and Hunger argue that sources of funding not only influence the strategic behaviour of public organisations but also they type of service clients would receive.[67] They argue that the type of service clients receive from organisations depends on the amount of funding they receive from them. If organisations get most of their funds from sponsors, they are likely to focus on the sponsors rather than on the clients. The key to understanding whose needs managers in public and nonprofit organisations would satisfy would depend on 'who pays for the delivered services'.

A framework to study strategies of public organisations

Boyne and Walker begin with an argument that existing typologies of strategies for both public and business organisations pose false contradictions between what they called **strategic stances** and **strategic actions**.[68] A strategic stance is a 'broad way in which an organization seeks to maintain or improve its performance'.[69] Strategic stances are relatively enduring and rarely change substantially in the short term. Strategic actions are the specific steps that an organisation takes to operationalise its stance. They are likely to change in the short term.[70]

They argue that strategies discussed in Miles and Snow[71] are really strategic stances while business-level strategies in Porter's[72] work, such as low cost, differentiation and focus are strategic actions. They argue that strategic actions occur within the strategic stances organisations take.

strategic stances
Broad and enduring perspectives that organisations adopt in relation to the environment they face

strategic actions
Specific and short-term actions that occur within a strategic stance

Miles and Snow proposed a typology of strategies that included four strategies: prospector, analyser, defender and reactor.[73] Defenders focus on a narrow product range and they need to be highly efficient to defend their market. Prospectors are innovative, seek new markets and emphasise change but they may not be very efficient. Reactors respond to the changes imposed on them by their environment. Analysers combine strategies of prospectors and defenders. On the one hand, they defend their market and on the other, they keep themselves open to new markets and innovative ideas. Boyne and Walker include three of them in their framework and exclude the analyser because it is an intermediate type.[74] Strategic actions, the second dimension of the typology, are five types of specific actions that organisations use to operationalise their stance. These concern changes in markets, services, revenues, the external organisation and the internal organisation.

Markets and services

A market may be defined geographically or through the characteristics of the clientele, for example, a particular age group or set of service needs. Public organisations can change their market by withdrawing from a particular geographic area, providing existing services to new groups of citizens and developing new services for a new type of clientele (e.g. hospitals providing service to HIV/AIDS patients). In Europe, housing associations have moved into such noncore areas as leisure and employment and training and education. Public services may be faced by new problems that require them to move to new markets. In the case of public organisations, markets and services become interchangeable because public organisations mostly provide services.[75]

Seeking revenues

Public organisations need to get revenues from their sponsors. For most public organisations, these revenues come from budgets. Recently, with the introduction of wide-ranging changes, public organisations have been allowed to raise money through such sources as charges, levies and donations. For example, Australian universities have been under pressure for quite some time to fund themselves. This had led them to reduce services provided, charging fees for services that were provided free of cost and engaging in recruiting students from foreign countries to raise revenue.[76]

External and internal organisation

Strategic actions in relation to the external and internal organisation become most important to public organisations that have constraints in changing their markets and finding novel ways to raise funds. This situation requires that they look at the internal organisation of their departments to save money or to provide better service by changing their internal structures, culture and values and introducing such human resources management techniques as performance-based pay. Externally, public organisations can also collaborate with business organisations, develop networks, consortia, joint ventures and also outsource to provide services more efficiently.[77]

Based on this analysis of strategic actions and strategic stances, Boyne and Walker (2004) identify three types of strategies for public organisations. **Prospectors** are innovative and proactive agencies. They are pioneers, search for new markets (i.e. clientele) and rapidly respond to changes in the environment. A prospector expands its budget and encroaches on the jurisdiction of other agencies. Prospectors are outward-looking organisations, which constantly scan the environment and respond to the market by developing new services, providing services to new clienteles and going into new jurisdictions. They change their markets and services while seeking revenues. They do not hesitate to change their internal and external organisations to align themselves with new environments.

prospectors
Organisations that always look for new business opportunities

Defenders are conservatives. They are not first movers. They are cautious. They adopt a product or service that has been tested and tried. They defend their current activities, jurisdiction and budget. They do not change their markets but modify their services and also modify their internal and external organisation to defend their market more efficiently and effectively.

Reactors do not have strategies of their own. External stakeholders impose their strategies on reactors. Reactors adjust to the ever changing demands of the stakeholders. They do not have the internal resources and capabilities of becoming prospectors or defenders.[78] Nor do they change their markets, nor do they introduce new products or services on their own volition. Their external stakeholders cajole or coerce them to change their markets, products and services.[79]

As always, the specific environment within which public organisations work plays a significant role in the success of strategies. Reactor strategy is considered lame but it could be more successful in the public sector because it can adjust to the changing demands and needs of the environment, particularly when the environmental forces are really strong. A study in the United States found that port authorities with a prospector stance performed best in a turbulent environment, while the authorities with a reactor stance were successful in a 'protected' environment.[80]

Boyne and Walker argue that public organisations are more likely to be reactors because they have very little discretion. As noted, they do have very little discretion to change their markets or clientele or the geographic area they serve, and very little autonomy to raise revenue. So it follows that they would be prospectors only if they have more freedom in choosing their markets and seeking revenue.[81]

This section has discussed the strategies public organisations pursue. It has argued that public organisations need to adopt strategies on two fronts: one set of strategies for their clients and recipients of their services and another for their sponsors who provide them with the budget to provide services to their clients. Findings of the empirical studies discussed show that sources of funding play a crucial role in the strategies that public organisations adopt. It has also discussed strategies that public organisations adopt to get more money from their sponsors.

defenders
Organisations that protect their current market by trying to increase efficiency

reactors
Organisations that respond to changes in their environment only under extreme pressure

Summary

This chapter has focused on the importance of studying strategic management of public organisations, has defined public organisations and has distinguished them from business organisations. The challenges faced by public organisations and also the responses that public sector organisations have adopted to meet them have been identified. The chapter has also discussed the theory and practice of strategic planning in public sectors, discussed strategies pursued by public organisations and concludes by discussing a framework to study strategies of public organisations. The following are the main points of the chapter:

▶ It is important to study the strategic management of public organisations because they are the largest employers and affect everyone in myriad ways.

▶ Most organisations have a 'public' character. No organisation is purely public or purely private. Instead of viewing public and private as dichotomous terms, they should be viewed as a continuum of publicness. Once this is done, discussion becomes more and more applicable not only to pure public organisations but also to others that possess various degrees of publicness. The number of nonprofit organisations is increasing every day. This discussion should also be applicable to nonprofit organisations because they display more similarity to public than to business organisations.

▶ Public organisations are fundamentally different from business organisations. The most important features of public organisation that distinguish them from business organisations include having coercive power and being nonmarket in character.

- Some of the concepts of strategic management are applicable to public organisations though. However, one must bear in mind the peculiar features of public organisations when doing so.
- Public organisations have been subjected to criticisms by governments, community groups and business organisations the world over that they are inefficient, ineffective, full of red tape, customer unfriendly and procedure rather than results oriented.
- The *Reinventing government* movement that originated in the United States and the new public management or managerialism popular in the Commonwealth countries prescribed public organisations to become catalytic, performance oriented and results oriented among other things.
- A series of reforms have been introduced by governments to public organisations and pressure has been put on them to apply strategic management approaches. These reforms included introduction of radical changes in how public managers are selected and recruited, emphasis on results and performance, decentralisation and delegation of power.
- Strategic planning processes recommended for public organisations include such steps as agreement on the planning effort, identification and clarification of the statutory framework, developing and clarifying mission and values, external and internal environmental assessment, identification of strategic issues, developing strategies to deal with the issues and describing what the organisation should look like in the near future.
- Experiences of implementing strategic planning suggest that public organisations need strong process champions and facilitators if they want to be successful. Other studies assessing implementation of strategic planning also indicate that strategic planning helps public organisations in identifying goals and in assessing internal and external environment among many other benefits.
- Empirical studies of strategies pursued by public organisations in the United States show the crucial importance of self generated funding in adopting strategies. They suggest that departments that are dependent on funding from the government adopt 'political' strategies while departments that are dependent on their own funding adopt 'developmental' strategies.
- To increase their current budget or to continue with their current budget, public organisations adopt strategies to influence the government and their clientele.
- A framework that has been developed to study strategies pursued by public organisations has also been discussed. The framework is interesting and promising because it brings Miles and Snow's framework, which has been extensively applied in the research on business organisations, to the public sector. This framework thus establishes a link between the public and private sector in the field of research on strategic management.

Practising strategic management

Review questions

1. List the benefits of studying the strategic management of public organisations.
2. Discuss the main recommendations of Osborne and Gaebler.
3. Define 'public organisation'.
4. Identify the findings of implementation of strategic planning approaches to public organisations.

Discussion questions

5. Strategy processes in private sector organisations are as ambiguous as strategy processes in public sector organisations. Do you agree with this statement? Justify your answer.
6. Do you agree with the findings of Johnstone and Marshall that there was lack of planning in the Australian universities?
7. There is very little incentive for public organisations to be responsive to their clients. Discuss.

Applied questions

8. Discuss the strategic planning framework adopted by the East Grampians Health Service outlined in the opening case of this chapter.
9. Discuss the strategic management issues generated by the Cornelia Rau case (Strategy in action 13.1).
10. Do you believe that the human resources management system evidenced by the termination of Paul Barratt (see Strategy in action 13.2) serves the public well?

Small-group exercises

Break into groups of three to five participants, and assess the implications of the recommendations of Osborne and Gaebler. In your assessment, answer the following questions.

1. List the recommendations of Osborne and Gaebler.
2. Identify the strategic management framework that their recommendations generate.
3. Identify the basic features of public organisations.
4. Identify the implications of the Osborne and Gaebler framework for a typical public organisation.

Article file

Find an example of a public organisation that has recently implemented a strategic planning process. Identify the problems the company faces and recommend measures to solve them.

Exploring the Web

Visiting a public organisation

Visit the website of the Department of Premier and Cabinet of the government of Western Australia (www.wa.gov.au/). Using the information available on the site, answer the following questions:

1. Has the Western Australian Government adopted a strategic planning framework?
2. If it has, describe the main features of the planning framework.
3. Discuss the issues the planning framework has generated for the government.

Strategic management project

Module 13

1. Discuss the environment your organisation is faced with.
2. Identify the strategies 'your organisation' is pursuing. Can you really call them strategies?
3. Identify the strategy process followed by 'your organisation'.

Additional resources

Bozeman, B. & Bretschneider, S 1994, 'The publicness puzzle in organizations theory: a test of explanations of differences between public and private organizations', *Journal of Public Administration Research and Theory*, vol. 4, no. 2, pp. 197–223. (Takes the discussion further regarding the differences between public and private organisations.)

Charih, M 2000, 'Government departmental strategies: a taxonomy of strategic behaviour in the Canadian government', *Management International*, vol. 5, no. 1, pp. 1–9. (An empirical study of the strategies that the strategies that the departments of the government of Canada pursue.)

Ellingson, DA & Wambsganss JR 2001, 'Modifying the approach to planning and evaluation in governmental entities: A 'Balanced Scorecard' approach, *Journal of Public Budgeting, Accounting and Financial Management*, vol. 13, no. 1, pp. 103–20. (Operationalises the four scorecards of the balanced scorecard for their application to public organisations.)

Lozeau, D, Langley, A & Jean-Louis, D 2002, 'The corruption of managerial techniques by organizations', *Human Relations*, vol. 55, no. 5, pp. 537–64. (Discusses the implications of implementing strategic planning in public hospitals.)

Mintzberg, H 1978, 'Patterns in strategy formation', *Management Science*, vol. 24, no. 3, pp. 934–48. (Compares and contrasts strategy process of public and private organisations.)

End notes

1. Wechsler, B & Backoff, RW 1986, 'Policy making and administration in state agencies: Strategic management approaches', *Public Administration Review*, vol. 55, no. 2, p. 321.
2. Emmet, MA & Crow, MM 1988, 'Public, private and hybrid organizations: An empirical examination of the role of publicness', *Administration and Society*, vol. 20, pp. 216–44.
3. Downs, A 1967, *Inside bureaucracy*, Little Brown and Company, Boston, Massachusetts, p. 29.
4. Nutt, PC & Backoff, RW 1993, 'Organizational publicness and its implications for strategic management, *Journal of Public Administration Research and Theory*, vol. 3, no. 2, p. 213.
5. ibid., p. 221.
6. Downs, op. cit., p. 30.
7. Nutt & Backoff, op. cit., p. 213.
8. ibid., p. 214.
9. ibid.
10. Boyne, GA & Walker, RM 2004, 'Strategy content and public service organizations', *Public Administration Research and Theory*, vol. 14, no. 2, p. 236.
11. Nutt & Backoff, op. cit., p. 218.
12. From Weber, M 1948, *Essays in sociology*, translated, edited and with an introduction by Gerth, HH & Wright Mills, C, Rutledge and Kegan Paul, London, p. 79.
13. Nutt & Backoff, op. cit., p. 219.
14. ibid., p. 220.
15. Montanari, JR & Bracker, JS 1986, 'The strategic management process at the public planning unit level', *Strategic Management Journal*, vol. 7, no. 3, p. 252.
16. Nutt & Backoff, op. cit., p. 220.
17. ibid., p. 223.
18. ibid., p. 224.
19. Wilenski, P 1983, 'Competing values in public administration', in Robert Banks (ed.), *Private values and public policy: the ethics of decision making in government administration*, Zodak Centre, Sydney, p. 16.
20. Emy, HV & Hughes, OE 1991, *Australian politics: realities in conflict*, 2nd edn, Macmillan, South Melbourne, p. 250.
21. McGary, A 2005, 'Mentally ill Aussie in detention centre, *The Australian*, 5 February.
22. ibid.
23. Montanari & Bracker, op. cit., p. 252.
24. Bryson, JM 1999, 'A strategic planning process for public and non-profit organizations', in JM Bryson (ed.), *Strategic management in public and voluntary services: a reader*, Pergamon, Amsterdam, pp. 2–3.
25. O'Faircheallaigh, C, Wanna, J & Weller, P 1999, *Public sector management in Australia: new challenges, new directions*, 2nd edn, Macmillan, Melbourne, pp. 21–34.
26. Berry, FS & Wechsler, BW 1995, 'State agencies experience with strategic planning: Findings from a national survey', *Public Administration Review*, vol. 55, no. 2, p. 161; Bryson, op. cit., pp. 2–3.
27. Osborne, D & Gaebler, T 1993, *Reinventing government: how the entrepreneurial spirit is transforming the public sector*, Plume, New York.
28. ibid., pp. 25–48.
29. Hughes, OE 1998, *Public management and administration: an introduction*, 2nd edn, Macmillan, Melbourne, p. 65.
30. ibid., pp. 108–37.
31. ibid., pp. 138–65.
32. Holmes, M & Shand, D 1995, 'Management reforms: Some practitioner perspectives on the past ten years', *Governance*, vol, 8, p. 564; Hughes op. cit., pp. 167–94.
33. Hughes, op. cit., pp. 195–218.
34. ibid.
35. Task Force on Management Improvement 1993, *The Australian public service reformed: an evaluation of a decade of management reform*, AGPS, Canberra, pp. 269–70.
36. ibid., pp. 250–1.
37. ibid., p. 168.
38. Pullin, LJ & Haidar, A 2003, 'Hiring and firing public managers: Returning authority to Australian politicians', *Employment Relations Record*, vol. 3, no. 1.
39. McGregor, R 1999, 'Ruling ratifies PM's power to hire and fire' *The Australian*, 20 August.
40. Bryson, op. cit., pp. 3–9. This model is based on the model that he outlines in 1988 in his Bryson, JM 1988, *Strategic planning for public and non-profit organisations*, Jossey Bass, San Francisco.
41. Wildavski, A 1979, *The politics of budgetary process*, Little Brown and Company, Boston, Massachusetts, chapter 6.
42. Johnston, J & Marshal, N 1995, 'Strategic management in Australian universities', in A Halachami & G Bouckaert (eds), *Public productivity through quality and strategic management*, IOS Press, vol. 1, pp. 201–2.
43. ibid., pp. 202–3.
44. ibid., pp. 204–5.
45. ibid., pp. 204–6.
46. ibid., p. 206.
47. ibid.
48. Bryson, JM & Roering, WD 1988, 'Initiation of strategic planning by Governments', *Public Administration Review*, vol. 48, no. 6, pp. 998–9.
49. ibid., p. 1001.
50. ibid., pp. 1001–2.
51. Quinn, JB & Voyer, J 2003, 'Logical incrementalism: Managing strategy formation', in Mintzberg, H, Lampel, J, Quinn, VB & Ghosal, S, *The strategy process: Concepts, contexts, cases*, 4th edn, Pearson, Essex, pp. 183–8.
52. Strieb, G & Poister, TH 1990, 'Strategic planning in US cities: Pattern of use, perceptions of effectiveness, and assessment of strategic capacity', *American Review of Public Administration*, vol. 20, no. 1, pp. 29–44.

53. Berry, FS & Wechsler, BW 1995, 'State agencies experience with strategic planning: findings from a national survey', *Public Administration Review*, vol. 55, no. 2, pp. 161–2.
54. ibid., pp. 162–3.
55. ibid., pp. 164–5.
56. Boyne & Walker, op. cit., p. 231.
57. Wechsler & Backoff, op. cit.
58. ibid. p. 323.
59. Boyne & Walker, op. cit., pp. 237–8.
60. Wechsler & Backoff, op. cit., pp. 323–4.
61. ibid., p. 323.
62. ibid., pp. 324–5.
63. ibid., p. 325.
64. Wildavski, op. cit.
65. Heclo, H & Wildavski, A 1974, *The private government of public money*, Macmillan, London.
66. Haidar, A 1988, 'Budget formulation and Max Weber's three types of dominations', *Indian Journal of Public Administration*, vol. 34, no. 4, pp. 1046–59.
67. Wheelen, TL & Hunger, JD 2004, *Strategic management and business policy*, 9th edn., Pearson, New Jersey, p. 328.
68. Boyne & Walker, op. cit., p. 239.
69. ibid., p. 232
70. ibid.
71. Miles, RE & Snow, CC 1978, *Organizational strategy, structure, and process*, McGraw–Hill, New York.
72. For a discussion of Porter's strategies, see chapter 6 of this book.
73. Miles & Snow, op. cit., p. 29.
74. Boyne & Walker, op. cit., p. 232.
75. ibid., pp. 241–2.
76. O'Faircheallaigh, Wanna & Weller, op. cit. pp. 27–8.
77. Boyne & Walker, op. cit., p. 243.
78. Miles & Snow, op. cit. p. 29.
79. ibid.
80. Boyne & Walker, op. cit., pp. 240–1.
81. ibid., pp. 244–7.

Cases in strategic management

Analysing a case study and writing a case study analysis

Case matrix

	Case title	Page	SME/MNC	Goods or service	Chapter(s)
Case 1	Kleenmaid: moving towards formal planning	C9	SME	Goods	1, 2, 3, 6
Case 2	Cooroy Mountain Spring Water: it is worth bottling	C16	SME	Goods	3
Case 3	Qantas: the high flyer of the airline industry?	C23	MNC	Service	3, 5, 6, 7
Case 4	Marlows Limited: a retrospective	C40	SME	Goods	3, 4, 5, 6, 7
Case 5	Bank of Queensland: bank different™	C51	MNC	Service	5, 6, 7
Case 6	Aldi in Australia	C60	MNC	Goods	6, 5
Case 7	Air New Zealand: challenges and opportunities	C69	MNC	Service	3, 7, 8
Case 8	Creating Fonterra: establishing New Zealand's largest business	C77	SME	Goods	7, 8
Case 9	Southcorp Limited: winemaker's winding road	C80	MNC	Goods	6, 7, 8, 9
Case 10	Fonterra's international strategy: developing strategy in New Zealand's largest business	C92	SME	Goods	7, 8
Case 11	Flying Kiwi Promotions Ltd: a kiwi flies	C100	SME	Not for profit	2, 3, 5, 10, 11

Introduction

Analysing a case study and writing a case study analysis

What is case study analysis?

Case study analysis is an integral part of a course in strategic management. The purpose of a case study is to provide students with experience of the strategic management problems faced by actual companies. A case study presents an account of what happened to a business or industry over some years. It chronicles the events that managers had to deal with, such as changes in the competitive environment, and charts the manager's response, which usually involved changing the business- or corporate-level strategy. The cases in part 5 of this book cover a wide range of issues and problems that managers have had to confront. Some cases are about finding the right business-level strategy to compete in changing conditions. Some are about companies that grew by acquisition, with little concern for the rationale behind their growth, and about how growth by acquisition affected their future profitability. Each case is different because each company is different. The underlying thread in all the cases, however, is the use of strategic management techniques to solve business problems.

Cases prove valuable in a strategic course for several reasons. First, cases provide you, the student, with experience of organisational problems that you probably have not had the opportunity to experience. In a relatively short time, you will have the chance to appreciate and analyse the problems faced by many different companies and to understand how managers tried to deal with those problems.

Second, cases illustrate the theory and content of strategic management — that is, all the information presented to you in the previous chapters of this book. This information has been collected, discovered and distilled from the observations, research and experience of managers and academicians. The meaning and implications of this information are made clearer when they are applied to case studies. The theory and concepts help reveal what is going on in the companies studied and allow you to evaluate the solutions that specific companies adopted to deal with their problems. Consequently, when you analyse cases, you will be like a detective who probes, with a set of conceptual tools, what happened and what or who was responsible, and then marshals the evidence that provides the solution. Top managers enjoy the thrill of testing their problem-solving abilities in the real world. It is important to remember that no-one knows what the right answer is. All that managers can do is make the best guess. Managers say repeatedly that they are happy if they are right only half the time in solving strategic problems. Strategic management is an uncertain game, and using cases to see how theory can be put into practice is one way of improving your skills of diagnostic investigation.

Third, case studies provide you with the opportunity to participate in class and gain experience in presenting your ideas to others. Instructors may sometimes call on students as a group to identify what is going on in a case; through classroom discussion, the issues in and solutions to the case problem will reveal themselves. In such a situation, you will have to organise your views and conclusions so you can present them to the class. Your classmates might have analysed the issues differently from you, and they will want you to argue your points before they will accept your conclusions, so be prepared for debate. This mode of discussion is an example of the dialectical approach to decision making that you may recall from chapter 1.

Instructors also may assign an individual, but more commonly a group, to analyse the case before the whole class. The individual or group probably will be responsible for a thirty- to forty-minute presentation of the case to the class. That presentation must cover the issues involved, the problems facing the company and recommendations for resolving the problems. The discussion then will be thrown open to the class, and the presenters will have to defend their ideas. Through such discussions and presentations, you will experience how to convey your ideas effectively to others. After all, a great deal of managers' time is spent in these kinds of situations, presenting their ideas and engaging in discussion with other managers, who have their own views about what is going on.

If you work in groups to analyse case studies, you also will learn about the group process involved in working as a team. When people work in groups, it is often difficult to schedule time and allocate responsibility for the case analysis. There are always group members who shirk their responsibilities and group members who are so sure of their own ideas that they try to dominate the group's analysis. Most strategic management takes place in groups, however, so it is best if you learn about these problems now.

Analysing a case study

The purpose of a case study is to allow you to apply the concepts of strategic management to a specific company or situation. Analysing a case study to determine which frameworks or tools (as covered in the theory section of this book) applies is an important skill. Each case study revolves around a different set of key success factors, so identifying the issues that are important and require analysis, versus less important issues, is a critical part of case analysis. For McDonald's, for example, it is important to understand the competitive environment in which the company operates, but not so much the industry structure, which does not drive the company's superior performance. To explain why McDonald's has been so successful would require an analysis of its internal strengths (probably in terms of the systems and processes used to provide superior customer value). Superior performance does not come from operating in a naturally attractive industry structure: McDonald's is facing ever increasing amounts of competition, which have led to price wars in some geographic areas where there is significant overcapacity. A key in analysing case studies, therefore, is to be able to differentiate the important drivers of performance (or lack of performance) from those factors that have little influence on the overall performance of the company.

Along with reading the case study several times, case analysis involves several steps. First, take the time to make a detailed exploration of the exhibits. The majority of exhibits are normally included in a case for a specific purpose. Conduct some financial analysis (covered later in this section). What stands out? What trends have you uncovered that seem interesting? Look for contradictory data and disputing trends. What do these mean? How may they be important? A case study is rarely simple, one-dimensional and designed with only one interpretation/solution in mind. If you can identify some of the complexities in a case study, then you will be well positioned to at least discuss key issues at a much deeper level than you could after the first reading of the case study.

To analyse a case study, consider the following steps:

1. analyse the environment
2. review the industry structure and the basis for competition
3. consider the key resources available to the company (including organisational capabilities) and how they differ from those of competitors
4. identify what it takes to be successful in the company's business and what the basic business model involves
5. identify the company strategy in place
6. determine the key issues facing the company
7. analyse what is driving these problems, as a pre-cursor to thinking about possible solutions
8. make recommendations
9. justify these recommendations.

The field of strategic management has built up a series of theories and frameworks that can help managers identify, evaluate and solve strategic issues facing a company. A straight application of theory, however, is unlikely to result in deep analysis. To an extent, students and managers alike looking at strategic issues need to think through how a company actually works and how certain actions or events are likely to play out. In the Aldi case for example, what do different customer groups want and, therefore, what determines where different customer groups do their shopping? In the Qantas case, it is important to think through the relative competitive positions of both Qantas and Virgin Blue to understand what options are available to these two competitors. In the Southcorp case, how will the unsuccessful merger/takeover of Rosemount affect the subsequent takeover of Southcorp by Foster's? And is consolidation of the wine industry the most appropriate strategy at present given existing market conditions? Sometimes, the issues are not obvious at the time — such as in the case of Flying Kiwi Promotions — and incorporate organisational structure, motivational and financial issues. In the end, the key to a good case study analysis is a detailed reading of the entire case, extensive thinking, considerable analysis and the development of recommendations that account for the possible contradictory or uncertain components of the case. A summary explanation of some of the steps noted for analysing case study material follows.

1. Analyse the environment

Chapter 3 discusses the need to conduct an analysis of the macro-environment in terms of trends that may affect the company. In analysing a case study, think about macro-environmental trends that are likely to significantly affect the company in the future. Rather than simply listing points under each major subheading (political/legal, economic and so on), identify just a few (if any) major factors that could significantly affect the company's operations.

2. Review the industry structure

Chapter 3 covers the five forces that determine an industry's structure. Attractive industry structures tend to provide above-average profits, while the reverse is true for unattractive industry structures. For most companies that do not have attractive industry structures, it is important to determine the industry factors that are limiting profitability. Are low barriers to entry, for example, stopping companies from raising their prices and earning higher returns? Remember, too, that industry structure is not static. How may it change in the future? Will this change benefit the local company? Can the company do anything to make the industry more attractive?

3. Consider the key resources available to the company

Chapter 4 discusses the role of resources and capabilities. The primary reasons for some companies being consistently high performers are (1) the set of resources they have at their disposal and (2) the way in which they deploy these resources. It is therefore important to identify the key resources available to the company (including tangible resources such as plant and equipment, intangible resources such as brand name, and organisational capabilities such as a distribution capability). It is also important to identify what makes the key resources 'sticky' to the company. In addition, how do the company's resources compare with the resources of competitors? Which company seems better placed to be able to meet the needs of customers? Why?

4. Identify what it takes to be successful in the company's business

What are the key success factors for the industry? Low price, innovative products, control of key distribution channels or something else, such as brand recognition? In essence, what is the secret of success in this business? This analysis normally involves an analysis of customers (who they are and what they want), so it may be necessary to segment the market to more clearly understand how different customer groups need to be served. Also important is an analysis of competition, including what drives competition, along what dimensions it takes place and how intense the competition is. Beating the competition may require significant economies of scale, access to rare and valuable inputs, the establishment of long-term relationships to control distribution or even the recruitment of the best and brightest employees.

5. Identify the company strategy in place

How does the company compete? How would you describe its strategy in just a few sentences? The company's strategy may be as simple as minimising the cost structure in every aspect of its operations to allow it to be the low-cost provider. Or it may be a little more complex, such as targeting one dimension of a niche market that highly values a set of product/service attributes. Comparing the company's strategy with those of other companies and considering how each company's strategy relates to the key success factors can be very revealing.

6. Determine the key issues facing the company

Most case studies feature issues or problems facing the company. It is important to identify these issues and their drivers. Lower sales at a takeaway food store, for example, may be a problem caused by increased competition and falling demand on the basis of consumers preferring healthier alternatives.

7. Analyse the problems

A considerable amount of theory is useful at this stage. Theory can help to explain why the company is in its position. The appropriate theory varies for every case study. The key is to select a theory that can explain what has driven the company to its present position, then use this analysis to develop appropriate recommendations.

8. Make recommendations

After completing the above analysis, you should be able to make recommendations on what the company should do. In some case studies, a number of recommendations will be possible (including some that are contradictory).

9. Justify the recommendations

The options put forward in step 8 need to be evaluated. You often will have thought of contradictory paths of action, so it is necessary to assess which is most appropriate and feasible. Doing this, you may rely on appropriate theory. Although there may be a theoretically superior option, this option may not be acceptable to the key decision maker(s) (such as the CEO). In this scenario, it is important to outline the theoretically optimal solution, explain why it may not be acceptable and then focus on justifying the next best recommendation.

After following all these stages, you will have performed a thorough analysis of the case study and you will be in a position to join in class discussion or present your ideas to the class, depending on the format used by your instructor. Remember that you must tailor your analysis to suit the specific issue discussed in the case study. In some case studies, you may omit one of the analysis steps because it is not relevant to the situation you are considering. You must be sensitive to the needs of the case study and not blindly apply the framework discussed in this section. The framework is meant only as a guide, not as an outline that you must use to do a successful analysis.

Writing a case study analysis

Often, as part of your course requirements, you need to present your instructor with a written case study analysis. This may be an individual or a group report. Whatever the situation, following certain guidelines in writing a case study analysis will improve the evaluation that your work receives from your instructor. Before using these guidelines, make sure that they do not conflict with any directions that your instructor has given you.

The structure of your written report is critical. Generally, if you follow the steps for analysis discussed in the previous section, you will already have a good structure for your written discussion. While this framework will provide a good structure for most written reports, it must be shaped to fit the individual case study being considered. Some case studies are about excellent companies experiencing no problems. In such instances, it is hard to write recommendations; instead, you can focus on analysing why the company is doing so well, using that analysis to structure the discussion. The following suggestions can help make a good analysis even better.

1. Do not repeat in summary form large pieces of factual information from the case study. (The instructor has read the case study and knows the story.) Rather, use the information in the case to illustrate your statements, defend your arguments or make salient points. Beyond the brief introduction to the company, you must avoid being descriptive; instead, you must be analytical.

2. Make sure the sections and subsections of your discussion flow logically and smoothly from one to the next. That is, try to build on what has gone before so the analysis of the case study moves towards a climax. This is particularly important for group analysis, because people in a group tend to split up the work and say, 'I'll do the beginning, you take the middle and I'll do the end'. The result is a choppy, stilted analysis because the parts do not flow from one to the next, and it is obvious to the instructor that no real group work has been done.

3. Avoid grammatical and spelling errors. They are evidence of sloppy work.

4. Sometimes instructors hand out questions for each case study to help you in your analysis. Use these questions as a guide for writing the case study analysis. They often illuminate the important issues that have to be covered in the discussion.

If you follow the guidelines in this section, you should be able to write a thorough and effective evaluation.

The role of financial analysis

Another important aspect of analysing a case study and writing a case study analysis is the role and use of financial information. A careful analysis of the company's financial condition immensely improves an analysis write-up. After all, financial data represent the concrete results of the company's strategy and structure. Although analysing financial statements can be quite complex, ratio analysis can be used to determine a general idea of a company's financial position. Financial performance ratios can be calculated from the statement of financial position and the income statement. These ratios can be classified into five subgroups: profit ratios, liquidity ratios, activity ratios, leverage ratios and shareholder return ratios. These ratios should be compared with the industry average or the company's performance in previous years. Deviation from the average, however, is not necessarily bad; it simply warrants further investigation. Young companies, for example, will have purchased assets at a different price and are likely to have a different capital structure than that of older companies. In addition to ratio analysis, a company's cash flow position is of critical importance and should be assessed. Cash flow shows how much actual cash a company possesses.

Profit ratios

Profit ratios measure the efficiency with which the company uses its resources. The more efficient the company, the greater is its profitability. It is useful to compare a company's profitability against that of its major competitors in its industry. Such a comparison shows whether the company is operating more or less efficiently than its rivals. In addition, the change in a company's profit ratios over time shows whether the company's performance is improving or declining.

Several different profit ratios can be used, each measuring a different aspect of a company's performance. The most commonly used profit ratios are as follows.

1. *Gross profit margin*. This ratio simply gives the percentage of sales available to cover general and administrative expenses and other operating costs. It is defined as follows:

$$\text{Gross profit margin} = \frac{\text{Sales revenue} - \text{Cost of goods sold}}{\text{Sales revenue}}$$

2. *Net profit margin*. This ratio gives the percentage of profit earned on sales. It is important because businesses need to make a profit to survive in the long term. It is defined as follows:

$$\text{Net profit margin} = \frac{\text{Net income}}{\text{Sales revenue}}$$

3. *Return on total assets*. This ratio measures the profit earned on the employment of assets. It is defined as follows:

$$\text{Return on total assets} = \frac{\text{Earnings before interest and tax}}{\text{Total assets}}$$

Note that this ratio is calculated before tax, whereas return on equity is calculated after tax.

4. *Return on equity*. This ratio measures the percentage of profit earned on the total shareholders' equity in the

company. This is a measure of the overall performance of the company. It is defined as follows:

$$\text{Return on equity} = \frac{\text{Profit after tax}}{\text{Total shareholders' fund (equity)}}$$

Liquidity ratios

A company's liquidity is a measure of its ability to meet short-term obligations. An asset is deemed liquid if it can be readily converted into cash. Liquid assets are current assets, such as cash, marketable securities, accounts receivable and so on. Two commonly used liquidity ratios are as follows.

1. *Current ratio*. This ratio measures the extent to which the claims of short-term creditors are covered by assets that can be quickly converted into cash. Most companies should have a ratio of at least 1, because failure to meet these commitments can lead to bankruptcy. The ratio is defined as follows:

$$\text{Current ratio} = \frac{\text{Current assets}}{\text{Current liabilities}}$$

2. *Quick ratio*. This ratio measures a company's ability to pay off the claims of short-term creditors without relying on the sale of its inventories. This is a valuable measure because the sale of inventories is often difficult. It is defined as follows:

$$\text{Quick ratio} = \frac{\text{Current assets} - \text{Inventory}}{\text{Current liabilities}}$$

Activity ratios

Activity ratios indicate how effectively a company is managing its assets. The following ratio is particularly useful.

1. *Inventory turnover*. This ratio measures the number of times that inventory is turned over, which is useful in determining whether a company is carrying excess stock in inventory. It is defined as follows:

$$\text{Inventory turnover} = \frac{\text{Cost of goods sold}}{\text{Inventory}}$$

The cost of goods sold is a better measure of turnover than sales is, because it is the cost of the inventory items. Inventory is taken at the date of the statement of financial position. Some companies choose to compute an average inventory, a beginning inventory and an ending inventory, but for simplicity use the inventory at the date of the statement of financial position.

Leverage ratios

A company is said to be highly leveraged if it uses more debt than equity, including stock and retained earnings.

The balance between debt and equity is called the *capital structure*. The optimal capital structure is determined by the individual company. Debt has a lower cost because creditors take less risk; they know they will get their interest and principal. Debt can be risky to the company, however, because bankruptcy can occur if not enough profit is made to cover the interest and principal payments.

Three commonly used leverage ratios are as follows:

1. *Debt-to-assets ratio*. This ratio is the most direct measure of the extent to which borrowed funds have been used to finance a company's investments. It is defined as follows:

$$\text{Debt-to-assets ratio} = \frac{\text{Total debt}}{\text{Total assets}}$$

Total debt is the sum of a company's current liabilities and its long-term debt, and total assets are the sum of fixed assets and current assets.

2. *Debt-to-equity ratio*. This ratio indicates the balance between debt and equity in a company's capital structure. It is perhaps the most widely used measure of a company's leverage. It is defined as follows:

$$\text{Debt-to-equity ratio} = \frac{\text{Total debt}}{\text{Total equity}}$$

3. *Times-covered ratio*. The times-covered ratio measures the extent to which a company's gross profit covers its annual interest payments. If the times-covered ratio falls to less than 1, then the company is unable to meet its interest costs and is technically insolvent. The ratio is defined as follows:

$$\frac{\text{Times-covered}}{\text{ratio}} = \frac{\text{Profit before interest and tax}}{\text{Total interest charges}}$$

Cash flow

Cash flow position is simply cash received minus cash distributed. The net cash flow can be taken from a company's statement of cash flows. Cash flow is important for what it tells us about a company's financing needs. A strong positive cash flow enables a company to fund future investments without having to borrow money from bankers or investors. This is desirable because the company avoids the need to pay interest or dividends. A weak or negative cash flow means that a company has to turn to external sources to fund future investments. Companies in strong-growth industries often find themselves in a poor cash flow position (because their investment needs are substantial), whereas successful companies based in mature industries generally find themselves in a strong cash flow position.

A company's internally generated cash flow is calculated by adding back its depreciation provision to profits after interest, taxes and dividend payments. If this figure is insufficient to cover proposed new investment expenditures, then the company has little choice but to (1) borrow funds to make up the shortfall or curtail investments. If this figure exceeds proposed new investments, then the company can use the excess to build up its liquidity (that is, through investments in financial assets) or repay existing loans ahead of schedule.

Conclusion

When evaluating a case, it is important to be systematic. Analyse the case studies in a logical manner. Using the framework suggested earlier in this section can help, but the key is to identify why a situation has arisen and what should be done about it. This process will normally involve using some of the theory covered in this book and, in some cases, undertaking further research. The most important part of a case study analysis is to be logical, so a reader can clearly follow your analysis from identification of the issues through to the recommendations. The reader should never be left wondering why you have made a particular recommendation or why you have introduced a specific framework. Remember, there are rarely right and wrong answers, so a logical approach and consistent arguments will determine how well you do in your case study analyses.

Kleenmaid: moving towards formal planning

By Bishnu Sharma, Kerry Scott, Paul Corcoran and Wayne Graham[1]

Introduction

Kleenmaid, a 100 per cent privately owned Australian company, has a commitment to the delivery of higher-quality, reliable home appliances (kitchen, laundry and lifestyle appliances) to its customers in Australia. The company's services are well supported by its aftersales service. In meeting its objectives of providing superior-quality products and services, the company uses the best manufacturers from around the world to produce Kleenmaid-branded products. Some of the products the company deals in include cooktops, ovens, rangehoods, microwaves, coffee machines, dishwashers, refrigerators, washing machines, dryers, vacuums, outdoor cooking centres, sinks, taps and accessories. Since its inception in 1985 by Andrew Young and Dick England, the company has made great strides with annual sales of more than $100 million through more than 30 stores across Australia. The company has been rated as one of the fastest-growing private companies in Australia and is regularly in the BRW Top 500 companies. Kleenmaid offers consumers a store with fully operational appliances, in which they can use the washing machines or cook up a storm in the kitchen. Major functions such as sales, marketing, customer service, finance, administration and information technology are managed from Kleenmaid's head office, which is located on the Sunshine Coast, Queensland.

As a part of its growth strategy, Kleenmaid bought the brand name and selected manufacturing equipment of liquidated company St George Appliances in 1999. St George, an Australian company for more than 50 years, used to export its products all over the world. The company was renamed as Kleenmaid St George after the purchase. After a period of growth and consolidation in 2004, Kleenmaid divested its interests in the St George brand and refocused on its core business of Kleenmaid appliances.

More than a million Australians use Kleenmaid appliances daily and as the largest Australian direct retailer of household appliances, the company claims that it is committed to bringing the world's best to its customers. The appliances that the company deals with have a reputation for unique design, outstanding performance, quality and reliability. Originally, products were sold using conventional retailers. However, to uphold Kleenmaid's commitment to providing unique products and exceptional service, it started selling directly to its customers through its own retail network in 1995.

In Kleenmaid's showrooms, customers can personally experience the appliances and the company's services first hand. Some of the extra rewards customers enjoy when dealing with this company are initiatives such as in-store competitor comparisons, in-store product trials, a national cooking program with in-store cooking demonstrations, dinners and events, a free in-store kitchen designer program and in-home product trials. In terms of customer service, it provides a very high level of protection to customers with five-year parts and labour warranty, a 'No Lemon Guarantee and unique Best Value Guarantee' (see figure C1.1).[2] The company claims to be the only Australian retailer to offer its customers this kind of outstanding protection.

Domestic appliances industry in Australia

The domestic appliances industry encompasses the manufacture of a range of electrical products including refrigerators, ovens and cooktops, washing machines, dryers, dishwashers, portable appliances and vacuum cleaners. Many of these products form a subset that is usually referred to as 'whitegoods'. The industry has seen a healthy growth in the volume of domestic electrical appliances sales with the rapid growth in housing development and an increase in new households in the past three or four years.[3]

The household appliances industry in Australia has been dominated by a few local players and some European brands. Recently, there has been a strong influx of Asian brands, most notably Samsung and LG, into the Australian market. Their ability to offer their products at lower prices than their competitors' has forced the existing manufacturers to discount their prices to position themselves in the current competitive market environment. Despite the increase in volume of sales, the downward pressure on prices has constrained the growth of the industry in value terms. The influx of cheaper brands into the market and the introduction of technological innovations have resulted in product differentiation. Consequently, the customers have a wider choice and the demand for differentiated products has grown, even in rural areas. The existing users have also taken the opportunity to replace their products, resulting in increased volume sales. Stainless steel and iridium finishes have proven to be increasingly popular types of premium products, as consumers have striven for the 'professional kitchen' look in their homes.[4]

Competitive intensity has increased both at the manufacturer and the retail level. In domestic electrical appliances in particular, Harvey Norman and Retravision have played a dominant role in the product distribution as they have a reputation for offering cheaper prices. Some of the factors that influence the demand for domestic appliances are consumer confidence, rate of product replacement, population growth and the growth of housing construction. The key players in this industry are Electrolux, Fisher & Paykel and GWA International.

Awards and recognition

Distribution of quality appliances has always been a core element of the Kleenmaid philosophy, and it has a passion for providing the products that not only look great but are also environmentally friendly. Recent successes acknowledging Kleenmaid's superior environmental positioning include the KFL1600 front-loading washing machine and the KFL850 front-loading washing machine both receiving the 2005 TESAW Award (Top Energy Saver Award from the Australian Government Greenhouse Office for the most energy-efficient appliances); the KFL1600 being five-star energy rated (the best energy rating of any washing machine in Australia or New Zealand) and also 5A water rated (one of the most water efficient washing machines in its class). For dishwashers, Kleenmaid's DW26i and DW25 are also both recipients of the 2005 TESAW Award. Additionally, all Kleenmaid ovens have A-class European ratings (there is no Australian standard) with a range of environmentally designed features including pyrolytic clean, eco-cooking modes, Easy Cook and all appliances being designed and selected with environmental considerations and energy efficiency.

Competition and competitive advantages

The Electrolux group, with sales of more than a billion dollars, dominates the appliance category in Australia.

This group bought Email and the brands associated with it (Westinghouse, Simpson and Dishlex). Fisher & Paykel and LG are the relatively new entrants in the market. In addition, there are a range of high-end brands, such as Miele, Maytag, Smeg, Gaggenau, Ilve and Blanco, all competing for the same premium dollar that Kleenmaid is targeting. Kleenmaid's major competition is with the overseas suppliers. Simpson and Westinghouse have a similar price and cater to the larger segment of the appliance market. Kleenmaid compares favourably with Miele in terms of price and quality and is regarded as the top-end product, while LG and Fisher & Paykel serve the top end of the mass market.

Kleenmaid's competitive advantage lies in:
- superior product design
- superior warranties
- superior in-store experience. This is evident in several key areas:
  - Salespeople are fully trained and have a better knowledge than that of their competitors' sales staff. Therefore, the customers are better informed about their product performance.
  - Kleenmaid's stores are *fully functional*, so customers can actually see a working demo (try before you buy).
  - Kleenmaid's national cooking program offers customers the opportunity to attend in-store dinners, VIP evenings and cooking lessons after their purchase.
  - Kleenmaid's in-store kitchen designer program offers a free kitchen design service (resulting in a tailored, colour 3D kitchen design for customers) and a comprehensive kitchen design service (a thorough design that can be presented to a cabinet maker).
  - Kleenmaid-owned and managed customer service and aftersales service to provide a complete 'Kleenmaid experience' of an exceptional level.

Fisher & Paykel (two-drawer dishwashers) and LG (Internet-enabled fridges) seem to be competing with the 'innovation' positioning platform. Kleenmaid believes that the 'service' positioning peak is vacant. Therefore, Kleenmaid believes this is a credible platform as its positioning strategy. The 'service' peak can extend itself from the shopping experience to free delivery and installation, to protecting the customers' investment for five years through to the guarantee of ensuring parts availability for at least the expected life of the product, plus managing aftersales and customer service.

Andrew Young: chairman and co-founder

Andrew Young, the co-founder, co-owner and chairman of Kleenmaid, commands high respect for steering the company to what it is today through his vision and his strategies and their successful execution. He was born in New Zealand and was a hard worker right from his early childhood.

At the age of eight, he was making money polishing shoes and often worked after school, weekends and school holidays for earnings. By 15, he had gained practical mechanical skills and owned his own plastic moulding business. At 22, Andrew established a partnership, 'Warringah Washer Service', which was sold a year later. Andrew then travelled overseas and on his return in 1978 founded a whitegoods spare parts company 'Anlin Spare Parts'.

After six years, he sold this business to Angus and Coote and moved to the Sunshine Coast, where, in 1987, he established Kleenmaid. Without any formal academic qualifications, Andrew uses his natural entrepreneurial ability to visualise opportunities that are often seen by his competitors as being considerably risky. Andrew believes in continuous improvement and is willing to accept the challenges that involves. He has a strong passion for customer service and sales. He says: 'If the customer is not well served, then we do not have a business and the process has fallen down'.

Along with his fellow directors, Andrew is committed to responding to customer and industry demands and maintaining customer service leadership in the whitegoods industry.

Mission statement

The following mission statement was established by Andrew Young and Dick England, the founding directors of the company, and has remained unchanged.

> We founded Kleenmaid with a commitment to introduce and maintain new levels of product quality and service within the major electrical appliance industry.
> We, together with our team at Kleenmaid, stand personally accountable to that founding commitment.
>
> *Andrew Young & Dick England*

Strategic planning

While Andrew remains a chief strategist, he is joined by the other directors and his management team in a consultative process for the growth and development of the business. The management team meets weekly to discuss existing projects and management issues with strategy implementation and review. The company has created an active working environment, which provides prompt action with a high level of flexibility in seizing market opportunities without much deviation in its proven core business approach. In addition, regular strategy sessions are held throughout the year and the members of the management team are empowered to lead the business with their relevant expertise in their areas of responsibility. Kleenmaid continues to hold staff meetings every month to discuss various strategic and operational issues.

The company has witnessed a big departure from its top-down approach to planning and decision-making to a participatory style over the past three years. In the past, Andrew used to act as the chief architect of the business strategy. In doing this, the staff members used to be consulted from time to time as required rather than holding regular (weekly or fortnightly) sit-down meetings. The specific departments used to provide necessary support to the managing director (Andrew Young) by providing relevant information when required.

Distribution of Kleenmaid stores

Kleenmaid has stores across Australia. Their distribution is:

- Victoria: Camberwell, Dandenong, Elsternwick, Geelong, Mitcham, Mornington and Thomastown
- Australian Capital Territory: Fyshwick
- New South Wales: Alexandria, Auburn, Brookvale, Castle Hill, Central Coast, Chatswood, Drummoyne, Liverpool, Penrith, Taren Point, Warners Bay, and Wollongong
- Queensland: Browns Plains, Capalaba, Fortitude Valley, Gold Coast, Jindalee, Sunshine Coast, Toowoomba and Virginia
- South Australia: Marion and Stepney
- Western Australia: Cannington, Joondalup, Myaree and Osborne Park
- Tasmania: Hobart.

Kleenmaid stores are called fully functional stores. In contrast to other whitegoods retailers, all the appliances in a Kleenmaid store are fully functional and can be demonstrated. Kleenmaid has the advantage of highly professional salespeople, who are trained in demonstrating the use and benefits of Kleenmaid products. It has also developed an extensive network of dealers in regional areas of Australia. Kleenmaid provides a comprehensive service for builders and developers. This can involve delivery, installation and full aftersales service at one competitive price. It takes care of all details including an on-site inspection and its staff carry out all installation and servicing if required.

Employee training and development

At Kleenmaid, there are 500 employees: 270 are Kleenmaid personnel while the remaining 230 work in stores owned by franchisees. In this company, there is a strong emphasis on staff support, encouragement and development. Each new staff member attends the Kleenmaid College to be inducted into the company and receive formal training in products, sales and customer service. More than $2 million is spent every year on training staff. Being a market-driven organisation, it has a practice of rewarding its staff with competitive remuneration. The employees in return are making a good contribution to the growth and the development of the company. The company is always looking for motivated, enthusiastic people to join its results-oriented and customer service-focused team. The directors present monthly meetings for head office staff, keeping them informed of business developments. All employees are provided with a full professional corporate uniform. Those working in the sales arena receive evaluation appliances (washing machine, dryer and dishwasher) valued at approximately $5000 and are required to report regularly on the products' performance. Head office personnel are provided with cooked lunches using the company products.

As a part of training and development, the company organises overseas tours and the employees' perceptions of these experiences are summarised in the following.

> While the factory tours, particularly General Electrics were extremely beneficial, the best aspect of the tour was the opportunity to share ideas and information with the other sales consultants and franchisees.
>
> There was a stage where we were all on a bus and the microphone was passed around to each of us so we could tell various sales stories. I found the experience to be extremely beneficial and motivating as it provided an opportunity to hear how other people handled various situations.

> The least I can do is to make sales so that this win–win situation continues and is profitable. — Vicki Thomas, Osborne Park, WA

Kleenmaid's franchising practices

As Australia's only direct retailer of kitchen and laundry appliances, Kleenmaid has earned a reputation for quality, service and performance. A large portion of Kleenmaid stores are franchised. With a product range sold exclusively through its stores, guaranteed margin and proven management systems developed over nearly 20 years, existing franchisees are enjoying outstanding financial success. For an investment of between $500 000 to $800 000 (including fixtures and fittings and stock, minimal goodwill), franchisees are averaging 50 per cent return on investment.

What does a typical Kleenmaid's franchisee think about Kleenmaid?

> Kleenmaid offers me a great opportunity to operate a business with a professional image, with the support of a forward thinking, young and enthusiastic team at head office. Being part of a franchised system means I can get on with the things that help sell and make money, without being weighed down with the daily issues of delivering a product. The overall product is excellent, the selling environment is exciting and the rewards are there if you work at it. Kleenmaid has managed to create space in a market usually dominated by large companies based on an honest, down to earth, enthusiastic approach to its product and customers. — Peter McMillan, Stepney, South Australia[5]

Customer service

Kleenmaid's slogan for customer service is 'We care about our customers!' Superior customer service has been a dominant factor in Kleenmaid's success. Kleenmaid was one of the first whitegoods companies to offer a five-year warranty but some of its competitors are now matching that.

It also offers 'Clever Kitchen Concept' seminars in which it provides advice on every aspect of kitchen design from the use of colour, lifestyle options, functionality and construction methods to all the latest international trends in appliances and materials. Experienced kitchen professionals conduct the seminars, which have proven to be the quickest and easiest way to create the customers' perfect kitchen, avoiding costly kitchen design mistakes and adding thousands of dollars in value to the customers' homes.

Kleenmaid also offers a complete range of interactive and informative services, as noted. To improve customer service further, Kleenmaid has formed alliances with some exclusive service partners. From this alliance, the customers can expect service within 48 hours for servicers who have spare parts and consumables on hand to ensure a higher first-time fix rate. The partners have well presented, highly skilled and qualified technicians. Mobile EFTPOS makes the payment convenient for customers and their service guarantees fixed price for 'out of warranty' service work. The customer call centres are open from 7 am to 7 pm Monday to Friday and 8 am to 4 pm on Saturday.

Information system and customer responsiveness

A system called 'Kleenmaid Integrated Software System (KISS)' based on Paradox software and capable of recording customer information had been in use since 1992. Owing to the rapid expansion of system users, the system capacity was not adequate and caused slow performance and frequent lockups. By the summer of 1997, a new in-house customer database system called 'Calls & Services' had been custom written to accommodate 50 users simultaneously. This system has since expanded to support more than 500 users and plays an important role in customer service. Customers contacting Kleenmaid are amazed at how quickly information is retrieved and the level of detail available. The networked system uses the industry approved 'MRG PRO' as its framework with improved servers to accommodate current and future expansion. Consistent reviewing of procedures and systems ensures Kleenmaid maintains its quest for excellence in the delivery of quality products and service. The company has recognised technology as a source of competitive advantage and employs a team of qualified professionals to work on continual technology improvements.

Service agents receive incentives for referring customers to Kleenmaid appliances. Referral business constitutes a vital part of Kleenmaid's sales and marketing strategy. It has established a network of some 1500 independent service agents nationally to provide aftersales service, as well as a spare parts operation located in Sydney to supply spare parts requirements to the service agent network and direct to the public. Customers requiring aftersales service phone a 1300 integrated voice system and after they enter their postcodes and the product requiring servicing, their calls are automatically directed to the local authorised service agent.

Customers' perceptions of Kleenmaid's products and services

Kleenmaid has a practice of monitoring customers' perceptions of Kleenmaid's products and services regularly. The results indicate a very high level of customer satisfaction and because of the superior service, most of its customers even remember the store consultant's name. Generally, the customers rate their products highly in terms of product performance in meeting their needs and they also tend to concur that Kleenmaid's appliance demonstration activities are highly beneficial to them.

Market segments and distribution practice

Kleenmaid distributes its products in three market segments across Australia:

1. Metropolitan and regional centre retail: through franchisee stores nationally, which exclusively sell Kleenmaid products. Kleenmaid does not distribute its product through any stores other than their own franchisee stores in metropolitan and major regional areas. Sales through this segment account for approximately 85 per cent of total national sales.
2. Country: through a range of retail outlets in country areas. Sales through this distribution medium account for about 4 per cent of total national sales. Distribution is not exclusive to its own stores in country areas.
3. Commercial: through developers and builders. Sales through this distribution medium account for about 11 per cent of total national sales.

New South Wales is the biggest market for Kleenmaid, followed by Victoria, Queensland, South Australia and Western Australia in terms of proportion of revenue. Generally, country wholesale has been in steady decline for the past few years. However commercial sales are growing substantially.

Kleenmaid has ambitious growth plans, principally through expanding its retail network of franchisees to gain better customer availability nationally. From 1987 to 1995,

Kleenmaid distributed through retailers such as Harvey Norman and Retravision. However, Kleenmaid felt that these retailers were not able to demonstrate the value of the product, so it decided to change its distribution strategy. As a result of this decision, it withdrew its products from these stores and established its own stores across Australia. Although sales improved considerably, the company felt that store managers lacked the drive and initiative to grow the business. Therefore, in 2000, it changed its strategy from owning its stores to franchising. In each of the franchised stores, sales have increased dramatically. Therefore, the company is determined to increase the availability of its product and expand the number of franchisees in new territories that are not currently serviced, and in some cases in existing territories in which the population densities warrant increased sales. Although the process of franchising is slow, it expects to continue its expansion plans for at least another two years.

Currently, the proportion of quotes that are converted to sales is about 33 per cent. The sales conversion, however, depends on[6] :

- existing customer (highest propensity)
- existing customer's referral to family or friend
- new customer predisposed to Kleenmaid brand
- trade referral (kitchen company, architect, opinion leader, service agent)
- price shoppers responding to 'sale' advertisements (lowest propensity).

More than 33 per cent of leads come from current customers and a further 27 per cent from customer referrals to family or friends. This suggests that there is a strong level of customer advocacy, which also indirectly indicates a high level of customer satisfaction. From a media perspective, the company targets all people 40 years and over in the socio-economic ABC class (the top 40 per cent of Australian households from an income perspective) with the secondary audience more narrowly defined as women 40 years and over. This is because media studies have indicated that about 56 per cent of decision makers who have renovated their homes are women.

From a market share perspective, Kleenmaid estimates that its 'any-product' penetration would be less than 5 per cent of all households.

Portfolio of product sales

There has been a major shift in Kleenmaid's product portfolio since the company commenced. As presented in table C1.1 in column 3, 23.8 per cent of all products purchased (1987–2005) were washing machines, but in the latest 12 months shown, washing machines constitute only 7.5 per cent of products purchased. This indicates an increasing trend to sell more ovens and cooktops versus the laundry category (washers and dryers). In terms of price, Kleenmaid's pricing structure positions the products above the top-of-the-range Australia- and New Zealand-manufactured brands but below the high-end European brands. The average life of whitegoods appliances is seven to 10 years but Kleenmaid's products last longer.

Table C1.1: Portfolio of product sales

Product	Number purchased 1987 to October 2005	%	Units sold November 2004 to October 2005 12 months	%
Oven	156 093	15.8	14 638	18.3
Cooktop	139 428	14.1	18 833	23.6
Rangehood	111 819	11.3	10 565	13.2
Dishwasher	117 100	11.9	8 526	10.7
Washing machine	234 669	23.8	5 997	7.5
Refrigerator	104 408	10.6	10 264	12.8
Sink	24 773	2.5	1 915	2.4
Tap	23 470	2.4	1 640	2.1
Cookware	15 204	1.5	2 170	2.7
Dryer	35 703	3.6	2 278	2.8
Microwave	10 774	1.1	1 945	2.4
Vacuum	9 646	1.0	651	0.8
Waste disposal	2 707	0.3	509	0.6
Total	985 794		79 931	

Source: Kleenmaid

Promotion of Kleenmaid's brand

The following practices are in place to promote Kleenmaid's brand and stores:

- TV advertising
- 'homemaker' and 'lifestyle' magazine advertising
- radio
- metropolitan, regional, suburban and local press

- direct marketing to their customer base and prospect lists
- industry stakeholder programs with service agents, kitchen companies, architects, designers and so on.

Kleenmaid has increased its budget for advertising, direct marketing and promotion considerably in recent years but this is way below the amount of money spent by retailers such as Harvey Norman and Retravision.

Strategic thinking as a response to business challenges

In the current competitive environment, sustaining the marketing and financial performance of the company would not be possible without promoting the Kleenmaid brand, which requires some serious strategic thinking. The brand development strategy needs further integration with the various components of corporate and business strategy such as supply chain management, market positioning, advertising and promotion, and expanding franchisees. Kleenmaid has an ambitious target of increasing its annual sales and being a brand of customers' choice. To respond to the changes in the business environment and achieve strategic and financial objectives, the company has actively been engaged in the introduction and management of various change initiatives. This has involved re-engineering how it does its business (e.g. business practices and business model). In this process, it has changed its planning practice from an informal top-down approach to a more of formal planning with increasing involvement of employees at different levels. Whether it will be successful in achieving what it intends to achieve is unknown but how it is launching its change initiatives and marshalling its resources show lots of promise.

Discussion questions

1. Identify the key business drivers that influence the success of the appliance industry.
2. Identify the key players of the industry and use strategic group mapping techniques for identifying the competitors of Kleenmaid, and discuss the extent of mobility barriers, if any, between the strategic groups.
3. Discuss whether the recent shift in the planning practice at Kleenmaid will be of any help in meeting its strategic and financial objectives. Provide sufficient evidence and justification to support your answer.
4. Use an appropriate framework to evaluate the level of attractiveness of the appliance industry in Australia.
5. What would you recommend to the top management to increase the company's competitive advantage and protect its current market position?

End notes

1. All the authors teach at University of the Sunshine Coast, Maroochydore DC QLD 4558, Australia. The authors wish to acknowledge the wonderful support and cooperation extended by the management of Kleenmaid, particularly Andrew Young, Tricia Grant and Nicole Moy, without which this study would not have been completed.
2. Kleenmaid n.d., accessed 8 November 2005, www.kleenmaid.com.au/guarantees.asp, viewed November 8, 2005.
3. *Euromonitor International* 2005, accessed 7 November 2005, www.euromonitor.com/Domestic_Appliances_In_Australia.
4. ibid.
5. Personal communication 2005.
6. Personal communication with the Kleenmaid staff 2005.

Cooroy Mountain Spring Water: it is worth bottling

By Wayne Graham, Paul Corcoran, Kerry Scott and Bishnu Sharma, University of the Sunshine Coast

Introduction

Cooroy Mountain Spring Water is a private company operating at the base of Cooroy Mountain, where a natural spring of water flows onto the third-generation family property. Cooroy Mountain is situated in the Sunshine Coast hinterland, 15 minutes inland from the popular beachside tourist destination of Noosa Heads and 90 minutes north of Brisbane. The business was established in 1991 after a local farmer responded to a request from Noosa Sheraton for the supply of high-quality water for their guests. In just 14 years, the business has grown rapidly and now delivers millions of bottles of water each year.

Cooroy Mountain Spring Water is a certified bottler of the Australasian Bottled Water Institute (ABWI). The business was awarded Best Water Bottling Plant by ABWI in 2001, 2002, 2003 and 2004, and an Order of Excellence in 2003 and 2004. The bottling facility is based on a hospital operating theatre, with pressurised, filtered and sterilised air maintaining a contaminant-free environment. Before being bottled, the spring water passes through a series of UV filtration and carbon filters, with the final filter being a 0.2-micron 'absolute membrane' filter to remove any bacteria. This process ensures bacteria-free water and, therefore, avoids the need to inject ozone into the bottled water. Tests by government and independent laboratories have analysed the water and found it to be of outstanding quality.

The supply of water from Cooroy Mountain is abundant. The plant currently uses less than 2 per cent of the available spring water from its underground spring at the base of the mountain. Even though the business bottles approximately 25 million litres of natural spring water yearly, the underground aquifer is barely affected in terms of its total available volume. With opportunities for contract fills, export markets and with the bottled water industry in Australia still in its infancy, Cooroy Mountain Spring Water is ideally suited for expansion and growth over the next few years of operation.

Products

The products are offered on the basis of three categories: retail, home and office delivery (HOD) and contract filling. Many different distributors deliver the retail products to supermarkets, shops, restaurants and other food outlets. The home and office range of products includes hot and cold dispensers, refrigerated coolers, stylish stoneware pottery crocks and fridge packs. Additionally, a range of timber stands is available to meet the specific needs of each customer. The retail and HOD range of bottled water products are shown in table C2.1. The delivery of the products is streamlined, with partnerships with distribution companies.

Table C2.1: Retail and HOD product range

Market segment	Size of bottles available
Retail	350 mL, 600 mL, 1 L (sports top), 1.5 L, 3 L, 10 L
Home and office delivery	11 L, 15 L, 19 L (all sizes are returnable and refillable)

The home and office product is delivered using ten contract drivers and three employee drivers. The vehicle fleet includes vans, small trucks and a semitrailer. The production patterns are seasonal, with three shifts operating in the summer months. It is during these months that the plant operates 24 hours a day, Monday to Friday. In the winter, production is reduced to one shift per day.

Community

Community support and sponsorship are important aspects of the business and Cooroy Mountain Spring Water has supported local and state events. Events sponsored include the Noosa Triathlon, the Caloundra Surf Classic, the Queensland Garden Expo, the King of the Mountain Festival and various community, charity and school events. In addition, the business provides support to organisations such as the Queensland Ballet and promotional products for local Sunshine Coast Radio Stations.

Organisational design

There are four levels in the hierarchy and more than 60 employees at Cooroy Mountain Spring Water. The managing director and owner has remained a 'hands-on' manager since inception. The general manager is responsible for the six functional areas: finance, customer service, sales, marketing, operations and logistics. Figure C2.1 depicts the Cooroy Mountain Spring Water organisational chart.[1]

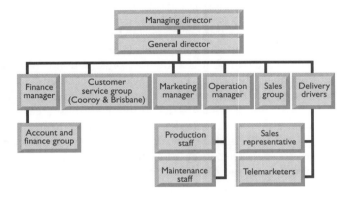

Figure C2.1: Cooroy Mountain Spring Water organisational chart

The bottled water industry in Australia

According to the Australian Consumers' Association, the Australian bottled water industry earns about $123 million per year.[2] In spite of Australia having safe drinking water, the bottled water industry has grown exponentially over the past five years. The largest segment of customers tends to be young females, particularly those between the ages of 14 and 35 years.[3] An online poll conducted by *Choice* magazine reported that 32 per cent of the respondents purchased bottled water because of a belief that it was healthier than available alternatives.[4] Of this group, 24 per cent bought bottled water because they believed that it was less likely to contain harmful bacteria and 8 per cent bought it because they believed it was less likely to contain harmful chemicals. The next highest group (29 per cent) bought bottled water because of the convenience. The bottle was given as the main reason for purchase by 22 per cent of respondents: the bottle could be reused (including filling it from a tap). Only 16 per cent indicated that they purchased bottled water because of its taste compared with that of tap water.[5]

Bottled water can be divided into two main categories: sparkling water, which is water that has undergone carbonation, and still water.[6] Bottled water can also be categorised by source: spring water, mineral water (usually spring water with a higher mineral content) or rainwater. Some water is bottled at the source, while other water may be transported to a processing and bottling plant. In Australia, mineral water seems to be the type most often carbonated. Some waters are subject to further processing. Products that are sold as purified water indicate that the water has been distilled or treated in some way. Improved water, sometimes called 'near' water, is water that has been flavoured or has had vitamins or minerals added.

Bottlers tend to target either the bulk water market (home and office delivery) or the individual consumer market (personal or table serves), although a few bottlers such as Cooroy Mountain Spring Water compete in both. The former group covers bottles or containers of 10 litres or larger. Brands such as Neverfail and Peats Ridge are the recognised national leaders in this group. The latter group covers cup sizes of between 110 mL and 330 mL and bottles of between 400 mL and 2 L. Here the leading brands include Mount Franklin, Frantelle, Pump, Cool Ridge and Summit. Recently, Mount Franklin has introduced its 'Lightly Sparkling' brand, which is only available at restaurants, cafes and hotels. This is a marked departure from the approaches usually seen in the bulk water and individual water markets.

In addition to the well-known brands, there is a multitude of boutique water bottlers. In all, it is estimated that there are more than 1000 water brands in Australia.[7] However, the Australian bottled water industry is dominated by a handful of brands. As table C2.2 shows, established food and beverage companies own many of these brands. The major player in the market is Coca-Cola Amatil (CCA), with two of the brand leaders, having acquired both Neverfail and Peats Ridge in 2003. However, competition in all areas of the market is intense. In the bulk water market (home and office delivery) the bottlers will usually hire coolers and stands and supply cups to customers. The personal market, on the other hand, is about availability. The larger food and beverage companies, with existing arrangements for product placement distribution, are in a better position than the boutique brands. Often the boutique companies are limited to operating at a regional level or on-selling their water (contract filling) to be bottled and branded by their better-known competitors.

For example, in Queensland, Cooroy Mountain Spring Water supplies spring water to a multinational company under a different label. The contract fill provides revenue to the company but at the same time the product becomes a competitor. Contract fills may also involve customised labelling and packaging. For example, a local business may wish to promote their label with the distribution of bottled water for a particular marketing campaign. Cooroy Mountain Spring Water responds to this request by supplying the product, printing and affixing the label, organising the packaging and delivering the final product.

Table C2.2: Major brands of bottled water

Parent company	Brand	Category of bottled water
Berri	Summit	Still spring
Bickford's	Aqua Pura	Still purified (pure as well as a flavoured variety)
Coca-Cola Amatil	Mount Franklin	Still spring
	Mount Franklin Lightly Sparkling	Sparkling spring
	Neverfail (acquired 2003)	Still spring
	Peats Ridge (acquired in 2003)	Still spring
	Deep Spring	Sparkling mineral (flavoured with fruit juices)
	Pump	Still purified
	Taurina Spa	Sparkling mineral
	BonAqua	Sparkling mineral
Danone Group (through Frucor)	Evian	Still spring
	H2go	Spring & mineral (pure and flavoured varieties)
	Mizone Sportswater	Pure water (with added vitamins and some fruit flavour)
Fosters	Torquay	Sparkling mineral (flavoured)
Nestlé	Perrier	Sparkling mineral
	San Pellegrino	Sparkling mineral (traditional as well as a new flavoured line)
	Vittel	Still mineral
Pure & Natural Beverages	Frantelle	Still spring
Schweppes	Cool Ridge	Still spring (various sources)

Source: Adapted from *Choice*, July 2005.

The bottled water industry became regulated in 2000 and is subject to the Food Standards Code established by Food Standards Australia New Zealand (FSANZ). Many of the regulations that are applied to the soft-drink industry also apply to bottled water. For example, *Standard 2.6.2*

Non-Alcoholic Beverages and Brewed Soft Drinks provides a definition of mineral and spring water as well as stating maximum levels of substances that packaged water is permitted to contain. Water must also meet *Standard 1.2 Labelling and Other Information Requirements*, which means that all ingredients must be listed.[8] There must even be a stated 'use by' date on the bottle.

The Australasian Bottled Water Institute (ABWI) is the peak body for bottled water producers in Australia, New Zealand and Oceania. It is a member organisation of the International Council of Bottled Water Associations. In addition to the Food Standards Code, the Institute speci- fies a further set of standards that its members must meet.[9] In some cases, these standards exceed the requirements of the Food Standards Code. Those bottlers who meet these standards, such as Cooroy Mountain Spring Water, are permitted to use the 'ABWI Certified Bottler' logo on their products and in their marketing.

At the moment there is no uniform process for approval of the source of bottled water. The ABWI is seeking co-operation from government agencies in all states and territories in Australia to establish regulations that specify, among other things, the analysis of the source water, the inspection procedures for the method of extraction and an approved Hazard Analysis Critical Control Point safety plan.[10]

The bottled water industry has not been without its problems. In the past few years, three major issues have arisen that might be of concern to bottlers and to consumers. First there were concerns over the level of bromates in bottled water, which exceeded the National Health and Medical Research Council's guidelines for tap water. A study conducted with the assistance of the Australian Water Quality Centre (AWQC) found that 12 of the 30 brands tested had bromate levels above the guideline.[11] However, the levels did not breach the Food Standards Code, because it does not specify minimum levels of bromate. Several disinfection techniques are used within the industry. However, it is only the process of ozonation that leads to the production of bromate.[12] The ABWI has applied to Food Standards Australia New Zealand for an amendment to the Food Standards Code to bring the packaged water requirements into line with the tap water requirements. Some bottlers, including Cooroy Mountain Spring Water, now highlight that they are bottled at the source and do not use ozonation in their bottling process.

The second major issue involved a belief that an increase in drinking bottled water would lead to an increase in tooth decay, particularly among young people. With the exception of Queensland and some local government areas in other states, municipal water contains added fluoride, which has been linked with a reduction in tooth decay. A reduction in drinking municipal water removes the protection offered by the fluoridated water. The Australian Institute of Health and Welfare is concerned that increased consumption of bottled spring water may affect oral health problems of future Australians. A recent study commissioned by the federal government found the incidence of tooth decay is increasing among children each year. However, the study also reports that the reduction in dental care funding and a change in dietary habits are also to blame.[13] Don Wilson from the Australian Dental Association states that although there is no firm evidence that the growth of bottled water consumption is linked to the rise in tooth decay, it could be a factor. Notwithstanding, he also claims that if consumers are swapping sugar-based, acidic, caffeine-laden drinks for water, then that is a good result.[14]

The third major issue relates to the cost of bottled water compared to tap water. Bottled water can cost anywhere between forty-six cents and $5 per litre depending on the size of the bottle. This is substantially more than the cost of production and marketing. The cost of tap water varies from area to area but it is unlikely that consumers are paying more than a fraction of $1 per 1000 L for their municipal supply.[15] According to the Australian Bureau of Statistics, 80 per cent of Australian households still rely on municipal water as their main drinking water supply.[16] Yet the price differential between tap water and bottled water does not seem to have created a consumer backlash. Rather, the bottled water industry continues to grow. Therefore, major beverage companies are attracted to the lucrative bottled water industry.

National and global trends towards healthy diets and remaining hydrated have prompted a growth in health beverages such as bottled water, especially over the past decade or so. The addition of chemicals such as chlorine in municipal water supplies has added to the growth of the sector. Chlorine is used to keep the pipes clean that connect houses to the treatment plants and town water users are now questioning whether there is any danger of drinking these additives.[17] This has also prompted a growth in the sale of tap filters in households. Tony Gentile from ABWI notes that bottled water is marketed as an alternative to soft drinks and juices. Gentile asserts that the industry does not sell natural spring water or mineral water on the basis of these products being superior to tap water.[18] Although many independent studies of municipal water have found that the mineral content of tap water is comparable with that of bottled spring water, there have been a few major exceptions. One such incident was in 1998, when the contaminants giardia and cryptosporidium were found in Sydney's water supply. This incident alone sparked a major boost in bottled water sales.[19]

The size of the industry is relatively small compared with that in other countries. Australians consume on average about 15 L of bottled water purchased from retail outlets every year, compared with 50 L in the United States, 110 L in France and 130 L in Italy.[20] Notwithstanding, the growth of the bottled water industry in Australia has risen rapidly in the past few years. This has resulted in significant acquisitions of small spring water businesses by major soft-drink companies. This has produced the proliferation of small spring water bottlers similar to Cooroy Mountain Spring Water. Bottlers of soft drink and alcoholic products are also adding water to their range.[21] Added to this, the industry has witnessed a growth in the number of treated water manufacturers. Rather than sourcing water from a spring, bottlers use existing town water and purify the water using a variety of treatments.[22]

The total retail still water market rose 3.8 per cent between 2003 and 2004, representing about 300 million L. This compares to almost 400 million L of juice-based drinks and a massive 1.8 billion L of carbonated soft drinks that are sold through retail outlets annually. In 2003, the total bottled water market represented 13 per cent of total beverage sales.[23] This means that on average every living Australian buys a 600 mL bottle of still water from a retail outlet every two weeks. The retail beverage market figures are shown in figure C2.2.

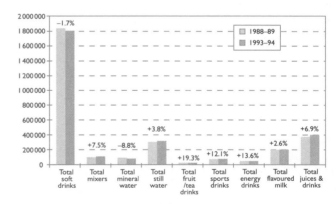

Figure C2.2: Retail beverage sales volume ('000 L)

Source: ACNielsen Dollars MAT 06/06/04 Combined Channels

The bottled water market has continued its strong growth pattern for the remaining part of 2004 and 2005. The Australian market is primarily a spring water market, with Australians showing a preference for a natural-tasting product of consistent quality. Other categories of bottled water in Australia include natural still mineral water, rain water and mineralised water. Mineral water that is carbonated and other similar products such as soda water are classified as carbonated soft drinks. 'Near' waters include such products as flavoured natural spring water without sugar, or waters that may contain low levels of sugars or other sweeteners, or may have added vitamins[24]. The total still water market is shown in figure C2.3.

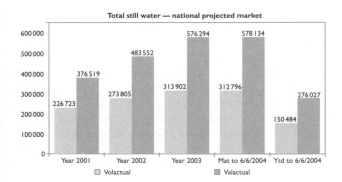

Figure C2.3: Retail still water market in Australia (volume in '000 L and value in dollars)

Source: ACNielsen Dollars MAT 06/06/04 Combined Channels

In terms of where Australians buy their bottled water, it should come as no surprise that the national grocery chains are the primary providers. All channels have shown an increase in sales in the last five years with the national grocers contributing to almost 50 per cent of the total retail sales of still water.[25] The still water market in Australia by channel is depicted in figure C2.4.

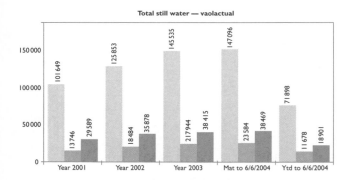

Figure C2.4: Still water market in Australia by channel (volume – '000 litres)

Source: ACNielson Dollars MAT 06/06/04 Combined Channels

The most popular size of still water bottles in the retail market segment is the 500–660 mL range. Interestingly, the next most popular is the 1.26–1.99 mL range. The product with the largest growth of sales between 2003 and 2004 is the more than 10 L range.[26] The still water market by product size is shown in table C2.3.

Table C2.3: Still water product sizes (volume share)

	Year 2003	MAT to 06/06/2004	YTD to 06/06/2004
Total still water 0–299 mL	0.1	0.1	0.1
Total still water 300–499 mL	1.0	1.2	1.2
Total still water 500–660 mL	27.6	27.5	26.9
Total still water 661–999 mL	15.6	15.6	15.4
Total still water 1–1.24 L	1.6	2.0	2.1
Total still water 1.25 L	0.8	0.9	1.0
Total still water 1.26–1.99 L	22.1	21.5	21.4
Total still water 2 L	2.6	2.5	2.4
Total still water 2.01–9.99 L	7.7	7.6	7.6
Total still water 10 L	13.8	12.1	11.9
Total still water over 10 L	7.1	9.0	10.0

Source: ACNielsen Dollars MAT 06/06/04 Combined Channels

The HOD market has continued its strong growth, although measuring the size of this market is difficult. The HOD market is currently estimated at more than 250 million L with huge potential for expansion given Australia's low level of market penetration. Approximately 1.5 per cent of households in Australia are delivered bottled water and 15 per cent of businesses. This compares with 10 per cent and 30 per cent in the United States. Similarly to Australia's, the New Zealand HOD market is still embryonic with large future potential.[27]

CCA and bottled water

CCA established a 35 per cent share of the retail bottled water market in 2004, led mainly by the Mount Franklin and Pump brands.[28] In 2000, CCA had noncarbonated beverage sales contributing 8 per cent of total sales. In 2004, the figure had risen to 20 per cent. A similar trend is occurring in CCA's operations in Indonesia, South Korea and New Zealand.[29]

In the HOD market segment, the Neverfail brand earned $20 million before interest and tax, representing a margin of 28 per cent. Home and office customer numbers rose by 16 per cent on the previous year and CCA plans to increase numbers further in 2005 by tackling the rise in household water filter sales.[30]

CCA is also likely to continue its aggressive acquisition strategy, particularly the purchase of established spring water sources. The water source could then be used to grow CCA's market share in the retail and HOD market segments simultaneously. With this large multinational company pursuing growth in the bottled water industry, consumers can expect continued high levels of competition resulting in price reduction, product development and market development. Private bottlers such as Cooroy Mountain Spring Water can probably expect attractive acquisition offers in the future.

Strategy at Cooroy Mountain Spring Water

The management team at Cooroy Mountain Spring Water acknowledges that luck has played a role in the success of the company. It acknowledges that the global trend towards healthy living has created a munificent environment, which has increased the demand for bottled water, particularly in the past five years. Notwithstanding, the managing director has taken an active role in generating success both for the business and the industry. As a board member of ABWI, he is able to keep abreast of developments in the industry and play a role in lobbying and influencing policies and industry-based legislation. He is also a member of the technical committee of ABWI. Additionally, the marketing manager is a member of the public relations committee of ABWI.

The company has established many alliances, being suppliers of product to the Australian defence force serving in the Solomon Islands, mining companies in Papua New Guinea and various units of the US military. Its export activities include the 'Australian Pure' brand that is sold in Singapore and Japan. Contracts also exist with Queensland Health, Queensland Rail, Queensland Fire & Rescue and Boral Quarries as well as aged homes and hospitals within the greater Sunshine Coast region.

Environmental threats against the industry have been identified by management as being improvements to the quality of town water supplies and the rising number of competitors. Management acknowledges that any beverage product is a potential competitor. It also notes the heightened competition from home water filters. Other threats include rising oil costs that affect the cost of packaging and delivery costs. Increasing fuel costs also influence household disposable incomes. This often results in consumers making decisions to eliminate 'luxury' products such as bottled water. Interestingly, these threats do not seem to be adversely affecting Cooroy Mountain Spring Water to date.

The environmental opportunities for the industry include the contamination of town water supplies. Globally, poor quality of water supplies of other countries caused by either pollution or lack of capabilities in the treatment of supplies could mean increasing sales, particularly to northern hemisphere countries during Australian winters, when production traditionally slows. Australian-based spring water is recognised globally as being of high quality, which could be a significant benefit to the export opportunities for Australian spring water companies.

Cooroy Mountain Spring Water is considering its future very carefully. Plans include changing the bottle range from a round shape to a square and 'curvy' shape. The square shape would increase packaging efficiency and the curves would help with appeal, especially in the retail segment. A possible contract with the Department of Agriculture and Fisheries could result in significant expansion of the facility. The company is also considering adding rainwater products to its range. Additionally, flavoured caps that release syrup into the water as the bottle is opened are being considered. Overall, the future looks bright for Cooroy Mountain Spring Water.

Discussion questions

1. What are the distinctive competencies that give Cooroy Mountain Spring Water a competitive advantage? Comment on its resource inimitability and substitutability.

2. Should Cooroy Mountain Spring Water expand globally? If so, why?

3. If Cooroy Mountain Spring Water were to choose the United States, China, Italy and New Zealand as potential markets, which entry modes should they choose for each location?

4. Identify the strategic groups operating in the bottled water industry in Australia using the information from the case and additional research.

5. Consider the macroenvironmental trends of the bottled water industry in Australia and develop three possible scenarios for the future of Cooroy Mountain Spring Water.

End notes

1. The information contained in the first four sections of this case study is based on company documentation, personal communications and interviews conducted with four senior managers at Cooroy Mountain Spring Water in September 2005.

2. Jackson, N 2005, 'Bottled water taps fears', *Sunday Herald-Sun*, 10 July, p. 22.

3. Australasian Bottled Water Institute, accessed 24 October 2005, www.bottledwater.org.au.
4. *Choice* 2005, 'Bottled water, a triumph of marketing', July.
5. ibid.
6. Australasian Bottled Water Institute, op. cit.
7. ibid.
8. ibid.
9. ibid.
10. ibid.
11. Magazinovic, R, Mulcahy, D, Davey, D & Nicholson, B n.d., 'Bromate formation in Australian bottled drinking water', paper presented at WaterTECH, Sydney.
12. Australian Water Quality Centre, accessed 25 October 2005, www.awqc.com.au.
13. ABC Premium News 2004, 'Bottled water blamed for increased tooth decay', 22 July, p. 1.
14. Strickland, K & Cresswell, A 2005, 'Bottled water found to be money down the drain', *Weekend Australian*, 26 March, p. 4.
15. *Choice* 2005, 'Bottled water, a triumph of marketing', July.
16. Australian Bureau of Statistics, accessed 25 October 2005, www.abs.gov.au.
17. Benson, S 2004, 'Truth filters through on bottled H$_2$O', *The Daily Telegraph*, 5 April, p. 13.
18. ibid.
19. Carter, F 2005, 'Water ways', *National Liquor News*, August, p. 27.
20. ibid.
21. Daily News 2005, 'Spirit-maker pours premier bottled water in to its range', 27 May, p. 5.
22. Benson, op. cit.
23. Australian Beverages Council Limited, accessed 26 October 2005, www.australianbeverages.org.
24. ibid.
25. ibid.
26. ibid.
27. Carter, op. cit.
28. Coca-Cola Amatil 2005, 'Fact book — October', accessed 28 October 2005, www.ccamatil.com.
29. Coca-Cola Amatil 2005, 'Annual report — 2004', accessed 28 October 2005, www.ccamatil.com.
30. Davis, T 2005, '2004 results presentation', accessed 30 October 2005, www.ccamatil.com.

Qantas: the high flyer of the airline industry?

By Stephane Tywoniak, Queensland University of Technology, and Peter Galvin, Curtin University of Technology

On 19 August 2004, Qantas announced record net profits of $648.4 million for the year ended 30 June, an increase of 89 per cent over 2003, despite a decline of 0.2 per cent in consolidated revenues to $11.4 billion (exhibit 5). Commenting on the results, the CEO of Qantas, Geoff Dixon, said the record full-year result, achieved in difficult conditions, was a tribute to Qantas staff and management: 'the group responded extremely well to the myriad challenges it has faced over the past 12 months.'

Qantas' record profits for 2003–04 were in sharp contrast with the financial performance of most airlines worldwide. After losses in 2001 and 2002, airline finances were dealt further blows in 2003 by the Iraq war, and the severe acute respiratory syndrome (SARS) epidemic, particularly in the Asia–Pacific region.[1,2] Estimates of consolidated losses in 2003 for the industry ranged between US$5.5 billion (*Air Transport World*) and US$6.5 billion (International Civil Aviation Organization).

The Australian airline industry

The market for air transport in Australia is disproportionately large: with a population of just under 20 million people, it has the world's fourth-largest market for domestic traffic, and the world's seventh-largest market overall. This situation is a reflection of the vast expanse of the Australian continent, the long distances between its major cities and the lack of alternative modes of transportation. The domestic Australian market is concentrated around a core network of high-density routes between its major cities: the ten busiest routes in 2003 accounted for 61.5 per cent of domestic traffic (measured in revenue passenger kilometres (RPKs).

From the 1950s to the early 1990s, the Australian airline industry was heavily regulated: domestic traffic was reserved to privately held Ansett Airlines and government-owned Australian Airlines, while Qantas (also government owned) operated internationally as Australia's 'flag-carrier'

airline. The domestic market was roughly equally shared between Ansett and Australian Airlines, though observers commented that the private operator was more efficient.[3] Deregulation was introduced in two stages.

Deregulation of domestic services: 1990–92

The domestic segment of the Australian market was defined by the *Airline Agreement Act 1981* as consisting of the trunk routes linking 18 major airports (other regional air services, representing a small fraction of the market, were regulated by separate legislation).[4] In 1990, domestic air services were liberalised, although Qantas and foreign carriers were still restricted to international flights. The Australian government expected that increased competition in the domestic market would increase customer choice and lower air fares.[5]

The first new entrant was Compass Airlines, based in Brisbane. It offered a 'no frills', single class service between Adelaide, Brisbane, Cairns, Melbourne, Sydney and Perth. Focusing on the city-pairs whose traffic density was highest allowed Compass to gain access to a large share of the market with a limited offering. The entrant sought to undercut the incumbents: its reduced infrastructure, 'no frills' service and focused operations gave it an operating cost advantage of around 40 per cent over Ansett and Australian. Compass set its fares 20 per cent below the full economy fare of the established operators, and quickly gained a 12 per cent market share.[6] But this was not sufficient for the new entrant to operate profitably: it registered a loss of $16.5 million in the year to November 1991 and ceased operations in December 1991.

Deregulation of international services and airline privatisation: 1992–95

Further deregulation occurred in 1992 when the Australian government privatised both Australian Airlines and Qantas, and opened up the domestic and international markets for competition. In 1990, the Australian government announced plans to sell 49 per cent of Qantas and 100 per cent of Australian Airlines. To maximise the proceeds, the government decided to sell Australian to Qantas, and then privatise the combined group.[7] In its bid for Australian, Qantas had argued that combining the two airlines would lead to savings of at least $100 million a year for the combined group.[8] The privatisation of Qantas proceeded in three stages. First, in December 1992, the government sold a 24.9 per cent stake in the airline to British Airways for $665 million. Second, in February 1993 the government recapitalised Qantas by $1.35 billion to reduce its debt and make the company more attractive to private investors.[9] Third, the company was floated on the Australian Stock Exchange on 31 July 1995, raising $1.45 billion for the government.

In parallel, the Australian government opened up competition on international air transport. In 1993, Ansett gained access to Asian destinations (Kuala Lumpur, Singapore, Hong Kong, Jakarta, Osaka, Bangkok), extending its competition with Qantas on lucrative international routes and improving its ability to feed its domestic network with international travellers, leading to a profits recovery in 1994.[10] In 1995, an 'open skies' agreement was signed between Australia and New Zealand, deregulating traffic between the two countries, and Air New Zealand acquired a 50 per cent stake in Ansett (from part owner TNT). Air New Zealand completed the purchase of Ansett in June 2000 when it purchased News Corporation's 50 per cent stake.[11]

After a period of change and turbulence, in the mid-1990s the Australian market had again settled into a duopoly situation. Ansett and Qantas were running operations of similar size in the Australian market, though Qantas was seen to have the advantage over Ansett: it had a more extensive international network feeding traffic to its domestic routes; after its recapitalisation and privatisation its finances were in better shape than those of Ansett.[12] The third chapter of the history of Australia's deregulated airline industry started in 2000.

Second wave of entry: 2000–01

The run-up to the 2000 Sydney Olympics — and the peak demand for travel that would ensue — was considered as a window of opportunity for new entrants.[13] Based in Newcastle (New South Wales), Impulse Airlines entered the fray in June, with services between Sydney and Melbourne, Canberra and Brisbane. It offered a single-class, 'no frills', low-cost service, charging $139 for a one-way trip between Sydney and Melbourne. All Impulse discounts were matched by Qantas and Ansett.[14]

Backed by UK entrepreneur Sir Richard Branson, Virgin Blue started operating in August 2000 from its base in Brisbane. It also offered a 'no frills', single-class service. Initially, Virgin Blue operated a smaller aircraft fleet than Impulse. Apart from Brisbane–Sydney, it avoided competing with the other entrant, focusing on other routes, such as Brisbane–Melbourne and Brisbane–Adelaide.[15] Its pricing policy was more progressive and Virgin Blue matched the heavily discounted fares on only a small proportion of its seats.[16]

By December 2000, the entrants had captured about 12 per cent of the domestic market. The discounted fares had stimulated demand and passenger volumes had increased by about 15 per cent overall, with a peak of in excess of 48 per cent on the Brisbane–Sydney route.[17] Increased capacity and lower fares had decreased profit margins for all competitors. Of the two incumbents, Ansett was hurt most: it had lost more market share to the entrants than Qantas, and it had higher operating costs because of its older and more diverse aircraft fleet.[18] By early 2001, Impulse was also running into financial trouble, and was bought out by Qantas in May.[19] The Australian Competition and Consumer Commission agreed to the deal on condition that Qantas ceded two-thirds of Impulse's takeoff and landing slots at Sydney Airport to Virgin Blue. The demise of Impulse opened opportunities for Virgin Blue, but did little for Ansett. Its planes had been grounded because of safety concerns in December 2000 and April 2001, damaging its reputation and finances.[20] By September 2001, Ansett was losing $1.3 million a day. The terrorist attacks of 11 September[21], and the collapse of air travel that ensued, gave its parent Air New Zealand no choice but to cut its losses and liquidate the failing airline.[22]

The main beneficiary of Ansett's collapse was Qantas. Although it competed with Virgin Blue on the busiest domestic routes, it was the sole operator of many secondary routes and serviced many more destinations than Virgin Blue. The demise of Ansett meant that Qantas faced increased demand on domestic routes at a time when international traffic slumped, providing an outlet for unused capacity.[23] By the end of 2001, the Australian domestic market for air travel had reverted to a duopoly, but one in which Qantas was now dominant with a market share in excess of 80 per cent. Although fare competition continued in the discount segment, the withdrawal of Ansett from the domestic market gave Qantas the opportunity to increase prices for business class and full economy passengers.[24]

The situation in 2004

Between 2000 and 2004, Virgin Blue had expanded its fleet from three to 44 aircraft (all Boeing 737s) and its network to cover all major domestic routes, capturing a 30 per cent share of the domestic market. It had set up Pacific Blue, an international low-cost airline, which had started services to New Zealand, and planned to fly to the West Coast of the USA.[25] To counter the threat of its low-cost rival, Qantas announced in 2003 the launch of its own low-cost operation, JetStar, which started in May 2004.

Virgin Blue

The low-cost airline, Virgin Blue, started operating in August 2000[26]. Sir Richard Branson's Virgin Group had reduced its stake in 2002 by selling 50 per cent of the stock to one of Australia's leading transportation and freight companies, Patrick Corporation. Sir Richard remained as president of the company, and Patrick Corporation's Managing Director Chris Corrigan took the chairmanship in 2003. After three profitable years (exhibit 8), 25 per cent of Virgin Blue's capital was floated in December 2003 on the Australian Stock Exchange, with Virgin Group reducing its stake to 25 per cent.[27]

In the space of less than four years, Australia's low-cost carrier had captured about one third of the domestic market. By end March 2004, Virgin Blue was flying to 20 destinations in Australia and two in New Zealand, concentrating on the high-volume domestic and trans-Tasman routes. The company was operating a low-cost model, with a twist.

Virgin Blue was operating according to the recipe of low-cost airlines:

- *Single type of aircraft:* all Virgin Blue planes were B737s, allowing a saving on maintenance and training. The airline had negotiated in 2002 a purchase agreement with Boeing, giving it the possibility to purchase 53 B737s at competitive prices. Ten planes had been acquired under the agreement, and Virgin Blue was planning to acquire more in 2004–05 (exhibit 8). To lower its fuel costs, Virgin had established a policy of reducing its cruising speed to mach 0.72, compared with an industry standard of mach 0.78, resulting in a 5 per cent fleetwide fuel burn reduction.[28]
- *Low-cost terminals:* dissimilarly to Europe and the United States, Australia had few secondary airports near its major cities — the main exception being Melbourne's Avalon airport where Qantas' JetStar was based. Virgin had initially been able to negotiate flexible, favourable terms for terminal access at the country's main airports (Brisbane, Sydney and Melbourne).
- *Ticketless distribution:* Virgin Blue claimed that almost 90 per cent of its fares were booked on the Internet. Customers could also make telephone bookings for a $10 fee.
- *Flexible working practices:* Virgin Blue working practices (e.g. cabin crew participating in cleaning up the aircraft) led to fast turnarounds at airports (30 minutes for Virgin, compared with a minimum of 35 minutes for Qantas domestic flights[29]) and more flight hours per day for each aircraft. Virgin Blue had been able to reduce the number of unions it dealt with down to three. This had enabled the company to introduce flexible working practices, reducing the distinctions between ground and cabin crews.

The twist in the low-cost recipe was Virgin Blue's 'user pays' concept. Customers who wanted to enjoy benefits not provided in the basic service could do so, for a fee. 'User pays' extras included:

- *Blue Zones:* on each flight, Virgin Blue proposed nine seats with extra legroom, located in the front row and near the emergency exits. For an additional $30 per sector, customers could enjoy 'business class'-like legroom.
- Inflight catering: passengers could purchase snacks and drinks from the 'a la carte' menu.
- *Blue Rooms:* for an annual fee of $199 (or $5 for a single admission), customers could use Virgin Blue's airport lounges at Brisbane, Sydney and Melbourne airports. The lounges provided traditional services, as well as massages and beauty treatments. The airline expected the Blue Rooms to be a profitable revenue centre by 2005.

According to Virgin Blue's head of sales, Tim Jordan, this strategy had allowed the low-cost airline to strike corporate deals with one-third of Australia's top 100 corporations.[30] But Virgin was still at a disadvantage to Qantas in the government market: the absence of a real business class and of an airport lounge at Canberra had hampered the ability of the low-cost airline to attract on its planes politicians and top civil servants, who remained attached to their traditional perks.[31]

Virgin Blue had established a service culture, and a relaxed working environment. This was symbolised by the casual uniforms of the staff (Virgin Blue pilots wore leather flying jackets) and the company's no-tie policy. The culture emphasised teamwork, flexibility and open communications: the airline's low-cost performance was not attributed to corporate managers' policies, but to the efforts of all staff. Staff commitment to the company was strong: 93 per cent of employees had become shareholders in the December 2003 IPO.[32] Passengers were not referred to as customers, but 'guests'. The quality of service was measured, among other, by the high level of on time departure (87 per cent). Virgin Blue had been awarded several prestigious industry awards in its relatively short history.

Opportunities and threats

International development: Virgin Blue had begun international services to New Zealand under the Pacific Blue brand (the company could not use the Virgin name outside

Australia). In September 2004, Pacific Blue had started services to Fiji and Vanuatu, and flights to the Cook Islands were scheduled to start in January 2005.[33] Further ahead, Virgin Blue had expressed interest in operating to the US west coast, one of Qantas' most profitable routes.[34]

Diversification: Virgin Blue had started to sell holiday packages through its Blue Holiday subsidiary. The development of this activity was seen by management as a growth opportunity.[35]

Alliances: Virgin Blue had started code-sharing agreements with United Airlines in 2004. It was expecting to enter similar agreements with Virgin Atlantic in late 2004, once its sister airline started to fly the 'kangaroo route' between the UK and Australia. A further possible development of the cooperation with Virgin Atlantic considered by Virgin Blue was the launch of a joint full-service airline to cover the Asia–Pacific market.

Profits under pressure: since its inception, Virgin Blue had had a remarkable profitability record, registering some of the highest profit rates in the airline industry. However, the outlook for the future pointed to a deteriorating performance. Competition from Qantas and JetStar had forced Virgin Blue to retreat from unprofitable routes (Sydney to Canberra and Alice Springs). Rising fuel costs were adding to operating costs, while the arrival of Jetstar had further increased capacity on the domestic market at a time when demand growth was slowing down. In addition, the airline faced increased charges at Sydney Airport, which had changed its pricing structure from a per aircraft load to a per passenger formula, resulting in increased costs. On 4 August 2004, Virgin Blue announced that profits for the first four months of its 2005 financial year were down 22 per cent on the same period the previous year, sending the share price down to $1.75, well below its $2.25 flotation level.[36] Virgin Blue management subsequently announced a fare review to halt the decline in margins, and a slowing down of capacity growth for the 2005 financial year. Although Virgin Blue had maintained low operating costs of 7.26 per cent in the half-year to September 2004 (exhibit 8), analysts feared that its cost structure would deteriorate with time as maintenance costs were expected to increase with the age of the fleet, and eventually reach the industry average of 15 per cent.[37] Industry observers also feared that the expansion of Virgin Blue's international and long-haul business would lead it to modify its service mix, and start offering in-flight catering and entertainment, compromising the low-cost formula.

Turbulence on board? The rapid growth of the airline had not always been well handled with regard to staff management and training. An increasing number of employees were reported to be unhappy about management's attitude, which was perceived to accept positive suggestions but suppress criticism, leading to a deterioration in motivation. Virgin Blue's lower wages had also been an easy target for Qantas' CEO Geoff Dixon, who had regularly portrayed his competitor's employees as 'Third World workers'.[38] Virgin Blue union representatives were under pressure from employees, who increasingly asked to obtain work arrangements comparable to those offered by Qantas, and the next round of collective bargaining (June to September 2005) was expected to be hotly contested.[39]

Qantas Airways Limited

In this continually changing industry environment that had become increasingly hard for traditional airlines, why was Qantas so much different from its international counterparts? But maybe more importantly, did Qantas have the strength and the sense of mind to continue to defy industry trends? What competitive strategy would give Qantas a sustained competitive advantage?

History

Qantas played a key role in the development of Australian and international aviation.[40] It is the world's second-oldest airline, and the oldest airline in the English-speaking world.

The deregulation of Australia's domestic airline industry in 1990 offered Qantas the opportunity to re-enter the domestic market after an absence of 40 years. The acquisition of Australian Airlines in 1992 provided Qantas with a strong domestic base which gave it a more equal competitive footing compared with its international competitors. The $1.35 billion recapitalisation strengthened its balance sheet, and the alliance with British Airways gave access to new markets and cost saving opportunities.

Qantas was listed on the Australian Stock Exchange on 31 July 1995. Since then it had reported a profit each year, a remarkable achievement for any airline. Between 1995 and 2004, Qantas had grown its activity (measured in RPKs) by 62 per cent, its revenue by 59 per cent, and its annual net profits had grown from $180 million to $684 million (exhibit 4).

Taking advantage of the 1995 deregulation between Australia and New Zealand, Qantas launched in 2001 a New Zealand domestic airline, Jetconnect, operating between the country's main cities of Auckland, Wellington, Christchurch and Queenstown.[41]

In 2002, Qantas relaunched the Australian Airlines brand as a single-class, full-service carrier linking its base in Cairns to holiday destinations in Asia.

In 2003, Qantas reorganised itself around a corporate centre (headquarters and Qantas Business Services) managing information technology (IT), property, procurement and aviation health services for the whole group. The operating subsidiaries involved three types of businesses: international and domestic flying businesses (Qantas International, Qantas Domestic, Qantaslink and Jetconnect, JetStar), flying services businesses (engineering technical operations and maintenance services, airports and catering), and associated businesses (Qantas Freight, Qantas Holidays, Qantas Defence Services).

After the reorganisation, the airline launched 'Sustainable Future', a cost reduction initiative aiming to reduce its cost base by $1.5 billion by 2006. The initiative was intended to bridge the gap between Qantas and Virgin Blue, which had an estimated 30 per cent cost advantage. One particular area targeted by Qantas CEO Geoff Dixon was work practices and salaries, intending to take a tough stance in his negotiations with Qantas' 14 unions to bring pay and conditions closer to that offered by its low-cost rival.[42] The company also sought to reduce its IT and communication costs through outsourcing contracts with respectively IBM and Telstra, worth $650 million and $750 million over ten years.[43] Delocalisation of staff was another source of cost savings: in June 2004, Qantas announced it would move 400 of its 4000 long-haul flight attendants offshore to London, in a move resulting in $20 million of annual savings. Ultimately, Qantas would aim to locate 20 per cent of its flight attendants offshore, in London, Bangkok, Auckland and other centres, reducing overseas accommodation costs and away-from-home allowances.[44]

In September 2004, British Airways (BA) announced it would sell its 18.25 per cent equity stake in Qantas. Although the two airlines would still cooperate within the OneWorld alliance and share the 'kangaroo route' to London, BA had its sights on European rather than global integration and needed to restructure its finances. From the point of view of the UK flag carrier, the investment in Qantas was no longer a strategic priority. The status of Qantas as one of the world's few profitable airlines meant that BA could sell its stake at a good price. For Qantas, the deal also meant that it could pursue its own strategy of alliances in the Asia–Pacific region.[45]

In July 2004, Qantas had unveiled plans to launch an Asian low-cost carrier based in Singapore, Jetstar Asia. Qantas would own 49.99 per cent of the equity in partnership with Temasek (19 per cent), an industrial holding company of the Singaporean government — which also owned 57 per cent of Singapore Airlines — and local businessmen Tony Chew (22 per cent) and FF Wong (10 per cent). JetStar Asia would start operating between Singapore and other Asian cities within five hours' flight by end 2004, and hoped to open a route to Beijing in 2005,

in time to benefit from the expected traffic boom of the 2008 Olympic games.[46] Commenting on the $50 million investment Qantas made in the venture, CEO Geoff Dixon declared: 'this is a modest investment for Qantas but it is an excellent opportunity to participate in the growing intra-Asian travel market'.[47]

The Qantas Group

Qantas was recognised as one of the world's leading long distance airlines, having pioneered services from Australia to North America and Europe. In 2003, Qantas ranked as the world's tenth largest airline (measured by RPKs — exhibit 2). At 30 June 2004, it employed about 34 000 staff, a fleet of 190 aircraft operating more than 5850 flights each week — 5000 in Australia, 300 in New Zealand and 560 international flights — to 60 ports in Australia, five in New Zealand, and 80 international destinations in 40 countries (exhibit 4).

After the 2003 reorganisation, the Qantas group comprised ten main operating subsidiaries, five passenger airlines (six once JetStar Asia would start in late 2004), two flying services support businesses, three airline-related associated businesses, and a corporate centre (Qantas Business Services).

Domestic passenger airlines

Qantas' domestic operations comprised three complementary airlines: Qantas, QantasLink and JetStar. The objective of the group was to maintain its combined share of the market at 65 per cent. In July 2004, Qantas estimated it had a 66.7 per cent share.[48]

Qantas Domestic

In the year to 30 June 2004, Qantas domestic flew 17.7 million passengers for 23 711 million RPKs. Qantas domestic represented 90 per cent of the group's domestic traffic. It primarily targeted business travellers, offering frequent services between main Australian airports ('Cityflyer': Melbourne, Sydney, Brisbane, Adelaide, Perth and Canberra). The full-service airline operated two-class flights on all its routes, offering in-flight meals and entertainment, and a network of Qantas Club airport lounges. In 2003–04, Qantas domestic accounted for 42 per cent of consolidated earnings before interest and tax (A$465.7 million).

QantasLink

QantasLink was the regional airline operation of Qantas in Australia, federating three wholly owned subsidiaries (Airlink, Eastern Australia Airlines and Sunstate Airline).

QantasLink operated a fleet of 43 small aircraft, employed about 1000 people, and flew more than 1900 flights each week to 50 metropolitan and regional destinations. In the year to 30 June 2004, it flew just under three million passengers, for 1931 million RPKs (7 per cent of Qantas domestic activity) providing a valuable feeder service for the Qantas domestic and international flights.[49] In addition, it had entered partnerships with ten other regional airlines in Australia, providing links to 60 other towns and cities. In 2003–04, QantasLink represented 9 per cent (A$97 million) of consolidated earnings before interest and tax.

JetStar

The new low-cost, domestic airline of the Qantas group began operating in May 2004. Its main base was Melbourne's airport at Avalon, which made it the first airline in Australia to operate scheduled flights from a secondary airport. In 2004, JetStar flew 800 times a week between Melbourne (Avalon and Tullamarine), Sydney, Brisbane and ten eastern Australian airports. It planned to extend its services to southern (Adelaide), central (Alice Springs), northern (Darwin) and western (Perth) cities in 2005. JetStar employed 650 staff, and operated a fleet of 14 B717s (acquired by the group with Impulse in 2001), to be replaced by 23 A320s by 2006.[50]

JetStar was conceived to complement the Qantas domestic services, targeting leisure travellers by offering 'no frills' services, a single class, and everyday low fares. It was supposed to compete with Virgin Blue on routes where the main full-service carrier was not competitive. In launching JetStar, Qantas risked cannibalising traffic on its own main routes, which was the cause of the demise of BA's Go low-cost subsidiary in Europe.[51]

By the end of 2004, it was probably too early to ascertain the full impact of JetStar on the balance of forces in the Australian domestic market. The new airline had certainly taken share away from Virgin Blue on certain routes (Virgin Blue discontinued its Sydney–Canberra service in late August 2004) and increased competition: Virgin Blue issued a statement that its profits had fallen by 22 per cent.[52] But there were signs that the Qantas domestic services were also experiencing lower yields,[53] and analysts remained cautious about the success of the new venture: until then, no network carrier in the world had been able to launch successfully a low-cost subsidiary.[54] Analysts perceived that the main strategic benefit of launching JetStar was to pre-empt the entry of another low-cost competitor in Australia.[55]

Qantas did not disclose JetStar's financial performance for 2003–04, but stated that the low-cost carrier had achieved a small operating profit in June 2004, and that

its cost structure of 8.25 per cent ASK was on target, and would decrease to 7.8 per cent ASK once the more economical A320 jets would be introduced.[56]

International and overseas passenger airlines

The international airline operations of the Qantas group consisted of three subsidiaries in 2004: Qantas, Australian Airlines and Jetconnect. JetStar Asia, expected to start in December 2004 would be the fourth international airline business of the group. International airline operations accounted for 41 per cent of group revenue in 2003–04.

Qantas International

Qantas international passenger traffic represented 64 per cent of group traffic in 2003–04 (51 910 million RPKs) and contributed 36 per cent of group earnings before interest and tax ($398 million).

Qantas had a 31 per cent share of international passenger traffic to and from Australia. While it held favourable positions on trans-Pacific routes — analysts estimated that Qantas earned 15 per cent of its profits on its route to the US west coast[57] — Qantas' position on routes to Europe was less favourable: the cooperation with British Airways protected it from a fare war on the 'kangaroo route', but the Australian flag carrier's inability to secure additional takeoff and landing slots at key European airports constrained its growth potential in the European Union (EU).[58] In August 2004, Qantas announced it had entered a code-share partnership with Air France on the route to Paris, whereby Qantas would cease to fly to the French capital, but would instead carry its passengers to Singapore where they would connect to an Air France plane. The airline felt it had better growth opportunities in Asia, introducing additional services to Hong Kong and Tokyo, and opening new routes to Mumbai and Shanghai.

According to analysts, the improvement in operating profits in 2003–04 was attributable to a rebound in business class traffic[59] — Qantas had introduced in 2003 its award-winning 'skybed' product on intercontinental business class flights, providing extra comfort to passengers.

Australian Airlines

Australian Airlines was Qantas' international leisure carrier. The strategic aim was to complement the Qantas international network in markets where the main airline, with its higher costs, could not profitably operate. Australian was targeting international holidaymakers in Australia and in Asia, flying Japanese tourists to Cairns and on to the Gold Coast, Darwin and Sydney, and Australian tourists to Asian destinations (Indonesia, Thailand, Malaysia, Singapore and Hong Kong). Based in Cairns, it employed about 400 staff, and had a fleet of six B767s, operating more than 100 flights per week. In 2003–04, Australian Airlines accounted for 4.3 per cent of group traffic (3485 million RPKs), had a load factor of 67.7 per cent (below the group average of 77.5 per cent) and generated $1.1 million of earnings before interest and tax.[60] According to industry analysts, this relatively modest performance was a reflection of competitive intensity in the leisure market.[61]

Jetconnect

Jetconnect operated regional flights in New Zealand, as well as some trans-Tasman services from Wellington and Christchurch.[62] It had a fleet of eight B373-300s, and was a full-service, single class airline. In 2003–04 Qantas generated 3 per cent of its revenues in New Zealand.

JetStar Asia

The new Singapore-based low-cost venture, in which Qantas held a 49.99 per cent share, was scheduled to start operating in December 2004, flying to Asian destinations within five hours. The airline would start to operate a fleet of four A320 planes, and had plans to expand it to 20 by 2007. Jetstar Asia was expecting to locate its operational base at the Singapore Changi airport's new low-cost terminal, once the facility opens in 2006.[63]

Flying services businesses

Qantas Engineering Technical Operations and Maintenance Services

Qantas operated one of the largest aircraft engineering and maintenance organisations in the Asia–Pacific region. With revenues in excess of $120 million, Qantas ETOMS had an international reputation for operational excellence and safety.

Airports and Catering

Qantas operated its own airport terminals in Sydney, Melbourne, Brisbane, Perth, Adelaide, Gold Coast, Hobart and Launceston. In 2003, Qantas had entered an agreement with Adelaide Airport Ltd to participate in the construction of a new $240 million passenger terminal in Adelaide, scheduled to open in 2005. In addition, Qantas operated facilities at more than 50 airports in Australia, and 25 overseas.

Qantas operated three catering businesses: Qantas Flight Catering, Caterair Airport Services Pty (catering), and Snapfresh (frozen meals). Together, they employed more than 4000 staff who prepared more than 50 million meals in 2003–04, for Qantas and more than 30 external customers, including airlines, rail and healthcare businesses. In 2003–04 the catering unit generated revenues of $537.2 million (32 per cent for external clients) and $90 million of operating profits.

Associated airline-related businesses

Qantas Freight

Although Qantas was primarily a passenger airline, air freight had been an integral part of its business from the start. Qantas Freight offered international and domestic freight and mail services, and domestic express parcel deliveries.[64] The activity employed about 700 people in 2004 for revenues in excess of $700 million.

Qantas Holidays

Qantas Holidays was Australia's largest travel wholesaler, serving more than 1.3 million customers per year worldwide.[65] It employed more than 1000 staff, and had a network of 100 sales agents worldwide. Under the brands Qantas Holidays and Viva! Holidays, it marketed an extensive range of holiday packages (35 brochures) covering 42 destinations in Australia and overseas. In 2003–04, the business generated revenues of $994 million and profits before interest and tax of $54 million, an increase of 24 per cent, reflecting the recovery of outbound leisure travel after the SARS and Iraq crises. It also held a 75 per cent stake in Holiday Tours and Travel, a Singaporean holiday wholesaler, which marketed a range of Asian holidays to the Australian market.

Corporate centre

The corporate centre comprised headquarters management and Qantas Business Services (QBS), which provided support to the operating subsidiaries in the areas of IT, human resources, property, procurement and health services.

Qantas Business Services

The aim of the creation of QBS was to bring commercial disciplines to the provision of traditional corporate services within the Qantas Group. QBS catered for the individual needs of each business area, at agreed cost and services levels. The reorganisation was expected to bring flexibility, effectiveness and greater cost efficiency in the delivery of corporate services.

Information Technology

Information Technology played a key role in the day-to-day operation of an airline, managing scheduling, reservations, pricing, frequent flyer accounts as well as traditional business functions, such as accounts and pay.[66] About 700 people are involved in Qantas' IT infrastructure, running 600 applications and linking 40 000 devices worldwide in real time. Qantas had outsourced some of its IT services to outside contractors. This strategy was seen as beneficial by Qantas because it guaranteed access to the latest technology without committing to large fixed costs in IT infrastructure.

Sales

Qantas sold its tickets to customers through a variety of channels.[67] It ran a 1300 staff telephone sales operation, with call centres in Melbourne, Brisbane, Hobart and 15 other countries worldwide. The call centres operated 24 hours a day, seven days a week, and provided support for travel agents and Internet sales, as well as direct bookings. Qantas.com, the group's Internet site was Australia's most popular travel website, with 5.5 million visits each month. Customers could buy tickets, redeem Frequent Flyer points on the site, as well as book hotel rooms, car rentals, and holidays. Qantas.com had become a major sales channel, providing 30 per cent of domestic bookings — although this was still much less than competitor Virgin Blue, which sold 80 per cent of its tickets online.[68] Most Qantas sales were still through travel agents. Qantas managed its own 17 travel centres in Australia, and had relationships with 4000 travel agents, linked to the airline through the Amadeus computer reservation system (Qantas also sold overseas through the competing Galileo and Sabre systems). Commissions paid to agents were estimated to run at about $100 million per annum.[69] Qantas wanted to substantially reduce this cost, and announced that from 1 January 2005 commissions would be reduced to 1 per cent (down from 5 per cent) on trans-Tasman and New Zealand flights, and to 7 per cent (down from 9 per cent) on international flights, commissions on domestic fares would fall from 1 July 2005 to 1 per cent (down from 5 per cent).[70] Finally, Qantas had teams dedicated to direct sales to major government and corporate customers, with a total staff of 490.

Marketing

Qantas was one of Australia's leading brands, with the kangaroo symbol representing reliability, safety, engineering excellence and customer service.[71] Qantas' reputation was acknowledged by numerous international and national industry awards, including:

- Airline of the year — *Air Transport World* (2004)
- Best airline to the Pacific, New Zealand and Australia — UK Travel Weekly Globe Awards (2004)
- Best airline, international, domestic and regional — National Travel Industry Awards (2004).

Spirit of Australia

The marketing slogan launched in 2000 featured prominently in all Qantas advertising. In August 2004, Qantas launched a follow-on TV commercial, 'I still call Australia home', featuring children from the National Boys Choir and the Australian Girls Choir, against the backdrop of some of the world's most spectacular landmarks.

Qantas Frequent Flyer

The premise behind frequent-flyer programs was brilliant: give empty seats on planes to loyal customers as free flights. Members accumulated points when they purchased airline tickets, but also through qualifying transactions with partner companies, such as car rental, hotels, and financial institutions. Over time, airlines had observed that only a fraction of the points were ever redeemed. The Qantas Frequent Flyer program had four million members and was the only Australia-based air travel loyalty scheme — in spite of suggestions by Sir Richard Branson, Virgin Blue had not introduced a competing program.[72] This monopoly situation had allowed Qantas to raise the membership joining fee ($82.5 in 2004) and tighten the conditions for earning points, in particular for economy passengers.[73] Members could accumulate points through flying with Qantas and OneWorld alliance airlines, and program partners including Hertz, Avis, Budget, Thrifty car rental, Telstra Telecard, Travelex Foreign Exchange and more than 4000 hotels worldwide. Points earned through loyalty programs of credit cards (Diners Club, American Express, ANZ Frequent Flyer Visa) and partner banks (CBA, NAB, AMP, Citibank, Westpac, St George, SunCorp) could also be converted to Qantas Frequent Flyer points. These partnerships were highly profitable to Qantas, who was estimated to sell about $400 million of points to financial institutions each year.[74] Members who accumulated higher levels of status credits within a year were granted Silver, Gold or Platinum status. At each status level, members would receive extra service benefits, including higher priority service numbers, check-in, baggage allowances, and for Gold and Platinum members, complimentary entrance to the Qantas Club and oneworld airport lounges. Qantas announced it would change in 2004–05 the accounting methodology for its frequent-flyer program. Although this would not have any effect on cash flow, the move was interpreted by analysts as giving Qantas a one-off opportunity to boost its earnings in 2004–05.[75]

Alliances

Qantas was a member of the oneworld alliance, and also had entered specific partnership with other airlines — some of which were not oneworld members.[76]

oneworld

Qantas was a founding member of the oneworld alliance (exhibit 1). Alliance membership provided customer benefits for customers who could earn and redeem frequent-flyer points with all alliance partners, and enjoy their frequent-flyer privileges across 390 lounges worldwide for top-tier card holders. Alliance members worked together to make travel across their combined networks as smooth as possible, coordinating connecting flights for the benefits of passengers, and also feeding traffic into each other's networks. Among global alliances, oneworld had been the first to commit to full e-ticket interlinking between its partners, on track for completion across all partners by the end of 2004.

Qantas and BA

Qantas and BA commenced a joint services agreement (JSA) in 1995. In August 2004, the ACCC approved a draft decision for the JSA to continue to operate on the 'kangaroo route' between Australia, Asia and Europe for another five years. The authorisation gave Qantas and BA the ability to coordinate schedules and pricing on their services. Qantas and BA shared a wide variety of resources through the alliance including sales and travel outlets, accommodation and other goods and services, and cooperated in fuel purchasing, ground handling, aircraft maintenance and catering. The partners code shared on each other's services between Australia, Singapore, Bangkok and the UK, BA services to UK domestic and European ports, Qantas Australian domestic, trans-Tasman and Auckland–Los Angeles services. The two airlines had integrated their operations in Singapore, Bangkok, Jakarta and Kuala Lumpur. They also had joint or co-located airport and sales offices in a number of locations around the world, and shared airport lounges in Hong Kong, Singapore, Los Angeles, Bangkok, Manila and Kuala Lumpur.

Qantas and American Airlines

Qantas and American Airlines cooperated under code-sharing agreements, reciprocal frequent-flyer programs and reciprocal lounge access arrangements. The relationship began in 1989 and was, at the time, the world's first commercial code-share agreement. The airlines code shared between Australia (Sydney, Melbourne, Brisbane) and the United States (13 destinations). Within Australia and New Zealand, American Airlines also code shared on some of Qantas' domestic services.

Other partnerships

In addition, Qantas had developed code-sharing agreements with 21 airlines to extend its network and/or offer more frequent services: Aircalin (Noumea), Air Niugini (Port Moresby), Air France (Paris), Air Pacific (Pacific Islands), Air Tahiti Nui (Papeete and Los Angeles), Air Vanuatu (Port Vila), Alaska Airlines (Seattle, Portland, Vancouver and Calgary), Asiana (Seoul), Cathay Pacific (Hong Kong and Rome), China Eastern Airlines (Shanghai), Eva Air (Taipei), Finnair (Helsinki, Bangkok and Singapore), Gulf Air (Singapore, Bahrain, Athens, Beirut and Dubai), Japan Airlines (Tokyo and Osaka), LAN (Auckland and Santiago),

Norfolk Jet Express (Norfolk Island), Polynesian Airlines (Apia), South African Airways (Johannesburg), Swiss (Singapore, Frankfurt and Zurich) and Vietnam Airlines (Ho Chi Minh City).

Yield management and pricing

A statement familiar to yield managers in the aviation industry was that 'no asset is more perishable than an airline seat'.[77] The reason was that when a flight departed with empty seats, the opportunity to sell them on that flight was lost forever. For 2003–04, Qantas reported an average load factor of 78 per cent. Airlines had adopted yield management systems, also called revenue management systems, to maximise revenues on each flight by setting the optimal price (which was not necessarily the highest) for each seat sold. Seat prices varied with time (early bookings were cheaper) and occupancy rates (prices increased as the aircrafts filled up). One feature of yield management that was poorly understood by travellers — because it occasionally generated high frustration — was overbooking. Airlines had noticed that on average a proportion of bookings would not be used ('no shows') and would customarily sell more tickets than seats available. This practice allowed airlines to maximise the number of seats they sold on each flight. Yield management required sophisticated and powerful computer systems to monitor sales and prices flight by flight. The trend since the startup of low-cost carriers had been to compare prices and search for the best deal — this also had been helped by the Internet. Qantas had adapted by modifying its product offering and pricing structure to respond to changing customer requirements.

Risk management

Airlines faced a very uncertain operating environment: world events could impact customer demand and input prices rapidly and unpredictably. Qantas faced three major risk categories.

1. Customer demand

Events such as the SARS epidemic and terrorist attacks could affect customer demand almost instantaneously. The integration of the domestic and international services, as well as prudent finance leases allowed Qantas to adjust capacity to demand quickly, and at little cost to the group.[78]

2. Fuel prices

International political and economic factors influenced the evolution of fuel prices. Qantas used options and swaps on aviation fuel and crude oil to hedge its exposure to price fluctuations. Seventy per cent of expected 2004–05 fuel needs were hedged at US$32 per barrel (crude oil equivalent),[79] but Qantas had indicated that it expected its fuel costs to increase by $400 million in 2004–05, in spite of its hedging strategy.[80] In May 2004, Qantas had introduced a fuel surcharge on its fares (increased in August 2004) to provide a cushion for 2004–05, once the cover in place expired. The company expected to phase the surcharge out once oil prices would decrease.

3. Currency risk

Qantas purchased its aircraft in US$, and was thus exposed to currency fluctuations on its capital expenditure. It also faced currency risks on its international operations' revenues and expenses. It sought to mitigate the currency risk by using a variety of long- and short-term hedging instruments. To avoid counterparty risk, the company also capped the maximum exposure to any one counterparty and dealt only with financial institutions with a minimum credit rating.[81]

Sustainable future program

Qantas' 2003–06 $1.5 billion cost reduction initiative, labelled 'Sustainable Future Program' had yielded $512 million of savings in 2003–04. An additional $1 billion was aimed at for 2004–06, with improvements expected as follows:

- labour productivity: $297 million
- fleet simplification, product initiatives and overheads: $528 million
- distribution initiatives: $175 million.

The company gave the following examples of cost reduction programs:

- fleet simplification: introduction of new, fuel-efficient aircraft, improved 'ontime' performance
- overheads: introduction of a group-wide IT 'backbone'
- labour productivity: reduction of manpower costs per ASK, new crew and training bases.[82]

The outlook

Margaret Jackson, chairman, and Geoff Dixon, CEO, concluded their review of Qantas operations in the 2003–04 annual report in these terms: 'provided market conditions do not deteriorate, the returns for the first few months of 2004–05, forward bookings and a continuation of efficiency gains lead Qantas to believe it improves on its 2003–04 result in 2004–05'.

However, investors reacted cautiously to Qantas' record performance in 2003–04: its share price fell by 2 per cent to $3.26 on 19 August 2004 (the day the results were announced). Financial analysts feared that the combination

of increased fuel costs and intense competition as additional capacity was planned to be brought in the market (both on international and domestic routes) would adversely affect results. The increased fares (fuel surcharge) may also dampen customer demand, further lowering yields. Qantas shares were thus expected to perform in line with the market average.[83]

Exhibits and additional information

Additional Information

Glossary of air industry terms

ASK: Available seat kilometres — the number of seats an airline provides multiplied by the number of kilometres they are flown; a measure of airline capacity

FTK: Freight tonnes kilometres — tonnes of freight carried over each stage multiplied by the stage distance

Load Factor: Revenue passenger-kilometres divided by available seat-kilometres

MTK: Mail tonnes kilometres — tonnes of mail carried over each stage multiplied by the stage distance

PKP: Performed passenger kilometres — the number of passengers multiplied by the number of kilometres they fly

RPK: Revenue passenger kilometres — the number of paying passengers multiplied by the number of kilometres they fly

RTK: Revenue tonnes kilometres — aggregate of revenue passenger, freight and mail tonne kilometres

Yield: Revenues divided by revenue passenger kilometres; it represents an aggregate of all the airfare and airline charges and is measured per kilometre.

Useful websites

www.qantas.com.au
www.virginblue.com.au
www.iata.com
www.icao.org
www.boeing.com
www.airbus.com
www.btre.gov.au
www.oneworldalliance.com
www.staralliance.com
www.skyteam.com

Exhibits

Exhibit 1: The three major airline alliances

oneworld	SkyTeam	Star Alliance
Partners: Aer Lingus, American Airlines, British Airways, Cathay Pacific, Finnair, Iberia, LanChile, Qantas	*Partners:* Aeromexico, Air France-KLM, Alitalia, Continental, CSA Czech Airlines, Delta, Korean Airlines, NorthWest Airlines	*Partners:* Air Canada, Air New Zealand, ANA, Asiana Airlines, Austrian, bmi, LOT Polish Airlines, Lufthansa, SAS, Singapore Airlines, Spanair, Thai Airways International, United, US Airways, VARIG
Links: 576 destinations in 134 countries	*Links:* 658 destinations in 137 countries	*Links:* 774 destinations in 133 countries
Combined fleet: 1574 aircraft	*Combined fleet:* 2032 aircraft	*Combined fleet:* 2153 aircraft
2003 market share (RPKs): 18.3 per cent	*2003 market share (RPKs):* 22.4 per cent	*2003 market share (RPKs):* 25.4 per cent

Sources: alliances websites

Exhibit 2: World top 20 airlines in 2003

Rank	Airline	Country	RPKs	Load factor (RPKs/ASKs)
1	American	United States	193 604	72.8%
2	United	United States	167 970	76.4%
3	Delta	United States	143 876	74.2%
4	Northwest	United States	110 637	77.2%
5	British Airways	UK	101 183	72.7%
6	Air France	France	99 590	75.6%
7	Continental	United States	92 661	75.7%
8	Lufthansa	Germany	90 027	73.1%
9	Southwest	United States	77 288	66.8%
10	Qantas	Australia	76 893	77.8%
11	Singapore	Singapore	63 817	73.3%
12	US Airways	United States	60 792	73.3%
13	Japan Airlines	Japan	59 160	64.6%
14	Thai	Thailand	44 396	69.6%
15	KLM	Netherlands	43 329	79.9%
16	Cathay Pacific	Hong Kong	42 774	72.2%
17	Iberia	Spain	42 100	75.0%
18	Korean Air	Rep. Korea	40 507	68.6%
19	America West	United States	34 247	76.4%
20	Alitalia	Italy	31 626	71.6%

Source: adapted from *Air Transport World: World airline report 2003* (www.atwonline.com), company accounts

Exhibit 3: Australian domestic market, 2003

Rank	City pairs	Revenue passengers	Revenue passenger kilometres	Available seat kilometres	Load factor	Aircraft trips
1	Melbourne–Sydney	5 625 444	3 971 563 464	4 899 159 618	81.1	33 665
2	Perth–Sydney	1 108 438	3 640 110 392	4 688 448 188	77.6	6 904
3	Brisbane–Melbourne	2 315 186	3 197 271 866	3 889 661 560	82.2	17 740
4	Melbourne–Perth	1 068 800	2 892 172 800	3 693 829 948	78.3	7 363
5	Brisbane–Sydney	3 735 918	2 813 146 254	3 514 149 223	80.1	26 290
6	Cairns–Sydney	838 090	1 651 875 390	2 041 781 519	80.9	4 648
7	Adelaide–Sydney	1 300 189	1 517 320 563	1 969 331 533	77.0	11 430
8	Brisbane–Cairns	894 544	1 244 310 704	1 559 670 931	79.8	7 357
9	Brisbane–Perth	301 271	1 089 094 665	1 299 774 279	83.8	2 181
10	Gold Coast–Melbourne	740 701	985 132 330	1 143 778 959	86.1	5 954
11	Adelaide–Melbourne	1 500 570	964 866 510	1 190 780 207	81.0	12 728
12	Adelaide–Perth	428 196	907 775 520	1 177 570 484	77.1	3 850
13	Gold Coast–Sydney	1 240 145	843 298 600	941 292 364	89.6	8 624
14	Adelaide–Brisbane	434 643	704 990 946	837 587 913	84.2	3 663
15	Brisbane–Townsville	595 143	661 799 016	816 431 008	81.1	5 189
16	Brisbane–Darwin	222 630	634 940 760	791 779 158	80.2	1 654
17	Hobart–Melbourne	877 474	542 278 932	691 259 360	78.4	9 029
18	Darwin–Sydney	151 106	476 739 430	614 751 078	77.5	1 132
19	Cairns–Melbourne	191 560	442 695 160	541 631 895	81.7	1 534
20	Canberra–Melbourne	765 201	359 644 470	486 474 243	73.9	9 842
21	Brisbane–Canberra	358 157	342 398 092	437 563 046	78.3	4 636
22	Brisbane–Mackay	359 957	286 885 729	380 321 729	75.4	3 854
23	Alice Springs–Sydney	136 455	275 912 010	359 568 391	76.7	1 250
24	Broome–Perth	145 248	243 580 896	322 075 265	75.6	2 004
25	Launceston–Melbourne	503 934	239 872 584	306 426 343	78.3	5 135
Total top 10			23 001 998 428	28 699 585 758		
Total top 39			32 386 238 214	40 609 441 893		
Other routes		5 380 231	5 045 544 968	7 176 891 072	70.3	213 460
Domestic Total		33 934 842	37 431 783 182	47 786 332 964	78.3	476 992

Source: adapted from Bureau of Transport and Regional Economics, *Digest of statistics 2002–03* (www.btre.gov.au/avstats/index.htm)

Exhibit 4: Qantas performance indicators 1995–2004

Year to 30/6	1995	1996	1997	1998	1999	2000	2001	2002	2003	2004
Revenue (A$m)	7162.9	7600.4	7834.4	8131.5	8448.7	9168.8	10188.2	10968.8	11374.9	11355.7
Net Profit (A$m)	180.1	246.2	252.7	304.8	421.6	517.3	415.4	428.0	343.5	684.4
Aircraft (#)	135	141	148	146	135	147	178	193	196	190
RPK (m)	50125	53358	57651	58619	59863	64149	70540	75314	77187	81276
Load factor (%)	72.0	72.1	72.9	71.9	73.2	75.4	75.9	78.3	77.6	78.0
Employees (FTE)	28565	29627	30080	28934	28226	29217	31632	33044	34872	33862

Source: Qantas annual reports

Exhibit 5: Qantas 2003–04 summary profit and loss account (year to 30 June)

	A$m
Sales and operating revenue	
Net passenger revenue	8978.30
Net freight revenue	469.70
Tours and travel revenue	711.10
Contract work revenue	502.60
Other sources	692.00
Total	11353.70
Expenditure	
Manpower and staff related	2938.50
Selling and marketing	466.10
Aircraft operating — variable	2226.80
Fuel and oil	1355.60
Property	309.80
Computer and communication	439.10
Depreciation and amortisation	1005.60
Non-cancellable operating lease rentals	263.50
Tours and travel	570.90
Capacity hire	287.40
Other	411.90
Share of net profit of associates and joint ventures	−19.70
Total	10255.50
Earnings before interest and tax	1098.20
Net borrowing costs	−133.60
Profit from ordinary activities before related income tax expense	964.60
Income tax expense relating to ordinary activities	−315.80
Net profit	648.80
Outside equity interests in net profit	−0.40
Net profit attributable to members of the company	648.40

Source: adapted from Qantas 2003–04 *Annual report*

Exhibit 6: Qantas 2003–04 performance by business segment

$m	Aircraft operations	Tours and travel	Catering	Eliminations	Consolidated
External sales	10 468.2	711.1	174.4	–	11 353.7
Inter-segment sales	129.0	283.3	362.8	–775.1	–
Total revenue	10 597.2	994.4	537.2	–775.1	11 353.7
Share of profit of joint ventures	19.7	–	–	–	19.7
EBIT	954.1	54.1	90.0	–	1098.2

Source: adapted from Qantas 2003–04 *Annual report*

Exhibit 7: Qantas 2003–04 earnings before interest and tax by activity

Qantas International	397.80
Qantas Domestic	465.70
Total airlines	**863.50**
Subsidiary businesses	
Qantas Holidays	54.10
QantasLink	97.00
Qantas Flight Catering	90.00
Australian Airlines	1.10
Qantas Defence Services	8.70
Equity accounted associates	19.70
Other subsidiaries	–35.90
Total subsidiary businesses	**234.70**
Consolidated	**1098.20**

Source: adapted from Qantas 2003–04 *Annual report*

Exhibit 8: Virgin Blue summary of performance 2001–05 (year to 31 March)

	2001 (*)	2002	2003	2004	H1 2005 (**)
Revenues (A$m)	74.8	338.3	914.6	1362.3	787
EBIT (A$m)	−0.3	44.5	146.4	218.3	90.1
NPAT (A$m)	−0.3(***)	34.8	107.8	158.5	63
Cash at end of period (A$m)	8.4	97	126.9	469.3	519.6
Employees	609	1421	2414	3440	n/a
Aircraft	6	17	31	40	48
PRKs (m)	664	3169	7194	11 584	7400
Load factor	73.9%	81.3%	79.3%	82.6%	76.80%
Cost per ASK (A¢)	8.42	8.82	8.46	8.16	7.26

(*) 7 months; (**) 6 months to 30/9/2004; (***) excludes A$10.6m start-up costs

Sources: Virgin Blue flotation prospectus (11/11/2003); Virgin Blue 2004 *Annual report*;
Virgin Blue Presentation to shareholders of H1 FY 2005 results; Virgin Blue H1 2005 results.

Exhibit 9: Virgin Blue operating costs, 2004

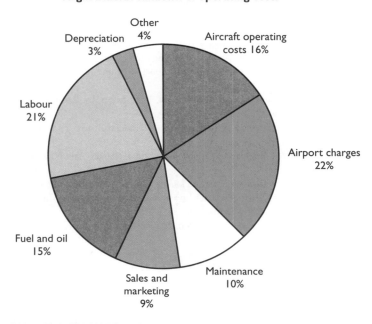

Virgin Blue: breakdown of operating costs

Source: Virgin Blue 2004 *Annual report*

Discussion questions

1. How have competitive dynamics evolved in the Australian airline industry since the early 1990s deregulation?
2. What makes the Australian airline industry different? Why do Qantas and Virgin Blue earn high profits when most airlines worldwide operate at a loss?
3. What is the strategy of Virgin Blue? Evaluate its competitive position.
4. What is the strategy of Qantas? Evaluate its competitive position.

References

1. *Air Transport World* 2004, 'Recovery 2004: gaining strength' January, pp. 28–34.
2. *Fortune International (Asia Edition)* 2003, 'Dead air: SARS sends aviation into a tailspin', 28 April.
3. *Wall Street Journal (Eastern Edition)* 1992, 'Australian carrier Ansett faces buffeting', 28 December.
4. The 18 cities and towns concerned were: Adelaide, Alice Springs, Brisbane, Cairns, Canberra, Coolangatta, Darwin, Gove, Hobart, Launceston, Mackay, Melbourne, Mount Isa, Perth, Proserpine, Rockhampton, Sydney and Townsville (*Airline Agreement Act 1981* 6(1)(e)).
5. Bureau of Transport Economics 1991, *Deregulation of domestic aviation: the first year*, report #73.
6. Bureau of Transport Economics, op. cit.
7. *Australian Financial Review* 1992, 'Qantas, Aust to merge as PM speeds changes', 1 June.
8. *Air Transport World* 1994, 'Re-creating Qantas', vol. 31, no. 5, pp. 74–78, May.
9. ibid.
10. *Business Review Weekly* 1993, 'Ansett challenges Qantas in Asia', 29 January.
11. *Australian Financial Review* 2000, 'Ansett deal launches Air NZ in big league', 19 February.
12. Forsyth, P 2003, 'Low cost carriers in Australia: experiences and impacts, *Journal of Air Transport Management*, vol. 9, pp. 277–84.
13. *Australian Financial Review* 2000, 'Virgin Blue starts before Olympics', 26 June.
14. *Australian Financial Review* 2000, 'All's fare in airline discount war', 14 August.
15. *Australian Financial Review* 2001, 'Airlines take aim as low-cost war heats up', 24 February.
16. Forsyth, op. cit.
17. *Australian Financial Review* 2001, 'Airlines take aim as low-cost war heats up', 24 February.
18. *Business Review Weekly* 2001, 'Sunshine in the open sky', 23 February.
19. *Business Review Weekly* 2001, 'Qantas gets a lift from Impulse deal', 25 May.
20. *Australian Financial Review* 2001, 'Out of order', 5 January; *Australian Financial Review* 2001, 'Ansett: the inside story of how safety came second', 21 April.
21. *Australian Financial Review* 2001, 'Nosedive: a tale of plummeting fortunes', 11 September.
22. *Business Review Weekly* 2001, 'Hard landing', 27 September.
23. *Business Review Weekly* 2001, 'Blue sky for Qantas', 27 September.
24. Forsyth, op. cit.
25. *Australian Financial Review* 2004, 'Trans-Tasman airline war leaves passengers sitting pretty', 27 March.
26. Data from Virgin Blue 2004 annual report, unless otherwise referenced.
27. *Australian Financial Review* 2004, 'Virgin targets small investors in $2.3bn float', 11 November.
28. *Aviation Week* 2004, 'Flying high: Virgin Blue enjoys huge success, seeks new places to expand', 12 July.
29. *Australian Financial Review* 2004, 'Limited downside on Jetstar', 26 February.
30. *Aviation Week* 2004, 'Flying high: Virgin Blue enjoys huge success, seeks new places to expand', 12 July.
31. *Australian Financial Review* 2004, 'Qantas gains height over Virgin Blue', 27 August.
32. *Business Review Weekly* 2004, 'Anything but blue skies', 26 August.
33. Presentation to shareholders of financial year 2005 first half results, 17 November 2004.
34. *Australian Financial Review* 2004, 'California dreamin' a Qantas nightmare', 8 July.
35. *Business Review Weekly* 2004, 'Anything but blue skies', 26 August.
36. *Business Review Weekly* 2004, 'Virgin's blue', 12 August.
37. *Business Review Weekly* 2004, 'Anything but blue skies', 26 August.
38. *Business Review Weekly* 2003, 'Mystery flight', 18 September.
39. *Business Review Weekly* 2004, 'Anything but blue skies', 2 August.
40. Qantas Factfile 2004, History.
41. Qantas Factfile 2004, Qantas in New Zealand and the Pacific.
42. *Business Review Weekly* 2003, 'Flight union dogfight', 26 June; *Business Review Weekly* 2003, 'The secret Qantas', 10 July.
43. *Australian Financial Review* 2004, 'Qantas contracts worth $1.4bn', 18 May.
44. *Australian Financial Review* 2004, 'Qantas books offshore tickets for crew', 23 June.
45. *Australian Financial Review* 2004, 'Dixon can now run his own race', 9 September.
46. *Aviation Week & Space Technology* 2004, 'Jetstar Asia looks east', 4 October.
47. *Aviation Week & Space Technology* 2004, 'New horizons; Qantas eyes growth outside its home market to take part in industry consolidation', 12 July.
48. Presentation of Qantas 2003/04 results to investors, 19 August 2004.
49. *Qantaslink*; Qantas Factfile 2004, Qantas 2004 Annual Report.
50. *JetStar*; Qantas Factfile 2004, Qantas 2004 Annual Report.
51. *Business Review Weekly* 2004, 'Fledgling flight plan', 2nd May.
52. *Australian Financial Review* 2004, 'Qantas gains height over Virgin Blue', 27 August.
53. *Australian Financial Review* 2004, 'Dixon's cleared for take-off', 11 September.
54. *Australian Financial Review* 2004, 'Jetstar rated a pretty short haul', 28 June.

55. *Australian Financial Review* 2004, 'Dixon looks for a dream run', 21 June.
56. Presentation of Qantas 2003/04 results to investors, 19 August.
57. *Australian Financial Review* 2004, 'California dreamin' a Qantas nightmare', 8 July.
58. *Australian Financial Review* 2004, 'Dixon's cleared for take-off', 11 September.
59. Qantas Airways: the lights are amber, Macquarie Research, 20 August 2004.
60. Qantas 2003/04 Annual Report.
61. Qantas Airways: the lights are amber, Macquarie Research, 20 August 2004.
62. Qantas Factfile 2004, Qantas in New Zealand and the Pacific.
63. *Aviation Week & Space Technology* 2004, 'Jetstar Asia looks east', 4 October.
64. Qantas Factfile 2004, Freight.
65. Qantas Factfile 2004, Qantas holidays.
66. Qantas Factfile 2004, Information technology.
67. Qantas Factfile 2004, Sales.
68. *Australian Financial Review* 2003, 'Blue sky ahead for airline internet bookings', 20 November.
69. *Australian Financial Review* 2004, 'Qantas to slash travel agents' commissions', 8 September.
70. *Australian Financial Review* 2004, 'Travel agents investors take flight', 9 September.
71. Qantas Factfiles 2004 and 2003/04 Annual Report.
72. '*Business Review Weekly* 2004, Anything but blue skies', 26 August.
73. *Australian Financial Review* 2003, 'Qantas frequent flyer points fly away', 23 December.
74. *Australian Financial Review* 2004, 'Display of aerobatics from Qantas', 20 August.
75. Qantas Airways: the lights are amber, Macquarie Research, 20 August 2004.
76. *Alliances*, Qantas Factfile 2004.
77. *Yield Management*, Qantas Factfile 2004.
78. Presentation of Qantas 2003/04 results to investors, 19 August, 2004.
79. Presentation of Qantas 2003/04 results to investors, 19 August, 2004.
80. *Australian Financial Review* 2004, 'Qantas seeks help to fight rivals', 20 August.
81. Qantas 2003–04 Annual Report.
82. Presentation of Qantas 2003–04 results to investors, 19 August 2004.
83. Macquarie Research 2004, Qantas Airways: the lights are amber, 20 August.

Marlows Limited: a retrospective

By Celia Dunlop, Corlia Kruger, Mark McPherson and Allen Smyth

Introduction

On a day in April 2002, Ray Della-Polina gazed out of his office window, contemplating the future of his company. Ray, co-founder and now executive chair of Marlows Limited, a Perth-based retailer in vehicle parts and accessories, sat with his managing director, Paul Wagner. Both had just come from a shareholder meeting, at which two major investors in this unlisted public company had made it clear that their investment timeframes did not coincide with Marlows' plans for growth. A family investor wanted to sell its equity within the year, while the venture capitalist was looking to relinquish its equity within three years.

Ray and Paul had a vision to grow Marlows' national market share of the auto aftermarket from 4 per cent to 15 per cent, hopefully within the next three to five years. Their plan was to develop a national retail footprint, expanding their geographic base by adding four stores each year. Both believed that Marlows' unique model gave the company a winning edge by attracting both do-it-yourself (DIY) and do-it-for-me (DIFM) customers.

For some years, Marlows had been the subject of industry speculation, with both a merger and public listing cited as potential future options for the company. Ray and Paul were only too aware of the financial difficulties of further expansion and were exploring options to realise their vision. The apparent instability among the shareholders was yet another obstacle in the path to Marlows' growth.

Aside from financing concerns, the choice of location of additional stores was crucial to the success of their plan. With a significant presence in both Western Australia and South Australia, Marlows was making inroads into the Victorian market. As expected, Marlows was not travelling the expansion road on its own, with many competitors in a similar frame of mind.

This case study was prepared under the supervision of Dr Peter Galvin of the Graduate School of Business, Curtin University of Technology. It is intended to be used as a basis for class discussion rather than as an illustration of either effective or ineffective handling of the situation.

A brief history of Marlows

From humble origins in 1974, with one employee and a single store (200 square metres) in the basement of Perth's City Arcade, Marlows had grown to be the largest independent specialist retailer of auto parts and accessories with vehicle servicing in Australia by 2001.

At the age of 36 years, Ray headed a group that purchased the business of Marlows in 1976. At the time, he formulated a twofold plan for Marlows:

1. to operate on the basic principle of offering a large range of quality products at prices equal to, or lower than, those of his competitors
2. to improve the prevailing public perception of parts shops by establishing high standards of service and in-store presentation.

After rapid early growth in Western Australia, the business consolidated in the mid-1980s. During that decade, Marlows relocated and enlarged some shops, added more workshops and even briefly expanded into New South Wales. Even though the expansion into New South Wales was unsuccessful (with the Parramatta store being sold in 1993), the company continued to grow. In August 1995, Marlows acquired the 33-year-old South Australian chain, Rocca Bros, in the largest takeover deal ever negotiated in the automotive parts industry in Australia at that time.

By 1997, the company had outgrown its head office and warehouses complex, and developed a new site at Malaga, which was an emerging industrial estate north of Perth. The custom-built facility (4200 square metres) was officially opened in March 1997, with a new general manager, Paul Wagner, appointed soon after. Recruited from Mobil Oil Australia, Paul was appointed managing director in July 1997, with Ray moving on to the position of executive chair.

Marlows had become a high-profile, successful and efficient retailer by 2001, with 520 employees and company stores, offices and warehouses occupying over 24 000 square metres in three states. Marlows' success and its contribution to the industry were formally recognised by the company's peers in 1984 — when the company was named Australian Automotive Aftermarket Association (AAAA) Retailer of the Year — and again in 1993 — when Ray received the AAAA Award for Outstanding Service to the Industry.

The philosophy behind Marlows' success to 2001 had been a focus on customers, employees, strict financial controls, creative marketing and the development of synergistic relationships with major suppliers.

The automotive industry

The auto aftermarket industry is a significant subsector of the automotive industry, encompassing the manufacture and sale of vehicles, parts and accessories, and the provision of fitting and repair services.

Trends in the automotive industry translate with a time delay to the aftermarket sector. Increases in the sales of new cars, for example, translate to increased demand for accessories in the short term and increased demand for parts and servicing in the longer term. Total new motor vehicle sales in Australia showed continuous growth over the eight years to 2002. The trend remained positive in 2002, with sales rising for the ninth consecutive month in February 2002. From September 2001, the sales of new passenger vehicles showed a monthly growth rate of approximately 1 per cent. New vehicle sales in February 2002 were 10.9 per cent higher than in February 2001.[1]

An estimated 11.7 million motor vehicles were registered in Australia (population of 19 million people) in 2002, with 9.84 million being passenger vehicles. The average age of the passenger motor vehicle fleet had increased from 1988 by 1.7 years to 10.3 years in 1999 — twice the average age of equivalent motor vehicles in Japan.

The growing age of the vehicle fleet creates opportunities for the sales of parts and accessories, and the servicing of those vehicles. This trend is particularly true of vehicles imported from Korea between 1995 and 2000. Once a vehicle's manufacturers' warranty expires, its owner is likely to purchase vehicle parts from the aftermarket industry.

The auto aftermarket industry

Industry profile

The automotive aftermarket industry comprises companies dealing in car batteries, vehicle air-conditioning (including installation), car sound systems (including installation), motor vehicle accessories (such as seat covers), motor vehicle parts (including servicing) and tyres.

The total automotive aftermarket for parts and accessories in Australia is estimated at $5 billion–6 billion per year (turnover). This includes both genuine parts from both original equipment manufacturers (OEMs) and nongenuine parts. There are various supply channels, with specialised wholesale/dealer networks undertaking OEM activity. In the nongenuine segment, supply occurs through wholesalers and retailers.

The overall market consists of dealer networks, retailers (DIY) and service centres (DIFM). The retail segment accounts for about $1.6 billion of total sales per year.

The United States is the largest source of automotive parts and accessories, supplying nearly 20 per cent of Australia's total imports. Other significant suppliers (in descending order) are Japan, Germany, Sweden and Italy. In 2000, imports accounted for 50 per cent of the Australian automotive parts and accessories market.

The US Department of State in 2001 forecast future growth for the export of automotive parts and accessories to Australia, predicting excellent opportunities for US suppliers of automotive mechanical and electrical parts and consumables.[2] The US automotive aftermarket dwarfs the Australian market in size, with some of the major US players turning over more in one quarter than the largest Australian player turns over in one year. AutoZone, the largest retailer of auto parts in north America,[3] opened 104 new stores in the United States and eight in Mexico in fiscal year 2001, bringing the company's total number of stores to 3040. AutoZone has made the most of the growing demand trends in the United States and used its strong cash flow to reduce long-term debt and repurchase company stock in fiscal year 2001.

Industry trends

Amos Bush, chair and managing director of Autobarn, one of the bigger competitors in the Australian aftermarket, recently bemoaned the lack of reliable industry statistics, stating 'We need proper research about where we are today, but we do not have facts to guide us in business decisions'.[4] He contrasted this lack with the depth of industry statistics available to companies in the United States.[5]

The US market is commonly regarded as a leading indicator of trends for the Australian industry. Automotive chains in the United States, which serve mainly DIY customers, had registered a five-year business growth of 3.9 per cent to 2001.[6] US research indicates that the following factors (in order of importance) influence where consumers shop: price, ability to see the product, availability, customer service, location of store and guarantee.

The move from DIY to DIFM

The US motor accessories market increased by 49.5 per cent from 1995 to 2001, dominated by appearance accessories (54.3 per cent), performance parts (21.2 per cent) and handling components (24.5 per cent).[7] The market for in-car entertainment products was growing fast too.[8]

The increasing complexity of modern motor vehicles, coupled with an increased willingness to pay for fitting services, has led to this growth in the DIFM market segment, while the DIY market is softening. This trend is bolstered by improvements in manufacturers' quality standards over the past 20 years, which have resulted in a greater reliability of automotive parts.

The demise of the desire to work on vehicles is reflected in the industry, which is seeing a net reduction in the volume of hard parts sold to retail customers. The positive consequence of this trend is evidenced in this group's increasing purchases of car care, performance dress-up and improvement products.

Other trends

The renewed customer focus and extended warranties offered by motor vehicle manufacturers are also creating new challenges for the aftermarket industry. Ford, Holden, Mitsubishi and Mazda all offer a standard three-year and 100 000-kilometre warranty to car owners, enticing owners back to the dealers for services and repairs. The rapid introduction of new technology in cars is changing the face of the aftermarket as well.[9] The servicing of computerised and electronic components, and also complex safety and luxury accessories, requires a major investment by outlets in expensive equipment and tools, and staff training. Large outlets such as dealerships and franchises, which can afford to invest in equipment, can benefit from these changes in technology.

Parts proliferation, due to the increasing diversity of vehicles in Australia, also continues.[10] This increases pressure on inventory, stock control and space in both service and distribution channels. Fast ('as needed') delivery is becoming a leading purchasing criterion in every market.

Last, the aftermarket is increasingly being affected by government regulations, ranging from vehicle safety and engine emission standards to noise regulations.[11] The enforcement of vehicle safety standards (by keeping unsafe vehicles off the road until they are brought up to an acceptable standard) is advantageous to the aftermarket industry because it increases demand for test-related services and parts. Australia enacted its first environmental standards for petrol and diesel in January 2002.

Economic indicators

The Australian economy is forecast to expand relatively slowly, compared with more than 4.9 per cent growth in gross domestic product in the previous decade. The growth rate of 2.3 per cent in 2002 was underpinned by strong consumer spending, which is growing at about 4 per cent per year. The Reserve Bank of Australia's monetary policy is to maintain inflation at 2–3 per cent.

Competition in the auto aftermarket industry

Although Marlows had an estimated 40 per cent of the retail market in Western Australia and South Australia, it was far from the biggest player in the national arena. Apart from specialist retailers, large generalist retailers such as Coles and Big W also compete within the same market.

The industry is extremely fragmented, with a large number of independent retailers holding almost 30 per cent of the market share. There is general consensus within the industry that the days of small owner-operated stores are numbered and that rationalisation of the industry has already progressed.

Figure C4.1 shows that Marlows' top three competitors, in terms of market share, are Super Cheap, Autobarn and Repco (part of the Automotive Parts Group [APG]). A number of smaller franchise groups are also expanding aggressively.

Coventry Group Limited (CGL)[12]

Coventry Group Limited's (CGL) automotive division consists of Coventrys in Western Australia, Motor Traders in South Australia and Coventry Auto Parts in New South Wales and Queensland. Coventrys in Western Australia is the largest automotive parts, tools and equipment distributor in the state, with 20 branches (nine in Perth and eleven in regional areas), carrying 130 000 different line items, including all the top brand names. Motor Traders commenced trading in 1925 and carries more than 75 000 stock items. It has eight outlets in Adelaide and three in regional areas of the state. Coventry Auto Parts — a joint venture with the Ford Motor Company of Australia — is CGL's first automotive parts operation in New South Wales (seven stores) and Queensland (four stores). It was restructured in August 2001 with the closure of its Victorian distribution activities, resulting from their failure to gain the genuine Ford parts distribution rights in Victoria. The joint venture lost $6.9 million in 2000–01. Divisional total revenue from sales in that year was $335.43 million, with a segment result of $5.65 million before tax.

Autobarn[13]

Autobarn is Australia's largest franchise retailer of automotive aftermarket accessories and parts, with over ninety stores throughout Victoria, Tasmania, South Australia, New South Wales, the Australian Capital Territory, Queensland and the Northern Territory. It experienced continuous growth over the 14 years to 2001, resulting in 91 franchises and one company-owned outlet. A total of ten new or extended stores were opened in Victoria (six), New South Wales (two), Queensland (two) and Tasmania (one) in the last six months of 2001, representing an investment of more than $4 million and adding another 6000 square metres to the total Autobarn floor space. Seven more Autobarn stores were set to open in the first half of 2002. Sales exceeded $140 million for the 2000–01 financial year. The franchise activity has a capital requirement of $440 000 to $545 000, with a 2 per cent royalty and 3 per cent advertising fee. Training and support include site selection, lease negotiations, store design and fitout, training, management, merchandising and ongoing advertising, marketing and management support.

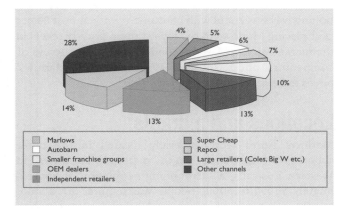

Figure C4.1: Auto aftermarket national market share

Source: from *Aftermarket*, February–March 2000. Reproduced with permission from the Australian Automotive Aftermarket Association

Repco/Automotive Parts Group (APG)[14]

APG was established in August 2001 to undertake a buyout of the Pacific Automotive Australia and New Zealand businesses, which were then a division of Pacific Dunlop Limited. The buyout imposed a debt of $276 million, of which $107 million had been repaid (from receivables at the time of purchase) by 2002. APG changed its name to Repco in 2002 to capitalise on the Repco brand name.

The individual businesses that comprise Repco are:

- Repco Australia (established 1922): with 304 stores across Australia and 2637 staff (as at November 2001), it is the automotive aftermarket leader in both retail and trade
- Repco New Zealand (established 1955): with 88 branches and 688 staff, it is the largest reseller of automotive aftermarket parts in New Zealand
- Ashdown (established 1999): it is a reseller in the automotive electrical market, with eighteen branches and 249 staff

- CarParts (established 1999): it is a wholesaler of domestically manufactured and imported replacement parts, with five branches and 123 staff
- Motospecs (established 2000): it is an importer/distributor of specialist products and a kitting specialist.

APG's interim financial report for 30 August 2001 to 31 December 2001 showed a net profit of $4.7 million on sales of $274.1 million.

Super Cheap Auto[15]

In 1976, Reg and Hazel Rowe started a small, home-based parts and mail order business. The company grew to comprise 37 stores based entirely in Queensland. The company's mission statement is 'To develop and grow our business to achieve the position of market leader in car accessories retailing in Australia. We will be recognised for our aggressive pricing, the largest "value for money" product range and our conveniently located stores'.

Since 1998, the business has gone through an extraordinary expansion: it opened 20 additional stores in New South Wales and the Australian Capital Territory in eighteen months, with fourteen of the new store openings in 2000 alone. In 1993, Super Cheap Auto operated only eight stores; by November 2001, it had a total of 89 stores. The average cost to open each store is $1 million.

Super Cheap Auto's success stems from its dynamic in-store retail merchandising strategy, extensive product range, outstanding customer service initiatives and 'superstore' warehouse-shopping environment (which averages 800 square metres). More than 10 000 products are available in every store. Achieving its highest ever annual turnover of $135 million in the 2000–01 financial year, Super Cheap Auto was forecasting turnover of $160 million in 2001–02.

Marlows — products and services

The principal products that Marlows sold to its customers are shown on the sales matrix in figure C4.2. Each store contained approximately 18 000-plus parts and accessories. The total inventory consisted of almost 50 000 product lines. One of the great attributes of Marlows was the depth of the product range available in a standard Marlows store.

Not only did Marlows offer one of the widest ranges of product lines, but it was also able to deliver the product to the customer. An email to Marlows from its web page guaranteed a response within four hours, indicating at which store the product is available. Regardless of the vagaries of various suppliers' performance, Marlows more often than not achieved an order fill rate of more than 98 per cent.

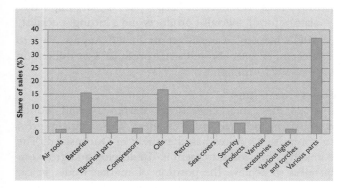

Figure C4.2: Marlows' sales matrix

Source: Marlows

A relatively recent addition to Marlows' product line in Western Australia were vehicle immobilisers. Marlows displayed initiative when legislation for the mandatory fitting of vehicle immobilisers was first contemplated in 1997, and it was closely involved in the initial preparation of the industry for the new requirements, training all of the state government inspectors and a large number of the fitters of immobilisers. Although the current market for immobilisers is softening, Marlows' market share increased significantly from 15 per cent in June 2000 to 27 per cent in June 2001. The company then used its trained electrical fitters to install in-car entertainment/sound systems.

Marlows again showed initiative in product development when it launched the 'Help Bits' program in 2000, with more than 2400 items (comprising automotive fixings, fasteners, seals and similar products) made available to customers for the first time as single units. Before the Marlows initiative, customers had no alternative but to buy such items in bulk. This unique offering by Marlows was not copied by competitors. The growth in sales for this program was strong, with customers welcoming the new product lines. The profit margins were also significantly higher for these types of product than for other products.

Marlows was the only competitor in the industry that combined its retail stores with full vehicle servicing. Each Marlows store had servicing bays right next to the retail store, where all types of vehicle servicing and repairs were undertaken (except full engine overhauls). The parts required for the repair of vehicles were sourced directly from the retail shop. Revenue from the DIFM segment grew steadily. Paul Wagner noted that fitting services represented 11 per cent of sales in 1996, compared with 14–15 per cent in 2001.

In an independent market survey that Marlows commissioned in 1999, the suppliers surveyed indicated that Marlows' fitting service was a key contributor to the company's success. [16] The company averaged almost 90 000 workshop jobs every year.

Cost/differentiation of products

Marlows' pricing policy was always to deliver products at the lowest possible price, without sacrificing quality. Marlows' reputation for low price and good quality was encapsulated in their marketing slogan: 'Up to double the range at down to half the price'. All stores also prominently displayed Marlows' 'pricing pledge', which committed Marlows to refunding twice the difference if a competitor offered a cheaper product within seven days. This positioning was successful with consumers, with almost 80 per cent placing Marlows in the lowest three price brackets in the market survey. Marlows conducted its own surveys of competitors' prices, and Paul Wagner believed Marlows' prices to be in the top end of the lower quartile.

Locations and markets

Marlows stores were generally located in the outer suburbs of Australia's major metropolitan areas. In Western Australia, a surrounding population of approximately 50 000 to 60 000 people was required for a store to achieve a profitable turnover. Marlows' 19 stores were located in three states: 11 stores in Western Australia (with most of the stores in the Perth metropolitan area, and two country stores in Rockingham and Mandurah), four stores in South Australia (located in metropolitan areas and within close proximity of each other) and four stores in Victoria (two in close proximity). All stores were open seven days a week, although the workshops were closed on Sundays. Marlows also had two distribution centres: one at Malaga in Perth and one in Regency Park in South Australia.

Market research conducted in late 1999 concluded that Marlows captured 39 per cent of the revenue spend in its particular segment of the Perth market and that Rocca Bros had 38.4 per cent of its market segment in Adelaide. [17]

Consumer profile

Marlows had a large retail customer base, with an estimated 2.15 million customers making purchases from Marlows stores in 2001. Customers (of whom 75 per cent were male) spent an average of $32 per visit.

According to Paul Wagner, 'hard' parts — which used to account for up to 60 per cent of sales — made up only 40 per cent of sales in 2001, with customers buying more car accessories than previously.[18]

According to a recent research report, consumers in the industry value: convenient services, including easy-access locations with onsite parking; longer opening hours; fast and reliable turnaround times for services; services on demand; transparent or preset prices; and service guarantees.[19] Because of the increase in young female motor vehicle ownership, the auto aftermarket is also experiencing a change in the traditional demographic profile of customers. Even though the biggest spenders on parts and accessories are males aged 45–55 years, the female customer sector is growing. Marlows appreciated that the female market segment is unlikely to be attracted to dimly lit parts counters serviced by disinterested employees, and it was one of the first retailers to re-evaluate the presentation standards within its stores.

Marlows was always sensitive to the needs of its customers, and it conducted regular customer satisfaction surveys, employing ex-RAC officials to ensure the independence of the surveys. Marlows boasted a customer complaint rate of only 0.12 per cent.[20]

Suppliers

Marlows had a large number of suppliers, both domestic and foreign. Almost 30 per cent of total products were sourced from overseas manufacturers and distributors, of which a large proportion were located in China and Taiwan. Paul Wagner pointed out that Marlows' reliance on these overseas suppliers made the company vulnerable in the case of relations between China and Taiwan becoming more problematic. Marlows was aware of the trend of consolidation among suppliers in the industry, and it endeavoured, where possible, to deal with manufacturers directly and limit its dependency on wholesalers. This was only possible, however, if Marlows continued to grow and offer suppliers a bigger market. As Paul commented, 'There are a huge number of retailers out there; we have to give suppliers a reason to do business with us, and we have to be able to source from them at competitive prices.'[21]

Marlows — the organisation

Marlows' mission statement emphasised a high level of customer service; being a progressive and professional business; and the importance of team members. The company credo focused on appropriately serving the needs of the various stakeholders, including customers, the community, team members, management, suppliers and shareholders.

Management and organisational structure

In July 1999, Paul Wagner was appointed chief executive officer of Marlows. The board of directors consisted of RL Della-Polina (executive chair), JB McAlwey, PA Della-Polina, WA James (director of Chieftain Securities Limited), GG Rocca (previous co-owner of Rocca Bros) and PS Wagner (managing director). The company's organisational structure was relatively flat (figure C4.3, page C8), reflecting its corporate culture of embracing teamwork and cooperation rather than hierarchy and direction.

Culture of teamwork and training

Marlows' straightforward business approach firmly established the company's integrity throughout the industry and was viewed by suppliers as a key contributor to Marlows' success.[22] True to the spirit of maintaining an honest workplace, Marlows had a strict policy on theft. Proof of this policy being a deterrent was shown in the company's inventory shrinkage rate of 0.85 per cent, which was well below the industry average.

Ray Della-Polina maintained a strong commitment to quality team–management relationships from the start. The Marlows Team Work Code was displayed prominently in the Malaga head office, testament to the company's belief in teamwork. In all company documentation, the employees were always referred to as 'team members'.

Approximately 80 per cent of Marlows' team members were nonunionised, and workplace agreements governed all employees' conditions of employment. The workplace agreements specifically linked remuneration to performance, with some employees' income determined by the number of customers served. The flexibility in working conditions derived from using workplace agreements encouraged productivity. Marlows had taken pre-emptive steps to protect the existing agreements from the legislative changes in Western Australia.

The turnover rate of staff was relatively low, mostly being about 3 per cent (except in Victoria, where new stores were still settling down).

Team training

All team members received training and the company made a conscious effort to do whatever it could to enhance the skills and knowledge of its people, for their own benefit as well as for customers. This ongoing commitment was

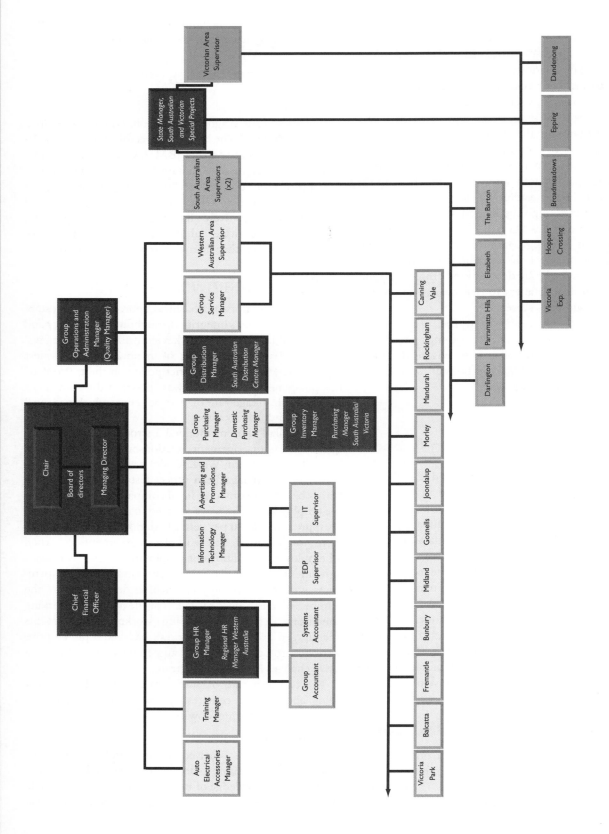

Figure C4.3: Marlows' organisational structure

Source: Marlows

rewarded with a Western Australian Government Employer Excellence Award for training in 1988. The company had a well-documented procedure — referred to as a 'Training Tree' — to record and publish a team member's training history with the company. All team members spent at least one week a year in training. Furthermore, the company encouraged attendance at external training courses and provided incentives in some cases (including part payment of course fees). Team members were trained to develop interpersonal and communication (selling) skills, in addition to possessing a high degree of technical knowledge. Marlows sales staff were reputed to have the best technical knowledge in the industry.

Systems and supply

Inventory management

In 1981, Marlows bought its first computer cash-register system so stock could be controlled by individual part number. From those early days, Marlows invested in developing custom-made inventory control and management systems. By 2002, the company managed the movement of more than 25 000 line items via individual stock-keeping unit (SKU) numbers, complete with both buying and retail pricing on file. Marlows believed that its home-built inventory management program was cutting edge for the industry and equal to anything in Australia.

A maximum five-minute delay behind real time allowed true cost reductions in inventory and storage facilities. The inventory system facilitated the transfer, on request, of stock held at other stores, further optimising inventory levels. It also accounted for seasonal fluctuations in demand and differentiated demand for SKU by location. Paul Wagner stated that Marlows' achieved 3.35–3.5 stock turns per year.[23]

As are all systems of this type, it was continually upgraded to enable Marlows to maintain its competitive advantage in this area of the business. The company adopted a new category management system within its purchasing department in 2001, to improve its management of stock levels. The company felt that the new management system resulted in less slow-moving and obsolete stock, with stock levels remaining constant even though new stores had opened.

Distribution/warehousing

Marlows had a distribution centre co-located at each headquarters in Western Australia and South Australia. (The Victorian stores did not have access to a central distribution centre.) Its product was sourced from no fewer than 12 overseas countries, direct from Australian manufacturers, as well as from local importers and wholesalers.

The central warehouse supplied, on a daily basis, about 70 per cent of the stores' requirements. The other 30 per cent was ordered from local wholesalers/distributors and delivered to the central warehouse daily, where each item was tagged with a barcode, checked against an invoice, then rechecked and packed into sealed crates, and distributed to the stores. The branches conducted no further checks of the goods received, because once the goods were processed, the central warehouse guaranteed counts to be entirely correct. Product was thus placed on the shelf within the store as expeditiously as possible (usually the same day).

All point-of-sale terminals were polled by 7 pm on normal nights and 11 pm on late night trading nights. Daily transactions were processed, and the sophisticated inventory management system concluded from the transactions the data items to be replenished to the stores. 'Picking slips' were generated for items that could be supplied from the bulk stocks, while 'order listings' for the other items were sent to the purchasing department, which ordered those items from local suppliers. The system also provided for the automatic stock reorder listings of the bulk store stocks.

Supply agreements and relationships

The company's central distribution facilities made delivery considerably easier for suppliers. All of the stores were company owned, so suppliers were confident that any deal with management would be implemented across all stores. This is rarely the case with franchise operations.

In the 1999 survey, the great majority of suppliers judged their relationship with Marlows to be 'good' or 'excellent'.[24] Most said that Marlows would be among the first companies that they would choose to deal with when a new product or service became available. Suppliers trusted Marlows to provide maximum exposure to their products and deliver effective merchandising.

Quality assurance

All the stores and workshops in Western Australia were ISO9002 accredited, and the workshops were RAC-approved repairers in Western Australia and RAA-approved repairers in South Australia. In 1995, Marlows embarked on a total quality management project, which was rolled out over 12 months. The company's quality management procedures controlled all of its processes, and a standardised format was used for all stores.

Marketing

The company's policy was to market aggressively. The company's advertising budget for 2000 amounted to $3.5 million, which represented 4.6 per cent of revenue — a ratio that had remained steady over the decade.

Marlows' marketing strategy uses different advertising channels: catalogues (which accounted for approximately half of the budget); newspapers; letterbox drops (used mostly for special promotions); television and radio (only in Western Australia and South Australia, where local star footballers acted as promoters of the Marlows brand); and sponsorships of motor racing events.

Marlows also maintained a presence on the Internet with two sites: www.marlows.com.au and www.theride.com. These sites included details of store locations, product offerings and motoring information, including car club contact details. A range of products could be purchased online from both websites, which were promoted in Marlows' mainstream advertising.

The 1999 survey confirmed that Marlows' marketing strategy was proving effective: 85 per cent of consumers surveyed in Western Australia recalled seeing some form of advertising for the company.[25]

Marlows' ideal model

Early in 1991, the company pulled out of the original City Arcade store, closed the Innaloo Shopping Centre outlet and opened a big new branch in Balcatta. The store formed the basis of the 'Marlows model' on which subsequent stores were based.

These moves indicated a significant redefinition of the company's marketing philosophy. Marlows then concentrated on bigger, specially designed stores, strategically placed in the major catchment areas but independent of shopping centres. The main motivations for this strategy were restrictive trading covenants that make seven-days-a-week trading impossible, as well as the difficulty of accommodating a workshop within the centre. Marlows did, however, co-locate its stores close to major shopping centres to benefit from the traffic flow.

Marlows developed its ideal model from its experiences and observations of successful companies overseas. Typically, a Marlows store was a bright, consumer-based, self-service store with a large fitting, service and repair workshop as standard. Of the 1000 square metres of store area, typically 75 per cent was allocated to retail and 25 per cent to service and fitting. A new store required an investment of about $2 million, of which $1.1 million was for land and building.

The company followed a strategy from the late 1990s of selling off the properties that it had developed and leasing those properties back for ten-year periods. This practice enabled the company to free capital for expansion in South Australia and Victoria.

Given the stand-alone model developed by the company, the company took on the role of de facto developer, because to achieve the specific requirements for the Marlows model, it was quicker and easier to buy and build than to adapt existing sites.

The headquarters at Malaga were built, sold and leased back in 1998. The Joondalup store was sold under a lease-back agreement in 1998, as were the Mandurah and Canning Vale properties in 2000. In June 2001, the Balcatta property was sold, also with a ten-year lease-back. The Broadmeadows and Werribee stores in Victoria were built in conjunction with property developers and leased back from inception.

Financials

The group sales revenue for the year ended 30 June 2001 amounted to more than $70 million. For shareholders, 2001 was not a good year because Marlows incurred a small operating loss compared with the profits of previous years. The main contributing factor to this state of affairs was the formation expenses of the e-commerce venture www.theride.com. Profitability had also been reduced as a result of establishing four stores in Victoria, the last of the four stores opening in Werribee in August 2001. The directors thus decided to pay no interim dividends out of the 2001 profits.

In 2001, sales growth of 4.2 per cent was achieved in Western Australia, compared with 0.74 per cent in South Australia. By June 2001, Marlows had invested $4 million in the Victorian expansion and was expecting a positive return on the first two stores opened there. The first two Victorian stores were expected to become cash positive during the 2002–03 financial year.

Marlows' biggest challenge for the future appeared to be how to finance further expansion activities. The company had sold off most of the property it still owned and did not have the cash to fund an aggressive expansion strategy. Its existing investment partner, Chieftain Securities Limited helped to fund the Rocca Bros acquisition. Chieftain Securities indicated, however, that its investment time-frame did not extend further than the next three years. Compounding this difficulty was the fact that one of the other major shareholders in Marlows might want to sell its shares in the company. The Delrai Family Trust held

54.1 per cent of Marlows shares, Chieftain Security held 31.1 per cent, the Della-Polina family trust held 5.5 per cent and smaller private investors made up the remainder of the shareholding. Two Marlows directors (Ray Della-Polina and JB McAlwey) were trustees and beneficiaries of the Delrai Trust. Some of the other trustees, however, wanted to exit from the investment in Marlows.

Ray and Paul Wagner were very concerned about the imminent trading of a huge percentage of the equity in the company. Paul admits that the automotive aftermarket is perceived as a somewhat 'unsexy backwater' for most mainline investors.[26] In the light of these financial uncertainties, the company's loss in 2001 further disheartened them, and the expansion plans appeared to be ill timed. Ray and Paul were considering approaching one of the major broking firms in Perth to help them to explore options for the future.

Growth initiatives

According to Ray Della-Polina, the company had a target of opening four new stores per year. Marlows' mission was to acquire a 15 per cent share of the national market and achieve market leadership. These expansion plans would have required annual funding of at least $8 million. The time from purchasing a property for development to the point at which a store became cash positive was about four to five years. Marlows maintained continuing research to identify suitable sites in the Melbourne area, where a store would require a surrounding population of 80 000 to 100 000 to be viable.

The Western Australian stores, developed in accordance with Marlows' model, were all quick off the mark, with most becoming cash positive and profit positive within 12 months (half of the initial projected time). Marlows' venture into the New South Wales market in the late 1980s was less successful. Two stores were established in Crows Nest and Parramatta only to be sold in 1987 and 1993 respectively. Even though Marlows spent almost $1 million in establishing an awareness of the Marlows brand on the east coast of Australia, the expansion failed. Management at the time attributed the failed expansion partly to the choice of location.

By 1995, Marlows was the dominant force in the Western Australian aftermarket. To grow the business, the company decided to expand into South Australia. The $7.2 million buyout of Rocca Bros in that state in 1995 was partly financed through a $4.5 million investment by Chieftain Securities Limited. The director of Chieftain, as well as Jim Rocca, joined the Marlows board.

A distribution centre was also added to the South Australian expansion, enabling Marlows to save costs on supply and distribution. The four South Australian stores continued to deliver good profitable returns. Annual sales were $20.6 million in the 2000–01 financial year. As in Western Australia, all the South Australian stores were cash positive and profit positive within 12 months, half the expected time.

Marlows' expansion into Victoria was initiated with the company's sixteenth store opening in Epping in October 1999. The second and third Victorian stores followed in close succession at Broadmeadows and Dandenong in 2000. The fourth store opened at Werribee in August 2001. The Victorian stores experienced a longer return period than that of the Western Australian and South Australian stores, and were expected to become cash positive two to three years after opening, and profitable after three to four years. Some of the problems experienced by the Victorian stores included the lack of a distribution centre and the absence of economies of scale in advertising.

Theride.com

Marlows' management was encouraged by their suppliers and investors, as well as a general industry sentiment, to develop an e-commerce site to complement the existing business. The site, www.theride.com, cost the company about $1.5 million to design and start up, and these expenses were the main contributing factor in the losses suffered by Marlows in 2001. The site's performance was disappointing, although not unique to Marlows, with the whole retail sector experiencing similar low returns. The site www.theride.com had an operating loss of $1.67 million in 2001.

Management decided to scale back its involvement in the e-commerce project, while retaining all rights for the intellectual property that had been developed. The new online presence, however, began experiencing a growth in sales, albeit from a small base. The site generated sales of $10 000 per month and had high growth. In addition, the site resulted in forty to fifty email queries per day. The online presence offered brand enhancement, and sales from this channel were expected to grow to 1–2 per cent of group sales within a few years.

The outcome

Marlows' goal was to develop to a national retail footprint throughout Australia, with a view to achieving 15 per cent market share of the national aftermarket. Bearing in mind the conflicting interests of their shareholders and Marlows' weak financial performance in 2001, Ray Della-Polina and Paul Wagner needed to consider the following issues in outlining a strategy in 2002 for Marlows' future:

- the factors external to Marlows that would have an impact on the company's choice of strategy, that is, the key success factors within the automotive aftermarket industry and important industry trends for Marlows to consider
- the success or otherwise of Marlows' strategy to date
- Marlows' key strengths and weaknesses, and the capabilities within the company that would contribute to its success in any future expansion
- a growth strategy and financing options for achieving Marlows' goal.

In 2003, however, Marlows was taken over by Super Cheap Auto.

Discussion questions

1. What are the industry's dominant economic features?
2. What is competition like and how strong is each of the competitive forces?
3. What is causing the industry's competitive structure and business environment to change?
4. Which companies are in the strongest/weakest positions?
5. What strategic moves are rivals likely to make next?
6. What are the key factors for competitive success?
7. What are Marlows' strengths, weaknesses, opportunities and threats?
8. What are Marlows' strategic capabilities that give competitive advantage?
9. What is Marlows' present strategy?
10. What strategic issues does the company face?
11. What strategic options does the company realistically have?
12. How can Marlows' finance growth initiatives?

End notes

1. Australian Bureau of Statistics, accessed June 2002, www.abs.gov.au.
2. US Department of State, *FY2001 country commercial guide*, www.corporateinformation.com/ausector/Automotive.html.
3. Autozone, accessed June 2002, www.autozone.com.
4. Bush, A 2001, Address to the AAPEX (Automotive Aftermarket Products Expo) SEMA (Specialty Equipment Market Association) Trade Show, Sydney, May.
5. 'How industry leaders see the retail future for the automotive aftersales market', 13 August 2001, www.ausauto.com.
6. ibid.
7. Kersting, C 2001, executive vice president, SEMA, 'The international experience: aftermarket retailing in the US', Paper presented at the inaugural AAPEX SEMA Trade Show, Sydney, 24 May.
8. ibid.
9. Diagonal Reports 2002, 'GAP 2002. Global Aftermarket Panel, Australia', www.diagonalreports.com/pdfs/gapau.pdf.
10. ibid.
11. Environment Australia, accessed June 2002, www.ea.gov.au/atmosphere/transport.
12. Coventrys, www.coventrys.com.au.
13. Autobarn, accessed June 2002, www.autobarn.com.au.
14. Automotive Parts Group, accessed June 2002, www.autopg.com.au/businesses/repcoaustralia.html.
15. Super Cheap Auto, accessed June 2002, www.supercheapauto.com.
16. Marlows Limited 2002, *Corporate profile*, 12 April.
17. ibid.
18. Wagner, P 2001, managing director, Marlows Limited, 'Challenges for the automotive parts and accessories retailer', paper presented at the inaugural AAAA Retail Conference, 24 May, Sydney.
19. Diagonal Reports, op. cit.
20. Marlows Limited, op. cit.
21. Wagner, op. cit.
22. Marlows Limited, op. cit.
23. Wagner, op. cit.
24. ibid.
25. ibid.
26. ibid.

Bank of Queensland: bank different™

By Kerry Scott, Paul Corcoran, Wayne Graham, Bishnu Sharma[1]

Introduction

Bank of Queensland (BOQ) is one of the oldest financial institutions in Queensland and one of Australia's fastest-growing retail banks. It began trading in 1874 as The Brisbane Permanent Benefit Building and Investment Society, the first permanent building society to be established in Queensland. The conversion from building society to savings bank occurred in 1887. This was followed by the conversion to trading bank in 1942, after mergers with other Queensland-based financial institutions. In 1970, the institution adopted the name 'Bank of Queensland', and in 1971, BOQ became a publicly listed company trading on the Australian Stock Exchange. BOQ began to expand its branch network beyond the boundaries of South-East Queensland in 1985, when it opened its first two regional branches in Cairns and Townsville, the two largest cities in far northern Queensland.

Today, BOQ is the second-largest Queensland-based financial institution (only Suncorp-Metway is larger), Queensland's fifth-largest listed company and Australia's tenth-largest bank, and is ranked in the top 150 companies on the Australian Stock Exchange with a market capitalisation of more than $1.6 billion. BOQ's operations take in both personal financial services and business banking, predominantly in the Queensland domestic market. In 2003, BOQ won the *Australian Banking & Finance* news magazine award for Best Regional Bank, beating rivals Adelaide Bank, Bank of Western Australia, Bendigo Bank, St George Bank, and Suncorp-Metway. Reflecting the progress made on the e-commerce side of its activities, Jennifer Heffernan, BOQ's general manager (operations and information technology), was voted Australia's Best CIO/eBanker in the same awards. In 2004, BOQ again took out the award for Best Regional Bank and also added the *AB&F* award for Best Website.[2]

Yet only a few years before, the situation for BOQ was looking less promising. By any standards, 2001 was a watershed for the bank. David Liddy was appointed as managing director in April 2001 after the retirement of John Dawson. David had previously been an executive with Westpac and had 33 years' experience in retail banking. However, on his fourth day as managing director, the Bank of Hawaii (which had been a significant long-term BOQ shareholder) announced its decision to sell its 17 per cent stake. Fortunately, there were others who believed in the potential of BOQ. Lindsay Fox, the founder of Fox Group Holdings, bought 9.6 per cent of the BOQ stock from Bank of Hawaii. The story goes that Lindsay rang David's previous boss at Westpac and asked him whether he would rehire him. On receiving a 'yes', Fox decided to buy the stock.[3] BOQ itself bought the remaining Bank of Hawaii stock. With this crisis resolved, David and the board could now concentrate on determining BOQ's strategic direction and its basis for competing in the Australian banking industry.

The Australian banking industry

The Australian banking industry plays a significant role in the operation and development of the Australian economy as a whole, and is integral to the proper functioning of Australia's financial system. The Australian financial system includes financial enterprises such as depository corporations (e.g. banks), life and other insurance corporations, pension funds, central borrowing authorities (established by state governments and the Northern Territory Government primarily to provide finance for public corporations and the like) and other financial intermediaries, such as mortgage unit trusts and economic development corporations. Exhibit 1 summarises the financial assets held by these various groups of financial enterprises 1999–2004. Banks are the largest deposit-taking institutions in Australia. The liabilities and financial assets of the Australian banking industry 2002–2004 are shown in exhibit 2. Nonbank deposit-taking institutions include building societies, credit unions, cash management trusts, money market corporations, pastoral finance companies, finance companies and general financiers.

The past four decades or so have seen the Australian financial system, and the banking industry in particular, transformed. Banks became licensed in 1941 and so came under the oversight of the Commonwealth Bank of Australia, which at that time performed the functions of Australia's central bank. During the 1940s and the 1950s, the Australian banking industry was highly regulated, with new entry to the industry impossible and controls on, for example, interest rate ceilings, the amount of money banks could lend and to whom they could lend. Much of this early regulation came about from recommendations for tighter controls over banking made by the 1937 Napier Royal Commission into the Monetary and Banking System. Widespread criticism had been levelled at the performance of banks during the Great Depression, and the prevalent sentiment supported increased government intervention.

During the late 1960s and early 1970s, economic thinking gradually swung in favour of free-market economics and market-oriented monetary policy. The general view became that a highly regulated financial system, including direct controls on banks, was hindering the development of Australia's economy in general, and of its financial system in particular. The process of deregulating the Australian banking industry began in earnest with the 1979 establishment by the coalition government of the Australian Financial System Inquiry (the Campbell Committee); and continued with the subsequent review of the Campbell Committee recommendations by the Martin Report (commissioned in 1983 by the newly elected Labor government). During the next five years, the Australian financial system was transformed to a virtually fully deregulated system: interest rate ceilings and controls on bank deposits were removed; new banks, including foreign banks, were permitted to enter the banking industry; the Australian dollar was floated; and most international transaction controls were removed.

At the same time as the Australian banking industry was subject to heavy government regulation before the 1980s, it had also been protected from international competition. Only two foreign banks were operating in Australia in 1984, the Bank of New Zealand and the Banque Nationale de Paris, both of which had been granted banking licences in 1945. (A third, the Taiwan-based Bank of China, had suspended its operations after the Australian government recognised the People's Republic of China in 1972. It was invited to recommence operations in 1985.) By contrast, between 1985 and 1992, six Australian and 16 overseas institutions were granted new banking licences.

The fourth major inquiry into the Australian financial system in 20 years was announced in 1996: the Financial System Inquiry (the Wallis Committee). The Wallis Committee released its final report, in which the trend towards financial market deregulation was essentially reaffirmed, in 1997. Arguably the major outcome of this inquiry was that the banking supervision function was transferred from the Reserve Bank of Australia

(established in 1959 as Australia's central bank and responsible for banking supervision since that time), to a new federal regulating authority, the Australian Prudential Regulation Authority (APRA), with effect from 1 July 1998. In addition to banks, APRA is responsible for the prudential supervision of building societies, credit unions, insurance companies and superannuation funds. At the same time, the Australian government established the 'four pillars policy', which prevents mergers among the four major banks. There is continuing speculation that a 'fifth pillar' could be created through a merger of two of the regional financial institutions.

At the end of October 2005, there were 53 banks operating in Australia. Of these, 14 were Australian-owned banks, 11 were foreign subsidiary banks and the remaining 28 were branches of foreign banks. A list of these banks is shown in exhibit 3. Four major banks, (the 'Big Four'): the Australia and New Zealand Banking Group, the Commonwealth Bank of Australia, the National Australia Bank, and the Westpac Banking Corporation, account for more than 50 per cent of the total assets of all banks in Australia. The Big Four banks provide widespread banking services and extensive retail branch networks across Australia. The remaining banks provide similar banking services, but through comparatively limited branch networks often located in specific regions.

The BOQ strategic blueprint

The 2000–01 annual report contained a new strategic blueprint for the expansion of BOQ. BOQ's values of teamwork, integrity, achievement, courage and passion were confirmed but the blueprint went further:

> We want to be the bank that looks after our staff, values and serves our customers, rewards our shareholders, and partners with our community.[4]

To pursue this approach BOQ established its 'Five Steps to Success', which identified key goals to be met.

Five steps to success

The five steps are outlined in figure C5.1.

BOQ also outlined the business strategy required to achieve the five steps, as shown in figure C5.2. The emphasis on the implementation of these has driven BOQ in the past few years.

Step 1: Organise around where we create value	To organise around where we create value we must understand our strengths and how we can make the most of them to grow our business. We can develop a real point of differentiation from our competitors by concentrating our efforts on our business division, retail operations, alliances and electronic banking.
Step 2: Being more efficient	We understand that an important part of any platform for growth is making sure we work efficiently. Finding efficiencies to further reduce our operating costs will enhance our revenue streams and give our customers and our shareholders the benefits of our increased competitive edge. However, we will not seek to reduce our costs at the expense of branch closures. Our efficiencies include revenue enhancement, expense management, sourcing alliances and our performance enhancement program.
Step 3: Finding new opportunities	We are always searching for new opportunities to grow our business. We believe we can access new opportunities by widening our reach, increasing our business scope, reconfiguring our business networks, and broadening our distribution network.
Step 4: Deepen and broaden customer relationships	We have our sights on improving our customer relationships. In addition to attracting new customers, we want to encourage our existing customers to do more business with us. We aim to offer them greater choice and convenience and continue to meet their changing needs. This means strengthening our relationship with them and better understanding their needs.
Step 5: Build the capabilities and culture to succeed	We need the right people in the right jobs, and we must enable them by providing them with the resources and skills they need to provide our customers with 'Service you wouldn't believe'. Our aim is to deliver every support to our staff to help them to perform their jobs even better and lead us to greater success. What we ask of our staff is superb execution of our business strategies.

Figure C5.1: BOQ's five steps to success

Source: Bank of Queensland 2001, *Annual report 2000–2001*, p. 7, www.boq.com.au/uploadedFiles/BOQ_Commentary2001.pdf

OUR BUSINESS STRATEGY

To achieve our growth objectives we will implement the following Business Strategy to breathe life into our Five Point Strategic Plan at an operational level. The elements of our business strategy are:

1. Our people We want the right people in the right jobs, being motivated by the right rewards.

2. Our processes We need to streamline our processes to improve efficiency and help us reduce our cost to income ratio.

3. Systems We need to improve our systems, particularly our loan application, consumer finance, general insurance, business lending, credit, and management information systems. This will give our people the information they need to make informed decisions about their business units.

4. Business banking We need to strengthen our business banking platform, and we plan to do this by increasing resources, improving new business performance and productivity, and understanding our portfolio segmentation.

5. Sales — Priority Direct and Alliances We need to refocus our Priority Direct division on Queensland business, and ensure it is a vehicle for business acquisition, not relationship management. We plan to introduce five key alliances and re-price our current alliance packages. And we also plan to introduce insurance and wealth creation products.

6. Retail banking We are looking to stimulate our retail banking results by expanding our retail network including branches, private agencies, business banking centres, ATMs, In-Store facilities, kiosks and mobile sales staff. We want to improve productivity by re-assessing our supply chains; we want to focus on training, to provide our staff with the skills they need to provide exceptional service we need to restructure our product range, to ensure we are meeting our customers' needs; and we also need to restructure our incentive program, to ensure the right staff are being rewarded.

Figure C5.2: BOQ's business strategy

Source: Bank of Queensland 2001, *Annual report 2000–2001*, p. 7, www.boq.com.au/uploadedFiles/BOQ_Commentary2001.pdf

The vision and goals of BOQ have been revisited and, where necessary, refined to reflect progress or emerging conditions. By 2005, the BOQ was aiming:

To be Australia's best regional bank, by:
- Advancing our already strong home base marketshare in Queensland;
- Establishing a national footprint through expanding our network interstate;
- Progressing the quality and breadth of our distribution channels and products;

- Creating shareholder value, in the short, medium and long term through people-focused profitable growth; and
- To further sharpen our focus on customer service and provide consumers with a genuinely differentiated enhanced-service delivery.[5]

Acquisitions

In 2002, David Liddy recognised that organic growth alone would not yield the level of results that would allow BOQ to compete with the major banks. Nonorganic growth through acquisitions would allow BOQ to expand its operations, and consequently its customer base, outside Queensland and at a much faster rate. In 2003, BOQ acquired the equipment finance business owned by UFJ Finance Australia (UFFA), which provided equipment and vendor-financing solutions to customers in Australia and New Zealand. The acquisition provided BOQ with UFFA's existing offices in Sydney, Melbourne, Perth, Canberra, Rockhampton, Townsville and Auckland. BOQ combined the acquired company with its existing equipment finance operations to form a new business unit, BOQ Equipment Finance. In the 2004–05 financial year, this side of its business recorded a 38 per cent rise in new sales over the previous year.

BOQ already owned 10 per cent of the shares in ATM Solutions Australasia and bought the remainder in September 2003. At the time, ATM Solutions was the second-largest third-party deployer of ATMs in Australia. Many of the ATMs were located in petrol stations and supermarkets throughout New South Wales and Victoria and in BOQ's home state of Queensland.

Alliances

In March 2002, BOQ entered into a ten-year $480 million outsourcing arrangement with global information technology company, EDS. Under the arrangement, EDS manages all BOQ information technology infrastructure, applications software and business processing services, including its Internet banking. Owing to its early success, the contract was extended in 2005 and will now continue through to 2014. David Liddy estimates that the alliance will provide savings to BOQ in the order of $120 million over the life of the contract.[6] Interestingly, the outsourcing was achieved without any loss of BOQ staff, although some were transferred to EDS. The outsourcing contract is underpinned by 51 critical service levels, which are monitored by BOQ management. The relationship involves much more than just operational matters though. EDS conducted the selection process and managed the project

for BOQ's new $40 million Core Banking System. EDS also enabled BOQ to become the first Australian financial institution to use NCR's new APTRAS Promote and APTRA Relate software. This software allows ATM marketing campaigns to be launched with the use of video, sound, graphics and promotional coupons targeted at different cardholders.

Having acquired ATM Solutions in 2003 for $18 million, BOQ sold the business to Macquarie Bank in mid-2005 for $64 million. The conditions of the sale maintain a strong link with BOQ. Under the deal, BOQ customers will still pay the concessional fee for using BOQ-branded ATMs. BOQ itself will continue to provide cash servicing to the ATMs and will receive a branding fee from Macquarie for the next five years. The ATM network now supplies more than 2100 ATMs (1200 with the BOQ logo).

In addition to these key alliances BOQ has also struck alliances to increase its range of products and services. David is on record as saying:

> … if we can't manufacture a market-leading product or service, we will find one in the market and distribute to our customers. Bank of Queensland is all about superior customer service, so it is important that we have a full range of products and services on offer, and that they are the best in the market.[7]

For example, BOQ's expansion in insurance products has been accomplished through relationships with Vero, St Andrews, OAMPS and CGU. BOQ has also developed a strategic partnership with Travelex to provide foreign currency exchange, traveller's cheques and debit cards at select BOQ branches. Most recently, BOQ has announced an alliance with Genesys Wealth Advisers (a subsidiary of Challenger Financial Services Group) to provide wealth management advice through the BOQ network. This alliance began in 2005 on a piloted basis in ten branches.

BOQ, however, is not afraid to forego alliances. In 2004, BOQ decided to withdraw from the mortgage broker market, which, at that time, was contributing 18 per cent of BOQ's new lending volumes. It was also a strong area of customer satisfaction. The Nielsen Annual Financial Institution Customer Monitor, which conducts the yearly survey of consumer views on mortgage products, reported a 90 per cent rating for BOQ.[8] This gave BOQ the second-highest rating of any Australian bank. David's view, however, was that the expanding BOQ branch network would provide a better option. To date, his optimism has been supported with continued growth in this area of the business.

Branch and head office expansion

In 2004, BOQ moved its 450 head office employees to new premises in the centre of the Brisbane CBD after negotiating naming rights to a new multistorey office building. The building has been renamed 'BOQ Centre'. The move will provide the bank with substantial floor space, allowing for the projected growth in head office operations. However, the growth at head office does not compare with the growth out in the branches.

In 2001, BOQ had 93 branches and, in February 2002, announced plans to expand into suburban, regional and rural areas in Queensland, with 34 new branches planned to be operational by 2004. By 2005, BOQ had expanded to 177 branches on the eastern seaboard. More than 20 new branches were opened in 2004 alone.[9] BOQ had 38 interstate branches (22 in New South Wales, 14 in Victoria and two in the ACT), most of which had been established using the Owner-Managed Branch™ model. In October 2005, BOQ announced plans to move into Western Australia and the Northern Territory. The bank had hoped to have opened 100 interstate branches (in New South Wales, Victoria and the ACT) by the end of 2006 but David Liddy has suggested that state government red tape is likely to slow the rollout of new branches and that the actual figure will be closer to 80.[10] BOQ currently has 193 branches, 53 outside Queensland.

The branch expansion pursued by BOQ runs counter to the approach generally taken in the Australian banking industry. Between 1993 and 2001, bank branches in Australia fell from 7064 to 4789. Of the Big Four banks, Westpac was the only one not to decrease the size of its branch network between 2001 and 2004. However, a recent survey by KPMG International suggests that retail banks are returning to business models that emphasise the personal touch.[11] This is illustrated by a resurgence in branch networks and moves away from automated telephone banking. Many banks, including the ANZ Bank, Commonwealth Bank and National Australia Bank, will find it challenging to return to the branch coverage that they once had. Many of the people who could contribute to the return are now working for their regional competitors.

BOQ's emphasis on customer–branch relationships has resulted in a slower takeup of some technological developments, such as Internet banking. In 1995, the Sydney-based Advance Bank (subsequently bought by St George in 1999) became the first Australian bank to provide the facility of Internet banking. However, it was not until the end of June 2002, that BOQ's 350 000 customers were able to log on to Internet banking for the first time. By that time, all the major banks had been offering electronic banking for at least five years. However, the strategic alliance with EDS is helping BOQ to catch (and it would say pass) the field.

The Owner-Managed Branch model

BOQ's growth has been almost entirely based on the Owner-Managed Branches (OMB); corporate branch numbers have stayed basically the same. OMB is essentially a franchise model, with franchisees required to find $150 000 up front to cover the initial startup costs. The BOQ model has seen experienced, entrepreneurial executives from other financial institutions adopt the role of franchisees. In most cases, these are executives with existing business and social networks within the communities in which they are located. The OMB model has not just contributed to interstate expansion. In the three years between August 2001 and August 2004, BOQ opened 44 new OMBs in Queensland.[12]

The OMB model gives BOQ centralised control over the brand, business policies and processes and over the key issue of credit control. Each branch is responsible for operational issues such as staffing and hours of operation. The branch is also responsible for determining its product range and local marketing. This allows the branch to demonstrate a local focus and sensitivity to local demand conditions.

At least one overseas bank is investigating the BOQ franchise arrangements with a view to using the model for its own operations. According to David Liddy, should the model be adopted, BOQ will receive payment for the use of the model and a further fee based on the number of branches opened.[13]

BOQ and the community

While concentrating on its business expansion, BOQ has also continued its role as a sponsor, donor and as a fundraiser. Even as a sponsor, BOQ is an award winner. In 2004, it won the *Australian Financial Review* Corporate Partnership Award for its association with the Queensland Reds rugby union team. The award is given for best practice in sponsor management. BOQ is also a sponsor of the Brisbane Lions Australian rules football team. Aside from team sponsorships, BOQ also provides assistance to individuals, such as triathlete Loretta Harrop.

In addition to its sporting focus, BOQ is involved in a range of charity work. Queensland's Royal Children's Hospital Foundation was supported through initiatives such as radio station B105's Christmas Appeal as well as an appeal through its own branch network, 'Banking on Our Kids'. The bank also became the first Australia-listed company to participate in the 'Investing in Hope' campaign, which enables shareholders to donate all or part of their dividend payments to children's hospital charities. Over the past few years, BOQ and its employees have supported campaigns by the Starlight Foundation, Leukaemia Foundation, Salvation Army, Careflight Queensland, Multiple Sclerosis Australia, Variety Club and Juvenile Diabetes Research Foundation.

Not all the decisions on sponsorship are taken at head office. BOQ's Local Communities and Branches Sponsorship Program, which commenced in 2003, allows branch management and staff to select local causes for support.

The future

BOQ is already developing new approaches to keep its existing customer base and to attract new customers. Its new deposit account — the Reverse Charges Account — pays the account holder a $2 per month 'reward', as well as waiving the monthly account fee, if the account balance is kept at or more than $2000 per month. There is also a new website — www.changemybank.com.au — which generates letters instructing the closure of accounts held at other banks and redirecting credits and debits.

According to David Liddy, any further consolidations of the financial services industry will increase the pressures on the smaller players.[14] In May 2004, the Commonwealth Bank sold its 12 per cent stake in BOQ, indicating that it thought it unlikely that it would be able to acquire BOQ. For its part, BOQ is more interested in expanding its business than in being part of another business's expansion. David is on record as supporting a removal of the government's four pillars policy.[15] He is more than happy to compete — and competition is hotting up, even among the regional banks. In 2005, BOQ lost out on the *AB&F* Best Regional Bank in the Australian Banking and Finance Awards to another Queensland local: Suncorp-Metway. You can be sure that BOQ is already planning a return to the number one position.

Discussion questions

1. Assume BOQ is assessing the success of its current strategic direction as part of its normal strategic management cycle. You work in the planning department at BOQ's head office in Brisbane and have been asked to prepare various strategic planning analyses and reports for presentation to the board of directors at its next meeting. Use the information in the case study to prepare the following reports:
   - an industry analysis of the Australian banking industry
   - a strengths, weaknesses, opportunities and threats (SWOT) analysis for the Bank of Queensland.

   Are there any other analyses/reports that would be useful?

2. Identify which of Porter's generic competitive strategies BOQ is pursuing. What does this mean for the bank in terms of generic building blocks, and in terms of product, market and distinctive competency choices?

3. What are the advantages and disadvantages of BOQ's choice of business-level strategy? What would you suggest to improve the bank's business-level strategy to improve its competitive position?

4. In what kind of industry environment (i.e. stage of industry lifecycle) does BOQ operate? What strategic implications does this have for the bank?

5. What new strategies would you advise BOQ to pursue to increase its competitive advantage? Do you think the bank will be able to maintain its competitive advantage in the future?

End notes

1. All the authors teach at University of the Sunshine Coast. The authors wish to acknowledge that much of the material for this case study came from publicly available Bank of Queensland documents and other sources are acknowledged in the text.
2. Australian Banking & Finance 2004 Awards, accessed 20 December 2005, www.charlton.com.au/events/banking/ABF_Awards_pages_A4.pdf.
3. *Courier-Mail* 2005, 'Little bank thinks big', 15 October.
4. Bank of Queensland 2001, *Annual report 2000–2001*, p. 5.
5. Bank of Queensland 2004, *Annual report*, p. 3.
6. ZDNet 2005, 'Bank of Queensland extends EDS contract', 5 May.
7. Bank of Queensland 2005, 'BOQ launches wealth management alliance', media release, 13 October.
8. Bank of Queensland 2004, *Annual report*, p. 3.
9. Bank of Queensland 2005, *Annual report*, p. 5.
10. *Herald-Sun* 2005, 'Sunshine and light at BoQ', 14 October, p. 71.
11. KPMG 2005, 'Retail banking survey — Customer satisfaction; at what price?', accessed 20 December 2005, www.kpmg.com.au/Default.aspx?TabID=67&KPMGArticleItemID=1242.
12. Bank of Queensland, accessed 20 December 2005, www.boq.com.au/aboutus_corporate_history.htm.
13. *Courier-Mail* 2005, 'Little bank thinks big', 15 October.
14. *The Cairns Post* 2005, 'Mergers way of the future, says bank', 14 October, p. 20.
15. ibid.

Exhibits

Exhibit 1: Financial assets of Australian financial institutions 1999–2004

FINANCIAL INSTITUTIONS, Financial assets

At 30 June	Depository corporations			Life insurance corporations $b	Pension funds $b	Other insurance corporations $b	Central borrowing authorities $b	Financial intermediaries $b	Consolidated financial sector $b
	Reserve Bank $b	Banks $b	Other $b						
1999	44.6	637.9	179.5	170.8	344.7	68.4	97.0	163.8	1 216.1
2000	51.1	728.6	197.0	185.7	423.9	72.9	91.3	214.3	1 400.3
2001	55.1	805.7	228.2	188.8	451.1	78.0	91.8	220.0	1 506.5
2002	54.7	875.3	245.5	190.7	451.2	77.5	93.9	240.3	1 600.5
2003	55.3	976.0	243.4	183.4	474.9	87.8	103.3	253.3	1 694.6
2004	62.3	1 116.0	233.0	193.1	572.1	90.4	101.2	324.4	1 946.1

Source: Australian Bureau of Statistics 2004, 'Financial enterprises', *Year book*, table 26.2 'Financial Institutions, Financial assets – 30 June', www.abs.gov.au

Exhibit 2: Financial assets and liabilities of Australian banks 2002–2004

BANKS (i), Financial assets and liabilities

	Amounts outstanding at 30 June		
	2002 $m	2003 $m	2004 $m
FINANCIAL ASSETS			
Currency and deposits	41 119	30 879	34 650
Acceptance of bills of exchange	77 783	76 984	83 398
One name paper	15 130	12 882	16 653
Bonds	26 161	28 776	34 941
Derivatives	41 089	57 276	58 290
Loans and placements	604 106	689 397	803 359
Equity	67 096	75 517	79 265
Prepayments of premiums and reserves	1 535	1 616	1 743
Other accounts receivable	1 319	2 645	3 728
Total (ii)	**875 338**	**975 972**	**1 116 027**
LIABILITIES			
Currency and deposits	450 250	504 533	567 084
Acceptance of bills of exchange	37 148	39 304	42 308
One name paper	88 391	113 464	145 645
Bonds	109 015	107 528	151 233
Derivatives	44 144	63 337	53 071
Loans and placements	43 040	45 898	39 789
Equity	181 787	171 717	180 002
Other accounts payable	3 560	3 280	2 528
Total	**957 335**	**1 049 061**	**1 181 660**

(i) Does not include the Reserve Bank of Australia
(ii) Excludes non-financial assets (e.g. fixed assets, property, inventories, etc.)

Source: Australian Bureau of Statistics 2004, 'Financial enterprises', *Year book*, table 26.4 'Banks(a) Financial assets and liabilities', www.abs.gov.au

Exhibit 3: Banks operating in Australia at end October 2005

Australian-owned banks
- Adelaide Bank
- AMP Bank Limited
- Australia and New Zealand Banking Group Limited
- Bank of Queensland Limited
- Bendigo Bank Limited
- Commonwealth Bank of Australia
- Commonwealth Development Bank of Australia (a subsidiary of Commonwealth Bank of Australia)
- Elders Rural Bank Limited
- Macquarie Bank Limited
- Members Equity Bank Pty Limited
- National Australia Bank Limited
- St George Bank Limited
- Suncorp-Metway Limited
- Westpac Banking Corporation

Foreign subsidiary banks
- Arab Bank Australia Limited
- Bank of China (Australia) Limited
- Bank of Cyprus Australia Pty Limited
- BankWest (the trading name of Bank of Western Australia Limited, a foreign subsidiary bank following its sale to Bank of Scotland in December 1995)
- Citibank Pty Limited (a subsidiary of Citibank N.A.)
- HSBC Bank Australia Limited
- ING Bank (Australia) Limited
- Laiki Bank (Australia) Limited
- NM Rothschild & Sons (Australia) Limited
- Rabobank Australia Limited (a subsidiary of Rabobank Nederland from October 1994)

Branches of foreign banks
- ABN Amro N.V.
- Bank of America, National Association
- Bank of China (subject to depositor protection provisions of the Banking Act 1959)
- Bank of Tokyo-Mitsubishi, Ltd
- Barclays Capital (the trading name of Barclays Bank plc)
- BNP Paribas
- Citibank N.A.
- Credit Suisse
- Deutsche Bank AG
- HBOS Treasury Services plc
- HSBC Bank plc
- ING Bank NV
- JPMorgan Chase Bank, National Association
- Mizuho Corporate Bank, Ltd
- Oversea-Chinese Banking Corporation Limited
- Rabobank Nederland (the trading name of Co-operative Central Raiffeisen-Boerenleenbank B.A.)
- Royal Bank of Canada
- Société Générale
- Standard Chartered Bank
- State Bank of India
- State Street Bank and Trust Company
- The International Commercial Bank of China
- The Royal Bank of Scotland Plc
- The Toronto-Dominion Bank
- Taiwan Business Bank
- UBS AG
- United Overseas Bank Limited
- WestLB AG

Source: Australian Prudential Regulatory Authority, accessed 20 December 2005, www.apra.gov.au/adi/ADIList.cfm#AOBC

Exhibit 4: Financial overview for Bank of Queensland 2001–2004

A$ millions	2001	2002	2003	2004
Total assets on balance sheet	4 222.0	5 280.2	7 203.8	9 927.6
Deposits	3 699.1	4 471.2	6 114.2	8 302.4
Borrowings and loan capital	217.4	423.8	541.7	818.3
Contributed equity	189.9	232.5	321.9	524.0
Reserves and retained profits	19.9	26.0	56.4	79.2
Total equity	209.8	258.5	378.3	603.2
Profit from ordinary activities before income tax and individually significant items	36.5	46.9	63.6	99.0
Less: Individually significant items	5.2	6.3	–	5.7
Profit from ordinary activities before income tax	31.3	40.6	63.6	93.3
Less: Income tax relating to ordinary activities	7.2	11.9	18.9	28.8
Profit from ordinary activities after tax and individually significant items	24.1	28.7	44.7	64.5

Source: adapted from Bank of Queensland 2004, *Annual report*, p. 4

Aldi in Australia

By Ingrid Bonn, School of Business, Bond University

Background

In 1948, the brothers Theo and Karl Albrecht opened the grocery store 'Albrecht Discounts' (Aldi) in Essen (Ruhr Valley), Germany. The store had a simple layout and offered a few products at a low price. The company grew rapidly, owning 13 stores in 1950 and about 300 stores in 1961 across Germany.

In 1961, Theo and Karl divided the company into Aldi North (run by Theo) and Aldi South (run by Karl). The reasons for this division, according to Dieter Brandes, a former managing director of Aldi in Schleswig-Holstein, Germany, were different views about how to develop the business. However, the brothers regularly exchanged information about a range of issues such as performance and cost figures, current and potential suppliers and they also conducted joint negotiations with suppliers.[1] In 2003, Theo and Karl stepped down as CEOs. Theo's son, Theo Albrecht Jr, now runs Aldi North, and Juergen Kroll and Norbert Podschlapp run Aldi South.

By the end of 2003, Aldi had become one of the world's biggest global food retailers with more than 7000 stores worldwide and estimated annual turnover of €36.2 billion.[2] Aldi's main market is Germany, which accounts for about two-thirds of sales, with Aldi having a 40 per cent share of the grocery market.[3]

Today, Aldi still operates in two divisions. Aldi North, based in Essen, manages operations in northern Germany, Belgium, Denmark, France, Luxembourg, the Netherlands and Spain. Aldi South, based in Muelheim, manages operations in southern Germany, Austria, the UK, Ireland, Switzerland, the United States and Australia.[4]

In Australia, the first Aldi store opened in Sydney in January 2001. The company came with $750 million in paid-up capital and plans to invest profits in further growth.[5] This all-cash approach to expansion keeps Aldi's risk levels low. In 2004, Aldi owned 44 stores in New South Wales, 20 in Victoria and eight in Queensland. With these stores, Aldi captured almost 5 per cent of total packaged grocery expenditure in New South Wales, 2.5 per cent in Victoria and 1.4 per cent in Queensland.[6] According to ACNielsen, Aldi could own more than 300 stores and capture 10 per cent of the Australian packaged grocery dollar market by 2010, if it achieves its planned store rollout program.[7]

Aldi's business strategy

Aldi is a typical 'hard discounter', pursuing a cost-leadership strategy (see figure C6.1 for characteristics of hard discounters). Its approach is to offer a limited number of good-quality products at low prices. Aldi stores stock about 700 products of the most popular everyday grocery and household items.[8] Having so few items is in stark contrast to a standard supermarket, which carries between 25 000 and 30 000 products. Aldi's products include frozen food, meat and dairy products, canned food, bakery products, household supplies, health and beauty products, nappies, cleaning products and a selection of fresh fruit and vegetables. In addition to household staples, Aldi also offers a selection of 'surprise buys', which change every week and are only available as long as the stocks last. These items include highly discounted hardware, electrical items, clothing, sports equipment and toys.

Aldi stocks a few national brands such as Vegemite, Kellogg's breakfast cereals, Milo and Nescafé, but 95 per cent of the products are Aldi's own brands. More than 80 per cent of its products are Australian made and many of its house-brand products are produced by well-known brand manufacturers. However, manufacturers seem reluctant to be openly associated with Aldi, fearing that they may jeopardise their relationship with other retailers. According to Walker, it is believed that Aldi's suppliers include George Weston's Tip Top Bakers, Arnotts, Goodman Fielder, Green's Foods, Kellogg Australia, Cadbury Schweppes' Cottees division, San Remo, Murray Goulburn, Golden Circle, Berri, Peats Ridge and Carter Holt Harvey.[9]

The Aldi website states that it focuses on its own brands to remain independent, enabling it to avoid the high marketing costs often associated with national brands and to set its own price, product and quality policies.[10] According to Shoebridge, however, house brands are attractive for grocery retailers because they cost 5–20 per cent less than national brands, depending on the category. In addition, a retailer's profit margin on house brands is about two percentage points higher than the margins on a national brand.[11]

Less than 1200 lines
Focus on dry grocery, although new categories are being added
Focus on own brands and 'exclusive' labels
Limited national brand presence
Strict focus on price
Limited in-store fixtures, product often bulk stacked on pallets

---

Figure C6.1: Characteristics of 'hard discounters'

Source: www.igd.com/cir.asp?cirid=463&search=1 (accessed 6 January 2005)

Having only a few products enables Aldi to use its impressive buying power and to control the cost of its products by buying in large quantities. According to Dieter Brandes, Aldi has 30 to 100 times the buying power of Wal-Mart.[12] Fewer products also mean that warehouses can be smaller, that shipping and handling is easier, and that the quality of the products can be controlled more rigorously. Aldi's products are tested and sampled regularly, both in-house and in independent food laboratories. The in-house tests involve blind tests by managers who compare their own products with those of leading brands. Aldi's website states that it would withdraw any product immediately if there were the slightest cause for concern.[13]

Minimising costs at all levels in the value chain is the key to Aldi's business strategy. Aldi stores are usually 1200 square metres in size; the biggest Coles supermarkets, by comparison, are about 5000 square metres.[14] This makes new sites cheaper and easier to find than it is for other supermarkets with their jumbo-sized stores. Aldi usually starts with locations in lower middle-class suburbs that have full employment. Once a store is profitable and attracts many customers, Aldi tends to open another store close by. Stores in Australia are either stand-alone or located in shopping centres, as opposed to Aldi's European stores, which are mostly stand-alone.

Aldi stores typically have only four or five employees per shop, compared with about 15 at a standard supermarket. They do not employ specialists such as bakers or butchers, because these products come prepacked. According to Michael Kloeters, group managing director Australia, Aldi pays store assistants $19.10 an hour plus bonuses, compared with the industry award rate of about $15 per hour. Employees are permanent full time or part time and have signed Australian workplace agreements. There are no casual staff or junior rates of pay.[15] However, despite the above-average pay rates, having fewer staff results in Aldi's labour costs being about 6 per cent of revenue, compared with about 12 to 16 per cent at a standard supermarket.[16]

Contributing to Aldi's relatively low labour costs are its restricted opening hours. Aldi in Labrador, Queensland, for example, had the following opening hours in January 2005: Monday to Wednesday 9 am – 6 pm, Thursday 9 am – 9 pm, Friday, 9 am – 7 pm, Saturday 8.30 am – 5 pm, and Sunday 10 am – 4 pm. In contrast, Woolworths, Coles, Bi-Lo and Action all had the following opening hours: Monday to Friday 8 am – 9 pm, Saturday 8 am – 5.30 pm, and Sunday 9 am – 6 pm. So, Aldi's stores are open for 19 hours less per week than the other supermarkets, which equates to a significant saving in labour costs.

The design of Aldi stores is simple and practical and all stores share similar layout and product presentations. The stores are usually bright, modern and have wide aisles. The products are displayed in specially designed cartons that can be stocked directly on to shelves or wheeled into place by using pallets. The placement of the pallets is based on logistic considerations, namely to improve workflow and productivity. Using pallets makes it easy to restock items: staff simply remove the old pallet and replace it with a new one. This approach helps to save on labour costs to stock shelves.

Aldi also saves costs by not providing free shopping bags. Customers are encouraged to bring their own bags or cardboard boxes. Alternatively, they can purchase new shopping bags at the checkout. Bags are not packed and payment with credit cards attracts a 1 per cent surcharge to cover additional costs. Furthermore, the use of a shopping trolley requires a $2 coin deposit, which is refunded when the customer returns the trolley to one of the designated trolley bays. Again, this approach saves costs because Aldi does not need to employ people to collect and return trolleys.

Marketing is another area where Aldi saves costs. Aldi has no marketing department and its marketing budget is about 0.3 per cent of revenue.[17] Advertising is minimal, relying on catalogues, local press advertising and Web updates. It focuses on product-oriented messages, predominantly about price and new 'surprise buys'. Aldi usually does not employ advertising agencies and does not spend money on market research. Instead, Aldi employees and managers explore what customers may need and stock it on a trial basis in three stores. Aldi's prices are uniform across each country, no matter where the stores are located. The prices for the 'surprise buys' are available on the Aldi website each week.

Despite minimal marketing, however, a study on 'best brands' by the Gesellschaft fuer Konsumforschung in 2004 showed that Aldi was the third most respected corporate brand in Germany, just behind electronics giant Siemens and car maker BMW (table C6.1). About 89 per cent of German households shopped at least once at Aldi in 2003.[18]

In addition to minimal marketing, Aldi spends nothing on public relations. Managers are usually discouraged from conducting interviews on Aldi themes. A rare public statement was made by Theo Albrecht in 1971, when he was released by kidnappers after three weeks in captivity and payment of US$13 million ransom.[19] At that time, it was the highest ransom ever paid in Germany.

Aldi does not use consultants and spends very little money on the development of sophisticated statistics and reports. Only the most important data are prepared for the internal control and information systems. In addition, there are no budgets or annual planning calculations.[20] This scrupulous attention to minimising costs, according to McKinsey and Co., has helped Aldi to achieve an operating margin of as high as 9.3 per cent in some regions of Germany.[21]

Table C6.1: Best corporate brands in Germany in 2004

Rank	Best corporate brands
1	Siemens
2	BMW
3	Aldi
4	VW
5	Adidas–Salomon
6	DaimlerChrysler
7	Bayer
8	Deutsche Telekom
9	Sparkasse
10	Allianz

Source: http://www.gfk.de/index.php?lang=de&contentpath=http%3A//www.gfk.de/presse/pressemeldung/contentdetail.php%3Fid%3D543 (accessed 7/1/2005)

Aldi's business strategy is based upon an idea of Theo's, which was developed into a successful business concept over the years. It has changed very little since its inception, except for minor adjustments based upon the changing internal and external conditions. Some of these changes involve the inclusion of milk and frozen products, the introduction of fresh fruit and vegetables and the addition of some non-food action articles. The introduction of new items, however, did not mean an extension of its product range. For example, when Aldi introduced 25 new frozen products, it eliminated 25 products that were considered 'weak', meaning that they lacked demand or did not fit into the product portfolio anymore. This approach ensures that Aldi stays with its concept of a limited product range, but adapts to the changing demands by modernising its product offerings.

Aldi's vision and guiding principles

Aldi has a clear business philosophy and guiding principles. The business philosophy can be summarised by the following statement: 'Top quality at incredibly low prices — guaranteed'.[22] In its advertising, Aldi elaborates on this philosophy by stating five main principles: (1) huge savings, (2) excellent quality, (3) outstanding value, (4) superb special buys and (5) buy with confidence (see figure C6.2).

Huge savings: Our grocery prices are set low and stay low every day. So you pay less on your weekly shopping.

Excellent quality: We ensure that our quality is as good, if not better, than the leading brands and own brands.

Outstanding value: When we combine incredibly low prices with the best quality products, you know that there is no better value grocery store.

Superb special buys: Every Thursday we introduce an exciting selection of 'special buys'. These are always extremely popular, and of course amazing value.

Buy with confidence: We are so confident in the quality of our products, that every store offers a 'total satisfaction or your money back' guarantee.

Figure C6.2: Aldi's pledge

Source: Advertising flyer by Aldi, 'Specials from 27 January [2005]'

Aldi's pledge outlines its key philosophy and principles, namely to offer its customers high-quality products at low prices. This is achieved by being cost conscious in every aspect of the organisation's value chain as outlined in the previous section. The approach is simple and clear, and it is well known throughout the organisation.

The second part of Aldi's key philosophy centres around a strong customer orientation. This involves focusing on meeting the basic needs of its customers by providing high quality products. Dieter Brandes argues that being credible to the customer is a key issue for Aldi. In his view, credibility involves 'walking the talk', which means that there needs to be a strong alignment between verbal messages, action and reality to gain the trust of the customers.[23] Dealing with complaints, for example, is one way in which to reinforce Aldi's message. If customers are unhappy with any of the products they have bought or if the products do not meet the required quality standards, Aldi refunds the money or provides customers with a substitute.

The third area in Aldi's philosophy involves the establishment of fair relationships with suppliers. Aldi guarantees payment terms of 30 days net and does not require suppliers to fund rebates or discounts, or to pay listing allowances. There are no negotiations after the deals have been made and Aldi does not have annual talks with suppliers, instead issues are dealt with on a needs basis. Suppliers have access to Aldi's international network, which potentially enables them to take their products to a global market.[24] To ensure fair dealings, Aldi managers are not allowed to accept gifts from suppliers.

Aldi's organisational culture

Aldi's culture has been strongly influenced by its founders. The cultural values and rules clearly reflect the organisation's philosophy, guiding principles and business strategy. Dieter describes Aldi's culture as one of 'simplicity'.[25] The Aldi model, which is based on a simple concept, namely the provision of high-quality products at low prices, is clearly understood by employees, managers and customers. Employees and managers at all levels of the organisation are very cost conscious and pay particular attention to economic efficiency. Waste is not tolerated. The aim is to avoid unnecessary costs wherever possible. For example, Theo is said personally to have switched off lights in offices when there was enough daylight from outside. The concept of 'cost-watching' extends into all areas of the value chain, including the development of new techniques for warehouse management or for the transport of goods.

The strong focus on economic efficiency is accompanied by a passion for detail. The aim is to find small improvements in all areas and to develop pleasure in achieving small successes. This culture of continual improvement is accompanied by a strong focus on the development and implementation of solutions. Aldi people, according to Dieter, are practitioners.[26] New ideas and solutions are tried, rather than being exposed to detailed analyses. If they prove to be successful, they are implemented quickly. New products, for example, are not subjected to elaborate market analyses, but are tested in three shops. If they are successful, meaning that they achieve a fast, predetermined minimum turnover, they are introduced into all other shops.

In addition to its focus on economic efficiency and continuous improvement, the organisational culture is also characterised by determination and persistence. As outlined, Aldi's business approach has been little changed since its foundation. Aldi has consequently pursued its business concept and has resisted temptations such as expanding the number of products, diversifying into other areas or changing its cost-leadership strategy. This is an important trait of its organisational culture, namely to continue doing what it does best.

The organisational culture is reinforced by Aldi's selection and recruitment approach. Aldi tends to select, develop and promote managerial talent carefully from inside the organisation. Important qualities for potential managers are a focus on economic efficiency, fairness towards others, including suppliers, modesty and reserve towards the public and the press. These behavioural characteristics are reinforced by job descriptions outlining clear goals and competencies. Aldi managers have usually been employed in different parts of the organisation, including the shops and the warehouse. They know how Aldi operates and have imbibed the organisational culture. Area managers, for example, go through a 12-month training program in which they learn about the structural and procedural elements of retail management, including store operations and trading rights, administration, logistics and property management. An important part of this program centres on Aldi's management system, including its focus on economic efficiency. The first part of the training takes place in a store where future area managers take over the role of a store manager for several months. This 'hands on' approach aims to acquaint them with Aldi's operations, but also its business philosophy and core values. During the second part of the training, future area managers work alongside experienced colleagues and learn about their role and responsibilities. This includes the tasks of recruitment, planning and organisation of the stores.[27]

Aldi's organisation structure

Aldi's business concept is supported by a decentralised organisation structure. The first, and probably most important decision to decentralise was when Aldi was divided into Aldi North (run by Theo Albrecht) and Aldi South (run by Karl Albrecht) in 1961. This decentralisation created two independent and autonomous organisations and enabled the brothers to pursue their own strategic ideas, rather than trying to compromise. The result of this decentralisation was that, for example, Aldi North stocked about 600 products, whereas Aldi South had only 450 products. Aldi North offered frozen products but Aldi South waited to see whether frozen products were successful in Aldi North before it included them in its own shops.[28] Decentralisation enabled the brothers to exchange experience, compare methods and results and implement the most successful approaches that the other Aldi had tested.

Adhering to the principle of decentralisation, an Aldi corporation looks after between 60 and 80 shops. If this number is reached within one region, a new Aldi corporation is founded. In 2004, for example, there were 65 autonomous regional entities in Germany — 35 in the Aldi North area and 30 in the Aldi South area.[29]

Aldi's organisation structure is flat and lean. For example, Aldi's headquarters in Germany employs fewer than 150 staff.[30] Aldi has no planning department and no central functions such as marketing, human resources, controlling, information systems or public relations. The responsibility lies with people in line functions who work on practical solutions and are responsible for their implementation as well as the results. Staff positions do not exist.

The principle of decentralisation is accompanied by a focus on delegation. It is based upon the so-called 'Harzburger Modell', a concept developed by Professor Reinhard Hoehn from the Fuehrungsakademie der Wirtschaft in Bad Harzburg, Germany. This model outlines three issues that should be delegated: the task, the necessary competencies to enable task implementation and the responsibility for implementation and results. Tasks that are delegated are those that (1) can be fulfilled in a better and more cost-effective way by others, (2) make the workplace more interesting for employees, (3) include responsibility, (4) are challenging and contribute to employees' professional development and (5) relieve superiors and allow them to concentrate on core tasks.[31]

Aldi delegates to the managers who are in charge of implementation. All managers have clearly defined job descriptions specifying the goals, responsibilities and authority of their positions. Control is exercised by random spot checks and by evaluating the results. The control system is also set up to provide information about whether managers comply with the cultural values of the organisation and whether they pass on the values and rules to their subordinates.

Aldi's principles of decentralisation and delegation, according to Dieter Brandes, mean that there is less bureaucracy and conflict due to the small size. Problems can be dealt with quicker and knowledge about the local market can be used to improve Aldi's approach. In addition, employees are more involved in the development of the organisation and they have greater potential for career advancement. Finally, the individual Aldi corporations can compete with each other in a healthy fashion.[32]

Aldi's competitive environment in Australia

The main players in Australia's food retail industry are Woolworths and Coles-Myer. In 2004, Woolworths' supermarkets division, trading as Woolworths and Safeway, was Australia's leading food retailer with 708 stores nationwide. Woolworths operating revenue for its supermarket segment at the end of the 2004 financial year was $24.19 billion, its earnings before interest and taxes $960 million. In comparison, the food, liquor and fuel segment of Coles-Myer contributed $21.28 billion to its operating revenue and $678 million to its net profit before interest and tax during the same period.[33] Woolworths has about 37 per cent of Australia's $66 billion grocery and retail alcohol market; Coles has a market share of about 32 per cent.[34]

Woolworths supermarket division comprises food, liquor and petrol. It also operates Internet food retailing through Homeshop (in Sydney, Melbourne and Canberra) and GreenGrocer (in Sydney and Melbourne). In 2004, the liquor operations included 536 Dan Murphy's, BWS (Beer, Wine, Spirits), First Estate and Woolworths/Safeway-attached liquor stores. In addition, Woolworths owned 50 per cent of the MGW liquor business (a joint venture with the Bruce Mathieson Group), which has 31 hotels and 110 liquor stores. The petrol division comprised 359 petrol sites, including 44 Woolworths/Caltex sites.[35]

Woolworths' general merchandise division consists of Big W discount department stores and the consumer electronic outlets Dick Smith Electronics, Dick Smith Electronics PowerHouse and Tandy. Other operations include Ezy-Banking, which offers banking products with backing from the Commonwealth Bank of Australia.[36] Woolworths also publishes three magazines, *Australian Good Taste*, *Woolworths Fresh*, and *Woolworths Australian Parents*.[37]

Woolworths has positioned itself as the 'The Fresh Food People', aiming to provide a wide range of fresh produce in addition to dry groceries and other merchandise. Many farmers in Australia grow their products exclusively for Woolworths, adhering to strict quality, food hygiene and safety standards. The 'Fresh Food People' strategy has been an important way of differentiating itself from major competitors, such as Coles-Myer. Woolworths actively advertises through magazines, newspapers, television and distributed leaflets, aiming to project an image of providing fresh, healthy and high quality products at a reasonable price. The second purpose of its advertising campaigns is to communicate a series of price specials. Woolworths (similar to other major chains) often promotes 'loss leader' specials to attract customers to the store. Prices are not uniform across Australia, but depend on the location and on the presence of competitors in the specific markets.

Woolworths' product range includes the 'Fresh Food' offer, well-established national brands, as well as its 'Homebrand' range, which, according to the company's annual report in 2004, is Australia's largest supermarket grocery brand by sales.[38]

In 1999, Woolworths launched 'Project Refresh', an Australiawide program that aimed to improve efficiency and to reduce costs by restructuring the company's supply chain, by adopting new technology and by introducing the new 'Every Day Low Price (EDLP)' strategy into its supermarkets. EDLP involved reducing prices for many national brands, pushing manufacturers to cut their prices. Level 1 of 'Project Refresh' has been completed and has resulted in an accumulated cost savings of 2.85 per cent of sales over the past five years. In dollar terms, this means a cumulative savings of $2.5 billion.[39]

The second stage of 'Project Refresh' is expected to deliver more cost savings over the next five years, in particular through improvements to its end-to-end supply chain program. This program aims to tackle store supply chain costs, the number, location and operation of distribution centres, transport management, process improvements and the development of integrated systems. For example, Woolworths plans to reduce its supermarket distribution centres from 31 distribution centres to nine regional distribution centres and two national distribution centres, aiming to reduce costs and stock levels and to optimise network efficiencies.

In addition to the strategies outlined above, Woolworths has also diversified into new sectors, such as petrol retailing and credit cards. Woolworths opened its first petrol outlet in Dubbo, New South Wales, in 1996. Customers who spend more than $30 dollars in one transaction at a Woolworths store receive a discount voucher of 4 cents per litre petrol. This approach has been very successful; Woolworths had 359 petrol sites across Australia by the end of the 2004 financial year. Its banking service Ezybanking was launched in 1999.[40]

Coles-Myer's largest division is also its food, liquor and fuel segment. The food division includes Coles and Bi-Lo. In 2004, Coles, a full-service supermarket, operated about 500 stores throughout Australia; Bi-Lo, a discount supermarket retailer had about 209 stores.[41] Coles also has an online shopping facility, Coles Online, which was available in Victoria and New South Wales in 2004.

Coles-Myer's liquor business includes 626 Liquorland, Vintage Cellars and Theo's stores. Coles Express, a commercial alliance between Coles-Myer and Shell, was Australia's largest fuel and convenience retail operation in 2004, with a national network of 598 stores.[42]

Coles-Myer's general merchandise and apparel brands comprise (1) Kmart, a discount department store, (2) Officeworks, a retailer of office and technology products, (3) Myer, a department store offering apparel, accessories, footwear, cosmetics, gifts and homewares, (4) Megamart, an electrical, furniture and homewares store and (5) Target, a low-margin, high-volume retailer.[43]

Similarly to Woolworths, Coles also is a full-service supermarket, offering fresh produce, dry groceries and other merchandise. Its strategy, however, is less succinct than Woolworths 'Fresh Food People' strategy. In March 2002, Coles announced a major restructuring program, aiming to cut costs by improving its supply chain management, implementing changes to its information technology and trying to achieve better synergies with the other segments in the Coles-Myer Corporation. The supply chain changes include restructuring its distribution centre

network and simplifying operations and processes in its stores and distribution centres. In addition, Coles planned to improve its loyalty programs.

Coles' 2004 annual report states three major goals: 'Being the Best Team so that we can Delight our Customers and Grow Shareholder Value'.[44] Delighting customers means ensuring that (1) shelves are fully stocked, (2) most-wanted products are available, (3) staff can focus on customer needs and (4) customers receive more information on product range and special offers.

Similarly to that of Woolworths, Coles' product range includes fresh food, an area that has been improved over the past few years, well-established national brands and house brands. Coles aims to concentrate more on the development of house brands and has set a target of increasing them to about 30 per cent.[45] Coles also aims to provide customers with more value for their money through competitive everyday prices and the promotion of price specials. Unlike Woolworths EDLP strategy for national brands, Coles promotes some products (mainly own brands) as EDLP, but still relies largely on its high-low pricing strategy for national brands. Prices at Coles vary across Australia, depending upon location and on the presence of competitors in the specific markets.

In May 2003, Coles-Myer formed an alliance with Shell to match the Woolworths petrol strategy. Similarly to Woolworths, customers receive a 4 cent discount per litre petrol if they spend more than $30 dollars in one transaction at a Coles or Bi-Lo store. By the end of the 2004 financial year, there was a national network of 598 stores, branded both Coles Express and Shell. Coles-Myer also formed an alliance with the National Australia Bank to include a credit card facility and revamped the company's long-running FlyBuys reward program.

Bi-Lo, a discount supermarket retailer that is owned by Coles-Myer, also aims to delight its customers. Their offer comprises fresh food, national brands and an extensive Bi-Lo house-brand range. Their target customers are those who want value for money. Bi-Lo tries to satisfy this segment by offering products at low prices. Bi-Lo's marketing included a 'Why Pay More?' campaign and the use of promotional initiatives such as 'Red Hot Sale'.

In addition to the major national chains, Woolworths and Coles-Myer, there are smaller regional players in the Australian food retail industry, namely Action (owned by Foodland Associated), IGA and Franklins.

Foodland Associated

Foodland Associated is a retailer and wholesaler of groceries in Western Australia, Queensland, northern

New South Wales and New Zealand. Foodland's largest division is its supermarket segment, which operated 230 supermarkets by the end of the 2004 financial year. Most of these supermarkets, 149, are in New Zealand. In Australia, Foodland runs 81 'Action' supermarkets, situated in Queensland and northern New South Wales (43) and Western Australia (38). Foodland's operating revenue at the end of the 2004 financial year for its Australian supermarket segment was $1.4 billion, its earnings before interest and taxes $39.1 million.[46]

Foodland's second division is its franchise and supply segment. Foodland is a grocery wholesaler to Western Australian independent supermarket operators including its own franchise banner groups Dewsons, Supa Valu, Foodland and Four Square. Foodland also operates three Cash & Carry branches and Foodlink, Western Australia's largest food service operator, supplying caterers, hotels, restaurants, cafes, institutions, schools and mine sites. In Australia, the franchise and supply division achieved operating revenue of $1 billion and earnings before interest and taxes of $45 million at the end of the 2004 financial year.[47]

Foodland's main strategies are to satisfy changing consumer demands by combining innovation with value and to reduce costs through greater efficiency and better use of technology. To achieve these strategies, Action supermarkets have upgraded their fresh food departments and continued to develop their own house brands. They have refurbished many of their existing supermarkets, tested new store formats and acquired new sites. In addition, Action has launched a customer loyalty program in Western Australia in November 2003. In Queensland, Action has entered into arrangements that will allow customers of 27 Action supermarkets access to petrol discount offers. Foodland has also agreed to purchase 16 Mobil service stations in the Perth, Western Australia, metropolitan area. In 2005, Foodland aims to continue improving its fresh food departments, its innovation in store design and its development of exclusive house brand ranges. In addition, the company plans to improve supply chain efficiencies, to make more effective and profitable use of store space and to better use new technologies, both at store and corporate level. Unlike Woolworths and Coles, which are centralising their distribution, Action aims to strengthen its ties with regional producers and wholesalers who are close to the regional retail centres and who can provide good-quality products at low prices. The purpose of this approach is to save on distribution costs required for long distances and to get quickly to the market with products that are very fresh.

IGA

IGA is another supermarket organisation with a regional presence in Australia. It has a market share of about 13.5 per cent.[48] IGA stands for Independent Grocers of Australia and was brought to Australia by Davids Holdings in 1988. IGA was originally founded in the United States in 1926 and represents an alliance between wholesalers, retailers and manufacturers. By the end of the 2004 financial year, there were 1138 IGA stores in Australia, located in Queensland, New South Wales, Victoria and South Australia. Davids name has changed to Metcash Trading Limited and the distribution side of the business is called IGA Distribution.[49]

All IGA stores are independently owned and operated. The IGA network unites formerly independent retailers that traded under many different names under one brand. This has led to better economies of scale and scope, better buying power and consistency in marketing, merchandising, information technology and store design. There are three types of IGA stores: Supa IGA; IGA and IGA Everyday; IGA X-press and Friendly Grocer IGA. Supa IGAs are full-service supermarkets, catering to customers who want to purchase all groceries and fresh food in one location. IGA and IGA Everyday are medium-format stores with a midsized supermarket range. IGA X-press and Friendly Grocer IGA are small-format stores, that attract a convenience market.[50]

The IGA Distribution business, owned by Metcash Trading, supplies the IGA stores as well as more than 3300 other independent grocers. Major achievements for IGA Distribution by the end of the 2004 financial year were sales of $3.96 billion and earnings before interest and tax of $131 million. In addition, IGA Distribution improved its customer service levels, reduced the costs of doing business and developed an innovative 'reverse' fuel offer.[51] Motorists can fill up at a petrol station of their choice and be reimbursed 4 cents per litre when they shop at an IGA store. IGA Distribution plans to undertake further cost reductions over the next few years by overhauling supply chain, distribution and technology arrangements. One key supply chain project for Metcash is setting up mega distribution centres in each capital city. Previously, Metcash had separate warehouses for liquor, dry groceries and perishables in three different suburbs. Central distribution centres will enable Metcash to take advantage of asset and labour sharing and is expected to result in substantial cost savings. Another major initiative is called 'Project Collaboration' and involves improving and streamlining Metcash's relationship with manufacturers, again with the aim of cutting costs. Finally, Metcash is in the process of implementing a freight movement efficiency program, which aims to fill transport vehicles to 95 per cent of capacity by consolidating orders, decreasing turnaround times and better managing delivery schedules.[52] At the time of writing, Metcash has launched a takeover bid for the Australian section of Foodland Associated. If successful, this acquisition would create Australia's third-largest food and liquor chain with annual wholesale and retail sales of $18.2 billion.[53]

Franklins

The third regional player in the Australian retail industry is Franklins, a discount supermarket chain, which was founded in 1941 by Frank Lindstrom. In 1954, Franklins was acquired by Harold Cornock and Norman Tieck and in the late 1970s, it was sold to Hong Kong company Dairy Farm International. In May 2001, Dairy Farm International left the business and many of the stores were sold to other retailers and wholesalers. Pick 'n' Pay, a South African retailer, purchased 50 stores and the rights to the Franklins and No Frills brands. Pick 'n' Pack relaunched the Franklins chain in May 2002. In the beginning of 2005, there were 77 Franklins supermarkets across New South Wales and in the ACT. Franklins' strategy concentrates on providing value for money, quality, friendly service, speedy checkouts and a good overall shopping experience.[54] As do all the other supermarkets, Franklins also aims to improve supply value chain management and update administration systems.

Summary

This discussion has shown the competitive environment in which Aldi operates. It is characterised by two major national chains, Woolworths and Coles, both full-service supermarkets that are trying to differentiate their product offerings and to provide more value for their customers by adding new retail services such as access to discounted petrol and to banking facilities. They offer house brands as a cheaper alternative to national brands and aim to increase the number of products they sell under brand names they own. Both Woolworths and Coles are in the process of overhauling their supply chain management, warehouse and distribution systems in an aggressive bid to cut costs. Price is an important issue and both claim to provide customers with competitive prices and more value for money.

The regional retail operators, Action, IGA and Franklins, pursue a similar approach. They are in the process of addressing supply chain efficiencies and improving logistic arrangements, also with the aim of cutting costs. Similar to Woolworths and Coles, all three regional operators offer house brands and are likely to increase their number

over the next few years. Price is also a major issue for the regional supermarkets and they all state that their prices are competitive and that they provide value for money.

Aldi's challenges

Since its entry into the Australian market in 2001, Aldi has been very successful. It has established 72 stores in New South Wales, Victoria and Queensland and is in the process of opening more stores in these states. Aldi's strategy of cost leadership seems to resonate with customers and supermarkets in close proximity to Aldi have tried to match their low prices for basic commodity-type items such as milk, flour, sugar and butter. The prices for more 'luxury' items, such as free-range eggs or bananas, however, were not matched, and Aldi was clearly cheaper (e.g. 12 extra large free-range eggs cost $3.99 at Aldi, $5.09 at Coles and $5.65 at Woolworths; 1 kg of bananas costs $1.69 at Aldi, $2.75 at Coles and $1.98 at Woolworths).[55] Since other supermarkets have taken up the price challenge, it is important for Aldi to ensure that its prices are lower or at least equal to the ones of its competitors and that its products develop a reputation for high quality. This is particularly important considering that the competition in the food retailing industry is likely to increase, due to a number of economic factors that may influence consumer confidence and consumer spending over the next few years. These factors include high levels of household debt, a low national rate of saving, falling house prices, high oil prices and possible increases in unemployment and interest rates. These factors are likely to have a negative impact on consumer spending and hence the competition for the consumer dollar is likely to become more intense.

A possible second challenge is the entry of other global players into the Australian market. According to international experts on global retailing, an entry of international players is unlikely in the short term; however, they predict that in the medium term, international players such as Wal-Mart (the US's largest retailer) or Tesco (the UK's largest retailer) might decide to move into Australia.[56] In addition, it is also possible that Aldi's major competitor in Europe, Lidl, decides to follow Aldi to Australia. Lidl, which belongs to the Schwarz Group, has copied the Aldi approach in many aspects. It also offers high-quality products at low prices, places great emphasis on economic efficiency and has minimised costs at all levels of the value chain. Apart from Germany, Lidl currently is present in the UK, Ireland, France, Portugal, Spain, the Netherlands, Belgium, Finland, Poland, Czech Republic, Austria, Italy and Greece.[57] Because of the similarity of its approach, an entry of Lidl into Australia would clearly present a major challenge to Aldi.

Discussion questions

1. What is Aldi's competitive advantage?
2. Discuss some of the trends in the Australian food retailing industry.
3. Is the industry in which Aldi operates attractive?
4. Should Aldi make changes to its current business strategy?
5. Should Aldi move into the other Australian states and territories: South Australia, Western Australia, Tasmania, ACT, Northern Territory?

References

1. Brandes, D 1998, *Konsequent einfach: eie ALDI-Erfolgsstory*, 3rd edn, Campus Verlag, Frankfurt.
2. http://english.lz-net.de/retailers/rankings/pages/show.prl?id=83.
3. ALDI group n.d., accessed 21 December 2004, www.hoovers.com/aldi/--ID__54910--/free-co-factsheet.xhtml.
4. Welcome to ALDI Australia, accessed 20 December 2004, http://australia.aldi.com.
5. Walker, J 2003, 'Inside Aldi', *Business Review Weekly*, 17–23 July, pp. 41–45.
6. ACNielsen 2004, *Grocery report*, accessed 20 December 2004, www.acnielsen.com.au/files/GroRptCon04.pdf.
7. ibid.
8. Welcome to ALDI Australia, op. cit.
9. Walker, op. cit.
10. Welcome to ALDI Australia, op. cit.
11. Shoebridge, N 2004, 'House-brand horrors', *Business Review Weekly*, 28 October–3 November, p. 59.
12. Hamson, L 2003, 'Inside Aldi', *The Grocer*, 29 November, pp. 28–30.
13. Welcome to ALDI Australia, op. cit.
14. Walker, op. cit.
15. ibid.
16. White, E & Ray, S 2004, 'Leadership (A special report); Bare-Bones shopping: Germany's discount retailers are among the world's most successful; Here's how one does it', *Wall Street Journal*, 10 May, p. R6.
17. Brandes, op. cit.
18. Ewing, J, Zammert, A, Zellner, W, Tiplady, E, Groves E & Eidam, M 2004, 'The next Wal-Mart? Like the US-based giant, Germany's Aldi boasts awesome margins and huge clout', *Business Week*, 26 April, p. 60.
19. Walker, op. cit.
20. Brandes, op. cit.
21. Ewing et. al., op. cit.
22. Advertising flyer by Aldi, 'Specials for 27 January [2005]'.
23. Brandes, op. cit.
24. Welcome to Aldi Australia, op. cit.
25. Brandes, op. cit.
26. ibid.
27. Area manager 2005, accessed 6 January 2005, http://uk.aldi.com/recruitment/recruitment_2.html.
28. Brandes, op. cit.
29. Brandes, D 2004, 'Uncompromisingly simple – the ALDI success story', ERA Packaging Conference, Freiburg, Germany, October.
30. Walker, op. cit.
31. Brandes 1998, op. cit.
32. ibid.
33. Woolworths Ltd, 2005, *Annual report 2004*; Coles-Myer Ltd 2005, *Annual report 2004*.
34. Metcash shareholders back Foodland bid, accessed 21 January 2005, www.xtramsn.co.nz/money/0,,5487-4034756,00.html.
35. Woolworths Ltd, op cit.
36. ibid.
37. Woolworths Ltd, Online shopping, accessed 21 January 2005, www.woolworths.com.au.
38. Woolworths Ltd 2005, *Annual report 2004*.
39. Ibid.
40. Woolworths Ltd, 2005, 'Our history', accessed 12 January 2005, www.woolworthslimited.com.au/aboutus/ourhistory/index.asp.
41. Coles-Myer Ltd, op cit.
42. ibid.
43. ibid.
44. ibid, p. 5.
45. Clow, R & Gluyas, R 2004, 'Food fight', *Weekend Australian*, 13–14 November, pp. 33 and 36.
46. Foodland Associated Ltd, *Annual report*, 2004.
47. ibid.
48. Lloyd, S 2004, 'Grocery growing pains', *Business Review Weekly*, 22–28 April, pp. 60–61.
49. IGA Australia, 'About us', accessed 18 January 2005, www.iga.net.au/info/aboutus.cfm; Metcash Trading Ltd, *Annual report 2004*.
50. IGA Australia, op. cit.
51. Metcash Trading Ltd, op cit.
52. Lloyd, op. cit.
53. Whyte, J 2005, 'Foodland readies response to Metcash', *Australian Financial Review*, 24 January, p. 12.
54. Franklins, 'About us', accessed 12 January 2005, www.franklins.com.au/aboutus.html.
55. The price comparison was done by the author on 22 January 2005 at Aldi, Coles and Woolworths in Labrador, Queensland.
56. IGD Retail Analysis 2005, Annual report, global retailing 2004, accessed 6 January 2005, www.igd.com/analysis.
57. *Manager Magazine* 2003, Angriff des Super-Kraemers', September, pp. 38–47.

Air New Zealand: challenges and opportunities

By Sussie Morrish, The University of Auckland, New Zealand

Introduction

On 24 August 2005, outgoing Air New Zealand CEO Ralph Norris gave an interview to Television New Zealand (TVNZ). In this interview, which aired during the prime time news, Ralph was less than complimentary to the New Zealand Commerce Commission, describing its approach to competition law as inflexible and out of touch.[1] Auckland-born Ralph was appointed as CEO in February 2002. Having left Air New Zealand in September 2005 to take on the post of CEO of the Australian Commonwealth Bank, he is confident that he leaves the airline financially sound, having successfully turned its business around. Air New Zealand suffered a near death experience in 2001, foiled only by the recapitalisation move of the New Zealand government, which saw the carrier move back to Crown ownership after it had been privatised in December 1988. Whereas Ralph can take satisfaction in Air New Zealand's financial success despite operating in a very difficult aviation environment, his main regret is the failure of the proposed alliance with Qantas Airways to gain the necessary approval from the competition authorities from both Australia and New Zealand. As he ponders the events that led to this outcome, he wonders what strategic options his successor might pursue in taking Air New Zealand into the next decade.

Background

Originally registered as Tasman Empire Airways Limited (TEAL) in 1940, with an original fleet of just two flying boats, Air New Zealand changed to its present name on 1 April 1965. As the country's flag carrier, it is regarded by Kiwis[2] as a symbol of national pride. It was privatised in December 1988, when a consortium headed by Brierly Investments Ltd took full ownership of the airline. However, to ensure that the majority shareholding is held by New Zealanders, the New Zealand government took a 'Kiwi' share, an instrument that gave it key veto powers.

Over the next 12 years, Air New Zealand shares were held by different private and institutional shareholders, including other airlines. Among these were Qantas Airways, Japan Airlines, American Airlines and Singapore Airlines. Air New Zealand also took shareholdings in other carriers. Its biggest shareholding was in Ansett Australia. In September 1999, it acquired 50 per cent of Ansett Holdings Ltd Group with an investment of NZ$540 million. This became a 100 per cent acquisition in June 2000, when the Foreign Investment Review Board of Australia approved its purchase, a move that briefly put the Air New Zealand and Ansett Group in the top 20 airline group. However, as the events of the succeeding months unfolded, this strategy was to prove almost fatal for Air New Zealand. They started with the grounding of the Ansett Boeing 767 fleet, after pylon cracks were found just before the Easter holidays in April 2001. The situation escalated and was widely played out in the media on both sides of the Tasman. The Ansett Group recorded huge losses and by 7 September, reached $1.3 million per day. Air New Zealand's troubles were exacerbated by the events of 11 September 2001 and the refusal of Qantas to buy the troubled Ansett Group for a token amount. This left Air New Zealand with no other option but to place Ansett into voluntary administration. The parent company itself recorded a net loss of NZ$1.425 billion for the financial year ending June 2001, attributed mainly to losses in its Ansett operations.

A rescue package worth NZ$885 million from the New Zealand government saved the airline from total collapse. This would see the government become the majority shareholder of the airline once again, with a shareholding of just more than 80 per cent. This also saw the restructuring of the airline, with new members on the board of directors. The directors' fees were also reduced after the recomposition. Air New Zealand's president and CEO at the time, Gary Toomey, resigned on 9 October.

What followed is one of the most amazing turnaround cases in the aviation industry. Under the leadership of the new chairman, John Palmer, and CEO, Ralph Norris, Air New Zealand embarked on a business transformation program that set new strategic directions for the company and achieved record savings and profits for the company in three years, despite the overall aviation industry suffering from very difficult circumstances that saw many bankruptcies.

Air New Zealand today

Air New Zealand is a full-service carrier flying to 25 domestic and 23 international destinations, covering Australia and the Pacific Islands, Asia, North America and Europe. In 2005, its operating fleet had a total of 89 aircraft, 45 of which it owns and 44 it leases. The fleet has an average age of 8.2 years.[3] It is one of the earliest members of the Star Alliance, now the biggest airline alliance, with 16 member airlines. Its membership of the Star Alliance network allows Air New Zealand passengers to connect to nearly 800 other destinations. In 2005, it carried 11.7 million passengers and had a worldwide workforce of 10 829 employees. It posted a profit of NZ$235 million and paid out a fully imputed dividend of 5 cents per share, finishing the year off with a NZ$1.1 billion cash balance. Five-year historical summaries of Air New Zealand's financial and operating statistics are contained in tables C7.1 and C7.2.

Table C7.1: Air New Zealand summary of financial performance

For the year ending 30 June	2001 $m	2002 $m	2003 $m	2004 $m	2005 $m
Total Operating Revenue	4025	3642	3617	3498	3616
Earnings Before Interest and Taxation	141	89	233	235	212
Net Surplus/(Deficit)	82	(319)	166	166	180
Financial Ratios	per cent	per cent	per cent	per cent	per cent
Return on Total Gross Assets	22.4	20.5	23.3	22.3	20.3
Return on Assets	(0.7)	(0.8)	6.3	6.1	5.2
Return on Equity	15.8	(36.1)	16.1	13.7	11.7

Source: Air New Zealand 2005, 'Five year statistical review', *Annual report*, pp. 89–91

Table C7.2: Air New Zealand key operating statistics

For the year ending 30 June (Group)	2001	2002	2003	2004	2005
Total Passengers Carried (000)	8716	9207	9809	10909	11690
Total Available Seat Kilometres (m)	22758	21776	23160	23937	25568
Total Passenger Load Factor per cent	72.6	73.3	75.5	74.8	75.9
Total Cargo Load Factor per cent	62.4	65.5	65.6	59.5	62.7
Total Employee Numbers	10761	9502	10165	10394	10829

Source: Air New Zealand 2005, 'Five year statistical review', *Annual report*, p. 92

These positive results were largely attributed to its business transformation program, which aims to achieve cost savings and revenue improvements starting with its domestic services.[4] Consider this statement from Air New Zealand Chairman John Palmer during the annual shareholder's meeting in Auckland on Wednesday, 22 October 2003:

> ...what may have seemed to many to be a counter-intuitive move, we started the change by reinventing the New Zealand domestic business. This will always be the core of our business and we will defend it vigorously. The best defence comes from a strong cost position and it is for this reason that we began our re-engineering with the domestic business.[5]

In its home country, Air New Zealand is a key sponsor of many major events such as rugby's National Provincial Championships, Fashion Week and Wine Awards. It also sponsors many groups, most notably the All Blacks. It also has a record of supporting charities through donations and travel assistance.

Air New Zealand consistently receives industry awards for its operations. For example, it is the recipient of the TTG 'Best Pacific Airline' award for six years running covering the period from 1998 to 2004. More recently, it received the 2005 *Air Transport World's*[6] Phoenix Award for what was described as 'a commercial rebirth through a life-changing transformation.'[7] In giving this award, judges commented that: 'Air New Zealand survived a near-death experience in 2001 to remake itself into a profitable and innovative competitor across different markets.' They further noted that Air New Zealand has become an industry leader in both product and culture in just three years after it hit extreme difficulty in 2001.[8]

Under Ralph's leadership, Air New Zealand launched the Express Class for its domestic operations, offering cheaper domestic fares of up to 50 per cent less than previous fare offerings. The program was launched on 1 November 2002 with a Boeing 767 flight from Auckland to Christchurch. Despite initial public concerns that Air New Zealand was going to become a downgraded airline, this strategy proved to be a huge success. The new service increased the domestic market significantly, so that by the time it celebrated its first anniversary, it had flown six million passengers. This was an increase of 22 per cent over the previous year. For a country of four million people, this was indeed significant. In a press release on 31 October 2003, Ralph said that Air New Zealand believed the growth was attributable to first-time fliers who found the lower fares attractive.[9] Alongside the Express Class, Air New Zealand also introduced Express Check kiosks, a technology that sped up the check-in process for Express Class customers in the key airports. Although some passengers were initially reluctant to use the kiosks, there is now a very high uptake among passengers who have grown accustomed to the process.

In its first year of operations, the Express Class product received numerous awards that included the 2003 New Zealand Tourism Awards for Innovation in Leadership and Strategic Planning; the 2003 NBR Advertising Campaign of the Year; and in the 2003 EFFIE Awards for Marketing Effectiveness, it won gold awards for its Consumer Services, Corporate Image and Corporate Reputation. It also won a silver award in the New Product category. These awards are given out by the Communication Agencies Association of New Zealand.[10]

Although it seems that Air New Zealand has found the right product and technology mix with its domestic services, its international operations offer more challenges. The long-haul operations are subject to very intense competition not only from other full-service airlines, but also from value-based airlines known in the industry as low-cost carriers. Air New Zealand's international operations account for 75 per cent of its revenues, while the domestic operations account for 25 per cent.

Alliances and the airline industry

The aviation industry is unique, mainly because it is governed by strict bilateral air services agreements between countries and negotiated freedom rights.[11] International carriers could only fly to countries where their home country has an agreement with a destination country. A more recent development in aviation is the 'open skies' agreement, which created a free market for aviation services.[12] This and tight economic regulation in the 1980s led jet and commuter operators in the United States to form alliances to develop markets jointly. As the industry was deregulated around the world, international partnerships were formed to pursue cost savings, market penetration and retention, financial injections, market stability and to circumvent infrastructure and institutional constraints.[13]

Among the earlier alliances were the Global Excellence Alliance between Delta, Swissair and Singapore Airlines formed in 1989; and the most enduring Northwest/KLM

alliance formed in the early 1990s.[14] This was followed by a spate of alliances between international airlines. Alliances allowed carriers to code-share with partner airlines and offer more destinations to their customers. To be truly global, it was considered necessary for an alliance grouping to have members from the three major regions: North America, Europe and Asia. Indeed, many of the alliances were initiated by carriers from these regions. Today, airline alliances are larger and offer many more benefits to member airlines. Their cooperation ranges from code-sharing, block-spacing and franchising to equity shareholdings among partners. Alliances can also offer some or all of the following benefits to member airlines: access to new markets by tapping into a partner's underused route rights or slots, and traffic feed into established gateways to increase load factors and to improve yield. They can also enable defence of current markets through seat capacity management of partners' shared operations. Furthermore, they allow for economies of scale through resource pooling across operational areas or cost centres such as sales and marketing, station and ground facilities and purchasing.[15]

The rise of global alliances alarmed many industry observers. Some warned that global alliances could lead to monopolies and higher airfares. Others argued that competition in the future will not be between airlines but between alliance groups. Consequently, this led to many carriers scrambling to join an alliance for fear that they would be at a competitive disadvantage if they were not aligned. But finding suitable partners to ally with is not always easy, mainly because alliances are not always easy to manage. Although many alliances were formed, the failure and dissolution rates were also very high, notably Qualiflyer, Wings, Alcazar and the KLM/Alitalia alliance. However, alliance groupings stabilised in the early 2000s. Today, there are three major global alliances, the largest of which is Star Alliance, formed in 1997. The other two alliances are oneworld and Sky Team. Table C7.3 shows these groupings.

Despite the monopoly concerns, however, airfares do not seem to have risen. Studies have found some fare lowering by alliance partners, especially on complementary routes.[17] While established carriers sought alliance partners, a new phenomenon arose with the advent of value-based or 'budget' airlines. Airlines such as Southwest, EasyJet and Ryanair entered the market and proved to be quite popular. In some markets, they are considered a threat to the survival of established carriers.

Table C7.3: Major airline alliances in 2005[16]

Star Alliance	oneworld alliance	Sky Team alliance
Air Canada	Aer Lingus	Aeromexico
Air New Zealand	American Airlines	Air France
ANA	British Airways	Alitalia
Asiana Airlines	Cathay Pacific	Continental
BMI	Finnair	TSA Czech Airlines
Austrian	Iberia	Delta
Lot Polish Airlines	LAN	KLM
Lufthansa	Qantas	Korean
SAS Scandinavian Airlines		NWA
Singapore Airlines		
Spanair		
TAP Portugal		
Thai Airways		
United		
US Airways		
Varig		

Air New Zealand and Qantas

New Zealand and Australia are the biggest economies in the Pacific Region and have always had healthy rivalry in many areas, especially in sporting pursuits such as rugby union, rugby league, cricket, netball, basketball and many others. This competition also extends to areas of business and the trans-Tasman skies have not been immune to this competition. Air New Zealand and Qantas have always been regarded as regional archrivals and for a long period have been the major carriers on the trans-Tasman route. Air New Zealand and its subsidiary Freedom Air hold about 52 per cent of the market, and Qantas about 39 per cent.[18]

This rivalry was evident when Qantas CEO Geoff Dixon was reported in *The Sydney Morning Herald* to have told his managers that Qantas wants to boost its trans-Tasman services and put Air New Zealand out of business. He was further quoted to have said: 'Qantas will be very aggressive in this regard.'[19] To this, Air New Zealand chairman John Palmer responded by acknowledging that threats from Qantas are not new to them and that Air New Zealand has been preparing for more aggressive competition. John added that: '... the only surprise this time is that they are actively seeking a damaging and costly battle on two fronts — the imminent introduction of additional competition from a revived Ansett in their home market and stronger competition offshore from a recapitalised Air New Zealand'.[20] What was, however, interesting about this report was Dixon saying that the New Zealand government eventually wanted Qantas to buy into its national airline. Although Dixon had denied this, Jim Anderton, the deputy prime minister at the time, indicated that the New Zealand government might eventually look for a cornerstone shareholder as it tried to relinquish some control over Air New Zealand and insinuated that some sort of partnership may be possible. Needless to say, a partnership with one party setting out to put the other out of business would not be a good strategic move.

More recently, other carriers have entered the market, including Emirates, the LCC Virgin Blue, and other Asian carriers. Although Air New Zealand and Qantas had traditionally operated the Trans-Tasman route as a virtual duopoly, there was concern that new entrants would lead to capacity dumping, making the service unsustainable.

In December 2002, in an unexpected move that surprised many observers, Air New Zealand and Qantas both submitted separate but interdependent applications to the NZ Commerce Commission. Qantas' application, made under section 67(1) of the *Commerce Act* sought approval to a 'share purchase agreement' for Qantas to acquire 22.5 per cent of Air New Zealand, worth NZ$550 million. For its part, Air New Zealand's application, made under section 58 of the *Commerce Act*, related to a proposed strategic alliance that would create a 'joint airline operation' between the two carriers.[21] A similar application was made to the Australian Competition and Consumer Commission (ACCC) at the same time.

The key features of this proposal involve joint operations on all Air New Zealand and Qantas flights to, from and within New Zealand. Through an advisory group comprised of three representatives from each party, both parties would also jointly coordinate virtually all aspects of their airline operation and cooperate on operations outside the scope of their joint airline operation. This arrangement would involve coordinating all aspects of their operations 'including passenger fares and freight rates, flight schedules, the amount of passenger and freight capacity provided on each sector, code-sharing, marketing, frequent flyer programs and profit sharing.'[22] In terms of governance, two representatives would sit on the Air New Zealand board while it in return would have one representative on the Qantas board.

The proposed alliance had its fair share of opposition and supporters. Professor Tim Hazledine of the department of economics at the University of Auckland argued that the proposed cooperation was not an alliance but effectively a cartel. His work provided some evidence and showed that without the 'independent competition,' fares would increase and competition would substantially lessen.[23]

In its draft determination in April 2003, the New Zealand Commerce Commission decided to turn down the proposal, saying that it was anticompetitive and could cost the New Zealand economy some NZ$430 million per year. The ACCC took a similar view. In an effort to reverse its initial ruling, Air New Zealand made submissions to the Commerce Commission in June 2003, arguing that the proposed alliance 'is the only way to secure substantial and long term benefits for New Zealand including tourism and job creation'.[24] In a statement released by Ralph Norris on 23 June 2003, he reiterated that Air New Zealand's future was dependent on the proposed alliance, combined with its Freedom Air operations, the Express Class and further continuous improvement of its international services.[25] All these elements he said were necessary for them to operate successfully.

> Air New Zealand has a short window of opportunity to solve the threat to its medium to long term survival. The only way it can do this is to be the remaining FSA in New Zealand, an outcome which it can achieve only through the platform of the Alliance. The Alliance provides a one-off opportunity to combine two strongly branded locally based airlines into a sustainable regional group. — Ralph Norris' evidence to the Commerce Commission hearing, 18 August 2003[26]

> Forcing the airlines to 'fight it out' will waste resources and will diminish the benefits that are available to the airlines and to the country, from allowing the Alliance. And if the structural changes force Air New Zealand into an ever more marginal role or, worse still, lead to its collapse, the opportunities both parties have today to secure a future in global markets, is likely to have been foregone, to the serious detriment of New Zealand. There is not likely to be a second chance. — John Palmer's closing address to the Commerce Commission hearing, 25 August 2003[27]

Meanwhile, across the Tasman, Australian Deputy Prime Minister John Anderson was also pushing for ACCC approval of the alliance, arguing that it was necessary for Qantas' future. He encouraged the two airlines to make concessions to tackle the anticompetitive nature of their proposal. Air New Zealand and Qantas offered substantial concessions in response to the draft determination featuring ten key undertakings that addressed key issues relating to possible anticompetitive activity, a new entrant's ability to compete and ensuring that the public benefits claimed by the airlines will eventuate. These covered such areas as trans-Tasman route scheduling, providing new entrants with access to slots, gates, counter facilities and other services, as well as limiting capacity, leasing aircrafts to new entrants and price cap provisions.[28]

On 9 September 2003, the ACCC made a final ruling that the proposed alliance was not in the public interest. Graham Samuel, ACCC chairman, said that 'the proposed alliance would be highly anticompetitive and offer little benefit to the Australian public'.[29] Air New Zealand and Qantas immediately appealed the decision and applied for a review of the ACCC decision with the Australian Competition Tribunal (ACT). After the announcement of the ruling, Air New Zealand's share price dropped eight cents to 47 cents, and Qantas shares by 19 cents to $3.33, 5.4 per cent lower than their opening price on the Australian Stock Exchange. On the New Zealand Exchange, from an opening high of NZ61 cents, Air New Zealand shares dropped by 13.3 per cent to NZ52 cents.

Despite these setbacks, when John Palmer addressed the annual shareholders' meeting on 22 October 2003 in Auckland, he was still hopeful of a successful outcome from the New Zealand authority and similarly from the ACT. He was optimistic that after gaining approval from both competition authorities and shareholders, the alliance could be implemented within the first six months of 2004. The following day, the Commerce Commission made a final ruling against the proposed alliance.

Alongside the appeal already before the ACT, Air New Zealand and Qantas went to the High Court in New Zealand to appeal against the Commerce Commission ruling.

On 20 September 2004, almost a year after the final Commerce Commission determination, the High Court turned down the appeal and upheld the decision to reject the proposed strategic alliance. The proponents were naturally disappointed with the decision, especially as it was widely known that the High Court did not agree with the Commerce Commission on many issues. About three weeks later, on 12 October, despite the High Court ruling, the ACT reached a different decision. It granted Australian regulatory approval for the proposed alliance to go ahead.

Although Air New Zealand and Qantas were somewhat vindicated by the ACT approval, they decided not to appeal the High Court decision in New Zealand. After reviewing the ruling, Qantas was of the view that an appeal 'would take too long, cost too much money and it was unlikely to succeed'.[30] Qantas CEO Geoff Dixon said in a statement that 'another 12 months of uncertainty, with the associated costs, is not in anyone's interest'.[31] The failure of the bid to gain approval from both countries meant that the proposal could not go ahead. Ralph Norris admitted that the proposal in its present form was dead.[32] Both airlines said it was 'time to move on' but they would continue to explore ways they could work together.

The stakeholders

In the period between the announcement of the proposed strategic alliance and the final ACT ruling (December 2002 to October 2004), many opinions were expressed by interested parties. A selection is featured in the following.

The New Zealand government

The proposed alliance was conditionally approved by the New Zealand government on 18 December 2002, subject to the approval of the regulatory bodies from both countries. It acknowledged that by granting Qantas consent to acquire 22.5 per cent of Air New Zealand, its shareholding in the national carrier would be reduced from 82 per cent to 64 per cent. Finance Minister Michael Cullen said that a strategic partner was necessary for Air New Zealand's long-term viability and survival and without a partner it could shrink to becoming a domestic carrier. The government warned that failure to gain Commerce Commission approval could mean that the airline faced an uncertain future. To this effect, New Zealanders, as shareholders, could in the future be asked to keep the airline solvent if it comes into difficulty. During the recently concluded election campaign, both Labour and National indicated that although they would not rule out selling part of the 82 per cent shareholding the government owned, they would keep a majority stake in the airline.[33]

Singapore Airlines

Originally a 25 per cent shareholder of Air New Zealand, Singapore Airlines was a rival bidder for Ansett Australia. When Air New Zealand was in trouble with its Ansett operations, Singapore Airlines sought to increase its shareholding to 49 per cent. This did not get government approval and the subsequent recapitalisation of Air New Zealand significantly reduced the value of its shareholding. On 23 January 2002, Dr CK Chong resigned from the board of Air New Zealand. In a final move to sever its shareholding in Air New Zealand, it sold its 6.3 per cent stake on 5 October 2004. Speculation was rife that Singapore Airlines would seek closer ties with Qantas when its majority shareholder, government investment agency Temasek Holdings, recently bought a 3 per cent stake in Qantas.[34] Both Air New Zealand and Singapore Airlines are members of the Star Alliance.

Interest groups

Groups that are likely to be affected by the proposed alliance made submissions to the Commerce Commission. In its submission in February 2003, the Inbound Tour Operators Council of New Zealand (ITOC), expressed its concern that 'the proposal would lessen competition, lead to declining standards and restrict the ability of new suppliers to enter the market'.[35] ITOC indicated that for it to support the proposal, appropriate conditions would need to be imposed to ensure the full removal of any risk of market dominance or intent to lessen competition.

In contrast to ITOC's position, the Australian Tourism Export Council (ATEC) was sympathetic to the proposed alliance and signalled its strong support for the deal. In a media release, its managing director, Peter Shelley, said that it was unacceptable for any of the regional carriers to have uncertainty about their commercial viability. National Chairman Andrew Burnes also expressed concerns and said that the carriers should not be expected to fly between Melbourne and Sydney for less than the taxi fare out of the airport.[36]

The aftermath

In a radio interview in Australia, Ralph Norris said that Air New Zealand may revisit the alliance plans in two or three years. The decision of the Australian regulatory body to grant approval creates the opportunity to look at a reapplication to the Commerce Commission.[37] Whether this will eventuate remains in the hands of new leadership at Air New Zealand. Presently, both airlines belong to competing alliance networks. The benefits of switching to another network must be weighed against the benefits of going into new partnerships.

The long and drawn-out process of seeking approval for the alliance was indeed costly for many parties. Claims for legal costs were filed before the High Court. On 2 August 2005, Air New Zealand was ordered by Justice Rodney

Hansen to pay more than NZ$2 million in legal costs to its opponents in its failed Qantas-alliance court case. Infratil, owner of two-thirds of Wellington Airport, and Gullivers Pacific, which owns the United Travel and Holiday Shoppe franchise brands, both opposed the proposed alliance. The Commerce Commission claim amounted to just under NZ$1.75 million. Air New Zealand does not think it should pay the Commission's legal costs.[38]

The day after this ruling, JetStar, a low-cost carrier, announced that it would start services to Christchurch from 1 December 2005. JetStar is owned by Qantas. It announced $39 one-way fares from Christchurch to Sydney, Melbourne, Brisbane and the Gold Coast, well below those of its parent company. JetStar is positioned against Virgin's Pacific Blue and Air New Zealand's Freedom Air. Observers are predicting a price war between the three low-cost carriers.

Conclusion

As globalisation continues, no other industry is more at the forefront than the aviation industry. Airlines will continue to operate in a dynamic and exciting but volatile environment. The period between 2000 and 2005 has delivered both disappointments and successes for Air New Zealand. Its business transformation program is not yet complete. Qantas is once again its main rival and Singapore Airlines is no longer a shareholder. Pacific Blue has entered the market and so has Emirates. The search for a new CEO continues. Air New Zealand has just taken delivery of the first of its B777s. This is the initial stage of its fleet upgrade that aims to make it more competitive internationally. It is continuing to expand its horizons with applications in place to commence direct service to Shanghai.

Air New Zealand is continuing to move on but must always be ready to take on the opportunities and challenges of the future.

Discussion questions

1. Discuss how barriers to entry in the airline industry have changed in the past decade.

2. In light of such lowering of barriers, what opportunities are there for Air New Zealand to pursue?

3. Air New Zealand must consider different stakeholders in its pursuit of corporate strategies. Identify the key stakeholders and their concerns.

4. The failure of its proposed collaboration with Qantas has positioned the two carriers as rivals again. Identify other ways they could cooperate without being anticompetitive.

5. In its domestic operations, Air New Zealand has used a cost-based strategy successfully with the Express Class. Discuss why the same strategy may not work in its long-haul services.

6. Air New Zealand is looking to develop its London route and poised to start flying to Shanghai in a few months. How can Air New Zealand differentiate itself from other carriers operating in these markets?

End notes

1. One News 2005, 'Ralph Norris fires parting shot', 24 August, accessed 28 December 2005, www.tvnz.co.nz/view/page/425823/606605.

2. The kiwi is a national icon of New Zealand but it is also a term popularly used to refer to New Zealanders.

3. Air New Zealand 2005, 'Five year statistical review', *Annual report*, pp. 89–91.

4. The full 2005 annual report is accessible through www.airnewzealand.co.nz.

5. Palmer J 2003, chairman's address, Air New Zealand's sixty-fourth annual shareholders' meeting, Air New Zealand, accessed 28 December 2005, www.airnz.co.nz/resources/chairman_address_22oct03.pdf.

6. *Air Transport World* is a leading aviation magazine and has been running these awards for more than 30 years.

7. Air New Zealand 2005, 'Air New Zealand wins industry award', 27 January, accessed 6 October 2005, www.airnewzealand.co.nz/aboutus/mediacentre/pressreleases/default.htm.

8. ibid.

9. Air New Zealand 2003 'Huge Success for First Year of Air New Zealand Express Class', 31 October, accessed 6 October 2005, www.airnewzealand.co.nz/aboutus/mediacentre/pressreleases_2003/default.htm.

10. ibid.

11. For a detailed explanation of the nine air freedom rights see: http://people.hofstra.edu/geotrans/eng/ch3en/conc3en/airfreedom.html.

12. See discussions on www.state.gov/e/eb/tra/c661.htm.

13. Morrish, S & Hamilton, R 2002, 'Airline alliances — who benefits?', *Journal of Air Transport Management*, vol. 8, no. 6, pp. 401–7.

14. Hamilton, R & Morrish, S 2005, 'Alliance size and performance', *Journal of International Business and Entrepreneurship*, vol. 2, no. 2, pp. 35–48.

15. See Morrish & Hamilton, op. cit.

16. Sources: www.staralliance.com/star_alliance/star/frame/main_10.html; www.oneworld.com/ and www.skyteam.com/skyteam.

17. See Morrish & Hamilton, op. cit. and Brueckner, JK 2001 'Airline alliances benefit consumers', *Policy Forum Institute of Government and Public Affairs*, University of Illinois, vol. 14, no. 3.

18. Samuel, G n.d., 'ACCC statement', accessed 12 October 2005, www.accc.gov.au/content/index.phtml/itemId/363616.

19. OneNews 2002, 'Air NZ fires back at Qantas', 4 February, accessed 12 October 2005, http://tvnz.co.nz/view/page/423466/79806.

20. ibid.

21. Commerce Commission n.d., 'Executive summary, proposed alliance between Air NZ and Qantas', accessed 6 October 2005, www.comcom.govt.nz/Businesscompetition.

22. ibid, p. i.

23. Hazledine, T 2004, 'Pie in the sky? The sequel (the proposed Air New Zealand — Qantas cartel)' , accessed 6 October 2005, www.nzae.org.nz/conferences/2004/87_Hazledine.pdf.

24. Air New Zealand n.d., 'History', accessed 6 October 2005, www.airnewzealand.co.nz/aboutus/corporateprofile/companyhistory/default.htm#history.

25. Air New Zealand 2003 'Air New Zealand alliance with Qantas preferable to failure, merger, or ongoing state subsidies', 23 June, accessed 6 October 2005, www.airnewzealand.co.nz/aboutus/mediacentre/pressreleases_2003/default.htm.

26. Air New Zealand 2003, 'Media advisory: summary of Air New Zealand CEO Ralph Norris's evidence presented to the Commerce Commission hearing', 18 August, accessed 24 November 2005, www.airnz.co.nz/aboutus/mediacentre/pressreleases_2003/media_advisory_200803.htm.

27. Palmer, J 2003, 'Closing address', Air New Zealand Limited, Commerce Commission hearing, 25 August, accessed 24 November 2005, www.comcom.govt.nz/BusinessCompetition/Anti-competitivePractices/Applications/ContentFiles/Documents/johnPalmer.pdf, p. 7.

28. For full details see: Air New Zealand 2003 'Air New Zealand and Qantas offer substantial concessions to Australian competition regulator', media release, 13 May, accessed 6 October 2005, www.airnewzealand.co.nz/aboutus/mediacentre/pressrelease.

29. Australian Competition and Consumer Commission n.d., accessed 12 October 2005, www.accc.gov.au/content/index.phtml/itemId/363616.

30. Flight International 2004, 'Alliance dropped', accessed 6 October 2005, www.flightinternational.com/Articles/2004/10/19/188885/Alliance+dropped+.html.

31. Reuters 2004, 'Air NZ says Australian regulator grants alliance appeal', 12 October, accessed 6 October 2005, www.news.airwise.com/stories/2004/10/1097578457.html.

32. *Airline Business* 2004, 'Appeal too little, too late,' 1 November, accessed 6 October 2005, www.airlinebusiness.com/Articles/2004/11/01/189096/Appeal+too+little per cent2c+too+late.html.

33. *The Christchurch Press* 2005, 'Government to retain majority stake in Air New Zealand', 3 August, p. C6.

34. Reuters 2004, 'Air NZ says Australian regulator grants alliance appeal', 12 October, accessed 6 October 2005, www.news.airwise.com/stories/2004/10/1097578457.html.

35. Inbound Tour Operators Council of New Zealand 2003, 'Comments to the New Zealand Commerce Commission on the proposed Air New Zealand/Qantas alliance', February, accessed 12 October 2005 www.comcom.govt.nz/businesscompetition.

36. ATEC n.d., 'ATEC supports Qantas/Air New Zealand deal', accessed 6 October 2005, www.atec.net.au/MediaRelease.

37. ABC Radio Australia News 2004, 'Air NZ to revisit Qantas alliance in two to three years', 13 October.

38. Travelbiz 2005, 'Air NZ faces $1.8m costs over QF-alliance case', 2 August, accessed 12 October 2005, www.travelbiz.com.au/articles/a1/0c0351a1.asp.

Creating Fonterra: establishing New Zealand's largest business

By Bob Hamilton and Paul Knott, College of Business and Economics, University of Canterbury, New Zealand

This case concerns the challenge of achieving a new industry structure against a background of powerful stakeholders with conflicting viewpoints. The case is set in the New Zealand dairy industry, which generates about 20 per cent of that country's exports. It concerns the proposal to merge the three major operators in that industry into one large organisation with the cohesion and scale to enable it to operate effectively in the international market. At the same time, the proposed merger would create a new entity, Fonterra, as the world's largest exporter of dairy products but one that also had huge dominance in the New Zealand domestic market for milk and related products. The case sets out the industry background and the prevailing anti-trust legislation in New Zealand and then outlines the pros and cons of the different industry structures. The question proposed is: how could the merger be achieved given the prevailing views of stakeholders, and under what conditions might it be allowed?

Industry background

New Zealand is a small country, with a population of about 4 million, that generates from its unsubsidised dairy farms a huge production surplus each year. Some 90–95 per cent of all milk produced is destined for overseas markets, representing more than 20 per cent by value of the country's exports. The main export products (and markets) are whole-milk powder (Central and South America); cheese (the United States, Japan, the European Union (EU)); butter (the UK and the EU); and skim-milk powder (the Middle East). The biggest markets by dollar value in 1999 were: the United States (NZ$635 million); Japan (NZ$388 million); and the UK (NZ$281 million).

The processing of raw milk in New Zealand had traditionally been done in local dairy factories owned cooperatively by the farmers supplying the milk. In the 1950s there were about 400 such factories of varying sizes dotted around the country, some within sight of each other. In 1923 the New Zealand government set up the New Zealand Dairy Board to be the sole exporter of dairy product. Over the years, the pursuit of greater efficiency and economies of scale brought about a dramatic reduction in dairy processors, until by the late 1990s only four were left: NZ Dairy Group, Kiwi Dairies, Tatua, and Westland. The 'big two' in this group were NZ Dairy Group and Kiwi, processing about 60 per cent and 30 per cent respectively of all the milk produced in the country in 1999. So the result of years of industry rationalisation was a structure of two large production cooperatives, each with a statutory requirement to channel their exports through the NZ Dairy Board.

The NZ Dairy Board was by no means an unsuccessful organisation, winning a New Zealand Export Award in 1999 when its growing export revenues were equivalent to 23 per cent of the country's. It was also New Zealand's largest business, managing its own marketing and distribution network in more than 100 countries and with more than 89 fully owned subsidiaries and associate companies around the world. The problem was that, as the two major processing companies grew in size, they had less need for the New Zealand Dairy Board to act as their export arm. The board was required to accept all the product from the processing companies and this led to competition through the board for access to export markets. The complexity of the negotiations between the board and the processors was beginning to hold the industry back and prevent it from responding quickly to market opportunities. The prospect that the dairy board had outlived its usefulness had been recognised in 1992 when a proposal was floated to merge it with the major dairy companies. This came to nothing at that time, but the idea gained strength through the 1990s as the industry continued its consolidation.

The case for change

As the New Zealand dairy industry consolidated, so too did the global industry, with one estimate suggesting that there will eventually be just ten major food retailers in the world. This means that suppliers also need scale to counteract the growing power of the buyers (even after the merger, Fonterra would still have only about one-third of the sales of Nestlé). There was also a perceived risk that the highly productive assets and expertise of the New Zealand industry could become part of global consolidation, with some loss of control over their use. The need for change was also backed by claimed benefits arising from cost savings; revenue increases; 'strategic gains' and rationalisation and other opportunities in Australia, totalling some NZ$310–332 million per year in additional pretax earnings, to be achieved in the third full year after the merger. Cost savings of NZ$120 million, mainly in overhead expenses, were to come from elimination of duplicated activities. Revenue increases of $NZ70 million were to flow from the better integration of manufacturing, marketing and distribution. The value of 'strategy gains' was to come from *harnessing synergies between different parts of the industry, providing fresh strategic impetus and broadening options to exploit new market, technology and biotech opportunities'* (from Fonterra press release). Given the uncertainty of this source of gain, the benefit was given as NZ$82–104 million per year. Fourth, a conservative estimate of the size of gains from further rationalisation and expansion of the Australian interests was put at NZ$38 million. On a different basis, some merger supporters also claimed that the creation of Fonterra would enable postmerger export earnings to grow from about NZ$8 billion to NZ$30 billion after ten years (by 2010), although this particular claim was not part of the official business case in support of the merger.

The merger proposal to achieve these claimed benefits was developed and sent to the dairy farmers in February 2001 and updated in April. In outline it involved the creation of a new cooperative business (Fonterra) that would subsume the assets of the NZ Dairy Board, the NZ Dairy Group and Kiwi Dairies, in effect amalgamating three of the five largest businesses in New Zealand. The dairy board would lose its statutory monopoly control over exports, with Fonterra assuming the rights to all foreign markets. It was also expected that the removal of the dairy board as the statutory body would facilitate World Trade Organisation negotiations to lower international trade barriers in which the New Zealand dairy industry has traditionally been attacked as a government-supported entity.

The merged operation would comprise two main business units:

NZ Milk Products (NZMP)[1]: the dairy companies' manufacturing and local market ingredients operations, and the ingredients business of the dairy board itself.

New Zealand Milk: the local market consumer operations of the NZ Group and Kiwi Dairies, plus the Dairy Board's consumer products division. It was expected that NZ Milk would purchase product at arm's length from NZMP.

The case against change

Arguments emerged against this proposal, including the power of the merged entity to blockade new entrants by withholding or restricting raw material supplies from them.

One obvious obstacle to the proposed move was the prospect that it would be opposed by the Commerce Commission, New Zealand's antitrust body. The commission is empowered by statute to assess the costs and benefits of all major takeovers and mergers and specifically to ensure that consumers are not exploited. The commission rebuffed a 1999 merger proposal along the lines of that being discussed here. In 1999, the commission found that the detriments of the merger exceeded the benefits and there was no evidence that either the public or the dairy farmers would be better off under a merged industry. The merger would in effect give one business control of more than 90 per cent of the domestic raw milk flow in the country, well above any measure of market dominance, and with the obvious consequence for higher domestic milk prices and producer surpluses. In 2000, McKinsey & Co. also put industry leaders on notice that a single entity would be better than two competing dairy cooperatives only if the risk of monopoly inefficiency were countered. Otherwise, the annual net benefit from having two contesting businesses was NZ$300 million. The same point was reinforced by a cabinet minister likely to be heavily involved in the issue:

> There are very good reasons why governments legislate against monopolies . . . with a monopoly processor, farmers would in effect have to accept the claims of managers that they are efficient. — Hon Jim Sutton, Minister of Agriculture and Forestry.

Government officials at the time were also strongly opposed to the merger, and in particular any attempt to bypass the Commerce Commission. The following extract summarises the advice to the cabinet:[2]

> Officials consider it likely that the evolution of two or more strong export-focussed co-operatives operating under a regulatory environment subject to the full provisions of the Commerce Act and other relevant commercial law could provide greater long-term gains than the proposed merger'

The reasons put forward by the officials were:

- Two or more companies will compete on the basis of two or more different business strategies. The spread of strategies should lessen the risk to the earnings of farmers and the nation.
- Having two or more competing companies is more likely to encourage innovation and best practice in production, marketing and exporting.
- Having two or more competing companies is likely to result in greater disciplines on the industry as a whole to be efficient. Over the long run, this should result in better earnings for farmers, lower prices for consumers and increased export earnings.

Others criticised the merger case on the basis that the cooperative form of organisation — one in which only the dairy farmers can be shareholders — was not suited to an international business with strong growth plans. It was seen as problematic as to whether enough commercial capital could be raised to fund rapid growth. The growth plan to boost export revenues to NZ$30 billion by 2010 would require rapid expansion in overseas markets with some additional risks attached. The single dominant provider model was also challenged on the grounds that it would hide inefficiency and chronic underperformance. One alternative suggestion was that a conventional limited company structure be formed with shares that could be traded in the normal way.

A final criticism was that the single business model being proposed would have no real incentive to innovate, particularly in the downstream product-market arena. The main incentive of the model was to encourage more milk to be produced at the farms, the lowest-margin part of the value chain.

The issue

In early 2001, a group of seven leading dairy industry executives had developed their second merger proposal for their industry, one that would in effect give a single company dominance in the industry. The outline of the proposal had already been sent to the farmers involved. An earlier and not dissimilar proposal in 1999 had been rebuffed by the Commerce Commission as being against the interests of consumers and not clearly in the interests of dairy farmers. The question now was how to proceed with this latest proposal to drastically change the structure of New Zealand's main export industry. Apart from any other consideration, the executives knew that they had to get the support of at least 75 per cent of 14 500 dairy farmers who would in effect own the new co-operative.

Discussion question

1. What strategies could be used to gather enough support from the dairy farmers?

End notes

1. NZ Milk Products was later renamed Fonterra Ingredients. We have retained the original name in use at the time of the merger discussions.
2. *The Independent* 2001, 11 April.

Disclaimer

This case study has been prepared by Paul Knott and Bob Hamilton of the Department of Management, University of Canterbury, from publicly available information. Although Fonterra Co-operative Group Limited has reviewed this case study, and has consented to its release, Fonterra makes no representations or warranties (express or implied) about the accuracy of any fact or statement in this case study, and accepts no responsibility for the information contained in the document. Any opinions expressed in this case study are those of the authors and are not those of Fonterra. This case study does not necessarily contain all relevant information and is not a complete statement or analysis of all the material facts and considerations. The information in this case study should therefore not be relied on for any purpose and should be used only as a basis for class discussion.

Southcorp Limited: winemaker's winding road

By Tatiana Zalan, The University of Melbourne

On 13 January 2005, Foster's Group, a leading Australian alcoholic beverages company, announced the purchase of an 18.8 per cent interest in Southcorp Limited, a major Australian wine producer, from Southcorp's largest shareholder, Reline Investments Pty Ltd, the Oatley family's investment vehicle. On 17 January 2005, Foster's revealed that it intended to launch a hostile takeover bid for the remaining Southcorp shares at a price of $4.17 per share in cash. The sale price, agreed with Reline Investments, was extended to all Southcorp shareholders and valued 100 per cent of the shares in Southcorp at $3.1 billion[1].

Frank Swan, chairman of Foster's, commented[2]:

> The acquisition of Southcorp is an excellent strategic fit. It will enhance Foster's long-term global growth prospects and deliver significant benefits to shareholders of both companies.

Foster's president and CEO, Trevor O'Hoy was also optimistic about the acquisition[3]:

> The combination of Foster's and Southcorp will transform the global wine industry and significantly enhance Australia's competitive position on the global stage. It will create an enhanced platform for growth and deliver long-term benefits to shareholders, employees, customers and consumers of the combined company. The breadth and quality of our two highly complementary wine portfolios — including brands such as Penfolds, Wolf Blass, Rosemount and Beringer — will position Foster's at the forefront of the global premium wine industry. Foster's will become the leading provider of premium Australian wine to customers and consumers in Australia, the US and the UK, with sales of over A$2.6 billion equating to around 39 million cases of wine annually.

The news of the takeover hardly took anyone by surprise: in recent years Southcorp's performance had been lacklustre and its share price tumbling (see exhibit 1 for Southcorp's historical financials and exhibit 2 for share price data). Regardless of the outcome of Foster's bid, it was clear that it was only a matter of time before Southcorp's premium brands would fall into the hands of another, more powerful industry player. Many observers pondered the strategic evolution of Southcorp, once a diversified industrial company and an aggressive acquirer itself, which became a single-purpose wine business and eventually an acquisition target.

Southcorp's strategic evolution

Early history

Southcorp began as a single-business brewer in 1888, when the South Australian Brewing, Malting, Wine and Spirits company was established in Adelaide, the capital of South Australia. Over the years, the company developed into a vertically integrated operation with brewing interests, wine and spirits wholesaling, retailing interests and hotel operations. Throughout the late 1970s and early 1980s brewing remained the company's primary activity. For more than 100 years, South Australian Brewing Holdings (SABH), as it became known, dominated the South Australian beer market, comfortably cashing up on the positional advantage. However, the strategy of the company was beginning to change in the mid-1980s in response to environmental and competitive threats. Beer production had peaked by 1981, and SABH's management realised that continued expansion opportunities would be limited within South Australia and would prove to be difficult beyond its borders.

During 1981–87, SABH grew through acquisitions and capital investment. At that time, the Australian capital markets were relatively inefficient, and many corporations, including SABH, were exploiting these capital market imperfections by increasing their earnings-per-share through successive acquisitions, and were rewarded by the stock market for growth. SABH's acquisitions in often unrelated businesses were largely opportunistic, debt funded and backed by cashflows from brewing operations. At that time, SABH had no idea of how to invest the cashflow from its core business into new activities and settled into the role of equity investor. Its portfolio read like a *Who's Who* of Adelaide business, including FH Faulding (22 per cent), Cooper & Sons Limited (26 per cent), Elders IXL (9 per cent) and CC Bottlers (20 per cent).[4] From 1985–87 (before the market crash), the value of this portfolio had grown from $157 million to $485 million, representing 67 per cent of SABH's total assets. In 1984, SABH also entered into the wine industry through a friendly takeover of one of Australia's oldest winemaking enter-prises B Seppelt & Sons Limited, who were on the edge of bankruptcy. This acquisition was not regarded as a serious entry into the industry but rather reflected a corporate fashion trend to own a winery.

The beer wars of the mid-1980s saw the emergence of Carlton United Breweries (CUB, which later became part of Foster's Group) and Bond Brewing as national brewers, both attempting to enter South Australia. Although SABH held almost 80 per cent of the local market share, beer volumes fell substantially, and so did the contribution of beer to the company's profits: although in 1981, brewing accounted for as much as 86 per cent of the business, in 1985, its contribution was reduced to 41 per cent.

Ross Wilson's era

In 1987 the 39-year old Ross Wilson, a former special projects officer at J Gadsden (acquired by SABH in 1986) who eventually went on to manage SABH's packaging division, became SABH's managing director. At that time, SABH was a strange hybrid with a near monopoly over the local brewing industry but not much else beyond Gadsden Packaging and minority investments in Elders, Pacific Dunlop and Coca-Cola Bottlers. In the next seven years, Ross transformed the conservative company. First, he made the timely decision to divest the share portfolio for $268 million ahead of the stock market crash in 1987, which left SABH cashed up for further growth. Second, he set the context for adopting a strategy to diversify the once provincial brewer into a substantial industrial company strong enough to withstand the emergence of the two national brewers. The essence of the strategy was to set up three core businesses in food and beverages, packaging, and household appliances — businesses that could achieve sustained market leadership in all products and services (being number one or two or else leaving the industry) — could either be grown locally and taken offshore or had a competitive edge to trade internationally from Australia. Consistent with this strategy, during the late 1980s and early 1990s, SABH made several acquisitions in packaging, wine, water heaters and appliances, turning packaging into a major contributor to the company's earnings.

Third, Ross changed SABH's purely domestic focus. For almost 100 years, SABH, as had many other traditional manufacturers, considered exports as a thankless and risky affair, and simply a way to get rid of surplus production that could not be sold locally. Ross forced executives to regard exports as the key to the company's success rather than a sideline. By the 1990s, with a market capitalisation of 1.01 billion and annual profit growth of 40 per cent during

1984–89, SABH was positioned as the seventeenth-largest company in Australia. Ross was viewed as having mapped out clear strategies and having made tough decisions on crucial matters such as debt, acquisitions and restruc-turing. He also introduced (in 1988) a new control system by tying executive remuneration to performance of their unit and the group as a whole. This system was believed to prevent managers from becoming too 'parochial'. Hopes of the business community for the company's international expansion plans ran high.

Southcorp's serious entry into the wine industry was the acquisition, in 1990, of Penfolds for $423 million. Penfolds, one of the finest Australian wine companies and the owner of the iconic Penfolds Grange, became part of the SABH's beverage and food division, adding such well-known labels as Kaiser Stuhl, Wynns Coonawarra Estate, Seaview, Killawarra, Tollana and Lindemans to its portfolio. Penfolds was an expensive acquisition (16 times earnings before interest and tax), and there were speculations that this move was more of an attempt to bail out a member of the Adelaide community. Buying Penfolds gave SABH the largest share, 32 per cent, of the domestic market, shared with Orlando Wyndham (20 per cent), Mildara (11–12 per cent) and Thomas Hardy (11–12 per cent).

The company's growth in the early 1990s stalled, in part because of the recession after the 1987 market crash. Since the late 1980s, SABH was actively looking for oppor-tunities to expand its brewing operations and implement its strategy of becoming either number one or two in the beer business nationally. In 1992, Ross developed plans to become part of an international brewing business and put forward a merger proposal to Foster's. The proposal was rejected because of Foster's concerns that the merger offered minimal synergies and did not fit its plans to become a single purpose international brewer. SABH even-tually sold its brewing, malting and hotel assets to Lion Nathan for $225 million.

The acquisition of the number two US hot water company Mor-Flo in July 1992 further compounded SABH's problems. The investment community responded to the acquisition by driving the share price down, assessing Ross' performance as less than glowing: he paid too much for some assets, lost a key canning contract with CUB and made some wrong decisions on packaging investments (see exhibit 3: Southcorp's performance in 1987–1994). Confronted with strong opposition, Wilson left in early 1994. The new managing director, Graham Kraehe, came in December 1994 from Pacific BBA to head Southcorp Holdings (the name was changed from SABH in 1993, after the disposal of the brewing assets).

Graham Kraehe's leadership

Although Graham had a formidable reputation for turning companies around, he had a tough job ahead of him. The packaging and water heaters groups had lost some major accounts, partly because of apparent personal friction between senior executives and major customers. The appliances group was involved in a price and warranty war with its competitors. The water heater business in the United States was losing money. The packaging business did not have any exposure to critical growth sectors of the industry.[5]

Graham continued the strategy of growth through acquisitions but took steps to divest noncore businesses and actively manage the portfolio. Southcorp focused on businesses with strong competitive advantages in brands, technology, scale and market position that could be expanded overseas, either through exports or foreign direct investment. The essence of the corporate strategy was, to some extent, a continuation of Ross Wilson's approach: to gain a number one or two position in each of the businesses in the company's portfolio or leave the industry. Despite these measures, by 1995 Southcorp's stock had reached an all time low of $2.80. Some critics argued that Southcorp was suffering a capital markets distrust of conglomerates along with other Australian diversified industrials.[6] Speculation was ripe that Foster's eyed Southcorp as a possible acquisition target.

In 1996–97, Graham regained the equity market confidence with remarkable rapidity, reflecting Southcorp's consolidation and refocusing its core businesses, with acquisitions designed to improve existing synergies. Southcorp's wine group strengthened its position as a global supplier of premium wines. Additionally, the purchase of Mildara Blass by Foster's at 30 times its earnings forced the market to rerate wine companies. The appliance group had grown and enjoyed a more successful 1997 year, helped by growing demand because of improvements in housing starts and the lower Australian dollar. The packaging group expanded operations in Australia and Asia, and was positioning itself in areas with stronger growth prospects. In 1996, a new advertising campaign 'Southcorp — the name behind the brands' was launched to use and further strengthen Southcorp's corporate image.

Nonetheless, many in the investment community believed that the most desirable course for the company was to slim down. In response, Graham contended that the stock offered investors an ideal group of businesses in terms of their exposure to cyclical and noncyclical elements of the domestic economy as well as geographical diversification and participation in wine.[7]

I don't see us as a conglomerate because we only have three businesses. Some conglomerates have 13 businesses and it is hard to know what they are doing. That really isn't the case with us. By having such diversification we reduce our exposure to various elements.

In response to shareholders' questions about the benefits of Southcorp's diversified structure with three businesses, the 1997 annual report stated the following[8]:

> Our approach to the Company's management is supported by international studies which have concluded that there is no statistical difference in total shareholder return between well managed diversified and non-diversified companies.
>
> We believe a well managed diversified company can create value for shareholders through an active program to maximise cross-business synergies, such as global communication system incorporating 3000 electronic mail users and a data network which is enabling the roll-out of common system across all Southcorp businesses. Other initiatives include group wide common purchasing projects and the transfer of best practice across the Corporation. These activities and a number of people initiatives [...] are facilitated by Corporate management.

Graham also worked hard at redefining the incentive system for senior managers, so that their performance was measured against the performance of each division and business within each division. The measure used was superior earnings growth, where the term 'superior' meant 'greater than average' growth in that industry. In addition to the divisions' monthly operational board meetings with the managing director, Southcorp's senior management met biannually to share ideas, network and communicate organisational objectives. In 1999, Southcorp organised an innovation conference, which encouraged idea generation. There was also a graduate recruitment program in place that ran at both the corporate and division levels, which included a two-year rotation throughout the company. Although there was no formal staff movement between divisions or corporate centre, vacant positions were advertised internally, which had resulted in movements over the years.

By the late 1990s, Southcorp Limited (which changed its name to more accurately reflect an active approach to corporate strategy) had three business units: packaging, water heating and wine. The EVA analysis, which was introduced by Graham in 1997–98, clearly indicated that while the wine and water heating divisions were value creators, the appliances and refrigeration units destroyed economic value. The whitegoods business, known for its Chef, Dishlex and Hoover brands, was sold to Email

Limited in early 1999, generating $145 million in cash after restructuring costs and write-down of assets. The heating and cooling business in Adelaide was sold to ILEC Investment Pty Ltd in July 1999, which completed Southcorp's exit from the appliances business. In each of the remaining businesses, Southcorp was number one or two in the Australian market, which provided strong cash-flow to support international growth initiatives, particularly in wine.

In 2000, SAP was implemented across the organisation, which was a key platform for moving toward integration of businesses. This initiative was intended to prepare the company for e-commerce, which was expected to include supply chain management, infrastructure and distribution improvements, and help to focus on cost reductions, such as moving from 20 payroll systems to one. An e-commerce group was established at the corporate level to provide leadership and knowledge transfer across divisions.

Southcorp's transformation

In 2000, Graham Kraehe retired from Southcorp and Tom Park, the executive general manager of Southcorp's wine division, took over. Tom had enjoyed a successful international career, including a 12-year tenure with Kraft Foods International. In 2001 Southcorp was trading on a price/earnings ratio of 14.7 times, which stood at a large discount to the All Industrials average of approximately 20 times. The media commented[9]:

> The market will be looking for more than visionary prose from Mr Park. It wants details about his strategy for delivering the Southcorp promise of creating the leading global branded wine company. It also wants reassurance the days of lacklustre returns are behind the company.

Southcorp's divestiture program continued. Unable to achieve a dominant position in the packaging business, in 2000, Southcorp sold the Australasian and Pacific assets for $800 million to Visy Industries, a major Australian paper and packaging company. The US packaging business was divested in management buyback in February 2001, for $175 million.

Feeling the pressure to deliver on its stated strategy of becoming a global player in wine, in the early 2000s, Southcorp was on the lookout for a suitable acquisition target, primarily in the United States. Failing to acquire Beringer Wine Estates (acquired by Foster's) and Kendall-Jackson, in early 2001, Southcorp merged with Rosemount Wine Estates, a premium Australian wine company owned by the Oatley family. Some commentators argued that the $1.5 billion acquisition was, in effect, a reverse takeover

of Southcorp by Rosemount, made possible because of Southcorp's inferior performance. Tom Park believed that the merger was entirely consistent with Southcorp's vision of becoming the leading branded wine company and provided a good strategic fit. The merger lifted Southcorp's market capitalisation to $4 billion, gave access to premium wine brands and created the world's largest premium-branded wine company. It improved what became known in the wine industry as 'The Southcorp model': a business based on a wide, although primarily Australia-based, portfolio of premium brands distributed through its international distribution network.

Tom's brief tenure effectively ended with the merger, and Keith Lambert of Rosemount assumed leadership of the merged company. The acquisition was share-based, so the Oatley family (of which Keith was part) became the largest shareholders of Southcorp. Keith continued the divestiture program. Southcorp's very profitable water heating business (which had 75 per cent of the market in Australia and New Zealand and 25 per cent of the market in the United States) and Goyen Valve Controls were eventually sold, and the once diversified industrial company became a single-purpose wine business. With the divestment of the cashflow-generating packaging and water heating businesses, raising funds in equity markets could be problematic and expensive, unless the company could develop a winning global wine strategy for its high-growth, high-risk wine business and demonstrate solid financial performance.

Southcorp's wine business

Throughout the 1990s, Southcorp's wine business had maintained leadership in the domestic market and led the restructuring of the wine industry through rapid consolidation. Both Ross Wilson and Graham Kraehe had been instrumental in moving the wine business from being a very strong national player to becoming a global business. Starting in 1993, the value of the wine business began to be fully realised. Premium and super-premium wine companies were added to its portfolio (e.g. Devil's Lair and Coldstream), and a $500 million injection of capital over five years boosted Southcorp's grape-growing capacity and modernised its winemaking facilities. Under new management, intensive cost-cutting measures were initiated: wineries had been merged, employees retrenched, stock levels trimmed and earning before interest and tax-to-sales margins lifted. Export-driven strategies were complemented, in the late 1990s, with investment through joint ventures in France, Moldova and California.

Southcorp achieved considerable success in establishing its brands and building its own distribution network in international markets. Much of this success was attributed to its flagship brand Penfolds Grange, which was acclaimed the best wine of the year in 1995 by the influential American magazine *Wine Spectator*, while the 1995 vintage Grange was named as one of the top 12 wines of the century. Lindemans, Southcorp's second brand with global potential, also received much acclaim. By the early 2000s, Southcorp became one of the top ten wine companies in the world, with 50 per cent of its production exported.

Southcorp Wines' formidable export success throughout the 1990s failed, however, to translate into superior financial performance in the late 1990s-early 2000s. Before Tom Park assuming leadership, return on capital in wine fell to 10 per cent (compared with the 15 per cent of major competitors).[10] Although the division was still the largest wine company in Australia, it was small compared with other alcoholic beverages companies and was considered inefficient and too diversified by international investors.[11] The merger with Rosemount, commitment to becoming a pure wine company and subsequent adoption of the Rosemount model had a positive effect on the share price. Rosemount had a truly impressive performance record: in the four years to 2001, it had compound revenue growth of almost 40 per cent, a return on capital of 30 per cent and a margin of 29 per cent.

According to the new CEO Keith Lambert, Southcorp's problems included a production-driven culture, an inability to track the success and failure of wine products and brands, the slow release of wine to the market and the inefficient use of capital. Costs associated with implementing the SAP computer system, resulting in supply chain inefficiencies, and Olympic sponsorship expenses exacerbated the situation.[12] Keith's first priorities were the introduction of a market-driven approach and implementing a materials requirement plan in Southcorp Wines, cutting staff numbers and finalising a joint venture agreement with Robert Mondavi, a premium Californian wine producer. Keith predicted initial synergies of $20 million, which in time would translate into $50 million to $100 million a year. Analysts, however, were less optimistic, arguing that the cultures of the two companies were too different and the problems with Southcorp too deep to expect smooth integration.

Keith showed unrelenting commitment to improving the merged company's performance but some of his actions proved more controversial. One was the inability (or perhaps unwillingness) to hold on to key Southcorp staff. Most of Southcorp's winemakers and viticulturalists were either retrenched or left the company (they were replaced by the Rosemount staff and fresh college graduates). Many of Southcorp's marketing executives in Australia, the UK and the United States also departed within a year of the merger. Rosemount distributors were given preference and those of Southcorp terminated. The results were devastating, particularly in the United States, where brands were squeezed because shelf space lacked. Therefore, the very popular Lindemans Bin 65, which had been growing at a double-digit rate in the United States in the 1990s, fell into single-digit growth and eventually declined into negative rates. The application of the Rosemount marketing approach to the Southcorp business model had a particularly disastrous effect. Rosemount had built its success on offering drinkable wines at relatively low prices, and there were questions in the trade whether the Rosemount style of wines contained residual sugar to make wines soft and more palatable (made possible because of Rosemount's microoxygenation technology, which made reds ready for the market within one year).[13] Some of the releases of cheaper Penfolds reds received poor reviews, and many observers called tinkering with a label such as Penfolds shortsighted.[14] Discounting ultrapremium St Michael and John Riddoch did further damage to the prestige of Southcorp's brands.

Large supermarket chains were major beneficiaries of this volume-driven approach: in 2001, supermarkets accounted for 29 per cent of Southcorp's business; a year later, it was 42 per cent. In the UK and Australia (where retail chains Coles and Woolworths controlled 50 per cent of the liquor market) supermarket chains pushed Lambert for bigger discounts. In the UK, for example, in 2002, Southcorp reduced its selling price to retailers by 30 per cent (compared with 2001's price). In a well-publicised move, UK supermarket Tesco returned a major shipment back to Southcorp because a promotional deal did not work out. The rest of the industry — Foster's, Orlando Wyndham and BRL Hardy — had no option but to follow Keith's price discounting (refer to exhibit 4 for wine market shares in Australia). The situation was exacerbated by record domestic vintages in Australia and the United States, which led to oversupply of grapes and, therefore, availability of cheap and mid-range wines in Southcorp's major international markets. The deteriorating global economic environment, industrywide consolidation and changes in consumer preferences added to Southcorp's problems. As a result, its profits and share price fell substantially, and Keith was compelled to issue profit warnings and write down inventory. In February 2003, the board forced Keith to resign, and John Ballard, a retired snackfood and retailing executive, was appointed the new CEO shortly afterwards. In September 2003, Southcorp announced more than $900 million in trading losses and write-downs, the tenth-largest loss in Australian corporate history, made worse by the problems plaguing the industry in general: profitless export growth (because of the rising Australian dollar) and the grape oversupply.

John was quick to announce what he termed Project Veraison, a program aimed at turning the company around.[15] He and his senior management team were credited with restoring investor confidence during his short tenure at the helm of Southcorp. Yet even John's enthusiasm could hardly protect Southcorp from losing its independent status: the media were speculating on which was to become the new corporate parent for Southcorp — Allied Domecq, Diageo or perhaps Foster's.

Foster's: the new corporate parent?

The strategic evolution of Foster's was somewhat similar to that of Southcorp and indeed many other diversified industrials in Australia. What eventually became a diversified alcoholic beverages company began in 1888 as a small lager brewer in Victoria. The brewery grew through amalgamation (in 1907, Foster's and five other Melbourne brewers amalgamated to form Carlton and United Breweries, or CUB), expansion of national reach and acquisition of major competitors. Its technological, brand-building and distribution capabilities combined with economies of scale were major factors in CUB establishing a marketing approach built around national brands and becoming an export success.

In 1983, CUB was acquired by Elders IXL, a highly diversified pastoral, trading and finance company. Elders' high gearing eventually led to the breakup and disposal of all its businesses except for the brewing interest, which in 1990 was renamed Foster's Brewing Group. After a period of extensive diversification by Elders, in the early 1990s, Foster's was labouring under more than $2 billion in debt and gearing levels in excess of 300 per cent. After a near-death experience and a massive sale of noncore assets, Foster's transformed itself from being a sprawling conglomerate with $15.4 billion of assets in finance, brewing, agribusiness and entrepreneurial investment businesses to a predominantly brewing group with assets of $7.4 billion. By the late 1990s, CUB was still the lowest-cost producer in the Australian brewing industry, controlling more than 56 per cent of the domestic market share (with Lion Nathan controlling 41 per cent). Its domestic strategy had been based on product innovations linked to consumer preferences, product quality, technical pre-eminence and national brand identity, first with Victoria Bitter, and subsequently with Foster's Light Ice and Carlton Cold.

Throughout the 1990s, CUB was highly successful in the domestic market, showing double-digit earnings growth for many consecutive years despite the declining volumes,
and developed an equally successful exporting business. By contrast, its international beer strategy based on foreign direct investment had failed to meet expectations: in 1990–2000, Foster's lost more than $250 million from its overseas operations in the UK, Canada and Asia. During those years, it poured the cashflow from its high-return domestic operations into acquisitions and joint ventures in foreign markets and then disposed of them to invest into more (usually unsuccessful) operations in the hope of sustaining revenue growth. It eventually sold off all UK and Canadian operations, while Foster's Asian operations (which comprised breweries in India, Vietnam and China) broke even in 2001 for the first time.

Foster's diversification into wine — in 1996, it purchased Mildara Blass, a premium Australian wine producer, for $482 million — was triggered by declining beer volumes in the domestic market and lack of success in its international beer strategy. At that time, Mildara Blass commanded 9 per cent of the bottled wine market, 25–30 per cent of the premium bottled wine market, 55 per cent of the sparkling wine market and about 6 per cent of the Australian export market, and was one of the most profitable wine producers in Australia. Despite being a profitable company, Mildara Blass' return on capital employed (ROCE; 8 per cent in 1996 lifted to 13 per cent in 2000) was considerably below the 16 per cent ROCE hurdle established by the corporate centre. The inability to achieve higher returns from the traditional wine business, at least in the short term, was the reason behind Mildara Blass' diversification into wine clubs with the acquisition of Cellarmaster's and into wine services. Opportunities to grow in the highly concentrated domestic market were, however, limited. The business expanded rapidly between 1998 and 2001 through acquisitions of traditional wine producers, wine clubs and contract services businesses in Europe, Japan and the United States and investments in vineyards and joint ventures in California and Chile. Mildara Blass' international strategy was focused on developing premium brands, improving margins, delivering capital efficiency and gaining better access to distribution. Foster's management contended to be the only major wine producer in the world that could lay claim to being market leaders in wine trade, wine clubs and wine services.[16] The sale of noncore parts of the business, including Australian Leisure and Hospitality Group and the Lensworth property division in 2003–04, marked Foster's shift to being a pure multibeverage organisation.

Mildara Blass' most important international acquisition occurred in 2000 with the purchase of Beringer Wine Estates, a premium Californian producer, for $2.6 billion, which created one of the largest premium winemakers in the world and firmly shifted the balance of Foster's assets from beer to wine. The wine business (renamed Beringer Blass Wine Estates) struggled in the early to mid-2000s: the wine clubs and services businesses were poor performers,[17] and there were significant integration problems with Beringer Blass Wine Estates. On balance, the wine business in Foster's portfolio proved to be a substantial value destroyer.[18]

When commenting on the takeover bid for Southcorp, Foster's CEO Trevor O'Hoy stated[19]:

> Our decision to proceed with this transaction has been made in the context of increasingly favourable industry trends, and greater confidence in the outlook for the North American wine market and New World wine markets generally.

Many industry observers, however, doubted the optimistic assessment of these trends and their implications for firm strategies in the industry, which had been undergoing dramatic structural change.

Trends in the global wine industry

One of the most pervasive trends was the consolidation of wine suppliers through domestic and crossborder mergers and acquisitions (see exhibit 5). Traditionally, the worldwide wine industry, estimated at more than US$100 billion (2003–04, retail), was very fragmented. There were more than a million wine companies around the world and none controlled more than 1 per cent of retail sales, with the top ten players commanding 11 per cent of global market share (based on volume). Industry consolidation was driven by a range of factors, including the capital-intensive nature of the industry and the consequent need to achieve economies of scale, a consolidating retail base, an increased interest in branded wines from both consumers and retailers, the threat of a global wine surplus which could put a pressure on margins, and the fear by the New World producers (such as Australia, Argentina, the United States and New Zealand) of retaliation by Old World countries (such as France, Italy and Spain). Consolidation of retailers, and, therefore, an increase in market power was particularly often cited by CEOs of alcoholic beverages companies and many analysts as a major driver of wine industry consolidation.

Two factors were believed crucial to competitive success in the wine industry: differentiation of the product offering and access to distribution. In the struggle to differentiate their products, wine producers adopted two

main approaches: labelling by region or terroir (as in the Old World) and branding (adopted primarily in the New World). It was unclear which approach was proving to be more successful or profitable. On the one hand, labelling by region had the advantage of imparting a sense of place, authenticity and even mystique. Branded wine, on the other hand, was a starting point for inexperienced consumers and had the prospect of creating customer loyalty and, therefore, higher sales volumes and profit margins. Access to distribution was a significant entry barrier in most international markets, which many wine firms tried to overcome through mergers and acquisitions. According to *Wine Spectator*, an influential US magazine[20]:

> Today, the problem isn't making fine wine. There is plenty of talent available. The problem now is selling fine wine … distribution, you see, is the real problem … we're seeing wine diversity slowly being strangled.

Not all industry observers believed in the espoused virtues of global scale and scope in the wine industry. Thus, on analysing the industry in depth, Michael Roberto of Harvard Business School made the following conclusion[21]:

> First, the size of the scale and scope economies appear to be modest in this industry. […] production economies are limited, sales force economies are questionable, and the geographic diversification of risk may be more effectively achieved by shareholders rather than wine producers. Second, institutional contexts in various nations are quite rigid, i.e., the French regulatory regime is not changing very quickly, nor is it likely to do so. In short, two sets of factors affect global industry structure: economic factors and institutional/contextual factors. While economic factors may be a catalyst for consolidation, contextual factors may be quite rigid and, therefore, may be constraining the trend toward consolidation in some regions of the world.

He then commented on the competitive strategies of alcoholic beverages firms who were driving industry consolidation, using Foster's as an example:

> The alcoholic beverages producers moving into the wine business have been quite explicit about the fact that they see premium wine as their next growth engine, given flat sales in their core businesses. Foster's Group provides the best example of this strategy. They have declared a vision of becoming 'a global wine company with a leading presence in every premium wine market worldwide'. In their 2001 annual report, the company actually

has a headline that reads 'Beer=Returns', while a second headline reads 'Wine=Growth'. In short, the companies are quite clear that they are deriving cash flow from the mature, but highly profitable, beer business; then, they are using that cash flow to subsidise a growth strategy in the wine business. This raises an important question: does this cross-subsidisation strategy enhance shareholder value? […] Thus, the only way that this corporate strategy adds value for shareholders is if the beer and wine businesses are somehow more valuable together than apart, i.e. if there are sizeable economies of scope. […] The economies appear to be mainly in the distribution area. Even then those economies seem to be limited to negotiating power, because there are serious questions about whether firms can consolidate the physical distribution of beer, wine and spirits without compromising product quality.

Other observers were equally sceptical about the globalisation potential of what appeared to be a collection of local industries, mainly because the structures of specific country markets varied considerably: the European Union had strong appellation control; the UK market was dominated by retailers' private labels; and the US market had an archaic three-tier distribution system, a remnant of the prohibition law in the 1930s. The geographical indication systems in France, Switzerland, Italy, Portugal, Spain and Greece were highly prescriptive and incorporated a tightly regimented series of laws and regulations that described the steps that must be followed from the moment of vine planting through to the bottling, labelling and selling of wines. Another big obstacle to globalisation was the parochialism of consumers in wine-producing countries: in France, for example, imports commanded less than 5 per cent of the market and the situation in Australia was no different. As a result of these differing market structures, the wine industry — contrary to the claims made by many executives and the media — did not have real global brands (with the exception of high-end champagnes).

These trends raised the question whether the proposed takeover, which would create the largest wine company to rival global leaders Pernod Ricard, Allied Domecq, Constellation and Diageo, made strategic sense. Foster's was yet to make a convincing case about the expected synergies between the two companies but some analysts and institutional shareholders had an uneasy feeling that the acquisition was a somewhat desperate attempt to make Fosters' struggling wine business work. They also wondered whether Southcorp's wine business would be better off under Foster's than it had ever been before.

Discussion questions

1. What corporate strategy did SABH pursue under Ross Wilson? Did it add value?
2. What corporate strategy did Graham Kraehe pursue and what was he trying to achieve? How effective was he as a corporate leader?
3. How was value created when Southcorp became a single-purpose wine firm?
4. What is your assessment of the takeover of Southcorp by Foster's? What is the strategic logic of this acquisition? And, more broadly, what do you think about the wine industry consolidation?
5. Will Foster's be a good corporate parent for Southcorp? How will value be added at the corporate level?

End notes

1. Foster's 2005, 'Foster's announces take over offer for Southcorp', company announcement, 17 January, accessed 17 October 2005, www.fosters.com.au/mediacentre/CB834B2977C0499093CD33 5492DF94E9.htm.
2. ibid.
3. ibid.
4. Wetherel, P 1988, 'The unsung brewer', Australian Business, 26 October, p. 94.
5. Fergusson, A 1996, 'Southcorp hits the comeback trail', BRW, 18 March, pp. 60–3.
6. Jemison, P 1995, 'Southcorp is losing some of its shine', Australian Financial Review, 5 May, p. 30.
7. Fergusson, op. cit.
8. Southcorp 1997, Annual report, chairman and CEO's review section.
9. Matterson, H 2001. 'Cometh the hour, focus is on Southcorp's man', The Australian, 12 February, p. 33.
10. ibid.
11. Ferguson, A 2001, 'Southcorp's magnum opus', Business Review Weekly, 11 May, pp. 56–9.
12. Matterson, H 2001, 'Vintage blend in wine merger', The Australian, 28 February, p. 20.
13. Ryan, C 2003, 'Blood on the vine', Australian Financial Review, 31 December, p. 11.
14. ibid.
15. Veraison is the French viticulture term which reflects the transformation process of grapes to realise their full potential.
16. Foster's 2000, Annual report, CEO questions and answers.
17. Business Review Weekly 2005, 'Foster's big gamble', 27 January – 2 February, pp. 13–17.
18. Kerin, P. 2005, 'Doing what comes naturally', Business Review Weekly, 27 January – 2 February, p. 10.
19. Foster's 2005, op. cit.
20. Wine Spectator 2001, October, cited in Roberto, MA 2003, 'The changing structure of the global wine industry', International Business and Economics Research Journal, vol. 2, no. 9, pp. 1–14.
21. Roberto, op. cit.

Exhibit 1: Southcorp's historical financials, 1995–2004

(in $ thousands)	1995	1996	1997	1998	1999	2000	2001	2002	2003	2004
Total sales	2360968	2549236	2555557	2735294	2807942	2595097	2492580	1999975	1104852	1062193
Operating profit (before income tax)	187048	189831	209103	235438	270226	267901	265971	368806	−941212	36744
Total assets	2383403	2720839	2840809	3092786	3163373	3418896	4390830	3747018	2656698	2463972
Shareholders' equity	1180972	1227546	1385756	1498748	1368619	1483662	2056256	2257711	1237554	1288574
Earnings per share (cents)°	20.4	20.6	22.8	25.5	29.0	32.9	32.3	42.2	−124.2	6.2
Return on equity	5.50	10.12	9.77	9.60	1.62	13.82	10.46	13.85	−74.57	3.59
Issue price/earning ratio	27.39	18.65	22.94	22.47	149.82	14.93	25.48	10.88	−2.18	69.08
Southcorp's businesses										
Assets										
Beverages (and food from 1987)									N/A	N/A
Packaging	735288	908404	996660	1069027	1084662	1133084			N/A	N/A
Wine	815011	871395	971192	1188185	1389339	1606873	3319772	3455494	N/A	N/A
Water heater						468968	580839		N/A	N/A
Appliances	763051	739794	727426	729786	545608				N/A	N/A
International									N/A	N/A
Dairy									N/A	N/A
Total segment	2313350	2519593	2695278	2986998	3019609	3208925	3906611	3455494	N/A	N/A
Unallocated items	70053	201246	145531	105788	143764	209971	490219		N/A	N/A
Total assets	2383403	2720839	2840809	3092786	3163373	3418896	4390830	3455494	N/A	N/A
Operating profit (before income tax)										
Beverages (and food from 1987)									N/A	N/A
Packaging	114847	132113	130463	117855	121035	102329	118518		N/A	N/A
Wine	68526	90047	106250	114189	137249	145506	158696	250480	N/A	N/A
Water heater						85632	76682	34181	N/A	N/A
Appliances	51632	37280	37736	62125	68325				N/A	N/A
International									N/A	N/A
Dairy									N/A	N/A
Segment total	235005	259440	274449	294169	326609	333467	353896	284661	N/A	N/A
Unallocated items/divestments	−11394	−8285	−8414	−8119	−10385	−4780	3135	149063	N/A	N/A
Total profit	223611	251155	266035	286050	316224	328687	357031	433724	N/A	N/A

Source: Worldscope

Exhibit 2: Southcorp's share price data

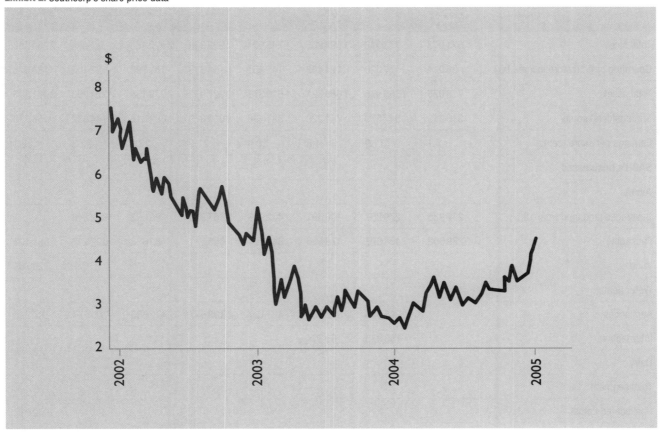

Source: Bloomberg, cited in *Business Review Weekly*, 27 January–2 February, 2005, p. 14

Exhibit 3: Southcorp's financials 1987–1994

(in $ thousands)	1987	1988	1989	1990	1991	1992	1993	1994
Total sales	571 073	773 948	1 538 905	1 745 924	1 933 966	2 022 455	N/A	2 254 288
Operating profit (before income tax)	36 014	77 620	124 463	145 451	164 318	183 892	192 402	186 576
Total assets	718 076	1 368 976	1 668 321	1 620 373	2 027 912	2 039 154	2 324 293	2 071 505
Shareholders' equity	310 219	547 579	754 220	831 496	1 019 679	1 062 816	1 146 832	1 156 379
Earnings per share (cents)°	7.1	11.9	21.8	20.9	21.9	22.3	22.3	22.1
SABH's businesses								
Assets								
Beverages (and food from 1987)	272 935	279 257	406 691	402 956	887 373	890 053	912 846	
Packaging	229 003	454 997	476 566	648 594	605 371	582 632	622 248	681 497
Wine								720 701
Water heater								
Appliances		270 045	347 408	457 127	493 547	472 686	705 374	590 295
International		150 933	165 304					
Dairy								
Total segment								
Unallocated items								79 012
Total assets	501 938	1 155 232	1 395 969	1 508 677	1 986 291	1 945 371	2 240 468	2 071 505
Operating profit (before income tax)								
Beverages (and food from 1987)	34 996	44 780	51 987	50 894	67 917	75 728	74 986	2 778
Packaging	23 629	39 021	66 995	89 897	97 316	97 431	104 363	113 117
Wine								61 834
Water heater								
Appliances		5 026	41 920	69 838	60 236	63 618	58 154	46 725
International		3 077	10 732					
Dairy	−856							
Segment total								
Unallocated items/divestments								−8 242
Total profit	57 769	91 904	171 634	210 629	225 469	236 777	237 503	216 212

Source: Southcorp's annual reports and Worldscope

Exhibit 4: Company shares of still light grape wine, Australia, 2002

Company	Market share
Southcorp Limited	25 per cent
Foster's Group	23 per cent
BRL Hardy	15 per cent
Orlando-Wyndham Group	12.5 per cent
McGuigan Simeon Wines	3.3 per cent
McWilliams Wines	2.3 per cent
Others	18.9 per cent

Source: Euromonitor, based on trade press (*Australian Liquor Retailer, Liquor Week, National Liquor Retailer*), company research, trade interviews, *Euromonitor* estimates. Still wines exclude sparkling wines and fortifieds.

Exhibit 5: Crossborder mergers and acquisitions in the wine industry

Acquirer	Year	Target	Consideration
Allied Domecq (UK)	2001	GH Mumm & Cie and Champagne Perrier Jouet (France)	€575 million
	2001	Montana Group (New Zealand)	NZ$1 billion
	2001	Buena Vista Winery (United States)	US$85.5 million
	2001	Bodegas y Vinedos and Vinedos y Bodegas (Argentina)	US$42.9 million
	2002	Bodegas y Bebidas S.A. (Spain)	US$42.9 million
	2004	Gray Farrell (United States)	N/A
Diageo (UK)	2001	Seagram, 62 per cent (with Pernod-Ricard)	£3.7 billion
	2004	Chalone Wine Group (United States)	US$260 million
Constellation (United)	2003/4	BRL Hardy (Australia)	US$1.14 billion
	2004	Ruffino (Italy)	US$80 million
	2004	Robert Mondavi	US$1.36 billion
Foster's (Australia)	2000	Windsor Vineyards (United States)	$50 million
	2000	Beringer Wine Estates (United States)	$2.6 billion
	2000	Castello di Gabbiano (Italy)	$35 million
	2001	Matua Wines, 51 per cent (NZ)	$9.3 million
	2001	Etude (United States)	N/A
	2001	International Wine Accessories (United States)	$35 million
Pernod Ricard (France)	2001	Seagram, 38 per cent (with Diageo)	£1.9 billion
	2005	Allied Domecq (in partnership with Fortune Brands)	US$17.8 billion

Source: Author, based on company reports and other public sources

Fonterra's international strategy: developing strategy in New Zealand's largest business

By Bob Hamilton and Paul Knott, College of Business and Economics, University of Canterbury, New Zealand

This case study is about developing an international growth strategy in a large New Zealand-owned business, operating in mainly commodity products in volatile markets. The case begins with a profile of the products and the international market situation. It sets out the performance objectives of the business and traces strategic moves in the first two years. The first two years' financial results are also included. This allows students to attempt to evaluate the early strategy of the new business and begin to shape a strategy for the next three to five years.

Introducing Fonterra

Fonterra is a large cooperatively owned dairy products business based in New Zealand. It was formed in June 2001 by the merger of the largest two remaining dairy processors, the NZ Dairy Group (NZDG) and Kiwi Dairies, and the New Zealand Dairy Board. The dairy board had been the sole exporter for New Zealand dairy products since 1923. NZDG and Kiwi were cooperatively owned dairy processors required to export through the dairy board. In the year 1999–2000, NZDG had sales of NZ$3.4 billion, processing 58 per cent of the raw milk supply in the country; Kiwi's sales were NZ$2.6 billion and it processed 30 per cent of the milk produced. The dairy board recorded export sales of NZ$7.65 billion, some 20 per cent of all New Zealand's exports. The dairy board was then New Zealand's largest business and one of its more successful, winning a coveted export award in 1999 for its success in marketing the country's huge surplus of dairy production to overseas markets. All rights to foreign market sales now reverted to

the new business, Fonterra. The creation of Fonterra was strongly supported by the dairy farmers, who are in effect the owners of the cooperative. It was also endorsed by the government of New Zealand, which decided to allow the merger in spite of the dominant position the merged business would have through its control of some 90 per cent of the raw-milk market in the country. The rationale for Fonterra's formation was that it would remove duplication of activities; allow better decisions to be made in the vital international markets; and provide the scale that was increasingly needed to operate effectively in these markets. The initial claim was that, through Fonterra, dairy exports would rise from about NZ$8 billion in 2001 to NZ$30 billion by 2010.

Products and markets

The growth ambitions of Fonterra are clearly well beyond what it could achieve in its home market, one that was defined by the company from the outset to be Australia and New Zealand. About 96 per cent of the raw milk produced in New Zealand is destined for export sales, and this makes up more than 20 per cent of the country's receipts from merchandise trade. Table C10.1 summarises the export slate of products and markets.

New Zealand is the largest exporter of casein products and is also moving ahead with a range of other sophisticated milk protein products that are highly specialised, high cost products with a myriad of potential uses.

The major dairy exporting nations are the European Union (EU) countries (where production is heavily subsidised), New Zealand and Australia. Along with smaller contributions from the United States and Canada, these three sources provide 90 per cent of the dairy-based product traded internationally. But only about 5 per cent of world production is actually traded internationally because, in contrast to New Zealand, most countries are either just self-sufficient or import. Therefore, the international market for dairy products is relatively small in comparison to world consumption.

In addition, 94 per cent of the world market has trade restrictions that allow Fonterra only very limited access. The EU and the United States in particular impose trade barriers and pay export subsidies that have a profound influence over the price of traded dairy products. Over the period 1986–2001, world dairy trade increased by one-third in real value terms, but it was flat or declining after 1995. World dairy prices fell in 1998 and 1999 especially for skim-milk powder and butter, reaching lows not seen for many years.

Table C10.1: Export products and markets

Product	Tonnes 1998–9	Tonnes 2002–3	Main destination markets
Whole-milk powder	347 308	502 376	Central & Sth America; SE Asia
Cheese	238 535	279 699	United States; Japan; EU countries
Butter	232 948	190 042	UK; EU countries
Skim-milk powder	172 611	218 156	Middle East
Casein products	86 653	116 915	USA; Japan; EU countries
Anhydrous milk fat	84 527	100 119	Not applicable

Source: data derived from NZ Official Yearbook, 2000, page 416; Fonterra

In the period 1994–1999, the total value of New Zealand dairy exports increased by 37 per cent and table C10.2 divides the main national markets into above- and below-average growth in this period. These national markets vary considerably in terms of relative economic and political stability. Arguably, less stable countries would include Russia, South America, South-East Asia and parts of the Middle East. In addition, as described above, only restricted access is available to some of the markets (EU countries, the United States). Under a free trade scenario, the prices obtainable by Fonterra on the international market would rise substantially, but currently such a scenario is a distant prospect at best.

Studies undertaken by the International Farm Comparison Network show that New Zealand farms have the lowest total costs per kg of milk solids produced. A few countries, including Australia, Bulgaria and Ukraine have only slightly higher total costs, but in many dairy-producing countries the production cost is more than double that in New Zealand (1996–97 data).

The global dairy industry has consolidated substantially in recent years. The main international companies are Nestlé (Switzerland), Kraft (United States), Parmalat (Italy) and Danone (France). At the time of its formation, Fonterra was the ninth largest in this league and so could not assume to have the scale on its own to dominate in this very competitive price-taking environment. Typical strategies employed by these firms in the 1990s included expansion into faster-growing developing country markets and seeking higher margins through value-added products.

Table C10.2: Faster- and slower-growing markets for NZ dairy exports 1994–99

Country	Above-average growth: NZ$m 1994	$m 1999	Country	Below-average growth: NZ$m 1994	$m 1999
United States	325	635	UK	383	281
Japan	254	388	Malaysia	218	245
Belgium	21	204	Mexico	199	195
Australia	114	185	Philippines	148	192
China	27	128	Taiwan	138	175
Thailand	75	117	Russia	97	130
Egypt	40	115	Venezuela	93	104
Sri Lanka	61	113	Germany	121	87
Saudi Arabia	74	113	Peru	87	86
Indonesia	54	84	Others	840	970
Vietnam	8	79			

Source: data derived from Statistics NZ

Fonterra's businesses

Fonterra operates through two distinct business units Fonterra Ingredients and New Zealand Milk (NZM). Fonterra Ingredients is the larger of the two in terms of revenue. It collects the raw milk from some 13 000 farms and processes it into a range of dairy ingredients for customers around the world (including Nestlé and Kraft) as well as supplying NZM. In 2002–03, its sales of 2.4 million tonnes were divided among the Americas (25 per cent), Asia (29 per cent), Oceania (21 per cent), and the rest of the world (25 per cent). While the bulk of the sales volume is represented by commodity dairy products, the business also supplies value-added ingredients including pharmaceutical lactose.

NZM is a fast-moving consumer goods business that supplies milk powders, cheese, liquid milks and yoghurts. It operates in 30 countries and manages a brand portfolio including Anchor, Anlene and Anmum. It has also been successfully pursuing opportunities in the food service sector. NZM accounted for 37 per cent of Fonterra's revenue in 2002–03.

By May 2002, Fonterra was manufacturing product at 29 sites in New Zealand, and 35 in other countries, with NZ$12 billion in total assets and 20 000 people around the world.

Research and development

Fonterra commits close to NZ$100 million to research and development (R&D) of both new products and improved processes, making it New Zealand's largest private sector investor in R&D. The expectation is that future growth and profitability will come increasingly from speciality hi-tech products with high value in both the local and exports markets. In 2002–03, some key initiatives were reported as follows:

- A joint venture with the University of Auckland to discover biologically active components in milk for application into new food ingredients, nutraceuticals and pharmaceuticals.
- A patent application for a process to improve the yield achieved in manufacturing cheese products.
- NZM's continuing focus on development and launch of new consumer products.
- Fonterra's biotechnology subsidiary, ViaLactia Biosciences, engaged in a number of projects aimed at long-term improvement of dairy production.
- A series of projects under the label JEDI aimed at improvements in productivity of the 'farm to customer' value chain through improved integration and logistics.

Paying the farmers

The creation of Fonterra was a bold move for the farmers who own it and for the New Zealand government, which allowed the merger despite serious concerns about the loss of competition, particularly in the domestic market for milk and derived products. The company must devise a strategy to remunerate the farmers because, as one commentator captured the sentiments of the farmers: 'Bloody hell, if this cooperative doesn't perform, farmers will leave in droves.' In other words, they would seek to sell their milk elsewhere (e.g. by founding new cooperatives) or even leave the dairy industry altogether.

Dairy farmers in New Zealand are paid by the cooperative they supply (and own in proportion to supply shares) and there have always been differences in the payout from each cooperative. The price to farmers is expressed as cents per kg of milk solids and reflects international commodity prices and the value of the New Zealand dollar, with a weaker currency generating a better nominal payout to the farmers. Recent prices are shown in table C10.3 and apply to the milking season ending 31 May for the year in question.

Fonterra's 2002 payout, from its first full year of operation, was supported by NZ$50 million paid out of reserves. A payout of 528 cents per kg would have allowed farmers to just break even for the year. When announcing the 2002 results, the company said that plunging overseas commodity markets had driven export prices for dairy products to 20-year lows, with world prices falling by 50 per cent between August 2001 and July 2002. In part, these price falls were driven by increased subsidies to dairy farmers in the United States and EU.

While Fonterra was drawing on reserves to support a payout of 533 cents per kg, one of the smaller dairy cooperatives that had refused to be part of the merger was paying 543 cents to its 282 farmer suppliers. Westland Milk Products, with about 3 per cent of the milk market, is located in the high rainfall area on the west coast of New Zealand's South Island. It produces milk powder, butter and casein from a modern factory that has just had a NZ$60 million upgrade. It is establishing its own international marketing network, after selling through Fonterra in 2002. The other remaining independent milk processing cooperative is Tatua Co-operative Dairy with just more than 1 per cent of the milk market. In 2002, Tatua paid its farmers 680 cents per kg of milk solids. Tatua operates a factory in the North Island producing nutritional ingredients such as casein, whey protein and lactoferrin. These are sold at premium prices to manufacturers of specialised nutritional and pharmaceutical products.

Year	1993	1994	1995	1996	1997	1998	1999	2000	2001	2002	2003
NZ Dairy Board payouts											
	325	290	300	360	318	300	325	335	460		
Total payouts (weighted average of all co-operatives)											
	366	332	340	399	363	342	358	378	501		
Fonterra payouts											
										533	**363**

Source: data derived from NZ Official Yearbooks; Livestock Improvement; Fonterra

Fonterra's initial strategic moves

The main early moves — as reported in the 2002 and 2003 annual reports — were as follows:

August 2001

Fonterra Ingredients signed an agreement with Dairy America, a marketing company representing the major US cooperatives, to export skim milk powder from the United States on commission using Fonterra Ingredients' marketing network, the biggest in the world.

December 2001

The purchase of the La Mesa and Eugenia businesses established Fonterra as the leading participant in Mexico's cheese market and number three in spreads. These businesses market a range of dairy products manufactured at three major sites across the country, both from local milk and imported dairy ingredients. Their major brands are La Mesa (cheese) and Eugenia and Delicia (spreads). The acquisition boosted New Zealand dairy sales in Mexico by more than NZ$200 million annually. Mexico, with a population of 99 million, is the second largest dairy market in Latin America after Brazil.

December 2001

Fonterra established a joint venture with Arla Foods AmbA, the largest dairy cooperative group in Europe, covering the UK and Europe. This brought Fonterra's Anchor brand together with Arla's Lurpak into one entity to improve their positioning in the declining, and so highly competitive, yellow fats market. The joint venture involved establishing a business responsible for marketing and distributing the brands in the UK, and developing new products for the yellow fats and spreads markets. The joint venture is 75 per cent Arla and 25 per cent Fonterra and is well placed to perform strongly in this difficult retail sector.

March 2002

Formally established an alliance with Nestlé to set up joint ventures in the dairy industry in North, Central and South America. The 50:50 alliance — Dairy Partners Americas — operates in all countries in the Americas and covers a range of branded consumer products, ingredients and milk processing. Joint ventures have now been established in Argentina, Brazil and Venezuela. The Americas represent an exciting opportunity and a challenge for Fonterra. In 2002, their combined dairy market was worth more than NZ$200 billion, of which Fonterra's share was less than 2 per cent.

March 2002

NZM entered the fast-growing Indian dairy market by establishing a joint venture with Britannia Industries Ltd based in Bangalore with an annual turnover of NZ$600 million. This joint venture will market processed cheese, butter, dairy whiteners, ghee and liquid milks. Britannia identified NZM as having the expertise and international marketing and product development experience needed to expand its dairy business rapidly. This alliance provided Fonterra with a strategic point of entry into a market of huge potential within the world's fourth-largest economy with a dairy market worth about NZ$50 billion per year.

March 2002

It established the first commercial production of milk protein concentrate in the United States (in New Mexico). This was done by extending the 50:50 DairiConcepts joint venture with Dairy Farmers of America to allow the expansion of the plant, which also produces infant formula and high-end cheese powders. This expansion was essential to meeting the needs of customers in the NAFTA agreement. Fonterra is said to have contributed its innovation capability and advanced R&D to the venture.

July 2002

It agreed with Bonlac Foods of Australia to merge the consumer food products operations of both companies in Australia and New Zealand. This created a strong, broadly based Australasian manufacturer and marketer, with a large portfolio of successful products and annual sales of more than NZ$2.3 billion. This significant merger in the 'home' market brought together the Mainland and Tip Top businesses in New Zealand with the Bonland, Peters and Browne businesses in Australia to create a strong growth platform. The merged business has a portfolio covering milk, ice-cream, cheese, butter, yoghurt, processed meats and convenience foods.

Future strategy

By May 2003, Fonterra was reporting its supply partnerships (including those with Bonlac, Dairy Farmers of America and Dairy Partners Americas) to be an integral part of its global business. Fonterra's payout for the year to 31 May 2003 was 363 cents per kg, a figure that was driven down by commodity price and exchange rate movements. Currency hedging reduced the immediate effect of the exchange rate, but no suitable hedging instruments were available for the commodity price. Meanwhile, the smaller cooperatives increased their payout differentials over Fonterra, with payments of 397 cents for Westland and 560 cents for Tatua. For purposes of comparison, the 2001 payouts were 500 cents for NZDG and Kiwi; 520 cents for Westland; and 550 cents for Tatua.

In September 2003, a new CEO, Andrew Ferrier, took up his post. He inherited the results of a strategic review undertaken during 2002, which sought to move the business strategy out five to 10 years into the future. It included analysis of trends in the international market and Fonterra's own strengths and expertise. The results of this review included a commitment to 13–15 per cent annual returns to its 13 000 farmer shareholders and a long-term strategy built on seven 'strategic themes'. These were:

1. lowest-cost supplier of commodity dairy products

2. leading price and inventory manager in the global commodity market

3. effective developer of dairy ingredients partnerships in selected markets

4. leading speciality milk components innovator and solutions provider

5. leading consumer nutritional milk marketer

6. leading dairy marketer to food service in key markets

7. develop integrated strategies for four key regional markets (China, eastern Europe, India and the economic grouping of Chile, Brazil and Argentina).

The challenge facing the new CEO and his team of executives was how to develop and implement these themes as a strategy capable of delivering the targeted financial performance. How should they proceed?

Discussion question

1. How should the CEO and team of executives develop the seven themes as a successful strategy?

Exhibit: Financial data

All figures refer to New Zealand dollars.

Consolidated profit and loss ($ million)

	Half-year to 31/11/01	Full year to 31/5/02	Half-year to 30/11/02	Full year to 31/5/03
Operating revenue	7034	**13924**	5980	**12474**
Operating expenses	4079	**8043**	4535	**8117**
Total payout to suppliers	2887	**5890**	1436	**4135**
Operating surplus (before interest and tax)	68	**(9)**	9	**222**
Taxation expense (credit)	(46)	**(22)**	9	**(62)**
Net surplus/(deficit)	22	**(31)**	18	**284**

Net surplus/(deficit) comprises:
    Parent interests
    Minority interests
	22	**(50)**
		19
			18	**257**
				27

Net surplus/(deficit)	22	**(31)**	18	**284**

Balance sheet ($ million)

	At 31/11/01	At 31/5/02	At 30/11/02	At 31/5/03
ASSETS				
Current				
Cash balance	497	**107**	245	**102**
Accounts receivable	1 822	**1 888**	1 867	**1 815**
Inventories	3 940	**3 554**	2 876	**2 751**
Other current	238	**223**	311	**182**
Noncurrent				
Property plant, equipment	3 681	**3 980**	3 961	**3 856**
Investments	528	**382**	348	**525**
Intangible assets	1 859	**1 587**	1 634	**1 499**
Other noncurrent	63	**79**	18	**16**
Total assets	12 618	**11 800**	11 260	**10 746**
LIABILITIES				
Current				
Borrowings	3 412	**3 024**	2 542	**1 771**
Accounts payable	1 127	**930**	1 220	**948**
Owing to suppliers	1 537	**1 015**	343	**375**
Other current	510	**207**	225	**124**
Noncurrent				
Term borrowings	443	**1 601**	2 027	**2 427**
Deferred taxation	271	**239**	115	**106**
Capital notes	200	**200**	286	**292**
Other noncurrent	–	**99**	71	**38**
Total liabilities	7 500	**7 315**	6 829	**6 081**
EQUITY				
Cooperative shares	3 644	**3 229**	3 216	**3 348**
Peak notes (See note 1)	1 115	**1 177**	1 152	**1 164**
Supply redemption rights (See note 2)	90	**67**	123	**188**
Reserves	1	**(307)**	(338)	**(185)**
Minority interests	268	**319**	278	**150**
TOTAL LIABILITIES + EQUITY	12 618	**11 800**	11 260	**10 746**

Statement of cash flows ($ million)

	Half-year to 31/11/01	Full year to 31/5/02	Half-year to 30/11/02	Full year to 31/5/03
Cash flow from operations				
Cash inflows	7 220	14 480	5 556	12 049
Cash outflows	(6 365)	(14 126)	(5 320)	(11 515)
Net cash flow — operations	855	354	236	534
Cash flow for investments				
Cash inflows	–	136	19	449
Cash outflows	(271)	(1 083)	(334)	(852)
Net cash flow — investments	(271)	(947)	(315)	(403)
Cash flows in financing				
Cash inflows	206	555	259	313
Cash outflows	(619)	(195)	(16)	(450)
Net cash flow — financing	(413)	360	243	(137)
Net increase (decrease) in cash held:	171	(233)	164	(6)
Opening cash balance	326	326	37	37
Effect of exchange rates on cash	–	(56)	(3)	(11)
Closing cash balances	497	37	198	20
Cash balances	497	107	245	102
Bank overdrafts (incl current borrowings)	–	(70)	(47)	(82)
Closing cash balances:	497	37	198	20
Reconciliation of net surplus to net cash flows from operations				
Net surplus/(deficit) from profit and loss	22	(31)	18	284
Adjustment for noncash items:				
Depreciation	211	440	215	535
Other noncash items	(5)	(51)	(115)	(83)
Movements in working capital	627	(408)	112	151
Items classified as investing and financing	–	404	6	(353)
Net cash flow from operating activities	855	354	236	534

Explanatory notes:

1. Each shareholder supplying milk to Fonterra in a season is required to hold a number of peak notes based on their milk supply during the season.
2. Issued to shareholders in exchange for shares required to be surrendered because the shareholder holds more shares than required in a season (based on actual supply of milk by that shareholder). Each supply redemption right may be exchanged for one fair value share when required due to increased production.

Flying Kiwi Promotions Ltd: a kiwi flies

By Mark Dibben, Lincoln University
Phil Garrett, Flying Kiwi Promotions Ltd

Figure C11.1: Celebrating the record with the volunteers at Chertsey. Front right to left: Phil Garrett, his wife and Glenn Hayward.

A kiwi 'flies' — almost

As if by some hidden cue, 30 people climb stiffly off a coach, while others get out of cars parked along the verge of a deserted road just outside Chertsey in Southern Canterbury on the South Island of New Zealand, one Monday morning in July 2005. It is 6.30 am, still dark. After a few minutes, the event manager motions everybody to gather around and introduces 'some key people', the two clerks of course, the chief timekeeper, who has brought the only officially certified timing equipment in New Zealand, the official delegate from the world governing body of motorcycle sport, the FIM (flown in the previous evening from Switzerland), the chief marshal and the chief engineer. Then he briefs everybody on the 'potentially very dangerous' events that are to take place and what happens should there be an accident. Finally, he calls out preassigned roles, such as wind speed measurement and marshalling, until every one of the volunteers knows his or her role, has signed the liability and insurance waiver forms and has picked up a bright orange safety jacket. A queue forms in front of a catering van that, along with an ambulance and a fire engine, has just arrived. Cars begin heading the short distance south along the base camp road to an intersection. They drive in different directions along a road that runs, dead straight, east–west. One of the cars

tows a trailer, on which sits a strange-looking, silver, cigar-shaped contraption: a 'world land speed record vehicle'.

Two of the cars head along the deserted road a short way to a point at which a nail has been hammered into the tarmac and circled with fluorescent orange paint. At the chief timekeeper's direction, two assistants begin unravelling wire from a dusty old drum, by ramming a broken broom handle through its centre and walking with it along the verge, the drum spinning until it runs out of wire. Surprised, they trudge back. After much discussion, they take another drum of wire and begin unrolling it from where they had left the first. They repeat the process until all the cable available runs to another point along the road at which a second nail has been hammered into the tarmac: the measured kilometre. The wires are connected up and small optical measuring beacons placed so that they line up pointing at each other from either side of the road parallel with the nails, and are connected up to small batteries.

More wires are run from one set of beacons at the designated 'entry' to a clock placed on a wooden picnic table behind the wire fence that runs alongside the verge, separating it from the trees beyond. Two men sit down behind the picnic table. One — the FIM delegate — places a large comb-bound block of timing sheets, specially prepared for this day, on the table, while the other — the chief timekeeper — fiddles with the clock, before going back over the fence to inspect the beacons and their battery. Another two people get into a small 4x4, head back to the other measuring beacons at the 'exit' of the kilometre, drive off the road into a field and park up.

A further group have by now driven east, stopping occasionally to let members off at prearranged locations. Each person carries a 'two-way radio,' a small, brand new anemometer and an air horn for scaring birds. The car they are travelling in reaches a bend in the road, stops and parks up, and the remainder of the occupants establish a 'turnaround point' for the record vehicle, two kilometres beyond the point at which the 4x4 sits in the field. While all this is happening at the east end, two kilometres beyond the picnic table to the west, a team of people have established a pits area, have unloaded the record vehicle from its trailer, have removed its fairing and are checking its brightly polished components.

At the base camp, the clerk of course steers his 'chase car' towards the intersection with the course road. Knowing the road is now closed, he ignores the 'Give Way' signs, turns left towards the pits area and roars off. He drives back and forth along the course, checking all is well with the people at either end and stopping at both sets of timing beacons to discuss progress. He radios back to base and guns the car to the west end. By the time the clerk of course — who was enjoying himself immensely until he looked at the fuel consumption readout on the course car's dashboard! — arrives back at the pits area, it is some two hours since the briefing, the wind is increasing and birds swoop over the fields. At base camp, the second clerk of course, who is in charge of all radio communications, uses a formal radio protocol to check that the course is safe and give the rider permission to start.

> Clerk of course — all stations. Course check please.
> Pits?
> Pits — okay
> Received. Chase car?
> Chase car — the course is clear.
> Received. Wind One?
> Wind One — okay. Wind speed is 1.6 metres per second.
> Received. Wind Two?
> Wind Two — okay. 1.5 metres per second.
> Received. Timing?
> Timing — okay.
> Received. Wind Three?

If the wind speed is greater than 2 metres per second, it is unsafe for the vehicle to run. After all stations have reported, the clerk of course declares:

> All stations, all stations. The course is open. No movement allowed.
> Clerk of course — pits.
> Pits — Go ahead.
> Is the rider and are all following vehicles ready?'
> Yes. All ready here.
> Thank you. The rider has permission to proceed.

The record vehicle, a 'one-off', purpose-built and highly tuned 1000cc Suzuki-engined motorcycle sidecar driven by Flying Kiwi director and first driver Phil Garrett, proceeds down the course, followed by the chase car, an ambulance and another van with mechanics on board. Once at the other end, they turn it around and Phil makes a return run. To break the world land speed record, two runs must be completed along the course in opposite directions within an hour, and the average time from both the 'out' and the 'return' run calculated to produce the ratified speed over the measured kilometre. Then it is the turn of the reserve driver Glenn Hayward.

It is now mid-morning, and Phil climbs back into the vehicle and makes a noticeably more rapid attempt. Phil clambers out of the vehicle and speaks to the FIM delegate on a two-way radio.

> How was that return run, Charles? — Over.
> Well, I timed it both directions with my watch and it's a record. Very fast — according to my timesheets

here, it must be well over 260 km/h average. But I cannot be sure. I cannot ratify it, because the clock did not start. Again. — Over.
> Thanks, Charles.

There is a long pause, before Phil is back on the radio.

> Everyone — Forget it. You'll have guessed from the radio traffic all morning the timing gear's not working. And it's not fixable quickly. I've not seen the official timing gear, obviously. But apparently the wire is broken somewhere. It's getting too windy now anyway. We'll have to come back tomorrow. Let's pack up and meet in Chertsey Hall in an hour. The locals have got some lunch for us. I really appreciate all your time and energy and that you've taken time off work to be here. But as you know, we've got the road from the council for the rest of the week and it's only our first day. It's not been a waste; we have learnt a lot. I'll talk to the timekeeper myself. We'll get all brand new wire for tomorrow in one length if possible. I'm sorry — I take full responsibility. The timing gear will be working tomorrow, I promise. But hey, the bike ran perfectly. And we did it with our first proper run.

He sighs.

> So there's no reason why we cannot do it again!

Discussion questions

1. Draw a schematised plan of the event, including the roads, pits, base camp and so on to help identify what aspects of the Flying Kiwi land speed record attempt required (a) operational planning, (b) control systems and (c) explicit organisational structure.

2. Broadly speaking, how would you go about taking this schematised drawing and making it into a reality?

3. What aspects of the project will have probably needed to be (a) hired in, (b) bought and (c) especially built?

4. Why might it have taken so much time after the initial briefing before the first record attempt run could take place?

5. Why did the clerk of course stop enjoying himself?

6. Has Flying Kiwi achieved (a) its overall mission and (b) its goals for the day?

7. What has gone wrong, what has gone right — and why do you suppose this is?

8. What implications might there be for the team from having to reconvene the next day?

9. As the director of Flying Kiwi, is Phil Garrett right to assume responsibility for what has happened, and why?

10. How long would it take you to go from the idea 'Let's break a world land speed record' to the reality of doing it? Days, months or years? How much might it cost, both monetarily and personally? What might be the implications of this?

How it started

Phil Garrett, an amateur sidecar racer who worked shifts at Placemakers in Christchurch, had just won the New Zealand South Island sidecar championship and taken his pit crew out to celebrate. As the evening progressed, his machine's top speed had risen in the telling. Someone had asked what the world land speed record was for sidecars. They had looked it up on the Internet, to discover that because of an FIM rule change, the world record stood at 222 km/h. The old record, set under old rules and therefore 'frozen', was 260 km/h. It had been set by Bob Burns, a New Zealander, not far from Christchurch in 1955. However, the New Zealand governing body, Motorcycling New Zealand, still recognised it as the official New Zealand record. 'I could beat 222! We could smash that. And we should be able to do more than 260 as well — something like 320 with a good engine.'

The idea stuck. A target of 320 km/h: the magic 200 m/h barrier. He searched the Internet, to discover that only about 150 people had ever broken it in land speed record attempts, in any sort of vehicle. 'All right then. I am going to beat that. How am I going to beat that?' He went to the FIM website (www.fim.ch) and downloaded the regulations. He discovered that apart from technical specifications of the machine, there was a requirement for a particular type of road, very straight and with a limited gradient. He had to find such a road and spent months searching land survey maps of New Zealand and found only one. As luck would have it, it happened to be only an hour's drive from his house. Now the idea seemed feasible.

With no experience of running a business of his own, Garrett soon realised he needed to separate the family's assets from the record attempt. In case anything did go wrong, he needed to protect his family. He bought a 'loss-attributable qualifying company' off the shelf, naming it Flying Kiwi Promotions Ltd. If it made a loss, he could set that loss against his personal tax allowance but still retain limited liability status. The company ethos would be the epitome of the never-give-up, Kiwi can-do attitude, and a sense of fun; the company's logo was a cartoon kiwi bird (the national icon of New Zealand) spinning its wheels. He covered his 4x4 with stickers with the name of the company, the expected speed and his mobile phone number. Having established the company, Phil needed to raise awareness money. He organised a website detailing everything about the project, with a supporters club people could join, plus displays of his racing sidecar at local motor shows and other public events, and the usual range of merchandise: posters, caps, T-shirts and jackets. He would ultimately give away more than 2500 posters.

The Flying Kiwi 320 Club would allow supporters to feel included, as well as raise some of the estimated NZ$250 000 the undertaking would require. For NZ$320, a member could 'buy' 1 km of the targeted 320 km/h and a sense of ownership of the event. In addition, members would receive posters, a certificate, a video, discount on merchandise, regular updates, their name on the website and in the supporter's chapter of a book being written about the record attempt and the chance to be involved in the running of the event itself, which would be closed to the public (primarily for safety reasons). The club would provide a unique opportunity to help make history and return a sporting record to Canterbury.

He received emails of support from as far away as the United States and the UK. Word spread quickly. Soon TV3, a New Zealand free-to-air broadcaster, had agreed to include Flying Kiwi on its Sunday afternoon sports program. Phil was always thinking how he could make the project work on television: he put cameras in the workshop to film everything that went on. Regular news spots followed and, in due course, TV3 would make an hour-long documentary.

Discussion questions

1. Visit the Flying Kiwi website at www.goflyingkiwi.co.nz. How important has Web-based marketing been for Flying Kiwi Promotions Ltd? What has been marketed?

2. What other methods has Phil Garrett used to raise awareness of Flying Kiwi? Do you consider this marketing strategy integral to the overall strategy of the company?

Gaining the resources — with no money to speak of

There was a danger in all this publicity. The more people who knew about it, the greater the chance somebody else would grab the idea and do it first. In motor racing terms, 320 km/h was well within the capability of many companies around the globe, including those in Formula 1 and the American IndyCar series, which annually design and build vehicles capable of similar speeds to stringent specifications and regulations. Flying Kiwi had to deliver and soon.

Phil needed more money than the 320 Club could provide, however. At one point, Flying Kiwi Promotions Ltd had NZ\$16 in the bank but NZ\$5000 in bills. He met with his bank manager, outlined his idea and asked whether the bank would sponsor the project by way of a short-term overdraft facility of NZ\$10 000 for four months. The interview was brief.

> How many of these bikes do you plan to make, Mr Garrett?
> One. It's a one-off.
> So why do people give you money then?!
> Well, because they want to.
> I'm sorry?
> Err, because they want to give me money.
> Oh, I see!

It was obvious he did not. Flying Kiwi Promotions Ltd never went overdrawn — it couldn't!

The problem of production was also recognised by others. He visited dozens of specialist motor parts companies and companies selling workshop equipment but with no money to spend he was always at a disadvantage. He could only talk his way into deals with possible suppliers to an extent. Other businesses were asking for similar components to build racing cars and powerboats and even other sorts of racing motorcycles, businesses that had a history and firm lines of credit, whose machines would be racing on New Zealand race circuits for years, giving their sponsors continued exposure for their support. His bike, on the other hand, would be a one-hit wonder.

Other problems also arose early on. The New Zealand motor racing industry is small when compared with Australia and particularly the UK and United States. There wasn't the depth of knowledge readily available to design and build a completely new machine; most were second hand, bought in from Europe at the end of their useful competitive life in that region. There also was not the ready cash available; motor sport in New Zealand was very much a shoestring affair. Phil was trying to build a unique world record-beating machine in the wrong country. Fortunately, Christchurch airport is home to a substantial aviation support industry, some of whose engineers happily got involved in the design work.

The engine is central to any motor vehicle. Phil briefly looked into the idea of using one from German manufacturer BMW, as a way of garnering substantial corporate backing. BMW had recently launched a new high-performance engine onto the market with its K1200S model and was seeking to move its brand image from manufacturer of rather staid motorcycles to one of technically advanced sports bikes. There was a risk in approaching a hi-tech company such as this, 'They could knock this bike together in an afternoon's smoko!' Nevertheless, he reasoned that the company might like to capitalise on their historical successes in sidecar racing during the 1950s, 1960s and 1970s to develop and promote both the new engine and their market position not only in New Zealand but elsewhere. The BMW New Zealand concessionaires were approached and the plan outlined but they never replied.

The Japanese manufacturer Suzuki was far more accommodating. Phil obtained an engine from Australia and Suzuki provided special tuning parts for free. New Zealand's market size problem was again highlighted, however, when it became clear these special parts were in very high demand and there was a limited supply. They were made overseas and there was not the overall bike sales volume in New Zealand to justify the investment necessary to support larger stocks. So although Suzuki offered all the engine support they possibly could, the most power available to Phil would be 180 bhp. Luckily, the design calculations predicted this state of tune was just enough to reach 320 km/h.

Another problem became apparent when Phil tried to procure materials, even to furnish the workshop. The New Zealand motor parts industry had supported previous 'mad ideas dreamt up in pubs'. However, businesses claimed they had been 'stung' by others in the past, giving materials for which they had never been paid. Everyone was wary of getting caught out. With no reputation of his own to work from, Phil was both up against other forms of motor sport in the competition for resources, and also the 'bad credit' reputation of others spooking the very businesses whose help he desperately needed.

The only way was to pay for everything before he took delivery. The 320 Club money, plus his own savings, made a start. He had a catchphrase: 'I haven't got the cash just now. When I do I'll come and pick it up.' While this stretched the business's limited funds, his reputation as one who actually paid *before* delivery grew so that businesses eventually recognised Flying Kiwi as legitimate, and relaxed. However, even when offered usual terms such as 30 days' credit, Phil refused, insisting wherever possible on paying in cash and upfront. The more this positive reputation grew, the more companies offered support, usually by giving products for free on a 'break the record and keep it' basis.

Six months from the scheduled attempt, Phil had written more than 200 sponsorship proposals to different companies. Often he visited the company first to discuss the project, so each was specifically tailored. As he grew more skilled at writing them they became shorter and more to the point. He emphasised the only thing he could, the kudos of a *world* land speed record that would reach 200 m/h. Some proposals sought cash support but most, such as the successful approach to American tools supplier Powerbuilt, suggested the company sponsor in materials — all the tool equipment for the project.

Every time anybody asked him how things were going, he would always say 'Really good!', or 'Excellent — having a great day today!' Even if this meant lying; he knew the response would always bring a smile, set a positive tone for the subsequent conversation, and go a long way to gaining support. He firmly believed in the adage 'in business, nothing succeeds like success'. Everywhere Phil went, he wore a Flying Kiwi shirt and hat and carried pictures of the technical drawings with him. He told everybody he met about the project, asking if they knew anyone who might help. Eventually, companies approached him unsolicited. It seemed a bush telegraph had started to operate in the industry: he would receive phone calls from companies he had never heard of, who just happened to have the very thing he then needed — and were happy to give him on the now customary 'get the record, keep the toys' terms.

Discussion questions

1. What do you make of Phil Garrett's meeting with his bank manager? What is the problem with the Flying Kiwi Promotions Ltd product? Why do people want to give money to Flying Kiwi?

2. Can you speculate about the possible reasons for BMW's lack of response? (A visit to www.bmw-motorrad.com may help.) How does this compare with Suzuki, and can you speculate why this might be the case? (Again Web research into Suzuki and its role in motor sport may be helpful.)

3. How would you assess Flying Kiwi Promotions Ltd's prospects for success given (a) an analysis of its competitive position in the motor sport industry and (b) an analysis of the New Zealand industry's technological position in comparison with other countries? (A visit to the websites of companies such as McLaren (www.mclaren.co.uk) may be helpful.)

4. How has Phil Garrett overcome the difficulties he faced in gaining the resources he needed?

Reaching the objective — setting goals, establishing a structure, and playing to the strengths of the people

The whole thing was beginning to take off. Phil Garrett found he could no longer work at Placemakers and devote enough time to Flying Kiwi. He negotiated leave of absence and a one-off payment as formal sponsorship. Phil now needed a clear idea of what was involved in achieving Flying Kiwi's mission. 'I hate doing things at the last minute and without a proper plan. It's altogether too random for me.' He searched the textbooks for a suitable model to base the business upon. He needed an organisation in which no-one was paid, everyone had specific jobs and the freedom to make decisions — so long as it didn't cost anything — and there was an inherent can-do culture. No-one was personally or legally responsible for anything except Phil but the goals could not be postponed, delayed or circumvented: they had to be met. With no template to work from, Phil devised 'an umbrella structure with me holding the umbrella'. He established six separate 'teams', totalling 28 people, comprising between two and 12 people each, responsible for build, design, administration, marketing and sponsorship, event management and engine development. Although a competent mechanic, and in spite of having already bought a suitable engine and having the parts necessary to tune it effectively, Phil gave the key job of rebuilding the engine to a local motorcycle dealership, the owner of which was a close personal friend, whose expertise he trusted. In return for their services, they were guaranteed a prominent — and free — advertising space on the bike.

In January 2005, Phil held the only formal meeting of the team leaders. He gave each six months to achieve their respective goals. Each team was responsible to him directly but had complete freedom and autonomy to deliver its goal by the set date in any way it wished. It did not matter if it set out on one course of action and then changed its mind, so long as the team's goal was met on time. If it needed anything, it should approach him directly; he would do his best to procure it somehow. As he remained in charge of advertising and sponsorship, rather than getting involved in the detail of specific aspects, he was now a general 'fixer', spending his time visiting companies: 'getting money and bits.' To this end, he found himself increasingly answerable to the team leaders for why things had not been done for *them*! Each team leader could approach any third party for assistance, so long as that third party understood there was no possibility of being paid unless personally agreed to by

Phil. He himself would be responsible for any mistakes; he would not hold any of his all-volunteer workforce to account. This, he reasoned, would engender an atmosphere of positive initiative with no fear of retribution. It would allow the creative thinking he needed to get around problems he could not yet envisage but knew would arise. Phil could not see how such a setup could work in any other organisation or with any paid group of people, but as time went on he was sure he had a winning structure.

Extensive use was made of knowledge and infrastructure in other organisations. Where necessary, he paid for services early on, such as NZ$10 000 for the design and build of 27 design prototypes and running 65 independent wind tunnel tests at Canterbury University engineering department. This eight-month research program provided many answers — and not just to aerodynamic problems. The findings also led to the specific engine power output required and the date for the attempts. The aerodynamicist forecast that the sidecar would be very sensitive to side wind. A search of weather records revealed the second week of July was historically the least windy week of the year in Chertsey. The date was set.

With only seven months left before the attempt, Phil increasingly needed a place away from the workshop, car and phone to discuss management issues with the event management team. With the help of a member of the 320 Club who worked there, a number of meetings were held in Lincoln University's commerce division. These meetings mainly consisted of brainstorming, 'worst-case scenario' planning, scoping out the health and life insurance requirements and costs, organising the road survey for the FIM, developing the safety plan for council approval, calculating how many volunteers would be needed on the day and the procedures and radio protocols that would be followed. By chance, the neighbour of another member of faculty in commerce was a highly respected motor sports manager. He was first approached informally by the two academics and, after some initial discussions, committed himself so fully that he eventually assumed the responsibility of clerk of course, driving the chase car during the attempts. A further source of assistance located through Lincoln was the 'Black Caps' New Zealand national cricket team's sports psychologist who worked at its training establishment based at the university. As well as providing input on preparing Phil for the psychological pressures involved in driving the bike on the day, he even secured a sponsorship deal with a local estate agent.

Of all the teams, the most fundamental was the build team. Phil picked 12 volunteers with sound mechanical knowledge, led by close friend and experienced motorcycle engineer Glenn Hayward, to work in groups most evenings and sometimes over the weekends to build the vehicle in accordance with the FIM technical regulations.

These dictated engine size, chassis dimensions, weight, safety systems and so on. Phil gave them six months and promised them beef stews! Some specialist components, such as the exhaust pipes, were subcontracted out but dates slipped by and the work schedule became more compressed because aspects of the build took longer than planned. People gave more of their time as they realised lives were at stake. They were committed to an ethos of quality, building — and rebuilding — the bike as if they themselves were to ride it.

The timeframe was reworked on countless occasions. Matters became more complicated as materials either turned up late or not at all, and had to be re-sourced. Every problem was unpacked and rethought, each aspect solved in sequence. Because of the wind requirements, the bike itself was 'reverse engineered'; they started with the right fairing and built the chassis to fit. Not surprisingly, the sidecar was only finally completed, its fairing painted and in place, the night before the attempts began. They would only really find out whether they had got it right when they made their first run at Chertsey.

Discussion questions

1. How did Phil Garrett overcome Flying Kiwi Promotions Ltd's lack of knowledge and resources in key areas?

2. How did Phil Garrett's role as director of Flying Kiwi Promotions Ltd develop over time? How does this compare to formal explanations of the role of directors as strategic thinkers, and with other businesses you know or have studied? What explanations can you give for any differences you observe?

3. How novel do you think Phil Garrett's organisational structure is as a means for achieving strategic and operational objectives? What might prevent it from being replicated in other organisations?

4. How important was planning in bringing the Flying Kiwi project to fruition? What might this say for the 'emergent' approach to strategy?

The record and its aftermath — Bonneville?

Phil Garrett had needed to break the record that very first morning. Every day spent at Chertsey cost $5000 in the hire of the emergency vehicles from the council, the chase car and its fuel, the bus to transport the volunteers, plus catering. The opportunity cost of two years' lost wages was NZ$150 000 but he had raised NZ$212 518 of sponsorship. Some of this was in cash from the 320 club and from a fund-raising evening. The 320 club had been invaluable, especially at the beginning when for example he had had to pay US$10 000 to the FIM just to apply formally to attempt the record. But most was in materials, components, workshop machinery and the like donated by companies who now all had their stickers on the bike. He had consequently broken even, more or less, getting the project to the starting line but Chertsey was a personal cost. Although he had set up Flying Kiwi Promotions Ltd to protect 'the family' from 'the project,' those 'lost wages' had meant using personal savings to supplement his wife's income to live day to day. This was getting serious. He rued his decision to allow the timekeeper to use the original timing wire. After lunch at the Chertsey Hall, at which the FIM delegate declared Flying Kiwi to be the best organised record attempt he had ever attended and everyone had at least tried to look pleased with the morning's work, Phil drove back to Christchurch to buy NZ$400 worth of new wire. But he sensed that the decision would cost him more than just money.

Tuesday, 12 July 2005, and the morning's weather forecast was not as good as Monday's. Thankfully, the whole crew had gone from having little or no experience of organising a motor sport event to seasoned pros in 24 hours. The two drivers had agreed they would take turns. Day two meant it was Glenn Hayward's turn to go first. Glenn had said he would do his run as a test and then hand the bike over to Phil but the weather was closing in. As the director of Flying Kiwi, Phil could justifiably have insisted on doing the first run himself but was happy to let his friend do it. After all, he reasoned, it was Glenn who had built the bike and had as much of a right to the record as he did.

Glenn got in and, after a moment's hesitation, went for it. Ten minutes later, the return run completed, he was the holder of the new world land speed record, at 272 km/h. The bike was prepared again, and Phil set off, knowing that with the record already in the bag, this was the last time the bike would ever be used. The weather 'window' was almost closed and they wouldn't be coming back. Apart from risking somebody getting hurt or damaging the bike, they couldn't afford to. Phil's average speed was 264 km/h, a New Zealand record.

Although they had broken the record, the bike had been designed to go much faster. This proved impossible because they needed a longer run-up to get it to its top speed than the Chertsey road could provide. Phil calculated that it had taken 15 000 hours of unpaid labour to build; it seemed a waste not to discover its true potential. Some weeks later, he announced that the bike would go to the salt flats at Bonneville in the United States. He soon changed his mind, however, because the regulations governing speed record attempts there (www.dlra.com) would require a different bike. This was 18 months' solid work, people were tired, the novelty had worn off and, even with more sponsorship

from Wynns Oils for the trip, he still would not be able to pay anybody. He had to make money himself to replenish family coffers and he had an incredibly patient wife to think about. Months spent working for a boss she hated, and then coming home to cook beef stew for a bunch of oil-stained hairy-backed blokes, before an evening alone in front of the telly was hardly a girl's idea of fun. He knew it was his turn to be the provider for a while. To this end Glenn, who had bought into the local Triumph motorcycle dealership, had arranged for Phil to take over his Wynns Oils sales agency, selling oil to garages and manufacturing plants in and around Christchurch.

Phil had a silent workshop filled with a redundant land speed record vehicle. Somehow, he had to get the bike off his property. He put it on display at various shows and malls and in the showrooms of companies who had sponsored the bike, just to get it out of the way. It was four years since Flying Kiwi Promotions Ltd had been founded, it had 'employed' more than 300 volunteers and had not made a dollar. Like many small companies, it was also 'asset rich, cash poor' and Phil seriously considered selling the bike, reasoning he would only keep it if he could turn it to good use for New Zealand. In the three months since they had broken the record, he had talked to clubs and schools as an 'inspirational speaker' but what he had hoped would be a replicable, long-term Flying Kiwi concept of pushing new frontiers, Kiwi ingenuity and being a 'good bastard' was well past its half-life. The world had seemingly moved on.

Discussion questions

1. How important do you think organisational learning and personal leadership were for Flying Kiwi Promotions Ltd? How do these relate to 'strategy'?
2. Did Phil Garrett's strategy for Flying Kiwi Promotions Ltd succeed? What factors affected this?
3. How might Phil Garrett be able to resolve his asset rich, cash poor situation? What should Phil do with Flying Kiwi Promotions Ltd now?

Glossary

absolute cost advantage: A superior cost position that is not related to the volume of product produced (p. 65)

absorptive capacity: A company's ability to identify, value, assimilate and use new knowledge (p. 117)

acquisitions: Purchases of existing businesses that become part of the purchasing company (p. 220)

adaptive cultures: Company cultures that are innovative and able to respond to change on the basis of giving middle management more responsibility (p. 308)

appropriability regimes: The mechanisms that a company can use to protect innovations from being copied by competitors (p. 150)

autonomy: The degree of freedom organisations have in pursuing their strategies (p. 394)

balanced scorecard: Evaluating strategies in terms of the financial, customer, internal business process, and innovation and learning perspectives (p. 369)

barriers to entry: Factors that make it costly for companies to enter an industry (p. 65)

benchmarking: The process of measuring a company against the products, practices and services of some of its most efficient global competitors (p. 122)

best industrial practice: Guidelines, or metrics, that define a best practice within a specific industry, for example defects per million parts for manufacturing companies (p. 121)

bottom-up change: A change process that is designed and implemented with the participation of managers and employees at several levels of the company (p. 354)

brand loyalty: Buyers' willingness to stay with a particular company's product for the brand and not the superior product attributes (p. 65)

broad differentiators: Companies that compete in a range of niche markets using a differentiation strategy (p. 168)

bureaucratic costs: The costs of running a company that tend to increase as the company grows, reflecting coordination costs (as more management is required) and the costs of inefficiencies that occur (p. 268)

business-level strategy: The plan of action that a company follows to gain a competitive advantage over other companies (p. 164)

business organisations: Organisations that sell their services and products in a competitive market environment (p. 393)

business process: Any company activity that is vital to delivering goods or services to customers quickly or promotes high quality or low costs (p. 337)

capabilities: A company's capacity to productively deploy resources, usually in combination, to bring about a desired end (p. 109)

capacity control strategies: Alternative ways of managing capacity that do not lead to price-based competition (p. 185)

cash cows: Businesses that have a high relative market share and are in low-growth industries (p. 216)

centralisation: When decisions are made at the upper levels of the organisational hierarchy (p. 273)

centrality: How central a department or division is to resource transfers or cross-divisional or cross-departmental activities (p. 350)

chaining: Gaining cost advantages from running multiple operations to outperform competitors on price (p. 176)

coercion: A situation in which an organisation, for example the government, can force its 'clients' to comply with its policies (p. 394)

cognitive biases: The decision-making errors that arise from how information is processed (p. 21)

company infrastructure: Structures, including the organisational structure, control systems and culture, that support all other value chain activities (p. 108)

competitive advantage: When a company is able to outperform its rivals, as commonly measured by the attainment of profits above the industry norm (p. 96)

complementary resources: Those resources that a company needs to access to be able to commercialise successfully and earn profits from a technology (p. 150)

complementors: Companies that supply complementary products or services that increase the inherent value of the focal product (p. 72)

consumer-oriented: Focusing on the consumer, in terms of who they are, what they seek and how their needs are satisfied (p. 36)

control: Using information gained through strategy evaluation to influence the behaviour of those implementing the strategy (by rewarding or punishing employees, for example) (p. 364)

core competencies: The central set of knowledge in a company that, when applied, allows the company to create superior value than can competitors (p. 217)

corporate development: Decisions concerned with which business opportunities a company should pursue and how it should pursue these opportunities, including how to exit from inappropriate businesses (p. 214)

corporate governance: The mechanisms used within an organisation to determine its strategic direction and ensure that it is consistent with the desires of key stakeholders (p. 32)

corporate-level strategy: Determining the businesses in which a company should be involved (p. 196)

cost-leadership strategy: Strategy based on having the lowest cost structure of all the companies in an industry (p. 8)

credible commitment: A commitment by two companies to an alliance in the form of a contract or expenditure that demonstrates their obligation to the alliance (p. 204)

critical success factors: Factors that invariably lead to the success of a strategy (p. 381)

customer defection rate: The percentage of customers who move to a competitor each year (p. 138)

customer perspective: How customers evaluate company products (p. 370)

customer response time: The time that it takes for a good to be delivered or a service to be performed (p. 105)

decentralisation: When decisions are made at different levels within the organisational hierarchy (p. 273)

defenders: Organisations that protect their current market by trying to increase efficiency (p. 409)

devil's advocacy: The critical analysis of a decision by considering all the potential downsides of the decision (p. 24)

dialectic inquiry: The process of debating two opposing approaches to an issue, so as to generate a single solution from the opposing views (p. 24)

differentiation strategy: Strategy based on achieving a competitive advantage through selling a unique product or service (p. 8)

distinctive competency: A unique strength that allows a company to achieve superior efficiency, quality, innovation or responsiveness to customers. It may be the skill to manage resources better than competitors do or the possession of a uniquely valuable resource and the ability to exploit that resource effectively. (p. 108)

diversification: The process by which an organisation operates in more than one business simultaneously (p. 8)

divestment strategy: Strategy of selling a business before an industry enters a severe decline (p. 188)

division of labour: Subdivision of tasks allowing employees to specialise in one subtask (p. 131)

division of work: How a company allocates people and resources to different tasks (p. 267)

dogs: Businesses that have a low relative market share and are in low-growth industries (p. 216)

dominant designs: Those versions of a product that dominate the industry and become a standard such that other versions struggle to compete in the industry (p. 150)

economic bottom line: The impact of organisational performance on the company's economic viability (p. 375)

economies of scale: Cost advantages that are obtained by spreading fixed costs over a greater number of units produced (p. 66)

economies of scope: The benefits that are derived when more than one business unit in the company can use the operations of a component of the value chain (p. 208)

emergent strategy: Strategy that evolves (that is, it is not planned) in an organisation on the basis of actions that the organisation takes in reaction to internal and external pressures (p. 15)

environmental bottom line: The impact of organisational performance on the natural environment (p. 375)

escalating commitment: The commitment of further resources, even when a project is failing, simply as a result of the resources that have already been committed (p. 22)

escalation: Continued use of a failed strategy (p. 378)

evaluation system design: Stipulation of matters that are important in evaluating the performance of strategies (p. 366)

ex ante **limits to competition:** Limited competition for resources before the company establishes a competitive advantage based on those resources (p. 113)

exit barriers: Factors that make it costly for companies to leave an industry (p. 69)

experience curve: The curve showing the reduction in unit cost for each additional unit produced, in which the efficiencies come from experience gained in producing the product (p. 132)

factor conditions: The factors of production, such as skilled labour and infrastructure, that a nation has to support an industry (p. 231)

financial perspective: How shareholders evaluate the performances of a company (p. 369)

first-mover disadvantages: The problems and costs that a company must bear as a result of being the first to enter an international market (p. 245)

flexible manufacturing: A system that allows a company to both attain economies of scale and customise the product somewhat (p. 136)

focus strategy: Strategy based on operating in a single segment of the market (p. 8)

foreign operations department: The department that organises the distribution and sales of goods produced in the company's home base for sales in other countries (p. 322)

fragmented industry: An industry that contains many small and medium-sized companies (p. 176)

franchising: Selling a brand name, systems and other aspects of a company's operations to others to be used in the same way, creating another business of the same type operating in the same way (p. 177)

full integration: Producing all of one input of the company entirely within the company, or disposing of all product output through company-owned channels (p. 198)

functional structure: An organisational structure in which employees are grouped into departments according to their functional role (p. 274)

global area structure: A structure in which all value creation activities are duplicated by a foreign division established in every country or region in which the company operates (p. 321)

global matrix structure: A structure in which a company has simultaneous product- and region-based lines of reporting (p. 324)

global product group structure: A structure in which the distribution and sales of a product to different countries are controlled at a product and then a country level (p. 323)

global web: The dispersal of different stages of a company's value chain around the world (p. 235)

goal: An objective that an organisation seeks to achieve at some point in the future (p. 38)

governance mechanisms: Mechanisms used within an organisation to ensure the direction set by top management matches that of key stakeholders (p. 42)

groupthink: A process in which all members of a group overlook important elements of information or contradictory views (p. 21)

harvest strategy: Strategy of maximising returns in an industry by eliminating investment and waiting for operations to become unprofitable (p. 188)

horizontal division of work: How tasks and functions are divided up within a company across the same level (p. 274)

horizontal specialisation: Division and allocation of functions or tasks among managers (p. 267)

human resources: Activities including employee recruitment, compensation, reward and training policies and programs (p. 108)

hypercompetition: Rapidly developing industries that do not achieve periods of maturity, so that patterns of competition are constantly changing (p. 81)

illusion of control: A belief that one can deal effectively with any events that arise from implementing a decision (p. 23)

illusive expectations: Managerial thinking that continuation with a failed strategy will lead to its success (p. 379)

impression management: Actions that managers adopt to hide their failures (p. 379)

incremental innovations: Innovations that build on existing technologies to improve them in some way (p. 148)

industry: A group of companies that offer products or services that are the same or close substitutes for each other (p. 64)

industry lifecycle model: A stylised model of how industries go through stages (p. 81)

inert cultures: Company cultures that do not change easily and are cautious and conservative (p. 308)

information systems: The hardware and software systems for inventory management, sales tracking, product pricing, product sales, customer service and other strategic and tactical functions of the company (p. 108)

innovation and learning perspective: The sustainability of a company over a long period of time (p. 371)

integration: How a company coordinates people and functions to accomplish organisational tasks (p. 267)

intended strategy: Planned strategy for the future that an organisation develops on the basis of a series of analyses (p. 15)

internal business process perspective: How processes related to cycle time, delivery speed, safety ratings and level of employee skills and knowledge, for example, match strategic requirements (p. 370)

internal governance: How top management manages the company (p. 207)

internal new venturing: Starting a new business from scratch (p. 220)

joint venture: A business that involves two or more companies operating in a cooperative manner (p. 222)

just-in-time inventory systems: The delivery of supplies just as they are needed for the production process (p. 140)

leadership strategy: Strategy of capturing the market share of companies leaving the industry (p. 187)

learning: Modifying a course of action after finding out about a strategy's outcomes and the processes that led to those outcomes (p. 364)

learning effects: The efficiencies that arise from employees learning, through repetition, to complete their tasks more efficiently (p. 132)

local demand conditions: The nature and level of demand for the industry's product or service (p. 231)

location economies: The economies that arise from either lowering the company's cost structure or creating a point of differentiation as a result of undertaking activities in the most conducive location in the world (p. 234)

logical incrementalism: A mode of strategic planning where organisations work with fixed goals and change their actions depending on the changes in the environment (p. 403)

macroenvironment: The broader environment that can affect a company through political, legal, technological, economic, sociocultural and demographic forces (p. 73)

major goals: Organisationwide goals for the medium term to long term (p. 5)

management by objectives: A system of measuring the performance of employees against established goals (p. 304)

managerialism: Importation of tools and practices of business organisations into public organisations (p. 397)

market development: The process of finding new markets for a company's products (p. 183)

market discipline: Instituting a process that ensures any supplies purchased through an alliance are comparable in price and quality with what is available in the market (p. 205)

market penetration: The process of actively seeking to increase a company's market share (p. 182)

market segmentation: The process of subdividing the market into customer groups based on customer preferences (p. 164)

marketing and sales: The activities necessary for the positioning, promotion and sale of the company's products and services (p. 107)

marketing strategy: A company's approach to its product pricing, promotion, design and distribution (or placement) (p. 138)

mass customisation: Flexible manufacturing that allows a company to both attain economies of scale and customise the product to meet consumer preferences (p. 136)

materials management: Activities that control the transmission of physical materials through the value chain (p. 108)

matrix structure: An organisational structure in which employees are grouped by both function and product orientation, resulting in two sets of reporting relationships (p. 280)

means–ends hierarchy: A series of actions to be undertaken to accomplish a goal (p. 366)

minimum efficient scale: The minimum plant size or production level that will allow a company to achieve significant economies of scale (p. 131)

mission: An organisation's unique purpose and the scope of its activities (p. 5)

modular products: Products for which the parts or components fit together in the same way over versions of the product (p. 137)

monitoring: Checking continually whether a strategy that is being implemented is on the right track (p. 363)

multidivisional structure: An organisational structure in which employees are grouped into divisions on the basis of common product markets or geographic markets (p. 277)

mutual dependence: When two or more companies rely on each other to act in each other's best interests, so the companies both benefit in the long term (p. 199)

network economics: The economic effects of a product's value being determined by the existence of complementary products or services (p. 85)

network structure: A structure in which a company links (horizontally or vertically) with other companies as an alternative to owning the business of those companies (p. 328)

new-venture division: A division that develops and trials new products and services away from existing operations (p. 327)

niche strategy: Strategy of focusing on a potentially profitable niche in an otherwise declining industry (p. 188)

nongovernmental organisation: Nonprofit group that combines resource mobilisation, information provision and activism to advocate for changes in certain areas (p. 50)

nonprice competition: When companies compete on nonprice dimensions (p. 179)

nonsubstitutability: How difficult it is to find a substitute for a resource (p. 116)

operating budget: A blueprint that states how managers intend to use organisational resources to achieve organisational goals most efficiently (p. 305)

organisational conflict: A struggle that occurs between two organisational groups (p. 343)

organisational culture: The collection of values and norms that are shared within a company, which influence the behaviour of company employees (p. 298)

organisational design: The combination of organisational structure and control systems that allows a company to implement its strategy effectively (p. 266)

organisational norms: Guidelines that develop from organisational values and reflect common expectations of employee behaviours (such as how things are done) (p. 306)

organisational politics: The tactics that managers use to obtain and use power to influence organisational goals or organisational activities (p. 346)

organisational routines: All the regular and predictable patterns of activity that make up the coordinated actions of a company's employees (p. 110)

organisational structure: The reporting relationships, communication channels and form of hierarchy within a company (p. 266)

organisational values: Beliefs and ideas about goals that the company should pursue and appropriate standards of behaviour (p. 306)

output control: A control system in which strategic managers estimate or forecast appropriate performance goals for managers at division, department and individual levels and then measure actual performance relative to these goals (p. 304)

outsourcing: The contracting out of activities normally undertaken by the company to outside suppliers (p. 205)

parallel sourcing policy: The acquisition of identical inputs from different suppliers (p. 205)

perceptual bias: Placing selective attention on the positive aspects of one's actions (p. 379)

personal control: The desire to shape and influence the behaviour of a manager in a face-to-face interaction in the pursuit of a company's strategies (p. 303)

power: Carrying through one's will even against resistance (p. 349)

power balance: When no single group dominates the direction or activities of a company (p. 352)

price cutting: A company's reduction of prices for strategic reasons (as opposed to simply discounting) (p. 179)

price leadership: Where a company sets prices for the entire industry on the basis of its pricing decision (p. 181)

price signalling: When companies make their pricing decisions known to competitors (p. 181)

prior hypothesis bias: The decision-making errors that arise from decision makers having strong beliefs about certain variables (p. 22)

product development: The process of creating new or improved products (p. 183)

product differentiation: When a product competes on the basis of some type of difference relative to other products in the market (p. 164)

product-oriented: Focusing on the product, in terms of what products are sold into which markets (p. 36)

product proliferation: When a company produces a range of products and services aimed at capturing different segments of the same market (p. 178)

production: The activities necessary for the creation of a good or service (p. 107)

program management and budgeting: A system in which an annual budget with clearly set out goals, programs, activities and tasks is formulated, and money allocated to these successive levels of budget (p. 399)

prospectors: Organisations that always look for new business opportunities (p. 408)

public organisations: Organisations that provide services and products free of charge working in an environment that provides very little competition (p. 393)

public relations: Using information gained through strategy evaluation to create a positive public image for a company (p. 365)

quantum innovations: Innovations that represent a completely new approach to solving a problem (p. 148)

question marks: Businesses that have a low relative market share and are in high-growth industries (p. 215)

quid pro quo: An exchange relationship in which a buyer pays for the services or products received (p. 393)

reactors: Organisations that respond to changes in their environment only under extreme pressure (p. 409)

realised strategy: Strategy that is implemented. It may be a combination of intended and emergent strategies. (p. 15)

reasoning by analogy: Decisions based on the application of simple analogies (p. 22)

re-engineering: The fundamental redesign of organisational structure or business processes to achieve dramatic improvements in competitiveness (p. 337)

Reinventing government: A movement that emphasises applying strategic management approaches to public organisations (p. 398)

related and supporting industries: Industries that are either upstream or downstream of the focus industry or link to the focus industry through other means such as complementary technologies (p. 232)

related diversification: A company's involvement in two or more businesses that are somehow linked or related (p. 207)

relative market share: The ratio of an SBU's market share to the market share held by the largest rival company in the industry (p. 215)

representativeness: Decisions based on knowledge of small samples or single occurrences (p. 23)

research and development (R&D): The activities necessary for the design of products and production processes (p. 106)

resource inimitability: How hard it is for competitors to imitate a resource (p. 114)

resource position barrier: A barrier that enables companies to sustain a resource-based competitive advantage (p. 114)

resource rareness: Possession of a resource by a few competitors (current or potential) or, ideally, by only one company (p. 114)

resource value: The value of a resource in helping a company to create or implement strategies that improve the company's efficiency, improve the ratio of value to cost of a product or service, or allow the company to either exploit its opportunities or neutralise threats arising from the external environment (p. 114)

resources: Factors that a company owns, controls and uses for the purpose of creating value (p. 109)

restructuring: Altering the form or management processes used within a business (in a corporate setting, sometimes reducing divisions, department or functional areas, as well as employees, to reduce operating costs) (p. 338)

risk of holdup: The risk that one company will act opportunistically when investments in specialised assets have been made (p. 200)

self-managing teams: Semiautonomous teams that manage themselves within the boundaries set by management (p. 141)

separation of powers: A situation in which the power of the organisation is divided among its constituent parts (p. 395)

service: The activities necessary for the provision of aftersales service and support (p. 107)

shareholder value model: A model of evaluating corporate performance in terms of the value created for shareholders (p. 368)

social justice bottom line: The impact of organisational operations on social institutions and people (p. 375)

span of control: The number of subordinates that a manager directly manages (p. 269)

specialised asset: An asset that is designed to perform a particular task and whose value is significantly reduced if it is used for an alternative task (p. 199)

stakeholders: Individuals or groups that have an interest, claim or stake in an organisation as a result of either their ability to affect, or their potential to be affected by, the organisation (p. 32)

standardisation: How much a company specifies how decisions are to be made so employees' behaviour becomes predictable (p. 305)

stars: Businesses that have a high relative market share and are in high-growth industries (p. 215)

strategic actions: Specific and short-term actions that occur within a strategic stance (p. 407)

strategic alliance: A partnership formed between organisations to further their common interests (p. 8)

strategic block: A cluster or network of companies that are somehow linked by alliances or other cooperative arrangements (p. 78)

strategic change: Altering a company's present state or activities to improve its competitiveness (p. 336)

strategic choice: The process of choosing from a range of strategic alternatives (p. 8)

strategic commitment: The level of resources and capabilities that a company commits to a particular strategic decision (pp. 117, 246)

strategic control: The process by which top management monitors the performances of managers implementing strategies on an ongoing basis (p. 298)

strategic group: A cluster of companies in an industry that follow similar strategies on the basis of similar resource endowments (p. 76)

strategic intent: The process of leveraging resources and capabilities to achieve a vision that is precise but very ambitious (p. 21)

strategic management process: The set of processes used to determine the strategies for the organisation (p. 4)

strategic stances: Broad and enduring perspectives that organisations adopt in relation to the environment they face (p. 407)

strategy: An action that an organisation takes to achieve its goals (p. 4)

strategy alternatives: Options that management has identified to achieve strategy objectives (p. 363)

strategy evaluation: Assessment of the performance of a strategy after it has been implemented (p. 362)

strategy formulation: The analysis process used to determine which strategies an organisation should use (p. 5)

strategy implementation: How strategies are executed, managed and reviewed (p. 5)

stuck in the middle: A description of companies that try to follow both cost-leadership and differentiation strategies simultaneously (p. 174)

support activities: The inputs that allow primary activities to take place (p. 108)

switching costs: The costs incurred in moving from one product or service to another product or service (p. 66)

SWOT: Strengths, weaknesses, opportunities and threats (p. 7)

taper integration: Buying input from independent suppliers as well as company-owned suppliers, or disposing of product output through independent channels as well as company-owned channels (p. 198)

technological myopia: When companies believe entirely in their technology and do not consider the market for the technology or alternative technologies (p. 148)

timing of entry: When a company enters an international market relative to the entry of international competitors (p. 245)

tit-for-tat strategy: When companies retaliate against the pricing decision of one competitor, so that enough iterations of retaliation can lead to a price war (p. 181)

top-down change: A change process that is designed and implemented from the top of the company (p. 354)

total quality management (TQM): A philosophy that focuses on constantly improving the quality of a company's products and services (p. 142)

transfer prices: Prices that one division or department within a company charges to supply inputs to another division or department in the same company (p. 282)

uniqueness: The ability of a company to gain a competitive advantage by either differentiating itself from its rivals and charging a premium for its product, or reducing its unit costs far below those of competitors (p. 104)

unrelated diversification: A company's involvement in two or more businesses that are not linked or related (p. 207)

value chain: The activities that are necessary for transforming inputs into outputs that customers value (p. 106)

vertical division of work: How authority is devolved within a company, creating tall or flat structures (p. 269)

vertical integration: The process by which an organisation controls either its own inputs (backward integration) or the distribution of its product or service (forward integration) (pp. 8, 197)

vertical specialisation: Division and allocation of authority among managers (p. 267)

virtual corporation: A company that outsources most of its activities (p. 206)

wholly owned subsidiary: A company that is completely owned by its parent company (p. 248)

Index

FRIENDS OF THE LIBRARY

· COLBY-SAWYER COLLEGE ·

This Book Is a Gift of

The Friends of
The Library

COLBY-SAWYER COLLEGE

Fourteen Families
in Pueblo Pottery

Fourteen Families in Pueblo Pottery

Rick Dillingham
Foreword by J. J. Brody

University of New Mexico Press
Albuquerque

Library of Congress-in-Publication Data
Dillingham, Rick.
    Fourteen families in Pueblo pottery / Rick Dillingham; foreword by J.J. Brody.—1st ed.
        p. cm
Rev. and expanded ed. of: Seven families in Pueblo pottery, 1974.
ISBN 0-8263-1498-8.   ISBN 0-8263-1499-6 (pbk).
1. Pueblo Indians—Pottery.
2. Pottery—Southwest, New.
I. Seven families in Pueblo pottery.
II. Title.
E99.P9D54   1994
738'.92'279—dc20
[B]
93-28021
    CIP
Copyright © 1994 by the University of New Mexico Press.

Third paperbound printing, 1997

Editor: Dana Asbury
Charts: Carol Cooperrider
Color photographs: Herbert Lotz
Design: Mary Shapiro

Printed in Hong Kong

(page 1) *Aerial view of (left) Hano Pueblo and (right) Sichomovi Pueblo, Hopi, Arizona, 1948. Photo by Cutter-Carr Flying Service, courtesy Museum of New Mexico, negative number 2605.* **(page 81)** *Acoma Pueblo, ca. 1935. Photo by T. Harmon Parkhurst, courtesy Museum of New Mexico, negative number 2050.* **(page 105)** *Zia Pueblo, ca. 1935. Photo by T. Harmon Parkhurst, courtesy Museum of New Mexico, negative number 45998.* **(page 119)** *Cochiti Pueblo, ca. 1905. Courtesy Museum of New Mexico, negative number 82570.* **(page 128)** *Santo Domingo Pueblo, ca. 1935. Photo by T. Harmon Parkhurst, courtesy Museum of New Mexico, negative number 4367.* **(page 144)** *Pottery vendors, Santa Clara Pueblo, ca. 1935. Photo by T. Harmon Parkhurst, courtesy Museum of New Mexico, negative number 4212.* **(page 239)** *San Ildefonso Pueblo, ca. 1925. Photo by T. Harmon Parkhurst, courtesy Museum of New Mexico, negative number 3810.*

This book is dedicated to those potters who have left a legacy for the world to enjoy. I especially want to acknowledge the friendships developed with Helen Naha (the Feather Woman) and Alma Tahbo, who both passed away while this book was being written.

Contents

Acknowledgments

Without the help and patience of the potters involved, this book would not have been possible. I am fortunate to have gotten to know many of these potters over the past twenty years or so and was happy to meet new potters on this project. Many of these potters bent over backward to help me by assembling family members to visit with me on my sojourns to the pueblos. To them I am deeply indebted. My hope was that this would be a fun project for many of these families, and I think it was successful in this respect. I am grateful to those potters who loaned me pottery and helped me locate photos of older or deceased members of their families. All pottery and photos are credited in the book. I also thank those potters whom I constantly bothered with visits and phone calls to make sure I had all the descendants in proper order. I especially wish to thank Gilbert Atencio from San Ildefonso for preparing a chart of his family. Even after checking and rechecking, I apologize if some family members are still misplaced in the genealogies.

I also wish to thank Ray and Judy Dewey and Dee Ann Menuez of Dewey Galleries, Ltd., in Santa Fe for access to their inventory. Andrea Fisher and Robb Lucas of the Case Trading Post at the Wheelwright Museum were very generous in loaning items from the inventory. Andrea Fisher in her new shop, Fisher Fine Pottery, also loaned to the book. Ron McGee and Brent McGee of McGee's Trading Post in Keams Canyon, Arizona, helped me find pottery by potters I had not met or had trouble locating; their assistance was most valuable. Also generous with their inventories were Bob Andrews of Andrews Pueblo Pottery and Alexander Anthony and Rob Perry of the Adobe Gallery, both in Old Town Albuquerque, and Anthony Whitman of Otowi Trading Company, Santa Fe. Richard Cannon of Packard's Indian Trading Company in Santa Fe purchased much of what is credited "Rick Dillingham inventory." His generosity here enabled me to acquire many pots, saving much time in the photographing and documenting. Rita Neal of the Old Territorial Shop in Scottsdale, Arizona, shipped me an important piece to complete the Chapella family section. Paul Speckled Rock of Merrock Galeria in Santa Clara Pueblo gave generously of his time and inventory and was very helpful in introducing me to new potters. Kenneth Tafoya of the Jemu Povi Gallery introduced me to members of his family and always pointed me in the right direction. Thanks also to Richard Myers of Agape Southwest Pueblo Pottery in Albuquerque and the Santa Fe Indian Trading Company in Santa Fe.

At institutions in Santa Fe, I wish to thank Michael J. Hering and Christy Hoffman of the Indian Arts Research Center at the School of American Research for access to the collections. Bruce Bernstein of the Museum of Indian Art and Culture/Laboratory of Anthropology went out of his way to assist me on short notice, and Jonathan Batkin of the Wheelwright Museum was also generous with his time.

It is always a pleasure to work with private collectors willing to open their homes. Among those who contributed to this project are George Buckner and Jay Lazarus, New York City; James and Barbara Kramer, Santa Fe; Jim Vigil, Jemez Pueblo; and Joe Accardo and Maureen McCarthy, Santa Fe. The many potters who loaned works from their personal collections are listed in the photo credits.

A very special note of thanks goes to photographer Herb Lotz for his patience and consistency throughout the preparation of this book. When pots became available, I needed shots done quickly so I could return the pieces to their owners. Herb's flexibility and professionalism with this project were much appreciated.

Joan O'Donnell, director of the School of American Research Press, who worked wonders with my *Acoma and Laguna Pottery* book published by that press, put in personal time to help me edit this text and the potters' comments. Thank you once again.

When I first called Beth Hadas, director of the University of New Mexico Press, about updating and expanding the *Seven Families in Pueblo Pottery* book, she was very enthusiastic and came to visit me immediately. Her support and enthusiasm never flagged throughout the course of the project. I thank her for giving me the opportunity to complete a project very dear to my heart.

I had an initial idea of how the book should look and be designed. My ideal was created better than I had imagined by Mary Shapiro, who has done an exceptional job. She shows great sensitivity in her design and has elevated the book to the status of a beautiful object. I thank her for her collaboration and wonderful effort.

Carol Cooperrider is responsible for making the genealogies legible, and this was no easy task. I thank her for her patience and perseverance with this project. I wish also to thank my personal assistant, Juliette Myers, for her help with details of this project and for putting up with me.

In May of 1974, the "Seven Families in Pueblo Pottery" exhibit opened at the Maxwell Museum of Anthropology at the University of New Mexico in Albuquerque. The show and its modest accompanying catalogue created a great deal of interest in Pueblo pottery and launched the careers of many potters who still enjoy that recognition today.

The show's opening was an event that can never be repeated. Potters, many of them now deceased, came from all over pueblo country, bringing their families to celebrate, to renew old friendships, and to forge new ones. To an avid collector like myself, the event—full of potters and suffused with goodwill—was magic.

The simple catalogue for the exhibit, its cover originally adorned with only a Frank Stella-like "7," became a guide to anyone interested in collecting Pueblo pottery. (The current version, still in print, has the work of Hopi/Tewa potter Dextra Quotskuyva Nampeyo on the cover.) Originally released by the Maxwell Museum, the catalogue was later published by the University of New Mexico Press; some 80,000 copies are currently in print. As one of a few books then available on the subject, the catalogue was unexpectedly influential. One of its flaws was that it did not include as many families of exceptional potters as I could have presented. Some of these families are included in this updated and expanded volume. But even here, many families from various pueblos are missing.

The original "Seven Families" exhibition had its roots in my own pottery collection. I found I was attracted to pottery that was done within certain families and in similar styles. It is interesting to note that some families are "destined" somehow to be creative and others have individuals that may excel in art. Those selections were purely personal, as are the selections in this new publication. I make no value judgments about the talents and skills of the individual potters or the relative importance of the different families. The selections are based on my personal tastes, my friendships with the potters, and the potters' desire to work with me to present their families in this publication.

Another flaw of the original "Seven Families" book was that it was *too* influential: some beginning collectors felt that if a potter wasn't in the catalogue his or her work wasn't "collectable." Nothing could be further from the truth. There are exceptionally talented potters everywhere, many of them not connected to "dynasties" of potters like those represented here. The main criteria for including potters in these books is that they belong to families in which at least three generations have been active potters and/or painters. Many noted potters from all pueblos work alone or with only one other member of their family. These potters unfortunately are not included in this book.

Pottery has changed a good deal since 1974. Attitudes about traditions and innovations among potters have changed, and so have the collectors. The buyers of Pueblo pottery today are mainly non-Indian collectors, and today's work is tailored to this market. Since the 1970s, collectors have increasingly sought specific pieces, which they would commission from potters, to round out their collections. Working

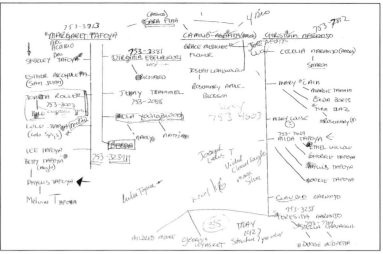

Top left: Opening day of the "Seven Families" exhibition at the Maxwell Museum of Anthropology, University of New Mexico, May 12, 1974. Left to right: Dextra Quotskuyva Nampeyo, Rachel Namingha Nampeyo, and Nellie Douma Nampeyo. Photo by Dick Dunatchik.

Top right: Original working drawing of part of the Tafoya family's genealogy, Santa Clara Pueblo, 1973–74.

Bottom: Four plaques from the original "Seven Families" exhibition at the Maxwell Museum of Anthropology in 1974. The potters made these pieces as nameplates for the cases that displayed their work (approximately 4 x 8 in.).

You are cordially invited
to the opening reception of

Families in Pueblo Pottery

a unique exhibition of contemporary pueblo pottery

May 12, 1974   11:30-5   Refreshments

Pottery demonstrations by Mary Cain and Christina Naranjo of Santa Clara Pueblo
Maxwell Museum of Anthropology, The University of New Mexico

Top left: Opening day of the "Seven Families" exhibition, Maxwell Museum of Anthropology, May 12, 1974. Left to right, top row: daughter of Emma Lewis Mitchell, Emma Lewis Mitchell, Delores Lewis Garcia, Carmel Lewis Haskaya, Rick Dillingham, unknown; bottom row: Clara Montoya, Maria Martinez, Lucy M. Lewis, Bernice Jones, unknown, Santana Martinez. Photo by Dick Dunatchik.

Bottom: Invitation to the original "Seven Families" exhibition, 1974.

Opposite: Mary Cain (left) and Christina Naranjo demonstrating at the opening of the "Seven Families" exhibition, May 12, 1974. Photographer unknown, courtesy of Mary Cain.

to order—to supply this growing market and earn a living—began cutting into potters' individual creativity. Some potters, then and now, resented these market pressures. Others have adapted their work to fit the market and have made strong commercial contributions.

The Indian art market is strong today, and creativity is blossoming all over the Pueblo world. Some potters, pushing the limits of a tradition they feel is antiquated, are making bold contemporary statements in clay. But tradition flourishes as well and has room for many individual creative statements. Many potters, deeply committed to traditional styles and methods, see in the newer work an upsetting erosion of tradition. Some members of the Tafoya family from Santa Clara Pueblo have chosen not to participate in this publication in protest of today's trend toward kiln-fired pottery and the practice of some potters misrepresenting nontraditional pottery to the buyer. Their gesture is noble but will not halt the relentless march into the future that nontraditional pottery represents. The book would have served as a vehicle for their individual statements of their preference for working in the styles they do. Instead, they gave me a statement from all involved.

Tradition itself is constantly being reinvented in Pueblo pottery. The distinctive carved pottery of Santa Clara and San Ildefonso was first made as recently as the 1920s. The sgraffito technique (sometimes erroneously termed "etched"—true etching involves an acid) is old to pottery in other parts of the world but very new to Pueblo pottery, begun by Popovi-Da and Tony Da at San Ildefonso in the mid- to late 1960s and carried to a pinnacle by Joseph Lonewolf and his family in the very early 1970s. In the 1990s potters from virtually every pueblo employ the sgraffito technique, and it is especially popular at Santa Clara. Using the technique on their slip-cast ware, Jemez, San Ildefonso, Acoma, and Laguna potters have created a whole new tourist market.

The black-on-black pottery made popular by Maria and Julian Martinez of San Ildefonso Pueblo was first made in the late teens of this century. The storyteller figures of Cochiti, though related to a figurative tradition of the latter part of the 1800s, were not made until the 1960s—spearheaded by Helen Cordero.

Hopi, Hopi/Tewa, and Zia potters like those in this book have carried on traditions that began centuries ago in their villages. But as commercialism becomes more prevalent in these villages, styles and tastes may change. Acoma Pueblo still keeps old stylistic traditions alive, but the electric kiln has all but supplanted the traditional outdoor sheep-manure firing.

The function of pottery has changed too—once made to be of practical use, it is now perceived as an art object. Service pottery and ceremonial pottery for personal and village use continue to be made today, and pottery is still traded among the pueblos as it has been for centuries. The difference in today's pottery manufacture is the Anglo desire to own unique and exceptional pieces. This has created divisions among potters and collectors alike.

We all—potter and collector alike—live in the late twentieth century, and I believe that to force Native American potters to remain, stylistically and technically, in the past is both unrealistic and patronizing. Traditional pottery may always have a solid place in the market and in Pueblo life, but as lifestyles change it also may be perceived by some as a limitation on innovation and individuality. Contemporary Native American artists may choose the less conservative path, pursuing their talent without worrying if their work will be accepted in the marketplace. Others value an anchor to the past, welcoming the continuity and timeless quality of traditional pottery. In the world of Pueblo pottery there seems to be room for both.

My interest in Pueblo pottery goes back to my early teens, as does my interest in ceramic art in general. Along with collecting and studying Pueblo pottery, I became a potter myself. This interest in collecting Indian pottery and learning ceramic art myself happened at roughly the same time. The quality of Pueblo pottery intrigued me because of its lack of slick technology. All the information came from the earth, as I hope my work conveys today. There is much more to clay than "mud." The clay, Mother Earth, is the vehicle that conveys potters' souls and is the glue that binds deep and lasting friendships. It is a tangible spiritual connection to life itself, and is not to be taken lightly. The clay is a great teacher, and many potters find joy in molding Mother Earth, listening to what She has to say, and attaining a center of peace while working. I have been very fortunate to know as many potters as I have, both Anglo and Native American. We all share a common ground.

Rick Dillingham
Santa Fe
June 1993

Foreword

The book you hold has its origins in a similar volume called *Seven Families in Pueblo Pottery*, which was originally published in 1974 by the Maxwell Museum of Anthropology as the catalogue of an exhibition of the same name; what you are reading now is as much an epilogue to the original as an introduction to its greatly expanded sequel. Though I worked at the Maxwell for many years before becoming its director in 1974, I can claim no credit for any part of *Seven Families*—neither the publication nor the exhibition which inspired it. Both came about when Professor John M. Campbell was its director and I was on leave, out of touch and out of the country. So I knew virtually nothing about either until the summer of 1974 and can talk about both as an almost disinterested party.

I have a first printing of *Seven Families* in front of me as I write this, and the credits listed on page 112 tell the initiated that almost the entire museum staff, including student employees such as Rick Dillingham and other part-time workers, contributed significantly to its creation. The staff was small and the project a corporate one produced by a talented group of people, most of whom simultaneously performed several different tasks. It is usual in such situations for those involved to lose track of their own contributions so that outsiders such as myself are entirely unable to credit individuals fairly for any particular part of the whole. The notion of "intellectual property" gets fuzzy around the edges, and the process is comparable in some ways to pottery making as it was, and sometimes still is, practiced by many of the extended families who were the subject of *Seven Families* as well as this book.

There is often a driving personality to these affairs, especially when the end product is strong and forceful, and in this instance Rick Dillingham appears to have filled that role. Rick was already an accomplished potter as well as a collector, student, and sometime dealer in Pueblo pottery. The exhibition and publication were largely his conception and shaped by his insights, which could well have been unique because of the many different ways in which he informed himself about Pueblo pottery and involved himself with it. It was a memorable show with a nicely complementary catalogue, and it took some time before I realized that we had a phenomenon on our hands.

Off-campus visitors kept coming, despite the frustrations of parking on the crowded campus of the University of New Mexico, and the catalogue kept selling, not only there, but also at Indian art and curio shops throughout the Southwest. I imagine we broke attendance records (for the most part we kept none in those days), and we certainly broke our catalogue sales records. Until then we had generally printed exhibition brochures or catalogues in editions of 2,000 or so, hoping to give away what did not sell only in the hundreds rather than the thousands. The first printing of *Seven Families* sold out, as did the second, and demand continued even after the exhibition closed. Having no desire to see the museum go into the book publishing business, I contracted with UNM Press to have them handle future printings which now number fifteen.

Phenomena occur with some regularity in the museum world and, like accidents, are defined by being unpredictable and explicable only after the fact, if at all. Why, for example, should one blockbuster exhibition about a historically obscure pharaoh named Tutankhamen play to great crowds, while another, equally well-produced and dramatizing with sex and violence the famed and sudden burial two millennia ago of Pompeii by volcanic ash, not excite the public imagination? Recognizing a phenomenon is not the same as understanding it, and periodically some of us speculated about *Seven Families* and why it had benefited from "the Tutankhamen effect." Its good title was certainly a factor, whose creator, though deserving of recognition, remains an anonymous member of that museum family. Timing was also important, and *Seven Families* was blessed by being sandwiched between the end of the family-commune–oriented hippie era, and the beginning of a burgeoning, worldwide interest in Native American art, life, and philosophy, which continues to this day. The reasons for that interest are many and varied and, in any case, can only have indirect bearing on the question for there have been many Pueblo pottery publications and exhibitions since, but few with its impact and longevity.

Title and timing tell only part of the story and then only if we look at what was novel about *Seven Families*. Its key innovation was the balance achieved between personal statements made by artists about their work and a focus on the cross-generational relationships between artists and their families. *Seven Families* projected the warm, personal qualities of the shared, corporate nature of creativity in the Pueblo world at the same time as it economically and effectively introduced many individual artists and their extended families to a wide audience. Those two themes of artist and community are greatly expanded in this new work, which also should intersect with a dynamic market for Pueblo pottery art in the outside world.

Euro-Americans have been collecting Pueblo Indian pottery in quantity since about 1880, but until the 1970s only two pottery artists, the Hopi-Tewa Nampeyo and Maria Martinez of San Ildefonso, had become at all well known to any but the most knowledgeable collectors. When large-scale collecting started, not only was most Pueblo pottery still made for household use rather than as something precious, but the notion of "pottery art" was almost as alien to the collectors as to the Pueblos. For the most part Pueblo potters and pottery painters were thought of as anonymous artisans producing useful and beautiful artifacts by conforming to prevailing community standards, and their works were interpreted as the products of particular places rather than the inventions of creative persons working within community traditions. Absence of signatures and other Euro-American markers of artistic individuality seemed only to confirm those judgments. By 1923, when Maria Martinez began systematically to sign her pottery, "pottery art" had become an established, if minor, fine art subcategory among Euro-Americans, and her work was thereafter accepted as a kind of art. But almost forty more years passed before most Pueblo pottery artists came to sign their works as a matter of course.

By the time of *Seven Families* most Pueblo pottery had long been made as a kind of art object for a non-Pueblo audience. Pots were essentially nonutilitarian, signed by their makers, and had come to signify—for many artists as well as their audience—both the creative individuality of an artist and the corporate values of the Pueblo communities within which they were made. That duality was perceived of only dimly then, for it was not often articulated and even now seems to be self-contradictory. Pueblo pottery traditions had changed markedly in almost every way imaginable since 1880, as had the Pueblos themselves, yet both somehow maintained their integrity and keen, creative relationships with the past. The new forms and traditions had dignity and seemed appropriate.

In 1974, Rick Dillingham—artist, student, scholar, collector, dealer—was led both by an ethical imperative and by the conviction of positive, practical market consequences to conceive of an exhibition and book that would give Pueblo pottery artists opportunity to be seen in equal part as creative individuals and as members of traditional communities. The *Seven Families* phenomenon was the result, and credit the Maxwell Museum and Jack Campbell and his staff as well as Dillingham for shaping the concept into a reality. Twenty years later, we have another imperative, another reality, and another book twice the size. Twenty years from now, we'll see.

J. J. Brody
September 1993

Subsistence

In the early seventies
I lived at Kha Pó'o Ōwengé*
with my Grandparents.
I sometimes stayed with my great Grandmother, Gía Kwijō,
who was a potter.
She taught me to make small pots and figurines
and we sold them to the tourists.
When we worked with the clay
it would dry on my hands, and
when I peeled it off
there were small white patches
where it had bleached my skin.
After a few minutes
my darker colored flesh returned;
it was the clay that showed me
who I really was.

Years have passed since Gía Kwijō died.
I still remember the strength of her hands
as she taught me
to shape the clay.
And I often wonder
about those small pots and figurines;
who bought them and
where they are now.
Sometimes I see Gía Kwijō's reflection
in the pots she made
that now sit
on my Grandparents' mantel.
It reminds me
that like all the women in my family, and
all things at Kha Pó'o Ōwengé,
I am made of clay, too.

RoseMary Diaz

*Original Tewa name for Santa Clara Pueblo

About the Photographs

All portraiture was done by Rick Dillingham unless otherwise noted. Photographs of deceased potters or of individuals who were away at the times I was photographing were borrowed from family members, rephotographed by Herbert Lotz, and cropped to fit this book. In some cases I was unable to schedule photo sessions and no existing portraits were available; these potters are not pictured here. A very few potters preferred not to be photographed.

All color photographs of the pottery in this book were taken by Herbert Lotz. The pieces pictured are from my personal collection, from other private collections both in the Southwest and across the country, from the potters' homes, and from stores, galleries, and museums.

Key to captions: The name of each potter is followed by the dimensions of the pictured pot (height x diameter), its date of manufacture, and its source.

About the Genealogy Charts

The charts that appeared in the original *Seven Families in Pueblo Pottery* book were used as a starting point for this publication. They were amended where necessary, as new generations of potters working today were included. The members of the original seven families and the additional seven families in this new publication helped create and double-check the charts to ensure as correct a lineage as possible.

I regret that I could not include everyone in these family trees. I tried to focus on potters' relatives but had to stray now and then to make as complete a family tree as possible. Many people listed as painters were instrumental in pottery decoration and styling. I wanted to present as much detail as possible, so the genealogies in this book are far more complex than in the earlier *Seven Families*. Despite the checking and double-checking, however, I'm sure some individuals have been left out. I have tried to bring each family up to the present, and with any luck the young people listed in this book will be pleased to see their connection in the family of pottery in the future. Some adopted children are listed both with their natural parents and with the adults who raised them. In some cases, adopted children are not specifically noted and are listed as children of the adopting parents. The last names listed are those the potters or their family members are using at present. Names change, and I apologize for any errors in that area. Deceased family members are listed with a (d.) following their names. Potters are noted with color in the charts. If someone is a noted painter or other craftsperson, I have tried to make note of it.

Map of the Pueblos

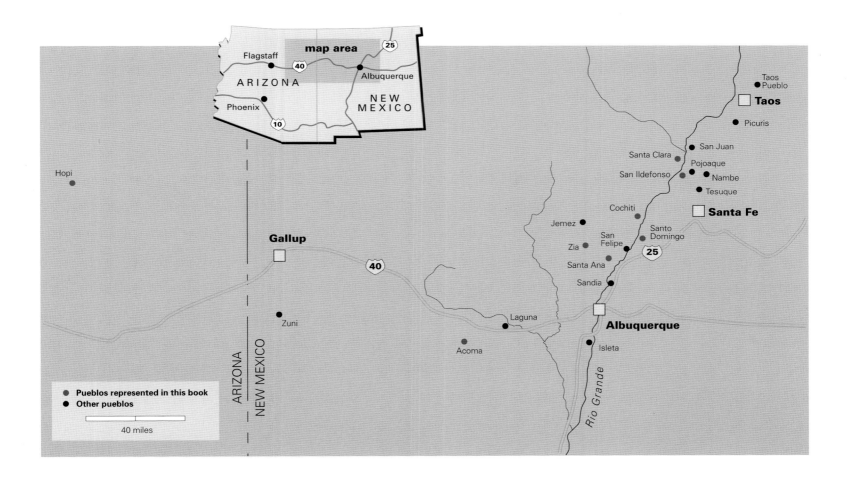

map area

Flagstaff
ARIZONA
Phoenix
NEW MEXICO
Albuquerque
40
25
10

Taos Pueblo
Taos
Picuris
San Juan
Santa Clara
Pojoaque
San Ildefonso
Nambe
Tesuque
Santa Fe
Cochiti
Jemez
Santo Domingo
Zia
San Felipe
25
Santa Ana
Sandia
Hopi
Gallup
40
Zuni
Laguna
Albuquerque
Acoma
Isleta
Rio Grande
ARIZONA
NEW MEXICO

● Pueblos represented in this book
● Other pueblos

40 miles

HOPI-TEWA

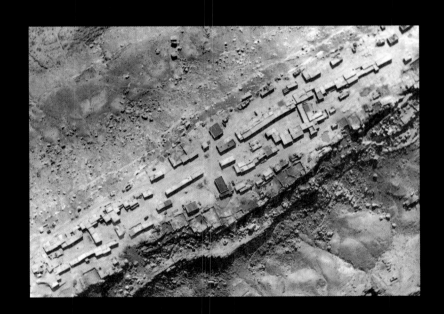

The Chapella Family

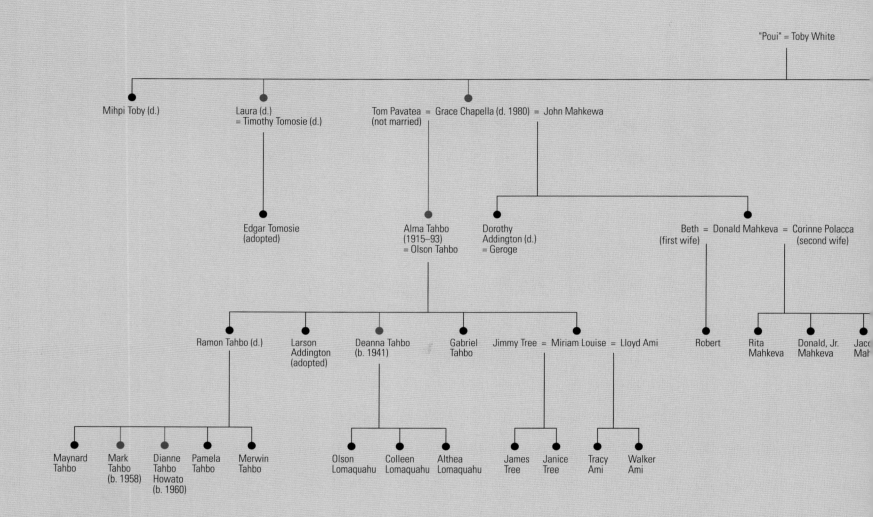

"Poui" = Toby White

Mihpi Toby (d.)

Laura (d.)
= Timothy Tomosie (d.)

Tom Pavatea = Grace Chapella (d. 1980) = John Mahkewa
(not married)

Edgar Tomosie
(adopted)

Alma Tahbo
(1915–93)
= Olson Tahbo

Dorothy
Addington (d.)
= Geroge

Beth = Donald Mahkeva = Corinne Polacca
(first wife)   (second wife)

Ramon Tahbo (d.)

Larson
Addington
(adopted)

Deanna Tahbo
(b. 1941)

Gabriel
Tahbo

Jimmy Tree = Miriam Louise = Lloyd Ami

Robert

Rita
Mahkeva

Donald, Jr.
Mahkeva

Jaco
Mah

Maynard
Tahbo

Mark
Tahbo
(b. 1958)

Dianne
Tahbo
Howato
(b. 1960)

Pamela
Tahbo

Merwin
Tahbo

Olson
Lomaquahu

Colleen
Lomaquahu

Althea
Lomaquahu

James
Tree

Janice
Tree

Tracy
Ami

Walker
Ami

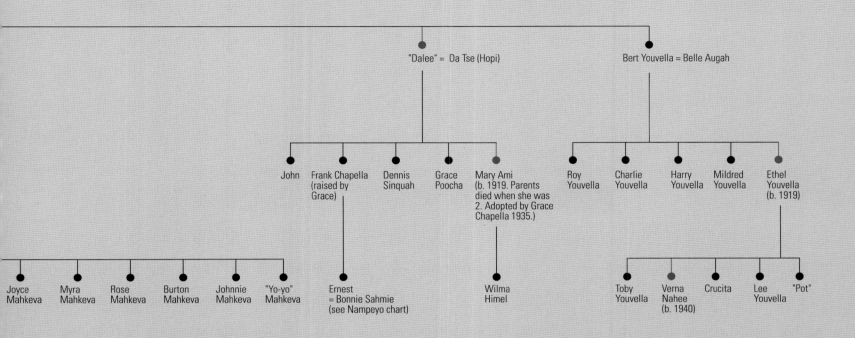

"Dalee" = Da Tse (Hopi)

Bert Youvella = Belle Augah

John

Frank Chapella
(raised by
Grace)

Dennis
Sinquah

Grace
Poocha

Mary Ami
(b. 1919. Parents
died when she was
2. Adopted by Grace
Chapella 1935.)

Roy
Youvella

Charlie
Youvella

Harry
Youvella

Mildred
Youvella

Ethel
Youvella
(b. 1919)

Joyce
Mahkeva

Myra
Mahkeva

Rose
Mahkeva

Burton
Mahkeva

Johnnie
Mahkeva

"Yo-yo"
Mahkeva

Ernest
= Bonnie Sahmie
(see Nampeyo chart)

Wilma
Himel

Toby
Youvella

Verna
Nahee
(b. 1940)

Crucita

Lee
Youvella

"Pot"

3

Opposite: Laura Tomosie (portrait not available). Pot 6 ¼ x 9 in., ca. 1965. Courtesy Old Territorial Shop, Scottsdale, Arizona.

Grace Chapella, ca. 1974 (photograph by Glenn Short). Pot 10 x 17 in., ca. 1955. Rick Dillingham collection.

Alma Tahbo, b. 1915
"I learned from my mother [Grace Chapella]. I used to just play with her pottery and make all kinds of things, then I started to make larger [pottery]. My mother took over these children of Dahlee: Frank, John, Dennis, Mary [Ami], and Grace. She had a hard time and started to work at Polacca Day School as a cook and a housekeeper. We were all raised with grandmother "Povi" Toby. In 1983 I had a stroke and was still making pottery up to then. The second stroke in 1986 really got me down.

All you think of is your pottery work. You don't care about cleaning the house. If you worried about other things when the pots were being fired, they would crack."

Deanna Tahbo, b. 1941
"I kind of just watched
Grandma [Grace Cha-
pella], and I started
molding little pieces,
and as the years went
by I added on and
made bigger pottery.
I give my credit for
inspiration to her."

*Opposite: Alma Tahbo. Pot 7 ½ x 11
in., 1981. Rick Dillingham collection.*

*Deanna Tahbo. Pot 4 ½ x 10 ½ in.,
1986. Rick Dillingham collection.*

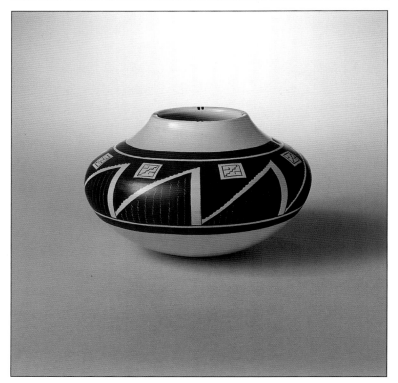

Mark Tahbo, b. 1958
"Grace [Chapella] was really a unique person. She was something special, and I've always admired her. She was a great inspiration to me. She was pretty old when I got interested [in pottery making], and she couldn't really give me all I needed to know. She was maybe 100, and her mind had slipped, so most was self-taught. I went through mistakes and errors. My pots today have a lot more 'being' than just a pot. To me they have life and sensitivity, just like a human being. When I create a pot I breathe life into it and hope it lives."

Dianna Tahbo Howato, b. 1960
"I consider the background of where [pottery making] came from, the family. I learned from observing. I learned most of what I know from Mark [Tahbo]. I was always interested in it since I first noticed pottery, and I got a lot of good feedback from Mark. I've grown to learn that pottery becomes a part of you . . . the feelings of that, and how I identify with it and how it identifies with me."

Top: Mark Tahbo. Pot 4 x 11 ¾ in., 1991. Rick Dillingham collection.

Bottom: Dianna Tahbo Howato. Pot 4 ½ x 7 in., 1991. Rick Dillingham collection.

Opposite: "Dalee" (portrait not available). Pot (identified by Grace Chapella, ca. 1972) 2 ½ x 4 ¾ in., ca. 1920s. Rick Dillingham collection.

Mary Ami, b. 1919
Mary Ami's mother, "Dahlee," died when Mary
was two years old. She was raised by Grace
Chapella, who then became her "mother."

*"When I was real little, I did the pottery with my
grandma (Grace and my mom's mother), and I
started pounding out pots on my elbow. Before I
got married (in 1945), I worked with my mother
[Grace]. Dahlee was living at the Bear House next
door to Nampeyo. She [Nampeyo] told me that
they worked together and Dahlee told her how to
make pottery. Nampeyo took care of me as a baby.
My grandmother worked with Nampeyo."*

Mary Ami signed her pottery "Mary Ami" until she
got married. She said that she changed the signa-
ture to "Buffalo Maiden" at the request of an uncle.

*Opposite: Mary Ami. Pot 6 ½ x 10 ½
in., ca. 1950. Rick Dillingham collection.*

10

Verna Nahee, b. 1940
"I like working with both types of the clay, red and gray [yellow]. With red I mainly do corrugated types. I enjoy making pottery. It means a lot. It gives me a good feeling when I work with clay. My mom learned from Grace Sayah [sayah is Tewa for grandmother] [Chapella], and I learned from both she and my mother. When we fire like this we think back on how she [Grace] did it. Ours is kind of 'broader' in design, others do finer designs. Making pottery isn't an easy thing. You have to have a clear mind. You have to be in the mood or they won't turn out. I like just to make to satisfy me. I don't take orders. To me taking orders is to satisfy someone else, and they never come out right."

Ethel Youvella, b. 1919
"I learned some from my mother's mother, Lela. I would mold little ones and she would fix them up for me. I used to go down to do pottery with Grace [Chapella] and Laura [Tomosie]. I learned to fire the red ones from Grace. I didn't get them to come out right until she helped. I didn't know how to do it [red pottery], so I did it her way and learned. If the paint doesn't stick I go over it and refire it. I hate to be selling it without the paint being right. Some tourists don't care, but I don't want to sell it that way."

Opposite: Verna Nahee. Pot 5 x 9 in., ca. 1980. Courtesy James and Barbara Kramer, Santa Fe.

Ethel Youvella. Pot 3 ½ x 4 in., ca. 1980. Courtesy James and Barbara Kramer, Santa Fe.

The Nampeyo Family

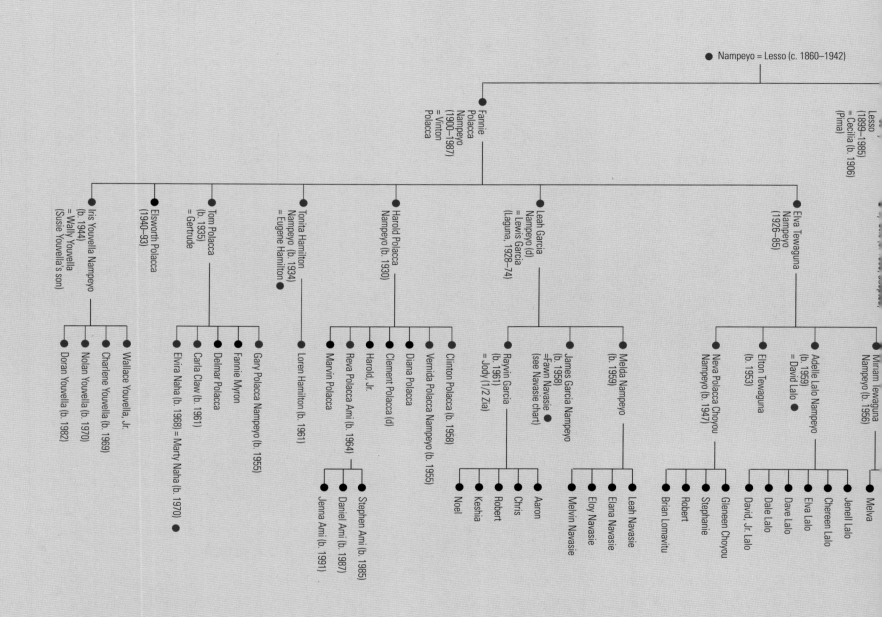

Nampeyo = Lesso (c. 1860–1942)

Lesso (1899–1985) = Cecilia (b. 1906) (Pima)

Fannie Polacca Nampeyo (1900–1987) = Vinton Polacca

Iris Youvella Nampeyo (b. 1944) = Wally Youvella (Susie Youvella's son)

Elsworth Polacca (1940–93)

Tom Polacca (b. 1935) = Gertrude

Tonita Hamilton Nampeyo (b. 1934) = Eugene Hamilton

Harold Polacca Nampeyo (b. 1930)

Leah Garcia Nampeyo (d) = Lewis Garcia (Laguna, 1928–74)

Elva Tewaguna Nampeyo (1926–85)

Doran Youvella (b. 1982)

Nolan Youvella (b. 1970)

Charlene Youvella (b. 1969)

Wallace Youvella, Jr.

Elvira Naha (b. 1968) = Marty Naha (b. 1970)

Carla Claw (b. 1961)

Delmar Polacca

Fannie Myron

Gary Polacca Nampeyo (b. 1955)

Loren Hamilton (b. 1961)

Marvin Polacca

Reva Polacca Ami (b. 1964)

Harold, Jr.

Clement Polacca (d)

Diana Polacca

Vernida Polacca Nampeyo (b. 1955)

Clinton Polacca (b. 1958)

Rayvin Garcia (b. 1961) = Jody (1/2 Zia)

James Garcia Nampeyo (b. 1958) = Fawn Navasie (see Navasie chart)

Melda Nampeyo (b. 1959)

Neva Polacca Choyou Nampeyo (b. 1947)

Elton Tewaguna (b. 1953)

Adelle Lalo Nampeyo (b. 1959) = David Lalo

Miriam Tewaguna Nampeyo (b. 1956)

Jenna Ami (b. 1991)

Daniel Ami (b. 1987)

Stephen Ami (b. 1985)

Noel

Keshia

Robert

Chris

Aaron

Melvin Navasie

Eloy Navasie

Elana Navasie

Leah Navasie

Brian Lomavitu

Robert

Stephanie

Gleneen Choyou

David, Jr. Lalo

Dale Lalo

Dave Lalo

Elva Lalo

Chereen Lalo

Jenell Lalo

Melva

14

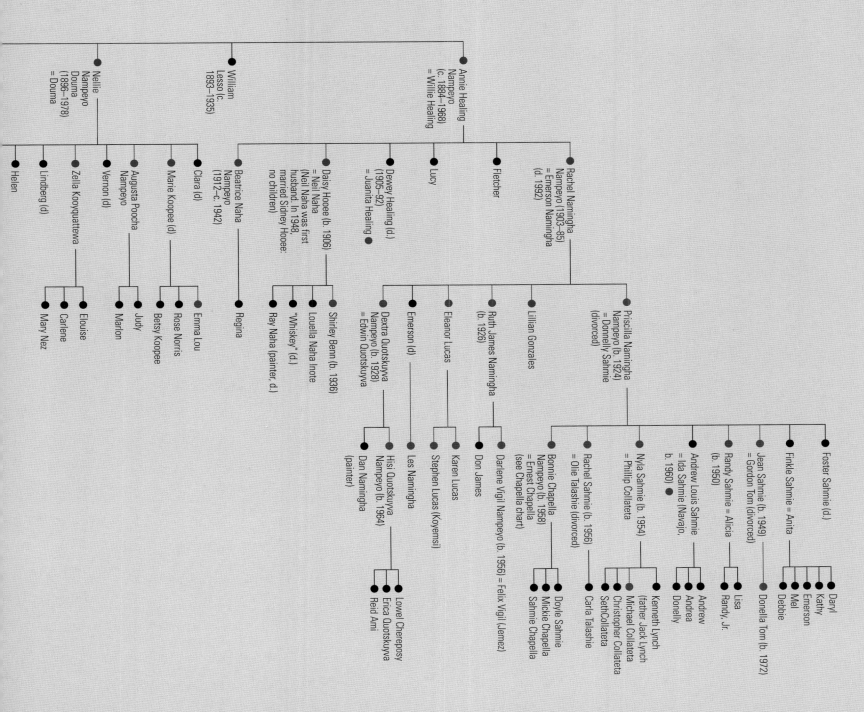

Nampeyo with her daughter Fannie (historic postcard, ca. 1930, courtesy Daisy Hooee). Pots: left: three-color polychrome, 5 x 10 ½ in., ca. 1900, Rick Dillingham collection; right: red-slipped polychrome, 8 x 15 in., ca. 1910–15; Rick Dillingham collection; opposite: white-slipped polychrome, 7 x 13 ½ in., ca. 1905, Rick Dillingham collection.

Tonita Hamilton Nampeyo, b. 1934
"I want to continue the traditional methods and designs. I don't want to deviate from what my mom [Fannie Polacca] and grandmother [Nampeyo] did and hand it down to the young ones. That's the most important thing, to keep tradition alive."

Opposite: Fannie Polacca Nampeyo, ca. 1972. Pot 7 x 11 in., ca. 1965. Rick Dillingham collection.

Tonita Hamilton Nampeyo. Pot 5 ½ x 3 ½ in., 1979. Rick Dillingham collection.

Eugene Hamilton
"I do some traditional, that's how I got in, and now I do the sgraffito, depending upon what mood I'm in."

Left: Eugene Hamilton. Pot 3 ¼ x 3 ½ in., 1992. Rick Dillingham inventory.

Right: Loren Hamilton. Pot 3 x 3 ½ in., 1992. Rick Dillingham inventory.

Opposite: Leah Garcia Nampeyo, ca. 1972. Pot 5 x 7 ¾ in., ca. 1965. Rick Dillingham collection.

Loren Hamilton, b. 1961
"[I learned] from being around the family, my grandmother [Fannie] and mom [Tonita]. I spent a year with Tom [Polacca] and learned from him. I started on my own and did the best I could. In the past year I started with sculpture, and a few months ago I started adding red slip.

"I strive to do my best and depict what we believe in on my pots. I try to take old designs and interpret them in my way. I've done it with moths and fine lines. I am working full time on potting now, and try to produce something people enjoy. As long as someone's happy, I'm happy."

Melda Navasie Nampeyo, b. 1959
"My grandma [Fannie Polacca] really told me to learn this. My little girls are starting to work on them, little pots, and they've sold a couple already. This is mostly the design I use, the black design. My mom [Leah Garcia] and grandmother painted for me. I've been working since 1985, I think, on my own."

Melda Nampeyo. Pot 3 x 3 ¼ in., 1992. Rick Dillingham inventory.

Opposite top: James Garcia Nampeyo. Pot 4 ½ x 9 in., 1992. Rick Dillingham inventory.

Opposite bottom: Rayvin Garcia. Pot 4 x 7 ½ in., 1992. Rick Dillingham inventory.

James Garcia
Nampeyo, b. 1958
"I carry on the tradition
of Nampeyo and got
started with my wife
[Fawn]. My grandmoth-
er [Fannie] really got
me started, and I used
to have her work with
me. I would mold them
and she would paint
them. Then she said I
had to get going on my
own, and I painted my
first pot in front of her.

"All the designs I do are
old traditional Nampeyo
designs. I haven't tried
anything new. Fawn
molds some of the larg-
er ones, and we work
together. I do the small-
er ones."

Rayvin Garcia, b. 1961
"I've been at it [pottery
making] about nine
years, since I've been
married, and it's mainly
my grandmother [Fan-
nie Polacca] who taught
me. I took her painting
style, and I don't want to
go into other designs.
This is the best way of
making a living for my
family."

Iris Youvella Nampeyo, b. 1944
"When I was just a little girl I would sit by my mother [Fannie Polacca] making little ladles, and I didn't know how to paint. My father said, 'Why don't you paint a corn on the ladle?' [the Nampeyo family belongs to the Corn Clan] and I thought he meant to build up a corn. Then I started painting, and then I got back to the reservation and saw all the traditional pots. And then I saw a pot with a corn on it and remembered what my dad said, and I thought I'd go in that direction. It was a Navajo pot. I feel a closeness to the corn because of my clan."

Iris Youvella Nampeyo. Pots: opposite: 4 1/2 x 6 in., 1992, courtesy Otowi Trading Co., Santa Fe; right: 2 1/4 x 4 1/2 in., ca. 1980, courtesy of the artist.

Nolan Youvella, b. 1970
"I first started out when I was about eleven. I used to make little pipes. After a while I started making pottery. I work with carving pottery, and later on I'll want to try painting. I was going to school for one and a half years and then I came back and started up with pots again."

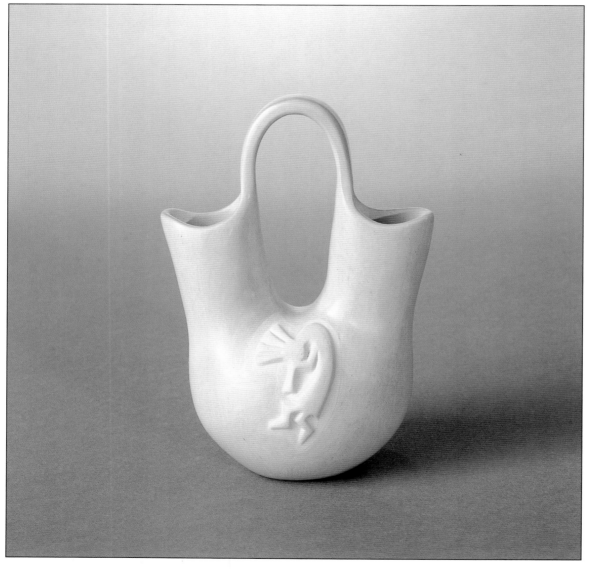

Nolan Youvella. Pot 5 x 3 ½ in., 1991. Courtesy Iris Youvella Nampeyo.

Opposite: Wallace Youvella (portrait not available). Pot 4 x 6 ¾ in., 1992. Courtesy McGees Indian Art, Keams Canyon, Arizona.

Charlene Youvella, b. 1969
"I would watch Fannie make pottery. I watched how she molded and fired. She gave me a chance to play with the clay she had, and that helped me to learn myself. I'll probably stay with miniatures. I've never tried painting. I'll stay with my mom's style. My dad helps me with them also."

Opposite: Wallace Youvella, Jr. (portrait not available). Pot 2 x 3 in., 1992. Courtesy Otowi Trading Co., Santa Fe.

Doran Youvella and Charlene Youvella. Doran Youvella pot 1 ¼ x 2 in., 1992, courtesy of the artist; Charlene Youvella pot ½ x 1 ¼ in., 1992, courtesy of the artist.

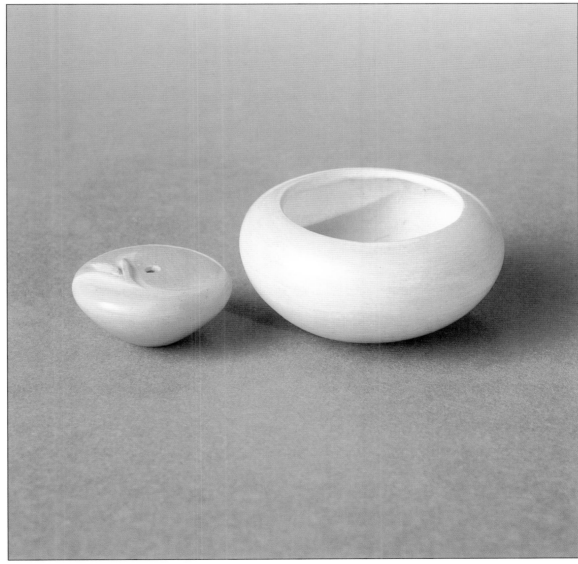

Vernida Nampeyo, b. 1955
"My pots, the pots I do, I only paint the fineline. I want to keep the tradition up, so I mainly stay with fineline. The main thing is keeping the tradition up. I fire the same way my Grandmother Fannie taught me. I do my baking [firing] in Polacca, not here in the canyon [Keams Canyon]. I worked with my dad [Harold Nampeyo] when he was well. He would make them and I would paint for him. I started learning how twelve years ago, and I learned all from Fannie.

"It means a lot to me to do painting. It's in a way like—it relaxes me—it's harmonious. Sometimes I'm not in the mood, and when I am the paint flows. If you're angry, lazy, your paint will fall off the pots. You have to want to do it and be in a good mood. Spiritually it helps you get going with pottery. It does bring in income, but I have another job on the side."

Opposite: Vernida Polacca Nampeyo. Pot 3 x 5 ½ in., 1992. Rick Dillingham inventory.

Harold Polacca Nampeyo (portrait not available). Pot painted by Fannie Nampeyo, 4 x 6 ½ in., ca. 1975. Rick Dillingham collection.

Reva Ami, b. 1964
"I learned mainly from Vernida [Nampeyo]. She's the one who kept push-ing me to start. I've only been potting since last July—1 year. I talked with Tonita [Hamilton Nampeyo] and Adelle [Nampeyo] and they have helped me quite a lot. I like doing it [pottery]. It's interesting. I'm sticking to the family's designs and I'm trying to get back into the older ones like my grandmother [Fannie Nampeyo]. I don't look far in the future, but I want to start making larger ones."

Clinton Polacca, b. 1958
"I learned from watching my grandmother, Fannie. I just starting doing pots by myself four years ago. I used to just make them, and she'd paint them. I have a respect for the designs. I usually just sell to people who really want them and connect with the design and respect it."

Opposite: Reva Polacca Ami. Pot 4 ⅞ x 9 in., 1993. Courtesy Merrock Galeria, Santa Clara Pueblo.

Left: Clinton Polacca. Pot 4 x 6 ¼ in., 1992. Rick Dillingham inventory.

Right: Tom Polacca Nampeyo (portrait not available). Pot 7 x 8 in., 1992. Rick Dillingham inventory.

33

Gary P. Nampeyo, b. 1955
"That style [carved pottery] was given to me by my father [Tom Polacca], and I've kind of come up with my own as well, different from his. I try to texture it with the scenery around here. If you look at rocks they're never all smooth. It gives the background a different look. The colors that go into it are similar to what surrounds us here at Hopi.

"I like to try to get across the ancientness of our people. That's what the style means to me. I try to tell a story with my pottery and use figures. Our people have been spread out across the Southwest with ruins, and when I use a flute player I try to bring back the past—what we see on pictographs.

"I use a carving knife—a kind of razor knife—and I use yucca paintbrushes and whatever I find to my liking."

34

Elvira Naha b. 1968
"I just learned from my dad [Tom Polacca], and he told me to try and I did. It's just a style [sgraffito] I stay with now. I use mostly kachina designs on my pots. I use all natural materials but fire mostly in a kiln."

Marty Naha, b. 1970
"I learned it off of Tom [Polacca] and his daughter Elvira. She's the one who really got me into it. We've been doing this for about two and a half years now. It's good money and we make a living with it. Tom invented this style [sgraffito]."

Carla Claw, b. 1961
"Mainly my work is kind of different from everybody's. I use a dark brown polished slip on plain seed pots done with sgraffito carving like my dad [Tom Polacca] does. It's kind of unique in a way—to me it's modern. That's the outlook now. Things that are different are more accepted, but they're done in traditional form that links us back to who we are."

Opposite: Gary Polacca Nampeyo. Pot 6 x 7 ½ in., 1992. Rick Dillingham inventory.

Elvira Naha. Pot not available.

Carla Claw. Pot 2 ½ x 1 ¾ in., 1992. Rick Dillingham inventory.

Miriam Tewaguna Nampeyo, b. 1956
"I feel good about doing pottery. It's the only thing I do now. It excites me to work. It took me quite a while after I got out of high school, four or five years. Then my mom [Elva Tewaguna] really started teaching me the pottery. Then I started on my own, not painting right off, especially the `fineline,' which was taught to me by my younger sister, Adelle."

Opposite: Elva Tewaguna Nampeyo, ca. 1972. Pot 6 ½ x 13 in., ca. 1980. Rick Dillingham collection.

Miriam Tewaguna Nampeyo. Pot 4 ½ x 5 in., 1992. Rick Dillingham inventory.

Adelle Lalo Nampeyo, b. 1959
Adelle's husband, David Lalo, has been potting in the carved style for two years.
"I guess I'm so glad I learned this from my mom [Elva Tewaguna] and grandma [Fannie Polacca], and now I'm trying to teach my girls. It means a lot to me to make pots, the spiritual way means a lot. I've tried some designs on my own but never really put it down on paper to continue them. I've tried them and let them go. I've stayed with designs in the family—fineline and black design [solid fineline or `migration pattern']."

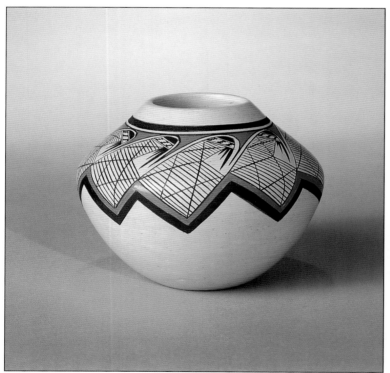

Left: Adelle Lalo Nampeyo. Pot 4 x 5 ¼ in., 1992. Rick Dillingham inventory.

Right: Neva Polacca Choyou Nampeyo (portrait not available). Pot 4 x 5 ⅜ in., ca. 1980. Courtesy James and Barbara Kramer, Santa Fe.

Opposite: Lynette Lesso. Two pots, each 3 ¼ in. tall, 1991. Courtesy of the artist.

Lynette Lesso, b. 1955
"My mom [Cecelia Lesso] told you in the first book that I would take over. She was my adopted mother, and she taught me so much that she learned from Nampeyo. She told me it would be a way to make a living, carrying it on.

"When I'm doing pottery I think good things. I let it go when there are ceremonies. I do all of it myself—clay, manure. I'm friends with some Navajos and they bring me the manure. From molding, sanding, polishing I do all of it myself. I teach my kids how to paint. I mix up designs—not in the order she [Cecelia] always used them.

"He [Wesley] helped my mom in gathering and in ideas with some of the designs, the manure, and clay. The rest she did on her own. He was there to back her up. When I'm doing this I think of my mom a lot."

Daisy Hooee, b. 1906
"My first husband was Neil Naha, and he left us and I came to Zuni to see the `doings' [ceremonies] to get happy. Then I got a job here cooking in Ramah and worked with 4-H boys and girls, lots of jobs. [She married Sidney Hooee, a Zuni in 1948; her children are with Neil Naha.]

"I taught pottery at the high school [Zuni], and I made it in the old way like my grandmother, Nampeyo. I learned from Nampeyo and so did my mother, Annie. Everybody painted for her—Nellie, Fannie, and my mother helped her a lot, painted those little fine lines. Rachel [Daisy's sister] painted for her, too. Her husband Lesso, he helped—he sure can paint, that old man too. [Documented examples of Lesso's painting are virtually nonexistent.] It was nice to have such a kind grandmother. She would never say `Don't bother the clay' when we wanted to make little things.

"They [Daisy's mother and father] had sheep and cows, and she [Annie] made pots too. She was a busy woman. The Navajo herded sheep for us, and she made all kinds of food, piki. She would herd sheep herself, and Grandma Nampeyo would come with her husband, and the old man herded sheep while she [Annie] painted pots.

"Nampeyo had trouble with her voice as well as her eyes, and at a point couldn't talk well, but she could laugh!

"I appreciate everything I've learned from you [Nampeyo], and I hope I can keep it up. She was laughing—I guess she was happy. I know we all love you. I hope some day we'll be doing like you're doing so that's why we help you. We all helped."

Opposite: Annie Healing Nampeyo (portrait not available). Pot 3 x 7 ½ in., ca. 1940s. Rick Dillingham collection.

Daisy Hooee Nampeyo, ca. 1975 (photographer unknown, courtesy Daisy Hooee Nampeyo). Pot 2 x 2 ½ in., ca. 1985. Courtesy Buckner/Lazarus collection, New York.

Shirley Benn, b. 1936

"I do three things. I make jewelry, I'm a seamstress, and I'm a potter. I like doing pottery sometimes to get away from the jewelry, and I can shape something while watching TV, just to relax. It is something I fall back on when I can't do jewelry. There are times when I get tired of doing jewelry and then I go to pottery. I like to sew also. I sew for my grandkids.

"I learned pottery making from my mom and my grandma, Annie. I lived with her [Annie] during the summers when school was out, and I used to play with her clay."

"My aunt [Rachel Namingha] and my grandma [Annie Healing] used to make pottery for a living. I used to stay in Polacca for the summers. I remember Priscilla [Namingha] made some pots. My mom [Daisy Hooee] was down here [at Zuni], and I wanted to make something for money. My grandma used to tell me to make little pots to sell. I was too small to paint them.

"When I was in Zuni (1955) I really got started in all aspects of pots. I learned jewelry making too. I made jewelry for a living and made pots on the side. A few years ago I started making larger pots."

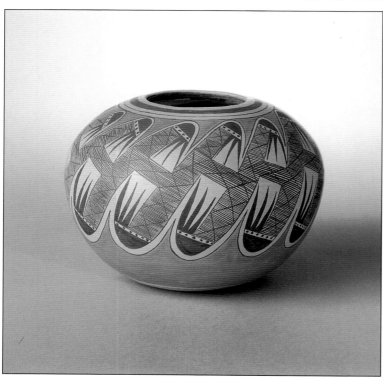

About Annie: "She used to garden at 'sand hills' during summer. She'd take me and my sister [Luella] up there, and she'd have some clay up there and we'd make little pots. Luella made some turtles not too long ago."

About Nampeyo: "I remember going from Zuni to Polacca to see her [Daisy's] grandmother. I remember her by the door, she was so small and white. She was playing with the dust by the windows. She was blind then."

"I learned most of my pottery from my grandmother, and when I got to doing more my mother helped with shaping. She taught me the ways to make them. The pottery maidens [Zuni Olla Maidens, a performance group that carries large water jars on their heads] would come in summertime, and she [Daisy] would help them make pottery. I learned to mix paint from my mom and learned about the designs, where they come from. I am also a silversmith, I do channel work, necklaces, bolos, and pins."

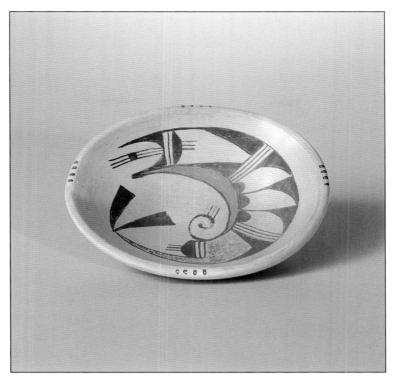

Opposite: Shirly Benn. Pot 4 x 6 in., ca. 1985. Courtesy Buckner/Lazarus collection, New York.

Top: Juanita Healing (portrait not available). Pot 1 ½ x 6 ½ x 7 ½ in., ca. 1978. Rick Dillingham collection.

Bottom: Cheryl Benn (portrait not available). Pot 4 x 4 in., ca. 1985. Courtesy Buckner/Lazarus collection, New York.

Right: Beatrice Naha Nampeyo (left), ca. 1930. Also pictured: Wesley Lesso (right), Rachel Namingha Nampeyo (center), and Priscilla Namingha Nampeyo (front). Courtesy Daisy Hooee Nampeyo. Pot not available.

Priscilla Namingha Nampeyo, b. 1924
"It's a good thing that I made pots, because it really helps—it helps my children, even my boys. I'm glad God created everything, and without Him we wouldn't be making pots. I always pray when I do my pots, and I tell my children to do the same thing. All of us are getting help from that.

"I learned some from Nampeyo because my grandmother [Annie Healing] didn't do much pottery and my mother [Rachel Namingha] worked with Nampeyo and would help paint and fire for her. Annie was with her [Nampeyo] all the time, and she painted for her too."

Opposite: Rachel Namingha Nampeyo, ca. 1972. Pot 4 1/4 x 8 1/2 in., 1979. Rick Dillingham collection.

Priscilla Namingha Nampeyo. Pot 7 1/2 x 12 in., 1987. Rick Dillingham collection.

Jean Sahme, b. 1949
(Why she leaves the `i' out of Sahmie: "It's simpler for me to spell it that way.")
"I have been happy doing my pottery. It's just gratifying that people enjoy what we do. I don't consider it work—it's something I like to do. We do suffer consequences working on it, but I like it. I share my thoughts in that way, through the pottery.

"What she [Nampeyo] left for us, we still enjoy it. Look how many years it's been since her death [1942], and we still enjoy it. I'm glad I came from an artistic family that can share these things."

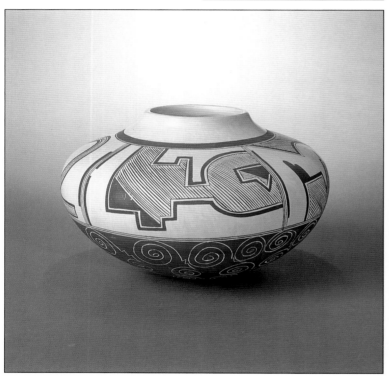

Left: Jean Sahme [note: this spelling is correct]. Pot 6 ½ x 9 ½ in., 1991. Rick Dillingham collection.

Right: Randy Sahmie (portrait not available). Pot 1 ¾ x 5 ¼ x 6 in., 1988. Rick Dillingham inventory.

Opposite: Donella Tom (portrait not available). Pot 1 x 6 in., 1992. Rick Dillingham inventory.

Ida Sahmie, b. 1960
"Personally, I feel I have a unique talent with pottery. It's a combination of both Hopi and Navajo, though I feel it should be more Navajo because I am a Navajo. I want to stick with more Navajo designs. The Yei figures are the most popular for me, secondly would be the rug designs, and third the sand painting designs."

Nyla Sahmie, b. 1954
"I had a great teacher and that's where I owe all my work—and that person is my mother [Priscilla Namingha]."

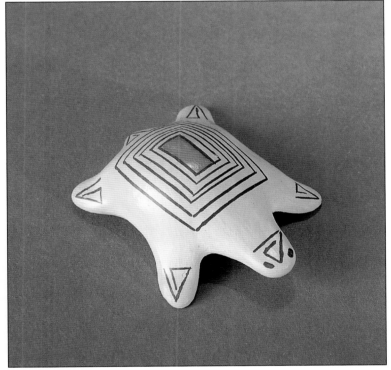

Opposite: Ida Sahmie. Pot 9 x 9 ½ in., 1990. Rick Dillingham collection.

Left: Nyla Sahmie. Pot 14 x 9 in., 1990. Courtesy of the artist.

Right: Michael Collateta (portrait not available). Turtle figure, 1 x 2 ½ in. Rick Dillingham inventory.

Rachel Sahmie, b. 1956
"It [pottery making] is part of my everyday. When you have a child, you make special time. It has automatically fit into everything I do. I don't feel complete if I don't do something on them every-day—even going on a walk for inspiration. It all just fits in, a member of the family."

Bonnie Chapella Nampeyo, b. 1958
"I'm just glad that my mom taught me to make pots, otherwise I don't know where I'd be now. She encouraged me all along. I don't think any-one could be as good a teacher as she."

Opposite: Rachel Sahmie. Pot 5 ½ x 4 in., 1980. Rick Dillingham collection.

Bonnie Chapella Nampeyo. Pot 3 ¼ x 4 in., 1992. Rick Dillingham inventory.

Ruth Namingha James, b. 1926
"First of all, I do some pottery, but all these years I was working for the federal government— twenty-seven years— and I didn't get back into it [pottery]. My other sisters got instruction from my mom, but I was always at work. My children—I had to be home to take care of them on weekends, so I never had time.

"I did do a little [pottery] work when I worked [for the government]. I never did the painting. I helped my mom mold, and she would paint them. I mainly do figurines and pottery with molded animals. I did do some painting on those. They were red clay. I also did some etching [sgraffito]."

Top: Eleanor Lucas (portrait not available). Pot 3 ¾ x 4 ⅝ in., ca. 1988. Courtesy Dewey Galleries, Ltd., Santa Fe.

Bottom: Karen Lucas (portrait not available). Pot 2 x 2 ½ in., 1992. Courtesy Otowi Trading Co., Santa Fe

Opposite: Ruth Namingha James (portrait not available). Storyteller figure, height 5 in., ca. 1985. Courtesy Jim Vigil, Jemez Pueblo.

*Darlene Vigil Nampeyo,
b. 1956
"Each pot that I create
gives me a special feel-
ing because I know it is
one of a kind and can
never be duplicated."*

*Top: Stephen Lucas, ca. 1980 (pho-
tographer unknown, courtesy Dextra
Quotskuyva). Opposite: Pot 5 ¼ x 6
in., 1992. Rick Dillingham inventory.*

*Bottom: Darlene Vigil Nampeyo. Four
tiles, 1992: triangle, 3 ½ in.; round,
4 ⅝ in. diameter; "bars," 4 ½ x 4 ½
in.; "manta," 4 ½ x 5 in.. Rick Dillingham collection.*

Les Namingha, b. 1967
(His mother is Zuni)
"Actually, I was looking at some of Dextra's designs and some were old Zuni designs. I want to do more with these designs. The Zuni potters now are using later designs with Spanish motifs. Not many are going back to the old designs from the ruins. I'd like to start doing a lot of these [designs in the Hawikuh book, The Excavation of Hawikuh, by Frederick Webb Hodge; Smith, Woodbury and Woodbury, Reprint, 1966, Musuem of the American Indian, Heye Foundation]. These designs and the designs from around here are an inspiration to me.

"I've been trying to experiment with my own designs, but Dextra says use the old ones first, they have a lot of power, then later add your own ideas. I'd like to incorporate some of the Zuni designs.

"I started four summers ago. My grandmother [Celecita Vicente] at Zuni was inspiring. I picked up something from her in terms of pottery, and four summers ago I really wanted to learn and Dextra offered to help. Dextra is a good teacher. Her work is of high quality, all parts of it. Steve [Lucas], Camille, and I have picked up her standards. We also got a lot of spiritual things from her. It was hard going back and forth to school, and I'd have to begin all over each summer."

Dextra Quotskuyva Nampeyo, b. 1928
"I think the pottery took over me and I can't get away from it. That's for sure. Clay is in my system. It's all the time, and you're happy with your pots. Camille has been doing real good. I was surprised, I thought she wouldn't continue."

Opposite: Les Namingha. Pot 6 ¾ x 6 ¼ in., 1992. Rick Dillingham inventory.

Dextra Quotskuyva Nampeyo. Pot 3 ¼ x 6 ¾ in., 1978. Rick Dillingham collection.

Camille Hisi Quotskuyva, b. 1964
"I've been doing pots seriously the past four years. I guess it's always been part of me, since I grew up with it. I guess it was only natural to do it. It was hard to learn, and at first I couldn't paint. Mom did the outlines until I could do it myself. I did sculptural stuff when I couldn't paint. Now I stick to traditional design—now that I can paint."

Top left: Hisi Quotskuyva Nampeyo. Pot 5 x 9 in., 1992. Rick Dillingham inventory.

Top right: Marie Koopee, ca. 1972. Pot not available.

Bottom right: Nellie Douma Nampeyo, ca. 1972. Opposite: Pot 3 ¼ x 7 ½ in., 1979. Rick Dillingham collection.

The Navasie Family

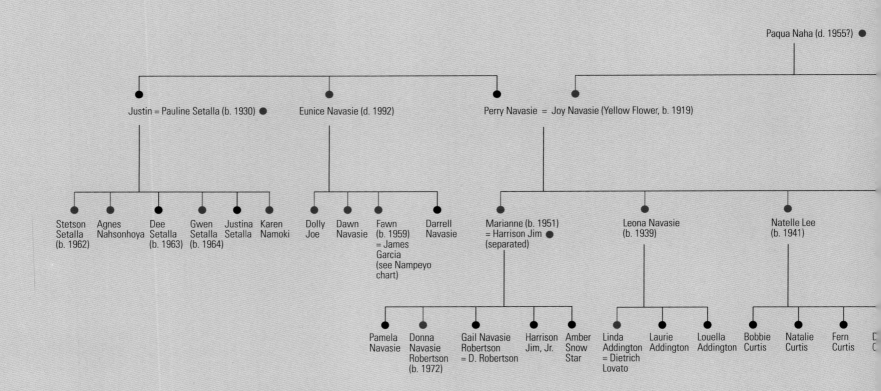

Paqua Naha (d. 1955?) ●

Justin = Pauline Setalla (b. 1930) ●   Eunice Navasie (d. 1992)   Perry Navasie = Joy Navasie (Yellow Flower, b. 1919)

Stetson Setalla (b. 1962) | Agnes Nahsonhoya | Dee Setalla (b. 1963) | Gwen Setalla | Justina Setalla (b. 1964) | Karen Namoki

Dolly Joe | Dawn Navasie | Fawn (b. 1959) = James Garcia (see Nampeyo chart) | Darrell Navasie

Marianne (b. 1951) = Harrison Jim ● (separated) | Leona Navasie (b. 1939) | Natelle Lee (b. 1941)

Pamela Navasie | Donna Navasie Robertson (b. 1972) | Gail Navasie Robertson = D. Robertson | Harrison Jim, Jr. | Amber Snow Star | Linda Addington = Dietrich Lovato | Laurie Addington | Louella Addington | Bobbie Curtis | Natalie Curtis | Fern Curtis

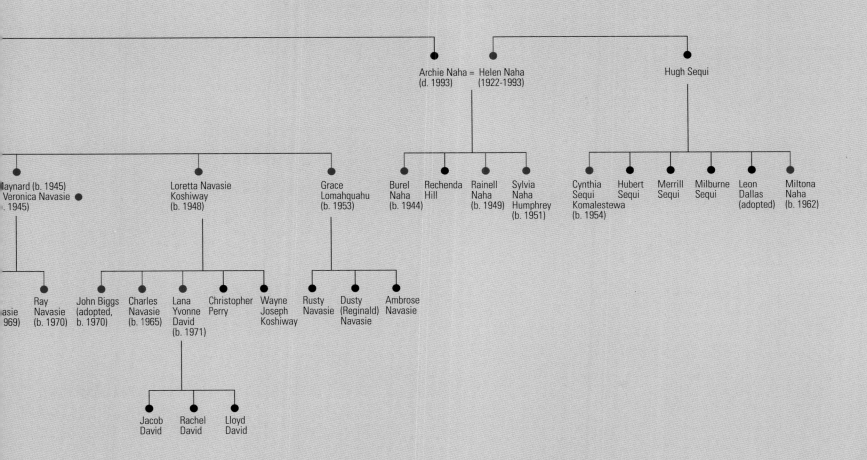

Archie Naha = Helen Naha
(d. 1993) (1922-1993)

Hugh Sequi

...aynard (b. 1945)
...Veronica Navasie
. 1945)

Loretta Navasie
Koshiway
(b. 1948)

Grace
Lomahquahu
(b. 1953)

Burel
Naha
(b. 1944)

Rechenda
Hill

Rainell
Naha
(b. 1949)

Sylvia
Naha
Humphrey
(b. 1951)

Cynthia
Sequi
Komalestewa
(b. 1954)

Hubert
Sequi

Merrill
Sequi

Milburne
Sequi

Leon
Dallas
(adopted)

Miltona
Naha
(b. 1962)

...asie
969)

Ray
Navasie
(b. 1970)

John Biggs
(adopted,
b. 1970)

Charles
Navasie
(b. 1965)

Lana
Yvonne
David
(b. 1971)

Christopher
Perry

Wayne
Joseph
Koshiway

Rusty
Navasie

Dusty
(Reginald)
Navasie

Ambrose
Navasie

Jacob
David

Rachel
David

Lloyd
David

Joy Navasie, b. 1919 ("But I have three birthdays, 1916 and 1918 also!")

She signs her pottery solely with the Frog symbol. "Every day we wake up to the same thing. It's a job we rely on, it's our livelihood. It's within us so much it just comes everyday. It's the only thing I'm really happy with. I enjoy my work. For a while I had to leave it when I got sick, and then the doctor said I could return to work.

"I've grown into the white slip [characteristic of the family's pottery] when my mother [Paqua] was alive. She did a beige and yellow pottery and started the white slip not long—three to four years— before she passed away. She didn't do much red. I did some little ones I remember in yellow clay. I used to put a flower drawing under my pot 'Yellow Flower' is my Indian name then I began to use my mother's trademark.

"When I was about twenty I started using the Frog. I made pottery before I married, I was a teenager— sixteen or seventeen. I feel good the slipped pottery has become recognized. It's hard to polish the slip. Everything is traditional—gathering the clay, the molding, coiling the pots, slipping, polishing, and painting them, and firing with sheep dung. The sheep manure is getting hard to get, but we haven't gotten into commercial stuff and I hope these girls don't do that. I want them to respect the Frog, my mother's work. I have pride in her Frog."

Joy Navasie. Pot 10 x 7 ½ in., 1981. Rick Dillingham collection.

Paqua Naha, ca. 1945? (photographer unknown, courtesy Maynard and Veronica Navasie). Opposite: Pot 8 ½ x 11 in., ca. 1950. Rick Dillingham collection.

Loretta Navasie Koshiway, b. 1948
She formerly signed her pottery with a Frog and the initial L.; now many carry just the Frog symbol. Joy Navasie does the painting.
"I still work closely with my mom. She outlines her own and I help her fill in and I'll help her mold. It's a process we go through, we'll pass them back and forth. I owe everything to her. She's taught me everything and without her we wouldn't have come this far. She taught us to thank the Mother Earth. All our work comes from nature."

Charles Navasie, b. 1965
"I owe it all to my grandmother [Joy Navasie]. She's the one who taught me. I kept working at it and I see an improvement in my work. The past three years she did my designing, and now I'm doing it. I'm trying to improve myself even further. My designs are similar to hers. I can never repay all my grandmother's help, and now I can help her. Putting back a little to help her out."

John Biggs, b. 1970
"I did some [pottery] in high school, it was a Native American art class. I learned to coil pottery and I came out here [Hopi] and kept on going. I was always drawing, since grade school and then I went to take art classes in Lawrence, Kansas. I started making pottery here with my mom and grandma. They inspired me and told me to keep up the good work and go to school."

Opposite left: Charles Navasie. Pot not available.

Opposite right: Loretta Navasie Koshiway. Pot 5 x 6 in., ca. 1988. Courtesy Buckner/ Lazarus collection, New York.

John Biggs (portrait not available). Pot 2 ½ x 3 ¼ in., 1992. Rick Dillingham inventory.

Leona Navasie, b. 1939
Her pottery in the recent past was signed with the Frog symbol and the initials L.N.

*"I think the reason I took interest in it—out of the family, my sisters anyway—
I knew my grandmother [Paqua Naha], and I stayed with her and saw the
work she did. It was a necessity at the time and wasn't appreciated as art. My
mom's [Joy Navasie] gotten to be pretty well known, and she talks to me of the
source of naturalness of the ingredients, the significance of everything, [from]
collecting clay to the preparation of the paints.*

*"I was raised off the reservation in the belagana world. I can see now looking
back I didn't appreciate my grandmother enough when she was alive. When
I came back home, when my mom was in her heyday—the eighties—lots of
shows, traveling, magazines—and that's when I got into potting with her. I
use it almost like therapy when I get a little depressed."*

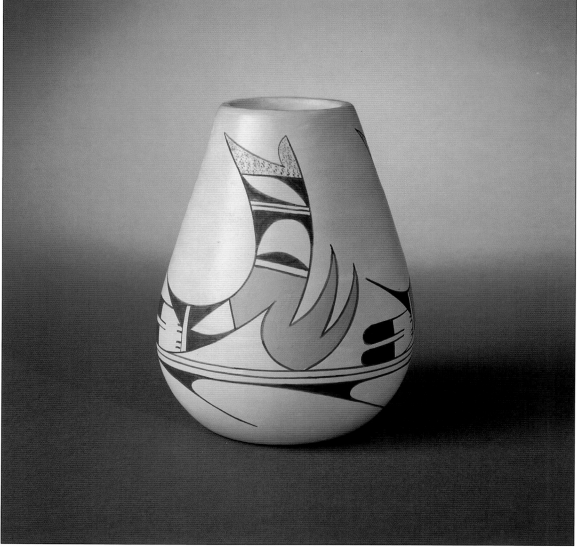

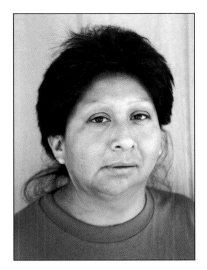

*Grace Lomahquahu,
b. 1953*
Her pottery has been
signed with the Frog
symbol and the initial G.
*"To tell the honest truth,
I've never had anything
to do with the yellow pottery. Doing the white
pots I learned from my
mother. The yellow would
come hard for me and
the white hard for them
[potters in the yellow
style], an exchange. I'm
always glad someone
wants to buy pottery.
You create it and it
feeds you. It's keeping
us alive and going.*

*"I guess mainly my
designs are similar to
hers [Joy Navasie]—
traditional. I try to keep
it similar to hers rather
than modernize it or
make it fancy."*

*Opposite: Leona Navasie. Pot 5 x 4
in., ca. 1987. Courtesy Buckner/
Lazarus collection, New York.*

*Grace Lomahquahu. Pot 6 x 7 in.,
1992. Rick Dillingham inventory.*

Maynard Navasie, b. 1945, and Veronica Navasie, b. 1945
They sign their pottery with a Frog and their initials.
Maynard: *"My mother-in-law [Laura Preston from Walpi] taught my wife, and I was really started by my mom [Joy Navasie] but the designing was my own. Ronnie [Veronica] has always done the molding, and I sand, polish, and paint. Pottery to our family is everything. It has paid for all our food and has helped in every way. It has also gotten us to know a lot of people who enjoy our work. I do the red slip when someone asks for it, but we usually do white-slipped pots. We use the Frog to carry the Navasie name."*

Bill Navasie, b.1969
He signs his pottery with a Frog, musical notes, and his initials.
"I just meet a lot of new people from the U.S., Japan, and Germany—people who travel a long way to look at Hopi art."

Maynard and Veronica Navasie.
Pots: tile, 6 ¼ in. tall, ca. 1982, Rick Dillingham collection; opposite: 7 x 6 in., 1990, Rick Dillingham inventory.

Marianne Navasie Jim, b. 1951
Her pottery in the recent past was signed with a Frog symbol and a tadpole drawing.
"As for me, I really enjoy my work. I used to sit here and watch my mom [Joy Navasie]. I wanted to learn the art of painting my own pottery, and it took a few years to learn [Joy would paint]. It relaxes my mind when I do it, although it can be tiring. I admire where it came from, from Paqua to my mom. I started when I was about twenty-five years old and my mother used to design them and we would sign them with a pollywog and M.N. [in addition to the family's Frog motif].

"There's too much contemporary [commercial and/or kiln-fired] pottery that we find hard to compete with. Even my girls have gotten into this contemporary work. We decided we needed to label them that way. My mother wants us to stick to traditional, stick to the old way."

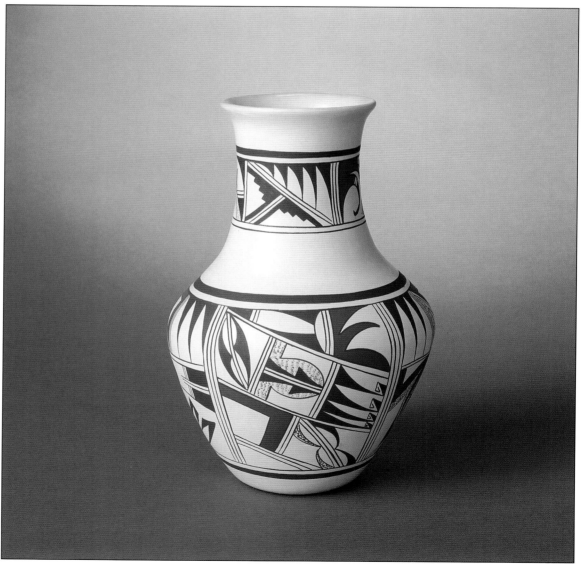

Donna Robertson,
b. 1972
"I got started when I was going to school. When I wanted something, my mom said, 'Go to work,' so I started making pottery—to work for what I want. I haven't tried anything else but the white style. It's the way I was taught. I haven't tried much out of the tradition, though I have done some small frog sculptures."

Opposite: Marianne Navasie. Pot 9 x 6 in., 1992. Rick Dillingham inventory.

Top: Cynthia Sequi Komalestewa. Pot 3 ½ x 3 ½ in., 1992. Courtesy Andrews Pueblo Pottery, Albuquerque.

Bottom: Miltona Naha (portrait not available). Pot 3 x 2 ½ in., 1992. Rick Dillingham inventory.

Cynthia Sequi, b. 1954
"I've been doing this for about six years. I kind of played around with clay when my maternal grandmother did it and I came down and worked with Sylvia [Naha], and then I started on my own. I would help her paint and then tried my own. I'm more Hopi than I am Tewa, so my pots are more Hopi style. Mine are a natural color and she [Sylvia] uses a white slip. I stayed with the brushes [commercial paintbrushes] after learning how to fill in with them."

Helen Naha (Feather Woman), b. 1922, d. 1993
"I started around 1945–46 because of financial problems we had after the war to support my family. It was hard for me to do it without a teacher. I had to teach myself. It took me a longer time to get used to it. The designs came from Awatovi ruins. Archie [her husband] and I used to put different designs together and came up with original combinations. He helped me with the clay, but I had to do the work all by myself. It took me six years for my pottery to start selling.

"I made a lot of mistakes because I taught myself. I like the black and white designs the best. I used to paint my pottery like Joy Navasie, and then I got my own designs from the sherds [at Awatovi ruin]. I watched Archie's mom, Paqua. I use a few designs with many variations."

Helen Ṅaha. Pot 5 ½ x 11 ½ in., ca. 1979. Rick Dillingham collection.

Opposite: Burel Naha. Pot 5 ½ x 8 ½ in., 1992. Rick Dillingham inventory.

Burel Naha, b. 1944
"As far as getting started, I owe it to my mother [Helen Naha]. I got started late because I had a teaching position. I used to work in the summer when school was out.

"The designs I was using earlier were my mom's, and a year and a half ago my daughter Cindy came home with a picture of a spider. She said they were doing [drawing] them at school. About two or three weeks later, at 3 a.m. with that on my mind, I couldn't find the drawing. When I found it, I started using spider designs on my pots. A lot of people call me Spider Man, and I've gone off with my own designs.

"It's refreshing to work with my hands. Being an art teacher got me going."

73

Sylvia Naha, b. 1951
She signs her pottery with a Feather and the initial S.
"A lot of my designs are in part some of Mom's
[Helen Naha] designs, and I just mix them. There
are about five designs of hers I use in different
ways. Sometimes I used to cover up crooked designs and fit others to it.

"I'm starting to mix my designs with more traditional
designs. A lot of people like the animal designs and
a lot like the traditional, so I mix them. People like
to see a lot of fineline, and others like the simplicity.
I like to bounce back and forth, to make something
eye pleasing. I don't understand what the design
meant before so I use them to make something someone will like."

Rainell (Rainy) Naha, b. 1949
"I've been around pots most all my life growing up. I
didn't see it as I do today. A young person sees things
differently. It was a burden to make finances come
together, so we helped our mom [Helen Naha]. It was
a chore, but at that time I really didn't understand it. I
left at eight and moved to Utah, and I'd come home
every summer. I didn't have too much social interaction with the villagers.

"I came back in 1989. I wanted to find my roots. I
needed to come home, and I wanted to learn this
[pottery making] while I had the greatest teacher
alive [Helen Naha]. There's been a tremendous
amount of growth, and I see myself as an artist in
traditional pots. I know what I need to stay within
those limits. I'm a potter, a competitive runner, I raise
cattle, and I volunteer at the high school. I tried my
hand at politics, and that only lasted a year!"

*Sylvia Naha Humphrey. Opposite: Pot
5 ½ x 5 in., 1992. Courtesy Andrews
Pueblo Pottery, Albuquerque.*

Rainelle Naha. Pot 4 ½ x 4 ¼ in., 1992. Rick Dillingham inventory.

Opposite: Dawn Navasie. Pot 5 x 8 in., 1992. Courtesy McGees Indian Art, Keams Canyon, Arizona.

Fawn Garcia, b. 1959
"I used to do the white pottery with my mom
[Eunice Navasie], and now I do the yellow style
with James. It's hard to get the white. I like doing
the white—it's harder. I still like to carry on my
mother's designs, since I learned from her. I try to
experiment with different types of designs. I do most
of the molding, I polish, then we do the painting
together. I think we're doing good and there's a lot
of improvement in our work. We'll get better at it!"

Pauline Setalla, b. 1930
"I learned from my mother-in-law, Agnes Navasie, my husband's mother, around 1954. His name is Justin. I do white pottery, but I got tired of white-washing, so now I'm doing some natural yellow and red clay. I taught all my children. I'm from Second Mesa and married here. I use mostly corn designs, yellow clouds, snow, and stairways. I also use pueblo houses [drawings of them] and lightning."

Dee Johnson Setalla, b. 1963
"I've been making since I was small. I learned everything from my mom. I quit when I went to school, and when I finished I started up again. Since I'm not working at a job I do pottery fulltime."

Opposite: Fawn Navasie Garcia. Pot 7 x 6 ¼ in., ca. 1988. Courtesy Dewey Galleries, Ltd., Santa Fe.

Top: Pauline Setalla. Pot not available.

Bottom: Dee Setalla. Pot not available.

Stetson Setalla (portrait not available). Pot 3 ½ x 9 ¾ in., 1992. Courtesy McGees Indian Art, Keams Canyon, Arizona.

ACOMA PUEBLO

The Chino Family

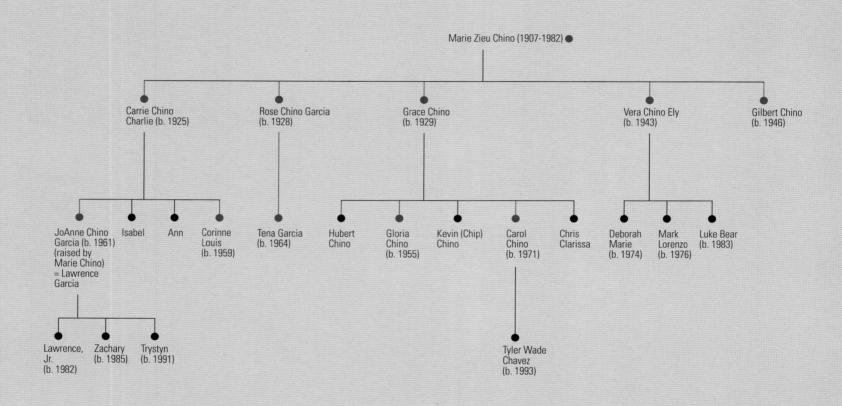

Marie Zieu Chino (1907-1982) ●

Carrie Chino Charlie (b. 1925)
Rose Chino Garcia (b. 1928)
Grace Chino (b. 1929)
Vera Chino Ely (b. 1943)
Gilbert Chino (b. 1946)

JoAnne Chino Garcia (b. 1961) (raised by Marie Chino) = Lawrence Garcia
Isabel
Ann
Corinne Louis (b. 1959)
Tena Garcia (b. 1964)
Hubert Chino
Gloria Chino (b. 1955)
Kevin (Chip) Chino
Carol Chino (b. 1971)
Chris Clarissa
Deborah Marie (b. 1974)
Mark Lorenzo (b. 1976)
Luke Bear (b. 1983)

Lawrence, Jr. (b. 1982)
Zachary (b. 1985)
Trystyn (b. 1991)
Tyler Wade Chavez (b. 1993)

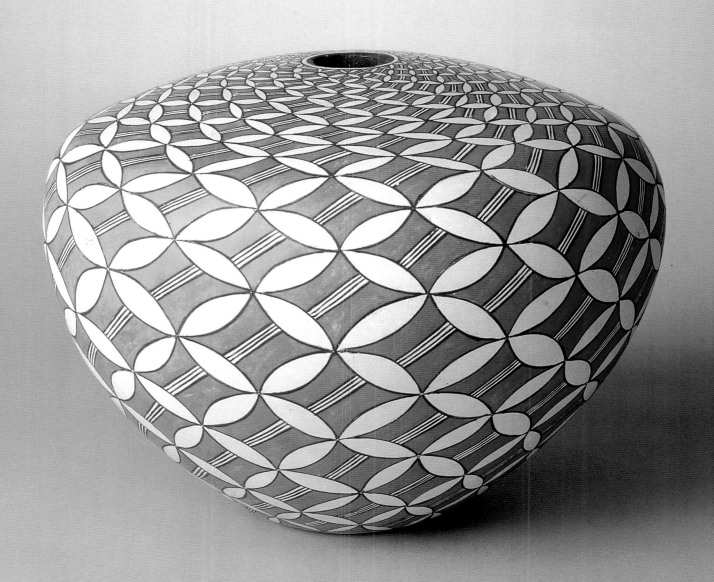

Tena Garcia, b. 1964
"I do miniatures. I like doing the Mimbres designs, and I do smaller pieces, and I help Rose [Chino Garcia] out on her bigger pieces. Rose taught me how to make pottery. I like making small seed pots and small versions of old jars. I want to learn how to make big pots in the future."

Previous page: Marie Zieu Chino. Pot 13 x 8 ½ in., 1979. Rick Dillingham collection.

Marie Zieu Chino, ca. 1972. Pot 9 x 11 ½ in., 1981. Rick Dillingham collection.

Tena Garcia. Pot not available.

Opposite: Rose Chino Garcia. Pot 7 x 8 in., 1992. Rick Dillingham inventory.

Rose Chino Garcia, b. 1928
"I enjoy doing it. I learned it from my mom [Marie Z. Chino] and just kept it up. She's no longer here. It's been doing real good for me and my daughter [Tena]. I'm trying to stick to Marie's designs. I always did the tall-necked shapes. I also do plates with potsherd designs. I've invented some designs myself. I want to continue doing pots and add on new designs and shapes when I can."

Carrie Chino Charlie, b. 1925
"I said, `Mom [Marie Z. Chino], show me how to make pottery,' and then she started teaching me. I was very interested in making, but I didn't learn it right away. I started helping her fill in her painting, then she started teaching me all of it. She started taking me to the markets, and then I began to teach my children. I learned the fineline design from my mom and have continued to use it. My daughters Isabel and Ann help me paint it now."

JoAnn Chino Garcia (portrait not available). Pot 4 ¼ x 4 ½ in., 1989. Rick Dillingham collection.

Opposite: Carrie Chino Charlie. Pot 8 ¼ x 11 ¼ in., ca. 1985. Rick Dillingham collection.

Gilbert Chino, b. 1946

"I value traditional pottery very much. It's a shame that some people have to mix commercial clay with real clay. From there it makes it difficult for those who use traditional stuff. During Indian Market it's like going to a flea market, because they really don't judge on traditional pottery. There's no way the colors you see are natural—we don't have those colors. We don't get as much as our work is worth when tourists don't know the difference between commercial and traditional. I do tell them what the difference is at the house when they come to buy. I want to be able to get what I put into it."

Opposite: Gilbert Chino. Pot with commercial black paint, 6 x 6 ½ in., 1989. Rick Dillingham collection.

Corrine Louis (portrait not available). Commercial ceramic pot, 7 x 2 ¾ in., ca. 1989. Courtesy Carrie Charlie.

Grace Chino, b. 1929

"When I first started it seemed easy, and now when I learned more it has become more enjoyable. I enjoy working. I like to work alone, with both the potting and painting. When I'm doing my pottery I think of mom [Marie Z. Chino] first, and that she could help me. I want to do like she does. She didn't need outlining, she just painted, and sometimes I do that now. I know the design and I just do it."

Grace Chino. Pot 8 ½ x 9 in., 1991, painted by Gloria Chino. Rick Dillingham inventory.

Top right: Gloria Chino (pot not available).

Bottom right: Vera Chino Ely (portrait courtesy Mark Ely). Opposite: Pot 7 x 8 ¼ in., ca. 1979, made by Marie Z. Chino and painted by Vera Chino Ely.

The Lewis Family

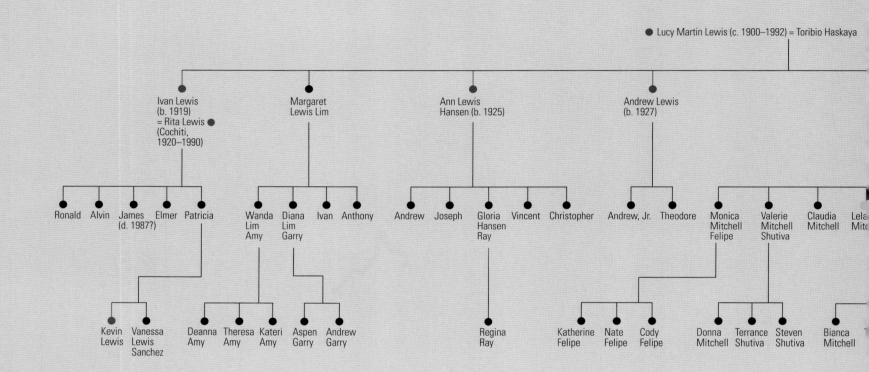

Lucy Martin Lewis (c. 1900–1992) = Toribio Haskaya

Ivan Lewis
(b. 1919)
= Rita Lewis
(Cochiti,
1920–1990)

Margaret
Lewis Lim

Ann Lewis
Hansen (b. 1925)

Andrew Lewis
(b. 1927)

Ronald Alvin James
(d. 1987?) Elmer Patricia

Wanda
Lim
Amy Diana
Lim
Garry Ivan Anthony

Andrew Joseph Gloria
Hansen
Ray Vincent Christopher

Andrew, Jr. Theodore Monica
Mitchell
Felipe Valerie
Mitchell
Shutiva Claudia
Mitchell Lela
Mit

Kevin
Lewis Vanessa
Lewis
Sanchez

Deanna
Amy Theresa
Amy Kateri
Amy Aspen
Garry Andrew
Garry

Regina
Ray

Katherine
Felipe Nate
Felipe Cody
Felipe Donna
Mitchell Terrance
Shutiva Steven
Shutiva Bianca
Mitchell

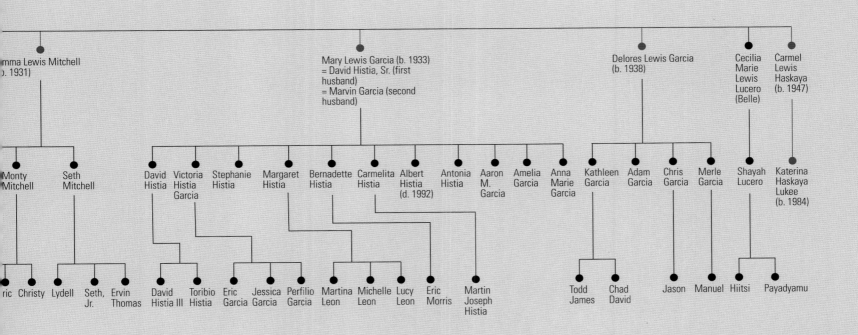

mma Lewis Mitchell
b. 1931)

Mary Lewis Garcia (b. 1933)
= David Histia, Sr. (first
husband)
= Marvin Garcia (second
husband)

Delores Lewis Garcia
(b. 1938)

Cecilia
Marie
Lewis
Lucero
(Belle)

Carmel
Lewis
Haskaya
(b. 1947)

Monty
Mitchell

Seth
Mitchell

David
Histia

Victoria
Histia
Garcia

Stephanie
Histia

Margaret
Histia

Bernadette
Histia

Carmelita
Histia

Albert
Histia
(d. 1992)

Antonia
Histia

Aaron
M.
Garcia

Amelia
Garcia

Anna
Marie
Garcia

Kathleen
Garcia

Adam
Garcia

Chris
Garcia

Merle
Garcia

Shayah
Lucero

Katerina
Haskaya
Lukee
(b. 1984)

ric   Christy

Lydell

Seth,
Jr.

Ervin
Thomas

David
Histia III

Toribio
Histia

Eric
Garcia

Jessica
Garcia

Perfilio
Garcia

Martina
Leon

Michelle
Leon

Lucy
Leon

Eric
Morris

Martin
Joseph
Histia

Todd
James

Chad
David

Jason

Manuel

Hiitsi

Payadyamu

93

Lucy Martin Lewis, 1980. Pots: 5 x 9 in., 1991, Rick Dillingham inventory; opposite: 5 x 6 ¼ in., ca. 1965, Rick Dillingham collection.

Ivan Lewis, b. 1919

"I never made Acoma pottery. When Rita's mother was getting older, she [Rita] took an interest in pottery. Her mother was a good potter and taught pottery making at the Indian schools in Santa Fe and Albuquerque. Rita learned from her mother, like my mother [Lucy M. Lewis] passed it to our family. We were married in 1944, and I moved to Cochiti. I was in the service and was discharged in 1946 or so. I decided to make my home here [at Cochiti]. Rita started [making pottery] around 1959. The dam [Cochiti Lake dam] started around 1965, and I worked on it for twelve years. I started pottery with her [Rita] around 1977. We used to work with silver, too. I didn't learn pottery from my mom, I learned from Rita. I started making different figures: cowboys, mermaids. I make them in the traditional way. I'm having a hard time getting the slip [white base slip], so sometimes I have to use some commercial paint when I don't have enough.

"You [Rick] got me started on mermaids with an order you gave me. People ask how I got started, and I tell them I used to talk to the mermaids at Cochiti Lake. They would come out around midnight. I'm the only one who knows where they are."

Lucy Martin Lewis, 1980. Two pieces: turkey figure, 4 in. high, 1991, and bird figure, 3 ½ in. long, 1991, both Rick Dillingham inventory.

Opposite: Ivan Lewis. Mermaid figure by Ivan and Rita Lewis, ca. 1987, 6 ½ x 10 ½ in.. Rick Dillingham collection.

Anne Lewis Hansen, b. 1925
"In 1935 or so, my brother and I used to sell the pottery with Mom [Lucy M. Lewis] along Route 66, before I went away to boarding school. I used to help Mom grind the sherds for clay. I started miniatures when she got the clay ready. In the 1950s I began to go to Indian Market and Gallup. Eventually, I got my own booth [after sharing with her mother].

"I left in 1944 and went to California, and I've lived there since. I come home every year. Now that Lucy is gone [d. 1991], I won't make it [home] as much. I like making pottery. I graduated from San Jose State with a history major. There's no problem working in California doing traditional Acoma pottery. I've helped jury shows in California, and I give classes and presentations on pottery."

Andrew Lewis, b. 1927

"When I first started, I figured it was only for women but I decided one day I wanted to make pottery. I asked my mom [Lucy Lewis] for some clay. She said, 'When it's gone, you know where it is to get your own.'

"As far as I know—or the stories I've heard—there was a man-woman [potter]. My late father knew him. I had an urge to make pottery, but my father didn't make. I use the Mimbres [designs], and mostly I stay with Acoma traditional designs. I'm trying to out-do some of the potters who do big pots. To date I've made one 22 inches in height and about 32 inches in diameter. I'm going to make bigger ones still."

Opposite: Anne Lewis Hansen. Pot 4 x 5 in., ca. 1982. Courtesy Delores Lewis Garcia.

Left: Kevin Lewis (Morningstar) (portrait not available). Animal figure 6 ½ x 9 in., 1992. Courtesy Buckner/ Lazarus collection, New York.

Right: Andrew Lewis. Pot 5 ½ x 6 ½ in., 1992. Rick Dillingham inventory.

Emma Lewis Mitchell, b. 1931
"I started about the 1960s. I found an old pot dated 1972 the other day. I'm sticking with the Mimbres designs. I want to keep them alive by continuing to use them—try to keep them as the Mimbres people painted them. I feel a spiritual connection to them. I think we're all connected some way. The archaeologists say, Where did the ancient people go? What about us? We're the new generation.

"There's a lot of good things to say about my mother. She was my inspiration, and without her encouragement, her help and guidance, I wouldn't be where I am today."

Mary Lewis Garcia, b. 1933
"I'm strictly sticking to traditional polychrome designs. Once in a while I'll do others—Chaco, Mesa Verde, or Mimbres—but I prefer to do Acoma Polychrome. I like to do the traditional olla form, miniatures, and large, and I like to make serving bowls and canteens. I also like to do Mesa Verde mugs and ladles and corrugated cooking pots.

"About commercial pottery: I wish they would go back to the traditional way of pottery making. It has more meaning. The materials are all there for us from the earth."

Opposite: Emma Lewis Mitchell. Pot 7 x 7 in., 1992. Rick Dillingham inventory.

Delores Lewis Garcia, b. 1938
"My greatest inspiration is from the ancient people, the Anasazi. If it weren't for them, we wouldn't be doing the pots. The best of all inspiration is my mom, Lucy. If it weren't for her, I wouldn't be making any pots. I think it's good we talk about our pottery [the family does a lot of public demonstration] because not everyone knows about Indian pottery. I think the non-Indian should hear it from a potter. From there, I think they understand the true feeling of Indian art, where the designs come from and where we came from—the Ancient People. Generation to generation, we keep the pottery rolling."

Opposite: Delores Lewis Garcia. Pot 3 x 5 in., 1991. Rick Dillingham inventory.

Carmel Lewis Haskaya with her daughter Katerina Haskaya Lukee. Pots: Left: Katerina Haskaya Lukee. 1 ½ x 1 ¾ in. (painted by Carmel). Right: Carmel Lewis Haskaya. Pot 4 x 6 in., 1991. Both Rick Dillingham inventory.

ZIA PUEBLO

The Medina Family

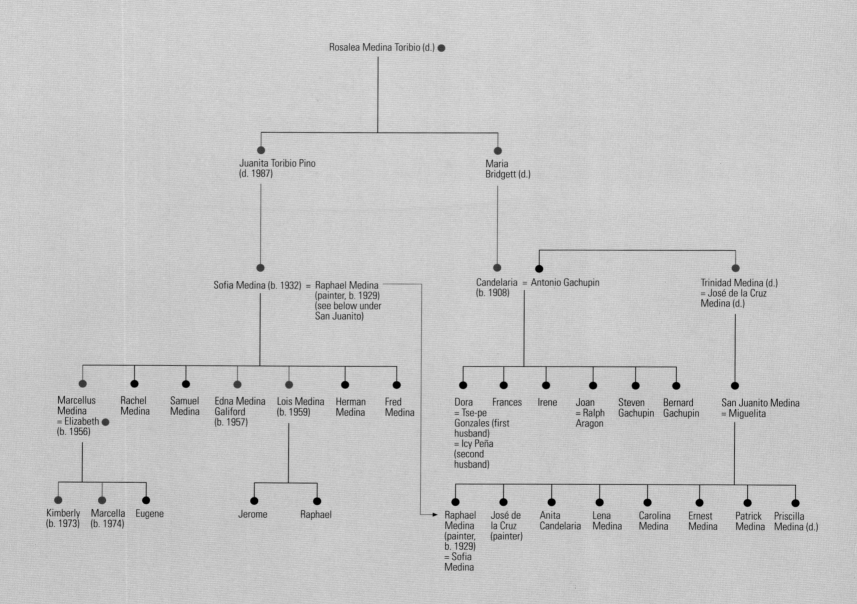

Rosalea Medina Toribio (d.) ●

Juanita Toribio Pino (d. 1987)

Maria Bridgett (d.)

Sofia Medina (b. 1932) = Raphael Medina (painter, b. 1929) (see below under San Juanito)

Candelaria (b. 1908) = Antonio Gachupin

Trinidad Medina (d.) = José de la Cruz Medina (d.)

Marcellus Medina = Elizabeth (b. 1956) ●

Rachel Medina

Samuel Medina

Edna Medina Galiford (b. 1957)

Lois Medina (b. 1959)

Herman Medina

Fred Medina

Dora = Tse-pe Gonzales (first husband) = Icy Peña (second husband)

Frances

Irene

Joan = Ralph Aragon

Steven Gachupin

Bernard Gachupin

San Juanito Medina = Miguelita

Kimberly (b. 1973)

Marcella (b. 1974)

Eugene

Jerome

Raphael

Raphael Medina (painter, b. 1929) = Sofia Medina

José de la Cruz (painter)

Anita Candelaria

Lena Medina

Carolina Medina

Ernest Medina

Patrick Medina

Priscilla Medina (d.)

Trinidad Medina, ca. 1925?, with Priscilla (deceased), Patrick, Ernest, Rose (deceased), Carolina and Trinidad (deceased). (Courtesy Sofia Medina, Zia.) Pot approximately 18 x 20 in., ca. 1925. Collection of Frank Sorauf, Minneapolis.

Opposite: J.D. (José de la Cruz) Medina (portrait not available). Pot made by Sofia Medina with acrylic painting by J. D. Medina, 8 x 10 ½ in., ca. 1975. Courtesy Margaret Gutierrez, Santa Clara Pueblo.

Top: Juanita Pino (portrait not available). Pot 10 ¼ x 11 in., 1950. Courtesy Museum of Indian Art and Culture/ Laboratory of Anthropology, Santa Fe.

Bottom: Sofia Medina. Pot 9 ½ x 11 in., 1992. Rick Dillingham inventory.

Sofia Medina, b. 1932
"I got into making potteries in 1963 after returning from California—I lived there a while. Raphael's [her husband] grandmother, Trinidad, started to show me how to make them. I started enjoying it. It made me feel that instead of sitting around, it was something I loved to do. I didn't do it for money. It was very consoling if I was depressed, and when I got back to pots it gave me a lot of relief. I talked to them. It's something that I hold in my heart. When I'm not doing my pottery, I'm not happy.

"In maybe 1954 I encouraged him [Raphael] to paint, and he did [acrylic] painting on paper. It was the same thing with him—he enjoyed painting, something he loved to do. I think he started painting on my pots in the seventies. He used natural pigments on only two of them."

"Spiritually, the pottery can ease your mind. I do sing a lot when I am working . . . worse than a radio!"

About Trinidad Medina: *"She always told me instead of sitting around after the children went to school to work on pottery. Pottery making was important. Financially she could depend on that. She said she'd teach me—but first, tell me and promise me whatever I teach you, pass it on to my grandchildren so in the future they will profit from it and in the future my work would continue."*

Sofia to her grandchildren: *"I've talked to them and explained to them, pottery is a hard job. And I told them, I don't know how long this pottery business will be good, so get an education. In case you are laid off a job, you will have something to fall back on, a financial backup."*

signed   by — Rafael Medina
tery made   by — Sofia P. Medina

Lois Medina, b. 1959
"I try to make my pottery distinctive in shape, form, and design, and I'm trying to do different styles and designs. I do a lot of research on my own, designs from other pueblos, and I mix them with mine. Then I go back to the old pottery and learn the meaning of each design.

"When I started working, my grandma [Sofia's mother, Juanita Pino] sat me down and told me the story behind pottery, how it was created—the true meaning behind it. She gave me everything—some old purse with old tools, gourds, brushes, black stone [for painting]—I won't use it, it's too precious. I had others made."

About Trinidad: "Trinidad had a lot of impact on me, though I didn't know her on a personal level well. Her design was so unique. I knew her as an old woman. I never really got to talk to her."

Rachel Medina, b. 1961
"Well, I went to school for a while, vocational school for a nursing degree, and I went to Eastern in Portales for a while. When I had my kids, I decided to do pots more seriously. Now I'm picking it up again.

"I stay down at old Santa Ana, where my fiancé is from, and I joked about reviving pottery there! I do the traditional style like my mom, but she tells me my designs are leaning to Santa Ana style, with more flowers and stuff. My mom told me they look Santa Ana. There's a lady teaching me the different Santa Ana designs, Eudora Montoya.

"With all the inspiration and guidance and support the family gives to one another, it's good to have them. It makes you feel you can do whatever you want in the art, and you feel successful."

Edna Galiford, b. 1957
"My work is very contemporary—I'm not traditional, I guess you could call it.
I try to keep a little tradition and keep with my father's style. I use a lot of contemporary bold designs, but the figures are traditional. I do painting on matte boards with bold colors, and the paintings I do on wood are more natural colors.

"On the pots, I do an in-between style. It's not very traditional—I mix everything up on the pots. I guess I'm trying to create my own style. I'm trying to make my own name—independence. I can't get away from the Medina name, everyone knows it.

"I have a degree in art education and commercial art. I taught two years at the Christian School and the public school in Gallup. Then I quit and started doing my art. I taught in Portales one year, too. I come home on special occasions—feast and Christmas."

Opposite: Lois Medina. Pot 10 ½ x 7 ¾ in., 1993. Rick Dillingham inventory.

Left: Rachel Medina. Pot not available.

Right: Edna Medina Galiford. Pot not available.

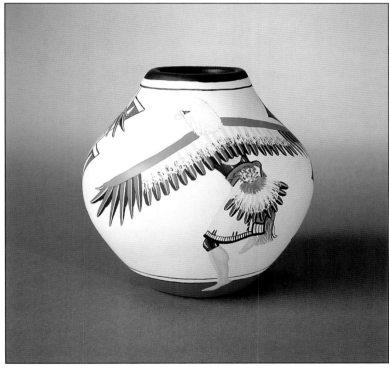

Marcellus Medina, b. 1954

"Me and Liz work with acrylic-painted pottery. She makes the pottery and fires it. After that stage, I take it, sand it, and work on it with acrylic paint. The natural [native pigment] ones I do are small—three to four inches—and I make the small ones. I don't produce them in huge quantity. I don't work on very large pieces.

"It was 1976 when I started. My father was teaching me, getting me used to painting figures on the pot itself. It's really hard. At the beginning I traced a figure of a dancer on a flat surface and then traced it on the pot, but the figure wasn't the same. It was all broken up—it didn't look right. It looked more like Picasso's figures! Instead of tracing, I sketch on the pot itself.

"My mom is really traditional. She really believes in traditional ways. For me and Liz it's half and half, part traditional and part contemporary. For an Indian artist to succeed they have to change with the times, and we have to appeal to Anglo art tastes. It's really difficult for my parents to understand, and we still debate it—old and new generations. We still believe in tradition but also in the new age."

Opposite: Elizabeth Medina. Pot 10 ½ x 11 in., 1992. Courtesy of the artist. Rachel Medina. Pot not available.

Marcellus Medina. Pot made by Elizabeth Medina and painted in acrylic by Marcellus Medina, 3 ¾ x 3 ½ in., 1990. Courtesy Buckner/ Lazarus collection, New York.

Elizabeth Medina, b. 1956
"I used to make pottery when I was a child, but
they were Jemez pottery [Liz was born at Jemez]. I
started making Zia pots after I was married in 1978
and got tribal permission. My mother-in-law, Sofia,
is my inspiration. She always gets the credit, and I
make sure she does!

"I still make the larger pots for Marcellus to paint. I
had to learn a lot, because it's different from the
Jemez pottery—the clay is different and so are the
paints.

"The black rock is what we use for temper. Basalt.
We pound it into chunks, then to powder. It's difficult to do. We bury chunks of rock by the river and
let freezing help deteriorate it. Once it's dug up, it's
a little easier to prepare. It's Mother Nature helping
with erosion. We leave them for two or three years.

"With our business, we're looking at a lot of changes,
and we want to make more and change the style
to something different where we can interest the
public."

*Kimberly Medina,
b. 1973*
"It's very interesting to learn about my family's history and where tradition came from—and that my family is still carrying on these traditions, passed from generation to generation. At first, when I started, it was exciting to do something different. Now that I'm older and going to school, I want to find out what's out there for me. I make during the summer when I'm not in school and when I need to make some extra money.

"It's hard for me to decide which direction to go. School is the most important thing for me now."

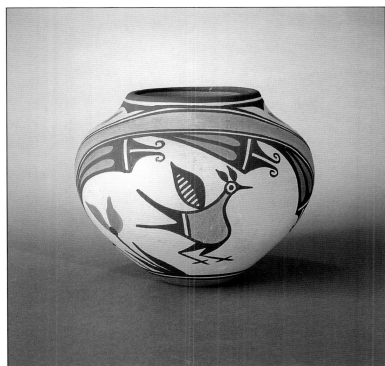

*Marcella Medina,
b. 1974*
"I only make small ones for spending money. Right now I'm not totally into pots, I'm still in high school. I do little traditional pots and sometimes I paint them. I wanted to do acrylic-painted pots, but it's hard. I don't have the patience."

COCHITI

The Herrera Family

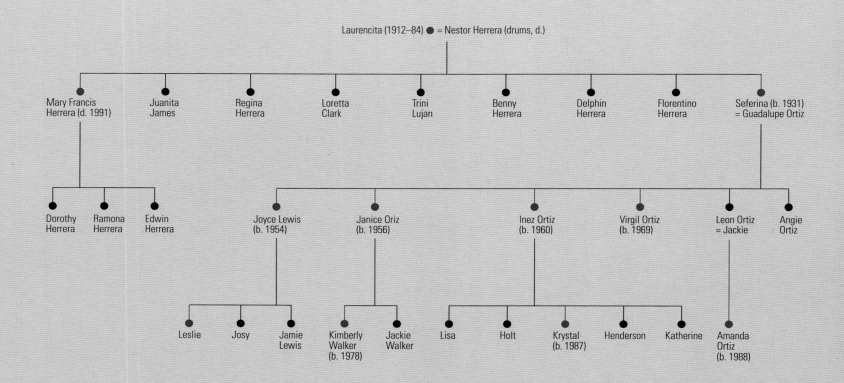

Laurencita (1912–84) ● = Nestor Herrera (drums, d.)

Mary Francis Herrera (d. 1991) | Juanita James | Regina Herrera | Loretta Clark | Trini Lujan | Benny Herrera | Delphin Herrera | Florentino Herrera | Seferina (b. 1931) = Guadalupe Ortiz

Dorothy Herrera | Ramona Herrera | Edwin Herrera | Joyce Lewis (b. 1954) | Janice Oriz (b. 1956) | Inez Ortiz (b. 1960) | Virgil Ortiz (b. 1969) | Leon Ortiz = Jackie | Angie Ortiz

Leslie | Josy | Jamie Lewis | Kimberly Walker (b. 1978) | Jackie Walker | Lisa | Holt | Krystal (b. 1987) | Henderson | Katherine | Amanda Ortiz (b. 1988)

Laurencita Herrera, b. 1912, d. 1984
On Seferina Ortiz: "She was one of a few making traditional pottery. She did all kinds of things: water jars, bowls, and figurines. I think she started the figurines in the 1960s. Just by watching her is how we learned. She would be the main inspiration on my part."

Laurencita Herrera, October 1958 (photographer unknown, courtesy Seferina Ortiz). Pots: left: female figure, height 9 ¾ in., 1958, IAF 2755, courtesy Indian Arts Research Center, School of American Research, Santa Fe; right: male figure, height 10 ¾ in., 1958, IAF 2756, courtesy Indian Arts Research Center, School of American Research, Santa Fe.

Seferina Ortiz, b. 1931
"I started making miniatures and gradually I started making larger ones. Now I make pots along with the figurines. I'm doing figures the traditional way. We started reviving the circus people, and we do nativities and I do the 'bathing beauties.' I like making the bears the most. My husband [Guadalupe] makes some, and he's learning to design. I make the black paint from the wild spinach (beeweed) plant. We have to dig the slip—ten to twelve feet underground until we found a layer."

Opposite: Laurencita Herrera. Story-teller, height 5 ¾ in., ca. 1975, Rick Dillingham inventory.

Seferina Ortiz. Bear figures: left: seated, height 4 ¾ in., 1992, Rick Dillingham inventory; right: standing, height 4 ¼ in., 1992, Rick Dillingham inventory.

Virgil Ortiz, b. 1969
"We were asked to revive the older figures, and we had pictures of old pieces. I started researching them and got more pictures. Everything I do is traditional. I still use the same designs, but I'll change them to add my own style. The first one [figure] I made is when I was six years old. I'm experimenting with pots, and I specialize in bears and circus people. I'm trying to revive the standing figures."

Joyce Lewis, b. 1954
"A lot of people wanted little things [pots], so I tried small. It seems I can make them better than big ones. Sometimes I make little tiny storytellers, too."

Joyce Ortiz Lewis. Nativity set, 1993, tallest figure 2 ½ in. Courtesy Seferina Ortiz.

Opposite: Virgil Ortiz. Figure, height 11 in., 1989. Rick Dillingham collection.

124

Janice Ortiz, b. 1956
"I range in anything from tiny miniature nativity sets to storytellers, plus the ceramics [commercial slipcast ware]. I do pots and mugs and little animals in ceramic. I do a lot of ceramic wedding vases also. I got everything from my mom—I use a lot of her designs. The designs were handed down in the family to the kids. I learned within the past year and a half, and I recently learned to paint with the yucca instead of brushes. I like it better than paint brushes, the lines are straight."

Inez Ortiz, b. 1960
"I make all kinds of things: bears, nativity sets, miniatures, story-tellers, owls, turtles, and clay drums. I mold the `couple' pieces [a man and woman together] in different sizes. I'm also into the ceramics to make some things easier. I go back to the traditional because people like it."

Opposite: Janice Ortiz. Storyteller, height 5 ½ in., 1992. Rick Dillingham inventory.

Inez Ortiz. Storyteller, height 2 ¾ in., 1992. Rick Dillingham inventory.

Group portrait: (Left to right) top row: Jamie Lewis, Kimberly Walker, Lisa Holt, bottom row: Krystal Henderson, Jackie Walker, and Amanda Ortiz.

SANTO DOMINGO

The Melchor Family

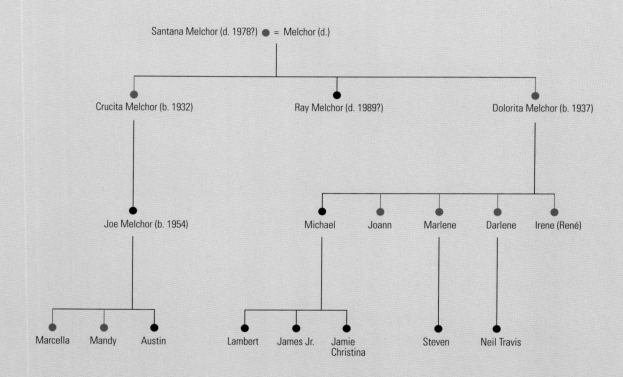

Santana Melchor (d. 1978?) ● = Melchor (d.)

Crucita Melchor (b. 1932)　　Ray Melchor (d. 1989?)　　Dolorita Melchor (b. 1937)

Joe Melchor (b. 1954)　　Michael　Joann　Marlene　Darlene　Irene (René)

Marcella　Mandy　Austin　　Lambert　James Jr.　Jamie Christina　　Steven　Neil Travis

Santana Melchor (courtesy Crucita and Dolorita Melchor). Pot: flag, 8 x 9 ½ in., 1976, Rick Dillingham collection.

Crucita Melchor, b. 1932
About her mother Santana Melchor: "She didn't go to school, she stayed home all the time. She was a housewife—cooking, making pottery and jewelry. She did mostly pottery she learned from her mother, Maria Garcia. She made small pots when she was very young, and at around twenty-five years old she was making big storage jars all by herself."

"I used to do designs when I was eighteen or so—I was still in school—and I'm still doing the painting.

"Its important for me that the kids carry on, because it's been in the family. It's a way to make a living."

Opposite: Santana Melchor. Pot: red birds, 12 ½ x 14 in., ca. 1975. Rick Dillingham collection.

Crucita Melchor. Pot 5 ½ x 13 in., ca. 1987. Rick Dillingham collection.

*Dolorita Melchor, b. 1937
"I fill in the blanks after Crucita has outlined the designs. We use old designs, what you see from the old pots."*

Top: Left: Mandy Melchor (portrait not available). Pot 2 x 3 in., 1986. Middle: Marlene Melchor (portrait not available). Pot 2 ½ x 3 in., 1979. Right: Ilene René Melchor (portrait not available). Pot 2 x 2 ¼ in., 1991. All pots courtesy Crucita Melchor.

Bottom: Dolorita Melchor. Pot made with Crucita Melchor, 5 ¼ x 8 ¼ in., ca. 1987. SAR 1990-16-1, courtesy Indian Arts Research Center, School of American Research, Santa Fe.

Opposite: Dolorita Melchor. Pot made with Crucita Melchor, 6 ¼ x 10 ¼ in., ca. 1988. SAR 1990-16-2, courtesy Indian Arts Research Center, School of American Research, Santa Fe.

The Tenorio Family

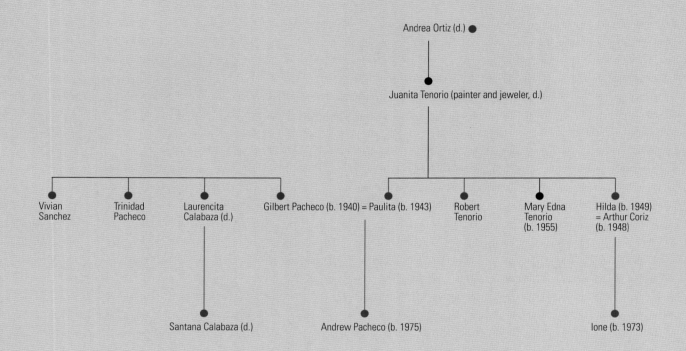

Andrea Ortiz (d.) ●

Juanita Tenorio (painter and jeweler, d.)

| Vivian Sanchez | Trinidad Pacheco | Laurencita Calabaza (d.) | Gilbert Pacheco (b. 1940) = Paulita (b. 1943) | Robert Tenorio | Mary Edna Tenorio (b. 1955) | Hilda (b. 1949) = Arthur Coriz (b. 1948) |

Santana Calabaza (d.)

Andrew Pacheco (b. 1975)

Ione (b. 1973)

Gilbert Pacheco, b. 1940, and Paulita Pacheco, b. 1943
Gilbert: "I used to help my mother as a youngster. I was interested in clay and we lived with grandmother in Sile at the ranch and would watch her make pots. We used to make tiny pots for the spirits to give us talent.

"I went through high school and after that I went into the army. Before we were married, Paulita worked with the handicapped at Head Start. After we got married, about five years, we got back together with pottery. It's been about twenty years of making pottery. We started with smaller pots, chili bowls, and sold to people here at the village or Santa Ana or Cochiti for traditional purposes. We started doing shows like Indian Market and we received awards. Now we're doing mostly bowls painted inside. Its all traditional and noncommercial. I do water jars, dough bowls, and pitchers. They went out of style, and now we're doing them.

"Mostly people are doing ceramic. We made two to show people the difference. Together we mix the clay, and we'll decide what we will make. We both form pots, and after they're dry [Paulita] sands and puts on the slip and I do the outlines on the painting [bowl interiors] and she fills them in. We both do the outside painting [bowl exteriors]."

Paulita Pacheco, on her son Andrew Pacheco, b. 1975
"He was going to Head Start and he learned by watching Robert [Tenorio]. He started playing with clay at five years old and at seven years started forming. At nine to ten he started dinosaur designs. It started with a project at school having to do with dinosaurs and he got real interested. We encouraged him to do stories about the pottery designs, and he would write them and put the paper inside the pots. He gives credit for his work to his Uncle Robert."

Previous page: Robert Tenorio (portrait not available). Pot 10 x 9 ½ in., 1987. SAR 1987-8-I, courtesy Indian Arts Research Center, School of American Research, Santa Fe.

Opposite: Paulita and Gilbert Pacheco. Pot 4 ¾ x 13 ¾ in., 1992. Rick Dillingham inventory.

Opposite: Andrew Pacheco. 8 ½ x 8 ½ in., 1990. SAR 1990-16-3, courtesy Indian Arts Research Center, School of American Research, Santa Fe.

Mary Edna Tenorio. Pot 3 x 8 ½ in., painted by Robert Tenorio, 1992. Courtesy Arthur and Hilda Coriz.

Arthur Coriz, b. 1948, and Hilda Coriz, b. 1949

Arthur: "I started making in 1975, nobody taught me how. I just learned by watching Robert [Tenorio] and Hilda. Robert used to paint for me, then a year or two later I started painting my own. I am learning to put on the white [slip]—it's always been Hilda's work. We both do the red [slip] and we both design. I mostly do stew bowls, dough bowls, water jars, and canteens.

"What we do on our pottery is nothing commercial, all is natural—clay, slip paint, and firing. It's all hand made, hand coiled."

Hilda: " My grandmothers both made pottery, and my mother made plain polished black and red pottery. I really learned from Robert, so I give him the credit. We made jewelry before pottery. Mary's been making since around 1983, and she has Robert do the painting. Ione also makes bowls with bird heads and tails."

Opposite: Hilda and Arthur Coriz.
Pots: bowl, 2 ¾ x 6 ¼ in., 1992,
courtesy of the artists; jar, 6 x 7 in.,
1992, courtesy of the artists.

Ione Coriz. Pot 4 x 4 in., 1992.
Courtesy Arthur and Hilda Coriz.

SANTA CLARA

The Chavarria Family

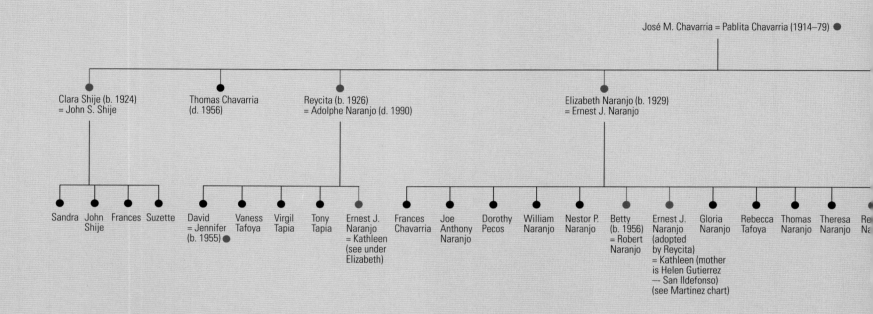

José M. Chavarria = Pablita Chavarria (1914–79) ●

Clara Shije (b. 1924)
= John S. Shije

Thomas Chavarria
(d. 1956)

Reycita (b. 1926)
= Adolphe Naranjo (d. 1990)

Elizabeth Naranjo (b. 1929)
= Ernest J. Naranjo

Sandra

John
Shije

Frances

Suzette

David
= Jennifer
(b. 1955) ●

Vaness
Tafoya

Virgil
Tapia

Tony
Tapia

Ernest J.
Naranjo
= Kathleen
(see under
Elizabeth)

Frances
Chavarria

Joe
Anthony
Naranjo

Dorothy
Pecos

William
Naranjo

Nestor P.
Naranjo

Betty
(b. 1956)
= Robert
Naranjo

Ernest J.
Naranjo
(adopted
by Reycita)
= Kathleen (mother
is Helen Gutierrez
— San Ildefonso)
(see Martinez chart)

Gloria
Naranjo

Rebecca
Tafoya

Thomas
Naranjo

Theresa
Naranjo

Re
Na

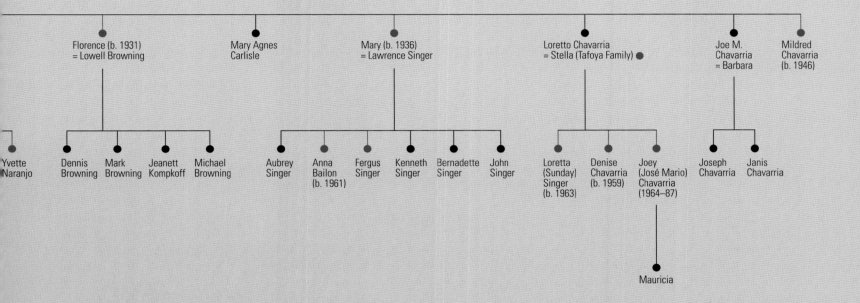

Florence (b. 1931)
= Lowell Browning

Mary Agnes
Carlisle

Mary (b. 1936)
= Lawrence Singer

Loretto Chavarria
= Stella (Tafoya Family)

Joe M.
Chavarria
= Barbara

Mildred
Chavarria
(b. 1946)

Yvette
Naranjo

Dennis
Browning

Mark
Browning

Jeanett
Kompkoff

Michael
Browning

Aubrey
Singer

Anna
Bailon
(b. 1961)

Fergus
Singer

Kenneth
Singer

Bernadette
Singer

John
Singer

Loretta
(Sunday)
Singer
(b. 1963)

Denise
Chavarria
(b. 1959)

Joey
(José Mario)
Chavarria
(1964–87)

Joseph
Chavarria

Janis
Chavarria

Mauricia

Clara Shije, b. 1924
"We all learned it from my mother [Pablita Chavarria]. We were with her all the time and we would watch. Mom passed away in 1979 [b. 1900]. I do baskets, wedding vases, and bowls. The basket handles are hard to do. We [Clara's mother and sisters] used to work together, but now we're on our own. I work sometimes with Florence because it takes two to fire. Everything is done by ourselves. I plan to stay with traditional style. I tried big pots, but decided to stay with smaller pieces."

Opposite: Pablita Chavarria, ca. 1965 (courtesy Elizabeth Naranjo). Pot 14 ¾ x 9 ½ in., ca. 1965. Courtesy Elizabeth Naranjo.

Clara Shije. Pot 5 ½ x 4 ½ in., 1992. Rick Dillingham inventory.

Reycita Naranjo, b. 1926

"The way I learned from my mom is the way I make my pots. I go after my own clay and I pick the big chunks. I pray before I take my clay and the sand I buy from Pojoaque [Pueblo]. I have to dry my clay real good in the sun before I soak them. Then I pound them into small chunks, about an inch, and then dry them in the oven—then they soak better. I sift my clay wet, then I mix the sand. My husband made a sifter out of screen—that's the reason I have no nails!

"I sift my sand and mix it with the clay. It has to be mixed real good, and then I set it out for a day. Then I start molding. I have little dishes for the bases of small ones, then coil them up. I shape them with gourds. I like the twisted handles, they're hard to do. I like the challenge. I only make two twisted-handle wedding vases a day, and I can make four or five bowls a day depending on the size. I've been getting a lot of orders. Since the weather got nice, I got some firing done."

Left: Elizabeth Naranjo. Opposite:
Pot 16 x 12 ½ in., ca. 1980. Rick Dillingham collection.

Right: Jennifer Naranjo. Figure (tallest point) 5 ¾ in., ca. 1990. Courtesy
Reycita Naranjo.

Jennifer Naranjo, b. 1955
"I learned from Reycita. I'm carrying on what she
taught me. My grandmother [Clara Sisneros] influenced me, but I was small when she passed away.
My mom is a nurse and I didn't learn [pottery] from
her. When I married David, I began to learn from
Reycita. I do mostly traditional black and nativity
sets. Mine are mostly smaller bowls, two to eight
inches. I'm still in that range, I haven't gone to the
big ones yet.

"I have done a lot of nativities. I start in the fall
for them. Both my daughters do their little pots. My
oldest [Melissa] is seventeen, and the little girl
[Amanda] is twelve. They're both interested."

Elizabeth Naranjo, b. 1929
"My mom [Pablita Chavarria] was my teacher.
I've been making pots 30 to 35 years. I started as
a young girl, learning, and after I got married I
really got into it. I paid attention to my mom and
watched her, and then I would help her when
she was older. She wasn't strong enough to polish, so I'd help her. I think you have to have more
patience with big pots than little ones. Betty is
the only one of my children who is working [with
pottery]. I did some redware, but it was hard using
the "fill-in" paint. It's different than the slip used for
black. You use the same slip on the black [for polishing and filled-in matte areas], and two different
ones for the red."

153

Betty Naranjo, b. 1956
"I love my work, I love to do it. It gives me enjoyment and pleasure to work with clay. I like to get my hands muddy. It gives me a livelihood to do during the day. I like the baskets [handled bowls], lamp bases, and bowls. Ernestine and Adrian [Betty's children] have begun to learn. I stick to the blackware. We say we will try red, but so far we've stayed with black."

Betty Naranjo. Pot 4 ½ x 3 ¾ in., 1992. Rick Dillingham inventory.

Opposite: Florence Browning. Pot 3 x 4 ¾ in., ca. 1990. Courtesy of the artist.

154

Florence Browning, b. 1931
"I haven't done anything since the market [Indian Market in August]. The last I did, I sold in Taos. I'd rather do pottery than anything else. I have to work, for the Indian Health Service, but am looking forward to retiring so I can work on pottery full-time.

"I sell at the markets. I also sell to dealers. I go to Bandelier every year, usually in the summer for two days. They bring a lot of school children from different states, and I do demos and answer questions. I meet lots of people there and I get to visit.

"Everything I know is from my mother. I started out when I was about ten, and we would fire my little pieces with hers. We're having trouble firing [now]. It's been a bad winter and everything is wet. It's the wind that's the most trouble."

Mildred Chavarria, b. 1946
"I do the medium-sized bowls—I haven't tried anything bigger. I started out seven years ago. I do pottery for income. I don't really go out to shows, I'm not into that. I prefer to make a group of pots and sell them to a dealer. I'm working at the same time [secretary to the Pueblo Governor]. Some people come by the house and I'll sell that way.

"I learned mostly from my mom [Pablita Chavarria], and I watched my sisters and picked it up and took it on my own. The first time was rough, not perfect—but as years have gone by, I'm doing pretty good. I don't think I'll get like my sisters, but my work is good too."

Mary Singer, b. 1936
"I learned from my mom. She's more or less the one who showed me how to make the clay and do polishing. We [my sisters and I] helped her when she was living to fire and do other things with her. She was going to teach us how to do red but we never did. We talked about it, but never did it. She mostly did larger and medium carved black pots. I like large pots, nice large ones where I can work them. I like to go and sell at the markets, but most of the time people call and order. I don't go to Eight Northern [the Indian craft market held in July]—it's too much work. I have gone in the past, but [with Indian Market in Santa Fe in August] it's too much work.

"I try to teach the kids pots. The boy [Fergus] knows how, and I taught my daughter [Anna] how to mix clay. I told them not to rush, do it slowly, you have to do it right from the beginning so they won't bust in the firing.

[About the current trend to kiln fire pottery] "I guess if that's what they want, but they shouldn't call it traditional. I've never seen a kiln."

Opposite: Mary Singer. Pot 14 x 10 in., ca. 1980. Courtesy Wheelwright Museum, Santa Fe.

Mildred Chavarria. Pot 2 ¾ x 4 ½ in., 1993. Rick Dillingham inventory.

The Gutierrez Family

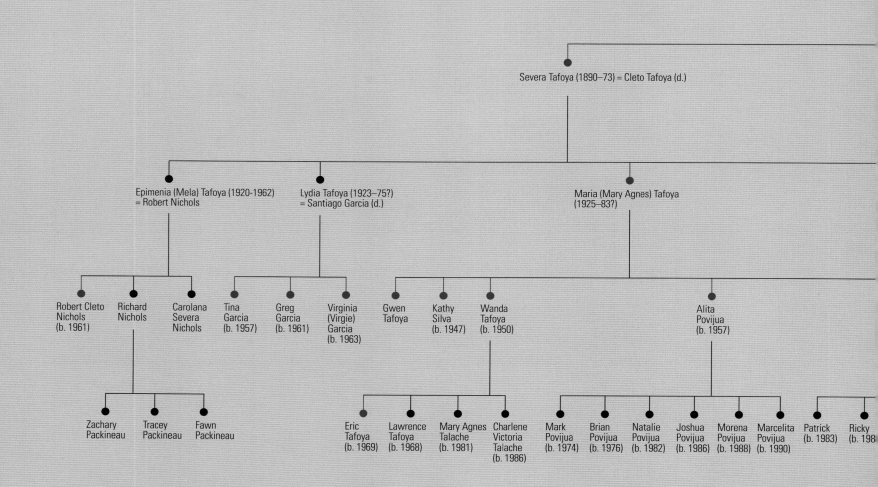

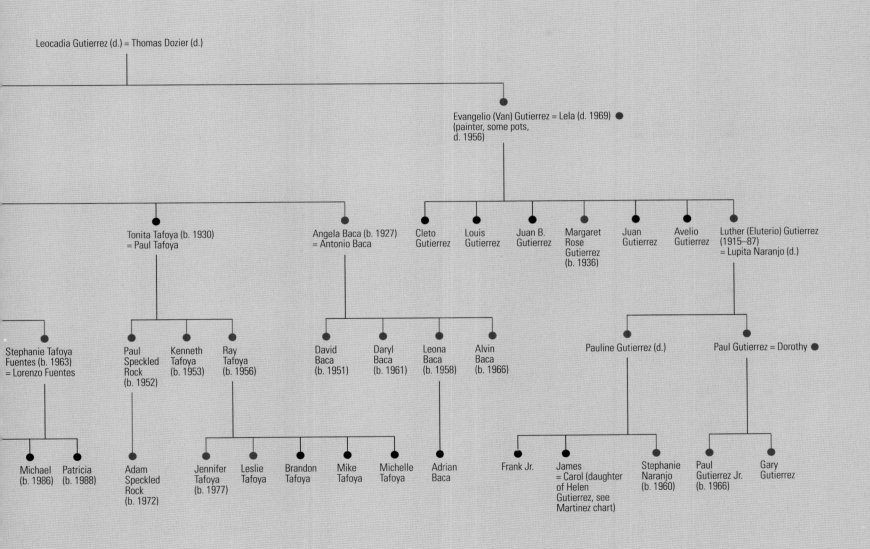

Leocadia Gutierrez (d.) = Thomas Dozier (d.)

Evangelio (Van) Gutierrez = Lela (d. 1969) ●
(painter, some pots,
d. 1956)

Tonita Tafoya (b. 1930)
= Paul Tafoya

Angela Baca (b. 1927)
= Antonio Baca

Cleto
Gutierrez

Louis
Gutierrez

Juan B.
Gutierrez

Margaret
Rose
Gutierrez
(b. 1936)

Juan
Gutierrez

Avelio
Gutierrez

Luther (Eluterio) Gutierrez
(1915–87)
= Lupita Naranjo (d.)

Stephanie Tafoya
Fuentes (b. 1963)
= Lorenzo Fuentes

Paul
Speckled
Rock
(b. 1952)

Kenneth
Tafoya
(b. 1953)

Ray
Tafoya
(b. 1956)

David
Baca
(b. 1951)

Daryl
Baca
(b. 1961)

Leona
Baca
(b. 1958)

Alvin
Baca
(b. 1966)

Pauline Gutierrez (d.)

Paul Gutierrez = Dorothy ●

Michael
(b. 1986)

Patricia
(b. 1988)

Adam
Speckled
Rock
(b. 1972)

Jennifer
Tafoya
(b. 1977)

Leslie
Tafoya

Brandon
Tafoya

Mike
Tafoya

Michelle
Tafoya

Adrian
Baca

Frank Jr.

James
= Carol (daughter
of Helen
Gutierrez, see
Martinez chart)

Stephanie
Naranjo
(b. 1960)

Paul
Gutierrez Jr.
(b. 1966)

Gary
Gutierrez

159

Robert Cleto Nichols, Tall Mountain, b. 1961
"I want to be original with my designs. I got turned off doing the standard feather and serpent designs. I use the melon design, parrot design—a design I came up with—kiva steps, and flowers. I saw a lot of flowers etched [sgraffito] on pottery, and I wanted to incorporate it in my work.

"I learned by watching everybody. It took me a while to learn to mix the clay. I started getting the clay myself. I started part-time when I worked at the Lab [Los Alamos], and what I did didn't come out. The polishing wasn't too hot. [I've been working] maybe since 1987. I'm not looking to be famous or anything, I just want to do it."

Opposite: Severa Tafoya (portrait not available). Pot 6 ¾ x 7 ¾ in., 1961. Courtesy Museum of Indian Art and Culture/Laboratory of Anthropology, Santa Fe.

Robert Cleto Nichols. Pot 4 x 5 ¼ in., 1993. Rick Dillingham inventory.

Virginia Garcia, b. 1963
"I mainly do traditional style because it's more beautiful. My grandmother [Severa Tafoya] started with traditional. My mother [Lydia Garcia] didn't do too much pottery. She did it when I grew up. Tina [Garcia, her sister] caught on, but I didn't get into pottery until 1987, then Tina and my boyfriend encouraged me to work. They kind of pushed, they wanted to see how well I could do. I was messing around at Tina's and she said I should continue. My first pots were pretty bad. I watched the different ways she worked. I work with water jar forms, round bear paw bowls, and wedding vases. I'm starting to get into melon bowls now. I do both black and red, and I don't do carving."

Opposite: Virginia Tafoya Garcia. Pot 7 ½ x 5 ¼ in., 1993. Courtesy Povi Jemu Indian Art, Santa Clara Pueblo.

Left: Tina Garcia. Pot 6 x 8 ¼ in., 1993. Courtesy Otowi Trading Company, Santa Fe.

Right: Greg Garcia (portrait not available). Pot 7 ⅛ x 5 ½ in., 1992. Rick Dillingham inventory.

Kathy Silva, b. 1947
"I used to sit with my grandma Severa and my mom used to help her make pottery. We all used to sit together. Severa passed away in 1973. I do the traditional, contemporary and incised [sgraffito].

I do miniatures, regular sizes and larger ones. She [Severa] was a great influence. We got most of our information from her. There are a lot of cousins doing pottery now. I've been potting since I was about six years old. I was teaching Lorenzo [Fuentes] when he married into our family, and his boys."

Wanda Tafoya, b. 1950
"I learned from my grandma, Severa [Tafoya], and took interest from her. My mom [Mary Agnes Tafoya] taught me as well. I do traditional miniatures—that's how I started. After that, we started etching-incised [sgraffito]. I work with my sons Eric and Lawrence. I have a daughter, Mary Agnes—she's one-half Nambe. She's starting to do micaceous pottery [traditional Nambe ware] and traditional Santa Clara. My other daughter, Charlene, is also doing micaceous pottery.

"I do big ones too, seed pots. I did several shows in Scottsdale, Kansas City, Missouri, and Tucson. I hope to do the Indian Market. The family has been doing Indian Market for about 35 years."

Stephanie Tafoya Fuentes, b. 1963
"I basically learned it from my mother [Mary Agnes Tafoya]. She was a potter and Severa's daughter. The pottery I do is mostly incised [sgraffito] type, and I mostly do miniatures. I don't do big ones because it's hard to finish and fire. We [Lorenzo Fuentes, her husband] do animals and flowers and hummingbirds [sculpture].

"I was too young to learn from Severa, and she was up in years at that time. Through my mother and my sisters, I got interested. I'm going to try to continue what I'm doing. I'm doing miniature wedding vases—they're hard. Smaller ones are easier for me. I think people really like the miniatures."

Lorenzo Fuentes [Stephanie Fuentes' husband], b. 1963
"My mother and grandmother are Santa Clara. I was born in California, and when I came back [to Santa Clara], Stephanie said, 'Why don't you try [pottery]?'

"Kathy [Silva] taught me how to get started. Kathy showed me the etching and two-tone firing. [Stephanie and I] have been married 8 years, and she helps me polish now and then. I collect the materials and fire myself. I'll probably go bigger with the pots in the future. I got a Third Place at the Eight Northern this year [1993]."

Alita Povijua, b. 1957
"I do incised [sgraffito] and traditional. I've been potting ten to fifteen years. My main influence was my mom [Mary Agnes Tafoya] and grandma [Severa Tafoya]. I do most the arts and crafts fairs and show my work there. I do some red as well as the black."

Opposite top: Kathy Silva. Pot 2 ⅞ x 2 in..

Opposite bottom: Eric Tafoya (portrait not available). Pot 3 ¼ x 3 ¼ in., 1993. Courtesy Povi Jemu Indian Art, Santa Clara Pueblo.

Stephanie Fuentes. Pot 1 ⅞ x 1 ¾ in., 1993. Courtesy Povi Jemu Indian Art, Santa Clara Pueblo.

Angela Baca, b. 1927
"I started making with my mother [Severa Tafoya]. She would say, 'Learn to make some, learn to make some, that way when I'm gone you'll know.' We used to live in Paul Speckled Rock's gallery [in the center of the plaza]. She was making a big pot for the Indian Market. 'Here, you polish it,' she said, and that was the first time. She said 'You did good work.' I don't remember what year that was. Then we both worked together. She was awarded a French government award along with Maria [Martinez], and they had to go to Gallup to receive it. Most people don't know about that. Pablita Velarde got one also.

"My mother makes melon bowls with bigger ridges, and one year I told her I'd like to try making them with smaller ridges. A lot of people started making melon bowls. When I started, I got a first prize at Indian Market. They've been making them [melon bowls] here along with the bear paw and black pots—it's Santa Clara traditional pottery. I used to make serpent designs, rain or water serpent.

"My father did all my mother's carving. Severa died in 1973. She was eighty-six. She made pottery up to a couple years before she died."

David Yellow Mountain Baca, b. 1951
"I started—it's about twelve years now. I didn't learn from my mom. I taught myself. My polishing is different from hers. I do traditional and contemporary, black and red. I also do clay peace pipes. The contemporary shapes are different from the traditional. What I'm known for is my squash design melon and seed pot melon. I've won awards at the Eight Northern Pueblos show, Indian Market, Gallup, and the Heard Museum. I got influenced at Eight Northern when it was here at Santa Clara. When I stayed in my mom's booth, people kept asking me questions, and I got into it then. My mom said, 'Why don't you try melons?' I was doing the etching [sgraffito] and contemporary work. Right now, hopefully, I'd like to have my work represented in the Smithsonian."

*Left: Angela Baca. Pot 3 ⅝ x 5 ¼
in., 1993. Courtesy Merrock Galeria,
Santa Clara Pueblo.*

*Right: David Baca. Pot 4 x 4 in., 1993.
Courtesy Povi Jemu Indian Art,
Santa Clara Pueblo.*

Leona Baca, b. 1958
"I was little when I started, ten or twelve years old. I do the exact thing my mom does, only miniatures. I do mostly black, but I do red sometimes. I work full-time [as an electronics technician] and work on weekends and when I find time. The only time I make a lot is for the shows—Eight Northern and Indian Market. Sometimes I have extra ones to sell. When I do make them I have my mother and brothers fire them, and sometimes I don't even see them before they're sold. I used to make bear paw [patterns on pottery forms] when I first started but I haven't made them in a long time. I have a son who is really interested. I guess I'll teach him how to do it."

Top: Leona Baca. Pot 2 x 2 ⅛ in., 1993. Courtesy of the artist.

Bottom: Daryl Baca (portrait not available). Pot 3 x 4 ¾ in., 1993. Courtesy Angela Baca.

Opposite: Alvin Baca. Pot 4 ⅜ x 3 ½ in., 1993. Courtesy of the artist.

Alvin Baca, b. 1966
"I learned from my mom, she taught me how to make pottery. We always sit together and make pots. I didn't know how, and she'd polish my first pots because I would break them. Mine are more like jars and hers are bowls. I don't know where I came up with the shape. I do both black and red. I make canteens too. They're hard to make and I do them for Indian Market. I started a new design with horizontal ridges. They look like a beehive."

169

Paul Speckled Rock, b. 1952
"My grandmother [Severa Tafoya] was my first inspiration. I made plain bowls and contemporary styles that I like. Of all the different things you can do with the clay, I don't like to stay with only traditional, though I use traditional methods. The bear fetishes I do are important to me. Larger pieces, pottery forms—that's what I'm doing now. I have supported his work [Adam Speckled Rock's], but he learned mostly from his mother [Rosemary Apple Blossom].

"I find selling other people's work [in my gallery] rewarding. I get to learn more about who my customers are. No two people are alike, and all have different tastes. I'd like to see my work in great collections, especially museums."

Paul Speckled Rock. Pot 2 ½ x 2 in., 1991. Courtesy Agape Southwest Pueblo Pottery, Albuquerque.

Opposite: Ray Tafoya. Pot 3 x 5 in., 1992. Courtesy Santa Fe Indian Trading Company, Santa Fe.

Ray Tafoya, b. 1956
"I started out as a silversmith in my teens. I was doing real good in silversmithing. I used to work for my father. He opened a little business doing jewelry. In around 1976 I started playing with clay, and in 1977 I got married to my wife Emily Suazo. She was making pottery. When silver prices went up in 1977, we incorporated our work together and started working in incised [sgraffito] pottery and continue to do so to this day.

"I'm kind of like a perfectionist. I used to work with eyeware and we couldn't make any mistakes because we were working with people's eyes. I applied what I learned to my creativity and firing. I make sure the preparations are just right. It [the firing] is the final judgment, and I don't loose any today. I don't fire a lot at a time, just a few so it's more controlled.

"The black is fired twice, black [firing], then etched [sgraffito], then I apply slips and fire again for a short period to set the slip. The red is fired once, the etching is done, slips applied and fired once.

"I have achieved a lot in my work, but I'm still not satisfied. In pottery the sky's the limit—what you put into it. I express this to my daughters, to do their best. I'm very pleased with what they've done with their art. I've seen interest in all my children to work with clay."

Kenneth Tafoya, b. 1953
"What I used to do was a lot of different shapes
with etching [sgraffito]. I still use traditional methods. I used to do wedding vases and seed pots,
but what I feel most comfortable with now are the
bear figures—I guess you can call them fetishes.
We have bears in our mountains here. We Indian
people are pushing the bear out of our areas because we are focusing more on the recreation of
the mountains. We are having trouble with co-exis-
tence. I would like to co-exist and that's why I focus
on this creature here. The BIA and Game and Fish
people, in order for the bears not to damage the
recreation areas, relocate them. I'm not happy
with this—they should stay in the mountains. They
should leave them be."

Jennifer Tafoya, b. 1977
"I've been working with clay since I was about six.
I was making bowls and little polished clay balls
with simple designs that were scratched in. I do
turtles and lizards and bears once in a while. They
are red and black. I think I'll go off in other directions. I'm still learning how to handle the clay. I'm
doing my own making, sanding, and polishing,
and my dad's teaching me how to fire."

Jennifer Tafoya. (Pot not available).

Opposite: Kenneth Tafoya. Bear fetish,
4 x 10 ½ in., 1993. Courtesy of the
artist.

Lela and Van Gutierrez, ca. 1933 (photographer unknown, courtesy Margaret Gutierrez). Pots: opposite: polychrome, ca. 1930, 7 x 7 ½, signed Lela and painted by Van, Rick Dillingham collection; left: black-on-black with orange pigment, 3 ¼ x 6 in. ca. 1930, signed by Lela and painted by Van, Rick Dillingham collection; right: polychrome, 9 ¼ x 9 in., 1932, IAF 1846, courtesy Indian Arts Research Center, School of American Research, Santa Fe .

Margaret Gutierrez, b. 1936

"They [Lela and Van Gutierrez] are the first ones who did the colors. I don't know how they came up with it—I never asked them. I guess by trial and error they came out with these colors—picking out clays and seeing what works and what doesn't work. Mom and Dad worked together, then Luther painted for her [during and after Van's death], and after she passed away I took over. When Pauline was alive she worked by herself. After Luther passed away, I signed the pottery by myself. My dad and Luther overlapped with painting.

"I still travel all over to get clays. I was over to the Grand Canyon and off to Denver. They're the only places I can find what I want. You can find it around here, too—La Bajada, Los Alamos. I go around and pick it up.

"Mom and Dad did some animals, but we just made them up. They didn't do as many as we did. Stephanie is doing figures.

"I'm working, working, working to try to finish some up. I do everything from start to finish now. I still fire outside. I lost a big turtle and wedding vase last week—oh, just crush it up! It's one of these things you have to chance. Now I fire one at a time, and I can pile up the animals, ten or so at a time. You have to get up so early in summer to fire, 4 or 5 a.m. Mostly everybody does the same thing here. Gosh, you can just smell it before the shows. Everybody's trying to do their things!

"Mom and Dad were potting before I was born and before Luther was born. They lost three kids before Luther was born—they had nine kids in all. Luther's kids, Paul and Pauline, were raised by Mom and Dad. We were like triplets."

Margaret Gutierrez. Polychrome pot 3 ¼ x 5 in., 1991. Rick Dillingham inventory.

Opposite: Pot by Margaret and Luther Gutierrez: polychrome, 9 x 9 ½ in., ca. 1970. Rick Dillingham collection.

Opposite: Lela and Luther Gutierrez: polychrome pot, 8 ³⁄₈ in. x 6 in., 1962, signed Lela and Luther (painted by Luther). IAF 2943, courtesy Indian Arts Research Center, School of American Research, Santa Fe. Lela and Luther Gutierrez, August 25, 1963, under the portal at the Palace of the Governors, Santa Fe (photo by Margaret and Paul Peters, courtesy Margaret Gutierrez).

Margaret and Luther Gutierrez: polychrome animal figure, height 4 ³⁄₈ in., ca. 1975, SAR 1989-7-298, courtesy Indian Arts Research Center, School of American Research, Santa Fe.

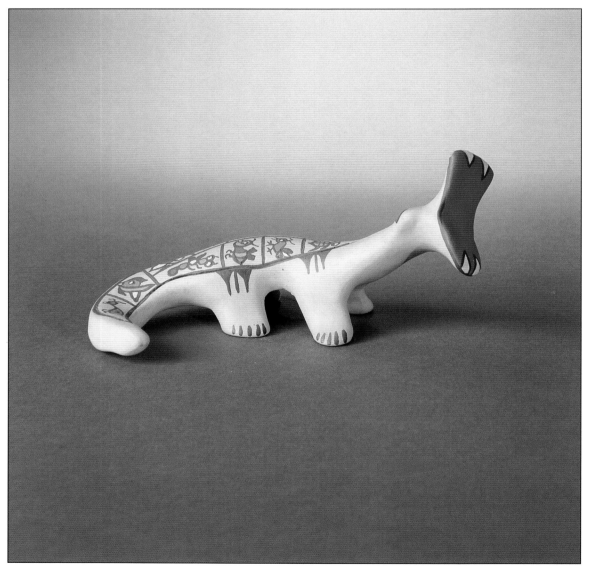

Stephanie Naranjo. Pot 2 ³/₄ x 6 in. long, ca. 1988. Courtesy Buckner/ Lazarus collection, New York.

Opposite: Pauline Gutierrez, ca. 1985 (photographer unknown, courtesy Margaret Gutierrez). Pot 3 ¹/₂ x 5 ¹/₄ in., ca 1987. Courtesy Stephanie Naranjo.

Paul Gutierrez, Sr., b. 1936, and Dorothy, b. 1940, [Navajo]
Paul Sr.: "That's how we make our living mostly. I learned from Margaret and Pauline, but I started with my grandmother [Lela]. But mostly we learned from Pauline and Margaret. We work in black; I don't have the patience to design. We do black and red, mostly figurines.

"Maybe later on we'll do the polychrome. Gary does some, he's a good designer. I'm not a good designer. My grandfather [Van] said he wanted to do polychrome. He went to different places getting colored clay [to make into slips] and see what would stick on pottery.

"Gary does everything alone. He's so picky he doesn't want anyone to monkey around with his pottery."

Dorothy: "We got married in 1965. I watched Pauline and Margaret. My mother is Navajo and makes rugs. We sell in Albuquerque and Santa Fe, Colorado, Arizona, the East, and California, different galleries. We sell at markets and to dealers. It's better to sell to everybody. All I do is make animals and nativities. I make and he [Paul Sr.] sands, polishes, and finishes, and he does the firing."

Paul Gutierrez, Sr.

Opposite: Paul Gutierrez, Jr. Pueblo sculpture, 5 ¾ x 4 in., ca. 1990. Courtesy of the artist.

Paul Gutierrez, Jr., b. 1966
"I watch her [Dorothy, his mother] make animals, mudheads, nativities, shaping the figurines. I haven't really done it seriously, but I want to continue. We used to visit Margaret and Luther, but I learned from my own family. I used to watch my grandfather [Luther] put designs on pots and I'd watch Margaret and Pauline sanding pottery. I do just blackware, like my mom. If you're going to make pottery you've got to be patient and happy with what you're doing."

The Tafoya Family

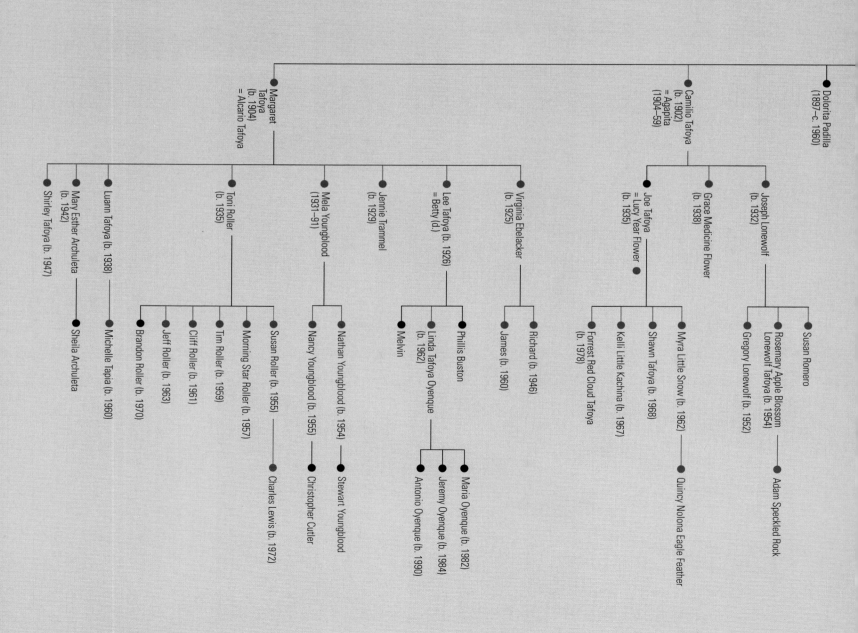

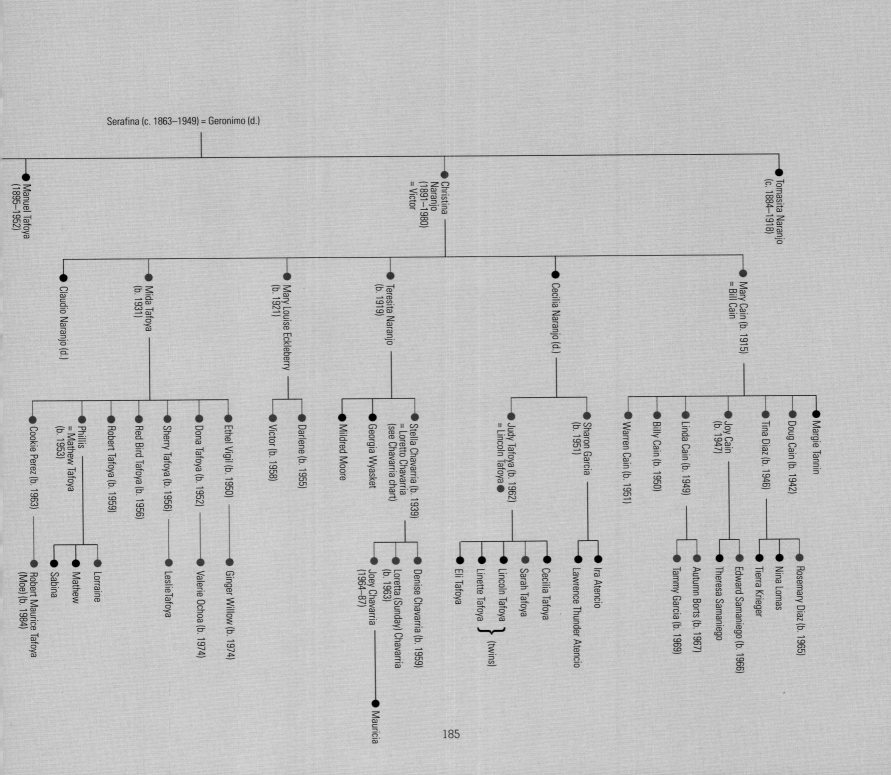

Serafina (c. 1863–1949) = Geronimo (d.)

Manuel Tafoya (1895–1952)

Christina Naranjo (1891–1980) = Victor

Tomasita Naranjo (c. 1884–1918)

Claudio Naranjo (d.)

Mida Tafoya (b. 1931)

Mary Louise Eckleberry (b. 1921)

Teresita Naranjo (b. 1919)

Cecilia Naranjo (d.)

Mary Cain (b. 1915) = Bill Cain

Cookie Perez (b. 1963)

Phillis = Mathew Tafoya (b. 1953)

Robert Tafoya (b. 1959)

Red Bird Tafoya (b. 1956)

Sherry Tafoya (b. 1956)

Dona Tafoya (b. 1952)

Ethel Vigil (b. 1950)

Victor (b. 1958)

Darlene (b. 1955)

Mildred Moore

Georgia Wyasket

Stella Chavarria (b. 1939) = Loretto Chavarria (see Chavarria chart)

Judy Tafoya (b. 1962) = Lincoln Tatoya

Sharon Garcia (b. 1951)

Warren Cain (b. 1951)

Billy Cain (b. 1950)

Linda Cain (b. 1949)

Joy Cain (b. 1947)

Tina Diaz (b. 1946)

Doug Cain (b. 1942)

Margie Tannin

Robert Maurice Tafoya (Moe) (b. 1984)

Sabina

Mathew

Lorraine

Leslie Tafoya

Valerie Ochoa (b. 1974)

Ginger Willow (b. 1974)

Joey Chavarria (1964–87)

Loretta (Sunday) Chavarria (b. 1963)

Denise Chavarria (b. 1959)

Eli Tafoya

Linette Tafoya

Lincoln Tafoya

} (twins)

Sarah Tafoya

Cecilia Tafoya

Lawrence Thunder Atencio

Ira Atencio

Tammy Garcia (b. 1969)

Autumn Borts (b. 1967)

Theresa Samaniego

Edward Samaniego (b. 1966)

Tierra Krieger

Nina Lomas

Rosemary Diaz (b. 1965)

Mauricia

185

Sarafina (Sara Fina or Serafina) Tafoya. Portrait: Geronimo and Sarafina Tafoya courtesy Mary Fredenburg and Lawrence and Mary Ellen Black. Pots: redware, ca. 1925, 4 x 10 in., courtesy Buckner/Lazarus collection, New York; opposite: blackware, 7 ¾ x 10 ¾ in., ca. 1922–23, IAF 2674, courtesy Indian Arts Research Center, School of American Research, Santa Fe.

Margaret Tafoya (portrait not available). Pots: opposite: redware wedding vase, 15 x 11 in., 1982; blackware, 7 1/4 x 9 1/2 in., 1976. Both Rick Dillingham collection.

The following is a statement prepared by Toni Roller, Mary Esther Archuleta, Virginia Ebelacker, Jennie Trammel, LuAnn Tafoya, and their mother Margaret Tafoya, February 1993.

"The Margaret Tafoya family did not wish to be included in the new or revised Seven Families in Pueblo Pottery, in protest against Indian potters who are using commercial materials in making pottery and firing in controlled kilns. We want to inform the public that this is going on while many claim their pottery is traditional. Being published in a book next to this type of potter shows our condoning that kind of work.

"There is room for every kind of potter, but they must specify that their work is nontraditional if they do not use natural materials or do not fire their pottery outdoors. We feel that when an Indian potter falsely presents his work to the public, it is outright fraud. The Tafoya family potters do not claim to be perfect, but we want to do our best to preserve our Indian culture and traditions."

Mary Esther Archuleta (portrait not available). Pot 4 1/2 x 7 1/2 in., ca. 1988. Courtesy Dewey Galleries, Ltd., Santa Fe.

Opposite: Toni Roller (portrait not available). Pot 9 1/2 in. diameter, 1979. Rick Dillingham collection.

Opposite: Jeff Roller (portrait not available). Pot 4 ¼ x 5 ½ in., 1991. Courtesy Case Trading Post/Wheelright Museum, Santa Fe.

Cliff Roller (portrait not available). Pot 4 x 5 ½ in., 1989. Rick Dillingham collection.

Left: Tim Roller (portrait not available). Pot 2 x 3 ½ in., 1992. Courtesy Toni Roller.

Right: Charles Lewis (portrait not available). Pot 4 ½ x 5 ¼ in., 1992. Rick Dillingham inventory.

Opposite: LuAnn Tafoya (portrait not available). Pot 16 x 14 ¼ in., 1992. Courtesy Case Trading Post/Wheelright Museum, Santa Fe.

Jennie Trammel (portrait not available). Pots: opposite: redware, 13 ½ x 9, ca. 1988, courtesy Dewey Galleries, Ltd., Santa Fe; bottom: blackware, 6 x 4 in., 1990, courtesy Case Trading Post/Wheelwright Museum, Santa Fe.

Top: Shirley Tafoya (portrait not available). Pot 2 ¾ x 3 ½ in., 1984. Rick Dillingham collection.

Top left: Lee and Betty Tafoya (Betty is deceased) (portrait not available). Pot 4 x 6 in., 1988. Courtesy Dewey Galleries, Ltd., Santa Fe.

Top right: Linda Tafoya Oyenque (portrait not available). Pot 5 ½ x 4 in., 1991, Rick Dillingham inventory.

Bottom left: Virginia Ebelacker (portrait not available). Pot 6 x 12 ½ in., ca. 1978. Rick Dillingham collection.

Bottom right: James Ebelacker (portrait not available). Pot 8 ½ x 8 ½ in., ca. 1988. Courtesy Buckner/Lazarus collection, New York.

Opposite: Richard Ebelacker (portrait not available). Pot 19 ¾ x 22 ½ in., 1992. Courtesy Museum of Indian Art and Culture/Laboratory of Anthropology, Santa Fe.

Nathan Youngblood, b. 1954
"Where I am right now, it's not easy to stay within traditional boundaries and challenge yourself. I get a lot of feedback from people who say, 'Why do you fire that way [traditional outdoor firing]? Why don't you fire in a kiln? Why do you prepare your clay? Why don't you go to the store and buy it? I guess the reason I don't want to go down that road is because when I lived with my grandparents [Margaret and Alcario Tafoya], the one thing they constantly tried to instill in me was that the way we do our pottery, the traditional way, was the way that was handed to us by the spirits that come before us. In order to show the proper respect for the clay and to the clay we need to continue doing it in the old way, and that means digging your own clays and mixing them together, hand-coiling, hand-burnishing, and outdoor firing."

Opposite: Mela Youngblood (portrait not available). Pot 8 ¾ x 7 ½ in., ca. 1988. Courtesy Dewey Galleries, Ltd., Santa Fe.

Nathan Youngblood. Pot 2 ½ x 11 in., 1988. Courtesy Buckner/Lazarus collection, New York.

Nancy Youngblood, b. 1955
"Everything's changed from when that book [Seven Families] was done. My career has advanced a lot. To some degree, winning ribbons at fairs got me motivated. Sometimes people who collect the work feel that it's important, it points them to an artist—and that's what it did for me. But after so many ribbons it's become less important. I've gotten the acknowledgment I've wanted. On any given day, awards could be given out differently. It's a matter of someone's taste.

"Could I live with this piece? Does it look good to me? That's when I realized what was important.

"I give Margaret Tafoya acknowledgment, that she was a major inspiration to me—not just her work, things like having faith. She would say, 'If you do the right thing, everything will turn out right.'

"Some ideas I've had stored in my mind for many years. Ideas I didn't think I could do. My brother [Nathan Youngblood] was a great inspiration. He said all that was limiting me was my mind, and if you can dream it you can make it. I have to challenge myself or I get lazy and repeat the same things. Another thing that is important to me is different cultures being remembered by their art. I wanted to be remembered for doing something rather than just taking up space in the world. I think of someone a hundred years from now thinking, 'Who was that? How did she do that?'"

Joseph Lonewolf, b. 1932
[From a prepared written statement:]
"My creativity, which is inspired by both my parents and the artistic heritage of my People—the Pueblo Indians—intertwines the traditional procedures used by ancestral potters with contemporary methods; and thus, it enables me to perfect my own individual style and means for personal expression. My teachings and our heritage of pottery making continues, today, in the creations of my three children and grandson."

Opposite left: Agapita Tafoya (portrait not available). Pot 4 ¼ x 6 in., ca. 1950. Courtesy Grace Medicine Flower, Santa Clara Pueblo.

Camilio Tafoya (portrait not available). Pots: Opposite top left: 1 ¾ x 1 ¾ in., 1991, courtesy Andrews Pueblo Pottery, Albuquerque; opposite right: 3 ½ x 4 ½ in., 1977, courtesy Grace Medicine Flower, Santa Clara Pueblo.

Joseph Lonewolf, ca. 1987 (photograph by Katheryn M. Favorite, courtesy the photographer, Santa Clara Pueblo). Pots: opposite top right: 1 ¾ x 1 ½ in., 1992, courtesy Andrews Pueblo Pottery, Albuquerque; 3 x 3 ½ in., 1977, SAR 1989-7-286, courtesy Indian Arts Research Center, School of American Research, Santa Fe.

Left: Susan Romero (portrait not available). Pot 2 x 1 ¾ in., 1991. Courtesy Andrews Pueblo Pottery, Albuquerque.

Middle: Rosemary Apple Blossom Lonewolf (1992, photographer unknown). Pot 2 ¾ x 2 ¼ in., 1981. Courtesy Buckner/Lazarus collection, New York.

Right: Gregory Lonewolf. Pot 1 ⅜ x 1 ⅛ in., 1992. Courtesy Andrews Pueblo Pottery, Albuquerque.

Rosemary Apple Blossom Tafoya, b. 1954
[Concerning her recent story-pots] "[They] serve to reflect my personal and unique life experiences. Subject matter ranges from (1) thoughts about a woman's body as a bearer of life, (2) my own pregnancy, (3) feelings about my mixed heritage, (4) what it means to live in the East as a Pueblo Indian, (5) reflections on the Columbus Quincentennary, and (6) even space exploration. In essence, I'm a modern Mimbres, commenting on my twentieth-century world just as those ancient potters did in illustrating their pots with vignettes of daily life. In summary, the themes of my pots are a unique blend of contemporary subjects based on traditional values."

[From the artist's printed statement:] "I am not, nor are my pieces, frozen in time. I am a contemporary Pueblo Indian woman facing complex issues in a rapidly changing world. Sometimes these issues present conflicts to 'traditional' Pueblo life. More often than not, however, the issues are the same personal and professional challenges any modern woman faces. It is these issues, then, that are explored and illustrated as the subject matter of my pots."

Gregory M. Lonewolf, b. 1952
"The first time I remember doing anything with clay and keeping it was a rolled slab of commercial clay in school with an imprint of my hand. My mother still has it.

"The whole family has been working on pottery a long time. I've always been interested in art, but other career things kept me from it until later when I worked in a frame shop and saw artwork coming in. My interest was heightened by talking to these artists and helping them with their work. I thought I'd give it a shot and see if I could sell my own work—etching, glass etching, woodwork, all sorts of media—I was never restricted by that.

"In 1984–85 I did my first show and sold three pieces. Within six months I decided to do this [artwork] full time. I do other artwork than just pottery.

"I got to see a lot of my father's work, but the first teaching I received was from Camilio [Tafoya, his grandfather] and Aunt Grace [Medicine Flower], and we did the traditional carved style. My 'internship' came from my father and sister Rosemary [Apple Blossom]. I learned a lot of different techniques from each member of the family and incorporated these methods into what I do now. I consider my father my mentor and hope someday to catch up with him, but I doubt I will."

[With regard to contemporary innovation at Santa Clara] "If you look at history with the Aztec, Inca, and in China, there was a period of time where the ruling party said, 'This is the way it will be.' Nothing changed, the creativity was stifled. To be a true artist you are always trying new things—from Indian or non-Indian sources. Sometimes you're able to incorporate it into your work. You're like a child, everything is new everyday."

Grace Medicine Flower, b. 1938
[I asked what had changed since the Seven
Families book:]
"Nothing's really changed except the age."

"I did sgraffito only in the seventies, and now I'm
combining deep carving and sgraffito. I'm also
doing bigger pots. I'm doing `cut-outs' or `sculp-
tured rims'—I don't have a name for it. I did some
work with my dad when I broke my wrist. He
works mostly with Joseph [Lonewolf]. He doesn't do
much anymore. He'll be ninety this year.

"You gotta change someways—the change has to
be. There are young ones with new ideas and you
have to look. Even traditional work is OK for going
off and doing new things. It makes the art exciting.
The traditional designs are kept, but you can
express in the way you design. If every so many
years you can come up with new ideas, it's exciting
to show them. Some galleries help artists do better
by pushing their work. You can repeat designs, but
they're never the same. I still enjoy it. I guess they
[Agapita and Camilio Tafoya] were making pottery before I was born. Mom used to do painted
pottery on red. Camilio later did carved pottery
and horse sculptures. Agapita passed away in
1959."

*Grace Medicine Flower. Opposite: by
Grace Medicine Flower and Camilio
Tafoya, 1971, 4 ¼ x 5 ¼ in., courtesy
Buckner/Lazarus collection, New
York.*

Quincy Tafoya, b. 1983
"I make turtles, dinosaurs, reptiles, snakes, bear, rabbits. I do them like Shawn [Tafoya]—red and white—and sometimes I do black. Black's too hard. I'm going to stick with pottery as I get older and do bigger and better ones."

Grace Medicine Flower. Pots left: 3 x 4 ¼ in., 1990, courtesy Andrews Pueblo Pottery, Albuquerque; right: 3 x 3 ¼ in., ca. 1975, courtesy Dewey Galleries, Ltd., Santa Fe.

Quincy Tafoya. Pot not available.

Opposite: Lucy Year Flower Tafoya. Pot 2 ¼ x 3 ½ x 3 in., ca. 1989. Courtesy Buckner/Lazarus collection, New York.

Lucy Year Flower Tafoya, b. 1935
*"I started in 1972. I picked it up from Camilio [Tafoya], but consider myself
self-taught. I learned to mix the clay myself, and all the pots popped until
I got the mixture right. I started with animals, then to little bowls. I did
miniatures for a while, and now I'm doing much larger work. I taught my
daughters. When I was working, they would play with the clay. Before I
knew it, they were making pots. They started getting more and more interested. It helps Myra, because she doesn't have to go to work. Kelli works
all the time on pottery."*

Myra Little Snow (portrait not available). Pot 3 x 3 ¾ in., 1992. Rick Dillingham inventory.

Christina Naranjo, ca. 1973 (photographer unknown, courtesy Mida Tafoya). Opposite: pot 13 ¾ x 11 ½ in., ca. 1975. Rick Dillingham collection.

Forrest Red Cloud
Tafoya, b. 1978
"I was nine or ten when I
got started. Shawn was
my main teacher. I do the
red and white type and I
did some turtles in black.
My favorite thing to draw
on the pots are animals,
dinosaurs, dogs, snakes."

Shawn Tafoya, b. 1968
"My work is different
because I want to do
something different than
the usual Santa Clara
carved ware. Right now
I'm doing red and buff,
and I want to go to the
older style, Tewa Poly-
chrome, and use it as an
inspiration for new work
and different designs.
My mother [Lucy Year
Flower] and aunt, Grace
Medicine Flower, were
my teachers. They really
influenced me. I did
blackware when I was
younger. I started experimenting with white slip
when I was twelve or
thirteen, and it took a
while to figure out how
to do it. It takes a longer,
hotter fire than the
black."

Opposite: Shawn Tafoya. Pot 6 x 9
in., 1993. Courtesy of the artist.

Top: Forrest Red Cloud. Pot 2 ¼ x 2 ½
in., 1992. Courtesy Buckner/Lazarus
collection, New York.

Bottom: Kelli Little Kachina (portrait
not available). Pot 4 x 3 ½ in., 1992.
Rick Dillingham inventory.

Mary Cain, b. 1915
"I guess mostly it [pottery making] came from my mother [Christina Naranjo]. When my grandmother [Serafina Tafoya] was living I was very young, and she would talk to us about it. When you're very young, you don't want to stay with it. When I started making later with my mom, I didn't want to stop. I started maybe in the late 1930s or early forties and signed some of them Mary Tafoya. We went to California from 1956 to 1973 and I went back and forth and worked with pottery because I wanted to stay with it. In the early 1970s I worked again with my mom.

"I don't want to leave the work. I just love to do it. It makes you feel so good—you're doing something for yourself, not dependent on others. It makes you feel happy.

"Later on, when the kids all came back out here [Santa Clara], I asked if they were interested in pottery and each started and now they're all 'in it.' After they got started, they got real interested and still do it."

Joy Cain, b. 1947
"When I first started, I didn't know anything. I just helped my mom [Mary Cain] and grandmother [Christina Naranjo]. I did all the dirty jobs for them, and then I got started learning from the bottom up. I made little, crooked, tiny bowls and threw most of them away. I learned the polishing from my mom, and heard, 'Do it over,' plenty of times. You've got to have a good stone to do the polishing. Now, I like to work on big bowls—they're a lot more fun. I enjoy the carving the best. It's like a big canvas, your bowl—draw on it and carve it out."

Top left: Joy Cain. Pot 4 ⅝ x 6 ¼ in., 1993. Courtesy of the artist.

Top right: Mary Cain. Opposite: Pot 9 x 7 ¼ in., 1992. Rick Dillingham inventory.

Edward Samaniego (Sunburst), b. 1966
"I like that it's passed down from generation to generation, and it shouldn't be lost. Knowing that fact will inspire me to make pottery, or to work on pottery every day. I like the water jar shape and I like the serpent design. I see great things to come with my art. I also paint in acrylic and oil. [Pottery and painting] are two separate types of art. I stick to the more traditional in pottery, and in the painting I can do anything."

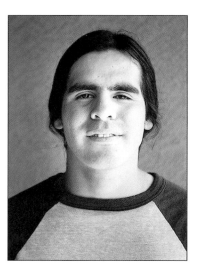

Edward Samaniego. Pot 4 x 4 ½ in., 1992. Courtesy of the artist.

Opposite left: Warren Cain (courtesy Mary Cain). Pot 3 x 5 in., 1993. Rick Dillingham inventory.

Opposite right: Doug Cain (portrait not available). Pot 3 ¼ x 5 ½ in., 1992. Courtesy of the artist.

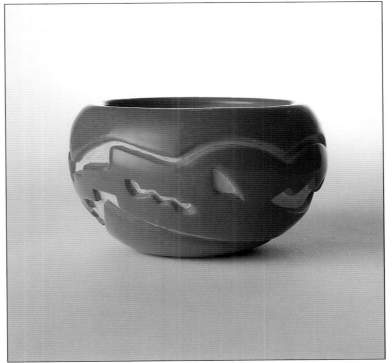

Tina Diaz, b. 1946
"I feel really proud and fortunate to be a part of this tradition that's being carried on. I love the clay, the people, the whole thing—especially the good-will."

RoseMary Diaz, b. 1965
"Although I am not a potter myself, being part of a family of potters has greatly influenced my work as a writer. I often incorporate certain aspects of pottery making into my writing—the dampness of the clay, the grit of the sand, the smell of the smoke when the pots are fired, and the smooth feel of their shiny surfaces when they're finished. In this way, and through the hands of my mother and her mother, I am connected to the clay."

Bill Cain, b. 1950

"Ten years ago my mother called me and asked if I wanted to learn pots. I was living in California at the time. She taught me how to mix the clay, make [the pottery], slip it, polish it, and fire it. It inspires one a lot, it relaxes me—it takes the tension away. I follow traditional design and add some contemporary. I can get inspired by the designs in the clouds. I like trying different types of clay for different colors. I do the serpent, bear paw, and whatever comes to mind."

Opposite left: RoseMary Diaz (photograph by Paul Keliiaa, 1993). Pot not available.

Opposite right: Tina Diaz. Pot 7 1/2 x 4 1/2 in., 1991. Rick Dillingham inventory.

Billy Cain. Pot 10 in. dia., 1992. Courtesy of the artist and Mary Cain.

*Autumn Borts, b. 1967
"I'm happy to know the
ways of the Santa Clara
people. I like to create
unusual and traditional
shapes that my mom
[Tina Diaz], grandmoth-
er [Mary Cain], and
other relatives have
taught and shown me.
I'm inspired by Mother
Earth and the things
that happen in life and
the things around me."*

*Top left: Autumn Borts. Pot 8 x 3 ½
in., 1992. Rick Dillingham inventory.*

*Top right: Linda Cain. Opposite: Pot
6 x 7 ¼ x 3 ¾ in., 1992. Courtesy of
the artist.*

Tammy Borts Garcia, b. 1969
"I've had a lot of inspiration from the older potters—and [then] mixing it with my own style. I'd say my style was traditional motifs with contemporary shapes. I learned from my mom [Linda Cain] and my grandmother [Mary Cain]. I want to continue doing pottery for as long as I live. I enjoy what I do, working with my hands. My main drive is that I really enjoy it. I enjoy working with the earth and using my mind to create new and different things."

Judy Tafoya, b. 1962
"I used to make small figurines when I was a child. I don't remember anything being finished. Then I left the pueblo when I was fourteen and I didn't return until I was twenty-one. I returned in 1983. My sister Sharon [Garcia] introduced me back into pottery making and helped me get my first pieces done. She helped me and my husband Lincoln Tafoya do our polishing and firing.

"I do traditional carved black pottery. I enjoy making nativity sets. I like to make pots that show something out of the normal. I like to make lidded pots, something I just started in the past year. I like to make the large storage vases.

"My carving is a little different than the rest of the family. I can spot my aunt's and cousin's work by their carving. I learned to create my own style. I didn't have anyone teach me to put the design on. I learned it myself, maybe from memory from when I was young.

"I believe the talent I have is a God-given talent. I'm able to be home with my children and to provide a good living. My husband is also a full-time potter. Lincoln does wildlife designs on his. It's a big responsibility to raise children and be there for them."

*Left: Tammy Garcia. Pot 6 x 5 in.,
1992. Rick Dillingham inventory.*

*Right: Judy Tafoya. Pot 11 ½ x 7 ¾
in. across spouts, 1993. Courtesy of
the artist.*

Sharon Naranjo Garcia, b. 1951
"I learned, of course, from my grandmother [Christina Naranjo]. She raised me. I admired her shapes and her traditional work. I like the water jar with bear paw, the double shoulder, there are many variations. I enjoy the traditional shapes and styles. I do everything by myself. I live in San Juan but continue to work in the Santa Clara style. My boys are picking it up now."

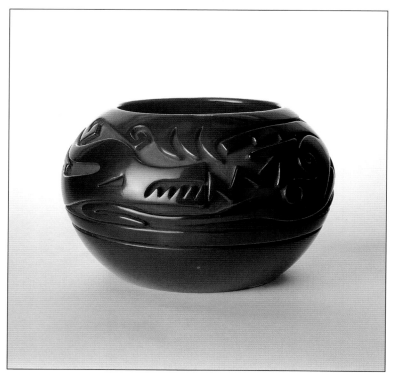

Left: Sharon Garcia. Pot 8 ¼ x 6 ¾ in., 1993. Courtesy Merrock Galeria, Santa Clara Pueblo.

Right: Teresita Naranjo. Pot 7 x 10 in., ca. 1965, IAF 3019. Courtesy Indian Arts Research Center, School of American Research, Santa Fe.

Teresita Naranjo, b. 1919 ("I think I'm 1,000 years old!")
"I used to tell Stella [Chavarria], look at the polishing, that's what shows. Don't work for money, work for a name."

[From a printed paper she prepared] *"I was born and raised in Santa Clara Pueblo and have lived there all my life. My parents were Victor and Christina Naranjo. I was born on May 1, 1919. On the fourth day I was given my Indian name by a midwife, she named me Bay-Po-Vi, which means Apple Blossom: then later on they baptized me in the Catholic Church and gave me my name Teresita Naranjo.*

"I did not know my grandparents on my father's side, they were dead before I was born, but on my mother's side my grandparents were Geronimo and Sarafina Tafoya. They have always done potteries all their lives. Of course, my grandfather was a very good farmer: he always raised his own crops and was always busy in the daytime, but when his work was done he would always do pottery work in the evenings to help my grandmother.

"My grandfather used to tell us the story about the waterdragon, which is called Avanyu in Tewa language which was spoken in his days. However the way he told it was the waterdragon brought luck, health, peace, joy, and happiness as well as rain and good crops to the Indian people and to all people on the earth. So he said whoever buys your pottery with the waterdragon design, he too will always have all those good things.

"Some people may say pottery making is a hobby; it is more than a hobby, thank God. It means my life. I have a business right in my home. I work to make a living. I have supported my children with pottery and given them their education and their needs since my husband died in 1950. Today my pottery means the handiwork of God."

Stella Chavarria, b. 1939
"I've been doing pots about thirty to thirty-two years. My two girls are both working on pots now, and one granddaughter and Joey [d. 1987] used to work. Mauricia is Joey's daughter, and at nine years old she is doing small ones. I learned from watching my mom [Teresita Naranjo] and used most of her traditional designs and those of my grandmother Christina. I enjoy working on pots, and I work every day. I wouldn't do anything else besides this."

Denise Chavarria, b. 1959
"I've been doing it for about twelve years, and it's been full time. It's still full time. I enjoy trying different shapes. I used to do small ones, and now I work a little bigger. My designs are different from my mom [Stella Chavarria] and sister [Loretta]. I learned it all from Mom, and I had to pay her—what—$50 per class! I hope it will make us as well known as my mom. We enjoy going to the different shows."

Opposite: Stella Chavarria. Pot 4 ½ x 3 ½ in., 1991. Rick Dillingham inventory.

Denise Chavarria. Pot 4 ½ x 3 ¾ in., 1992. Rick Dillingham inventory.

Left: Joey Chavarria (portrait not available). Pot 3 ½ x 3 ⅜ in., ca. 1983. Courtesy Otowi Trading Co., Santa Fe.

Middle: Loretta (Sunday) Chavarria. Pot 3 ¼ x 3 ¼ in., 1992. Rick Dillingham inventory.

Right: Mida Tafoya. Pot 3 ¼ x 7 in., ca. 1989. Courtesy Dewey Galleries, Ltd., Santa Fe.

Loretta (Sunday) Chavarria, b. 1963
"I seriously started about four to five years ago. Last year I started doing the etched [sgraffito], and I still do the carved. I watched my mom and learned from her. I mostly work on small ones. I guess I never really tried big ones— smaller ones are easier for me. I also have a full-time job at Los Alamos. I'm a computer operator there."

Mida Tafoya, b. 1931
"I love working with clay. Mother Earth—she's been good to me. To me, pottery making means a lot. Mother Earth never let me down. Whatever I make, wedding vases, bowls, all come out good. I enjoy working with you [referring to unfinished pottery on the table], and people will be happy to have the pots in their homes.

"I enjoy doing shows. I enjoy meeting people and talking about the pottery. I let them touch the clay so they can feel how it is. It's been around thirty years of work, and I learned from Christina [Naranjo]. Me and her used to work together. She showed me how to make pottery, talk with Mother Earth and be good to her—not to be mad—talk to her, how to mold the clay, how to make big ones and take care of myself and the clay.

"My son Robert and his girlfriend do painted red pottery, and he does a lot of small carved ones which he learned from me. My son Mike does the carving like me. Him and his wife work together. She does the polishing, she's from San Ildefonso. He also learned from me. Donna does pottery too, and she works for Pojoaque Pueblo but still helps me with pottery. She does some on her own, but works mostly with me."

[Grandson Robert Maurice (Moe) Tafoya (b. 1984), son of daughter Cookie, said while I was there: *"Grandma, can I make a pottery?"*]

Phyllis M. Tafoya, b. 1953
"I started making pottery when I was about twelve, and I learned from my grandmother Christina Naranjo and grandmother Lucaria Tafoya. I first started making animals and bowls that had painted designs. The next step I took was making medium-size bowls that were carved. I hung in that area when I was in college. It was after college that I started on my own, my own direction. Now I'm working on traditional black wedding vases and traditional red bowls. I guess I could say I came from little pieces to big stuff. I'm more comfortable making large pots now. With my boyfriend, we make contemporary stuff. I make the bowl and he does the sgraffito design. I'm doing a lot of contemporary . . . they are traditional black and red but use sgraffito design. They are dance pieces with buffalo and deer dancers."

Opposite: Phyllis Tafoya. Pot 9 x 10 ½ in., 1993. Courtesy of the artist.

Sherry Tafoya (portrait not available). Pot 7 ⅞ x 5 ¼ in., 1993. Courtesy Merrock Galeria, Santa Clara Pueblo.

Ethel Vigil, b. 1950
"I take great pride in putting out quality pieces. I sign them, and what I have my name on I want to be proud of. I take great pride in doing the work. It's a money-making thing, but it's also a handed-down art that we learn. I do the red and the black carved pottery. I learned on my own. My mother [Mida Tafoya] did it, and I watched her. I picked it up because I was interested. My work is different from my mother's. I'm trying to teach my four daughters, but the patience isn't there for them yet."

Dona Tafoya, b. 1952
"It's a good source of income. It's extra income, and it also gives you a satisfaction that you can do something with your hands that someone else can appreciate. I don't do it as much now because I have a full-time job—mostly for shows and special events. My mother [Mida Tafoya] and grandmother [Christina Naranjo] were my main teachers."

Cookie Tafoya, b. 1963
"I grew up with it [pottery], watching my grandmother [Christina Naranjo]. I would go to her house after school and cut newspapers to put in her bowls to start pottery. As I got older, I watched my mom. She taught me to polish, carve, and design. My mom basically taught me, and then I developed my own designs—which is important to me because you have your own personality and I like to show mine. I don't like to use the same designs and shapes over and over; I like to try new things. It depends on my mood. Sometimes I can be real creative and sometimes I go with more traditional pots: wedding vases, water pots, and seed pots."

Opposite: Ethel Vigil. Pot 4 ¾ x 3 ½ in., 1993. Courtesy Merrock Galeria, Santa Clara Pueblo.

Dona Tafoya. Pot not available.

Cookie Perez (portrait not available). Pot 1 ½ x 2 ¼ in., 1993. Rick Dillingham inventory.

Valerie Ochoa, b. 1974
"I've been doing it [pottery making] since I was about nine. I think it's important because it helps to keep the tradition of potters in our family alive. I do simple little carved bowls, and some uncarved. I enjoy making them, you have a reason to get dirty! I learned everything from my grandma [Mida Tafoya]."

Mary Louise Eckleberry, b. 1921
"Since I was little, we [Mary Louise and her sisters] helped Mom [Christina Naranjo] with the potteries. We made little ones, but they wanted to save their clay. We lived in Indiana from 1946, and we returned here [Santa Clara] in 1982. After I came back to live here I started up again. Mom used to make birds and turtles, so I make them also. The melon bowls—people were looking for it, and you just try to do it. I also do some wedding vases."

Victor Eckleberry, b. 1958, and Naomi Eckleberry, b. 1961
Naomi: "Victor does storage jars and `eggs,' and I do wedding vases and bowls."
[From a printout she gave me] "To create my pieces—inspiration, enthusiasm, patience, and creativity come from within. My hands and a few simple tools do the rest."

Victor [no photo]: "It's how I feed my kids. I work part-time on construction and go fishing in the canyon. Life revolves around my work—almost every day. It's art, but it's also a part of you. You're always thinking about it. It doesn't go away. It's intense and not just a one-day thing. It's everything. Mixing the clay, firing, there's a lot that goes into a final piece that people don't see."

Opposite: Valerie Ochoa. Pot not available.

Left: Mary Louise Eckleberry. Pot 2 ¾ x 3 ¾ in., ca. 1990. Courtesy of the artist.

Right: Victor Eckleberry (portrait not available). Pot 3 ½ x 2 ¾ in., 1992. Courtesy of the artist.

SAN ILDEFONSO

The Gonzales Family

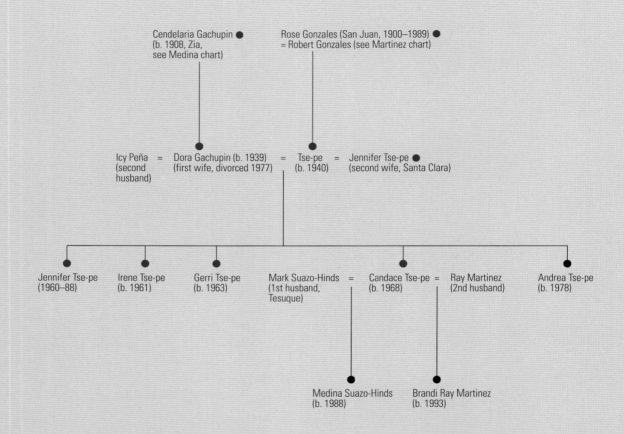

Cendelaria Gachupin ●
(b. 1908, Zia,
see Medina chart)

Rose Gonzales (San Juan, 1900–1989) ●
= Robert Gonzales (see Martinez chart)

Icy Peña = Dora Gachupin (b. 1939) = Tse-pe = Jennifer Tse-pe ●
(second (first wife, divorced 1977) (b. 1940) (second wife, Santa Clara)
husband)

Jennifer Tse-pe
(1960–88)

Irene Tse-pe
(b. 1961)

Gerri Tse-pe
(b. 1963)

Mark Suazo-Hinds = Candace Tse-pe = Ray Martinez
(1st husband, (b. 1968) (2nd husband)
Tesuque)

Andrea Tse-pe
(b. 1978)

Medina Suazo-Hinds
(b. 1988)

Brandi Ray Martinez
(b. 1993)

Rose Gonzales, ca. 1973 (photo by Dick Dunatchik). Pots: previous page: red, 4 ½ x 9 in., ca. 1935, IAF 2089, courtesy Indian Arts Research Center, School of American Research, Santa Fe; black, 9 ½ x 10 ½ in., ca. 1975, courtesy Dora Tse-Pe Peña, San Ildefonso Pueblo.

Opposite: Tse-Pe. Pot 13 ¾ in. diameter, 1990. Rick Dillingham inventory.

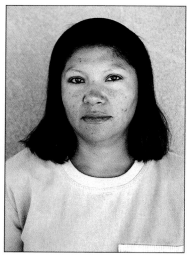

Tse-Pe, b. 1940

"With the changing of times, I'm finding still I have a strong urge in wanting to and continuing what Mother Earth has let me do—that is, her allowing me to make her as pretty as I can.

"I find myself feeling probably the strongest that I have felt in all these years I've been molding the beautiful clay. I have fun and different innovative feelings since I have started working with my wife, Jennifer. She in her own pottery-making right comes from a grandmother and mother who are accomplished potters [San Juan]. We try not to separate too much. We both gather clay and clean it, and after it's set [Mother Earth] takes some first, and we see what the mood sets up, who sits at the workbench first.

"We do all stages together: cleaning, making, polishing. I do the designs and she [Jennifer] helps, she's very much involved. We both fire together. The finishing we both do, adding stones and whatever. The end results are shared, we give a lot of thanks. My thoughts and my prayers and thankfulness have all been fulfilled and it all leads to my late mother Rose [Gonzales]. She was my inspiration, something that will never be forgotten. My everyday thanksgiving goes to those—and all who have been a part of me in the pottery world or anywhere."

Jennifer Tse-Pe, b. 1960

"In the past three years I would consider myself a potter. I saw my grandmother and mother doing it as I was growing up, but it was just a thing I saw. I saw them happy working and enjoying it. I didn't actually learn from them but experienced it growing up. It all fell into place, I didn't find it hard or a chore.

"I saw Tse-Pe enjoying it and working with it. It wasn't a chore. Somewhere there, Tse-Pe deserves a lot of credit, including [from] myself, who admire his work."

Tse-Pe.

Jennifer Tse-Pe. Pot not available.

Opposite: Candelaria Gachupin. Pot 7 1/2 x 11 1/2 in., ca. 1970. Courtesy Dora Tse-Pe Peña, San Ildefonso Pueblo.

Candelaria Gachupin, b. 1908
"I started since the 1930s and I'm still doing little pieces. I have some made, and I've always worked in traditional style. I use two backgrounds [slips] like her [referring to a photo of Rosalea Medina], and I do the same. I learned from Rosalea. My mother was a potter, but she passed away when I was a little girl. People asked her to make cooking pots because there wasn't the market there is now. They used them for serving dishes—there weren't so many store-bought dishes then. I taught Dora to do Zia style before she got married, then she started making black pottery after her mother-in-law, Rose [Gonzales]."

245

Dora Tse-Pe Peña, b. 1939
Married in 1961 to Tse-Pe and divorced in 1977
"The most important thing [at Zia Pueblo], along
with working with my mother [Candelaria Gachu-
pin], was the way she taught me spirituality, the
sacredness of clay and respect for the clay. By
the time I started work here [San Ildefonso], I
already knew all that. I knew how to make pots,
and Grandma Rose [Gonzales] helped me to adapt
to the San Ildefonso clay. From her I learned to do
the polishing, which isn't done at Zia. I call what I
have a gift—it was almost an overnight success. In
1971 at Gallup [Inter-Tribal Ceremonial] I got a
Best of Class competing with the 'greats.' It was a
great inspiration.

"I hope and pray that my girls will continue with
their pots, and they learn all they can from me
while I'm here. I encourage them to do the carving,
like Grandma Rose and me. Not many are doing
the carving now. To me it's important to respect and
care for the pots. I don't make many. I would rather
work on quality than quantity."

Opposite: Dora Tse-Pe Peña. Pot 6 x 4
in., 1992. Rick Dillingham inventory.

Tse-Pe and Dora. Pot 4 ½ x 7 ¾ in.,
1972. Courtesy Adobe Gallery,
Albuquerque.

Irene Tse-Pe, b. 1961
"I feel fortunate to have grown up among good potters and pottery. My early memories of my grandmothers [Rose Gonzales and Candelaria Gachupin] have always been of them working with pottery. I was around Grandma Rose more. She was always so peaceful working on pots. I remember focusing on her hands, watching her work on pots. I want to carry on the carving tradition that Grandma Rose did. Some people say it's not real creative by not trying other things, but that's what I want to do."

Opposite: Irene Tse-Pe. Pot 3 ½ x 3 ¼ in., ca. 1987. Courtesy Dora Tse-Pe Peña, San Ildefonso Pueblo.

Candace Tse-Pe. Pot 2 ¼ x 2 ½ in., 1992. Courtesy of the artist.

The Martinez Family

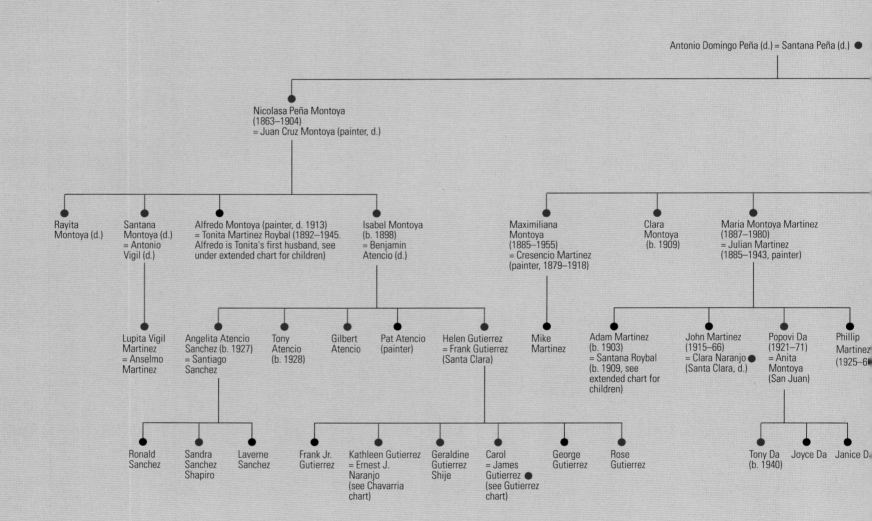

Antonio Domingo Peña (d.) = Santana Peña (d.)

Nicolasa Peña Montoya
(1863–1904)
= Juan Cruz Montoya (painter, d.)

Rayita
Montoya (d.)

Santana
Montoya (d.)
= Antonio
Vigil (d.)

Alfredo Montoya (painter, d. 1913)
= Tonita Martinez Roybal (1892–1945.
Alfredo is Tonita's first husband, see
under extended chart for children)

Isabel Montoya
(b. 1898)
= Benjamin
Atencio (d.)

Maximiliana
Montoya
(1885–1955)
= Cresencio Martinez
(painter, 1879–1918)

Clara
Montoya
(b. 1909)

Maria Montoya Martinez
(1887–1980)
= Julian Martinez
(1885–1943, painter)

Lupita Vigil
Martinez
= Anselmo
Martinez

Angelita Atencio
Sanchez (b. 1927)
= Santiago
Sanchez

Tony
Atencio
(b. 1928)

Gilbert
Atencio

Pat Atencio
(painter)

Helen Gutierrez
= Frank Gutierrez
(Santa Clara)

Mike
Martinez

Adam Martinez
(b. 1903)
= Santana Roybal
(b. 1909, see
extended chart for
children)

John Martinez
(1915–66)
= Clara Naranjo
(Santa Clara, d.)

Popovi Da
(1921–71)
= Anita
Montoya
(San Juan)

Phillip
Martinez
(1925–6

Ronald
Sanchez

Sandra
Sanchez
Shapiro

Laverne
Sanchez

Frank Jr.
Gutierrez

Kathleen Gutierrez
= Ernest J.
Naranjo
(see Chavarria
chart)

Geraldine
Gutierrez
Shije

Carol
= James
Gutierrez
(see Gutierrez
chart)

George
Gutierrez

Rose
Gutierrez

Tony Da
(b. 1940)

Joyce Da

Janice D

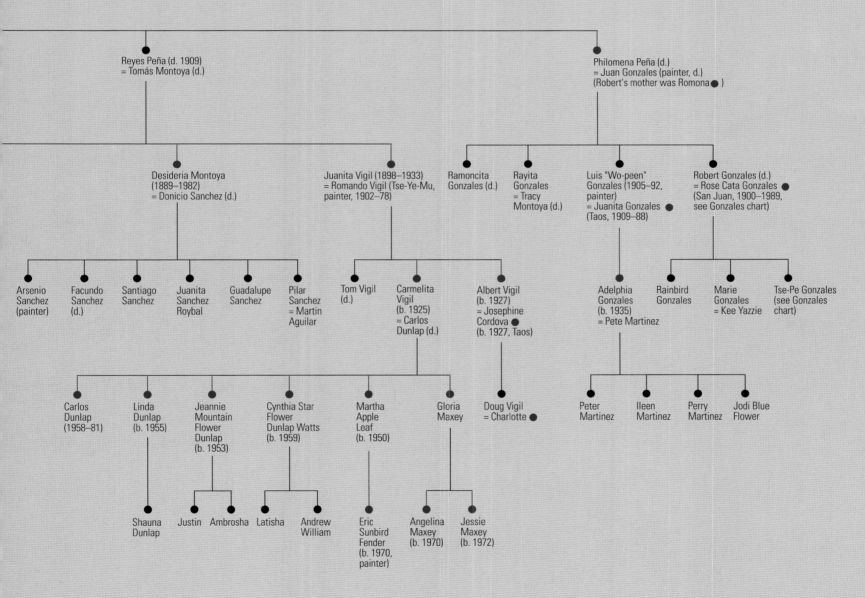

Reyes Peña (d. 1909)
= Tomás Montoya (d.)

Philomena Peña (d.)
= Juan Gonzales (painter, d.)
(Robert's mother was Romona ●)

Desideria Montoya
(1889–1982)
= Donicio Sanchez (d.)

Juanita Vigil (1898–1933)
= Romando Vigil (Tse-Ye-Mu,
painter, 1902–78)

Ramoncita
Gonzales (d.)

Rayita
Gonzales
= Tracy
Montoya (d.)

Luis "Wo-peen"
Gonzales (1905–92,
painter)
= Juanita Gonzales ●
(Taos, 1909–88)

Robert Gonzales (d.)
= Rose Cata Gonzales ●
(San Juan, 1900–1989,
see Gonzales chart)

Arsenio
Sanchez
(painter)

Facundo
Sanchez
(d.)

Santiago
Sanchez

Juanita
Sanchez
Roybal

Guadalupe
Sanchez

Pilar
Sanchez
= Martin
Aguilar

Tom Vigil
(d.)

Carmelita
Vigil
(b. 1925)
= Carlos
Dunlap (d.)

Albert Vigil
(b. 1927)
= Josephine
Cordova ●
(b. 1927, Taos)

Adelphia
Gonzales
(b. 1935)
= Pete Martinez

Rainbird
Gonzales

Marie
Gonzales
= Kee Yazzie

Tse-Pe Gonzales
(see Gonzales
chart)

Carlos
Dunlap
(1958–81)

Linda
Dunlap
(b. 1955)

Jeannie
Mountain
Flower
Dunlap
(b. 1953)

Cynthia Star
Flower
Dunlap Watts
(b. 1959)

Martha
Apple
Leaf
(b. 1950)

Gloria
Maxey

Doug Vigil
= Charlotte ●

Peter
Martinez

Ileen
Martinez

Perry
Martinez

Jodi Blue
Flower

Shauna
Dunlap

Justin

Ambrosha

Latisha

Andrew
William

Eric
Sunbird
Fender
(b. 1970,
painter)

Angelina
Maxey
(b. 1970)

Jessie
Maxey
(b. 1972)

The Martinez (extended) Family

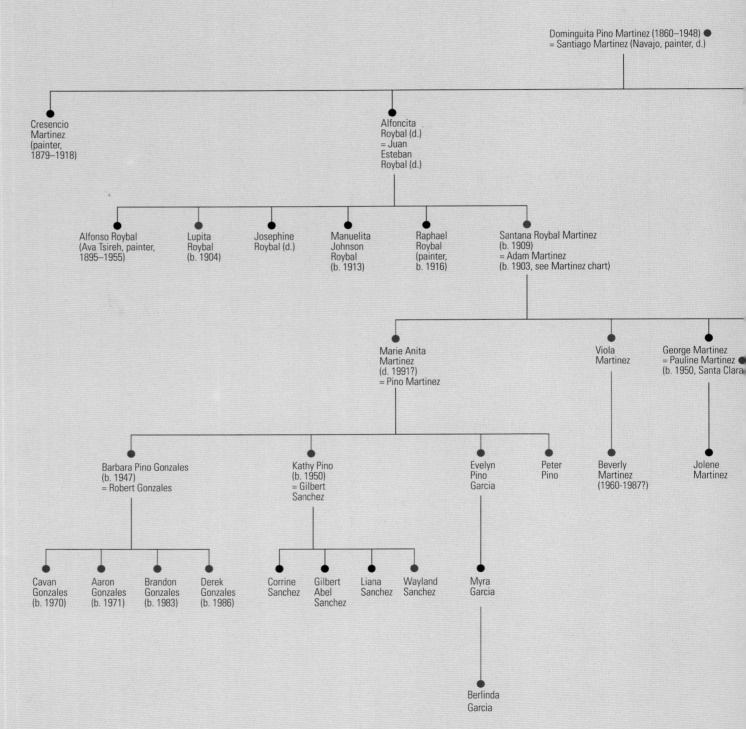

Dominguita Pino Martinez (1860–1948) ●
= Santiago Martinez (Navajo, painter, d.)

Cresencio
Martinez
(painter,
1879–1918)

Alfoncita
Roybal (d.)
= Juan
Esteban
Roybal (d.)

Alfonso Roybal
(Ava Tsireh, painter,
1895–1955)

Lupita
Roybal
(b. 1904)

Josephine
Roybal (d.)

Manuelita
Johnson
Roybal
(b. 1913)

Raphael
Roybal
(painter,
b. 1916)

Santana Roybal Martinez
(b. 1909)
= Adam Martinez
(b. 1903, see Martinez chart)

Marie Anita
Martinez
(d. 1991?)
= Pino Martinez

Viola
Martinez

George Martinez
= Pauline Martinez
(b. 1950, Santa Clara)

Barbara Pino Gonzales
(b. 1947)
= Robert Gonzales

Kathy Pino
(b. 1950)
= Gilbert
Sanchez

Evelyn
Pino
Garcia

Peter
Pino

Beverly
Martinez
(1960-1987?)

Jolene
Martinez

Cavan
Gonzales
(b. 1970)

Aaron
Gonzales
(b. 1971)

Brandon
Gonzales
(b. 1983)

Derek
Gonzales
(b. 1986)

Corrine
Sanchez

Gilbert
Abel
Sanchez

Liana
Sanchez

Wayland
Sanchez

Myra
Garcia

Berlinda
Garcia

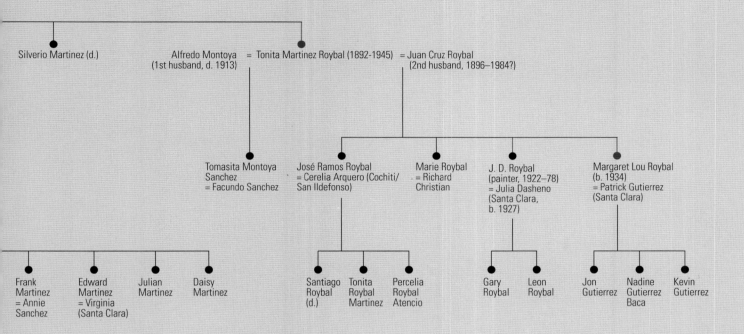

Silverio Martinez (d.)

Alfredo Montoya
(1st husband, d. 1913)

= Tonita Martinez Roybal (1892-1945) = Juan Cruz Roybal
(2nd husband, 1896–1984?)

Tomasita Montoya
Sanchez
= Facundo Sanchez

José Ramos Roybal
= Cerelia Arquero (Cochiti/
San Ildefonso)

Marie Roybal
= Richard
Christian

J. D. Roybal
(painter, 1922–78)
= Julia Dasheno
(Santa Clara,
b. 1927)

Margaret Lou Roybal
(b. 1934)
= Patrick Gutierrez
(Santa Clara)

Frank
Martinez
= Annie
Sanchez

Edward
Martinez
= Virginia
(Santa Clara)

Julian
Martinez

Daisy
Martinez

Santiago
Roybal
(d.)

Tonita
Roybal
Martinez

Percelia
Roybal
Atencio

Gary
Roybal

Leon
Roybal

Jon
Gutierrez

Nadine
Gutierrez
Baca

Kevin
Gutierrez

Maximiliana Montoya (portrait not available). Black-on-black pot, 5 ½ x 6 ¾ in., ca. 1955. SAR 1988-6-80, courtesy Indian Arts Research Center, School of American Research, Santa Fe.

Top: Desideria Sanchez (with Maria Martinez), ca. 1973. Opposite: black-on-black pot, 6 x 9 ¼ in., ca. 1940. Courtesy Carmelita Dunlap.

Albert and Josephine Vigil
Josephine, b. 1927 (Taos)
"I didn't get to know her [Juanita Vigil], but from
our Aunt Maria [Martinez]. What we [Albert and
Josephine] do is cream-on-red pottery, and that's
our main work. I used to do black, and I saw Aunt
Maria doing some red and I decided to work more
with the red. I think it's over twenty years we've
been working on pots. I do all the work, and he
[Albert] does the painting. He painted before on
paper and let that go. Then he started with painting pottery.

"My mom [from Taos] used to do the mica pots
but never sold them. She made them for use. Her
work is a lot different than what we are doing
here. We were in L.A. for fifteen years, and when
we returned [to San Ildefonso] we made pottery
for a living. I used to watch Aunt Maria, and she
encouraged me to work with pottery. My husband
works, and he paints when he has time.

"I started learning polishing from Clara [Montoya].
She was the one—we used to get together and she
would teach me. I wanted to try the polychrome. I
noticed some of the red pottery is fired in kilns. We
do the open firing."

Opposite: Albert Vigil and Josephine
Vigil. Pot 8 ¼ x 6 ¼ in., 1992. Courtesy Andrews Pueblo Pottery, Albuquerque.

Carmelita Dunlap, b. 1925
My Aunt Maria and Desideria—I learned from them by just watching them.
They used to tell me to sit down and watch so I could learn. My mother
[Juanita Vigil] passed away when I was small—Maria and Desideria raised
us. We stay with the traditional ways—the black-on-black. I do polychrome,
too, the cream color, and I do red-on-black and brown ware, which is our
invention. Carlos found out about it.

"I learned a lot of things from Desideria and some things from Aunt Maria
too. I think they all used to work together, the sisters, and Desideria used to
work by herself. We called her Grandma. We would stay with Desideria for a
couple months, and then stay with Aunt Maria a couple months.

"I used to make real small ones and little animals. We returned from California
in the mid 1950s and I really started up with pottery."

Opposite: Carmelita Dunlap. Black-on-black pot, 4 ¼ x 7 ¾ in., 1992. Courtesy Merrock Galeria, Santa Clara Pueblo.

Carlos Dunlap, ca. 1978 (courtesy Carmelita Dunlap). Polychrome pot 3 x 13 in., ca. 1975. Courtesy Margaret Gutierrez.

Linda Dunlap, b. 1955
"I would say the same thing as my mother. What I'm doing is traditional pottery, and I learned from Mom and Carlos. We all have different shapes we do. I'm trying to make bigger ones, but I usually work in smaller sizes. I learned the making mostly from my mom, and with Carlos I learned about painting and firing. I want to keep on and see how far I can take it. I have a daughter and will help her with it."

Jeannie Mountain Flower Dunlap, b. 1953
"I'm following in my mom's [Carmelita Dunlap's] footsteps, and I'm helping her when I can with her work. Ever since Carlos died, I've been helping her. Linda [Dunlap], Mom, and I fire our pots and work together here at the house. It was hard for her to do the big pots, so I started helping her."

Cynthia Star Flower Dunlap Watts, b. 1959
"On my work I try to take my time and not rush, because if you rush they don't come out good. I used to watch Carmelita and Carlos [Dunlap]. They would encourage me. I started with little ones and got to larger ones. I do all my work myself.

"I live in Cortez [Colorado], and I work there. My husband started encouraging me more after I moved to Colorado. He encouraged me to keep it up. He's making buffalos and bears, and my daughter Latisha makes small ones, and my son Andrew makes and paints his pots.

"Everybody likes my polishing and painting. It's coming out a lot better now than before. My mom made me do it and keep trying."

Opposite: Linda Dunlap. Pot 8 ½ x 8 in., 1991. Courtesy of the artist.

Jeannie Mountain Flower Dunlap. Pot not available.

Cynthia Star Flower Dunlap Watts. Pot 18 x 11 ½ in., 1992. Courtesy of the artist.

Martha Apple Leaf Fender, b. 1950
"[My main influences were] Maria and Desideria, I remember I grew up with her [Desideria] and later I worked with Carlos. I learned how to really make them [pottery] from him. He would help make them for us and then he would smash them down and get us to make them ourselves. I enjoy the black and also do green on red, it's different—but I haven't worked on those lately. It was supposed to be white like Uncle Albert [Vigil] but it cooled to green. I got the color from Uncle Tse-Pe. I like working with it— it's something new. Erik [Fender] learned from my mom and I and now he does most of the painting for me—so much easier."

Erik Sunbird Fender (Than Tsideh), b. 1970
"When I got into doing the pottery, it was from watching Grandmother [Carmelita Dunlap], Mom [Martha], and Uncle Carlos. I guess it just rubbed off on me. I got into experimenting with different kinds of clay and firing techniques, and from there I developed my styles now. [My preference is] between black-on-black, polychrome, and black-on-red. There's nobody here at the pueblo who does black-on-red—it's a lost technique. I'm trying to revive it in a way, I guess. Now I'm looking at old photos of pots and I get inspiration from them . . . especially my shapes now. I love to look at old polychrome pieces for ideas."

Opposite left: Martha Apple Leaf (portrait not available). Pot 4 ⅜ x 5 ¾ in., 1992. Courtesy Merrock Galeria, Santa Clara Pueblo.

Opposite right: Erik Sunbird Fender (Than Tsideh). Pot 2 x 11 ¾ in., 1991. Courtesy of the artist and Carmelita Dunlap.

Maria Martinez, ca. 1973. Pots: black, signed "Marie," 5 x 8 ½ in., ca. 1925, IAF 1889, courtesy Indian Arts Research Center, School of American Research, Santa Fe; opposite: red carved, signed "Marie and Julian," 6 x 7 in., ca. 1925–30, Rick Dillingham collection.

Maria Martinez. Pots: top: Marie and Julian polychrome, unsigned, 10 x 10 ½ in., ca. 1915–20, IAF 2637, courtesy Indian Arts Research Center, School of American Research, Santa Fe; bottom: Marie and Julian polychrome plaque, signed "Marie," 10 in. diameter, ca. 1920–25, courtesy Buckner/Lazarus collection, New York; opposite: black-on-black, signed "Marie and Julian," ca. 1940, 7 x 9 in., Rick Dillingham inventory.

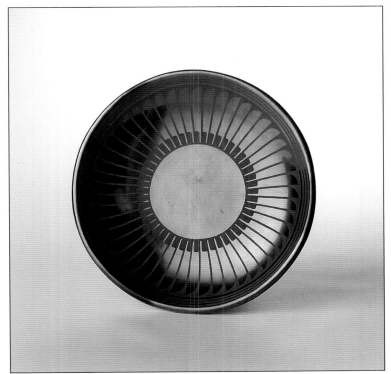

Maria Martinez. Pots: opposite: black with no design, signed "Marie and Santana," 3 ½ x 13 ¾ in., ca. 1950, IAF 2819, courtesy Indian Arts Research Center, School of American Research, Santa Fe; top: plain black-ware, signed "Maria Poveka," 6 x 13 in., April, 1967 ("467"), IAF 3129, courtesy Indian Arts Research Center, School of American Research, Santa Fe; bottom: black-on-black, signed "Maria and Popovi," plate 2 x 11 ¼ in., October 1970 ("1070"), Rick Dillingham collection.

Popovi Da and Maria Martinez, ca.
1960 (photograph by Maurice Eby,
courtesy Anita M. Da). Pots: black-
on-black, 4 x 5 in., March 1971
("371"), courtesy Buckner/Lazarus
collection, New York; opposite:
made by Maria Martinez and finished by Popovi Da and Tony Da, 2 ¼
x 7 ½ in., June 1970 ("670"), courtesy Buckner/Lazarus collection,
New York.

Tony Da, ca. 1970 (photograph by Laura Gilpin, courtesy Anita M. Da). Opposite: redware pot, 7 x 7 in., ca. 1970–72, Rick Dillingham inventory; bear figure, 3 x 5 ½ in. long, ca. 1968, courtesy Anita M. Da.

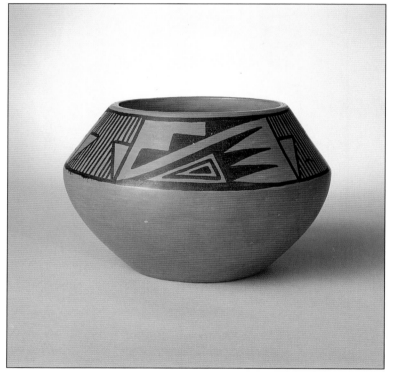

Tonita Roybal and Juan Cruz Roybal. Pots: left: white and red-on-red, ca. 1925, 7 ¾ x 9 ¼ in., IAF 2087, courtesy Indian Arts Research Center, School of American Research, Santa Fe; right: black-on-red, ca. 1923, 6 x 8 ½ in., Rick Dillingham inventory.

Opposite: Dominguita Pino (mother) and Tonita Roybal, 11 ½ x 12 ½ in., ca. 1910–14. Rick Dillingham collection.

Santana Martinez, b. 1909
"I like my work, but I'm taking it kind of easy. I can't do too much. Right now I'm trying to finish some small pots. I feel very happy about the young children doing the work, and I'm trying to help them. They're doing pretty good.

"I feel I was lucky to have Maria and Julian help me—Maria with my pots, and Julian with decoration. I have my own family—my mother, grandmother, and aunt—who were also potters. I have only one daughter, Anita, working.

"Clara [Montoya] still polishes for us, but she won't polish the big pieces anymore.

"When I started decorating, I signed Marie and Santana, and then I started just signing my name, not with Adam then. Some white people were here and said they had seen one of my pots in a grocery store—it was a Santo Domingo pot with `Santana' on it. That's when we started signing Santana and Adam."

Santana and Adam Martinez (portrait of Santana only). Opposite: pot 5 ½ x 5 ½ in., 1979. Rick Dillingham collection.

Margaret Lou Gutierrez, b. 1934.
"My dad [Juan Cruz Roybal] was my main teacher.
He wanted me to try and make pottery like they
did when mother [Tonita Roybal] was still living.
He encouraged the black-on-black. My dad said,
'Stick to traditional,' and I always did. I've tried the
red [pottery], but I like the black. He [Juan Cruz
Roybal] taught me how to paint different styles of
designs that he used to make, also J. D. Roybal
helped me with painting.

"I moved to Santa Clara in 1957 when I got married. I started potting in around 1971–72. I was still
small, I was ten when she [Tonita Roybal] died. I
remember going to Indian Market when they had
it under the portal. I remember her making pottery
and my dad painting.

"My favorite style is the feather design from San
Ildefonso. I came across some of my mother's pottery and a lot of people tell me they [my pots]
resemble her pots a lot."

Opposite: Tonita Roybal and Juan
Cruz Roybal. Pot black-on-black, ca.
1930–35, 8 ½ x 8 in., IAF 2091,
courtesy Indian Arts Research Center, School of American Research,
Santa Fe.

Margaret Lou Gutierrez. Pot painted
by Elvis Torres. Courtesy Torres
Indian Arts, San Ildefonso Pueblo.

Opposite: Marie Anita Martinez (d. 1992) (portrait not available). Pot 6 x 5 in., 1991. Courtesy Anita M. Da.

Barbara Gonzales (Tahn-Moo-Whe). Pot 2 x 4 in., 1980. Courtesy Andrews Pueblo Pottery, Albuquerque.

Cavan Gonzalez, b. 1970

"I just got my B.F.A. from Alfred University in upstate New York. I went to school there to get a different approach to the art world rather than staying in the Southwest and being taught what everyone else already knew. I want to go on for my M.F.A., and my future is to teach college-level intaglio and/or ceramics. I'm having fun with etchings, zinc plate, and woodcuts. Now I'm experimenting with polychrome pottery. It seems like a lost or forgotten tradition. It was traditional before black pots."

 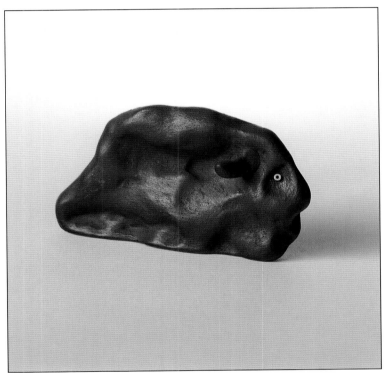

*Opposite: Cavan Gonzales. Pot 3 x
11 ¾ in., 1992. Courtesy Dewey
Galleries, Ltd., Santa Fe.*

*Left: Derek Gonzales. Figure 1 ⅛ x
2 ¼ in., 1992. Courtesy Pat Lollar.*

*Right: Brandon Gonzales. Figure
2 ¼ x 4 in., 1992. Courtesy Pat Lollar.*

Pauline Martinez, b. 1950

"I am from Santa Clara and did pottery with my mother [Crecencia Tafoya]. When I married George Martinez in 1970, I moved to San Ildefonso. I continued to work with my mom. I began to work with Santana [Martinez], and she used to paint for me. Clara [Montoya] helped polish the bigger ones and did the small ones.

"I've stayed with traditional feathers and avanyu designs. I do wedding vases, melon bowls, and black-on-black pottery. I'll probably continue what I'm doing now and hopefully will do bigger pots. I'm doing my own painting now."

Kathy Sanchez, b. 1950
"I think pottery making is a very important pathway to relate to the earth. The earth is the one that nurtures you, and you want to relate to it, acknowledge its importance in your life, acknowledge it every day. Working with clay reminds you of the connectedness of everything. I was married in 1970 and began potting then, also after I finished college.

"You learn all of life's messages from the pathway of working with clay. I like to relate to the spiritual side. Pottery has become so commercial, you tend to be physically oriented rather than spiritually oriented. It's easy to loose focus."

Opposite left: Pauline Martinez. Pot 3 ¼ x 3 ½ in., 1990. Rick Dillingham inventory.

Opposite right: Kathy Sanchez (portrait not available). Bear fetish: height 4 in., 1992. Courtesy Torres Indian Arts, San Ildefonso.

Isabel Montoya Atencio. (portrait not available). Pot 6 x 8 in.,ca. 1965. Courtesy Gilbert Atencio.

286

Adelphia Martinez, b. 1935
"My influences would be from my mother after she came down from Taos.
She did some black and red [pottery] with my aunt, Rose Gonzales. The other
influence was my father. He was a watercolor artist. He did horses and
dancers. He always encouraged us to do our best. My Taos grandmother did
the micaceous pottery and I use some mica in my work and incorporate Taos
and San Ildefonso. I do sgraffito and carving and work both in black and red.
My mom and Aunt Rose did a lot of carving and I learned from them. Their
styles were similiar and I've been told mine looks like theirs."

Opposite: Juanita Gonzales and
"Wo-peen" Gonzales. Plate 7 ½ in.
diameter, ca. 1955. Courtesy Andrew
Fisher Fine Pottery, Santa Fe.

Adelphia Martinez. Wedding vase 9
x 6 in., 1993. Courtesy of the artist.

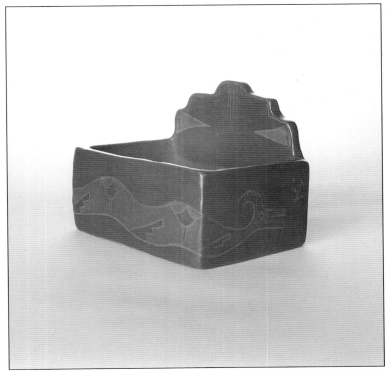

Opposite: Gilbert Atencio. Plate 10 in. diameter, ca. 1980. Courtesy of the artist.

Left: Helen Gutierrez. Plate 10 in. diameter, ca. 1988. Courtesy Torres Indian Arts, San Ildefonso Pueblo.

Right: Romona Gonzales (portrait not available). Pseudo-ceremonial box 5 x 6 ¾ in., ca. 1930.